Three timex in a row

Three timex in a row

Prentice Hall Mathematics

ALGEBRA READINESS

Charles
McNemar
Ramirez

Boston, Massachusetts • Chandler, Arizona • Glenview, Illinois • Upper Saddle River, New Jersey

Acknowledgments appear on pages 807–808, which constitute an extension of this copyright page.

ISBN-13: 978-0-13-372118-8
ISBN-10:   0-13-372118-3
10 11 12 13 14   V011   20 19 18 17 16

Authors

Series Author

Randall I. Charles, Ph.D., is Professor Emeritus in the Department of Mathematics and Computer Science at San Jose State University, San Jose, California. He began his career as a high school mathematics teacher, and he was a mathematics supervisor for five years. Dr. Charles has been a member of several NCTM committees and is the former Vice President of the National Council of Supervisors of Mathematics. Much of his writing and research has been in the area of problem solving. He has authored more than 75 mathematics textbooks for kindergarten through college.

Authors

Bonnie McNemar is a mathematics educator with more than 30 years of experience in Texas schools as a teacher, administrator, and consultant. She began her career as a middle school mathematics teacher and served as a supervisor at the district, county, and state levels. Ms. McNemar was the director of the Texas Mathematics Staff Development Program, now known as TEXTEAMS, for five years, and she was the first director of the Teachers Teaching with Technology (T^3) Program. She remains active in both of these organizations as well as in several local, state and national mathematics organizations, including NCTM.

Alma Ramirez is co-director of the Mathematics Case Project at WestEd, a nonprofit educational institute in Oakland, California. A former bilingual elementary and middle school teacher, Ms. Ramirez has considerable expertise in mathematics teaching and learning, second language acquisition, and professional development. She has served as a consultant on a variety of projects and has extensive experience as an author for elementary and middle-grades texts. In addition, her work has appeared in the 2004 NCTM Yearbook. Ms. Ramirez is a frequent presenter at professional meetings and conferences.

Contributing Authors

David M. Davison, Ph.D.
Professor of Mathematics Education
Montana State University
Billings, Montana

Leah McCracken
Educational Technology Consultant
Billings, Montana

Marsha Landau, Ph.D.
Retired Professor of Mathematics Education
National-Louis University
Evanston, Illinois

Linda Thompson
Consultant
Warrenton, Oregon

Mathematics Program Advisors

Prentice Hall wishes to thank the following educators for their ongoing advice in the development of this Edition of Prentice Hall Mathematics. Their valuable insights have helped ensure that this mathematics series meets the needs of students and their teachers.

Consultants

Ann Bell
Mathematics
Prentice Hall Consultant
Franklin, Tennessee

Blanche Brownley
Mathematics
Prentice Hall Consultant
Olney, Maryland

Joe Brumfield
Mathematics
Prentice Hall Consultant
Altadena, California

Linda Buckhalt
Mathematics
Prentice Hall Consultant
Derwood, Maryland

Andrea Gordon
Mathematics
Prentice Hall Consultant
Atlanta, Georgia

Eleanor Lopes
Mathematics
Prentice Hall Consultant
New Castle, Delaware

Sally Marsh
Mathematics
Prentice Hall Consultant
Baltimore, Maryland

Bob Pacyga
Mathematics
Prentice Hall Consultant
Darien, Illinois

Judy Porter
Mathematics
Prentice Hall Consultant
Fuquay-Varena, North Carolina

Rose Primiani
Mathematics
Prentice Hall Consultant
Harbor City, New Jersey

Jayne Radu
Mathematics
Prentice Hall Consultant
Scottsdale, Arizona

Pam Revels
Mathematics
Prentice Hall Consultant
Sarasota, Florida

Barbara Rogers
Mathematics
Prentice Hall Consultant
Raleigh, North Carolina

Michael Seals
Mathematics
Prentice Hall Consultant
Edmond, Oklahoma

Margaret Thomas
Mathematics
Prentice Hall Consultant
Indianapolis, Indiana

Reviewers

Chandler Cox
White Knoll Middle School
West Columbia, South Carolina

Fred Ferguson
Yough High School
Herminie, Pennsylvania

Nancy Hughes
Indian Hills Middle School
Shawnee Mission, Kansas

Dorothy (Dot)
Johnson-Manning
Siwell Road Middle School
Jackson, Mississippi

Ellice P. Martin, Ed.D.
Lanier County Middle School
Lakeland, Georgia

Desireé Marcelin McNeal
Susan Miller Dorsey High School
Los Angeles, California

Vocabulary Development Consultants

Kate Kinsella Kate Kinsella, Ed.D., is a faculty member in the Department of Secondary Education at San Francisco State University. A specialist in second-language acquisition and adolescent literacy, she teaches coursework addressing language and literacy development across the secondary curricula. Dr. Kinsella earned her master's degree in TESOL from San Francisco State University and her Ed.D. in Second Language Acquisition from the University of San Francisco.

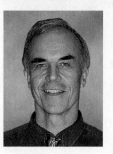

Kevin Feldman Kevin Feldman, Ed.D., is the Director of Reading and Early Intervention with the Sonoma County Office of Education (SCOE) and an independent educational consultant. At the SCOE, he develops, organizes, and monitors programs related to K-12 literacy. Dr. Feldman has a master's degree from the University of California, Riverside, in Special Education, Learning Disabilities, and Instructional Design. He earned his Ed.D. in Curriculum and Instruction from the University of San Francisco.

Contents in Brief

Mathematics Student Handbook

Algebraic Expressions and Integers

Solving One-Step Equations and Inequalities

Decimals and Equations

Factors, Fractions, and Exponents

Operations With Fractions

Student Support

Ratios, Proportions, and Percents

Solving Equations and Inequalities

Linear Functions and Graphing

Spatial Thinking

CHAPTER 10

Area and Volume

Student Support

Instant Check System

Check Your Readiness 498
Check Skills You'll Need 500, 507, 512, 519, 527, 534, 539, 544, 548, 552
Quick Check 501, 507, 508, 509, 513, 514, 520, 527, 528, 529, 535, 536, 540, 545, 548, 549, 552, 553
Check Your Understanding 502, 510, 515, 521, 530, 537, 541, 550, 554
Checkpoint Quiz 517, 547

Vocabulary ◀))

New Vocabulary 500, 507, 519, 527, 534, 539, 552
Vocabulary Tip 501, 521, 522
Vocabulary Review 557

GO Online

Video Tutor Help 513, 535, 548
Active Math 501, 529, 535
Homework Video Tutor 502, 511, 516, 522, 531, 538, 541, 546, 551, 555
Lesson Quizzes 503, 511, 517, 523, 531, 537, 541, 547, 551, 555
Vocabulary Quiz 557
Chapter Test 560

Standards Mastery and Assessment

CHAPTER
11

Irrational Numbers and Nonlinear Functions

Student Support

Instant Check System

Check Your Readiness 564
Check Skills You'll Need 566, 570, 579, 586, 591
Quick Check 566, 567, 571, 572, 580, 581, 587, 591, 592
Check Your Understanding 568, 573, 582, 594
Checkpoint Quiz 575, 595

Vocabulary 🔊

New Vocabulary 566, 570, 579, 591
Vocabulary Tip 570, 581
Vocabulary Review 597, 601

GO Online

Active Math 567, 572
Homework Video Tutor 569, 574, 583, 588, 594
Lesson Quizzes 569, 573, 583, 589, 595
Vocabulary Quiz 597
Chapter Test 600

✓ **Check Your Readiness** 564

11-1 Square Roots and Irrational Numbers 566

11-2 The Pythagorean Theorem 570
• **Activity Lab** The Pythagorean Theorem and Circles, 576
✓ **Checkpoint Quiz 1** 575

11-3 Distance and Midpoint Formulas 579
• **Activity Lab** Multiplying and Dividing Square Roots, 578
• **Guided Problem Solving** Understanding Math Problems, 584
• **Mathematical Reasoning** Area of an Equilateral Triangle, 585

11-4 Reasoning Strategy: Write a Proportion 586

11-5 Graphing Nonlinear Functions 591
• **Activity Lab** Monomials, 590
✓ **Checkpoint Quiz 2** 595

Standards Mastery and Assessment

• Test-Taking Strategies: Using a Variable, 596
• Chapter Review, 597
• Chapter Test, 600
• Multiple Choice Practice, 569, 575, 583, 589, 595, 596
• Standards Mastery Cumulative Practice, 601

CHAPTER 12

Data Analysis

Learning the
Standards

Your *Prentice Hall Algebra-Readiness* textbook is designed to help you fully understand and learn the tools and skills necessary to succeed in Algebra. Here are some features of your textbook that will support your learning throughout the year.

Instant Check System

Look for the ✓ in each lesson. These questions are opportunities for you and your teacher to make sure you understand the mathematics – so you can be successful with each day's lesson.

GO for Help

Look for this Go for Help arrow throughout every lesson to point you to where you can get help or review important concepts. Be an independent learner – and go for help when you're having trouble.

Get Ready to Learn

1-2 The Order of Operations

Introduce Add, subtract, multiply, and divide rational numbers.
Develop Determine when and how to break a problem into simpler parts.
Use the correct order of operations to evaluate algebraic expressions.

What You'll Learn
• To use the order of operations
• To use grouping symbols

. . . And Why
To find the value of an expression with more than one operation

☑ **Check Skills You'll Need**

Find each quotient.

1. 164 ÷ 2 **2.** 344 ÷ 8

3. 284 ÷ 4 **4.** 133 ÷ 7

5. 182 ÷ 13 **6.** 650 ÷ 25

GO for Help
Skills Handbook, p. 683

🔊 **New Vocabulary**
• order of operations

Using the Order of Operations

Standards Investigation
Experimenting With Order

In most languages, the meaning of words depends on their order. For example, "sign the check" is not the same as "check the sign."

Similarly, order is important in the language of mathematics.

1. Mental Math Find the value of the expression $3 + 5 \times 2$.

2. What answer do you get to Question 1 if you multiply before adding? If you add before multiplying?

3. Reasoning How does the order in which you do the operations affect your answer?

The order in which you perform operations can affect the value of an expression. To avoid confusion, mathematicians have agreed on an **order of operations.** Multiply and divide first. Then add and subtract.

To *simplify* a numerical expression, you use the order of operations and replace the expression with the simplest name for its value.

2 EXAMPLE Using the Order of Operations

Simplify $3 \cdot 5 - 8 \div 4 + 6$.

$$3 \cdot 5 - 8 \div 4 + 6$$
$$15 \quad - \quad 2 \quad + \quad 6 \quad \text{Multiply and divide from left to right.}$$
$$13 + 6 \quad \text{Add and subtract from left to right.}$$
$$19 \quad \text{Add.}$$

☑ **Quick Check**

2. Simplify each expression.
a. $4 - 1 \cdot 2 + 6 \div 3$ **b.** $5 + 6 \cdot 4 \div 3 - 1$

Using Grouping Symbols

Grouping symbols, such as parentheses, ( ), and brackets, [ ], indicate order. A fraction bar also is a grouping symbol, since $\frac{4+2}{3} = (4+2) \div 3$. Always work inside grouping symbols first.

Take Note / Order of Operations

1. Work inside grouping symbols.
2. Multiply and divide in order from left to right.
3. Add and subtract in order from left to right.

3 EXAMPLE Simplifying With Grouping Symbols

Multiple Choice Which procedure is correct for simplifying $24 \div [6 - (2 \cdot 2)]$?

Ⓐ $24 \div [6 - (2 \cdot 2)] = 4 - 2 \cdot 2 = 4 - 4 = 0$
Ⓑ $24 \div [6 - (2 \cdot 2)] = 24 \div 2 = 24 \div 8 = 3$
Ⓒ $24 \div [6 - (2 \cdot 2)] = 4 - 2 \cdot 2 = 2 \cdot 2 = 4$
Ⓓ $24 \div [6 - (2 \cdot 2)] = 24 \div (6 - 4) = 24 \div 2 = 12$

Choice D follows the order of operations by working inside the grouping symbols first. Choice D is correct.

Vocabulary Tip

Grouping symbols say "do this first." Inside grouping symbols, multiply and divide before adding and subtracting.

☑ **Quick Check**

3. Simplify the expression $1 + \frac{10 - 2}{4}$.

Content Standards

Your textbook identifies which standards you'll be covering each day. You'll also know whether you are being introduced to this standard for the first time, developing your understanding of it, or showing your mastery of it.

☑ Check Skills You'll Need

These questions make sure you're ready to start the lesson by reviewing important skills and vocabulary words you'll need. Need help? Go for Help points you to the lesson you can review.

☑ Quick Check

These questions, after every example, help you and your teacher make sure you understand the example – and the standards being taught.

Standards Mastery in Your Book

Practicing the
Standards

Your *Prentice Hall Algebra-Readiness* textbook gives you plenty of opportunities to practice, with plenty of homework help along the way.

✓ Check Your Understanding

These exercises give you and your teacher a chance to review the entire lesson before you begin your homework. Put everything you just learned together!

Standards Practice

Each lesson's Standards Practice gives you different levels of exercises.

A Practice by Example: These exercises give you practice with the examples you just learned. Go for Help points you back to the example for easy reference.

B Apply Your Skills: These exercises give you a chance to practice everything you learned in the day's lesson.

C Challenge: This problem extends your learning and gives you a more challenging problem.

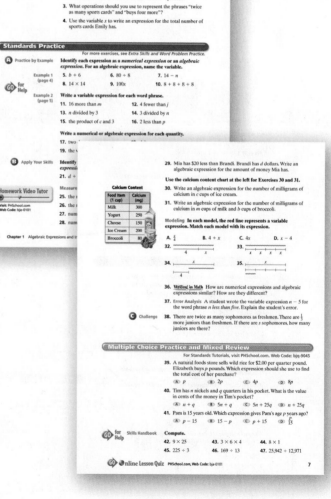

Homework Video Tutor

What if you need help with your homework? These tutorials show real teachers reviewing each lesson. Your Prentice Hall textbook gives you a unique source for more help – called Homework Video Tutors. Log on to PHSchool.com and enter the Web Code provided – you'll get the homework help you need!

Mastering the
Standards

Your *Prentice Hall Algebra-Readiness* textbook provides opportunities for you to ensure you've mastered the standards after every lesson and every chapter in your textbook.

Standards Mastery After Every Lesson

Multiple Choice Practice and Mixed Review

The final part of each day's exercises includes practice with multiple choice problems and a chance to review skills you learned earlier in your course. This will help keep your skills sharp and help you receive lots of practice with multiple choice questions. All questions are correlated to the standards.

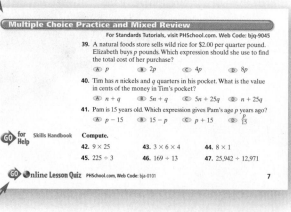

Multiple Choice Practice and Mixed Review

For Standards Tutorials, visit PHSchool.com. Web Code: bjq-9045

39. A natural foods store sells wild rice for $2.00 per quarter pound. Elizabeth buys p pounds. Which expression should she use to find the total cost of her purchase?
    Ⓐ p Ⓑ $2p$ Ⓒ $4p$ Ⓓ $8p$

40. Tim has n nickels and q quarters in his pocket. What is the value in cents of the money in Tim's pocket?
    Ⓐ $n + q$ Ⓑ $5n + q$ Ⓒ $5n + 25q$ Ⓓ $n + 25q$

41. Pam is 15 years old. Which expression gives Pam's age p years ago?
    Ⓐ $p - 15$ Ⓑ $15 - p$ Ⓒ $p + 15$ Ⓓ $\frac{p}{15}$

GO for Help   Skills Handbook   **Compute.**

42. 9×25 43. $3 \times 6 \times 4$ 44. 8×1

45. $225 \div 3$ 46. $169 \div 13$ 47. $25,942 \div 12,971$

GO Online Lesson Quiz   PHSchool.com, Web Code: bja-0101   7

GO for Help

The Go for Help arrow points to the lesson you can review. You can also go online and take a lesson quiz – another chance to make sure you've mastered the standards you learned.

Standards Mastery after Every Chapter

After every chapter, Standards Mastery Cumulative Practice provides an opportunity to demonstrate your understanding of all the standards covered so far.

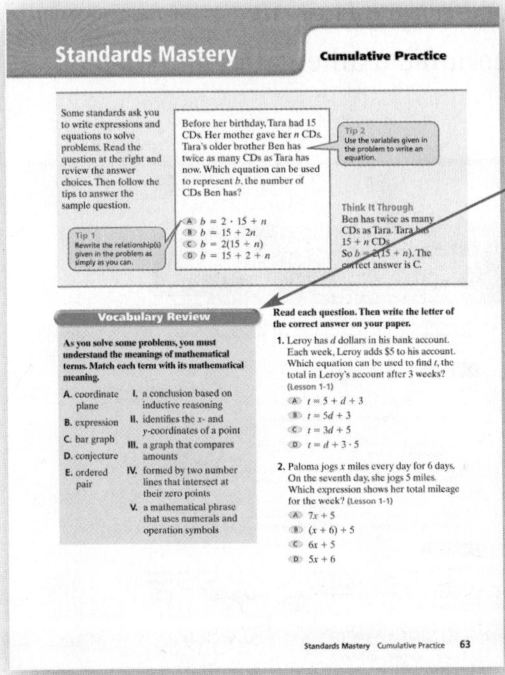

Standards Mastery

Cumulative Practice

Some standards ask you to write expressions and equations to solve problems. Read the question at the right and review the answer choices. Then follow the tips to answer the sample question.

Before her birthday, Tara had 15 CDs. Her mother gave her n CDs. Tara's older brother Ben has twice as many CDs as Tara has now. Which equation can be used to represent b, the number of CDs Ben has?

- A $b = 2 \cdot 15 + n$
- B $b = 15 + 2n$
- C $b = 2(15 + n)$
- D $b = 15 + 2 + n$

Tip 1
Rewrite the relationship(s) given in the problem as simply as you can.

Tip 2
Use the variables given in the problem to write an equation.

Think It Through
Ben has twice as many CDs as Tara. Tara has $15 + n$ CDs. So $b = 2(15 + n)$. The correct answer is C.

Vocabulary Review

As you solve some problems, you must understand the meanings of mathematical terms. Match each term with its mathematical meaning.

A. coordinate plane
B. expression
C. bar graph
D. conjecture
E. ordered pair

I. a conclusion based on inductive reasoning
II. identifies the x- and y-coordinates of a point
III. a graph that compares amounts
IV. formed by two number lines that intersect at their zero points
V. a mathematical phrase that uses numerals and operation symbols

Read each question. Then write the letter of the correct answer on your paper.

1. Leroy has d dollars in his bank account. Each week, Leroy adds $5 to his account. Which equation can be used to find t, the total in Leroy's account after 3 weeks? (Lesson 1-1)
   - A $t = 5 + d + 3$
   - B $t = 5d + 3$
   - C $t = 3d + 5$
   - D $t = d + 3 \cdot 5$

2. Paloma jogs x miles every day for 6 days. On the seventh day, she jogs 5 miles. Which expression shows her total mileage for the week? (Lesson 1-1)
   - A $7x + 5$
   - B $(x + 6) + 5$
   - C $6x + 5$
   - D $5x + 6$

Standards Mastery Cumulative Practice 63

Review key mathematical vocabulary from each chapter.

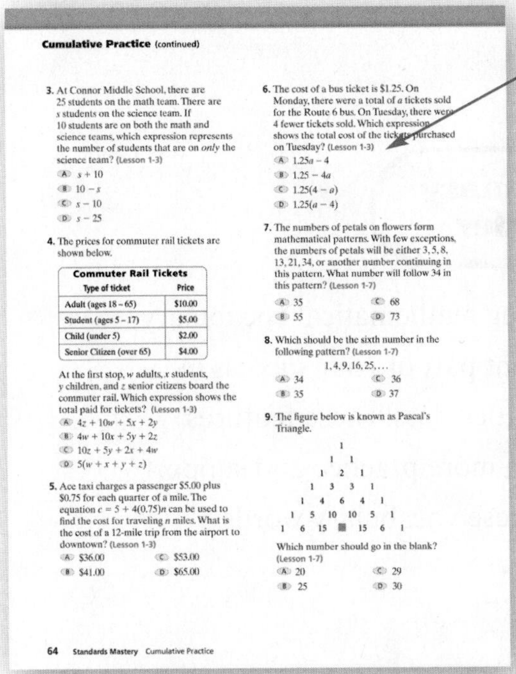

Cumulative Practice (continued)

3. At Connor Middle School, there are 25 students on the math team. There are s students on the science team. If 10 students are on both the math and science teams, which expression represents the number of students that are on *only* the science team? (Lesson 1-3)
   - A $s + 10$
   - B $10 - s$
   - C $s - 10$
   - D $s - 25$

4. The prices for commuter rail tickets are shown below.

Commuter Rail Tickets	
Type of ticket	Price
Adult (ages 18 – 65)	$10.00
Student (ages 5 – 17)	$5.00
Child (under 5)	$2.00
Senior Citizen (over 65)	$4.00

   At the first stop, w adults, x students, y children, and z senior citizens board the commuter rail. Which expression shows the total paid for tickets? (Lesson 1-3)
   - A $4z + 10w + 5x + 2y$
   - B $4w + 10x + 5y + 2z$
   - C $10z + 5y + 2x + 4w$
   - D $5(w + x + y + z)$

5. Ace taxi charges a passenger $5.00 plus $0.75 for each quarter of a mile. The equation $c = 5 + 4(0.75)n$ can be used to find the cost for traveling n miles. What is the cost of a 12-mile trip from the airport to downtown? (Lesson 1-3)
   - A $36.00
   - B $41.00
   - C $53.00
   - D $65.00

6. The cost of a bus ticket is $1.25. On Monday, there were a total of a tickets sold for the Route 6 bus. On Tuesday, there were 4 fewer tickets sold. Which expression shows the total cost of the tickets purchased on Tuesday? (Lesson 1-3)
   - A $1.25a - 4$
   - B $1.25 - 4a$
   - C $1.25(4 - a)$
   - D $1.25(a - 4)$

7. The numbers of petals on flowers form mathematical patterns. With few exceptions, the numbers of petals will be either 3, 5, 8, 13, 21, 34, or another number continuing in this pattern. What number will follow 34 in this pattern? (Lesson 1-7)
   - A 35
   - B 55
   - C 68
   - D 73

8. Which should be the sixth number in the following pattern? (Lesson 1-7)
   1, 4, 9, 16, 25, . . .
   - A 34
   - B 35
   - C 36
   - D 37

9. The figure below is known as Pascal's Triangle.

   1
   1 1
   1 2 1
   1 3 3 1
   1 4 6 4 1
   1 5 10 10 5 1
   1 6 15 ■ 15 6 1

   Which number should go in the blank? (Lesson 1-7)
   - A 20
   - B 25
   - C 29
   - D 30

64 Standards Mastery Cumulative Practice

Go for Help references point to where you can go to review previous lessons.

Standards Mastery in Your Book

Mastering the
Standards

There are other types of features in your *Prentice Hall Algebra-Readiness* textbook that will help you learn the mathematics and be successful in your class.

These features provide opportunities for you to engage with the mathematics being taught. Each feature states the standards being covered.

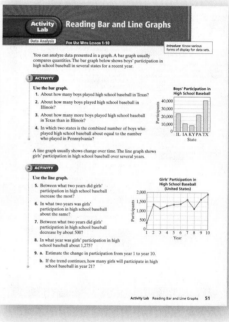

Understanding mathematical vocabulary is an important part of your success in any mathematics class. These features give you even more practice and support in learning these vocabulary words.

GPS Guided Problem Solving

These features give you more support in becoming a good problem solver.

- We provide a great model for talking through the problem-solving process.
- "Think It Through" questions get more in-depth.

- The first two exercises present the steps you should take to solve the problem. They often contain a visual model of the problem.
- The remaining exercises provide independent practice.

GPS Guided Problem Solving

FOR USE WITH PAGE 11, EXERCISE 24

Understanding Math Problems Read the problem below. Then let Daria's thinking guide you through the solution. Check your understanding with the exercises at the bottom of the page.

Simplify $2[8 + (5 - 3)] - 8$.

What Daria Thinks

What Daria Thinks	What Daria Writes
There are two sets of grouping symbols, square brackets and parentheses: $[8 + (5 - 3)]$.	$2[8 + (5 - 3)] - 8$
I need to begin by working inside the innermost grouping symbols, the parentheses: $(5 - 3)$.	$2[8 + (2)] - 8$
Now I need to work inside the next pair of grouping symbols, the square brackets, to find $[8 + 2]$.	$2[10] - 8$
Multiply before subtracting.	$20 - 8$
Now subtract.	12
The simplified expression is 12.	

EXERCISES

Simplify each expression.

1. $2[(13 - 4) \div 3]$
2. $1 + \frac{11 - 3}{4}$
3. $3[(8 + 4) \div 6]$
4. $\frac{6 + 9}{3} - 2$
5. $4[3 + (2 \cdot 3)]$
6. $16 \div (8 - 4) - 2$
7. $3(8 - 2) + 12$
8. $2[4(7 - 2) + 3]$
9. $6 - \frac{4 - 10}{2}$
10. $25 \div (15 \div 3) \cdot 2$
11. $\frac{17 - 12}{5} + (4 - 2)$
12. $7(12 \div 3 - 3)$

Guided Problem Solving Understanding Math Problems **13**

Algebra-Readiness
Student Center

Your Prentice Hall Student Center is your one-stop spot for reviewing the math you learned in class and completing your homework.

Interactive Text

Your complete textbook – electronically! Also includes:

- Stepped examples for you to review
- Activities and Videos to review your lesson
- Self-Check tests to make sure you're on the right track.

Student Worksheets

All the additional resources your teacher might assign you to extend your learning.

Web Resources

Links out to helpful sites to extend your understanding of math concepts.

Student Center available online and on CD-ROM

Go Online

Throughout this book you will find links to the Prentice Hall Web site. Use the Web Codes provided with each link to gain direct access to online material. Here's how to *Go Online*:

1. Go to PHSchool.com
2. Enter the Web Code
3. Click Go!

Lesson Web Codes

Lesson Quiz Web Codes: There is an online quiz for every lesson. Access these quizzes with Web Codes bja-0101 through bja-1206 for Lesson 1-1 through Lesson 12-6.

Homework Video Tutor Web Codes: For every lesson, there is additional support online to help students complete their homework. Access the Homework Video Tutors with Web Codes bje-0101 through bje-1206 for Lesson 1-1 through Lesson 12-6.

Lesson Quizzes
Web Code format: bja-0204
02 = Chapter 2   04 = Lesson 4

Homework Video Tutor
Web Code format: bje-0605
06 = Chapter 6   05 = Lesson 5

Chapter Web Codes

Chapter	Vocabulary Quizzes	Chapter Tests	Chapter Projects
1	bjj-0151	bja-0152	bjd-0161
2	bjj-0251	bja-0252	bjd-0261
3	bjj-0351	bja-0352	bjd-0361
4	bjj-0451	bja-0452	bjd-0461
5	bjj-0551	bja-0552	bjd-0561
6	bjj-0651	bja-0652	bjd-0661
7	bjj-0751	bja-0752	bjd-0761
8	bjj-0851	bja-0852	bjd-0861
9	bjj-0951	bja-0952	bjd-0961
10	bjj-1051	bja-1052	bjd-1061
11	bjj-1151	bja-1152	bjd-1161
12	bjj-1251	bja-1252	bjd-1261

Additional Web Codes

Video Tutor Help:
Use Web Code bje-0775 to access engaging online instructional videos to help bring math concepts to life.

Data Updates:
Use Web Code bjg-9041 to get up-to-date government data for use in examples and exercises.

Entry-Level Assessment

Read each question. Then write the letter of the correct answer on your paper.

1. Which of the following lists of numbers is in order from least to greatest?

   Ⓐ $\frac{4}{5}, -2, 0, -\frac{1}{3}, 0.75$

   Ⓑ $-\frac{1}{3}, \frac{4}{5}, 0.75, 0, -2$

   Ⓒ $-2, 0, -\frac{1}{3}, 0.75, \frac{4}{5}$

   Ⓓ $-2, -\frac{1}{3}, 0, 0.75, \frac{4}{5}$

2. Which point on the number line below corresponds to the number $-1\frac{2}{3}$?

   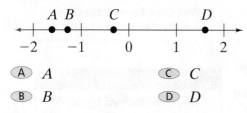

   Ⓐ A   Ⓒ C

   Ⓑ B   Ⓓ D

3. There are 5 dogs, 8 cats, and 2 birds for sale at the pet store. What is the ratio of birds to cats?

   Ⓐ 8 to 5   Ⓒ 8 : 2

   Ⓑ 2 : 8   Ⓓ 5 to 2

4. The distance from home plate to the centerfield fence in a local baseball field is 137 yards. The length of a football field, including the end zones, is 120 yards. What is the ratio of the distance from home plate to the centerfield fence in the baseball field to the length of a football field?

   Ⓐ 120 : 137   Ⓒ 137 to 120

   Ⓑ $\frac{37}{120}$ Ⓓ 120 : 37

5. Solve the following proportion for x.
   $$\frac{4}{7} = \frac{16}{x}$$

   Ⓐ 1.75   Ⓒ 16

   Ⓑ 9.2   Ⓓ 28

6. The two triangles below are similar. What is the measure of $\overline{FE}$?

   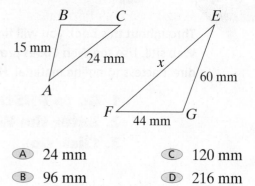

   Ⓐ 24 mm   Ⓒ 120 mm

   Ⓑ 96 mm   Ⓓ 216 mm

7. Amber bought a shirt on sale for $12. The original price was $15. Find the percent of the discount.

   Ⓐ 20%   Ⓒ 27%

   Ⓑ 24%   Ⓓ 30%

8. Trey pays $34.25 for dinner. If he leaves a 15% tip, how much will he spend on dinner and the tip?

   Ⓐ $37.69   Ⓒ $39.08

   Ⓑ $38.94   Ⓓ $39.39

9. Simplify.
   $$(2 \cdot 7 + 2 \cdot 3) - 2(-3 + 3)$$

   Ⓐ 2   Ⓑ 8   Ⓒ 20   Ⓓ 32

10. A mountain climber begins climbing at 1,200 feet above sea level. He climbs 4,000 feet and then descends 900 feet to camp. What is his final elevation above sea level?

    Ⓐ 900 feet   Ⓒ 4,300 feet

    Ⓑ 4,000 feet   Ⓓ 6,100 feet

11. Marco weighs $137\frac{1}{4}$ lb. Carlos weighs $165\frac{2}{3}$ lb. How much more does Carlos weigh than Marco?

    Ⓐ $28\frac{1}{7}$ lb   Ⓒ $32\frac{1}{7}$ lb

    Ⓑ $28\frac{5}{12}$ lb   Ⓓ $32\frac{1}{12}$ lb

12. Gina ran $5\frac{3}{4}$ km on Monday, $6\frac{1}{2}$ km on Tuesday, $5\frac{1}{3}$ km on Wednesday, and $6\frac{4}{5}$ on Thursday. About how many kilometers did Gina run in all?

- (A) 22 km
- (C) 26 km
- (B) 25 km
- (D) 28 km

13. Which word phrase can be modeled by the following algebraic expression?

$$4t - 9$$

- (A) nine less than four times a number
- (B) nine minus the product of four and a number
- (C) the product of a number and four is less than nine
- (D) four less nine times a number

14. Bill's job pays $12.75 per hour. Which algebraic expression represents Bill's pay, in dollars, for working h hours?

- (A) $12.75 + h$
- (C) $12.75h$
- (B) $12.75 - h$
- (D) $\dfrac{h}{12.75}$

15. What is the solution to the following equation?

$$a - 7 = 13$$

- (A) $a = 6$
- (C) $a = 20$
- (B) $a = 7$
- (D) $a = 91$

16. Jill saw 7 more wrens on her bird feeder today than she did yesterday. She saw 11 wrens today. Which equation can you use to find the number of wrens x Jill saw yesterday?

- (A) $x + 7 = 11$
- (B) $x - 7 = 11$
- (C) $x + 11 = 7$
- (D) $x - 11 = 7$

17. Solve the following equation for s.

$$\frac{s}{-36} = 8$$

- (A) -288
- (C) -4.5
- (B) -144
- (D) $-0.\overline{2}$

18. Simplify.

$$2^3 \cdot (9 - 6)^4$$

- (A) 216
- (C) 648
- (B) 324
- (D) 864

19. Which operation do you perform first when simplifying the following expression?

$$10 - 5^2 \div 3 + 2$$

- (A) Raise 5 to the second power.
- (B) Add 3 and 2.
- (C) Subtract 5 from 10.
- (D) Divide 5 by 3.

20. Derek can type approximately 4,800 words in 2 hours 30 minutes. What is his average typing rate?

- (A) 32 words per minute
- (B) 48 words per minute
- (C) 32 words per hour
- (D) 48 words per hour

21. Sonja is shopping for apples. Which rate is equivalent to the lowest unit price for apples?

- (A) $\dfrac{\$.89}{1 \text{ lb}}$
- (C) $\dfrac{\$3.15}{3 \text{ lb}}$
- (B) $\dfrac{\$1.55}{2 \text{ lb}}$
- (D) $\dfrac{\$3.89}{4 \text{ lb}}$

22. In professional baseball, the circular pitcher's mound has a diameter of 18 feet. What is the circumference of the pitcher's mound? Use 3.14 as an approximation for π.

- (A) 28.26 feet
- (C) 44.74 feet
- (B) 32.78 feet
- (D) 56.52 feet

23. Mr. Li placed a birdbath in the middle of his flower garden. The base of the birdbath is a circle. How much area is left in the garden for the flowers? Use 3.14 as an approximation for π.

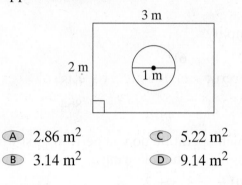

3 m

2 m

1 m

Ⓐ 2.86 m²   Ⓒ 5.22 m²

Ⓑ 3.14 m²   Ⓓ 9.14 m²

24. What is the volume of the box shown below?

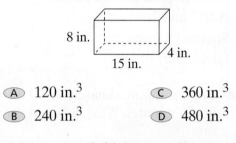

8 in.

4 in.

15 in.

Ⓐ 120 in.³   Ⓒ 360 in.³

Ⓑ 240 in.³   Ⓓ 480 in.³

25. A large can of chicken noodle soup has a height of 5 inches and a diameter of 3 inches. What is the volume of this soup can to the nearest cubic inch? Use 3.14 as an approximation for π.

Ⓐ 35 in.²   Ⓒ 45 in.²

Ⓑ 37 in.²   Ⓓ 47 in.²

26. The smallest angle in a right triangle measures 36°. What is the measure of the second smallest angle in the triangle?

Ⓐ 46°   Ⓒ 52°

Ⓑ 48°   Ⓓ 54°

27. The ramp below is installed at the front door of Lucy's school. What is the value of x?

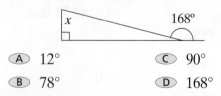

x 168°

Ⓐ 12°   Ⓒ 90°

Ⓑ 78°   Ⓓ 168°

28. What is the mean of the following set of data?

15, 15, 22, 10, 18, 22

Ⓐ 13   Ⓒ 17

Ⓑ 15   Ⓓ 22

29. Listed below are the salaries for the employees in one department of a company.

Salaries

$34,000	$21,500	$89,000
$36,000	$24,000	$24,000
$48,300	$28,000	$39,000
$29,500	$33,500	$32,600
$18,250	$42,700	$49,600

Which salary is most likely to be considered an outlier?

Ⓐ $18,250   Ⓒ $49,000

Ⓑ $32,000   Ⓓ $89,000

30. Alex conducted a survey to find out about his classmates' reading habits. To conduct his survey, he went to the library after school and asked every student there how many hours they read per week. What choice best explains why this a biased sample?

Ⓐ Alex is more likely to run into his friends at the library.

Ⓑ Students at the library after school are likely to read more than those not at the library.

Ⓒ There are also other people at the library besides students.

Ⓓ People may also be doing other things at the library besides reading.

31. Which of the following is a biased question?

    Ⓐ Do you prefer to exercise or to watch television?

    Ⓑ What type of snack do you prefer?

    Ⓒ What is your favorite movie?

    Ⓓ Would you rather listen to boring classical music or upbeat hip-hop?

32. Joanne has four shirts, three pairs of pants, and two belts to choose from. How many different outfits can she make using one shirt, one pair of pants, and one belt?

    Ⓐ 8   Ⓒ 16

    Ⓑ 12   Ⓓ 24

33. The tree diagram below shows the possible outcomes for tossing a coin three times. In the diagram, T represents landing on tails and H represents landing on heads. What is the probability that the coin will land on heads exactly one time?

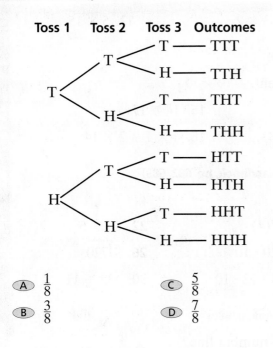

Toss 1   Toss 2   Toss 3 Outcomes

    Ⓐ $\frac{1}{8}$ Ⓒ $\frac{5}{8}$

    Ⓑ $\frac{3}{8}$ Ⓓ $\frac{7}{8}$

34. In a class of 27 students, there are 15 boys and 12 girls. If the teacher randomly selects a student to go to the board to solve a problem, what is the probability that the student chosen is a girl?

    Ⓐ $\frac{3}{5}$ Ⓒ $\frac{5}{9}$

    Ⓑ $\frac{4}{9}$ Ⓓ $\frac{5}{3}$

35. A box contains 8 plain bagels, 6 blueberry bagels, and 4 garlic bagels. Allison likes plain and blueberry bagels, but not garlic bagels. If she takes a bagel at random from the box, what is the probability that she will get a bagel that she likes?

    Ⓐ $\frac{1}{5}$ Ⓒ $\frac{2}{5}$

    Ⓑ $\frac{3}{10}$ Ⓓ $\frac{7}{9}$

36. Each of the letters in the word MENDOCINO is written on a card, and the cards are mixed thoroughly. You draw one card and replace it. You draw a second card. Find the probability that the first card is E and the second card is N.

    Ⓐ $\frac{1}{36}$ Ⓒ $\frac{1}{24}$

    Ⓑ $\frac{1}{3}$ Ⓓ $\frac{4}{9}$

37. There are 6 red marbles and 4 blue marbles in a jar. You remove one marble, and then remove another marble without replacing the first one. What is the probability that you remove 2 red marbles?

    Ⓐ $\frac{2}{15}$ Ⓒ $\frac{9}{25}$

    Ⓑ $\frac{1}{3}$ Ⓓ $\frac{2}{3}$

Algebraic Expressions and Integers

What You've Learned

Solve addition, subtraction, multiplication, and division problems, including those arising in concrete situations, that use positive and negative integers and combinations of these operations. *Grade Six*

Write and evaluate an algebraic expression for a given situation, using up to three variables. *Grade Six*

✓ Check Your Readiness

GO for Help to the Lesson in green.

Multiplying and Dividing Whole Numbers (Skills Handbook, pp. 682, 683)

Find each product or quotient.

1. $7 \div 7$ **2.** $99 \div 9$ **3.** $44 \div 4$ **4.** $57 \div 3$

5. $65 \div 5$ **6.** 5×8 **7.** $68 \div 4$ **8.** 11×4

9. 22×8 **10.** 2×14 **11.** 83×2 **12.** 5×15

Comparing Whole Numbers (Skills Handbook, p. 680)

Compare. Use $>$, $<$, or $=$ to complete each statement.

13. $5 \blacksquare 2$ **14.** $1 \blacksquare 0$ **15.** $14 \blacksquare 17$

16. $6 + 12 \blacksquare 7 + 13$ **17.** $10 - 2 \blacksquare 27 - 18$ **18.** $4 \times 7 \blacksquare 2 \times 14$

Multiplying and Dividing Whole Numbers (Skills Handbook, pp. 682, 683)

Find each product or quotient.

19. $36 \div 3$ **20.** 10×3 **21.** $7(4)$ **22.** $25 \div 5$

23. $12 \cdot 8$ **24.** $7 \overline{)35}$ **25.** $20 \cdot 10$ **26.** $9 \overline{)720}$

27. $124 \div 4$ **28.** $12 \overline{)156}$ **29.** $4 \cdot 12 \cdot 10$ **30.** $132 \div 11$

Reading Numbers on a Number Line (Skills Handbook, p. 680)

What is the distance of each point from zero on the number line?

31. A **32.** B

33. C **34.** D

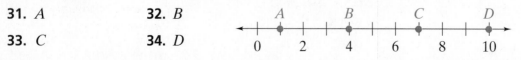

What You'll Learn Next

Add, subtract, multiply, and divide rational numbers.

Understand the meaning of the absolute value of a number; determine the absolute value of real numbers.

Use variable and appropriate operations to write an expression.

▲ You can use integers to describe elevations above and below sea level such as the elevation of Mount Shasta.

New Vocabulary

◄)) **English and Spanish Audio Online**

- **absolute value** (p. 19)
- **additive inverses** (p. 24)
- **algebraic expression** (p. 4)
- **conjecture** (p. 35)
- **coordinate plane** (p. 52)
- **counterexample** (p. 37)
- **deductive reasoning** (p. 57)
- **evaluate** (p. 14)

- **inductive reasoning** (p. 35)
- **integers** (p. 19)
- **Inverse Property of Addition** (p. 24)
- **opposites** (p. 19)
- **order of operations** (p. 8)
- **ordered pair** (p. 52)
- **origin** (p. 52)

- **quadrants** (p. 52)
- **variable** (p. 4)
- **x-axis** (p. 52)
- **x-coordinate** (p. 52)
- **y-axis** (p. 52)
- **y-coordinate** (p. 52)

Academic Vocabulary

- **justify** (p. 57)

Variables and Expressions

Introduce, Develop Use variables and appropriate operations to write an expression.

Introduce Use algebraic terminology (e.g., variable, expression) correctly.

What You'll Learn

- To identify variables, numerical expressions, and algebraic expressions
- To write algebraic expressions for word phrases

. . . And Why

To use the language of algebra to model real-world problems

✓ Check Skills You'll Need

Complete each equation.

1. 1 week = ■ days

2. 1 foot = ■ inches

3. 1 nickel = ■ cents

4. 1 gallon = ■ quarts

5. 1 yard = ■ feet

GO for Help
Table 1, p. 699

◄)) New Vocabulary

- variable
- algebraic expression

Identifying Numerical and Algebraic Expressions

How many miles can you drive on ten gallons of gas? The answer depends on the type of vehicle you drive. The table shows some typical data.

Vehicle Type	Miles	Gallons	Miles per Gallon
Subcompact	330	10	$330 \div 10$
Compact	300	10	$300 \div 10$
Mid-size sedan	245	10	$245 \div 10$
Sport utility vehicle	175	10	$175 \div 10$
Pickup truck	160	10	$160 \div 10$

The last column gives a *numerical expression* for each vehicle's miles per gallon.

If you don't know the number of miles, you can use a *variable* to stand for the number. Then you can write an *algebraic expression* for miles per gallon.

variable → m ← miles on 10 gallons

algebraic expression → $m \div 10$ ← miles per gallon

A **variable** is a letter that stands for a number.

An **algebraic expression** is a mathematical phrase that uses variables, numerals, and operation symbols. Algebraic expressions are sometimes called *variable expressions*.

Online active math

For: Variable Expressions Activity
Use: Interactive Textbook, 1-1

1 EXAMPLE Identifying Expressions

Identify each expression as a *numerical expression* or an *algebraic expression*. If the expression is an algebraic expression, name the variable.

a. $5 - 5$

numerical expression

b. $c - 5$

Algebraic expression; c is the variable.

✅ Quick Check

1. Identify each expression as a *numerical expression* or an *algebraic expression*. For an algebraic expression, name the variable.

  a. $8 \div x$ **b.** 100×6 **c.** $d + 43 - 9$

Writing Algebraic Expressions

You can translate word phrases into algebraic expressions.

Word Phrase	Algebraic Expression
Nine more than a number y	$y + 9$
4 less than a number n	$n - 4$
A number z times three	$z \cdot 3$ or $3z$ or $3(z)$
A number a divided by 12	$a \div 12$ or $\frac{a}{12}$
5 times the quantity 4 plus a number c	$5 \cdot (4 + c)$ or $5(4 + c)$

Vocabulary Tip

You can translate many words for operations into operation symbols.

total	$+$
more than	$+$
increased by	$+$
difference	$-$
fewer than	$-$
less than	$-$
decreased by	$-$
product	$\times$ or $\cdot$ or ( )
times	$\times$ or $\cdot$ or ( )
quotient	$\div$ or —
divided by	$\div$ or —

An algebraic expression is an efficient way to express a mathematical relationship.

2 EXAMPLE   Writing an Algebraic Expression

The maximum speed allowed in a solar car race is 65 mi/h. Write an algebraic expression for the distance a solar car could travel in a given time at an average speed of 65 mi/h.

Words   65   times   number of hours

             Let h = number of hours.

Expression   65   · h

The algebraic expression $65 \cdot h$, or $65h$, describes the distance in miles a solar car could travel in h hours.

✅ Quick Check

2. a. Bagels cost $.50 each. Write an algebraic expression for the cost of b bagels.

  b. **Measurement** Write an algebraic expression for the number of hours in m minutes.

Complete Exercises 1–4 to solve the problem below.

Emily has twice as many sports cards as Jose. Then she buys four more for $2 each. Use the variable x to write an expression for the total number of sports cards Emily has.

1. What given information is *not* needed to write an expression for the total number of cards?

2. What unknown information will the variable represent?

3. What operations should you use to represent the phrases "twice as many sports cards" and "buys four more"?

4. Use the variable x to write an expression for the total number of sports cards Emily has.

Standards Practice

For more exercises, see *Extra Skills and Word Problem Practice.*

A Practice by Example

Example 1
(page 4)

GO for Help

Example 2
(page 5)

Identify each expression as a *numerical expression* or an *algebraic expression*. For an algebraic expression, name the variable.

5. $b + 6$ 6. $80 \div 8$ 7. $14 - n$

8. 14×14 9. $100x$ 10. $8 + 8 + 8 + 8$

Write a variable expression for each word phrase.

11. 16 more than m 12. 4 fewer than j

13. n divided by 3   14. 3 divided by n

15. the product of c and 3   16. 2 less than p

Write a numerical or algebraic expression for each quantity.

17. two dozen eggs   18. d dozen eggs

19. the value in cents of 7 nickels   20. the value in cents of n nickels

B Apply Your Skills

Identify each expression as a *numerical expression* or an *algebraic expression*. For a variable expression, name the variable.

21. $d + 53$ 22. $12 - 7$ 23. $\frac{g}{9}$ 24. $4(5)$

Measurement **Write an expression for each quantity.**

25. the number of days in 4 weeks

26. the number of days in w weeks

27. number of pounds in 160 ounces

28. number of pounds in z ounces

Homework Video Tutor

Visit: PHSchool.com
Web Code: bje-0101

29. Mia has \$20 less than Brandi. Brandi has d dollars. Write an algebraic expression for the amount of money Mia has.

Use the calcium content chart at the left for Exercises 30 and 31.

30. Write an algebraic expression for the number of milligrams of calcium in c cups of ice cream.

31. Write an algebraic expression for the number of milligrams of calcium in m cups of milk and b cups of broccoli.

Calcium Content

Food Item (1 cup)	Calcium (mg)
Milk	300
Yogurt	250
Cheese	150
Ice Cream	200
Broccoli	80

Modeling **In each model, the red line represents a variable expression. Match each model with its expression.**

A. $\frac{x}{4}$ **B.** $4 + x$ **C.** $4x$ **D.** $x - 4$

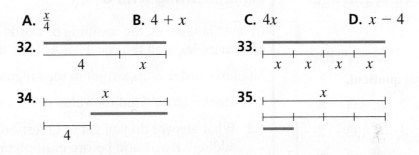

32. _____
  4   x

33. _____
  x x x x

34. _____ x
  |___|
  4

35. _____ x
  |__|

36. Writing in Math How are numerical expressions and algebraic expressions similar? How are they different?

37. Error Analysis A student wrote the variable expression $n - 5$ for the word phrase *n less than five*. Explain the student's error.

C Challenge **38.** There are twice as many sophomores as freshmen. There are $\frac{1}{3}$ more juniors than freshmen. If there are s sophomores, how many juniors are there?

Multiple Choice Practice and Mixed Review

For Standards Tutorials, visit PHSchool.com. Web Code: bjq-9045

39. A natural foods store sells wild rice for \$2.00 per quarter pound. Elizabeth buys p pounds. Which expression should she use to find the total cost of her purchase?

(A) p (B) $2p$ (C) $4p$ (D) $8p$

40. Tim has n nickels and q quarters in his pocket. What is the value in cents of the money in Tim's pocket?

(A) $n + q$ (B) $5n + q$ (C) $5n + 25q$ (D) $n + 25q$

41. Pam is 15 years old. Which expression gives Pam's age p years ago?

(A) $p - 15$ (B) $15 - p$ (C) $p + 15$ (D) $\frac{p}{15}$

GO for Help **Skills Handbook** **Compute.**

42. 9×25 **43.** $3 \times 6 \times 4$ **44.** 8×1

45. $225 \div 3$ **46.** $169 \div 13$ **47.** $25,942 \div 12,971$

The Order of Operations

Introduce Add, subtract, multiply, and divide rational numbers.
Develop Determine when and how to break a problem into simpler parts.
Use the correct order of operations to evaluate algebraic expressions.

What You'll Learn

- To use the order of operations
- To use grouping symbols

. . . And Why

To find the value of an expression with more than one operation

✓ **Check Skills You'll Need**

Find each quotient.

1. $164 \div 2$ 2. $344 \div 8$

3. $284 \div 4$ 4. $133 \div 7$

5. $182 \div 13$ 6. $650 \div 25$

GO for Help
Skills Handbook, p. 683

🔊 **New Vocabulary**

- order of operations

Using the Order of Operations

Standards Investigation
Experimenting With Order

In most languages, the meaning of words depends on their order. For example, "sign the check" is not the same as "check the sign."

Similarly, order is important in the language of mathematics.

1. **Mental Math** Find the value of the expression $3 + 5 \times 2$.

2. What answer do you get to Question 1 if you multiply before adding? If you add before multiplying?

3. **Reasoning** How does the order in which you do the operations affect your answer?

The order in which you perform operations can affect the value of an expression. To avoid confusion, mathematicians have agreed on an **order of operations.** Multiply and divide first. Then add and subtract.

To *simplify* a numerical expression, you use the order of operations and replace the expression with the simplest name for its value.

GO Online

Video Tutor Help
Visit: PHSchool.com
Web Code: bje-0775

---

1 EXAMPLE   **Simplifying Expressions**

Simplify $4 + 15 \div 3$.

$$4 + 15 \div 3$$

$$4 + 5 \qquad \text{First divide.}$$

$$9 \qquad \text{Then add.}$$

✓ **Quick Check**

1. Simplify each expression.

   a. $2 + 5 \times 3$ **b.** $12 \div 3 - 1$ **c.** $10 - 1 \cdot 7$

When operations have the same rank in the order of operations, do them from left to right.

---

2 EXAMPLE Using the Order of Operations

Simplify $3 \cdot 5 - 8 \div 4 + 6$.

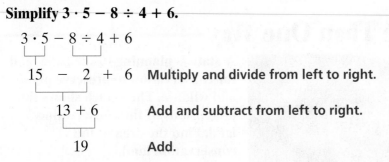

$3 \cdot 5 - 8 \div 4 + 6$

$15 \quad - \quad 2 \quad + \quad 6$ Multiply and divide from left to right.

$13 + 6$ Add and subtract from left to right.

19 Add.

✔ Quick Check

2. Simplify each expression.

    a. $4 - 1 \cdot 2 + 6 \div 3$ **b.** $5 + 6 \cdot 4 \div 3 - 1$

Using Grouping Symbols

Grouping symbols, such as parentheses, ( ), and brackets, [ ], indicate order. A fraction bar also is a grouping symbol, since $\frac{4 + 2}{3} = (4 + 2) \div 3$. Always work inside grouping symbols first.

Take Note **Order of Operations**

1. Work inside grouping symbols.
2. Multiply and divide in order from left to right.
3. Add and subtract in order from left to right.

---

3 EXAMPLE Simplifying With Grouping Symbols

Multiple Choice **Which procedure is correct for simplifying**
$24 \div [6 - (2 \cdot 2)]$**?**

  Ⓐ $24 \div [6 - (2 \cdot 2)] = 4 - 2 \cdot 2 = 4 - 4 = 0$

  Ⓑ $24 \div [6 - (2 \cdot 2)] = 24 \div 4 \cdot 2 = 24 \div 8 = 3$

  Ⓒ $24 \div [6 - (2 \cdot 2)] = 4 - 2 \cdot 2 = 2 \cdot 2 = 4$

  Ⓓ $24 \div [6 - (2 \cdot 2)] = 24 \div (6 - 4) = 24 \div 2 = 12$

Choice D follows the order of operations by working inside the grouping symbols first. Choice D is correct.

✔ Quick Check

3. Simplify the expression $1 + \frac{10 - 2}{4}$.

You can use the order of operations to find the area of an irregular figure by more than one method.

More Than One Way

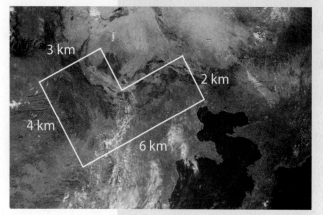

A state is planning to set aside land for conservation to preserve plants and wildlife. The sketch shows the dimensions of the conservation land. Find the area of the conservation land.

Kevin's Method

Divide the figure into rectangles. Then add their areas.

$$\text{Area} = \text{Area} \textcircled{1} + \text{Area} \textcircled{2}$$
$$= 4 \cdot 3 + (6 - 3) \cdot 2$$
$$= 4 \cdot 3 + 3 \cdot 2$$
$$= 12 + 6$$
$$= 18$$

The land's area is 18 km^2.

Tina's Method

Visualize attaching a small rectangle to complete a large rectangle. Then subtract the small area from the large area.

$$\text{Area} = \text{Area of large rectangle} - \text{Area of small rectangle}$$
$$= 6 \cdot 4 - (6 - 3) \cdot (4 - 2)$$
$$= 6 \cdot 4 - 3 \cdot 2$$
$$= 24 - 6$$
$$= 18$$

The land's area is 18 km^2.

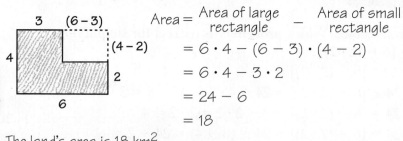

Choose a Method

1. Which method would you use to find the town's area? Explain.

2. Can you think of another way to solve the problem? Explain.

Match each expression with the first step in simplifying the expression.

1. $3(4 + 7) - 5$

2. $3(4) + 7 - 5$

3. $3(4) + (7 - 5)$

4. $3(4 + 7 - 5)$

A. $12 + 7 - 5$

B. $3(11 - 5)$

C. $3(11) - 5$

D. $3(4) + 2$

Standards Practice

For more exercises, see *Extra Skills and Word Problem Practice*.

A Practice by Example

Examples 1 and 2
(pages 8–9)

GO for Help

Example 3
(page 9)

Simplify each expression.

5. $3 + 6 \times 4$

6. $35 \div 7 - 2$

7. $8 - 2 \cdot 3$

8. $12 - 8 \div 2 + 3$

9. $21 \div 7 + 14 \times 2$

10. $2 \cdot 2 + 0 \cdot 4$

11. $7 + 3 \cdot (8 \div 4)$

12. $2(15 - 9) \cdot 9$

13. $[2 + (6 \cdot 8)] - 1$

14. $2(6) + \frac{7 + 8}{3}$

15. $12 \div (3 - 2) + 1$

16. $(21 + 3) \div 4 \div 2$

17. $3(7 + 4)$

18. $6 + \frac{6 + 2}{4}$

19. $\frac{21 + 15}{3 + 6}$

B Apply Your Skills

20. Error Analysis A student found the value of the expression $30 \div 6 - 1$ to be 6. Explain the student's error.

21. Writing in Math Why do we need to agree on an order of operations?

Simplify each expression. Justify each step.

22. $(56 - 5) \div 17$

23. $60 \div 4 + 9$

24. $2[8 + (5 - 3)] - 8$

25. $12 \div 3 \times 4$

26. $36 - 27 \div 9 \div 1$

27. $6(4 + 1) - 5$

GO for Help

For a guide to solving
Exercise 24, see
page 13.

Compare. Use **>, <,** or **=** to complete each statement.

28. $15 \cdot 3 - 2$ ■ $15 \cdot (3 - 2)$

29. $18 - 6 \div 3$ ■ $(18 - 6) \div 3$

30. $12 \div 3 + 9 \cdot 4$ ■ $12 \div (3 + 9) \cdot 4$

31. $(19 - 15) \div (3 + 1)$ ■ $19 - 15 \div 3 + 1$

Insert grouping symbols to make each number sentence true.

32. $7 + 4 \cdot 6 = 66$

33. $7 \cdot 8 - 6 + 3 = 17$

34. $3 + 8 - 2 \cdot 5 = 45$

Homework Video Tutor

Write a numerical expression for each phrase. Then simplify.

35. five added to the product of four and nine

36. twenty-one minus the sum of fifteen and five

37. seventeen minus the quotient of twenty-five and five

38. Multiple Choice Insert grouping symbols to make the number sentence $3 + 8 - 2 \cdot 5 = 45$ correct.

  Ⓐ $(3 + 8) - 2 \cdot 5 = 45$ Ⓒ $[3 + (8 - 2)] \cdot 5 = 45$

  Ⓑ $3 + (8 - 2) \cdot 5 = 45$ Ⓓ $3 + [8 - (2 \cdot 5)] = 45$

39. A part-time employee worked 4 hours on Monday and 7 hours each day for the next 3 days. Write and simplify an expression that shows the total number of hours worked.

Write two expressions you could use to find the area of each shaded figure. Find the area.

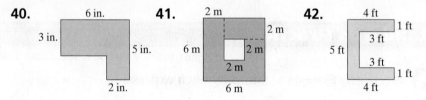

40. **41.** **42.**

43. Open-Ended Write a word problem for the numerical expression $3(4 + 3) + 2$. Then simplify the expression.

Ⓒ Challenge   **44. Number Sense** Use the digits 1–9 in order. Insert operation signs and grouping symbols to get a value of 100.

Multiple Choice Practice and Mixed Review

For Standards Tutorials, visit PHSchool.com. Web Code: bjq-9045

45. Bob pays the phone company $5.00 per month plus $0.05 per minute for every phone call he makes. Which expression can he use to calculate his bill in a month when he uses m minutes?

  Ⓐ $5 + 0.05$ Ⓒ $5 + 0.05m$

  Ⓑ $5m + 0.05$ Ⓓ $(5 \times 0.05)m$

46. A garden is in the shape of a square, with 2 foot-by-2 foot squares removed from each corner. Which expression gives the area of the garden?

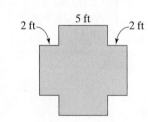

  Ⓐ $4(2 + 5) + 5 \cdot 5$

  Ⓑ $(2 + 5 + 2) \cdot (2 + 5 + 2) - 4(2 \cdot 2)$

  Ⓒ $(2 + 5 + 2) - (2 \cdot 2)$

  Ⓓ $4(2 \cdot 2) + 4(5 \cdot 2) + 5 \cdot 5$

47. Which expression represents the phrase "two more than twelve times a number"?

  Ⓐ $n + 2$ Ⓑ $2n$ Ⓒ $\frac{n}{12} + 2$ Ⓓ $12n + 2$

GO for Help   Lesson 1-1   **Write a variable expression for each word phrase.**

48. the product of a number n and 8

49. k divided by 20

50. six less than a number h

51. the value, in cents, of d dimes

Understanding Math Problems Read the problem below. Then let Daria's thinking guide you through the solution. Check your understanding with the exercises at the bottom of the page.

Simplify $2[8 + (5 - 3)] - 8$.

What Daria Thinks

There are two sets of grouping symbols, square brackets and parentheses: $[8 + (5 - 3)]$.

I need to begin by working inside the innermost grouping symbols, the parentheses: $(5 - 3)$.

Now I need to work inside the next pair of grouping symbols, the square brackets, to find $[8 + 2]$.

Multiply before subtracting.

Now subtract.

The simplified expression is 12.

What Daria Writes

$2[8 + (5 - 3)] - 8$

$2[8 + (2)] - 8$

$2[10] - 8$

$20 - 8$

12

EXERCISES

Simplify each expression.

1. $2[(13 - 4) \div 3]$

2. $1 + \frac{11 - 3}{4}$

3. $3[(8 + 4) \div 6]$

4. $\frac{6 + 9}{3} - 2$

5. $4[3 + (2 \cdot 3)]$

6. $16 \div (8 - 4) - 2$

7. $3(8 - 2) + 12$

8. $2[4(7 - 2) + 3]$

9. $6 - \frac{4 - 10}{2}$

10. $25 \div (15 \div 3) \cdot 2$

11. $\frac{17 - 12}{5} + (4 - 2)$

12. $7(12 \div 3 - 3)$

Writing and Evaluating Expressions

What You'll Learn

- To evaluate algebraic expressions
- To solve problems by evaluating expressions

...And Why

To solve real-world problems involving packaging and shopping

✓ **Check Skills You'll Need**

Simplify each expression.

1. $6(9 + 1)$

2. $17 - 2 + 3$

3. $9 + 8 \cdot 2 + 4$

4. $[3(5) + 1] \cdot 2$

GO **for Help**
Lesson 1-2

🔊 **New Vocabulary**

- evaluate

Develop Use variables and appropriate operations to write an expression.

Introduce Use the correct order of operations to evaluate algebraic expressions.

Evaluating Algebraic Expressions

To **evaluate** an algebraic expression, you first replace each variable with a number. Then, you use the order of operations to simplify.

1 EXAMPLE Evaluating an Expression

Evaluate $4y - 15$ for $y = 9$.

$$
\begin{aligned}
4y - 15 &= 4(9) - 15 && \text{Replace } y \text{ with 9.} \\
&= 36 - 15 && \text{Multiply.} \\
&= 21 && \text{Subtract.}
\end{aligned}
$$

✓ **Quick Check**

1. Evaluate each expression.

    a. $63 - 5x$, for $x = 7$ **b.** $4(t + 3) + 1$, for $t = 8$

Sometimes expressions have more than one variable.

2 EXAMPLE Replacing More Than One Variable

Evaluate $3ab + \dfrac{c}{2}$ for $a = 2$, $b = 5$, and $c = 10$.

$$
\begin{aligned}
3ab + \frac{c}{2} &= 3 \cdot 2 \cdot 5 + \frac{10}{2} && \text{Replace the variables.} \\
&= 3 \cdot 2 \cdot 5 + 5 && \text{Work within grouping symbols.} \\
&= 6 \cdot 5 + 5 && \text{Multiply from left to right.} \\
&= 30 + 5 && \text{Multiply.} \\
&= 35 && \text{Add.}
\end{aligned}
$$

✓ **Quick Check**

2. Evaluate each expression.

    a. $6(g + h)$, for $g = 8$ and $h = 7$

    b. $2xy - z$, for $x = 4$, $y = 3$, and $z = 1$

    c. $\dfrac{r + s}{2}$, for $r = 13$ and $s = 11$

Solving Problems by Evaluating Expressions

You can write and evaluate algebraic expressions to solve problems.

3 EXAMPLE Evaluating an Expression

Eggs can come in cartons of 18 eggs.
a. Write an algebraic expression for the number of cartons a restaurant should order to get *e* eggs.
b. Evaluate the expression for 108 eggs.

Eggs are often sold in cartons of 6, 12 or 18.

a. *e* **eggs**

$\frac{e}{18}$ ← eggs wanted
← number in carton

b. **108 eggs**

$\frac{e}{18} = \frac{108}{18}$ Evaluate for e = 108.

$= 6$ Divide.

The restaurant should order six cartons to get 108 eggs.

✓ Quick Check

3. A store pays $29 for a case of drinks. Write an algebraic expression for the cost of *c* cases. Find the cost of five cases.

4 EXAMPLE Evaluating an Expression

An online music store charges $14 for each CD. Shipping costs $6 per order. Write an algebraic expression for the cost of ordering CDs. Find the cost of ordering eight CDs.

Table

Number of CDs	Cost of CDs	Shipping ($)	Total Cost ($)
1	$1 \cdot 14$	6	$1 \cdot 14 + 6 = 20$
2	$2 \cdot 14$	6	$2 \cdot 14 + 6 = 34$
4	$4 \cdot 14$	6	$4 \cdot 14 + 6 = 62$

Let *n* = number of CDs.

Expression   14   ·   *n*   +   6

Evaluate the expression for *n* = 8.

$14 \cdot n + 6 = 14 \cdot 8 + 6$ **Replace n with 8.**

$= 112 + 6 = 118$ **Multiply. Then add.**

It costs $118 to order eight CDs.

Problem Solving Tip

In Example 4, the phrase *for each* implies multiplication. So *$14 for each CD* means "$14 times the number of CDs."

✓ Quick Check

4. Find the cost of ordering ten CDs.

The steps for simplifying an expression are shown. Justify each step by stating the applicable part of the order of operations.

$$10 - (15 - 3) \div 4 \cdot 2 + 2$$

1. $10 - 12 \div 4 \cdot 2 + 2$ _?_

2. $10 - 3 \cdot 2 + 2$ _?_

3. $10 - 6 + 2$ _?_

4. $4 + 2$ _?_

5. 6 _?_

Standards Practice

For more exercises, see *Extra Skills and Word Problem Practice.*

A **Practice by Example**

Example 1 (page 14)

GO **for Help**

Evaluate each expression.

6. $7b$, for $b = 5$ **7.** $5 - c$, for $c = 3$ **8.** $x \div 8$, for $x = 40$

9. $3n + 2$, for $n = 7$ **10.** $41 - 4h$, for $h = 10$ **11.** $5a + 7$, for $a = 20$

Example 2 (page 14)

Evaluate each expression for $x = 2$, $y = 3$, and $z = 10$.

12. xyz **13.** $8y \div x$ **14.** $\frac{z}{5} + 2$ **15.** $4y - x$

16. $2z + xy$ **17.** $\frac{9 + y}{x}$ **18.** $4xy - z$ **19.** $5(y + z)$

Examples 3 and 4 (page 15)

20. An office assistant types 55 words per minute.
  a. Write an algebraic expression for the number of words the office assistant types in m minutes.
  b. Evaluate the expression for 20 minutes.

B **Apply Your Skills**

Evaluate each expression.

21. $2a + 5$, for $a = 5$ **22.** $105z$, for $z = 7$

23. $6 \div a + 8$, for $a = 2$ **24.** $19 - (a - 4)$, for $a = 8$

25. $13ab$, for $a = 1$ and $b = 7$ **26.** $16 - 4mn$, for $m = 0$ and $n = 3$

27. $j(5 + k)$, for $j = 11$ and $k = 4$ **28.** rst, for $r = 5$, $s = 5$, and $t = 5$

29. $\frac{150}{z + y}$, for $y = 25$ and $z = 50$ **30.** $\frac{x - y}{4}$, for $x = 52$ and $y = 12$

Homework Video Tutor

Visit: PHSchool.com
Web Code: bje-0103

31. Data Analysis Use the chart to find how many calories a 100-lb person uses in an hour of moderate walking.
  a. Write an expression for the number of calories a 100-lb person uses in moderate walking for w hours.
  b. Evaluate the expression to find the number of calories a 100-lb person uses in moderate walking for 2 hours.

Calories per Hour Used by a 100-lb Walker

Type of Walking	Calories
Slow	110
Moderate	153
Brisk	175
Racing	295

SOURCE: www.nutristrategy.com

By *porpoising* (jumping clear of the water), dolphins can travel as fast as 26 km/h.

32. Write an expression for the number of kilometers a dolphin travels in *d* hours swimming at 8 km/h. Then find the number of kilometers the dolphin travels in 3 hours.

33. Error Analysis Your friend evaluates $(10 - k) \div 5$ for $k = 5$ and gets 9 for an answer. Explain your friend's error.

Evaluate each expression for $a = 3$ and $b = 4.2$.

34. $4a - b + \dfrac{b}{2}$

35. $\dfrac{a}{6} + 3a - \dfrac{b}{7}$

36. $b(10 + a)$

37. $(2b + 0.6) - 3a$

38. A fitness club requires a $100 initiation fee and dues of $25 each month. Write an expression for the cost of membership for *n* months. Then find the cost of membership for one year.

39. Writing in Math Write a word problem that could be solved by evaluating the expression $3x - 5$ for $x = 5$.

 Challenge

40. A carnival charges $5 for admission plus $2 per ride.
a. Write an expression for the cost of admission plus *r* rides.
b. How many rides can you afford if you have $15 to spend?

Multiple Choice Practice and Mixed Review

For Standards Tutorials, visit PHSchool.com. Web Code: bjq-9045

Every minute, about 145 babies are born in the world. Use this information for Exercises 41–43.

41. Which expression shows how many babies are born in the world in *m* minutes?
Ⓐ 60*m*
Ⓒ 60*m* + 145
Ⓑ 145*m* + 60
Ⓓ 145*m*

42. About how many babies are born in the world in 6 minutes?
Ⓐ 360 babies
Ⓒ 870 babies
Ⓑ 505 babies
Ⓓ 930 babies

43. About how many babies are born in the world in one day?
Ⓐ 3,480 babies
Ⓒ 104,400 babies
Ⓑ 86,400 babies
Ⓓ 208,800 babies

 Lesson 1-1

Write a variable expression for each word phrase.

44. *t* fewer than 19

45. *d* divided by 20

Lesson 1-2 **46. Error Analysis** Valerie has test grades of 96, 82, 78, and 76. Using a calculator, she found her average grade to be 275. Is Valerie's answer reasonable? Explain Valerie's error.

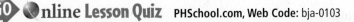

1-4 Integers and Absolute Value

Develop, Master Understand the meaning of the absolute value of a number; interpret the absolute value as the distance of the number from zero on a number line; and determine the absolute value of real numbers.

Develop Use a variety of methods, such as diagrams, to explain mathematical reasoning.

What You'll Learn

- To graph and order integers
- To find opposites and absolute values

. . . And Why

To represent real-world quantities that are less than zero, such as temperatures and scores

✓ **Check Skills You'll Need**

Write an expression for each description.

1. three less than *m*

2. 8 divided by 2

3. 8 plus seven

GO for Help

Lesson 1-1

◀)) **New Vocabulary**

- opposites
- integers
- absolute value

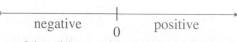
Comparing Integers

Antifreeze is mixed with the water in a car's radiator to prevent the water from freezing. Pure water freezes at about 32 degrees Fahrenheit (°F) *above* zero. A mixture of equal parts water and antifreeze freezes at about 32 degrees *below* zero.

Freezing Points

Substance	Freezing Temperature (°F)
Water	32
Antifreeze and water	−32
Seawater	28
Gasoline	−36

You can write 32 degrees above zero as +32°F or 32°F. You can write 32 degrees below zero as −32°F. Read the numbers 32 and −32 as "*positive* 32" and "*negative* 32," respectively.

A number line helps you compare numbers and arrange them in order.

Numbers increase in value from left to right.

negative   0   positive

0 is neither positive nor negative.

To compare and order numbers, you can use symbols for "is less than" (<), "is less than or equal to" (≤), "is greater than" (>), and "is greater than or equal to" (≥).

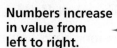
1 EXAMPLE Graphing on a Number Line

Three friends score −1, 4, and −5 in a game of miniature golf. Compare the scores and order them from least to greatest.

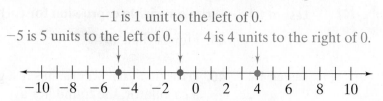

−1 is 1 unit to the left of 0.
−5 is 5 units to the left of 0.   4 is 4 units to the right of 0.

−5 is to the left of −1, and −1 is to the left of 4, so $-5 < -1 < 4$. From least to greatest, the scores are −5, −1, 4.

✅ Quick Check

1. Graph 0, 2, and −6. Compare the numbers and order the numbers from least to greatest.

Finding Absolute Value

Numbers that are the same distance from zero on a number line but in opposite directions are called **opposites.**

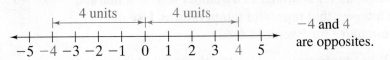

−4 and 4 are opposites.

Vocabulary Tip

Recall: The <u>whole numbers</u>, 0, 1, 2, 3, 4, . . . , are the counting numbers and zero.

Integers are the whole numbers and their opposites. A number's distance from zero on the number line is called its **absolute value.** You write *the absolute value of 3* as $|3|$. Two numbers *a* and *b* are close to each other if $|a - b|$ is small.

2 EXAMPLE **Finding Absolute Value**

Use a number line to find $|-3|$ and $|3|$.

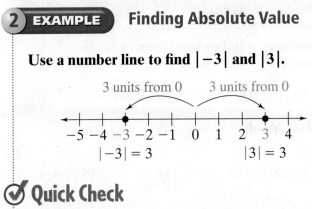

$|-3| = 3$ $|3| = 3$

✅ Quick Check

2. Write $|-10|$ in words. Then find $|-10|$.

Treat absolute value symbols as grouping symbols when using the order of operations.

3 EXAMPLE **Simplifying an Expression**

Simplify $14 - |9 + 4|$.

$14 - |9 + 4| = 14 - |13|$ **Work within grouping symbols.**

$= 14 - 13$ **Find the absolute value.**

$= 1$ **Simplify.**

✅ Quick Check

3. Simplify $5|-4|$.

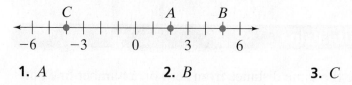
Write the number represented by each point on the number line.

```
        C           A       B
←—+—+—•—+—+—+—+—•—+—+—•—+—→
  -6   -3    0    3    6
```

1. *A*   **2.** *B*   **3.** *C*

A thermometer is similar to a number line. It is marked
with integers that represent temperatures. Use the
thermometer for Exercises 4–6.

4. What temperature does the thermometer model?

5. Which temperature is warmer: 5°C or −5°C?

6. Which integer is greater: 5 or −5?

—5°C

—0

—−5°C

For more exercises, see Extra Skills and Word Problem Practice.

A **Practice by Example**

Example 1
(page 18)

GO for Help

**Graph each set of numbers on a number line. Then order the
numbers from least to greatest.**

7. −2, 8, −9   **8.** −3, −12, −9   **9.** 0, 6, −6

Examples 2 and 3
(page 19)

**Use a number line to find the absolute values of the integers in
each pair.**

10. 1, −1 **11.** −2, 2 **12.** −8, 8 **13.** −7, 7 **14.** 6, −6 **15.** −4, 4

Simplify each expression.

16. $|18|$ **17.** $|-3|$

18. $|-6| + 2 \cdot 7$ **19.** $|10 + 9| - 2$

B **Apply Your Skills**

Open-Ended **Describe a quantity each integer could represent.**

20. −1,000   **21.** 28   **22.** −126

Write the integer represented by each point.

```
      D             B       C       A
←—+—•—+—+—+—+—•—+—+—•—+—+—•—+—→
      -5        0        5
```

23. *A*   **24.** *B*   **25.** *C*   **26.** *D*

Simplify each expression.

27. $|0|$ **28.** $|-1,000|$ **29.** $-|-13|$

30. $|-56|$ **31.** $-|-23|$ **32.** $-|12|$

Compare. Use >, <, or = to complete each statement.

33. $-8 \blacksquare 0$ **34.** $4 \blacksquare -25$ **35.** $-9 \blacksquare -2$

36. $|-1| \blacksquare |50|$ **37.** $|-6| \blacksquare |-12|$ **38.** $|10| \blacksquare |-10|$

39. $|-2| + 4 \blacksquare 6$ **40.** $5 \blacksquare -|-6|$ **41.** $|-8| \blacksquare -|-8|$

Write an expression to represent each quantity.

42. a loss of $\frac{1}{3}$ of an investment of d dollars

43. n degrees Fahrenheit above $r°$F room temperature

Read the passage below before doing Exercises 44 and 45.

Finding Famous Ships

Scientist-explorer Robert D. Ballard led the expeditions that found two famous ships deep in the North Atlantic Ocean.

In 1912, the luxury passenger liner *Titanic* struck an iceberg. It came to rest 12,500 ft below sea level. *Titanic* was 882 ft long and 92 ft wide.

In 1941, the mighty warship *Bismarck* sank in battle. *Bismarck* was 823 ft long and 118 ft wide.

Star Hercules, only 269 ft long, towed the underwater camera sled that found *Bismarck* under 15,617 ft of water.

44. Write integers to represent the positions of *Titanic* and *Bismarck*.

45. A friend says that *Bismarck*'s resting place is higher than *Titanic*'s since 15,617 is higher than 12,500. Explain your friend's error.

Complete each sentence with a word that makes it true.

46. An integer is negative, positive, or ? .

47. The opposite of a ? number is negative.

48. The absolute value of an integer is never ? .

Record Low Temperatures for Three States

State	Temperature (°C)
California	−45
Nevada	−50
Georgia	−17

SOURCE: *U.S. National Climatic Data Center*

49. a. Data Analysis Use a number line to graph the data at the left. Label each temperature with the name of the state.
   b. Which state recorded the lowest temperature?

50. Writing in Math How can you use integers to describe elevations above and below sea level?

51. Reasoning Explain why $|x + y|$ and $|x| + |y|$ are not the same. Give examples to show that $|x + y| = |x| + |y|$ for some values of x and y, and $|x + y| \neq |x| + |y|$ for other values of x and y.

Challenge

Open-Ended Name two consecutive integers between the given integers.

52. $-6, 2$ **53.** $0, -4$ **54.** $-8, -12$

For Standards Tutorials, visit PHSchool.com. Web Code: bjq-9045

55. Which expression has the value -90?

  Ⓐ $|-90|$ Ⓑ 90 Ⓒ $|90|$ Ⓓ $-|90|$

56. A gift shop owner uses the expression $15m - 50$ to calculate the profit, in dollars, from selling m mugs. What is the profit from selling 45 mugs?

  Ⓐ $75   Ⓒ $625
  Ⓑ $525   Ⓓ $675

57. Complete $6 + 8 \div 2 \blacksquare 4 + 5$.

  Ⓐ $<$ Ⓑ $>$ Ⓒ $=$ Ⓓ $\leq$

58. A sign in a shoe store reads, Buy 2 pairs, get the third pair at half price. A customer bought 3 pairs, each originally marked $36. Which expression cannot be used to find the total cost?

  Ⓐ $3 \cdot 36 \div 2$ Ⓒ $36 + 36 + 36 \div 2$
  Ⓑ $(36 + 36) + (36 \div 2)$ Ⓓ $2 \cdot 36 + 36 \div 2$

GO for Help

Lesson 1-3

Evaluate each expression.

59. $p - 5$, for $p = 19$ **60.** $3d + 3$, for $d = 7$ **61.** $55y$, for $y = 8$

Lesson 1-2

Compare. Use >, <, or = to complete each statement.

62. $5 + 10 \div 5 \blacksquare (5 + 10) \div 5$

63. $(9 - 6) \div (2 + 1) \blacksquare 9 - 6 \div 2 + 1$

Lesson 1-1

64. Suppose you have c CDs. Your friend has 6 more CDs than you do. Write an expression for the number of CDs your friend has.

✓ Checkpoint Quiz 1

Write a variable expression for each word phrase.

  1. 23 more than f **2.** g divided by 34   **3.** product of 9 and p

Simplify each expression.

  4. $17 + 16 - 13$ **5.** $70 \div [5(3 + 4)]$ **6.** $9 \times 6 \div 3 + 1$

Evaluate each expression for $x = 4$, $y = 6$, and $z = 12$.

  7. $2x - 8$ **8.** $3(z + y)$ **9.** $4y - z + \frac{z}{x}$

10. On Monday, the average temperature was $-10°F$. On Tuesday, it was $-15°F$. On Wednesday, it was $-13°F$. On Thursday, it was $0°F$.
  a. Graph the temperatures on a number line.
  b. Write the days in order from coldest to warmest.

Modeling Integers

> **Develop** Use a variety of methods, such as models, to explain mathematical reasoning.
> Add and subtract rational numbers (integers).

You can use models to represent integers.
Use ▢ to represent a positive integer.
Use ▣ to represent a negative integer.

1 ACTIVITY

Use models to represent the integers 3, −1, and −4.

▢▢▢ 3   ▣ −1   ▣▣▣▣ −4

An equal number of yellow squares and red squares combine to make zero.

This is a *zero pair.* ⟶ ▢▣ represents zero, or ▢ + ▣ = 0.

You can remove zero pairs to simplify integer models.

2 ACTIVITY

Write the integer that is represented by ▣▣▣▣▣▢▢.

▣▣▣▣▣▢▢

▣▣▣▣▣
▢▢

Group the zero pairs.
Then remove them.

▣▣▣ −3

Write the integer that the simplified model represents.

EXERCISES

Draw a model of each integer.

1. −3   **2.** 5   **3.** −2   **4.** 7

5. 0   **6.** −6   **7.** 2   **8.** −8

Write an integer for each model.

9. ▢▢

10. ▣▣▣▣▣▣

11. ▣▣

12. ▢▢▢▢▢▢

13. ▣▣▢
      ▢▣▣

14. ▣▣▣▢▢
      ▢

15. ▢▣▢▢▢
      ▢▣▣

16. ▣▣▢▢▢▣▣

17. a. Describe how you would model the integers −15 and 25.
   b. Reasoning Suppose you combine the models from part (a). How many zero pairs could you make? How many squares would be left after you removed the zero pairs?

Adding Integers

Introduce Add rational numbers (integers).

Introduce Simplify numerical expressions by applying properties of rational numbers and justify the process used.

Develop Use a variety of methods, such as models, to explain mathematical reasoning.

What You'll Learn

- To use models to add integers
- To use rules to add integers

. . . And Why

To use integers to solve real-world problems in Earth Science

✓ Check Skills You'll Need

Compare. Use $>$, $<$, or $=$ to complete each statement.

1. -6 ■ -3

2. 2 ■ -15

3. -5 ■ $|5|$

4. $|10|$ ■ $|-10|$

5. $|9|$ ■ $|-2|$

6. $|-8|$ ■ $|0|$

 for Help

Lesson 1-4

◄)) New Vocabulary

- additive inverses
- Inverse Property of Addition

Using Models to Add Integers

If a car goes forward 20 ft and then backs up 20 ft, it ends where it started. Using opposite integers, you can represent this situation as $20 + (-20) = 0$.

When you add opposites, the sum is zero. So, opposites are also called **additive inverses**.

Take Note   Inverse Property of Addition

The sum of an integer and its additive inverse is zero.

Arithmetic	Algebra
$1 + (-1) = 0$	$x + (-x) = 0$
$-1 + 1 = 0$	$-x + x = 0$

You can model the addition of integers. One positive unit and one negative unit combine to make a zero pair since ■ + ■ = 0.

To model addition, group the zero pairs that can be removed. Write the integer that the simplified model represents.

1 EXAMPLE   Using Models to Add Integers

Use models to find $2 + (-5)$.

$2 + (-5)$ ■■ + ■■■ ■■   Model the sum.

-3 ■■ ■■■ ■   Group and remove zero pairs. Write the integer that the simplified model represents.

$2 + (-5) = -3$

✓ Quick Check

1. Draw a model and find each sum.
   a. $-1 + 4$ b. $7 + (-3)$ c. $-2 + (-2)$

A number line is another model that you can use to add integers, as shown in Example 2.

GO **O**nline

Video Tutor Help
Visit: PHSchool.com
Web Code: bje-0775

2 EXAMPLE Using a Number Line

On two plays, a football team first loses 8 yd and then gains 3 yd. Find −8 + 3 to find the result of the two plays.

Start at 0. To represent −8, move left 8 units. To add positive 3, move right 3 units to −5.

$-8 + 3 = -5$

The result of the two plays is a loss of 5 yd.

✓ Quick Check

2. Use a number line to find each sum.

   a. $2 + (-6)$ **b.** $-4 + 9$ **c.** $-5 + (-1)$

Using Rules to Add Integers

You can also use rules to find the sum of two integers.

Take Note Adding Integers

Same Sign The sum of two positive integers is positive. The sum of two negative integers is negative.

Different Signs To add two integers with different signs, find the difference of their absolute values. The sum has the sign of the integer with the greater absolute value.

3 EXAMPLE Applying Rules to Add Integers

Find each sum.

a. −12 + (−31)

   $-12 + (-31) = -43$ Since both integers are negative, the sum is negative.

b. 7 + (−18)

   $|-18| - |7| = 18 - 7$ Find the difference of the absolute values.

            $= 11$ Simplify.

   $7 + (-18) = -11$ Since −18 has the greater absolute value, the sum is negative.

✓ Quick Check

3. Find each sum.

    a. $-22 + (-16)$ **b.** $60 + (-13)$ **c.** $-125 + 35$

4 EXAMPLE Adding Integers

A worldwide network of monitors keeps track of earthquake activity.

Earth Science The earthquake monitor in Hockley, Texas, is located in a salt mine at an elevation of -416 m. The elevation of a monitor in Parkfield, California, is 1,580 m higher than the one in Hockley. Find the elevation of the monitor in Parkfield.

$-416 + 1,580$	Write an expression.
$\|1,580\| - \|-416\| = 1,580 - 416$	Find the difference of the absolute values.
$= 1,164$	Simplify.
$-416 + 1,580 = 1,164$	Since 1,580 has the greater absolute value, the sum is positive.

The elevation of the monitor in Parkfield is 1,164 m.

✓ Quick Check

4. The elevation of a monitor in Piñon Flat, California, is 1,696 m higher than the monitor in Hockley, Texas. Find the elevation of the monitor in Piñon Flat.

To add several integers, use the order of operations.

5 EXAMPLE Using the Order of Operations

Find $-12 + (-6) + 15 + (-2)$.

$-12 + (-6) + 15 + (-2)$	Add from left to right.
$-18 \quad + \quad 15 + (-2)$	The sum of two negative integers is negative.
$-3 \quad + \quad (-2)$	$\|-18\| - \|15\| = 3$. Since -18 has the greater absolute value, the sum is negative.
-5	The sum of two negative integers is negative.

$-12 + (-6) + 15 + (-2) = -5$

✓ Quick Check

5. Find each sum.

    a. $1 + (-3) + 2 + (-10)$ **b.** $-250 + 200 + (-100) + 220$

Match each integer with its additive inverse.

1. 3

2. −3

3. |−2|

4. −2

5. 0

A. −2
B. 0
C. −3
D. 2
E. 3

Mental Math Without adding, determine whether each sum is a positive or negative integer.

6. $-10 + (-2)$ **7.** $5 + (-3)$ **8.** $9 + (-15)$

For more exercises, see *Extra Skills and Word Problem Practice.*

A Practice by Example

Examples 1 and 2
(pages 24 and 25)

GO for Help

Modeling Write an expression for each model. Find the sum.

9. ■ ■ ■ ■ +
■ ■ ■ ■ ■ ■

10. ■ ■ ■ ■ ■ + ■ ■

11.

12.

Draw a model and find each sum.

13. $2 + (-5)$ **14.** $-5 + 2$ **15.** $5 + (-2)$ **16.** $-5 + (-2)$

Example 3
(page 25)

Find each sum.

17. $14 + (-11)$ **18.** $0 + (-9)$ **19.** $-6 + (-7)$

20. $-18 + 4$ **21.** $-40 + 93$ **22.** $-26 + (-39)$

Example 4
(page 26)

23. Geography The highest peak at Mt. Ellsworth in Montana is 3,275 m lower than the highest peak of Mt. Kilimanjaro in Kenya, at 5,895 m. Find the elevation of the highest peak at Mt. Ellsworth.

Example 5
(page 26)

Find each sum.

24. $19 + (-9) + 45 + (-32)$ **25.** $-3 + 2 + (-7) + 7 + 13$

26. $-94 + 68 + (-22) + (-13)$ **27.** $-20 + (-89) + 112 + 9$

B Apply Your Skills

Compare. Use >, <, or = to complete each statement.

28. $-6 + 1 \blacksquare 5 + 1$ **29.** $0 + 3 \blacksquare -2 + 0$

30. $49 + (-21) \blacksquare |-18|$ **31.** $|-20| + (-7) \blacksquare -11 + (-11)$

Mental Math **Find each sum.**

32. $-5 + 20$ **33.** $9 + (-9)$ **34.** $10 + (-3)$ **35.** $-5 + 5 + 16$

Reasoning **Without adding, tell whether each sum is positive, negative, or zero. Explain how you found your answer.**

36. $-4 + (-10)$ **37.** $11 + (-3)$ **38.** $6 + (-6)$ **39.** $-4 + (-2)$

Evaluate each expression for $n = -15$.

40. $n + (-7) - n$ **41.** $15 + n + (-8)$ **42.** $n + (-15) + n$

Write a numerical expression. Then find the sum.

43. You borrow $20, and then pay back $18.

44. You save $200, and then spend $75.

45. A man deposits $120, and then writes a check for $25.

46. A submarine at 35 ft below sea level moves up 10 ft.

Use the order of operations to find each sum.

47. $4 + (-6) + 3$ **48.** $-72 + 36 + (-6) + (-18)$

49. Maria had $123. She spent $35, loaned $20 to a friend, and received her $90 paycheck. How much does she have now?

50. **Error Analysis** A friend says that the value of $-17 + 5$ is -22. Explain how your friend may have made this error.

51. **Writing in Math** A friend is having trouble finding the sum of -84 and 28. What explanation would you give to help your friend?

Reasoning **For Exercises 54–57, use the number line and tell whether the value of each expression is positive or negative.**

<!-- number line with points a, b, 0, c -->

$$a \qquad\qquad b \quad 0 \qquad\qquad c$$

52. $a + b$ **53.** $b + c$ **54.** $a + a$ **55.** $|a + b + c|$

C **Challenge**   **56.** Is $a + |-b| = a + b$ true *sometimes*, *always*, or *never*? Explain.

Multiple Choice Practice and Mixed Review

For Standards Tutorials, visit PHSchool.com. Web Code: bjq-9045

57. Which is an example of the Inverse Property of Addition?

     A $xy = yx$ **C** $x + y = y + x$

     B $x[y + (-y)] = x(0)$ **D** $x\left(\dfrac{y}{y}\right) = x(1)$

58. Refer to the map at the right. The lowest temperature recorded in South America is 54 degrees higher than the lowest temperature recorded in North America. What is the lowest temperature recorded in South America?

Ⓐ $-135°F$ Ⓒ $-17°F$

Ⓑ $-27°F$ Ⓓ $-138°F$

Lowest Recorded Temperatures

North America $-81°F$

Europe $-67°F$

Africa $-11°F$

South America ■°F

Source: *The World Almanac*

59. Jason plans to save $15 each week. Which expression shows how much he will have saved after w weeks?

Ⓐ $15 - w$ Ⓒ $w + 15$

Ⓑ $15w$ Ⓓ $\frac{15}{w}$

GO for Help   Lesson 1-4

Compare. Use >, <, or = to complete each statement.

60. -90 ■ -6

61. -2 ■ -7

62. $|-15|$ ■ -15

Mathematical Reasoning

Develop Test conjectures using inductive and deductive reasoning.

Sometimes, Always, Never

Some mathematical statements, such as "the sum of two positive integers is positive" are always true. Sometimes a mathematical statement is true only under certain conditions. You use reasoning to decide whether statements are *sometimes*, *always*, or *never* true.

EXAMPLE

Decide whether the statement is *sometimes*, *always*, or *never* true:
The expression $-|a| + a$ is equal to 0 for all values of a.

Test values of a to see whether the statement is true. Start with a positive integer and a negative integer.

For $a = 1$, $-|1| + 1 = 0$. The statement is true.

For $a = -1$, $-|-1| + (-1) = -2$. The statement is false.

Because the statement is false for $a = -1$, you can conclude that the statement is only *sometimes* true.

EXERCISES

1. Decide whether the statement is *sometimes*, *always*, or *never* true: The perimeter of a square with side length a is less than the perimeter of a rectangle with side lengths a and b.

1-6 Subtracting Integers

Introduce Subtract rational numbers (integers).

Develop Use a variety of methods, such as models, to explain mathematical reasoning.

What You'll Learn

• To use models to subtract integers

• To use a rule to subtract integers

. . . And Why

To use integers to solve real-world problems involving weather

✓ Check Skills You'll Need

Find each sum.

1. $8 + (-9)$

2. $-11 + (-18)$

3. $-4 + (-6)$

4. $14 + (-3)$

5. $6 + (-6)$

6. $-13 + (-10)$

GO for Help
Lesson 1-5

Using Models to Subtract Integers

You can use models to help you understand subtraction of integers.

1 EXAMPLE   Using Models to Subtract Integers

Find $-6 - (-2)$.

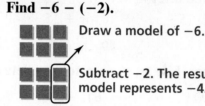

Draw a model of -6.

Subtract -2. The resulting model represents -4.

$$-6 - (-2) = -4$$

✓ Quick Check

1. Use models to find each difference.

   a. $-7 - (-2)$ **b.** $-4 - (-3)$ **c.** $-8 - (-5)$

You can use a number line to subtract a larger integer from a smaller integer.

2 EXAMPLE   Using a Number Line to Subtract Integers

Find $3 - 5$.

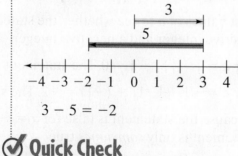

Start at 0. To represent 3, move right 3 units. To subtract 5, move left 5 units to -2.

$$3 - 5 = -2$$

✓ Quick Check

2. Use a number line to find each difference.

   a. $4 - 8$ **b.** $-1 - 5$ **c.** $-2 - (-7)$

Using a Rule to Subtract Integers

You can use models to show the relationship between adding and subtracting integers.

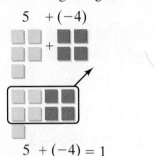

$5 + (-4)$

$5 + (-4) = 1$

$5 - 4$

$5 - 4 = 1$

Both $5 + (-4)$ and $5 - 4$ equal 1. So, $5 + (-4) = 5 - 4$.

Online
active math

For: Integers Activity
Use: Interactive Textbook, 1-6

The models suggest the following rule for subtracting integers.

Take Note   **Subtracting Integers**

To subtract an integer, add its opposite.

Arithmetic	Algebra
$2 - 5 = 2 + (-5) = -3$	$a - b = a + (-b)$
$2 - (-5) = 2 + 5 = 7$	$a - (-b) = a + b$

---

3 **EXAMPLE**   **Using a Rule to Subtract Integers**

In January, 1916, the temperature in Browning, Montana, dropped 100 degrees overnight. The initial temperature was 44°F. What was the final temperature?

$44 - 100$ Write an expression.

$44 - 100 = 44 + (-100)$ To subtract 100, add its opposite.

$\qquad\quad = -56$ Simplify.

The final temperature was -56°F.

✓ Quick Check

3. Find each difference.
   a. $32 - (-3)$ **b.** $-40 - 66$ **c.** $2 - 48$
   d. The lowest temperature ever recorded on the moon was about -170°C. The lowest temperature ever recorded in Antarctica was -89°C. Find the difference in the temperatures.

The lowest temperature ever recorded on Earth was -129°F (-89°C) in Vostok, Antarctica. Scientists there are taking ice-core samples to depths of $-3,600$ m.

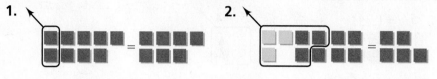

Check Your Understanding

Write a number sentence for each model.

1.

2.

Rewrite each expression using only addition.

3. $6 - 4$ **4.** $-5 - (-10)$ **5.** $14 - (-2)$

6. $20 - 4 + 7$ **7.** $1 - 18 - (-3)$ **8.** $-2 + (-3) - 5$

Standards Practice

For more exercises, see *Extra Skills and Word Problem Practice.*

A Practice by Example

Examples 1 and 2
(page 30)

Modeling Use models to help you find each difference.

9. $-7 - (-3)$ **10.** $-15 - (-7)$ **11.** $-5 - (-6)$

12. $9 - (-8)$ **13.** $-14 - (-8)$ **14.** $-7 - (-7)$

15. $2 - 3$ **16.** $-2 - 3$ **17.** $-10 - 2$

Example 3
(page 31)

Write each difference as a sum. Then simplify.

18. $6 - 2$ **19.** $6 - (-2)$ **20.** $-6 - 2$ **21.** $2 - 6$

22. $2 - (-6)$ **23.** $-2 - 6$ **24.** $5 - 11$ **25.** $75 - (-25)$

26. Suppose you have a score of 35 in a game. You get a 50-point penalty. What is your new score?

B Apply Your Skills

Find each difference.

27. $-49 - 75$ **28.** $-65 - 15$ **29.** $16 - (-3)$

30. $120 - (-50)$ **31.** $989 - 76$ **32.** $-35 - 25$

33. $-92 - (-9)$ **34.** $-81 - (-13)$ **35.** $36 - 88$

Simplify.

36. $-90 - (-80) - 20$ **37.** $810 - 30 - (-70)$

38. $23 - (-15) - 28$ **39.** $-17 + 25 - (-58)$

Open-Ended Use positive and negative integers to write two different subtraction number sentences for each difference.

SAMPLE ■ − ■ = −5 $17 - 22 = -5$
$-20 - (-15) = -5$

40. ■ − ■ = 0 **41.** ■ − ■ = 10 **42.** ■ − ■ = −6

43. ■ − ■ = −15 **44.** ■ − ■ = $|-3|$ **45.** ■ − ■ = $|11|$

Homework Video Tutor

Visit: PHSchool.com
Web Code: bje-0106

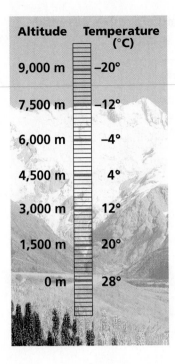

Altitude	Temperature (°C)
9,000 m	−20°
7,500 m	−12°
6,000 m	−4°
4,500 m	4°
3,000 m	12°
1,500 m	20°
0 m	28°

The graph at the left shows how temperature changes with altitude. Use this graph for Exercises 46–48.

46. As the altitude increases, what happens to the temperature?

47. What is the change in temperature from 1,500 m to 6,000 m?

48. **Multiple Choice** Find the change in temperature for every 1,500-meter increase in altitude.

    Ⓐ 12°C   Ⓑ 8°C   Ⓒ −8°C   Ⓓ −12°C

Mental Math Simplify each expression.

49. $-6 - (-8)$ **50.** $-45 - 15$ **51.** $-7 - (-7) + (-7)$

52. $100 - (-50)$ **53.** $20 - (-10) - 20$ **54.** $-11 + 22 - (-55)$

55. $3 - (-3) + 6$ **56.** $-32 + 2 + (-10)$ **57.** $-87 + (-3) + 90$

58. $6 - (-6) + 6$ **59.** $0 + (-15) - 15$ **60.** $-13 - 17 + 10$

Write a numerical expression for each phrase. Then simplify and answer the question.

61. You are $2 in debt. You borrow $4 more. What is the total amount of your debt?

62. An airplane takes off, climbs 3,000 ft, and then descends 600 ft. What is the airplane's current height?

63. From 0°F, the temperature increases 15 degrees and then drops 25 degrees. What is the current temperature?

Estimation Round each number. Then estimate the sum or difference.

    SAMPLE $-2{,}216 - 488 \approx -2{,}200 - 500 = -2{,}700$

64. $-41 - (-86)$ **65.** $-227 - 49$ **66.** $-398 - 67$

67. $-86 - 22$ **68.** $288 - 59$ **69.** $63 - (-21)$

70. a. Writing in Math A thermometer is like a vertical number line. Use the one at the right to write a subtraction problem.
    b. Write and simplify a numerical expression for your problem.

71. a. Patterns Copy and complete. The first one is done for you.

    $8 - (-4) = 12$
    $12 - (-4) = \blacksquare$
    $16 - (-4) = \blacksquare$
    $20 - (-4) = \blacksquare$
    $24 - (-4) = \blacksquare$

    b. If you begin at 8 and subtract −4 five times, the result is $\blacksquare$.
    c. Begin at 0 and subtract −4 six times. What is the result?

72. Reasoning For what values of a is each statement true? Give an example, if possible.
    a. $|a - 5| = |a| - 5$ **b.** $|a - 5| > |a| - 5$ **c.** $|a - 5| < |a| - 5$

Challenge In each number square, the rows, columns, and diagonals have the same sum. Copy and complete each number square.

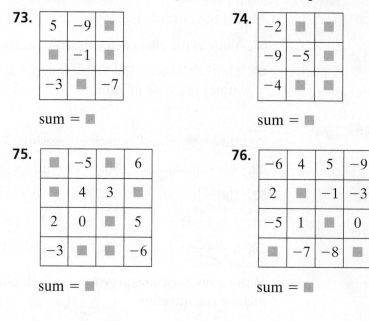

73.

5	−9	■
■	−1	■
−3	■	−7

sum = ■

74.

−2	■	■
−9	−5	■
−4	■	■

sum = ■

75.

■	−5	■	6
■	4	3	■
2	0	■	5
−3	■	■	−6

sum = ■

76.

−6	4	5	−9
2	■	−1	−3
−5	1	■	0
■	−7	−8	■

sum = ■

Multiple Choice Practice and Mixed Review

For Standards Tutorials, visit PHSchool.com. Web Code: bjq-9045

77. Three of the four expressions below have the same value. Which one has a different value?

  (A) $6 + (−4)$ (C) $|4 − 6|$
  (B) $6 − 4$ (D) $−6 − 4$

78. What is the value of $−23 + |−15| + |−17| + (−35)$?

  (A) $−56$ (C) $|−26|$
  (B) $−26$ (D) 56

79. Sam and Sally play a trivia game. After 4 turns, Sam's score is $−25$. On the fifth turn, he scores 8 points. Which expression shows how to find Sam's score?

  (A) $−25 − 8$ (B) $−25 + 8$ (C) $−25 \cdot 8$ (D) $−25 ÷ 8$

GO for Help

Lesson 1-5   **Find each sum.**

80. $−17 + 12$ **81.** $−8 + 15$ **82.** $−9 + (−4) + 7$

83. $−6 + (−5)$ **84.** $13 + (−7)$ **85.** $3 + 9 + (−1)$

Lesson 1-4   **Open-Ended Complete each statement with an integer.**

86. $−5 > ■$ **87.** $■ < 6$ **88.** $|−1| > ■$ **89.** $|■| < 8$

Lesson 1-1   **90.** Write an expression for the phrase *one hundred plus the product of six and nine.* Simplify the expression.

1-7 Inductive Reasoning

Develop Formulate and justify mathematical conjectures based on a general description of the mathematical question or problem posed.
Develop Make conjectures by using inductive reasoning.
Develop Use words to explain mathematical reasoning.

What You'll Learn

- To write rules for patterns
- To make predictions and test conjectures

. . . And Why

To use inductive reasoning in finding patterns and in making conjectures about economic data

✓ Check Skills You'll Need

Find each difference.

1. $-3 - 4$ **2.** $-7 - 4$

3. $-11 - 4$ **4.** $-15 - 4$

 for Help

Lesson 1-6

🔊 New Vocabulary

- inductive reasoning
- conjecture
- counterexample

Writing Rules for Patterns

Inductive reasoning is making conclusions based on patterns you observe. A conclusion you reach by inductive reasoning is a **conjecture.**

1 EXAMPLE Reasoning Inductively

Visual Patterns Use inductive reasoning. Make a conjecture about the next figure in the pattern. Then draw the figure.

Observation: The shaded triangle is rotating clockwise around the square.

Conjecture: The next figure will have a shaded triangle in the bottom-right corner.

✓ Quick Check

1. Make a conjecture about the next figure in the pattern at the right. Then draw the figure.

For a number pattern, a conjecture can be a rule that explains how to make the pattern. The three dots in a pattern tell you that the pattern continues.

2 EXAMPLE Writing Rules for Patterns

Number Patterns Write a rule for each number pattern.

a. 30, 25, 20, 15, . . .	Start with 30 and subtract 5 repeatedly.
b. 2, −2, 2, −2, . . .	Alternate 2 and its opposite.
c. 1, 3, 4, 12, 13, . . .	Start with 1. Alternate multiplying by 3 and adding 1.

✓ Quick Check

2. Write a rule for the pattern 4, 9, 14, 19, ...

3 EXAMPLE **Extending a Pattern**

Number Patterns Write a rule for the number pattern
640, 320, 160, 80, . . . Find the next two numbers in the pattern.

640,   320,   160,   80   The first number is 640. The next
     ÷2   ÷2   ÷2   numbers are found by dividing by 2.

The rule is *Start with 640 and divide by 2.* The next two numbers
in the pattern are 80 ÷ 2 = 40 and 40 ÷ 2 = 20.

✓ Quick Check

3. Write a rule for the pattern 1, 3, 5, 7, . . . Find the next two
numbers in the pattern.

Predictions and Counterexamples

With sufficient information, you can make predictions based on
reasonable conjectures. Such predictions will probably—but not
necessarily—turn out to be accurate.

4 EXAMPLE **Analyzing a Prediction**

See the graph below. Is a conjecture that average hourly earnings in
the year 2010 will be about $18.25 reasonable?

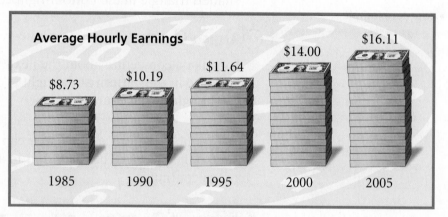

Average hourly earnings appear to increase by $1.40 to $2.40
every five years. The conjecture of $18.25 in 2010 is reasonable,
since it is about $2.00 more than the earnings for 2005.

✓ Quick Check

4. You toss a coin four times, and it comes up heads each time. Is
the conjecture *The coin will come up heads on every toss*
reasonable? Explain.

An example that proves a statement false is a **counterexample.**
You need only one counterexample to prove that a conjecture
is incorrect.

5 EXAMPLE Analyzing Conjectures

Inductive Reasoning Is each conjecture correct or incorrect? If it
is incorrect, give a counterexample.

a. **Every four-sided figure is a rectangle.**
The conjecture is incorrect. The figure below has four sides, but
it is not a rectangle.

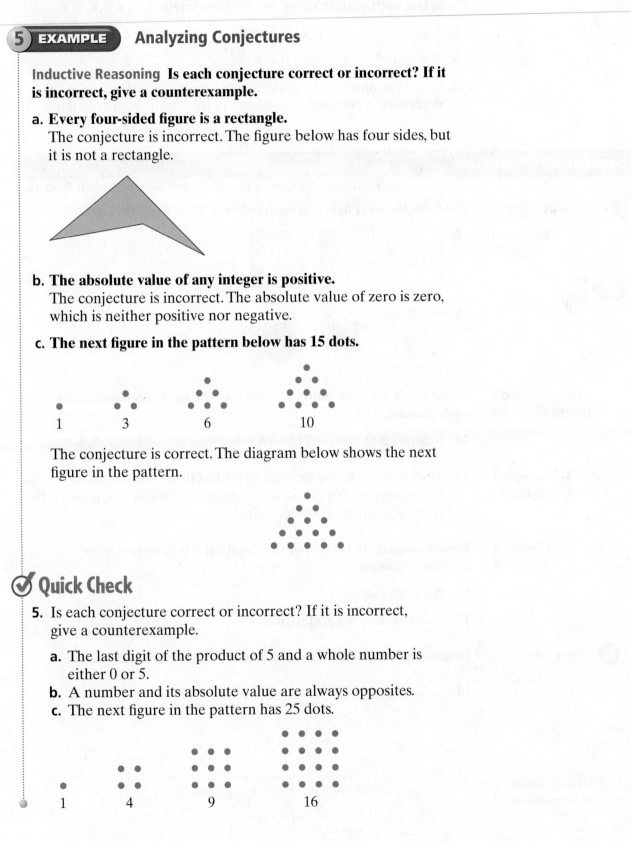

b. **The absolute value of any integer is positive.**
The conjecture is incorrect. The absolute value of zero is zero,
which is neither positive nor negative.

c. **The next figure in the pattern below has 15 dots.**

The conjecture is correct. The diagram below shows the next
figure in the pattern.

✅ Quick Check

5. Is each conjecture correct or incorrect? If it is incorrect,
give a counterexample.

a. The last digit of the product of 5 and a whole number is
either 0 or 5.
b. A number and its absolute value are always opposites.
c. The next figure in the pattern has 25 dots.

Complete each pattern using one of these integers: 3, 4, 5, 6, 7, 8.

1. 1, 2, ■, 4   **2.** 2, 4, ■, 8   **3.** 2, 4, ■, 16

4. 2, 4, ■, 11   **5.** 1, 2, ■, 7   **6.** 9, 7, ■, 3

7. Do two examples of a pattern provide enough information to determine a pattern? Use examples to support your reasoning.

Standards Practice

For more exercises, see *Extra Skills and Word Problem Practice.*

A Practice by Example

Example 1
(page 35)

Go for Help

Describe the next figure in each pattern. Then draw the figure.

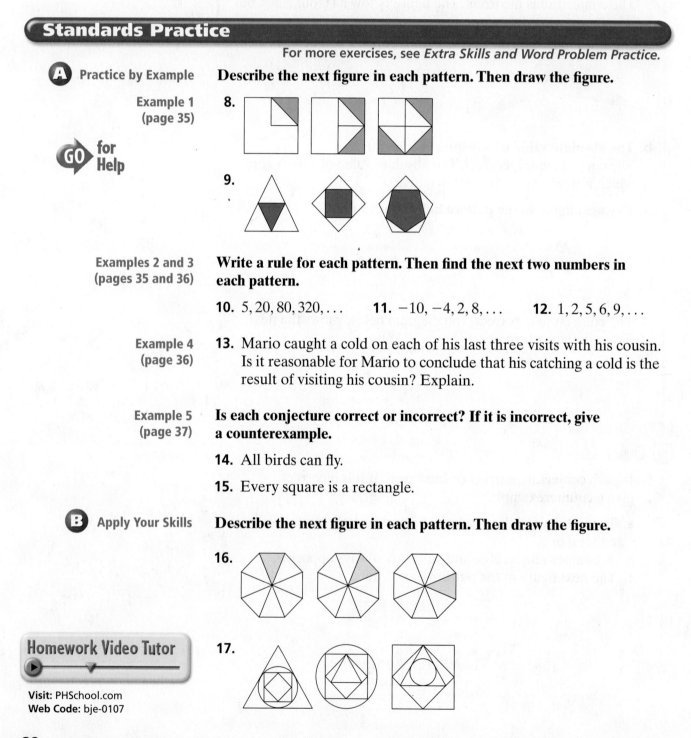

8.

9.

Examples 2 and 3
(pages 35 and 36)

Write a rule for each pattern. Then find the next two numbers in each pattern.

10. 5, 20, 80, 320, . . .   **11.** −10, −4, 2, 8, . . .   **12.** 1, 2, 5, 6, 9, . . .

Example 4
(page 36)

13. Mario caught a cold on each of his last three visits with his cousin. Is it reasonable for Mario to conclude that his catching a cold is the result of visiting his cousin? Explain.

Example 5
(page 37)

Is each conjecture correct or incorrect? If it is incorrect, give a counterexample.

14. All birds can fly.

15. Every square is a rectangle.

B Apply Your Skills

Describe the next figure in each pattern. Then draw the figure.

16.

17.

Homework Video Tutor

Visit: PHSchool.com
Web Code: bje-0107

18. a. Writing in Math Use the graph at the right. Write a conjecture about the unemployment rate in 2005. Justify your reasoning.

b. How could you test your conjecture?

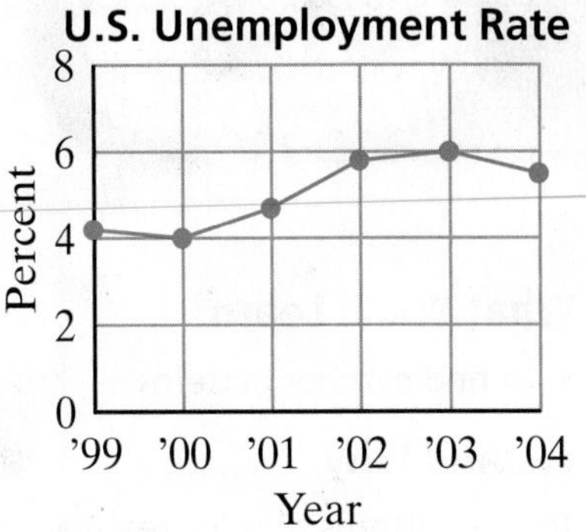

U.S. Unemployment Rate

Reasoning Is each conjecture correct? If incorrect, give a counterexample.

19. Every clover has three leaves.

20. The sum of two numbers is always greater than either of the two numbers.

21. A whole number is divisible by 3 if the sum of its digits is divisible by 3.

Write a rule for each pattern. Then find the next three numbers in the pattern.

22. $1, 1.5, 2, 2.5, 3, \ldots$

23. $-1.1, -2.2, -3.3, \ldots$

24. $1, 4, 10, 22, 46, 94, \ldots$

25. $1, -2, 4, -5, 7, -8, \ldots$

C Challenge

26. Predict the sum of the numbers in the ninth row of the pattern.

```
            1
          1 2 1
        1 2 3 2 1
      1 2 3 4 3 2 1
```

Multiple Choice Practice and Mixed Review

For Standards Tutorials, visit PHSchool.com. Web Code: bjq-9045

27. Ms. Smith's eighth grade class had a fundraiser. On Monday, they made $12. On Tuesday, they made $15. On both Wednesday and Thursday, they made $21. On Friday, their sales slowed to $17. Each day, they had spent $2.00 for supplies. Which expression can be used to find the profit that the students made?

Ⓐ $p = 12 + 15 + 2(21) + 17 - 2$

Ⓑ $p = 12 + 15 + 2(21) - 2(5)$

Ⓒ $p = 12 + 15 + 21 + 17 - 2$

Ⓓ $p = 12 + 15 + 2(21) + 17 - 2(5)$

28. During a football game, a team gained 5 yards, lost 6 yards, gained 14 yards, and lost 2 yards. What was the total net yards the team moved?

Ⓐ 27 yd   Ⓑ 15 yd   Ⓒ 13 yd   Ⓓ 11 yd

Find each difference.

GO for Help Lesson 1-6

29. $1 - 8$

30. $-4 - (-9)$

31. $86 - (-17)$

Reasoning Strategy: Look for a Pattern

Develop Analyze problems by identifying relationships and observing patterns.

What You'll Learn

• To find number patterns

. . . And Why

To use patterns to solve real-world problems involving communication

Check Skills You'll Need

Write a rule for each pattern. Find the next three numbers.

1. 8, 11, 14, 17, . . .

2. 1, 5, 4, 8, 7, . . .

3. 3, 5, 10, 12, 24, . . .

4. 1, 4, 7, 10, . . .

GO for Help
Lesson 1-7

Finding Number Patterns

Math Strategies in Action
What do songs on the radio, computer code, and your body's DNA have in common?

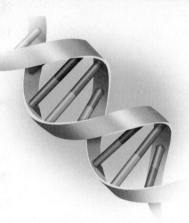

All are based on patterns. Radio uses patterns of electromagnetic waves. Computer code consists of patterns of numbers. Your DNA is made up of molecules that repeat in special patterns.

You can solve many types of problems by finding and using patterns. Making predictions from patterns is a form of inductive reasoning.

1 EXAMPLE Finding a Number Pattern

News spreads quickly at Riverdell High. Each student who hears a story repeats it 15 minutes later to two students who have not yet heard it and then tells no one else.

Suppose one student hears some news at 8:00 A.M. How many students will know the news at 9:00 A.M.?

Understand Understand the problem.

1. How many students does each student tell?

2. How long does the news take to reach the second and third students?

Plan Make a plan to solve the problem.

Make a table to organize the numbers. Then look for a pattern.

3. How many *new* students will hear the news at 8:15 A.M.?

4. How many 15-minute periods are there between 8:00 A.M. and 9:00 A.M.?

Carry Out Carry out the plan.

The pattern is to add the number of new students to the number who already know.

$$1 + 2 = 3 \quad \text{the number who know at 8:15}$$
(One student talks to 2.)

$$3 + 4 = 7 \quad \text{the number who know at 8:30}$$
(Two students talk to 4.)

Make a table and extend the pattern to 9:00.

Time	8:00	8:15	8:30	8:45	9:00
Number of new students told	1	2	4	8	16
Number of students who know	1	1 + 2 = 3	3 + 4 = 7	7 + 8 = 15	15 + 16 = 31

By 9:00 A.M., 31 students will know the news.

Check Check the answer to be sure it is reasonable.

One way to check whether a solution is reasonable is to solve the problem by another method. You can use a *tree diagram* to show the pattern visually.

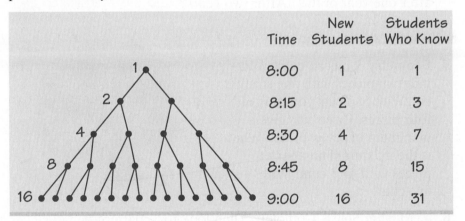

	Time	New Students	Students Who Know
1	8:00	1	1
2	8:15	2	3
4	8:30	4	7
8	8:45	8	15
16	9:00	16	31

5. Describe two ways to find the number of students who will know the news at 9:15 A.M.

6. Suppose you want to continue the pattern beyond 9:15. Which would work better, a table or a tree diagram? Explain.

7. There are 251 students at Riverdell High. By what time will every student know the news?

✓ Quick Check

8. Suppose each student who hears the story repeats it in 10 minutes. How many students will know the news at 9:00 A.M.?

1-8   Look for a Pattern   **41**

For more exercises, see *Extra Skills and Word Problem Practice*.

A Practice by Example

Example 1
(page 40)

GO for
Help

***Look for a Pattern* to help you solve each problem.**

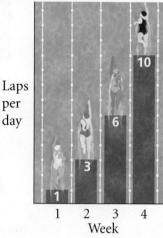

1. **Data Analysis** Caroline is training for a swim meet. The graph shows the number of laps per day she swims each week. If she stays with this training pattern, how many laps per day will Caroline swim in week 8?

2. Students are to march in a parade. There will be one first grader, two second graders, three third graders, and so on, through the twelfth grade. How many students will march in the parade?

3. Suppose that every day you save twice as many pennies as you saved the day before. You start by saving one penny on January 1. How much money will you have in all on January 10?

4. An old clock started to lose one minute each day. It was too fragile to fix, but too beloved to stop. How slow was the clock after one year of this? After two years?

B Apply Your Skills

Solve using any strategy.

5. **Geometry** You can cut a pizza into two pieces with one straight cut. With two cuts you can get four pieces. Three cuts give a maximum of seven pieces. What is the maximum number of pieces with four cuts? With five cuts?

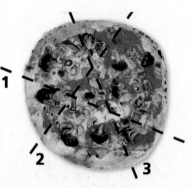

6. **a. Number Sense** Complete. Then look for a pattern.

   $2 \cdot 2 = \blacksquare$ $3 \cdot 3 = \blacksquare$
   $1 \cdot 3 = \blacksquare$ $2 \cdot 4 = \blacksquare$
   Difference $= \blacksquare$ Difference $= \blacksquare$

   $4 \cdot 4 = \blacksquare$ $5 \cdot 5 = \blacksquare$
   $3 \cdot 5 = \blacksquare$ $4 \cdot 6 \doteq \blacksquare$
   Difference $= \blacksquare$ Difference $= \blacksquare$

   b. Which is greater, $10 \cdot 12$ or $11 \cdot 11$? What is the difference?

   c. Reasoning Suppose you know that $47 \cdot 47 = 2{,}209$. Use this to find $46 \cdot 48$.

   d. Suppose you know that $64 \cdot 66 = 4{,}224$. Use this to find $65 \cdot 65$.

STRATEGIES

- Act It Out
- Draw a Diagram
- Try, Test, Revise
- Look for a Pattern
- Make a Model
- Make a Table
- Simulate the Problem
- Solve by Graphing
- Use Multiple Strategies
- Work a Simpler Problem
- Work Backward
- Write an Equation
- Write a Proportion

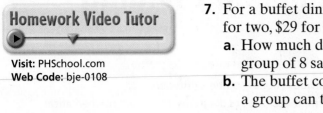

Visit: PHSchool.com
Web Code: bje-0108

7. For a buffet dinner, a restaurant charges $10 for one person, $20 for two, $29 for three, $37 for four, $44 for five, and so on.
   a. How much does a buffet dinner for 8 cost? How much does a group of 8 save by eating together rather than separately?
   b. The buffet costs the restaurant $6 per person. How large a group can the restaurant serve without losing money?

8. Jayne has 3 quarters, 2 dimes, a nickel, and 2 pennies in her pocket. How many different amounts of money can she make using some or all of these coins?

C Challenge

9. A woman jogging at 6 mi/h passes a man biking in the opposite direction at 12 mi/h. If they maintain their speeds, how far from each other will they be 10 minutes after passing?

Multiple Choice Practice and Mixed Review

For Standards Tutorials, visit PHSchool.com. Web Code: bjq-9045

10. One yeast cell "buds" into 2 cells (the original cell and one new cell) at a rate of once per hour. How many yeast cells will be present after 8 hours?
   Ⓐ 128   Ⓑ 256   Ⓒ 512   Ⓓ 1,024

11. Sue is raising money for charity by walking. The table shows the amount she earns as she walks. Which equation can be used to determine a, the amount earned by walking w miles?

Number of Miles	1	2	3
Dollars Earned	14.50	19.00	23.50

   Ⓐ $a = 10 + 4.50w$ Ⓑ $a = 14.50w$
   Ⓒ $a = 14.50 + 4.50w$ Ⓓ $a = 5.50 + 4.50w$

 for Help   Lesson 1-7

Visual Patterns Describe the next figure in each pattern. Then draw the figure.

12.
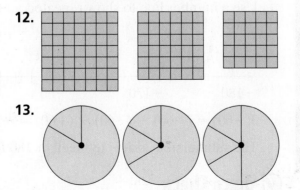

13.

Multiplying and Dividing Integers

What You'll Learn

- To multiply integers using repeated addition, patterns, and rules
- To divide integers using rules

. . . And Why

To solve real-world problems involving deep-sea exploration and currency

✓ Check Skills You'll Need

Simplify each expression.

1. $5 \cdot 4$ **2.** $3 \cdot 8$

3. $5 \cdot 5$ **4.** $14 \cdot 2$

5. $6 \cdot 5$ **6.** $20 \cdot 7$

GO▶ for Help

Skills Handbook, p. 682

Multiplying Integers

Standards Investigation
Preparing to Multiply Integers

1. Copy and complete the table. The first row is done for you.

Multiplication	Repeated Addition	Sum
$3 \cdot (-5)$	$-5 + (-5) + (-5)$	-15
$5 \cdot (-4)$	■	■
$2 \cdot (-8)$	■	■
$4 \cdot (-10)$	■	■

2. What do you notice about the signs of the sums?

3. **Inductive Reasoning** What does the pattern suggest about the product of a positive integer and a negative integer?

You can think of multiplication as repeated addition.

1 EXAMPLE   Using a Number Line

After it is launched from a boat, a submersible descends 60 ft/min. Where is it in relation to sea level 3 minutes after its launch?

Use a number line to show repeated addition.

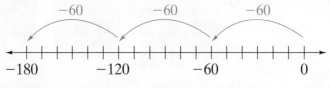

$3(-60) = (-60) + (-60) + (-60) = -180$

The submersible is at -180 feet, or 180 feet below sea level.

✓ Quick Check

1. Simplify each product.

    a. $2(-6)$ **b.** $4(-3)$ **c.** $7(-2)$

You can use patterns to simplify the product of a negative number and a positive number, or the product of two negative numbers.

2 EXAMPLE Using Patterns to Multiply Integers

Patterns Use a pattern to find each product.

a. $-2(5)$

$2(5) = 10$	**Start with products you know.**
$1(5) = 5$	
$0(5) = 0$	
$-1(5) = -5$	**Continue the pattern.**
$-2(5) = -10$	

b. $-2(-5)$

$2(-5) = -10$
$1(-5) = -5$
$0(-5) = 0$
$-1(-5) = 5$
$-2(-5) = 10$

✓ Quick Check

2. Patterns Use a pattern to simplify $-3(-4)$.

By inductive reasoning, the patterns from Example 2 suggest rules for multiplying integers.

Take Note — Multiplying Integers

The product of two integers with the same sign is positive.
The product of two integers with different signs is negative.
The product of zero and any integer is zero.

Examples

$$3(4) = 12 \qquad 3(-4) = -12$$
$$-3(-4) = 12 \qquad -3(4) = -12$$
$$3(0) = 0 \qquad -4(0) = 0$$

3 EXAMPLE Using Rules to Multiply Integers

Multiple Choice Which procedure is correct for multiplying $-3 \cdot 5(-4)$?

- Ⓐ $-3 \cdot 5(-4) = 15(-4) = -60$
- Ⓑ $-3 \cdot 5(-4) = -3(1) = -3$
- Ⓒ $-3 \cdot 5(-4) = -3(-1) = 3$
- Ⓓ $-3 \cdot 5(-4) = -15(-4) = 60$

Multiply from left to right. The product of a negative integer and a positive integer is negative. The product of two negative integers is positive. The product is 60. The answer is D.

✓ Quick Check

3. Simplify each product.

a. $-4 \cdot 8(-2)$ **b.** $6(-3)(5)$ **c.** $-7 \cdot (-14) \cdot 0$

Dividing Integers

The rules for dividing integers are similar to those for multiplying.

> **Take Note** **Dividing Integers**
>
> The quotient of two integers with the same sign is positive.
> The quotient of two integers with different signs is negative.
> Remember that division by zero is undefined.
>
> **Examples**
> $$12 \div 3 = 4 \qquad 12 \div (-3) = -4$$
> $$-12 \div (-3) = 4 \qquad -12 \div 3 = -4$$

4 EXAMPLE **Dividing Integers**

Find the average of the differences in the values of a Canadian dollar and a U.S. dollar for 2001–2005.

Value of Dollars (U.S. Cents)

Year	Canadian Dollar	U.S. Dollar	Difference
2001	65	100	–35
2002	64	100	–36
2003	71	100	–29
2004	77	100	–23
2005	83	100	–17

Source: *U.S. Federal Reserve*

$$\frac{-35 + (-36) + (-29) + (-23) + (-17)}{5}$$ Write an expression for the average.

$$= \frac{-140}{5}$$ Use the order of operations. The fraction bar acts as a grouping symbol.

$$= -28$$ The quotient of a negative integer and a positive integer is negative.

For 2001–2005, the average difference was −28¢. The Canadian dollar was worth an average of 28¢ less than the U.S. dollar.

✓ Quick Check

4. Simplify each quotient.

    a. $-32 \div 8$ **b.** $-48 \div (-6)$ **c.** $-56 \div (-4)$

    d. Find the average of $4, -3, -5, 2,$ and -8.

1. Write a number sentence for the product shown on the number line.

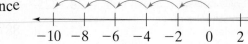

$$-10 \quad -8 \quad -6 \quad -4 \quad -2 \quad 0 \quad 2$$

Write each sum as a product. Simplify the product.

2. $(-9) + (-9) + (-9) + (-9)$

3. $(-5) + (-5) + (-5) + (-5) + (-5)$

Mental Math **Without computing, tell whether each product or quotient is *positive* or *negative*. Explain your reasoning.**

4. $-6(-20)$ 5. $7(-83)$ 6. $39 \div (-3)$ 7. $-3(8)(-24)$

Standards Practice

For more exercises, see *Extra Skills and Word Problem Practice.*

A Practice by Example

8. The temperature dropped 5 degrees each hour for 7 h. Use an integer to represent the total change in temperature.

Example 1
(page 44)

GO for Help

Simplify each product.

9. $3(-3)$ 10. $4(-11)$ 11. $3(-8)$

12. $5(-10)$ 13. $6(-3)$ 14. $2(-15)$

Examples 2 and 3
(page 45)

15. $9(-9)$ 16. $3(-24)$ 17. $8(-6)$

18. $-5(-3)$ 19. $-6 \cdot 10$ 20. $-10 \cdot 0$

Example 4
(page 46)

21. $-9(-8)(-5)$ 22. $0(-12) \cdot 4$ 23. $8 \cdot 3(-4)$

Find each quotient.

24. $24 \div (-24)$ 25. $18 \div (-1)$ 26. $-120 \div 12$

27. $56 \div (-8)$ 28. $-72 \div 12$ 29. $-100 \div (-10)$

For each group, find the average.

30. temperatures: $-9°C, -12°C, 9°C, 4°C, -2°C$

31. football yardage: 10 yd, -5 yd, 7 yd, 9 yd, -11 yd

32. golf scores: $-3, 4, 2, 1, -4, -1, 3, -2$

33. bank balances: $325, -\$150, \$130, \$200, -\$45$

B Apply Your Skills

Name the point on the number line that is the graph of each product.

$$D \quad F \quad C \qquad A \qquad\quad B \qquad\quad E$$
$$-8 \quad -6 \quad -4 \quad -2 \quad 0 \quad 2 \quad 4 \quad 6 \quad 8$$

34. $-2 \cdot 0$ 35. $4(-2)$ 36. $2(-2)$ 37. $|-2| \cdot |-2|$

Use repeated addition, patterns, or rules to simplify each product or quotient.

38. $225 \div (-15)$ **39.** $|-2| \cdot (-7)$ **40.** $-59(-79)$

41. $243(-88)$ **42.** $-200 \div -25$ **43.** $-18(-12)$

44. $38(-2)$ **45.** $1{,}000 \div (-50)$ **46.** $24(-16)(-32)$

47. The price of one share of a stock fell $3 each day for 12 days.
  a. Write an integer to represent the total change in price of a share of the stock.
  b. The original stock price was $76 per share. What was the price after the drop?

Compare. Use >, <, or = to complete each statement.

48. $(-9)(-6)$ ■ $8(-10)$ **49.** $5(-2)$ ■ $(-6)(-1)$

50. $-10 \div (-2)$ ■ $25 \div (-5)$ **51.** $-|-28| \div 7$ ■ $-28 \div (-7)$

52. $|-25| \div |-5|$ ■ $|-25 \div (-5)|$ **53.** $-(-15 \div 5)$ ■ $-100 \div (-20)$

Number Sense Use integer rules and other math facts to answer each question.

54. What integer and -8 have the product -96?

55. What integer and 9 have the product -135?

56. What integer and -3 have the quotient 9?

57. What two integers have a sum of -10 and a product of -75?

Open-Ended Simplify each pair of expressions. Then write an integer that is between the values of the expressions.

58. $-2 \cdot (-2)$ and $2 \cdot 4$ **59.** $10 + (-7)$ and $10 \div (-5)$

60. $50 + (-48)$ and $80 \div (-20)$ **61.** $121 \div (-11)$ and $|-7| - |7|$

62. a. Inductive Reasoning Will the sign be positive or negative for the product of three negative integers? Of four negative integers? Of five negative integers?
  b. Writing in Math Use inductive reasoning to write a rule for the sign of the product of more than two negative integers.

63. Reasoning If a and b are positive integers, and x and y are negative integers, what is the sign of $\frac{a+b}{x+y}$? Explain.

64. Jerry owns 20 shares of stock valued at $23 each. One day, the price of the stock rose $2. It fell $1 on each of the next three days. The stock price rose $4 on the next day. What was the total value of Jerry's stock at the end of this time period?

C Challenge **65. a.** Use models to find $\frac{1}{4}(2)$.
  b. Describe how you can find $\frac{1}{4}\left(\frac{1}{2}\right)$.

For Standards Tutorials, visit PHSchool.com. Web Code: bjq-9045

66. A scuba diver descended to a depth of 50 feet in 25 seconds. Which integer indicates the average number of feet per second the diver traveled?

 Ⓐ -50 Ⓑ -25 Ⓒ -2 Ⓓ -1

67. Rosie's bank balance at the start of the week was $254. She made 3 withdrawals for $25 each. How much did she have in her account after the three withdrawals?

 Ⓐ $25   Ⓑ $75   Ⓒ $179   Ⓓ $329

68. In the equation $a - b = c$, if b is not zero, is a always greater than c? Which answer and reasoning are correct?

 Ⓐ Yes. If $a - b = c$, then $a = b + c$, and the sum of 2 numbers is always greater than either of the other numbers.

 Ⓑ No. If b is negative, then c is greater than a.

 Ⓒ Yes. Subtraction means to take away. If b objects are taken away from a objects, the result must be a number smaller than a.

 Ⓓ No. If b is a fraction, then c is greater than a.

GO for Help

Lesson 1-8   **69. Reasoning** How many whole numbers from 10 to 200 have exactly two identical digits?

Lessons 1-5, 1-6   **Compare. Use >, <, or = to complete each statement.**

70. $-3 + (-8) \blacksquare 12 - (-6)$

71. $-9 + 13 \blacksquare 24 - 30$

72. $|-6| - |12| \blacksquare -8 + |-12|$

Lesson 1-1   **Write a variable expression for each word phrase.**

73. 50 decreased by a number n **74.** the product of y and 60

✓ Checkpoint Quiz 2

Simplify each expression.

1. $3 + (-11)$ **2.** $12 - (-8)$

3. $-9 \cdot 5$ **4.** $-64 \div (-8)$

5. $|3| \cdot 8 \div (-2)$ **6.** $-8(-3)(3)$

Open-Ended Use integers to complete each equation.

7. $\blacksquare + \blacksquare = -7$ **8.** $\blacksquare - (-20) = \blacksquare$ **9.** $\blacksquare \cdot \blacksquare = -40$

Patterns Find the next three numbers in each pattern.

10. $-7, -2, 3, 8, \ldots$ **11.** $1, 3, 9, 27, \ldots$

Develop Use algebraic terminology correctly.

You can learn new vocabulary by building your own index-card word list.

- Write the term. Then write the definition.
- Include any math symbols related to the term.
- Give an example that shows how the term is used.
- Give a nonexample showing how the term might *not* apply.

EXAMPLE

Make an index card for the vocabulary term *algebraic expression*.

Algebraic Expression	Write the term.
Definition: An algebraic expression is a mathematical phrase that uses variables, numerals, and operation symbols.	Write the definition.
Example: $h + 5$　　$f - 7$　　$3a$　　$\frac{x}{2}$	Give examples.
Nonexamples: 5　　$25 - 4$　　13　　-21	Give nonexamples.

EXERCISES

Make an index card like the one shown above for each vocabulary term. Include any helpful everyday meanings.

1. variable
2. order of operations
3. evaluate
4. opposites
5. integers
6. absolute value
7. conjecture
8. inductive reasoning
9. counterexample

10. **Error Analysis** A student wrote the definition of *integers* at the right. Which parts are correct? Which parts are incorrect? Explain.

Integers

Definition: Integers are all the counting numbers and their opposites.

Examples: $-8, 4, -1, 5, 10, -12$

Nonexamples: $\frac{1}{2}, 0, -\frac{3}{4}, -1.5$

Activity Lab

Reading Bar and Line Graphs

> **Introduce** Know various forms of display for data sets.

You can analyze data presented in a graph. A bar graph usually compares quantities. The bar graph below shows boys' participation in high school baseball in several states for a recent year.

1 ACTIVITY

Use the bar graph.

1. About how many boys played high school baseball in Texas?

2. About how many boys played high school baseball in Illinois?

3. About how many more boys played high school baseball in Texas than in Illinois?

4. In which two states is the combined number of boys who played high school baseball about equal to the number who played in Pennsylvania?

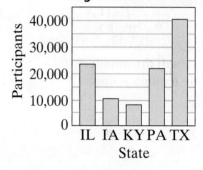

Boys' Participation in High School Baseball

A line graph usually shows change over time. The line graph shows girls' participation in high school baseball over several years.

2 ACTIVITY

Use the line graph.

5. Between what two years did girls' participation in high school baseball increase the most?

6. In what two years was girls' participation in high school baseball about the same?

7. Between what two years did girls' participation in high school baseball decrease by about 500?

8. In what year was girls' participation in high school baseball about 1,275?

9. **a.** Estimate the change in participation from year 1 to year 10.

   b. If the trend continues, how many girls will participate in high school baseball in year 21?

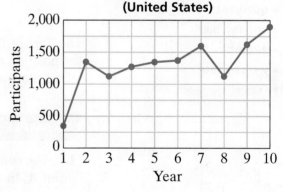

Girls' Participation in High School Baseball (United States)

The Coordinate Plane

What You'll Learn

- To name coordinates and quadrants in the coordinate plane
- To graph points in the coordinate plane

. . . And Why

To solve real-world problems involving geography

☑ **Check Skills You'll Need**

Graph the numbers on a number line.

1. $-2, 1, -5$

2. $0, 2, -4$

3. $-3, 3, -2$

4. $-1, -5, -8$

GO for Help
Lesson 1-4

🔊 **New Vocabulary**

- coordinate plane
- *x*-axis   • *y*-axis
- quadrants • origin
- ordered pair
- *x*-coordinate
- *y*-coordinate

Introduce Use coordinate graphs to plot simple figures.
Students graph and interpret linear and some nonlinear functions.

Naming Coordinates and Quadrants

A **coordinate plane** is formed by the intersection of two number lines. The horizontal number line is called the **x-axis** and the vertical number line is called the **y-axis**.

The *x*- and *y*-axes divide the coordinate plane into four **quadrants**.

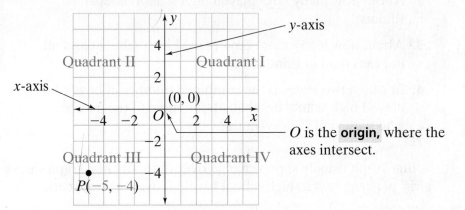

An **ordered pair** gives the coordinates and location of a point. The ordered pair $(-5, -4)$ identifies point P in Quadrant III above.

$$(-5, -4)$$

The **x-coordinate** shows the position right or left of the *y*-axis.

The **y-coordinate** shows the position above or below the *x*-axis.

---

1 EXAMPLE   **Naming Coordinates and Quadrants**

Use the coordinate plane at the left. Write the coordinates of point A. In which quadrant is point A located?

Point A is located 2 units to the left of the *y*-axis. So the *x*-coordinate is -2. The point is 1 unit above the *x*-axis. So the *y*-coordinate is 1.

The coordinates of point A are $(-2, 1)$. Point A is located in Quadrant II.

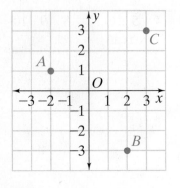

☑ **Quick Check**

1. Write the coordinates of B and C.

Online
active math

For: Coordinate Plane Activity
Use: Interactive Textbook, 1-10

To graph a point $A(x, y)$ in a coordinate plane, you graph the ordered pair (x, y).

2 EXAMPLE **Graphing Points**

Graph point $R(3, -4\frac{1}{2})$.

Step 1
Start at the origin.

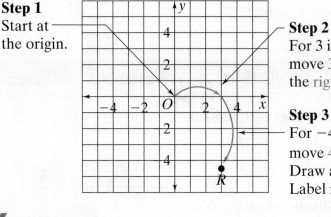

Step 2
For 3 in $R(3, -4\frac{1}{2})$, move 3 units to the right.

Step 3
For $-4\frac{1}{2}$ in $R(3, -4\frac{1}{2})$, move $4\frac{1}{2}$ units down. Draw a dot. Label it R.

✓ Quick Check

2. Graph point $S(-4\frac{1}{2}, 3)$.

You can use a coordinate plane to plot geometric figures.

3 EXAMPLE **Plotting a Figure**

Graph a figure with vertices $T(1, -2)$, $U(-3, -2)$, $V(-3, 2)$, and $W(1, 2)$. Name the figure.

Plot and label each point on a coordinate plane. Connect the points with lines.

The figure is a square.

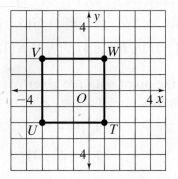

Vocabulary Tip

The *vertex* of a polygon is the point where two sides meet. *Vertices* is the plural of vertex.

✓ Quick Check

3. Graph a figure with vertices $K(3, 1)$, $L(-2\frac{1}{2}, 1)$, and $M(-2, -4)$. Name the figure.

1. Vocabulary What ordered pair names the origin?

A student is graphing the point $(-5, 4)$.

2. The x-coordinate is ■.

3. The integer 4 is the __?__ .

4. a. To graph the point, start at the __?__ .
   b. Then move ■ units left.
   c. Then move 4 units __?__ .

For more exercises, see *Extra Skills and Word Problem Practice*.

Ⓐ Practice by Example

Example 1
(page 52)

GO for Help

In which quadrant does each point lie?

5. J **6.** V **7.** M

8. K **9.** P **10.** Q

Write the coordinates of each point.

11. T **12.** G **13.** R

14. Q **15.** P **16.** M

Example 2
(page 53)

Draw a coordinate plane. Then graph each point.

17. $A(-1, 3)$ **18.** $B(-4, -1)$ **19.** $C(2, 5)$ **20.** $D(2, -2)$

21. $E(0, 6)$ **22.** $F(-3, 2)$ **23.** $G(6, 0)$ **24.** $H(1, 7)$

Example 3
(page 53)

Graph and name the figure with the given vertices.

25. $A(2, 3), B(3, -1), C(-1, -1)$

26. $D(3, 3), E(5, 3), F(5, 1)\ G(3, 0)$

27. $H(-2, 1), I(-3, 3), J(0, 4)\ K(1, 2)$

Ⓑ Apply Your Skills

Homework Video Tutor

Visit: PHSchool.com
Web Code: bje-0110

Name the point with the given coordinates.

28. $(3, 2)$ **29.** $(0, -5)$

30. $(2, 3)$ **31.** $(-2, -3)$

Write the coordinates of each point.

32. A **33.** B

34. C **35.** D

36. Mental Math Write the coordinates of the point on the y-axis 4 units below the x-axis.

In which quadrant or on which axis does each point lie?

37. $W(x, y)$ if $x = 0, y > 0$

38. $Z(x, y)$ if $x > 0, y < 0$

39. $B(0, |-2|)$

40. $R(x, y)$ if $x < 0, y > 0$

Geometry **Graph and connect the points in the order given. Connect the last point to the first. Name the figure.**

41. $(-4, 1), (1, 1), (-3, -1)$

42. $(2\frac{1}{2}, 2), (2\frac{1}{2}, -1), (-5, -1), (-5, 2)$

43. $(-1, 2), (1, 5), (7, 5), (5, 2)$

44. $(2, -4), (7, -1), (4, 4), (-1, 1)$

Geometry **$PQRS$ is a square. Find the coordinates of S.**

45. $P(-5, 0), Q(0, 5), R(5, 0), S(\blacksquare, \blacksquare)$

46. $P(-1, 3), Q(4, 3), R(4, -2), S(\blacksquare, \blacksquare)$

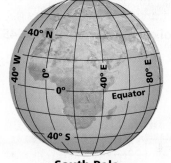

North Pole

South Pole

Latitude and longitude are measurements in a coordinate system that locates every point on Earth's surface.

Geography **On a map, coordinates are given in degrees of longitude and latitude. Use the map below for Exercises 47–50.**

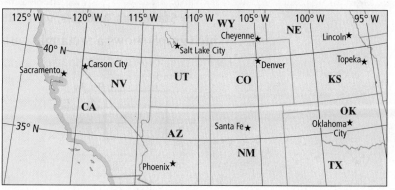

47. Find the longitude and latitude of Sacramento, California.

48. Find the longitude and latitude of Topeka, Kansas.

49. What city is located near 120° W, 40° N?

50. What city is located near 106° W, 35° N?

Geometry **Use one coordinate plane for Exercises 51–53.**

51. Graph the points $(-2, 1), (-2, 3), (1, 3)$, and $(1, 1)$. Connect them in the order given. Connect the last point to the first.

52. Change the coordinates of Exercise 51 as described below. Graph and connect the points for each new set of coordinates. Use a different color for each set.
  a. Multiply each x-coordinate by -1.
  b. Multiply each y-coordinate by -1.
  c. Multiply each coordinate by -1.

53. Writing in Math Compare each figure in Exercise 52 to the figure in Exercise 51. Write a short paragraph describing your results.

Mental Math In which quadrant does $P(x, y)$ lie?

54. x is positive, y is negative   **55.** x is positive, y is positive

56. x is negative, y is positive   **57.** x is negative, y is negative

58. Open-Ended Draw a dot-to-dot picture on a coordinate grid. Write the coordinates of the points in order. Exchange coordinates with a classmate and draw the other's picture.

59. Reasoning Assume that $a \neq b$. Do (a, b) and (b, a) describe the same point? Explain.

C Challenge

60. Write the coordinates of four points in the coordinate plane that are 3 units from the origin. Graph the points.

61. The formula for the area of a triangle is $A = \frac{1}{2} bh$. Find the area of a triangle with vertices $(2, 0)$, $(6, 0)$, and $(4, 4)$.

Multiple Choice Practice and Mixed Review

For Standards Tutorials, visit PHSchool.com. Web Code: bjq-9045

62. Which graph shows a rectangle with one vertex at $(3, -2)$?

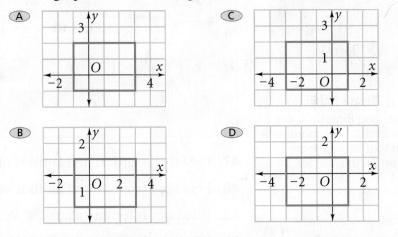

63. Ann deposited $35.75 into her bank at the start of the month. Over the next few weeks, she wrote checks for $64.23 and $21.58. She also withdrew $50.00. What other information is needed to find Ann's balance after these transactions?

  Ⓐ Ann's starting balance
  Ⓑ The check numbers
  Ⓒ The length of time Ann has had an account
  Ⓓ The name of the bank

GO for Help   **Lesson 1-4**   **Write the value of each expression.**

64. $|-8|$ **65.** $-|-95|$ **66.** the opposite of 12

67. $|16| + 4$ **68.** $|-6| - 2$ **69.** the opposite of -3

Justifying Each Step

By justifying each step in a solution, you show that you fully understand how to reach the answer. You can also go back to solutions to review concepts and to check for errors.

One way to justify each step is to write each step on a separate line with the reason for the step. Be sure that each reason or explanation clearly indicates what operations to use.

When you reason logically from given facts to a conclusion, you are using **deductive reasoning.**

Develop Simplify numerical expressions and justify the process used.
Develop Express the solution clearly and logically by using the appropriate mathematical notation and terms and clear language.
Develop Note the method of deriving the solution.

1 EXAMPLE

Evaluate $x + |-7 \cdot 8|$ for $x = -3$. Justify each step.

Make one column to show each step in the solution. Make another column to show the reason for the step.

Step	Reason
$x + |-7 \cdot 8| = -3 + |-7 \cdot 8|$	Substitute.
$= -3 + |-56|$	Multiply inside grouping symbols.
$= -3 + 56$	Simplify absolute value.
$= 53$	Add.

2 EXAMPLE

A student simplified the expression $-16 \div 4 \cdot 2 + 3$. The student's work is shown at the right. Is the solution complete? If not, write a complete solution.

The first step combines several operations. Because more than one operation is shown at a time, the student can't easily check the answer.

Step	Reason
$-16 \div 4 \cdot 2 + 3$	
$-8 + 3$	Simplify.
5	Add.

Rewrite the solution showing the operation at each step.

Step	Reason
$-16 \div 4 \cdot 2 + 3 = -4 \cdot 2 + 3$	Divide first.
$= -8 + 3$	Multiply.
$= -5$	Add.

EXERCISES

1. Simplify $12 - 4 \cdot |5|$. Justify each step. Check your answer.

2. Explain how noting each step can help you check your answer.

When you solve a problem, you sometimes must identify missing information needed to solve the problem. First figure out how you would solve the problem. Then look at the given information. Decide what information you still need.

EXAMPLE

Mrs. Hernandez is ordering supplies for her department. She orders 5 boxes of pencils at $2.89 each, 2 boxes of blank CDs at $9.49 each, and 4 boxes of computer paper at $14.89 each. She has a coupon for a discount on the cost of the supplies. What other information does she need to find the cost of the supplies?

Ⓐ The date on which the supplies were purchased
Ⓑ The number of CDs in a box
Ⓒ The value of the discount coupon
Ⓓ The price of each pencil

Multiply the cost of each item by the number of boxes purchased, find the sum, and then subtract the value of the coupon. The information needed is the value of the coupon. So the correct answer is C.

Multiple Choice Practice

Read each question. Then write the correct answer on your paper.

1. Celia sells used CDs for $3 and used DVDs for $5. A customer buys 5 CDs and 3 DVDs. What other information is needed to find the customer's correct change?
   Ⓐ The types of music on the CDs
   Ⓑ The total number of CDs and DVDs
   Ⓒ The length of the movies on the DVDs
   Ⓓ The amount the customer gave Celia for the purchase

2. Mr. Bonner is ordering new band uniforms. The first ten uniforms ordered cost $89.45 each. The rest cost $79.00 each. The school will cover half of the cost. What other information is necessary to find the amount of money the school has to pay for the uniforms?
   Ⓐ The number of students in the band
   Ⓑ The amount each student will have to contribute
   Ⓒ The number of fundraisers needed to buy the uniforms
   Ⓓ Each band student's size

Chapter 1 Review

Choose the vocabulary term that correctly completes the sentence.

1. The ordered pair $(0, 0)$ represents the location of the __?__ .

2. A letter that stands for a number in an expression is a(n) __?__ .

3. The vertical axis in the coordinate plane is known as the __?__ .

4. The coordinate plane is divided into four __?__ .

5. All whole numbers and their opposites are __?__ .

6. In the ordered pair $(-5, 2)$, the number -5 is the __?__ .

7. The distance that a number is from zero on a number line is the __?__ of the number.

Go Online
PHSchool.com
For: Vocabulary quiz
Web Code: bjj-0151

Skills and Concepts

Lesson 1-1

- To identify variables, numerical expressions, and algebraic expressions
- To write algebraic expressions for word phrases

A **variable** is a letter that stands for a number. An **algebraic expression** uses variables, numerals, and operation symbols.

Write an algebraic expression for each word phrase.

8. twenty-five less than x

9. the product of n and 3

10. ten decreased by t

11. a number x divided by 4

12. a number n increased by 5

13. two more than y

Lesson 1-2

- To use the order of operations
- To use grouping symbols

To simplify a numerical expression, follow the **order of operations.**

1. Work inside grouping symbols.

2. Multiply and divide in order from left to right.

3. Add and subtract in order from left to right.

Simplify each expression.

14. $3 \cdot 7 + 6 \div 2$

15. $(4 + 8) \div 2 \cdot 2$

16. $9 \cdot 5 - 4(12 \div 6)$

Lesson 1-3
- To evaluate algebraic expressions
- To solve problems by evaluating expressions

To **evaluate** an algebraic expression, substitute a number for each variable. Use the order of operations to simplify.

Evaluate each expression.

17. $3x + 4$, for $x = 5$

18. $15 + 10 \div n$, for $n = 5$

19. $(y - 6)2$, for $y = 16$

20. $4(4 + m)$, for $m = 6$

21. $15t \cdot 10$, for $t = 3$

22. $z + [15 - (z - 1)]$, for $z = 4$

Lesson 1-4
- To graph and order integers
- To find opposites and absolute values

Integers are the set of whole numbers and their **opposites**. The **absolute value** of an integer is its distance from zero on a number line. On a number line, the integer farther to the right is the greater integer.

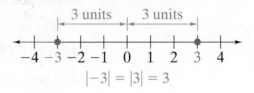

$|-3| = |3| = 3$

Simplify each expression.

23. the opposite of 17

24. $|-1{,}000|$

25. the absolute value of negative 9

26. the opposite of the absolute value of 12

Compare. Use >, <, or = to complete each statement.

27. $-7 \blacksquare -9$ **28.** $0 \blacksquare -3$ **29.** $-6 \blacksquare 2$ **30.** $|-5| \blacksquare |5|$

31. A slide at a water park is 30 ft high. What integer represents your change in elevation when you go down the slide?

Lessons 1-5 and 1-6
- To use models to add integers
- To use rules to add integers
- To use models to subtract integers
- To use rules to subtract integers

To add integers with the *same* sign, add their absolute values. The sum has the same sign. To add integers with *different* signs, find the difference of their absolute values. The sum has the sign of the integer with the greater absolute value. To subtract an integer, add its opposite.

Simplify each expression.

32. $8 + (-15)$ **33.** $-9 + 21$ **34.** $9 - (-5)$

35. $14 + (-9) + (-20)$ **36.** $-62 - (-59) - 24$

37. $-7 - 4$ **38.** $-4 + 12 + (-3) + (-6)$

39. An eagle leaves her nest on the side of a cliff. She soars upward 60 ft and then dives 80 ft. What is her change in elevation after leaving the nest?

Lesson 1-7

- To write rules for patterns
- To make predictions and test conjectures

Inductive reasoning is making conclusions based on patterns you observe. A conclusion reached by inductive reasoning is a **conjecture.**

Write a rule for each pattern. Find the next three numbers in the pattern.

40. $0, 6, 12, 18, \ldots$ **41.** $-18, -9, 0, 9, \ldots$ **42.** $\frac{1}{2}, 1, 1\frac{1}{2}, 2, \ldots$

Lesson 1-8

- To find number patterns

You can use patterns to solve problems.

43. Suppose you plan to save $12 per week. You have already saved $7.50. In how many weeks will you have saved at least $100?

44. A four-line classified ad costs $28 for a week. Each additional line costs $10.50. What is the weekly cost of a 12-line ad?

Lesson 1-9

- To multiply integers using repeated addition, patterns, and rules
- To divide integers using rules

To multiply or divide integers, multiply or divide the absolute values of the integers. If the integers have the same sign, the product or quotient is positive. If the integers have different signs, the product or quotient is negative.

Multiply or divide.

45. $7(-6)$ **46.** $250 \div (-50)$ **47.** $(-9)(-8)$

48. $-56 \div (-8)$ **49.** $-120 \div 40$ **50.** $-15(11)$

51. $\frac{-64}{8}$ **52.** $(-5)(-7)$ **53.** $(-6)(-17)$

Lesson 1-10

- To name coordinates and quadrants in the coordinate plane
- To graph points in the coordinate plane

A **coordinate plane** is formed by the intersection of two number lines. The *x*-axis and the *y*-axis divide the coordinate plane into four **quadrants.** An **ordered pair** gives the coordinates of a point. The *x*-coordinate shows the position right or left of the *y*-axis. The *y*-coordinate shows the position above or below the *x*-axis.

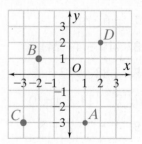

Write the coordinates of each point.

54. A **55.** B **56.** C **57.** D

Write an expression for each phrase.

1. a number n increased by nineteen

2. ten less than negative three

3. the product of x and negative five

4. 5 more than the opposite of y

Evaluate each expression for the given values of the variables.

5. $3a + 5$, for $a = -5$

6. $5m + 9 + 7n$, for $m = 8$ and $n = 1$

7. $3|x - y| + x$, for $x = 1$ and $y = 8$

8. $20 - 2(a - b)$, for $a = 3$ and $b = 2$

Simplify each expression.

9. $|-5|$

10. opposite of -9

11. opposite of 7

12. $|15|$

Use >, <, or = to complete each sentence.

13. $-6 \blacksquare -5$

14. $8 \blacksquare -10$

15. $-3 \blacksquare 3$

16. $0 \blacksquare -7$

Simplify each expression.

17. $15 + (-7)$

18. $-8 - (-12)$

19. $-9(-7)$

20. $54 \div (-6)$

21. $-6 \cdot 48$

22. $\frac{-56}{-7}$

23. $119 - (-24)$

24. $-47 + (-21)$

25. $-83 + 17$

26. $5(-12)(-3)(-1)$

27. $2 \cdot |14 - (-9)|$

28. $8 \cdot 6 \div (2 + 1)$

29. $4 + 7 \cdot 2 + 8$

30. $16 - 2 \cdot (5 + 3)$

In which quadrant or on which axis does each point lie?

31. $(-5, 7)$

32. $(0, -4)$

33. $(-8, -6)$

Write the coordinates of each point.

34. F

35. G

36. H

37. J

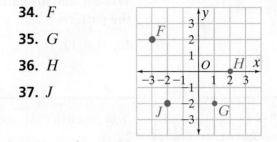

38. A shirt costs $15 and jeans cost $25.
   a. Write an expression for the cost of j jeans and s shirts.
   b. Evaluate the expression to find the cost of three pairs of jeans and five shirts.
   c. How many pairs of jeans can you buy for $60?

39. Which statement is *always* true?
   A. The absolute value of an integer is equal to the opposite of the integer.
   B. The absolute value of an integer is greater than zero.
   C. An integer is greater than its opposite.
   D. A positive integer is greater than a negative integer.

40. A submarine was 250 m below sea level. It rose 75 m. Use an integer to describe the new depth of the submarine.

41. Write a rule for the pattern below. Find the next three numbers in the pattern.
   $100, 90, 85, 75, 70, 60, \ldots$

42. You are in an elevator on the seventh floor. You go down 4 floors and then up 8 floors. Then you go down 3 floors and up 9 floors. The elevator goes down again 2 floors, and you get off. According to the pattern, on which floor are you now?

43. **Writing in Math** Describe how to order the integers $2, -6, 9, 0,$ and -13 from least to greatest.

Standards Mastery

Some standards ask you to write expressions and equations to solve problems. Read the question at the right and review the answer choices. Then follow the tips to answer the sample question.

Tip 1
Rewrite the relationship(s) given in the problem as simply as you can.

Before her birthday, Tara had 15 CDs. Her mother gave her n CDs. Tara's older brother Ben has twice as many CDs as Tara has now. Which equation can be used to represent b, the number of CDs Ben has?

Ⓐ $b = 2 \cdot 15 + n$
Ⓑ $b = 15 + 2n$
Ⓒ $b = 2(15 + n)$
Ⓓ $b = 15 + 2 + n$

Tip 2
Use the variables given in the problem to write an equation.

Think It Through
Ben has twice as many CDs as Tara. Tara has $15 + n$ CDs. So $b = 2(15 + n)$. The correct answer is C.

Vocabulary Review

As you solve some problems, you must understand the meanings of mathematical terms. Match each term with its mathematical meaning.

A. coordinate plane

B. expression

C. bar graph

D. conjecture

E. ordered pair

I. a conclusion based on inductive reasoning

II. identifies the x- and y-coordinates of a point

III. a graph that compares amounts

IV. formed by two number lines that intersect at their zero points

V. a mathematical phrase that uses numerals and operation symbols

Read each question. Then write the letter of the correct answer on your paper.

1. Leroy has d dollars in his bank account. Each week, Leroy adds $5 to his account. Which equation can be used to find t, the total in Leroy's account after 3 weeks? (Lesson 1-1)

   Ⓐ $t = 5 + d + 3$
   Ⓑ $t = 5d + 3$
   Ⓒ $t = 3d + 5$
   Ⓓ $t = d + 3 \cdot 5$

2. Paloma jogs x miles every day for 6 days. On the seventh day, she jogs 5 miles. Which expression shows her total mileage for the week? (Lesson 1-1)

   Ⓐ $7x + 5$
   Ⓑ $(x + 6) + 5$
   Ⓒ $6x + 5$
   Ⓓ $5x + 6$

3. At Connor Middle School, there are 25 students on the math team. There are *s* students on the science team. If 10 students are on both the math and science teams, which expression represents the number of students that are on *only* the science team? **(Lesson 1-3)**

   Ⓐ $s + 10$

   Ⓑ $10 - s$

   Ⓒ $s - 10$

   Ⓓ $s - 25$

4. The prices for commuter rail tickets are shown below.

Commuter Rail Tickets	
Type of ticket	**Price**
Adult (ages 18 – 65)	$10.00
Student (ages 5 – 17)	$5.00
Child (under 5)	$2.00
Senior Citizen (over 65)	$4.00

   At the first stop, *w* adults, *x* students, *y* children, and *z* senior citizens board the commuter rail. Which expression shows the total paid for tickets? **(Lesson 1-3)**

   Ⓐ $4z + 10w + 5x + 2y$

   Ⓑ $4w + 10x + 5y + 2z$

   Ⓒ $10z + 5y + 2x + 4w$

   Ⓓ $5(w + x + y + z)$

5. Ace taxi charges a passenger $5.00 plus $0.75 for each quarter of a mile. The equation $c = 5 + 4(0.75)n$ can be used to find the cost for traveling *n* miles. What is the cost of a 12-mile trip from the airport to downtown? **(Lesson 1-3)**

   Ⓐ $36.00   Ⓒ $53.00

   Ⓑ $41.00   Ⓓ $65.00

6. The cost of a bus ticket is $1.25. On Monday, there were a total of *a* tickets sold for the Route 6 bus. On Tuesday, there were 4 fewer tickets sold. Which expression shows the total cost of the tickets purchased on Tuesday? **(Lesson 1-3)**

   Ⓐ $1.25a - 4$

   Ⓑ $1.25 - 4a$

   Ⓒ $1.25(4 - a)$

   Ⓓ $1.25(a - 4)$

7. The numbers of petals on flowers form mathematical patterns. With few exceptions, the numbers of petals will be either 3, 5, 8, 13, 21, 34, or another number continuing in this pattern. What number will follow 34 in this pattern? **(Lesson 1-7)**

   Ⓐ 35   Ⓒ 68

   Ⓑ 55   Ⓓ 73

8. Which should be the sixth number in the following pattern? **(Lesson 1-7)**

   $$1, 4, 9, 16, 25, \ldots$$

   Ⓐ 34   Ⓒ 36

   Ⓑ 35   Ⓓ 37

9. The figure below is known as Pascal's Triangle.

   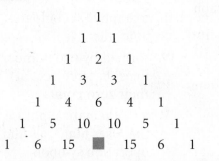

   Which number should go in the blank? **(Lesson 1-7)**

   Ⓐ 20   Ⓒ 29

   Ⓑ 25   Ⓓ 30

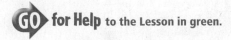

Standards Mastery

10. Points $A(1, 2)$, $B(3, 5)$, and $C(4, 1)$ form a triangle. If the x-coordinate of each point is multiplied by -1, which of the following is true? **(Lesson 1-2)**

- Ⓐ The new triangle is to the left of the original triangle.
- Ⓑ The new triangle is to the right of the original triangle.
- Ⓒ The new triangle is directly above the original triangle.
- Ⓓ The new triangle is directly below the original triangle.

11. Which graph shows a triangle with one vertex at $(3, -1)$? **(Lesson 1-10)**

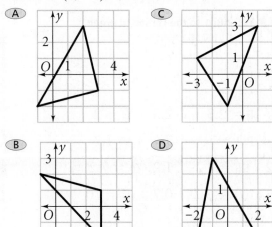

12. Luiz, Dan, and Camila participated in a fundraiser. Dan got 3 times as many pledges as Luiz. If Camilla got 23 more pledges than Luiz, and Luiz got 33 pledges, how many total pledges did they get? **(Lesson 1-2)**

- Ⓐ 224
- Ⓑ 188
- Ⓒ 155
- Ⓓ 138

13. Kim's aunt gave her $35 towards the cost of a printer. Kim makes $24 per week baby-sitting. How much has Kim saved after five weeks? **(Lesson 1-2)**

- Ⓐ $59
- Ⓑ $120
- Ⓒ $155
- Ⓓ $295

14. The *Titanic* ship sank to a depth of $-12,600$ feet. The *Edmund Fitzgerald* ship sank to a depth of -530 feet. What is the difference in depths between the two sunken ships? **(Lesson 1-2)**

- Ⓐ 530 feet
- Ⓑ 730 feet
- Ⓒ 12,070 feet
- Ⓓ 14,130 feet

15. The video store charges a $10 membership fee and $3 for every video rented. For the summer months of June, July, and August, the store runs a special. Each customer gets a free video after every 10 videos rented. Jane joins the store in June. Over the summer, she rents a total of 26 videos. How much does she pay in total? **(Lesson 1-2)**

- Ⓐ $72
- Ⓑ $78
- Ⓒ $82
- Ⓓ $88

Solving One-Step Equations and Inequalities

CHAPTER

2

What You've Learned

Add, subtract, multiply, and divide rational numbers (integers, fractions, and terminating decimals) and take positive rational numbers to whole-number powers.

Use variables and appropriate operations to write an equation that represents a verbal description.

 **Check Your Readiness** **GO** **for Help** to the Lesson in green.

Related Equations (Skills Handbook, pp. 687–692)

Complete the related equations.

1. $2.0 - \blacksquare = 0.9$ $0.9 + \blacksquare = 2.0$ **2.** $2 + \blacksquare = 2.3$ $2.3 - \blacksquare = 2$

3. $2.0 - \blacksquare = 1.3$ $1.3 + \blacksquare = 2.0$ **4.** $\blacksquare + 1.2 = 7$ $7 - \blacksquare = 1.2$

5. $3 \cdot \blacksquare = 7.5$ $7.5 \div \blacksquare = 3$ **6.** $7.2 \div \blacksquare = 1.2$ $1.2 \cdot \blacksquare = 7.2$

7. $3.6 \div \blacksquare = 6$ $6 \cdot \blacksquare = 3.6$ **8.** $\blacksquare \cdot (10) = 0.7$ $0.7 \div \blacksquare = 10$

Comparing Numbers (Lessons 1-5, 1-6, and 1-9)

Compare. Use $>$, $<$, or $=$ to complete each statement.

9. $6 \blacksquare 16$

10. $5 \blacksquare -5$

11. $-52 \blacksquare -21$

12. $0 \blacksquare -8$

13. $-7 \blacksquare 3$

14. $12 + 3 \blacksquare 19 - 4$

15. $-2 \cdot 6 \blacksquare 4 \cdot (-3)$

16. $27 \div 9 \blacksquare 6 \cdot 2$

17. $18 - 27 \blacksquare -34 + 12$

18. $8(-5) \blacksquare 100 - 65$

19. $6 \div (10 - 8) \blacksquare 1 + 5$

20. $3(-2)(-4) \blacksquare 4(-3)(2)$

Order of Operations With Integers (Lesson 1-2)

Simplify each expression.

21. $5 \cdot 2 + 5 \cdot 3$

22. $7(6 - 2)$

23. $10 \cdot 3 - 5 \cdot 3$

24. $-(34 + 76)$

25. $4(6) + 4(3)$

26. $-4(12 - 16)$

27. $7(8) - 10(8)$

28. $11 \cdot 9 - 6 \cdot 9$

29. $-2 \cdot 3 - 2 \cdot 7$

30. $6 \cdot (-9) - 3(-9)$

31. $-5(3) - (-5)(2)$

32. $(72 - 81)(5)$

What You'll Learn Next

Simplify numerical expressions by applying properties of rational numbers (e.g., identity, inverse, distributive, associative, commutative) and justify the process used.

Use algebraic terminology (e.g., term, coefficient, constant) correctly.

▲ You can use the properties of numbers to solve problems involving fund-raising.

New Vocabulary

🔊 **English and Spanish Audio Online**

- **additive identity** (p. 69)
- **Associative Properties of Addition and Multiplication** (p. 68)
- **coefficient** (p. 78)
- **Commutative Properties of Addition and Multiplication** (p. 68)
- **constant** (p. 78)
- **Distributive Property** (p. 73)
- **equation** (p. 82)
- **inequality** (p. 102)
- **inverse operations** (p. 88)
- **like terms** (p. 78)
- **multiplicative identity** (p. 69)
- **open sentence** (p. 82)
- **simplify an algebraic expression** (p. 78)
- **solution of an equation** (p. 83)
- **solution of an inequality** (p. 102)
- **term** (p. 78)

Academic Vocabulary
- **determine** (p. 115)
- **explain** (p. 115)
- **identify** (p. 115)

Properties of Numbers

Introduce Simplify numerical expressions by applying properties of rational numbers (e.g., identity, associative, commutative) and justify the process used.

Develop Express the solution clearly and logically by using the appropriate mathematical notation and terms and clear language.

What You'll Learn

- To identify properties of addition and multiplication
- To use properties to solve problems

... And Why

To find answers quickly using mental math

✓ Check Skills You'll Need

Simplify.

1. $-18 + (-7)$

2. $32 - (-3)$

3. $(-13) + 6$

4. $2 - 48$

GO for Help

Lessons 1-5 and 1-6

🔊 New Vocabulary

- Commutative Properties
- Associative Properties
- additive identity
- multiplicative identity
- Identity Properties

Identifying Properties

The sum of 6 and 4 is the same as the sum of 4 and 6. Similarly, the product of 9 and 5 is the same as the product of 5 and 9. These suggest the following properties.

Take Note ✎ Commutative Properties of Addition and Multiplication

Changing the order of the values you are adding or multiplying does not change the sum or product.

Arithmetic	Algebra
$6 + 4 = 4 + 6$	$a + b = b + a$
$9 \cdot 5 = 5 \cdot 9$	$a \cdot b = b \cdot a$

You can also change the grouping of the values before you add or multiply them.

Take Note ✎ Associative Properties of Addition and Multiplication

Changing the grouping of the values you are adding or multiplying does not change the sum or product.

Arithmetic	Algebra
$(2 + 7) + 3 = 2 + (7 + 3)$	$(a + b) + c = a + (b + c)$
$(9 \cdot 4)5 = 9(4 \cdot 5)$	$(a \cdot b)c = a(b \cdot c)$

1 EXAMPLE Using the Associative Property of Addition

Carlos rented a set of golf clubs for $7 and a golf cart for $12. He paid a greens fee of $23. Find his total cost.

You can use the Associative Property of Addition to find the total cost in two different ways.

$(7 + 12) + 23 = 19 + 23 = 42$ **Add 7 and 12 first.**
$7 + (12 + 23) = 7 + 35 = 42$ **Add 12 and 23 first.**

Carlos's total cost was $42.

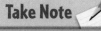

Quick Check

1. You spend $6 for dinner, $8 for a movie, and $4 for popcorn. Find your total cost. Explain which property or properties you used.

When you add a number and 0, the sum equals the original number. The **additive identity** is 0. When you multiply a number and 1, the product equals the original number. The **multiplicative identity** is 1.

Vocabulary Tip

In mathematics, an identity leaves the value of other numbers unchanged.

Take Note Identity Properties of Addition and Multiplication

The sum of any number and zero is the original number. The product of any number and 1 is the original number.

Arithmetic	Algebra
$12 + 0 = 12; 10 \cdot 1 = 10$	$a + 0 = a; a \cdot 1 = a$

2 EXAMPLE   Identifying Properties

Name each property shown.

a. $5 \cdot 7 = 7 \cdot 5$ Commutative Property of Multiplication

b. $c \cdot 1 = c$ Identity Property of Multiplication

c. $7 + a = a + 7$ Commutative Property of Addition

d. $5(xy) = (5x)y$ Associative Property of Multiplication

Quick Check

2. Name each property shown.

   a. $3 + 6 = 6 + 3$ b. $8 = 1 \cdot 8$ c. $(3z)m = 3(zm)$

Using Properties

When numbers are easy to compute mentally, you can use properties and mental math to find sums.

Problem Solving Tip

Look for combinations that equal 10 or a multiple of 10, since they are easier to use in calculating mentally.

3 EXAMPLE   Using Mental Math With Addition

Use mental math to simplify $(81 + 6) + 9$.

$(81 + 6) + 9$

$= (6 + 81) + 9$ Use the Commutative Property of Addition.

$= 6 + (81 + 9)$ Use the Associative Property of Addition.

$= 6 + 90$ Work within grouping symbols.

$= 96$ Add.

✅ Quick Check

3. Use mental math to simplify each expression.

    a. $6 + 7 + 14$ **b.** $8 + 0 + 2 + (-7)$

    c. $5 + 12 + 18 + 5$ **d.** $19 + (-30) + 21$

---

4 EXAMPLE **Using Properties**

$.35

$.85

$1.65

Suppose you buy the school supplies shown at the left. Use mental math to find the cost of the supplies.

$1.65 + 0.85 + 0.35$

$= 0.85 + 1.65 + 0.35$	**Use the Commutative Property of Addition.**
$= 0.85 + (1.65 + 0.35)$	**Use the Associative Property of Addition.**
$= 0.85 + 2.00$	**Work within grouping symbols.**
$= 2.85$	**Add.**

The cost of the school supplies is $2.85.

✅ Quick Check

4. Use the supermarket receipt and mental math to find the cost of the groceries.

> 4321XXXX21
> **SOUTH STREET MARKET**
> ITEMS
> 1 GALLON MILK $2.30
> BREAD $1.80
> APPLES $2.20

Quick Tip

For a guide to adding decimals, see Skills Handbook, page 687.

You can also use mental math to help you find products.

---

5 EXAMPLE **Using Mental Math With Multiplication**

Use mental math to simplify $(4 \cdot 9) \cdot 5$.

$(4 \cdot 9) \cdot 5 = (9 \cdot 4) \cdot 5$	**Use the Commutative Property of Multiplication.**
$= 9 \cdot (4 \cdot 5)$	**Use the Associative Property of Multiplication.**
$= 9 \cdot 20$	**Multiply within parentheses.**
$= 180$	**Multiply.**

✅ Quick Check

5. Use mental math to simplify each expression.

    a. $25 \cdot (3 \cdot 4)$ **b.** $3 \cdot 1 \cdot -5 \cdot 8$

    c. $2(-8)(-15)$ **d.** $5 \cdot 9 \cdot 6 \cdot (-2) \cdot (-1)$

Name each property shown.

1. ◆ + ● = ● + ◆

2. ■ · (◆ · ●) = (■ · ◆) · ●

Which two numbers would you combine first? Explain.

3. $5 + 36 + 95$

4. $2 \cdot 17 \cdot 5$

5. Critical Thinking How do reordering and regrouping help you to add mentally? Include examples.

Standards Practice

For more exercises, see *Extra Skills and Word Problem Practice*.

A Practice by Example

Example 1
(page 68)

Go for Help

Use the Associative Property to write two different expressions that you could use to find each sum.

6. Add 1, 3, and 25.

7. Add 5, 91, and 11.

8. On a road trip, your family spends $120 for gas, $15 for bottled water, and $80 for food. Find your family's total cost. Explain which property or properties you used.

Example 2
(page 69)

Name each property shown.

9. $7 + 6 = 6 + 7$

10. $0 + 8 = 8$

11. $(6 \cdot 15)2 = 6(15 \cdot 2)$

12. $(12r)s = 12(rs)$

13. $999 \cdot 1 = 999$

14. $ab = ba$

Example 3
(page 69)

Mental Math Use mental math to simplify each expression.

15. $(5 + 23) + 65$

16. $9 + (14 + 1)$

17. $31 + 0 + (-2)$

Examples 4 and 5
(page 70)

18. $(0.50 + 34) + 3.50$

19. $(4.55 + 27) + 5.45$

20. $1.50 + (3.17 + 6.50)$

21. $-0.25 + 4.88 + 3.25$

22. $6 \cdot 3 \cdot 5$

23. $5 \cdot 7 \cdot (-2)$

24. $25 \cdot 4 \cdot 8$

25. $8 \cdot 4 \cdot (-10)$

26. Mental Math Loryn is flying roundtrip from Dallas, Texas, to Minneapolis, Minnesota. The fare for her ticket is $308. Each airport charges a $16 airport fee. There is also a tax of $12 on the fare. What is the total cost of Loryn's ticket?

B Apply Your Skills

Simplify each expression.

27. $25 + 157 + (-75)$

28. $140 + 17 + (-60)$

29. $5 \cdot 50 \cdot 20 \cdot (-2)$

30. $125 + 18 + 75 + 162$

Homework Video Tutor

Visit: PHSchool.com
Web Code: bje-0201

31. Writing in Math Which two numbers would you combine first to simplify $3 + 6 + 27$? Explain.

$15.20

$7.65

$1.35

32. Lance has purchased some supplies to start his new garden. Use the prices shown at the left and mental math to find the cost of the supplies.

Mental Math Evaluate each expression.

33. $x(y \cdot z)$, for $x = 4$, $y = 27$, and $z = 5$

34. $a + b + c$, for $a = 14$, $b = 252$, and $c = 26$

35. **Reasoning** Are there commutative and associative properties for subtraction and division? Justify your answer.

C Challenge

36. **Reasoning** Can you use $4 + 2 = 6$ as your first step in simplifying $3 \cdot 4 + 2 \div (-2)$? Explain.

37. For what values of a and c is the equation $ab + 2c = b$ true?

Multiple Choice Practice and Mixed Review

For Standards Tutorials, visit PHSchool.com. Web Code: bjq-9045

38. Which equation shows the Associative Property of Addition?

Ⓐ $8 + 6 + 7 = 8 + 7 + 6$

Ⓑ $(10 + 5) + 15 = 10 + (5 + 15)$

Ⓒ $9 + 0 + (-1) = 9 + (-1)$

Ⓓ $(-2) \cdot 1 \cdot 9 = (-2) \cdot 9$

39. You spent $3.00 on milk, $1.00 on apples, and $2.00 on granola bars. You have a coupon for $0.50 off the total. There is no tax. What information is needed to find the amount of change you receive?

Ⓐ The amount of money in your wallet

Ⓑ The amount of money given to the cashier

Ⓒ The number of granola bars you bought

Ⓓ The weight of the apples

40. Triangle ABC is shown in the graph. Which are the coordinates of Point B?

Ⓐ $(2, 2)$

Ⓑ $(-2, 2)$

Ⓒ $(-2, -2)$

Ⓓ $(2, -2)$

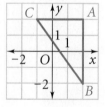

Lesson 1-10

In which quadrant does the graph of each ordered pair lie?

41. $(-6, -3)$ **42.** $(8, -1)$ **43.** $(-4, 17)$ **44.** $(-1, 4)$

Lesson 1-9

45. Lin worked 4 hours per day for 3 days to build a model bridge. How many hours did she spend on the project?

Develop Simplify numerical expressions by applying properties of rational numbers (e.g., distributive) and justify the process used.

Develop Use a variety of methods, such as models, to explain mathematical reasoning.

What You'll Learn

• To use the distributive property with numerical expressions

• To use the distributive property with algebraic expressions

. . . And Why

To solve real-world multiplication problems using mental math

✓ Check Skills You'll Need

Simplify each expression.

1. $3 \cdot 7 - 9$

2. $(9 - 5)6$

3. $8 + 2 \cdot 6$

4. $2(6 - 3)$

5. $4 \cdot 5 - 4 \cdot 3$

6. $3 \cdot 2 - 1 \cdot 2$

 for Help
Lesson 1-2

🔊 New Vocabulary

• Distributive Property

Numerical Expressions

Standards Investigation

Exploring the Distributive Property

You can find the total area of two rectangles by two methods.

1. Method 1: Find the area of each rectangle. Then find the sum of the areas.

2. Method 2: Combine the two rectangles into one large rectangle. Find its length. Find its width. Then find its area.

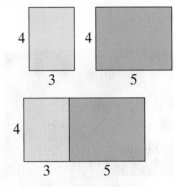

3. On a piece of paper, draw two rectangles with the same width, and lengths different from those above. Label the dimensions. Repeat Method 1 and Method 2 with your pair of rectangles. What do you notice about your results?

The Activity above shows different ways to find the sum of the areas of two rectangles. It suggests the *Distributive Property,* which combines multiplication with addition and subtraction.

Take Note   Distributive Property

To multiply a sum or difference, multiply each number within the parentheses by the number outside the parentheses.

Arithmetic	Algebra
$3(2 + 6) = 3(2) + 3(6)$	$a(b + c) = ab + ac$
$(2 + 6)3 = 2(3) + 6(3)$	$(b + c)a = ba + ca$
$6(7 - 4) = 6(7) - 6(4)$	$a(b - c) = ab - ac$
$(7 - 4)6 = 7(6) - 4(6)$	$(b - c)a = ba - ca$

You can use the Distributive Property to multiply mentally.

1 EXAMPLE   **Using the Distributive Property I**

Use the Distributive Property to find 20(102) mentally.

$$20(102) = 20(100 + 2)$$ **Write 102 as (100 + 2).**

$$20(100 + 2) = 20 \cdot 100 + 20 \cdot 2$$ **Use the Distributive Property.**

$$= 2,000 + 40$$ **Multiply.**

$$= 2,040$$ **Add.**

✓ Quick Check

1. Find the product $9 \cdot 199$ mentally.

2 EXAMPLE   **Using the Distributive Property II**

Multiple Choice **At a fund-raising sale, a library sold 397 books for the price shown at the left. How much money did the library make?**

ⓐ $1,600   ⓑ $1,588   ⓒ $401   ⓓ $397

$$(397)4 = (400 - 3)4$$ **Write 397 as (400 − 3).**

$$= 400 \cdot 4 - 3 \cdot 4$$ **Use the Distributive Property.**

$$= 1,600 - 12$$ **Multiply.**

$$= 1,588$$ **Subtract.**

The library made $1,588. The answer is B.

✓ Quick Check

2. Your club sold calendars for $7. Club members sold 204 calendars. How much money did they raise?

3 EXAMPLE   **Using the Distributive Property III**

Simplify 8(15) − 8(5).

$$8(15) - 8(5) = 8(15 - 5)$$ **Use the Distributive Property.**

$$= 8(10)$$ **Work within grouping symbols.**

$$= 80$$ **Multiply.**

✓ Quick Check

3. Simplify each expression.

   a. $7(21) + 7(9)$ **b.** $12(52) - 12(62)$ **c.** $(16)7 - (11)7$

You can model the Distributive Property with algebraic expressions.

4 EXAMPLE **Using Models to Multiply**

Use a model to multiply $3(2x + 5)$.

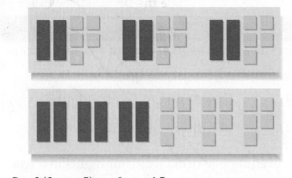

Model three groups
of $2x + 5$.

Use the Commutative
Property of Addition
to regroup.

Problem Solving Tip

▌ represents x.

▢ represents 1.

▐ represents -1.

So, $3(2x + 5) = 6x + 15$.

✓ Quick Check

4. Use a model to multiply.

    a. $4(2x - 3)$ **b.** $3(x + 4)$ **c.** $(3x + 1)2$

In Example 4, notice that 3 multiplies both $2x$ and 5.
That is, $3(2x + 5) = 3(2x) + 3(5)$.

5 EXAMPLE **Using the Distributive Property IV**

Multiply.

a. $-5(4x - 3)$

    $-5(4x - 3) = -5(4x) - (-5)(3)$ **Use the Distributive Property.**

               $= -20x - (-15)$ **Multiply.**

               $= -20x + 15$ **Simplify.**

b. $(2x + 5)7$

    $(2x + 5)7 = (2x)7 + (5)7$ **Use the Distributive Property.**

            $= 14x + 35$ **Multiply.**

Vocabulary Tip

When you distribute
papers in class, you
give some to each
classmate. Similarly,
when you <u>distribute</u> a
number over a sum
or difference, you
multiply each value
within the parentheses
by that number.

✓ Quick Check

5. Multiply.

    a. $2(7 - 3d)$ **b.** $(6m + 1)(3)$ **c.** $-3(5t - 2)$

Copy and complete each statement.

1. $12(3 + 5) = \blacksquare \cdot 3 + \blacksquare \cdot 5$ **2.** $(y - 6)z = y \cdot \blacksquare - 6 \cdot \blacksquare$

3. $a(3 - b) = \blacksquare 3 - \blacksquare b$ **4.** $6 \cdot b + 12 \cdot b = (6 + 12)\blacksquare$

Standards Practice

For more exercises, see *Extra Skills and Word Problem Practice.*

A Practice by Example

Examples 1 and 2
(page 74)

GO for Help

Mental Math Use the Distributive Property to simplify.

5. $6(23)$ **6.** $5(18)$ **7.** $7(48)$ **8.** $13(101)$

9. $(104)(9)$ **10.** $6(52)$ **11.** $8(98)$ **12.** $(208)4$

13. A theater sold out its evening performances four nights in a row. The theater has 294 seats. How many people attended the theater in the four nights?

Example 3
(page 74)

Simplify each expression.

14. $7(3) + 7(5)$ **15.** $2(9) - 3(9)$ **16.** $6(4) + 6(8)$

17. $9(3) - 2(3)$ **18.** $(12)27 - (12)24$ **19.** $(3)5 + (27)5$

Example 4
(page 75)

Write an expression using parentheses for each model. Then multiply.

20.

21.

Multiply. Use models as needed.

22. $2(t - 5)$ **23.** $(v - 3)4$ **24.** $3(2h - 1)$ **25.** $-2(7z + 3)$

Example 5
(page 75)

Multiply.

26. $7(b - 3)$ **27.** $12(a + 3)$ **28.** $(2 + 3d)5$ **29.** $-5(m + 6)$

30. $3(5 - 3w)$ **31.** $-7(t - 4)$ **32.** $4(b + 5)$ **33.** $(y - 6)2$

B Apply Your Skills

Mental Math Use the Distributive Property to simplify.

34. $5(1,005)$ **35.** $-32 \cdot 6 + 29 \cdot 6$

36. $4 \cdot 19 - 4 \cdot (11)$ **37.** $(-8) \cdot 10 + 3 \cdot (-8)$

Mental Math Solve using mental math.

38. Every day, Lila eats a bowl of cereal that has 193 Calories. What is the total number of Calories in cereal that Lila eats in a week?

39. The trip from Roberto's house to his aunt's house is 896 miles. How long is the round trip?

Use the Distributive Property to multiply.

40. $-3(2t + 6)$ **41.** $-7(-3n + 2)$ **42.** $(4 - t)(-7)$

43. $-5(-m + 6)$ **44.** $-8(6 - c)$ **45.** $(5y + 8)(-3)$

Name each property shown.

46. $m[t + (-t)] = mt + m(-t)$ **47.** $m[t + (-t)] = m(-t + t)$

48. $m[t + (-t)] = [t + (-t)]m$ **49.** $m + [t + (-t)] = (m + t) + (-t)$

50. **Writing in Math** Explain how to use the Distributive Property to multiply $6(3r + 4s)$.

51. **Error Analysis** Suppose your friend wrote $7(2m + t) = 14m + t$. What error did your friend make?

52. **Reasoning** Explain why $c(a + b) = (a + b)c$.

C Challenge   **53.** Write an expression in the form $a(b + c)$ that simplifies to $21x + 24$.

Multiple Choice Practice and Mixed Review

For Standards Tutorials, visit PHSchool.com. Web Code: bjq-9045

54. There are 7 squares on a piece of paper. Juan places 1 penny in the first square, 2 pennies in the second, 4 in the third, and 8 in the fourth. He keeps doubling the number of pennies he places in each square. How many pennies are there in all 7 squares?
  Ⓐ 63   Ⓑ 64   Ⓒ 127   Ⓓ 128

55. Which equation correctly illustrates the Distributive Property?
  Ⓐ $18(100 + 4) = (18 \cdot 100) + 4$
  Ⓑ $18(100 + 4) = (18 + 100) \cdot (18 + 4)$
  Ⓒ $18(100 + 4) = (18 + 100) \cdot 4$
  Ⓓ $18(100 + 4) = (18 \cdot 100) + (18 \cdot 4)$

 for Help   Lessons 1-5 and 1-6   **56.** You have $120 in your checking account. In one month, you deposit $30, write a check for $21, withdraw $20, and deposit $45. Find your balance at the end of the month.

Lesson 1-3   **Evaluate each expression.**

57. $7 - m$, for $m = 6$ **58.** $6t + 1$, for $t = -2$ **59.** $c \div 3 - 5$, for $c = 6$

2-3 Simplifying Algebraic Expressions

Develop Simplify numerical expressions by applying properties of rational numbers and justify the process used.

Introduce Use algebraic terminology (e.g. term, coefficient, constant) correctly.

What You'll Learn

- To identify parts of an algebraic expression
- To simplify expressions

. . . And Why

To extend addition and subtraction skills to include variables

Check Skills You'll Need

Simplify each expression.

1. $5(b + 4)$
2. $-3(2x + 5)$
3. $4(-8 - 3q)$
4. $-6(2b - 7)$

GO for Help Lesson 2-2

New Vocabulary

- term
- constant
- like terms
- coefficient
- simplify an algebraic expression

Identifying Parts of an Algebraic Expression

The diagram shows the possible parts of an algebraic expression.

A **term** is a number or the product of a number and variable(s).

$7a + 4a + 3b - 6$ ← A **constant** is a term that has no variable.

Like terms have identical variables.

A **coefficient** is a number that multiplies a variable.

Rewriting subtraction as addition can help you identify the coefficient(s) and constant(s) in an expression.

$5x - 3y + z - 2$

$= 5x + (-3y) + z + (-2)$ **Rewrite subtraction as adding opposites.**

$= 5x + (-3y) + 1z + (-2)$ **Identity Property of Multiplication**

The coefficients are 5, −3, and 1. The constant is −2. Notice that the sign between terms in the original expression determines whether a coefficient or constant is positive or negative.

1 EXAMPLE Identifying Parts of an Expression

Name the coefficients, the like terms, and the constants in $3m - 2n + n - 4$.

Coefficients: 3, −2, 1 Like terms: $-2n$ and n Constant: −4

Quick Check

1. Name the coefficients, the like terms, and the constants.

a. $6 + 2s + 4s$ b. $-4x$ c. $9m + 2r - 2m + r$

Simplifying Algebraic Expressions

You **simplify an algebraic expression** by replacing it with an equivalent expression that has as few terms as possible. You can use models to help you simplify.

2 EXAMPLE Using Models to Simplify

Simplify $2x + 4 + 3x$**.**

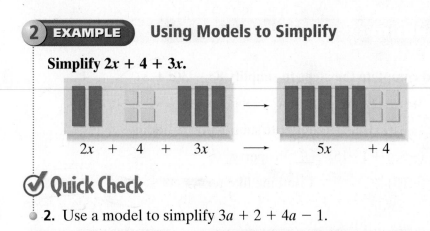

$2x + 4 + 3x \longrightarrow 5x + 4$

✓ Quick Check

2. Use a model to simplify $3a + 2 + 4a - 1$.

You can also use the Distributive Property to combine like terms.

3 EXAMPLE Combining Like Terms

Simplify $5y + y$**.**

$5y + y = 5y + 1y$	**Use the Identity Property of Multiplication.**
$= (5 + 1)y$	**Use the Distributive Property.**
$= 6y$	**Simplify.**

GO Online

Video Tutor Help
Visit: PHSchool.com
Web Code: bje-0775

✓ Quick Check

3. Simplify each expression.

   a. $3b - b$ **b.** $-4m - 9m$ **c.** $p + 6p - 4p$

Deductive reasoning is the process of reasoning logically from given facts to a conclusion. As you justify the steps in a problem, you are using deductive reasoning.

4 EXAMPLE Using Deductive Reasoning

Evaluate $4g + 9 + 3g$ **for** $g = 5$**. Justify each step.**

$4g + 9 + 3g = 4g + 3g + 9$	**Commutative Property of Addition**
$= (4 + 3)g + 9$	**Distributive Property**
$= 7g + 9$	**Simplify.**
$= 7(5) + 9$	**Substitute.**
$= 44$	**Simplify.**

✓ Quick Check

4. Simplify $6y + 4m - 7y + m$. Justify each step.

Copy and complete the steps to simplify $8c - 3(c + 5)$.

$8c - 3(c + 5)$

1. $8c + (-3)(c + 5)$ Rewrite subtraction as adding   ? .

2. $8c + (-3c) + (-15)$? Property

3. $\blacksquare + (-15)$ Combine like terms.

Standards Practice

For more exercises, see *Extra Skills and Word Problem Practice*.

Ⓐ Practice by Example

Example 1
(page 78)

GO for Help

Name the coefficients, the like terms, and the constants.

4. $3x + 5y - 3$ **5.** $2x - 7$ **6.** $4x - 7x + 3x$

7. $6xy - 5xy$ **8.** $-3x$ **9.** $a + 2a + 3a - 4a$

Example 2
(page 79)

Use a model to simplify each expression.

10. $x + 2 + 3x + 5 + x + 3 + 2x$

11. $2x + 1 + x - 4 + 4x + 1$

12. $x + 2 + 3x$ **13.** $2x + 1 + 6x - 4$

Example 3
(page 79)

Simplify each expression.

14. $12a + a$ **15.** $5a + 8a$ **16.** $-2b + b$

17. $7w - w$ **18.** $2r - 5 + 6r$ **19.** $4a - 3 + 5a$

Example 4
(page 79)

Simplify each expression. Justify each step.

20. $2g + 3(g + 5)$ **21.** $-3z + 8(z + y)$

22. $4m + 3d - 5m + d$ **23.** $t - 3 + 2(t + 2)$

Ⓑ Apply Your Skills

Simplify each expression.

24. $8z + 8y + 3z$ **25.** $t - 3t + 2t + 4$ **26.** $18 + 6(9k - 13)$

27. $r + 3 - 6r + r$ **28.** $-4(a + 3) - a$ **29.** $4m + 3 - 5m + m$

30. $3(g + 5) + 2g$ **31.** $2b - 6 + 3b - b$ **32.** $-5 + 3x + 3 + 2$

33. Juan bought supplies for his new gecko. He bought four plants for p dollars each. He also bought a 10-gallon tank for $10 and a water dish for $3. Write an expression Juan could use to find the total cost of the supplies.

34. Error Analysis Your friend simplified $x + y + xy$ to $2xy$. What error did your friend make?

35. Writing in Math The expression $10bc$ has two variables. Explain why $10bc$ is not two terms.

C Challenge

Simplify each expression. Justify each step.

36. $(2t + 4)3 + 6(-5t) - (-8)$ **37.** $-12(5x) + 3(-7x) - x$

38. $w + 3w + 4(5 + w - 3w)$ **39.** $18u - 6(9k - 7 - 10u) + 4k$

Multiple Choice Practice and Mixed Review

For Standards Tutorials, visit PHSchool.com. Web Code: bjq-9045

40. Which expression has exactly two like terms?

Ⓐ $3t + 1 - t$ Ⓑ $7 + 2m$ Ⓒ $8q + 3p$ Ⓓ $6r + r - 9r$

41. Which statement is always true?

Ⓐ The absolute value of an integer is equal to the opposite of the integer.

Ⓑ The absolute value of an integer is greater than zero.

Ⓒ An integer is greater than its opposite.

Ⓓ The absolute value of a is equal to the absolute value of $-a$.

 for Help   Lesson 1-8

42. A pair of rock climbers start up a 1,000-ft cliff. After one hour, they have gone up 160 ft. After two hours, they have gone up 320 ft. If they continue at this rate, how far up will they be after five hours?

✓ Checkpoint Quiz 1

Name each property shown.

1. $3 \cdot (-6) = -6 \cdot 3$ **2.** $(3a)b = 3(ab)$

3. $17 \cdot 1 = 17$ **4.** $6 + 0 = 0 + 6$

5. $(3 + 2)(4) = (4)(3 + 2)$ **6.** $4(3 - 2) = 4(3) - 4(2)$

Simplify each expression.

7. $3(a + 2a)$ **8.** $9y - 3y + 12y$ **9.** $7(2w) + 2(w - 3)$

Variables and Equations

Develop Use variables and appropriate operations to write an equation that represents a verbal description.

Develop Use algebraic terminology correctly.

What You'll Learn

- To classify types of equations
- To check equations using substitution

. . . And Why

To check solutions of real-world equations involving weights

✓ Check Skills You'll Need

Write an algebraic expression for each phrase.

1. the sum of x and 46

2. four less than g

3. t decreased by five

4. the quotient of z and 26

GO for Help

Lesson 1-1

🔊 New Vocabulary

- equation
- open sentence
- solution of an equation

Classifying Types of Equations

An **equation** is a mathematical sentence with an equal sign. Here are three of the ways you might see equations written.

$9 + 2 = 11$	a numerical expression equal to a numerical expression
$x + 7 = 37$	an algebraic expression equal to a numerical expression
$a + (-3) = 2a + 5$	an algebraic expression equal to an algebraic expression

An equation with a numerical expression equal to another numerical expression is either *true* or *false*. An equation with one or more variables is an **open sentence**.

1 EXAMPLE Classifying Equations

State whether each equation is *true, false,* or an *open sentence*.

a. $6 + 12 = 18$ true, because $18 = 18$

b. $6 = 4 + 3$ false, because $6 \neq 7$

c. $6y = -3 + 5y$ an open sentence, because there is a variable

✓ Quick Check

1. Explain whether each equation is *true, false,* or an *open sentence*.

    a. $9 - 7 = 3$ **b.** $8 + x = 2$ **c.** $4 \cdot 5 = 20$

You can write a mathematical word sentence as an equation.

2 EXAMPLE Writing an Equation

Write an equation for *Nine times the opposite of five is forty-five*. State whether the equation is *true, false,* or an *open sentence*.

Words	nine	times	the opposite of five	is	forty-five
	9	times	-5	is	45
Equation	9	$\cdot$	(-5)	$=$	45

The equation is false. $9 \cdot (-5) = -45$, and $-45 \neq 45$.

Vocabulary Tip

The verb <u>is</u> between two quantities suggests writing the equal sign.

✅ Quick Check

2. Write an equation for *Twenty minus x is three.*
   Is the equation true, false, or an open sentence? Explain.

Checking Equations Using Substitution

A solution of an equation is a value for a variable that makes an equation true. You substitute a number for a variable to determine whether the number is a solution of the equation.

Vocabulary Tip

≠ shows that two values are not equal.
≟ asks whether two values are equal.

3 EXAMPLE   Substituting to Check

Is 30 a solution of the equation 170 + x = 200?

$$170 + x = 200$$
$$170 + 30 \stackrel{?}{=} 200 \qquad \textbf{Substitute 30 for } x.$$
$$200 = 200$$

Yes, 30 is a solution of the equation.

✅ Quick Check

3. Is the given number a solution of the equation?

   a. $8 + t = 2t; 1$ **b.** $9 - m = 3; 6$

4 EXAMPLE   Substituting to Check

On a mule ride, a rider's gear weighs 10 lb. The rider plus the gear weighs 145 lb. Can the rider's weight be 160 lb?

Words	weight of rider	plus	weight of gear	is	145 lb

Let w = weight of rider.

Equation	w	+	10	=	145

$$w + 10 = 145$$
$$160 + 10 \stackrel{?}{=} 145 \qquad \textbf{Substitute 160 for the variable.}$$
$$170 \neq 145$$

No, the rider's weight cannot be 160 lb.

On a Grand Canyon mule ride, a rider and pack must weigh less than 200 lb.

✅ Quick Check

4. A tent weighs 6 lb. Your backpack and the tent together weigh 33 lb. Use an equation to find whether the backpack weighs 27 lb.

Is the statement *true* or *false*? Explain.

1. An equation can be false.

2. $3w - 7$ is an open sentence.

3. An open sentence must contain a variable.

4. Some open sentences are true for all variable values.

5. What is the difference between an algebraic equation and an algebraic expression?

Standards Practice

For more exercises, see *Extra Skills and Word Problem Practice.*

Ⓐ Practice by Example

Example 1
(page 82)

GO for Help

State whether each equation is *true, false,* or an *open sentence.* Explain.

6. $5 + 9 = 14$ **7.** $4x - 8 = 25$ **8.** $x - 10 = 22 - x$

9. $6 + 1 = 5 + 3$ **10.** $20 = 2 \cdot 10$ **11.** $3 \cdot 9 = 30$

Example 2
(page 82)

Write an equation for each sentence. State whether the equation is *true, false,* or an *open sentence.* Explain.

12. Four times the opposite of five equals negative twenty.

13. Twenty-five equals a number v plus fifteen.

Example 3
(page 83)

Is the given number a solution of the equation?

14. $c + 5 = 3; -2$ **15.** $24 = c + 29; -2$ **16.** $4 + d = 6; 2$

17. $20 - c = 12; 8$ **18.** $8 = a + 3; 10$ **19.** $3 + 2t = 7; 4$

Example 4
(page 83)

Write an equation. Is the given value a solution?

20. A veterinarian weighs 140 lb. When she steps on a scale while holding a dog, the scale shows 192 lb. Let d represent the weight of the dog. Does the dog weigh 52 lb?

21. A family's expenses are $1,200. One parent makes $850. Must the other earn $400 for both incomes to equal expenses?

Ⓑ Apply Your Skills

State whether each equation is *true, false,* or an *open sentence.* Explain.

22. $-24(-2) = 18(4 + 2)$ **23.** $-9 + x = 50 \div 10 + 3$

24. $6[-3 - (-5)] = 2(-4 + 10)$ **25.** $4[2 + (-6)] = 2[x - (-12)]$

Write an equation for each sentence. State whether each equation is *true, false,* or an *open sentence.* Explain.

26. The product of negative twenty and nine is negative eleven.

27. The sum of fifteen and a number n is fifty.

Which of the numbers are reasonable substitutions for each variable? Justify your reasoning.

28. Let p represent the number of passengers on a fifty-passenger school bus. Can p be 30? $27\frac{1}{2}$? -5? 48?

29. Let d represent the day of a month. Can d be 15? 56? 28? 0?

Visit: PHSchool.com
Web Code: bje-0204

30. **Writing in Math** Equations can be true or false. Can an expression be true or false? Explain.

Is the given number a solution of the equation? Explain.

31. $\frac{c}{2} - 8 = 3(-3); -2$ **32.** $14 = 28 \div x; 14$

33. $-x - 5 = 6; 1$ **34.** $3b \div 18 = 2; 12$

Challenge   **Language Arts** Some word sentences are similar to equations. Exercises 35–37 are about word sentences.

35. The sentence *Abraham Lincoln was an American president* is true. Write two other true sentences.

36. The sentence *Eleanor Roosevelt was an American president* is false. Write two other false sentences.

37. The sentence *He is a professional baseball player* is open. It is not clear to whom the word *he* refers. Write two other open sentences.

Multiple Choice Practice and Mixed Review

For Standards Tutorials, visit PHSchool.com. Web Code: bjq-9045

38. Josh wants to raise his test average to 91. So far, he has earned an 87 and a 90 on tests. Which equation can be used to determine the score, s, Josh needs on his third test?

   Ⓐ $\frac{87 + 90 + s}{3} = 91$ Ⓒ $\frac{87 + 90 + 91}{3} = s$

   Ⓑ $\frac{87 + 90}{2} + s = 91$ Ⓓ $\frac{87 + 90}{2} + 91 = s$

39. Which equation is false?

   Ⓐ $3 + (-7) = 10$ Ⓒ $8 \cdot 2 - 15 = 1$

   Ⓑ $6 \div 2 = 3$ Ⓓ $7w = 3w + 12$

GO for Help

Lesson 2-3   **Simplify each expression.**

40. $6m + 7 - 2m$ **41.** $-8t + 4t - 19$ **42.** $3w + 5k - 4w + k$

Lesson 1-8   **43.** Larissa ran 15 mi in her first week of training. In the second week she ran 17 mi. In the third week she ran 19 mi. If she continued her pattern, how far did she run the fourth week?

Lesson 1-3   **Evaluate each expression for $a = 3$ and $b = 2$.**

44. $a - b + 15$ **45.** $(3b - 2a) \div 4$ **46.** $3(b + 2) - 4$

Using Models With Equations

You can model an equation by drawing a balance scale. In the examples below, a green rectangle represents the variable.

Equation 1   **Equation 2**

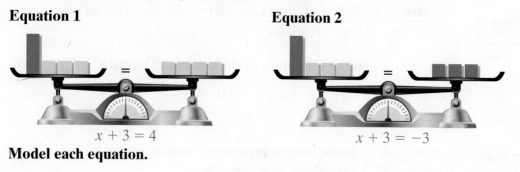

$x + 3 = 4$ $x + 3 = -3$

Model each equation.

1. $x + 3 = 5$ **2.** $z + 2 = -6$ **3.** $y + 1 = 4$

To solve an equation, get the variable alone on one side of the equal sign. To do this, remove the same number of units from each side.

Here's how to solve $x + 3 = 7$.

Model the equation.   **Solve by removing 3 units from each side. The solution is 4.**

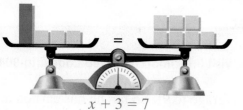

$x + 3 = 7$ $x = 4$

Check $x + 3 = 7$

$4 + 3 \stackrel{?}{=} 7$ Replace x with 4.

$7 = 7$ ✔

Solve each equation. Check your result.

4. $x + 3 = 6$ **5.** $m + 2 = 8$ **6.** $1 = 1 + d$

7. $-4 + y = -7$ **8.** $-1 + p = -5$ **9.** $w - 2 = -3$

The models below are simpler versions of the balance scale model. The vertical line represents the equal sign. Write and solve the equation for each model.

10.   **11.**   **12.**

Sometimes you cannot remove the same number of units from each side.
You may need to add units to form zero pairs. Here's how to solve
$x + 2 = -4$.

$x + 2 = -4$

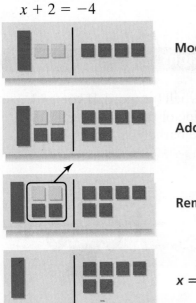

Model the equation.

Add –2 to each side.

Remove zero pairs.

$x = -6$

Check $x + 2 = -4$

$-6 + 2 \stackrel{?}{=} -4$ Replace x with –6.

$-4 = -4$ ✔

Solve each equation. Check your result.

13. $y + 2 = -2$ **14.** $x + 5 = 2$ **15.** $n + 7 = 1$

16. $-1 = k + 3$ **17.** $x - 4 = 5$ **18.** $2 = z - 3$

Write and solve the equation for each model.

19.   **20.**   **21.**

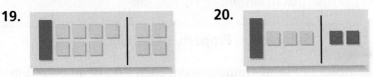

22. Open-Ended Write two different equations that have the
solution modeled at the right.

23. Number Sense Give an example of an equation model that
has the same color unit squares on each side but still requires
zero pairs to solve. Explain why zero pairs are needed.

Solving Equations by Adding or Subtracting

Develop Use variables and appropriate operations to write an equation that represents a verbal description.

Develop Simplify numerical expressions by applying properties of rational numbers and justify the process used.

Develop Make precise calculations and check the validity of the results from the context of the problem.

Using Subtraction to Solve Equations

Solving an equation is like keeping a barbell balanced. If you add weight to or subtract weight from one side of the bar, you must do the same on the other side. You keep the barbell balanced when you remove the same weight from each side.

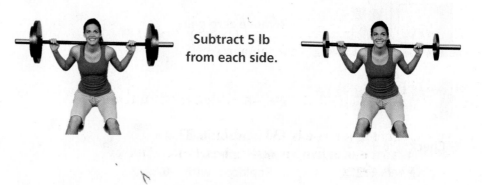

Subtract 5 lb from each side.

In previous math courses, you used related equations like $3 + 5 = 8$ and $8 - 3 = 5$. These equations show that addition and subtraction undo each other.

When you solve an equation, your goal is to get the variable alone on one side of the equation. The value on the other side tells you the solution of the original equation. You use **inverse operations,** which undo each other, to get the variable alone. You use inverse and identity properties to simplify expressions.

Take Note ✏️   Subtraction Property of Equality

You can subtract the same number from each side of an equation.

Arithmetic	Algebra
$10 = 2(5)$	If $a = b$,
$10 - 5 = 2(5) - 5$	then $a - c = b - c$.

After you solve an equation, use your result in the original equation (as shown in Example 1) to check that your solution is correct.

1 EXAMPLE Subtracting to Solve an Equation

Solve $x + 6 = 4$.

Method 1

$$x + 6 = 4$$
$$x + 6 - 6 = 4 - 6 \quad \text{Subtract 6 from each side.}$$
$$x + 0 = -2 \quad \text{Inverse Property of Addition}$$
$$x = -2 \quad \text{Identity Property of Addition}$$

Check $\quad x + 6 = 4$
$$-2 + 6 \overset{?}{=} 4 \quad \text{Replace } x \text{ with } -2.$$
$$4 = 4 ✓$$

Method 2

$$x + 6 = \quad 4$$
$$\underline{-6 \quad -6}$$
$$x = -2$$

✅ Quick Check

1. Solve each equation.

   a. $x + 8 = 3$ **b.** $5 = d + 1$ **c.** $c + (-4) = -5$

To check a solution to a real-world problem, decide whether your solution is correct using the original problem.

2 EXAMPLE Subtracting to Solve an Equation

Fred's target heart rate is 130 beats/min. This is 58 beats/min more than his resting heart rate. Find his resting heart rate.

Words   target rate   is   58   more than   resting rate

         Let r = resting heart rate.

Equation   130   =   58   + r

$$130 = 58 + r$$
$$130 = r + 58 \quad \text{Use the Commutative Property of Addition.}$$
$$130 - 58 = r + 58 - 58 \quad \text{Subtract 58 from each side.}$$
$$72 = r \quad \text{Simplify.}$$

Fred's resting heart rate is 72 beats per minute.

Check The resting heart rate plus 58 beats per minute should be 130 beats per minute.
$72 + 58 = 130$ ✓

Here is one method for estimating your target heart-rate range: Begin by subtracting your age from 220. Then multiply the result by 0.6 and 0.8 to find the lower and upper limits of your heart-rate range.

✅ Quick Check

2. Cora measures her heart rate at 123 beats per minute. This is 55 beats per minute more than her resting heart rate r. Write and solve an equation to find Cora's resting heart rate.

Using Addition to Solve Equations

When you solve an equation involving subtraction, *add* the same number to each side of the equation.

Take Note   **Addition Property of Equality**

You can add the same number to each side of an equation.

Arithmetic	Algebra
$8 = 2(4)$	If $a = b$,
$8 + 3 = 2(4) + 3$	then $a + c = b + c$.

For: Equations Activity
Use: Interactive Textbook, 2-5

3   **EXAMPLE**   **Adding to Solve an Equation**

Solve $b - 12 = -49$.

$$b - 12 = -49$$
$$b - 12 + 12 = -49 + 12 \quad \text{Add 12 to each side.}$$
$$b = -37 \qquad\qquad \text{Simplify.}$$

✓ Quick Check

3. Solve each equation.

   a. $y - 5 = 8$ **b.** $p - 30 = 42$ **c.** $98 = x - 14$

---

4   **EXAMPLE**   **Adding to Solve an Equation**

Multiple Choice   **Your friend's DVR cost $328 less than her TV. Her DVR cost $179. About how much did her TV cost?**

   Ⓐ   about $175   Ⓒ   about $325
   Ⓑ   about $300   Ⓓ   about $500

$$\$328 \approx \$325$$
$$\$179 \approx \$175 \qquad \text{Round to numbers that are easy to compute.}$$
$$175 \approx t - 325 \qquad\qquad \text{Write an equation.}$$
$$175 + 325 \approx t - 325 + 325 \qquad \text{Add 325 to each side.}$$
$$500 \approx t \qquad\qquad\qquad \text{Simplify.}$$

Your friend's TV cost about $500. The answer is D.

✓ Quick Check

4. A used book costs $17 less than the same book new. The used book costs $9. About how much does the new book cost?

Write an equation for each sentence.

1. Negative six plus y equals eighteen.

2. The number a minus five is twenty-three.

State the first step in solving each equation.

3. $a + 8 = 12$ **4.** $54 + x = 98$ **5.** $34 = c - 19$

Copy and complete the steps for solving each equation.

6.
$$35 + b = -90$$
$$35 - \blacksquare + b = -90 - \blacksquare$$
$$b = \blacksquare$$

7.
$$y - 86 = -322$$
$$y - 86 + \blacksquare = -322 + \blacksquare$$
$$y = \blacksquare$$

Standards Practice

For more exercises, see *Extra Skills and Word Problem Practice*.

A **Practice by Example**

GO for Help

Example 1
(page 89)

Solve each equation.

8. $a + 8 = 12$ **9.** $t + (-3) = 8$ **10.** $3 = n + 4$

11. $d + (-4) = -7$ **12.** $c + 9 = 37$ **13.** $q + (-10) = -25$

Example 2
(page 89)

14. The average distance from the sun to Jupiter is 778 million km. This distance is 550 million km greater than the average distance from the sun to Mars. Write and solve an equation to find the average distance d that Mars is from the sun.

Quick Tip

For a guide to reading and solving Exercise 15, see page 93.

15. The speed of sound through steel is 5,200 meters per second (m/s). This is 2,520 m/s faster than the speed of sound through silver. Write and solve an equation to find the speed of sound s through silver.

Example 3
(page 90)

Solve each equation.

16. $d - 4 = -7$ **17.** $c - 34 = 20$ **18.** $a - 4 = -18$

19. $r - 3 = 8$ **20.** $z - 100 = 100$ **21.** $5 = d - 1$

Example 4
(page 90)

22. Venus's average distance from the sun is 108 million km. This distance is 42 million km less than the average distance from the sun to Earth. Write and solve an equation to find Earth's average distance d from the sun.

B **Apply Your Skills**

Solve each equation.

23. $54 + x = 98$ **24.** $e - 43 = -45$ **25.** $47 = 7 + y$

26. $450 = a - 325$ **27.** $h + 35 = 15$ **28.** $298 + n = 294$

29. Multiple Choice In one year, 487 million people across the world spoke English. This was 512 million people fewer than the number who spoke Mandarin Chinese. Which equation could you use to find the number of people n who spoke Mandarin Chinese?

- Ⓐ $487 = n - 512$
- Ⓒ $487 = n \times 512$
- Ⓑ $487 = 512 - n$
- Ⓓ $487 = 512 \div n$

30. This year, the Tigers won six more games than the Panthers. What other fact would you need to know in order to use the equation $p + 6 = 22$ to find the number of games, p, that the Panthers won?

Mental Math Use mental math to solve each equation.

31. $b + 15 = -5$ **32.** $130 = 30 + s$ **33.** $x + 800 = 500$

34. Error Analysis A student solved the equation $x - 6 = -6$. His solution was -12. What error did the student make?

35. Writing in Math To solve $x + 25 = -22$, one student subtracted 25 from each side. Another student added -25 to each side. Will both methods work? Explain.

Ⓒ Challenge **Solve each equation.**

36. $-45 = x + (-3) + 50$ **37.** $-215 + e + (-43) = -145$

38. $n - 29 - 16 = 246$ **39.** $34 + p + 112 = 78 - 7$

40. $183 + k - 20 = -15$ **41.** $328 = z - 31 + 219$

Multiple Choice Practice and Mixed Review

For Standards Tutorials, visit PHSchool.com. Web Code: bjq-9045

42. Which statement is false?

- Ⓐ The equation $4 + (7 + 2) = (4 + 7) + 2$ shows the Associative Property of Addition.
- Ⓑ The additive inverse of -9 is 9.
- Ⓒ The equation $5(3 + 6) = 5(3) + 5(6)$ shows the Commutative Property of Addition.
- Ⓓ The multiplicative identity is 1.

GO for Help   Lesson 2-4

State whether each equation is *true*, *false*, or an *open sentence*. Explain.

43. $x + 2 = 4$ **44.** $4 = 6 - 2$ **45.** $5 - 3 = 7 - 4$

Lesson 1-8   **46. Patterns** Deric studied 30 min for his first math test. He studied 45 min for the second test and 60 min for the third test. If he continues this pattern, how long will he study for the fifth test?

Understanding Word Problems Read the problem below. Then let Tom's thinking guide you through the solution. Check your understanding with the exercise at the bottom of the page.

The speed of sound through steel is 5,200 meters per second (m/s). This is 2,520 m/s faster than the speed of sound through silver. Write and solve an equation to find the speed of sound s through silver.

What Tom Thinks

I'll read the problem and write down the important information.

Where to start? Well, it's always helpful to look for a relationship in the problem.

The speed is greater through steel. I will either have to subtract from the speed through steel to get the speed through silver, or add to the speed through silver to get the speed through steel. I'll add.

Since I know the speed through steel, I have to name only one variable.

Now I can write the equation.

I can solve the equation by using the Subtraction Property of Equality.

I have to state what was asked for in the problem.

What Tom Writes

Speed of sound through steel = 5,200 m/s. The speed through steel is 2,520 m/s faster than the speed through silver.

The speed through steel is 2,520 m/s faster than the speed through silver.

Steel speed = silver speed + 2,520

Let s = speed of sound through silver.

$$5,200 = s + 2,520$$

$$5,200 - 2,520 = s + 2,520 - 2,520$$
$$2,680 = s$$

The speed of sound through silver is 2,680 m/s.

EXERCISE

1. Pamela can run the 300-m hurdles in 52.3 s. Elaine takes 2.8 s more than Pamela to make the same run. How long does it take Elaine to run the 300-m hurdles?

2-6

Solving Equations by Multiplying or Dividing

Develop Simplify numerical expressions by applying properties of rational numbers and justify the process used.

Develop Make precise calculations and check the validity of the results.

What You'll Learn

- To solve one-step equations using division
- To solve one-step equations using multiplication

. . . And Why

To solve real-world problems involving population growth

✓ Check Skills You'll Need

Simplify each quotient.

1. $\frac{18}{18}$ 2. $\frac{-7}{7}$

3. $\frac{21}{-21}$ 4. $\frac{-13}{-13}$

GO for Help
Lesson 1-9

Using Division to Solve Equations

Division and multiplication are inverse operations. You can solve a multiplication equation by using the Division Property of Equality.

Take Note   **Division Property of Equality**

If you divide each side of an equation by the same nonzero number, the two sides remain equal.

Arithmetic	Algebra
$6 = 3(2)$	If $a = b$ and $c \neq 0$,
$\frac{6}{3} = \frac{3(2)}{3}$	then $\frac{a}{c} = \frac{b}{c}$.

1 EXAMPLE Dividing to Solve an Equation I

The United States population in 2005 was twice the population in 1949. Find the 1949 population in millions.

U.S. Population Growth

Words

| 2005 population | was | twice | 1949 population |

Let p = population in 1949.

Equation   296   =   2 · p

$296 = 2p$

$\frac{296}{2} = \frac{2p}{2}$ **Divide each side by 2.**

$148 = 1p$ **Simplify.**

$148 = p$ **Use the Identity Property of Multiplication.**

The United States population in 1949 was 148 million people.

Check Is the answer reasonable? Twice the 1949 population should be the 2005 population. Since $148 \cdot 2 = 296$, the answer is reasonable.

✓ Quick Check

1. Solve the equation $4x = 84$.

2 EXAMPLE Dividing to Solve an Equation II

Solve $5r = -20$.

$$5r = -20$$

$$\frac{5r}{5} = \frac{-20}{5} \quad \text{Divide each side by 5.}$$

$$r = -4 \quad \text{Simplify.}$$

Check
$$5r = -20$$
$$5 \cdot (-4) \stackrel{?}{=} -20 \quad \text{Replace } r \text{ with } -4.$$
$$-20 = -20 \checkmark$$

Video Tutor Help
Visit: PHSchool.com
Web Code: bje-0775

✓ Quick Check

2. Solve each equation.

a. $-3b = 24$ **b.** $96 = -8n$ **c.** $-4d = -56$

Using Multiplication to Solve Equations

When you multiply each side of an equation by the same number, the two sides remain equal.

Take Note **Multiplication Property of Equality**

You can multiply each side of an equation by the same number.

Arithmetic	Algebra
$12 = 3(4)$	If $a = b$,
$12 \cdot 2 = 3(4) \cdot 2$	then $ac = bc$.

3 EXAMPLE Multiplying to Solve an Equation

Solve $\frac{x}{-9} = -3$.

$$\frac{x}{-9} = -3$$

$$-9\left(\frac{x}{-9}\right) = -9(-3) \quad \text{Multiply each side by } -9.$$

$$x = 27 \quad \text{Simplify.}$$

✓ Quick Check

3. Solve each equation.

a. $\frac{r}{-5} = 10$ **b.** $\frac{s}{6} = 54$ **c.** $-30 = \frac{t}{20}$

Write an equation for each sentence.

1. The value of x divided by 25 is 125.

2. The product of -15 and t is -75.

State the first step in solving each equation.

3. $6x = 96$ **4.** $32 = c \cdot 3$ **5.** $\frac{r}{5} = -4$

Mental Math **Is -3 a solution of each equation? Explain.**

6. $\frac{b}{-3} = 1$ **7.** $\frac{-18}{k} = -6$ **8.** $3t = 9$

Standards Practice

For more exercises, see *Extra Skills and Word Problem Practice.*

A Practice by Example

Examples 1 and 2
(pages 94 and 95)

GO for Help

Solve each equation.

9. $6x = 96$ **10.** $108 = 9x$ **11.** $8y = 112$

12. $45 = 9a$ **13.** $5w = 95$ **14.** $15c = 90$

15. $8x = -48$ **16.** $4a = 28$ **17.** $-60 = 12m$

18. $-2b = 30$ **19.** $-10d = 100$ **20.** $162 = -18t$

21. Carol earns \$8/h. How many hours must she work to earn \$288?

22. At a rate of \$15 per month, how long does saving \$135 take?

Example 3
(page 95)

Solve each equation.

23. $6 = \frac{a}{7}$ **24.** $\frac{w}{12} = 2$ **25.** $\frac{n}{15} = 7$ **26.** $\frac{b}{-6} = 20$

27. $-2 = \frac{d}{8}$ **28.** $\frac{v}{3} = -4$ **29.** $-\frac{m}{20} = -2$ **30.** $\frac{r}{-5} = -4$

B Apply Your Skills

Solve each equation.

31. $39 = c \cdot 3$ **32.** $25x = -125$ **33.** $\frac{v}{3} = 14$ **34.** $\frac{m}{-4} = 13$

35. $-50 = \frac{n}{-6}$ **36.** $72 = 8n$ **37.** $22p = 110$ **38.** $\frac{r}{-9} = -18$

39. **Reasoning** You can divide each side of an equation by the same nonzero value. Explain what would result from the equation $4 \cdot 0 = 5 \cdot 0$ if you could divide each side by zero, and if $\frac{0}{0} = 1$.

Write an equation for each sentence. Solve the equation.

40. The product of negative twenty and y is one hundred.

41. The value n divided by ten is one hundred.

U.S. School Enrollment

Grades	Millions of Students
Kindergarten	■
1–8	33
9–12	17

SOURCE: U.S. Department of Education.
Go to **PHSchool.com** for a data update.
Web Code: bjg-9041

42. Seven multiplied by k is negative one hundred sixty-eight.

43. One of the world's tallest office buildings is in Malaysia. The building has 88 stories. The height of the 88 stories is 1,232 ft. What is the height of one story?

   Ⓐ 9 ft   Ⓑ 11 ft   Ⓒ 14 ft   Ⓓ 88 ft

44. Use the table at the left. The number of students in grades 1–8 is 3.6 times the number of students in kindergarten. Write and solve an equation to find the number of students s in kindergarten. Round to the nearest million.

45. **Writing in Math** How are the procedures to solve $3x = 9$ and $x + 3 = 9$ alike? How are they different?

46. **Open-Ended** Write a question that can be solved using the equation $5x = 45$.

Mental Math Solve each equation.

47. $75m = -7,500$ **48.** $\dfrac{v}{-50} = 300$ **49.** $3,823 = \dfrac{s}{100}$

 Challenge

For what values of x is each equation true?

50. $|x| = 7$ **51.** $-3|x| = -9$ **52.** $\dfrac{|x|}{3} = 2$

53. $x - a = b$ **54.** $a + x = b$ **55.** $ax = b$

Multiple Choice Practice and Mixed Review

For Standards Tutorials, visit PHSchool.com. Web Code: bjq-9045

56. Write an algebraic expression for the phrase *eight less than the absolute value of a number*.

   Ⓐ $8 - |x|$ Ⓑ $x - |8|$ Ⓒ $|x| - 8$ Ⓓ $|8| - x$

57. Simplify $(3x + 4)2 + 3(-2x)$.

   Ⓐ $-3x + 8$ Ⓑ $-3x + 4$ Ⓒ $12x + 8$ Ⓓ 8

58. Which property is shown? $(ab)c = a(bc)$

   Ⓐ associative   Ⓒ commutative

   Ⓑ identity   Ⓓ distributive

 for Help

Lesson 2-5

Solve each equation.

59. $-4 = a + 7$ **60.** $n - 5 = 12$ **61.** $t - (-4) = -15$ **62.** $y + 10 = 12$

Lesson 1-5

63. Suppose you start hiking from a point 92 ft below sea level and break for lunch on a hilltop that is 1,673 ft above sea level. What is your change in elevation?

Lesson 1-1

Write a variable expression for each phrase.

64. three less than a **65.** 7 times a number n

2-7

Reasoning Strategy: Try, Test, Revise

Develop Formulate and justify mathematical conjectures based on a general description of the mathematical question or problem posed.

Develop Make and test conjectures by using both inductive and deductive reasoning.

What You'll Learn

- To solve a problem using the Try, Test, Revise strategy

. . . And Why

To solve real-world problems involving money

 **Check Skills You'll Need**

Simplify.

1. $158 + 20$

2. $158 + 30$

3. $158 + 25$

4. $158 + 22$

5. In Exercises 1–4, which result came closest to 181?

GO **for Help**
Lesson 1-5

Try, Test, Revise

Math Strategies in Action Did you know that meteorologists use weather balloons to collect data? They use the temperature, humidity, and other data in mathematical models to bring you the daily weather forecast. As more data become available—from weather balloons and satellites, for example—the models, and therefore the weather reports, become more accurate.

Similarly, in math problems, you can make an initial conjecture. You can test your conjecture. If it is not the right answer, you can use what you learn from your first conjecture to make a better, second conjecture.

1 EXAMPLE Using Try, Test, Revise

The theater club at school put on a play. For one performance, the club sold 133 tickets and raised $471. Tickets cost $4 for adults and $3 for students. How many student tickets and how many adult tickets did the club sell?

Understand **Understand the problem.**

Look at the given information to make an informed conjecture.

1. How much does each type of ticket cost?

2. How many tickets did the club sell for the performance?

3. How much money did the club raise from ticket sales for this performance?

Plan **Make a plan to solve the problem.**

Make a conjecture and then test it. Use what you learn from your conjecture to make a better, second conjecture.

4. When you make a conjecture for how many adult tickets were sold, how can you use your conjecture to find how many student tickets could have been sold?

5. By what number do you multiply your conjecture of adult tickets sold to find how much money was made on adult tickets?

Carry Out **Carry out the plan.**

You can organize conjectures in a table. As a first conjecture, try making about half the tickets adult tickets.

Adult Tickets	Student Tickets	Total Money (in dollars)	
60	133 − 60 = 73	60(4) + 73(3) = 240 + 219 = 459	The total is too low. Increase the number of adult tickets.
80	133 − 80 = 53	80(4) + 53(3) = 320 + 159 = 479	The total is too high. Decrease the number of adult tickets.
70	133 − 70 = 63	70(4) + 63(3) = 280 + 189 = 469	The total is very close. Increase the number of adult tickets.
72	133 − 72 = 61	72(4) + 61(3) = 288 + 183 = 471	The total is correct.

There were 72 adult tickets and 61 student tickets sold.

Check **Check the answer to be sure it is reasonable.**

To check the answer for reasonableness, solve the problem another way. Consider using logical reasoning.

- The less expensive ticket is $3. So the theater club would get $133 \cdot \$3 = \$399$ if all the tickets sold were student tickets.

- $\$471 − \$399 = \$72$. The theater club actually raised $72 more than if they had sold only student tickets.

- Since adult tickets are $1 more than student tickets, there must have been 72 adult tickets sold.

- $133 − 72 = 61$. There were 61 student tickets sold.

- Since $72 \cdot 4 + 61 \cdot 3 = 471$, the solution 72 adult tickets and 61 student tickets is correct.

 Quick Check

6. Suppose the club sold the same number of tickets but raised $452. How many tickets of each type did the theater club sell?

For more exercises, see *Extra Skills and Word Problem Practice*.

A Practice by Example

Example 1
(page 98)

Use the *Try, Test, Revise* strategy to solve each problem.

1. Bonnie has 16 coins in her pocket worth $1.50. What are two different combinations of coins she could have in her pocket?

2. A cashier's drawer has some $5 bills, some $10 bills, and some $20 bills. There are 15 bills worth a total of $185. How many $5 bills, $10 bills, and $20 bills are there?

3. The Smiths have two children. The sum of their ages is 23. The product of their ages is 132. How old are the children?

4. The sum of Mr. and Mrs. Bergen's ages is 100. The difference between their ages is 10. How old are Mr. and Mrs. Bergen?

B Apply Your Skills

Solve using any strategy.

STRATEGIES

- **Act It Out**
- **Draw a Diagram**
- **Try, Test, Revise**
- **Look for a Pattern**
- **Make a Model**
- **Make a Table**
- **Simulate the Problem**
- **Solve by Graphing**
- **Use Multiple Strategies**
- **Work a Simpler Problem**
- **Work Backward**
- **Write an Equation**
- **Write a Proportion**

5. Geometry A rectangular vegetable garden has a length of 8 ft and a width of 5 ft. The width is increased by 2 ft. By how many square feet does the area increase?

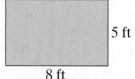

5 ft

8 ft

6. Trains leave New York for Boston every 40 min. The first train leaves at 5:20 A.M. What departure time is closest to 12:55 P.M.?

7. Number Theory A number multiplied by itself and then by itself again gives −1,000. What is the number?

8. In a group of quarters and nickels, there are four more nickels than quarters. How many nickels and quarters are there if the coins are worth $2.30?

9. The sum of the page numbers on two facing pages is 245. The product of the numbers is 15,006. What are the page numbers?

10. A student bought some compact discs for $12 each and some books for $5 each. She spent $39 in all on five items. How many of each item did she buy?

11. Two runners ran as a team in a 5,000-m relay race. The first runner ran 500 m farther than the second runner. How many meters did each run?

Homework Video Tutor

Visit: PHSchool.com
Web Code: bje-0207

12. Ron puts three pennies in a jar. His father offers to triple the total amount of money in Ron's jar at the end of each day. How much is in the jar at the end of one week?

C Challenge

13. A certain bacteria doubles the number of its cells every 20 min. A scientist puts 50 cells in a culture dish. How many cells will be in the culture dish after 2 h?

Multiple Choice Practice and Mixed Review

For Standards Tutorials, visit PHSchool.com. Web Code: bjq-9045

14. Teresa's parents put an addition on their house. Their living room was originally 12 feet long and w feet wide. The room is now 10 feet wider than it was originally. Which equation can be used to find the area A of the room?

Ⓐ $A = 12w + 10$ Ⓒ $A = 12w + 120$

Ⓑ $A = w + 120$ Ⓓ $A = 22w$

15. A photograph is 6 in. $\times$ 4 in. If you make a copy of the photograph with double the length and width, what is the area of the copy?

Ⓐ 96 in.^{2} Ⓑ 48 in.^{2} Ⓒ 24 in.^{2} Ⓓ 20 in.^{2}

GO for Help

Lesson 2-6   **[Algebra]** Solve each equation.

16. $\frac{m}{4} = 52$ **17.** $3x = -18$ **18.** $63 = \frac{t}{-3}$ **19.** $-32 = -16y$

Lesson 2-1   **Identify each property shown.**

20. $8 + (6 + 17) = (8 + 6) + 17$ **21.** $1{,}879 \cdot 1 = 1{,}879$

Lesson 1-9   **22.** The sound of thunder travels about one mile in five seconds. Suppose a bolt of lightning strikes 3 mi away. How long does it take for the sound of the thunder to reach you?

Mathematical Reasoning

Develop Analyze problems by identifying relationships.

Equation Puzzles

Equations are written using numbers and symbols. You can use the numbers 1, 2, 5, and 8 and the symbols $-$, $\div$, and $=$ to write an equation. Start by writing and evaluating expressions involving a single operation. Then write an equation using the expressions. Since $8 \div 2 = 4$ and $5 - 1 = 4$, that means $8 \div 2 = 5 - 1$.

EXERCISES

Write an equation using each number and symbol only once.

1. 5 7 8 16 = $-$ $\div$

2. 2 4 7 13 = $+$ $-$

3. 5 8 8 24 = $-$ $\div$

4. 3 4 4 5 7 = $+$ $+$ $\times$

5. 2 3 3 4 5 = $+$ $-$ $\times$

Inequalities and Their Graphs

Develop Use variables and appropriate operations to write an inequality that represents a verbal description.

Develop Use algebraic terminology (e.g., inequality) correctly.

Develop Solve two-step linear inequalities.

What You'll Learn

• To graph inequalities
• To write inequalities

...And Why

To solve real-world problems involving nutrition

✓ Check Skills You'll Need

Graph each set of numbers on a number line. Order the numbers from least to greatest.

1. $-3, 7, -9$

2. $-2, -10, -8$

3. $0, 3, -5$
4. $3, -6, 10$

GO for Help
Lesson 1-2

◀ New Vocabulary

• inequality
• solution of the inequality

Graphing Inequalities

An **inequality** is a mathematical sentence that contains $>, <, \geq, \leq$, or $\neq$. Some inequalities contain a variable.

Any number that makes an inequality true is a **solution of the inequality.** For example, -4 is a solution of $y \geq -5$ because $-4 \geq -5$.

You can graph the solutions of an inequality on a number line.

1 EXAMPLE   Graphing Solutions of Inequalities

Graph the solutions of each inequality on a number line.

a. $y < 3$

An open dot shows that 3 is *not* a solution.

Shade all the points to the left of 3.

b. $x > -1$

An open dot shows that -1 is *not* a solution.

Shade all the points to the right of -1.

c. $a \leq -2$

A closed dot shows that -2 *is* a solution.

Shade all the points to the left of -2.

d. $-6 \leq g$

A closed dot shows that -6 *is* a solution.

Shade all the points to the right of -6.

✓ Quick Check

1. Graph the solutions of each inequality.
  a. $z < -2$ **b.** $4 > t$ **c.** $a \geq -5$ **d.** $2 \geq c$

Writing Inequalities

You can write an inequality for a graph.

2 EXAMPLE   Writing Inequalities to Describe Graphs

Write the inequality shown in each graph.

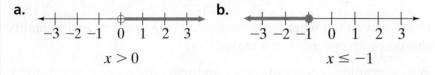

a.

$$x > 0$$

b.

$$x \le -1$$

✓ Quick Check

2. Write an inequality for the graph below.

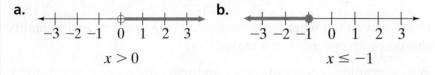

You can write an inequality to describe a real-world situation. Keep in mind that *at most* means "no more than," and hence, "less than or equal to." *At least* means "no less than," and hence, "greater than or equal to."

3 EXAMPLE   Writing an Inequality

Food can be labeled *low sodium* only if it meets the requirement established by the federal government. Use the table to write an inequality for this requirement.

Label	Definition
Sodium-free food	Less than 5 mg per serving
Very low sodium food	At most 35 mg per serving
Low-sodium food	At most 140 mg per serving

Words

a serving of low-sodium food	has at most	140 mg sodium

Let s = number of milligrams of sodium in a serving of low-sodium food.

Inequality

s	$\le$	140

✓ Quick Check

3. Use the table in Example 3. A certain food is labeled *sodium free*. Write an inequality for *n*, the number of milligrams of sodium in a serving of this sodium-free food.

Match each inequality with its graph.

1. $x \geq -4$ **2.** $x \leq -4$ **3.** $x > -4$ **4.** $x < -4$

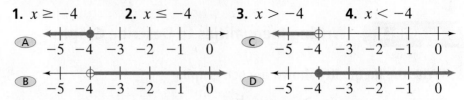

5. How can you tell whether the endpoint of a graph of an inequality should be an open dot or a closed dot?

6. Why is graphing the solutions of an inequality more efficient than listing all the solutions of the inequality?

Standards Practice

For more exercises, see *Extra Skills and Word Problem Practice*.

Ⓐ **Practice by Example**

Example 1
(page 102)

GO for Help

Graph the solutions of each inequality on a number line.

7. $x < 7$ **8.** $y > 2$ **9.** $a < 3$ **10.** $c < 1$

11. $-3 < z$ **12.** $x > 1$ **13.** $m \leq -4$ **14.** $b \geq 6$

Example 2
(page 103)

Write an inequality for each graph.

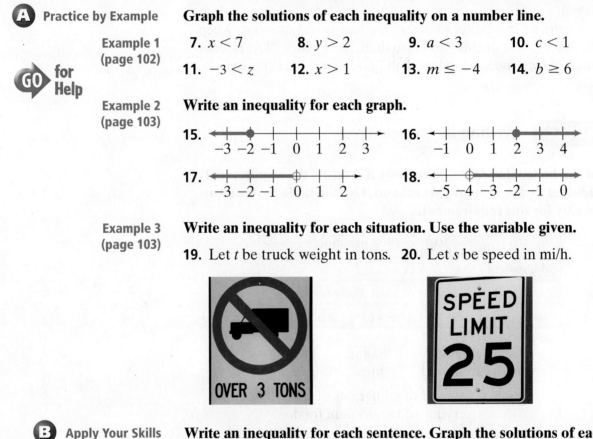

Example 3
(page 103)

Write an inequality for each situation. Use the variable given.

19. Let t be truck weight in tons. **20.** Let s be speed in mi/h.

Ⓑ **Apply Your Skills**

Write an inequality for each sentence. Graph the solutions of each inequality on a number line.

21. x is less than 5. **22.** y is greater than -3.

23. A number c is at least 12. **24.** r is not greater than five.

25. The total t is greater than 7. **26.** p is not more than 30.

Write an inequality for each graph.

27.

28.

29.

30.

31. Writing in Math Describe a situation that you could represent with an inequality. Then write the inequality.

32. Write an inequality to describe this situation. A student pays for three movie tickets with a twenty-dollar bill and gets change back. Let t be the cost of a movie ticket.

33. High-fiber foods have at least 5 g of fiber per serving. Write an inequality to represent this situation. Let f be the number of grams of fiber per serving of high-fiber food.

34. Compare. Use $>$ or $<$ to complete each statement.
a. If $a < b$, then b ■ a.
b. If $x > y$ and $y > z$, then x ■ z.

35. Number Sense No more than 50 students walked in a walkathon. Let s be the number of students. Determine which numbers are reasonable values for s: 40, $45\frac{1}{2}$, 50, and 55.

C Challenge **36.** What is the largest integer value of x that is a solution of the inequality $x - 7 < 8$?

37. Solve the inequality $y + b > a$ for y.

Multiple Choice Practice and Mixed Review

For Standards Tutorials, visit PHSchool.com. Web Code: bjq-9045

38. Which inequality best represents the following sentence?
A number t is greater than or equal to -8.
Ⓐ $-8 \le t$ Ⓑ $t > -8$ Ⓒ $t \le -8$ Ⓓ $-8 \ge t$

39. A game-board designer has to design a board that is at least 5 feet wide. Let w be the width of the board. Which inequality describes this situation?
Ⓐ $w < 5$ Ⓑ $w > 5$ Ⓒ $w \le 5$ Ⓓ $w \ge 5$

40. A recipe calls for 4 cups of flour. Tameeka has 20 cups of flour. Let r represent the flour she has left after making the recipe. Which equation represents this situation?
Ⓐ $r - 20 = 4$ Ⓑ $20 - 4 = r$ Ⓒ $r - 4 = 16$ Ⓓ $r - 4 = 20$

GO for Help Lessons 2-5 and 2-6

Solve each equation.

41. $x - 5 = 29$ **42.** $7y = 35$ **43.** $t \div 12 = 6$

Lesson 2-3

Simplify each expression.

44. $6 - 5s + 4s + 3$ **45.** $n + (n + 2) + (n + 4)$

2-9

Solving One-Step Inequalities by Adding or Subtracting

What You'll Learn

- To solve one-step inequalities using subtraction
- To solve one-step inequalities using addition

. . . And Why

To solve real-world problems involving camera memory

 **Check Skills You'll Need**

Solve each equation.

1. $m + 7 = 5$

2. $k - 8 = 11$

3. $12 + h = 21$

4. $6 = n - 23$

GO for Help
Lesson 2-5

Develop Use variables and appropriate operations to write an inequality that represents a verbal description.

Develop Solve two-step linear inequalities.

Solving Inequalities by Subtracting

Solving an inequality is similar to solving an equation. You want to get the variable alone on one side of the inequality.

If you subtract 2 from each side of the inequality $-1 < 2$, the resulting inequality $-3 < 0$ is also true.

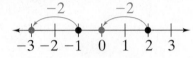

Take Note   **Subtraction Property of Inequality**

You can subtract the same number from each side of an inequality.

Arithmetic	Algebra
$7 > 4$, so $7 - 3 > 4 - 3$	If $a > b$, then $a - c > b - c$.
$6 < 9$, so $6 - 2 < 9 - 2$	If $a < b$, then $a - c < b - c$.

1 EXAMPLE   **Subtracting to Solve an Inequality**

Solve each inequality. Graph the solutions.

a. $n + 8 \geq 19$

$$n + 8 \geq 19$$
$$n + 8 - 8 \geq 19 - 8 \quad \text{Subtract 8 from each side.}$$
$$n \geq 11 \quad\quad\quad \text{Simplify.}$$

```
←—+—+—+—+—+—+—+—●—+—→
  0   2   4   6   8   10  12
```

b. $-26 > y + 14$

$$-26 > y + 14$$
$$-26 - 14 > y + 14 - 14 \quad \text{Subtract 14 from each side.}$$
$$-40 > y \text{ or } y < -40 \quad \text{Simplify.}$$

```
←—+—○—+—+—+—+—+—→
 -50 -40 -30 -20 -10  0  .10
```

✓ **Quick Check**

1. Solve each inequality. Graph the solutions.
  a. $m + 3 > 6$ **b.** $8 + t < 15$ **c.** $-3 \leq x + 7$

2 EXAMPLE **Subtracting to Solve an Inequality**

Nearly 512 megabytes (MB) of memory are available in your digital camera. If you have used 128 MB, how much memory is available for taking more pictures?

Words | memory used | plus | memory for taking more pictures | is less than | total memory |

Let m = memory available for taking more pictures.

Inequality | 128 | + | m | < | 512 |

$$128 + m < 512$$
$$128 - 128 + m < 512 - 128 \qquad \text{Subtract 128 from each side.}$$
$$m < 384 \qquad \text{Simplify.}$$

Less than 384 MB of memory is available for other pictures.

You can increase the memory of a digital camera by adding a memory card. These cards have extra memory in multiples of 128 megabytes.

✓ Quick Check

2. An airline lets you check up to 65 lb of luggage. One suitcase weighs 37 lb. How much can another suitcase weigh?

Using Addition to Solve Inequalities

To solve an inequality involving subtraction, use addition.

Take Note **Addition Property of Inequality**

You can add the same number to each side of an inequality.

Arithmetic

$7 > 3$, so $7 + 4 > 3 + 4$
$2 < 5$, so $2 + 6 < 5 + 6$

Algebra

If $a > b$, then $a + c > b + c$.
If $a < b$, then $a + c < b + c$.

---

3 EXAMPLE **Adding to Solve an Inequality**

Solve $n - 15 < 3$.

$$n - 15 < 3$$
$$n - 15 + 15 < 3 + 15 \qquad \text{Add 15 to each side.}$$
$$n < 18 \qquad \text{Simplify.}$$

✓ Quick Check

3. Solve each inequality.
  a. $m - 13 > 29$ **b.** $v - 4 \leq 7$ **c.** $t - 5 \geq 11$

Online active math

For: Inequalities Activity
Use: Interactive Textbook, 2-9

The steps for solving an inequality are shown. Justify each step.

$$6 + x + 4 < 16$$

1. $6 + 4 + x < 16$ ____?____

2. $10 + x < 16$ ____?____

3. $10 - 10 + x < 16 - 10$ ____?____

4. $x < 6$ ____?____

Standards Practice

For more exercises, see *Extra Skills and Word Problem Practice*.

A Practice by Example

Example 1
(page 106)

Solve each inequality. Graph the solutions.

5. $w + 5 < 12$ **6.** $2 > 9 + a$ **7.** $x + 6 \geq 7$ **8.** $18 \leq 20 + w$

9. $2 + m \leq 2$ **10.** $-7 < 5 + x$ **11.** $30 \geq t + 45$ **12.** $p + 22 \geq -10$

Example 2
(page 107)

13. The total weight limit for a truck is 100,000 lb. The truck weighs 36,000 lb empty. What is the most that the truck's load can weigh?

14. You are saving to buy a bicycle that will cost at least $120. Your parents give you $45 toward the bicycle. How much money will you have to save?

Example 3
(page 107)

Solve each inequality.

15. $x - 5 \geq 6$ **16.** $n - 12 \leq 3$ **17.** $r - 4 \leq 3$

18. $x - 7 < 15$ **19.** $c - 9 > 5$ **20.** $h - 10 \geq 6$

21. $w - 8 < 3$ **22.** $12 \geq y - 5$ **23.** $4 \geq y - 4$

B Apply Your Skills

What do you do to the first inequality to get the second inequality?

24. $x + 8 \leq 11; x \leq 3$ **25.** $x - 3 > 9; x > 12$

Solve each inequality. Graph the solutions.

26. $x - 8 > -2$ **27.** $6 < y + 19$ **28.** $3 \leq y - 5$

29. $-8 \geq k - 3$ **30.** $-3 + y > 4$ **31.** $a - 0.5 < 2.5$

32. $7 + r > 11$ **33.** $9 < b + 4$ **34.** $u - 3 \geq 9$

Write an inequality for each sentence. Then solve the inequality.

35. Thirteen plus a number n is greater than fifteen.

36. The sum of a number w and 3 is less than or equal to ten.

37. Jim has $87. He spends $6 for socks and at least $32 for shoes. How much does he have left to spend for shirts?

Reasoning **Justify each step.**

38. $4 + a + 3 > 16$
$4 + 3 + a > 16$
$7 + a > 16$
$7 - 7 + a > 16 - 7$
$a > 9$

39. $m - 2(8 - 5) \le -9$
$m - 2(3) \le -9$
$m - 6 \le -9$
$m - 6 + 6 \le -9 + 6$
$m \le -3$

40. <u>Writing in Math</u> Which of the inequalities $m > -2$, $m < -2$, $-2 < m$, and $-2 > m$ are solutions to $m + 4 > 2$? Explain.

C Challenge

41. You have $50.00. You want to buy DVDs and see a movie. Admission to the movie is $8.00. Each DVD costs $12.00. Write and solve an inequality to find how many DVDs you can buy.

Multiple Choice Practice and Mixed Review

For Standards Tutorials, visit PHSchool.com. Web Code: bjq-9045

42. Which expression is equivalent to $3b - (6b + 8) + 3$?
Ⓐ $9b + 11$ Ⓑ $-3b + 11$ Ⓒ $3b + 11$ Ⓓ $-3b - 5$

43. Find $|-7| - |-8|$.
Ⓐ -15 Ⓑ -1 Ⓒ 1 Ⓓ 15

GO for Help

Lesson 2-8 **Graph the solutions of each inequality.**

44. $x < 2$ **45.** $x \ge -5$ **46.** $y \le 4$ **47.** $m > 0$

Lesson 2-3 **Simplify each expression.**

48. $4x + 6 - 2x + 6$ **49.** $-4 - 5t + t - 10$

Lesson 1-4 **50.** Write an integer to represent a debt of $35.

✓ Checkpoint Quiz 2

State whether the equation is *true, false,* or an *open sentence.* Explain.

1. $4 + 15 = 27 - 8$ **2.** $-30 = 9w$ **3.** $|9 - 10| = 8 - 9$

Solve each equation or inequality.

4. $y - 3 = -7$ **5.** $x + 4 = 8$

6. $7t = 42$ **7.** $m \div 8 = -4$

8. $-90 = 10f$ **9.** $9 \le 3 + a$

10. $r - 12 < 7$ **11.** $m + 15 > -4$

12. You have some quarters, dimes, and pennies—eight coins worth $.77 altogether. How many of each type of coin do you have?

Solving One-Step Inequalities by Multiplying or Dividing

What You'll Learn

- To solve one-step inequalities using division
- To solve one-step inequalities using multiplication

. . . And Why

To solve real-world problems involving weight limits

✓ Check Skills You'll Need

Solve each equation.

1. $6x = 24$

2. $63 = -7v$

3. $\frac{x}{-2} = 10$

4. $\frac{t}{6} = 48$

GO for Help
Lesson 2-6

Solving Inequalities Using Division

Standards Investigation
Solving Inequalities

Explore what happens when you divide each side of an inequality by a number.

1. Simplify each expression at the right. Replace each ■ with $>$ or $<$.

2. Patterns Does the direction of the inequality symbol stay the same as you divide each side of an inequality by the given numbers? Explain your reasoning.

$6 \div 3 \ \blacksquare \ 12 \div 3$
$6 \div 2 \ \blacksquare \ 12 \div 2$
$6 \div 1 \ \blacksquare \ 12 \div 1$
$6 \div (-1) \ \blacksquare \ 12 \div (-1)$
$6 \div (-2) \ \blacksquare \ 12 \div (-2)$
$6 \div (-3) \ \blacksquare \ 12 \div (-3)$

You can solve an inequality that involves multiplication by dividing each side of the inequality by a nonzero number.

Take Note / Division Properties of Inequality

If you divide each side of an inequality by a positive number, you leave the inequality symbol unchanged.

Arithmetic	**Algebra**
$3 < 6$, so $\frac{3}{3} < \frac{6}{3}$	If $a < b$ and c is positive, then $\frac{a}{c} < \frac{b}{c}$.
$8 > 2$, so $\frac{8}{2} > \frac{2}{2}$	If $a > b$ and c is positive, then $\frac{a}{c} > \frac{b}{c}$.

If you divide each side of an inequality by a negative number, *you reverse the inequality symbol.*

Arithmetic	**Algebra**
$6 < 12$, so $\frac{6}{-3} > \frac{12}{-3}$	If $a < b$ and c is negative, then $\frac{a}{c} > \frac{b}{c}$.
$16 > 8$, so $\frac{16}{-4} < \frac{8}{-4}$	If $a > b$ and c is negative, then $\frac{a}{c} < \frac{b}{c}$.

1 **EXAMPLE** **Using Division to Solve an Inequality**

Express elevators can travel as fast as 1,800 ft/min.

An elevator can carry up to 2,500 lb. Suppose the weight of an average adult is 150 lb. At most how many average-sized adults can safely ride the elevator at the same time?

Words | the number of adults | times | 150 lb | is less than or equal to | 2,500 lb

Let x = the number of adults.

Inequality $\qquad x \qquad \cdot \qquad 150\text{ lb} \qquad \le \qquad 2{,}500$

$$150x \le 2{,}500$$

$$\frac{150x}{150} \le \frac{2{,}500}{150}$$ **Divide each side by 150.**

$$x \le 16.\overline{6}$$ **Simplify. Round the answer down to find a whole number of people.**

At most 16 average adults can safely ride the elevator at one time.

Check Is the answer reasonable? The total weight of 16 average adults is $16(150) = 2{,}400$ lb. This is less than 2,500 lb but so close that another adult could not ride. The answer is reasonable.

STATE INSPECTION CERTIFICATE
Department of Public Safety
Certificate for the Use of Elevator
LOCATION: 221 Pat Street
SPEED: 150 ft per min
CAPACITY: 2,500 lb
ISSUED ON: 06/06/09
EXPIRES: 06/06/10

✓ **Quick Check**

1. Solve each inequality.

a. $4x > 40$ **b.** $-21 > 3m$ **c.** $36 > -9t$

Solving Inequalities Using Multiplication

You can solve inequalities that involve division.

Take Note **Multiplication Properties of Inequality**

If you multiply each side of an inequality by a positive number, you leave the inequality symbol unchanged.

Arithmetic   **Algebra**

$3 < 4$, so $3(5) < 4(5)$ If $a < b$ and c is positive, then $ac < bc$.

$7 > 2$, so $7(6) > 2(6)$ If $a > b$ and c is positive, then $ac > bc$.

If you multiply each side of an inequality by a negative number, *you reverse the inequality symbol.*

Arithmetic   **Algebra**

$6 < 9$, so $6(-2) > 9(-2)$ If $a < b$ and c is negative, then $ac > bc$.

$7 > 5$, so $7(-3) < 5(-3)$ If $a > b$ and c is negative, then $ac < bc$.

Online
active math

For: Inequalities Activity
Use: Interactive Textbook, 2-10

EXAMPLE 2 — Multiplying to Solve an Inequality

Solve $\frac{t}{-4} \geq 7$.

$$\frac{t}{-4} \geq 7$$

$$-4\left(\frac{t}{-4}\right) \leq -4(7)$$ Multiply each side by −4 and reverse the inequality symbol.

$$t \leq -28$$ Simplify.

✓ Quick Check

2. Solve each inequality.

   a. $\frac{m}{4} \geq 2$ b. $\frac{t}{-3} < 7$ c. $5 < \frac{r}{7}$

More Than One Way

Solve $-3x < 12$.

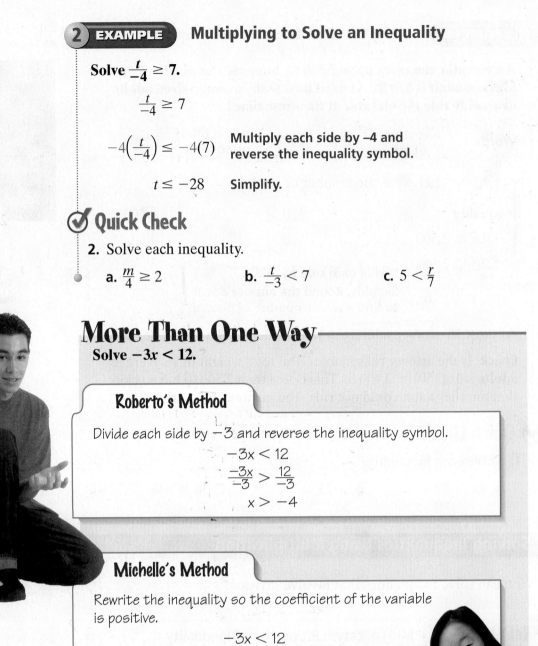

Roberto's Method

Divide each side by −3 and reverse the inequality symbol.

$$-3x < 12$$
$$\frac{-3x}{-3} > \frac{12}{-3}$$
$$x > -4$$

Michelle's Method

Rewrite the inequality so the coefficient of the variable is positive.

$$-3x < 12$$
$$-3x + 3x < 12 + 3x$$
$$0 < 12 + 3x$$
$$0 - 12 < 3x + 12 - 12$$
$$-12 < 3x$$
$$\frac{-12}{3} < \frac{3x}{3}$$
$$-4 < x, \text{ or } x > -4$$

Choose a Method

1. Which method would you use to solve this inequality? Explain.

2. Solve $18 < -6x$ using Roberto's Method or Michelle's Method.

What happens to the inequality symbol when you do the following to each side of an inequality?

1. Subtract a negative number.   **2.** Multiply by a positive number.

3. Divide by a negative number.   **4.** Multiply by a negative number.

What was done to the first inequality to get the second?

5. $4x \geq 48; x \geq 12$ **6.** $8 > -4x; -2 < x$

Standards Practice

For more exercises, see *Extra Skills and Word Problem Practice*.

Ⓐ Practice by Example

Example 1
(page 111)

GO for Help

Solve each inequality.

7. $3t > 21$ **8.** $-2x < 14$ **9.** $8 > -4x$ **10.** $6m > 24$

11. $9x \leq 27$ **12.** $18 < -2m$ **13.** $64 \leq -8k$ **14.** $7m > 28$

15. Paul earns $9 per hour. How many hours must Paul work to earn at least $645?

Example 2
(page 112)

Solve each inequality.

16. $\frac{x}{-6} > 3$ **17.** $\frac{m}{6} \leq -18$ **18.** $\frac{x}{3} \geq 5$ **19.** $\frac{y}{4} > 3$

20. $\frac{r}{-4} > 2$ **21.** $6 > \frac{q}{-3}$ **22.** $20 < \frac{v}{6}$ **23.** $\frac{b}{4} \geq 3$

Ⓑ Apply Your Skills

Solve each inequality.

24. $-4x < -16$ **25.** $-r \geq 21$ **26.** $\frac{1}{2}x \geq -3$ **27.** $\frac{b}{3} \geq -31$

28. $-3 \geq \frac{g}{-7}$ **29.** $3 > \frac{b}{-6}$ **30.** $4x > -8$ **31.** $-6x \leq -24$

32. Marnie pays $.06 per kilowatt-hour for electricity. She has budgeted $72 for her electricity. What is the greatest number of kilowatt-hours Marnie can use and stay within her budget?

33. Error Analysis Your friend solved $3x > -12$ as shown at the left. What error did your friend make?

$$3x > -12$$
$$\frac{3x}{3} \diagdown \frac{-12}{3}$$
$$x < -4$$

34. Multiple Choice Sue worked at least 13 hours last week. She earns $5.75 per hour. What is the least amount she earned?

Ⓐ $75   Ⓑ $74.75   Ⓒ $65   Ⓓ $7.50

Homework Video Tutor

Write an inequality for each sentence. Then solve the inequality.

35. A number t multiplied by seven is less than or equal to 21.

36. A number b divided by 4 is greater than or equal to 3.

37. The quotient of a number v divided by -5 is less than 9.

38. Writing in Math Explain how solving $-4t < 32$ is different from solving $4t < -32$.

Reasoning Justify each step.

39. $2g \geq -18$
$\dfrac{2g}{2} \geq \dfrac{-18}{2}$
$g \geq -9$

40. $-7m \leq -28$
$\dfrac{-7m}{-7} \geq \dfrac{-28}{-7}$
$m \geq 4$

41. $\dfrac{a}{3} > 12$
$\left(\dfrac{a}{3}\right)(3) > 12(3)$
$a > 36$

42. Open-Ended Write a problem that you would solve using the inequality $5m \leq 15$.

43. For every 18 four-year-old children in day care there must be at least one teacher. At one day-care center, 56 four-year-olds are signed up for next year. At least how many teachers must the center have to teach four-year-olds next year?

C Challenge

44. Reasoning The rules for multiplying and dividing both sides of an inequality do not mention zero. Discuss why.

45. Miquel solved the inequality $-3 > \dfrac{x}{-4}$ and got $12 < x$. Linnea solved the same inequality and got $x > 12$. Are they both correct? Explain.

Multiple Choice Practice and Mixed Review

For Standards Tutorials, visit PHSchool.com. Web Code: bjq-9045

46. Simplify $8 + (-20) \div 4 \cdot 3$.
Ⓐ -7　　　Ⓑ 3　　　Ⓒ 21　　　Ⓓ 23

47. What number completes the pattern?
$1, 3, 4, \blacksquare, 11, 18, 29$
Ⓐ 5　　　Ⓑ 6　　　Ⓒ 7　　　Ⓓ 9

48. Leslie participated in a walkathon. Her mother pledged $1.50 per mile and a friend pledged $0.25 per mile. Leslie walked 9 miles. How many dollars did she earn?
Ⓐ 1.75　　　Ⓑ 2.25　　　Ⓒ 13.50　　　Ⓓ 15.75

GO for Help

Lesson 2-9

Solve each inequality.

49. $6 + t > 17$　　　**50.** $-9 \geq r + 5$　　　**51.** $11 > v - 12$

Lessons 2-1 and 2-2

Name each property shown.

52. $-12(100 - 3) = -12(100) - (-12)(3)$

53. $102 + 34 + 98 = 102 + 98 + 34$

Lesson 1-6

54. The high temperature one day in January was $34°F$, and the low temperature was $27°F$. What was the difference between the high and the low temperatures that day?

High-use academic words are words that you will see often in textbooks and on tests. These words are not math vocabulary terms, but knowing them will help you succeed in mathematics.

Words to Learn: Direction Words

Some words tell you what to do in a problem. You need to understand what these words are asking so that you give the correct answer.

Word	Meaning
Determine	Find out by investigating or calculating.
Explain	Give facts and details to make an idea easy to understand.
Identify	Tell the name of or describe the characteristics of something.

EXERCISES

Determine whether each statement is *true* or *false*.

1. The owner's manual for a car explains how to drive.

2. The weatherman determines what kind of storm will arrive.

3. This week's supermarket flyer identifies items that are on sale.

Identify each property shown.

4. $7 + a = a + 7$

5. $3(x - 4) = 3x - 12$

Explain how to use zero pairs to solve each equation.

6.

7.

8. a. Word Knowledge Think about the word **justify**. Choose the letter for how well you know the word.
   A. I know its meaning.
   B I have seen it, but I do not know its meaning.
   C. I do not know it.

   b. Look up **justify** in a dictionary or online. Write its definition.

   c. Write a sentence involving mathematics and using the word **justify**.

Using Mental Math

You can solve many problems quickly using mental math and proven "shortcut" methods. Use mental math techniques when an exact answer is needed and the calculations are not complicated. Change a numerical expression into a simpler equivalent expression by using the associative, commutative, or distributive properties of numbers.

1 EXAMPLE

Solve the equation $x - 476 = 325$.

  (A) -151 (B) 151 (C) 791 (D) 801

What you think

The difference between a number and 476 is positive, so I know choice A is not correct. I know I must add 325 and 476. I can make the problem easier by splitting 325 into 300 and 25 and splitting 476 into 400 and 75 and 1. Then I group numbers that are easy to add together: $300 + 400 = 700$ and $25 + 75 = 100$. Finally, I add $700 + 100 + 1$, which equals 801.

Why it works

$x = 325 + 476$

$x = (300 + 25) + (400 + 75 + 1)$ **Think of numbers that are easy to add.**

$x = 300 + 400 + 25 + 75 + 1$ **Commutative Property of Addition**

$x = (300 + 400) + (25 + 75) + 1$ **Associative Property of Addition**

$x = 700 + 100 + 1$ **Work within grouping symbols.**

$x = 801$ **Add.**

Choice D is the correct answer.

Multiple Choice Practice

Use number sense and mental math to solve.

1. $x + 48 = 293$

  (A) 241   (B) 245   (C) 255   (D) 341

2. $6x = 312$

  (A) 52   (B) 306   (C) 318   (D) 502

3. You brought $50 with you to the mall. You came home with $15. How much did you spend?

  (A) $15   (B) $35   (C) $45   (D) $65

Chapter 2 Review

Vocabulary Review

🔊 English and Spanish Audio Online

additive identity (p. 69)
Associative Properties of Addition and Multiplication (p. 68)
coefficient (p. 78)
Commutative Properties of Addition and Multiplication (p. 68)
constant (p. 78)

Distributive Property (p. 73)
equation (p. 82)
Identity Properties of Addition and Multiplication (p. 69)
inequality (p. 102)
inverse operations (p. 88)
like terms (p. 78)
multiplicative identity (p. 69)

open sentence (p. 82)
simplify an algebraic expression (p. 78)
solution of an equation (p. 83)
solution of an inequality (p. 102)
term (p. 78)

For each numbered definition given below, write the letter of the word or phrase being defined.

1. a value that makes an equation true
2. a term that has no variable
3. a number or the product of a number and variable(s)
4. the number that multiplies a variable
5. the number zero
6. terms with identical variables
7. an equation with one or more variables
8. a mathematical sentence with an equal sign
9. the number one
10. a mathematical sentence with $>, <, \geq, \leq,$ or $\neq$

A. coefficient
B. constant
C. additive identity
D. solution of an equation
E. term
F. equation
G. multiplicative identity
H. like terms
I. inequality
J. open sentence

Go Online
PHSchool.com
For: Online vocabulary quiz
Web Code: bjj-0251

Skills and Concepts

Lesson 2-1
- To identify properties of addition and multiplication
- To use properties to solve problems

Use the **Commutative Property** to change order. Use the **Associative Property** to change grouping. Adding zero to an expression does not change its value. Multiplying an expression by 1 does not change its value.

Simplify each expression. Justify each step.

11. $58 + 16 + 2 + 4$
12. $4 \cdot 7 \cdot 25 \cdot 1$
13. $125 + 347 + 75$
14. $(20 \cdot 65) \cdot 5$
15. $10 \cdot 15 \cdot 2$
16. $37 + 0 + (5 + 63)$

Lesson 2-2

- To use the Distributive Property with numerical expressions
- To use the Distributive Property with algebraic expressions

Use the **Distributive Property** to multiply a number outside parentheses by each term of a sum or difference.

Mental Math Use the Distributive Property to simplify.

17. $9(96)$ **18.** $8(62)$ **19.** $(43)(9)$

Use the Distributive Property to multiply.

20. $4(w + 9)$ **21.** $(2 + 4a)12$ **22.** $-7(6 - 2m)$

23. Explain why $5x + 15 = 5(x + 3)$.

Lesson 2-3

- To identify parts of an algebraic expression
- To simplify expressions

To **simplify** an algebraic expression, replace it with an equivalent expression with as few terms as possible.

Simplify each expression.

24. $8a + 7 - 11a$ **25.** $3(w + 3) + 4w$

26. $6 + x - 4x + 3$ **27.** $19 - 4(5n + 1) - 4n$

28. $10 + 7k - 2(3k + 5)$ **29.** $-7(2r - 1) + 3(8 - r)$

30. Explain how to determine whether terms are like terms.

Lesson 2-4

- To classify types of equations
- To check equations using substitution

You can write an **equation** to model a situation. An equation with numerical expressions is true or false. An equation with at least one variable is an **open sentence**. A **solution** of an open-sentence equation is a value of a variable that makes the equation true.

Write an equation for each sentence. Is each equation *true, false,* or an *open sentence?*

31. Thirty-two plus five equals the product of six and six.

32. A number t divided by seventeen equals the opposite of three.

33. The product of four and twenty equals eighty.

34. The admission price to an art museum increased by $1.75 to $6.50. Let p be the original admission price. Write an equation to model the situation.

Lessons 2-5 and 2-6

- To solve one-step equations using subtraction
- To solve one-step equations using addition
- To solve one-step equations using division
- To solve one-step equations using multiplication

To solve an equation, use an **inverse operation** and the **properties of equality** to get the variable alone on one side of the equation.

Solve each equation.

35. $6 + y = 17$ **36.** $-2 = a - 10$ **37.** $3x = -15$

38. $\frac{m}{9} = 3$ **39.** $\frac{w}{4} = 32$ **40.** $40 = -5b$

Lesson 2-7

- To solve a problem using the Try, Test, Revise strategy

You can solve some problems by trying an answer. Use each incorrect conjecture to make a better conjecture.

41. Marcella and Danilo went to a bookstore. Marcella bought 2 notebooks and 3 pens for $14.50. Danilo bought 1 notebook and 2 pens for $7.50. How much does 1 notebook cost?

Lesson 2-8

- To graph inequalities
- To write inequalities

To graph an **inequality**, use a number line. Use an open dot for $>$ and $<$. Use a closed dot for $\geq$ and $\leq$.

Graph the solutions of each inequality.

42. $m > -13$ **43.** $t \geq -2$ **44.** $0 < r$ **45.** $w \leq 6$

Write an inequality for each sentence.

46. The temperature t is less than zero degrees.

47. The height h is greater than twelve feet.

Lessons 2-9 and 2-10

- To solve one-step inequalities using subtraction
- To solve one-step inequalities using addition
- To solve one-step inequalities using division
- To solve one-step inequalities using multiplication

To solve a one-step inequality, use inverse operations and the **properties of inequality** to get the variable alone on one side of the inequality. When multiplying or dividing each side of an inequality by a negative number, *reverse* the direction of the inequality symbol.

Solve each inequality.

48. $n - 4 > 10$ **49.** $-5 \leq k - 7$ **50.** $6s \leq 18$

51. $\frac{m}{3} < -2$ **52.** $-d > 14$ **53.** $\frac{c}{-4} \geq -9$

Go Online PHSchool.com **For:** Chapter Test **Web Code:** bja-0252

Is each equation *true, false,* **or an** *open sentence*? **Explain.**

1. $24 = 3(-8)$

2. $5x + 28 = 153$

3. $18(-7 \div 7) = (-2)(9)$

4. $-6 + 15 = (120 \div 20) - (5 - 8)$

Simplify. Use the commutative and the associative properties.

5. $50 \cdot 38 \cdot 2$

6. $45 + 62 + 55$

7. $2 \cdot 27 \cdot 5$

8. $99 + (-7) + 101$

9. **Open-Ended** Write a number sentence that illustrates the Associative Property of Addition.

Simplify each expression.

10. $2(x + y) - 2y$

11. $5a + 2b + 3a - 7b$

12. $3(2r - 5) + 8(r + 2)$

13. $(-2c + 3d)(-5) + 3(-2c) - (-8d)$

Solve each equation.

14. $k - 23 = 17$

15. $\frac{t}{-5} = 15$

16. $y \div 12 = -3$

17. $7w = -217$

18. $-9 + a = 11$

19. $n - 2 = 13$

20. $120 = 38 + p$

21. $w \cdot (-2) = 14$

22. $r + 6 = 30$

23. $m - 7 = -3$

24. $9t = 18$

25. $-3f = -42$

26. $5 = \frac{s}{-7}$

27. $\frac{h}{12} = 12$

For Exercises 28 and 29, write and solve an equation.

28. Thirty-six sections of fencing, all the same length, are joined to form a fence 180 m long. How long is each section of fencing?

29. Brian bought a used bike for $25 less than its original price. He paid a total of $88 for the bike. What was the original price of the bike?

30. **Writing in Math** How are the rules for solving inequalities similar to those for solving equations? How are they different?

Write an inequality for each situation. Graph the solutions.

31. The total t is greater than 5.

32. The perimeter p is less than 64.

33. The number of passengers p on the bus is no more than 45.

34. The number of students s that ran in the road race was not less than 55.

35. The number of questions q answered correctly is at most 49.

Solve each inequality.

36. $5 \le x + 1$

37. $\frac{a}{3} > 4$

38. $y - 6 < 9$

39. $-2n \le 10$

40. $3b \ge 3$

41. $\frac{p}{-2} < -5$

42. $r + 8 > 12$

43. $j - 7 \le 24$

44. $h - 5 \ge -16$

45. $8 + b < -3$

46. $3k \le -27$

47. $\frac{h}{4} > 16$

48. $9 < \frac{a}{6}$

49. $-7z < 21$

Some problems ask you to write an expression or equation that can be used to solve a problem. Read the question at the right and review the answer choices.

Georgia received a $15 gift certificate for her birthday. She used it as she purchased new clothes for school. She purchased a pair of jeans for $30, 3 T-shirts for $9 each, and a pair of shoes for $25. Which equation can be used to find t, the total Georgia will pay before sales tax is added?

- Ⓐ $t = 30 + 9 + 25 + 15$
- Ⓑ $t = 30 + 9 + 25 - 15$
- Ⓒ $t = 30 + 3 \cdot 9 - 15$
- Ⓓ $t = 30 + 3 \cdot 9 + 25 - 15$

Tip
Write an equation and compare it with the answer choices.

Think It Through
Write the items purchased and an expression for the sum.

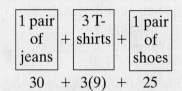

$$30 \quad + \quad 3(9) \quad + \quad 25$$

Subtract the amount of the gift certificate.

$$30 + 3(9) + 25 - 15$$

The correct answer is D.

Vocabulary Review

As you solve problems, you must understand the meanings of mathematical terms. Match each term with its mathematical meaning.

A. conjecture

B. expression

C. equation

D. origin

E. ordered pair

I. A mathematical phrase that uses numerals and operation symbols

II. Identifies the x- and y-coordinates of a point

III. Where the axes intersect on a coordinate plane

IV. A conclusion based on inductive reasoning

V. A mathematical sentence with an equal sign

Read each question. Then write the letter of the correct answer on your paper.

1. The bar graph shows the number of hours of sleep required by children. Which would be a reasonable conjecture for the number of hours of sleep needed by a 13-year-old? **(Lesson 1-7)**

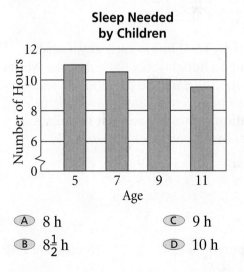

- Ⓐ 8 h
- Ⓑ $8\frac{1}{2}$ h
- Ⓒ 9 h
- Ⓓ 10 h

2. Which number should be the fifth number in the pattern 1, 4, 16, 64 . . . ? **(Lesson 1-7)**

- Ⓐ 128
- Ⓑ 192
- Ⓒ 256
- Ⓓ 512

Cumulative Practice (continued)

3. Measure each of the line segments in centimeters. How long should the seventh line segment in this pattern be? (Lesson 1-7)

Segment 1 ___
Segment 2 _____
Segment 3 _____
Segment 4 _____

Ⓐ 8 cm   Ⓒ 12 cm
Ⓑ 16 cm   Ⓓ 32 cm

4. Elaine rents a car for one day from Best Rental Cars and drives 80 miles. Which expression could be used to determine the cost of Elaine's rental? (Lesson 1-2)

Best Rental Cars
Rates
| $30.00 per day | $0.25 per mile |

Ⓐ $30 + 80 \cdot 0.25$
Ⓑ $30 \cdot 80 + 0.25$
Ⓒ $(30 + 80) \cdot 0.25$
Ⓓ $(30 + 0.25) \cdot 80$

5. Shana works 2 hours each day, Tuesday through Thursday. On Saturday, she works 5 hours. She earns $6 per hour on weekdays and $9 per hour on Saturday. Which equation shows the amount in dollars, a, she earns in one week? (Lesson 1-2)

Ⓐ $a = 2 \cdot 6 + 5 \cdot 9$
Ⓑ $a = 2 \cdot 3 \cdot 6 + 5 \cdot 9$
Ⓒ $a = 2(3 + 6) + 5 \cdot 9$
Ⓓ $a = 2 \cdot 3 \cdot 6 \cdot 5 \cdot 9$

6. Simplify $|-6 - 4| \div |-7 - 13|$. (Lesson 1-4)

Ⓐ -2 Ⓒ 2
Ⓑ 0.5   Ⓓ 10

7. The temperature was 10°F at midnight. It dropped 1°F per hour for the next 5 hours and 2°F per hour for the next 3 hours. Which equation can be used to find the temperature, t, at 8:00 A.M.? (Lesson 1-2)

Ⓐ $t = 10 - 5(-1) + 3(-2)$
Ⓑ $t = 10 + 5(-1) + 3(-2)$
Ⓒ $t = 10 + 5(1) + 3(2)$
Ⓓ $t = 10 - 5(-1) - 3(-2)$

8. Which property does the equation $3 + (7 + 2) = (3 + 7) + 2$ show? (Lesson 2-1)

Ⓐ Commutative Property of Addition
Ⓑ Identity Property of Addition
Ⓒ Distributive Property
Ⓓ Associative Property of Addition

9. At 6 A.M., the temperature was −2°F. At noon, it was 15 degrees warmer. By 7 P.M., the temperature had fallen 4 degrees from the noontime temperature. What was the temperature at 7 P.M.? (Lesson 1-5)

Ⓐ $-17°F$ Ⓒ 13°F
Ⓑ 9°F   Ⓓ 21°F

10. Which equation shows the Associative Property of Multiplication? (Lesson 2-1)

Ⓐ $9 \cdot 7 \cdot 8 = 9 \cdot 8 \cdot 7$
Ⓑ $(8 \cdot 3) \cdot 13 = 8 \cdot (3 \cdot 13)$
Ⓒ $12 + (-4) + 0 = 12 + (-4)$
Ⓓ $19 \cdot (-3) \cdot 1 = 19 \cdot (-3)$

11. On Friday, s students attended a play. On Saturday, 128 students attended the play. Seventeen more students attended on Saturday than on Friday. Which equation represents this situation? (Lesson 2-4)

Ⓐ $s + 17 = 128$
Ⓑ $s = 17 + 128$
Ⓒ $s - 17 = 128$
Ⓓ $s - 128 = 17$

Standards Mastery

12. Which of the following is true for all integer values of a? (Lesson 2-8)

Ⓐ $|a| > 0$
Ⓑ $|a| < 0$
Ⓒ $|a| = -a$
Ⓓ $|-a| = |a|$

13. Which graph shows a rectangle with one vertex at $(-2, 2)$ and two on the y-axis?
(Lesson 2-10)

Ⓐ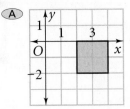

Ⓑ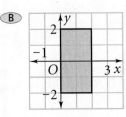

Ⓒ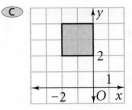

Ⓓ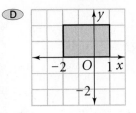

14. Which ordered pair represents a point inside the triangle?
(Lesson 1-10)

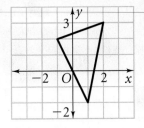

Ⓐ $(-1, 2)$
Ⓑ $(-2, -1)$
Ⓒ $(2, 1)$
Ⓓ $(1, 2)$

15. For a science project, Beth Ann grew a kudzu plant. She measured the plant's length each day.

Day	Length
1	48 cm
2	52 cm
3	57 cm
4	63 cm

Based on the information in the table, what is a reasonable prediction for the length on Day 7? (Lesson 1-3)

Ⓐ Between 65 and 74 inches
Ⓑ Between 74 and 83 inches
Ⓒ Between 83 and 92 inches
Ⓓ Between 92 and 101 inches

Decimals and Equations

What You've Learned

Compare rational numbers.

Add, subtract, multiply, and divide rational numbers (integers).

Use variables and appropriate operations to write an equation.

Make and test conjectures by using both inductive and deductive reasoning.

Check Your Readiness **GO for Help** to the Lesson in green.

Rounding Numbers (Skills Handbook, p. 681)

Round each number to the nearest ten.

1. 37　　　　**2.** 9　　　　**3.** 2　　　　**4.** 602　　　　**5.** 834　　　　**6.** 6,009

Comparing and Ordering Decimals (Skills Handbook, p. 685)

Compare. Use $>$, $<$, or $=$ to complete each statement.

7. 0.96 ▪ 1.32 　　　　　　**8.** 7.641 ▪ 7.593 　　　　　**9.** 6.3 ▪ 6.38

10. 5.001 ▪ 5.02 　　　　　**11.** -9.871 ▪ -10.3 　　　**12.** -27.619 ▪ -27.7

Order each group of decimals from least to greatest.

13. 8.35, 8.349, 8.351, 9.25 　　　　**14.** 0.02, 0.017, 0.201, 0.0201

15. $-1.4, -1.04, -1.401, -14.1$ 　　**16.** $-2.3, -3.2, -3.19, -2.8$

Operations With Decimals (Skills Handbook, pp. 687–693)

Simplify.

17. $3.4 + 8.09$ 　　**18.** $8 - 4.93$ 　　**19.** $0.59 + 3.06$ 　　**20.** $2.19 - 0.984$

21. $(1.001)(6.7)$ 　**22.** $40.02 \div 5.8$ 　**23.** $10.4 \cdot 5.3$ 　　**24.** $\dfrac{77.38}{7.3}$

Multiplying and Dividing by Powers of 10 (Skills Handbook, p. 691)

Simplify.

25. $9.87 \cdot 10$ 　　**26.** $5.32 \cdot 100$ 　　**27.** $0.3 \cdot 1,000$ 　　**28.** $15.407 \cdot 10,000$

29. $0.8 \div 10$ 　　**30.** $8.42 \div 100$ 　　**31.** $16.1 \div 1,000$ 　　**32.** $12.09 \div 10,000$

*Baranois de thon rubané à la tomate et à l'ail confit 1.
Tuna "baranois" stuffed with mashed tomatoes and candied gar

* Rosace de st jacques, coulis de tomates et basilic. 11 €⁹⁰
Sea scallops pie with a tomatoes and basil "coulis"

* Moules frites (marinière, poulette ou curry). 16 €⁰⁰
Fresh mussels and fries (white wine, cream or curry).

* Vivanneau entier et son coulis de poivrons jaunes. 18 €⁹⁰
Whole red snapper with a yellow sweet peppers sauce.

*Filet mignon de porc en croûte

What You'll Learn Next

Add, subtract, multiply, and divide rational numbers (terminating decimals).
Compare weights, capacities, geometric measures, times, and temperatures within measurement systems.
Use estimation to verify the reasonableness of calculated results.

▲ You can use estimation and decimals to decide whether the cost of multiple items is reasonable.

Writing and Comparing Decimals

Each digit in a decimal has both a place and a value. The value of any place is one-tenth the value of the place to its left. A place-value chart like the one at the right can help you read and write decimals.

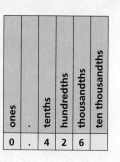

ones	.	tenths	hundredths	thousandths	ten thousandths
0	.	4	2	6	

1 EXAMPLE

a. Express 0.426 using words.

The last digit, 6, is in the thousandths place. So, 0.426 ends with the word *thousandths*.

0.426 is four hundred twenty-six thousandths.

b. Write *two and three hundredths* as a decimal.

And represents the decimal point. The hundredths place is the second place to the right of the decimal point.

Two and three hundredths is 2.03.

You can use decimal squares to model and compare decimals.

2 EXAMPLE

a. Model 0.6.

b. Model 0.58.

c. Model 1.05.

d. Compare 0.6 and 0.58. The models show that 0.6 > 0.58.

EXERCISES

Express each decimal using words.

1. 0.23   **2.** 0.624   **3.** 3.081   **4.** 58.36

Write each as a decimal.

5. three and two tenths   **6.** five and forty-one hundredths   **7.** fourteen ten-thousandths

Model and compare each pair of decimals.

8. 0.2 and 0.12   **9.** 0.89 and 0.9   **10.** 0.53 and 0.5   **11.** 1.35 and 1.4

Rounding and Estimating

Develop Add and subtract rational numbers.
Develop Use estimation to verify the reasonableness of calculated results.
Develop Indicate the relative advantages of exact and approximate solutions.

What You'll Learn

- To round decimals
- To estimate sums and differences

. . . And Why

To understand and apply appropriate estimation strategies in real-world situations such as grocery shopping

✓ Check Skills You'll Need

Use the number 27.3865. Write the value of the given digit.

1. 2   **2.** 3

3. 8   **4.** 6

GO for Help

Skills Handbook, p. 684

Rounding Decimals

Standards Investigation
Estimating in the Real World

Some real-world problems require only an estimate for an answer. Others require an exact answer. Decide whether each situation needs an estimate or an exact answer. Explain your reasoning.

1. a headline noting the number of people living in China

2. the amount of money a baby sitter charges per hour

3. the width of a window screen

4. the distance from Earth to the moon

5. the hours at soccer practice in one month

6. the number of tickets to sell for a play

You can round decimal numbers when you don't need exact values.

For: Comparing Decimals Activity
Use: Interactive Textbook, 3-1

1 EXAMPLE   Rounding Decimals

a. Round 4.2683 to the nearest tenth.

┌─ tenths place
4.2683
└─ 5 or greater
⬇
┌─ Round up to 3.
4.3

b. Round 4.2683 to the nearest one.

┌─ ones place
4.2683
└─ less than 5
⬇
┌─ Do not change.
4

✓ Quick Check

1. Identify the underlined place. Then round each number to that place.

     a. 38.4<u>1</u>   **b.** <u>0</u>.7772   **c.** 7,098.5<u>6</u>

     d. 274.94<u>3</u>4   **e.** 5.<u>0</u>25   **f.** 9.8<u>5</u>1

Estimating Sums and Differences

Vocabulary Tip

Read the symbol ≈ as "is approximately equal to."

You can estimate a result before you calculate. Then, if your answer is close to your estimate, you know that it is probably correct.

Write $126   ≈ $130

Read $126 is approximately equal to $130.

One way to estimate is to round all numbers to the same place.

2 EXAMPLE Rounding to Estimate

Problem Solving Tip

When rounding to estimate, keep in mind whether the estimate will be higher or lower than the exact answer.

Estimate to find whether each answer is reasonable.

a. Calculation   Estimate   **b.** Calculation   Estimate

$$
\begin{array}{rcl}
\$135.95 & \approx & \$140 \\
\$15.90 & \approx & \$20 \\
+\ \$24.05 & \approx & +\ \$20 \\
\hline
\$275.90\ \text{✗} & & \$180
\end{array}
\qquad
\begin{array}{rcl}
464.90 & \approx & 460 \\
-\ 125.73 & \approx & -\ 130 \\
\hline
339.17\ \text{✔} & & 330
\end{array}
$$

The answer is not close to the estimate. It is *not* reasonable.

The answer is close to the estimate. It is reasonable.

✓ Quick Check

2. Estimate by rounding.

     a. 355.302 + 204.889   **b.** 453.56 − 230.07

A *front-end estimate* is often closer to the exact sum than an estimate you find by rounding. First add the front-end digits. Round to estimate the sum of the remaining digits. Then combine estimates.

$1.73

$1.10

$2.71

3 EXAMPLE Using Front-End Estimation

The costs of carrots, peppers, and broccoli are shown at the left. Estimate the total cost of the vegetables.

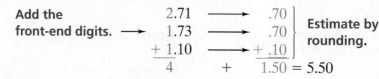

Add the front-end digits. ⟶

$$
\begin{array}{rcl}
2.71 & \longrightarrow & .70 \\
1.73 & \longrightarrow & .70 \\
+\ 1.10 & \longrightarrow & +\ .10 \\
\hline
4 & + & 1.50 = 5.50
\end{array}
$$

Estimate by rounding.

The total cost is about $5.50.

✓ Quick Check

3. Estimate using front-end estimation.

     a. 6.75 + 2.2 + 9.58   **b.** $1.07 + $2.49 + $7.40

You can also use *clustering* to estimate the sum of several numbers that are all close to the same value.

4 EXAMPLE Using Clustering

Estimate the total charge for the bills shown at the right.

four months

The values cluster around $15. ⟶ $15 \cdot 4 = 60$

The total long-distance charge is about $60.00.

Phone Bill

May Total	**$15.35**
June Total	**$16.05**
July Total	**$14.90**
August Total	**$15.05**

✓ Quick Check

4. Estimate $26.7 + 26.2 + 24.52 + 25.25 + 23.9$ using clustering.

You can use estimation to find an approximate answer quickly. When you choose a method of estimation, consider how close to the exact answer your estimate should be.

More Than One Way

Four items are priced at $4.39, $3.75, $4.96, and $2.40. You have $14. Can you purchase the items?

Nicole's Method

Round each price to the nearest dollar. Then add.
$4.39 + $3.75 + $4.96 + $2.40
$4 + $4 + $5 + $2 = $15
No, $14 is not enough.

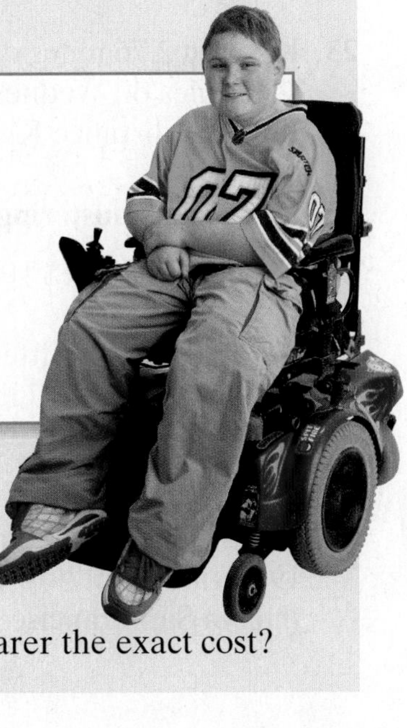

Eric's Method

Use front-end estimation.

$4.39	⟶	$.40
3.75	⟶	.80
4.96	⟶	1.00
+ 2.40	⟶	+ .40
$13	+	$2.60 = $15.60

No, $14 is not enough.

Choose a Method

1. Which method would you use to estimate the cost of the items? Explain.

2. Find the exact cost. Which estimate is nearer the exact cost?

Decide whether each situation represents an estimate or an exact value. Explain.

1. A server adds up the cost of four friends' meals at a restaurant.

2. An organizer finds the number of people likely to attend an event.

3. You find the number of times you blink in an hour.

4. A track-and-field judge finds the distance of a long jump.

Standards Practice

For more exercises, see *Extra Skills and Word Problem Practice.*

A Practice by Example

Example 1
(page 127)

GO for Help

Identify the underlined place. Then round each number to that place.

5. 27.3856   6. 0.9122   7. 1,045.98   8. 74.879

Round to the underlined place.

9. 345.678   10. 3.14159   11. 214.76   12. 2.9437

Example 2
(page 128)

Estimate by rounding.

13. $37.99 − $27.32   14. 1.58 + 17.0244   15. 172.98 − 128.301

16. $4.89 + $3.87   17. $16.81 + $11.49   18. $565 − $225

Example 3
(page 128)

Estimate using front-end estimation.

19. $6.04 + $3.45 + $4.43   20. $5.92 + $4.07

21. 9.89 + 2.43 + 8.37   22. 14.39 + 79.12

23. Kim ran 2.76 miles on Monday, 2.34 miles on Tuesday, and 1.97 miles on Wednesday. Use front-end estimation to estimate the total distance Kim ran.

Example 4
(page 129)

Estimate using clustering.

24. $9.50 + $8.45 + $9.08   25. 15.4 + 16 + 15.9 + 16.25 + 15.7

B Apply Your Skills

26. Rico's dog has a litter of four puppies. The puppies weigh 2.33 lb, 2.70 lb, 2.27 lb, and 2.64 lb. Use clustering to estimate the total weight of the puppies.

Homework Video Tutor

Visit: PHSchool.com
Web Code: bje-0301

27. Mobile, Alabama, has an average annual rainfall of 63.96 in. The average annual rainfall in San Francisco, California, is 19.70 in. About how much more rain falls each year in Mobile than in San Francisco?

28. Open-Ended Describe a situation in which a rounded answer is appropriate. Describe one in which an exact answer is necessary.

Estimate. Use a method of your choice.

29. $8.974 + 2.154$ **30.** $600 - 209.52$ **31.** $\$412.44 + \$72.23$

32. $\$8.99 + \$8.01$ **33.** $2.3 + 2.3 + 4.56$ **34.** $\$89.90 - \$49.29$

35. $800 + 810.5 + 807.3 + 791.1$ **36.** $54.23 + 56.12 + 57.98 + 55.55$

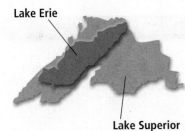

Lake Erie

Lake Superior

37. Lake Superior, the largest of the Great Lakes, has an area of about 31,760 mi². Lake Erie, the smallest of the Great Lakes, has an area of about 9,920 mi². About how much larger is Lake Superior than Lake Erie?

38. Writing in Math You have $11.50 to buy two presents. You find one item that costs $7.43. Another item costs $4.41. What estimation strategy will help you decide whether you have enough money to buy both? Explain.

39. Error Analysis You used a calculator to find $383.8 - 21.9$. Your estimate was 360, but your display reads 164.8. How could you have gotten 164.8 on your calculator?

C Challenge

40. Estimate the solution to $x + 3.2 = 0.75$. Without solving, decide whether your estimate is greater than or less than the exact answer.

Multiple Choice Practice and Mixed Review

For Standards Tutorials, visit PHSchool.com. Web Code: bjq-9045

41. Karen bought 3 pencils for $.59 each, 2 glue sticks for $3.35 each, and an eraser for $.99. The clerk charged her $5.46. How should Karen estimate the total cost to check the clerk's calculation?

  Ⓐ Round each item's cost to the nearest $.50 and add.

  Ⓑ Round each item's cost to the nearest $1 and add.

  Ⓒ Round each item's cost to the nearest $2 and add.

  Ⓓ Add the costs of one of each item and multiply by 3.

42. The school store sells pencils for $.25 and pens for $.50. On Monday, 41 pencils and 29 pens were sold. How much money did the school store collect in pen and pencil sales on Monday?

  Ⓐ $24.75   Ⓒ $26.75

  Ⓑ $25.75   Ⓓ $27.75

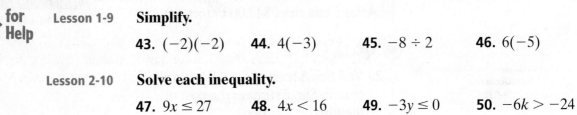

GO for Help

Lesson 1-9   **Simplify.**

43. $(-2)(-2)$ **44.** $4(-3)$ **45.** $-8 \div 2$ **46.** $6(-5)$

Lesson 2-10   **Solve each inequality.**

47. $9x \le 27$ **48.** $4x < 16$ **49.** $-3y \le 0$ **50.** $-6k > -24$

Estimating Decimal Products and Quotients

Develop Multiply and divide rational numbers (decimals).

Develop Use estimation to verify the reasonableness of results.

Develop Indicate the relative advantages of exact and approximate solutions to problems and give answers to a specified degree of accuracy.

What You'll Learn

- To estimate products
- To estimate quotients

. . . And Why

To determine the reasonableness of answers to real-world problems involving mass

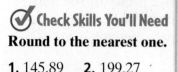 Check Skills You'll Need

Round to the nearest one.

1. 145.89   **2.** 199.27

3. 101.06   **4.** 28.45

 for Help

Lesson 3-1

New Vocabulary

- compatible numbers

Estimating Products

You can use mental math to estimate products and quotients. It is a good idea to estimate answers to check your calculations.

1 EXAMPLE Estimating the Product

Estimate 7.65 · 3.2.

$7.65 \approx 8$ $3.2 \approx 3$ **Round to the nearest one.**

$\qquad 8 \cdot 3 = 24$ **Multiply.**

$7.65 \cdot 3.2 \approx 24$

✓ Quick Check

1. Estimate each product.

   a. $4.72 \cdot 1.8$ **b.** $17.02 \cdot 3.78$ **c.** $8.25 \cdot 19.8$

2 EXAMPLE Checking Calculations

Arlene bought 6 yd of fabric to make a quilt. The fabric cost $6.75/yd. The sales clerk charged Arlene $45.90 before tax. Did the clerk make a mistake? Explain.

$6.75 \approx 7$ **Round to the nearest dollar.**

$7 \cdot 6 = 42$ **Multiply 7 times 6, the number of yards of fabric**

The sales clerk made a mistake. Since $6.75 < 7$, the actual cost should be less than the estimate. The clerk should have charged Arlene less than $42.00 before tax.

Fabric is usually sold by the yard but can be cut to the nearest inch.

✓ Quick Check

2. You buy 8 rolls of film. Each roll costs $4.79. Estimate the cost of the film before tax.

Estimating Quotients

When dividing, remember these names for the parts of a division sentence.

$$6 \div 3 = 2$$

dividend — quotient — divisor

When dividing, you can use *compatible numbers* to estimate quotients. **Compatible numbers** are numbers that are easy to divide mentally. When you estimate a quotient, first round the divisor, and then round the dividend to a compatible number.

3 EXAMPLE Using Compatible Numbers

Measurement A bowling ball has a mass of 5.61 kg. Each bowling pin has a mass of 1.57 kg. How many bowling pins are about equal to the bowling ball in mass? Estimate 5.61 ÷ 1.57.

$1.57 \approx 2$	Round the divisor.
$5.61 \approx 6$	Round the dividend to a multiple of 2 that is close to 5.61.
$6 \div 2 = 3$	Divide.

The mass of three bowling pins is about equal to that of the bowling ball.

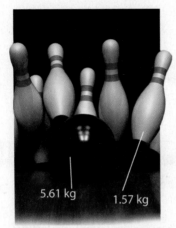

5.61 kg 1.57 kg

The masses of ten-pin bowling balls range from 3.63 kg to 7.26 kg.

✓ Quick Check

3. Estimate each quotient.

a. $38.9 \div 1.79$ **b.** $11.95 \div 2.1$ **c.** $82.52 \div 4.25$

You can estimate to determine the reasonableness of results.

4 EXAMPLE Estimating to Determine Reasonableness

Number Sense Is 2.15 a reasonable quotient for 17.931 ÷ 8.34?

$8.34 \approx 8$	Round the divisor.
$17.931 \approx 16$	Round the dividend to a multiple of 8 that is close to 17.931.
$16 \div 8 = 2$	Divide.

Since 2.15 is close to the estimate 2, it is reasonable.

✓ Quick Check

4. Use estimation. Is each quotient reasonable? Explain.

a. $1.564 \div 2.3 = 0.68$ **b.** $26.0454 \div 4.98 = 52.3$

Problem Solving Tip

You can sometimes use estimation to eliminate answer choices on a multiple choice test.

What is 8.19 ÷ 2.1?

Ⓐ 39   Ⓒ 3.9

Ⓑ 4.1   Ⓓ 0.41

If you estimate $8 \div 2 \approx 4$, then you know you can eliminate choices A and D.

Complete Exercises 1–4 to solve the problem below.

You review your sales slip after buying 4 CDs that cost $14.95 each. The total before tax was $77.80. Is this total correct?

1. What expression represents the total cost of the CDs?

2. Would you use rounding or compatible numbers to estimate the total? Explain.

3. Estimate the cost of 4 CDs.

4. Compare your estimate to the total on the sales slip. Is the total on the sales slip reasonable?

5. Suppose you bought 6 CDs for $14.95 each. Would the total $77.80 before tax be reasonable? Explain.

Standards Practice

For more exercises, see *Extra Skills and Word Problem Practice.*

A Practice by Example

Examples 1 and 2
(page 132)

GO for Help

Estimate each product.

6. $4.56 \cdot 7.02$ 7. $11.15 \cdot 4.44$ 8. $6.3 \cdot 9.2$

9. $24.5 \cdot 4.2$ 10. $3.29 \cdot 58$ 11. $0.08 \cdot 40.05$

12. The cost of 6 hamburgers for $2.89 each

13. The cost of 5 soccer balls for $12.29 each

Example 3
(page 133)

Estimate each quotient using compatible numbers.

14. $3.9 \div 2.1$ 15. $3.86 \div 1.95$ 16. $19.56 \div 0.71$

17. $\$585 \div 11.75$ 18. $18.2 \div 3.4$ 19. $57.1 \div 7.2$

20. Marshall buys a sack of peaches for $5.98. The peaches weigh 2.77 pounds. About what price per pound did Marshall pay?

Example 4
(page 133)

Use estimation. Is each quotient reasonable? Explain.

21. $102.6 \div 22.5 = 45.6$ 22. $\$32.40 \div 4.80 = \$67.50$

B Apply Your Skills

Estimate each product or quotient.

23. $193.7 \cdot 1.78$ 24. $7.95 \div 2.1$ 25. $9.392 \div 2.9$

26. $876.66 \cdot 39.64$ 27. $\$75.45 \div 12.48$ 28. $16.33 \cdot 3.5$

Use estimation. Is each product or quotient reasonable? Explain.

29. $-46.82(-1.5) = 702.3$ 30. $-71.5071 \div (-11.9) = 6.009$

Data Analysis Use the table below for Exercises 31–33.

Selected Wages (40-h week)

Occupation	Detroit, MI	Lincoln, NE
Elementary School Teacher	$1,820.80	$1,298.00
Secretary	$723.20	$508.00
Truck Driver	$685.20	$636.80

SOURCE: U.S. Department of Labor

31. Estimate the hourly wage for each staff position.

32. Estimate the yearly (52 weeks) salary for each staff position.

33. How much more per hour does a secretary in Detroit, Michigan, make than a secretary in Lincoln, Nebraska?

34. Shari is planning a 450-mi car trip. Her car can travel about 39 mi on a gallon of gasoline. Gasoline costs $1.89/gal. About how much will the gas cost for her trip?

35. **Writing in Math** You estimate $21.2 \div 3.75$ to be 5. Your friend estimates the quotient to be 7. Explain how the two estimates can be different and yet both be reasonable.

C Challenge

36. Humans breathe about 15 breaths in a minute. The average breath at rest contains 0.76 liter of air. About how many liters of air will you breathe while at rest for 25 minutes?

Multiple Choice Practice and Mixed Review

For Standards Tutorials, visit PHSchool.com. Web Code: bjq-9045

37. Based on his list, Diego determines the cost of groceries is $12.21. How can he make an estimate to check his calculation?

Bread	$1.49
Milk	$3.05
Juice	$2.49
Spaghetti	$1.09
Cereal	$4.09

Ⓐ Multiply the cost of the least expensive item by 5.

Ⓑ Multiply the cost of the most expensive item by 5.

Ⓒ Add the dollars. Round the cents to the nearest $0.1 and add.

Ⓓ Round each item up to the next whole dollar and add.

38. Ms. Jones uses the expression $0.75t + 0.25h$ to calculate her students' grades where t is the test average and h is the homework average. What is Kelly's grade if her test average is 92 and her homework average is 96?

Ⓐ 92　　　　Ⓑ 93　　　　Ⓒ 94　　　　Ⓓ 95

GO for Help　Lesson 1-8

39. A bus trip from Sacramento to Los Angeles takes 7 h 40 min. You depart at 11:40 A.M. At what time will you arrive in Los Angeles?

Read the exercise below and then read how the needed data are found in the table. Follow along as the problem is solved. Check your understanding by solving the exercise at the bottom of the page.

Use the table. How much more per hour does a registered nurse in San Jose, CA, make than a registered nurse in Washington, D.C.?

The title of the table tells you that the table entries are wages for a 40-h week.

Occupations: Look down for registered nurse.

Cities: Look across for San Jose and Washington.

The table tells you that in a 40-h week:

A registered nurse in San Jose makes $1,691.20.

A registered nurse in Washington makes $1,227.20.

Selected Wages (40-h week)

Occupation	San Jose, CA	Washington, D.C.
Registered Nurse	$1,691.20	$1,227.20
Radiology Technician	$1,350.00	$1,065.20
Orderly	$622.00	$495.20

SOURCE: U.S. Department of Labor

Estimate:

A San Jose registered nurse makes about
$1,700 − $1,220 = $480 more in a 40-h week.

That's about $480 ÷ 40 = $12 more per hour.

Calculate — Method 1

$1,691.20 − 1227.20 = 464$ **Subtract to find the difference in weekly wages.**

$464 ÷ 40 = 11.6$ **Divide to find the difference in hourly wages.**

Calculate — Method 2

$1,691.20 ÷ 40 = 42.28$ **Divide to find the Washington hourly wage.**

$1,227.20 ÷ 40 = 30.68$ **Divide to find the San Jose hourly wage.**

$42.28 − 30.68 = 11.60$ **Subtract to find the difference in hourly wages.**

A San Jose registered nurse makes $11.60/h more than one in Washington.

This is close to the estimate of $12/h.

EXERCISES

1. How much less per hour does an orderly in Washington make than an orderly in San Jose?

2. How much less per hour does a radiology technician in San Jose make than a nurse in San Jose?

Using Formulas

Develop Use the correct order of operations to evaluate algebraic expressions such as $3(2x + 5)^2$.

Introduce Use formulas routinely for finding the perimeter and area of basic two-dimensional figures.

What You'll Learn

- To substitute into formulas
- To use the formula for the perimeter of a rectangle

. . . And Why

To use formulas to solve real-world problems involving distances, temperatures, and perimeters

✓ Check Skills You'll Need

Evaluate each expression for $x = 3$ and $y = 4$.

1. $2x + 2y$ 2. $2x + y$

3. $2(x + y)$ 4. $\dfrac{x + y}{2}$

GO for Help
Lesson 1-3

◀)) New Vocabulary

- formula
- perimeter

Substituting Into Formulas

A **formula** is an equation that shows a relationship between quantities that are represented by variables.

An important formula in math and science is $d = rt$, where d is the distance, r is the rate or speed, and t is the time spent traveling.

1 EXAMPLE   Using the Rate Formula

Suppose you travel 162 miles in 3 hours. Use the formula $d = rt$ to find your average speed.

$d = rt$	Write the formula.
$162 = (r)(3)$	Substitute 162 for d and 3 for t.
$\dfrac{162}{3} = \dfrac{3r}{3}$	Divide each side by 3.
$54 = r$	Simplify.

Your average speed is 54 mi/h.

✓ Quick Check

1. Use the formula $d = rt$. Find d, r, or t.

   a. $d = 273$ mi, $t = 9.75$ h   b. $d = 540.75$ in., $r = 10.5$ in./yr

2 EXAMPLE   Substituting Into a Formula

You can estimate the temperature outside using the chirps of a cricket. Use the formula $F = \frac{n}{4} + 37$, where n is the number of times a cricket chirps in one minute, and F is the temperature in degrees Fahrenheit. Estimate the temperature when a cricket chirps 100 times in a minute.

$F = \dfrac{n}{4} + 37$	Write the formula.
$F = \dfrac{100}{4} + 37$	Replace n with 100.
$F = 25 + 37$	Divide.
$F = 62$	Add.

The temperature is about 62°F.

✓ Quick Check

2. Use the formula $F = \frac{n}{4} + 37$ to estimate the temperature in degrees Fahrenheit for each situation.

    a. 96 chirps/min   **b.** 88 chirps/min   **c.** 66 chirps/min

Using a Perimeter Formula

Vocabulary Tip

Think of peRIMeter as the distance around the "rim" of a figure.

The **perimeter** of a figure is the distance around the figure. You can find the perimeter of a rectangle by adding the lengths of the four sides, or by using the formula $P = 2\ell + 2w$, where ℓ is the length, and w is the width. For rectangles, it does not matter which dimension you choose to be the length or the width.

3 EXAMPLE   **Finding Perimeter**

Problem Solving Tip

Read and solve the problem before looking for the correct answer.

Multiple Choice Use the formula for the perimeter of a rectangle, $P = 2\ell + 2w$. What is the perimeter of the rectangle?

  Ⓐ 60 ft   Ⓑ 61 ft   Ⓒ 62 ft   Ⓓ 64 ft

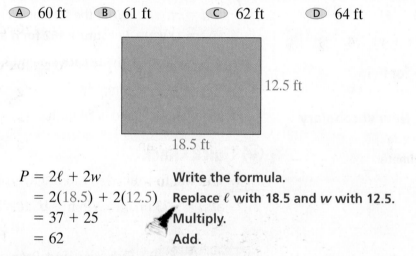

$$
\begin{aligned}
P &= 2\ell + 2w & &\text{Write the formula.}\\
&= 2(18.5) + 2(12.5) & &\text{Replace } \ell \text{ with 18.5 and } w \text{ with 12.5.}\\
&= 37 + 25 & &\text{Multiply.}\\
&= 62 & &\text{Add.}
\end{aligned}
$$

The perimeter of the rectangle is 62 ft. The correct choice is C.

✓ Quick Check

3. Find the perimeter of each rectangle.

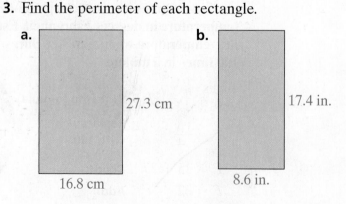

a. 27.3 cm, 16.8 cm

b. 17.4 in., 8.6 in.

Complete Exercises 1–4 to solve the problem below.

A plane travels 2,730 miles in 9.75 hours. Use the formula $d = rt$ to find the plane's average speed.

1. What number should you substitute for d?

2. What variable is unknown in the formula?

3. What operation should you use to solve the formula?

4. What is the plane's average speed?

Standards Practice

For more exercises, see *Extra Skills and Word Problem Practice*.

A Practice by Example

Example 1
(page 137)

GO for Help

Use the formula $d = rt$. Find d, r, or t.

5. $r = 38.5$ mi/h, $t = 12.5$ h

6. $d = 2,730$ mi, $t = 9.75$ h

7. $d = 596.39$ cm, $r = 2.3$ cm/s

8. $d = 10.2$ ft, $r = 0.5$ ft/h

9. $r = 65$ mi/h, $t = 8.3$ h

10. $d = 57$ yd, $r = 3$ yd/s

Example 2
(page 137)

Use the formula $F = \frac{n}{4} + 37$ to estimate each temperature.

11. 120 chirps/min

12. 80 chirps/min

13. 92 chirps/min

14. 64 chirps/min

15. 60 chirps/min

16. 78 chirps/min

Example 3
(page 138)

Use the formula $P = 2\ell + 2w$. Find the perimeter of each rectangle.

17.

11.2 mm

16.5 mm

18.

6.2 m

7.3 m

B Apply Your Skills

Given that C is the temperature in degrees Celsius, use the formula $F = 1.8C + 32$ to find each temperature F in degrees Fahrenheit.

19. $C = 58$

20. $C = -4$

21. $C = 72$

22. $C = 56$

23. $C = -89$

24. $C = -18$

Geometry Use the formula $P = 2\ell + 2w$. Find the perimeter of each rectangle. Then use the formula $A = \ell w$ to find each area.

25.

3.7 m

7.3 m

26.

11.2 cm

25.8 cm

Homework Video Tutor

Visit: PHSchool.com
Web Code: bje-0303

Modoc County, California, is nearly rectangular in shape. Use the map at the right for Exercises 27 and 28.

Modoc County
Alturas
56 mi
—75 mi—

27. Use the formula for area. Find the approximate area of Modoc.

28. Use the formula for perimeter. Find the approximate perimeter of Modoc.

29. Multiple Choice The area of the rectangle is 27.8 square feet. Which is the best estimate of the length of the rectangle?

4 ft

Ⓐ 5 ft   Ⓒ 7 ft
Ⓑ 6 ft   Ⓓ 8 ft

C Challenge

30. The top surface of a world-record rectangular strawberry shortcake was 175.33 ft long and 48 in. wide. Use the formula for perimeter. Find the approximate perimeter of the cake.

31. Find the approximate area of the top of the cake in Exercise 25.

Multiple Choice Practice and Mixed Review

For Standards Tutorials, visit PHSchool.com. Web Code: bjq-9045

32. Evaluate $b(3a - 2)$ for $a = -7$ and $b = 3.5$.

Ⓐ -80.5 Ⓑ -75.5 Ⓒ -28 Ⓓ -23

33. Which of the following is equivalent to $6x + 15$?

Ⓐ $\frac{2}{x}$ Ⓑ $3(2x + 5)$ Ⓒ $6(x + 15)$ Ⓓ $6x + 9$

34. You want to put a fence around a rectangular garden with side lengths of 12 feet and 14 feet. How much fencing do you need?

Ⓐ 26 feet   Ⓑ 38 feet   Ⓒ 52 feet   Ⓓ 168 feet

GO for Help   Lesson 1-7

35. Patterns Which equation, $n = 2t$ or $t = n \cdot 2$, describes the relationship between the variables in the table? Explain.

n	14	16	18	20
t	7	8	9	10

Checkpoint Quiz 1

Round each number to the underlined place value.

1. 15.6<u>5</u>71   **2.** 0.89<u>1</u>4   **3.** 7,0<u>2</u>2.56   **4.** 345.<u>6</u>78

Estimate.

5. $3.7 \cdot 8.06$ **6.** $17.25 + 6.66$ **7.** $8.7 - 9.6$ **8.** $11.7 \div 1.8$

9. Jennifer drives at an average speed of 54 mi/h. At this rate, how long does it take Jennifer to drive 459 miles?

Understanding Math Problems Read the problem below. Then let Joe's thinking guide you through the solution. Check your understanding with the exercises at the bottom of the page.

Geometry Use the formula $P = 2\ell + 2w$. Find the perimeter of the rectangle. Then use the formula $A = \ell w$ to find the area.

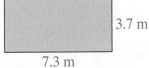
3.7 m

7.3 m

What Joe Thinks	What Joe Writes
I need to use the formula for perimeter.	$P = 2\ell + 2w$
Substitute 7.3 for ℓ and 3.7 for w.	$P = 2(7.3) + 2(3.7)$
I can use the Distributive Property to make the work easier.	$P = 2(7.3 + 3.7)$
Add within parentheses.	$P = 2(11)$
Now multiply.	$P = 22$
Next, I need to use the formula for area.	$A = \ell w$
Substitute 7.3 for ℓ and 3.7 for w. Multiply.	$A = 7.3(3.7) = 27.01$
Now I need to write the units. Don't forget that area is in square units.	Perimeter is 22 m. Area is 27.01 m².

EXERCISES

Geometry Use the formula $P = 2\ell + 2w$. Find the perimeter of each rectangle. Then use the formula $A = \ell w$ to find each area.

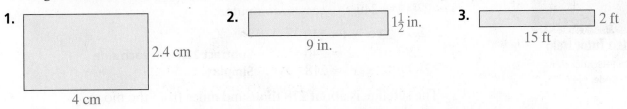

1.

2.4 cm

4 cm

2.

9 in.

$1\frac{1}{2}$ in.

3.

15 ft

2 ft

Solving Equations by Adding or Subtracting Decimals

What You'll Learn

- To solve one-step decimal equations involving addition
- To solve one-step decimal equations involving subtraction

. . . And Why

To solve real-world problems involving astronomy and money management

✓ **Check Skills You'll Need**

Simplify.

1. $2.8 + 7.06$

2. $0.65 + 1.8$

3. $4.52 - 2.48$

4. $3.7 - 0.62$

 **for Help**

Skills Handbook, p. 687

Develop Add and subtract rational numbers (terminating decimals).

Using Subtraction to Solve Equations

In Lesson 2-5, you used the Subtraction Property of Equality to solve equations involving integers. You can also use this property to solve equations with decimals. Remember to subtract the same number from each side of the equation.

1 EXAMPLE **Subtracting to Solve an Equation**

Solve $n + 4.5 = -9.7$.

$$n + 4.5 = -9.7$$
$$n + 4.5 - 4.5 = -9.7 - 4.5 \quad \text{Subtract 4.5 from each side.}$$
$$n = -14.2 \quad \text{Simplify.}$$

Check $\quad n + 4.5 = -9.7$
$$-14.2 + 4.5 \stackrel{?}{=} -9.7 \quad \text{Replace } n \text{ with } -14.2.$$
$$-9.7 = -9.7 ✓$$

✓ **Quick Check**

1. Solve each equation.

a. $x + 4.9 = 18.8$ **b.** $14.73 = -24.23 + b$

2 EXAMPLE **Estimating a Solution**

Astronomy Use the diagram below. A communications satellite is circling Earth. About how far is the satellite from the moon?

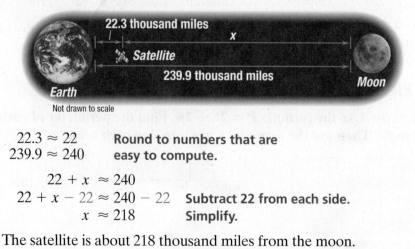

22.3 thousand miles

x

Satellite

239.9 thousand miles

Earth

Moon

Not drawn to scale

$$22.3 \approx 22 \quad \text{Round to numbers that are}$$
$$239.9 \approx 240 \quad \text{easy to compute.}$$

$$22 + x \approx 240$$
$$22 + x - 22 \approx 240 - 22 \quad \text{Subtract 22 from each side.}$$
$$x \approx 218 \quad \text{Simplify.}$$

The satellite is about 218 thousand miles from the moon.

 **nline**

Video Tutor Help

Visit: PHSchool.com
Web Code: bje-0775

✓ Quick Check

2. A store's cost plus markup is the price you pay for an item. Suppose a pair of shoes costs a store $35.48. You pay $70. Write and solve an equation to find the store's markup.

GO for Help

For help with adding and subtracting decimals, see Skills Handbook, page 687.

Using Addition to Solve Equations

You can also use the Addition Property of Equality to solve an equation involving decimals. Remember to add the same number to each side of the equation.

3 EXAMPLE   Adding to Solve an Equation

Solve $k - 14.4 = -18.39$.

$$k - 14.4 = -18.39$$
$$k - 14.4 + 14.4 = -18.39 + 14.4 \quad \text{Add 14.4 to each side.}$$
$$k = -3.99 \quad \text{Simplify.}$$

Online active math

For: Decimal Equations Activity
Use: Interactive Textbook, 3-4

✓ Quick Check

3. Solve each equation.

  a. $n - 5.85 = 15.25$ b. $-10 = c - 2.6$

4 EXAMPLE   Adding to Solve an Equation

Danzel wrote a check for $76.85. His new account balance is $235.15. What was his previous balance?

Words   │ previous balance │ minus │ check │ is │ new balance

Let p = previous balance.

Equation p $-$ 76.85 $=$ 235.15

$$p - 76.85 = 235.15$$
$$p - 76.85 + 76.85 = 235.15 + 76.85 \quad \text{Add 76.85 to each side.}$$
$$p = 312 \quad \text{Simplify.}$$

Danzel's previous balance was $312.

✓ Quick Check

4. You spent $14.95 for a new shirt. You now have $12.48. Write and solve an equation to find how much money you had before you bought the shirt.

Check Your Understanding

Determine whether $x = 3.3$ is a solution of each equation.

1. $x + 3.7 = 7$ **2.** $6.3 - x = 3.3$ **3.** $10.2 + x = 13.5$

Complete the steps for each equation. Justify each step.

4. $x + 1.2 = 15$ **5.** $y - 3.33 = 12.42$
     $x + 1.2 - \blacksquare = 15 - \blacksquare$ $y - 3.33 + \blacksquare = 12.42 + \blacksquare$
         $x = \blacksquare$ $y = \blacksquare$

Standards Practice

For more exercises, see *Extra Skills and Word Problem Practice.*

A   Practice by Example

Examples 1 and 2
(page 142)

Solve each equation.

6. $c + 9 = 3.7$ **7.** $b + 7.6 = 23$ **8.** $43.6 = n + 17.5$

9. $6.35 + b = 9.89$ **10.** $12.13 = n + 1.4$ **11.** $x + 0.35 = 9.15$

12. Astronomy The planet Mars takes 599.01 days longer than Mercury to orbit the sun. In all, the Mars orbit takes 686.98 days. Write and solve an equation to find about how long it takes Mercury to orbit the sun.

Examples 3 and 4
(page 143)

Solve each equation.

13. $d - 4.9 = 18.8$ **14.** $c - 19.2 = 24$ **15.** $-2.5 = q - 1.7$

16. $-5.6 = y - 8$ **17.** $4.3 = g - 1$ **18.** $a - 108.8 = -203$

19. Rachel wrote a check for $161.15. Her new account balance is $423.28. What was her previous account balance?

B   Apply Your Skills

Hares are generally larger and have longer hind legs and longer ears than rabbits.

20. Michael Johnson's world record in the 200-m sprint is 19.32 s. His 400-m world record is 23.86 s slower than his 200-m record. Write and solve an equation to find Johnson's 400-m record.

21. Biology A hare travels about 17.83 mi/h faster on land than a giant tortoise. A hare can hop at about 18 mi/h. Write and solve an equation to find about how fast a giant tortoise can travel on land.

Solve each equation.

22. $4.035 = a - 3.25$ **23.** $h - (-1.5) = 1.5$ **24.** $e + (-7.8) = -6.7$

Mental Math Use mental math to solve each equation.

25. $1.60 = 0.40 + s$ **26.** $x + 8.8 = 9.9$ **27.** $5.5 = x - 5.5$

28. David wants to start a baseball card collection, so he takes his piggy bank to the store, picks a pack of cards and puts all his change on the counter. If David has $7.14 in change, and the cards cost $1.89, how much does David have left?

Homework Video Tutor

Visit: PHSchool.com
Web Code: bje-0304

29. David doesn't want to put any pennies back into his bank. What other amount of change would he have needed to get only nickels, dimes and quarters back from the store clerk? Justify your answer.

30. Error Analysis A student solved an equation as shown at the left. Explain the student's error.

$$x - 1.6 = -6$$
$$x - 1.6 + 1.6 = -6 - 1.6$$
$$x = -7.6$$

31. Writing in Math Explain how you would use the Addition (not Subtraction) Property of Equality to solve $x + 1.8 = -4.7$.

32. Reasoning Without solving, tell how the solutions of the equations $x + 14 = 15$, $x + 1.4 = 1.5$, and $x + 0.14 = 0.15$ compare. Explain.

C Challenge   **Solve each equation.**

33. $143.587 + x - 22.96 = 156.4$ **34.** $-924.87 - 1,237 + b = 86.125$

Multiple Choice Practice and Mixed Review

For Standards Tutorials, visit PHSchool.com. Web Code: bjq-9045

35. Which statement describes how to solve $x + 0.042 = 0.826$?

    Ⓐ Add 0.042 to each side.

    Ⓑ Add 0.826 to each side.

    Ⓒ Subtract 0.042 from each side.

    Ⓓ Subtract 0.826 from each side.

36. What is the area of the rectangle below?

    Ⓐ 11.9 cm²   Ⓒ 20.58 cm²

    Ⓑ 18 cm²   Ⓓ 23.8 cm²

2.1 cm

9.8 cm

GO for Help   Lesson 3-3

Use the formula $A = \ell w$. Find A.

37. $\ell = 23.4$ in., $w = 15.8$ in.   **38.** $\ell = 5.5$ cm, $w = 7$ cm

Solving Equations by Multiplying or Dividing Decimals

What You'll Learn

- To solve one-step decimal equations involving multiplication
- To solve one-step decimal equations involving division

. . . And Why

To solve real-world problems in oil production

✓ Check Skills You'll Need

Find each product.

1. 2.6(4.5)

2. 3.2(0.15)

3. 11.03(0.6)

4. 8.003(0.6)

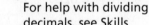 **for Help**

Skills Handbook, p. 688

Develop Multiply and divide rational numbers (terminating decimals).

Using Division to Solve Equations

In Lesson 2-6, you used the Division Property of Equality to solve equations involving integers. You can also use this property to solve equations with decimals. Remember to divide each side of the equation by the same nonzero number.

1 EXAMPLE Dividing to Solve an Equation

Solve $0.9r = -5.4$.

$$0.9r = -5.4$$

$$\frac{0.9r}{0.9} = \frac{-5.4}{0.9} \qquad \text{Divide each side by 0.9.}$$

$$r = -6 \qquad \text{Simplify.}$$

Check $\qquad 0.9r = -5.4$

$\qquad\qquad 0.9(-6) \overset{?}{=} -5.4 \qquad$ **Replace r with –6.**

$\qquad\qquad\quad -5.4 = -5.4 \checkmark$

✓ Quick Check

1. Solve each equation.

    a. $0.8x = -1.6$ **b.** $1.15 = 2.3x$ **c.** $-81.81 = -0.9n$

2 EXAMPLE Dividing to Solve an Equation

An oil field produces an average of 16.8 thousand barrels of crude oil per day. About how many days will it take to produce 200 thousand barrels?

Words	daily barrel production	times	number of days	equals	200 thousand barrels

Let d = number of days.

Equation	16.8	·	d	=	200

$$16.8d = 200$$

$$\frac{16.8d}{16.8} = \frac{200}{16.8} \qquad \text{Divide each side by 16.8.}$$

$$d = 11.904 \ldots \quad \text{Simplify.}$$

$$d \approx 12 \qquad\qquad \text{Round to the nearest whole number.}$$

It will take about 12 days to produce 200 thousand barrels.

GO for Help

For help with dividing decimals, see Skills Handbook, page 692.

2. You paid $7.70 to mail a package that weighed 5.5 lb. Write and solve an equation to find the cost per pound.

Using Multiplication to Solve Equations

To solve an equation involving division, multiply each side by the same nonzero number.

Quick Tip

Remember to maintain the balance: Whatever you do to one side of an equation you must do to the other side.

3 EXAMPLE Multiplying to Solve an Equation

Solve $\frac{m}{-7.2} = -12.5$.

$$\frac{m}{-7.2} = -12.5$$

$$\frac{m}{-7.2}(-7.2) = -12.5(-7.2) \quad \text{Multiply each side by } -7.2.$$

$$m = 90 \quad \text{Simplify.}$$

✅ **Quick Check**

3. Solve each equation.

   a. $\frac{r}{-6.0} = 0.5$ **b.** $\frac{s}{2.5} = 5$ **c.** $-80 = \frac{t}{4.5}$

4 EXAMPLE Multiplying to Solve an Equation

Multiple Choice The 1923 baseball season was one of Babe Ruth's best. He was at bat 522 times and had a batting average of 0.393, rounded to the nearest thousandth. The batting average formula is $a = \frac{h}{n}$, where a is the batting average, h is the number of hits, and n is the number of times at bat. How many hits did Babe Ruth make?

   Ⓐ 522 hits   Ⓑ 393 hits   Ⓒ 206 hits   Ⓓ 205 hits

$$a = \frac{h}{n}$$

$$0.393 = \frac{h}{522} \quad \text{Replace } a \text{ with } 0.393 \text{ and } n \text{ with } 522.$$

$$(0.393)(522) = \frac{h}{522}(522) \quad \text{Multiply each side by } 522.$$

$$h = 205.146 \quad \text{Simplify.}$$

$$h \approx 205 \quad \begin{array}{l}\text{Since } h \text{ (hits) represents an integer,} \\ \text{round to the nearest integer.}\end{array}$$

Babe Ruth made 205 hits. The answer is D.

✅ **Quick Check**

4. Suppose your batting average is 0.222. You have batted 54 times. How many hits do you have?

Use estimation to decide if each solution is reasonable for the given equation.

1. $4x = 8.8;\ x = 2.2$

2. $\frac{y}{2.5} = 0.6;\ y = 15$

3. $136 = b(9);\ b = 10.4$

4. $\frac{p}{4} = 1.95;\ p = 7.8$

$2.7x = 30$

$3x \approx 30$

$x \approx 90$

5. Error Analysis A student estimated the solution of an equation as shown at the left. What error did the student make?

Standards Practice

For more exercises, see *Extra Skills and Word Problem Practice.*

Ⓐ **Practice by Example**

Examples 1 and 2
(page 146)

GO for Help

Solve each equation.

6. $0.8s = -6.4$

7. $0.8x = 0.48$

8. $-0.5y = -0.73$

9. $2x = -4.88$

10. $2.21 = 1.7w$

11. $3.2n = 27.52$

12. $-0.3y = 7.53$

13. $1.92 = 1.6s$

14. $0.7x = 2.8$

15. A factory produces an average of seven thousand televisions per day. About how many days will it take to produce 63.5 thousand televisions?

Examples 3 and 4
(page 147)

Solve each equation.

16. $\frac{n}{2.3} = -4.8$

17. $0.97 = \frac{c}{-2}$

18. $\frac{n}{1.7} = 0.22$

19. $120 = \frac{v}{3.8}$

20. $9 = \frac{a}{1.5}$

21. $\frac{m}{7.08} = -100$

22. $\frac{b}{7} = -8$

23. $\frac{k}{2.01} = 0.04$

24. $200 = \frac{f}{4}$

25. During the 1954 baseball season with the New York Yankees, Yogi Berra was at bat 584 times and had a batting average of 0.307. Use the batting-average formula in Example 4 to find the number of hits Berra made.

Ⓑ **Apply Your Skills**

Solve each equation.

26. $6.4x = 0.2816$

27. $0.004m = 0.12$

28. $4.5 = m \div (-3.3)$

29. $-33.04 = \frac{z}{-0.03}$

30. $5.1z = -11.73$

31. $-0.45 = x \div 12$

32. a. Error Analysis Harry found 324.8 as a solution for the equation $4x = 81.2$. What was Harry's error?

b. Estimation How could Harry have used estimation to check whether his answer was reasonable?

Write an equation for each sentence. Solve for the variable.

33. The product of a number n and -7.3 is 30.66.

34. The quotient of a number n divided by -4.5 equals 200.6.

Homework Video Tutor

Visit: PHSchool.com
Web Code: bje-0305

35. a. Your batting average is 0.244, and you have been at bat 82 times. How many hits do you have?
   b. **Writing in Math** Why is it necessary to round your answer in part (a) to the nearest integer?

36. Jan pays $\$.08$ per kilowatt-hour for electricity. Her electric bill is $\$59.22$. Write and solve an equation to find how many kilowatt-hours of electricity Jan used.

37. Number Sense The weight of a record-setting onion was 12.25 lb. An average-sized onion weighs 0.5 lb. About how many average-sized onions have a total weight equal to the record-setting onion?

38. Measurement If you know a length ℓ in meters, you can multiply the length by 3.28 to find the length in feet f.
   a. Write an equation to model this situation.
   b. A tree is 7.5 m tall. Use your equation to find this height in feet.
   c. A bookshelf is 6 ft tall. What is this height in meters?
   d. A room is 12 ft long and 15 ft wide. Use your equation and the formula for the area of a rectangle to find the area of the room in square meters. Round to the nearest tenth.

Challenge

39. Reasoning Find values for x and y that satisfy $xy = 0.42$ and $x + y = 1.3$.

Multiple Choice Practice and Mixed Review

For Standards Tutorials, visit PHSchool.com. Web Code: bjq-9045

40. Omar bought 3.5 pints of strawberries for $\$8.75$. What is the cost of one pint of strawberries?
   Ⓐ $\$2.50$ Ⓑ $\$2.75$ Ⓒ $\$5.25$ Ⓓ $\$12.25$

41. Doug sketches $\triangle ABC$ on a graph as displayed at the right. What are the coordinates of a vertex of the triangle? 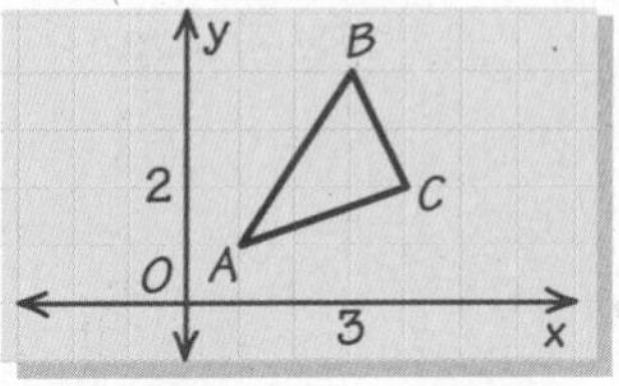
   Ⓐ $(2, 4)$ Ⓒ $(4, 3)$
   Ⓑ $(-1, 1)$ Ⓓ $(1, 1)$

42. A group of friends goes out for dinner. The bill is $\$36.81$. If they share the cost equally and each person's share is about $\$7.35$, how many people are in the group?
   Ⓐ 4 Ⓑ 5 Ⓒ 6 Ⓓ 7

for Help   Lesson 3-4

Solve each equation.

43. $c + 9 = 3.7$ **44.** $-5.6 = y - 8$ **45.** $4.035 = a - 3.25$

Using the Metric System

Introduce Compare weights, capacities, and geometric measures within measurement systems.

What You'll Learn

- To identify appropriate metric measures
- To convert metric units

. . . And Why

To solve real-world problems involving metric measures

☑ **Check Skills You'll Need**

Find each product or quotient.

1. 5×100

2. $14.06 \div 1,000$

3. 0.294×10

4. $0.9 \div 100$

GO **for Help**

Skills Handbook, p. 691

Identifying Appropriate Metric Measures

Knowing the approximate size of each metric unit of measure will allow you to choose an appropriate unit.

Take Note ✎ **Metric Units of Measurement**

	Unit	Reference Example
Length	millimeter (mm)	about the thickness of a dime
	centimeter (cm)	about the width of a thumbnail
	meter (m)	about the distance from a doorknob to the floor
	kilometer (km)	a little more than one half mile
Capacity	milliliter (mL)	about 5 drops of water
	liter (L)	a little more than a quart of milk
Mass	milligram (mg)	about the mass of a speck of sawdust
	gram (g)	about the mass of a paper clip
	kilogram (kg)	about one half the mass of this math book

① **EXAMPLE** **Choosing an Appropriate Unit**

Choose an appropriate metric unit. Explain your choice.

a. height of a classroom chalkboard

Meter; the height of a chalkboard is about twice the distance from the floor to a doorknob.

b. mass of a backpack filled with books

Kilogram; the mass of a backpack filled with books is many times the mass of this textbook.

c. capacity of a birdbath

Liter; several quart bottles of water would fill a birdbath.

☑ **Quick Check**

1. Choose an appropriate metric unit. Explain your choice.

a. length of a broom **b.** the mass of an energy bar
c. mass of a horse **d.** capacity of a car's gas tank

Estimating With Metric Units

Estimation Choose a reasonable estimate. Explain your choice.

a. capacity of a juice box: 200 mL or 200 L

200 mL; the juice box holds less than a quart of milk.

b. length of a new pencil: 15 cm or 15 m

15 cm; the length of a pencil would be about 15 widths of a thumbnail.

c. mass of a small tube of toothpaste: 100 g or 100 kg

100 g; the mass is about the same as a box of paper clips.

✅ Quick Check

2. Choose a reasonable estimate. Explain your choice.

   a. distance between two cities: 50 mm or 50 km
   b. amount of liquid that an eyedropper holds: 10 mL or 10 L

Converting Metric Units

The metric system uses a decimal system to relate different units to each other. Look at the metric-units chart below. The units highlighted in yellow are the units most often used. From left to right, each unit is $\frac{1}{10}$ of the size of the unit before it.

	kilo-	hecto-	deka-	UNIT	deci-	centi-	milli-
Length	kilometer (km)	hectometer (hm)	dekameter (dam)	meter (m)	decimeter (dm)	centimeter (cm)	millimeter (mm)
Capacity	kiloliter (kL)	hectoliter (hL)	dekaliter (daL)	liter (L)	deciliter (dL)	centiliter (cL)	milliliter (mL)
Mass	kilogram (kg)	hectogram (hg)	dekagram (dag)	gram (g)	decigram (dg)	centigram (cg)	milligram (mg)

You can convert from one unit to another by multiplying or dividing by 10; 100; 1,000; and so on.

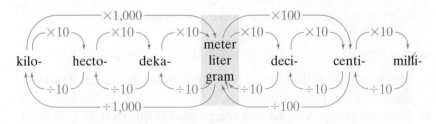

Vocabulary Tip

The prefixes, such as *milli*, *centi*, and *deci*, denote the relative sizes of the units.

To convert from one unit to another in the metric system, find the relationship between the two units.

Remember:
* Multiply if you are going from a larger unit to a smaller unit since there will be more of the smaller units.
* Divide if you are going from a smaller unit to a larger unit since there will be fewer of the larger units.

3 EXAMPLE **Converting Between Metric Units**

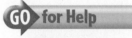

GO for Help

For a guide to multiplying and dividing decimals by powers of ten, see Skills Handbook, page 691.

Mental Math **Complete each statement.**

a. **4.35 L = ▪ mL**

$4.35 \cdot 1,000 = 4,350$ To convert liters to milliliters, multiply by 1,000.

$4.35 \text{ L} = 4,350 \text{ mL}$

b. **914 cm = ▪ m**

$914 \div 100 = 9.14$ To convert centimeters to meters, divide by 100.

$914 \text{ cm} = 9.14 \text{ m}$

✓ Quick Check

3. Complete each statement.

   a. $35 \text{ mL} = ▪ \text{ L}$ b. $▪ \text{ g} = 250 \text{ kg}$ c. $▪ \text{ cm} = 60 \text{ m}$

4 EXAMPLE **Converting Between Metric Units**

The ancient city of Machu Picchu (c. 1450–1550) is located in Peru's Andes Mountains.

Geography The ancient Incan city of Machu Picchu is located in Peru. Its altitude is about 2,300 m above sea level. What is Machu Picchu's altitude in kilometers?

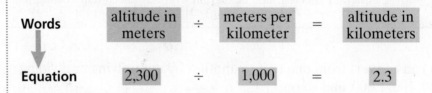

Words	altitude in meters	÷	meters per kilometer	=	altitude in kilometers
Equation	2,300	÷	1,000	=	2.3

Machu Picchu is about 2.3 km above sea level.

✓ Quick Check

4. a. The record for the highest a kite has flown is 3.8 km. Find the height of the kite in meters.
   b. **Number Sense** You have a recipe that requires 0.25 L of milk. Your measuring cup is marked only in milliliters. How many milliliters of milk do you need?

Match each quantity with an appropriate metric unit. Explain your choice.

1. length of your thumb
2. mass of a book
3. length of a soccer field
4. amount of water in a fishbowl
5. mass of an eraser
6. amount of fluid in a straw

A. gram
B. meter
C. centimeter
D. milliliter
E. liter
F. kilogram

Standards Practice

For more exercises, see *Extra Skills and Word Problem Practice.*

A Practice by Example

Example 1
(page 150)

GO for Help

Choose an appropriate metric unit of measure. Explain your choice.

7. mass of a banana
8. depth of Lake Michigan
9. length of a small calculator
10. mass of a car
11. width of a highway
12. quantity of water in a spoon

Example 2
(page 151)

Choose a reasonable estimate. Explain your choice.

13. the mass of a small dog: 5 g or 5 kg
14. amount of liquid you should drink daily: 2,000 mL or 2,000 L
15. the mass of a box of cereal: 350 mg or 350 g

Example 3
(page 152)

Mental Math Complete each statement.

16. $54 \text{ m} = \blacksquare \text{ cm}$
17. $\blacksquare \text{ L} = 234 \text{ mL}$
18. $12 \text{ g} = \blacksquare \text{ kg}$
19. $\blacksquare \text{ m} = 3.01 \text{ km}$
20. $0.25 \text{ m} = \blacksquare \text{ cm}$
21. $\blacksquare \text{ mL} = 7.3 \text{ L}$
22. $595 \text{ g} = \blacksquare \text{ kg}$
23. $35 \text{ m} = \blacksquare \text{ km}$
24. $\blacksquare \text{ mg} = 0.27 \text{ g}$

Example 4
(page 152)

25. Elgin Street, in Bacup, England, is the shortest street in the world. It is 518 cm long. How many meters long is it?

26. A shrew, the mammal with the fastest metabolism, has a mass of only 0.004 kg. What is its mass in grams?

B Apply Your Skills

27. **Error Analysis** One of the world's largest pearls had a mass of 6,392 g. Camille wrote in her report that the pearl had a mass of 6,392,000 kg. What was her error?

Write the metric unit that makes each statement true.

28. $9.03 \text{ m} = 9,030 \blacksquare$
29. $890 \text{ cm} = 8.9 \blacksquare$
30. $130,000 \blacksquare = 1.3 \text{ km}$

31. The maximum recorded flow of water over Yosemite Falls was 48,000,000 mL/s.

    a. About how many liters of water flow over Yosemite Falls each second at its maximum?

    b. At its maximum, about how many liters of water flow over the falls in a minute?

Estimation **Choose a reasonable estimate. Explain your choice.**

32. the width of a sidewalk: 150 cm or 150 m

33. the length of 24 city blocks: 2 m or 2 km

34. the mass of a thumbtack: 1 mg or 1 g

Mental Math **Complete each statement.**

35. 90,050 mL = ▪ L   **36.** ▪ m = 875 cm   **37.** 620 m = ▪ km

38. 9,120 mg = ▪ g   **39.** 900 km = ▪ m   **40.** 5 g = ▪ kg

41. ▪ cm = 13 km   **42.** 301 kg = ▪ mg   **43.** ▪ km = 562,300 cm

44. A world-record grapefruit had a mass of 3,068 g. What was its mass in kilograms?

45. A hippopotamus is so large that it has a stomach 304.8 cm long, yet it is agile enough to outrun a human. How long is the stomach of a hippopotamus in meters?

Number Sense **Match each measurement with its equivalent measurement from the table.**

46. 0.015 km   **47.** 1,500 cm   **48.** 150,000 mg

49. 0.15 L   **50.** 15 L   **51.** 1,500 g

A. 15,000 mL	B. 150 cm	C. 150 g
D. 1.5 kg	E. 15 m	F. 150 mL
G. 150 kg	H. 0.15 mL	I. 1,500 mm

52. <u>Writing in Math</u> The prefix kilo- means "one thousand," and the prefix milli- means "one thousandth." What do the prefixes tell you about kilometer and kilogram, and milliliter and milligram?

53. Suppose you walk about 3 mi/h.

    a. Approximately how many kilometers can you walk in an hour?

    b. How many meters can you walk in an hour?

C Challenge   **54.** A square with sides of length 2 m has area 4 m^2. What should you multiply 4 m^2 by to convert the area to square kilometers?

Yosemite Falls

Homework Video Tutor

Visit: PHSchool.com
Web Code: bje-0306

Multiple Choice Practice and Mixed Review

For Standards Tutorials, visit PHSchool.com. Web Code: bjq-9045

55. Bill drinks 267 milliliters of water from his 1-liter water bottle. How many liters does he have left?

   (A) 0.733 L   (B) 7.33 L   (C) 73.3 L   (D) 733 L

56. Charlotte earns $6 per hour. She wants to save $40 to buy a new sweater. She already has $8 saved. Which equation can be used to determine n, the number of hours Charlotte needs to work to have enough money to buy the sweater?

   (A) $6n - 8 = 40$ (C) $6n = 40 + 8$

   (B) $6n + 8 = 40$ (D) $n + 8 = \frac{40}{6}$

57. Which of the following is a term in the expression $2x + 4a + 7$?

   (A) x (B) 4   (C) 7   (D) $2x + 4a$

for Help

Lesson 3-5

58. Clinton Bailey, Sr., holds the record for knot tying. He tied six different rope knots in 8.1 s. Write and solve an equation to find his average time per knot.

Lesson 3-2

Estimate each product or quotient.

59. $28.134 \div 3.75$ **60.** $8.517 \cdot 9.82$ **61.** $101.49 \div 9.51$

Lessons 2-9 and 2-10

Solve each inequality.

62. $a - 5 \geq 16$ **63.** $n + 8 < -7$ **64.** $-3r \leq 21$

✓ Checkpoint Quiz 2

Solve each equation.

1. $0.5m = 0.125$ **2.** $d \div 0.3 = 28.5$ **3.** $y - 135.43 = -5.43$

4. $12.2 = 4x$ **5.** $29.25 = 4.5w$ **6.** $k + 870.9 = 1,000.5$

Choose the most reasonable estimate. Explain your choice.

7. height of a standard house window: 1.5 cm or 1.5 m

8. capacity of a shampoo bottle: 500 mL or 500 L

Complete each statement.

9. 95 mL = ■ L   **10.** ■ cm = 76.5 km

11. ■ km = 675 m   **12.** 7.1 kg = ■ g

13. The world's smallest horse had a mass of only 9.1 kg. What was the mass of the horse in grams?

The pin below measures about 5 cm. A more precise measurement is 4.5 cm. An even more precise measurement is 46 mm. The smaller the units on the scale of a measuring instrument, the more precise the measurement is.

1 EXAMPLE

Which measurement is more precise 5 g or 8 mg?

Since a milligram is a smaller unit of measure than a gram, 8 mg is more precise than 5 g.

A calculation will be only as precise as the least precise measurement used in the calculation. So, round your results to match the precision of the least precise measurement.

2 EXAMPLE

Add the lengths 6.31 m, 5.447 m, and 2.8 m.

$6.31 + 5.447 + 2.8 = 14.557$ The least precise measurement
                                  is 2.8 m. Round the sum to the
Rounded to tenths $\approx$ 14.6 m   nearest tenth of a meter.

Digits that represent an actual measurement are **significant digits.** Nonzero digits (1–9) are always significant. The rules below will help you decide whether a zero is a significant digit.

Type of Number	Which Zeros Are Significant	Example
decimal numbers between 0 and 1	Zeros to the left of *all* the nonzero digits are not significant. All other zeros are significant.	significant digits 0.006040 not significant digits
positive integers	Zeros to the right of *all* the nonzero digits are not significant (unless specifically known to be). Zeros between nonzero digits are significant.	significant digits 203,400 not significant digits
noninteger decimal numbers greater than 1	All zeros are significant.	significant digits 350.07050

3 EXAMPLE

How many significant digits are in 0.0504 m?

The 5 and the 4 are significant. The zero between them is significant.
The other zeros are not significant. There are three significant digits.

When you multiply or divide measurements, round your answer to
match the least number of significant digits in the problem.

4 EXAMPLE

A plot for a new house measures 152.6 m by 121 m.
What is the area of the plot? Use significant digits.

┌─── 3 significant digits

$152.6 \cdot 121 = 18,464.6$ ◄─── **Multiply.**

└─── 4 significant digits

The area is 18,500 m². ◄─── **Round the area to 3 significant digits.**

EXERCISES

Choose the more precise measurement.

1. 3 m or 5.2 m   **2.** 8 mL or 9.5 L   **3.** 1.89 km or 8.7 cm   **4.** 1.9 kg or 1.87 kg

5. Error Analysis Your friend says that 4.35 km is more precise
than 5.2 cm because a hundredths unit is a smaller unit than a
tenths unit. What mistake did your friend make?

Find each sum or difference. Round to the place value of the less
precise measurement.

6. $5.6 g + 8 g$ **7.** $8.35 kg + 6.2 kg$ **8.** $8.2 km - 1.75 km$ **9.** $9 cm - 2.3 cm$

Determine the number of significant digits in each measurement.

10. 0.069 m   **11.** 100.5 L   **12.** 3,400 kL   **13.** 5.2100 km

Find each product or quotient. Use significant digits.

14. 1,234 in. · 31 in.   **15.** 0.0702 ft · 227 ft   **16.** 16,250 m ÷ 14.5 s   **17.** 132.5 cm · 43.2 cm

3-7

Reasoning Strategy: Act It Out

Develop Analyze problems by sequencing and prioritizing information.
Develop Apply strategies and results from simpler problems to more complex problems.

What You'll Learn

- To solve problems by acting them out

. . . And Why

To solve real-world problems involving motion

✓ Check Skills You'll Need

Write a rule for each number pattern. Find the next three numbers in the pattern.

1. 0, 6, 12, 18, . . .

2. −18, −9, 0, 9, . . .

3. 0, 2, 1, 3, 2, 4, 3, . . .

4. 7, 6, 8, 7, 9, 8, 10, . . .

GO for Help
Lesson 1-7

Act It Out

Math Strategies in Action
Have you ever wondered how public speakers manage to talk to large audiences in a relaxed manner? Many public speakers brainstorm their topic ahead of time. Then they act out their speech by practicing in front of a mirror. You can *Act It Out* to solve math problems. Here is a well-known problem that can be solved by acting it out.

1 EXAMPLE Using Act It Out

A snail is trying to escape from a well 10 ft deep. The snail can climb 2 ft each day, but each night it slides back 1 ft. How many days will the snail take to climb out of the well?

Understand Understand the problem.

A snail needs to climb 10 ft to escape from a well. It can climb 2 ft per day. At night the snail slides back 1 ft.

1. How far up the well will the snail be after the first day and the first night?

2. How far up the well will the snail be after the second day?

3. How far up the well will the snail be after the second day and the second night?

Plan Make a plan to solve the problem.

At first you might think that the snail progresses 1 ft each day and will therefore take 10 days to escape. This answer is wrong, however, because it leaves out an important part of the problem.

To act out the problem, stand up and follow these steps:

- Move forward two steps to *simulate*, or model, the snail's climb during the day.

- Then move backward one step to simulate the snail's slide back during the night.

Carry Out **Carry out the plan.**

Act out the problem, keeping track of your progress in a table like the one below.

Time	Progress
Day 1	Up 2 ft from bottom
Night 1	Up 1 ft from bottom
Day 2	Up 3 ft from bottom

4. Copy and complete the table, acting out the rest of the problem. How many days will it take for the snail to make it out of the 10-ft well?

Check **Check the answer to be sure it is reasonable.**

You can check whether your answer is reasonable by drawing a diagram.

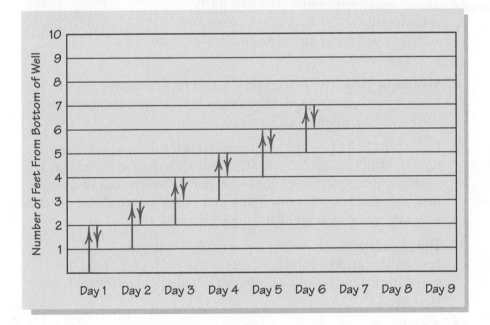

✓ Quick Check

5. Copy and complete the diagram to check your answer.

For more exercises, see *Extra Skills and Word Problem Practice*.

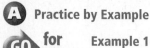

A Practice by Example

GO for Help Example 1 (page 158)

Solve by acting out each problem.

1. In a tennis tournament, each athlete plays one match against each of the other athletes. There are 12 athletes scheduled to play in the tournament. How many matches will be played?

2. A rancher wants to build a fence for a square lot with dimensions of 50 yd by 50 yd. He wants to install a fence post every 5 yd with a post at each corner. How many fence posts will he need?

3. Four candidates run for president of the student council. Three other candidates run for vice-president. In how many different ways can the two offices be filled?

B Apply Your Skills

STRATEGIES

- Act It Out
- Draw a Diagram
- Try, Test, Revise
- Look for a Pattern
- Make a Model
- Make a Table
- Simulate the Problem
- Solve by Graphing
- Use Multiple Strategies
- Work a Simpler Problem
- Work Backward
- Write an Equation
- Write a Proportion

Solve using any strategy.

4. The school store buys pencils for $.20 each. It sells the pencils for $.25 each. How much profit does the store make if it sells five dozen pencils?

5. To accommodate a wheelchair, a builder installed countertops that are 0.75 ft lower than the original ones. The new countertops are 2.5 ft high. How high were the original countertops?

6. What is the total number of squares in the figure at the right?

7. There are 10 girls and 8 boys at a party. A cartoonist wants to sketch a picture of each boy with each girl. How many sketches are required?

8. **Writing in Math** The houses on your street are numbered 1 to 120. No numbers are skipped. How many house numbers contain at least one 5? Explain your strategy.

9. Before the use of computers, typesetters used metal pieces of type to print each letter in a word and each digit in a number. For example, three pieces of type—1, 4, and 8—were used to create the page number 148. How many pieces of type would be needed to set the page numbers 1 through 476?

10. The population of Rancho Cucamonga, California, is 151,640 people. The area of Rancho Cucamonga is 37.4 mi^2. Find the population density—the number of people per square mile. Show your work.

C Challenge

11. Ana, Brian, Carla, David, and Eric are friends. They go to a movie but cannot find five seats together. They have to split up into a group of three and a group of two. How many different ways can the friends organize themselves into these two groups?

Homework Video Tutor

Visit: PHSchool.com
Web Code: bje-0307

Multiple Choice Practice and Mixed Review

For Standards Tutorials, visit PHSchool.com. Web Code: bjq-9045

12. There are 10 people in a room. Each person shakes hands with every other person once. How many handshakes take place?
 Ⓐ 10 Ⓑ 45 Ⓒ 55 Ⓓ 100

13. What is the seventh number in the pattern below?
$-3, 6, -12, 24, \ldots$
 Ⓐ -192 Ⓑ -48 Ⓒ 96 Ⓓ 172

14. How many milliseconds are in one second?
 Ⓐ 0.1 Ⓑ 10 Ⓒ 100 Ⓓ 1,000

GO for Help Lesson 3-6

Measurement **Complete each statement.**

15. 27 cm = ▮ m **16.** 5,200 km = ▮ m **17.** 2,000 mg = ▮ g

18. 0.5 L = ▮ mL **19.** 3 m = ▮ cm **20.** 6 kg = ▮ mg

Mathematical Reasoning

Evaluating Reasonableness

There are many ways to check a solution for reasonableness. For some problems, you can quickly evaluate whether or not the solution makes sense when you consider the context of the problem.

EXAMPLE

Decide if the solution shown below is reasonable for the following problem: A fruit punch recipe calls for 2.5 L of juice. The juice is sold in 946-mL bottles. How much juice should you buy to make the fruit punch?

> I need 2.5 L, or 2,500 mL.
>
> I'll divide 2,500 mL by the volume of a bottle.
>
> $\dfrac{2{,}500 \text{ mL}}{946 \text{ mL}} = 2.64$
>
> I need to buy 2.64 bottles.

You cannot buy 2.64 bottles of juice. The answer is not reasonable.

EXERCISE

1. Fencing comes in 3-m pieces. How many pieces should you buy to enclose a square with 7-m sides?

Not all questions ask you to find the solution to a problem. Some questions simply ask how you would solve a problem.

EXAMPLE

At a market, Sara buys a package containing 12 cans of green beans for $10.68. Each can weighs 14.5 ounces and makes 3.5 servings. Which process could she use to find the total number of servings in the package of green beans?

Ⓐ Multiply the price per can times the number of cans per package.
Ⓑ Multiply the weight of each can by the number of cans per package.
Ⓒ Multiply the number of cans per package by the number of servings per can.
Ⓓ Divide the number of cans per package by the number of servings per can.

This problem has more information than needed to find the total number of servings. The necessary information is that there are 12 cans in a package and each can has $3\frac{1}{2}$ servings. To find the total number of servings, you multiply the number of cans per package by the number of servings per can. So the correct answer is C.

Multiple Choice Practice

Read each question. Then write the letter of the correct answer on your paper.

1. Manny used a $10 bill to pay for 3 muffins and 2 bottles of milk. Each muffin cost $.79, and each bottle of milk cost $.99. To find the total cost, Manny first multiplied 3 times $.79 and 2 times $.99. What should he do next?
   Ⓐ Add the two products.
   Ⓑ Subtract the two products.
   Ⓒ Multiply the two products.
   Ⓓ Divide the two products

2. Mr. Giddings' restaurant has 36 tables that seat 6 people each. Mr. Giddings ordered 15 boxes of glasses. Each box holds 8 glasses. Which process can he use to find whether he ordered enough glasses for all the tables?
   Ⓐ Add the product of 36 and 6 to the product of 15 and 8.
   Ⓑ Compare the product of 36 and 6 with the product of 15 and 8.
   Ⓒ Multiply the product of 36 and 6 by the product of 15 and 8.
   Ⓓ Divide 36 by 6 and then multiply the quotient by 8.

Chapter 3 Review

Choose the vocabulary word that completes each sentence.

1. Digits that represent an actual measurement are __?__.

2. Numbers that are easy to divide are called __?__.

3. An equation that shows a relationship between quantities that are represented by variables is a __?__.

4. The distance around a figure is the __?__.

Go Online
PHSchool.com
For: Vocabulary quiz
Web Code: bjj-0351

Skills and Concepts

Lesson 3-1
• To round decimals
• To estimate sums and differences

You can estimate the sum of decimals by rounding, front-end estimating, or clustering.

You can estimate the difference of decimals by rounding.

Estimate each sum or difference. State which method you used.

5. $3.14 + 6.952$

6. $10.2538 - 6.095$

7. $14.451 + 9.736$

8. $14.27 - 4.268$

9. $20.681 + 19.39 + 20.56$

10. $12.814 - 6.3791$

11. $9.0426 + 2.7182$

12. $21.9384 - 15.639$

13. $6.257 + 6.129 + 6.34$

14. $19.83 - 14.268$

15. Explain when you would use each estimation method named above to estimate a sum of decimals. Use examples.

16. Last year Lake Jones rose to 672.42 feet during the spring floods. This year Lake Jones rose to 711.36 feet. About how much higher did the lake rise this year?

Lesson 3-2

- To estimate products
- To estimate quotients

You can estimate a product by rounding. You can estimate a quotient of two decimals by using **compatible numbers.**

Estimate each product or quotient.

17. 8.15(6.04)   **18.** $19.28 \div 5.439$

19. $1.9 \cdot 4.92$ **20.** $25.1 \div 4.87$

21. $12.497 \cdot 0.894$ **22.** $59.3581 \div 11.5304$

23. 3.59(−2.3291)   **24.** $-17.45 \div 3.059$

25. (−2.0936)(−5.6892)   **26.** (4.175)(6.2)

Lesson 3-3

- To substitute into formulas
- To use the formula for the perimeter of a rectangle

A **formula** is an equation that shows a relationship between quantities that are represented by variables. You can use formulas to find such things as **perimeter,** area, and distance.

Evaluate each formula for the values given.

27. distance: $d = rt$
   when $r = 35$ mi/h and
   $t = 2$ h

28. area of a rectangle: $A = \ell w$
   when $\ell = 16$ mm and
   $w = 24$ mm

29. circumference: $C = 2\pi r$
   when $r = 6$ in. Use 3.14 for π.

30. perimeter of a square: $P = 4s$
   when $s = 13$ cm

Lesson 3-4

- To solve one-step decimal equations involving addition
- To solve one-step decimal equations involving subtraction

To solve a one-step equation involving addition or subtraction of decimals, use an inverse operation and either the Subtraction or the Addition Property of Equality to get the variable alone on one side of the equation.

Solve each equation.

31. $n + 3.8 = 10.9$ **32.** $y - 6.72 = 2.53$

33. $h + 0.67 = -1.34$ **34.** $t - 2.7 = 23.5$

35. $12.9 + x = 3.8$ **36.** $5.7 = b - 4.9$

37. On Monday a stock is worth $3.20 per share. By Friday the stock is worth $2.64 per share.
   a. Write an equation to model the change in price.
   b. Solve the equation to find the amount by which the price changed.

Lesson 3-5

- To solve one-step decimal equations involving multiplication
- To solve one-step decimal equations involving division

To solve a one-step equation involving multiplication or division of decimals, use an inverse operation and either the Division or the Multiplication Property of Equality to get the variable alone on one side of the equation.

Solve each equation.

38. $6.3m = 15.75$

39. $a \div 4.9 = 8.33$

40. $v \cdot 7.1 = 80.23$

41. $c \div 12.5 = 77.5$

42. $-5.7z = 110.58$

43. $d \div 4.75 = -38.95$

44. You paid $5.60 to mail a package that weighed 3.5 lb.
  a. Write an equation to model the cost per pound.
  b. Solve the equation to find the mailing cost per pound.

Lesson 3-6

- To identify appropriate metric measures
- To convert metric units

The **metric system** of measurement uses a decimal system to relate units to one another. To measure, you must choose an appropriate unit of measure.

Choose an appropriate metric unit of measure. Explain each choice.

45. height of a building

46. mass of a bicycle

47. amount of milk in a glass

Mental Math Complete each statement.

48. $0.85 \text{ m} = \blacksquare \text{ cm}$

49. $160 \text{ mL} = \blacksquare \text{ L}$

50. $2.3 \text{ m} = \blacksquare \text{ cm}$

51. $1.6 \text{ kg} = \blacksquare \text{ g}$

52. $0.62 \text{ L} = \blacksquare \text{ mL}$

53. $80 \text{ g} = \blacksquare \text{ kg}$

54. Explain why centimeters would be an inappropriate unit to measure the height of a mature oak tree.

Lesson 3-7

- To solve problems by acting them out

You can solve some problems by acting them out.

55. Mike, Don, Tameka, and Rosa sit in the four desks in the last row of desks. Each day they sit in a different order. How many days can they do this before they repeat a seating pattern?

56. You are hiking with three friends. You pass a group of six hikers going the other way. Each person in one group greets each person in the other group. How many greetings are there? Explain.

Chapter 3 Test

Go Online
PHSchool.com

For: Chapter Test
Web Code: bja-0352

Estimate each value.

1. $6.43 - 4.079$ **2.** $2.06 + 3.91$

3. $5.97 - 1.674$ **4.** $6.025 + 0.35$

5. $8.54 + 2.3$ **6.** $6.25 \cdot 9.87$

7. $12.89 \div 3.04$ **8.** $1.76 \cdot 3.93$

9. $4.96 \div 2.49$ **10.** $3.2 \cdot 14.69$

Evaluate each formula for the given values.

11. area of a rectangle: $A = \ell w$
when $\ell = 3.8$ in. and $w = 1.5$ in.

12. perimeter of a square: $P = 4s$
when $s = 4.7$ cm

13. perimeter of a rectangle: $P = 2\ell + 2w$
when $\ell = 2.9$ m and $w = 6.05$ m

14. distance: $d = rt$
when $r = 55$ mi/h and $t = 6$ h

15. temperature in degrees fahrenheit:
$F = 1.8C + 32$ when $C = 35$

Solve each equation.

16. $x + 7.8 = 12.5$

17. $n - 5.9 = 0.5$

18. $4.1 + c = -1.2$

19. $d - 6.3 = 11$

20. $-9.7 + h = 10.3$

21. $m \div 2.7 = 14.58$

22. $h \cdot 4.7 = 30.55$

23. $b \div (-7.8) = -79.56$

24. $-3.4t = 30.94$

Write an appropriate metric unit of measure for each quantity.

25. the height of a truck

26. the capacity of a standard shampoo bottle

27. the mass of a pineapple

28. the width of a paperback book

Complete.

29. 4.5 m = ■ cm   **30.** 68 mL = ■ L

31. 90 kg = ■ g   **32.** $6{,}700$ cm = ■ m

33. 4 L = ■ mL   **34.** 50.2 g = ■ kg

For Exercises 35 and 36, write an equation, and then solve.

35. You spend $6.50 on a pair of gloves. You now have $7.00. How much money did you have originally?

36. The fastest speed recorded for a reptile on land is 9.7 m/s for a spiny-tailed iguana. At this rate, how long would it take this iguana to travel 116.4 m?

37. Geography Madrid and Barcelona are cities in Spain. The distance between them is 636,000 m. What is this in kilometers?

38. A mechanical toy on a circular track goes forward 3 in. and then backward 2 in. How many moves does the toy take to complete one 15-in. revolution of the track?

39. You have an 18-ft metal pipe. How many cuts must you make to cut the pipe into 2-ft-long pieces?

40. **Writing in Math** Are all formulas equations? Are all equations formulas? Explain.

Standards Mastery

Some problems ask you to use estimation to verify the reasonableness of calculated results. Read the question at the right and review the answer choices. Then follow the tip to answer the sample question.

Tip
Write the expression represented by each choice.

Mrs. Ortiz bought some nature books at $6.50 each and 6 novels at $4.75 each. There is no tax. She bought a total of 8 books. Her receipt only shows a total of $41.50. How can she quickly estimate to make sure this total is reasonable?

- **A** Add 4.75 and 6.50. Then multiply by 8.
- **B** Round 4.75 to 5. Round 6.50 to 7. Add 5 + 7 and multiply by 8.
- **C** Round the costs to 5 and multiply by 8.
- **D** Round the costs to 7 and multiply by 8.

Think It Through
You can eliminate choices A and B because these methods will give a total for purchasing 8 books of each type.

Choice D is not reasonable because she only bought 2 books at $6.50 each. Choice C is the most reasonable because most of the books cost close to $5, so 5 × 8 is a reasonable estimate.

Vocabulary Review

As you solve problems, you must understand the meanings of mathematical terms. Choose the vocabulary term that correctly completes the sentence.

A. A (coefficient, constant) is a term that has no variables.

B. The (x-axis, y-axis) is the horizontal axis in the coordinate plane.

C. (Perimeter, Area) indicates the distance around a figure.

D. The (expression, solution) is the value that makes an equation true.

Read each question. Then write the letter of the correct answer on your paper.

1. Simplify $-4 - |4 + 11|$. **(Lesson 1-4)**
   - **A** -19
   - **B** 3
   - **C** 11
   - **D** 19

2. Simplify $|12 + 16| - |-9 - 7|$. **(Lesson 1-4)**
   - **A** 12
   - **B** 26
   - **C** 30
   - **D** 44

3. Which statement is true for all positive whole numbers a? **(Lesson 1-4)**
   - **A** $|a + 4.5| > |a - 4.5|$
   - **B** $|a - 4.5| > |a + 4.5|$
   - **C** $|2.3 + a| < |-2.3 - a|$
   - **D** $|-2.3 - a| < |-2.3 + a|$

4. Evaluate $ab + c$ for $a = 4.3$, $b = -8$, and $c = 0.5$. **(Lesson 1-3)**
   - **A** -33.9
   - **B** -4.88
   - **C** 12.8
   - **D** 34.9

5. Evaluate $c - b - a$ for $a = 24.3$, $b = -75$, and $c = -14.6$. (Lesson 1-3)

- (A) −113.9
- (C) 36.1
- (B) −84.7
- (D) 65.3

6. What is the perimeter of a rectangular field that has a width of 10.4 m and a length of 12.3 m? (Lesson 3-3)

- (A) 22.7 m
- (C) 35 m
- (B) 33.1 m
- (D) 45.4 m

7. Hair grows at a rate of about 1.02 cm per month. Find the number of meters hair grows in 12 months. (Lesson 3-6)

- (A) about 0.1224 m
- (B) about 1.47 m
- (C) about 12.24 m
- (D) about 13.02 m

8. Which list shows the decimals in order from least to greatest? (Lesson 3-1)

- (A) 0.3, 0.03, 0.13, 0.035
- (B) 0.03, 0.3, 0.13, 0.035
- (C) 0.035, 0.03, 0.3, 0.13
- (D) 0.03, 0.035, 0.13, 0.3

9. Ms. Perez hands her students the index cards below. She asks her students to place the cards on a number line.

Which card should be placed farthest to the left? (Lesson 3-1)

- (A) 0
- (B) 3
- (C) −2
- (D) −2.5

10. The heights of Shawn's friends are listed in the table. Who is the shortest? (Lesson 3-1)

Height's of Shawn's Friends

Name	Height (inches)
Ed	64.0
Lisa	62.5
Melissa	62.25
Jason	60.25
Alex	60.3

- (A) Lisa
- (C) Jason
- (B) Melissa
- (D) Alex

11. Danielle's parents loaned her $80 for car repairs and $150 to buy a new suit for an interview. She promises to pay them back in 8 equal monthly payments of $30. How can you quickly check to see that Danielle's total is reasonable? (Lesson 3-2)

- (A) Add 80 and 150 then multiply by 8.
- (B) Subtract 150 and 80 then multiply by 8.
- (C) Add 80 and 150 then divide by 8.
- (D) Subtract 150 and 80 then divide by 8.

12. Leah has $2.00 in her pocket. Which of the following can she buy? (Lesson 3-1)

Item	Cost ($)
Pen	0.45
Pencil	0.15
Eraser	0.65
Glue Stick	0.88
Ruler	1.09
Protractor	0.98
Pencil Sharpener	0.59

- (A) Ruler and protractor
- (B) Ruler, pencil, and eraser
- (C) Protractor, pen, and glue stick
- (D) Protractor, eraser, and pencil sharpener

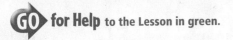
13. Rita has a 6 ft-by-8 ft garden. She builds a fence around her garden with posts every 2 feet. How many fence posts are used? **(Lesson 3-7)**

  Ⓐ 10   Ⓒ 14

  Ⓑ 12   Ⓓ 18

14. Mr. Simons is measuring a room to determine the amount of paint he needs. Two walls of the room are 15 ft by 9 ft and two walls are 10 ft by 9 ft. There are 4 windows that are 3 ft by 5 ft each and a doorway that is $7\frac{1}{2}$ ft by 3 ft. Which procedure should be used to find the area to be painted? **(Lesson 3-7)**

  Ⓐ Find the area of a wall and subtract the window area and the doorway area.

  Ⓑ Find the total area of the four walls.

  Ⓒ Find the total perimeter of the walls and subtract the total perimeter of the windows and doorway.

  Ⓓ Find the total area of the walls and subtract the total of the area of the windows and doorway.

15. Which of the following coordinates are within $\triangle PQR$? **(Lesson 1-10)**

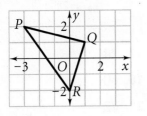

  Ⓐ $(-2, 1\frac{1}{2})$

  Ⓑ $(2, 1\frac{1}{2})$

  Ⓒ $(-1\frac{1}{2}, 2)$

  Ⓓ $(1\frac{1}{2}, -2)$

16. Helen drives 55 miles per hour. She is traveling 245 miles. Which equation can be used to find h, the number of hours she drives? **(Lesson 1-3)**

  Ⓐ $h = 245 \times 55$

  Ⓑ $h = 2 - 5545$

  Ⓒ $h = 245 \div 55$

  Ⓓ $h = 245 + 55$

17. Nate walks 4 miles per hour. Which equation could be used to find how many miles Nate walked after 2.5 hours? **(Lesson 2-4)**

  Ⓐ $m = 4 + 2.5$

  Ⓑ $m = 4 - 2.5$

  Ⓒ $m = 4(2.5)$

  Ⓓ $m = 4 \div 2.5$

18. Which statement is true? **(Lesson 2-1)**

  Ⓐ The equation $6(5 + 4) = 6(5) + 6(4)$ shows the Commutative Property of Addition.

  Ⓑ The equation $a + 0 = a$ shows the Identity Property of Addition.

  Ⓒ The equation $(3 + 7) + 9 = 9 + (3 + 7)$ shows the Associative Property of Addition.

  Ⓓ The equation $8(x + 4) = 8(x) + 8(4)$ shows the Associative Property of Multiplication.

Factors, Fractions, and Exponents

What You've Learned

Compare rational numbers in general.

Add, subtract, multiply, and divide rational numbers (integers, fractions, and terminating decimals) and take positive rational numbers to whole-number powers.

Simplify numerical expressions by applying properties of rational numbers (e.g., identity, associative, commutative) and justify the process used.

Use algebraic terminology (e.g., term, coefficient, inequality, expression, constant) correctly.

 **Check Your Readiness**　　**GO for Help** to the Lesson in green.

Multiplying Three or More Factors (Lesson 1-9)

Find each product.

1. $12 \cdot 12 \cdot 12$ 　　**2.** $(-4)(-4)(-4)$ 　　**3.** $9 \cdot 9 \cdot 9 \cdot 9$

4. $5 \cdot 5 \cdot 5 \cdot 5 \cdot 5 \cdot 5$ 　　**5.** $8 \cdot 8 \cdot 8$ 　　**6.** $(-2)(-2)(-2)(-2)(-2)(-2)$

Multiplying Whole Numbers (Skills Handbook, p. 682)

Write two numbers that, when multiplied, result in each product.

7. 12 　　**8.** 45 　　**9.** 18 　　**10.** 63 　　**11.** 24

12. 50 　　**13.** 32 　　**14.** 81 　　**15.** 54 　　**16.** 60

17. 28 　　**18.** 56 　　**19.** 44 　　**20.** 36 　　**21.** 72

Dividing Whole Numbers (Skills Handbook, p. 683)

Find each quotient.

22. $720 \div 8$ 　　**23.** $7{,}200 \div 8$ 　　**24.** $6\overline{)132}$

25. $3\overline{)147}$ 　　**26.** $\frac{189}{9}$ 　　**27.** $\frac{450}{10}$

28. $424 \div 2$ 　　**29.** $700 \div 5$ 　　**30.** $92 \div 4$

31. $5\overline{)135}$ 　　**32.** $\frac{273}{3}$ 　　**33.** $10\overline{)1{,}300}$

What You'll Learn Next

Read, write, and compare rational numbers in scientific notation (positive and negative powers of ten), compare rational numbers in general.

Understand negative whole-number exponents. Multiply and divide expressions involving exponents with a common base.

Multiply, divide, and simplify rational numbers by using exponent rules. Multiply and divide monomials.

▲ You can use exponents to express very small numbers, such as the mass of a cicada.

New Vocabulary

◀)) English and Spanish Audio Online

- **base** (p. 178)
- **composite number** (p. 182)
- **divisible** (p. 172)
- **equivalent fractions** (p. 188)
- **exponents** (p. 178)
- **factor** (p. 173)

- **greatest common divisor (GCD)** (p. 183)
- **greatest common factor (GCF)** (p. 183)
- **power** (p. 178)
- **prime factorization** (p. 183)

- **prime number** (p. 182)
- **rational number** (p. 197)
- **scientific notation** (p. 210)
- **simplest form** (p. 188)
- **standard notation** (p. 211)

Academic Vocabulary
- **explain** (p. 172)

4-1 Divisibility and Factors

What You'll Learn

- To use divisibility tests
- To find factors

. . . And Why

To solve real-world problems involving arrangements

✓ Check Skills You'll Need

Find each quotient.

1. $480 \div 3$ 2. $365 \div 5$

3. $459 \div 9$ 4. $288 \div 6$

5. $\dfrac{354}{2}$ 6. $\dfrac{354}{3}$

GO for Help

Skills Handbook, p. 683

🔊 New Vocabulary

- divisible
- factor

Vocabulary Tip

When you explain, you give details that make a thought easy to understand.

Add and subtract fractions by using factoring to find common denominators.

Using Divisibility Tests

One integer is **divisible** by another if the remainder is 0 when you divide. Because $18 \div 3 = 6$, 18 is divisible by 3. You can test for divisibility using mental math.

Take Note 🖊 **Divisibility Rules for 2, 5, and 10**

An integer is divisible by

- 2 if it ends in 0, 2, 4, 6, or 8.
- 5 if it ends in 0 or 5.
- 10 if it ends in 0.

Even numbers end in 0, 2, 4, 6, or 8 and are divisible by 2.
Odd numbers end in 1, 3, 5, 7, or 9 and are not divisible by 2.

---

1 EXAMPLE   Divisibility by 2, 5, and 10

Is the first number divisible by the second? Explain.

a. 567 by 2   No; 567 does not end in 0, 2, 4, 6, or 8.

b. 1,015 by 5   Yes; 1,015 ends in 5.

c. 111,120 by 10   Yes; 111,120 ends in 0.

✓ Quick Check

1. Is the first number divisible by the second? Explain.

   a. 160 by 5   **b.** 56 by 10   **c.** 53 by 2   **d.** 1,118 by 2

To see a pattern for divisibility by 3 and 9, compare the answers to the questions asked in this table.

Number	Sum of digits	Is the sum divisible by 3?	Is the sum divisible by 9?	Is the number divisible by 3?	Is the number divisible by 9?
282	$2 + 8 + 2 = 12$	Yes	No	Yes	No
468	$4 + 6 + 8 = 18$	Yes	Yes	Yes	Yes
215	$2 + 1 + 5 = 8$	No	No	No	No
1,017	$1 + 0 + 1 + 7 = 9$	Yes	Yes	Yes	Yes

The pattern in the table suggests the following rules for divisibility by 3 and 9.

Vocabulary Tip

The words <u>divisibility</u>, <u>divisor</u>, and <u>dividend</u> are all related to the verb <u>divide</u>.

Take Note / **Divisibility Rules for 3 and 9**

An integer is divisible by
- 3 if the sum of its digits is divisible by 3.
- 9 if the sum of its digits is divisible by 9.

2 EXAMPLE **Divisibility by 3 and 9**

Is the first number divisible by the second? Explain.

a. 567 by 3   Yes; $5 + 6 + 7 = 18$. 18 is divisible by 3.

b. 1,015 by 9   No; $1 + 0 + 1 + 5 = 7$. 7 is not divisible by 9.

✓ Quick Check

2. Is the first number divisible by the second? Explain.

   a. 64 by 9   **b.** 472 by 3   **c.** 174 by 3   **d.** 43,542 by 9

Finding Factors

You can form the three rectangles at the right with 12 squares. Each rectangle has an area of 12 square units. Their dimensions, 1, 2, 3, 4, 6, and 12, are the *factors* of 12. One integer is a **factor** of another nonzero integer if it divides that integer with remainder zero.

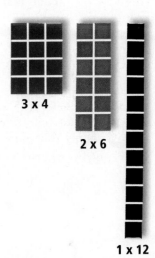

3 x 4

2 x 6

1 x 12

3 EXAMPLE **Finding Factors**

There are 20 students singing at a school concert. Each row of singers must have the same number of students. If there are at least 5 students in each row, what are all the possible arrangements?

$1 \cdot 20$, $2 \cdot 10$, $4 \cdot 5$ **Find the factors of 20.**

There can be 1 row of 20 students, 2 rows of 10 students, or 4 rows of 5 students.

✓ Quick Check

3. List the positive factors of each integer.

   a. 10   **b.** 21   **c.** 24   **d.** 31

   e. What are the possible arrangements for Example 3 if there are 36 students singing at the concert?

Write a number for each description.

1. an odd number

2. a number divisible by 3

3. an even number divisible by 5

4. a number divisible by 5 but less than 10

5. an even factor of 14

For more exercises, see *Extra Skills and Word Problem Practice.*

A Practice by Example

Example 1
(page 172)

GO for Help

Example 2
(page 173)

Is the first number divisible by the second? Explain.

6. 37 by 2   7. 240 by 2   8. 1,468 by 2   9. 2,005 by 10

10. 20 by 10   11. 45 by 5   12. 60 by 5   13. 123 by 2

14. 78 by 9   15. 69 by 3   16. 108 by 9   17. 258 by 3

18. 3,694 by 9   19. 5,751 by 9   20. 123 by 3   21. 456 by 3

Example 3
(page 173)

List the positive factors of each integer.

22. 4   23. 8   24. 23   25. 75

26. There are 32 students in the school drill team performance. Each row of team members must have the same number of students. If there are at least 8 students in each row, what are all the possible arrangements?

B Apply Your Skills

State whether each number is divisible by 2, 3, 5, 9, 10, or none. Explain. Some numbers may have more than one divisor.

27. 52   28. 891   29. 4,805   30. 437,684

31. a. Which of the following numbers are divisible by both 2 and 3?
    10   66   898   4,710   975
    b. Which of the numbers above are divisible by 6?
    c. Using your results, write a divisibility rule for 6.

Show all possible ways that each integer can be written as the product of two positive factors.

32. 25   33. 28   34. 32   35. 35

36. 37   37. 50   38. 53   39. 72

Write the missing digit to make each number divisible by 9.

40. 22■,034   41. 3■,817   42. 2,03■,371   43. 1■,111

44. Writing in Math If a number is divisible by 9, is it also divisible by 3? Explain how you reached your conclusion.

45. Reasoning John made oatmeal cookies for a class bake sale. The cookies need to be distributed equally on 2 or more plates. If each plate gets at least 7 cookies, what are the possible combinations for the totals below?

   a. 42 cookies   **b.** 56 cookies

   c. 60 cookies   **d.** 144 cookies

46. Reasoning If a is divisible by 2, what can you conclude about $a + 1$? Justify your answer.

47. a. Copy and complete the table.

Number	Last two digits	Are last two digits divisible by 4?	Is the number divisible by 4?
136	36	Yes	Yes
1,268	68	Yes	Yes
314	14	No	No
1,078	■	■	■
696	■	■	■

   b. Reasoning Write a divisibility rule for 4.

C Challenge   **Open-Ended** **Write three numbers greater than 20 for each description.**

48. divisible by 5, but not divisible by 10

49. divisible by 3, but not divisible by 5, 9, or 10

50. divisible by 2, 3, 5, and 10, but not divisible by 9

Multiple Choice Practice and Mixed Review

For Standards Tutorials, visit PHSchool.com. Web Code: bjq-9045

51. Which statement describes how to convert grams to kilograms?

   Ⓐ Divide the number of grams by 100.

   Ⓑ Multiply the number of grams by 100.

   Ⓒ Multiply the number of grams by 1,000.

   Ⓓ Divide the number of grams by 1,000.

52. A scuba diver swims at a depth of -44 yards. Coral sea bushes are located directly below him at a depth of -90 yards. How many yards does the scuba diver have to swim to reach the bushes?

   Ⓐ 136 yd   Ⓒ -56 yd

   Ⓑ -46 yd   Ⓓ -136 yd

GO for Help   Lesson 3-6   **Complete each statement.**

53. 24 ■ = 24,000 mg   **54.** 18.2 km = 1,820,000 ■

Develop Use algebraic terminology correctly.

One way to show connections among ideas is to draw a diagram called a concept map. The lines in a concept map connect related ideas.

EXAMPLE

Make a concept map with the terms from Chapter 4 related to factors.

composite number
divisible
factor
greatest common factor
prime factorization
prime number

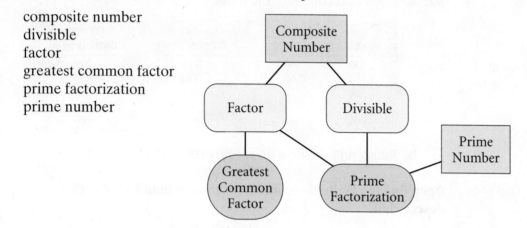

EXERCISES

1. Copy the concept map at the right. Fill in the ovals using the appropriate terms listed below.

    axes
    coordinate plane
    ordered pair
    origin
    quadrants
    x-axis
    x-coordinate
    y-axis
    y-coordinate

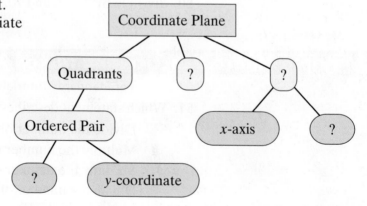

2. Use the list below to make a concept map for exponents.

    base
    exponent
    power
    scientific notation

> **Develop** Formulate mathematical conjectures based on a general description of the mathematical question or problem posed.
> **Develop** Make conjectures by using inductive reasoning.
> Take positive rational numbers to whole-number powers.

1. Fold a sheet of paper in half as shown below. Count the number of sections made by the fold.

2. Fold it in half again. Count the number of sections made by the two folds.

3. Continue folding the paper. Copy and complete the first two columns of the table below.

Number of Times You Fold the Paper in Half	Number of Sections the Folds Make	Written as Multiplication of 2
1	2	2
2	▦	2 · 2
3	▦	▦
4	▦	▦

4. You can rewrite each value in the second column by multiplying 2 several times, as shown in the third column. Copy and complete the third column of the table.

5. Extend your table for 5, 6, and 7 folds.

6. **Reasoning** What do you notice about the number of folds in the first column and the number of times you write the number 2 in the third column?

7. You can write the expressions in the third column using *exponents*. For example, $2 = 2^1$, where the exponent, 1, indicates the number of times you use the number 2. Similarly, $4 = 2 \cdot 2 = 2^2$. Add a fourth column to your table. Write the expression from the third column using exponents.

8. **Predict** Look at the patterns that are developing in your table. What is the digit in the ones' place for the value of 2^{15} expressed without an exponent?

9. a. You can rewrite the equation $\frac{32}{2} = 16$ as $\frac{2^5}{2} = 2^4$. What is the value of $\frac{2^3}{2}$?

   b. **Make a Conjecture** What is the value of 2^0?

Exponents

Introduce Take positive rational numbers to whole-number powers.
Develop Use the correct order of operations to evaluate algebraic expressions.
Introduce Interpret positive whole-number powers as repeated multiplication.
Evaluate expressions that include exponents.

What You'll Learn

- To use exponents
- To use the order of operations with exponents

... And Why

To solve real-world problems involving magnification

✓ Check Skills You'll Need

Find each product.

1. $3 \cdot 3 \cdot 3 \cdot 3$

2. $-12 \cdot (-12)$

3. $(-4)(-4)(-4)$

4. $10 \cdot 10 \cdot 10 \cdot 10$

GO for Help
Lesson 1-9

◀)) New Vocabulary

- exponents
- power
- base

Using Exponents

You can use **exponents** to show repeated multiplication.

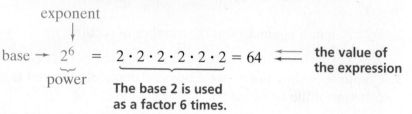

A **power** has two parts, a **base** and an exponent. The expression 2^6 is read as "two to the sixth power." Depending on the situation, you may decide to communicate an idea using either a power or the value of the power.

Power	Verbal Expression	Value
12^1	*Twelve to the first power*	12
6^2	*Six to the second power, or six squared*	$6 \cdot 6 = 36$
$(0.2)^3$	*Two tenths to the third power, or two tenths cubed*	$(0.2)(0.2)(0.2) = 0.008$
-7^4	*The opposite of the quantity seven to the fourth power*	$-(7 \cdot 7 \cdot 7 \cdot 7) = -2,401$
$(-8)^5$	*Negative eight to the fifth power*	$(-8)(-8)(-8)(-8)(-8) = -32,768$

GO Online

Video Tutor Help
Visit: PHSchool.com
Web Code: bje-0775

1 EXAMPLE Using an Exponent

Write the expression using an exponent.

a. $(-5)(-5)(-5)$

$(-5)^3$ Include the negative sign within parentheses.

b. $-2 \cdot a \cdot b \cdot a \cdot a$

$-2 \cdot a \cdot a \cdot a \cdot b$ commutative and associative properties

$-2a^3b$ Write $a \cdot a \cdot a$ using exponents.

✓ Quick Check

1. Write using exponents.   **a.** $6 \cdot 6 \cdot 6$ **b.** $4 \cdot y \cdot x \cdot y$

2 EXAMPLE Simplifying a Power

A microscope can magnify a specimen 10^3 times. How many times is that?

$10^3 = 10 \cdot 10 \cdot 10$ The exponent indicates that the base 10 is used as a factor 3 times.

$= 1,000$ Multiply.

The microscope can magnify the specimen 1,000 times.

✓ Quick Check

2. a. Simplify 7^2.   **b.** Evaluate $-a^4$ and $(-a)^4$, for $a = 2$.

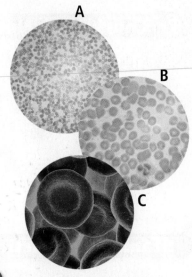

Human blood cells are shown here magnified (A) 10^2 times, (B) 10^3 times, and (C) 10^4 times.

Using the Order of Operations With Exponents

You can extend the order of operations to include exponents.

Take Note Order of Operations

1. Work inside grouping symbols.
2. Simplify any terms with exponents.
3. Multiply and divide in order from left to right.
4. Add and subtract in order from left to right.

3 EXAMPLE Using the Order of Operations

a. Simplify $4(3.7 + 2)^2$.

$4(3.7 + 2)^2 = 4(5.7)^2$ Work within parentheses first.

$= 4 \cdot 32.49$ Simplify $(5.7)^2$.

$= 129.96$ Multiply.

b. Evaluate $-2x^3 + 4y$, for $x = 2$ and $y = 3$.

$-2x^3 + 4y = -2(2)^3 + 4(3)$ Replace x with 2 and y with 3.

$= -2(8) + 4(3)$ Simplify $(2)^3$.

$= -16 + 12$ Multiply from left to right.

$= -4$ Add.

✓ Quick Check

3. a. Simplify $2 \cdot 5^2 + 4 \cdot (-3)^3$.
   b. Evaluate $3a^2 + 6$, for $a = -5$.

Online
active math

Order of Operations

Simplify the expression shown below.
Click on the blue parts of the expression to perform the associated operation.

$(2^2 \cdot 20 - 16) \div 16$

For: Order of Operations Activity
Use: Interactive Textbook, 4-2

Fill in the blanks with the correct term.

1. A(n) __?__ is an expression that has two parts, a base and a(n) __?__.

2. In the expression x^3, the __?__ is 3.

3. In the expression 6^4, the __?__ is 6.

4. **Reasoning** Are -8^2 and $(-8)^2$ equal? Explain.

Standards Practice

For more exercises, see *Extra Skills and Word Problem Practice*.

A Practice by Example

Example 1
(page 178)

GO for Help

Write using exponents.

5. $r \cdot r \cdot r \cdot r \cdot s \cdot s$ 6. $5 \cdot 5 \cdot a \cdot a$ 7. $9 \cdot 9 \cdot 9 \cdot 9 \cdot 9$

8. $8 \cdot 8 \cdot 8$ 9. $-7 \cdot a \cdot a \cdot b$ 10. $(-5)(-5)(-5)(-5)$

Example 2
(page 179)

Simplify.

11. 10^4 12. 4^3 13. 2^6 14. $(-4)^3$ 15. -4^3 16. $(-6)^3$

17. **Science** An electron microscope can magnify a specimen about 10^6 times. How many times is that?

Example 3
(page 179)

Simplify.

18. $49 - (4 \cdot 2)^2$ 19. $-3^2 + 5 \cdot 2^3$ 20. $2 \cdot (-2)^4 + 10^1$

Evaluate.

21. $3a^2 - 2$, for $a = 5$ 22. $c^3 + 4$, for $c = 2.3$

23. $-4y^2 + y^3$, for $y = 3$ 24. $2m^2 + n$, for $m = 1.5, n = 4$

B Apply Your Skills

Write using exponents.

25. $-5 \cdot x \cdot x \cdot 3 \cdot y$ 26. d cubed   27. $-2 \cdot a \cdot (-4) \cdot b \cdot b$

28. **Error Analysis** A student gives ab^3 as an answer when asked to write $ab \cdot ab \cdot ab$ using exponents. What is the student's error?

Homework Video Tutor

Visit: PHSchool.com
Web Code: bje-0402

Simplify.

29. $15 + (4 + 6)^2 \div 5$ 30. $(4 + 8)^2 \div 4^2$ 31. $(12 - 3)^2 \div (2^2 - 1^2)$

Evaluate each expression.

32. $-6m^2$, for $m = 2$ 33. $5k^2$, for $k = 1.2$

34. $8 - x^3$, for $x = 2$ 35. $3(2m + 5)^2$, for $m = 2$

36. $4(2y - 3)^2$, for $y = 5$ 37. $y^2 + 2y + 5$, for $y = 0.4$

n	$4n$	4^n	n^4
1	▪	▪	▪
2	▪	▪	▪
3	▪	▪	▪
4	▪	▪	▪

38. a. Copy and complete the table at the left.
   b. For what value(s) of n is each sentence true?
   $$4^n = n^4 \qquad 4^n < n^4 \qquad 4^n > n^4$$

39. a. A certain microscope can magnify a specimen about 10^4 times. How many times is that?
   b. Would you use 10^4 or your answer to part (a) to compare the power of the microscope to other microscopes? Explain.

40. Reasoning Does $-a^2 = (-a)^2$ for any values of a? Explain.

Geometry Exercises 41–44 involve cubes made from smaller cubes, like the one at the left. Suppose such a cube has edges of length 5 cm.

41. What is the area of a face?   **42.** What is the volume?

Find the length of an edge of a cube that has each measurement.

43. face area of 64 in.^{2} **44.** a volume of 64 in.^{3}

45. Reasoning Describe all pairs of values of x and y for which $5x^2y = 5xy^2$. Justify your answer.

46. Given that $2^{10} = 1{,}024$, find 2^{11} mentally.

47. Language Arts Why do you think *squared* and *cubed* are used to indicate the second power and the third power?

48. Writing in Math Evaluate $(-1)^m$ for $m = 2, 4,$ and 6. Then evaluate $(-1)^m$ for $m = 1, 3,$ and 5. Write a conjecture about the sign of an even power of a negative number. Then write a conjecture about the sign of an odd power of a negative number.

C Challenge   **49.** If $3^4 = 81$, $3^3 = 27$, $3^2 = 9$, and $3^1 = 3$, what do 3^0 and 3^{-1} equal?

Edge length $s = 3$ in.
Area of Face $= s^2$
$\qquad\qquad = 9$ in.^{2}
Volume $= s^3$
$\qquad\qquad = 27$ in.^{3}

Multiple Choice Practice and Mixed Review

For Standards Tutorials, visit PHSchool.com. Web Code: bjq-9045

50. Owen earned $950 doing yard work from March to June. He earned $\frac{2}{5}$ of the total in March and April. Which equation can be used to find a, the amount he earned in May and June?

   Ⓐ $a = 950 - \frac{2}{5}(950)$ Ⓒ $a = \frac{2}{5}(950) - 950$

   Ⓑ $a = \frac{2}{5}(950) - 95$ Ⓓ $a = \frac{2}{5}(950) + 950$

51. Find the perimeter of the triangle.

   Ⓐ 30.3 m   Ⓒ 40.5 m

   Ⓑ 36.9 m   Ⓓ 42 m

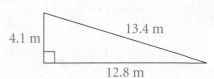

4.1 m   13.4 m   12.8 m

 for Help   **Lesson 4-1**   **State whether each number is divisible by 2, 3, 5, 9, 10, or none.**

52. 36   **53.** 135   **54.** 171   **55.** 190

Prime Factorization and Greatest Common Divisor

What You'll Learn

- To find the prime factorization of a number
- To find the greatest common divisor (GCD) of two or more numbers

. . . And Why

To solve real-world problems involving organization

✓ Check Skills You'll Need

List the positive factors of each number.

1. 15   **2.** 35   **3.** 7

4. 20   **5.** 100   **6.** 121

GO for Help

Lesson 4-1

◀)) New Vocabulary

- prime number
- composite number
- prime factorization
- greatest common factor (GCF)
- greatest common divisor (GCD)

Add and subtract fractions by using factoring to find common denominators.

Finding Prime Factorizations

Standards Investigation
Exploring Prime Numbers

The diagram shows the only rectangle you can make with integer side lengths and an area of 5 square units. Work with a partner. Find the number of rectangles you can make with each number of unit squares: 2, 3, 4, 5, 6, 7, 8, 9, and 10.

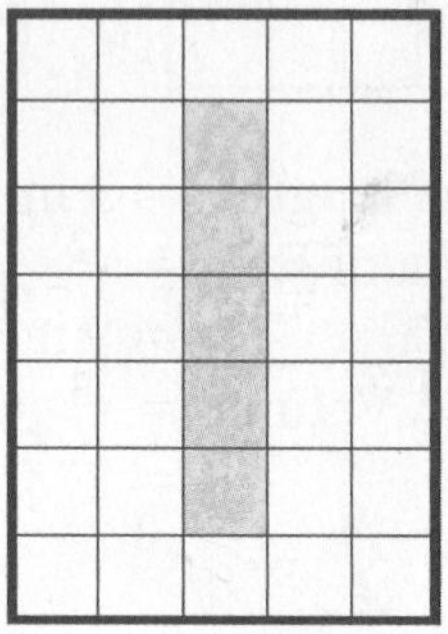

1. For which numbers of squares is only one rectangle possible?

2. For which numbers of squares is more than one rectangle possible?

3. List the dimensions of the rectangles you can make with each of the following numbers of unit squares: 13, 15, 17, 19, and 21.

A **prime number** is an integer greater than 1 with exactly two positive factors, 1 and the number itself. The numbers 2, 3, 5, and 7 are prime numbers.

A **composite number** is an integer greater than 1 with more than two positive factors. The numbers 4, 6, 8, 9, and 10 are composite numbers. The number 1 is neither prime nor composite.

1 EXAMPLE   Prime or Composite?

State whether each number is *prime* or *composite*. Explain.

a. 23   Prime; it has only two factors, 1 and 23.

b. 129   Composite; it has more than two factors, 1, 3, 43, and 129.

✓ Quick Check

1. Which numbers from 10 to 20 are prime? Which are composite?

Writing a composite number as a product of its prime factors shows the **prime factorization** of the number. You can use a *factor tree* to find prime factorizations. Write the final factors in increasing order from left to right. Use exponents to indicate repeated factors.

Problem Solving Tip

To check whether a number is prime, look for prime factors in order, starting with 2. When you get to a prime whose square is greater than the original number, you can stop.

2 EXAMPLE Writing the Prime Factorizations

Use a factor tree to write the prime factorization of 825.

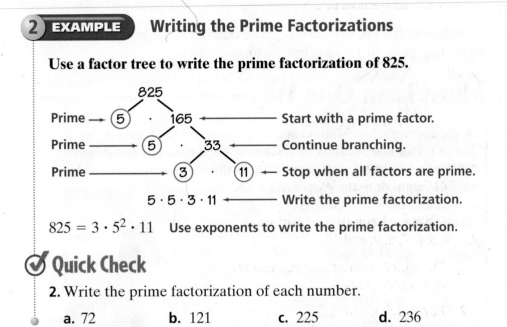

Prime → ⑤ · 165 ← Start with a prime factor.
Prime → ⑤ · 33 ← Continue branching.
Prime → ③ · ⑪ ← Stop when all factors are prime.
5 · 5 · 3 · 11 ← Write the prime factorization.

$825 = 3 \cdot 5^2 \cdot 11$ Use exponents to write the prime factorization.

✓ Quick Check

2. Write the prime factorization of each number.

   a. 72   **b.** 121   **c.** 225   **d.** 236

Finding the Greatest Common Divisor

Factors that are the same for two or more numbers or expressions are *common factors*. The greatest of these common factors is called the **greatest common factor (GCF)** or the **greatest common divisor (GCD).** You can use prime factorization to find the GCD of two or more numbers or expressions. If there are no prime factors and variable factors in common, the GCD is 1.

Vocabulary Tip

A factor is a number that divides evenly into another number with a remainder of zero. For example, 2 and a are factors of $2a$ because $2 \cdot a = 2a$.

3 EXAMPLE Finding the Greatest Common Divisor

Find the GCD of each pair of numbers or expressions.

  a. 40 and 60   **b. $6a^3b$ and $4a^2b$**

$40 = 2^3 \cdot 5$ Write the prime $6a^3b = 2 \cdot 3 \cdot a^3 \cdot b$
$60 = 2^2 \cdot 3 \cdot 5$ factorizations. $4a^2b = 2 \cdot 2 \cdot a^2 \cdot b$

           Find the common factors.

$GCD = 2^2 \cdot 5$ Use the lesser power of $GCD = 2 \cdot a^2 \cdot b$
      $= 20$ the common factors. $= 2a^2b$

The GCD of 40   The GCD of $6a^3b$
and 60 is 20.   and $4a^2b$ is $2a^2b$.

3. Use prime factorizations to find each GCD.

    a. 8, 20   **b.** 12, 87   **c.** $12r^3, 8r$ **d.** $15m^2n, 45m$

You can find the GCD of two or more numbers or expressions by listing factors or by using prime factorizations.

More Than One Way

A parade organizer wants each of three marching bands to have the same number of band members in each row. The bands have 48, 32, and 56 band members. What is the greatest number of band members possible for each row?

Jasmine's Method

List the factors of each number. Then find the greatest factor the numbers have in common.

48: 1, 2, 3, 4, 6, ⑧ 12, 16, 24, 48

32: 1, 2, 4, ⑧ 16, 32

56: 1, 2, 4, 7, ⑧ 14, 28, 56

The GCD of 48, 32, and 56 is 8. The greatest possible number of band members in each row is 8.

Daryl's Method

Find the prime factorization of each number. Then find the least power of all common prime factors.

48: $2^4 \cdot 3$
32: 2^5
56: $2^3 \cdot 7$

The GCD of 48, 32, and 56 is 2^3, or 8. The greatest possible number of band members in each row is 8.

Choose a Method

1. Which method do you prefer to find the GCD? Explain why.

2. Which method would you use to find the GCD of 4, 8, and 24? Of 54, 27, and 36? Explain why.

1. Find two prime numbers between 30 and 40.

2. Find two composite numbers between 40 and 50.

3. **Critical Thinking** Two students began prime factorizations of 225 as shown below. Complete both factor trees. Are both solutions valid? Explain.

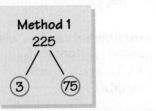
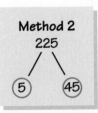

Standards Practice

For more exercises, see *Extra Skills and Word Problem Practice.*

A Practice by Example

Example 1
(page 182)

State whether each number is prime or composite. Explain.

| **4.** 27 | **5.** 31 | **6.** 38 | **7.** 53 |
| **8.** 45 | **9.** 19 | **10.** 87 | **11.** 93 |

Example 2
(page 183)

Write the prime factorization of each number.

| **12.** 42 | **13.** 360 | **14.** 115 | **15.** 186 |
| **16.** 8 | **17.** 49 | **18.** 34 | **19.** 621 |

Example 3
(page 183)

Use prime factorization to find the greatest common divisor.

20. 10, 45   **21.** 57, 84   **22.** $3y^2, 24y^3$ **23.** $6m^3n, 8mn^2$

B Apply Your Skills

Is each number prime, composite, or neither? For each composite number, write the prime factorization.

24. 17   **25.** 1   **26.** 49   **27.** 522

28. A math teacher and a science teacher combine their first-period classes for a group activity. The math class has 24 students and the science class has 16 students. The teachers need to divide the students into groups of the same size. Each group must have the same number of math students. Find the greatest number of groups possible.

Find the GCD of each.

29. 42, 65   **30.** 54, 144   **31.** 8, 16, 20   **32.** 12, 18, 21

33. $180a^2, 210a$ **34.** a^3b, a^2b^2 **35.** c^3df^2, c^2d^2f **36.** a^2b, b^2c, ac^2

37. Multiple Choice Factors of 6 less than 6 are 1, 2, and 3.
Factors of 8 less than 8 are 1, 2, and 4.
6 is a perfect number: $1 + 2 + 3 = 6$
8 is not a perfect number: $1 + 2 + 4 \neq 8$
Which of the following is a perfect number?

    (A) 24   (B) 26   (C) 28   (D) 30

Homework Video Tutor

Visit: PHSchool.com
Web Code: bje-0403

38. Organizers for a high school graduation put 126 chairs for graduates in the front section and 588 chairs for guests in the back section. If all rows have the same number of chairs, what is the greatest number of chairs possible for a row?

Two numbers are *relatively prime* if their GCD is 1. Are the numbers in each pair below relatively prime? Explain.

SAMPLE   8, 17   Yes, 8 and 17 are relatively prime. The GCD is 1.
               7, 35   No, 7 and 35 are not relatively prime. The GCD is 7.

39. 3, 20   **40.** 9, 42   **41.** 13, 52   **42.** 24, 47

43. 52, 65   **44.** 63, 74   **45.** 15, 22   **46.** 42, 72

47. Writing in Math Explain how to find the prime factorization of 50.

C Challenge   **48.** Find the GCD of $220a^3b^2c$, $363a^2b^2c^2$, and $462bc^3$.

Multiple Choice Practice and Mixed Review

For Standards Tutorials, visit PHSchool.com. Web Code: bjq-9045

49. Tyler installs carpet in two bedrooms. His bedroom is 14 feet by 14 feet, and his friend's bedroom is 14 feet by 16 feet. Which expression could be used to find the total number of square feet of carpet Tyler needs?

    (A) $2^{14} + 14 \cdot 16$ (C) $14^3 + 16$
    (B) $14 \cdot 3 + 16$ (D) $14^2 + 14 \cdot 16$

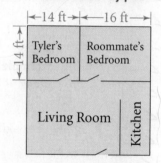

50. Mora walked x miles on Monday. On Tuesday, she walked $x + 1$ miles. On Wednesday, she walked $x + 2$ miles. Every day she adds a mile. Which expression shows the total number of miles Mora has walked Monday through Saturday?

    (A) $5x + 15$ (B) $5x + 21$ (C) $6x + 15$ (D) $6x + 21$

GO for Help   Lesson 4-2   **Evaluate for $x = 2$ and $y = 5$.**

51. x^2y **52.** xy^2 **53.** $x^2 + y^2$ **54.** $x^4 - y$

Lesson 3-5   **Solve each equation.**

55. $3x = 5.4$ **56.** $-0.5a = 4.35$

57. $4.32 = 1.6y$ **58.** $-8m = -74.4$

Develop Know various forms of display for data sets.
Develop Use a variety of methods, such as diagrams, to explain mathematical reasoning.

In a **Venn diagram** you use circles to represent collections of objects. The intersection, or overlap, of two circles indicates what is common to both collections.

1 EXAMPLE

School coaches plan to send notices to all students playing fall or winter sports. How many notices do they need to send?

Students in Sports

Season	Students
Fall	155
Winter	79
Both fall and winter	28

number who played only a fall sport
155 − 28 = 127

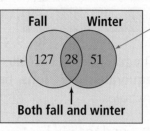

number who played only a winter sport
79 − 28 = 51

Both fall and winter

Add all three numbers to find the number of notices needed.

127 + 28 + 51 = 206

The coaches need to send 206 notices.

You can use a Venn diagram to find the GCD of two numbers.

2 EXAMPLE

Find the GCD of 30 and 84.

Include the common prime factors of 30 and 84 in the intersection.

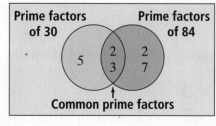

Prime factors of 30   Prime factors of 84

5   2 3   2 7

Common prime factors

The GCD is the product of the factors in the intersection.

The GCD is 2 · 3, or 6.

EXERCISES

1. In a class of 38 students, 32 are wearing jeans, 21 are wearing T-shirts, and 15 are wearing both. How many students are wearing jeans and something other than a T-shirt?

Draw a Venn diagram to find the GCD of each pair of numbers.

2. 24, 56   3. 35, 49   4. 36, 84   5. 72, 108

Simplifying Fractions

Convert fractions to decimals and percents.
Be able to convert terminating decimals into reduced fractions.

What You'll Learn

- To find equivalent fractions
- To write fractions in simplest form

. . . And Why

To solve real-world problems involving statistics

☑ **Check Skills You'll Need**

Find each GCD.

1. 14, 21   **2.** 48, 60

3. $5mn, 15m^2n$

4. $63r^2, 48s^3$

GO for Help
Lesson 4-3

🔊 **New Vocabulary**

- equivalent fractions
- simplest form

Finding Equivalent Fractions

Each fraction model below represents one whole. The blue model is divided into four equal parts. The orange model is divided into twelve equal parts.

$\frac{3}{4}$ of the model is shaded.

$\frac{9}{12}$ of the model is shaded.

$$\frac{3}{4} = \frac{3 \cdot 3}{4 \cdot 3} = \frac{9}{12}$$

The fraction models show that $\frac{3}{4} = \frac{9}{12}$. The fractions $\frac{3}{4}$ and $\frac{9}{12}$ are **equivalent fractions** because they describe the same part of a whole.

You can find equivalent fractions by multiplying or dividing the numerator and denominator by the same nonzero factor.

1 EXAMPLE Finding an Equivalent Fraction

Find two fractions equivalent to $\frac{4}{12}$.

a. $\frac{4}{12} = \frac{4 \cdot 3}{12 \cdot 3}$ **b.** $\frac{4}{12} = \frac{4 \div 4}{12 \div 4}$

$= \frac{12}{36}$ $= \frac{1}{3}$

The fractions $\frac{12}{36}$ and $\frac{1}{3}$ are both equivalent to $\frac{4}{12}$.

☑ **Quick Check**

1. Find two fractions equivalent to each fraction.

  a. $\frac{5}{15}$ **b.** $\frac{10}{12}$ **c.** $\frac{14}{20}$

Vocabulary Tip

Most fraction names are made by adding *th* or *ths* to the denominator. You read $\frac{1}{4}$ as "one fourth," $\frac{2}{5}$ as "two fifths," and $\frac{8}{10}$ as "eight tenths." Halves and thirds are two exceptions.

Writing Fractions in Simplest Form

A fraction is in **simplest form** when the numerator and the denominator have no common factors other than 1. You can use the GCD to write a fraction in simplest form. In some situations, you may need to choose between simplest form and an equivalent fraction.

② EXAMPLE Simplifying a Fraction

Use the photo at the right. Write the fraction of adolescent milk-drinkers who drink 2% or whole milk in simplest form. Which fraction best communicates the survey results? Why?

The GCD of 8 and 12 is 4.

$$\frac{8}{12} = \frac{8 \div 4}{12 \div 4}$$ **Divide the numerator and denominator by the GCD, 4.**

$$= \frac{2}{3}$$ **Simplify.**

Of adolescent milk-drinkers, $\frac{2}{3}$ drink 2% or whole milk. The fraction $\frac{2}{3}$ best communicates the survey results because most people have a mental picture of $\frac{2}{3}$ but not of $\frac{8}{12}$.

A survey of adolescent milk-drinkers in California found that about 8 out of 12, or $\frac{8}{12}$, drink 2% or whole milk.

✓ Quick Check

2. Write each fraction in simplest form.

   a. $\frac{6}{8}$ **b.** $\frac{9}{12}$ **c.** $\frac{28}{35}$

You can often simplify a fraction that contains a variable. In this book, you may assume that no expression for a denominator equals zero.

Problem Solving Tip

To make sure a fraction is simplified, check that the numerator and denominator do not have a common factor.

③ EXAMPLE Simplifying a Fraction With a Variable

Write in simplest form.

a. $\dfrac{y}{xy}$

$$\frac{y}{xy} = \frac{y^1}{xy_1}$$ **Divide the numerator and denominator by the common factor, y.**

$$= \frac{1}{x}$$ **Simplify.**

b. $\dfrac{3ab^2}{12ac}$

$$\frac{3ab^2}{12ac} = \frac{3 \cdot a \cdot b \cdot b}{2 \cdot 2 \cdot 3 \cdot a \cdot c}$$ **Write as a product of prime factors.**

$$= \frac{3^1 \cdot a^1 \cdot b \cdot b}{2 \cdot 2 \cdot {}_1 3 \cdot {}_1 a \cdot c}$$ **Divide the numerator and denominator by the common fac—**

$$= \frac{b \cdot b}{2 \cdot 2 \cdot c}$$ **Simplify.**

$$= \frac{b \cdot b}{4 \cdot c}$$

$$= \frac{b^2}{4c}$$

✓ Quick Check

3. Write in simplest form.   **a.** $\dfrac{b}{abc}$ **b**

190

Visit: PHSchool.com
Web Code: bje-0404

Chapter 4 Factors, Fractions, and Exponents

4-5: Open—

Homework Video

Copy and complete each model to represent $\frac{1}{3}$.

1.

2.

3.

4. Which expression is equivalent to $\frac{12a^8}{4a^2}$?

Ⓐ $3a^4$ Ⓑ $3a^6$ Ⓒ $8a^4$ Ⓓ $8a^6$

Standards Practice

For more exercises, see *Extra Skills and Word Problem Practice*.

Ⓐ Practice by Example

Example 1
(page 188)

GO for Help

Example 2
(page 189)

Find two fractions equivalent to each fraction.

5. $\frac{2}{8}$ 6. $\frac{8}{10}$ 7. $\frac{3}{9}$ 8. $\frac{8}{36}$ 9. $\frac{6}{18}$ 10. $\frac{20}{22}$

Write each fraction in simplest form.

11. $\frac{3}{9}$ 12. $\frac{4}{10}$ 13. $\frac{12}{48}$ 14. $\frac{2}{10}$ 15. $\frac{4}{12}$ 16. $\frac{6}{15}$

17. Doctors suggest that most people need about 8 h of sleep each night to stay healthy. What fraction of the day is this? Write your answer in simplest form.

Example 3
(page 189)

Write in simplest form.

18. $\frac{2x}{3x}$ 19. $\frac{4km^2}{12k}$ 20. $\frac{b}{bc}$ 21. $\frac{24x}{16}$

22. $\frac{8pr}{12p}$ 23. $\frac{14a^2}{24a}$ 24. $\frac{4bc}{16b}$ 25. $\frac{40ab^2}{5ab}$

Ⓑ Apply Your Skills

Find two fractions equivalent to each fraction.

26. $\frac{4}{8}$ 27. $\frac{4}{10}$ 28. $\frac{5}{20}$ 29. $\frac{10}{16}$ 30. $\frac{25}{100}$

31. **Error Analysis** A student claims $\frac{65}{91}$ is in simplest form. Do you agree? Explain.

GO for Help

For a guide to reading and solving Exercise 31, see page 192.

Write in simplest form.

32. $\frac{8}{14}$ 33. $\frac{18}{32}$ 34. $\frac{20}{30}$ 35. $\frac{12}{16}$ 36. $\frac{15^3}{15^2}$ 37. $\frac{56pq}{7pq}$

38. $\frac{5c^2d}{15c}$ 39. $\frac{4r^3st}{36st^2}$ 40. $\frac{5t}{10t^2}$ 41. $\frac{x^2y}{3yz}$ 42. $\frac{12gh}{8g^2h^2}$ 43. $\frac{6m^2n^2}{9mn^2}$

44. In a survey, 27 out of 45 students say that chocolate is their favorite flavor of frozen yogurt.
   a. Write the fraction $\frac{27}{45}$ in simplest form.
   b. **Reasoning** When might you want to use the fraction $\frac{27}{45}$?

     Ended Write two fraction that simplify to $\frac{3x}{5}$.

Tutor

46. Writing in Math Does $\frac{1}{2}$ of one pizza represent the same amount as $\frac{1}{2}$ of another pizza? Justify your answer.

PC and On Line Households in the U.S. (millions)

Households	2001	2003
Total households	110	112
Households with PCs	56	62
Households with Internet access	50	56

Source: U.S. Census Bureau

The table shows the number of households with personal computers (PCs) and Internet access in the United States. For Exercises 47–49, write each fraction in simplest form.

47. In 2001, what fraction of U.S. households had PCs?

48. In 2001, what fraction of U.S. households with PCs had Internet access? (Assume that a household with Internet access had a PC.)

49. a. In 2003, what fraction of U.S. households with PCs had Internet access? (*Hint:* See Exercise 48.)
b. Was the fraction greater in 2001 or 2003? Explain.

50. Write the numerator and denominator of $\frac{24}{32}$ as products of prime factors. Then use the prime factors to write the fraction in simplest form.

 Challenge

51. Write the rational number 7.32 as a fraction in simplest form.

Multiple Choice Practice and Mixed Review

For Standards Tutorials, visit PHSchool.com. Web Code: bjq-9045

52. Yesterday, the low temperature was $-4°C$ and the high was $6°C$. In degrees Celsius, what was the difference in temperatures?
   (A) -10 (B) -2 (C) 2 (D) 10

53. Evaluate xy^{-2} for $x = -9$ and $y = 3$.
   (A) -54 (B) -1 (C) 1 (D) 54

GO for Help Lesson 3-4

Solve each equation.

54. $y + 3.23 = 5.85$ **55.** $b - 2.13 = 9.9$ **56.** $12.8 + z = 6.47$

✓ Checkpoint Quiz 1

State whether each number is divisible by 2, 3, 5, 9, 10, or none.

1. 30   **2.** 54   **3.** 48   **4.** 161   **5.** 2,583

Evaluate each expression.

6. x^2, for $x = 8$ **7.** a^3, for $a = 5$ **8.** $-2z^2$, for $z = -3$

Write in simplest form.

9. $\frac{8}{16}$ **10.** $\frac{14}{21}$ **11.** $\frac{16}{28}$ **12.** $\frac{3a}{12a}$ **13.** $\frac{2xy}{x}$

14. Open-Ended Write two expressions whose GCD is $5a^2$.

> **Develop** Use a variety of methods, such as numbers, to explain mathematical reasoning.

Analyzing Errors **Read the problem below. Then let Tina's thinking guide you through the solution. Check your understanding with the exercises at the bottom of the page.**

A student claims $\frac{65}{91}$ is in simplest form. Do you agree? Explain.

What Tina Thinks

Do I agree? The wording of the problem suggests that the student is wrong.

What does simplest form mean for a fraction?

First I'll factor 65.

Is 5 a factor of 91?

Is 13 a factor of 91?

Aha! I'll finish and show the simplest form of the fraction.

I'm done!

What Tina Writes

No.

A fraction is in simplest form when the numerator and denominator have no common factor other than 1.

Since 65 ends in 5, 5 is a factor of 65. $65 = 5 \cdot 13$.

5 is not a factor of 91. So, 5 cannot be a common factor.

$91 = 7 \cdot 13$. Therefore, 13 is a common factor of 65 and 91.

$$\frac{65}{91} = \frac{5 \cdot \overset{1}{\cancel{13}}}{7 \cdot \underset{1}{\cancel{13}}} = \frac{5}{7}$$

$\frac{5}{7}$ is the simplest form for the fraction.

EXERCISES

Use what you know about factors to decide whether each fraction is in simplest form. If not, simplify.

1. $\frac{17}{51}$ 2. $\frac{39}{91}$ 3. $\frac{51}{57}$ 4. $\frac{57}{76}$ 5. $\frac{57}{87}$

Reasoning Strategy: Solve a Simpler Problem

Develop Determine when and how to break a problem into simpler parts.

What You'll Learn

- Solve complex problems by first solving simpler cases

. . . And Why

To solve real-world problems involving photography

✓ Check Skills You'll Need

Compare. Use < or > to complete each statement.

1. 3 ■ 0

2. −16 ■ −25

3. 0 ■ 1

4. −30 ■ −20

GO for Help
Skills Handbook, p. 698

Solve a Simpler Problem

Math Strategies in Action Scientists often encounter problems that are very complicated. When they work to develop a new vaccine or develop a new method to fight disease, they usually work on smaller or simpler pieces of the problem first. Sometimes when you solve a problem, it helps to solve other problems that have similar conditions. Here is a problem that shows you how to use this strategy.

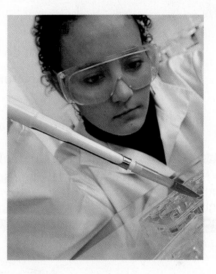

1 EXAMPLE Solving a Simpler Problem

Mandy, Jim, Keisha, Darren, Lin, Chris, and Jen are friends. They want to take pictures of themselves with two people in each picture. How many pictures do they need to take?

Understand Understand the problem.

1. What do you need to find?

2. How many people are there in all?

3. How many people will be in each photograph?

Plan Make a plan to solve the problem.

To make sure that you account for every pair of friends, make an organized list.

Carry out the plan.

Solve a simpler problem. Change the problem to a simpler one based on three friends, and then try four friends to see if there is a pattern.

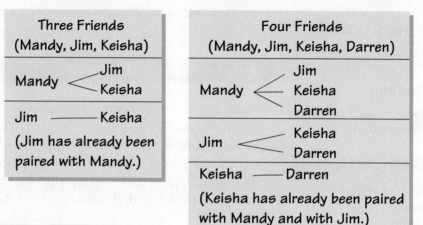

Three Friends (Mandy, Jim, Keisha)
Mandy < Jim, Keisha
Jim ——— Keisha
(Jim has already been paired with Mandy.)

Four Friends (Mandy, Jim, Keisha, Darren)
Mandy < Jim, Keisha, Darren
Jim < Keisha, Darren
Keisha ——— Darren
(Keisha has already been paired with Mandy and with Jim.)

4. What pattern do you see?

5. How many pictures do they need to take?

Check Check the answer to be sure it is reasonable.

Problem Solving Tip

Drawing a diagram can help you organize information to check an answer.

You can check to make sure your answer is reasonable by drawing a diagram. Draw line segments to show all possible pairs of friends.

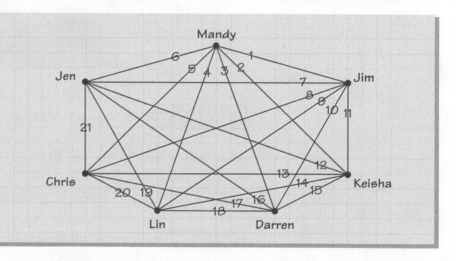

There are 21 line segments. This shows there are 21 pairs of friends.

✓ Quick Check

6. Suppose Mandy and nine friends pair up for pictures. Use the pattern suggested above and find how many pictures there will be.

194 Chapter 4 Factors, Fractions, and Exponents

For more exercises, see *Extra Skills and Word Problem Practice.*

A Practice by Example

Example 1
(page 193)

GO for Help

Solve each problem by solving a simpler problem.

1. You decide to number the 58 pages in your journal from 1 to 58. How many digits do you have to write?

2. **Geometry** What is the total number of triangles in the figure at the right?

3. You have pepperoni, mushrooms, onions, and green peppers. How many different pizzas can you make by using one, two, three, or four of the toppings?

B Apply Your Skills

STRATEGIES

- Act It Out
- Draw a Diagram
- Try, Test, Revise
- Look for a Pattern
- Make a Model
- Make a Table
- Simulate the Problem
- Solve by Graphing
- Use Multiple Strategies
- Work a Simpler Problem
- Work Backward
- Write an Equation
- Write a Proportion

Solve using any strategy.

4. Eight people are at a party. Everyone shakes hands once with everyone else. How many handshakes are there altogether?

5. **Geometry** You have 24 feet of fence to make a rectangular garden. Each side will measure a whole number of feet. How many different-sized rectangular gardens can you make?

6. You throw three darts at the board shown at the right. If each dart hits the board, what possible point totals can you score?

7. **Multiple Choice** The bottom row of a stack of blocks contains 11 blocks. The row above it contains 9 blocks. The next higher row contains 7 blocks. The rows continue in this pattern, and the top row contains a single block. How many blocks does the stack contain in all?

   Ⓐ 66 blocks   Ⓑ 36 blocks   Ⓒ 28 blocks   Ⓓ 20 blocks

8. A sandwich shop serves turkey, ham, chicken, and egg salad sandwiches. You can have any sandwich on white, wheat, or rye bread. How many different sandwiches could you order?

Homework Video Tutor

Visit: PHSchool.com
Web Code: bje-0405

9. A car manufacturer offers exterior colors of white, blue, red, black, and silver. The manufacturer offers interior colors of black and silver. How many different color combinations are there?

10. You have one penny, one nickel, one dime, and one quarter. How many different amounts of money can you make using one or more of these coins?

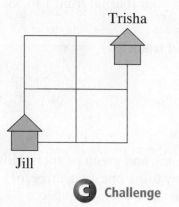

Trisha

Jill

11. Copy the diagram at the left. Using the paths shown, Jill can walk to Trisha's house in many different ways. Draw each route that is four blocks long. How can you be sure that you have found all possible routes?

12. **Geometry** How many different rectangles are there with an area of 36 cm^2 if the side lengths of each, in centimeters, are whole numbers?

C Challenge

13. Darius, Tyrek, and Zeroy earn a total of $150 by washing cars. Each earns a different amount. They agree to share equally. Darius divides half of his money equally between Tyrek and Zeroy. Tyrek then has too much money, so he gives Darius and Zeroy each $10. Finally Zeroy gives Darius $2, and they now have equal amounts. How much did they each earn originally?

Multiple Choice Practice and Mixed Review

For Standards Tutorials, visit PHSchool.com. Web Code: bjq-9045

14. Which of the following is equivalent to 4 L?

Ⓐ 40 mL

Ⓒ 4,000 mL

Ⓑ 400 mL

Ⓓ 40,000 mL

15. Three friends compare the length of model planes. Emma's model is $\frac{4}{5}$ as long as Ryan's model. Delu's model, which is 210 cm long, is 1.5 times as long as Ryan's model. How long is Emma's model?

Ⓐ 3.94 m   Ⓑ 2.52 m   Ⓒ 1.75 m   Ⓓ 1.12 m

16. Evaluate $3y^2 - 2x^3$, for $x = -1.7$ and $y = 2.3$.

Ⓐ 6.044   Ⓑ 6.056   Ⓒ 22.696   Ⓓ 25.696

17. Simplify $\left[\frac{2}{3}\right]^3$.

Ⓐ $\frac{6}{27}$ Ⓑ $\frac{8}{27}$ Ⓒ $\frac{6}{9}$ Ⓓ $\frac{8}{9}$

GO for Help

Lesson 4-4

Write in simplest form.

18. $\frac{6}{12}$ **19.** $\frac{10}{40}$ **20.** $\frac{6a^2}{15}$ **21.** $\frac{14a^3}{28a^2}$

Lesson 1-7

Write a rule for each pattern.

22. $10, 20, 30, \ldots$ **23.** $8, 5, 2, -1, \ldots$ **24.** $2, 6, 18, 54, \ldots$

Rational Numbers

Develop Compare rational numbers.

Master Use the correct order of operations to evaluate algebraic expressions. Know that every rational number is either a terminating or repeating decimal.

What You'll Learn

- To identify and graph rational numbers
- To evaluate fractions containing variables

. . . And Why

To solve real-world problems involving rates

 Check Skills You'll Need

Write in simplest form.

1. $\frac{2}{10}$ **2.** $\frac{14}{21}$

3. $\frac{28}{35}$ **4.** $\frac{6}{8}$

GO **for Help**
Lesson 4-4

🔊 **New Vocabulary**

- rational number

Identifying and Graphing Rational Numbers

A **rational number** is any number you can write as a quotient $\frac{a}{b}$ of two integers, where b is not zero. The diagram below shows relationships among rational numbers.

Notice that all integers are rational numbers. This is true because you can write any integer a as $\frac{a}{1}$.

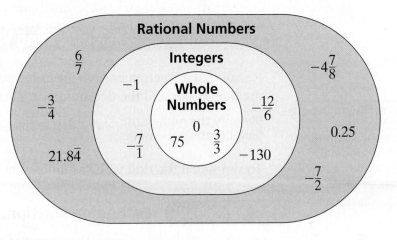

Here are three ways you can write a negative rational number.

$$-\frac{7}{9} = \frac{-7}{9} = \frac{7}{-9}$$

For each rational number, there is an unlimited number of equivalent fractions.

Quick Review

The quotient of two integers with the same sign is positive.

1 **EXAMPLE**   **Writing Equivalent Fractions**

Write two lists of fractions equivalent to $\frac{1}{2}$.

$\frac{1}{2} = \frac{2}{4} = \frac{3}{6} = \cdots$ Numerators and denominators are positive.

$\frac{1}{2} = \frac{-1}{-2} = \frac{-2}{-4} = \cdots$ Numerators and denominators are negative.

✓ **Quick Check**

1. Write three fractions equivalent to $-\frac{4}{5}$.

You can graph rational numbers on a number line.

Comparing and Ordering Rational Numbers

Use a number line to order the numbers $\frac{1}{2}$, $-\frac{8}{10}$, 1, and -0.2 from least to greatest.

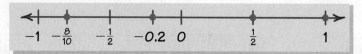

The order of the points from left to right gives the order of the numbers from least to greatest. So, $-\frac{8}{10} < -0.2 < \frac{1}{2} < 1$.

✓ Quick Check

2. Use a number line to order the numbers $-\frac{1}{2}$, $-\frac{4}{10}$, -2, and 0.9 from least to greatest.

Evaluating Fractions Containing Variables

Recall that a fraction bar is a grouping symbol, so you first simplify the numerator and the denominator. Then, simplify the fraction.

Simplify the numerator. ⟶ $\dfrac{1 + 9 + 2}{2 - 5} = \dfrac{12}{-3} = -4$ ⟵ simplest form
Simplify the denominator. ⟶

To simplify a fraction with variables, first substitute for the variables.

> **Quick Tip**
>
> To change a fraction to an integer or decimal, divide the numerator by the denominator.

Evaluating Fractions With Variables

The speed of a car changes from 37 ft/s to 102 ft/s in five seconds. What is its acceleration in feet per second per second (ft/s²)?
Use the formula $a = \dfrac{f - i}{t}$ where a is acceleration, f is final speed, i is initial speed, and t is time.

$$a = \frac{f - i}{t}$$ Use the acceleration formula.

$$= \frac{102 - 37}{5}$$ Substitute for the variables.

$$= \frac{65}{5}$$ Subtract.

$$= 13$$ Write in simplest form.

The car's acceleration is 13 ft/s².

The world's fastest car, the *Thrust SSC*, can go from 0 ft/s to 880 ft/s in 16 s.

✓ Quick Check

3. Evaluate for $a = 6$ and $b = -5$. Write in simplest form.

   a. $\dfrac{a + b}{-3}$ b. $\dfrac{7 - b}{3a}$ c. $\dfrac{a + 9}{b}$

Write the rational number represented by each point.

$$\begin{array}{ccccccc} A & D & & B & & C & \\ \bullet & \bullet & | & \bullet & | & \bullet & \\ -1 & & & 0 & & & 1 \end{array}$$

1. A **2.** B **3.** C **4.** D

State whether the given fraction is equivalent to $\frac{-5}{6}$.

5. $\frac{5}{-6}$ **6.** $\frac{-15}{18}$ **7.** $-\frac{20}{24}$ **8.** $\frac{-5}{-6}$

Standards Practice

For more exercises, see *Extra Skills and Word Problem Practice.*

A Practice by Example

Example 1
(page 197)

GO for Help

Example 2
(page 198)

Write three fractions equivalent to each fraction.

9. $\frac{1}{6}$ **10.** $\frac{3}{5}$ **11.** $-\frac{5}{9}$ **12.** $-\frac{4}{4}$ **13.** $-\frac{2}{3}$ **14.** $\frac{4}{7}$

Use a number line to order each set of numbers from least to greatest.

15. $\frac{1}{10}, -\frac{3}{5}, 2, -0.3, -0.75, \frac{2}{3}$

16. $\frac{1}{2}, \frac{3}{4}, -0.5, \frac{9}{10}, 0, -0.1$

Example 3
(page 198)

Evaluate for $a = -4$ and $b = -6$. Write in simplest form.

17. $\frac{a}{b}$ **18.** $\frac{a + 9}{b}$ **19.** $\frac{b + a}{3a}$

20. $\frac{2a + b}{20}$ **21.** $\frac{b + 7}{2a}$ **22.** $\frac{b - a}{3b}$

23. The speed of a racing boat changes from 0 ft/s to 264 ft/s in six seconds. What is the acceleration of the boat in ft/s^2? Use the acceleration formula given in Example 3.

B Apply Your Skills

Write a rational number that is between each pair of numbers.

24. $0, -1$ **25.** $0.9, 1.1$ **26.** $\frac{-1}{5}, \frac{-4}{5}$

Evaluate. Write in simplest form.

27. $\frac{y}{-x}$, for $x = 5$ and $y = -4$

28. $\frac{m}{n}$, for $m = -2$ and $n = 8$

29. $\frac{m - n}{-12}$, for $m = -3$ and $n = 6$

30. $\frac{6b - 16}{3c}$, for $b = 8$ and $c = 12$

31. $\frac{-2y}{x^2}$, for $x = 9$ and $y = 3$

32. $\frac{3m - 11}{n}$, for $m = 7$ and $n = 14$

33. a. Open-Ended Write two rational numbers between 0 and $\frac{1}{2}$.
b. How many other rational numbers are between 0 and $\frac{1}{2}$? Explain.

34. Reasoning What are three fractions equivalent to $\frac{a}{b}$? Explain.

35. The formula $s = \dfrac{1{,}600}{d^2}$ gives the strength s of a radio signal at a distance d miles from the transmitter. What is the strength at 5 mi? Write your answer in simplest form.

36. Writing in Math Explain why a whole number is an integer and an integer is a rational number.

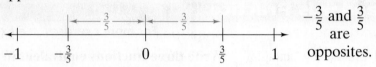

Homework Video Tutor

Visit: PHSchool.com
Web Code: bje-0406

Write the opposite and the absolute value of each number.

SAMPLE Find the opposite and the absolute value of $-\frac{3}{5}$.

Opposite:

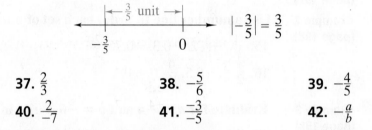

$-\frac{3}{5}$ and $\frac{3}{5}$ are opposites.

Absolute value:

$$\left|-\frac{3}{5}\right| = \frac{3}{5}$$

37. $\frac{2}{3}$ **38.** $-\frac{5}{6}$ **39.** $-\frac{4}{5}$

40. $\frac{2}{-7}$ **41.** $\frac{-3}{-5}$ **42.** $-\frac{a}{b}$

C Challenge

Reasoning Tell whether each statement is true for all positive integers a and b. If the statement is not always true, give a counterexample.

43. $\dfrac{a^2}{b} > \dfrac{a}{b}$ **44.** $\dfrac{3a}{3b} = \dfrac{a}{b}$ **45.** $\dfrac{a^2}{b^2} > \dfrac{a}{b}$

Multiple Choice Practice and Mixed Review

For Standards Tutorials, visit PHSchool.com. Web Code: bjq-9045

46. Which pair of numbers is between -3 and -2?
   Ⓐ $-2\frac{1}{2}, -2\frac{1}{3}$ Ⓑ $-3\frac{1}{2}, -3\frac{1}{3}$ Ⓒ $-2, \pi$ Ⓓ $-2\frac{1}{2}, -3$

47. Allison bought 2 meters of rope for her science fair project. She used 87 centimeters of it. How many meters did she have left?
   Ⓐ 0.0113 m   Ⓑ 0.113 m   Ⓒ 1.13 m   Ⓓ 113 m

48. What is the simplest form of $\dfrac{y(xy-7)}{10}$ when $x = 6$ and $y = 2$?
   Ⓐ 3   Ⓑ $\frac{30}{10}$ Ⓒ 1   Ⓓ $\frac{10}{10}$

 for Help

Lesson 4-5

49. Patterns Lucia has 4 pairs of slacks, 5 shirts, and 2 sweaters. How many different three-piece outfits can she make?

Exponents and Multiplication

Introduce, Develop Multiply expressions involving exponents with a common base.

Introduce Multiply and simplify rational numbers by using exponent rules.

Develop Simplify and evaluate expressions that include exponents.

Introduce Multiply monomials.

What You'll Learn

- To multiply powers with the same base
- To find a power of a power

. . . And Why

To learn the rules for operating with exponents

☑ Check Skills You'll Need

Write using exponents.

1. $k \cdot k \cdot k \cdot k$

2. $m \cdot n \cdot m \cdot n$

3. $2 \cdot 2 \cdot 2 \cdot 2$

4. $5 \cdot 5 \cdot 5$

GO for Help
Lesson 4-2

Multiplying Powers With the Same Base

In Lesson 4-2, you learned how to use exponents to indicate repeated multiplication. What happens when you multiply two powers with the same base, such as 7^2 and 7^3?

$$7^2 \cdot 7^3 = (7 \cdot 7) \cdot (7 \cdot 7 \cdot 7) = 7^5$$

Notice that $7^2 \cdot 7^3 = 7^5 = 7^{2+3}$. In general, when you multiply powers with the same base, you can add the exponents.

Take Note | Multiplying Powers With the Same Base

To multiply numbers or variables with the same base, add the exponents.

Arithmetic	**Algebra**
$2^3 \cdot 2^4 = 2^{3+4} = 2^7$	$a^m \cdot a^n = a^{m+n}$, for positive integers m and n.

You *simplify* an expression by doing as many of the indicated operations as possible.

1 EXAMPLE Multiplying Powers

Simplify each expression.

a. $(0.3) \cdot (0.3)^3$

$(0.3)^1 \cdot (0.3)^3 = (0.3)^{1+3}$ — Add the exponents of powers with the same base.

$= (0.3)^4$

$= 0.0081$ — Simplify.

b. $a^5 \cdot a \cdot b^2$

$a^5 \cdot a^1 \cdot b^2 = a^{5+1}b^2$ — Add the exponents of powers with the same base.

$= a^6 b^2$ — Simplify.

☑ Quick Review

Recall that $3 = 3^1$ and $a = a^1$ because a base with exponent 1 is equal to the base itself.

☑ Quick Check

1. Simplify each expression.   **a.** $(0.2)^2 \cdot (0.2)^3$ **b.** $m^5 \cdot m^7$

Problem Solving Tip

When in doubt, write it out! If you are unsure about the rules for multiplying powers, write the powers out. For instance, write $x^2 \cdot x^5$ as $(x \cdot x) \cdot (x \cdot x \cdot x \cdot x \cdot x)$. This simplifies to x^7.

Simplify $-2x^2 \cdot 3x^5$.

$$-2x^2 \cdot 3x^5 = -2 \cdot 3 \cdot x^2 \cdot x^5 \qquad \text{Use the Commutative Property of Multiplication.}$$
$$= -6x^{2+5} \qquad \text{Add the exponents.}$$
$$= -6x^7 \qquad \text{Simplify.}$$

✓ **Quick Check**

2. Simplify each expression.

   a. $6a^3 \cdot 3a$ **b.** $-5c^2 \cdot -3c^7$ **c.** $4x^2 \cdot 3x^4$

Finding a Power of a Power

You can find the power of a power by using the rule of Multiplying Powers With the Same Base.

$$(7^2)^3 = (7^2) \cdot (7^2) \cdot (7^2) \qquad \text{Use } 7^2 \text{ as a base 3 times.}$$
$$= 7^{2+2+2} \qquad \begin{array}{l}\text{When multiplying powers with the}\\\text{same base, add the exponents.}\end{array}$$
$$= 7^6 \qquad \text{Simplify.}$$

Notice that $(7^2)^3 = 7^6 = 7^{2 \cdot 3}$. You can raise a power to a power by multiplying the exponents.

Take Note **Finding a Power of a Power**

To find a power of a power, multiply the exponents.

Arithmetic	Algebra
$(2^3)^4 = 2^{3 \cdot 4} = 2^{12}$	$(a^m)^n = a^{m \cdot n}$, for positive integers m and n.

Online active math

For: Exponent Activity
Use: Interactive Textbook, 4-7

3 **EXAMPLE** **Simplifying Powers of Powers**

Simplify each expression.

a. $(3^2)^3$

$$(3^2)^3 = (3)^{2 \cdot 3} \quad \longleftarrow \text{Multiply the exponents.} \longrightarrow$$
$$= (3)^6 \quad \longleftarrow \text{Simplify the exponent.} \longrightarrow$$
$$= 729 \quad \longleftarrow \text{Simplify.}$$

b. $(a^6)^2$

$$(a^6)^2 = a^{6 \cdot 2}$$
$$= a^{12}$$

✓ **Quick Check**

3. Simplify each expression.

   a. $(2^4)^2$ **b.** $(c^5)^4$ **c.** $(m^3)^2$

Match each expression with its equivalent.

1. $12y^{12} \cdot 2y^6$

2. $5y \cdot 2y^8$

3. $6y^6 \cdot 4y^3$

4. $(2y^6)^3$

A. $8y^{18}$
B. $10y^9$
C. $24y^9$
D. $24y^{18}$

Standards Practice

For more exercises, see *Extra Skills and Word Problem Practice*.

Ⓐ **Practice by Example**

Example 1
(page 201)

Ⓖⓞ for Help

Example 2
(page 202)

Example 3
(page 202)

Simplify each expression.

5. $\left(\frac{1}{4}\right)^2 \cdot \frac{1}{4}$

6. $a^2 \cdot a^5$

7. $x^4 \cdot y \cdot x^5 \cdot y$

8. $m^{50} \cdot m^2$

9. $(3)^2 \cdot (0.2)^3 \cdot 3$

10. $x \cdot y \cdot y \cdot x^5 \cdot y^3$

11. $7b^3 \cdot 4b^4$

12. $-9c^2 \cdot -2c^8$

13. $5x^3 \cdot 2x^6$

14. $-7x^6 \cdot -5x^8$

15. $-5d^5 \cdot 6d^2$

16. $4b^4 \cdot 12b^7$

17. $(10^3)^2$

18. $(m^6)^4$

19. $(2^2)^3$

20. $(c^2)^8$

21. $(x^5)^7$

22. $(0^5)^8$

Ⓑ **Apply Your Skills**

Homework Video Tutor
▶ ————————

Visit: PHSchool.com
Web Code: bje-0407

Complete each equation.

23. $8^2 \cdot 8^\blacksquare = 8^9$

24. $c^\blacksquare \cdot c^4 = c^{11}$

25. $(9^\blacksquare)^4 = 9^{16}$

26. $5^6 \cdot 5^\blacksquare = 5^{14}$

27. $x^\blacksquare \cdot x^{12} = x^{15}$

28. $(a^\blacksquare)^9 = a^{27}$

Compare. Use >, <, or = to complete each statement.

29. $25^2 \;\blacksquare\; (5^2)^2$

30. $(2^7)^7 \;\blacksquare\; (2^{25})^2$

31. $(4^3 \cdot 4^2)^3 \;\blacksquare\; 4^9$

32. **Open-Ended** A megabyte is 2^{20} bytes. Use exponents to write 2^{20} in four different ways.

33. **Writing in Math** Explain why $x^8 \cdot x^2$ has the same value as $x^5 \cdot x^5$.

Geometry Find the area of each rectangle.

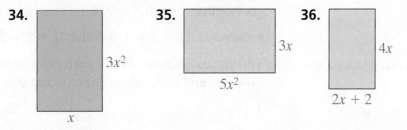

34.
$3x^2$
x

35.
$3x$
$5x^2$

36.
$4x$
$2x + 2$

37. **Error Analysis** Marcos thinks $x^4 + x^4$ simplifies to $2x^4$. Doug thinks $x^4 + x^4$ simplifies to x^8. Which result is correct? Explain.

38. Reasoning Does $-(2^3)^2$ have the same value as $(-2^3)^2$? Justify your answer.

 Challenge

39. a. Use exponents to write an expression in simplest form for the numerator of $\left(\frac{a}{b}\right)^{12}$.

b. Simplify $\left(\frac{a}{b}\right)^n$.

Multiple Choice Practice and Mixed Review

For Standards Tutorials, visit PHSchool.com. Web Code: bjq-9045

40. What is the value of $(0.4)^2$?

Ⓐ 0.16   Ⓑ 0.08   Ⓒ 0.8   Ⓓ 1.6

41. Which expression is equivalent to 2^{13}?

Ⓐ $(2^3)^{10}$ Ⓑ $2^5 \cdot 2^8$ Ⓒ $2^1 \cdot 2^{13}$ Ⓓ 8,190

42. Leslie states that $a^3 \geq a$ for all integer values of a. Is she correct?

Ⓐ Yes; integers are the set of numbers, $\ldots -2, -1, 0, 1, 2, \ldots$

Ⓑ Yes; cubing a number means multiplying it by itself 3 times, which will always result in a larger number.

Ⓒ No; cubing a fraction results in a smaller number.

Ⓓ No; cubing a negative number results in a smaller number.

GO for Help Lesson 4-6

Evaluate. Write in simplest form.

43. $\frac{mn}{m-6}$, for $m = 4$ and $n = 2$ **44.** $\frac{g+gh}{h-g}$, for $g = -3$ and $h = -5$

Mathematical Reasoning

Develop Justify mathematical conjectures.

Goldbach's Conjecture

In 1742, the mathematician Christian Goldbach made a conjecture involving prime numbers that has yet to be proved or disproved.

Goldbach's Conjecture: Every even number greater than 2 is the sum of two prime numbers.

Examples: $10 = 7 + 3$ and $24 = 11 + 13$

Goldbach's conjecture leads to a second conjecture: Every odd number greater than or equal to 9 is the sum of three prime numbers.

Examples: $11 = 3 + 3 + 5$ and $21 = 2 + 2 + 17$

Test the conjectures. Write each even number as the sum of two prime numbers and each odd number as the sum of three prime numbers.

1. 16

2. 25

3. 32

4. 47

4-8 · Exponents and Division

Master Understand negative exponents. Divide expressions involving exponents with a common base.

Develop Multiply, divide, and simplify rational numbers by using exponent rules.

Develop Simplify and evaluate expressions that include exponents.

Develop Multiply monomials.

What You'll Learn

- To divide expressions containing exponents
- To simplify expressions with integer exponents

. . . And Why

To solve real-world problems involving science

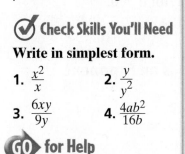

Check Skills You'll Need

Write in simplest form.

1. $\dfrac{x^2}{x}$ 2. $\dfrac{y}{y^2}$

3. $\dfrac{6xy}{9y}$ 4. $\dfrac{4ab^2}{16b}$

for Help
Lesson 4-4

Dividing Expressions Containing Exponents

In Lesson 4-7, you learned that you add exponents to multiply powers with the same base. To divide powers with the same base, you subtract exponents. Here's why.

$$\frac{7^8}{7^3} = \frac{7 \cdot 7 \cdot 7 \cdot 7 \cdot 7 \cdot 7 \cdot 7 \cdot 7}{7 \cdot 7 \cdot 7}$$ Expand the numerator and denominator.

$$= \frac{7^1 \cdot 7^1 \cdot 7^1 \cdot 7 \cdot 7 \cdot 7 \cdot 7 \cdot 7}{1^7 \cdot 1^7 \cdot 1^7}$$ Divide common factors.

$$= 7^5$$

Notice that $\dfrac{7^8}{7^3} = 7^5 = 7^{8-3}$. This suggests the following rule.

Take Note Dividing Powers With the Same Base

To divide numbers or variables *with the same nonzero base,* subtract the exponents.

Arithmetic

$$\frac{4^5}{4^2} = 4^{5-2} = 4^3$$

Algebra

$$\frac{a^m}{a^n} = a^{m-n}, \text{for } a \neq 0 \text{ and positive integers } m \text{ and } n.$$

---

1 EXAMPLE Dividing a Power by a Power

Simplify each expression.

a. $\dfrac{3^8}{3^5}$ b. $\dfrac{a^4}{a^2}$

$\dfrac{3^8}{3^5} = 3^{8-5}$ ⟵ Subtract the exponents. ⟶ $\dfrac{a^4}{a^2} = a^{4-2}$

$\quad = 3^3$ ⟵ Simplify the exponent. ⟶ $\quad = a^2$

$\quad = 27$ ⟵ Simplify.

Quick Check

1. Simplify each expression.   a. $\dfrac{10^7}{10^4}$ b. $\dfrac{x^{25}}{x^{18}}$

What happens when you divide powers with the same base and get zero as an exponent? Consider $\frac{3^4}{3^4}$.

$$\frac{3^4}{3^4} = 3^{4-4} = 3^0 \qquad\qquad \frac{3^4}{3^4} = \frac{\cancel{3}^1 \cdot \cancel{3}^1 \cdot \cancel{3}^1 \cdot \cancel{3}^1}{\cancel{3}_1 \cdot \cancel{3}_1 \cdot \cancel{3}_1 \cdot \cancel{3}_1} = \frac{1}{1} = 1$$

Notice that $\frac{3^4}{3^4} = 3^0$ and $\frac{3^4}{3^4} = 1$. This suggests the following rule.

Take Note ✐ **Zero as an Exponent**

Arithmetic	**Algebra**
$3^0 = 1$	$a^0 = 1$, for $a \neq 0$.

---

2 **EXAMPLE** **Simplifying When Zero Is an Exponent**

Simplify each expression.

a. $\dfrac{(-8)^2}{(-8)^2}$

$\dfrac{(-8)^2}{(-8)^2} = (-8)^{2-2}$ **Subtract the exponents.**

$= (-8)^0$ **Simplify.**

$= 1$

b. $\dfrac{6b^3}{18b^3}$

$\dfrac{6b^3}{18b^3} = \dfrac{1}{3}b^0$ **Subtract the exponents. Simplify $\frac{6}{18}$.**

$= \dfrac{1}{3} \cdot 1$ **Simplify b^0.**

$= \dfrac{1}{3}$ **Multiply.**

✅ **Quick Check**

2. Simplify each expression.

   a. 43^0 **b.** $\dfrac{5^2 x^6}{5x^6}$ **c.** $\dfrac{x^5 y^6}{x^5 y^3}$ **d.** $\dfrac{1}{5}x^0$

What happens when you divide powers with the same base and get a negative exponent? Consider $\frac{3^2}{3^4}$.

$$\frac{3^2}{3^4} = 3^{2-4} = 3^{-2} \qquad\qquad \frac{3^2}{3^4} = \frac{\cancel{3}^1 \cdot \cancel{3}^1}{\cancel{3}_1 \cdot \cancel{3}_1 \cdot 3 \cdot 3} = \frac{1}{3^2}$$

In the examples above, 3^{-2} indicates repeated division by 3. These results suggest the rule at the top of page 207.

Arithmetic	Algebra
$3^{-2} = \dfrac{1}{3^2}$	$a^{-n} = \dfrac{1}{a^n}$, for $a \neq 0$.

A hummingbird has a mass of about 10^{-2} kg, or $\dfrac{1}{10^2}$ kg. To simplify 10^{-2}, you write $\dfrac{1}{100}$ or 0.01. So the hummingbird has a mass of 0.01 kg. To simplify an expression such as x^{-2}, you write it as $\dfrac{1}{x^2}$, using no negative exponents.

3 EXAMPLE Using Positive Exponents

Simplify each expression.

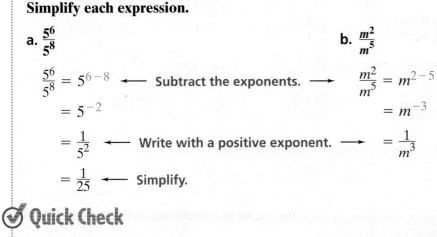

a. $\dfrac{5^6}{5^8}$

$\dfrac{5^6}{5^8} = 5^{6-8}$ ⟵ Subtract the exponents. ⟶

$= 5^{-2}$

$= \dfrac{1}{5^2}$ ⟵ Write with a positive exponent. ⟶

$= \dfrac{1}{25}$ ⟵ Simplify.

b. $\dfrac{m^2}{m^5}$

$\dfrac{m^2}{m^5} = m^{2-5}$

$= m^{-3}$

$= \dfrac{1}{m^3}$

The Calliope hummingbird, which is found in the western United States and Canada, has an average mass of 0.002 kg.

☑ **Quick Check**

3. Simplify each expression.
   a. $\dfrac{4^5}{4^7}$ b. $\dfrac{a^4}{a^6}$ c. $\dfrac{3y^8}{9y^{12}}$

You can also write an expression such as $\dfrac{1}{x^2}$ so that there is no fraction bar.

4 EXAMPLE Using Negative Exponents

Write $\dfrac{x^2 y^3}{x^3 y}$ without a fraction bar.

$\dfrac{x^2 y^3}{x^3 y} = x^{2-3} y^{3-1}$ Use the Rule for Dividing Powers With the Same Base.

$= x^{-1} y^2$ Subtract the exponents.

Online
active math

For: Exponent Activity
Use: Interactive Textbook, 4-8

☑ **Quick Check**

4. Write each expression without a fraction bar.
   a. $\dfrac{b^3}{b^9}$ b. $\dfrac{m^3 n^2}{m^6 n^8}$ c. $\dfrac{x y^5}{x^5 y^3}$

Write out the factors of each expression. Simplify using a single exponent.

1. $\dfrac{2^6}{2^5}$　　2. $\dfrac{\left(\frac{1}{3}\right)^4}{\left(\frac{1}{3}\right)^2}$　　3. $\dfrac{(0.08)^5}{(0.08)^2}$

4. Explain how you know 3^{-2} is not a negative number.

Standards Practice

For more exercises, see *Extra Skills and Word Problem Practice*.

A Practice by Example

Example 1
(page 205)

GO for Help

Example 2
(page 206)

Example 3
(page 207)

Example 4
(page 207)

Simplify each expression.

5. $\dfrac{2^5}{2^2}$　　6. $\dfrac{h^6}{h^2}$　　7. $\dfrac{10y^7}{6y^2}$　　8. $\dfrac{10b^8}{2b^6}$

9. $\dfrac{6^2}{6^1}$　　10. $\dfrac{11^5}{11^3}$　　11. $\dfrac{x^7}{x^3}$　　12. $\dfrac{a^{27}}{a^{19}}$

13. $(-4)^0$　　14. $\dfrac{w^8z^{15}}{w^8z^8}$　　15. $\dfrac{b^3c^2}{b^3c}$　　16. $\dfrac{2y^3}{8y^3}$

17. $\dfrac{4a^3}{20a^6}$　　18. $\dfrac{100m^{100}}{200m^{200}}$　　19. $\dfrac{b^5}{b^8}$　　20. $\dfrac{a^2}{a^7}$

Write each expression without a fraction bar.

21. $\dfrac{y^4}{y^7}$　　22. $\dfrac{a^2b^4}{a^8b^2}$　　23. $\dfrac{m^5n^6}{m^7n^8}$　　24. $\dfrac{xy^2}{x^4y^9}$

B Apply Your Skills

25. **Error Analysis** A student wrote that $-5^0 = 1$. What was the student's error?

Loma Prieta, California

26. The *magnitude* of an earthquake is a measure of the amount of energy released. An earthquake of magnitude 6 releases about 30 times as much energy as an earthquake of magnitude 5. The magnitude of the 1989 earthquake in Loma Prieta, California, was about 7. The magnitude of the 1933 earthquake in Sanriku, Japan, was about 9. Simplify $\dfrac{30^9}{30^7}$ to find how many times as much energy was released in the Sanriku earthquake.

You can use the rules for exponents to simplify rational numbers. Simplify each expression.

SAMPLE $\dfrac{8}{32} = \dfrac{2^3}{2^5} = \dfrac{1}{2^2} = \dfrac{1}{4}$

27. $\dfrac{36}{216}$　　28. $\dfrac{27}{81}$　　29. $\dfrac{16}{64}$　　30. $\dfrac{125}{625}$

Complete each equation.

31. $\dfrac{x^6}{x^{\blacksquare}} = x^4$　　32. $\dfrac{14x^5}{7x^3} = 2x^{\blacksquare}$　　33. $\dfrac{10^5}{10^{\blacksquare}} = 1$

34. **Open-Ended** Write three different quotients that equal 5^{-7}.

35. Writing in Math Is -3^{-2} positive or negative? Justify your answer.

Write each expression without a fraction bar.

36. $\dfrac{x^3}{x^5}$ **37.** $\dfrac{a^9b^3}{a^7b^8}$ **38.** $\dfrac{m^9n^3}{m^2n^{10}}$ **39.** $\dfrac{b^{14}c^2}{b^9c^{11}}$

40. $\dfrac{5x^2}{x^{-5}}$ **41.** $\dfrac{5b^{-7}}{5b^{-2}}$ **42.** $\dfrac{4^2 + 6^2}{2^2}$ **43.** $\dfrac{r^{-5}}{r^{-2}}$

C Challenge

To *square* a number n means to evaluate the expression n^2. The inverse of squaring a number is finding a *square root*. The square root of 36 is 6 because $6^2 = 36$. Find the square root of the following terms.

44. 64 **45.** $\dfrac{16}{25}$ **46.** $\dfrac{a^4}{b^6}$ **47.** $\dfrac{x^{10}}{y^{16}}$

Multiple Choice Practice and Mixed Review

For Standards Tutorials, visit PHSchool.com. Web Code: bjq-9045

48. Brad separates a large bag of apples into 1.5-pound bags. He ends up with 6 bags. Which equation can be used to find p, the number of pounds of apples in the large bag?

   Ⓐ $1.5p = 6$ Ⓒ $p - 1.5 = 6$

   Ⓑ $p + 1.5 = 6$ Ⓓ $\dfrac{p}{1.5} = 6$

49. Which list shows the expressions in order from least to greatest?

   Ⓐ $2^3, 3^2, 3^{-3}, (-2)^2$ Ⓒ $3^{-2}, (-2)^2, 3^2, 2^3$

   Ⓑ $3^{-2}, (-2)^2, 2^3, 3^2$ Ⓓ $(-2)^2, 3^{-2}, 2^3, 3^2$

GO for Help   Lesson 4-7

Simplify each expression.

50. $5^2 \cdot 5$ **51.** $x^7 \cdot x^2$ **52.** $2a^9 \cdot 8a^7$

✓ Checkpoint Quiz 2

Write three fractions equivalent to each given fraction.

1. $\dfrac{3}{12}$ **2.** $\dfrac{12}{36}$ **3.** $\dfrac{49}{70}$ **4.** $\dfrac{18}{28}$ **5.** $\dfrac{4}{5}$

Evaluate for $a = 4$ and $b = -6$. Write in simplest form.

6. $\dfrac{a}{2b}$ **7.** $\dfrac{b + a}{a}$ **8.** $\dfrac{a - b}{15}$ **9.** $\dfrac{b - a}{a^2}$ **10.** $\dfrac{3a + b}{24}$

Graph the rational numbers below on the same number line.

11. -0.8 **12.** $\dfrac{1}{2}$ **13.** 0.6 **14.** $-\dfrac{2}{10}$ **15.** $\dfrac{9}{10}$

Simplify each expression.

16. $2^3 \cdot 2^4$ **17.** $(x^5)^{10}$ **18.** $\dfrac{18a^4}{3a^2}$ **19.** $\dfrac{x^3}{x^8}$ **20.** $\dfrac{a^3b^5}{a^9b^5}$

Scientific Notation

Develop Read, write, and compare rational numbers in scientific notation (positive and negative powers of ten), compare rational numbers in general.

What You'll Learn

- To write and evaluate numbers in scientific notation
- To calculate with scientific notation

. . . And Why

To solve real-world problems involving weight and mass

✓ Check Skills You'll Need

Write each expression with a single exponent.

1. $10^3 \cdot 10^5$

2. $10^7 \cdot 10^9$

3. $10^5 \cdot 10^{-3}$

4. $10^{-6} \cdot 10^3$

GO for Help
Lesson 4-7

◀)) New Vocabulary

- scientific notation
- standard notation

Writing and Evaluating Scientific Notation

Standards Investigation
Exploring Prime Numbers

1. Copy and complete the chart below.

5×10^4	$= 5 \times 10,000$	$= 50,000$
5×10^3	$= 5 \times 1,000$	$= \blacksquare$
5×10^2	$= 5 \times \blacksquare$	$= \blacksquare$
5×10^1	$= 5 \times \blacksquare$	$= \blacksquare$
5×10^0	$= 5 \times \blacksquare$	$= \blacksquare$
5×10^{-1}	$= 5 \times \frac{1}{10}$	$= 5 \times 0.1 \quad = 0.5$
5×10^{-2}	$= 5 \times \blacksquare$	$= 5 \times 0.01 = 0.05$
5×10^{-3}	$= 5 \times \blacksquare$	$= 5 \times \blacksquare \quad = 0.005$
5×10^{-4}	$= 5 \times \blacksquare$	$= 5 \times \blacksquare \quad = \blacksquare$

2. Patterns Describe any related patterns that you see in your chart.

3. a. Based on the patterns you see, simplify 5×10^7.
   b. Simplify 5×10^{-6}.

GO for Help

For a guide to multiplying by powers of ten, see Skills Handbook, page 691.

Scientific notation provides a way to write numbers using powers of 10. You write a number in scientific notation as the product of two factors.

Second factor is a power of 10.

$$7,500,000,000,000 = 7.5 \times 10^{12}$$

First factor is greater than or equal to 1, but less than 10.

Scientific notation lets you know the size of a number without having to count digits. For example, if the exponent of 10 is 6, the number is in the millions. If the exponent is 9, the number is in the billions.

1 EXAMPLE Writing in Scientific Notation

Multiple Choice The world's largest tree has been named "General Sherman." Its weight in pounds is about 2,770,000. Write this number in scientific notation.

Ⓐ 2.77×10^{-6} Ⓒ 2.77×10^{6}

Ⓑ 2.77×10^{6} Ⓓ 2.77×10^{7}

Sequoia National Park

2,770,000   Move the decimal point to get a decimal
6 places   greater than 1 but less than 10.

2.77   Drop the zeros after the 7.

2.77×10^{6} You moved the decimal point 6 places. The original number is greater than 10. Use 6 as the exponent of 10.

The answer is B.

✓ Quick Check

1. Write in scientific notation.   **a.** 54,500,000   **b.** 723,000

In scientific notation, you use a negative exponent to write a number between 0 and 1.

2 EXAMPLE Writing in Scientific Notation

Write 0.000079 in scientific notation.

0.000079   Move the decimal point to get a decimal
5 places   greater than 1 but less than 10.

7.9   Drop the zeros before the 7.

7.9×10^{-5} You moved the decimal point 5 places. The original number is less than 1. Use −5 as the exponent of 10.

✓ Quick Check

2. Write in scientific notation.   **a.** 0.00021   **b.** 0.00000005

You can change expressions from scientific notation to **standard notation** by simplifying the product of the two factors.

3 EXAMPLE Writing in Standard Notation

Write each number in standard notation.

a. 8.9×10^{5} b. 2.71×10^{-6}

8.90000   Write zeros while moving the decimal point.   000002.71

890,000   Rewrite in standard notation.   0.00000271

> **Quick Tip**
>
> When multiplying by a power of 10, move the decimal point to the right. When dividing by a power of 10, move the decimal point to the left.

   3. Write each number in standard notation.

   a. 3.21×10^7 **b.** 5.9×10^{-8} **c.** 1.006×10^{10}

For a number to be in scientific notation, the digit in front of the decimal must be 1 or between 1 and 10.

4 EXAMPLE   **Changing to Scientific Notation**

Write each number in scientific notation.

a. 0.37×10^{10}

$0.37 \times 10^{10} = 3.7 \times 10^{-1} \times 10^{10}$ **Write 0.37 as 3.7×10^{-1}.**

$= 3.7 \times 10^9$ **Add the exponents.**

b. 453.1×10^8

$453.1 \times 10^8 = 4.531 \times 10^2 \times 10^8$ **Write 453.1 as 4.531×10^2.**

$= 4.531 \times 10^{10}$ **Add the exponents.**

✓ **Quick Check**

   4. Write each number in scientific notation.

   a. 16×10^5 **b.** 0.203×10^6 **c.** $7,243 \times 10^{12}$

You can compare and order numbers using scientific notation. First compare the powers of 10, and then compare the decimals.

5 EXAMPLE   **Comparing and Ordering Numbers**

Order 0.064×10^8, 312×10^{-4}, and 0.58×10^7 from least to greatest.

Write each number in scientific notation.

0.064×10^8 312×10^{-4} 0.58×10^7

$\downarrow$ $\downarrow$ $\downarrow$

6.4×10^6 3.12×10^{-2} 5.8×10^6

Order the powers of 10. Arrange the decimals with the same power of 10 in order.

3.12×10^{-2} 5.8×10^6 6.4×10^6

Write the original numbers in order.

   $312 \times 10^{-4}, 0.58 \times 10^7, 0.064 \times 10^8$

✓ **Quick Check**

   5. Order from least to greatest.

   a. $526 \times 10^7, 18.3 \times 10^6, 0.098 \times 10^9$
   b. $8 \times 10^{-9}, 14.7 \times 10^{-7}, 0.22 \times 10^{-10}$

Calculating With Scientific Notation

You can multiply numbers in scientific notation using the rule for Multiplying Powers with the Same Base.

6 EXAMPLE Multiplying With Scientific Notation

Multiply 3×10^{-7} and 9×10^3. Express the result in scientific notation.

$$(3 \times 10^{-7})(9 \times 10^3) = 3 \times 9 \times 10^{-7} \times 10^3$$ Use the Commutative Property of Multiplication.

$$= 27 \times 10^{-7} \times 10^3$$ Multiply 3 and 9.

$$= 27 \times 10^{-4}$$ Add the exponents.

$$= 2.7 \times 10^1 \times 10^{-4}$$ Write 27 as 2.7×10^1.

$$= 2.7 \times 10^{-3}$$ Add the exponents.

Video Tutor Help
Visit: PHSchool.com
Web Code: bje-0775

✓ Quick Check

6. Multiply. Express each result in scientific notation.

    a. $(4 \times 10^4)(6 \times 10^6)$ **b.** $(7.1 \times 10^{-8})(8 \times 10^4)$

7 EXAMPLE Using Scientific Notation

The Great Pyramid of Giza in Egypt contains about 2.3×10^6 blocks of stone. On the average, each block of stone weighs about 5×10^3 lb. About how many pounds of stone does the Great Pyramid contain?

$$(2.3 \times 10^6)(5 \times 10^3)$$ Multiply number of blocks by weight of each.

$$= 2.3 \times 5 \times 10^6 \times 10^3$$ Use the Commutative Property of Multiplication.

$$= 11.5 \times 10^6 \times 10^3$$ Multiply 2.3 and 5.

$$= 11.5 \times 10^9$$ Add the exponents.

$$= 1.15 \times 10^1 \times 10^9$$ Write 11.5 as 1.15×10^1.

$$= 1.15 \times 10^{10}$$ Add the exponents.

The Great Pyramid contains about 1.15×10^{10} lb of stone.

The Great Pyramid of Giza

✓ Quick Check

7. A hydrogen atom has a mass of 1.67×10^{-27} kg. What is the mass of 6×10^3 hydrogen atoms? Express the result in scientific notation.

1. The first digit of a number written in scientific notation must be greater than or equal to ■ and less than 10.

2. Will the number 2.34×10^5 have five zeros when written in standard form? Explain.

3. Will 24.7×10^{-3} be greater than or less than zero? Explain.

4. What number is greater, 3×10^0 or 0.003×10^3? Explain.

5. Explain how the Commutative Property of Multiplication helps you multiply numbers in scientific notation.

Standards Practice

For more exercises, see *Extra Skills and Word Problem Practice*.

A   Practice by Example

Examples 1 and 2
(page 211)

GO for Help

In Exercises 6–12, write each number in scientific notation.

6. 8,900,000,000   7. 555,900,000   8. 0.000631

9. 0.000006   10. 0.209   11. 0.00409

12. Pluto is about 5 billion km from the sun.

Example 3
(page 211)

Write each number in standard notation.

13. 5.94×10^7 14. 2.104×10^{-8} 15. 1.2×10^5

16. 7.2×10^{-4} 17. 2.75×10^8 18. 6.0502×10^{-3}

Example 4
(page 212)

Write each number in scientific notation.

19. 0.09×10^{12} 20. 0.72×10^{-4}

21. 52.8×10^9 22. $3,508 \times 10^{-7}$

Example 5
(page 212)

Order from least to greatest.

23. $16 \times 10^9, 2.3 \times 10^{12}, 0.065 \times 10^{11}$

24. $253 \times 10^{-9}, 3.7 \times 10^{-8}, 12.9 \times 10^{-7}$

25. $65 \times 10^4, 432 \times 10^3, 2.996 \times 10^4$

Example 6
(page 213)

Multiply. Express each result in scientific notation.

26. $(5 \times 10^6)(6 \times 10^2)$ 27. $(4.3 \times 10^3)(2 \times 10^{-8})$

28. $(9 \times 10^{-3})(7 \times 10^8)$ 29. $(3 \times 10^2)(2 \times 10^2)$

Example 7
(page 213)

30. An ant weighs about 2×10^{-5} lb. There are about 10^{15} ants on Earth. How many pounds of ants are on Earth?

In Exercises 31–33, write each number in standard notation.

31. 9×10^2 **32.** 8.43×10^6 **33.** 6.02×10^{-7}

34. One light-year is 5.88×10^{12} mi.

35. The Death Stalker scorpion can release 2.19×10^{-5} oz of venom in a sting. How is this weight expressed in standard notation?
  Ⓐ 0.00000219 oz   Ⓒ 21,900 oz
  Ⓑ 0.0000219 oz   Ⓓ 219,000 oz

Death Stalker scorpion

Order from least to greatest.

36. $55.8 \times 10^{-5}, 782 \times 10^{-8}, 9.1 \times 10^{-5}, 1,009 \times 10^2, 0.8 \times 10^{-4}$

37. **Writing in Math** Explain how to write each number in scientific notation. **a.** 0.00043   **b.** 523.4×10^5

Solve. Write each result in scientific notation.

38. The population density of India is about 8.33×10^2 people per square mile. The area of India is 1.2×10^6 mi^2. What is the approximate population of India?

39. In the year 2010, the population of the United States is expected to be about 315 million. Health expenditures will be about $8,754 per person. In total, about how much will the United States spend on health care in 2010?

Homework Video Tutor

Visit: PHSchool.com
Web Code: bje-0409

C Challenge   **40.** Simplify. Express the result in scientific notation.
$$\frac{(1.2 \times 10^{-5})(0.035 \times 10^7)}{(4.7 \times 10^3)(5.2 \times 10^{-8})}$$

Multiple Choice Practice and Mixed Review

For Standards Tutorials, visit PHSchool.com. Web Code: bjq-9045

41. Earth is 93,000,000 miles away from the sun. Which of the following represents this distance in scientific notation?
  Ⓐ 9.3×10^{-7} Ⓒ 93×10^6
  Ⓑ 9.3×10^6 Ⓓ 9.3×10^7

42. At a pet store, Max knows that the expression $205.5p + 102.5k$ represents the cost of p puppies and k kittens. If Max wants to buy 3 puppies and 4 kittens, what is the total cost of the pets?
  Ⓐ $94.13   Ⓑ $315.00   Ⓒ $1,026.50   Ⓓ $1,129.50

43. What is the simplest form of $a^{10} \cdot a \cdot a^2$?
  Ⓐ $a^{10} \cdot a$ Ⓑ a^{12} Ⓒ a^{13} Ⓓ a^{20}

GO for Help   Lesson 4-8   **Simplify each expression.**

44. $\dfrac{10^7}{10^9}$ **45.** $\dfrac{x^3 y}{xy}$ **46.** $\dfrac{15b^2}{10b^5}$ **47.** $\dfrac{9m^7}{3m^5 n}$

Reading-comprehension questions require that you read and understand information given to you in print in order to use mathematics to solve the problem.

EXAMPLE

Read the passage below. Then answer the questions based on what is stated or implied in the passage.

> The sun is the largest object in our solar system. It contains approximately 98% of the total solar-system mass. The interior of the sun can hold over 1.3 million Earths. The mass of Earth is 5.98×10^{24} kg. The sun is approximately 330,000 times the mass of Earth.

What is the mass of the sun?

You read, "The sun is approximately 330,000 times the mass of Earth."

$$\begin{aligned}
\text{Mass of sun} &\approx 330{,}000 \times \text{mass of Earth.} \\
M &\approx 330{,}000 \times 5.98 \times 10^{24} \\
&\approx 3.3 \times 10^5 \times 5.98 \times 10^{24} \\
&\approx 19.734 \times 10^{29} \\
&\approx 1.97 \times 10^{30}
\end{aligned}$$

The mass of the sun is about 1.97×10^{30} kg.

Multiple Choice Practice and Mixed Review

Read each question. Then write the letter of the correct answer on your paper.

1. The diameter of Jupiter is 142,800 kilometers. How is this length expressed in scientific notation?

- Ⓐ 1.428×10^5 km
- Ⓒ 1.428×10^{-5} km
- Ⓑ 14.28×10^4 km
- Ⓓ 1.428×10^6 km

2. The mass of Jupiter is about 318 times the mass of Earth. Use the information in the Example above. What is the approximate mass of Jupiter in scientific notation?

- Ⓐ 19×10^{24} kg
- Ⓒ 1.9×10^{28} kg
- Ⓑ 1.9×10^{27} kg
- Ⓓ 1.9×10^{-27} kg

3. A human hair is approximately 1×10^{-4} meters thick. Which of the following represents the thickness in standard notation?

- Ⓐ 0.01 m
- Ⓒ 0.0001 m
- Ⓑ 0.001 m
- Ⓓ 0.00001 m

Chapter 4 Review

Choose the vocabulary term that correctly completes each sentence.

1. One integer is a(n) __?__ of another integer if it divides that integer with remainder zero.

2. A fraction is in __?__ when the numerator and denominator have no factors in common other than 1.

3. A number that you can write as the quotient $\frac{a}{b}$ of two integers, where b is not zero, is a(n) __?__.

4. You can write numbers using powers of 10 in a shorthand way called __?__.

5. You can show repeated multiplication with __?__.

6. If a positive integer greater than 1 has exactly two factors, 1 and the integer itself, the integer is a(n) __?__.

Go Online
PHSchool.com

For: Vocabulary quiz
Web Code: bjj-0451

Skills and Concepts

Lesson 4-1
• To use divisibility tests
• To find factors

One integer is **divisible** by another if the remainder is zero when you divide. Divisibility tests help you find factors. One integer is a **factor** of another integer if it divides that integer with remainder zero.

List the positive factors of each number.

7. 12   8. 30   9. 42   10. 72   11. 111   12. 252

Lesson 4-2
• To use exponents
• To use the order of operations with exponents

To simplify an expression that has an **exponent,** remember that the **base** is the number used as a factor. The exponent shows the number of times the base is used as a factor.

Simplify each expression.

13. 2^3

14. $3(10 - 7)^2$

15. $28 + (1 + 5)^2 \cdot 4$

16. -5^2

Evaluate each expression.

17. x^2, for $x = 11$

18. $7m^2 - 5$, for $m = 3$

19. $(2a + 1)^2$, for $a = -4$

20. b^2, for $b = -4$

Lesson 4-3

- To find the prime factorization of a number
- To find the greatest common divisor (GCD) of two or more numbers

A **prime number** is an integer greater than 1 with exactly two positive factors, 1 and itself. An integer greater than 1 with more than two factors is a **composite number**. The **prime factorization** of a composite number is the product of its prime factors.

The **greatest common divisor (GCD)** of two or more numbers or expressions is the greatest factor that the numbers or expressions have in common. You can list factors or use prime factorization to find the GCD of two or more numbers or expressions.

Is each number *prime*, *composite*, or *neither*? For each composite number, write the prime factorization. Use exponents where possible.

21. 13   **22.** 20   **23.** 73   **24.** 110   **25.** 87

Find the GCD.

26. $16, 60$ **27.** $36, 81, 27$ **28.** $15, 17, 30$

29. $3x^2y, 9x^2$ **30.** $8a^2b, 14ab^2$ **31.** $3cd^4, 12c^3d, 6c^2d^2$

32. Reasoning Why is the GCD of two or more positive integers never greater than the least of the numbers?

Lesson 4-4

- To find equivalent fractions
- To write fractions in simplest form

Equivalent fractions describe the same part of a whole. A fraction is in **simplest form** when the numerator and the denominator have no common factors other than 1. You can use the GCD of the numerator and denominator to write a fraction in simplest form.

Write in simplest form.

33. $\frac{3}{15}$ **34.** $\frac{10}{20}$ **35.** $\frac{16}{52}$ **36.** $\frac{28}{40}$ **37.** $\frac{21}{33}$ **38.** $\frac{9}{54}$

39. $\frac{xy}{y}$ **40.** $\frac{25m}{5m}$ **41.** $\frac{2y}{8y}$ **42.** $\frac{2c}{5c}$ **43.** $\frac{9x^2}{27x}$ **44.** $\frac{36bc}{9c}$

Lesson 4-5

- To solve complex problems by first solving simpler cases

When a problem is complicated, you can solve related simpler problems to better understand the problem.

45. Reasoning A school's lockers are numbered 1 to 100. One hundred students enter the school one at a time. The first student opens the lockers. The second student closes the even-numbered lockers. The third student either closes or opens every third locker. The remaining students continue the pattern. After all the students have passed the lockers, which lockers are open?

Lesson 4-6

- To identify and graph rational numbers
- To evaluate fractions containing variables

A **rational number** is any number you can write as a quotient $\frac{a}{b}$ of two integers, where b is not zero.

Graph the rational numbers below on the same number line.

46. 2 **47.** -0.6 **48.** $-\frac{5}{10}$ **49.** $\frac{2}{10}$

Evaluate each expression for $a = -5$ and $b = -2$. Write in simplest form.

50. $\frac{b}{a}$ **51.** $\frac{a + b}{4b}$ **52.** $\frac{b - a}{a - b}$ **53.** $\frac{b^2}{a}$

Lessons 4-7 and 4-8

- To multiply powers with the same base
- To find a power of a power
- To divide expressions containing exponents
- To simplify expressions with integer exponents

To multiply numbers or variables with the same base, add the exponents. To raise a power to a power, multiply the exponents. To divide numbers or variables with the same nonzero base, subtract the exponents.

Simplify each expression.

54. $2^4 \cdot 2^3$ **55.** $7a^4 \cdot 3a^2$ **56.** $b \cdot c^2 \cdot b^6 \cdot c^2$ **57.** $(x^3)^5$

58. $(y^4)^5$ **59.** $\frac{4^8}{4^2}$ **60.** $\frac{b^2}{b^4}$ **61.** $\frac{28xy^7}{32xy^{12}}$

Lesson 4-9

- To write and evaluate numbers in scientific notation
- To calculate with scientific notation

Scientific notation provides a way to write numbers as the product of two factors, a power of 10 and a decimal greater than or equal to 1, but less than 10. To multiply numbers in scientific notation, multiply the decimals, multiply the powers of ten, and then put the result into scientific notation.

Write each number in scientific notation.

62. 2,000,000 **63.** 458,000,000 **64.** 0.0000007 **65.** 0.0000000059

Write each number in standard notation.

66. 8×10^{11} **67.** 3.2×10^{-6} **68.** 1.119×10^7 **69.** 5×10^{-12}

Order from least to greatest.

70. $3{,}644 \times 10^9, 12 \times 10^{11}, 4.3 \times 10^{10}$

71. $58 \times 10^{-10}, 8 \times 10^{-10}, 716 \times 10^{-10}$

Multiply. Express each result in scientific notation.

72. $(4 \times 10^9)(6 \times 10^6)$ **73.** $(5 \times 10^7)(3.6 \times 10^3)$

Chapter 4 Test

State whether each number is divisible by 2, 3, 5, 9, or 10.

1. 36   **2.** 100   **3.** 270

4. 84   **5.** 555   **6.** 49

List all the factors of each number.

7. 16   **8.** 30   **9.** 41

10. 23   **11.** 55   **12.** 64

Simplify each expression.

13. 5^3 **14.** $2^0 \cdot 2^3$ **15.** $3^2 + 3^3$

16. $4^2 \cdot 1^3$ **17.** $(-9)^2$ **18.** $(7 - 6)^4$

19. $-2(3 + 2)^2$ **20.** $-6^2 + 6$

21. **Writing in Math** A number written in scientific notation is doubled. Must the exponent of the power of 10 change? Explain.

Evaluate for $a = -2$ and $b = 3$.

22. $(a \cdot b)^2$ **23.** $a^2 b$ **24.** $b^3 \cdot b^0$

25. $(a + b)^5$ **26.** $b^2 - a$ **27.** $2(a^2 + b^3)$

Is each number *prime* or *composite*? For each composite number, write the prime factorization.

28. 24   **29.** 17   **30.** 42

31. 54   **32.** 72   **33.** 100

Find the GCD.

34. 56, 96   **35.** 36, 60   **36.** 14, 25

37. $15x, 24x^2$ **38.** $14a^2 b^3, 21ab^2$

Simplify.

39. $\frac{4}{16}$ **40.** $\frac{44}{52}$ **41.** $\frac{15}{63}$

42. $\frac{a^3}{a^2}$ **43.** $\frac{5b^4}{b}$ **44.** $\frac{8m^4 n^2}{40mn}$

Graph the numbers on the same number line.

45. $\frac{1}{10}$ **46.** -0.3 **47.** $-\frac{1}{2}$ **48.** 1

49. You have an 18-ft metal pipe. How many cuts must you make to cut the pipe into 2-ft-long pieces?

Evaluate for $x = 4$ and $y = -3$. Write in simplest form.

50. $\frac{2y}{x^2}$ **51.** $\frac{xy}{5x}$ **52.** $\frac{(x + y)^3}{x}$

53. $\frac{x + 3y}{10}$ **54.** $\frac{y^2 - x}{5}$ **55.** $\frac{x - y}{x + y}$

Simplify each expression.

56. $a^4 \cdot a$ **57.** $(y^3)^6$ **58.** $x^3 \cdot x^6 \cdot y^2$

59. $(a^3)^2$ **60.** $6b^7 \cdot 5b^2$ **61.** $\frac{9^8}{9^2}$

62. $\frac{6a^7}{15a^3}$ **63.** $\frac{b^8}{b^{11}}$ **64.** $\frac{2x^2 y^5}{8x^3 y^5}$

Write each number in scientific notation.

65. 43,000,000   **66.** 6,000,000,000

67. 0.0000032   **68.** 0.00000000099

Write each number in standard notation.

69. 5×10^5 **70.** 3.812×10^{-7}

71. 9.3×10^8 **72.** 1.02×10^{-9}

Order from least to greatest.

73. $3 \times 10^{10}, 742 \times 10^7, 0.006 \times 10^{12}$

74. $85 \times 10^{-7}, 2 \times 10^{-5}, 0.9 \times 10^{-8}$

Multiply. Express each result in scientific notation.

75. $(3 \times 10^{10})(7 \times 10^8)$

76. $(8.3 \times 10^6)(3 \times 10^5)$

Some problems ask you to use scientific notation. Scientific notation is used as a way to write very large or very small numbers.

Tip 1
In scientific notation, you use negative exponents for numbers less than 1 and positive exponents for numbers greater than or equal to 10.

A scientist measures the length of a bacterium. It is about 0.0000537 meter long. Which expression represents this number in scientific notation?

- (A) 5.37×10^{-4}
- (B) 5.37×10^{-5}
- (C) 5.37×10^{4}
- (D) 5.37×10^{5}

Think It Through
To write 0.0000537 in scientific notation, move the decimal point 5 decimal places to the right. The result, 5.37, is greater than 1 but less than 10. The original number is less than 1, so use -5 as the exponent of 10. The answer is B.

Vocabulary Review

As you solve problems, you must understand the meanings of mathematical terms. Choose the vocabulary term that correctly completes the sentence.

A. (Scientific, Standard) notation is the usual form for representing a number.

B. You can use (exponents, rational numbers) to show how many times a base is used as a factor.

C. A (rational number, median) can be written as a quotient of two integers.

Read each question. Then write the letter of the correct answer on your paper.

1. A red blood cell is 9×10^{-6} meter in diameter. Which expression represents this diameter in standard notation? (Lesson 4-9)

- (A) 0.00009 m
- (B) 0.000009 m
- (C) 0.0000009 m
- (D) 9,000,000 m

2. The speed of light is approximately 186,000 miles per second. This number can be written in scientific notation as 1.86 times a power of 10. What is the exponent? (Lesson 4-9)

- (A) -5
- (B) -4
- (C) 4
- (D) 5

3. The table shows the sizes of various objects in scientific notation. Which of the following represents the size of a plant cell in standard notation? (Lesson 4-9)

Objects Under Microscope

Object	Size (m)
Bacterium	1×10^{-6}
Large Virus	1×10^{-7}
Plant Cell	1×10^{-4}
Animal Cell	1×10^{-5}

- (A) 0.000001 m
- (B) 0.0000001 m
- (C) 0.0001 m
- (D) 0.00001 m

4. A large pizza is cut into 12 slices. Rachel and her friends eat 9 slices, or $\frac{9}{12}$ of the pizza. In the choices below, all the pizzas are the same size. In which situation was the same amount of pizza eaten? (Lesson 4-4)

- (A) 5 out of 8 slices
- (B) 3 out of 4 slices
- (C) 10 out of 16 slices
- (D) 4 out of 6 slices

5. Greg averages 50 miles per hour. How long will it take him to drive 425 miles? (Lesson 3-3)

- (A) $7\frac{1}{2}$ h
- (C) $8\frac{1}{4}$ h
- (B) $7\frac{2}{3}$ h
- (D) $8\frac{1}{2}$ h

6. Austin, Jackson, Zoe, and Sydney go bowling. The total cost was $34. Austin paid $\frac{1}{4}$ of the cost, Jackson paid 0.3 of the cost, Zoe paid $7.50, and Sydney paid the rest. Who paid the least amount? (Lesson 3-5)

- (A) Austin
- (B) Jackson
- (C) Zoe
- (D) Sydney

7. What is the next number in the pattern below? (Lesson 1-9)
$-0.5, -1, -2, -4, -8, \ldots$

- (A) -16
- (B) -12
- (C) -10
- (D) -8.5

8. Simplify $5a^2b \cdot 2ab^2$. (Lesson 4-2)

- (A) $10a^2b$
- (C) $10a^3b^3$
- (B) $3a^2b$
- (D) $3a^3b^3$

9. Simplify $(2)^{-3}$. (Lesson 4-8)

- (A) 8
- (C) $-\frac{1}{8}$
- (B) $\frac{1}{8}$
- (D) -8

10. Simplify $\left(\frac{1}{3}\right)^{-4}$. (Lesson 4-8)

- (A) 81
- (C) $-\frac{1}{81}$
- (B) $\frac{1}{81}$
- (D) -81

11. Which statement describes how to convert meters to centimeters? (Lesson 3-6)

- (A) Divide the number of meters by 10.
- (B) Multiply the number of meters by 10.
- (C) Multiply the number of meters by 100.
- (D) Divide the number of meters by 100.

12. What is the perimeter of a rectangle with width 3.4 cm and length is 9.7 cm? (Lesson 3-3)

- (A) 12.1
- (C) 22.8
- (B) 13.1
- (D) 26.2

13. Evaluate $4x^5y^2$ for $x = 2$ and $y = 7$. (Lesson 4-2)

- (A) 56
- (C) 1,960
- (B) 560
- (D) 6,272

14. Which expression is equivalent to $\frac{r^5s^2}{r^3s^7}$? (Lesson 4-8)

- (A) r^2s^{-5}
- (C) r^2s^5
- (B) $r^{-2}s^{-5}$
- (D) $r^{-2}s^5$

15. Which sentence is true? (Lesson 2-8)

   (A) $(-6 \cdot 5) - (7 + 4) \geq 0$

   (B) $(-5)^2 = (2)^{-5}$

   (C) $-16 - 4 = (-2)(10)$

   (D) $3 \cdot 4 \leq 15 - 6$

16. The prices for the amusement park and water park are shown on the sign. The cashier sold a total of 18 tickets in the last half hour for a total of $336. How many tickets for just the amusement park were sold? (Lesson 2-7)

> **Admission Prices**
>
> \$14 Amusement Park
>
> \$20 Amusement Park and Water Park

   (A) 4   (B) 9   (C) 14   (D) 16

17. In the rectangular room below, the length is 3 times the width. If the perimeter is 48 feet, what is the length of the closet? (Lesson 3-3)

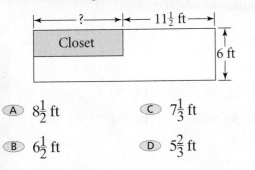

   (A) $8\frac{1}{2}$ ft   (C) $7\frac{1}{3}$ ft

   (B) $6\frac{1}{2}$ ft   (D) $5\frac{2}{3}$ ft

18. Find the perimeter of a rectangle with sides of length 3 cm and 50 mm. (Lesson 3-3)

   (A) 53 mm

   (B) 106 mm

   (C) 150 mm

   (D) 160 mm

19. What is the simplest form of $\dfrac{a^9 b^7 z^4}{a^{12} b^3 z}$? (Lesson 4-8)

   (A) $a^4 b^4 z^4$

   (B) $\dfrac{b^4 z^3}{a^3}$

   (C) $a^{21} b^{10} z^5$

   (D) $\dfrac{b^4 z^4}{abz}$

20. Evaluate $\dfrac{3m^2 - 12}{n}$ for $m = 8$ and $n = 4$. (Lesson 4-2)

   (A) 3   (C) 45

   (B) 9   (D) 51

21. Louise is 1,620 millimeters tall. What is her height in meters? (Lesson 3-6)

   (A) 1.62   (C) 162

   (B) 16.2   (D) 1,620

22. Yesterday, the temperature in the morning was $-8°C$. Today, the temperature in the morning was $9°C$. What was the increase in temperature in degrees Celsius? (Lesson 1-6)

   (A) -17 (C) 1

   (B) -1 (D) 17

Operations With Fractions

What You've Learned

Add, subtract, multiply, and divide rational numbers (integers and terminating decimals) and take positive rational numbers to whole-number powers.

Use variables and appropriate operations to write an expression or an equation that represents a verbal description.

Compare weights, capacities, and geometric measures within measurement systems.

✓ Check Your Readiness   **GO for Help** to the Lesson in green.

Solving Equations (Lessons 3-4 and 3-5)

Solve each equation.

1. $x + 1.8 = 3$ **2.** $n - 41 = 19$ **3.** $a \div (-3) = 15$ **4.** $-19 = p + 21$

5. $6t = 9$ **6.** $40 = z - 34$ **7.** $8d = 64$ **8.** $-0.89 = \frac{x}{2}$

Finding the Greatest Common Divisor (Lesson 4-3)

Find the GCD of each group of numbers.

9. $3, 15$ **10.** $16, 20$ **11.** $12, 36$ **12.** $11, 30$ **13.** $30, 40, 210$

14. $45, 80$ **15.** $27, 72$ **16.** $15, 121$ **17.** $30, 500$ **18.** $14, 28, 84$

Reading and Writing Fractions (Lesson 4-4)

Write two equivalent fractions to describe each model.

19.    **20.**   **21.**

Writing Fractions and Decimals (Lesson 4-6)

Write each fraction in simplest form.

22. $\frac{10}{12}$ **23.** $\frac{8}{20}$ **24.** $\frac{-32}{16}$ **25.** $\frac{25}{100}$ **26.** $-\frac{120}{125}$ **27.** $\frac{15}{45}$

28. $\frac{-20}{-75}$ **29.** $\frac{16}{124}$ **30.** $-\frac{18}{81}$ **31.** $-\frac{10}{65}$ **32.** $\frac{14}{84}$ **33.** $\frac{55}{77}$

Divide. Write each quotient as a decimal.

34. $27 \div 5$ **35.** $6 \div 10$ **36.** $10 \div 16$ **37.** $9 \div 12$ **38.** $15 \div 40$

What You'll Learn Next

Add, subtract, multiply, and divide rational numbers.

Know that every rational number is either a terminating or a repeating decimal and be able to convert terminating decimals into reduced fractions.

Add and subtract fractions by using factoring to find common denominators.

▲ You can use fractions to represent the length of a musical note or to describe the rhythm of a song.

New Vocabulary

◀)) **English and Spanish Audio Online**

- **dimensional analysis** (p. 248)
- **Inverse Property of Multiplication** (p. 244)
- **least common denominator (LCD)** (p. 228)
- **least common multiple (LCM)** (p. 226)

- **multiple** (p. 226)
- **multiplicative inverses** (p. 244)
- **reciprocals** (p. 244)
- **repeating decimal** (p. 232)
- **terminating decimal** (p. 231)

Academic Vocabulary
- **compare** (p. 228)
- **order** (p. 228)

Comparing and Ordering Rational Numbers

What You'll Learn

• To find the least common multiple
• To compare fractions

. . . And Why

To solve real-world problems involving team records

✓ **Check Skills You'll Need**

Write the prime factorization of each number.

1. 20   **2.** 125   **3.** 45

4. 186   **5.** 621   **6.** 1,575

GO **for Help**
Lesson 4-3

🔊 **New Vocabulary**

• multiple
• least common multiple (LCM)
• least common denominator (LCD)

Develop Compare rational numbers in general.
Add and subtract fractions by using factoring to find common denominators.

Finding the Least Common Multiple

A **multiple** of a number is the product of that number and any nonzero whole number.

Multiples of 4: 4, 8, ⑫, 16, 20, ㉔, 28, 32, ㊱, . . .

Multiples of 6: 6, ⑫, 18, ㉔, 30, ㊱, 42, . . .

The numbers 12, 24, and 36 are *common multiples* of 4 and 6. The common multiple 12 is their **least common multiple (LCM)**.

1 **EXAMPLE**   **Finding the LCM**

Today, both the school baseball and school soccer teams had games. The baseball team plays every 6 days. The soccer team plays every 5 days. When will both teams have games on the same day again?

6, 12, 18, 24, ㉚, 36, . . . List the multiples of 6.

5, 10, 15, 20, 25, ㉚, . . . List the multiples of 5.

The LCM is 30. In 30 days both teams will have games again.

✓ **Quick Check**

1. Find the LCM.

    a. 3, 4   **b.** 4, 5   **c.** 3, 4, 5

You can also use prime factorization to find the LCM.

2 **EXAMPLE**   **Using Prime Factorization**

Find the LCM of 12 and 40.

$$\left.\begin{array}{l} 12 = 2^2 \cdot ③ \\ 40 = ②^3 \cdot ⑤ \end{array}\right\}$$ Write the prime factorizations.

LCM $= 2^3 \cdot 3 \cdot 5$ Use the greatest power of each factor.

     $= 120$ Multiply.

The LCM of 12 and 40 is 120.

✓ Quick Check

2. Use prime factorization to find the LCM.

    a. 6, 16   **b.** 9, 15   **c.** 12, 15, 18

You can find the LCM of a variable expression.

3 EXAMPLE Finding the LCM of Variable Expressions

Find the LCM of $6a^2$ and $18a^3$.

$$\left. \begin{array}{l} 6a^2 = \boxed{2} \cdot 3 \cdot a^2 \\ 18a^3 = 2 \cdot \boxed{3^2} \cdot \boxed{a^3} \end{array} \right\} \quad \text{Write the prime factorizations.}$$

$$\text{LCM} = 2 \cdot 3^2 \cdot a^3 \qquad \text{Use the greatest power of each factor.}$$

$$= 18a^3 \qquad \text{Multiply.}$$

The LCM of $6a^2$ and $18a^3$ is $18a^3$.

✓ Quick Check

3. Find the LCM.

    a. $12x, 15xy$ **b.** $8m^2, 14m^4$ **c.** $25y^2, 15x$

Comparing Fractions

You can use a number line to compare fractions. As with integers, graph positive fractions to the right of zero and negative fractions to the left of zero.

4 EXAMPLE Using a Number Line

Graph and compare the fractions in each pair.

a. $\dfrac{9}{11}, \dfrac{6}{11}$ **b.** $-\dfrac{1}{2}, -\dfrac{1}{10}$

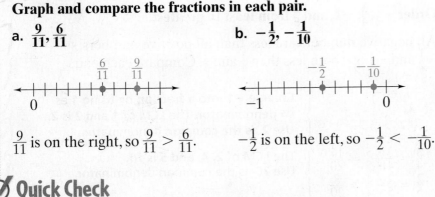

$\dfrac{9}{11}$ is on the right, so $\dfrac{9}{11} > \dfrac{6}{11}$. $-\dfrac{1}{2}$ is on the left, so $-\dfrac{1}{2} < -\dfrac{1}{10}$.

Online active math*

For: Fractions Activity
Use: Interactive Textbook, 5-1

✓ Quick Check

4. Use a number line to compare the fractions in each pair.

    a. $\dfrac{4}{9}, \dfrac{2}{9}$ **b.** $-\dfrac{4}{9}, -\dfrac{2}{9}$ **c.** $-\dfrac{4}{9}, \dfrac{2}{9}$

When fractions have different denominators, rewrite the fractions with a common denominator. Then compare the numerators. The **least common denominator (LCD)** of two or more fractions is the LCM of the denominators. The LCD is sometimes called the *lowest common denominator*.

5 EXAMPLE Using the LCD

The math team won $\frac{5}{8}$ of its competitions and the debate team won $\frac{7}{10}$ of its competitions. Which team won the greater fraction of competitions?

Step 1 Find the LCM of 8 and 10.

$$8 = 2^3 \text{ and } 10 = 2 \cdot 5$$
$$\text{LCM} = 2^3 \cdot 5 = 40$$

Step 2 Write equivalent fractions with a denominator of 40.

$$\frac{5 \cdot 5}{8 \cdot 5} = \frac{25}{40}$$
$$\frac{7 \cdot 4}{10 \cdot 4} = \frac{28}{40}$$

Step 3 Compare the fractions.

$$\frac{25}{40} < \frac{28}{40}, \text{ so } \frac{5}{8} < \frac{7}{10}.$$

The debate team won the greater fraction of competitions.

Debate teams can have as few as 8 debates and as many as 20 debates in a school year.

✓ **Quick Check**

5. Compare the fractions in each pair.

    a. $\frac{6}{7}, \frac{4}{5}$ **b.** $\frac{2}{3}, \frac{3}{4}$ **c.** $-\frac{3}{4}, -\frac{7}{10}$

6 EXAMPLE Ordering Fractions

Order $-\frac{1}{2}, \frac{3}{4}, -1,$ and $\frac{2}{5}$ from least to greatest.

All negative numbers are less than all positive numbers, so $-\frac{1}{2}$ and -1 are both less than $\frac{3}{4}$ and $\frac{2}{5}$. Compare each pair.

$$-1 = \frac{-1}{1}$$
$$\frac{-1}{1} \cdot \frac{2}{2} = \frac{-2}{2}$$

Change -1 into a fraction by using 1 as its denominator. The LCM of 1 and 2 is 2. Use 2 as the common denominator.

$$\frac{3}{4} = \frac{3 \cdot 5}{4 \cdot 5} = \frac{15}{20}$$
$$\frac{2}{5} = \frac{2 \cdot 4}{5 \cdot 4} = \frac{8}{20}$$

The LCM of 2, 4, and 5 is 20. Use 20 as the common denominator.

$$-\frac{2}{2} < -\frac{1}{2} \text{ and } \frac{8}{20} < \frac{15}{20}, \text{ so } -1 < -\frac{1}{2} < \frac{2}{5} < \frac{3}{4}.$$

✓ **Quick Check**

6. Order $\frac{2}{3}, \frac{1}{6}, 1,$ and $\frac{5}{12}$ from least to greatest.

Vocabulary Tip

When you <u>compare</u> items, you tell how they are alike or different. When you <u>order</u> items, you put them in a specific arrangement.

Complete Exercises 1–4 to solve the problem below.

Salt shakers come in boxes of 30 and pepper shakers come in boxes of 24. How many whole boxes of each must you buy to get an equal number of salt and pepper shakers?

   1. List the first six multiples of 30 and the first six multiples of 24.

   2. What do the multiples represent in the context of the problem?

   3. What does the least common multiple represent?

   4. How many boxes must you buy?

Standards Practice

For more exercises, see *Extra Skills and Word Problem Practice.*

Ⓐ Practice by Example

Example 1
(page 226)

GO for Help

Find the LCM of each pair by listing multiples.

5. $10, 36$ **6.** $7, 12$ **7.** $5, 6$ **8.** $5, 6, 7$

   9. Both the football and volleyball teams have games today. The football team plays every 7 days. The volleyball team plays every 3 days. When will both teams have games on the same day again?

Examples 2 and 3
(pages 226 and 227)

Find the LCM.

10. $15, 27$ **11.** $5, 12, 15$ **12.** $12x, 40y$ **13.** $6a^3, 8a$

Examples 4 and 5
(pages 227 and 228)

Compare the fractions in each pair.

14. $\frac{4}{5} \blacksquare \frac{2}{5}$ **15.** $-\frac{2}{3} \blacksquare -\frac{1}{3}$ **16.** $\frac{5}{8} \blacksquare -\frac{5}{8}$ **17.** $\frac{11}{12} \blacksquare \frac{7}{12}$

18. $\frac{5}{6} \blacksquare \frac{3}{4}$ **19.** $\frac{6}{8} \blacksquare \frac{7}{9}$ **20.** $\frac{1}{6} \blacksquare \frac{1}{8}$ **21.** $-\frac{5}{18} \blacksquare -\frac{1}{3}$

   22. At the track meet, Maria placed first in $\frac{4}{5}$ of her events and Carla placed first in $\frac{2}{3}$ of her events. Who placed first in the greater fraction of events?

Example 6
(pages 228)

Order from least to greatest.

23. $\frac{7}{9}, \frac{3}{9}, \frac{5}{9}$ **24.** $\frac{1}{2}, \frac{1}{3}, \frac{1}{4}$ **25.** $\frac{2}{5}, \frac{2}{3}, \frac{2}{7}, 2$ **26.** $\frac{2}{5}, -\frac{3}{8}, -\frac{1}{3}, \frac{2}{4}$

Ⓑ Apply Your Skills

Mental Math Compare. Use $>$, $<$, or $=$ to complete each statement.

27. $-\frac{3}{19} \blacksquare \frac{1}{200}$ **28.** $\frac{-1}{-3} \blacksquare \frac{1}{3}$ **29.** $\frac{9}{11} \blacksquare \frac{7}{11}$ **30.** $\frac{-2}{-7} \blacksquare \frac{4}{14}$

31. $\frac{8}{8} \blacksquare \frac{3}{3}$ **32.** $\frac{2}{10} \blacksquare \frac{2}{100}$ **33.** $\frac{2}{5} \blacksquare 3\frac{2}{5}$ **34.** $\frac{-4}{-17} \blacksquare -\frac{5}{2}$

Find the LCM.

35. $45, 120, 150$ **36.** $2, 5, 12, 15$ **37.** $12x, 40$ **38.** $7ab, 8a^3b^2, 10a^4$

39. $8x, 18xy$ **40.** $9b^3, 12bc^2$ **41.** $4g^2, 10j^4$ **42.** $2x^3, 5y^2, 15xy^2$

43. The manager of Frank's Snack Shop buys hot dogs in packages of 36. He buys hot dog buns in packages of 20. He cannot buy part of a package. What is the least number of packages of each product he can buy to have an equal number of hot dogs and buns?

Homework Video Tutor

Visit: PHSchool.com
Web Code: bje-0501

Compare. Use >, <, or = to complete each statement.

44. $\frac{7}{14}$ ■ $\frac{3}{6}$ **45.** $-\frac{7}{9}$ ■ $-\frac{2}{3}$ **46.** $\frac{8}{5}$ ■ $\frac{3}{2}$ **47.** $-\frac{19}{24}$ ■ $-\frac{5}{6}$

48. $-\frac{3}{8}$ ■ $-\frac{6}{16}$ **49.** $\frac{10}{11}$ ■ $\frac{4}{5}$ **50.** $\frac{1}{2}$ ■ $\frac{2}{4}$ **51.** -3 ■ $-\frac{12}{36}$

52. <u>**Writing in Math**</u> Jeremy and Fran want to compare $\frac{5}{8}$ to $\frac{9}{12}$. Jeremy writes equivalent fractions with a denominator of 96. Fran writes equivalent fractions with a denominator of 24. Which method would you prefer? Explain.

53. **Geometry** You have tiles that measure 4 in. by 5 in. What is the smallest square region you can cover without cutting or overlapping the tiles? Explain.

© Challenge **54.** Two positive integers have an LCM of 120. They do not have any common factors. What pairs of integers satisfy this description?

Multiple Choice Practice and Mixed Review

For Standards Tutorials, visit PHSchool.com. Web Code: bjq-9045

55. The table at the right shows the fraction of games won by four basketball teams. Which two schools won the same fraction of games?

Team	Games Won	Games Played
McCarthy	10	16
Edwards	8	14
Porter	12	21
Robinson	10	15

Ⓐ McCarthy and Porter
Ⓑ McCarthy and Robinson
Ⓒ Edwards and Robinson
Ⓓ Edwards and Porter

56. The average distance between Earth and the moon is about 385,000 kilometers. Which of the following represents this distance in scientific notation?

Ⓐ 3.85×10^{-6} km Ⓒ 3.85×10^{5} km
Ⓑ 3.85×10^{-5} km Ⓓ 3.85×10^{6} km

57. Which list has the numbers in order from least to greatest?

Ⓐ 14.07, 14.7, 14.68, 14.9 Ⓒ 14.07, 14.7, 14.9, 14.68
Ⓑ 14.7, 14.07, 14.9, 14.68 Ⓓ 14.07, 14.68, 14.7, 14.9

 for Help **Lesson 4-9**

Write in scientific notation.

58. 5,000,000 **59.** 0.001394 **60.** 8,900,000 **61.** 0.000005

5-2

Fractions and Decimals

Master Compare rational numbers in general.

Introduce Convert fractions to decimals.

Introduce, Develop Know that every rational number is either a terminating or a repeating decimal and be able to convert terminating decimals into reduced fractions.

What You'll Learn

- To write rational numbers as decimals
- To write terminating and repeating decimals as fractions

. . . And Why

To solve real-world problems involving buying food

✓ Check Skills You'll Need

Write the decimals in order from least to greatest.

1. 2.41, 0.241, 24.1, 12.4

2. 1.030, 13.03, 1.300, 1.003

3. 0.1, 0.01, −0.1, −0.01

GO for Help

Skills Handbook, p. 685

◀)) **New Vocabulary**

- terminating decimal
- repeating decimal

Writing Rational Numbers as Decimals

You can write a fraction as a decimal by dividing the numerator by the denominator. When the division ends with a remainder of zero, the quotient is called a **terminating decimal.**

$$\frac{5}{8} \text{ or } 5 \div 8 \longrightarrow 8\overline{)5.000} \quad \begin{array}{r} 0.625 \leftarrow \text{quotient} \\ \underline{-4\,8} \\ 20 \\ \underline{-16} \\ 40 \\ \underline{-40} \\ 0 \leftarrow \text{remainder} \end{array}$$

The division process for $5 \div 8$ ends with a remainder of zero. So 0.625 is a terminating decimal.

① EXAMPLE Writing a Terminating Decimal

A customer at a delicatessen asks for $\frac{1}{4}$ lb of potato salad. Use the scale at the right. Is the customer getting the amount of potato salad she requested? Explain.

$$\frac{1}{4} = 1 \div 4 = 0.25$$

Since $\frac{1}{4} = 0.25$, the customer is getting the right amount of potato salad.

✓ Quick Check

1. Write each fraction or mixed number as a decimal.

　a. $\frac{3}{4}$　　　**b.** $1\frac{7}{8}$

　c. $3\frac{3}{10}$　　**d.** $\frac{3}{5}$

Video Tutor Help

Visit: PHSchool.com
Web Code: bje-0775

In a **repeating decimal,** the same block of digits repeats infinitely many times. The block of digits that repeats can be one digit or more than one digit. You can write every rational number as a fraction. You can write every fraction as a decimal that terminates or repeats. So, you can write every rational number as a decimal that terminates or repeats.

2 EXAMPLE **Writing a Repeating Decimal**

Write each rational number as a decimal. State the block of digits that repeats.

a. $\frac{2}{3}$ **b.** $\frac{15}{11}$

$2 \div 3 = 0.66666\ldots$ ←Divide.→ $15 \div 11 = 1.36363\ldots$

                       Place a bar over the

$= 0.\overline{6}$ ←**block of digits**→ $= 1.\overline{36}$
                     that repeats.

$\frac{2}{3} = 0.\overline{6}$; the digit
that repeats is 6. $\frac{15}{11} = 1.\overline{36}$; the
block of digits that
repeats is 36.

✓ Quick Check

2. Write each rational number as a decimal. State whether the decimal is *terminating* or *repeating*. If the decimal repeats, state the block of digits that repeats.

a. $\frac{7}{9}$ **b.** $\frac{21}{22}$ **c.** $\frac{11}{8}$ **d.** $\frac{8}{11}$

Quick Tip

To write $-\frac{3}{5}$ as a decimal, you can evaluate $-3 \div 5$, $3 \div (-5)$, or $-(3 \div 5)$.

When you compare and order decimals and fractions, it may be helpful to first write the fractions as decimals.

3 EXAMPLE **Ordering Fractions and Decimals**

Write the numbers in order from least to greatest.

$$\frac{1}{4}, -0.2, -\frac{3}{5}, 1.1$$

$\left.\begin{array}{l} 1 \div 4 = 0.25 \\ -3 \div 5 = -0.6 \end{array}\right\}$ **Change the fractions to decimals.**

$-0.6 < -0.2 < 0.25 < 1.1$ **Compare the decimals.**

From least to greatest, the numbers are $-\frac{3}{5}$, -0.2, $\frac{1}{4}$, and 1.1.

✓ Quick Check

3. Order 0.2, $\frac{4}{5}$, $\frac{7}{10}$, and 0.5 from least to greatest.

Writing Decimals as Fractions

Reading a decimal correctly provides a way to write a fraction.

Decimal	Read	Fraction
0.43	"forty-three hundredths"	$\frac{43}{100}$

If a decimal is greater than 1, you can write it as a mixed number.

4 EXAMPLE Writing a Decimal as a Fraction

Write 1.12 as a mixed number in simplest form.

$1.12 = 1\frac{12}{100}$ **Keep the whole number 1. Write twelve hundredths as a fraction.**

$= 1\frac{12 \div 4}{100 \div 4}$ **Divide the numerator and denominator of the fraction by the GCF, 4.**

$1.12 = 1\frac{3}{25}$ **Simplify.**

✓ Quick Check

4. Write as a fraction or a mixed number in simplest form.

    a. 1.75   **b.** 2.32   **c.** 0.65

You can use algebra to write a repeating decimal as a fraction.

5 EXAMPLE Writing a Repeating Decimal as a Fraction

Write the repeating decimal $0.\overline{72}$ as a fraction in simplest form.

$n = 0.\overline{72}$ **Let the variable n equal the decimal.**

$100n = 72.\overline{72}$ **Multiply each side by 10^2, or 100.**

$\begin{aligned}100n &= 72.\overline{72} \\ -n &= -0.\overline{72} \\ \hline 99n &= 72\end{aligned}$ **The Subtraction Property of Equality lets you subtract the same value from each side of the equation.**

$\frac{99n}{99} = \frac{72}{99}$ **Divide each side by 99.**

$n = \frac{72 \div 9}{99 \div 9}$ **Divide the numerator and denominator by the GCF, 9.**

$= \frac{8}{11}$ **Simplify.**

As a fraction in simplest form, $0.\overline{72} = \frac{8}{11}$.

✓ Quick Check

5. Write each decimal as a fraction in simplest form.

    a. $0.\overline{7}$ **b.** $0.\overline{54}$ **c.** $0.\overline{213}$

Vocabulary Tip

Properties of Equality allow you to change both sides of an equation in the same way.

1. Vocabulary Every __?__ number can be written as a terminating or repeating decimal.

Match each rational number with an equivalent fraction or decimal.

2. 0.2

3. $\frac{1}{3}$

4. 1.3

5. 0.12

6. $\frac{2}{5}$

A. $0.\overline{3}$

B. $\frac{3}{25}$

C. 0.4

D. $\frac{1}{5}$

E. $1\frac{3}{10}$

Standards Practice

For more exercises, see *Extra Skills and Word Problem Practice.*

A Practice by Example

Example 1
(page 231)

Go for Help

Write each fraction or mixed number as a decimal.

7. $\frac{7}{25}$ **8.** $\frac{3}{5}$ **9.** $1\frac{9}{20}$ **10.** $6\frac{1}{4}$

11. Randy and Becky measure a carpet. Becky says the carpet's length is $10\frac{5}{16}$ ft. Randy writes "10.3125 ft." Did Randy write the correct measurement? Explain.

Example 2
(page 232)

Write each rational number as a decimal. State whether the decimal is *terminating* or *repeating*. If the decimal repeats, state the block of digits that repeats.

12. $-\frac{5}{8}$ **13.** $-\frac{1}{6}$ **14.** $\frac{2}{9}$ **15.** $\frac{9}{11}$

Example 3
(page 232)

Order from least to greatest.

16. $1.2, \frac{3}{5}, -0.5, \frac{9}{10}$ **17.** $\frac{1}{2}, \frac{3}{2}, \frac{5}{2}, 0.3$

18. $-\frac{1}{4}, -\frac{1}{8}, -0.75, -0.625$ **19.** $\frac{3}{2}, \frac{2}{5}, \frac{6}{5}, 0.06$

Examples 4 and 5
(page 233)

Write each decimal as a fraction or a mixed number in simplest form.

20. 2.25   **21.** 3.4   **22.** 0.08   **23.** 7.15

24. $0.\overline{5}$ **25.** $0.\overline{126}$ **26.** $0.\overline{27}$ **27.** $-0.\overline{3}$

B Apply Your Skills

Mental Math Compare. Use >, <, or = to complete each statement.

28. $\frac{1}{2}$ ■ 1.2   **29.** $\frac{7}{8}$ ■ 0.875   **30.** $\frac{3}{5}$ ■ 0.25   **31.** $\frac{1}{8}$ ■ 0.375

32. Number Sense A carpenter has a bolt with diameter $\frac{5}{32}$ in. Will the bolt fit in a hole made by a drill bit with diameter 0.2 in.? Explain.

33. Batting averages are usually expressed as decimals. Sarah got 32 hits in 112 times at bat. Lizzie got 26 hits in 86 times at bat.
   a. Data Analysis Find their batting averages to the nearest thousandth.
   b. Probability Based on their batting averages, who is more likely to get a hit? Explain.

34. Number Sense Copy and complete this table of some commonly used fractions and decimals. Write the fractions in simplest form.

Fraction	■	■	$\frac{3}{8}$	$\frac{1}{2}$	■	$\frac{3}{4}$	$\frac{7}{8}$
Decimal	0.125	0.25	■	■	0.625	■	■

Write as a fraction or a mixed number in simplest form.

35. $0.0\overline{6}$ **36.** $0.18\overline{3}$ **37.** 0.272727 **38.** $1.1\overline{9}$

39. **Writing in Math** Is $3.010010001\dots$ a repeating decimal? Explain.

40. Number Sense The number of digits that repeat in a repeating decimal is called the *period* of the decimal. The period of $0.\overline{3}$ is 1.
   a. Write $\frac{5}{7}, \frac{4}{13}$, and $\frac{7}{15}$ as decimals.
   b. What is the period of each decimal you wrote in part (a)?

41. Reasoning Seth had just finished a division problem on his calculator when the telephone rang. He got distracted. When he looked back at the calculator, all he could see was the display 0.04040404. What might have been the division problem? Explain.

⬤ **Challenge**   **42.** Describe a method you can use to generate a decimal that does not terminate or repeat. Is the decimal a rational number?

Multiple Choice Practice and Mixed Review

For Standards Tutorials, visit PHSchool.com. Web Code: bjq-9045

43. A bird flies 1,605 miles from Montreal, Canada, to Houston, Texas. The equation $\frac{k}{1.61} = 1{,}605$ can be used to find the approximate distance k in kilometers. What is the distance in kilometers?
   Ⓐ 997 km   Ⓑ 1,603 km   Ⓒ 1,607 km   Ⓓ 2,584 km

44. Which decimal is equivalent to $\frac{2}{3}$?
   Ⓐ 0.230   Ⓑ 0.233   Ⓒ 0.667   Ⓓ $0.\overline{6}$

45. Write 1.625 as a mixed number.
   Ⓐ $1\frac{1}{6}$ Ⓑ $1\frac{1}{4}$ Ⓒ $1\frac{5}{8}$ Ⓓ $1\frac{6}{25}$

GO for Help   Lesson 4-9   **46. Geography** Lake Mead, located between Arizona and Nevada, has a capacity of 34,850,000,000 m³. Write this number in scientific notation.

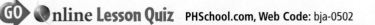

Estimating With Fractions and Mixed Numbers

FOR USE WITH LESSON 5-3

Develop Add, subtract, multiply, and divide rational numbers.
Develop Use estimation to verify the reasonableness of calculated results.

You can round to estimate sums and differences involving fractions and mixed numbers. In one method, you round the fraction or the fraction part of a mixed number to $0, \frac{1}{2},$ or 1.

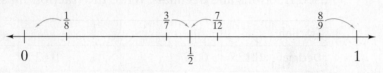

Round to 0 when the numerator is less than half of the denominator.

Round to $\frac{1}{2}$ when the numerator is about half the denominator.

Round to 1 when the numerator and denominator are almost equal.

1 EXAMPLE

Eva bought $\frac{2}{3}$ lb of Swiss cheese, $\frac{1}{4}$ lb of jack cheese, and $\frac{3}{8}$ lb of cheddar. The scale showed a total of 1.29 lb. Is the total reasonable?

$\frac{2}{3} \approx 1 \qquad \frac{1}{4} \approx 0 \qquad \frac{3}{8} \approx \frac{1}{2}$ ◄—— **Round each fraction.**

$1 + 0 + \frac{1}{2} = 1\frac{1}{2}$ ◄—— **Add.**

Eva bought about $1\frac{1}{2}$ lb, or 1.5 lb, of cheese. The total is reasonable.

You can get reasonable estimates when multiplying by first rounding to the nearest whole number. For division, use compatible numbers.

2 EXAMPLE

a. Estimate $4\frac{1}{8} \cdot 1\frac{9}{10}$.

$4\frac{1}{8} \cdot 1\frac{9}{10}$ If the fractional part is greater than $\frac{1}{2}$, round up.

$\downarrow \qquad \downarrow$

$4 \cdot 2 = 8$ **Multiply.**

b. Estimate $16\frac{1}{5} \div 2\frac{3}{4}$.

$16\frac{1}{5} \div 2\frac{3}{4}$ $2\frac{3}{4}$ rounds to 3. A number compatible with 3 and close to $16\frac{1}{5}$ is 15.

$\downarrow \qquad \downarrow$

$15 \div 3 = 5$ **Divide.**

EXERCISES

Estimate the value of each expression.

1. $\frac{2}{3} + \frac{7}{8}$

2. $5\frac{1}{12} - 2\frac{7}{9}$

3. $\frac{11}{12} \cdot 4$

4. $6\frac{8}{9} \div 1\frac{1}{5}$

5. Ira bought $\frac{5}{8}$ lb roast beef and $\frac{3}{4}$ lb of turkey. About how much more turkey did he buy than roast beef?

5-3 Adding and Subtracting Fractions

Develop Add and subtract rational numbers (fractions).
Introduce, Develop Add and subtract fractions by using factoring.

What You'll Learn

- To add and subtract fractions
- To use factoring to find common denominators

. . . And Why

To solve real-world problems involving cooking

✓ Check Skills You'll Need

Find the LCM of each group of numbers or expressions.

1. $4, 8$ 2. $9, 18$

3. $2n, 5$ 4. $3, 6, 9$

5. $8, 5, 4$ 6. $10, n$

for Help
Lesson 5-1

Adding and Subtracting Fractions

The sum (or difference) of fractions with like denominators is the sum (or difference) of the numerators. The denominators do not change.

1 EXAMPLE **Simplifying With Like Denominators**

Find each sum or difference. Simplify if possible.

a. $\frac{1}{8} + \frac{3}{8}$

$$\frac{1}{8} + \frac{3}{8} = \frac{1+3}{8}$$ Add or subtract the numerators.

$$= \frac{4}{8} = \frac{1}{2}$$ Simplify.

b. $\frac{9}{x} - \frac{7}{x}$

$$\frac{9}{x} - \frac{7}{x} = \frac{9-7}{x}$$

$$= \frac{2}{x}$$

✓ Quick Check

1. Find each sum.   a. $\frac{3}{7} + \frac{1}{7}$ b. $\frac{2}{k} + \frac{3}{k}$

To add or subtract fractions with unlike denominators, write the fractions with a common denominator. The method below works for addition and subtraction.

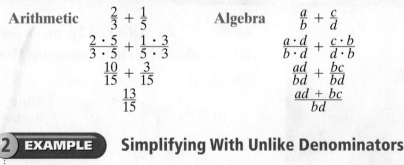

Arithmetic $\frac{2}{3} + \frac{1}{5}$

$$\frac{2 \cdot 5}{3 \cdot 5} + \frac{1 \cdot 3}{5 \cdot 3}$$

$$\frac{10}{15} + \frac{3}{15}$$

$$\frac{13}{15}$$

Algebra $\frac{a}{b} + \frac{c}{d}$

$$\frac{a \cdot d}{b \cdot d} + \frac{c \cdot b}{d \cdot b}$$

$$\frac{ad}{bd} + \frac{bc}{bd}$$

$$\frac{ad + bc}{bd}$$

2 EXAMPLE **Simplifying With Unlike Denominators**

Simplify each difference.

a. $\frac{1}{8} - \frac{5}{6}$

$$\frac{1}{8} - \frac{5}{6} = \frac{1 \cdot 6 - 8 \cdot 5}{8 \cdot 6}$$ Use a common denominator.

$$= \frac{6 - 40}{48} = -\frac{17}{24}$$ Simplify.

b. $\frac{1}{8} - \frac{5x}{6}$

$$\frac{1}{8} - \frac{5x}{6} = \frac{1 \cdot 6 - 8 \cdot 5x}{8 \cdot 6}$$

$$= \frac{6 - 40x}{48}$$

✓ Quick Check

2. Find each sum or difference.   a. $-\frac{7}{8} + \frac{3}{4}$ b. $\frac{3}{7} - \frac{2}{m}$

Online
active math

For: Fractions Activity
Use: Interactive Textbook, 5-3

Using Factoring to Find Common Denominators

You can use factoring to find the LCD of two fractions before you add or subtract.

3 EXAMPLE **Using Factoring**

Find $\frac{3}{8} + \frac{5}{12}$.

$\frac{3}{8} + \frac{5}{12} = \frac{3}{2^3} + \frac{5}{2^2 \cdot 3}$ Write the prime factorizations of the denominators.

$= \frac{3 \cdot 3}{2^3 \cdot 3} + \frac{5 \cdot 2}{2^2 \cdot 3 \cdot 2}$ Rewrite the fractions using the LCD, $2^3 \cdot 3$.

$= \frac{9}{24} + \frac{10}{24}$ Simplify.

$= \frac{19}{24}$ Add the numerators.

✓ Quick Check

3. Find each sum or difference.   **a.** $\frac{5}{8} - \frac{5}{6}$ **b.** $\frac{7}{12} - \frac{5}{9}$

Before you add or subtract mixed numbers, write the mixed numbers as improper fractions.

4 EXAMPLE **Adding Mixed Numbers**

Multiple Choice Ali hiked $2\frac{1}{10}$ mi on the Pacific Crest Trail and then another $1\frac{3}{4}$ mi to his campsite. How far did he hike in all?

Ⓐ $\frac{7}{20}$ mi   Ⓑ $1\frac{8}{20}$ mi   Ⓒ $2\frac{9}{20}$ mi   Ⓓ $3\frac{17}{20}$ mi

$2\frac{1}{10} + 1\frac{3}{4} = \frac{21}{10} + \frac{7}{4}$ Write mixed numbers as improper fractions.

$= \frac{21}{2 \cdot 5} + \frac{7}{2^2}$ Write the prime factorizations of the denominators.

$= \frac{21 \cdot 2}{2 \cdot 5 \cdot 2} + \frac{7 \cdot 5}{2^2 \cdot 5}$ Rewrite the fractions using the LCD, $2^2 \cdot 5$.

$= \frac{42}{20} + \frac{35}{20}$ Simplify.

$= \frac{77}{20}$ Add the numerators.

$= 3\frac{17}{20}$ Write the fraction as a mixed number.

Ali hiked $3\frac{17}{20}$ mi in all. The answer is D.

Pacific Crest Trail in California

4. Find each sum or difference. Simplify if possible.

  a. $5\frac{3}{4} + \frac{7}{8}$ **b.** $5\frac{2}{9} - 3\frac{1}{6}$ **c.** $2\frac{3}{12} - \frac{7}{9}$

You can add and subtract mixed numbers in more than one way.

More Than One Way

Banana Bread

5 ripe bananas	3½ cups flour
4 eggs	2 tsp baking soda
1 cup shortening	1 tsp salt
2½ cups sugar	1½ cups chopped walnuts, optional
3 tsp vanilla	

You are making banana bread for a bake sale, using the recipe at the right. You have $1\frac{3}{4}$ c of sugar left in a bag of sugar. How much more sugar do you need?

Tina's Method

You write both mixed numbers as improper fractions.

$$2\frac{1}{2} - 1\frac{3}{4} = \frac{5}{2} - \frac{7}{4}$$

$$= \frac{5}{2} - \frac{7}{2^2}$$

$$= \frac{5 \cdot 2}{2 \cdot 2} - \frac{7}{2^2}$$

$$= \frac{10}{4} - \frac{7}{4}$$

$$= \frac{3}{4}$$

You need $\frac{3}{4}$ c more sugar.

Kevin's Method

You write $2\frac{1}{2}$ as $2\frac{2}{4}$ and then rewrite it as $1\frac{6}{4}$ before subtracting.

$$2\frac{1}{2} - 1\frac{3}{4} = 2\frac{2}{4} - 1\frac{3}{4}$$

$$= 1\frac{6}{4} - 1\frac{3}{4}$$

$$= (1 - 1) + \left(\frac{6}{4} - \frac{3}{4}\right)$$

$$= \frac{3}{4}$$

You need $\frac{3}{4}$ c more sugar.

Quick Tip

To add or subtract fractions, they must have the same denominator. Sometimes you may only have to rename one fraction, but sometimes you may need to rename both.

Choose a Method

  1. For the problem above, which method do you prefer? Explain.

  2. Which method would you use to find $2\frac{4}{7} - 1\frac{9}{14}$? Which method would you use to find $-1\frac{1}{2} - 1\frac{3}{4}$? Explain your choices.

Match each expression with an equivalent expression.

1. $\frac{1}{2} + \frac{3}{4}$

2. $\frac{8}{9} + \frac{5}{12}$

3. $\frac{2}{6} + 1$

4. $\frac{1}{21} + \frac{11}{15}$

5. $\frac{7}{21} + \frac{4}{6}$

A. $\frac{1}{3} + \frac{2}{3}$

B. $\frac{32}{36} + \frac{15}{36}$

C. $\frac{1}{3} + \frac{3}{3}$

D. $\frac{2}{4} + \frac{3}{4}$

E. $\frac{5}{105} + \frac{77}{105}$

Standards Practice

For more exercises, see *Extra Skills and Word Problem Practice*.

A Practice by Example

Example 1
(page 237)

Example 2
(page 237)

Examples 3 and 4
(page 238)

Find each sum or difference. Simplify if possible.

6. $\frac{3}{16} + \frac{7}{16}$ 7. $\frac{6}{z} + \left(-\frac{2}{z}\right)$ 8. $\frac{15}{q} - \frac{8}{q}$ 9. $\frac{5}{11} + \frac{4}{11}$

10. $\frac{11}{12} - \frac{7}{12}$ 11. $\frac{7}{8} + \frac{5}{8}$ 12. $\frac{3}{10} - \frac{7}{10}$ 13. $\frac{2}{x} + \frac{3}{x}$

Simplify each sum or difference.

14. $\frac{3}{4} - \frac{2}{3}$ 15. $\frac{12}{20} - \frac{1}{4}$ 16. $-\frac{3}{10} - \frac{5}{100}$ 17. $\frac{6}{x} - \frac{2}{5}$

Find each sum or difference. Simplify if possible.

18. $3\frac{3}{4} + 2\frac{1}{4}$ 19. $\frac{4}{16} + \frac{3}{8}$ 20. $10\frac{1}{18} + 3\frac{3}{4}$ 21. $\frac{5}{8} + \frac{7}{12}$

22. $1\frac{5}{9} - 1\frac{2}{9}$ 23. $5\frac{3}{4} - 2\frac{1}{8}$ 24. $1\frac{5}{6} - \frac{7}{9}$ 25. $1\frac{7}{8} - 2\frac{3}{4}$

26. Kim works on social studies homework for $2\frac{2}{5}$ h. Then she works on math homework for $1\frac{1}{4}$ h. How many hours total does Kim spend doing homework?

B Apply Your Skills

Homework Video Tutor

Visit: PHSchool.com
Web Code: bje-0503

Estimation Estimate each sum or difference.

27. $2\frac{1}{3} + 7\frac{1}{8}$ 28. $25\frac{5}{18} - 9\frac{11}{17}$ 29. $15\frac{3}{4} + 31\frac{1}{2}$ 30. $-4\frac{7}{8} + 15\frac{1}{10}$

31. **Writing in Math** Describe why estimating a sum or difference before adding or subtracting is useful.

32. A doll artist cuts a piece of lace $8\frac{5}{8}$ in. long from a piece $10\frac{1}{2}$ in. long. How many inches of lace are left?

Find each sum or difference.

33. $\frac{12}{15} + 0.5$ 34. $\frac{3}{n} + \left(-\frac{3}{10}\right)$ 35. $\frac{7}{10} + \frac{2d}{3}$ 36. $\frac{5}{6} - \left(-\frac{7}{9}\right)$

Mental Math Find each sum.

37. $\frac{3}{4} + \frac{3}{8} + \frac{1}{4}$ **38.** $2\frac{5}{7} + 1\frac{2}{5} + 3\frac{2}{7}$ **39.** $\frac{2}{7} + \frac{x}{2} + \left(-\frac{2}{7}\right)$

40. There were three snowstorms last winter. The storms dropped $3\frac{1}{2}$ in., $6\frac{1}{16}$ in., and $10\frac{3}{4}$ in. of snow. What was the combined snowfall of the three storms?

Use prime factors to find the LCD. Then simplify each expression.

41. $\frac{7}{24} - \frac{15}{90}$ **42.** $\frac{-5}{66} + \frac{-7}{99}$ **43.** $\frac{2}{28} + \frac{1}{49}$

 Challenge   **44.** Dora and Paul have a collection of x marbles. Dora has $\frac{x}{3}$ marbles. What fraction of the marbles does Paul have?

Multiple Choice Practice and Mixed Review

For Standards Tutorials, visit PHSchool.com. Web Code: bjq-9045

45. Simplify $5\frac{1}{4} + 3\frac{1}{2} + 2$.

   Ⓐ $8\frac{3}{4}$ Ⓑ $9\frac{1}{4}$ Ⓒ $10\frac{3}{4}$ Ⓓ $12\frac{1}{2}$

46. A teacher asked four students how long they studied for a test. Who studied longest?

   Ⓐ Marsha   Ⓒ Pedro
   Ⓑ Cora   Ⓓ Darcy

Name	Time (hours)
Marsha	$2\frac{1}{8}$
Cora	2.2
Pedro	2.15
Darcy	$2\frac{2}{5}$

47. Roger has played basketball for $5\frac{3}{4}$ years. Cindy has played for $2\frac{5}{6}$ years. What is a reasonable estimate for how much longer Roger has played than Cindy?

   Ⓐ $1\frac{1}{2}$ years   Ⓑ 2 years   Ⓒ $2\frac{1}{2}$ years   Ⓓ 3 years

 for Help   Lesson 5-2   **Order from least to greatest.**

48. $\frac{5}{8}, \frac{4}{7}, \frac{3}{6}$ **49.** $\frac{2}{3}, 0.6, 0.66$ **50.** $\frac{10}{9}, \frac{9}{10}, -\frac{9}{10}, -\frac{10}{9}$

✓ Checkpoint Quiz 1

Compare. Use >, <, or = to complete each statement.

1. $\frac{2}{3} \blacksquare \frac{2}{5}$ **2.** $2\frac{2}{3} \blacksquare 2\frac{4}{6}$ **3.** $-\frac{1}{5} \blacksquare -\frac{1}{8}$ **4.** $-1.65 \blacksquare -1\frac{5}{8}$

Write each fraction or mixed number as a decimal and each decimal as a fraction in simplest form.

5. $\frac{51}{100}$ **6.** 0.012 **7.** $1\frac{1}{4}$ **8.** $0.\overline{3}$ **9.** $\frac{5}{6}$ **10.** $0.\overline{51}$

Find each sum or difference. Simplify if possible.

11. $\frac{6}{13} + \frac{5}{13}$ **12.** $\frac{11}{12} - \frac{7}{9}$ **13.** $1\frac{3}{5} + 2\frac{7}{8}$ **14.** $4\frac{1}{7} - 3\frac{10}{21}$

5-4

Multiplying and Dividing Fractions

Develop Multiply and divide rational numbers (fractions).

Develop Simplify numerical expressions by applying properties of rational numbers (e.g., inverse).

What You'll Learn

- To multiply fractions
- To divide fractions

. . . And Why

To solve real-world problems involving area

 **Check Skills You'll Need**

Write each mixed number as an improper fraction.

1. $2\frac{1}{3}$ **2.** $3\frac{3}{10}$ **3.** $1\frac{4}{9}$

4. $4\frac{4}{5}$ **5.** $7\frac{7}{8}$ **6.** $5\frac{1}{7}$

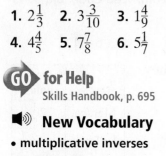 **for Help**

Skills Handbook, p. 695

🔊 **New Vocabulary**

- multiplicative inverses
- reciprocals
- Inverse Property of Multiplication

Multiplying Rational Numbers

Standards Investigation
Modeling Multiplication of Fractions

Use paper folding to find $\frac{2}{3}$ of $\frac{1}{4}$, or $\frac{2}{3} \cdot \frac{1}{4}$.

1. Fold a sheet of paper into fourths as shown. Shade $\frac{1}{4}$ of it.

2. Now unfold the paper and fold it into thirds as shown in the second picture. Shade $\frac{2}{3}$ of it.

3. **a.** Count the small rectangles.
   b. How many did you shade twice?
   c. What fraction of the small rectangles is this?

4. Use your model to complete:
   $$\frac{2}{3} \cdot \frac{1}{4} = \frac{\blacksquare}{\blacksquare}$$

5. **Modeling** Use paper folding and shading to find $\frac{3}{4} \cdot \frac{1}{2}$.

To multiply fractions, first multiply their numerators and multiply their denominators. Then write the result in simplest form.

---

1 EXAMPLE Multiplying Fractions

Find $\frac{3}{7} \cdot \frac{4}{5}$. Simplify if possible.

$$\frac{3}{7} \cdot \frac{4}{5} = \frac{3 \cdot 4}{7 \cdot 5} \qquad \begin{array}{l}\longleftarrow \text{ Multiply the numerators.} \\ \longleftarrow \text{ Multiply the denominators.}\end{array}$$

$$= \frac{12}{35} \qquad \longleftarrow \text{ Simplify.}$$

✓ Quick Check

1. Find each product. Simplify if possible.

a. $\frac{2}{5}\left(\frac{1}{3}\right)$ **b.** $-\frac{5}{6} \cdot \frac{2}{3}$ **c.** $\frac{7}{8} \cdot \frac{5}{9}$ **d.** $-\frac{1}{4}\left(-\frac{3}{8}\right)$

For: Fractions Activity
Use: Interactive Textbook, 5-4

When a numerator and a denominator have common factors, you can simplify before multiplying.

2 EXAMPLE **Simplifying Before Multiplying**

Quick Tip

If either the numerator or denominator is negative, or if the negative sign is in front of the fraction, then the entire fraction is negative. $\frac{-17}{24} = -\frac{17}{24}$

a. Find $\frac{9}{15} \cdot \frac{-5}{9}$.

$\frac{9}{15} \cdot \frac{-5}{9} = \frac{1\cancel{9}}{3\cancel{15}} \cdot \frac{-1\cancel{-5}}{1\cancel{9}}$ Divide the common factors.

$= -\frac{1}{3}$ Multiply.

b. Find $\frac{y}{4} \cdot \frac{8}{11}$.

$\frac{y}{4} \cdot \frac{8}{11} = \frac{y}{1\cancel{4}} \cdot \frac{8^2}{11}$ Divide the common factors.

$= \frac{2y}{11}$ Multiply.

✓ Quick Check

2. Find each product. Simplify if possible.

   a. $\frac{2}{3} \cdot \frac{6}{7}$ b. $-\frac{5}{15} \cdot \frac{21}{25}$ c. $\frac{2x}{9} \cdot \frac{3}{4}$

To multiply mixed numbers, first write them as improper fractions. Then simplify before multiplying, if possible.

3 EXAMPLE **Multiplying Mixed Numbers**

Geometry The area of Golden Gate Park in San Francisco can be estimated using a rectangle $3\frac{2}{5}$ mi long and $\frac{1}{2}$ mi wide. What is the approximate area of Golden Gate Park?

$A = 3\frac{2}{5} \cdot \frac{1}{2}$ Area of a rectangle = length · width.

$= \frac{17}{5} \cdot \frac{1}{2}$ Write $3\frac{2}{5}$ as an improper fraction, $\frac{17}{5}$.

$= \frac{17}{10}$ Multiply.

$= 1\frac{7}{10}$ Write as a mixed number.

The area of Golden Gate Park is about $1\frac{7}{10}$ mi².

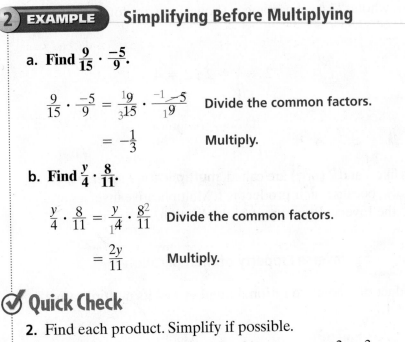

Golden Gate Park

✓ Quick Check

3. Find each product. Simplify if possible.

   a. $3\frac{3}{4} \cdot \frac{2}{5}$ b. $\frac{2}{3} \cdot 1\frac{2}{7}$ c. $\left(-2\frac{5}{6}\right) \cdot 1\frac{3}{5}$

Dividing Rational Numbers

Asking "What is $2 \div \frac{1}{2}$?" is the same as asking "How many halves are in two wholes?" As the oranges show, there are four halves in two wholes.

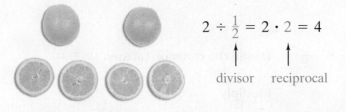

$$2 \div \frac{1}{2} = 2 \cdot 2 = 4$$

divisor   reciprocal

Numbers like $\frac{1}{2}$ and 2 (or $\frac{2}{1}$) are called **multiplicative inverses,** or **reciprocals,** because their product is 1. Multiplicative inverses are related to the Inverse Property of Multiplication.

Take Note   **Inverse Property of Multiplication**

The product of a nonzero rational number and its multiplicative inverse is 1.

Arithmetic	Algebra
$2 \cdot \frac{1}{2} = 1$	$a \cdot \frac{1}{a} = 1$
$\frac{1}{2} \cdot 2 = 1$	$\frac{1}{a} \cdot a = 1$

To divide fractions, rewrite the division as a related multiplication in which you multiply by the reciprocal of the divisor.

4 EXAMPLE   **Dividing Fractions**

a. Find $\frac{2}{9} \div \frac{2}{5}$.

$\frac{2}{9} \div \frac{2}{5} = \frac{2}{9} \cdot \frac{5}{2}$ Multiply by the reciprocal of the divisor.

$= \frac{2^1}{9} \cdot \frac{5}{1\,2}$ Divide the common factors.

$= \frac{5}{9}$ Simplify

b. Find $\frac{x}{3} \div \frac{x}{4}$.

$\frac{x}{3} \div \frac{x}{4} = \frac{x}{3} \cdot \frac{4}{x}$

$= \frac{x^1}{3} \cdot \frac{4}{1\,x}$

$= \frac{4}{3} = 1\frac{1}{3}$

✓ Quick Check

4. Find each quotient. Simplify if possible.

   a. $-\frac{1}{4} \div \frac{1}{2}$ **b.** $\frac{5a}{8} \div \frac{2}{3}$ **c.** $\frac{3b}{7} \div \frac{6}{7}$

As with multiplication, to divide mixed numbers, change the mixed numbers to improper fractions before multiplying by the reciprocal of the divisor.

1. **Vocabulary** A reciprocal is also called a(n) _?_ .

Write the reciprocal of each rational number.

2. $\frac{2}{3}$ 3. -2 4. $\frac{1}{3}$ 5. $-\frac{1}{3}$ 6. $-1\frac{4}{5}$

Copy and complete each equation.

7. $\frac{7}{8} \cdot \frac{8}{7} = \blacksquare$

8. $\frac{2}{5} \cdot \blacksquare = 1$

9. $\blacksquare \cdot 4 = 1$

10. $\frac{9}{2} \cdot \blacksquare = 1$

For more exercises, see *Extra Skills and Word Problem Practice.*

Ⓐ **Practice by Example**

Examples 1 and 2
(pages 242 and 243)

GO for Help

Example 3
(page 243)

Find each product. Simplify if possible.

11. $\frac{2}{3} \cdot \frac{1}{5}$ 12. $-\frac{1}{2}\left(\frac{3}{8}\right)$ 13. $-\frac{4}{7} \cdot -\frac{3}{5}$ 14. $\left(-\frac{2}{3}\right)\left(\frac{11}{13}\right)$

15. $\left(-\frac{7}{8}\right)\left(-\frac{4}{5}\right)$ 16. $\frac{12y}{25} \cdot \frac{5}{6}$ 17. $\frac{9}{10} \cdot \frac{15x}{3}$ 18. $\frac{5}{9}\left(\frac{9}{10}\right)$

19. $5\frac{7}{8} \cdot \frac{6}{7}$ 20. $2\frac{3}{4} \cdot 1\frac{1}{5}$ 21. $-1\frac{2}{5} \cdot 2\frac{2}{7}$ 22. $-3\frac{2}{5} \cdot -1\frac{2}{3}$

23. Jim spends $\frac{3}{4}$ of an hour on homework. His older sister Gina spends $1\frac{2}{3}$ times as much on her homework as Jim spends on his. How much time does Gina spend doing her homework?

Example 4
(page 244)

Find each quotient. Simplify if possible.

24. $\frac{1}{2} \div \frac{1}{3}$ 25. $\frac{5}{8} \div \frac{3}{4}$ 26. $-\frac{3}{4} \div \frac{1}{3}$ 27. $\frac{11}{12} \div \left(-\frac{7}{8}\right)$

28. $\frac{3}{4} \div \frac{8}{9}$ 29. $\frac{3}{4} \div \frac{1}{2}$ 30. $\frac{2t}{5} \div \frac{2}{5}$ 31. $\frac{1}{x} \div \frac{3}{x}$

32. $\frac{2}{5} \div \frac{15}{16}$ 33. $-\frac{6n}{7} \div \frac{n}{3}$ 34. $\frac{2}{9} \div \frac{w}{3}$ 35. $\frac{3}{8} \div \frac{6}{32}$

Ⓑ **Apply Your Skills**

Find each product or quotient. Simplify if possible.

36. $\frac{6x}{7} \cdot \frac{1}{3}$ 37. $-\frac{2}{3} \cdot \frac{9}{10}$ 38. $\frac{8}{9} \cdot \frac{15}{28}$ 39. $-1\frac{1}{4} \cdot 6\frac{2}{3}$

40. $-\frac{1}{2} \div \frac{2}{3}$ 41. $\frac{10}{13} \div \frac{15}{26}$ 42. $6\frac{3}{4} \div \frac{9}{10}$ 43. $1\frac{4}{5} \div \left(-1\frac{1}{2}\right)$

44. **Number Sense** One granola bar weighs $1\frac{1}{2}$ oz. What is the weight of six granola bars?

Simplify each expression.

45. $\dfrac{\frac{2}{3} - \frac{1}{3}}{\frac{3}{4}}$ 46. $\frac{5}{6} \cdot \left(\frac{1}{4} + \frac{5}{12}\right)$ 47. $\dfrac{\frac{3}{4} + \frac{5}{6}}{\frac{3}{5} \cdot \frac{4}{5}}$

Mental Math Simplify each expression.

48. $\frac{1}{2} \cdot \frac{2}{5}$ **49.** $\frac{1}{2} \div \frac{2}{5}$ **50.** $10 \cdot \frac{1}{4}$ **51.** $10 \div \frac{1}{4}$

52. $\frac{5}{8} \cdot \frac{3}{5}$ **53.** $\frac{5}{8} \div \frac{3}{5}$ **54.** $\frac{3}{7} \cdot \frac{12}{21}$ **55.** $\frac{3}{7} \div \frac{12}{21}$

56. Multiple Choice A cable television crew has to install cable along a road $1\frac{1}{2}$ mi long. The crew takes a day to install each $\frac{1}{4}$ mi of cable. How many days will the installation take?

 Ⓐ 6 days Ⓑ $1\frac{3}{4}$ days Ⓒ $\frac{3}{4}$ day Ⓓ $\frac{3}{8}$ day

Visit: PHSchool.com
Web Code: bje-0504

57. a. Write an expression for the following: The product of $\frac{1}{2}a$ and 3 is decreased by the quotient $a \div (-4)$.
 b. Evaluate your expression for $a = 3$.

58. A cheetah can run as fast as 64 mi/h. At that speed, how far could a cheetah run in $\frac{1}{16}$ h? $\frac{1}{30}$ h?

59. You are hiking along a trail that is $13\frac{1}{2}$ mi long. You plan to rest every $2\frac{1}{4}$ mi. How many rest stops will you make?

60. Writing in Math Why must you change mixed numbers to improper fractions before multiplying or dividing them?

61. a. Patterns Find each quotient: $\frac{1}{2} \div 2$, $\frac{1}{2} \div 3$, $\frac{1}{2} \div 4$, and $\frac{1}{2} \div 5$.
 b. Explain what happens to the quotients as the divisors increase in value.

62. Reasoning Write a multiplication equation and a division equation that you could use to show the result of cutting four melons into eight equal slices each.

Ⓒ **Challenge**

63. Open-Ended Find two fractions greater than $\frac{1}{2}$ with a product less than $\frac{1}{2}$.

Multiple Choice Practice and Mixed Review

For Standards Tutorials, visit PHSchool.com. Web Code: bjq-9045

64. A soup recipe calls for $\frac{3}{4}$ cup of beans. Matt wants to triple the recipe. How many cups of beans are needed?

 Ⓐ $\frac{9}{12}$ cup Ⓑ $2\frac{1}{4}$ cups Ⓒ $2\frac{1}{2}$ cups Ⓓ $3\frac{3}{4}$ cups

65. Which number is the greatest?

 Ⓐ 6.03×10^3 Ⓒ 6.3×10^3
 Ⓑ 6.003×10^2 Ⓓ 6.303×10^2

66. A battery needs to be replaced every 15 months. How many times will the battery need to be replaced in 10 years?

 Ⓐ 6 Ⓑ 7 Ⓒ 8 Ⓓ 9

 Lesson 5-3 **Add or subtract.**

67. $\frac{4}{5} + \frac{6}{7}$ **68.** $\frac{10}{13} - \frac{25}{26}$ **69.** $-\frac{3}{10} + \frac{3}{5}$ **70.** $\frac{16}{21} - \frac{5}{7}$

Using Customary Units of Measurement

What You'll Learn

- To identify appropriate customary units
- To convert customary units

. . . And Why

To solve real-world problems involving consumer issues

✓ Check Skills You'll Need

Find each product.

1. $4 \cdot \frac{1}{12}$ **2.** $3\frac{1}{4} \cdot \frac{16}{1}$

3. $1\frac{1}{4} \cdot \frac{8}{1}$ **4.** $4\frac{1}{2} \cdot \frac{1}{3}$

GO for Help
Lesson 5-4

🔊 New Vocabulary

- dimensional analysis

Develop Compare weights, capacities, and geometric measures within measurement systems.

Introduce, Develop Use measures expressed as rates to solve problems; and use dimensional analysis to check the reasonableness of the answer.

Identifying Appropriate Units of Measure

Most people in the United States use the *customary system* of measurement.

Customary Units of Measure

Type	Length	Capacity	Weight
Unit	inch (in.) foot (ft) yard (yd) mile (mi)	fluid ounce (fl oz) cup (c) pint (pt) quart (qt) gallon (gal)	ounce (oz) pound (lb) ton (t)
Equivalents	1 ft = 12 in. 1 yd = 3 ft 1 mi = 5,280 ft	1 c = 8 fl oz 1 pt = 2 c 1 qt = 2 pt 1 gal = 4 qt	1 lb = 16 oz 1 t = 2,000 lb

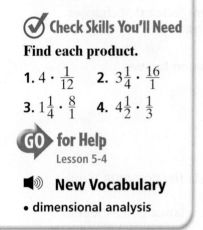

In order to measure an object, you should choose an appropriate unit of measure.

1 EXAMPLE Choosing a Unit of Measure

Choose an appropriate unit of measure. Explain your choice.

a. weight of a truck
Measure its weight in tons because a truck is very heavy.

b. length of a hallway rug
Measure its length in feet or yards because the length is too great to measure in inches.

✓ Quick Check

1. Choose an appropriate unit of measure. Explain.

a. length of a swimming pool **b.** weight of a baby
c. length of a pencil **d.** capacity of an eyedropper

Converting Customary Units

You use *conversion factors* to change from one unit of measure to another. You use equivalent units to write a conversion factor. For example, $\frac{12 \text{ in.}}{1 \text{ ft}} = 1$, so you can use $\frac{12 \text{ in.}}{1 \text{ ft}}$ to convert from feet to inches. **Dimensional analysis** is a method of manipulating units to determine the units of the result.

2 EXAMPLE   Using Conversion Factors

Convert 10 quarts to gallons.

$$10 \text{ qt} = \frac{10 \text{ qt}}{1} \cdot \frac{1 \text{ gal}}{4 \text{ qt}} \qquad \text{Use a conversion factor that changes quarts to gallons.}$$

$$= \frac{{}^5 10 \text{ qt} \cdot 1 \text{ gal}}{{}_2 4 \text{ qt}} \qquad \text{Divide the common factors.}$$

$$= \frac{5}{2} \text{ gal} = 2\frac{1}{2} \text{ gal} \quad \text{Simplify.}$$

There are $2\frac{1}{2}$ gal in 10 qt.

Check Use dimensional analysis to divide the common units.

Since $\frac{\text{qt} \cdot \text{gal}}{\text{qt}} = \text{gal}$, the units check. The answer is reasonable.

✔ Quick Check

2. Complete the equation 14 oz = ▪ lb.

Converting units can help you make comparisons.

3 EXAMPLE   Comparing Units

Store A

Store B

Store A and Store B each sell bags of cashew nuts as shown at the left for the same price. Which store gives you more cashews for your money?

$$4\frac{1}{4} \text{ lb} = \frac{17}{4} \text{ lb} \cdot \frac{16 \text{ oz}}{1 \text{ lb}} \qquad \text{Use a conversion factor that changes pounds to ounces.}$$

$$= \frac{17}{{}_1 4} \text{ lb} \cdot \frac{{}^4 16 \text{ oz}}{1 \text{ lb}} \qquad \text{Divide the common factors. Use dimensional analysis to check the units.}$$

$$= 68 \text{ oz} \qquad\qquad\qquad \text{Multiply.}$$

Since 76 oz > 68 oz, Store B gives you more for your money.

✔ Quick Check

3. Complete the equation $3\frac{1}{2}$ yd = ▪ ft.

Number Sense Match each measurement from the first group with an equivalent amount from the second group.

1. 15 mi   A. 30,000 lb

2. 15 t   B. $\frac{3}{400}$ t

3. 15 in.   C. $1\frac{1}{4}$ ft

4. 15 fl oz   D. $7\frac{1}{2}$ pt

5. 15 c   E. $7\frac{1}{2}$ qt

6. 15 lb   F. $1\frac{7}{8}$ c

7. 15 pt   G. 79,200 ft

Compare. Use >, <, or = to complete each statement.

8. 1 pt ▪ 1 qt   9. 2 t ▪ 2,200 lb   10. 36 in. ▪ 3 ft

Standards Practice

For more exercises, see *Extra Skills and Word Problem Practice.*

A Practice by Example

GO for Help

Example 1 (page 247)

Choose an appropriate unit of measure. Explain your choice.

11. weight of a paper clip   12. capacity of a baby bottle

13. distance to Australia   14. length of a sports field

Examples 2 and 3 (page 248)

Complete each equation.

15. 3 qt = ▪ gal   16. 3 gal = ▪ qt   17. 1,000 lb = ▪ t

18. $\frac{1}{2}$ yd = ▪ ft   19. $\frac{1}{2}$ mi = ▪ ft   20. $10\frac{1}{2}$ lb = ▪ oz

21. Julia clears $9\frac{1}{2}$ ft in the pole vault. Maya clears 112 in. Which vaulter clears the greater height?

B Apply Your Skills

Estimation Match each indicated measurement with a possible value.

22. height of a 7-year-old   A. 4 lb

23. weight of a bag of apples   B. 4 ft
                                  C. 4 c

24. width of your palm   D. 4 oz

25. amount of water in a vase   E. 4 in.

26. weight of a peach

27. You are hiking a 2-mi-long trail. You pass by a sign showing that you have hiked 1,000 ft. How many feet are left?

Is each item likely to be measured by *length, weight,* **or** *capacity*?

28. a hair ribbon   **29.** a package of meat

30. a bottle of juice   **31.** a bag of oranges

32. a zipper   **33.** the contents of an eyedropper

Choose an appropriate unit of measure. Explain your choice.

34. capacity of a cooking pot   **35.** weight of a medium-sized fish

36. weight of a sheet of paper   **37.** capacity of a swimming pool

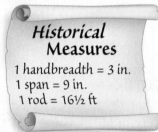

Historical
Measures
1 handbreadth = 3 in.
1 span = 9 in.
1 rod = 16½ ft

38. People once measured lengths in *handbreadths, spans,* and *rods.*
  a. How many are there: handbreadths in 1 span? Handbreadths in 1 rod? Spans in 1 rod?
  b. **Open-Ended** Measure the length of an object. Give the length in *handbreadths, spans,* and *rods.*
  c. **Writing in Math** Consider the measurements you made in part (b). Which unit of measure is the most appropriate for the item you chose? Explain.

39. a. Geography The Mississippi River is about 19,747,200 ft long. What is a better unit of measure? Find the length of the Mississippi using the better unit of measure.
  b. Choose a historical measure from Exercise 38. Find the length of the Mississippi in that unit.

Estimation Is each measurement reasonable? If not, give a reasonable measurement.

40. A textbook weighs 2 oz.   **41.** The street is 25 ft wide.

42. You drink about 10 gal of liquid per day.   **43.** A sewing needle is about 2 ft long.

44. Reasoning A student converted 8 cups to pints. His answer was 16 pints. Use dimensional analysis to determine whether the student's answer is reasonable.

Use estimation, mental math, or paper and pencil to complete each statement.

45. 28 in. = ■ ft   **46.** 5 c = ■ pt   **47.** 5 t = ■ lb

48. 2,640 ft = ■ mi   **49.** 3,000 lb = ■ t   **50.** 13 pt = ■ qt

51. Error Analysis Suzanne claims a quarter-pound hamburger is heavier than a 6-oz hamburger. Explain why she is incorrect.

Homework Video Tutor

Visit: PHSchool.com
Web Code: bje-0505

 Challenge

Complete each equation.

52. $2\frac{1}{4}$ yd = $6\frac{3}{4}$ ■   **53.** 6 qt = $1\frac{1}{2}$ ■   **54.** 100 lb = $\frac{1}{20}$ ■

Multiple Choice Practice and Mixed Review

For Standards Tutorials, visit PHSchool.com. Web Code: bjq-9045

55. Mandy bought 2 pounds of walnuts. She gave 12 ounces to a friend, used 5 ounces when she was baking, and ate 3 ounces. How many pounds of walnuts does she have left?

   Ⓐ 1.8 lb   Ⓑ 1.5 lb   Ⓒ 1 lb   Ⓓ 0.75 lb

56. Rachel runs a five-mile race. How many yards is the race?

   Ⓐ 26,400 yd   Ⓑ 15,840 yd   Ⓒ 8,800 yd   Ⓓ 15 yd

GO for Help   Lesson 5-4   **Multiply or divide.**

57. $\frac{9}{11} \div 2\frac{7}{11}$ **58.** $1\frac{5}{7} \cdot 1\frac{1}{2}$ **59.** $\frac{9}{10} \div \frac{3}{4}$ **60.** $2\frac{2}{5} \cdot 3\frac{2}{3}$

Mathematical Reasoning

Develop Use measures expressed as rates; and use dimensional analysis to check the reasonableness of the answer.

Using Dimensional Analysis

Dimensional analysis is a method of manipulating units in calculations to check the units of the result. Dimensional analysis is most helpful when you have several conversion factors.

EXAMPLE

Convert 30 mi/h to ft/s.

Use the conversion factors $\frac{5,280 \text{ ft}}{1 \text{ mi}}$, $\frac{1 \text{ h}}{60 \text{ min}}$, and $\frac{1 \text{ min}}{60 \text{ s}}$.

$$\frac{30 \text{ mi}}{1 \text{ h}} = \frac{30 \text{ mi}}{1 \text{ h}} \cdot \frac{5,280 \text{ ft}}{1 \text{ mi}} \cdot \frac{1 \text{ h}}{60 \text{ min}} \cdot \frac{1 \text{ min}}{60 \text{ s}}$$

$$= \frac{44 \text{ ft}}{1 \text{ s}} \qquad \text{Simplify.}$$

Use dimensional analysis to check the units of the answer. Divide common units just as you would divide numbers or variables.

$$\frac{\text{mi}}{\text{h}} \cdot \frac{\text{ft}}{\text{mi}} \cdot \frac{\text{h}}{\text{min}} \cdot \frac{\text{min}}{\text{s}} = \frac{\cancel{\text{mi}} \cdot \text{ft} \cdot \cancel{\text{h}} \cdot \cancel{\text{min}}}{\cancel{\text{h}} \cdot \cancel{\text{mi}} \cdot \cancel{\text{min}} \cdot \text{s}} \qquad \begin{array}{l}\text{Write the expression} \\ \text{using only units.}\end{array}$$

$$= \frac{\text{ft}}{\text{s}} \qquad \text{Simplify.}$$

The units of the result check, so the answer is reasonable.

EXERCISE

1. To convert 78 km/h to m/s, a student simplified the expression $\frac{78 \text{ km}}{1 \text{ h}} \cdot \frac{60 \text{ min}}{1 \text{ h}} \cdot \frac{60 \text{ s}}{1 \text{ min}} \cdot \frac{1 \text{ km}}{1,000 \text{ m}}$ and got 280.8 m/s. Is the answer reasonable? Explain.

Greatest Possible Error

Develop Compare measures within a measurement system.
Develop Give answers to a specified degree of accuracy.

Measurement is not exact. To the nearest centimeter, each segment below measures 3 cm.

When a measurement is rounded to the nearest centimeter, it can vary from the actual length by as much as one half centimeter. The *greatest possible error* of a measurement is half the unit used for measuring.

EXAMPLE

Find the greatest possible error for each measurement.

a. $1\frac{1}{2}$ **in.** The measurement is to the nearest $\frac{1}{2}$ in.

Since $\frac{1}{2} \cdot \frac{1}{2} = \frac{1}{4}$, the greatest possible error is $\frac{1}{4}$ in.

b. 15.6 L The measurement is to the nearest tenth of a liter.

Since $\frac{1}{2} \cdot 0.1 = 0.05$, the greatest possible error is 0.05 L.

c. 3.004 mm The measurement is to the nearest 0.001 mm.

Since $\frac{1}{2} \cdot 0.001 = 0.0005$, the greatest possible error is 0.0005 mm.

EXERCISES

Find the greatest possible error for each measurement.

1. 45.98 mg　　　　**2.** $12\frac{1}{4}$ in.　　　　**3.** 54.4 cm　　　　**4.** $1\frac{3}{4}$ c

5. 3 ft　　　　**6.** 9 g　　　　**7.** 12.3 L　　　　**8.** 15.575 mm

9. $24\frac{1}{2}$ yd　　　　**10.** 512 m　　　　**11.** $10\frac{1}{8}$ oz　　　　**12.** $3\frac{1}{16}$ in.

13. A carpenter is cutting a table leg that is $2\frac{1}{4}$ ft long.
　　a. What is the greatest possible error?
　　b. **Writing in Math**　Is the greatest possible error acceptable in this situation? Explain.

What unit should be used to make a measurement with the given greatest possible error?

14. $\frac{1}{16}$ in.　　　　**15.** $\frac{1}{4}$ c　　　　**16.** 5 mm　　　　**17.** 5 dg

5-6 Work Backward

Develop Use a variety of methods, such as numbers and models, to explain mathematical reasoning.

Work Backward

Math Strategies in Action The Longleat hedge maze in England was designed in 1975. The hedges are so high you can't see over them unless you stand on one of the wooden staircases placed throughout the maze. Once you find the center of the maze in its 1.7 miles of pathways, you have to remember the path you followed and work backward to get out.

Working backward from known information will sometimes help you solve a problem.

1 EXAMPLE   Working Backward

You are planning to go to a baseball game that starts at 1:00 P.M. You want to arrive half an hour early. Your walk to the train station is about 10 minutes long. The train ride to the city takes $\frac{3}{4}$ of an hour. After you arrive in the city, you will need to walk for about 10 more minutes to get to the stadium. What time should you plan to leave?

Understand **Understand the problem.**

Think about the information you are given.

1. What do you want to find?

2. What is your arrival time?

3. How much time will you spend walking to the train?

4. How much time will you spend on the train?

5. How much time will you spend walking from the train?

Plan Make a plan to solve the problem.

You know that the series of events must end at 1:00 P.M. Work backward to find when the events must begin.

Carry Out Carry out the plan.

Move the hands of a clock to find your departure time.

6. Write the starting time for each event.

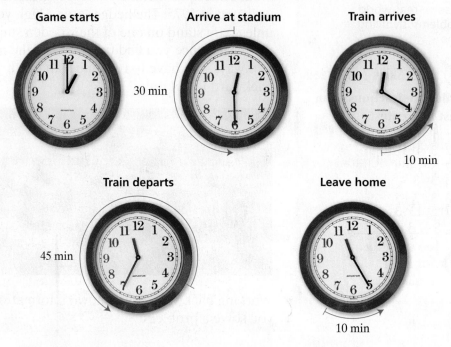

Game starts   Arrive at stadium   Train arrives

30 min   10 min

Train departs   Leave home

45 min   10 min

You should leave home at 11:25 A.M.

Check Check the answer to be sure it is reasonable.

Check whether the departure time is reasonable. Find the total time needed.

10 min + 45 min + 10 min + 30 min = 95 min

Add 95 minutes to your departure time.

$$\begin{array}{r} 11:\ 25 \\ +\ 0:\ 95 \\ \hline 11:120 \end{array}$$ **120 min = 2 h**

11:120 = 2 hours after 11:00, or 1:00 P.M.

Since the game starts at 1 P.M., your departure time is reasonable.

☑ Quick Check

7. Suppose you must be home by 6:00 P.M. If the return trip takes the same amount of time, how long can the game run in order for you to be at home on time?

For more exercises, see *Extra Skills and Word Problem Practice.*

 A Practice by Example

Example 1
(page 253)

STRATEGIES

- Act It Out
- Draw a Diagram
- Try, Test, Revise
- Look for a Pattern
- Make a Model
- Make a Table
- Simulate the Problem
- Solve by Graphing
- Use Multiple Strategies
- Work a Simpler Problem
- Work Backward
- Write an Equation
- Write a Proportion

Work backward to solve each problem.

1. Eduardo wants to finish mowing lawns at 3:00 P.M. on Saturday. It takes $1\frac{1}{2}$ h to mow the first lawn and twice as long to mow the lawn next door. The lawn across the street takes $1\frac{1}{2}$ h to mow. Eduardo plans to take a $\frac{1}{2}$-h break between the second and third lawns. What time should he plan to start mowing?

2. Siobhan's family is planning a trip to the Grand Canyon. It will take 5 h of driving along with three $\frac{1}{2}$-h stops. They want to arrive at 3:30 P.M. What time should they plan to leave?

3. Korin is going to a movie. The movie begins at 1:00 P.M. She has a 15-minute walk to the bus from her home and a 5-minute walk from the bus to the movie. The bus ride takes 38 min. What is the latest bus she can take to make the movie?

★ BUS DEPARTURE TIMES 🚌

10:10 A.M.	12:05 P.M.
10:30 A.M.	12:15 P.M.
11:00 A.M.	12:25 P.M.
11:35 A.M.	12:40 P.M.

B Apply Your Skills

Solve using any strategy.

4. **Number Sense** Use the equation at the right. Choose from the numbers 1, 2, 3, 5, and 6, and make four different true equations.
$$\frac{\blacksquare}{\blacksquare} + \frac{\blacksquare}{\blacksquare} = \frac{\blacksquare}{\blacksquare}$$

5. You have two nickels, three dimes, and a quarter. Using at least one of each coin, how many different amounts of money can you make? Explain.

6. **Geometry** Zach's rectangular garden measures 12 ft by 10 ft. He puts a stake in each corner and one every 2 ft along each side. How many stakes are there in all?

7. You spent half of your money at the amusement park and had $15 left. How much money did you have originally?

8. Describe the pattern of the numbers below. Then find the next three numbers in the pattern.
$\frac{2}{3}, 1\frac{5}{12}, 2\frac{1}{6}, 2\frac{11}{12}, \blacksquare, \blacksquare, \blacksquare, \ldots$

Homework Video Tutor

Visit: PHSchool.com
Web Code: bje-0506

 **for Help**

For a guide to reading and describing the pattern in Exercise 8, see page 257.

9. Several freshmen tried out for the school track team.

After Round 1, $\frac{1}{2}$ of the freshmen were eliminated.

After Round 2, $\frac{1}{3}$ of those remaining were eliminated.

After Round 3, $\frac{1}{4}$ of those remaining were eliminated.

After Round 4, $\frac{1}{5}$ of those remaining were eliminated.

After Round 5, $\frac{1}{6}$ of those remaining were eliminated.

The 10 freshmen who remained made it onto the track team. How many freshmen originally tried out?

 Challenge

10. Pump A can fill five identical tanks in 60 min. Pump B can fill three tanks that same size in 60 min.
   a. How long does it take pump A to fill one tank?
   b. How long does it take pump B to fill one tank?
   c. How long does it take pumps A and B together to fill one tank?

Multiple Choice Practice and Mixed Review

For Standards Tutorials, visit PHSchool.com. Web Code: bjq-9045

11. Abby wants to finish her homework before dinner at 7:00 P.M. Her math homework will take $\frac{3}{4}$ hour, her science homework will take $\frac{1}{2}$ hour, and her English homework will take 1 hour. What is the latest she can start her homework in order to be done by 7:00 P.M.?
   Ⓐ 4:30 P.M.   Ⓑ 4:45 P.M.   Ⓒ 5:00 P.M.   Ⓓ 5:15 P.M.

12. You spent $\frac{1}{2}$ of your money at the theater and $\frac{1}{4}$ at an arcade. You have $17.50 left. How much did you have originally?
   Ⓐ $70   Ⓑ $35   Ⓒ $17.50   Ⓓ $13.12

13. What is the next number in this pattern? $\frac{3}{4}, 1\frac{1}{2}, 2\frac{1}{4}, 3, \ldots$
   Ⓐ $3\frac{1}{4}$ Ⓑ $3\frac{1}{2}$ Ⓒ $3\frac{3}{4}$ Ⓓ 4

14. What are the coordinates of Point A of the triangle below?

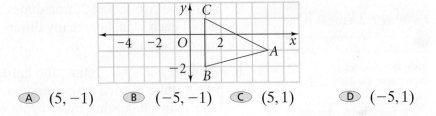

   Ⓐ $(5, -1)$ Ⓑ $(-5, -1)$ Ⓒ $(5, 1)$ Ⓓ $(-5, 1)$

 for Help Lessons 5-4 and 1-9

Simplify each expression.

15. $\frac{1}{3} \div \frac{5}{6}$ 16. $1\frac{2}{3} \div 1\frac{1}{9}$ 17. $-\frac{1}{6} \cdot (-12)$

18. $-8 \cdot 5$ 19. $2 \cdot 3 \cdot (-4) \cdot 5$ 20. $-100 \div (-10)$

Lesson 3-2   21. **Estimation** You want to buy three shirts for $15.95 each. Estimate the total cost of the shirts.

Develop Add and subtract rational numbers.
Develop Analyze problems by observing patterns.
Develop Make and test conjectures by using inductive reasoning.

Understanding Math Problems **Read the problem below. Then let Greg's thinking guide you through the solution. Check your understanding with the exercise at the bottom of the page.**

Describe the pattern of the numbers below. Then find the next three numbers in the pattern.

$\frac{2}{3}, 1\frac{5}{12}, 2\frac{1}{6}, 2\frac{11}{12}, \blacksquare, \blacksquare, \blacksquare, \ldots$

What Greg Thinks

I must find what kind of pattern this is so that I can describe it. I'll check the differences between terms.

The differences are the same, $\frac{3}{4}$. I can describe the pattern.

Now I have to find the next three numbers.

First I have to find $2\frac{11}{12} + \frac{3}{4}$.

Next, $3\frac{2}{3} + \frac{3}{4}$.

Finally, $4\frac{5}{12} + \frac{3}{4}$.

I'm done!

What Greg Writes

$1\frac{5}{12} - \frac{2}{3} = \frac{17}{12} - \frac{2}{3} = \frac{17}{12} - \frac{8}{12} = \frac{9}{12}$, or $\frac{3}{4}$

$2\frac{1}{6} - 1\frac{5}{12} = \frac{13}{6} - \frac{17}{12} = \frac{26}{12} - \frac{17}{12} = \frac{9}{12}$, or $\frac{3}{4}$

$2\frac{11}{12} - 2\frac{1}{6} = 2\frac{11}{12} - 2\frac{2}{12} = \frac{9}{12}$, or $\frac{3}{4}$

Start with $\frac{2}{3}$ and add $\frac{3}{4}$ repeatedly.

$2\frac{11}{12} + \frac{3}{4} = 2\frac{11}{12} + \frac{9}{12}$
$\qquad = 2\frac{20}{12} = 3\frac{8}{12} = 3\frac{2}{3}$

$3\frac{2}{3} + \frac{3}{4} = \frac{11}{3} + \frac{3}{4}$
$\qquad = \frac{44}{12} + \frac{9}{12} = \frac{53}{12} = 4\frac{5}{12}$

$4\frac{5}{12} + \frac{3}{4} = 4\frac{5}{12} + \frac{9}{12}$
$\qquad = 4\frac{14}{12} = 5\frac{2}{12} = 5\frac{1}{6}$

The next three numbers are $3\frac{2}{3}, 4\frac{5}{12}$, and $5\frac{1}{6}$.

EXERCISE

1. Describe the pattern of the numbers below.
   Then find the next three numbers in the pattern.

   $1\frac{3}{4}, 3, 4\frac{1}{4}, 5\frac{1}{2}, \blacksquare, \blacksquare, \blacksquare, \ldots$

Solving Equations by Adding or Subtracting Fractions

What You'll Learn

- To solve equations by subtracting fractions
- To solve equations by adding fractions

. . . And Why

To solve real-world problems involving recycling

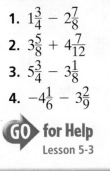

Check Skills You'll Need

Find each sum or difference.

1. $1\frac{3}{4} - 2\frac{7}{8}$

2. $3\frac{5}{8} + 4\frac{7}{12}$

3. $5\frac{3}{4} - 3\frac{1}{8}$

4. $-4\frac{1}{6} - 3\frac{2}{9}$

GO for Help

Lesson 5-3

Develop Add and subtract rational numbers (fractions).

Develop Convert fractions to decimals and use these representations in computations and applications.

Develop, Master Add and subtract fractions by using factoring to find common denominators.

Using Subtraction to Solve Equations

You solve equations with fractions the same way you solve equations with integers and decimals, by using inverse operations and the Properties of Equality.

1 EXAMPLE Subtracting a Fraction to Solve an Equation

In 2003, the average household in the United States recycled about $\frac{3}{10}$ of its solid waste. The Environmental Protection Agency (EPA) has set a goal of recycling about $\frac{1}{3}$ of solid waste. By how much would the average U.S. household need to increase its recycling to meet the EPA goal?

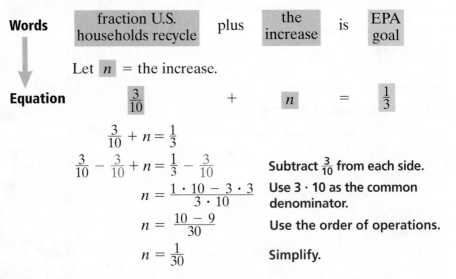

Words

| fraction U.S. households recycle | plus | the increase | is | EPA goal |

Let n = the increase.

Equation $\frac{3}{10}$ $+$ n $=$ $\frac{1}{3}$

$$\frac{3}{10} + n = \frac{1}{3}$$

$$\frac{3}{10} - \frac{3}{10} + n = \frac{1}{3} - \frac{3}{10} \qquad \text{Subtract } \frac{3}{10} \text{ from each side.}$$

$$n = \frac{1 \cdot 10 - 3 \cdot 3}{3 \cdot 10} \qquad \text{Use } 3 \cdot 10 \text{ as the common denominator.}$$

$$n = \frac{10 - 9}{30} \qquad \text{Use the order of operations.}$$

$$n = \frac{1}{30} \qquad \text{Simplify.}$$

To meet the EPA goal, the average U.S. household needs to recycle $\frac{1}{30}$ more of its waste.

Check Is the answer reasonable? The present fraction of solid waste that is recycled plus the increase must equal the goal. Since $\frac{3}{10} + \frac{1}{30} = \frac{9}{30} + \frac{1}{30} = \frac{10}{30} = \frac{1}{3}$, the answer is reasonable.

✓ Quick Check

1. Solve and check. $y + \frac{8}{9} = \frac{5}{9}$

You can use addition to solve an equation involving subtraction.

2 EXAMPLE **Adding a Fraction to Solve an Equation**

Solve $n - \frac{3}{4} = -\frac{5}{8}$.

$$n - \frac{3}{4} = -\frac{5}{8}$$

$$n - \frac{3}{4} + \frac{3}{4} = -\frac{5}{8} + \frac{3}{4}$$ Add $\frac{3}{4}$ to each side.

$$n = \frac{-5 + 3 \cdot 2}{2^3}$$ Use 2^3 as the common denominator.

$$n = \frac{-5 + 6}{8}$$ Use the order of operations.

$$n = \frac{1}{8}$$ Divide the common factors and simplify.

> **Quick Tip**
>
> For a guide to the order of operations, see page 179.

✓ **Quick Check**

2. Solve and check the equation $\frac{6}{7} = x - \frac{2}{7}$.

Sometimes you might find it helpful to convert a fraction or mixed number to a decimal.

3 EXAMPLE **Using a Mixed Number to Solve an Equation**

Henry cut $1\frac{3}{8}$ yards from a piece of wood. Afterward, it was $2\frac{1}{4}$ yards long. The equation $p - 1\frac{3}{8} = 2\frac{1}{4}$ models this situation. How long was the piece of wood before Henry cut it?

Method 1 (mixed numbers)

$$p - 1\frac{3}{8} = 2\frac{1}{4}$$
$$p - 1\frac{3}{8} + 1\frac{3}{8} = 2\frac{1}{4} + 1\frac{3}{8}$$
$$p = 2\frac{2}{8} + 1\frac{3}{8}$$
$$p = 3\frac{5}{8}$$

Method 2 (decimals)

$$p - 1\frac{3}{8} = 2\frac{1}{4}$$
$$p - 1.375 = 2.25$$
$$p - 1.375 + 1.375 = 2.25 + 1.375$$
$$p = 3.625$$

The piece of wood was $3\frac{5}{8}$ yards, or 3.625 yards, long.

✓ **Quick Check**

3. a. Solve $3\frac{7}{18} = z + 1\frac{1}{3}$.

b. Which method did you use to solve the equation in part (a)? Explain.

Copy and complete each step in the solution of the equation below.

$$x - \frac{3}{4} = \frac{1}{6}$$

1. $x - \frac{3}{4} + \frac{3}{4} = \frac{1}{6} + \frac{3}{4}$?

2. $x = \frac{1}{\blacksquare} + \frac{3}{2^2}$ Factor the denominators.

3. $x = \frac{1 \cdot 2}{2 \cdot 3 \cdot 2} + \frac{3 \cdot 3}{2^2 \cdot 3}$?

4. $x = \frac{2}{12} + \blacksquare$ Simplify.

5. $x = \blacksquare$ Add the numerators.

Standards Practice

For more exercises, see *Extra Skills and Word Problem Practice.*

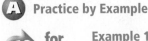 **A** Practice by Example

GO for Help Example 1 (page 258)

Solve and check each equation.

6. $b + \frac{4}{5} = \frac{9}{10}$ **7.** $g + \frac{9}{10} = \frac{7}{10}$ **8.** $m + \frac{3}{4} = \frac{1}{4}$

9. Jarrel's goal is to be half finished with the book he is reading by Friday. By Wednesday he has read $\frac{1}{3}$ of the book. How much more does he need to read to meet his goal?

Example 2 (page 259)

Solve and check each equation.

10. $a - \frac{1}{8} = \frac{5}{8}$ **11.** $t - \frac{2}{3} = \frac{4}{9}$ **12.** $c - \frac{9}{10} = \frac{1}{3}$

13. $\frac{1}{2} = n - \frac{5}{8}$ **14.** $a - \frac{5}{8} = \frac{7}{12}$ **15.** $3 = j - \frac{5}{8}$

Example 3 (page 259)

16. $x + 1\frac{1}{4} = 4\frac{3}{4}$ **17.** $5\frac{1}{4} = w + 2\frac{1}{2}$ **18.** $10\frac{1}{2} = x + 1\frac{1}{2}$

19. $z + 7\frac{5}{9} = 7\frac{5}{9}$ **20.** $c - 2\frac{1}{12} = 3\frac{1}{12}$ **21.** $y + 4\frac{7}{8} = 2$

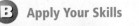 **B** Apply Your Skills

Number Sense **Without solving each equation, state whether** x **is** *positive, negative,* **or** *zero.* **Justify your response.**

22. $x + 2\frac{9}{11} = 2\frac{9}{11}$ **23.** $x + \frac{9}{10} = \frac{1}{2}$ **24.** $x + 4\frac{1}{5} = 5\frac{1}{2}$

25. A restaurant chef needs $8\frac{1}{2}$ lb of salmon. To get a good price, he buys more than he needs. He ends up with $4\frac{7}{8}$ lb too much. How much salmon did he buy?

26. A carpenter used $3\frac{3}{16}$ lb of nails for a job. After the job was over, the remaining nails weighed $1\frac{1}{16}$ lb. How many pounds of nails did the carpenter have at the beginning of the job?

The average weight of a Coho salmon is about $35\frac{1}{2}$ lb.

27. At the beginning of the school year, Jamie's height was $62\frac{1}{2}$ inches. During the school year she grew $1\frac{3}{4}$ inches, $\frac{1}{8}$ inch more than she grew the previous year.
    a. What was Jamie's height at the end of the school year?
    b. How tall was Jamie at the start of the previous school year?

Solve and check each equation.

28. $p - 3\frac{2}{3} = 1\frac{1}{3}$ 29. $1\frac{3}{8} = b + 2\frac{1}{6}$ 30. $y - 4\frac{7}{8} = \frac{3}{4}$

31. $x + \frac{2}{3} - \frac{1}{3} = 3\frac{1}{3}$ 32. $x - \frac{3}{4} + \frac{1}{6} = 1\frac{5}{12}$ 33. $x - 2\frac{2}{5} + 3\frac{1}{10} = \frac{3}{5}$

34. **Error Analysis** A student solved an equation as shown at the right. What is the student's error?

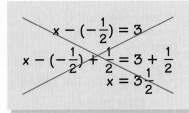

$x - (-\frac{1}{2}) = 3$
$x - (-\frac{1}{2}) + \frac{1}{2} = 3 + \frac{1}{2}$
$x = 3\frac{1}{2}$

C Challenge 35. **Writing in Math** Write a problem that you could solve with the equation $x + \frac{1}{2} = 7$. Solve your problem.

36. During a recent wet spell, the water level in Jasper's Pond rose $2\frac{3}{4}$ in. The depth of the pond was then 10 ft 3 in. What was the depth of the water in the pond before the wet spell?

Multiple Choice Practice and Mixed Review

For Standards Tutorials, visit PHSchool.com. Web Code: bjq-9045

37. Brent worked $7\frac{1}{2}$ hours on Monday, $6\frac{1}{4}$ hours on Tuesday, and $5\frac{2}{3}$ hours on Friday. How many total hours did he work?

    Ⓐ $19\frac{5}{12}$ h   Ⓑ $19\frac{1}{4}$ h   Ⓒ $18\frac{3}{4}$ h   Ⓓ $18\frac{5}{12}$ h

38. A tree is $10\frac{1}{2}$ feet tall. Which equation can be used to find the initial height of the tree t before it grew 8 inches in the last year?

    Ⓐ $t + \frac{8}{12} = 10\frac{1}{2}$ Ⓒ $t - \frac{8}{12} = 10\frac{1}{2}$

    Ⓑ $t + 10\frac{1}{2} = \frac{8}{12}$ Ⓓ $t - 10\frac{1}{2} = \frac{8}{12}$

39. Which expression can be used to express the perimeter p, in inches, of the rectangular figure below?

    Ⓐ $p = 18 \cdot 12$

    Ⓑ $p = 18 \cdot \frac{1}{12}$

    Ⓒ $p = 36 \cdot \frac{1}{12}$

    Ⓓ $p = 36 \cdot 12$

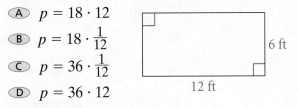

6 ft

12 ft

GO for Help Lesson 5-5

Complete each statement.

40. $2\frac{2}{3}$ ft = 32 ▓   41. $1\frac{1}{2}$ ▓ = 12 fl oz   42. 9 pt = $4\frac{1}{2}$ ▓

43. $\frac{1}{2}$ ▓ = $\frac{1}{4}$ qt   44. 750 lb = $\frac{3}{8}$ ▓   45. $1\frac{2}{3}$ ▓ = 5 ft

Solving Equations by Multiplying Fractions

What You'll Learn

- To solve equations by multiplying fractions
- To solve equations by multiplying mixed numbers

... And Why

To solve real-world problems involving carpentry

☑ **Check Skills You'll Need**

Find each product.

1. $\frac{4}{7} \cdot \frac{5}{8}$
2. $\frac{9}{10} \cdot \left(-\frac{5}{3}\right)$
3. $-1\frac{1}{4} \cdot \left(-\frac{5}{1}\right)$
4. $4\frac{1}{2} \cdot \frac{2}{3}$

GO for Help
Lesson 5-4

Develop Multiply rational numbers (fractions).

Develop Simplify numerical expressions by applying properties of rational numbers (e.g., inverse) and justify the process used.

Using Multiplication to Solve Equations

You know how to undo multiplication by dividing each side of an equation by the same number. You can also multiply each side of an equation by the same fraction to undo multiplication.

1 EXAMPLE Multiplying by a Reciprocal

Solve $5a = \frac{1}{7}$.

$$5a = \frac{1}{7}$$

$\frac{1}{5} \cdot (5a) = \frac{1}{5} \cdot \frac{1}{7}$ **Multiply each side by $\frac{1}{5}$, the reciprocal of 5.**

$1a = \frac{1}{35}$ **Inverse Property of Multiplication**

$a = \frac{1}{35}$ **Identity Property of Multiplication**

☑ **Quick Check**

1. Solve $2y = \frac{7}{9}$.

When a numerator and a denominator have common factors, you can divide the common factors to help you multiply.

Quick Tip

To review reciprocals, see page 244.

2 EXAMPLE Simplifying Before Multiplying

Solve $\frac{4}{5}m = \frac{9}{10}$.

$$\frac{4}{5}m = \frac{9}{10}$$

$\frac{5}{4} \cdot \frac{4}{5}m = \frac{5}{4} \cdot \frac{9}{10}$ **Multiply each side by $\frac{5}{4}$, the reciprocal of $\frac{4}{5}$.**

$m = \frac{\overset{1}{5}}{4} \cdot \frac{9}{\underset{2}{10}}$ **Divide common factors.**

$m = \frac{9}{8}$ **Simplify.**

$m = 1\frac{1}{8}$ **Write as a mixed number.**

☑ **Quick Check**

2. Solve $\frac{5}{4} = \frac{5}{4}d$.

3 EXAMPLE **Multiplying by the Negative Reciprocal**

Solve $-\frac{14}{25}k = \frac{8}{15}$.

$$-\frac{14}{25}k = \frac{8}{15}$$

$$-\frac{25}{14}\left(-\frac{14}{25}k\right) = -\frac{25}{14}\left(\frac{8}{15}\right) \quad$$ Multiply each side by $-\frac{25}{14}$, the reciprocal of $-\frac{14}{25}$.

$$k = -\frac{\overset{5}{2}5 \cdot \overset{4}{8}}{\underset{7}{1}4 \cdot 1\underset{3}{5}} = -\frac{20}{21} \quad$$ Divide common factors and simplify.

Video Tutor Help
Visit: PHSchool.com
Web Code: bje-0775

✓ **Quick Check**

3. Solve each equation.

a. $-\frac{6}{7}r = \frac{3}{4}$ b. $-\frac{10}{13}b = -\frac{2}{3}$ c. $-6n = \frac{3}{7}$

Solving Equations With Mixed Numbers

Change mixed numbers to improper fractions before multiplying.

4 EXAMPLE **Solving an Equation With Mixed Numbers**

Multiple Choice Your teacher needs a shelf to hold a set of textbooks each $1\frac{5}{8}$ in. wide. How many books will fit on a 26-in.-long shelf?

Ⓐ 13 books   Ⓑ 16 books   Ⓒ 40 books   Ⓓ 42 books

Words	width of each book	times	the number of books	is	width of bookshelf

Let n = the number of books.

Equation	$1\frac{5}{8}$	·	n	=	26

$$1\frac{5}{8} \cdot n = 26$$

$$\frac{13}{8}n = 26 \quad$$ Write $1\frac{5}{8}$ as $\frac{13}{8}$.

$$\frac{8}{13} \cdot \frac{13}{8}n = \frac{8}{13} \cdot 26 \quad$$ Multiply each side by $\frac{8}{13}$, the reciprocal of $\frac{13}{8}$.

$$n = \frac{8 \cdot \overset{2}{26}}{\underset{1}{1}3 \cdot 1} = 16 \quad$$ Divide common factors and simplify.

Your teacher can fit 16 books on the shelf. The answer is B.

Quick Tip

Remember to ask yourself whether your answer is reasonable. If your answer to "How many books?" is $2\frac{1}{2}$, make sure you round down to "2 books."

✓ **Quick Check**

4. Solve each equation.

a. $3\frac{1}{2}n = 28$ b. $-\frac{7}{20} = 1\frac{1}{6}r$ c. $-2\frac{3}{4}h = -12\frac{1}{2}$

1. **Error Analysis** A student solved an equation as shown at the right. Find the student's error. What is the correct solution?

$$-\frac{7}{10}h = 5\frac{3}{5}$$

$$\frac{10}{7} \cdot \left(-\frac{7}{10}h\right) = \frac{10}{7} \cdot 5\frac{3}{5}$$

$$h = \frac{\overset{2}{\cancel{10}}}{\cancel{7}_1} \cdot \frac{\overset{4}{\cancel{28}}}{\cancel{5}_1}$$

$$h = 8$$

Number Sense Without solving each equation, state whether x is *positive*, *negative*, or *zero*.

2. $17x = -\frac{11}{30}$ 3. $\frac{1}{57}x = 2$

4. $\frac{4}{13}x = 0$ 5. $-6\frac{1}{2}x = 0$

For more exercises, see *Extra Skills and Word Problem Practice*.

A Practice by Example

Examples 1–3
(pages 262 and 263)

GO for Help

Solve each equation.

6. $6p = \frac{5}{8}$ 7. $5x = \frac{2}{3}$ 8. $2k = \frac{5}{6}$ 9. $7z = \frac{3}{8}$

10. $2y = \frac{1}{3}$ 11. $3b = \frac{4}{7}$ 12. $7c = \frac{3}{4}$ 13. $9y = \frac{5}{7}$

14. $\frac{2}{3}d = \frac{5}{8}$ 15. $\frac{5}{8} = \frac{5}{8}k$ 16. $\frac{5}{9} = \frac{1}{8}h$ 17. $\frac{1}{7}x = \frac{4}{7}$

18. $\frac{3}{4}d = \frac{3}{8}$ 19. $\frac{10}{27} = \frac{5}{9}t$ 20. $\frac{2}{7}a = \frac{5}{8}$ 21. $\frac{1}{9}p = \frac{5}{6}$

22. $-\frac{2}{3}t = -2$ 23. $-5s = \frac{5}{7}$ 24. $\frac{8}{9} = -6d$ 25. $\frac{2}{3}x = -8$

Example 4
(page 263)

26. A sheet of plywood is $\frac{3}{4}$ in. thick. Write and solve an equation to find how many sheets of plywood are in a stack 9 in. high.

Solve each equation.

27. $3 = 1\frac{1}{2}b$ 28. $2\frac{1}{2}x = \frac{2}{5}$ 29. $2\frac{1}{3}m = \frac{7}{12}$ 30. $-1\frac{6}{7}g = -\frac{13}{15}$

31. $\frac{1}{15} = -1\frac{1}{10}t$ 32. $2\frac{1}{8}k = 7$ 33. $1\frac{1}{2}n = 3\frac{4}{9}$ 34. $-9\frac{1}{3} = -1\frac{1}{4}t$

B Apply Your Skills

35. Tomás calculates that he will need 86 hours to build a boat. He can work on the boat $8\frac{3}{5}$ hours per week. How many weeks will it take Tomás to build the boat?

36. A small airplane coming in for a landing descends $\frac{5}{66}$ mi/min. About how long does it take to descend 4,000 ft? (*Hint:* 1 mi = 5,280 ft)

37. **Astronomy** The Chandra satellite telescope views X-rays in space. It orbits as much as 87,000 miles above Earth. This is about $\frac{1}{3}$ of the distance to the moon. About how far away is the moon?

Homework Video Tutor

Visit: PHSchool.com
Web Code: bje-0508

Solve each equation.

38. $-\frac{5}{7}x = \frac{9}{10}$ **39.** $\frac{9}{13} = -\frac{6}{11}s$ **40.** $-3b = \frac{2}{3}$

41. $-\frac{12}{13} = -\frac{1}{4}w$ **42.** $3\frac{1}{9}a = \frac{3}{7}$ **43.** $2\frac{3}{4} = -6\frac{3}{5}y$

44. $1\frac{1}{2}m = 1\frac{3}{4}$ **45.** $3\frac{3}{5}p = -4\frac{4}{9}$ **46.** $\frac{1}{8}d = \frac{1}{4}$

47. $\frac{1}{3}y = 2$ **48.** $\frac{3}{7}x = 1$ **49.** $\frac{7}{8}z = 3\frac{1}{2}$

Kudzu

50. Biology In ideal conditions, the kudzu plant can grow at least $1\frac{3}{20}$ ft per week. At this rate, how many weeks would it take a kudzu plant to grow 23 ft?

51. Writing in Math Describe how you would solve and check the equation $\frac{2}{3}x = 3$.

52. Reasoning By what would you multiply each side of the equation $ax = 27$ to solve for x? By what would you multiply each side of the equation $\frac{1}{a}x = 27$ to solve for x?

53. Rates A sailfish can swim about $11\frac{1}{3}$ mi in 10 min. About how many miles can a sailfish swim per minute? At that speed, about how many feet does a sailfish swim in one second?

54. Critical Thinking One student says, "You solve the equation $\frac{1}{b} = \frac{1}{15}$ by multiplying each side by b." Another student replies, "No, you solve the equation by dividing each side by $\frac{1}{b}$." Who is correct? Justify your answer.

C Challenge   **Solve each equation.**

55. $-\frac{3}{4}x + \frac{1}{4}x = -6$ **56.** $\frac{5}{8}x - 6\frac{3}{8}x = 1\frac{1}{2}$ **57.** $\frac{-5}{-7}x + \left(-\frac{1}{5}x\right) = -\frac{3}{5}$

Multiple Choice Practice and Mixed Review

For Standards Tutorials, visit PHSchool.com. Web Code: bjq-9045

58. The copy of a photo is $6\frac{1}{2}$ inches long. This is $\frac{3}{4}$ of the length of the original photo. Which equation can be used to determine ℓ, the length of the original photo?

   Ⓐ $6\frac{1}{2}\ell = \frac{3}{4}$ Ⓑ $6\frac{1}{2} = \frac{3}{4}\ell$ Ⓒ $6\frac{1}{2} + \ell = \frac{3}{4}$ Ⓓ $6\frac{1}{2} - \ell = \frac{3}{4}$

59. The Jones family uses an average of 1 quart of milk each day. At this rate, how many days will it take the family to use $5\frac{1}{2}$ gallons of milk?

   Ⓐ $19\frac{1}{2}$ Ⓑ 20   Ⓒ $21\frac{1}{2}$ Ⓓ 22

60. A single copy of a book is $2\frac{3}{4}$ in. thick. A shipping box will hold a stack of books up to $16\frac{3}{4}$ in. tall. How many copies of the book can you stack in the box?

   Ⓐ 6   Ⓑ 8   Ⓒ 32   Ⓓ 45

Lesson 5-7   **Solve each equation.**

61. $j + \frac{3}{4} = \frac{7}{8}$ **62.** $\frac{4}{5} = y - \frac{3}{5}$ **63.** $6\frac{1}{2} = m + 2\frac{7}{8}$

Lesson 5-3   **64.** One bag of popcorn holds $1\frac{5}{8}$ oz. Another holds $1\frac{3}{4}$ oz.
     a. Which bag holds more popcorn?
     b. How much more?
     c. How much popcorn can the two bags hold in all?

Lessons 4-7 and 4-8   **Simplify each expression.**

65. $3r \cdot r^4$ **66.** $\frac{6x^3}{2x}$ **67.** $10s^2 \cdot 10s^3$

68. $\frac{20a^5}{4a^2}$ **69.** $x^3 \cdot x^{10}$ **70.** $q^5 \cdot 3q$

✓ Checkpoint Quiz 2

Multiply or divide.

1. $\frac{2}{3}(21)$ **2.** $\frac{4}{5} \cdot \frac{5}{8}$ **3.** $-\frac{4}{9}\left(\frac{1}{3}\right)$

4. $\frac{2}{5} \div \frac{3}{10}$ **5.** $-\frac{3}{4} \div \frac{3}{8}$ **6.** $8\frac{1}{2} \div \frac{1}{4}$

Complete each statement.

7. ■ t = 4,500 lb   **8.** $2\frac{1}{2}$ yd = ■ in.

9. 24 oz = ■ lb   **10.** ■ mi = 1,760 ft

Solve each equation.

11. $y + \frac{2}{5} = \frac{3}{5}$ **12.** $t - \frac{3}{4} = \frac{7}{8}$ **13.** $x - 4\frac{1}{2} = 6\frac{3}{4}$

14. $4t = \frac{24}{35}$ **15.** $\frac{5}{7}y = \frac{1}{3}$ **16.** $5\frac{1}{3} + v = -12$

17. $-\frac{8}{9}g = \frac{3}{5}$ **18.** $\frac{9}{10} = \frac{1}{4}w$ **19.** $1\frac{1}{2}d = \frac{5}{22}$

20. A jetliner is cruising at an altitude of 31,680 ft. What is the altitude in miles?

21. A car is travelling $\frac{11}{12}$ miles per minute. What is the speed of the car in miles per hour?

22. You spend $\frac{1}{3}$ of your money on lunch. Your friend then pays back a loan of $2.50. Later, you spend $4 on a movie ticket and $1.25 for a snack. You have $5.25 left. How much money did you have before lunch?

23. Open-Ended Describe an object you might measure using the customary system of measurement. Choose a unit of measure and estimate the measurement of the object using that unit.

Choosing Fractions or Decimals to Solve a Problem

> *Develop* Convert fractions to decimals and use these representations in computations and applications.
> *Develop* Apply strategies and results from simpler problems to more complex problems.

When you solve real-world problems involving fractions or decimals, you can choose to use either fractions or decimals to find the solution. The example below shows two methods to solve the same problem. Consider which method you would use.

EXAMPLE

A football stadium has 110 seating sections. Of these, 0.3 of the sections are lower-level seating close to the field, and $\frac{2}{5}$ are mid-level seating. The rest of the sections are upper-level seating. Find the number of upper-level sections.

Method 1 Using a fraction

Find the portion of seating sections that are lower and mid level.

$0.3 = \frac{3}{10}$ **Write the decimal as a fraction.**

$\frac{3}{10} + \frac{2}{5} = \frac{3}{10} + \frac{4}{10}$ **Use a common denominator.**

$= \frac{7}{10}$ **Simplify.**

Find the number of seating sections in the lower and mid levels.

$\frac{7}{10} \cdot 110 = 77$

Method 2 Using a decimal

$\frac{2}{5} = 0.4$ **Write the fraction as a decimal.**

$0.3 + 0.4$

0.7

$0.7 \cdot 110 = 77$

Find the number of seating sections in the upper level.
Since $110 - 77 = 33$, there are 33 upper-level sections.

EXERCISES

1. **Reasoning** Which method would you use in the Example above? Explain.

2. A garden has 200 square feet. You use $\frac{1}{5}$ of the garden for corn, 0.6 of the garden for tomatoes, and the rest for lettuce and herbs. How many square feet do you use for lettuce and herbs?

3. A husband, a wife, and their two children use about 300 gallons of water daily. The husband uses 0.15 of the water and the wife uses $\frac{1}{4}$ of the water. How many gallons do the children use?

Develop Add, subtract, multiply, and divide rational numbers and take positive rational numbers to whole-number powers.
Develop Apply strategies and results from simpler problems to more complex problems.

Some problems ask you to perform operations with multiple operations or with different forms of rational numbers. Although these problems may look difficult, you can use the order of operations to break the problems into smaller problems. By applying what you already know about operations with rational numbers, you can reason through more complex problems.

1 EXAMPLE

Simplify $\dfrac{\frac{1}{3}}{\frac{4}{5}} - \dfrac{\left(\frac{1}{2}\right)^{-3}}{1\frac{1}{2}}$.

The problem involves fractions, division, subtraction, and exponents. Break the problem into several smaller problems.

Step 1 Using the order of operations, simplify the exponent first.

$\left(\dfrac{1}{2}\right)^{-3} = \dfrac{1}{\frac{1}{2} \cdot \frac{1}{2} \cdot \frac{1}{2}}$ **Write the exponent as repeated division.**

$= \dfrac{1}{\frac{1}{8}}$ **Simplify.**

$= 1 \div \dfrac{1}{8}$ **Rewrite the fraction as a division expression.**

$= 1 \cdot 8 = 8$ **Multiply by the reciprocal.**

Step 2 Next, simplify the first division expression.

$\dfrac{\frac{1}{3}}{\frac{4}{5}} = \dfrac{1}{3} \div \dfrac{4}{5}$ **Rewrite the fraction as a division expression.**

$= \dfrac{1}{3} \cdot \dfrac{5}{4}$ **Multiply by the reciprocal.**

$= \dfrac{5}{12}$ **Simplify.**

Step 3 Use the simplified exponent from Step 1 to simplify the second division expression.

$\dfrac{\left(\frac{1}{2}\right)^{-3}}{1\frac{1}{2}} = \dfrac{8}{1\frac{1}{2}}$ **Substitute the simplified exponent.**

$= 8 \div 1\dfrac{1}{2}$ **Rewrite the fraction as a division expression.**

$= 8 \div \dfrac{3}{2}$ **Write the mixed number as a fraction.**

$= 8 \cdot \dfrac{2}{3}$ **Multiply by the reciprocal.**

$= \dfrac{16}{3}$ **Simplify.**

Step 4 Use your results from Steps 2 and 3 to write a simpler problem.

$$\frac{\frac{1}{3}}{\frac{4}{5}} - \frac{\left(\frac{1}{2}\right)^{-3}}{1\frac{1}{2}} = \frac{5}{12} - \frac{16}{3}$$ Substitute the simplified division expressions.

$$= \frac{5}{12} - \frac{64}{12}$$ Use the LCD, 12.

$$= -\frac{59}{12} = -4\frac{11}{12}$$ Simplify. Write the fraction as a mixed number.

When a computation involves several forms of rational numbers, choose the forms at each step that make the calculations simplest.

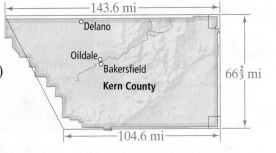

2 EXAMPLE

Kern County in California is approximately trapezoidal in shape. Use the formula $A = \frac{1}{2}h(b_1 + b_2)$ to find the approximate area of Kern.

To find the area, you need to simplify the expression $\frac{1}{2} \cdot 66\frac{2}{3}(143.6 + 104.6)$.

$$\frac{1}{2} \cdot 66\frac{2}{3}(143.6 + 104.6) = \frac{1}{2} \cdot 66\frac{2}{3}(248.2)$$ Add in parentheses. Both numbers are already decimals, so do not change their forms.

$$= \frac{1}{2} \cdot \frac{100}{3} \cdot \frac{2,482}{10}$$ Write all the numbers in the same form. In this case, multiplying fractions is simpler than decimals.

$$= \frac{1 \cdot 100 \cdot 2,482}{2 \cdot 3 \cdot 10}$$ Multiply.

$$= \frac{248,200}{60}$$ Simplify.

$$= \frac{12,410}{3} = 4,136\frac{2}{3}$$ Simplify. Write the fraction as a mixed number.

The area is about $4,136\frac{2}{3}$ square miles, or $4,136.\overline{6}$ square miles.

EXERCISES

Simplify each expression.

1. $\left(\frac{2}{3}\right)^{-2} + \frac{\frac{3}{5}}{\frac{6}{7}}$

2. $\frac{2}{3}\left(\frac{1.5 + \frac{1}{5}}{2}\right)$

3. $2.4\left(\frac{1}{2}\right) + \frac{1}{5}(0.2)^{-2}$

Powers of Products and Quotients

What You'll Learn

- To find powers of products
- To find powers of quotients

. . . And Why

To solve real-world problems involving area

✓ **Check Skills You'll Need**

Simplify each expression.

1. $(2^2)^3$ **2.** $(3^2)^2$ **3.** $(1^5)^4$

4. $(x^3)^6$ **5.** $(b^2)^5$ **6.** $(a^7)^4$

GO for Help
Lesson 4-7

Develop Take positive rational numbers to whole-number powers.

Master Multiply, divide, and simplify rational numbers by using exponent rules.

Master Interpret negative whole-number powers as repeated multiplication by the multiplicative inverse. Simplify expressions that include exponents.

Develop Multiply monomials; extend the process of taking powers to monomials.

Finding Powers of Products

You can use the Commutative and Associative Properties of Multiplication to find a pattern in products raised to a power.

$$(4 \cdot 2)^3 = (4 \cdot 2) \cdot (4 \cdot 2) \cdot (4 \cdot 2) \quad \text{Write the factors.}$$
$$= 4 \cdot 4 \cdot 4 \cdot 2 \cdot 2 \cdot 2 \quad \text{Commutative Property}$$
$$= (4 \cdot 4 \cdot 4) \cdot (2 \cdot 2 \cdot 2) \quad \text{Associative Property}$$
$$= 4^3 \cdot 2^3 \quad \text{Write the powers.}$$

This result suggests a rule for simplifying products raised to a power.

Take Note / **Rule for Raising a Product to a Power**

To raise a product to a power, raise each factor to the power.

Arithmetic	**Algebra**
$(5 \cdot 3)^4 = 5^4 \cdot 3^4$	$(ab)^m = a^m b^m$,
	for any positive integer m

To simplify an expression, you should eliminate as many parentheses as possible.

1 **EXAMPLE** **Simplifying a Power of a Product**

Simplify $(4x^2)^3$.

$$(4x^2)^3 = 4^3 \cdot (x^2)^3 \quad \text{Raise each factor to the third power.}$$
$$= 4^3 \cdot x^{2 \cdot 3} \quad \text{Use the Rule for Raising a Power to a Power.}$$
$$= 4^3 \cdot x^6 \quad \text{Multiply exponents.}$$
$$= 64x^6 \quad \text{Simplify.}$$

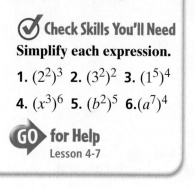

Quick Review

Rule for Raising a Power to a Power:
$(a^m)^n = a^{m \cdot n}$

✓ **Quick Check**

1. Simplify each expression.

a. $(2(3))^3$ **b.** $(2p)^4$ **c.** $(xy^2)^5$ **d.** $(5x^3)^2$

The location of a negative sign affects the value of an expression.

2 **EXAMPLE** **Working With a Negative Sign**

a. Simplify $(-5x)^2$.

$$(-5x)^2 = (-5)^2(x)^2$$
$$= 25x^2$$

b. Simplify $-(5x)^2$.

$$-(5x)^2 = (-1)(5x)^2$$
$$= (-1)(5)^2(x)^2$$
$$= -25x^2$$

✓ **Quick Check**

2. Simplify each expression. **a.** $(-2y)^4$ **b.** $-(2y)^4$

Finding Powers of Quotients

You can use repeated multiplication to write a power of a quotient.

Take Note ✏️ **Raising a Quotient to a Power**

To raise a quotient to a power, raise both the numerator and denominator to the power.

Arithmetic

$$\left(\frac{2}{3}\right)^3 = \left(\frac{2}{3}\right)\left(\frac{2}{3}\right)\left(\frac{2}{3}\right) = \frac{2^3}{3^3}$$

Algebra

$$\left(\frac{a}{b}\right)^m = \frac{a^m}{b^m}, \text{ for } b \neq 0$$
and any positive integer m

Vocabulary Tip

You read $\left(\frac{2}{3}\right)^4$ as "two thirds to the fourth power." You read $\frac{2}{3^4}$ as "two divided by three to the fourth power."

3 **EXAMPLE** **Raising a Quotient to a Power**

Geometry **Find the area of the square tile.**

$$A = s^2 \qquad s = \text{length of a side}$$
$$= \left(\frac{3}{b}\right)^2$$
$$= \frac{3^2}{b^2} = \frac{9}{b^2}$$

The area of the tile is $\frac{9}{b^2}$ square units.

✓ **Quick Check**

3. Simplify each expression. **a.** $\left(-\frac{2}{3}\right)^4$ **b.** $\left(\frac{2x^2}{3}\right)^3$

You have described negative exponents as repeated division. You can use the rule for raising a quotient to a power to describe negative exponents as repeated multiplication by the multiplicative inverse.

$$a^{-2} = \frac{1}{a^2} = \frac{1^2}{a^2} = \left(\frac{1}{a}\right)^2$$

Complete Exercises 1–4 to solve the problem below.

The side length of a square tablecloth is $5x^2$ cm. Will the tablecloth completely cover a square tabletop with area $20x^4$ cm?

1. Use exponents to write an expression for the area of the tablecloth.

2. Write an expression for the area of the tablecloth without using exponents. Simplify the expression.

3. Use exponent rules to simplify the expression you wrote in Exercise 1. Does the result match the result from Exercise 2?

4. Compare the coefficient for the area of the tablecloth to the coefficient for the area of the tabletop. Will the tablecloth cover the tabletop? Explain.

Standards Practice

For more exercises, see *Extra Skills and Word Problem Practice.*

A Practice by Example

Simplify each expression.

Example 1
(pages 270)

5. $(3(2))^2$ **6.** $(3j)^3$ **7.** $(rs^3)^4$ **8.** $(7t^2)^3$

9. $(4a^5)^2$ **10.** $(2c^2)^5$ **11.** $(2x^2)^3$ **12.** $(a^2b^4)^3$

13. $(2a^5)^3$ **14.** $(c^3)^2$ **15.** $(2b)^3$ **16.** $(ac^2)^2$

Example 2
(page 271)

17. $(-10x^3)^4$ **18.** $-(xy)^2$ **19.** $(-5b)^3$ **20.** $-(3x)^2$

21. $(-5c^3)^2$ **22.** $-(x^2y^2)^2$ **23.** $(-3a^4b)^3$ **24.** $-(m^2 \cdot n)^4$

Example 3
(page 271)

Simplify each expression.

25. $\left(\frac{2}{5}\right)^2$ **26.** $\left(-\frac{2}{5}\right)^3$ **27.** $\left(\frac{4}{7y}\right)^2$ **28.** $\left(\frac{3x^2}{10}\right)^4$ **29.** $\left(\frac{4}{9}\right)^2$

30. $\left(-\frac{3}{7}\right)^2$ **31.** $\left(-\frac{m}{b^3}\right)^6$ **32.** $\left(\frac{1}{3x^2}\right)^4$ **33.** $\left(-\frac{3}{4}\right)^3$ **34.** $\left(\frac{3t^2}{5}\right)^2$

B Apply Your Skills

Number Sense **Complete each equation.**

35. $(5 \cdot 2)^{\blacksquare} = 25 \cdot 4$ **36.** $(a^2)^{\blacksquare} = a^2$ **37.** $(4m)^{\blacksquare} = 256m^4$

38. $\left(-\frac{1}{2}\right)^{\blacksquare} = -\frac{1}{8}$ **39.** $\left(\frac{b^{\blacksquare}}{5}\right)^2 = \frac{b^{10}}{25}$ **40.** $\left(\frac{3}{7}\right)^{\blacksquare} = \frac{27}{343}$

Evaluate for $a = -1$, $b = 3$, and $c = \frac{1}{2}$.

41. $(-b^2)^2$ **42.** $\left(\frac{a}{b}\right)^3$ **43.** $(4c^2)^2$ **44.** $(a^2b)^2$

Homework Video Tutor

Visit: PHSchool.com
Web Code: bje-0509

45. Geometry Find the area of a square with side length $4c$ units.

46. A square table has sides that measure $3x^2$ ft. Write an expression for the area of the tabletop. Simplify your expression.

Geometry Use the formula $V = s^3$, where s is the length of a side, to find the volume of each cube.

47. **48.** **49.**

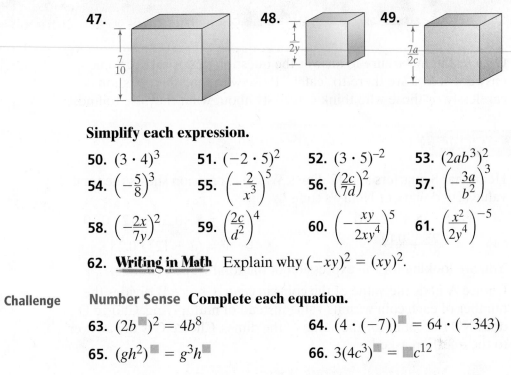

Simplify each expression.

50. $(3 \cdot 4)^3$ **51.** $(-2 \cdot 5)^2$ **52.** $(3 \cdot 5)^{-2}$ **53.** $(2ab^3)^2$

54. $\left(-\frac{5}{8}\right)^3$ **55.** $\left(-\frac{2}{x^3}\right)^5$ **56.** $\left(\frac{2c}{7d}\right)^2$ **57.** $\left(-\frac{3a}{b^2}\right)^3$

58. $\left(-\frac{2x}{7y}\right)^2$ **59.** $\left(\frac{2c}{d^2}\right)^4$ **60.** $\left(-\frac{xy}{2xy^4}\right)^5$ **61.** $\left(\frac{x^2}{2y^4}\right)^{-5}$

62. **Writing in Math** Explain why $(-xy)^2 = (xy)^2$.

C Challenge

Number Sense Complete each equation.

63. $(2b^{\blacksquare})^2 = 4b^8$ **64.** $(4 \cdot (-7))^{\blacksquare} = 64 \cdot (-343)$

65. $(gh^2)^{\blacksquare} = g^3 h^{\blacksquare}$ **66.** $3(4c^3)^{\blacksquare} = \blacksquare c^{12}$

Multiple Choice Practice and Mixed Review

For Standards Tutorials, visit PHSchool.com. Web Code: bjq-9045

67. Which of the following is equal to $(2)^{-5}$?

Ⓐ -32 Ⓑ $-\frac{1}{32}$ Ⓒ $\frac{1}{32}$ Ⓓ 32

68. Which expression does not simplify to a^{36}?

Ⓐ $(a^2)^{18}$ Ⓑ $(a^3)^6$ Ⓒ $(a^6)^6$ Ⓓ $(a^9)^4$

69. Simplify $(2x^3)^4$.

Ⓐ $8x^7$ Ⓑ $8x^{12}$ Ⓒ $16x^7$ Ⓓ $16x^{12}$

70. Gabrielle has 12 socks in her drawer. Of the socks, $\frac{1}{3}$ are white, $\frac{1}{2}$ are green, and the rest are black. She reaches in and grabs socks without looking. How many socks must she grab before she is certain she has two socks of the same color?

Ⓐ 3 Ⓑ 4 Ⓒ 6 Ⓓ 12

71. What is the first step in simplifying $\frac{1}{6} + \frac{3}{4}$ using the least common denominator?

Ⓐ $\left(\frac{1}{6} \cdot \frac{1}{2}\right) + \left(\frac{3}{4} \cdot \frac{1}{3}\right)$ Ⓒ $\left(\frac{1}{6} \cdot \frac{1}{4}\right) + \left(\frac{3}{4} \cdot \frac{1}{6}\right)$

Ⓑ $\left(\frac{1}{6} \cdot \frac{2}{2}\right) + \left(\frac{3}{4} \cdot \frac{3}{3}\right)$ Ⓓ $\left(\frac{1}{6} \cdot \frac{4}{4}\right) + \left(\frac{3}{4} \cdot \frac{6}{6}\right)$

GO for Help Lesson 5-8 **Solve each equation.**

72. $\frac{2}{7}h = \frac{7}{8}$ **73.** $7c = 1\frac{5}{9}$ **74.** $\frac{5}{8} = \frac{10}{12}x$ **75.** $10\frac{3}{4} = -5\frac{1}{2}y$

On a test item, be sure to answer the question that is asked. Some answer choices are there to "catch" those who read the question carelessly, or those who think carelessly about what they are to find.

1 EXAMPLE

Henry has 8 quarters and 12 dimes. Which expression shows the total value v, in dollars, of Henry's coins?

- **A** $v = 8 \cdot 25 + 12 \cdot 10$
- **B** $v = \frac{0.25}{8} + \frac{0.10}{12}$
- **C** $v = 8 \cdot 0.25 + 12 \cdot 0.10$
- **D** $v = (8 + 12) \cdot 0.25$

You are looking for the expression of the total value in *dollars*.

Choice A finds the value of the coins in *cents*. Choice B divides the number of each coin with its value instead of multiplying. Choice D does NOT account for the value of the dimes. Choice C is the answer to the question asked.

2 EXAMPLE

Stan needed 6 lb of potatoes for the school picnic. He bought potatoes in 3-lb bags for $1.89 per bag. Zorn bought 10 lb of potatoes to make potato salad for the picnic. He paid $2.59 per 5-lb bag. How much more did Zorn pay for potatoes than Stan?

- **A** $.70
- **B** $1.40
- **C** $5.18
- **D** $8.96

Choice A is how much more Zorn paid *per bag* of potatoes.

Choice C is how much Zorn paid for 10 lb of potatoes.

Choice D is how much Zorn and Stan paid in all for potatoes.

Choice B is the answer to the question asked.

Multiple Choice Practice

Read each question. Then write the letter of the correct answer on your paper.

1. Michelle buys a sweater originally priced at $39 that is $\frac{1}{3}$ off the original price. What is the sale price?
   - **A** $13
   - **B** $26
   - **C** $38.33
   - **D** $38.66

2. Dante, a landscaper, purchased three trees. The first was $38.99. A second was $54.99. His total bill before tax was $152.98. How much more did he pay for the third tree than for the second one?
   - **A** $93.98
   - **B** $59.00
   - **C** $16.00
   - **D** $4.01

Chapter 5 Review

Vocabulary Review

🔊 **English and Spanish Audio Online**

dimensional analysis (p. 248)
Inverse Property of Multiplication
   (p. 244)
least common denominator (LCD)
   (p. 228)

least common multiple (LCM)
   (p. 226)
multiple (p. 226)
multiplicative inverses (p. 244)

reciprocals (p. 244)
repeating decimal (p. 232)
terminating decimal (p. 231)

Match each word or phrase with its description.

1. For $\frac{5}{6}$ and $\frac{4}{9}$, this is equal to 18.

2. The pair of fractions $-\frac{13}{45}$ and $-\frac{45}{13}$ are these.

3. For 5, 6, and 12, this is equal to 60.

4. You can convert the fraction $\frac{1}{9}$ to one of these.

5. For 7, one of these is 35.

6. This allows you to check the units of a calculation.

7. You can convert the fraction $\frac{4}{5}$ to one of these.

a. least common multiple (LCM)

b. repeating decimal

c. reciprocals

d. dimensional analysis

e. terminating decimal

f. least common denominator (LCD)

g. multiple

Go Online
PHSchool.com

For: Vocabulary quiz
Web Code: bjj-0551

Skills and Concepts

Lesson 5-1

- To find the least common multiple
- To compare fractions

A **multiple** of a number is the product of that number and any nonzero whole number.

A *common multiple* of any group of numbers is a number that is a multiple of all the numbers. The common multiple with the least value is the **least common multiple (LCM)** of the numbers.

To compare fractions, use the LCM as the **least common denominator (LCD)** and write equivalent fractions.

Find the LCM of each group of numbers or expressions.

8. 12, 18   9. $8m^2, 14m$ 10. 3, 5, 7   11. $6x, 15y$

Compare. Use >, <, or = to complete each statement.

12. $\frac{5}{9} \blacksquare \frac{5}{11}$ 13. $\frac{2}{3} \blacksquare \frac{3}{4}$ 14. $-\frac{4}{5} \blacksquare -\frac{7}{8}$ 15. $\frac{1}{3} \blacksquare \frac{4}{12}$

Lesson 5-2

- To write rational numbers as decimals
- To write terminating and repeating decimals as fractions

To write a fraction as a decimal, divide the numerator by the denominator. If the division has a remainder of zero, the decimal is a **terminating decimal.** If the division produces a repeating block of digits, the decimal is a **repeating decimal.** The repeating part of the decimal is written with an overbar.

Reading a decimal correctly provides one way to write it as a fraction. To write a repeating decimal as a fraction, use algebra to eliminate the repeating part.

Write each fraction as a decimal.

16. $\frac{3}{5}$ **17.** $\frac{1}{6}$ **18.** $\frac{5}{8}$ **19.** $\frac{3}{10}$ **20.** $\frac{7}{100}$

Write each decimal as a fraction or mixed number.

21. 0.25 **22.** $0.8\overline{3}$ **23.** 5.6 **24.** $2.\overline{04}$

Lesson 5-3

- To add and subtract fractions
- To use factoring to find common denominators

To add or subtract fractions and mixed numbers, write them with a common denominator. Then you can add or subtract the numerators. Change a mixed number to an improper fraction before adding or subtracting.

Add or subtract.

25. $2\frac{1}{3} + \frac{3}{4}$ **26.** $16\frac{4}{5} - 9\frac{2}{3}$ **27.** $\frac{6}{x} + \frac{3}{5}$ **28.** $1\frac{1}{2} - \frac{5}{8}$

29. An upholsterer cuts a piece of cording $1\frac{2}{3}$ ft long from a piece $2\frac{1}{4}$ ft long. How much cording is left?

Lesson 5-4

- To multiply fractions
- To divide fractions

To multiply fractions, multiply their numerators and their denominators. To divide fractions, multiply the first fraction by the **reciprocal** of the second fraction.

To multiply or divide mixed numbers, write them as improper fractions before multiplying or dividing.

Find each product or quotient.

30. $\frac{1}{4} \cdot \frac{7}{10}$ **31.** $-\frac{2}{3} \div \frac{5}{6}$ **32.** $1\frac{3}{5} \cdot \frac{3}{4}$ **33.** $9\frac{3}{4} \div 2\frac{3}{5}$ **34.** $\frac{3x}{5} \div \frac{6x}{5}$

Lesson 5-5

- To identify appropriate customary units
- To convert customary units

To convert units of measure in the customary system of measurement, use conversion factors.

Complete each statement.

35. 30 in. = ■ ft **36.** ■ lb = 54 oz **37.** 20 yd = ■ ft

38. ■ fl oz = $1\frac{1}{2}$ pt **39.** 12 gal = ■ pt **40.** $2\frac{3}{4}$ t = ■ lb

Lesson 5-6

- To solve problems by working backward

To solve some problems, you have to work backward.

41. Your family is planning a 4-h car trip. Along the way, you are planning to make three $\frac{1}{2}$-h stops. At what time should you leave home to arrive at the destination by 8:00 P.M.?

42. Buses bound for Los Angeles leave the station every hour from 6:00 A.M. to 8:00 P.M. How many buses is that in one day?

43. You sell used CDs at a local flea market. It costs $15 to rent a booth for the day. You spend $8 on lunch, and you make $140 selling CDs. If you have $162.50 at the end of the day, how much money did you have at the start of the day?

Lessons 5-7 and 5-8

- To solve equations by subtracting fractions
- To solve equations by adding fractions
- To solve equations by multiplying fractions
- To solve equations by multiplying mixed numbers

To solve equations with fractions, use inverse operations to undo addition or subtraction. You can undo multiplication by multiplying each side of the equation by the same fraction, usually a reciprocal of a fraction in the equation.

Solve each equation.

44. $\frac{1}{8} + x = 2\frac{1}{2}$ **45.** $x - \frac{1}{3} = \frac{4}{5}$ **46.** $x + 4\frac{2}{3} = 6$

47. $6x = \frac{1}{9}$ **48.** $-\frac{3}{4}x = \frac{2}{7}$ **49.** $2\frac{2}{5}x = \frac{8}{15}$

Lesson 5-9

- To find powers of products
- To find powers of quotients

To raise a product to a power, raise each factor to the power. To raise a quotient to a power, raise both the numerator and the denominator to the power.

Simplify each expression.

50. $(2d)^4$ **51.** $(-3(2))^2$ **52.** $(a^2b)^5$

53. $\left(-\frac{1}{2}\right)^3$ **54.** $\left(\frac{x}{3}\right)^2$ **55.** $\left(\frac{2a}{c^2}\right)^4$

Go Online
PHSchool.com

For: Chapter Test
Web Code: bja-0552

Find the LCM of each pair.

1. $24, 36$

2. $50, 100$

3. $3x, 2y$

4. $16, 20$

Compare. Use $>$, $<$, or $=$ to complete each statement.

5. $\frac{7}{8} \blacksquare \frac{7}{9}$

6. $\frac{2}{3} \blacksquare \frac{10}{15}$

7. $\frac{7}{10} \blacksquare 0.71$

8. $2\frac{3}{5} \blacksquare 2\frac{2}{3}$

9. $-0.87 \blacksquare -\frac{7}{8}$

10. $\frac{3}{4} \blacksquare \frac{14}{20}$

Order from least to greatest.

11. $0.5, \frac{1}{10}, 0, -\frac{1}{4}$

12. $-\frac{3}{5}, -0.\overline{6}, \frac{1}{6}, \frac{2}{3}$

Write each decimal as a fraction.

13. 0.4

14. $0.\overline{7}$

15. $12.\overline{36}$

16. 5.2

17. 0.002

18. $7.\overline{1}$

Write each fraction as a decimal.

19. $\frac{4}{15}$

20. $-\frac{2}{3}$

21. $\frac{3}{8}$

22. $\frac{1}{2}$

23. $\frac{6}{7}$

24. $\frac{5}{9}$

Add or subtract.

25. $\frac{1}{8} + \frac{3}{4}$

26. $\frac{2}{3} - \frac{1}{9}$

27. $-\frac{1}{6x} + \frac{1}{4}$

28. $11\frac{5}{6} - 5\frac{3}{8}$

29. $\frac{2}{3} - \left(-\frac{8y}{9}\right)$

30. $2\frac{1}{5} - \frac{3}{4}$

Multiply or divide.

31. $\frac{3}{5} \cdot \frac{1}{2}$

32. $-\frac{3}{4} \cdot \frac{5}{8}$

33. $\frac{5}{8x} \div \frac{7}{16}$

34. $\frac{4}{m} \div \frac{5m}{9}$

35. $3\frac{3}{4} \cdot 2\frac{4}{5}$

36. $-1\frac{1}{3} \div \left(-\frac{5}{9}\right)$

Complete each equation.

37. $10 \text{ yd} = \blacksquare \text{ ft}$

38. $20 \text{ oz} = \blacksquare \text{ lb}$

39. $\blacksquare \text{ lb} = 1\frac{3}{4} \text{ t}$

40. $6 \text{ pt} = \blacksquare \text{ qt}$

41. $3\frac{1}{2} \text{ qt} = \blacksquare \text{ c}$

42. $\blacksquare \text{ in.} = 1\frac{3}{4} \text{ yd}$

Solve each equation.

43. $m - \frac{2}{3} = \frac{1}{4}$

44. $h + \frac{3}{5} = \frac{9}{10}$

45. $x - \frac{5}{6} = -\frac{5}{6}$

46. $\frac{3}{5}a = 9$

47. $n + \frac{7}{8} = \frac{1}{3}$

48. $2\frac{1}{2}n = 3\frac{3}{4}$

49. $-5b = 3\frac{1}{3}$

50. $\frac{3}{8}y = -15$

Simplify each expression.

51. $(3(4))^2$

52. $(2a)^3$

53. $\left(\frac{3}{4}\right)^3$

54. $(3x^2)^3$

55. $-(2x^2y)^4$

56. $\left(\frac{2y}{5x}\right)^3$

Solve.

57. **Number Sense** Suppose you take a number, subtract 8, multiply by 7, add 10, and divide by 5. The result is 9. What is the original number?

58. You spend $\frac{3}{4}$ of your money on clothes and have $21 left. How much did you have before you bought the clothes?

59. **Writing in Math** Write a word problem for the equation $x - 1\frac{1}{4} = 5$.

60. Two packages each weigh $1\frac{7}{8}$ lb. How much do they weigh altogether?

61. You rode your bicycle a mile and a half to school. Then you rode to a friend's house. Altogether you rode $2\frac{1}{10}$ miles. Write and solve an equation to find how far it is from school to your friend's house.

Some problems ask you to interpret a data display. Venn diagrams allow you to compare categories.

The class sponsored surveyed 40 students about their after school activities on a certain day. The results are in the diagram below. Which statement is supported by the diagram?

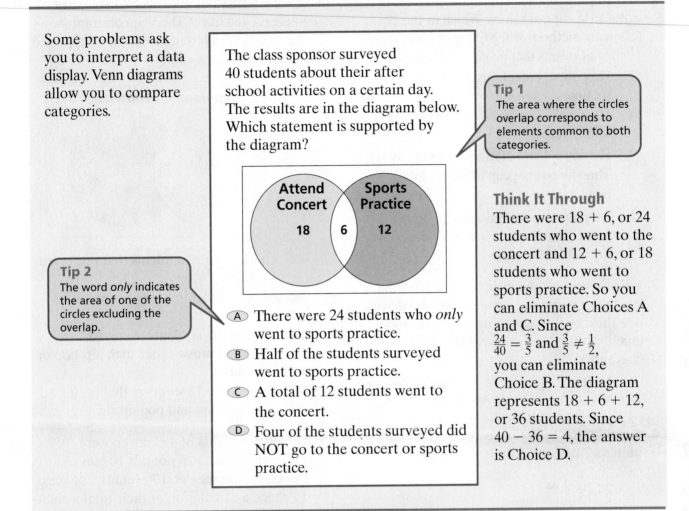

Tip 1
The area where the circles overlap corresponds to elements common to both categories.

Tip 2
The word *only* indicates the area of one of the circles excluding the overlap.

Ⓐ There were 24 students who *only* went to sports practice.

Ⓑ Half of the students surveyed went to sports practice.

Ⓒ A total of 12 students went to the concert.

Ⓓ Four of the students surveyed did NOT go to the concert or sports practice.

Think It Through
There were $18 + 6$, or 24 students who went to the concert and $12 + 6$, or 18 students who went to sports practice. So you can eliminate Choices A and C. Since $\frac{24}{40} = \frac{3}{5}$ and $\frac{3}{5} \neq \frac{1}{2}$, you can eliminate Choice B. The diagram represents $18 + 6 + 12$, or 36 students. Since $40 - 36 = 4$, the answer is Choice D.

Vocabulary Review

As you solve problems, you must understand the meanings of mathematical terms. Choose the vocabulary term that correctly completes the sentence.

A. The (area, perimeter) of a figure is the distance around the figure.

B. A mathematical sentence with an equal sign is an (expression, equation).

C. You use (estimation, perimeter) to check computations with decimal numbers.

D. In a (bar graph, Venn diagram), the overlap of two circles indicates what is common to both collections.

Read each question. Then write the letter of the correct answer on your paper.

1. Andre orders $\frac{1}{2}$ pound of sliced turkey at a deli. Look at the deli scale. Which expression can be used to find how much more than $\frac{1}{2}$ pound is on the scale? **(Lesson 5-2)**

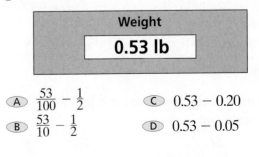

Weight
0.53 lb

Ⓐ $\frac{53}{100} - \frac{1}{2}$ Ⓒ $0.53 - 0.20$

Ⓑ $\frac{53}{10} - \frac{1}{2}$ Ⓓ $0.53 - 0.05$

2. August prepares a recipe in a large bowl that calls for $1\frac{1}{2}$ cups of raisins. Which of the following methods will NOT give him the $1\frac{1}{2}$ cups of raisins that he needs? (Lesson 5-2)

   Ⓐ He pours $\frac{1}{4}$ cup of raisins into the bowl six times.

   Ⓑ He pours $\frac{1}{2}$ cup of raisins into the bowl four times.

   Ⓒ He pours 1 cup of raisins into the bowl. Then he pours $\frac{1}{4}$ cup of raisins into the bowl twice.

   Ⓓ He pours $\frac{1}{4}$ cup of raisins in the bowl twice. Then he pours $\frac{1}{3}$ cup of raisins into the bowl three times.

3. Julie drives half the distance of a 168-mile trip. After stopping at a rest stop, she drives one third of the remaining distance. How much farther does she have to drive? (Lesson 2-5)

   Ⓐ 112 mi   Ⓒ 52 mi

   Ⓑ 56 mi   Ⓓ 28 mi

4. Which of the following is NOT a rational number? (Lesson 5-2)

   Ⓐ $\frac{42}{61}$

   Ⓑ $2.21\overline{5}$

   Ⓒ $0.010010001\ldots$

   Ⓓ $1.131313\ldots$

5. Which fraction is equivalent to 0.625? (Lesson 5-2)

   Ⓐ $\frac{5}{8}$ Ⓒ $\frac{1}{16}$

   Ⓑ $6\frac{1}{4}$ Ⓓ $\frac{3}{5}$

6. Simplify $a^3 \div a^2$. (Lesson 4-8)

   Ⓐ a^6 Ⓒ a^2

   Ⓑ a^5 Ⓓ a

7. Which of the following is equal to 3^{-3}? (Lesson 4-8)

   Ⓐ -27 Ⓒ $\frac{1}{27}$

   Ⓑ -9 Ⓓ $\frac{1}{9}$

8. A survey asks 100 students, "What type of music do you like?" The Venn diagram shows the results. Which statement is best supported by the diagram? (Page 187)

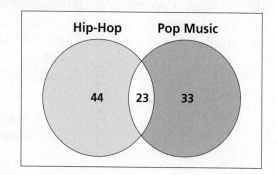

   Ⓐ There were 33 students that preferred hip-hop.

   Ⓑ All the students surveyed preferred pop music.

   Ⓒ Most of the students surveyed preferred music other than hip-hop or pop music.

   Ⓓ There were 23 students that preferred both hip-hop and pop music.

9. The birth weights of 4 children were 7 pounds 2 ounces, 6 pounds 10 ounces, 8 pounds 5 ounces, and 7 pounds 9 ounces. To check a calculation of their total weight, Luis estimated the total weight of the babies at birth was 30 pounds. Which best describes his estimate? (Lesson 5-5)

   Ⓐ More than the actual weight because he rounded to the nearest ounce

   Ⓑ Less than the actual weight because he rounded to the nearest ounce

   Ⓒ Less than the actual weight because he rounded to the nearest pound

   Ⓓ More than the actual weight because he rounded to the nearest pound

10. A company wants to make 16 equal payments for a new computer that costs $2,229.99 including tax and for a fax machine that costs $109.99 including tax. What is a reasonable estimate that the company can use to check the calculated amount of each payment? **(Lesson 5-2)**

  Ⓐ $202   Ⓒ $120

  Ⓑ $146   Ⓓ $100

11. The four most populated cities in the United States in 2005 are shown in the table below.

Most Populated U.S. Cities

City	Population (millions)
New York	8.10
Los Angeles	3.85
Chicago	2.86
Houston	2.01

Between which two cities was the difference in population about 800,000 people? **(Lesson 3-1)**

  Ⓐ Chicago and Los Angeles

  Ⓑ New York and Los Angeles

  Ⓒ Chicago and Houston

  Ⓓ Houston and New York

12. Maureen forgets to turn a faucet off. After a minute, 1.5 gallons of water comes out of the faucet. Which equation can be used to find the number of gallons, g, that comes out of the faucet after 2 hours? **(Lesson 2-6)**

  Ⓐ $g = 1.5 \cdot \frac{1}{30}$ Ⓒ $g = 1.5 \cdot 120$

  Ⓑ $g = 1.5 \cdot \frac{1}{120}$ Ⓓ $g = 1.5 \cdot 604$

13. A train travels at a rate of 40 miles per hour for 3 hours. The train engineer wants to make the trip back in $2\frac{1}{2}$ hours. Which equation can be used to find r, the rate the train has to travel on the trip back? **(Lesson 3-3)**

  Ⓐ $r = 40 \cdot \frac{3}{2.5}$

  Ⓑ $r = 40 \cdot 3 \cdot 2.5$

  Ⓒ $r = 40 \cdot \frac{2.5}{3}$

  Ⓓ $r = 40 \cdot 2.5$

14. A package of 6 stickers costs $1.50. What is the total cost to give a sticker to 296 children? **(Lesson 2-6)**

  Ⓐ $75.50   Ⓒ $74

  Ⓑ $75   Ⓓ $73.50

15. A book is $1\frac{3}{4}$ inches thick. There are 8 copies of the same book stacked in a bookstore. How tall is the stack? **(Lesson 5-4)**

  Ⓐ $\frac{2}{3}$ ft   Ⓒ 6 ft

  Ⓑ $1\frac{1}{6}$ ft   Ⓓ 14 ft

16. Tami is cutting an $8\frac{1}{2}$-inch-wide piece of paper into strips for an art project. How many $\frac{5}{8}$-inch strips can she cut? **(Lesson 5-4)**

  Ⓐ 4   Ⓒ 13

  Ⓑ 5   Ⓓ 14

Ratios, Proportions, and Percents

What You've Learned

Add, subtract, multiply, and divide rational numbers.

Add and subtract fractions by using factoring to find common denominators.

Compare weights, capacities, and geometric measures within measurement systems.

✓ **Check Your Readiness**   **GO for Help** to the Lesson in green.

Solving Equations by Multiplying or Dividing (Lessons 2-6, 3-5, and 5-8)

Solve each equation.

1. $3x = 48$

2. $94.5 = 7r$

3. $\frac{3}{7}t = \frac{3}{8}$

4. $0.5y = 1.25$

5. $\frac{4}{5}x = 1$

6. $38.5 = 1.4m$

Simplifying Fractions (Lesson 4-4)

Find two fractions equivalent to each fraction.

7. $\frac{1}{4}$

8. $\frac{4}{10}$

9. $\frac{6}{14}$

10. $\frac{2}{9}$

11. $\frac{3}{8}$

12. $\frac{5}{6}$

Write each fraction in simplest form.

13. $\frac{2}{8}$

14. $\frac{6}{24}$

15. $\frac{12}{15}$

16. $\frac{6}{16}$

17. $\frac{18}{42}$

18. $\frac{25}{200}$

19. $\frac{80}{96}$

20. $\frac{40}{1,000}$

Writing Fractions and Decimals (Lesson 5-2)

Write each fraction as a decimal. Write each decimal as a fraction or a mixed number in simplest form.

21. $\frac{7}{20}$

22. 0.06

23. $\frac{30}{8}$

24. 0.35

25. 0.875

26. $3\frac{3}{5}$

27. 1.07

28. $\frac{12}{18}$

29. $11\frac{1}{9}$

30. 0.8

31. $\frac{100}{16}$

32. 3.98

▲ You can use percents to describe changes in a city's population.

What You'll Learn Next

Calculate the percentage of increases and decreases of a quantity.

Solve problems that involve discounts, markups, commissions, and profit.

Solve multistep problems involving rate, average speed, distance, and time.

Use measures expressed as rates (e.g., speed, density) and measures expressed as products (e.g., person-days) to solve problems; check the units of the solutions; and use dimensional analysis to check the reasonableness of the answer.

New Vocabulary

🔊 **English and Spanish Audio Online**

- **commission** (p. 312)
- **cross products** (p. 290)
- **discount** (p. 320)
- **indirect measurement** (p. 296)
- **markup** (p. 320)

- **percent** (p. 301)
- **percent of change** (p. 316)
- **proportion** (p. 290)
- **rate** (p. 284)
- **ratio** (p. 284)

- **scale drawing** (p. 296)
- **similar figures** (p. 295)
- **unit rate** (p. 284)

Academic Vocabulary
- **multi-step** (p. 325)
- **reasonable** (p. 304)

Ratios and Unit Rates

What You'll Learn

- To find rates and unit rates
- To use measures expressed as rates and products to solve problems

. . . And Why

To solve real-world problems involving unit prices, gas mileage, and speed

✓ Check Skills You'll Need

Write in simplest form.

1. $\frac{30}{35}$ 2. $\frac{24}{40}$

3. $\frac{54}{60}$ 4. $\frac{12}{15}$

5. $\frac{14}{42}$ 6. $\frac{40}{24}$

GO for Help
Lesson 4-4

🔊 New Vocabulary

- ratio
- rate
- unit rate

For: Exploring Ratios Activity
Use: Interactive Textbook, 6-1

Develop, Master Compare weights, capacities, geometric measures, times, and temperatures within and between measurement systems (e.g., miles per hour and feet per second, cubic inches to cubic centimeters).

Develop, Master Use measures expressed as rates (e.g., speed, density) to solve problems; check the units of the solutions; and use dimensional analysis to check the reasonableness of the answer.

Introduce Solve multistep problems involving rate.

Finding Rates and Unit Rates

A **ratio** is a comparison of two quantities by division. You can write a ratio in different ways.

Arithmetic	Algebra
10 to 15 10 : 15 $\frac{10}{15}$	a to b $a : b$ $\frac{a}{b}$, for $b \neq 0$

A **rate** is a ratio that compares quantities in different units. A **unit rate** is a rate that has a denominator of 1. Examples of unit rates include unit cost, gas mileage, and speed.

1 EXAMPLE   Finding Unit Rates

Multiple Choice The table shows prices for different sizes of the same dish detergent. Which size has the lowest unit cost?

Ⓐ Trial   Ⓒ Family
Ⓑ Regular   Ⓓ Economy

Detergent Prices

Size	Volume (fl oz)	Price
Trial	6	$.78
Regular	12	$1.20
Family	28	$2.24
Economy	40	$3.60

Trial: $\frac{\text{price}}{\text{volume}} \rightarrow \frac{\$.78}{6 \text{ fl oz}} = \$.13/\text{fl oz}$

Regular: $\frac{\text{price}}{\text{volume}} \rightarrow \frac{\$1.20}{12 \text{ fl oz}} = \$.10/\text{fl oz}$

Family: $\frac{\text{price}}{\text{volume}} \rightarrow \frac{\$2.24}{28 \text{ fl oz}} = \$.08/\text{fl oz}$ Find the unit costs.

Economy: $\frac{\text{price}}{\text{volume}} \rightarrow \frac{\$3.60}{40 \text{ fl oz}} = \$.09/\text{fl oz}$

The family size has the lowest unit cost. The answer is C.

✓ Quick Check

1. A car goes 425 mi on 12.5 gal of gas. Find the unit rate.

When converting rates, you can use dimensional analysis to check the reasonableness of the answer.

EXAMPLE ## Converting a Rate

A turtle swims at a rate of 10 mi/h. How many feet will it swim in 5 min?

$$10 \text{ mi/h} = \frac{10 \text{ mi}}{1 \text{ h}} \cdot \frac{5,280 \text{ ft}}{1 \text{ mi}} \cdot \frac{1 \text{ h}}{60 \text{ min}}$$

Convert miles to feet and hours to minutes.

$$= \frac{880 \text{ ft}}{\text{min}}$$

Simplify.

$$\frac{880 \text{ ft}}{\text{min}} \cdot 5 \text{ min} = 4,400 \text{ ft}$$

Multiply to find the distance.

The turtle will swim 4,400 ft in 5 min.

Check Use dimensional analysis.

Since $\frac{\text{mi} \cdot \text{ft} \cdot \text{h}}{\text{h} \cdot \text{mi} \cdot \text{min}} = \frac{\text{ft}}{\text{min}}$ and $\frac{\text{ft}}{\text{min}} \cdot \text{min} = \text{ft}$, the units check.

> **Quick Tip**
>
> When a problem involves two different units, make sure you express your answer in the correct unit.

✓ Quick Check

2. Complete: 3.5 qt/min = ■ gal/h.

Finding Rates Expressed as Products

Some measures are expressed as products. For example, person-days are a measure of the amount of time needed for a number of people to complete a job.

If a job takes 2 people working for 1 day, then it takes (2 persons) · (1 day) = 2 person-days. The same job can be completed by 1 person in 2 days. In other words, 1 person can complete $\frac{1}{2}$ of the work in 1 day.

> **Vocabulary Tip**
>
> You can use a hyphen to write the product of two units. For example, write *person times days* as "person-days."

3 **EXAMPLE** ## Finding Rates Expressed as Products

A company has a job that will take 240 person-days to complete. How many workers are needed to complete the job in 30 days?

It takes 240 workers to complete the job in 1 day. To find the number of workers needed to complete the job in 30 days, divide.

$$\frac{240 \text{ person-days}}{30 \text{ days}} = 8 \text{ persons}$$

Divide the number of person-days by the number of days.

The company needs 8 persons, or 8 workers, to complete the job in 30 days.

Check Since $\frac{\text{person} \cdot \text{days}}{\text{days}} = \text{person}$, the units check.

✓ Quick Check

3. A contractor has a job that requires 540 person-days. How many workers are needed to complete the job in 60 days?

Favorite Type of TV Show	
Drama	Comedy
ℍℍ ℍℍ ℍℍ	ℍℍ ℍℍ
ⅠⅠⅠⅠ	ℍℍ Ⅰ

The table at the left shows the results of a survey. Write each ratio in simplest form.

1. Drama to Comedy

2. Comedy to the total

3. A 45-min long-distance phone call costs $2.25. What is the cost per minute?

4. Calculate the number of person-days to complete a job if 15 people work for 21 days.

For more exercises, see *Extra Skills and Word Problem Practice.*

A Practice by Example

Example 1
(page 284)

GO for Help

Find each unit rate.

5. A skydiver falls 144 ft in 3 s.

6. A pump moves 42 gal in 7 min.

7. A car travels 676 mi in 13 h.

8. 20 c of water evaporate in 5 d.

Example 2
(page 285)

Complete each statement.

9. 720 m/day = ■ m/min

10. 1.5 gal/min = ■ qt/h

11. 32 yd/min = ■ in./s

12. 0.85 km/s = ■ m/min

13. 80 mi/h = ■ ft/s

14. 20 fl oz/min = ■ qt/day

Example 3
(page 285)

15. A painting project will take a total of 360 person-days to complete.
   a. How many days will it take to complete the project if 30 people work on the project?
   b. If the project must be completed in 10 days, how many people must be employed?

B Apply Your Skills

16. Shampoo A is priced at $3.79 for 12 oz. Shampoo B is priced at $4.89 for 14.5 oz. Which brand has the lower unit cost?

17. A stock investment of 160 shares paid a dividend of $584. At this rate, what dividend would be paid on 270 shares of stock?

18. Anna and Julia take a bicycle trip. Anna rides 20 miles in $1\frac{1}{3}$ hours. Julia rides 246 miles in 16 hours. Which rider has the slower unit rate? By how much?

Homework Video Tutor

Visit: PHSchool.com
Web Code: bje-0601

19. What is the rate in meters per second of a jetliner that is traveling at a rate of 846 km/h?

20. Error Analysis A student converts 100 ft/min to 500 in./s. Use dimensional analysis to explain why the student's result is not reasonable.

Boys in Two Classes

Class	Number of Boys	Number of Students
A	6	30
B	4	24

Use the table at the left for Exercises 21 and 22.

21. For each class, write the ratio of the number of boys to the total number of students.

22. Which class has the greater ratio of boys to students?

23. Writing in Math A student claims that a ratio remains unchanged if 1 is added to both the numerator and the denominator of the fraction. Does $\frac{a}{b}$ equal $\frac{a+1}{b+1}$? Write an explanation, and give an example or a counterexample.

Watt-hours are used to measure energy used. One watt-hour (1 Wh) is equal to one watt (1 W) of power used for one hour (1 h).

24. Two 100-W light bulbs used a total of 400 Wh of energy. For how many hours did the light bulbs use power?

25. A stereo system requiring 200 watts of power used 1,500 watt-hours of energy. For how many hours did the stereo use power?

26. Density is the ratio of a substance's mass to its volume. A volume of 20 cubic centimeters of gold has a mass of 386 grams. Express the density of gold as a unit rate.

C Challenge **27.** Patrice and Tatiana share baby-sitting duties. The ratio comparing the amount of time each one works is 6 : 5. They earn a total of $77. If Patrice works longer, how much should each receive?

Multiple Choice Practice and Mixed Review

For Standards Tutorials, visit PHSchool.com. Web Code: bjq-9045

28. A 50-pound bag of Glossy Coat Horse Feed costs $23.50. A 25-pound bag costs $15.50. How much money per pound would you save by buying the bag with the lower unit price?

Ⓐ $0.15   Ⓑ $0.51   Ⓒ $0.62   Ⓓ $1.09

29. Karla and her dad were nailing up plywood. They started at 10:00. Karla drove 30 nails in 10 min, the time it took her dad to drive 50 nails. At that rate for each, when did they finish driving 392 nails in all?

Ⓐ 10:30   Ⓑ 10:39   Ⓒ 10:45   Ⓓ 10:49

30. Which fraction is equivalent to 2.5?

Ⓐ $\frac{9}{4}$ Ⓑ $\frac{5}{2}$ Ⓒ $\frac{26}{5}$ Ⓓ $\frac{21}{4}$

GO for Help Lesson 5-9

Simplify each expression.

31. $(-3 \cdot 4)^3$ **32.** $(2x^2y)^4$ **33.** $\left(-\frac{ab^3}{a^2b}\right)^3$

Estimating to Convert Between Measurement Systems

Master Compare weights and capacities within and between measurement systems.
Master Use measures expressed as rates (e.g., speed, density) and measures expressed as products to solve problems; check the units of the solutions; and use dimensional analysis to check the reasonableness of the answer.

Suppose you are traveling in a country that uses the metric system. You can use conversion factors to convert a unit of measure from one system to another. For example, since 1 mi ≈ 1.61 km, you can use $\frac{1\ mi}{1.61\ km}$ and $\frac{1.61\ km}{1\ mi}$ as conversion factors. The table shows some useful conversion factors.

Customary Units and Metric Units	Conversion Factors
1 in. = 2.54 cm	$\frac{1\ in.}{2.54\ cm}$ or $\frac{2.54\ cm}{1\ in.}$
1 mi ≈ 1.61 km	$\frac{1\ mi}{1.61\ km}$ or $\frac{1.61\ km}{1\ mi}$
1.06 qt ≈ 1 L	$\frac{1.06\ qt}{1\ L}$ or $\frac{1\ L}{1.06\ qt}$
1 oz ≈ 28.4 g	$\frac{1\ oz}{28.4\ g}$ or $\frac{28.4\ g}{1\ oz}$
2.20 lb ≈ 1 kg	$\frac{2.20\ lb}{1\ kg}$ or $\frac{1\ kg}{2.20\ lb}$

In general, a conversion between systems results in an approximate measurement.

1 ACTIVITY

Suppose you and your family have rented a car in France. You see a sign that says "Paris 60 km." Is it more or less than 60 mi to Paris?

Since 1 mi ≈ 1.61 km, you know that

1 mi > 1 km

so 60 mi > 60 km.

It is less than 60 miles to Paris.

2 ACTIVITY

Use the information from Activity 1. About how many miles is it to Paris?

$60\ km \approx 60\ km \cdot \frac{1\ mi}{1.61\ km}$ Use a conversion factor that changes kilometers to miles.

$= 60\ \cancel{km} \cdot \frac{1\ mi}{1.61\ \cancel{km}}$ Divide the common units. Use dimensional analysis to check the units.

$= \frac{60\ mi}{1.61}$ Multiply.

$\approx 37\ mi$ Divide.

It is about 37 miles to Paris.

Sometimes you may need to use a conversion factor more than once.

3 ACTIVITY

Convert 572 in.^{2} to cm^2.

You need to convert square inches to square centimeters. Use the conversion factor 1 in. = 2.54 cm twice to convert in. to cm.

$$572 \text{ in.}^2 = 572 \cdot \text{in.} \cdot \text{in.}$$

$$572 \text{ in.}^2 = 572 \cdot \text{in.} \cdot \text{in.} \cdot \frac{2.54 \text{ cm}}{1 \text{ in.}} \cdot \frac{2.54 \text{ cm}}{1 \text{ in.}} \qquad \text{Convert in.}^2 \text{ to cm}^2.$$

$$\approx 3{,}690.3 \text{ cm}^2 \qquad \text{Multiply.}$$

An area of 572 in.^{2} is about 3,690.3 cm^2.

Check Use dimensional analysis.

Since $\dfrac{\text{in.} \cdot \text{in.} \cdot \text{cm} \cdot \text{cm}}{\text{in.} \cdot \text{in.}} = \text{cm}^2$, the units check.

EXERCISES

Convert. Where necessary, round to the nearest tenth.

1. 8 in. ≈ ■ cm
2. 16 cm^2 ≈ ■ in.^{2}
3. ■ mi^2 ≈ 20 km^2
4. ■ km^2 ≈ 100 mi^2
5. ■ L ≈ 50 qt
6. ■ g ≈ 15 oz
7. 15 L ≈ ■ qt
8. ■ lb ≈ 14 kg
9. 44 lb ≈ ■ kg
10. 100 oz ≈ ■ kg
11. ■ L ≈ 212 pt
12. 500 g ≈ ■ lb
13. 1,000 cm^2 ≈ ■ in.^{2}
14. ■ gal ≈ 20 L
15. ■ km/h ≈ 10 mi/h

16. Gasoline is sold by the liter in Europe. Suppose your family car has a 20-gal gas tank. How many liters would fill the gas tank? (*Hint:* Change gallons to quarts and quarts to liters.)

17. London, England, is about 414 km from Paris, France. Dallas, Texas, is about 250 miles from Houston, Texas. Which distance is longer? How much longer is it?

18. A recipe calls for 8 oz of figs. The figs come in packages of 100 g. How many packages should you buy?

19. **Writing in Math** Explain how you would estimate the number of kilometers in 19 miles.

20. In Exercise 15 above, you may have found that 10 mi/h ≈ 16.1 km/h. Also, 10 mi/h = 880 ft/min (Example 2, p. 285). Convert both 16.1 km/h and 880 ft/min to meters per second and compare.

6-2 Proportions

What You'll Learn

- To solve proportions
- To use proportions to solve problems

. . . And Why

To solve real-world problems involving science

✓ **Check Skills You'll Need**

Solve each equation.

1. $4x = 52$ **2.** $3y = 18$

3. $5b = 75$ **4.** $7k = 21$

GO for Help

Lesson 2-6

🔊 **New Vocabulary**

- proportion
- cross products

Calculate the percentage of increases and decreases of a quantity.

Solving Proportions

A **proportion** is an equality of two ratios—for example, $\frac{6}{9} = \frac{8}{12}$. You can use the Multiplication Property of Equality to show an important property of all proportions.

$$\text{If } \frac{a}{b} = \frac{c}{d}$$

$$\text{then } \frac{a}{b} \cdot bd = \frac{c}{d} \cdot bd \quad \textbf{Multiplication Property of Equality}$$

$$\frac{ab^1d}{_1b} = \frac{cbd^1}{_1d} \quad \frac{b}{b} = \textbf{1} \text{ and } \frac{d}{d} = \textbf{1}$$

and $ad = cb$, or $ad = bc$.

The products ad and bc are called the **cross products** of the proportion $\frac{a}{b} = \frac{c}{d}$.

Take Note **Cross Products**

In a proportion, the cross products are equal.

Arithmetic	Algebra
$\frac{6}{9} = \frac{8}{12}$	$\frac{a}{b} = \frac{c}{d}$
$6 \cdot 12 = 9 \cdot 8 = 72$	$ad = bc$

To solve a proportion that contains a variable, you find the value that makes the equation true.

GO Online

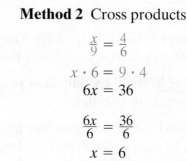

Video Tutor Help

Visit: PHSchool.com
Web Code: bje-0775

---

1 EXAMPLE **Multiplying to Solve a Proportion**

Solve $\frac{x}{9} = \frac{4}{6}$.

Method 1 Multiplication Property of Equality

$$\frac{x}{9} = \frac{4}{6}$$

$$\frac{x}{9} \cdot 9 = \frac{4}{6} \cdot 9$$

$$x = \frac{36}{6}$$

$$x = 6$$

Method 2 Cross products

$$\frac{x}{9} = \frac{4}{6}$$

$$x \cdot 6 = 9 \cdot 4$$

$$6x = 36$$

$$\frac{6x}{6} = \frac{36}{6}$$

$$x = 6$$

---

290   Chapter 6 Ratios, Proportions, and Percents

✅ Quick Check

1. Solve each proportion.

    a. $\frac{h}{9} = \frac{2}{3}$ **b.** $\frac{4}{5} = \frac{t}{55}$ **c.** $\frac{22}{d} = \frac{6}{21}$

Two ratios form a proportion if their cross products are equal.

2 EXAMPLE   Testing for a Proportion

Do the ratios $\frac{4}{6}$ and $\frac{10}{14}$ form a proportion? Explain.

    $\frac{4}{6} \overset{?}{=} \frac{10}{14}$ **Test by writing as a proportion.**

    $4 \cdot 14 \overset{?}{=} 6 \cdot 10$ **Write the cross products.**

      $56 \neq 60$ **Simplify.**

The ratios do not form a proportion. Cross products are not equal.

✅ Quick Check

2. Tell whether the two ratios form a proportion. Explain.

    a. $\frac{6}{9}, \frac{4}{6}$ **b.** $\frac{15}{20}, \frac{5}{7}$ **c.** $\frac{7}{12}, \frac{17.5}{30}$

Using Proportions to Solve Problems

You can write and solve proportions for many real-world problems.

3 EXAMPLE   Solving a Problem Using a Proportion

Multiple Choice One hundred nautical miles equals about 115 standard, or statute, miles. How many statute miles equal 381 nautical miles? Round your answer to the nearest whole number.

  Ⓐ 30   Ⓑ 331   Ⓒ 438   Ⓓ 571

This photo was tak⟨ ⟩ an altitude of 38⟨ ⟩ miles.

Let d = distance in statute miles.

$$\text{distance in nautical miles} \longrightarrow \frac{100}{115} = \frac{381}{d} \longleftarrow \text{distance in nautical miles}$$
$$\text{distance in statute miles} \qquad\qquad\qquad\qquad \longleftarrow \text{distance in statute miles}$$

    $100d = 115(381)$ **Write the cross products.**

       $d = \frac{115(381)}{100}$ **Divide each side by 100.**

        ≈ 438 **A calculator may be useful.**

381 nautical miles is about 438 statute miles. The answer is C.

✅ Quick Check

3. To the nearest mile, how far in nautical miles is 100 statute miles?

Complete Exercises 1–3 to solve the problem below.

To make lemonade, you need 6 lemons and 8 cups of ice water. How many lemons do you need if you have 24 cups of ice water?

1. What is the ratio of lemons to cups of water?

2. Write a proportion using an equivalent ratio of lemons to 24 cups of water.

3. How many lemons are needed for 24 cups of water?

4. **Error Analysis** Fancy ribbon costs $3 for 15 in. Your friend wants to find the cost of 3 ft of ribbon. He uses the proportion $\frac{3}{15} = \frac{x}{3}$ and gets an answer of $.60. Explain your friend's error.

Standards Practice

For more exercises, see *Extra Skills and Word Problem Practice.*

A Practice by Example

Example 1
(page 290)

GO for Help

Solve each proportion.

5. $\frac{2}{v} = \frac{1}{8}$

6. $\frac{z}{42} = \frac{25}{70}$

7. $\frac{4}{h} = \frac{8}{10}$

8. $\frac{4}{16} = \frac{s}{8}$

9. $\frac{4}{11} = \frac{x}{22}$

10. $\frac{2}{9} = \frac{r}{36}$

11. $\frac{12}{n} = \frac{2}{12}$

12. $\frac{1}{15} = \frac{3}{p}$

13. $\frac{4}{15} = \frac{a}{75}$

14. $\frac{3}{4} = \frac{21}{b}$

15. $\frac{13}{c} = \frac{39}{60}$

16. $\frac{3}{6} = \frac{7}{d}$

Example 2
(page 291)

Tell whether the two ratios form a proportion. Explain.

17. $\frac{2}{3}$ and $\frac{10}{20}$

18. $\frac{25}{80}$ and $\frac{5}{16}$

19. $\frac{4}{7}$ and $\frac{20}{25}$

20. $\frac{2}{3}$ and $\frac{10}{16}$

21. $\frac{3}{4}$ and $\frac{12}{15}$

22. $\frac{3}{8}$ and $\frac{21}{56}$

23. $\frac{9}{24}$ and $\frac{15}{40}$

24. $\frac{20}{32}$ and $\frac{12}{20}$

Example 3
(page 291)

25. At the Copy Shoppe, 18 copies cost $1.08. At that rate, how much will 40 copies cost?

26. Three tea bags are needed to make a gallon of iced tea. How many tea bags are needed to make four gallons?

27. Three posters cost $9.60. At that rate, how many posters can you buy for $48?

ly Your Skills

Tell whether the two ratios form a proportion. Explain.

28. $\frac{3.9}{5.4}$ and $\frac{13}{18}$

29. $\frac{54}{60}$ and $\frac{118}{110}$

30. $\frac{27}{72}$ and $\frac{48}{128}$

31. $\frac{144}{120}$ and $\frac{75}{145}$

32. $\frac{27}{54}$ and $\frac{22}{44}$

33. $\frac{95}{100}$ and $\frac{285}{300}$

34. $\frac{72}{73}$ and $\frac{36}{37}$

35. $\frac{1.5}{4.5}$ and $\frac{3}{1}$

ntal Math Solve by mental math.

$\frac{1}{6} = \frac{a}{72}$

37. $\frac{120}{24} = \frac{y}{2}$

38. $\frac{10}{v} = \frac{3}{1.5}$

39. $\frac{n}{12} = \frac{12}{2}$

6-2 Pr

, and Percents

40. On a recent day, the exchange rate for U.S. dollars to European euros was 1.32 dollars per euro. On that day, about how many euros would you get for 25 dollars?

Solve each proportion. Where necessary, round to the nearest tenth.

41. $\frac{4}{3} = \frac{b}{21}$ **42.** $\frac{6}{25} = \frac{e}{80}$ **43.** $\frac{4}{9} = \frac{f}{15}$ **44.** $\frac{3}{8} = \frac{50}{g}$

45. $\frac{24}{17} = \frac{109}{h}$ **46.** $\frac{7}{9} = \frac{j}{22.5}$ **47.** $\frac{6}{13} = \frac{7.8}{m}$ **48.** $\frac{20}{27} = \frac{1.1}{n}$

Estimation   **Estimate the solution of each proportion.**

49. $\frac{3}{2} = \frac{29}{d}$ **50.** $\frac{20}{3.9} = \frac{s}{6}$ **51.** $\frac{1.5}{p} = \frac{2.1}{4.1}$ **52.** $\frac{f}{4} = \frac{12}{49}$

53. At the rate shown in the picture, how much would five potatoes cost?

Potatoes
3 for $22

54. A microchip inspector found three defective chips in a batch containing 750 chips. At that rate, how many defective chips would there be in 10,000 chips?

55. **Reasoning** If $\frac{a}{b} = \frac{c}{d}$, will $\frac{a}{c} = \frac{b}{d}$? Assume that $b \neq 0$, $c \neq 0$, and $d \neq 0$. Explain your reasoning.

56. **Geometry** A rectangle that is 20 cm long and 28 cm wide is the same shape as one that is 9 cm long and z cm wide. Find z.

57. **Multiple Choice** Your team scores 4 runs in the first three innings of a 9-inning baseball game. If the team continues at that rate, how many runs will it score in the game?

   Ⓐ 8 runs   Ⓑ 12 runs   Ⓒ 13 runs   Ⓓ 16 runs

For Exercises 58–61, use the table.

58. How many times does an adult's heart beat in 270 s?

59. In how many seconds will a newborn's heart beat 35 times?

60. In how many seconds will a 12-year-old's heart beat 17 times?

61. In 45 s, how many more times does a newborn's heart beat than a 6-year-old's heart?

Human Heart Rates

Age (years)	Beats per Minute
newborn	140
1	120
6	100
10	90
12	85
adult	80

In Exercises 62–69, write a proportion for each situation. Then solve.

62. 20 lb for $27.50; 12 lb for x dollars

63. 25 yd in $2\frac{1}{2}$ s; 100 yd in x seconds

64. 3 miles in 2.8 minutes; 33.3 miles in x minutes

65. $3\frac{1}{2}$ pounds in 4 cubic inches; x pound in 1 cubic inch

66. 5 km in 18 min 36 s; 8 km in v minutes

67. 96 oz for $2; y pounds for $10

68. 4 oz for $1.85; 1 lb for t dollars

69. $5.76 for 2 lb 4 oz; c dollars for 1 pound

70. **Writing in Math** A truck driver estimates that it will take him 12 h to drive 1,160 km. After 5 h, he has driven 484 km. Is he on schedule? Explain.

C Challenge **71.** You make a sketch of your bedroom that is 4 in. wide and 5 in. long. The ratio $\frac{\text{dimension of sketch}}{\text{actual dimension}}$ is $\frac{1\,\text{in.}}{3\,\text{ft}}$. What are the actual dimensions of the room?

Multiple Choice Practice and Mixed Review

For Standards Tutorials, visit PHSchool.com. Web Code: bjq-9045

72. Four children have lemonade stands. Use the tables below to find which child sells lemonade at a constant unit price.

Sydney's Prices		Herman's Prices		Carmen's Prices		Arthur's Prices	
Number of Cups	Price	Number of Cups	Price	Number of Cups	Price	Number of Cups	Price
1	$1.00	1	$0.50	1	$0.50	1	$1.00
2	$1.50	2	$1.00	2	$1.00	2	$2.00
3	$2.00	3	$1.50	3	$1.25	3	$2.75
4	$2.50	4	$2.00	4	$1.50	4	$3.75

Ⓐ Sydney Ⓑ Herman Ⓒ Carmen Ⓓ Arthur

73. Amoebas are tiny one-celled organisms. They may be as small as 1×10^{-2} inch. Which of the following represents this size in standard notation?

Ⓐ 0.001 in. Ⓑ 0.01 in. Ⓒ 0.1 in. Ⓓ 100 in.

74. Solve the equation $k + 2\frac{1}{5} = 1\frac{1}{4}$ for k.

Ⓐ $-3\frac{9}{20}$ Ⓑ $\frac{-19}{20}$ Ⓒ $\frac{19}{20}$ Ⓓ $3\frac{9}{20}$

GO for Help Lesson 6-1 **Write each ratio as a fraction in simplest form.**

75. ten per thousand **76.** 30 to 55 **77.** 125 : 70

Similar Figures and Scale Drawings

What You'll Learn

- To solve problems that involve similar figures
- To solve problems that involve scale drawings

...And Why

To solve real-world problems involving maps

✓ Check Skills You'll Need

Solve each proportion. Round to the nearest tenth where necessary.

1. $\frac{2}{3} = \frac{f}{21}$ 2. $\frac{3}{8} = \frac{50}{p}$

3. $\frac{9}{4} = \frac{15}{p}$ 4. $\frac{16}{3} = \frac{19}{g}$

GO for Help

Lesson 6-2

New Vocabulary

- similar figures
- indirect measurement
- scale drawing

For: Similar Figures Activity
Use: Interactive Textbook, 6-3

Introduce, Develop Construct and read drawings and models made to scale.

Using Similar Figures

Similar figures have the same shape, but not necessarily the same size. Similar figures have *corresponding angles* and *corresponding sides*.

The symbol ~ means "is similar to." At the right, $\triangle ABC \sim \triangle XYZ$.

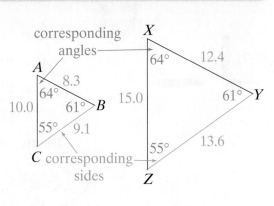

Take Note ✏ Similar Figures

Similar figures have two properties.

- The corresponding angles have equal measures.
- The lengths of corresponding sides are in proportion.

1 EXAMPLE Using Similar Figures

Parallelogram $ABCD \sim$ parallelogram $EFGH$. Find the value of x.

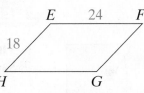

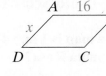

Write a proportion for corresponding sides.

Side DA corresponds to side HE.	$\frac{x}{18} = \frac{16}{24}$	Side AB corresponds to side EF.
	$x \cdot 24 = 18 \cdot 16$	Write cross products.
	$\frac{24x}{24} = \frac{18 \cdot 16}{24}$	Divide each side by 24.
	$x = 12$	Simplify.

✓ Quick Check

1. Parallelogram $KLMN$ is similar to parallelogram $ABCD$ in Example 1.
If $KL = 21$, find KN. Round to the nearest tenth.

You can use similar figures to compute distances that are difficult to measure directly. Such a process is called **indirect measurement.**

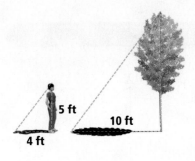

5 ft

4 ft

10 ft

2 EXAMPLE — Using Indirect Measurement

A tree casts a shadow 10 ft long. A 5-ft woman casts a shadow 4 ft long. The triangle shown for the woman and her shadow is similar to the triangle shown for the tree and its shadow. How tall is the tree?

$\dfrac{4}{10} = \dfrac{5}{x}$ Corresponding sides of similar triangles are in proportion.

$4x = 10 \cdot 5$ Write cross products.

$\dfrac{4x}{4} = \dfrac{10 \cdot 5}{4}$ Divide each side by 4.

$x = 12.5$ Simplify.

The tree is 12.5 ft tall.

✓ Quick Check

2. A building 70 ft high casts a 150-ft shadow. A nearby flagpole casts a 60-ft shadow. Draw a diagram. Use similar triangles to find the height of the flagpole.

Using Scale Drawings

A **scale drawing** is an enlarged or reduced drawing that is similar to an actual object or place. The ratio of a distance in the drawing to the corresponding actual distance is the *scale* of the drawing.

3 EXAMPLE — Using Scale Drawings

The scale of the map is 1 in. : 44 mi. About how far from Sacramento is Santa Rosa?

Map distance = $1\frac{1}{2}$ in. or 1.5 in.   Measure the map distance.

$\dfrac{\text{map (in.)}}{\text{actual (mi)}} \rightarrow \dfrac{1}{44} = \dfrac{1.5}{d} \leftarrow \dfrac{\text{map (in.)}}{\text{actual (mi)}}$ Write a proportion.

$1 \cdot d = 44 \cdot 1.5$ Write cross products.

$d = 66$ Simplify.

Sacramento is about 66 mi from Santa Rosa.

✓ Quick Check

3. The distance from Sacramento to San Jose is about 121 mi. What is the approximate map distance between these two cities?

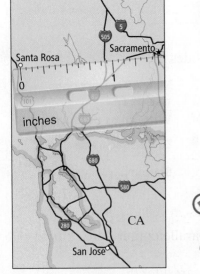

The rectangles below are similar. Find the missing length.

1.

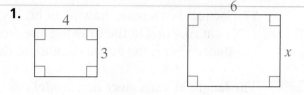

2. A scale drawing has a scale of 1 in. : 10 ft. What is the distance on the drawing for an actual distance of 45 ft?

3. **Critical Thinking** A note at the bottom of a map says "not to scale." Explain why that is important information.

Standards Practice

For more exercises, see *Extra Skills and Word Problem Practice*.

(A) **Practice by Example**

GO for Help
Example 1
(page 295)

Trapezoid *EFGH* ~ trapezoid *MNOP*. Find the indicated value.

4. x

5. y

6. z

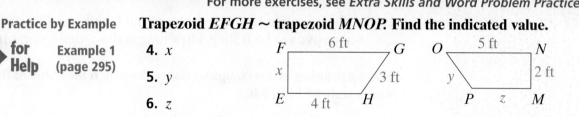

The triangles in each pair are similar. Find the missing length. Round to the nearest tenth where necessary.

7.

8.

9.

10.

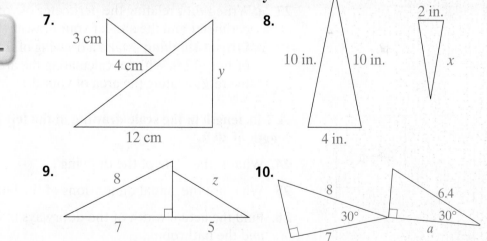

Homework Video Tutor

Visit: PHSchool.com
Web Code: bje-0603

Example 2
(page 296)

11. **Indirect Measurement** A tree casts a shadow 8 ft long. A 6-ft man casts a shadow 4 ft long. The triangle formed by the tree and its shadow is similar to the triangle formed by the man and his shadow. How tall is the tree?

12. An image on a slide is similar to its projected image. The slide is 35 mm wide and 21 mm high. Its projected image is 85 cm wide. To the nearest centimeter, how high is the image?

Example 3
(page 296)

The scale of a map is 1 cm : 12 km. Find the actual distance for each map distance.

13. 1.5 cm   **14.** 12 cm   **15.** 4.25 cm   **16.** 8.3 cm

17. Jacques has a scale drawing of his bedroom with a scale of 1 cm : 0.4 m. On the drawing, the front window is 3 cm from the door. What is the actual distance in the room?

B   **Apply Your Skills**

The length of each piece in a model railroad built on the HO scale is $\frac{1}{87}$ of the actual length. Another popular model is the N scale, for which the scale is $\frac{1}{160}$.

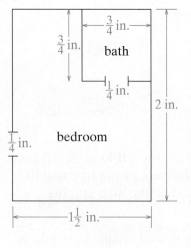

18. In the photograph are HO and N models of the same locomotive. Which type of model is labeled A? Which type of model is labeled B?

19. Each car on a full-size passenger train is 80 ft long. What is the length in inches of a model passenger car in the HO scale? In the N scale?

20. In the O scale, a length is $\frac{1}{48}$ the actual length. An O-scale locomotive is 1.05 ft long. How long is the actual locomotive?

Make a drawing of a rectangular dance floor 90 ft long and 72 ft wide with a scale of 1 in. : 9 ft.

21. What is the perimeter of your drawing?

22. What is the area of your drawing?

23. a. Write ratios relating the perimeter of your drawing to the actual perimeter and the area of your drawing to the actual area.
    b. Critical Thinking Make a drawing of the dance floor with a scale of 1 in. : 12 ft. Without calculating the area of your drawing, find the ratio relating the area of your drawing to the actual area.

A 2-in. length in the scale drawing at the left represents an actual length of 20 ft.

24. What is the scale of the drawing?

25. What are the actual dimensions of the bath?

26. Find the actual width of the doorways that lead into the bedroom and the bathroom.

27. Find the actual area of the bedroom.

28. Can a bed 6 ft long and 3 ft wide fit into the narrow section of the bedroom? Justify your answer.

A scale drawing has a scale of $\frac{1}{2}$ in. : 10 ft. Find the length on the drawing for each actual length.

29. 40 ft   **30.** 5 ft   **31.** 35 ft   **32.** $3\frac{1}{2}$ ft

33. Open-Ended Choose a room in your home. Make a scale drawing of the length and width of the room. Be sure to include your scale in the drawing.

 Challenge

34. <u>Writing in Math</u> Explain why all squares are similar. For what other shape can you say that all figures are similar? Explain.

35. A boxcar on a freight train is 40 ft long. A model boxcar is 3 in. long. In which scale, HO, N, or O, was the model built? (*Hint:* See Exercises 18–20.)

36. You are building a display shelf for your model train. You have 12 cars. Each car is 1.2 ft long. You want 1.2 in. of space between cars. How long must the shelf be?

Multiple Choice Practice and Mixed Review

For Standards Tutorials, visit PHSchool.com. Web Code: bjq-9045

37. The triangles shown are similar. Find *l*, the length of $\overline{XY}$.

Ⓐ 16 units   Ⓒ 9 units
Ⓑ 10.5 units   Ⓓ 4.7 units

38. Abe does 40 sit-ups in 60 seconds. Catherine does 25 sit-ups in 50 seconds. Based on these rates, which statement is true?

Ⓐ Abe's rate is less than Catherine's rate.
Ⓑ Both rates are equal.
Ⓒ Abe's rate is greater than Catherine's rate.
Ⓓ If Abe's rate is constant, he will do 120 sit-ups in 2.5 min.

GO for Help

Lesson 6-2 **Solve each proportion.**

39. $\frac{x}{5} = \frac{32}{80}$ **40.** $\frac{3}{8} = \frac{r}{15}$ **41.** $\frac{40}{w} = \frac{50}{3}$ **42.** $\frac{24}{16} = \frac{204}{c}$

Lesson 5-2 **Write each fraction as a decimal.**

43. $\frac{3}{8}$ **44.** $\frac{4}{9}$ **45.** $\frac{7}{16}$ **46.** $\frac{5}{12}$

✓ Checkpoint Quiz 1

Write each phrase as a unit rate.

1. 20 mi in 5 h   **2.** 42 gal in 7 min   **3.** a fall of 144 ft in 3 s

4. Geometry The figures (left) are similar. Find the missing length.

5. A person blinks 112 times in 4 min. At that rate, how many times does the person blink in 1.5 min?

6. A photo is 3 in. wide by 5 in. high. Find the width of an enlargement that is 11 in. high.

Develop Construct and read drawings and models to scale.

You can use geometry software to make a scale drawing, or **dilation,** of a figure. First choose the Dilate command. Then choose a center of dilation and a scale, which is also known as a **scale factor.**

ACTIVITY

Draw a triangle. Then draw a dilation with scale factor 3.

Use geometry software. Draw $\triangle ABC$. Draw point D on one side of the triangle. Choose D as the center of a dilation with scale factor 3.

The result is an image like the one at the right. Each side of the dilation is 3 times as long as the corresponding side of $\triangle ABC$.

If you move point D, the dilation also will move. If instead you move A, B, or C, the dilation will change as $\triangle ABC$ changes.

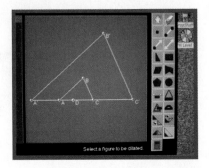

EXERCISES

Use geometry software to draw $\triangle PQR$.

1. **a.** Draw a point S *outside* $\triangle PQR$. Draw a dilation of $\triangle PQR$ with center S and scale factor 2.5. Label the dilation $\triangle XYZ$. $\triangle XYZ$ is similar to $\triangle PQR$. Angle X corresponds to angle P, angle Y corresponds to angle Q, and angle Z corresponds to angle R.
   b. Compare the location of $\triangle XYZ$ to the location of $\triangle PQR$. Does the dilation lie inside the original triangle? Outside the triangle? Do the triangles overlap?
   c. Now move S *inside* $\triangle PQR$. Once again, compare the locations of the two triangles. How did moving the center of dilation change the relative locations of the triangles?

2. Change the location of point S so that $\triangle PQR$ and $\triangle XYZ$ have the given number of points in common. Print an example of each case.
   a. 0   **b.** 1   **c.** 2   **d.** more than 2

3. With S inside $\triangle PQR$, change the scale factor to 0.5. Describe the relative locations of the two triangles.

4. **a.** Keep the scale factor of the dilation at 0.5. Use the Area tool to find the area of $\triangle PQR$. Use the Area tool again to find the area of $\triangle XYZ$. Write a ratio to compare the areas.
   b. Move P, Q, or R to see how the area of $\triangle XYZ$ changes as the area of $\triangle PQR$ changes. Does the ratio of the areas change?
   c. **Reasoning** What do your results suggest about the areas of similar triangles that have a scale factor of 0.5?

6-4

Fractions, Decimals, and Percents

What You'll Learn

- To write percents as fractions and decimals
- To write decimals and fractions as percents

. . . And Why

To solve real-world problems involving statistics

✓ Check Skills You'll Need

Write each fraction as a decimal.

1. $\frac{5}{8}$ 2. $\frac{9}{20}$ 3. $\frac{3}{4}$

4. $\frac{5}{6}$ 5. $\frac{2}{3}$ 6. $\frac{8}{11}$

GO for Help
Lesson 5-2

◄)) New Vocabulary
- percent

Develop Convert fractions to decimals and percents and use these representations in estimations, computations, and applications.

Writing Percents as Fractions and Decimals

A **percent** is a ratio that compares a number to 100. Therefore, you can write a percent as a fraction with a denominator of 100.

1 EXAMPLE **Writing a Percent as a Fraction**

Write each percent as a fraction or a mixed number.

a. **5%**

$\frac{5}{100}$ ◄—— Write as a fraction with a denominator of 100. ——► $\frac{125}{100}$

$\frac{1}{20}$ ◄—— Simplify. ——► $\frac{5}{4}$

Write as a mixed number. ——► $1\frac{1}{4}$

b. **125%**

✓ Quick Check

1. Write each percent as a fraction or mixed number in simplest form.

    a. 58%   b. 72%   c. 144%

To write a percent as a decimal, write the percent as a fraction with a denominator of 100. Then divide to convert the fraction to a decimal.

2 EXAMPLE **Writing a Percent as a Decimal**

The California valley quail population in California increases about 1.5% each year. Write 1.5% as a decimal.

$1.5\% = \frac{1.5}{100}$ Write as a fraction with a denominator of 100.

$= 001.5$ Divide by moving the decimal point left two places. You may need to write one or more zeros.

$= 0.015$

✓ Quick Check

2. a. Write 62.5% as a decimal.
   b. About 45% of the people in the United States have type O blood. Write this percent as a decimal and as a fraction in simplest form.

The California valley quail is the state bird of California.

Writing Decimals and Fractions as Percents

for Help

For a guide to writing decimals as fractions, see Lesson 5-2.

To write a decimal as a percent, rewrite the decimal as a fraction with a denominator of 100. Then write the fraction as a percent.

Another way to change a decimal to a percent is to multiply the decimal by 100 and add a percent sign. When you multiply by 100, you move the decimal point two places to the right.

3 EXAMPLE **Writing a Decimal as a Percent**

Write 0.333 as a percent.

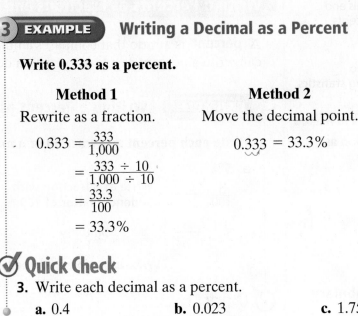

Method 1
Rewrite as a fraction.

$$0.333 = \frac{333}{1,000}$$

$$= \frac{333 \div 10}{1,000 \div 10}$$

$$= \frac{33.3}{100}$$

$$= 33.3\%$$

Method 2
Move the decimal point.

$$0.333 = 33.3\%$$

✓ Quick Check

3. Write each decimal as a percent.

a. 0.4   **b.** 0.023   **c.** 1.75

To write a fraction as a percent, divide the numerator by the denominator. Then convert the decimal quotient to a percent.

4 EXAMPLE **Writing a Fraction as a Percent**

Five out of sixteen families in the United States own dogs. What percent of families own dogs?

$\frac{5}{16}$ Write a fraction.

0.3125   Divide the numerator by the denominator.

31.25%   Write as a percent.

About 31% of families own dogs.

✓ Quick Check

4. Three out of eleven families in the United States own cats. To the nearest percent, what percent of families own cats?

Match each percent with an equivalent fraction or decimal.

1. 4%
2. 14%
3. 40%
4. 200%

A. 0.4
B. $\frac{50}{25}$
C. 0.14
D. $\frac{1}{25}$

5. Which is greater, 0.5 or 4%? Explain.

Standards Practice

For more exercises, see *Extra Skills and Word Problem Practice.*

A Practice by Example

Example 1
(page 301)

GO for Help

Write each percent as a fraction or mixed number in simplest form.

6. 40%   7. 28%   8. 39%   9. 55%   10. 20%

11. 6%   12. 98%   13. 315%   14. 220%   15. 102%

Example 2
(page 301)

Write each percent as a decimal.

16. 36%   17. 4.4%   18. 1%   19. 6.3%   20. 133%

21. 79.7%   22. 350%   23. 52%   24. 31.4%   25. 0.03%

26. In one year, women made up 40% of freshmen studying computer science at a certain university. Write this percent as a decimal and as a fraction in simplest form.

Example 3
(page 302)

Write each decimal as a percent.

27. 1.68   28. 0.36   29. 0.70   30. 0.002   31. 0.06

32. 1.88   33. 2.59   34. 1.11   35. 0.156   36. 0.043

Example 4
(page 302)

Write each fraction as a percent. Round to the nearest tenth of a percent where necessary.

37. $\frac{23}{100}$ 38. $\frac{1}{4}$ 39. $\frac{11}{20}$ 40. $\frac{3}{5}$ 41. $\frac{5}{8}$

42. $\frac{4}{19}$ 43. $\frac{1}{6}$ 44. $\frac{7}{20}$ 45. $\frac{2}{9}$ 46. $\frac{7}{18}$

47. In the United States, about one person in eight lives in California. To the nearest percent, what percent of people in the United States live in California?

B Apply Your Skills

Write each fraction as a percent. Round to the nearest tenth of a percent where necessary.

48. $\frac{8}{13}$ 49. $\frac{5}{6}$ 50. $\frac{111}{100}$ 51. $\frac{9}{2}$ 52. $\frac{12}{5}$

Compare. Use >, <, or = to complete each statement.

53. 0.05% ▇ 50%   **54.** $\frac{7}{12}$ ▇ 60%   **55.** $\frac{140}{130}$ ▇ 104%

Estimation **About what percent of each flag is red?**

56.

California

57.

North Carolina

Homework Video Tutor

Visit: PHSchool.com
Web Code: bje-0604

Copy and complete the table.

	Fraction	Decimal	Percent
58.	$\frac{4}{5}$	▇	▇
59.	▇	0.10	▇
60.	▇	0.5	▇
61.	$\frac{3}{4}$	▇	▇
62.	▇	▇	67%
63.	▇	▇	25%

Vocabulary Tip

A reasonable statement is one that makes sense.

Reasoning **Is the statement reasonable? Explain.**

64. Each year, about 18% of Americans go camping. About 82% of Americans do not go camping.

65. A student correctly answered 200% of the items on a test.

66. Today a runner ran 150% of the distance she ran yesterday.

67. On a test, a student missed 12 items and correctly answered 96% of all items.

Order each set of numbers from least to greatest.

68. $0.63, -0.72, 69\%, -\frac{3}{4}, 78\%$ **69.** $11\%, -1\%, \frac{1}{8}, -0.09, 0.093$

70. A map has a scale of 0.01%. Write the scale as a fraction.

71. Jeanette answered 32 questions correctly on a 45-question test. The passing grade was 70%. Did Jeanette pass? Justify your answer.

72. A scale drawing has a scale of 1 : 12. Write the scale as a percent.

73. **Writing in Math** Explain how to write a decimal as a percent. Give examples.

74. a. On his last math assignment, Kyle answered 5% of the questions incorrectly, or 1 question. How many questions did Kyle answer correctly?

b. On the same test, Diana answered 16 questions correctly. What percent of the questions did she answer incorrectly?

75. Reasoning Explain why 0.25 is different from 0.25%.

76. A crowd filled the 8,000 seats in a stadium. There were 1,400 children and 4,800 men present. Write a ratio and a percent to describe how many seats were filled by women.

C Challenge **77.** The results of a survey indicate that "32% of students surveyed prefer chicken." Forty of the students surveyed prefer chicken. How many students were surveyed in all?

Multiple Choice Practice and Mixed Review

For Standards Tutorials, visit PHSchool.com. Web Code: bjq-9045

78. If 12% of an iceberg is above water, what fraction is below the water?

A $\frac{3}{25}$
B $\frac{12}{88}$
C $\frac{22}{25}$
D $1\frac{3}{25}$

79. Which graph shows a triangle with one vertex at $(0, 3)$ and another in the second quadrant?

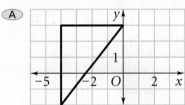
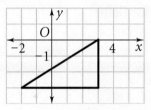

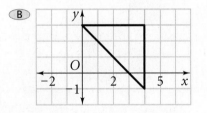
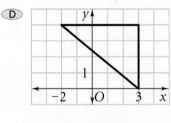

80. $\triangle EFG$ was dilated to form $\triangle MNP$. Which number best represents the scale factor used to change $\triangle EFG$ into $\triangle MNP$?

A 6
B 3
C $\frac{1}{3}$
D $\frac{1}{6}$

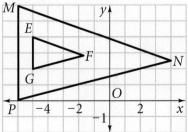

 for Help   Lesson 3-5   **Solve each equation.**

81. $0.85x = 39.95$

82. $\frac{b}{-25} = 1.8$

6-5 Proportions and Percents

Develop Convert fractions to decimals and percents and use these representations in estimations, computations, and applications.

Solve problems that involve discounts and markups.

What You'll Learn

- To find part of a whole
- To find a whole amount

. . . And Why

To solve real-world problems involving business data

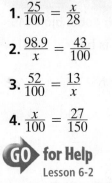

Check Skills You'll Need

Solve each proportion.

1. $\frac{25}{100} = \frac{x}{28}$

2. $\frac{98.9}{x} = \frac{43}{100}$

3. $\frac{52}{100} = \frac{13}{x}$

4. $\frac{x}{100} = \frac{27}{150}$

GO for Help
Lesson 6-2

Finding Part of a Whole

You can solve a percent problem by writing and solving a proportion.

A model can help you write a proportion. This model shows that 30 is 75% of 40.

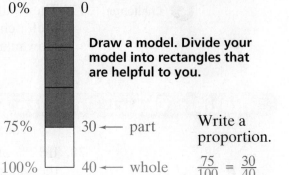

Draw a model. Divide your model into rectangles that are helpful to you.

Write a proportion.

$\frac{75}{100} = \frac{30}{40}$

1 EXAMPLE Finding Part of a Whole

Find 65% of 245.

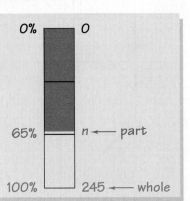

$\frac{65}{100} = \frac{n}{245}$ **Write a proportion.**

$65(245) = 100n$ **Write cross products.**

$\frac{65(245)}{100} = \frac{100n}{100}$ **Divide each side by 100.**

$159.25 = n$ **Simplify.**

65% of 245 is 159.25.

Quick Check

1. Draw a model and write a proportion. Then solve.

a. 25% of 124 is ■.   **b.** 43% of 230 is ■.   **c.** 12.5% of 80 is ■.

What percent of 60 is 52? Round to the nearest tenth of a percent.

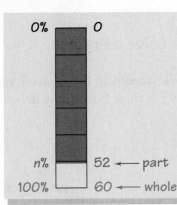

$$\frac{n}{100} = \frac{52}{60}$$ Write a proportion.

$$60n = 100(52)$$ Write cross products.

$$\frac{60n}{60} = \frac{100(52)}{60}$$ Divide each side by 60.

$$n = 86.\overline{6}$$ Simplify.

$$\approx 86.7$$ Round.

52 is approximately 86.7% of 60.

Quick Check

2. Round to the nearest tenth.

    a. What percent of 250 is 138?   **b.** 14 is what percent of 15?

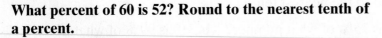
Finding a Whole Amount

Sometimes you know the percent that a part represents, and you want to find the whole amount. For example, your class fundraising committee might announce, "We've collected $207 so far, which is 46% of our goal!" You can use a proportion to calculate the goal.

3 **EXAMPLE**   Finding a Whole Amount

207 is 46% of what number?

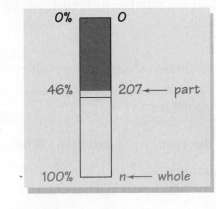

$$\frac{46}{100} = \frac{207}{n}$$ Write a proportion.

$$46n = 100(207)$$ Write cross products.

$$\frac{46n}{46} = \frac{100(207)}{46}$$ Divide each side by 46.

$$n = 450$$ Simplify.

207 is 46% of 450.

Online
active math

For: Proportions Activity
Use: Interactive Textbook, 6-5

✅ Quick Check

3. Round to the nearest tenth.

    a. 19 is 75% of what number?   **b.** 310 is 99% of what number?

4 **EXAMPLE**   **Using Percents to Solve a Problem**

In 2005, the number of drive-in movie screens in the United States was about 84% of the number in 1995. About how many drive-in screens were there in 1995?

Drive-In Movies

Year	Number of Screens
1995	■
2000	717
2005	709

Source: Motion Picture Association of America

$\dfrac{84}{100} = \dfrac{709}{n}$ Write a proportion.

$84n = 100(709)$ Write cross products.

$\dfrac{84n}{84} = \dfrac{100(709)}{84}$ Divide each side by 84.

$n \approx 844$ Round to the nearest whole number.

There were about 844 drive-in screens in 1995.

Check Is the answer reasonable? The original problem says that the number of screens in 2005 was 84% of the number in 1995. Check by estimating:

84% of 844 $\approx 0.9 \times 800 = 720$, which is close to 709, the number for 2005. So the answer is reasonable.

✅ Quick Check

4. Refer to the table in Example 4. In 2000, the number of drive-in movie screens was about 20.1% of the number in 1980. Find the number of drive-in screens in 1980.

Here is a summary of how to use proportions to solve percent problems.

Take Note   **Percents and Proportions**

Finding the Percent	Finding the Part	Finding the Whole
What percent of 40 is 6?	What number is 15% of 40?	6 is 15% of what number?
$\dfrac{n}{100} = \dfrac{6}{40} \leftarrow \text{part} \atop \leftarrow \text{whole}$	$\dfrac{15}{100} = \dfrac{n}{40} \leftarrow \text{part} \atop \leftarrow \text{whole}$	$\dfrac{15}{100} = \dfrac{6}{n} \leftarrow \text{part} \atop \leftarrow \text{whole}$

Match each question with the correct proportion.

1. 42 is 60% of what number?

2. What number is 42% of 60?

3. 42 is what percent of 60?

A. $\frac{42}{60} = \frac{x}{100}$

B. $\frac{42}{m} = \frac{60}{100}$

C. $\frac{42}{100} = \frac{x}{60}$

4. Draw a model to represent the percent of 75 that is 30.

Standards Practice

For more exercises, see *Extra Skills and Word Problem Practice*.

A Practice by Example

For Exercises 5–26, write and solve a proportion to find the unknown amount. Where necessary, round to the nearest tenth.

Example 1
(page 306)

Go for Help

5.

0%   0

75%   *n*

100%   560

6.

0%   0

85%   *n*

100%   20

7. 80% of 20 is ▪.

8. 40% of 60 is ▪.

9. 53% of 70 is ▪.

10. 18% of 150 is ▪.

11. 16% of 75 is ▪.

12. 92% of 625 is ▪.

Example 2
(page 307)

13.

0%   0

n%   16

100%   20

14.

0%   0

n%   18

100%   75

15. ▪% of 40 is 30.

16. ▪% of 20 is 4.

17. ▪% of 25 is 13.

18. 75 is ▪% of 250.

19. ▪% of 92 is 17.

20. ▪% of 80 is 14.

Example 3
(page 307)

21. 8 is 25% of ▪.

22. 14 is 35% of ▪.

23. 31 is 49% of ▪.

24. 45 is 93% of ▪.

25. 1 is 2% of ▪.

26. 6 is 98% of ▪.

Example 4
(page 308)

27. In 1950, the population of Alaska was about 128,535. That was about 19.4% of the population of Alaska in the year 2005. About how many people lived in Alaska in the year 2005?

28. A bicycle cost $250 last year. It now costs 20% less. How much does the bicycle cost now?

State	Sales Tax
Nevada	6.5%
Kansas	5.3%
Pennsylvania	6%
New Mexico	5%
California	7.25%

Write and solve a proportion. Where necessary, round to the nearest whole amount.

29. Find 300% of 50.

30. $12\frac{1}{2}$% of ■ is 50.

31. Find 60% of 15.

32. 40,571 is ■% of 76,550.

33. 35% of ■ is 52.5.

34. 121.8 is ■% of 105.

35. The table shows sales tax rates for different states. For each state, find the following amount on a $15,000 car.
 a. the amount of sales tax   **b.** the car's total cost

36. You invested some money and made a profit of $55. Your profit was 11% of your investment. How much did you invest?

37. Nineteen members, or 38%, of the ski club are going on a ski trip. Find the total number of members in the club.

38. **Error Analysis** Your class has 26 students, which represents 5% of your school's enrollment. Your friend uses the proportion $\frac{5}{100} = \frac{n}{26}$ to find the number of students in your school. Explain your friend's error.

39. **Writing in Math** At Pics, all posters are 30% off. At Pacs, all posters are marked $\frac{1}{3}$ off. Which is the greater discount rate? Explain.

40. **Reasoning** Do a% of b and b% of a represent the same amount? Justify your answer.

C Challenge

41. You have 264 points, or 88%, in four rounds of a five-part competition. How many points do you need to score in the next round to raise your score to 90%?

Multiple Choice Practice and Mixed Review

For Standards Tutorials, visit PHSchool.com. Web Code: bjq-9045

42. Your school is having a homecoming dinner dance and offers three choices for dinner. One fifth of the students order steak, and $\frac{2}{3}$ order chicken. What fraction of the students order fish?
 Ⓐ $\frac{2}{15}$ Ⓑ $\frac{3}{8}$ Ⓒ $\frac{1}{2}$ Ⓓ $\frac{13}{15}$

43. There are 500 students who voted in an election at school. Of those students, 25% voted for Li, $\frac{2}{5}$ voted for Mae, and the rest voted for Marg. How many students voted for Marg?
 Ⓐ 125   Ⓑ 175   Ⓒ 205   Ⓓ 325

44. Stan drives 165 miles in 3 hours. If he continues at the same rate, how many miles will he drive in 5 hours?
 Ⓐ 53 mi   Ⓑ 55 mi   Ⓒ 275 mi   Ⓓ 495 mi

GO for Help Lesson 6-4

Write each number as a percent.

45. 0.08   **46.** 0.523   **47.** $\frac{7}{12}$ **48.** 4.56

Percents and Equations

Introduce Solve problems that involve commissions.

What You'll Learn

- To write and solve percent equations
- To use equations to solve percent problems

. . . And Why

To solve real-world problems involving earnings and surveys

✓ **Check Skills You'll Need**

Write each percent as a decimal.

1. 48%   **2.** 5%

3. 23.8%   **4.** 72.25%

5. 136%   **6.** 178.5%

GO for Help

Lesson 6-4

🔊 **New Vocabulary**

- commission

Writing and Solving Percent Equations

You can solve a percent problem by writing and solving an equation. When you use a percent in an equation, write it as a decimal.

Take Note ✏️ **Percent Equations**

Finding the Percent	Finding the Part	Finding the Whole
What percent of 40 is 6?	What is 15% of 40?	6 is 15% of what?
$n \cdot 40 = 6$	$n = 0.15 \cdot 40$	$6 = 0.15 \cdot n$

1 **EXAMPLE** **Solving a Percent Equation**

What is 85% of 62?

$n = 0.85 \cdot 62$ Write an equation. Write the percent as a decimal.

$n = 52.7$ Simplify.

85% of 62 is 52.7.

✓ **Quick Check**

1. Write and solve an equation.

   a. 0.96 is what percent of 10?   **b.** 19.2 is 32% of what?

You can also write and solve equations having percents greater than 100%.

2 **EXAMPLE** **Percents Greater Than 100%**

What percent of 48 is 54?

$n \cdot 48 = 54$ Write an equation.

$\dfrac{48n}{48} = \dfrac{54}{48}$ Divide each side by 48.

$n = 1.125$ Simplify.

$= 112.5\%$ Change the decimal to a percent.

54 is 112.5% of 48.

✓ **Quick Check**

2. Write and solve an equation.

   a. What is 145.5% of 20?   **b.** 380 is 125% of what number?

GO **Online**

Video Tutor Help
Visit: PHSchool.com
Web Code: bje-0775

Using Equations to Solve Percent Problems

Some sales jobs pay an amount based on how much you sell. This amount is called a **commission.**

3 EXAMPLE Solving a Commission Problem

A real-estate agent makes a 4.5% commission on property she sells. How much commission does she make on the sale of a house for $132,500?

Words | amount of commission | is | 4.5% | of | $132,500

Let c = amount of commission.

Equation c = 0.045 · 132,500

$$c = 0.045 \cdot 132,500$$
$$= 5,962.50$$

The agent's commission is $5,962.50.

✓ Quick Check

3. A singer receives a 5% royalty on each CD sale. To the nearest cent, find his royalty for a CD that sells for $16.99.

4 EXAMPLE Solving a Percent Problem

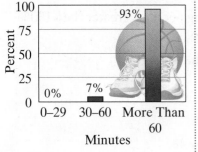

Responses to "How many minutes per day should you exercise?"

The graph shows the results of a survey. There were about 1,130 people who answered "more than 60 minutes." How many people were surveyed?

Words | 1,130 | is | 93% | of | number surveyed

Let n = number surveyed.

Equation | 1,130 | = | 0.93 | · | n

$$0.93n = 1,130$$
$$\frac{0.93n}{0.93} = \frac{1,130}{0.93}$$
$$n = 1,215.0537\ldots$$

You cannot have 0.0537... of a person. About 1,215 people were surveyed.

✓ Quick Check

4. In a survey, 952 people, or 68%, preferred smooth peanut butter to crunchy. How many people were surveyed?

1. **Mental Math** 14 is 50% of what number?

2. **Reasoning** Suppose that 44 is 20% of some number. Is the unknown number greater than or less than 44? Explain.

3. Explain two ways to find 32% of a number.

4. A real estate agent received a $7,000 commission for a sale of $175,000. Find the percent of commission.

Standards Practice

For more exercises, see *Extra Skills and Word Problem Practice*.

A Practice by Example

Write an equation and solve.

Example 1
(page 311)

GO for Help

5. Find 30% of 30.
6. What percent of 40 is 25?
7. 120 is 15% of what number?
8. What percent of 20 is 11?
9. Find 56% of 75.
10. 85% of z is 106,250. What is z?

Example 2
(page 311)

11. What percent of 4 is 9?
12. Find 500% of 12.
13. What percent of 150 is 96?
14. 3.5% of d is 0.105. What is d?
15. What percent of 1 is 4.7?
16. Find 15% of 150.

Example 3
(page 312)

17. Julius writes novels and receives 12% of the price for each book sold. To the nearest cent, find the royalty Julius receives for a book price of $7.99.

18. An agent makes 16% commission on an athlete's signing bonus. If the bonus is $26,000, what is the agent's commission?

Example 4
(page 312)

For Exercises 19 and 20, the table gives information about videocassette recorders (VCRs) in the United States.

19. The number of households with VCRs in 2000 was about 90% of the number with VCRs in 2005. About how many households had VCRs in 2005?

20. The number of households with VCRs in 1990 was about 87.5% of the number with VCRs in 1993. About how many households had VCRs in 1993?

Households With VCRs

Year	Households (millions)
1990	63
1995	77
2000	88
2005	■

SOURCE: Statistical Abstract of the United States. Go to **PHSchool.com** for a data update. Web Code: bjg-9041

B Apply Your Skills

21. Decide whether each statement is true or false. Explain.

   a. The number of households with VCRs in 1990 was less than 10% of the number in 2000.

   b. The number of households with VCRs in 2000 was more than 50% of the number in 1990.

Write and solve an equation. Where necessary, round to the nearest tenth or tenth of a percent.

22. What percent of 45 is 24?   23. Find 5.5% of 44.

24. What percent of 8 is 20?   25. 9.2% of b is 27.6. What is b?

26. 135% of t is 63. What is t?   27. What is 264% of 12?

28. A salesperson receives 5.4% commission. On one sale, she received $6.48. What was the amount of the sale?

29. **Reasoning** Describe a situation in which you would use a percent greater than 100%.

Visit: PHSchool.com
Web Code: bje-0606

Mental Math Use mental math.

30. What percent of 60 is 30?   31. 100% of t is 100. What is t?

32. Find 5% of 10.   33. What percent of 55 is 11?

34. 50% of g is 24. What is g?   35. Find 15% of 12.

C Challenge   36. You pay a real estate agent a 4% commission for selling your house. After paying the commission, you receive $302,900. What was the actual selling price of the house?

Multiple Choice Practice and Mixed Review

For Standards Tutorials, visit PHSchool.com. Web Code: bjq-9045

37. Jill's model car is shown in the diagram. The model represents an actual car that is 16 feet long. Jill wants to calculate the roof length of the actual car. What other information is necessary to find the length of the actual roof?

$1\frac{1}{2}$ in.

3 in.

   Ⓐ The actual roof height   Ⓒ The model roof length
   Ⓑ The model roof height   Ⓓ The model door width

38. You receive a 3% commission on all sales. How much do you earn for selling a refrigerator that costs $789.00?

   Ⓐ $23.67   Ⓒ $765.33
   Ⓑ $236.70   Ⓓ $812.64

 for Help   Lesson 6-5   **Write a proportion. Then solve.**

39. ■% of 360 is 45.   40. 35% of 60 is ■.   41. 45 is 1.5% of ■.

Lesson 4-7   **Simplify each expression.**

42. $10^2 \cdot 10^4$ 43. $9y^4 \cdot y^5$ 44. $(x^3)^7$

Estimating With Percents

Develop Convert fractions to decimals and percents and use these representations in estimations and applications.

When you want to estimate the solution to a percent problem, you often want to convert the percents to decimals or fractions. For example, knowing that 78% is a little more than $\frac{3}{4}$ and a little less than 0.8 can help you choose compatible numbers.

ACTIVITY

About 8% of people are left-handed. 8% is almost 10%, or $\frac{1}{10}$, or 0.1, and 8% is also about $\frac{1}{12}$. Which estimate for 8% is more reasonable for each situation?

a. **In a group of 72 people, about how many would you expect to be left-handed?**

The fraction $\frac{1}{12}$ is compatible with 72, so use 8% $\approx \frac{1}{12}$.

$$\frac{1}{12} \cdot 72 = 6$$

About 6 people in the group would be left-handed.

b. **About 55,000 people attended a football game. About how many of them would you expect to be left-handed?**

The decimal 0.1 allows you to use mental math, so use 8% $\approx$ 0.1.

$0.1 \cdot 55,000 = 5,500$ **Move the decimal point left one place.**

About 5,500 people at the football game would be left-handed.

c. **Twenty people are riding an elevator. About how many of them would you expect to be left-handed?**

The fraction $\frac{1}{10}$ is compatible with 20, so use 8% $\approx \frac{1}{10}$.

$$\frac{1}{10} \cdot 20 = 2$$

About 2 people riding the elevator would be left-handed.

EXERCISES

Without solving, choose a compatible number for the percent in each problem. Justify your choice.

1. 23% of 64   **2.** 11% of 350   **3.** 4% of 80   **4.** 67% of 120

Use compatible numbers to solve each problem.

5. 652 students attend Tippitt Middle School. 49% live less than three miles from school. About how many students is this?

6. Mr. Ross's bill for lunch at a restaurant was $22.60. He wants to leave a 15% to 20% tip. Should he leave $2.75, $3.25, or $4? Explain your reasoning.

6-7 Percent of Change

Introduce, Develop Calclulate the percentage of increases and decreases of a quantity.

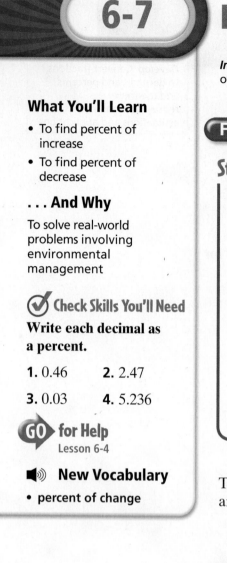

What You'll Learn

- To find percent of increase
- To find percent of decrease

. . . And Why

To solve real-world problems involving environmental management

✓ Check Skills You'll Need

Write each decimal as a percent.

1. 0.46   **2.** 2.47

3. 0.03   **4.** 5.236

GO for Help
Lesson 6-4

🔊 New Vocabulary

- percent of change

Finding Percent of Increase

Standards Investigation
Exploring Percent of Change

1. Find the change in population from 1990 to 2000 for each state.

2. Which state had the greater change in population?

3. Write the ratio $\frac{\text{change in population}}{\text{1990 population}}$ for each state. Then write each ratio as a percent.

4. Compare the two percents. Which state had the greater population change in terms of percent?

Populations of Two States

State	1990	2000
California	29,786,000	33,872,000
Nevada	1,202,000	1,998,000

The percent a quantity increases or decreases from its original amount is the **percent of change.**

$$\text{percent of change} = \frac{\text{amount of change}}{\text{original amount}}$$

1 EXAMPLE   Finding Percent of Increase

Find the percent of increase from 4 to 7.5.

amount of increase = 7.5 − 4 = 3.5

percent of increase = $\frac{\text{amount of increase}}{\text{original amount}}$

$= \frac{3.5}{4}$

$= 0.875 = 87.5\%$

The percent of increase from 4 to 7.5 is 87.5%.

✓ Quick Check

1. Find each percent of increase.

a. from 100 to 114   **b.** from 2.0 to 3.2   **c.** from 4,000 to 8,500

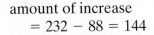

EXAMPLE **Finding Percent of Increase**

The annual production of municipal solid waste in the United States has more than doubled since 1960. Find the percent of increase from 1960 to 2000.

Municipal Solid Waste

88 million tons — 1960
121 million tons — 1970
152 million tons — 1980
205 million tons — 1990
232 million tons — 2000

SOURCE: Environmental Protection Agency.
Go to **PHSchool.com** for a data update.
Web Code: bjg-9041

amount of increase
$= 232 - 88 = 144$

percent of increase
$= \dfrac{\text{amount of increase}}{\text{original amount}}$

$= \dfrac{144}{88}$

$= 1.6\overline{3} \approx 163\%$

The percent of increase from 1960 to 2000 was about 163%.

✓ Quick Check

2. Find the percent of increase in solid-waste production from 1970 to 1980. Round to the nearest percent.

Finding Percent of Decrease

You also can find percent of decrease.

EXAMPLE **Finding Percent of Decrease**

Find the percent of decrease from 1,500 to 1,416.

amount of decrease $= 1,500 - 1,416 = 84$

percent of decrease $= \dfrac{\text{amount of decrease}}{\text{original amount}}$

$= \dfrac{84}{1,500}$

$= 0.056 = 5.6\%$

The percent of decrease is 5.6%.

✓ Quick Check

3. Find each percent of decrease. Where necessary, round to the nearest tenth of a percent.

a. from 9.6 to 4.8   **b.** from 202 to 192   **c.** from 854.5 to 60.6

1. **Vocabulary** The percent of change is the percent a quantity increases or decreases from its ___?___ amount.

Find each percent of change. Tell whether the change is an increase or decrease.

2. from 30 to 39   3. from 60.3 to 48.9   4. from −7 to −10

5. **Error Analysis** Jessi's first step in finding the percent of change from 7 to 8 was to write $\frac{8-7}{8} = \frac{1}{8}$. Explain Jessi's error.

Standards Practice

For more exercises, see *Extra Skills and Word Problem Practice*.

Ⓐ Practice by Example

Examples 1 and 2
(pages 316, 317)

GO for
Help

Find each percent of increase.

6. from 30 to 39   7. from 50 to 66   8. from 4 to 4.5

9. from 48 to 60   10. from 32 to 76   11. from 5 to 5.5

12. from 55 to 176   13. from 38 to 95   14. from 2.5 to 3

15. In the United States in the 20th century, average life expectancy increased from about 47 years to about 77 years. Find the percent of increase to the nearest percent.

Example 3
(page 317)

Find each percent of decrease. Where necessary, round to the nearest tenth of a percent.

16. from 60 to 48   17. from 180 to 54   18. from 180 to 108

19. from 280 to 126   20. from 240 to 90   21. from 42 to 35

22. from 64 to 24   23. from 6.5 to 4.8   24. from 7.4 to 2.4

25. A computer that cost $1,099 last year costs $999 this year.

26. A racing bicycle that cost $1,500 new costs $845 used.

Ⓑ Apply Your Skills

Find each percent of change. Tell whether the change is an increase or a decrease. Where necessary, round to the nearest tenth of a percent.

27. from 96 to 78   28. from 90 to 75   29. from 80 to 95

30. from 45 to 105   31. from 27 to 72   32. from 120 to 95

33. from 87 to 108   34. from 59 to 127   35. from 77 to 13

36. The average cost of a gallon of gasoline was $1.29 in 1997 and $2.96 in 2006. Find the percent of increase.

Homework Video Tutor

▶ ─────────▽─────────

Visit: PHSchool.com
Web Code: bje-0607

The giant panda Su Lin was born at the San Diego Zoo in August 2005. She weighed 13 oz.

37. Su Lin weighed 3.29 lb at one month, and 47 lb at one year. Find each percent of increase of weight. Round to the nearest percent.
   a. from birth to one month
   b. from one month to one year
   c. from birth to one year
   d. **Writing in Math** Explain why the sum of the percent increase from birth to one month and from one month to one year does not equal the percent increase from birth to one year.

Mental Math Use mental math to find each percent of change. Tell whether the change is an increase or a decrease.

38. from 25 to 30   39. from 40 to 45   40. from 50 to 45

41. from 100 to 101.1 42. from 40 to 20   43. from 15 to 12

C Challenge

44. a. **Reasoning** 100 is increased by 10%. The result is decreased by 10%. Is the final result 100? Explain.
   b. Compare the final result in part (a) to 100, the original number. Find the percent of change.

45. The number of students on the honor roll for term 2 is 552. This is a 20% increase from the previous term. Find the number of students who were on the honor roll during term 1.

Multiple Choice Practice and Mixed Review

For Standards Tutorials, visit PHSchool.com. Web Code: bjq-9045

46. What is the percent of change from 148 to 37?
   Ⓐ 3%   Ⓑ 25%   Ⓒ 75%   Ⓓ 111%

47. Mimi was 36 inches tall two years ago. If she is 17% taller this year, how tall is she? Round your answer to the nearest inch.
   Ⓐ 53 in.   Ⓑ 42 in.   Ⓒ 39 in.   Ⓓ 37 in.

48. $\triangle KLM$ is similar to $\triangle PRS$. What scale factor was used to dilate $\triangle KLM$ to $\triangle PRS$?
   Ⓐ 3.5
   Ⓑ 0.75
   Ⓒ 0.50
   Ⓓ 0.25

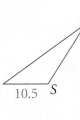

GO for Help   Lesson 6-4

49. The Space Surveillance Center in Colorado tracks about 8,500 objects in orbit around Earth. All but about 500 objects are junk from past space missions. What percent are junk? Round to the nearest percent.

Lesson 4-2

Evaluate each expression.

50. $3x^2$ for $x = -5$ 51. $[(3 + 12)4]^2$ 52. $(7 + 4y)^2$ for $y = -2$

Markup and Discount

Develop Calculate the percentage of increases and decreases of a quantity.
Develop Solve problems that involve discounts, markups, and commissions.

What You'll Learn

- To find markups
- To find discounts

. . . And Why

To solve real-world problems involving price, markups, and discounts

✓ Check Skills You'll Need

Write an equation and solve. Round to hundredths as needed.

1. What is 75% of $82?

2. What is 42% of $170?

3. What is 5.5% of $24?

4. What is 80% of $15.99?

GO for Help
Lesson 6-5

🔊 New Vocabulary

- markup
- discount

Finding Markups

To make a profit, stores charge more for merchandise than they pay for it. The amount of increase is called the **markup.** The percent of increase is the *percent of markup*.

1 EXAMPLE Finding Markup

A music store's percent of markup is 67%. A CD costs the store $10.15. Find the markup.

markup = percent of markup · store's cost

$= 0.67 \cdot 10.15$

≈ 6.80 **Simplify. Round to the nearest cent.**

The markup is $6.80.

✓ Quick Check

1. A clothing store pays $56 for a jacket. The store's percent of markup is 75%. Find the markup for the jacket.

The store's cost plus the markup equals the *selling price*.

2 EXAMPLE Finding Selling Price

A computer store pays $6 for a computer mouse. The percent of markup is 75%. Find the mouse's selling price.

$0.75 \cdot 6 = 4.50$ **Multiply to find the markup.**

$6.00 + 4.50 = 10.50$ **Cost + markup = selling price.**

The selling price is $10.50.

✓ Quick Check

2. A $5 cap has a 70% markup. Find the selling price.

Finding Discounts

When an item goes on sale, the amount of the price decrease is the **discount.** The percent of decrease is the *percent of discount*.

sale price = regular price − discount

Finding Discount

Athletic shoes that regularly sell for $85.99 are on sale for 20% off. Find the discount.

$$\text{discount} = \text{percent of discount} \cdot \text{regular price}$$
$$= 0.20 \cdot 85.99$$
$$\approx 17.20 \qquad \textbf{Simplify. Round to the nearest cent.}$$

The discount is $17.20.

✅ Quick Check

3. Pants priced at $21.99 are marked 15% off. Find the discount.

Here are two ways to use percent of discount to find a sale price.

More Than One Way

A video game that regularly sells for $39.95 is on sale for 20% off. What is the sale price?

Eric's Method

Find the discount. Then find the sale price.

$$\text{discount} = \text{percent of discount} \cdot \text{regular price}$$
$$= 0.20 \cdot 39.95$$
$$= 7.99$$
$$\text{sale price} = \text{regular price} - \text{discount}$$
$$= 39.95 - 7.99$$
$$= 31.96$$

The sale price is $31.96.

Michelle's Method

Find the sale price directly. The sale price equals 100% of the regular price minus 20% of the regular price.

$$\text{sale price} = (100\% - 20\%) \cdot \text{regular price}$$
$$= 80\% \cdot \text{regular price}$$
$$= 0.80(39.95)$$
$$= 31.96$$

The sale price is $31.96.

Choose a Method

1. Which method do you prefer? Explain.

2. Find the sale price if the percent of discount is 25%. Round to the nearest cent.

Vocabulary Match the term with its meaning.

1. discount
2. sale price
3. selling price
4. markup

A. regular price minus the discount
B. amount of increase
C. amount of the price decrease
D. cost plus the markup

5. What is the selling price of a $25.50 item with a markup of 26%?

Standards Practice

For more exercises, see *Extra Skills and Word Problem Practice.*

A Practice by Example

Example 1
(page 320)

GO for Help

For Exercises 6–8, find each markup.

6. cost: $1.50
   percent of markup: 70%

7. cost: $38
   percent of markup: 58%

8. A beach store pays $11.40 for each beach umbrella. The store's percent of markup is 75%.

Example 2
(page 320)

For Exercises 9–11, find each selling price.

9. cost: $6
   percent of markup: 75%

10. cost: $149.99
    percent of markup: 100%

11. A clothing store pays $15 for a shirt. The percent of markup is 85%.

Example 3
(page 321)

For Exercises 12–14, find each discount and sale price.

12. regular price: $100
    percent of discount: 27%

13. regular price: $8.49
    percent of discount: 5%

14. boots regularly $125 that are on sale for 30% off

B Apply Your Skills

Find each selling price. Where necessary, round to the nearest cent.

15. regular price: $14.99
    percent of discount: 15%

16. cost: $15
    percent of markup: 15%

GO for Help

For a guide to solving Exercise 17, see page 324.

17. An $11 shirt is on sale for 10% off.
    a. Describe two different methods of finding the sale price.
    b. Use one of the methods to find the sale price.

18. Store A is selling a video for 20% off the store's regular price of $25.95. Store B is selling the same video for 30% off the store's regular price of $29.50. Which store's sale price is lower? How much lower is it?

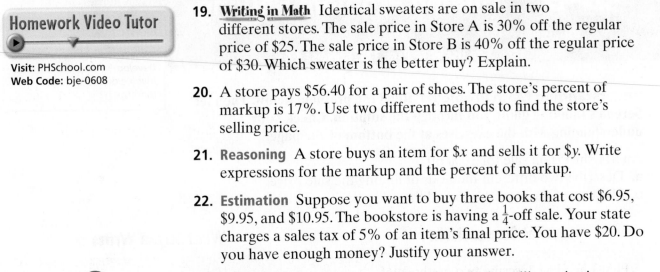
19. Writing in Math Identical sweaters are on sale in two different stores. The sale price in Store A is 30% off the regular price of $25. The sale price in Store B is 40% off the regular price of $30. Which sweater is the better buy? Explain.

20. A store pays $56.40 for a pair of shoes. The store's percent of markup is 17%. Use two different methods to find the store's selling price.

21. Reasoning A store buys an item for $x and sells it for $y. Write expressions for the markup and the percent of markup.

22. Estimation Suppose you want to buy three books that cost $6.95, $9.95, and $10.95. The bookstore is having a $\frac{1}{4}$-off sale. Your state charges a sales tax of 5% of an item's final price. You have $20. Do you have enough money? Justify your answer.

C Challenge **23.** Find the price a store paid for an item, if the selling price is $501 with a $37\frac{1}{2}$% markup.

Multiple Choice Practice and Mixed Review

For Standards Tutorials, visit PHSchool.com. Web Code: bjq-9045

24. The sale price of a coat is 40% off its regular price of $59.50. Which equation can be used to find s, the sale price of the coat?

A $s = 59.50 - 59.50(0.40)$ C $s = 59.50 - 59.50(0.60)$

B $s = 59.50 + 59.50(0.40)$ D $s = 59.50 + 59.50(0.60)$

25. Loretta bought a new computer for $1,849, a new printer for $159, and new software for $289, including tax. She plans to make equal payments of 10% of the total amount. What is a reasonable amount for each payment?

A $20   B $23   C $230   D $2,100

for Help **Lesson 6-7** **Find each percent of decrease. Round to the nearest tenth.**

26. from 90 to 70   **27.** from 44.4 to 14.8   **28.** from 1,750 to 1,125

✓ Checkpoint Quiz 2

Compare. Use >, <, or = to complete each statement.

1. $\frac{14}{25}$ ■ 56%   **2.** 1.1% ■ 0.11   **3.** $\frac{3}{11}$ ■ 27%

Write and solve an equation.

4. Find 33% of 120.   **5.** Find 125% of 42.

6. What percent of 5.6 is 1.4?   **7.** 15% of q is 9.75. What is q?

8. A car originally priced at $12,000 is sold at a 20% discount. Find the sale price.

GPS Guided Problem Solving

FOR USE WITH PAGE 322, EXERCISE 17

Develop Solve problems that involve discounts and markups.

Understanding Math Problems Read the problem below. Then let Serena's thinking guide you through the solution. Check your understanding with the exercises at the bottom of the page.

An $11 shirt is on sale for 10% off.
a. Describe two different methods of finding the sale price.
b. Use one of the methods to find the sale price.

What Serena Thinks

First I need to describe two methods of finding the sale price. Then I need to find the sale price.

One way to find the sale price is to find 10% of the price and subtract it.

Another way is to find 90% of the original price.

I need to choose one of the methods. Multiplying by 0.9 is faster than multiplying by 0.1 and then subtracting, so that's the method I'll use.

Now I need to write my answers.

What Serena Writes

Two methods:

price − (0.1 × price) = sale price

0.9 × price = sale price

0.9 × 11 = 9.9

a. Method 1: Find the amount of the 10% discount and subtract it from the original price.
Method 2: Find 90% of the original price.
b. The sale price is $9.90.

EXERCISES

Find each sale price.

1. $25 sweater; 15% off

2. $325 stereo; 20% off

3. $85 sneakers; 25% off

4. $15 T-shirt; 10% off

5. $520 TV; 18% off

6. $14 book; 12% off

Applications of Rational Numbers

What You'll Learn

- To apply rational numbers
- To estimate percents using fractions and decimals

. . . And Why

To solve real-world problems involving rates and probability

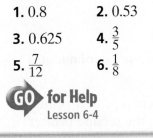 **Check Skills You'll Need**

Write each decimal or fraction as a percent.

1. 0.8   **2.** 0.53

3. 0.625   **4.** $\frac{3}{5}$

5. $\frac{7}{12}$ **6.** $\frac{1}{8}$

GO for Help
Lesson 6-4

Vocabulary Tip

Multi-step means "more than two steps."

Develop Add, subtract, multiply, and divide rational numbers.

Develop Convert fractions to decimals and percents and use these representations in estimations, computations, and applications.

Develop Solve multistep problems involving rate, average speed, distance, and time.

Applying Rational Numbers

You can use rational numbers in the form of fractions, decimals, and percents to solve multi-step problems. When you work with rational numbers, it is often helpful to write all the numbers in the same form.

1 EXAMPLE   Comparing Rational Numbers

A family drove 800 mi from Oakland, California, to Seattle, Washington. They drove $\frac{5}{16}$ of the trip on the first day, 0.2 of the trip on the second day, 30% of the trip on the third day, and 150 mi on the last day. On which day did they drive the farthest?

Method 1 Find the distance traveled each day. Compare.

$\frac{5}{16} \cdot 800 \text{ mi} = 250 \text{ mi}$ They drove $\frac{5}{16}$ of 800 mi on the first day.

$0.2 \cdot 800 \text{ mi} = 160 \text{ mi}$ They drove 0.2 of 800 mi on the second day.

$0.30 \cdot 800 \text{ mi} = 240 \text{ mi}$ They drove 30% of 800 mi on the third day.

150 mi They drove 150 mi on the fourth day.

They drove the farthest, 250 mi, on the first day.

Method 2 Write the four parts of the trip in the same form. Compare.

$\frac{5}{16} = 0.3125$ Write the fraction for the first day as a decimal.

0.2 The part of the trip on the second day is a decimal.

$30\% = 0.30$ Write the percent for the third day as a decimal.

$\frac{150}{800} = 0.1875$ Divide 150 by 800 for the fourth day.

Compare the decimals: $0.3125 > 0.30 > 0.2 > 0.1875$. They drove the farthest on the first day.

✓ Quick Check

1. An event planner has a $2,000 budget for an event. She spends 32% of the budget on chair rentals, 0.4 of the budget on food, $\frac{1}{5}$ of the budget on door prizes, and $160 on decorations. On which part does she spend the most?

You can use rational numbers to solve multi-step rate problems.

2 EXAMPLE Using Rational Numbers and Rates

Printer Sale

Prints 300 pages
in 10 minutes

Refer to the picture at the left. A second printer prints 40% more pages in 12 min. Which printer is faster?

Step 1 Find the rate of the first printer.

$\frac{300}{10} = 30$ Divide the number of pages by the number of minutes printing.

The first printer prints 30 pages/min.

Step 2 To find the rate of the second printer, first find the number of pages the second printer prints in 12 min.

40% of 300 = 0.40 · 300   **Write 40% as a decimal.**
= 120   **Multiply.**

Step 3 The second printer prints 40% *more* pages. Add.

300 + 120 = 420

The second printer prints 420 pages in 12 mins.

Step 4 Find the rate of the second printer.

$\frac{420}{12} = 35$ Divide the number of pages by the number of minutes printing.

The second printer prints 35 pages/min. The second printer prints more pages per minute than the first printer, so the second printer is faster.

✓ Quick Check

2. A copier makes 225 copies in 5 min. Another copier makes 20% fewer copies in 3 min. Which copier is faster?

Estimating Rational Numbers

You can use rational numbers to estimate when an exact answer is not needed. Estimation is useful in problems involving tips, sales tax, and sale prices. To estimate, change a percent to a fraction or decimal that is close to its value. The table below lists some common fraction, decimal, and percent equivalents.

Fraction	$\frac{1}{10}$	$\frac{1}{4}$	$\frac{1}{3}$	$\frac{2}{5}$	$\frac{1}{2}$	$\frac{2}{3}$	$\frac{3}{4}$	$\frac{4}{5}$	$\frac{9}{10}$	1
Decimal	0.1	0.25	$0.\overline{3}$	0.4	0.5	$0.\overline{6}$	0.75	0.8	0.9	1
Percent	10%	25%	$33\frac{1}{3}\%$	40%	50%	$66\frac{2}{3}\%$	75%	80%	90%	100%

3 EXAMPLE Estimating Percents Using Fractions

Use the nutrition label for macaroni at the left. The "% Daily Value" column gives the percent of the Reference Daily Intake (RDI) in one serving. The RDI for calcium is 1,000 mg. About how many milligrams of calcium are in one serving?

$$23\% \approx \frac{1}{4}$$ Use a fraction close to 23%.
Since 23% is close to 25%, use $\frac{1}{4}$.

$$23\% \text{ of } 1{,}000 \approx \frac{1}{4} \cdot 1{,}000$$ Estimate.

$$= 250$$ Multiply.

There are about 250 mg of calcium in one serving.

Nutrition Facts

Serving Size 1 cup (228g)
Servings Per Container 2

Amount Per Serving

Calories 250   Calories from Fat 110

	% Daily Value
Total Fat 12g	18%
Saturated Fat 3g	15%
Trans Fat 3g	
Cholesterol 30mg	10%
Sodium 470mg	20%
Total Carbohydrates 31g	10%
Dietary Fiber 0g	0%
Sugars 5g	
Protein 5g	
Vitamin A	4%
Vitamin C	2%
Calcium	23%
Iron	6%

✓ Quick Check

3. The RDI for iron is 18 mg. About how many milligrams of iron are in one serving of macaroni?

4 EXAMPLE Estimating Percents Using Decimals

A jacket is on sale for 35% off of $49.95. After the discount, 7.75% sales tax is added. Is $30.00 enough money to buy the jacket?

Step 1 Estimate the discount on the jacket.

$$35\% \approx 0.4$$ Use a decimal close to 35%.

$$49.95 \approx 50$$ Round the regular price.

$$35\% \text{ of } 49.95 \approx 0.4 \cdot 50$$ Estimate.

$$= 20$$ Multiply.

The discount is about $20.

Step 2 Subtract to find the sale price of the jacket.

$$\$50 - \$20 = \$30$$

The sale price of the jacket is about $30.

Step 3 Estimate the amount of tax.

$$7.75\% \approx 0.1$$ Use a decimal close to 7.75%.

$$7.75\% \text{ of } 30 \approx 0.1 \cdot 30$$ Estimate.

$$= 3$$

The amount of tax is about $3.

Step 4 Add the tax to the sale price: $30 + $3 = $33.

The total cost is about $33. So $30 is not enough.

✓ Quick Check

4. A computer is on sale for 15% off the regular price of $399.95. After the discount, 8.25% sales tax is added. Is $350 enough money to buy the computer? Justify your answer.

Complete Exercises 1–3 to solve the problem below.

The Lopez family drove $\frac{11}{20}$ of a 270-mi trip. The Brown family drove 52% of a 300-mi trip. Which family drove farther? How many miles farther?

1. How many miles did the Lopez family drive?

2. How many miles did the Brown family drive?

3. Which family drove farther? How many miles farther?

4. **Error Analysis** What is the error in the estimate at the right? Correct the error. Show your work.

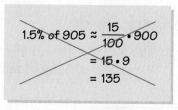

$$1.5\% \text{ of } 905 \approx \frac{15}{100} \cdot 900$$
$$= 15 \cdot 9$$
$$= 135$$

Standards Practice

For more exercises, see *Extra Skills and Word Problem Practice.*

A Practice by Example

Example 1
(page 325)

GO for Help

5. A family drove 1,250 mi to a vacation spot. They drove $\frac{1}{3}$ of the trip before dinner. After dinner, they drove 0.2 of the trip. The next day they drove 25% of the trip before lunch and drove the remaining 200 mi afterward. During which part of the trip did the family drive the farthest?

6. Out of 80 students surveyed about their favorite school lunch, 10% prefer hamburgers, 0.45 prefer chicken, and $\frac{3}{8}$ prefer spaghetti. The remaining 6 students chose sandwiches. Which meal do the greatest number of students prefer?

Example 2
(page 326)

7. **Rates** One worker packages 52 products in 8 h. A second worker packages 20% more products in 9 h. Which worker packages more products per hour?

8. Suppose you can type 412 words in 5 min. Your friend can type $\frac{3}{4}$ as many words in 3 min. Who types faster?

Examples 3 and 4
(page 327)

9. You want to buy a shirt that costs $24.95. Your parents agree to pay 23% of the cost. Estimate the amount your parents will contribute.

10. Estimate a 15% tip on a dinner bill of $29.70.

B Apply Your Skills

Homework Video Tutor

11. Fuel efficiency is the number of miles a vehicle can travel per gallon of gasoline. The less gas a car uses per mile, the more efficient it is. A mid-size car can travel 238 mi on 7 gal of gasoline. A minivan can travel 30% more miles on 12 gal. Which vehicle has greater fuel efficiency?

Visit: PHSchool.com
Web Code: bje-0609

Calories of Breakfast Foods

Food	Calories
apple	72
orange	62
1 c 2% milk	121
1 oz cereal	110
wheat bagel	260

12. Use the table at the left. The average person's daily caloric intake should be about 2,000 Calories. After eating a wheat bagel and an apple for breakfast, and a bag of crackers for a snack, a person has consumed 27% of the daily caloric intake. Estimate the number of Calories in the bag of crackers.

Mental Math Estimate 8.5% sales tax for each purchase.

13. $8.95   **14.** $11.63   **15.** $28.55

16. In a survey of 237 people, about 42% said green is their favorite color. About $\frac{3}{16}$ more people said blue is their favorite color. Estimate the number of people who prefer the color blue.

Orchestra Sections

Use the chart at the left for exercises 17–18.

17. Estimate the number of musicians in the woodwind section of a 96-member orchestra.

18. Estimate the number of musicians in the brass and percussion sections if the orchestra has 120 musicians.

Number Sense Use >, <, or = to complete each statement.

19. 27% of 156 ■ $\frac{5}{16}$ of 209   **20.** $\frac{2}{9}$ of 357 ■ 0.2 of 186

C Challenge

21. Rates Two people set out on a 10-mile bike race. Ron maintained an average speed of 20 mi/h. Isabella's speed for the first 5 miles was 25% greater than Ron's. For the rest of the race, she could manage only $\frac{3}{5}$ of her initial speed. Who won the race?

Multiple Choice Practice and Mixed Review

For Standards Tutorials, visit PHSchool.com. Web Code: bjq-9045

22. During one year, a video store rented an average of about 120 videos per day. During the following year, the number of videos rented dropped by 15%. During the second year, about how many videos were rented per day?

    Ⓐ 18   Ⓑ 102   Ⓒ 105   Ⓓ 128

23. A radio that usually sells for $59.99 is on sale for $\frac{1}{5}$ off. Which expression can you use to estimate your discount?

    Ⓐ 0.002 × 60   Ⓑ 0.05 × 60   Ⓒ 0.20 × 60   Ⓓ 0.50 × 60

24. You receive a discount of 6% on a TV that costs $195.50. How much do you pay for the TV?

    Ⓐ $178.20   Ⓑ $183.77   Ⓒ $207.23   Ⓓ $312.80

GO for Help   Lesson 6-3   **25.** The scale of a map is 3 in. : 20 mi. Find the actual distance for a map distance of 4.2 in.

6-10

Reasoning Strategy: Make a Table

What You'll Learn

- To solve problems by making a table

. . . And Why

To solve real-world problems involving population estimates

 **Check Skills You'll Need**

Solve.

1. For two weeks, you double the amount of money you saved the previous day. You save $.01 the first day. How much money will you have at the end of the two weeks?

GO for Help
Lesson 1-8

Make a Table

Have you ever watched a baseball game at a field that didn't have a scoreboard? It's hard to keep track of the score!

A scoreboard is a type of table. You can use tables to organize information. Tables are particularly helpful in solving problems that require several steps.

1 EXAMPLE Making a Table

At the beginning of the year 2000, the population of the United States was about 273.5 million. The rate of population growth was about 0.85% per year. If that rate continues, what will the population be at the beginning of 2010?

Understand Understand the problem.

Read the problem carefully.

1. What information are you asked to find?

2. What information will you need to use to solve the problem?

Plan Make a plan to solve the problem.

Decide on a strategy. You can use the percent of increase to predict the population increase for each year from 2000 to 2010. You can make a table to organize your predictions for each year.

3. How can you find the increase in population from the beginning of 2000 to the end of that year?

4. How can you find the population at the beginning of 2001?

5. The percent of increase is the same each year. Does that mean that the increase in population also will be the same each year? Explain your reasoning.

Carry Out Carry out the plan.

Copy and complete the table below.

6. Find the numbers for Column 4 by multiplying the numbers in Columns 2 and 3. Round to the nearest tenth of a million.

7. Find the numbers for Column 5 (and, hence, the next Column 2 entries) by adding the numbers in Columns 2 and 4.

1	2	3	4	5
Year	Population at Beginning of Year (millions)	Rate of Increase (0.85%)	Increase in Population (millions)	Population at End of Year (millions)
2000	273.5	0.0085	2.3	275.8
2001	275.8	0.0085	2.3	278.1
2002	278.1	0.0085	2.4	280.5
2003	280.5	0.0085	2.4	282.9
2004	282.9	0.0085	2.4	285.3
2005	285.3	0.0085	2.4	287.7
2006	287.7	0.0085	2.4	290.1
2007	290.1	0.0085	▪	▪
2008	▪	0.0085	▪	▪
2009	▪	0.0085	▪	▪
2010	▪			

8. Sometimes the number in Column 4 changes from one year to the next, and sometimes it does not change. Explain.

9. What is your prediction for population at the beginning of 2010?

Check Check the answer to be sure it is reasonable.

10. Your friend says that she knows a quicker way to find the answer. Simply multiply 273.5 · 0.0085 · 10 to find the increase for the ten-year period 2000 to 2010. Do you agree with your friend's approach? Explain your reasoning.

✓ Quick Check

11. Suppose the annual percent of increase in population is 0.9%. At that rate, what will the population be at the beginning of 2010?

For more exercises, see *Extra Skills and Word Problem Practice*.

A Practice by Example

 **for Help** Example 1 (page 330)

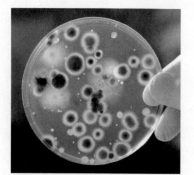

Microbe cultures grow on agar gel in petri dishes.

Make a table to solve each problem.

1. The population of a town increases at the rate of 1% each year. Today the town's population is 8,500. What will the population be in five years?

2. A microbe population increases 100% every 10 min. If you start with 1 microbe, how many will you have at the end of 1 h?

3. Cher has forgotten the combination to her locker. She knows it consists of four numbers—3, 5, 7, and 9—but she can't recall the order. She decides to try every possible order until she gets the right one. How many possible orders are there?

4. At the beginning of the year 2000, Bob put $100 in a savings account. The bank pays Bob 5% interest on his total savings at the end of each year, including all interest added to the account. Assume the interest rate continues and Bob does not deposit any additional money in the account. How much will he have in his savings account, to the nearest cent, after 5 interest payments?

B Apply Your Skills

STRATEGIES

- Act It Out
- Draw a Diagram
- Try, Test, Revise
- Look for a Pattern
- Make a Model
- Make a Table
- Simulate the Problem
- Solve by Graphing
- Use Multiple Strategies
- Work a Simpler Problem
- Work Backward
- Write an Equation
- Write a Proportion

Use any strategy to solve each problem.

5. Paco has four pairs of jeans and four T-shirts. How many outfits of a T-shirt and a pair of jeans can Paco make?

6. **Geometry** The length of a rectangle is twice the width. The perimeter of the rectangle is 42 cm. Find the length and width.

7. **Number Sense** The difference of two numbers is 18. The sum of the two numbers is 34. What are the two numbers?

8. You fill a container $\frac{3}{4}$ full of water. The amount of water now in the container is 6 quarts. How much can the container hold?

9. A family went to the movies. Tickets cost $4 for each child and $6 for each adult. The total admission charge for the family was $26. List all the possible numbers of adults and children in the family.

10. **Number Sense** A number n is multiplied by $\frac{5}{8}$. The product is subtracted from $\frac{2}{3}$. The result is $\frac{7}{12}$. What is n?

Homework Video Tutor

Visit: PHSchool.com
Web Code: bje-0610

11. Water for irrigation is measured in *acre-feet*. One acre-foot is the volume of water that would cover one acre of land to a depth of one foot. How many acre-feet of water would it take to cover 600 acres to a depth of one inch?

C Challenge

12. **Geometry** The height of a triangle is half the length of its base. The area of the triangle is 12.25 cm². Find the height.

Multiple Choice Practice and Mixed Review

For Standards Tutorials, visit PHSchool.com. Web Code: bjq-9045

13. Jenny deposited $300 in a savings account at the start of 2004. Her bank pays 3% interest on her total savings at the end of each year. She does not deposit or withdraw any money. To the nearest cent, how much money is in the account at the end of 2008?

   Ⓐ $309.00   Ⓑ $345.72   Ⓒ $347.78   Ⓓ $390.21

14. What is the percent of increase from 1.32 to 1.44, rounded to the nearest percent?

   Ⓐ 8%   Ⓑ 9%   Ⓒ 12%   Ⓓ 15%

15. A store pays $50.00 for a coat. Its markup is 25%. Later, it puts the coat on sale at 20% off. What is the sale price of the coat?

   Ⓐ $40.00   Ⓑ $50.00   Ⓒ $52.50   Ⓓ $62.50

 for Help   Lesson 6-1

16. A car travels 264 mi on 12 gal of gas. Find the unit rate in miles per gallon.

Mathematical Reasoning

Develop Develop generalizations of the results obtained and the strategies used and apply them to new problem situations.

Multi-Step Rate Problems

You often solve multi-step problems by breaking them into parts. Sometimes you can apply a strategy repeatedly to solve a problem.

EXAMPLE

You and your friend ride bicycles in opposite directions. You travel at 4.5 mi/h. Your friend travels at 6 mi/h. After 3 hours, how many miles apart are you and your friend?

Step 1 Use the distance formula to find the distance you travel.

$d = 4.5 \times 3$ **Substitute 4.5 for the rate and 3 for the time.**

$d = 13.5$ **Multiply.**

Step 2 Use the distance formula to find the distance your friend travels.

$d = 6 \times 3$ **Substitute 6 for the rate and 3 for the time.**

$d = 18$ **Multiply.**

Step 3 Add to find the number of miles apart.

13.5 mi + 18 mi = 31.5 mi

EXERCISE

1. A bus leaves the bus and rail terminal and travels north at 55 mi/h. A train leaves the terminal at the same time and travels south at 90 mi/h. How far apart will they be after 5 hours?

Estimation may help you find an answer, check an answer, or eliminate answer choices. If, however, an incorrect choice is very close to the correct choice, you will still have to find the exact answer.

EXAMPLE

A coat regularly priced at $89.95 is on sale at 40% off. What is the sale price of the coat?

   Ⓐ $35.98   Ⓑ $49.95   Ⓒ $53.97   Ⓓ $54.03

$89.95 \approx \$90$

40% is less than half. The discount will be less than $45, which is half of $90. So, the sale price will be more than $45.

This eliminates choice A.

40% of $90 = 0.4 \cdot 90$

$\qquad\qquad\quad = 36$

$90 - 36 = 54$, so the sale price is about $54. This eliminates choice B.

Choices C and D are both very close to $54, so you have to compute to find that the answer is choice C.

Multiple Choice Practice and Mixed Review

Read each question. Then write the letter of the correct answer on your paper.

1. A store pays $8.50 for a case of scented candles. The percent of markup is 110% at the store. What price will the store charge for the case of candles?

   Ⓐ $9.35   Ⓑ $16.15   Ⓒ $17.85   Ⓓ $18.15

2. Juan makes a scale model of a building. The actual building has a width of 30 yd and a height of 55 yd. His model has a width of 1.3 ft. What is a good estimate of the height of the model?

   Ⓐ 0.7 ft   Ⓑ 2.4 ft   Ⓒ 16 ft   Ⓓ 24 ft

3. An entomologist noted that in the past five years, in the local forest preserve, the population of bees decreased by 35%. In her study, she recorded that the number of active hives five years ago was 60. If the number of active hives decreased at the same rate as the bee population, how many hives are active today?

   Ⓐ 21 hives   Ⓒ 35 hives

   Ⓑ 25 hives   Ⓓ 39 hives

Chapter 6 Review

Match the vocabulary terms with their descriptions.

1. a comparison of two quantities by division

2. a ratio that compares a number to 100

3. the amount charged for an item above the cost

4. the amount of a price decrease

5. a ratio that compares quantities in different units

6. a rate that has a denominator of 1

7. two equal ratios

A. markup
B. percent
C. ratio
D. discount
E. unit rate
F. proportion
G. rate

Go **O**nline
PHSchool.com

For: Vocabulary quiz
Web Code: bjj-0651

Skills and Concepts

Lesson 6-1
- To find rates and unit rates
- To use measures expressed as rates and products to solve problems

A **ratio** is a comparison of two quantities by division. A **rate** is a ratio that compares quantities in different units. A **unit rate** is a rate that has a denominator of 1.

Write each ratio as a unit rate.

8. 150 mi in 3 h   **9.** $9.45 for 5 lb   **10.** 270 words in 3 min

Convert each measure. Round to the nearest tenth, if necessary.

11. 90 in./min = ■ ft/min   **12.** 12 cm/day = ■ cm/h

Lesson 6-2
- To solve proportions
- To use proportions to solve problems

A **proportion** is an equality of ratios. To solve a proportion, write the cross products and then solve.

Solve. Round to the nearest tenth where necessary.

13. $\frac{5}{6} = \frac{n}{42}$ **14.** $\frac{53}{2} = \frac{18}{x}$

15. $\frac{15}{a} = \frac{30}{98}$ **16.** $\frac{m}{150} = \frac{21}{25}$

Chapter Review (continued)

Lesson 6-3

- To solve problems that involve similar figures
- To solve problems that involve scale drawings

Similar figures have the same shape, but not necessarily the same size. In similar figures, the corresponding angles have equal measures and the corresponding sides are proportional.

A **scale drawing** is an enlarged or reduced drawing of an object.

The figures in each pair are similar. Find *x*.

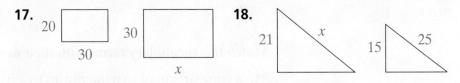

17.

18.

19. A map has a scale of 1 cm : 75 km. What is the distance on the map for an actual distance of 37.5 km?

Lesson 6-4

- To write percents as fractions and decimals
- To write decimals and fractions as percents

A **percent** is a ratio that compares a number to 100.

Write each percent as a fraction in simplest form and as a decimal.

20. 24%

21. 72%

22. 8%

23. 0.5%

Write each number as a percent. Round to the nearest tenth of a percent.

24. 0.3

25. 0.33

26. $\frac{1}{3}$

27. 0.35

28. $\frac{16}{18}$

29. 0.021

30. $\frac{120}{50}$

31. 0.0064

Lessons 6-5 and 6-6

- To find part of a whole
- To find a whole amount
- To write and solve percent equations
- To use equations to solve percent problems

Solve percent problems by using a proportion or an equation.

Write and solve a proportion.

32. Find 15% of 48.

33. 20% of *x* is 30. What is *x*?

34. What percent of 300 is 90?

35. 125% of *y* is 100. What is *y*?

Write and solve an equation.

36. 35% of *a* is 70. What is *a*?

37. Find 68% of 300.

38. What percent of 180 is 9?

39. What percent of 56 is 3.5?

Lessons 6-7 and 6-8

- To find percent of increase
- To find percent of decrease
- To find markups
- To find discounts

A **percent of change** is the percent by which a quantity increases or decreases from its original amount.

$$\text{percent of change} = \frac{\text{amount of change}}{\text{original amount}}$$

Markup is a real-world application of percent of increase. **Discount** is a real-world application of percent of decrease.

Find each percent of change. Tell whether the change is an increase or a decrease.

40. 120 to 90   **41.** 148 to 37   **42.** 285 to 342   **43.** 1,000 to 250

44. A cap that cost a retailer $5 was marked up by 75%. Find the selling price.

45. Peaches that are usually priced at $2/lb are on sale for 15% off. Find the sale price.

Lesson 6-9

- To apply rational numbers
- To estimate percents using fractions and decimals

You can use rational numbers in the form of fractions, decimals, and percents to solve multi-step problems.

46. A class voted on how to donate $550 they raised for charity. They gave $165 to the town conservation fund, 20% to the preschool, $\frac{2}{5}$ to the soup kitchen, and 0.1 to the humane society. Which group received the most money? Explain.

Use fractions or decimals to estimate each percent.

47. 23% of 64   **48.** 98% of 77   **49.** 34% of 123

Lesson 6-10

- To solve problems by making a table

Make a table to organize information or to solve problems that have several steps.

50. Alicia bikes 25% of a 100-mi trip on the first day. She bikes $\frac{1}{3}$ of the remaining distance on the second day. On the third day, she bikes 40% of the remaining distance. Make a table to find the number of miles left in Alicia's trip.

51. Describe how you could use a table together with another problem-solving strategy that you have studied. Justify your answer with an example.

Find each unit rate.

1. A car travels 84 mi on 3 gal of gas.

2. A car travels 220 mi in 4 h.

Write = or ≠ to complete each statement.

3. $\frac{7}{8} \blacksquare \frac{40}{42}$

4. $\frac{3}{5} \blacksquare \frac{45}{75}$

5. $\frac{12}{18} \blacksquare \frac{18}{12}$

6. $\frac{5}{9} \blacksquare \frac{25}{81}$

Solve each proportion.

7. $\frac{x}{8} = \frac{90}{120}$

8. $\frac{0.8}{90} = \frac{5.6}{y}$

Write a proportion to describe each situation. Then solve.

9. Three cans of dog food sell for 99¢. Find the cost of 15 cans.

10. A photo that measures 5 in. by 7 in. is enlarged to 7.5 in. by b in.

11. A student reads 45 pages in 2 h and x pages in 3 h.

For Exercises 12–14, use the drawing below. The length of the kitchen in the drawing is $1\frac{1}{4}$ in. The actual length is 20 ft.

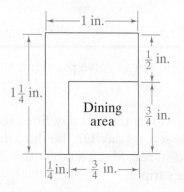

12. What is the scale of the drawing?

13. What is the actual width of the kitchen?

14. What are the actual length and width of the dining area?

Write each decimal as a percent.

15. 0.37

16. 0.005

17. 1.02

Write each fraction as a percent.

18. $\frac{5}{8}$

19. $\frac{7}{16}$

20. $\frac{5}{4}$

Solve.

21. What percent of 400 is 20?

22. Find 45% of 12.

23. 20% of c is 24. What is c?

24. What percent of 3 is 15?

25. Find 125% of 50.

26. 60% of y is 75. What is y?

Find each percent of change. Tell whether the change is an increase or a decrease. Round to the nearest tenth of a percent.

27. from 60 to 36

28. from 18 to 24

29. from 15 to 25

30. from 85 to 50

31. from 8.8 to 30

32. from 1.2 to 0.2

33. A salesperson made a $128 commission selling merchandise. His commission rate was 5%. Find the dollar amount of his sales.

34. A bicycle that usually sells for $230 is on sale for 15% off. Find the sale price.

35. You read 52 pages in 2 h. Your friend reads $\frac{1}{4}$ more pages in $2\frac{1}{2}$ h. Who reads faster? Explain.

36. Estimate the total cost of a bike selling for $195.99 plus a 7.25% sales tax.

37. **Writing in Math** Explain the difference between a markup and a discount.

38. In how many ways can you make $.35 in change without using pennies?

Some questions ask you to find a missing length from a scale drawing. You can use a proportion to solve these problems.

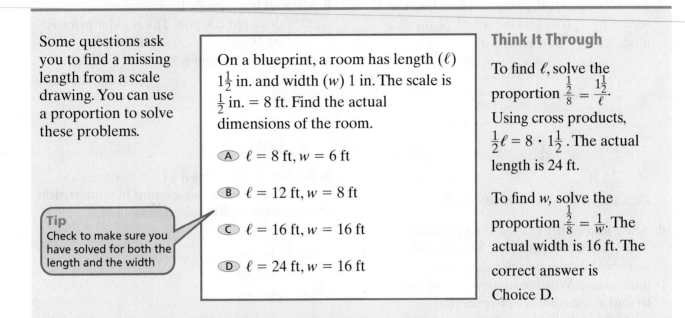

On a blueprint, a room has length (ℓ) $1\frac{1}{2}$ in. and width (w) 1 in. The scale is $\frac{1}{2}$ in. = 8 ft. Find the actual dimensions of the room.

- Ⓐ $\ell = 8$ ft, $w = 6$ ft
- Ⓑ $\ell = 12$ ft, $w = 8$ ft
- Ⓒ $\ell = 16$ ft, $w = 16$ ft
- Ⓓ $\ell = 24$ ft, $w = 16$ ft

Tip
Check to make sure you have solved for both the length and the width

Think It Through

To find ℓ, solve the proportion $\frac{\frac{1}{2}}{8} = \frac{1\frac{1}{2}}{\ell}$.
Using cross products, $\frac{1}{2}\ell = 8 \cdot 1\frac{1}{2}$. The actual length is 24 ft.

To find w, solve the proportion $\frac{\frac{1}{2}}{8} = \frac{1}{w}$. The actual width is 16 ft. The correct answer is Choice D.

Vocabulary Review

As you solve some problems, you must understand the meanings of mathematical terms. Match each term with its mathematical meaning.

A. unit rate

B. proportion

C. similar figures

D. rate

E. percent

I. a ratio that compares quantities in different units

II. The lengths of the corresponding sides are proportional and the corresponding angles have equal measures.

III. a ratio that has a denominator of 1

IV. an equality of two ratios

V. a ratio that compares a number to 100

Read each question. Then write the letter of the correct answer on your paper.

1. A map of the United States has a scale of 1 in. : 250 mi. The cities of Los Angeles, California, and Dallas, Texas, are $5\frac{3}{4}$ inches apart on the map. Find the actual distance between these two cities. **(Lesson 6-3)**

- Ⓐ 43.5 mi
- Ⓒ 1,335 mi
- Ⓑ 260.75 mi
- Ⓓ 1,437.5 mi

2. Rectangle *RSTV* is similar to rectangle *ABCD*. What is *k*, the length of $\overline{ST}$? **(Lesson 6-3)**

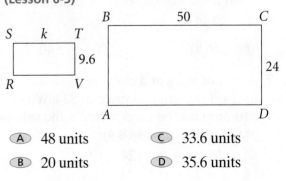

- Ⓐ 48 units
- Ⓒ 33.6 units
- Ⓑ 20 units
- Ⓓ 35.6 units

3. $\triangle FGH$ is a scale drawing of a flag. Use the scale 1 in. : $\frac{1}{4}$ ft to find the length of the side modeled by $\overline{FG}$. **(Lesson 6-3)**

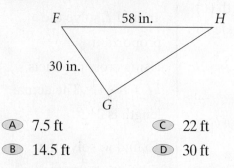

- Ⓐ 7.5 ft
- Ⓑ 14.5 ft
- Ⓒ 22 ft
- Ⓓ 30 ft

4. Andy and Cathy ran for class president. There were 598 votes, but 36 of the votes were withdrawn because they were unreadable. Which equation can be used to find n, the number of votes that represent a tie? **(Lesson 5-8)**

- Ⓐ $n = \frac{1}{2}(598 - 36)$
- Ⓑ $n = \frac{1}{2}(598 + 36)$
- Ⓒ $n = \frac{1}{2}(598)$
- Ⓓ $n = 598 - 36$

5. Your job is to paint $\frac{1}{4}$ of the lockers in the school. Your friend agrees to share the job equally with you. What fraction of the lockers will each of you paint? **(Lesson 5-4)**

- Ⓐ $\frac{1}{16}$
- Ⓑ $\frac{1}{8}$
- Ⓒ $\frac{1}{4}$
- Ⓓ $\frac{1}{2}$

6. Shoes cost a store $56.40. Find the store's profit if the markup is 17%. **(Lesson 6-9)**

- Ⓐ $9.59
- Ⓑ $46.81
- Ⓒ $65.99
- Ⓓ $73.40

7. A pair of jeans at a clothing store is on sale for $\frac{1}{5}$ off the original price of $24. Which equation can be used to find s, the sale price of the jeans? **(Lesson 6-9)**

- Ⓐ $s = 24 - 0.8 \cdot 24$
- Ⓑ $s = 24 - 0.2 \cdot 24$
- Ⓒ $s = 24 + 0.2 \cdot 24$
- Ⓓ $s = 24 + 0.8 \cdot 24$

8. Michael buys a new lawn mower with a 20% discount coupon. The regular price is $359.99. What is the discounted price before tax? **(Lesson 6-9)**

- Ⓐ $20.00
- Ⓑ $72.00
- Ⓒ $287.99
- Ⓓ $339.99

9. A sales agent earns a 12.5% commission on all sales. Find the amount of commission earned on a $500 sale. **(Lesson 6-9)**

- Ⓐ $62.50
- Ⓑ $354.16
- Ⓒ $437.50
- Ⓓ $562.50

10. Jared spent $75 in June. In July, he spent $\frac{1}{5}$ more money than he did in June. Which procedure can be used to determine the money he spent in July? Find the amount of money spent. **(Lesson 5-4)**

- Ⓐ Add $\frac{1}{5}$ and 75; $75.20.
- Ⓑ Multiply $\frac{1}{5}$ and 75 and then add 75; $90.
- Ⓒ Multiply $\frac{1}{5}$ and 75; $15.
- Ⓓ Divide $\frac{1}{5}$ by 75. Then subtract the result from 75; $74.99.

11. The table below lists the cost of various sizes of juice.

Size	Cost
16 oz	$2.29
32 oz	$3.69
48 oz	$3.99
64 oz	$6.99

Which size juice is the best buy? **(Lesson 6-1)**

- Ⓐ 16 oz
- Ⓑ 32 oz
- Ⓒ 48 oz
- Ⓓ 64 oz

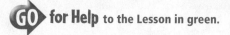

Standards Mastery

12. A lion's heart beats 12 times in 16 seconds. Use the unit rate of the lion's heartbeat to find the number of beats in 60 seconds. **(Lesson 6-1)**

(A) 5 (C) 88

(B) 45 (D) 192

13. Cheryl buys 16 balloons for her friend. At the rate given in the sign below, how much does she pay? **(Lesson 6-1)**

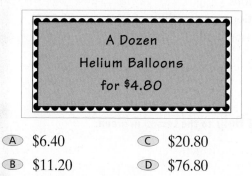

A Dozen
Helium Balloons
for $4.80

(A) $6.40 (C) $20.80

(B) $11.20 (D) $76.80

14. Two fifths of the students in the school play are eighth-graders, 0.25 are seventh-graders, $\frac{1}{3}$ are sixth-graders, and the rest are fifth-graders. There are 60 total students in the play. Which grade has the most students in the play? **(Lesson 6-5)**

(A) fifth grade

(B) sixth grade

(C) seventh grade

(D) eighth grade

15. A plant is originally priced at $35. It is now on sale for 25% off. Which proportion can be used to find d, the discount on the price of the plant? **(Lesson 6-9)**

(A) $\frac{d}{25} = \frac{100}{35}$ (C) $\frac{d}{35} = \frac{25}{100}$

(B) $\frac{d}{35} = \frac{75}{100}$ (D) $\frac{d}{25} = \frac{100}{75}$

16. You run $1\frac{1}{2}$ mi on Monday, $\frac{3}{4}$ mi on Tuesday, and $2\frac{1}{10}$ mi on Wednesday. Find the total distance you run on those days. **(Lesson 5-3)**

(A) $3\frac{5}{16}$ mi

(B) $3\frac{7}{20}$ mi

(C) $3\frac{1}{2}$ mi

(D) $4\frac{7}{20}$ mi

17. A cook needs $3\frac{1}{2}$ cups of flour. The cook has $\frac{3}{8}$ of a cup. How many more cups of flour does the cook need? **(Lesson 5-3)**

(A) $2\frac{1}{8}$ (C) $3\frac{1}{8}$

(B) $2\frac{1}{3}$ (D) $3\frac{7}{8}$

18. You sell one of your CDs for $11.30. This is $3.75 more than you originally paid. If a represents the amount you originally paid, which equation *cannot* be used to find this amount? **(Lesson 2-5)**

(A) $a + 3.75 = 11.30$

(B) $11.30 - a = 3.75$

(C) $11.30 = 3.75 + a$

(D) $a - 3.75 = 11.30$

19. Betty is drawing a map with a scale in which 1 centimeter represents 5 kilometers. In her drawing, her house is 9.5 centimeters away from the lake. What is the actual distance from her house to the lake? **(Lesson 6-3)**

(A) 475 km (C) 45 km

(B) 47.5 km (D) 4.5 km

CHAPTER 7

Solving Equations and Inequalities

What You've Learned

Add, subtract, multiply, and divide rational numbers.

Convert fractions to decimals and percents and use these representations in estimations, computations, and applications.

Use variables and appropriate operations to write an equation or inequality.

Simplify numerical expressions by applying properties of rational numbers and justify the process used.

✓ **Check Your Readiness**   **GO** ▶ **for Help** to the Lesson in green.

Writing Variable Expressions (Lesson 1-1)

Write a variable expression for each situation.

1. three more than p points

2. six fewer than q questions

3. the number of months in y years

4. the value in cents of d dimes

5. twice as many as b baskets

6. eight fewer than n nickels

Simplifying Expressions (Lesson 2-3)

Simplify each expression.

7. $3n + n$

8. $5b + 10 - 8b$

9. $12c + 9 + 7c + 4$

10. $3x + 2y - 7y - 10x$ **11.** $2(a + 3)$

12. $5(m - 7) + 4m$

Solving Equations (Lessons 2-5, 2-6)

Solve each equation.

13. $a - 3 = 8$

14. $-9 = 12 + x$

15. $\frac{m}{7} = -14$

16. $-10 = -2b$

17. $y \div 2 = 4$

18. $6.8 = c - 2.2$

19. $\frac{x}{-4} = 8$

20. $-40 = 5a$

Solving Inequalities (Lessons 2-9, 2-10)

Solve and graph each inequality.

21. $c + 6 \geq 7$

22. $y - 8 < -6$

23. $5b < 20$

24. $-3x < 0$

25. $12 \leq x + 18$

26. $-\frac{x}{3} \geq -5$

27. $b - 15 \leq 4$

28. $\frac{m}{4} \geq 20$

What You'll Learn Next

Compute simple and compound interest.

Use variables and appropriate operations to write an equation or inequality. Solve two-step linear equations and inequalities in one variable over the rational numbers, interpret the solution or solutions in the context from which they arose, and verify the reasonableness of the results.

▲ You can use an inequality to express a range in elevation or depth.

New Vocabulary

🔊 English and Spanish Audio Online

- **balance** (p. 372)
- **compound interest** (p. 372)
- **consecutive integers** (p. 349)

- **interest** (p. 371)
- **interest rate** (p. 371)

- **principal** (p. 371)
- **simple interest** (p. 371)

Academic Vocabulary
- **model** (p. 345)

7-1 Solving Two-Step Equations

Introduce, Develop Solve two-step linear equations in one variable over the rational numbers, interpret the solution or solutions in the context from which they arose, and verify the reasonableness of the results.

What You'll Learn

- To solve two-step equations
- To use two-step equations to solve problems

. . . And Why

To solve problems involving savings

✓ Check Skills You'll Need

Solve each equation.

1. $9 + k = 17$

2. $d - 10 = 1$

3. $y - 5 = -4$

4. $x + 16 = 4$

5. $b + 6 = -4$

GO for Help
Lesson 2-5

Using Properties to Solve Two-Step Equations

Models can help you understand the algebra behind solving the equation $2x + 1 = 5$.

$2x + 1 = 5$ **Model the equation.**

$2x + 1 - 1 = 5 - 1$
$2x = 4$ **Remove 1 square from each side.**

$\dfrac{2x}{2} = \dfrac{4}{2}$ **Divide each side into two equal groups.**

$x = 2$ **Simplify.**

To solve a two-step equation, first undo addition or subtraction. Then undo multiplication or division.

1 EXAMPLE   Undoing an Operation

For: Two-Step Equation Activity
Use: Interactive Textbook, 7-1

Solve $3n - 6 = 15$.

$3n - 6 = 15$

$3n - 6 + 6 = 15 + 6$ **Add 6 to each side.**

$3n = 21$ **Simplify.**

$\dfrac{3n}{3} = \dfrac{21}{3}$ **Divide each side by 3.**

$n = 7$ **Simplify.**

Check $3n - 6 = 15$

$3(7) - 6 \overset{?}{=} 15$ **Replace n with 7.**

$21 - 6 \overset{?}{=} 15$ **Multiply.**

$15 = 15$ ✓   **Simplify.**

Quick Check

1. Solve each equation.

   a. $15x + 3 = 48$ **b.** $\frac{t}{4} - 10 = -6$

---

2 EXAMPLE   **Negative Coefficients**

Solve $5 - x = 17$.

$$5 - x = 17$$
$$-5 + 5 - x = -5 + 17 \quad \text{Add } -5 \text{ to each side.}$$
$$0 - x = 12 \quad \text{Simplify.}$$
$$-x = 12 \quad 0 - x = -x$$
$$-1(-x) = -1(12) \quad \text{Multiply each side by } -1.$$
$$x = -12 \quad \text{Simplify.}$$

Quick Check

2. Solve each equation.

   a. $-a + 6 = 8$ **b.** $-9 - \frac{y}{7} = -12$

Solving Problems With Two-Step Equations

You can use two-step equations to model real-world situations.

Vocabulary Tip

To <u>model</u> a situation, represent it in another form, such as a drawing or an equation.

3 EXAMPLE   **Using Two-Step Equations**

Lynne wants to save $900 to go to Puerto Rico. She saves $45 each week and now has $180. To find how many more weeks w it will take to have $900, solve $180 + 45w = 900$.

$$180 + 45w = 900$$
$$180 + 45w - 180 = 900 - 180 \quad \text{Subtract 180 from each side.}$$
$$45w = 720 \quad \text{Simplify.}$$
$$\frac{45w}{45} = \frac{720}{45} \quad \text{Divide each side by 45.}$$
$$w = 16 \quad \text{Simplify.}$$

It will take Lynne 16 more weeks to have $900.

Check Is the answer reasonable? $180 + 45(16) = 900$, so the answer is reasonable.

San Juan, Puerto Rico

Quick Check

3. Jacob bought four begonias in 6-in. pots and a $19 fern at a fundraiser. He spent a total of $63. Solve the equation $4p + 19 = 63$ to find the price p of each begonia.

Match each equation with the first step in solving the equation.

1. $10 - 3z = 22$

2. $10w + 3 = 9$

3. $2y + 9 = 3$

4. $10z = 30$

A. Subtract 9 from each side.
B. Subtract 3 from each side.
C. Subtract 10 from each side.
D. Divide each side by 10.

5. The order of operations tells you the order to do operations when simplifying expressions. How is the order of operations related to the order in which you do operations to solve an equation?

Standards Practice

For more exercises, see *Extra Skills and Word Problem Practice.*

A Practice by Example

Examples 1 and 2
(pages 344 and 345)

GO for Help

Solve each equation.

6. $2d - 8 = -10$ 7. $9x - 15 = 39$ 8. $\frac{x}{3} + 2 = 0$

9. $12 - 11a = 45$ 10. $-8c + 1 = -3$ 11. $5 = -\frac{x}{3} + 10$

12. $18 = -a + 2$ 13. $4 - \frac{m}{5} = 18$ 14. $-75 - k = -95$

Example 3
(page 345)

15. Jose bought a new computer that cost $1,200. He paid $400 down and will pay $50 per week until the balance is paid off. Solve the equation $400 + 50w = 1,200$ to find the number of weeks it will take Jose to pay off the computer.

B Apply Your Skills

Solve and check each equation.

16. $15 = -11b + 4$ 17. $-35 = 4h + 1$ 18. $10 = 3 + \frac{b}{2}$

19. $12y - 6 = 138$ 20. $2x + 3 = 15$ 21. $-6t + (-4) = 14$

22. You bought a CD for $16.95 and eight blank videotapes. The total cost was $52.55 before the sales tax was added. Solve the equation $8t + 16.95 = 52.55$ to find the cost of each blank videotape.

Mental Math **Solve each equation.**

23. $\frac{n}{6} + 2 = -8$ 24. $4a - 1 = 27$ 25. $\frac{k}{5} + 3 = 6$

Homework Video Tutor

▶

Visit: PHSchool.com
Web Code: bje-0701

26. A building contractor buys 525 metal bars. Because he is buying more than 500 bars, the wholesaler gives him a discount of $420. The total price is $3,780. Solve the equation $525b - 420 = 3,780$ to find the cost of each metal bar.

27. Carmela wants to buy a digital camera for $249. She has $24 and is saving $15 each week. Solve the equation $15w + 24 = 249$ to find how many weeks w it will take Carmela to save enough to buy the digital camera.

28. Error Analysis A student solved the equation $\frac{x}{4} + 5 = 1$ without showing all the work. The student's solution is incorrect. What error did the student make?

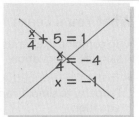

$$\frac{x}{4} + 5 = 1$$
$$\frac{x}{4} = -4$$
$$x = -1$$

29. Writing in Math Explain how the processes of solving $\frac{x}{4} - 2 = 8$ and $\frac{x}{4} = 8$ are different.

Solve and check each equation.

30. $1.5x + 1.2 = 5.7$

31. $-1.7 = 2.2b - 6.1$

32. $3c - 3.2 = 4.6$

33. $\frac{y}{4} + 4.7 = 8.2$

C Challenge

34. A soccer player wants to eat no more than 700 Calories at a meal that includes a Reuben sandwich and pickles. The sandwich has 464 Calories, and the pickles have 7 Calories each.
  a. Solve the equation $464 + 7f = 700$ to find the number of pickles the soccer player can eat.
  b. Suppose the soccer player drinks a 200-Calorie sports drink with the meal. Write and solve an equation to find the number of pickles the soccer player can eat now.

Multiple Choice Practice and Mixed Review

For Standards Tutorials, visit PHSchool.com. Web Code: bjq-9045

35. Bret buys game tokens for $.25 each. He spends $7.50 for food and $14.00 in all. The equation $0.25t + 7.50 = 14$ represents the number of tokens t he buys. Find the number of tokens he buys.
  Ⓐ 6.5   Ⓑ 26   Ⓒ 48.5   Ⓓ 86

36. What is the solution of $\frac{x}{6} - 8 = 7$?
  Ⓐ −6   Ⓑ 6   Ⓒ 15   Ⓓ 90

37. Which of the following is NOT a rational number?
  Ⓐ −5   Ⓑ 1.3485…   Ⓒ −1.25   Ⓓ $\frac{7}{8}$

38. Using a 10%-off coupon for CDs, what is the total cost, before sales tax, of 3 CDs that are regularly priced at $16.99, $12.99, and $14.85?
  Ⓐ $4.48   Ⓑ $40.35   Ⓒ $43.35   Ⓓ $44.83

 for Help   Lesson 6-8

Find each percent of markup.

39. wholesale price: $34
selling price: $42.50

40. wholesale price: $45.95
selling price: $82.71

7-2 Solving Multi-Step Equations

What You'll Learn

- To combine like terms to simplify an equation
- To use the Distributive Property to simplify an equation

. . . And Why

To solve problems involving consecutive integers

✓ Check Skills You'll Need

Simplify each expression.

1. $2x + 4 + 3x$

2. $5y + y$

3. $8a - 5a$

4. $2 - 4c + 5c$

5. $4x + 3 - 2(5 + x)$

GO for Help
Lesson 2-3

◀)) New Vocabulary
- consecutive integers

Master Simplify numerical expressions by applying properties of rational numbers and justify the process used.

Develop Evaluate the reasonableness of the solution in the context of the original situation.

Students simplify expressions before solving linear equations.

Combining Like Terms

Standards Investigation
Simplifying Equations

The model below represents the equation $2x + 7 + x = 16$

1. How does this equation differ from others you have seen?

2. **a.** Regroup so that all the green rectangles are together. This is the same as combining like terms. Write an equation to represent the model after you regroup.
   b. Solve your equation. Check your solution.

Combine like terms to simplify an equation before you solve it.

---

1 EXAMPLE   Combining Like Terms

Jake and Suki collect model airplanes. Suki has four fewer than twice as many model airplanes as Jake. Together they have 14 models. Solve the equation $m + 2m - 4 = 14$. Find the number of models each person has.

$$m + 2m - 4 = 14$$

$3m - 4 = 14$	Combine like terms.
$3m - 4 + 4 = 14 + 4$	Add 4 to each side.
$3m = 18$	Simplify.
$\frac{3m}{3} = \frac{18}{3}$	Divide each side by 3.
$m = 6$	Simplify.

Jake has 6 models. Suki has $2(6) - 4 = 8$ models.

Check Is the solution reasonable? Jake and Suki have a total of 14 models. Since $6 + 8 = 14$, the solution is reasonable.

1. One basketball team defeated another by 13 points. The total number of points scored by both teams was 171. Solve the equation $p + p - 13 = 171$ to find the number of points p scored by the winning team.

When you count by 1's from any integer, you are counting **consecutive integers.**

two consecutive integers   three consecutive integers

120, 121   −5, −4, −3

2 **EXAMPLE**   **Finding Consecutive Integers**

Number Sense **The sum of three consecutive integers is 96. Find the integers.**

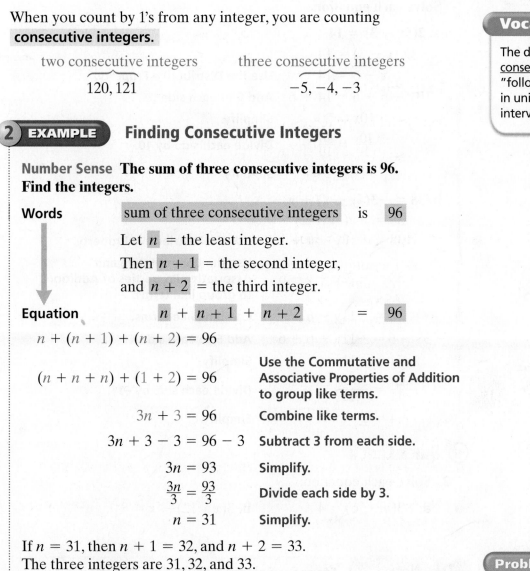

Words   sum of three consecutive integers   is   96

Let n = the least integer.

Then $n + 1$ = the second integer,

and $n + 2$ = the third integer.

Equation $n + n + 1 + n + 2$ =   96

$n + (n + 1) + (n + 2) = 96$

$(n + n + n) + (1 + 2) = 96$ Use the Commutative and Associative Properties of Addition to group like terms.

$3n + 3 = 96$ Combine like terms.

$3n + 3 - 3 = 96 - 3$ Subtract 3 from each side.

$3n = 93$ Simplify.

$\dfrac{3n}{3} = \dfrac{93}{3}$ Divide each side by 3.

$n = 31$ Simplify.

If $n = 31$, then $n + 1 = 32$, and $n + 2 = 33$.
The three integers are 31, 32, and 33.

Check Is the solution reasonable? Yes, because $31 + 32 + 33 = 96$.

✅ **Quick Check**

2. **a. Number Sense** Find four consecutive integers with a sum of 358.
   b. For *consecutive even integers,* the first is n, and the second is $n + 2$. Find two consecutive even integers with a sum of 66.

Using the Distributive Property

Sometimes you may need to use the Distributive Property when you solve a multi-step equation.

3 **EXAMPLE**   Using the Distributive Property

Solve each equation.

a. $2(5x - 3) = 14$

$2(5x - 3) = 14$	
$10x - 6 = 14$	Use the Distributive Property.
$10x - 6 + 6 = 14 + 6$	Add 6 to each side.
$10x = 20$	Simplify.
$\dfrac{10x}{10} = \dfrac{20}{10}$	Divide each side by 10.
$x = 2$	Simplify.

b. $38 = -3(4y + 2) + y$

$38 = -3(4y + 2) + y$	
$38 = -12y - 6 + y$	Use the Distributive Property.
$38 = -12y + y - 6$	Use the Commutative and Associative Properties of Addition to group like terms.
$38 = -11y - 6$	Combine like terms.
$38 + 6 = -11y - 6 + 6$	Add 6 to each side.
$44 = -11y$	Simplify.
$\dfrac{44}{-11} = \dfrac{-11y}{-11}$	Divide each side by –11.
$-4 = y$	Simplify.

✓ Quick Check

3. Solve each equation.

   a. $-3(m - 6) = 4$ **b.** $3(x + 12) - x = 8$

Take Note   Steps for Solving a Multi-Step Equation

Step 1 Use the Distributive Property, if necessary.

Step 2 Combine like terms.

Step 3 Undo addition or subtraction.

Step 4 Undo multiplication or division.

Justify each step in the solution of the equation below.

$$-2(-a + 3) - a = 0$$

1. $2a + (-6) - a = 0$ ___?___

2. $2a - a + (-6) = 0$ ___?___

3. $a + (-6) = 0$ ___?___

4. $a + (-6) - (-6) = 0 - (-6)$ ___?___

5. $a = 6$ ___?___

For more exercises, see *Extra Skills and Word Problem Practice.*

A Practice by Example

Example 1
(page 348)

GO for Help

Solve each equation.

6. $8a + 4a = 144$ **7.** $4a + 1 - a = 19$ **8.** $18 = b - 7b$

9. Bill and Jasmine together have 94 glass marbles. Bill has 4 more than twice as many marbles as Jasmine. If Jasmine has m marbles, then Bill has $2m + 4$ marbles. Solve the equation $m + 2m + 4 = 94$. Find how many glass marbles each has.

Example 2
(page 349)

Number Sense Find the integers.

10. The sum of two consecutive integers is 131.

11. The sum of three consecutive even integers is 60.

Example 3
(page 350)

Solve each equation.

12. $3(n - 2) = 36$ **13.** $4(y - 1) = 36$

14. $3(2x + 1) + x = -39$ **15.** $m + 4(2m - 3) = -3$

B Apply Your Skills

Solve and check each equation.

16. $5x - x = -12$ **17.** $-6 = a + a + 4$

18. $-9 - b + 8b = -23$ **19.** $36 = y - 5y - 12$

20. $21 = 2(4a + 2)$ **21.** $8 - 3(x - 4) = 4$

Homework Video Tutor

Visit: PHSchool.com
Web Code: bje-0702

Number Sense Find the integers.

22. The sum of four consecutive integers is -22.

23. The sum of five consecutive integers is -65.

24. Error Analysis A student solved the equation $7x - 5 - 5x = 15$ and found $x = 5$. What might be the student's error?

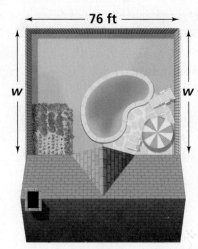

76 ft

w   w

25. Multiple Choice A carpenter is building a fence around a swimming pool, as shown at the left. The carpenter will use 120 feet of fencing. What is the unknown dimension of the enclosed area?

  Ⓐ 22 ft   Ⓑ 44 ft   Ⓒ 76 ft   Ⓓ 120 ft

26. Number Sense Two numbers are w and $3w - 5$. Their sum is 23. Solve the equation $w + 3w - 5 = 23$ to find the numbers.

27. Writing in Math Explain how to solve $3(9 + 4a) - 19 = 32$.

28. Together, Donal, Yolanda, and Iris made 27 birdhouses for a school fair. Yolanda made n birdhouses. Donal made one more birdhouse than Yolanda, and Iris made one more than Donal. Solve the equation $n + (n + 1) + (n + 1 + 1) = 27$. Find the number of birdhouses each one made.

Geometry For each rectangle, the area is 20 cm². Find the value of x.

29.

4 cm

$(x + 3)$ cm

30.

$(2x - 4)$ cm

10 cm

Ⓒ **Challenge**   **Solve and check each equation.**

31. $\frac{1}{3}[2(x - 8) + 1] = 19$

32. $3 = \frac{1}{4}(m - 4) + \frac{1}{4}m$

Number Sense **Find the integers.**

33. The sum of four consecutive odd integers is -72.

34. The sum of five consecutive even integers is 0.

Multiple Choice Practice and Mixed Review

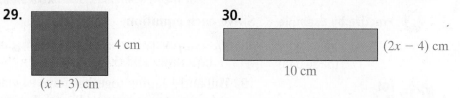

For Standards Tutorials, visit PHSchool.com. Web Code: bjq-9045

35. $3(2x + 5) = \underline{\ \ ?\ \ }$

  Ⓐ $5x + 5$ Ⓑ $6x + 5$ Ⓒ $6x + 8$ Ⓓ $6x + 15$

36. The table shows the lowest recorded temperature in four states. What is the difference between the highest and the lowest temperature?

  Ⓐ $57°F$ Ⓒ $82°F$
  Ⓑ $78°F$ Ⓓ $92°F$

State	Lowest Temperature (°F)
Alaska	−80
Florida	−2
Texas	−23
Hawaii	12

GO for Help   Lesson 7-1   **Solve each equation.**

37. $10a - 32 = -28$ **38.** $5 - 2d = 15$ **39.** $\frac{c}{4} - 7 = 5$

Two-Step Equations With Fractions and Decimals

Master Add, subtract, multiply, and divide rational numbers.

Develop Solve two-step linear equations in one variable over the rational numbers, interpret the solution or solutions in the context from which they arose, and verify the reasonableness of results.

What You'll Learn

- To solve two-step equations with fractions
- To solve two-step equations with decimals

. . . And Why

To solve problems involving cost of phone service

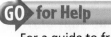 **Check Skills You'll Need**

Solve each equation.

1. $2n + 53 = 47$

2. $4m - 37 = -28$

3. $-26x - 4 = 100$

4. $-3a + 15 = 13$

GO for Help
Lesson 7-1

GO for Help

For a guide to fractions and reciprocals, see pages 244, 262, and Skills Handbook page 697.

GO Online

Video Tutor Help

Visit: PHSchool.com
Web Code: bje-0775

Solving Two-Step Equations With Fractions

Remember, when the coefficient of a variable in an equation is a fraction, you can use the reciprocal to solve the equation.

$$\frac{4}{5}x = 12$$
$$\frac{5}{4} \cdot \frac{4}{5}x = \frac{5}{4} \cdot 12 \quad \text{Multiply each side by } \tfrac{5}{4}, \text{ because } \tfrac{5}{4} \cdot \tfrac{4}{5} = 1.$$
$$x = 15$$

When you have a two-step equation, gather the variables on one side of the equation and the constants on the other before multiplying by the reciprocal.

1 EXAMPLE **Using the Reciprocal**

Solve $\frac{2}{3}n - 6 = 22$.

$$\frac{2}{3}n - 6 = 22$$
$$\frac{2}{3}n - 6 + 6 = 22 + 6 \qquad \text{Add 6 to each side.}$$
$$\frac{2}{3}n = 28 \qquad \text{Simplify.}$$
$$\frac{3}{2} \cdot \frac{2}{3}n = \frac{3}{2} \cdot 28 \qquad \text{Multiply each side by } \tfrac{3}{2}, \text{ the reciprocal of } \tfrac{2}{3}.$$
$$n = \frac{3 \cdot 28^{14}}{1^2} \qquad \text{Divide common factors.}$$
$$n = 42 \qquad \text{Simplify.}$$

Check $\frac{2}{3}n - 6 = 22$

$$\frac{2}{3}(42) - 6 \stackrel{?}{=} 22 \qquad \text{Replace } n \text{ with 42.}$$
$$\frac{2 \cdot 42^{14}}{1^3} - 6 \stackrel{?}{=} 22 \qquad \text{Divide common factors.}$$
$$28 - 6 \stackrel{?}{=} 22 \qquad \text{Multiply.}$$
$$22 = 22 \checkmark$$

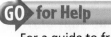 **Quick Check**

1. Solve each equation.

    a. $-\frac{7}{10}k + 14 = -21$ **b.** $\frac{2}{3}m - 4 = 3$

You can use the Multiplication Property of Equality to simplify the solving of an equation involving fractions. Use the LCM of the denominators to clear the equation of fractions.

GO **for Help**

For a guide to finding the least common multiple (LCM), see Lesson 5-1.

2 EXAMPLE **Using the LCM**

Solve $\frac{2}{5}x + 2 = \frac{3}{4}$.

$$\frac{2}{5}x + 2 = \frac{3}{4}$$

$20\left(\frac{2}{5}x + 2\right) = 20\left(\frac{3}{4}\right)$ Multiply each side by 20, the LCM of 5 and 4.

$8x + 40 = 15$ Use the Distributive Property. Simplify.

$8x + 40 - 40 = 15 - 40$ Subtract 40 from each side.

$8x = -25$ Simplify.

$\frac{8x}{8} = \frac{-25}{8}$ Divide each side by 8.

$x = -3\frac{1}{8}$ Simplify.

✓ Quick Check

2. Solve the equation $-\frac{7}{12} + y = \frac{1}{6}$.

Solving Two-Step Equations With Decimals

You can use the properties of equality to solve decimal equations.

3 EXAMPLE **Using Properties of Equality**

Suppose your cell phone plan is $20 per month plus $.15 per minute. Your bill is $37.25. How many minutes are on your bill?

Words   monthly charge $+$ cost per minute $\cdot$ minutes $=$ total cost

Let m = minutes on your bill.

Equation 20 $+$ 0.15 $\cdot$ m $=$ 37.25

$20 + 0.15x = 37.25$

$20 - 20 + 0.15x = 37.25 - 20$ Subtract 20 from each side.

$0.15x = 17.25$ Simplify.

$\frac{0.15x}{0.15} = \frac{17.25}{0.15}$ Divide each side by 0.15.

$x = 115$ Simplify.

There are 115 minutes on your bill.

✓ Quick Check

3. Solve $1.5x - 3.6 = 2.4$.

You can solve two-step decimal equations in more than one way.

More Than One Way

For local telephone service, the McNeils pay $9.95/month plus $.035/min for local calls. Last month, they paid $12.75 for local service. Find the minutes m of local calls.

Nicole's Method

I will solve the equation $0.035m + 9.95 = 12.75$. I can work with decimals as I have before.

$$0.035m + 9.95 = 12.75$$
$$0.035m + 9.95 - 9.95 = 12.75 - 9.95$$
$$0.035m = 2.8$$
$$\frac{0.035m}{0.035} = \frac{2.8}{0.035}$$
$$m = 80$$

The McNeils made 80 min of local calls.

Daryl's Method

Solve the equation $0.035m + 9.95 = 12.75$. Use multiplication to clear the decimals. Use the decimals with the greatest number of decimal places to decide what power of 10 to use.

$$0.035m + 9.95 = 12.75$$
$$1,000(0.035m + 9.95) = 1,000(12.75)$$
$$35m + 9,950 = 12,750$$
$$35m + 9,950 - 9,950 = 12,750 - 9,950$$
$$35m = 2,800$$
$$\frac{35m}{35} = \frac{2,800}{35}$$
$$m = 80$$

The McNeils made 80 min of local calls.

Choose a Method

1. Which method would you use to find the number of minutes? Explain.

2. In Daryl's method, why was each side of the equation multiplied by 1,000?

Match each equation with an equation that has the same solution.

1. $\frac{1}{9} - \frac{2}{3}x = 3$

2. $1.3x - 1.75 = 0.4$

3. $\frac{1}{2}x + \frac{1}{4} = \frac{1}{2}$

4. $0.1x + 1.5 = 10$

5. $4 - 3.25x = 1.4$

A. $x + 15 = 100$
B. $400 - 325x = 140$
C. $2x + 1 = 2$
D. $1 - 6x = 27$
E. $130x - 175 = 40$

Standards Practice

For more exercises, see *Extra Skills and Word Problem Practice.*

A Practice by Example

Example 1
(page 353)

GO for Help

State the first step in solving each equation. Do not solve.

6. $\frac{1}{4}x + 3 = 2$ **7.** $-\frac{1}{5}y + 2 = -3$ **8.** $\frac{1}{2}n - 4 = 6$

Solve each equation.

9. $\frac{5}{8}c - 8 = 12$ **10.** $-8 + \frac{3}{5}g = -2$ **11.** $\frac{3}{4}b + 6 = 15$

Example 2
(page 354)

Mental Math By what number would you multiply each equation to get an equation without denominators? Do not solve.

12. $\frac{1}{2}h - 1 = \frac{3}{8}$ **13.** $\frac{1}{5}y + 3 = \frac{2}{3}$ **14.** $\frac{7}{10}c - 10 = \frac{2}{5}$

Solve each equation.

15. $\frac{1}{4}c + 2 = \frac{3}{4}$ **16.** $8 - \frac{w}{10} = \frac{3}{5}$ **17.** $\frac{2}{3}a - 2 = \frac{1}{3}$

Example 3
(page 354)

18. $0.7c - 10 = 0.5$ **19.** $1.2n + 3.4 = 10$

20. $-0.8k - 3.1 = -8.3$ **21.** $0.4b + 9.2 = 10$

22. $0.9x + 2.3x = -6.4$ **23.** $-2d + 4.3 = 10.7$

24. Dwayne is taking a drawing class. The drawing pencils cost $.97 apiece and a sketchbook costs $5.95. Dwayne spent a total of $11.77. Write and solve an equation to find the number n of pencils he bought.

B Apply Your Skills

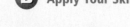

Homework Video Tutor

Visit: PHSchool.com
Web Code: bje-0703

Solve and check each equation.

25. $\frac{5}{8}p - 2\frac{1}{2} = 2$ **26.** $1\frac{1}{3}p + 1 = 1\frac{2}{3}$ **27.** $0.07x + 9.95 = 12.47$

28. $-\frac{3}{4}y + \frac{1}{4} = \frac{1}{2}$ **29.** $-\frac{5x}{4} = -\frac{1}{2}$ **30.** $2.4b + 5.6 = -11.2$

31. $4x + 2 = -28.4$ **32.** $-\frac{1}{3}x + 3 = -1$ **33.** $\frac{2}{7}k - \frac{1}{14}k = -3$

34. $0.4(a + 2) = 2$ **35.** $\frac{1}{2}(x - 1) = \frac{1}{2}$ **36.** $1.2c + 2.6c = 4.56$

White-water rafts carry as few as 2 or as many as 16 passengers.

37. Six friends hire a raft and guide to go white-water rafting in Colorado. Each person also buys a souvenir photo of the trip for $25.75. The total each person pays is $90.30. Write and solve an equation to find the cost c of the raft and guide.

38. Writing in Math At a 15%-off sale, a customer pays $11.01 for a video. Explain how to solve the equation $p - 0.15p = 11.01$ to find the original price p of the video.

39. A pair of athletic shoes is on sale for $\frac{1}{4}$ off the original cost. The sale price is $49.95. Solve the equation $c - \frac{1}{4}c = 49.95$ to find the original cost c of the shoes.

40. Geometry Use the rectangle at the right.
  a. Find the value of x if the area is 15 square units.
  b. Find the value of x if the perimeter is 24 units.

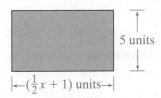

5 units

$\left(\frac{1}{2}x + 1\right)$ units

C **Challenge** **Solve and check each equation.**

41. $12p + 7 = -15 + 6.5p$ **42.** $5(t - 0.4) = -6t$

Multiple Choice Practice and Mixed Review

For Standards Tutorials, visit PHSchool.com. Web Code: bjq-9045

43. What is the solution of $7.1 = 3.8h + 5.2$?
  (A) 0.5   (B) 0.63   (C) 1.9   (D) 3.3

44. Eva can run 3 miles in 24 minutes. At this rate, how long will it take her to run 5 miles?
  (A) 36 min   (B) 38 min   (C) 40 min   (D) 42 min

45. If you enlarge the photograph at the right to triple its dimensions, what is the area of the enlargement?
  (A) 180 in.^{2} (C) 540 in.^{2}
  (B) 216 in.^{2} (D) 600 in.^{2}

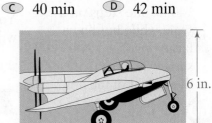

6 in.

10 in.

Lesson 7-2

Solve each equation.

46. $-9 = 3(y + 4)$ **47.** $x + 7 - 3x = 7$ **48.** $5(t - 8) = 10$

49. $w - 3 + 2w = 9$ **50.** $4(5 + 2a) = -4$ **51.** $2(3b - 5) = 8$

Lesson 6-2

52. Mrs. Milton travels 60 mi round-trip to work. She works five days a week. Her car gets about 25 mi/gal of gasoline. About how many gallons of gasoline does Mrs. Milton's car use during her weekly commute?

Reasoning Strategy: Write an Equation

Develop Use variables and appropriate operations to write an equation.
Develop Solve two-step linear equations, interpret the solution in the context from which it arose, and verify the reasonableness of the results.
Develop Solve multi-step problems involving rate.
Develop Use estimation to verify the reasonableness of calculated results.

What You'll Learn

To write an equation to solve a problem

... And Why

To solve problems about rates

✓ Check Skills You'll Need

Write an equation to represent each situation.

1. Pierre bought a puppy for $48. This is $21 less than the original price. What was the original price of the puppy?

2. A tent weighs 6 lb. Together, your backpack and the tent weigh 33 lb. How much does your backpack weigh?

3. A veterinarian weighs 140 lb. She steps on a scale while holding a large dog. The scale shows 192 lb. What is the weight of the dog?

GO for Help
Lesson 2-4

Write an Equation

Math Strategies in Action Stephen Hawking used equations to describe black holes. Scientists write and use equations and formulas every day. Banks use equations to calculate interest and loan information. Statisticians use equations to find sports and population statistics. Doctors use equations to calculate correct doses.

You have written one-step equations for word problems. Now you will extend your skills to more complex situations.

1 EXAMPLE Writing an Equation

To rent a moving van costs $29.95/day plus $.12/mi. Ms. Smith's bill for a two-day rental was $70.46. How many miles did she drive?

Understand **Understand the problem.**

1. What is the goal of this problem?

2. For how long did Ms. Smith rent the van?

3. What does the van cost without mileage?

4. What is the mileage charge?

Plan Make a plan to solve the problem.

Write an equation.

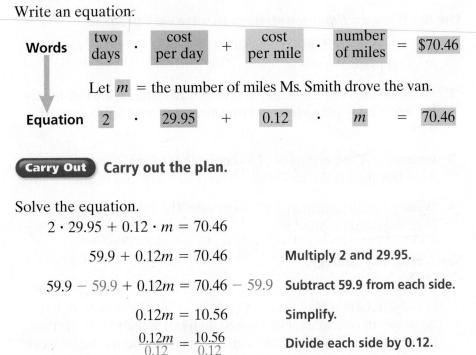

Words two days · cost per day + cost per mile · number of miles = $70.46

Let m = the number of miles Ms. Smith drove the van.

Equation 2 · 29.95 + 0.12 · m = 70.46

Carry Out Carry out the plan.

Solve the equation.

$2 \cdot 29.95 + 0.12 \cdot m = 70.46$

$59.9 + 0.12m = 70.46$	**Multiply 2 and 29.95.**
$59.9 - 59.9 + 0.12m = 70.46 - 59.9$	**Subtract 59.9 from each side.**
$0.12m = 10.56$	**Simplify.**
$\dfrac{0.12m}{0.12} = \dfrac{10.56}{0.12}$	**Divide each side by 0.12.**
$m = 88$	**Simplify.**

Ms. Smith drove the van 88 mi.

Check Check the answer to be sure it is reasonable.

You can estimate to check the reasonableness of the answer.

$$29.95 \approx 30$$
$$0.12 \approx 0.1 \quad \Big\} \quad \textbf{Round each number.}$$
$$88 \approx 90$$

$2 \cdot 30 + 0.1 \cdot 90 = 60 + 9$	**Multiply.**
$= 69$	**Simplify.**

Since $69 \approx 70.46$, 88 mi is a reasonable answer.

✓ Quick Check

5. **a.** Suppose that Ms. Smith's bill for the two-day rental was $76.34. How would the equation change? Explain.
   b. Solve the new equation to find how many miles Ms. Smith drove the van.
   c. Estimate to check the reasonableness of your answer to part (b).

6. Mr. Jones rented the same van for three days. His bill was $104.49. How many miles did he drive?

For more exercises, see *Extra Skills and Word Problem Practice*.

 **Practice by Example**

 for Help Example 1 (page 358)

Use the *Write an Equation* strategy to solve each problem.

1. The sale price of a sweater is $48. The price is 20% less than the original price. What was the original price?

2. Elena has $240 in the bank. She withdraws $15 each week to pay for her weekly piano lesson. How many lessons can she afford with her savings?

3. Geometry The perimeter of a rectangle is 64 cm. The length is 4 cm less than twice the width. Find the length and width.

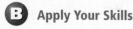 **GO for Help**

For a guide to solving Exercise 4, see page 362.

4. Wendy bought a drill at a 10%-off sale. The sale price was $75.60. Find the original price *p*.

 Apply Your Skills

Solve using any strategy.

5. Lamar's summer job is mowing lawns for a landscaper. His pay is $7.50/h. Lamar also makes $11.25/h for any time over 40 h that he works in one week. He worked 40 h last week plus *n* overtime hours and made $339.38. How many overtime hours did he work?

STRATEGIES

- Act It Out
- Draw a Diagram
- Try, Test, Revise
- Look for a Pattern
- Make a Model
- Make a Table
- Simulate the Problem
- Solve by Graphing
- Use Multiple Strategies
- Work a Simpler Problem
- Work Backward
- Write an Equation
- Write a Proportion

6. Number Sense Find two whole numbers with a sum of 15 and a product of 54.

7. A farmer drew the diagram of a square pen at the right. He plans to put one post at each corner and one post every 3 ft in between. How many posts will he use?

21 ft

8. It takes 8 painters 6 hours to paint the walls of a gymnasium.
   a. How many person-hours does this job require?
   b. How many hours will 12 painters take to paint the gymnasium?

9. Cathy has a collection of dimes and quarters. The number of dimes equals the number of quarters. She has a total of $2.80. How many of each coin does Cathy have? (*Hint:* Let *n* = the number of dimes. Since each dime has a value of 10¢, the value of *n* dimes is 10*n*. Since the number of quarters is also *n*, the value of *n* quarters is 25*n*. Also change the value of $2.80 to its value in cents.)

 Challenge

10. Physics The weight of an object on Venus is about $\frac{9}{10}$ of its weight on Earth. The weight of an object on Jupiter is about $\frac{13}{5}$ times its weight on Earth.
   a. If a rock weighs 23 lb on Venus, how much would it weigh on Earth?
   b. If the same rock were on Jupiter, how much would it weigh?

Homework Video Tutor

Visit: PHSchool.com
Web Code: bje-0704

11. Amber leaves home on her bicycle, riding at a steady rate of 8 mi/h. Her brother Eduardo leaves home on his bicycle half an hour later, following Amber's route. He rides at a steady rate of 12 mi/h. How long after Amber leaves will Eduardo catch up?

Multiple Choice Practice and Mixed Review

For Standards Tutorials, visit PHSchool.com. Web Code: bjq-9045

12. Which list has the numbers in order from least to greatest?

Ⓐ $\frac{1}{5}, 25\%, 0.85, 90\%, 0.6$ Ⓒ $25\%, \frac{1}{5}, 0.6, 0.85, 90$

Ⓑ $\frac{1}{5}, 0.6, 0.85, 25\%, 90\%$ Ⓓ $\frac{1}{5}, 25\%, 0.6, 0.85, 90\%$

13. The bar graph shows whether Lucy's classmates prefer to paint, write, or design Web pages as a hobby. Which statement is supported by the bar graph?

Ⓐ There are 26 students in her class.

Ⓑ More girls prefer to paint than boys.

Ⓒ Six boys prefer to write.

Ⓓ Four girls say they prefer to design Web pages.

Lesson 7-3

Solve each equation.

14. $\frac{3}{5}k + \frac{1}{5}k = 4$ 15. $1.4x + 8.8 = 92.8$

Checkpoint Quiz 1

Solve each equation.

1. $12n + 60 = 300$ 2. $5y - 9 - 3y = 13$ 3. $-44 = 3x + 10$

4. $\frac{a}{4} - \frac{3}{4} = \frac{1}{4}$ 5. $\frac{4}{7}x - 3 = 13$ 6. $-\frac{x}{6} - 8 = 0$

7. $0.6x + 1.9x = 5$ 8. $10(5 + m) = 63$ 9. $2c + 4 + 3c = -26$

10. $\frac{1}{5}(x + 10) = 2$ 11. $7(2y - 1) = 7$ 12. $3a + 9 = 27$

Write an equation for each situation. Then solve.

13. Gloria bought a suit at a 25%-off sale. The sale price was $82.50. Find the original price.

14. **Number Sense** Three consecutive integers have a sum of 132. Find the integers.

FOR USE WITH PAGE 360, EXERCISE 4

Understanding Math Problems Read through the problem below. Then let Elena's thinking guide you through the solution. Check your understanding with the exercise at the bottom of the page.

> **Develop˜** Solve problems that involve discounts. **Develop˜** Use variables and appropriate operations to write an equation.

Wendy bought a drill at a 10%-off sale. The sale price was $75.60. Find the original price p.

What Elena Thinks

What information is given in the problem? I'll write it down.

What am I trying to find out? I'll write out the question.

I know that 10% off means that you subtract 10% of the original price from the original price. I'll write this as an equation in words.

I'll use a variable for the original price. And I'll write 10% as the decimal 0.1.

I can write p as $1p$ so that I can subtract like terms. Then I will simplify.

To finish solving the equation, I divide both sides by 0.9.

Is $84.00 a reasonable answer? 10% of 84 is about 8, and $84 - 8$ is 76. This is close to $75.60. Yes, my answer is reasonable.

What Elena Writes

A drill was on sale for 10% off. The sale price was $75.60.

What was the original price?

Original price minus 10% of the original price is the sale price, $75.60.

$$p - 0.1p = 75.60$$

$$1p - 0.1p = 75.60$$

$$0.9p = 75.60$$

$$\frac{0.9}{0.9}p = \frac{75.60}{0.9}$$

$$p = 84$$

The original price of the drill was $84.00.

EXERCISE

1. Tanya got a 5% raise at her job at the video store. She now makes $6.51 per hour. How much did she make per hour before the raise?

7-5 Solving Two-Step Inequalities

What You'll Learn

• To solve two-step inequalities

• To use two-step inequalities to solve problems

. . . And Why

To solve problems involving camping and jobs

✓ **Check Skills You'll Need**

Solve each inequality. Graph the solutions.

1. $w + 4 \geq -5$

2. $7 < z - 3$

3. $4 > a + 6$

4. $x - 5 \leq -6$

GO for Help
Lesson 2-9

Develop Use variables and appropriate operations to write an inequality.

Introduce, Develop Solve two-step linear inequalities over the rational numbers, interpret the solution or solutions in the context from which they arose, and verify the reasonableness of the results.

Develop Make precise calculations and check the validity of the results.

Solving Two-Step Inequalities

You solve two-step inequalities and equations using similar steps.

1 EXAMPLE **Undoing Operations**

Solve and graph $2y - 3 \leq -5$.

$$2y - 3 \leq -5$$

$2y - 3 + 3 \leq -5 + 3$ **Add 3 to each side.**

$2y \leq -2$ **Simplify.**

$\dfrac{2y}{2} \leq \dfrac{-2}{2}$ **Divide each side by 2.**

$y \leq -1$ **Simplify.**

```
<----+----+----+----+----+----+----+---->
    -6   -4   -2    0    2    4    6
```

✓ **Quick Check**

1. Solve and graph $-10 \geq \frac{1}{2}x - 6$.

Remember to reverse the direction of the inequality symbol when you multiply or divide by a negative number.

2 EXAMPLE **Reversing the Inequality Symbol**

Solve $-9 > -\frac{1}{3}x + 6$.

$$-9 > -\tfrac{1}{3}x + 6$$

$-9 - 6 > -\tfrac{1}{3}x + 6 - 6$ **Subtract 6 from each side.**

$-15 > -\tfrac{1}{3}x$ **Simplify.**

$-3(-15) < -3\left(-\tfrac{1}{3}x\right)$ **Multiply each side by −3. Reverse the direction of the inequality symbol.**

$45 < x$, or $x > 45$ **Simplify.**

✓ **Quick Check**

2. Solve and graph $-2m + 4 \leq 34$.

Quick Tip

You can write the solution to an equation or inequality in the form $\{x : x > 45\}$. Read it as "all values of x such that x is greater than 45."

Now that you know how to solve two-step inequalities, you can use them to solve real-world problems.

3 EXAMPLE Using Two-Step Inequalities

An expedition leader estimates that a group of showshoers can carry less than 550 lb of food and equipment. The group must carry 336 lb of equipment as well as 25 lb of food for each climber. What is the greatest possible number of people in the expedition?

Words

| 336 lb of equipment | + | 25 lb of food/ person | times | number of people | is less than | 550 lb |

Let p = the number of people in the expedition.

Inequality 336 $+$ 25 $\cdot$ p $<$ 550

Solve the inequality.

$$336 + 25p < 550$$
$$336 + 25p - 336 < 550 - 336 \qquad \text{Subtract 336 from each side.}$$
$$25p < 214 \qquad \text{Simplify.}$$
$$\frac{25p}{25} < \frac{214}{25} \qquad \text{Divide each side by 25.}$$
$$p < 8.56 \qquad \text{Simplify.}$$

You cannot have 0.56 of a person. The greatest possible number of people in the expedition is 8.

Check Is the answer reasonable? The original problem states that the total of the equipment plus 25 lb of food per person is less than 550 lb. Since $336 + 25(8) = 536$ and $336 + 25(9) = 561$, the greatest whole number that satisfies the inequality is 8. The answer is reasonable.

A pint of water weighs 1 lb. You need about a gallon of water per person per day.

Quick Tip

Since $p < 8.56$, the "greatest number of people" must be the greatest whole number less than 8.56.

✓ Quick Check

3. **Commissions** A stereo salesperson earns a salary of $1,900 per month, plus a commission of 4% of sales. The salesperson wants to maintain a monthly income of at least $2,200. How much must the salesperson sell each month?

Complete Exercises 1–4 to solve the problem below.

You divide a number x by -4. Then you subtract 2 from the quotient. The result is at most -18. What are the possible solutions?

1. Write an expression to represent the description "You divide a number x by -4. Then you subtract 2 from the quotient."

2. If your expression from Exercise 1 is the left side of an inequality, what inequality symbol will you use to represent "at most"?

3. Write and solve the inequality described in the problem.

4. Is -12 a possible solution?

Standards Practice

For more exercises, see *Extra Skills and Word Problem Practice*.

Ⓐ Practice by Example

Tell what you can do to the first inequality in order to get the second. Be sure to list *all* steps.

Example 1
(page 363)

5. $4x - 2 \leq 6; x \leq 2$ 6. $\frac{1}{2}a - 1 < 3; a < 8$

GO for Help

Solve and graph each inequality.

7. $10 + 4a < -6$ 8. $2m + 8 > 0$ 9. $6 + 3y > 5$

10. $4x - 9 > -7$ 11. $\frac{1}{3}a - 4 \geq -1$ 12. $4 + 7a \geq 32$

Example 2
(page 363)

13. $-2x - 1 < 11$ 14. $-\frac{b}{7} + 7 \leq 6$ 15. $2.1 - 0.6y \geq 0.9$

16. $10 \leq -8x - 6$ 17. $-5y + 3 \geq 28$ 18. $-21 - 3m < 0$

Example 3
(page 364)

19. **Average Speed** On a trip from Louisiana to Florida, your family wants to travel at least 420 miles in 8 hours of driving. Write and solve an inequality to find what your average speed must be.

20. **Number Sense** You divide a number x by -3. Then you subtract 1 from the quotient. The result is at most 5. Write and solve an inequality to find all possible solutions.

Ⓑ Apply Your Skills

Solve each inequality.

21. $-\frac{1}{9}c + 13 \geq 5$ 22. $\frac{x}{3} + 11 < 31$ 23. $6y - 10 - y > 14$

24. $-\frac{x}{6} - 2 < 4$ 25. $\frac{1}{2}c - \frac{1}{4} < -\frac{3}{4}$ 26. $-4(2a + 7) \leq -12$

27. **Error Analysis** A student solved and graphed the inequality $-12x + 40 > 4$. What error did the student make?

Homework Video Tutor

Visit: PHSchool.com
Web Code: bje-0705

Photo Lab

Photo Price List

Size	Price
3 in. × 5 in.	$.40
4 in. × 6 in.	$.45
5 in. × 7 in.	$1.95
8 in. × 10 in.	$4.95
8 in. × 12 in.	$6.45
11 in. × 14 in.	$7.00
16 in. × 20 in.	$13.95
20 in. × 30 in.	$16.95

C Challenge

Write an inequality for each situation. Then solve.

28. Maureen is ordering photographic reprints and enlargements. She can spend at most $11. She wants to order an 11-in. × 14-in. enlargement and some 3-in. × 5-in. reprints. How many reprints can she order using the price list at the left?

29. You want to spend at most $10 for a taxi ride. Before you go anywhere, the taxi driver sets the meter at the initial charge of $2. The meter then adds $1.25 for every mile driven. If you plan on a $1 tip, what is the farthest you can go?

30. **Writing in Math** A friend was absent from class today. Write a letter to your friend telling how to solve two-step inequalities.

31. Corey's parents agree to loan Corey $182 to help pay for the school's spring music trip to Florida. Corey agrees to monthly payback amounts of $2, $4, $6, $8, and so on. How long will it take Corey to pay back the $182?

32. You and a friend want to spend at most $20 each on a horse-carriage sightseeing ride. There is an initial charge of $5 and then $2.50 for each quarter-mile driven. You plan on giving a $6 tip. For how many miles can you ride in the carriage?

Multiple Choice Practice and Mixed Review

For Standards Tutorials, visit PHSchool.com. Web Code: bjq-9045

33. The rectangles are similar. The area of the smaller rectangle is 32 square units. What is the area of the larger rectangle?

4

8

5

- Ⓐ 12.5 units²
- Ⓒ 40 units²
- Ⓑ 25.6 units²
- Ⓓ 50 units²

34. Emma wants to get large photos printed in color. She compared prices from four print shops. Which shop's prices are based on a constant unit price?

Ⓐ **Print Shop 1**

Photos	2	4	6	8
Cost ($)	7.5	15	22.5	30

Ⓒ **Print Shop 3**

Photos	2	4	6	8
Cost ($)	7.5	14	28	56

Ⓑ **Print Shop 2**

Photos	2	4	6	8
Cost ($)	2	6	10	14

Ⓓ **Print Shop 4**

Photos	2	4	6	8
Cost ($)	2	4	8	16

 for Help

Lesson 6-6

35. A stereo costs $262.99. The sales tax rate is 5%. What is the total cost of the stereo?

7-6 Transforming Formulas

Develop Solve multistep problems involving rate, average speed, distance, and time.

Develop Use formulas routinely for finding the perimeter and area of basic two-dimensional figures.

What You'll Learn

- To solve a formula for a given variable
- To use formulas to solve problems

. . . And Why

To find travel times in real-world situations

✓ Check Skills You'll Need

Use each formula for the values given.

1. Use the formula $d = rt$ to find d when $r = 80$ km/h and $t = 4$ h.

2. Use the formula $P = 2\ell + 2w$ to find P when $\ell = 9$ m and $w = 7$ m.

3. Use the formula $A = \frac{1}{2}bh$ to find A when $b = 12$ ft and $h = 8$ ft.

for Help
Lesson 3-3

For: Solving Formulas Activity
Use: Interactive Textbook, 7-6

Solving Formulas for a Given Variable

Remember that a formula shows the relationship between two or more quantities. You can use the properties of equality to transform a formula to represent one quantity in terms of another.

1 EXAMPLE **Transforming in One Step**

Solve the area formula $A = \ell w$ for ℓ.

$$A = \ell w$$

$$\frac{A}{w} = \frac{\ell w}{w} \qquad \text{Divide each side by } w.$$

$$\frac{A}{w} = \ell, \text{ or } \ell = \frac{A}{w} \qquad \text{Simplify.}$$

✓ Quick Check

1. Solve for the variable indicated in red.

   a. $p = s - c$ b. $h = \frac{k}{j}$ c. $I = prt$

Sometimes you need to use more than one step.

2 EXAMPLE **Using More Than One Step**

Solve the perimeter formula $P = 2\ell + 2w$ for ℓ.

$$P = 2\ell + 2w$$

$$P - 2w = 2\ell + 2w - 2w \qquad \text{Subtract } 2w \text{ from each side.}$$

$$P - 2w = 2\ell \qquad \text{Simplify.}$$

$$\frac{1}{2}(P - 2w) = \frac{1}{2}(2\ell) \qquad \text{Multiply each side by } \frac{1}{2}.$$

$$\frac{1}{2}P - w = \ell \qquad \text{Use the Distributive Property and simplify.}$$

✓ Quick Check

2. Solve for the variable indicated in red.

   a. $5a + 7 = b$ b. $P = 2\ell + 2w$ c. $y = \frac{x}{3} + 8$

Using Formulas to Solve Problems

You can transform formulas to solve real-world problems.

3 EXAMPLE Using a Distance Formula

Antelope Valley California
Poppy Reserve

You plan a 425-mi trip to Antelope Valley California Poppy Reserve. You estimate you will average 50 mi/h. To find about how long the trip will take, solve the distance formula $d = rt$ for t. Then substitute to find the time.

$$d = rt$$

$$\frac{d}{r} = \frac{rt}{r} \qquad \text{Divide each side by } r.$$

$$\frac{d}{r} = t, \text{ or } t = \frac{d}{r} \qquad \text{Simplify.}$$

$$t = \frac{425}{50} = 8.5 \qquad \text{Replace } d \text{ with 425 and } r \text{ with 50. Simplify.}$$

It will take you about 8.5 h to complete the trip.

✓ Quick Check

3. Solve the distance formula in Example 3 for r.

4 EXAMPLE Using a Temperature Formula

Multiple Choice An exchange student in your class wants to know the Celsius equivalent of 77°F. Use the formula $F = \frac{9}{5}C + 32$. What is the Celsius equivalent of 77°F?

  Ⓐ 81°C   Ⓑ 60.6°C   Ⓒ 45°C   Ⓓ 25°C

$$F = \frac{9}{5}C + 32$$

$$F - 32 = \frac{9}{5}C + 32 - 32 \qquad \text{Subtract 32 from each side.}$$

$$F - 32 = \frac{9}{5}C \qquad \text{Simplify.}$$

$$\frac{5}{9}(F - 32) = \frac{5}{9} \cdot \frac{9}{5}C \qquad \text{Multiply each side by } \frac{5}{9}.$$

$$\frac{5}{9}(F - 32) = C, \text{ or } C = \frac{5}{9}(F - 32) \qquad \text{Simplify and rewrite.}$$

$$C = \frac{5}{9}(77 - 32) = 25 \qquad \text{Replace } F \text{ with 77. Simplify.}$$

77°F is 25°C. The answer is D.

Quick Tip

Formulas can appear in many different forms on a test. Make sure you use the form that will give you the correct answer.

✓ Quick Check

4. Solve the batting average formula, $a = \frac{h}{n}$, for h. Find the number of hits h a batter needs in 40 times at bat n to have an average of 0.275.

Complete the steps to solve each equation for the variable indicated in red.

1. $a = 6c + 3$

$a - \blacksquare = 6c + 3 - 3$

$a - \blacksquare = 6c$

$\dfrac{a - 3}{\blacksquare} = \dfrac{6c}{\blacksquare}$

$\dfrac{a - 3}{\blacksquare} = \blacksquare$

2. $g = \dfrac{h}{j}$

$\blacksquare g = j\left(\dfrac{h}{j}\right)$

$jg = \blacksquare$

$\dfrac{jg}{\blacksquare} = \dfrac{h}{g}$

$\blacksquare = \dfrac{h}{g}$

For more exercises, see Extra Skills and Word Problem Practice.

Ⓐ Practice by Example

Examples 1 and 2
(page 367)

Examples 3 and 4
(page 368)

Solve for the variable indicated in red.

3. $V = \ell wh$ **4.** $P = 4s$ **5.** $q = \dfrac{p}{d}$

6. $r = 2s - 8$ **7.** $\dfrac{2}{3}m - 5 = n$ **8.** $m = \dfrac{a + b}{2}$

9. Commissions LaTanya sells business suits and gets a 4% commission on her sales. Last week, she received a paycheck that included $196 in commissions. Solve the formula $C = 0.04s$ for s, where C is the amount of commission and s is the amount of sales. Substitute to find LaTanya's sales.

10. You have $12.00 to rent a pair of in-line skates. They rent for $3.00 plus $1.50 per hour. To determine the maximum length of time you can rent the in-line skates, solve the formula $C = 3 + 1.5h$ for h. Then substitute 12 for C.

Ⓑ Apply Your Skills

Solve for the variable indicated in red.

11. $V = \dfrac{1}{2}\pi r^2 h$ **12.** $d^2 = \dfrac{3}{2}h$ **13.** $A = \dfrac{1}{2}(a + b)h$

14. a. Bricklayers use the formula $N = 7LH$ to estimate the number of bricks N needed in a wall. L is the length of the wall and H is the height. Solve the formula for H.
    b. If 1,134 bricks are used to build a wall that is 18 ft long, how high is the wall?

Homework Video Tutor

Visit: PHSchool.com
Web Code: bje-0706

15. Writing in Math A formula for the perimeter of a rectangle is $P = 2(b + h)$. Explain how you would find the height of the rectangle if you knew the perimeter and the base.

16. a. You can use the formula $C = \pi d$ to find the circumference C of a circle with diameter d. Solve the formula for d.
    b. Use 3.14 for π. Find d when $C = 15.7$.

Challenge

17. a. Joe uses the formula $p = wh + 1.5wv$ to figure his weekly pay. In the formula, p is the weekly pay, w is the hourly wage, h is the number of regular hours, and v is the number of overtime hours. Solve the formula for v.

b. Joe's hourly wage is \$6.24/h. If he earned \$282.36 last week working 40 regular hours plus overtime, how many hours overtime did he work?

Multiple Choice Practice and Mixed Review

For Standards Tutorials, visit PHSchool.com. Web Code: bjq-9045

18. Which of the following shows the next step in simplifying $\frac{7}{9} + \frac{5}{6}$ using the least common denominator?

  Ⓐ $\left(\frac{7}{9} \cdot \frac{4}{4}\right) + \left(\frac{5}{6} \cdot \frac{6}{6}\right)$ Ⓒ $\left(\frac{7}{9} \cdot \frac{6}{6}\right) + \left(\frac{5}{6} \cdot \frac{4}{4}\right)$

  Ⓑ $\left(\frac{7}{9} \cdot \frac{2}{2}\right) + \left(\frac{5}{6} \cdot \frac{3}{3}\right)$ Ⓓ $\left(\frac{7}{9} \cdot \frac{6}{6}\right) + \left(\frac{5}{6} \cdot \frac{9}{9}\right)$

19. What are the coordinates of one of the vertices of the figure?

  Ⓐ $(7, -3)$

  Ⓑ $(-7, -3)$

  Ⓒ $(3, 6)$

  Ⓓ $(-3, 6)$

20. Which expression is equivalent to $8^3 \cdot 8^7$?

  Ⓐ 8^{10} Ⓒ 64^{10}

  Ⓑ 8^{21} Ⓓ 64^{21}

GO for Help

Lesson 7-5 **Solve each inequality.**

21. $3x - 12 > -6$ **22.** $17 \le -4a + 5$ **23.** $-\frac{b}{2} + 9 < -3$

Lesson 6-5 **Write and solve an equation.**

24. What percent of 20 is 15?   **25.** 80% of what is 25?

Checkpoint Quiz 2

Solve each equation or inequality.

  1. $-8a - 6 = 10$ **2.** $9b + 42 = -12$ **3.** $2c + 6 + 7c = 8$

  4. $0 = -6y + 24$ **5.** $5 = 7x - 16$ **6.** $9m - 48 = -3$

  7. $15 - 10y < 24$ **8.** $23 > -\frac{x}{2} - 5$ **9.** $1.8x - 3.4 > 5.6$

Solve for the variable indicated in red.

  10. $s = g + h$ **11.** $3r + 4 = k$ **12.** $I = prt$

7-7 Simple and Compound Interest

Develop, Master Compute simple and compound interest.

What You'll Learn

- To solve simple-interest problems
- To solve compound-interest problems

. . . And Why

To find interest paid on investments using simple and compound interest

✓ **Check Skills You'll Need**

Find each amount.

1. 6% of $400

2. 55% of $2,000

3. 4.5% of $700

4. $5\frac{1}{2}$% of $325

GO for Help
Lesson 6-6

🔊 **New Vocabulary**

- principal
- interest
- interest rate
- simple interest
- compound interest
- balance

Simple Interest

When you first deposit money in a savings account, your deposit is called **principal.** The bank takes the money and invests it. In return, the bank pays you **interest** based on the **interest rate.** **Simple interest** is interest paid only on the principal.

Take Note ✏️   Simple-Interest Formula

$$I = prt,$$
where I is the interest, p is the principal,
r is the interest rate per year, and t is the time in years.

① EXAMPLE   Finding Simple Interest

Suppose you deposit $500 in a savings account. The interest rate is 4% per year.

a. Find the simple interest earned in six years. Find the total of principal plus interest.

$I = prt$	Use the simple-interest formula.
$I = 500 \cdot 0.04 \cdot 6$	Replace p with 500, r with 0.04, and t with 6.
$I = 120$	Simplify.
total $= 500 + 120 = 620$	Find the total.

The account will earn $120 in six years. The total of principal plus interest will be $620.

b. Find the interest earned in three months. Find the total of principal plus interest.

$t = \frac{3}{12} = \frac{1}{4} = 0.25$	Write the months as part of a year.
$I = prt$	Use the simple-interest formula.
$I = 500 \cdot 0.04 \cdot 0.25$	Replace p with 500, r with 0.04, and t with 0.25.
$I = 5$	Simplify.
total $= 500 + 5 = 505$	Find the total.

The account will earn $5 in three months. The total of principal plus interest will be $505.

✅ Quick Check

1. Find the simple interest.

   a. principal = $250
   interest rate = 4%
   time = 3 years

   b. principal = $250
   interest rate = 3.5%
   time = 6 months

Compound Interest

Quick Review

To write a percent as a decimal, move the decimal point two places to the left.

When a bank pays interest on the principal and on the interest an account has earned, the bank is paying **compound interest.** The principal plus the interest is the **balance,** which becomes the principal on which the bank figures the next interest payment.

2 EXAMPLE Using a Table

Multiple Choice **You deposit $400 in an account that earns 5% interest compounded annually (once per year). What is the balance in your account after 4 years? In your last calculation, round to the nearest cent.**

Ⓐ $510.51   Ⓑ $486.20   Ⓒ $480.00   Ⓓ $463.05

Principal at Beginning of Year	Interest	Balance
Year 1: $400.00	400.00 · 0.05 = 20.00	400 + 20 = 420.00
Year 2: $420.00	420.00 · 0.05 = 21.00	420 + 21 = 441.00
Year 3: $441.00	441.00 · 0.05 = 22.05	441 + 22.05 = 463.05
Year 4: $463.05	463.05 · 0.05 = 23.1525	463.05 + 23.1525 ≈ 486.20

After four years, the balance is $486.20. The answer is B.

✅ Quick Check

2. Make a table and find the balance. The interest is compounded annually.

   a. principal = $500
   interest rate = 3%
   time = 2 years

   b. principal = $625
   interest rate = 2%
   time = 4 years

Vocabulary Tip

Interest periods:
Annual—1 per year
Semiannual—2 per year
Quarterly—4 per year
Monthly—12 per year
Daily—360 per year
          (not 365)

You can find a balance using compound interest in one step with the compound interest formula and a calculator. An *interest period* is the length of time over which interest is calculated. The interest period can be a year or less than a year.

Take Note ✏️   Compound-Interest Formula

$$B = p(1 + r)^n,$$
where B is the final balance, p is the principal,
r is the interest rate for each interest period, and
n is the number of interest periods.

You can use this formula to solve Example 2.

$B = p(1 + r)^n$

$B = 400(1 + 0.05)^4$ **Replace p with 400, r with 0.05, and n with 4.**

$B \approx 486.20$ **Round to the nearest cent.**

The balance is $486.20. Using the formula means there are fewer calculations and fewer chances for mistakes.

When interest is compounded semiannually (twice per year), you must *divide* the interest rate by the number of interest periods, which is 2.

$$\frac{6\% \text{ annual}}{\text{interest rate}} \div \frac{2 \text{ interest}}{\text{periods}} = \frac{3\% \text{ semiannual}}{\text{interest rate}}$$

To find the number of payment periods, *multiply* the number of years by the number of interest periods per year.

3 EXAMPLE   Using the Compound Interest Formula

Find the balance on a deposit of $1,000 that earns 4% interest compounded semiannually for 5 years.

The interest rate r for compounding semiannually is $0.04 \div 2$, or 0.02. The number of payment periods n is 5 years $\times$ 2 interest periods per year, or 10.

$B = p(1 + r)^n$ **Use the compound-interest formula.**

$B = 1,000(1 + 0.02)^{10}$ **Replace p with 1,000, r with 0.02, and n with 10.**

$B \approx 1,218.99$ **Round to the nearest cent.**

The balance is $1,218.99.

Online
active math

For: Calculating Interest Activity
Use: Interactive Textbook, 7-7

✅ Quick Check

3. Find the balance for each account.
Amount deposited: $900, annual interest: 2%, time: 3 years

   a. compounding annually   **b.** compounding semiannually

Vocabulary Match each term with its meaning.

1. interest
2. balance
3. interest rate
4. principal

A. initial amount of investment
B. principal plus earned interest
C. money paid on an investment
D. percent of the investment an account earns

5. One account has a principal of $1,000 and earns 4% simple interest per year. Another account has a principal of $1,000 and earns 4% interest compounded annually. Which account has the greater balance at the end of four years? Explain.

Standards Practice

For more exercises, see *Extra Skills and Word Problem Practice.*

A Practice by Example

Example 1
(page 371)

Find the simple interest. Then find the total of principal plus interest.

6. principal = $200
   interest rate = 4%
   time = 2 years

7. principal = $870
   interest rate = 3%
   time = 9 months

Example 2
(page 372)

Complete each table. Compound the interest annually. In your last calculation, round to the nearest cent.

8. $3,000 at 4% for 3 years

Principal at Start of Year	Interest	Balance
Year 1: $3,000	▦	▦
Year 2: ▦	▦	▦
Year 3: ▦	▦	▦

9. $10,000 at 6% for 3 years

Principal at Start of Year	Interest	Balance
Year 1: $10,000	▦	▦
Year 2: ▦	▦	▦
Year 3: ▦	▦	▦

Example 3
(page 373)

Find each balance.

10. $495 at 4% compounded annually for 2 years

11. $15,600 at 3% compounded semiannually for 3 years

B Apply Your Skills

12. You deposit $600 in a savings account for 3 years. The account pays 8% annual interest compounded quarterly.
    a. What is the quarterly interest rate?
    b. What is the number of payment periods?
    c. Find the final balance in the account.

Find each balance.

13. $54,500 at 3% compounded semiannually for 9 years

14. $900 at a simple-interest rate of 3.25% for 3 months

15. Multiple Choice Calculate the amount of simple interest on $9,000 deposited at an interest rate of 5% for 2 years.

Ⓐ $900   Ⓑ $922.50   Ⓒ $9,900   Ⓓ $9,922.50

16. Open-Ended Choose an amount of money to be invested and an interest rate. Find the value of the investment after 5 years if the interest is simple interest; if the interest is compounded annually.

17. Writing in Math Explain the difference between simple interest and compound interest.

18. A student borrows $800 at 5.3% annual interest compounded semiannually. He makes no payments.
   a. How much will he owe after four years?
   b. How much interest will he owe in four years?

Ⓒ Challenge

19. Ling invests $1,000 in an account paying 8% interest.
   a. Compare the account balances after 5 years of simple interest and after 5 years of interest compounded annually.
   b. After how many years of compounded interest will the account balance be about twice Ling's initial investment?
   c. Reasoning What would the simple interest rate have to be for the investment to double in the same amount of time?

Multiple Choice Practice and Mixed Review

For Standards Tutorials, visit PHSchool.com. **Web Code:** bjq-9045

20. Robert invests $5,000 at 14% simple interest for one year. About how much interest does he earn for half the year?

Ⓐ $5,700   Ⓑ $2,850   Ⓒ $700   Ⓓ $350

21. Where does the number -2^{-3} belong on the number line?

Ⓐ Between 0 and $-\frac{1}{4}$

Ⓑ Between $-\frac{1}{4}$ and $-\frac{1}{2}$

Ⓒ Between $-\frac{1}{2}$ and $-\frac{3}{4}$

Ⓓ Between $-\frac{3}{4}$ and -1

$$\begin{array}{ccccc} -1 & -\frac{3}{4} & -\frac{1}{2} & -\frac{1}{4} & 0 \end{array}$$

22. Aiko plans to sell 2-pound bags of mixed nuts for $8.50. Which person sells the mixed nuts for the same price per pound?

Ⓐ Vanessa:
3 lb for $12.75

Ⓑ Fabio:
4 lb for $15.00

Ⓒ Ainsley:
1 lb for $4.50

Ⓓ Laken:
5 lb for $23.75

GO for Help · Lesson 7-6

Solve for the variable indicated in red.

23. $f = \frac{15m}{a}$ **24.** $y = 4x - 9$ **25.** $d = \frac{5}{8}k + 1$

Before you do all the work involved in solving a multiple-choice problem, you usually can eliminate some answer choices. This can save you time in finding the correct answer.

1 EXAMPLE

On her baseball team, Wanda uses the formula $a = \frac{h}{n}$, where a is her batting average, h is the number of hits, and n is the number of times at bat. How many hits does she get if her batting average is 0.240 and the number of times at bat is 25?

Ⓐ 28   Ⓑ 7   Ⓒ 6   Ⓓ 0

When a batting average is between 0 and 1, the number of hits is always greater than 0 and less than the number of times at bat. So you can eliminate choices A and D. Then substitute $a = 0.240$ and $n = 25$ to find that choice C is the correct answer.

2 EXAMPLE

The perimeter of a triangle is 32 centimeters. One side is 11 centimeters long. The other two sides are the same length. What is the length of one of the other sides?

Ⓐ 9.5 cm   Ⓑ 10.5 cm   Ⓒ 11 cm   Ⓓ 21 cm

The expression $32 - 11$, or 21, represents the sum of the lengths of the two other sides. So you can eliminate choice J. If you divide 21 by 2, you find the length of another side, 10.5. The correct answer is choice B.

Multiple Choice Practice

Read each question. Then write the letter of the correct answer on your paper.

1. On a field trip to the zoo, 21 students voted to have sandwiches for lunch. This represents $\frac{7}{8}$ of the class. How many students are in the class?

     Ⓐ 24   Ⓑ 25   Ⓒ 38   Ⓓ 40

2. The area of a rectangle is 64 in.^{2}. If the area is increased by 25%, which of the following could be the dimensions of the new rectangle?

     Ⓐ 6 in. by 8 in.   Ⓒ 10 in. by 10 in.
     Ⓑ 10 in. by 8 in.   Ⓓ 8 in. by 8 in.

3. It costs $6.00 to get 20 pictures developed. At this rate, how much will it cost to get 35 pictures developed?

     Ⓐ $3.41   Ⓑ $10.50   Ⓒ $21.00   Ⓓ $41.00

Chapter 7 Review

Choose the vocabulary term that correctly completes the sentence.

1. A bank pays __?__ when it pays interest on the principal and on the interest an account has earned.

2. The amount of money first deposited into a savings account is called the __?__.

3. The principal plus the interest is the __?__ of the account.

4. When you count by 1s from any integer, you are counting __?__.

5. A bank pays interest based on its advertised __?__.

6. __?__ is paid only on the principal of an account.

7. A bank pays you __?__ for the use of your money.

Go Online
PHSchool.com

For: Vocabulary quiz
Web Code: bjj-0751

Skills and Concepts

Lesson 7-1
• To solve two-step equations
• To use two-step equations to solve problems

To solve two-step equations, undo addition and subtraction, then undo multiplication and division.

Solve each equation.

8. $2a - 7 = -15$ 9. $3 = -6x + 15$ 10. $\frac{c}{4} + 10 = 22$

11. $1.5y + 3.4 = 7.9$ 12. $\frac{2}{3}y - 9 = 5$ 13. $8 = 9x - 7$

Lesson 7-2
• To combine like terms to simplify an equation
• To use the Distributive Property to simplify an equation

To solve multi-step equations, remove grouping symbols and combine like terms first. Then follow the steps for solving two-step equations.

Solve each equation.

14. $8m - 3m = 4$ 15. $6 - 2y - y = 12$

16. $2(b - 7) = 16$ 17. $-2(5 + 6c) + 16 = -90$

18. **Number Sense** Find four consecutive integers with a sum of -66.

Chapter Review (continued)

Lesson 7-3

- To solve two-step equations with fractions
- To solve two-step equations with decimals

When the coefficient of the variable in an equation is a fraction, gather the variables on one side of the equation and use the reciprocal to solve. Use the properties of equality to solve equations involving decimals.

Solve each equation.

19. $\frac{2}{3}q + 5 = \frac{3}{4}$ **20.** $\frac{1}{6}b - 1 = 1\frac{2}{3}$

21. $10 = 5 + \frac{4}{5}w$ **22.** $1.2x + 2.7 = 6.3$

23. $3.75x - 5.1 = 6.12$ **24.** $-13.1 - 5.4x = -20.38$

25. A cable TV company charges $24.95 per month for basic service and $6.95 per month for each premium channel. A customer's bill for one month is $45.80. Write and solve an equation to find the number of premium channels the customer receives.

Lesson 7-4

- To write an equation to solve a problem

One strategy for solving problems is to write an equation and then solve the equation.

Write an equation. Then solve.

26. A pair of jeans is on sale for 15% off the original price. The sale price of the jeans is $29.74. What was the original price?

27. A bank teller is counting his money and notices that he has an equal number of tens and twenties. He also has $147 in other bills. If the total value of the bills he has is $1,167, how many tens and twenties does he have?

28. Jalisha invested some money and made an 8% profit. The current value of her investment is $1,296. How much did she invest initially?

Lesson 7-5

- To solve two-step inequalities
- To use two-step inequalities to solve problems

Solving two-step inequalities involves the same steps as solving two-step equations. Reverse the direction of the inequality symbol when you multiply or divide by a negative number.

Solve and graph each inequality.

29. $2a - 3 > 11$ **30.** $9y + 13 \le -14$

31. $-6c + 12 \ge 8$ **32.** $23 < 7 - 4x$

33. $\frac{8}{9}x + 5 < -3$ **34.** $-\frac{b}{2} + 14 > 13$

35. $-17 > \frac{x}{3} - 19$ **36.** $x + 4x + 9 \ge 6$

37. Last year's computer model is on sale for $799. You can add more memory to the computer. Each chip of 8 megabytes of memory costs $25. How many megabytes of memory can you add if you have at most $1,000 to spend? Write and solve an inequality.

Lesson 7-6

- To solve a formula for a given variable
- To use formulas to solve problems

Use the properties of equality to transform a formula.

Solve for the variable indicated in red.

38. $r = 6km$

39. $8x = 6y$

40. $Q = gp$

41. $a = b - 2c$

42. $w = 3a + 5n$

43. $e = \frac{h}{6} + 11$

Lesson 7-7

- To solve simple-interest problems
- To solve compound-interest problems

You can calculate **simple interest** using the formula $I = prt$, where I is the interest, p is the **principal** (original amount deposited), r is the **interest rate** per year, and t is the time in years.

Compound interest is interest paid on both the principal and interest. It is found using the formula $B = p(1 + r)^n$, where B is the final **balance,** p is the principal, r is the interest rate for each interest period, and n is the number of interest periods.

Find the simple interest.

44. $150 deposited at an interest rate of 4.5% for 2 years

45. $2,525 deposited at an interest rate of 2.5% for 4 years

46. $6,000 deposited at an interest rate of 3% for 6 months

Find each balance.

47. $8,000 at 2% compounded annually for 3 years

48. $17,500 at 4.25% compounded annually for 6 years

49. $22,000 at 3% compounded semiannually for 8 years

50. $33,800 at 3.5% compounded semiannually for 5 years

51. The more interest periods there are, the more interest you make on an investment. Do you agree with this statement? Explain.

Go Online For: Chapter Test
PHSchool.com Web Code: bja-0752

Solve each equation.

1. $3x + 4 = 19$ **2.** $5 + \frac{c}{9} = -31$

3. $2y - 15 = 11$ **4.** $8a + 3 = -12.2$

5. $\frac{3}{5}b - 8 = 4$ **6.** $\frac{m}{2} - 5 = 7$

7. $-83 = 9x - 2$ **8.** $18 - \frac{a}{4} = -5$

9. $\frac{3}{5}y + \frac{2}{5} = \frac{4}{5}$ **10.** $-23 - c = -19$

11. $3x + 4x = 21$ **12.** $\frac{1}{2}(10y + 4) = 17$

13. $2(7b - 6) - 4 = 12$

14. $2m - 6 = m$

15. $\frac{2}{3}a - 5 + \frac{8}{9}a = -19$

16. $0.015x + 3.45 = 4.65$

17. $3y + 3 = -15$

18. $2b + 18 = -8$

Write an equation. Then solve.

19. Number Sense Find three consecutive integers with a sum of 267.

20. A rental car company charges $35 a day plus $.15/mi for a mid-size car. A customer owes $117.15 for a three-day rental. How many miles did the customer drive?

21. Rates A moving truck leaves a house and travels 240 mi. The family leaves the house 1 h later following the same route in a car. They travel at a steady rate of 60 mi/h. How long after the moving truck leaves the house will the car have traveled the same distance?

22. The Jaspers collect nickels, dimes, and quarters in a jar. When they count the change in the jar, there are twice as many nickels as there are quarters. If there is $15.30 in dimes and $74.80 in all, how many quarters are there?

Solve and graph each inequality.

23. $7m - 8 > 6$ **24.** $2x - 6 \geq -9$

25. $-9a - 1 \leq 26$ **26.** $22 < 6c + 4$

27. $\frac{b}{3} + 12 > -3$ **28.** $-\frac{2}{3}x + 8 \leq 2$

29. $11 > -3y + 2$ **30.** $16 - 4a > 8$

31. Commissions An insurance salesperson earns a salary of $4,200 per month plus a commission of 3% of sales. How much must the salesperson sell to have a monthly income of at least $4,500?

32. Writing in Math How is solving a two-step inequality different from solving a two-step equation?

Solve for the variable indicated in red.

33. $H = 3w + 2$ **34.** $g = cst$

35. $R = 6n + 4p$ **36.** $y = \frac{x}{5} - 4$

Find the simple interest.

37. $800 deposited at an interest rate of 1.5% for 3 years

38. $1,050 deposited at an interest rate of 2% for 9 months

39. $2,500 deposited at an interest rate of 4.25% for 5 years

Find each balance.

40. $12,000 at 4% compounded annually for 4 years

41. $1,950 at 5% compounded annually for 2 years

42. $18,500 at 4.5% compounded semiannually for 5 years

43. $75,000 at 3% compounded semiannually for 8 years

Some problems ask you to identify an equation that matches a particular situation.

An eighth-grade class raised $634 for a field trip to a museum. The museum charged $4.75 for each admission. There was $26 left over. Which equation could be used to find n, the number of people that went on the field trip?

- Ⓐ $634 = 4.75n - 26$
- Ⓑ $634 = 4.75n + 26$
- Ⓒ $634 = \frac{n}{4.75} - 26$
- Ⓓ $634 = \frac{n}{4.75} + 26$

Think It Through

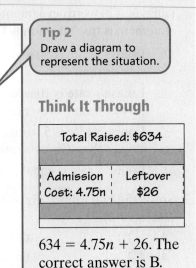

Total Raised: $634	
Admission Cost: 4.75n	Leftover $26

$634 = 4.75n + 26$. The correct answer is B.

Vocabulary Review

As you solve problems, you must understand the meanings of mathematical terms. Match each term with its mathematical meaning.

A. equation

B. scale drawing

C. integers

D. unit price

E. consecutive integers

I. is similar to an actual object or place

II. a sequence obtained by counting by ones from any integer

III. a rate that gives the cost of one item

IV. the whole numbers, zero, and their opposites

V. a mathematical sentence with an equal sign

Read each question. Then write the letter of the correct answer on your paper.

1. The tables show how four farmers sell ears of corn. Which table is based on a constant unit price? **(Lesson 6-1)**

Ⓐ
Number of Ears	Cost ($)
1	0.75
2	1.00
3	1.25
4	1.50

Ⓒ
Number of Ears	Cost ($)
2	1.75
4	2.50
6	3.75
8	5.25

Ⓑ
Number of Ears	Cost ($)
3	1.00
6	2.00
9	4.00
12	8.00

Ⓓ
Number of Ears	Cost ($)
4	1.25
8	2.50
12	3.75
16	5.00

2. Louise can type 70 words in 2 minutes. Corey can type 120 words in 3 minutes. Which statement is true? **(Lesson 6-1)**

Ⓐ Louise's rate is 50 words per minute slower than Corey's rate.

Ⓑ Louise's rate is 10 words per minute slower than Corey's rate.

Ⓒ Louise's rate is 5 words per minute slower than Corey's rate.

Ⓓ Louise's rate is equal to Corey's rate.

3. Solve the equation $2.35x + 4 = 6.82$.
(Lesson 7-3)

Ⓐ -1.1 Ⓒ 2.82
Ⓑ 1.2 Ⓓ 4.47

4. What is the first step in solving the equation $2 = 5\frac{1}{2} - \frac{1}{3}b$? **(Lesson 7-3)**

Ⓐ Subtract $5\frac{1}{2}$ from each side.

Ⓑ Add $\frac{1}{3}$ to each side.

Ⓒ Multiply each side by -3.

Ⓓ Subtract 2 from each side.

5. The table shows weight estimates of dinosaur species. Which dinosaur weighed about 5.27×10^7 g less than a *Brachiosaurus*?
(Lesson 3-6)

Dinosaur	Weight (kg)
Stegosaurus	1,800
Brachiosaurus	54,500
Allosaurus	4,500
Tyrannosaurus	6,000
Rhabdodon	450

Ⓐ *Allosaurus*   Ⓒ *Tyrannosaurus*
Ⓑ *Rhabdodon*   Ⓓ *Stegosaurus*

6. Cheng drives 25 miles on a highway at a constant rate of 60 miles per hour. How much time does the trip take? **(Lesson 3-3)**

Ⓐ 25 minutes   Ⓒ 85 minutes
Ⓑ 35 minutes   Ⓓ 1,500 minutes

7. The table represents the favorite activities of 150 people surveyed at a resort.

Boutique Shopping	Jet Boat Skiing	Rafting	Massage at Spa
35	49	24	42

Which bar graph best represents the data? **(page 51)**

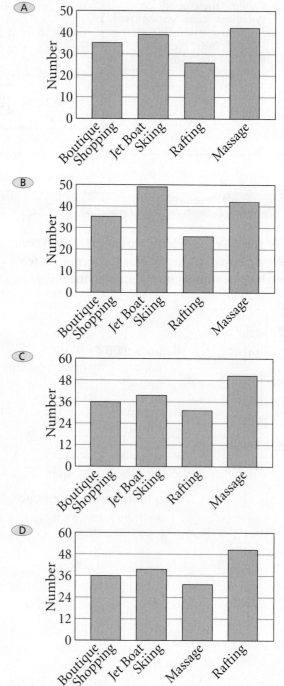

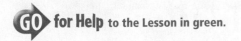
8. The table below shows the number of hours Ellen baby-sits from April to June. Which line graph best represents the data? **(page 51)**

Number of Hours Babysitting

April	May	June
64	35	104

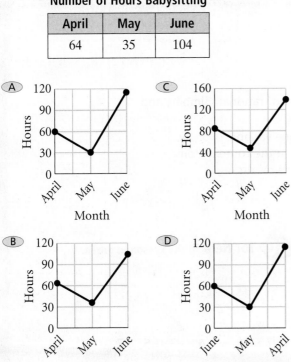

9. Figure *KLMN* was dilated to form figure *PRST*. What is the scale factor used to change figure *KLMN* to figure *PRST*? **(page 308)**

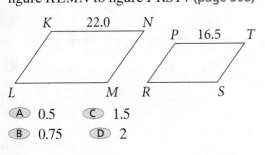

(A) 0.5   (C) 1.5
(B) 0.75   (D) 2

10. For a field trip, a principal collected $300 per grade from grades 5, 6, 7, and 8, as well as $3.50 from each student. The principal collected $4,700.

Which equation can you solve to find the number of students *s*? **(Lesson 7-3)**

(A) $300 + 3.50s = 4,700$

(B) $(300 + 3.50)s = 4,700$

(C) $300 \cdot 4 + 3.50s = 4,700$

(D) $300 \cdot 4 + 3.50 \cdot 4s = 4,700$

11. Figure *WXYZ* is similar to figure *STUV*. What scale factor was used to dilate figure *WXYZ* to figure *STUV*? **(page 308)**

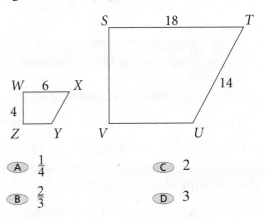

(A) $\frac{1}{4}$ (C) 2

(B) $\frac{2}{3}$ (D) 3

12. Molly buys a 5-foot-long sterling chain. She uses 16 inches for her own necklace and 18 inches for a chain she gives to a friend. How many inches of chain are left? **(Lesson 5-5)**

(A) 94 inches   (C) 26 inches
(B) 29 inches   (D) 18 inches

Linear Functions and Graphing

What You've Learned

Compute simple and compound interest.

Simplify numerical expressions by applying properties of rational numbers and justify the process used.

Solve two-step linear equations and inequalities in one variable over the rational numbers, interpret the solution or solutions in the context from which they arose, and verify the reasonableness of the results.

 **Check Your Readiness**   **GO for Help** to the Lesson in green.

Describing Number Patterns (Lesson 1-7)

Write the next two numbers in each pattern.

1. $8, 5, 2, -1, \ldots$ **2.** $43, 37, 31, 25, \ldots$ **3.** $4.5, 6, 7.5, 9, \ldots$ **4.** $-3, -5, -7, -9, \ldots$

Graphing Points (Lesson 1-10)

Write the coordinates of each point.

5. A **6.** B **7.** C

8. D **9.** E **10.** F

Draw a coordinate plane. Graph each point.

11. $M(0, -2)$ **12.** $H(-2, 4)$ **13.** $J(6, 1)$

14. $K(5, -3)$ **15.** $L(-4, -3)$ **16.** $G(3, 0)$

Simplifying Fractions (Lesson 4-4)

Write each fraction in simplest form.

17. $\dfrac{-5 - (-4)}{12 - (-6)}$ **18.** $\dfrac{15 - (-12)}{17 - 8}$ **19.** $\dfrac{-4 - 1}{-7 - (-2)}$ **20.** $\dfrac{4.3 - 3.5}{7.1 - 4.7}$

Transforming Equations (Lesson 7-6)

Solve each equation for y.

21. $4x + y = 3$ **22.** $y - 4 = -2x$ **23.** $2x - y = 6$ **24.** $8 + y + 6x = 0$

25. $12 - y = x$ **26.** $2y + x = 5$ **27.** $5y - 20 = x$ **28.** $3x + 4y = 12$

What You'll Learn Next

Use variables and operations to write a system of equations or inequalities.

Use algebraic terminology correctly.

Represent quantitative relationships graphically.

Graph linear functions, noting that the vertical change per unit of horizontal change is always the same and know that the ratio is called the slope of a graph.

Plot the values of quantities whose ratios are always the same. Fit a line to the plot and understand that the slope of the line equals the ratio of the quantities.

▲ You can use a linear function to relate total cost to the number of items purchased.

New Vocabulary

🔊 **English and Spanish Audio Online**

- **constant of variation** (p. 405)
- **direct variation** (p. 405)
- **domain** (p. 388)
- **function** (p. 388)
- **linear equation** (p. 394)
- **linear inequality** (p. 420)

- **range** (p. 388)
- **relation** (p. 388)
- **slope** (p. 399)
- **slope-intercept form** (p. 401)
- **solution** (p. 393)
- **system of linear equations** (p. 414)

- **system of linear inequalities** (p. 422)
- **vertical-line test** (p. 389)
- **_y_-intercept** (p. 401)

Activity Lab

Relating Graphs to Events

FOR USE WITH LESSON 8-1

> *Introduce* Represent quantitative relationships graphically and interpret the meaning of a specific part of a graph in the situation represented by the graph.

You can use graphs to show real-world relationships visually. Labels can help explain the parts of a graph.

1 EXAMPLE

The graph at the right shows one trip from home to school and back. The trip combines walking and getting a ride from a neighbor. Tell what the graph shows by labeling each part.

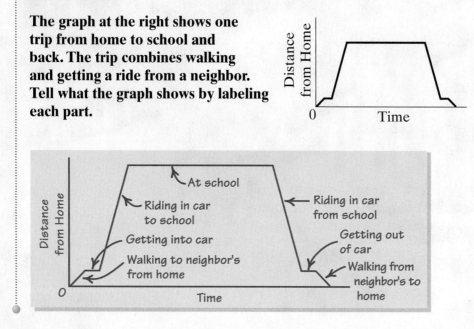

Label the parts of each graph.

1.

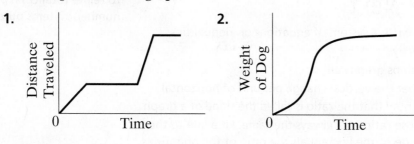

2.

3. The graph at the right is a *step graph*. It shows the prices at a parking garage.
   a. How much does parking cost for an hour or less?
   b. How much does parking cost for 4 hours and 20 minutes?
   c. A receipt from the parking garage is for $7. What is the greatest length of time the car could have been in the garage?

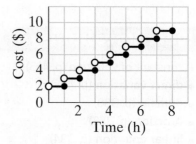

4. **Reasoning** Use the graph at the right. Jolene and Tamika were sprinting. Which girl ran faster? Explain.

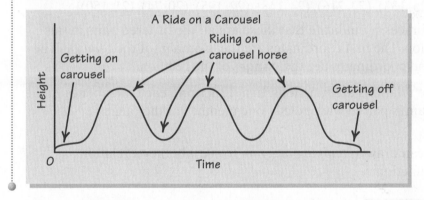

When you draw a graph without actual data, you are making a sketch. A sketch can help you visualize relationships.

2 EXAMPLE

You go to an amusement park and ride a moving horse on a carousel. Sketch a graph to show your height above the ground. Identify your axes and include labels for each part.

A Ride on a Carousel

Getting on carousel

Riding on carousel horse

Getting off carousel

Height

Time

Sketch a graph for each situation. Identify your axes and include labels for each part.

5. the temperature outside during one 24-hour period

6. your speed as you take a trip on a train

7. the total distance you travel as you go to a concert and return home

8. the distance above ground of a pole vaulter's feet at a track meet

9. You pour water at a constant rate into the container shown at the right. Sketch a graph of the water level as you fill the container.

Relations and Functions

Master Use algebraic terminology correctly.
Graph linear functions.

What You'll Learn

- To determine whether a relation is a function
- To graph relations and functions

. . . And Why

To solve real-world problems involving cooking

✔ Check Skills You'll Need

Graph each point.

1. $A(3, 4)$ 2. $B(-3, 1)$

3. $F(2, 0)$ 4. $D(2, -2)$

5. $C(-4, -3)$

6. $E(0, -4)$

GO for Help
Lesson 1-10

◀)) New Vocabulary

- relation
- domain
- range
- function
- vertical-line test

Identifying Relations and Functions

The table shows the results of a canned-food drive.

You can write the data in the table as a **relation,** a set of ordered pairs. The first coordinate of each ordered pair is the number of students in a homeroom. The second coordinate is the number of cans the students in that homeroom collected.

Food for Life Canned-Food Drive

Homeroom	Number of Students	Number of Cans
101	25	133
102	22	216
103	24	148
104	22	195
105	20	74
106	21	150

Here is the relation represented by the table:

$$\{(25, 133), (22, 216), (24, 148), (22, 195), (20, 74), (21, 150)\}$$

The braces, { }, indicate that these are all the ordered pairs in this relation. The first coordinates are the **domain** of the relation. The second coordinates are the **range** of the relation.

Some relations are functions. In a **function,** each member of the domain is paired with exactly one member of the range.

You can draw a *mapping diagram* to see whether a relation is a function.

1 EXAMPLE Identifying a Function

Is each relation a function? Explain.

a. {(0, 1), (1, 2), (1, 3), (2, 4)}

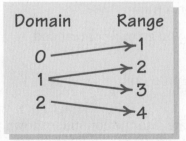

List the domain values and the range values in order.

Draw arrows from the domain values to their range values.

There are two range values for the domain value 1. This relation is *not* a function.

b. {(0, 1), (1, 2), (2, 2), (3, 4)}   **c.** {(0, 1), (1, 3), (2, 2), (3, 4)}

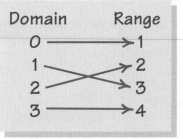

There is one range value for each domain value. This relation is a function.

There is one range value for each domain value. This relation is a function.

✓ Quick Check

1. Is each relation a function? Explain.

    a. {(−2, 3), (2, 2), (2, −2)}   **b.** {(−5, −4), (0, −4), (5, −4)}

Functions can model many everyday situations when one quantity depends on another. One quantity *is a function of* the other.

2 EXAMPLE   **Identifying a Function**

Is the time needed to cook a turkey a function of the weight of the turkey? Explain.

The time the turkey cooks (range value) is determined by the weight of the turkey (domain value). This relation is a function.

✓ Quick Check

2. a. For the United States Postal Service, is package weight a function of the postage paid to mail the package? Explain.
    b. Is the cost of postage a function of package weight? Explain.

You can estimate the cooking time of a turkey: 20 minutes per pound unstuffed, or 30 minutes per pound stuffed.

Graphing Relations and Functions

Graphing a relation on a coordinate plane gives you a visual way to tell whether the relation is a function. If the relation is a function, then any vertical line passes through at most one point on the graph. If you can find a vertical line that passes through two points on the graph, then the relation is *not* a function. This method is called the **vertical-line test.**

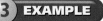 **EXAMPLE** **Using the Vertical-Line Test**

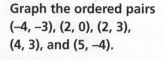

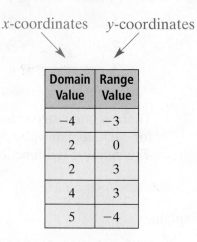

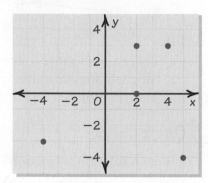

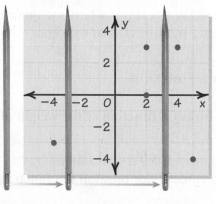

Vocabulary Tip

The first value in an ordered pair, the <u>x-coordinate</u>, shows horizontal position.

The second value in an ordered pair, the <u>y-coordinate</u>, shows vertical position.

a. Graph the relation shown in the table.

x-coordinates   *y*-coordinates

Domain Value	Range Value
−4	−3
2	0
2	3
4	3
5	−4

Graph the ordered pairs (–4, –3), (2, 0), (2, 3), (4, 3), and (5, –4).

b. Use the vertical-line test. Is the relation a function? Explain.

Pass a pencil across the graph as shown. Keep the pencil vertical (parallel to the *y*-axis) to represent a vertical line.

The pencil held vertically would pass through both (2, 0) and (2, 3), so the relation is *not* a function.

✓ Quick Check

3. **[Algebra]** Graph the relation shown in each table. Use the vertical-line test. Is the relation a function? Explain.

a.
x	y
−6	−5
−3	−2
0	−2
1	0
4	3
5	7

b.
x	y
−7	4
−2	6
−1	−1
−1	3
0	5
1	5

c.
x	y
−5	4
−4	4
−3	4
0	0
1	4
2	4

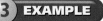

Use the graph for Exercises 1–3.

1. What is the domain of the relation?

2. What is the range of the relation?

3. Is the relation a function?

Suppose the point (1, 2) is added to the relation.

4. Does the domain of the relation change? If so, how?

5. Does the range of the relation change? If so, how?

6. Is the new relation a function?

Standards Practice

For more exercises, see *Extra Skills and Word Problem Practice*.

Ⓐ Practice by Example

Example 1
(page 388)

GO for Help

Is each relation a function? Explain.

7. Domain Range   8. Domain Range   9. Domain Range

$$\begin{array}{cc} -5 \\ -2 \longrightarrow -2 \\ 2 \longrightarrow 3 \\ 5 \end{array}$$

$$\begin{array}{cc} & -5 \\ -4 \longrightarrow -1 \\ -3 \longrightarrow 2 \\ & 6 \end{array}$$

$$\begin{array}{cc} 3 \longrightarrow -5 \\ 6 < \begin{array}{c} -2 \\ 0 \end{array} \\ 7 \longrightarrow 1 \end{array}$$

Example 2
(page 389)

10. Is the time you take to go to the library a function of the distance to the library? Explain.

11. Is the price of a one-year subscription to your favorite magazine a function of the age of the subscriber? Explain.

Example 3
(page 390)

Graph each relation shown. Use the vertical-line test. Is the relation a function? Explain.

12. $\{(-1, 3), (-1, 2), (0, -4), (4, 2)\}$ 13. $\{(3, -1), (2, -1), (-4, 0), (2, 4)\}$

Ⓑ Apply Your Skills

Graph each relation. Is the relation a function? Explain.

14. $\{(0, 1), (3, 5), (2, 2), \left(-\frac{1}{2}, -\frac{4}{5}\right)\}$ 15. $\{(-1, 9), (0, -1), (-1, 4), (4, 9)\}$

16. $\{(-1, 1), (-2, 1), (-2, 2), (0, 2)\}$

17.
x	y
−5	6
−2	3
3	2
6	4

18.
x	y
3	−7
1	−5
−1	−5
−3	−7

19.
x	y
−7	3
−5	1
−5	−1
−7	−3

20.
x	y
6	−2
1	−1
0	−2
−1	−3

Homework Video Tutor

Visit: PHSchool.com
Web Code: bje-0801

21. Writing in Math Is every relation a function? Is every function a relation? Explain.

22. Geometry Explain why the area of a square is a function of the length of a side of the square.

23. Error Analysis Your friend says that a relation is not a function when two ordered pairs have the same *y*-coordinate. Explain your friend's error.

C Challenge **Patterns In each function below, there is a pattern to how the range values relate to the domain values. Describe the pattern.**

24. $\{(-2, 0), (0, 2), (3, 5), (8, 10)\}$ **25.** $\{(-5, 5), (-1, 1), (0, 0), (3, -3)\}$

26. $\{(-1, -0.5), (2, 1), (7, 3.5)\}$ **27.** $\{(1, 1), (2, 4), (3, 9), (4, 16)\}$

28. a. Open-Ended Write two different relations for which the domain is $\{-1, 0, 1\}$ and the range is $\{1, 2\}$.

   b. Graph your relations. Use the vertical-line test to tell whether each relation is a function.

For Standards Tutorials, visit PHSchool.com. Web Code: bjq-9045

For Exercises 29 and 30, which choice best explains why the relation is or is NOT a function?

29. $\{(-5, 7), (-2, -1), (0, 3), (4, 7)\}$

   Ⓐ A function; only one range value exists for each domain value.
   Ⓑ A function; two domain values exist for range value 7.
   Ⓒ Not a function; the relation passes the vertical line test.
   Ⓓ Not a function; two domain values exist for range value 7.

30. $\{(-8, -4), (-2, 0), (1, 3), (-2, 6)\}$

   Ⓐ A function; only one range value exists for each domain value.
   Ⓑ A function; two range values exist for domain value -2.
   Ⓒ Not a function; the relation passes the vertical line test.
   Ⓓ Not a function; two range values exist for domain value -2.

31. Order $-\frac{1}{4}, \frac{3}{2}, -0.3, 0.6,$ and $-\frac{7}{8}$ from least to greatest.

   Ⓐ $-\frac{1}{4}, \frac{3}{2}, -0.3, 0.6, -\frac{7}{8}$ Ⓒ $\frac{3}{2}, -\frac{1}{4}, -\frac{7}{8}, -0.3, 0.6$
   Ⓑ $-\frac{1}{4}, -0.3, \frac{3}{2}, 0.6, -\frac{7}{8}$ Ⓓ $-\frac{7}{8}, -0.3, -\frac{1}{4}, 0.6, \frac{3}{2}$

 Lesson 7-7 **32.** You invest $1,200 in an account that earns 3.5% interest compounded annually. Find the account balance after four years.

Lessons 7-1 and 7-3 **Solve each equation.**

33. $-42 + 3c = -6$ **34.** $\frac{3}{2}t - 4 = \frac{1}{2}$ **35.** $2m - 4.9 = -3.6$

Equations With Two Variables

What You'll Learn

- To find solutions of equations with two variables
- To graph linear equations with two variables

... And Why

To solve real-world problems involving meteorology and oceanography

✓ Check Skills You'll Need

Evaluate each expression for $x = 2$.

1. $2 + x$ **2.** $x - 12$

3. $8x - 13$ **4.** $24 \div 2x$

GO for Help
Lesson 1-3

🔊 New Vocabulary

- solution
- linear equation

Finding Solutions of Two-Variable Equations

In previous chapters, you solved equations with one variable, such as $2x + 5 = 7$. In this chapter, you will find solutions of equations with two variables, such as $y = 3x + 4$. An ordered pair that makes such an equation a true statement is a **solution** of the equation.

① EXAMPLE   Finding a Solution

Find the solution of $y = 3x + 4$ for $x = -1$.

$y = 3x + 4$

$y = 3(-1) + 4$ **Replace x with –1.**

$y = -3 + 4$ **Multiply.**

$y = 1$ **Add.**

A solution of the equation is $(-1, 1)$.

✓ Quick Check

1. Find the solution of each equation for $x = -3$.

   a. $y = 2x + 1$ **b.** $y = -4x + 3$ **c.** $y = 0x - 4$

You can use two-variable equations to model real-world situations.

② EXAMPLE   Using Substitution to Find a Solution

The equation $t = 21 - 0.01n$ models the normal low July temperature in degrees Celsius at Mount Rushmore, South Dakota. In the equation, t is the temperature at n meters above the base of the mountain. Find the normal low July temperature at 300 m above the base.

$t = 21 - 0.01n$

$t = 21 - 0.01(300)$ **Replace n with 300.**

$t = 21 - 3$ **Multiply.**

$t = 18$ **Subtract.**

A solution of the equation is $(300, 18)$. The normal low July temperature at 300 m above the base of the mountain is 18°C.

Mt. Rushmore is 1,745 m tall.

✓ Quick Check

2. Find the normal low July temperature at 700 m above the base of Mount Rushmore.

Graphing Equations With Two Variables

An equation with two variables can have many solutions. One way to show these solutions is to graph them, which also gives a graph of the equation. A **linear equation** is any equation whose graph is a line. All the equations in this lesson are linear equations.

3 EXAMPLE   **Graphing a Linear Equation**

Graph $y = -\frac{1}{2}x + 3$. Is $(2, 2)$ a solution?

Step 1 Make a table of values to show ordered-pair solutions.

x	$-\frac{1}{2}x + 3$	(x, y)
-2	$-\frac{1}{2}(-2) + 3 = 1 + 3 = 4$	(-2, 4)
0	$-\frac{1}{2}(0) + 3 = 0 + 3 = 3$	(0, 3)
4	$-\frac{1}{2}(4) + 3 = -2 + 3 = 1$	(4, 1)

Step 2 Graph the ordered pairs. Draw a line through the points.

The point $(2, 2)$ appears on the graph, so it is a solution.

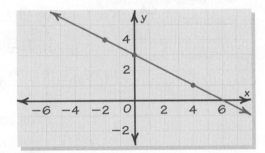

Check Substitute $(2, 2)$ in the original equation. Since $2 = -\frac{1}{2} \cdot 2 + 3$, $(2, 2)$ is a solution.

✓ Quick Check

3. Graph each linear equation. Is the given point a solution?
   a. $y = 2x + 1; (-1, -1)$ **b.** $y = 3x - 2; (-2, 0)$

GO ⦿nline

Video Tutor Help

Visit: PHSchool.com
Web Code: bje-0775

If you use the vertical-line test on the graph in Example 3, you see that every x-value has exactly one y-value. This means that the relation $y = -\frac{1}{2}x + 3$ is a function. A linear equation is a linear function *unless* its graph is a vertical line.

4 EXAMPLE   Graphing $y = a$ and $x = b$

Graph each equation. Is the equation a function?

a. $y = 2$

For every value of x, $y = 2$.

This is a horizontal line.
The equation $y = 2$ is
a function.

b. $x = 2$

For every value of y, $x = 2$.

This is a vertical line.
The equation $x = 2$ is
not a function.

✓ Quick Check

4. Graph each equation. Is the equation a function?

a. $x = 1$ **b.** $y = -4$ **c.** $x = 0$

You may find it helpful to solve an equation for y before you find
solutions and graph the equation.

5 EXAMPLE   Graphing by Solving for y

Solve $3x + y = -5$ for y. Then graph the equation.

Solve the equation for y.

$$3x + y = -5$$
$$3x + y - 3x = -5 - 3x \quad \text{Subtract 3x from each side.}$$
$$y = -3x - 5 \quad \text{Simplify.}$$

Make a table of values.

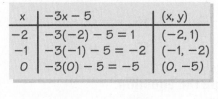

x	$-3x - 5$	(x, y)
-2	$-3(-2) - 5 = 1$	$(-2, 1)$
-1	$-3(-1) - 5 = -2$	$(-1, -2)$
0	$-3(0) - 5 = -5$	$(0, -5)$

Graph.

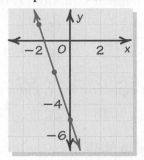

✓ Quick Check

5. Solve each equation for y. Then graph the equation.

a. $2x + y = 3$ **b.** $y - x = 5$ **c.** $-3x + 2y = 6$

The equation $F = 1.8C + 32$ is used to convert a temperature C in degrees Celsius to a temperature F in degrees Fahrenheit. Use this equation for Exercises 1–5.

1. Copy and complete the table below.

Degrees Celsius, C	0	15	20	25
Degrees Fahrenheit, F				

2. Graph the points. Plot C-values on the x-axis and F-values on the y-axis. Connect the points with a line.

3. Does $(5, 20)$ appear on the graph?

4. Is $(5, 20)$ a solution of the equation?

5. Is the equation a function?

Standards Practice

For more exercises, see *Extra Skills and Word Problem Practice*.

Ⓐ Practice by Example

Example 1
(page 393)

GO for Help

Find the solution of each equation for $x = -5$.

6. $y = 4x + 2$ **7.** $y = -3x - 1$ **8.** $y = 8x$

Find the solution of $y = -x - 3$ for the given value of x.

9. -2 **10.** 0 **11.** 2

Example 2
(page 393)

The equation $k = 1.6d$ gives an approximate relationship between d miles and k kilometers. Express each distance in kilometers.

12. the 430 miles between Boise, Idaho, and Reno, Nevada

13. the 665 miles between Columbus, Ohio, and Des Moines, Iowa

Examples 3 and 4
(pages 394 and 395)

Graph each linear equation. Is the equation a function?

14. $y = x - 3$ **15.** $y = -x - 2$ **16.** $y = \frac{2}{3}x - 2$

17. $y = 2x - 1$ **18.** $x = 7$ **19.** $y = 0$

Example 5
(page 395)

Solve each equation for y. Then graph the equation.

20. $-4x + y = 16$ **21.** $-3y = 3x - 9$ **22.** $2x - 4y = 12$

Ⓑ Apply Your Skills

23. Writing in Math Explain how you can determine from a linear equation whether the solutions of the equation form a function.

Homework Video Tutor

Visit: PHSchool.com
Web Code: bje-0802

Find the solutions of each equation for $x = -2, 1,$ and 4.

24. $y = 7 - 3x$ **25.** $y = \frac{1}{4}x + 6$ **26.** $y = \frac{3}{5}x - 6$

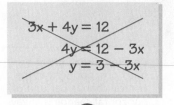

$3x + 4y = 12$

$4y = 12 - 3x$

$y = 3 - 3x$

27. Error Analysis A student solved $3x + 4y = 12$ for y. Her work is at the left. What error did the student make?

28. José is driving on a highway. The equation $d = 55t$ relates the number of miles d and the amount of time in hours t. About how many hours does José spend driving 100 mi?

C **Challenge**

29. If you swim the backstroke, you burn 9 cal/min (calories per minute). If you swim the butterfly stroke, you burn 12 cal/min. The equation $9x + 12y = 360$ models how you can burn 360 cal by swimming the backstroke for x min and the butterfly for y min.
  a. Find the solutions of the equation for $x = 0$ and then $y = 0$. Explain what your solutions mean.
  b. Graph the solutions you found in part (a). Draw a line through the two points.
  c. Vocabulary The solutions you found in part (a) are the *y-intercept* and the *x-intercept* of the line. Explain why these names are appropriate.
  d. Use your graph from part (b). If you swim the butterfly stroke for 10 min, how long should you swim the backstroke to burn a total of 360 calories?

Multiple Choice Practice and Mixed Review

For Standards Tutorials, visit PHSchool.com. Web Code: bjq-9045

30. Which graph best represents the equation $y = 2x + 4$?

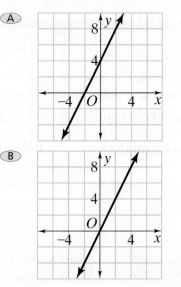
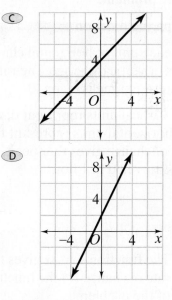

31. Which relation is a function?
  Ⓐ $\{(1, 2), (2, 1), (2, 3), (4, 1)\}$ Ⓒ $\{(0, 1), (1, 1), (2, 1), (3, 1)\}$
  Ⓑ $\{(1, 0), (1, 1), (1, 2), (2, 0)\}$ Ⓓ $\{(1, 2), (2, 1), (1, 3), (4, 1)\}$

GO for Help Lesson 8-1

Is each relation a function? Explain.

32. $\{(2, 4), (3, 6), (-3, 6), (1, 2)\}$ **33.** $\{(0, 3), (2, 1), (-7, 2), (1, 1)\}$

In 1 centimeter, there are 10 millimeters. In 2 centimeters, there are 20 millimeters. The number of millimeters changes by 10 as the number of centimeters changes by 1. You can represent the relationship between millimeters and centimeters with a ratio.

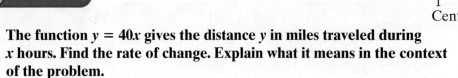

$$\frac{\text{change in number of millimeters}}{\text{change in number centimeters}} = \frac{10}{1}$$

A ratio comparing two changing quantities is called a *rate of change.* You can find the rate of change from a graph such as the one at the right.

Notice that the rate of change is the ratio of the vertical change to the horizontal change. In a linear function, this ratio is the same between any two points.

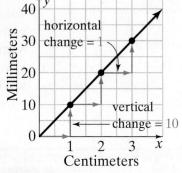

EXAMPLE

The function $y = 40x$ gives the distance y in miles traveled during x hours. Find the rate of change. Explain what it means in the context of the problem.

Graph the function.

For each unit of horizontal change, there are 40 units of vertical change. The rate of change of distance to time is $\frac{40}{1}$, or 40.

The vertical units represent distance traveled and the horizontal units represent time in hours. So the rate of change gives the speed, or the number of miles traveled in 1 hour.

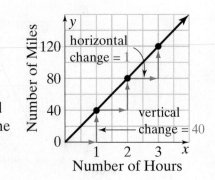

EXERCISES

1. The function $y = 3x$ gives the number of feet y in x yards. Find the rate of change for the function. Explain what it means in the context of the problem.

2. Find the rate of change modeled by the equation $y = 0.6x - 1$.

3. A function of x has value 4 when $x = -5$, 2 when $x = -2$, and 0 when $x = 1$. Is it a linear function?

4. A function of x has value -2 when $x = -3$, 0 when $x = 1$, and 3 when $x = 2$. Is it a linear function?

Slope and *y*-intercept

Introduce, Develop Represent quantitative relationships graphically.

Develop Graph linear functions, noting that the vertical change per unit of horizontal change is always the same and know that the ratio is called the slope of a graph.

Develop Plot the values of quantities whose ratios are always the same. Fit a line to the plot and understand that the slope of the line equals the ratio of the quantities.

What You'll Learn

• To find the slope of a line

• To use slope-intercept form in graphing a linear equation

. . . And Why

To solve real-world problems involving the incline of a ramp or the slant of a roof

✓ Check Skills You'll Need

Find each difference.

1. $-4 - 5$ **2.** $3 - (-2)$

3. $6 - 9$ **4.** $-1 - (-1)$

GO for Help

Lesson 1-6

◀») New Vocabulary

• slope

• *y*-intercept

• slope-intercept form

Finding the Slope of a Line

Standards Investigation
Understanding Slope

1. a. Graph $y = x$, $y = 2x$, and $y = 3x$ on one coordinate plane.
   b. How does the graph of $y = kx$ change as k, the coefficient of x, increases?

2. a. Graph $y = x$ and $y = -x$ on the same coordinate plane.
   b. How are the graphs of $y = x$ and $y = -x$ alike? Different?

The ratio that describes the tilt of a line is its slope. If a line slants upward from left to right, it has positive slope. If it slants downward, it has negative slope. To calculate slope, you use this ratio.

$$\textbf{slope} = \frac{\text{vertical change}}{\text{horizontal change}} = \frac{\text{rise}}{\text{run}}$$

The slope of a line is the same between any two points on the line.

① EXAMPLE Using Rise and Run to Find Slope

Find the slope of each line.

a.

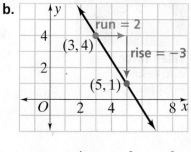

$$\text{slope} = \frac{\text{rise}}{\text{run}} = \frac{2}{4} = \frac{1}{2}$$

b.

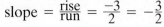

$$\text{slope} = \frac{\text{rise}}{\text{run}} = \frac{-3}{2} = -\frac{3}{2}$$

✓ Quick Check

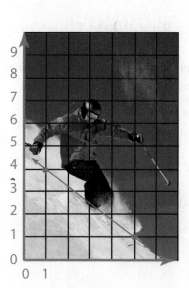

1. What is the slope of the ski trail at the left?

If you know two points of a line, you can find the slope of the line using the following formula.

$$\text{slope} = \frac{\text{difference in } y\text{-coordinates}}{\text{difference in } x\text{-coordinates}}$$

The y-coordinate you use first in the numerator must correspond to the x-coordinate you use first in the denominator.

Horizontal and vertical lines are special cases for slope.

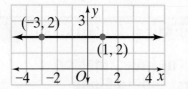

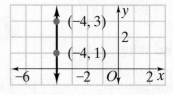

Vocabulary Tip

You may say that a vertical line has *no slope*. But be sure that you do not confuse *no slope* with *slope 0*.

$$\text{slope} = \frac{2-2}{1-(-3)} = \frac{0}{4} = 0$$

Slope is 0 for a horizontal line.

$$\text{slope} \frac{1-3}{-4-(-4)} = \frac{-2}{0}$$

Division by zero is undefined. Slope is *undefined* for a vertical line.

2 EXAMPLE   Using Coordinates to Find Slope

Find the slope of the line through $C(-2, 6)$ and $D(4, 3)$.

$$\text{slope} = \frac{\text{difference in } y\text{-coordinates}}{\text{difference in } x\text{-coordinates}} = \frac{3-6}{4-(-2)} = \frac{-3}{6} = \frac{-1}{2} = -\frac{1}{2}$$

✓ Quick Check

2. Find the slope of the line through $V(8, -1)$, $Q(0, -7)$.

Video Tutor Help
Visit: PHSchool.com
Web Code: bje-0775

The ratios between the quantities in some real-world relations are equal. The slope of the line representing the relation equals the ratio.

3 EXAMPLE   Interpreting Slope in a Real-World Situation

A store sells sugar in bulk for 25 cents per pound. Graph the relation (pounds of sugar, cost). Compare the slope of the line through the points on your graph to the ratio $\dfrac{\text{cost}}{\text{pounds of sugar}}$.

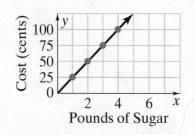

Use two points to find the slope.

$$\text{slope} = \frac{75-25}{3-1} = \frac{50}{2} = \frac{25}{1}$$

$$\frac{\text{cost}}{\text{pounds of sugar}} = \frac{25}{1}$$

The slope equals the ratio.

✓ Quick Check

3. Find the slope of the line determined by the relation (inches, feet).

Here is the graph of $y = -\frac{1}{2}x + 3$.

The slope of the line is $\frac{-2}{4}$, or $-\frac{1}{2}$.

The **y-intercept** of the line is the point where the line crosses the y-axis. The constant in the equation is the y-intercept.

$$y = -\frac{1}{2}x + 3$$

slope y-intercept

(graph showing line through (0, 3) and (4, 1) with rise = -2 and run = 4)

Vocabulary Tip

The word <u>intercept</u> sounds like <u>intersect</u>, which means "to cross." Think of the y-intercept as where the line crosses the y-axis.

Take Note   **Slope-Intercept Form**

The equation $y = mx + b$ is the **slope-intercept form.** In this form, m is the slope of the line, and b is the y-intercept.

You can use slope-intercept form to help you graph an equation.

4 EXAMPLE   Graphing a Linear Equation

A ramp slopes from a warehouse door down to a street. The equation $y = -\frac{1}{3}x + 2$ models the ramp, where x is the horizontal distance in feet from the bottom of the door and y is the height in feet above the street. Graph the equation.

Step 1 Since the y-intercept is 2, graph $(0, 2)$.

Step 2 Since the slope is $-\frac{1}{3}$ or $\frac{-1}{3}$, move 1 unit down from $(0, 2)$. Then move 3 units right to graph a second point.

Step 3 Draw a line through the points.

(graph showing line through (0, 2) and (3, 1))

For: Writing Equations Activity
Use: Interactive Textbook, 8-3

✓ Quick Check

4. Graph each equation.

a. $y = 2x - 3$ **b.** $y = -x + 4$

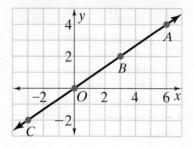

Use the graph at the left for Exercises 1–3.

1. Copy and complete the solution below to find the slope of the graph using points A and B.

   slope $= \dfrac{2 - \blacksquare}{\blacksquare - 6}$

   $= \dfrac{\blacksquare}{\blacksquare}$

2. Use Points B and C to find the slope of the graph.

3. Based on your answers to Exercises 1 and 2, does the graph represent a linear equation? Explain.

Standards Practice

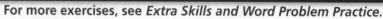

For more exercises, see *Extra Skills and Word Problem Practice*.

Ⓐ **Practice by Example**

Example 1
(page 399)

GO for Help

Find the slope of each line.

4.

5.

Example 2
(page 400)

Find the slope of the line through each pair of points.

6. $A(2, 6), B(8, 1)$

7. $E(1, -2), F(4, -8)$

8. $N(-5, 2), Q(1, -4)$

9. $G(3, 4), H(6, 10)$

Example 3
(page 400)

Find the slope of the line determined by each relation.

10. (time in hours, distance traveled at 50 mi/h)

11. (number of pens, cost at $.65/pen)

Example 4
(page 401)

Identify the slope and y-intercept of the graph of each equation. Then graph the equation.

12. $y = 7x + 3$

13. $y = -x$

14. $y = \frac{1}{2}x - 8$

15. $y = 2x + 1$

16. $y = -3x - 1$

17. $y = x - 4$

18. $y = 4$

19. $y = -3x + 3$

20. $y = -\frac{3}{2}x + 6$

Ⓑ **Apply Your Skills**

21. **Error Analysis** A student said that the slope of the line through $(8, 4)$ and $(2, 2)$ is 3. What error could this student have made?

22. **Open-Ended** Write equations for five different lines that intersect at $(0, 3)$.

Find the slope of each line.

23. 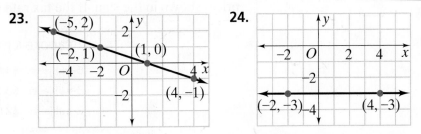 **24.**

25. The slope of a roof is its *pitch*. You indicate the pitch of a roof by a ratio $a : b$, where a is the number of feet of rise for every b feet of run. In the photos at the left, which house has the roof with a steeper pitch? Explain.

26. **Multiple Choice** Find the slope of the line through $(0, -4)$ and $(3, -3)$.

Ⓐ $\frac{3}{4}$ Ⓑ $\frac{2}{3}$ Ⓒ $\frac{1}{3}$ Ⓓ -1

Find the slope of the line through each pair of points.

27. $C\left(\frac{1}{2}, \frac{3}{4}\right), D\left(\frac{1}{4}, \frac{3}{4}\right)$ **28.** $L(7, -6.3), M(5, -1.3)$

29. $J(2.1, 3), K(2.1, 4.2)$ **30.** $A\left(\frac{2}{3}, 2\frac{2}{3}\right), B\left(2\frac{2}{3}, \frac{2}{3}\right)$

Solve each equation for y. Then graph the equation.

31. $y - 2x = 4$ **32.** $y + 3 = 5x$ **33.** $2y + 2x = 2$

34. $3y + 2x = 3$ **35.** $y - \frac{1}{2}x = 0$ **36.** $y + 3 = 0$

37. $2y = x - 8$ **38.** $-4y = x + 48$ **39.** $3y - 2x = 15$

40. Does the point $(-3, 4)$ lie on the graph of $y = -2x + 1$? Explain.

41. Does the point $(-2, -4)$ lie on the graph of $2y - 6x = 4$? Explain.

42. Graph the line with no slope that passes through $(4, -2)$.

43. **a.** Graph the groups of equations on three coordinate planes.

Group 1	Group 2	Group 3
$y = 2x - 5$	$y = -3x - 1$	$y = -6$
$y = 2x$	$y = -3x$	$y = 1$
$y = 2x + 3$	$y = -3x + 4$	$y = 4.5$

     b. **Writing in Math** How are the lines in each group related to each other? Explain.

     c. **Reasoning** What is the coefficient of x in the equation of a graph that has slope 0?

Ⓒ Challenge

44. The slope of a road is its *grade*. What do you think it means for the grade of a road to be 4%?

For more exercises, see *Extra Skills and Word Problem Practice*.

45. Bert buys a 5-subject notebook and a 2-subject notebook at the prices shown in the sign. If the tax rate is 8%, what is the total cost?

> NOTEBOOKS & PAPER
>
> 5-subject: $4.50
> 3-subject: $3.00
> 2-subject: $2.50

  Ⓐ $5.94   Ⓑ $7.00   Ⓒ $7.56   Ⓓ $8.10

46. Bessie wants to run toy train tracks from the couch to a table. The distance from the couch to the table is 2 meters. Each track is 20 centimeters long. So far, she has put down 9 tracks. How much space is left?

  Ⓐ 0.2 m   Ⓑ 0.8 m   Ⓒ 1 m   Ⓓ 1.8 m

GO for Help

Lesson 7-5   **Solve and graph each inequality.**

47. $4x + 5 < 17$ **48.** $18 \le 5 - 2x$ **49.** $-x + 6 > 31$

Lesson 6-7   **Find each percent of change. Tell whether the change is an increase or a decrease.**

50. from 10 to 9   **51.** from 20 to 30   **52.** from 52 to 39

Lesson 6-6   **53.** During the 2004 season, New York theater goers bought 11.3 million tickets for a total of $749.0 million. Theater goers spent a total of 3.2% more than the year before. What was the total amount spent during 2003?

✓ Checkpoint Quiz 1

1. Find three solutions of $9x - 2y = 18$.

2. Graph $3x - y = 5$ on a coordinate plane.

3. Is $\{(-2, 0), (-1, 3), (0, -2), (3, -1)\}$ a function? Explain.

4. **Writing in Math** Explain how to use the vertical-line test to determine whether a relation is a function.

Find the slope of the line through the given points.

5. $A(1, 5), B(3, 15)$ **6.** $D(-2, -4), F(0, -6)$

7. $G(-3, 4), H(-3, -6)$ **8.** $J(1.5, 4), K(-2, -3)$

9. What are the slope and the y-intercept of $y = -2x + 5$?

Direct Variation

Master Graph linear functions.

Master Plot values of quantities whose ratios are always the same. Fit a line to the plot and understand that the slope of the line equals the ratio of the quantities.

Master Solve multistep problems involving direct variation.

Finding the Constant of Variation

A **direct variation** is a linear function modeled by the equation $y = kx$, where $k \neq 0$. The coefficient k is the **constant of variation.** You can find k using a graph.

1 EXAMPLE **Finding the Constant of Variation**

The table of values models a direct variation. Graph the direct variation. Find the constant of variation.

x	y
0	0
2	3
4	6
6	9

Plot the points on a coordinate plane. Connect the points.

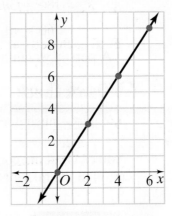

Use a point to find the constant of variation.

$y = kx$	**Use the equation for a direct variation.**
$3 = k \cdot 2$	**Use (2, 3). Substitute.**
$\frac{3}{2} = k$	**Solve for k.**

The constant of variation is $\frac{3}{2}$.

☑ Quick Check

x	y
0	0
3	4
6	8
9	12

1. The table at the left models a direct variation. Graph the direct variation. Find the constant of variation.

Notice that the ratio $\frac{y}{x}$ is $\frac{3}{2}$ for any point on the line in Example 1. The slope of the line is also $\frac{3}{2}$. In a direct variation, the ratio $\frac{y}{x}$ is the same for any point on the line and is equal to the slope of the line.

Writing a Direct Variation

Vocabulary Tip

A direct variation is sometimes called a *direct proportion*. You can also say "*y* is directly proportional to *x*."

You can use the constant of variation to write a direct variation. In a direct variation, you say "*y* varies directly with *x*."

2 EXAMPLE Writing a Direct Variation

Your weight *w* on Earth's surface varies directly with your weight *m* on Mars. A person weighing 120 lb on Earth weighs about 40 lb on Mars. About how much does a person weighing 180 lb on Earth weigh on Mars?

Step 1 Find the constant of variation.

$w = km$ Write the equation for a direct variation.

$120 = k \cdot 40$ Substitute 120 for *w* and 40 for *m*.

$3 = k$ Divide each side by 40. Simplify.

Step 2 Find the weight of a 180-lb person on Mars.

$w = km$ Write the equation for a direct variation.

$180 = 3m$ Substitute 3 for *k* and 180 for *w*.

$60 = m$ Divide each side by 3. Simplify.

A person weighing 180 lb on Earth weighs about 60 lb on Mars.

✓ Quick Check

2. How much does a person weighing 75 lb on Mars weigh on Earth?

You can find the constant of variation using any ordered pair (x, y) in the relation where $y \neq 0$.

3 EXAMPLE Writing a Direct Variation Using a Point

Write an equation for the direct variation that includes $A(-4, 3)$.

Step 1 Find the constant of variation.

$y = kx$ Write the equation for a direct variation.

$3 = k(-4)$ Substitute 4 for *x* and 3 for *y*.

$k = -\frac{3}{4}$ Divide each side by −4. Simplify.

Step 2 Write the equation using the value of *k*.

$y = kx$ Write the equation for a direct variation.

$y = -\frac{3}{4}x$ Replace *k* with $-\frac{3}{4}$.

✓ Quick Check

3. Write an equation for the direct variation that includes $B(3, -5)$.

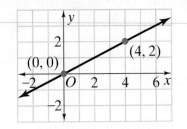

(0, 0)
(4, 2)

1. Use the graph at the left. Find the constant of variation.

Complete Exercises 2–4 to solve the problem below.

The number of liters y in container varies directly with the number of quarts x in the container. A carton contains 2 qt, or 1.89 L, of juice. Find the number of liters in 8 quarts.

2. Find the constant of variation.

3. Write a direct variation that describes the situation.

4. How many liters of juice are in 8 qt of juice?

Standards Practice

For more exercises, see *Extra Skills and Word Problem Practice*.

A **Practice by Example**

Example 1
(page 405)

Each table models a direct variation. Graph the direct variation. Find the constant of variation.

5.

x	y
−2	−5
0	0
2	5
4	10

6.

x	y
−1	−2
0	0
1	2
2	4

7.

x	y
−3	−2
0	0
3	2
6	4

Example 2
(page 406)

8. The number of gallons of gas a vehicle uses varies directly with the number of miles traveled. You travel 120 miles and use 5 gallons of gas. Write an equation to model the situation.

9. The amount of money you earn varies directly with the number of hours you work. You work for 6 h and earn $43.50. How many hours do you need to work to earn $246.50?

Example 3
(page 406)

Write an equation for a direct variation that includes each point.

10. $C(4, 3)$ **11.** $D(6, -3)$ **12.** $E(-3, -5)$

B **Apply Your Skills**

GO for Help

For a guide to solving Exercise 13, see page 409.

13. The distance d a spring stretches varies directly with the force f applied to it. A certain spring stretches 31.5 in. when a weight is attached to it, as shown.
  a. Write an equation to model this situation.
  b. Find the distance the spring will stretch if a 15-lb weight is attached.

31.5 in

9 lb

14. The equation $V = kT$ models the volume and temperature of air in a balloon. Use the data in the table to find the temperature when the volume is 12.6 L.

Air in a Balloon

Volume *V* (liters)	Temperature *T* (kelvins)
125	▪
300	400

15. A recipe for 12 cupcakes uses $\frac{2}{3}$ c sugar. The number of cupcakes is directly proportional to the amount of sugar. How many cupcakes can you make with 3 c sugar?

C Challenge

16. The distance a spring stretches is directly proportional to the force applied to the spring. A 2-lb weight stretches a spring to 15 in. A 12-lb weight stretches the same spring to 20 in. Find the length of the spring with no weight attached.

Multiple Choice Practice and Mixed Review

For Standards Tutorials, visit PHSchool.com. Web Code: bjq-9045

17. A worker earns $38.85 for 7 hours of work. About how much will the worker earn for working 37 hours?

Ⓐ $150 Ⓑ $205 Ⓒ $300 Ⓓ $1,400

18. Little Grocery sells 60 paper cups for $2.40. Which rate has the same price per cup?

Ⓐ 50 cups for $2.50 Ⓒ 100 cups for $3.00
Ⓑ 40 cups for $2.00 Ⓓ 80 cups for $3.20

GO for Help Lesson 8-3

Find the slope of the line through each pair of points.

19. $C(0, -2), D(2, 1)$ **20.** $J(3, -1), K(6, 1)$ **21.** $G(12, 8), H(6, 2)$

Mathematical Reasoning

Develop Evaluate the reasonableness of the solution in the context of the original situation.

Evaluating for Reasonableness

When you use a graph to find a solution, you must evaluate your solution for reasonableness in the context of the original situation.

The equation $y = 10 - 2x$ models the gallons of water y in a 10-gal tank after x hours. Use the graph of $y = 10 - 2x$ at the left for Exercises 1–5.

1. When y is 12, what does the value of x represent in this situation? Is it a reasonable solution in the context of the situation?

2. When x is 8, what does the value of y represent in this situation? Is it a reasonable solution in the context of the situation?

3. Reasoning What is the water level in the tank after 8 hours?

4. What values of y are reasonable in the context of the situation?

5. Redraw the graph to show all the solutions that are reasonable.

FOR USE WITH PAGE 407, EXERCISE 13

Master Solve multistep problems involving direct variation.

Understanding Math Problems Read through the problem below. Then follow along with what Juan thinks as he solves the problem. Check your understanding with the exercises at the bottom of the page.

The distance d a spring stretches varies directly with the force f applied to it. A certain spring stretches a distance of 31.5 in. when a weight is attached to it, as shown.

a. Write an equation to model this situation.

b. Find the distance the spring will stretch if a 15-lb weight is attached.

31.5 in

9 lb

What Juan Thinks

The equation will have the form $d = kf$.

The diagram shows that a 9-lb weight stretches the spring 31.5 in. I can use this information to find k.

Now I can write an equation using 3.5 for k.

For part (b) of the problem, I will substitute 15 for f in the equation.

I'll write my answer to part (b) and include the units.

What Juan Writes

$d = kf$

$31.5 = k(9)$
$\frac{31.5}{9} = k$
$3.5 = k$

The direct variation is $d = 3.5f$.

$d = 3.5(15)$
$d = 52.5$

The spring will stretch 52.5 in. when a 15-lb weight is attached.

EXERCISES

1. A certain spring stretches 5 in. when a 15-lb weight is attached. How far will the spring stretch when a 24-lb weight is attached?

2. The weight w that you can lift with a lever varies directly with the force f that you apply to the lever. Suppose you can lift a 42-lb weight by applying 18 lb of force to a certain lever.
   a. Write a direct variation equation to model this situation.
   b. How much force would you need to apply to the lever to lift a 140-lb weight?

Reasoning Strategy: Use Multiple Strategies

What You'll Learn

- To solve problems by combining strategies

. . . And Why

To solve problems about building a kite

 **Check Skills You'll Need**

Write an equation for each statement.

1. Seven times the opposite of twelve is negative 84.

2. Eleven times a number is 132.

3. A number divided by 45 is three.

GO for Help
Lesson 2-4

Master Solve two-step linear equations.
Develop Use diagrams to explain mathematical reasoning.
Develop Develop generalizations of the results obtained and the strategies used and apply them to new problem situations.

Combining Strategies

Math Strategies in Action
After a natural disaster such as a flood, relief workers help to rescue survivors. They also bring supplies to people who need them. Relief organizers use multiple strategies as they coordinate their efforts.

In many situations in your own life, you have already combined multiple strategies. Remember when you learned how to ride a bike or fly a kite. The more you practiced, the less you had to think about the steps required to be successful.

In mathematics, you can combine strategies to solve problems. The more strategies you learn and the more you use them, the better problem solver you will be. Solving problems can become as easy as riding a bike or flying a kite!

1 EXAMPLE Using Multiple Strategies

Suppose you receive instructions for building a kite. The writer of the instructions presents them as a puzzle:

> I fly above the clouds with my tail flowing behind me.
> My tail is 12 ft plus twice my length. Together, our length is 21 ft. How long am I? How long is my tail?

Understand Understand the problem.

Read the problem carefully.

1. What do you want to find?

2. What is the relationship between the length of the kite's tail and the length of the kite's body?

Plan **Make a plan to solve the problem.**

To get a visual picture of the problem, draw a diagram. Then write an equation to solve the problem.

Carry Out **Carry out the plan.**

Draw a diagram.

Let b = length of the body of the kite.

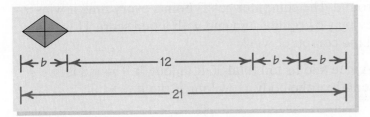

Write an equation.

$3b + 12 = 21$	Use the diagram to write an equation.
$3b + 12 - 12 = 21 - 12$	Subtract 12 from each side.
$3b = 9$	Simplify.
$\dfrac{3b}{3} = \dfrac{9}{3}$	Divide each side by 3.
$b = 3$	

The kite is 3 ft long. Now find the length of the tail.

length of tail $= 2b + 12$	Use the diagram to write an expression for the length of the tail.
$= 2(3) + 12$	Replace b with the length of the kite's body.
$= 18$	Simplify.

The tail is 18 ft long.

Check **Check the answer to be sure it is reasonable.**

It is always good procedure to check your result in the context of the original problem.

✓ Quick Check

3. The original problem says that the tail must be 12 ft plus twice the length of the kite's body. Show that the lengths found meet this condition.

4. The length of the kite's body plus the length of its tail must be 21 ft. Show that the lengths found meet this condition.

For more exercises, see *Extra Skills and Word Problem Practice*.

A Practice by Example

Example 1
(page 410)

GO for Help

Combine multiple strategies to solve each problem.

1. **Rates** A bus traveling 40 mi/h left Freetown at noon. A car following the bus at 60 mi/h left Freetown at 1:30 P.M.
   a. At what time did the car catch up with the bus?
   b. How many miles were the car and the bus from Freetown when the car caught up with the bus?

2. A student playing a computer chess game gets 5 points every time he wins a round. The computer gets 3 points every time it wins a round. They play 64 rounds and end with a tied score. How many rounds did the computer win?

3. **Algebra** A kite and its tail total 36 ft in length. The tail is five times the length of the body. How long is the kite's tail?

B Apply Your Skills

Solve using any strategy.

4. A student has $8 to spend on a phone call. The cost of a call is $.34 for the first minute and $.24 for each additional minute. How long can the student talk on the phone?

5. A student weighs her hamsters two at a time. Sandy and White Ears weigh 209 g together. White Ears and Sport weigh 223 g together. Sandy and Sport weigh 216 g together. How much does each hamster weigh?

STRATEGIES

- Act It Out
- Draw a Diagram
- Try, Test, Revise
- Look for a Pattern
- Make a Model
- Make a Table
- Simulate the Problem
- Solve by Graphing
- Use Multiple Strategies
- Work a Simpler Problem
- Work Backward
- Write an Equation
- Write a Proportion

6. **Geometry** There are 27 white cubes assembled to form a large cube as shown. The outside surface of the large cube is painted green. The large cube is then separated into the 27 smaller cubes. How many of the small cubes will have green paint on exactly the following number of faces?

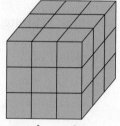

   a. three faces   b. two faces   c. one face   d. no face

7. You decide to purchase a new telephone. You can choose from 8 different models, 2 different cord lengths, and 4 different colors. How many possible choices do you have?

8. **Geometry** A lot measures 50 ft by 100 ft. The house on the lot measures 25 ft by 50 ft. What is the area of the lawn?

9. **Algebra** A student spends $\frac{1}{3}$ of her money on a movie and $\frac{1}{4}$ of the remaining amount on a snack after the movie. She now has $12 left. How much money did she have originally?

10. A shopper spends $78 on computer supplies. He gives the clerk a $100 bill. In how many ways can the clerk make change without giving the customer more than seven $1 bills?

11. A clerk starts working at a beginning salary of $10,400 with an annual increase of $400. An assistant clerk who starts at the same time has a starting salary of $9,600 per year with an annual increase of $600.
    a. Who earns more after 3 years?
    b. After how many years will the assistant be earning more money than the clerk?

C Challenge

12. **Geometry** You have three pieces of string, each 60 cm long. You form a circle with one piece, a square with another, and an equilateral triangle with the third piece. How do the areas of the three figures compare? Explain.

13. Each face of a cube can be painted either red or yellow. How many different ways can you paint the cube?

Multiple Choice Practice and Mixed Review

For Standards Tutorials, visit PHSchool.com. Web Code: bjq-9045

14. A house lot measures 7,533 ft². How many square yards is the lot?
    A 628 yd²   C 2,511 yd²
    B 837 yd²   D 6,777 yd²

15. What is the tenth term in the number pattern below?
    $0.75, 1.5, 2.25, 3, \ldots$
    A 6   B 6.25   C 7.5   D 8

16. Danny had $18\frac{1}{2}$ inches of ribbon. He used $9\frac{3}{4}$ inches when he wrapped a present for his mother. How many inches of ribbon does he have left?
    A $8\frac{1}{4}$ in.   B $8\frac{1}{2}$ in.   C $8\frac{3}{4}$ in.   D $9\frac{1}{4}$ in.

17. Bottled water costs $3 for four bottles. Which graph shows this relationship?

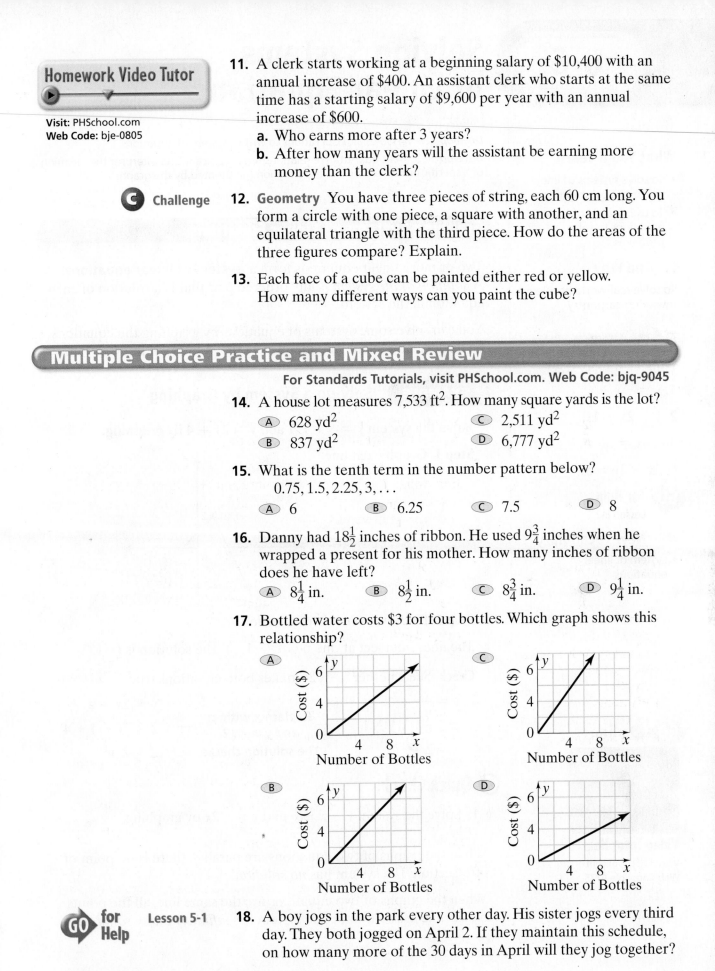

18. A boy jogs in the park every other day. His sister jogs every third day. They both jogged on April 2. If they maintain this schedule, on how many more of the 30 days in April will they jog together?

GO for Help   Lesson 5-1

Solving Systems of Linear Equations

Develop Use variables and operations to write a system of equations.

Develop Represent quantitative relationships graphically and interpret the meaning of a specific part of a graph in the situation represented by the graph.

Graphing Systems of Linear Equations

Two or more linear equations form a **system of linear equations.** A *solution of the system* is any ordered pair that is a solution of each equation in the system.

You can solve some systems of equations by graphing the equations on a coordinate plane and identifying the point(s) of intersection.

1 EXAMPLE **Solving a System by Graphing**

Solve the system $y = -x + 1$ and $y = 2x + 4$ by graphing.

Step 1 Graph each line.

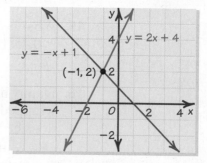

Step 2 Find the point of intersection.

The lines intersect at one point, $(-1, 2)$. The solution is $(-1, 2)$.

Check See whether $(-1, 2)$ makes both equations true.

$$y = -x + 1$$
$$2 \stackrel{?}{=} -(-1) + 1$$
$$2 = 2 ✔$$

← Replace x with -1 and y with 2. →
The solution checks.

$$y = 2x + 4$$
$$2 \stackrel{?}{=} 2(-1) + 4$$
$$2 = 2 ✔$$

✓ Quick Check

1. Solve the system $y = x - 6$ and $y = -2x$ by graphing.

When the graphs of two equations are parallel, there is no point of intersection. The system has *no solution*.

When the graphs of two equations are the same line, all the points on the line are solutions. The system has *infinitely many solutions*.

2) EXAMPLE **Solving Special Systems**

Solve each system of equations by graphing.

a. $x + y = 1; y = -x + 3$

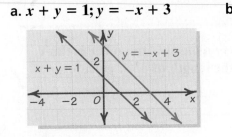

b. $x - 2y = 4; 2x - 4y = 8$

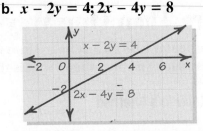

The lines are parallel.
They do not intersect.
There is no solution.

The graphs are the same line.
There are infinitely many
solutions.

✅ Quick Check

2. Solve each system by graphing.

a. $y = x - 6$
　　$x - y = 6$

b. $y = x + 4$
　　$y = x$

Using Systems of Linear Equations

You can write and graph systems of equations to solve problems.

3) EXAMPLE **Using a System of Equations**

Find two numbers with a sum of 6 and a difference of 4.

Step 1 Write equations.

Let x = the greater number.
Let y = the lesser number.

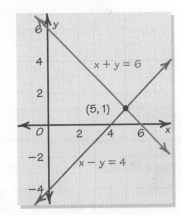

Equation 1 Sum　is　6.
　　　　　$x + y$　=　6

Equation 2 Difference　is　4.
　　　　　$x - y$　　=　4

Step 2 Graph the equations.

The lines intersect at $(5, 1)$.
The numbers are 5 and 1.

Check Since the sum of 5 and 1 is 6 and the difference of 5 and 1
is 4, the answer is correct.

✅ Quick Check

3. Find two numbers with a difference of 2 and a sum of -8.

You can solve some problems involving two variables by writing and graphing a system of equations, or you may be able to use one variable to write and solve an equation.

More Than One Way

A carpenter cuts an 8-ft board into two pieces. One piece is three times as long as the other. What is the length of each piece?

Roberto's Method

Write and graph a system of equations.

Let x = length of longer piece; y = length of shorter piece.

Equation 1   Longer piece is three times shorter piece.

$$x = 3 \cdot y$$

Equation 2   Sum of lengths is eight.

$$x + y = 8$$

Graph the equations.

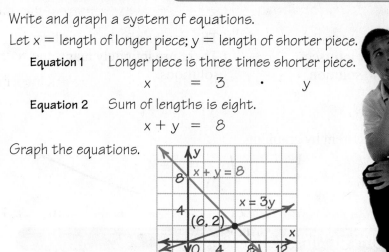

The lines intersect at (6, 2). The lengths are 6 ft and 2 ft.

Michelle's Method

Write a one-variable equation.

Let x = length of shorter piece; 3x = length of longer piece.

Equation   Shorter piece plus longer piece is 8 feet.

$$x + 3x = 8$$
$$4x = 8$$
$$x = 2$$

The shorter piece is 2 ft, and the longer piece is 3(2) = 6 ft.

Choose a Method

1. Which method would you use to find the lengths? Explain.

2. In Roberto's Method, suppose x = length of shorter piece. What difference would this make in the equations and the graph?

Complete Exercises 1–5 to solve the problem below.

A four-foot-long wooden rod is cut into two pieces to make a kite. One piece is three times as long as the other. Let x equal the length of the shorter piece and y equal the length of the longer piece.

1. Write an equation to represent the phrase "a four-foot-long wooden rod is cut into two pieces."

2. Write an equation to represent the phrase "one piece is three times as long as the other."

3. Graph the equations on the same coordinate plane.

4. What does the point where the lines intersect represent?

5. What is the length of each piece?

Standards Practice

For more exercises, see *Extra Skills and Word Problem Practice.*

A Practice by Example
Example 1
(page 414)

GO for Help

Check whether $(-1, 5)$ is a solution of each system of equations. Show your work.

6. $x + y = 4$
   $x - y = 6$

7. $y = -2x + 3$
   $y = x - 4$

8. $2x = y - 7$
   $2y = -x + 9$

Solve each system of equations by graphing. Check each solution.

9. $y = x + 1$
   $y = 3x - 7$

10. $y = 2x + 5$
    $x + y = 8$

11. $y = 2x - 2$
    $y = 6$

Example 2
(page 415)

12. $-3x + y = 5$
    $y = 3x - 7$

13. $y = -x - 3$
    $y = -x + 2$

14. $y = -6 - 2x$
    $2x + y = -6$

Example 3
(page 415)

15. Find two numbers with a sum of -8 and a difference of 4. Let x be the greater number and y be the lesser number.

B Apply Your Skills

Is each ordered pair a solution of the given system of equations? Show your work.

16. $2x + 5y = 3$
    $y = 7.5x; (1.5, 0.2)$

17. $6x - 6y = 2$
    $3x + 9y = -7; \left(-\frac{1}{3}, -\frac{2}{3}\right)$

Solve each system of equations by graphing. Check each solution.

18. $x + y = 3$
    $2x = 10 - 2y$

19. $x - y = -4$
    $x + y = 6$

20. $2x - 4y = 4$
    $y = 0.5x - 1$

21. **Geometry** The perimeter of a rectangle is 24 ft. Its length is five times its width. Let x be the length and y be the width. What is the area of the rectangle?

22. There are 11 animals in a barnyard. Some are chickens and some are cows. There are 38 legs in all. Let x be the number of chickens and y be the number of cows. How many of each animal are in the barnyard?

23. One sales position pays $200/wk plus 10% commission. Another sales position pays $150/wk plus 20% commission.
  a. For each job, write an equation that relates the amount of sales x for one week to the money earned y.
  b. Solve the system to find the amount of sales in a week that will earn the same amount from each job. Show your work.
  c. If weekly sales at each job are about $600, at which job can you earn more money? Explain.

24. One plane leaves Los Angeles traveling at 500 mi/h. Another plane leaves an hour later, following the same route at 600 mi/h.
  a. How many hours will the second plane take to catch up to the first plane?
  b. How far from Los Angeles will the planes be when the second plane catches up to the first?

25. a. Graph each system of equations on a separate coordinate plane.

$$y = 3x + 1 \qquad\qquad y = -2x - 1$$
$$y = 3x - 2 \qquad\qquad y = -2x + 4$$

  b. **Writing in Math** Based on part (a), write a conjecture about solutions to systems of equations that have the same slope.

26. Geometry The graphs of $y = 3$, $y = 7$, $x = 2$, and $x = 5$ contain the sides of a rectangle. Find the area of the rectangle.

C Challenge

Open-Ended **Write a system of equations with the given number of solutions.**

27. no solution **28.** one solution **29.** infinitely many

30. Solve the system $y = x + 2$, $y = 4x + 11$, and $y = -2x - 7$.

Multiple Choice Practice and Mixed Review

For Standards Tutorials, visit PHSchool.com. Web Code: bjq-9045

31. Hazel buys a sweater originally priced at $34.99 that is 10% off. She also buys a T-shirt that is 20% off its $12.00 price and a coat for 30% off its $99.99 price. She pays 7% tax for the 3 items. What other information is needed to determine the change she receives from the cashier?
  Ⓐ the sale price of the coat
  Ⓑ the amount Hazel gave the cashier
  Ⓒ the total price for the 3 items before tax
  Ⓓ the sale price of the 3 items after tax

32. Rectangle A is similar to rectangle B. The area of rectangle A is 1,000 square feet. Find the area of rectangle B.

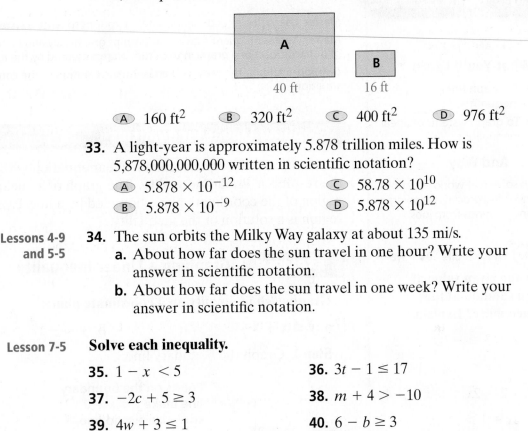

Ⓐ 160 ft²   Ⓑ 320 ft²   Ⓒ 400 ft²   Ⓓ 976 ft²

33. A light-year is approximately 5.878 trillion miles. How is 5,878,000,000,000 written in scientific notation?

Ⓐ 5.878×10^{-12} Ⓒ 58.78×10^{10}

Ⓑ 5.878×10^{-9} Ⓓ 5.878×10^{12}

GO for Help   **Lessons 4-9 and 5-5**

34. The sun orbits the Milky Way galaxy at about 135 mi/s.
  a. About how far does the sun travel in one hour? Write your answer in scientific notation.
  b. About how far does the sun travel in one week? Write your answer in scientific notation.

Lesson 7-5   **Solve each inequality.**

35. $1 - x < 5$ **36.** $3t - 1 \le 17$

37. $-2c + 5 \ge 3$ **38.** $m + 4 > -10$

39. $4w + 3 \le 1$ **40.** $6 - b \ge 3$

✓ Checkpoint Quiz 2

1. Write an equation for the direct variation that includes the point $A\left(-\frac{1}{2}, 4\right)$.

2. Write an equation for the direct variation shown in the table at the right.

x	y
4	−12
5	−15
6	−30
7	−35

Solve each system by graphing.

3. $y = -4x$
$y = -x + 6$

4. $x - y = 1$
$x + y = -7$

5. $6x + 2y = 12$
$y = 3x$

6. $y = x + 1$
$y = -x - 3$

7. Measurement The number of cubic inches a liquid occupies varies directly with the number of gallons. Two gallons of liquid occupy 462 cubic inches. Write a direct variation relating cubic inches c to gallons g.

8. Find two numbers with a sum of −4 and a difference of 10.

Linear Inequalities

Master Use variables and appropriate operations to write a system of inequalities.

Master Represent quantitative relationships graphically and interpret the meaning of a specific part of a graph in the situation represented by the graph.

Develop Evaluate the reasonableness of the solution in the context of the situation.

Graphing Linear Inequalities

If you replace the equal sign in a linear equation with $>$, $<$, $\geq$, or $\leq$, the result is a **linear inequality.** The graph of a linear inequality is a region of the coordinate plane bounded by a line. Every point in the region is a solution of the inequality.

1 EXAMPLE Graphing a Linear Inequality

Graph each inequality on a coordinate plane.

a. $y \leq x + 2$ **b.** $y < -2x$

Step 1 Graph the boundary line.

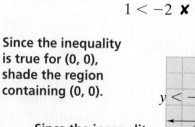

Points on the boundary line make $y \leq x + 2$ true. Use a solid line.

Points on the boundary line do *not* make $y < -2x$ true. Use a dashed line.

Step 2 Test a point not on the boundary line.

Test $(0, 0)$ in the inequality.

$$y \leq x + 2$$
$$0 \overset{?}{\leq} 0 + 2 \quad \text{Substitute.}$$
$$0 \leq 2 \quad ✔ \quad \text{true}$$

Test $(1, 1)$ in the inequality.

$$y < -2x$$
$$1 \overset{?}{<} -2(1) \quad \text{Substitute.}$$
$$1 < -2 \quad ✘ \quad \text{false}$$

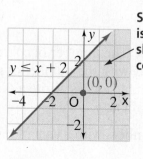

Since the inequality is true for (0, 0), shade the region containing (0, 0).

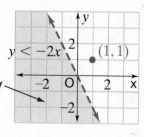

Since the inequality is false for (1, 1), shade the region that does *not* contain (1, 1).

✓ Quick Check

1. Graph each inequality on its own coordinate plane.

    a. $y \geq 3x - 1$ **b.** $y > -x + 3$ **c.** $y < 2x - 4$

2 EXAMPLE **Using a Linear Inequality**

Use the photo of a farmer's market at the right. Suppose you want to buy strawberries and lemons. You plan to spend no more than $10. How many pounds of each can you buy?

Step 1 Write an inequality.

Words	cost of strawberries	plus	cost of lemons	is at most	ten dollars

Let x = number of pounds of strawberries.

Let y = number of pounds of lemons.

Inequality	$3x$	+	y	≤	10

Step 2 Write the equation of the boundary line in slope-intercept form.

$3x + y \leq 10$

$\quad y \leq -3x + 10$

$\quad y = -3x + 10$

Step 3 Graph $y = -3x + 10$ in Quadrant I since weight is not negative.

Step 4 Test $(1, 1)$.

$y \leq -3x + 10$

$1 \overset{?}{\leq} -3(1) + 10$

$1 \leq 7$ ✔

The inequality is true. $(1, 1)$ is a solution.

Step 5 Shade the region containing $(1, 1)$.

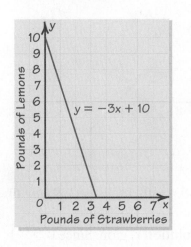

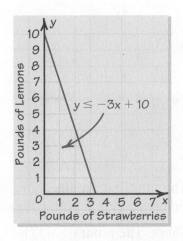

The graph shows the possible solutions. For example, you could buy 1 pound of strawberries and 5 pounds of lemons.

✓ Quick Check

2. Adult tickets to the school play cost $4. Children's tickets cost $2. Your goal is to sell tickets worth at least $30. Let x be the number of children's tickets and y be the number of adult tickets. Graph a linear inequality to show how many of each type of ticket you must sell to earn at least $30.

Graphing Systems of Linear Inequalities

Two or more linear inequalities form a **system of linear inequalities.** A *solution of a system of linear inequalities* is any ordered pair that makes each inequality in the system true. To solve a system, graph the inequalities on one coordinate plane.

3 EXAMPLE   Solving a System of Linear Inequalities

One number is greater than a second number. Their sum is less than or equal to two. What could the two numbers be?

Step 1 Write the inequalities.
Let x = the first number. Let y = the second number.

Inequality 1 First number   is greater than   second number.
$$x \qquad\qquad > \qquad\qquad y$$

Inequality 2 Sum   is less than or equal to   two.
$$x + y \qquad\qquad \leq \qquad\qquad 2$$

Step 2 Graph $x > y$ on a coordinate plane.

Step 3 Graph $x + y \leq 2$ on the same coordinate plane.

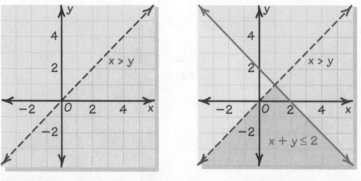

The solutions are the coordinates of all the points in the region that is shaded in both colors.

Check The point $(0, -1)$ is in the solution region. Since $0 > -1$, and $0 + (-1) \leq 2$, the point makes both inequalities true. The solution checks.

✓ Quick Check

3. Solve the system $y \leq -2x - 5$ and $y < \frac{1}{2}x$ by graphing.

Choose a linear inequality to match each graph.

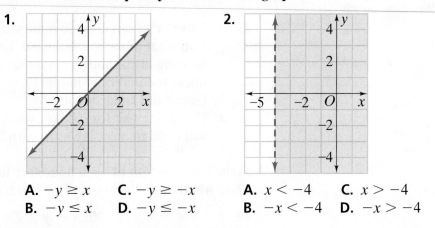

1.

2.

A. $-y \geq x$ **C.** $-y \geq -x$

B. $-y \leq x$ **D.** $-y \leq -x$

A. $x < -4$ **C.** $x > -4$

B. $-x < -4$ **D.** $-x > -4$

The graph of each inequality is bounded by a line. State whether the boundary line is solid or dashed.

3. $y > x$ **4.** $y \leq -x + 1$ **5.** $y \geq x - 1$

Standards Practice

For more exercises, see *Extra Skills and Word Problem Practice.*

A Practice by Example

Example 1
(page 420)

Go for Help

Example 2
(page 421)

Graph each inequality on its own coordinate plane.

6. $y > x - 6$ **7.** $y \leq -x + 8$ **8.** $y > x + 2$

9. $y \geq 2x - 1$ **10.** $y < -\frac{1}{3}x + 1$ **11.** $y \leq 2x + 1$

Solve each inequality for y.

12. $4x + y < -3$ **13.** $-y \leq 2x$ **14.** $2x + 3y \leq 7$

For Exercises 15–16, show all the solutions by writing and graphing a linear inequality.

15. A number is greater than or equal to three times another number. What are the numbers?

16. Melissa has a collection of dimes and nickels with a total value of less than one dollar. Let x be the number of dimes and y be the number of nickels. How many of each type does she have?

Example 3
(page 422)

Solve each system of inequalities by graphing. Use a point on the x- or y-axis to check each solution.

17. $y > -x$ **18.** $y \leq x$ **19.** $y > -x$ **20.** $y \leq -x + 1$
     $y < x + 6$ $y \geq -x - 4$ $y > 2x + 3$ $y > x - 5$

B Apply Your Skills

21. <u>Writing in Math</u> Describe the difference between the graph of $y < -x$ and the graph of $-y < x$.

Graph each inequality on its own coordinate plane.

22. $x - y > 10$ **23.** $y \leq 5$ **24.** $y \geq -\frac{2}{3}x$

25. $9x + 3y < 3$ **26.** $x - 2y \geq -12$ **27.** $-6x - 4y > 8$

28. a. Rates You can earn $6/h mowing lawns and $3/h baby-sitting. You want to earn at least $45. Let x = number of hours mowing lawns and y = number of hours baby-sitting. Write a linear inequality to model this situation.

   b. Graph the linear inequality.

   c. If you baby-sit for 6 hours, what is the number of hours you will need to mow lawns to earn $45?

Write the equation of each boundary line in slope-intercept form. State whether the boundary line is solid or dashed.

29. $x + y < -3$ **30.** $x - y \geq 7$ **31.** $-y > 4x$

32. $-y \leq -\frac{1}{2}x$ **33.** $5x + 3y \leq 9$ **34.** $4x - 2y > 10$

35. Medium drinks cost $2 and large drinks cost $3. A vendor wants to have at least $60 in sales. Let x be the number of medium drinks sold and y be the number of large drinks sold. Write an inequality to describe the situation.

Solve each system of inequalities by graphing.

36. $2x + y \leq 4$ **37.** $x + y > -3$ **38.** $x < 6$
$y + 1 \geq -2x$ $x - y < 5$ $y \leq 2x$

39. $y < 4$ **40.** $-2x + y > 1$ **41.** $3x + y > 5$
$x > -5$ $x + 2y < 2$ $y \geq -2$

42. Writing in Math How is graphing an inequality on a coordinate plane similar to graphing an inequality on a number line? How is it different?

C Challenge   **Open-Ended** Write a system of inequalities with the number of solutions indicated. If such a system is not possible, tell why.

43. no solutions   **44.** all real numbers   **45.** the points of a line

Reasoning Write a system of inequalities to describe each graph.

46. 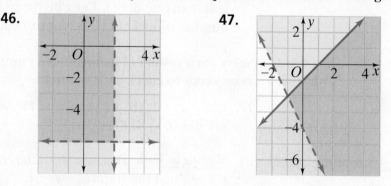   **47.**

Multiple Choice Practice and Mixed Review

For Standards Tutorials, visit PHSchool.com. Web Code: bjq-9045

48. You want to spend less than $20 on asparagus and green beans. Asparagus costs $3.00 per pound and green beans cost $.50 per pound. Let *a* represent the number of pounds of asparagus and *g* represent the number of pounds of green beans. Which inequality models what you can spend?

   Ⓐ $3a + 0.5g > 20$ Ⓒ $3a + 0.5g < 20$

   Ⓑ $3a + 0.5g \geq 20$ Ⓓ $3a + 0.5g \leq 20$

49. You plan to sell hand-made bracelets. The more bracelets you sell, the greater your profit will be. The graph shows your profit *y* for making and selling *x* bracelets. Describe the situation represented by the *x*-intercept.

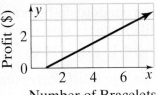

Number of Bracelets

   Ⓐ   When you sell 0 bracelets, your profit is $0.

   Ⓑ   When you sell 1 bracelet, your profit is $0.

   Ⓒ   When you sell 3 bracelets, your profit is $1.

   Ⓓ   When you sell 5 bracelets, your profit is $2.

50. Mr. Parker buys store gift cards for his students. Each card costs $2.50. He has a coupon for $5.00 off any purchase at the store. The equation $2.50g - 5 = c$ can be used to determine the cost *c* when he buys *g* gift cards. What is the cost of 90 gift cards?

   Ⓐ $230.00   Ⓑ $220.00   Ⓒ $87.50   Ⓓ $38.00

GO for Help

Lesson 8-6   **Solve each system of equations by graphing. Check each solution.**

51. $x + y = 8$ **52.** $y = 2x - 1$ **53.** $3y = -2x - 3$
$x - y = -2$ $2x - y = 3$ $3y = x - 12$

Lesson 6-6   **54.** In 2005, there were 242 California condors. Of these birds, 132 were in captivity, 61 were living free in California, and 49 were living free in Arizona.

   a. What percent of the condors were living free in Arizona? Round your answer to the nearest tenth of a percent.

   b. What percent of the condors were living free in all? Round your answer to the nearest tenth of a percent.

Lessons 5-7 and 5-8   **Solve each equation.**

55. $m - \frac{2}{3} = \frac{1}{6}$ **56.** $\frac{5}{4}c = \frac{3}{2}$ **57.** $\frac{3}{4} + w = \frac{9}{10}$

Lesson 4-6   **Evaluate each expression for $c = 4$ and $m = -3$.**

58. $\frac{c + m}{5}$ **59.** $\frac{m - c}{2}$ **60.** $\frac{2c - m}{-4}$ **61.** $\frac{4m}{2 - c}$

To get the correct answer in multiple-choice tests, you can use the strategy *Work Backward* if a problem asks you to find an initial value.

EXAMPLE

Ellen wants to serve dinner at 6:00 P.M. The table shows activities she needs to do before she serves dinner. What is the latest time Ellen should start the activities to serve dinner on time?

Ⓐ 2:15 P.M.　　Ⓑ 1:50 P.M.　　Ⓒ 1:30 P.M.　　Ⓓ 1:00 P.M.

You can *Work Backward* from the time dinner is served.

$$6:00 - 2 \text{ h} = 4:00$$
$$4:00 - 30 \text{ min} = 3:30$$
$$3:30 - 45 \text{ min} = 2:45$$
$$2:45 - 1\frac{1}{4} \text{ h} = 1:30$$

Ellen should start at 1:30 P.M. The correct answer is choice C.

Ellen's Activities

Activity	Duration
Clean Apartment	2 hours
Shop for Dinner	30 minutes
Travel Time	45 minutes
Prepare Dinner	$1\frac{1}{4}$ hours

Multiple Choice Practice

Read each question. Then write the letter of the correct answer on your paper.

1. Erica is $2\frac{3}{4}$ inches taller than Todd. Todd is twice as tall as his younger sister Lily. If Lily is 25 inches tall, how tall is Erica?
   Ⓐ $27\frac{3}{4}$ in.　　Ⓑ $47\frac{1}{4}$ in.　　Ⓒ $52\frac{3}{4}$ in.　　Ⓓ $55\frac{1}{2}$ in.

2. Seth took $20 out of his savings account 2 weeks ago. He then took out 20% of his account yesterday. He now has $40 in the account. How much money did he have in the account originally?
   Ⓐ $53.33　　Ⓑ $60.80　　Ⓒ $68.00　　Ⓓ $70.00

3. During a speech, half the audience leaves in the first 30 minutes. In the next 30 minutes, $\frac{1}{3}$ of the remaining people leave. Twelve more people leave near the end of the speech. If 20 people stay for the entire speech, how many people were originally in the audience?
   Ⓐ 48　　Ⓑ 96　　Ⓒ 112　　Ⓓ 192

4. Connor arrived in Dallas and took 45 minutes to go to the post office. Afterward, it took him 2 hours and 40 minutes to walk to a play, see the play, and eat dinner at a nearby restaurant. If it is currently 10:00 P.M., what time did he arrive in Dallas?
   Ⓐ 6:10 P.M.　　Ⓑ 6:15 P.M.　　Ⓒ 6:35 P.M.　　Ⓓ 6:55 P.M.

Chapter 8 Review

constant of variation (p. 405)	range (p. 388)	system of linear
direct variation (p. 405)	relation (p. 388)	equations (p. 414)
domain (p. 388)	slope (p. 399)	system of linear
function (p. 388)	slope-intercept	inequalities (p. 422)
linear equation (p. 394)	form (p. 401)	vertical-line test (p. 389)
linear inequality (p. 420)	solution (p. 393)	y-intercept (p. 401)

Choose the vocabulary term that correctly completes the sentence.

1. The tilt or slant of a line is its __?__ .

2. To determine whether the graph shows a function, use the __?__ .

3. A linear function modeled by the equation $y = kx$, where $k \neq 0$, is a __?__ .

4. When each member of a relation's domain is paired with exactly one member of the range, the relation is a __?__ .

5. Any equation whose graph is a line is a __?__ .

6. The first coordinates in a set of ordered pairs is the __?__ of the relation.

7. The second coordinates in a set of ordered pairs is the __?__ of the relation.

8. An ordered pair that makes an equation a true statement is a __?__ of the equation.

Go Online
PHSchool.com

For: Vocabulary quiz
Web Code: bjj-0851

Skills and Concepts

Lesson 8-1

- To determine whether a relation is a function

- To graph relations and functions

Any set of ordered pairs is a **relation.** The **domain** of a relation is the set of first coordinates of the ordered pairs. The **range** is the set of second coordinates. A **function** is a relation in which no two ordered pairs have the same first coordinate.

Is each relation a function? Explain.

9. $\{(2, 3), (4, 3), (0, 1), (-2, 3)\}$

10.
x	−3	4	−1	−4
y	0	2	0	1

11.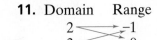
   Domain   Range

12. Is the amount of a long-distance telephone bill a function of time spent talking on the telephone? Explain.

Lesson 8-2

- To find solutions of equations with two variables
- To graph linear equations with two variables

A solution of an equation with two variables is any ordered pair that makes the equation true. The graph of a **linear equation** is a line.

Find the solutions of each equation for $x = -3, 0,$ and 2.

13. $y = x + 5$ **14.** $y = -4x$ **15.** $y = \frac{1}{2}x + 3$ **16.** $y = 6 - 2x$

Lesson 8-3

- To find the slope of a line
- To use slope-intercept form in graphing a linear equation

Slope is a measure describing the tilt of a line, which you can calculate using the ratio $\frac{\text{vertical change}}{\text{horizontal change}}$, or $\frac{\text{difference in } y\text{-coordinates}}{\text{difference in } x\text{-coordinates}}$. One form of a linear equation is the slope-intercept form, $y = mx + b$, where m is the slope and b is the y-intercept.

Identify the slope and y-intercept of each equation. Then graph each equation.

17. $x + y = 7$ **18.** $x - y = -2$

19. $2x + 5y = 10$ **20.** $3x - 2y = 12$

Find the slope of each line.

21.   **22.**   **23.**

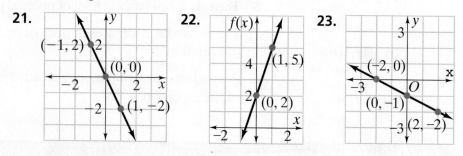

Lesson 8-4

- To find the constant of variation
- To write a direct variation

A **direct variation** is a linear function modeled by the equation $y = kx$, where $k \neq 0$. The coefficient k is the constant of variation. You can find k using a graph.

Find the constant of variation for each direct variation.

24.   **25.**

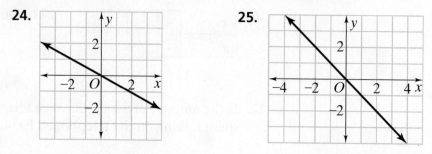

26. A segment measures 5 in. or 12.7 cm. The number of inches varies directly with the number of centimeters. Find the number of centimeters in 24 in.

Lesson 8-5

- To solve problems by combining strategies

You can combine multiple strategies to solve problems.

27. A gardener plans to use 196 feet of fencing to enclose a garden. What is the largest possible area of the garden?

28. Explain your choice of strategies for Exercise 27.

Lesson 8-6

- To solve systems of linear equations by graphing
- To use systems of linear equations to solve problems

Two or more linear equations with the same variables form a **system of linear equations.** A solution of a system of equations is any ordered pair that makes each equation true.

Solve each system by graphing.

29. $y = \frac{1}{2}x - 3$
$y = -\frac{1}{2}x + 1$

30. $3x + 2y = 6$
$x + 4y = -8$

31. $y = x - 5$
$y = -2x + 1$

32. $x + 4 = y$
$y = 5x$

33. Explain why it is possible for a system of linear equations to have no solutions.

Lesson 8-7

- To graph linear inequalities
- To graph systems of linear inequalities

Two or more linear inequalities with the same variables form a **system of linear inequalities.** A solution of a system of inequalities is any ordered pair that makes both inequalities true. You can solve a system by graphing.

Graph each inequality.

34. $y > 2x + 5$

35. $y \leq -x + 1$

36. $y \geq \frac{1}{2}x - 3$

37. $y < 3x - 2$

Solve each system by graphing.

38. $y < 3x + 2$
$y > 3x - 1$

39. $y > 6x$
$y \leq x + 3$

Is each relation a function? Explain.

1. $\{(-2, -12), (-2, 0), (-2, 4), (-2, 11)\}$

2. $\{(8, 1), (4, 1), (0, 1), (-15, 1)\}$

3. $\{(-4, -6), (-3, -2), (1, -2), (1, 0), (1, 3)\}$

4. $\{(0, 1), (0, 2), (1, 2), (1, 3), (3, 1), (4, 2)\}$

Graph each equation.

5. $y = 2x$

6. $y = -x - 2$

7. $2x - y = 4$

8. $3y = x - 6$

Find the slope of the line through each pair of points.

9. $C(0, 1)$ and $D(-5, 1)$

10. $M(-4, 1)$ and $N(6, 3)$

11. $J(-1, -2)$ and $K(2, 7)$

12. $P(4, 9)$ and $Q(-6, 12)$

13. $S(5, 9)$ and $T(3, 7)$

14. $W(-6, 4)$ and $Z(0, 1)$

15. $A(-4, -3)$ and $B(-10, -9)$

Each table models a direct variation. Find the constant of variation.

16.

x	y
−2	−3
0	0
2	3
4	6

17.

x	y
−3	4
0	0
3	−4
6	−8

18. The number of kilowatt-hours of electricity used in a home varies directly with the total cost of electricity. The cost for 315 kilowatt-hours is $22.52. Find the cost of using 530 kilowatt-hours.

Graph each inequality.

19. $y \geq 3x - 1$

20. $y < -x + 5$

Solve each system by graphing.

21. $y = x - 1$
    $x = 2y$

22. $x + y = 4$
    $2x + 2y = 8$

23. $x + y = 3$
    $y = x - 5$

24. $y = x + 1$
    $y = -x + 3$

25. $y = x + 5$
    $y = -2x + 8$

26. $y = -2x + 1$
    $2x + y = -1$

27. $y = 3x$
    $-y = -3x$

28. $y \leq 3x - 2$
    $y > x + 4$

29. **Writing in Math** Is the amount of sales tax paid a function of the labeled price of a taxable item? Explain.

30. **Writing in Math** Is a person's age a function of his or her height? Explain.

31. A class is selling calendars for a fundraiser. It costs $5 for each calendar plus $25 to ship the order. The class will sell each calendar for $5.50. How many calendars must the class sell for the cost to equal the earnings?

32. The sum of two numbers is 6. The result when the greater number is decreased by twice the lesser is 9. Let x be the greater number and y be the lesser number. Find the numbers.

33. The distance a car travels varies directly with the time it travels. A car travels 115 mi in 2 h. Find the number of miles the car travels in 7 h.

34. **Open-Ended** The slope of a line through the origin is $-\frac{2}{3}$. Find the coordinates of two points on the line.

Some problems ask you to interpret a graph. Read the question at the right and review the answer choices. Then follow the tips to answer the sample question.

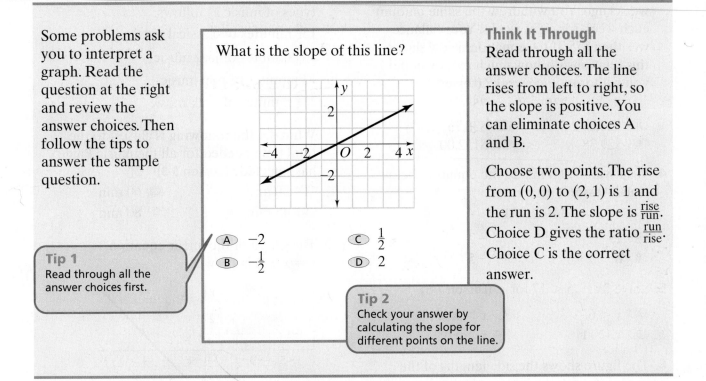

What is the slope of this line?

A −2

B −$\frac{1}{2}$

C $\frac{1}{2}$

D 2

Tip 1
Read through all the answer choices first.

Tip 2
Check your answer by calculating the slope for different points on the line.

Think It Through
Read through all the answer choices. The line rises from left to right, so the slope is positive. You can eliminate choices A and B.

Choose two points. The rise from (0, 0) to (2, 1) is 1 and the run is 2. The slope is $\frac{\text{rise}}{\text{run}}$. Choice D gives the ratio $\frac{\text{run}}{\text{rise}}$. Choice C is the correct answer.

Vocabulary Review

As you solve problems, you must understand the meanings of mathematical terms. Match each term with its mathematical meaning.

A. relation

B. domain

C. range

D. slope

E. y-intercept

I. a ratio that describes the tilt of a line

II. the second coordinates of a relation

III. a set of ordered pairs

IV. the y-coordinate of the point where the line crosses the y-axis

V. the first coordinates of a relation

Read each question. Then write the letter of the correct answer on your paper.

1. On his vacation, Marc has a total of $260 to spend. He spends $\frac{1}{4}$ of the total at a gift shop, 30% at a fishing store, and $78.60 at a toy store. How much money does he have left? **(Lesson 6-9)**

   A $38.40   C $78.00

   B $65.00   D $117.00

2. In a school survey of 380 students, 15% voted for a bull mascot, $\frac{2}{5}$ voted for an eagle mascot, and the rest voted for a wolf mascot. How many students voted for the wolf mascot? **(Lesson 6-9)**

   A 57   C 171

   B 152   D 209

3. You had $235 in your savings account nine weeks ago. You withdrew the same amount each week for eight weeks. Your balance was then $75. If the equation below shows this relationship, how much money m did you withdraw each week? **(Lesson 7-1)**

$$235 - 8m = 75$$

    Ⓐ $20.00   Ⓒ $38.75

    Ⓑ $29.38   Ⓓ $152.00

4. What value of a makes the equation below true? **(Lesson 7-1)**

$$\frac{a}{5} + 2 = 1$$

    Ⓐ 15   Ⓒ -2

    Ⓑ 8   Ⓓ -5

5. Solve $2x + 5 < 17$ for x. **(Lesson 7-5)**

    Ⓐ $x < 6$ Ⓒ $x > 6$

    Ⓑ $x < 11$ Ⓓ $x > 11$

6. The figure shows the side lengths of the square base of the Khafre pyramid in Giza. What is a reasonable estimate of the perimeter of the base? **(Lesson 3-3)**

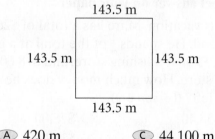

    Ⓐ 420 m   Ⓒ 44,100 m

    Ⓑ 600 m   Ⓓ 46,225 m

7. A gallon of paint can cover about 250 square feet. Stacy wants to paint 2 walls that are each 8 feet by 16 feet and a ceiling that is 14 feet by 16 feet. About how many gallons of paint will she need? **(Lesson 2-7)**

    Ⓐ Less than 1   Ⓒ From 2 to 3

    Ⓑ From 1 to 2   Ⓓ From 3 to 4

8. Paige wants to make a CD using various types of music as follows:

$15\frac{4}{5}$ minutes of classical music

$20\frac{1}{4}$ minutes of jazz music

13 minutes of pop music

$28\frac{2}{5}$ minutes of rock music

Which of the following is closest to the total time needed for all the music Paige has selected? **(Lesson 5-3)**

    Ⓐ 30 min   Ⓒ 60 min

    Ⓑ 45 min   Ⓓ 80 min

9. The graph of the linear equation $y = x - 3$ is shown.

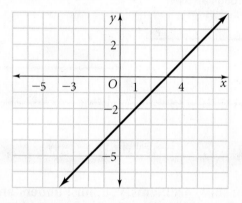

Which table of ordered pairs contains only points on this line? **(Lesson 8-2)**

Ⓐ

x	−2	0	4	3
y	−5	−3	1	0

Ⓑ

x	−5	−3	0	4
y	−2	0	3	1

Ⓒ

x	−1	0	1	2
y	−4	−3	2	1

Ⓓ

x	−1	0	2	3
y	−4	−3	−2	−1

10. Which line graph below best represents the table of values? **(Lesson 8-2)**

x	-2	0	2	3
y	2	1	0	$-\frac{1}{2}$

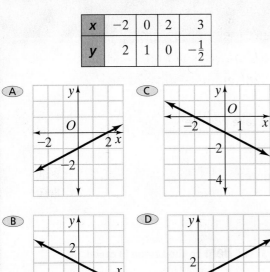

11. What is the slope of this line? **(Lesson 8-3)**

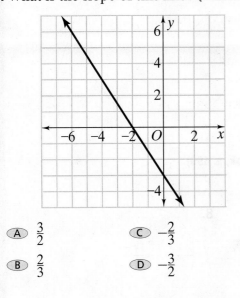

Ⓐ $\frac{3}{2}$ Ⓒ $-\frac{2}{3}$

Ⓑ $\frac{2}{3}$ Ⓓ $-\frac{3}{2}$

12. What is the perimeter of a rectangular picture frame with width 10 in. and length 14 in.? **(Lesson 3-3)**

Ⓐ 14 in. Ⓒ 28 in.
Ⓑ 20 in. Ⓓ 48 in.

13. A canoe is on sale for $348.75. You have a coupon for $\frac{1}{5}$ off the sale price. Which expression can you use to estimate the discount on the canoe? **(Lesson 6-4)**

Ⓐ 0.0020 × $350.00

Ⓑ 0.05 × $350.00

Ⓒ 0.20 × $350.00

Ⓓ 0.50 × $350.00

14. A commercial airplane increases its altitude from 500 ft to 1,400 ft in 2 minutes. A postal airplane increases its altitude at the same rate. How long does it take the postal airplane to increase its altitude from 1,200 ft to 2,400 ft? **(Lesson 4-6)**

Ⓐ $2\frac{2}{3}$ min

Ⓑ $2\frac{2}{5}$ min

Ⓒ $1\frac{1}{2}$ min

Ⓓ $\frac{2}{3}$ min

What You've Learned

Add, subtract, multiply, and divide rational numbers, and take positive rational numbers to whole-number powers.

Construct and read drawings made to scale.

Understand and use coordinate graphs to plot simple figures.

✓ Check Your Readiness   **GO for Help** to the Lesson in green.

Finding Perimeters (Lesson 3-3)

Find the perimeter of each figure.

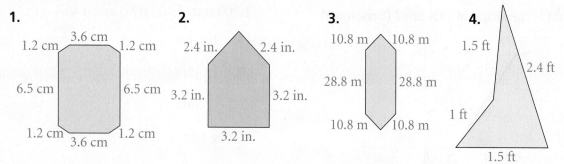

1. 1.2 cm · 3.6 cm · 1.2 cm · 6.5 cm · 6.5 cm · 1.2 cm · 3.6 cm · 1.2 cm

2. 2.4 in. · 2.4 in. · 3.2 in. · 3.2 in. · 3.2 in.

3. 10.8 m · 10.8 m · 28.8 m · 28.8 m · 10.8 m · 10.8 m

4. 1.5 ft · 2.4 ft · 1 ft · 1.5 ft

Dividing Decimals by Whole Numbers (Skills Handbook, p. 690)

Find the radius of each circle.

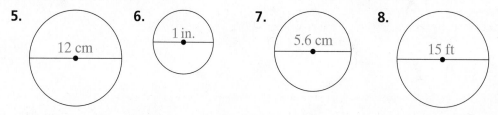

5. 12 cm

6. 1 in.

7. 5.6 cm

8. 15 ft

Graphing on the Coordinate Plane (Lesson 1-10)

Graph each point on the same coordinate plane.

9. $A(0, 7)$ **10.** $B(-2, 5)$ **11.** $E(4, 0)$ **12.** $D(2, -4)$ **13.** $C(-3, -1)$

14. $F\left(1\frac{1}{2}, -3\right)$ **15.** $G(0, 0)$ **16.** $J(0, -1)$ **17.** $I(-4, -5)$ **18.** $H(-5, -5)$

▲ Astronomers use angle measures to position telescopes.

What You'll Learn Next

Identify and construct basic elements of geometric figures.

Understand and use coordinate graphs to plot simple figures and determine their image under translations and reflections.

Demonstrate an understanding of conditions that indicate two geometrical figures are congruent and what congruence means about the relationships between the sides and angles of the two figures.

435

Introduction to Geometry: Points, Lines, and Planes

Introduce Identify and construct basic elements of geometric figures.
Introduce Describe how two or more objects are related in space (e.g., skew lines).

Points, Lines, and Planes

Geometric shapes are evident in many human-made and natural structures. Notice the intersecting lines that form the spider's web in the photo below. Two other examples of geometry in nature are the spiral structure of a snail's shell and the shape of a snowflake.

Basic Geometric Figures

Name	Sample	Symbolic Name	Description
Point	• *A*	Point *A*	A **point** is a location in space. It has no size.
Line	*A* *B* *n*	$\overleftrightarrow{AB}$, $\overleftrightarrow{BA}$, or *n*	A **line** is a series of points that extends in opposite directions without end. A lowercase letter can name a line.
Plane	*A* *B* *M* *D* *C*	*ABCD* or *M*	A **plane** is a flat surface with no thickness. It contains many lines and extends without end in the directions of all its lines.
Line segment or segment	*Q* *P*	$\overline{PQ}$, or $\overline{QP}$	A **segment** is a part of a line. It has two endpoints. *PQ* represents the length of $\overline{PQ}$.
Ray	*C* *R*	$\overrightarrow{CR}$	A **ray** is a part of a line. It has exactly one endpoint. Name its endpoint first.

You can combine the basic geometric figures to create many other geometric figures.

1 EXAMPLE Naming Geometric Figures

Name each figure in the diagram.

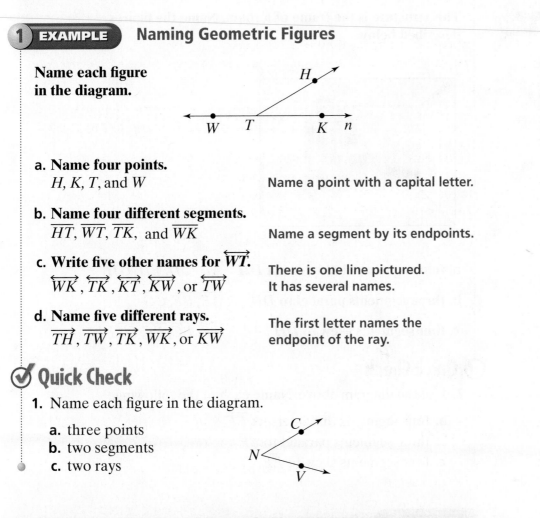

a. Name four points.
$H, K, T,$ and W Name a point with a capital letter.

b. Name four different segments.
$\overline{HT}, \overline{WT}, \overline{TK},$ and $\overline{WK}$ Name a segment by its endpoints.

c. Write five other names for $\overleftrightarrow{WT}$.
$\overleftrightarrow{WK}, \overleftrightarrow{TK}, \overleftrightarrow{KT}, \overleftrightarrow{KW},$ or $\overleftrightarrow{TW}$ There is one line pictured. It has several names.

d. Name five different rays.
$\overrightarrow{TH}, \overrightarrow{TW}, \overrightarrow{TK}, \overrightarrow{WK},$ or $\overrightarrow{KW}$ The first letter names the endpoint of the ray.

✓ Quick Check

1. Name each figure in the diagram.

   a. three points
   b. two segments
   c. two rays

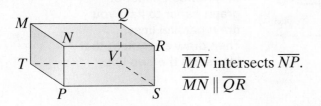

Intersecting, Parallel, and Skew Lines

Two lines *intersect* if they have exactly one point in common. Two lines that lie in the same plane and do not intersect are **parallel.** You use the symbol ∥ to indicate "is parallel to." Segments and rays are parallel if they lie in parallel lines.

$\overline{MN}$ intersects $\overline{NP}$.
$\overline{MN} \parallel \overline{QR}$

> **Vocabulary Tip**
>
> The symbol ∥ used for "parallel" looks like two parallel lines.

Skew lines are lines that do not lie in the same plane. They are not parallel, and they do not intersect. Skew segments must be parts of skew lines. In the diagram above, $\overline{MN}$ and $\overline{RS}$ are skew.

This structure is the frame of a room. Name the figures described below.

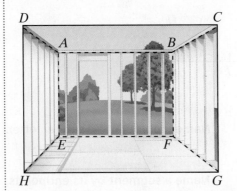

a. four segments that intersect $\overline{DH}$ $\overline{AD}, \overline{CD}, \overline{EH}, \overline{GH}$

b. three segments parallel to $\overline{DH}$ $\overline{AE}, \overline{BF}, \overline{CG}$

c. four segments skew to $\overline{DH}$ $\overline{AB}, \overline{BC}, \overline{EF}, \overline{FG}$

✓ Quick Check

2. Use the diagram above. Name each of the following.

   a. four segments that intersect $\overline{EF}$
   b. three segments parallel to $\overline{EF}$
   c. four segments skew to $\overline{EF}$

3 EXAMPLE   **Drawing Lines**

For: Lines and Planes Activity
Use: Interactive Textbook, 9-1

Draw two parallel lines. Then draw a segment that intersects the parallel lines.

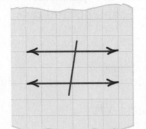

Use the lines on a piece of notebook paper or graph paper to help you draw parallel lines. Then draw a segment that intersects the two lines.

✓ Quick Check

3. Use notebook paper or graph paper. Draw the figures indicated.

   a. three parallel segments
   b. a ray that intersects the parallel segments of part (a)
   c. a segment, $\overline{AB}$ **d.** a ray, $\overrightarrow{QR}$ **e.** a line, $\overleftrightarrow{LM}$

Name the indicated figures in each diagram.

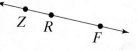

1. three points
2. three different segments
3. four different rays

4. all points
5. all segments
6. all lines

7. Is it possible for two lines that are not in the same plane to be parallel? Explain.

Standards Practice

For more exercises, see *Extra Skills and Word Problem Practice*.

A Practice by Example

Example 1
(page 437)

GO for Help

Name the indicated figures in each diagram.

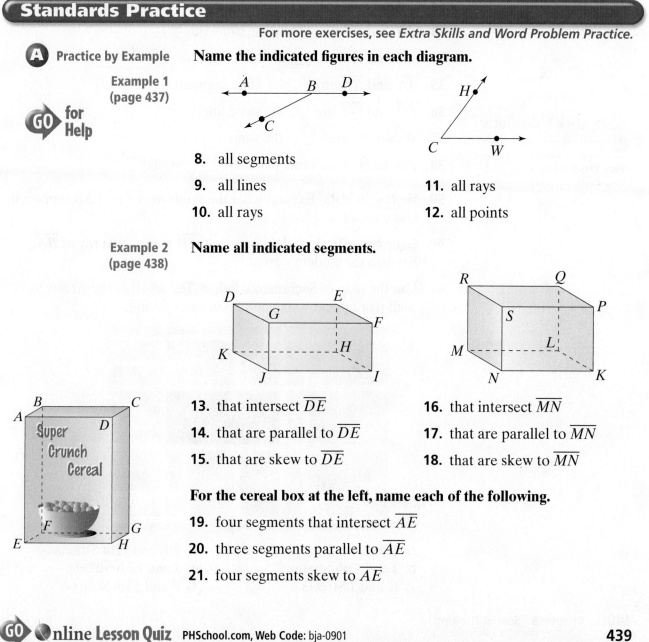

8. all segments
9. all lines
10. all rays

11. all rays
12. all points

Example 2
(page 438)

Name all indicated segments.

13. that intersect $\overline{DE}$
14. that are parallel to $\overline{DE}$
15. that are skew to $\overline{DE}$

16. that intersect $\overline{MN}$
17. that are parallel to $\overline{MN}$
18. that are skew to $\overline{MN}$

For the cereal box at the left, name each of the following.

19. four segments that intersect $\overline{AE}$
20. three segments parallel to $\overline{AE}$
21. four segments skew to $\overline{AE}$

Example 3
(page 438)

22. Use notebook paper or graph paper. Draw three segments that are parallel to each other. Draw a line that intersects the parallel segments.

23. Draw two parallel rays.　　**24.** Draw $\overrightarrow{VB}$.

25. Draw $\overleftrightarrow{CD}$ so that it intersects two segments, $\overline{FG}$ and $\overline{HJ}$.

B **Apply Your Skills**　**Modeling** **Draw each of the following. If not possible, explain.**

26. $\overleftrightarrow{PQ} \parallel \overleftrightarrow{RS}$　　**27.** $\overrightarrow{AB} \parallel \overrightarrow{BC}$　　**28.** $\overrightarrow{JK}$ skew to $\overleftrightarrow{LM}$

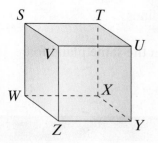

Use the figure at the left. Name a segment to make each statement true.

29. ■ $\parallel \overline{XY}$　　　　　　**30.** ■ $\parallel \overline{YZ}$

31. ■ $\parallel \overline{WX}$　　　　　　**32.** ■ $\parallel \overline{SV}$

Complete with *always, sometimes,* or *never* to make a true statement.

33. $\overrightarrow{AB}$ and $\overrightarrow{BC}$ are ___?___ on the same line.

34. $\overrightarrow{AB}$ and $\overrightarrow{AC}$ are ___?___ the same ray.

35. $\overline{AX}$ and $\overline{XA}$ are ___?___ the same segment.

36. $\overleftrightarrow{TQ}$ and $\overleftrightarrow{QT}$ are ___?___ the same line.

37. Skew lines are ___?___ in the same plane.

38. Two lines in the same plane are ___?___ parallel.

39. **Writing in Math** Explain what the symbols $\overline{AB}$ and AB represent. Use examples.

40. **Error Analysis** A student says that $\overrightarrow{AB}$ is the same ray as $\overrightarrow{BA}$. Explain the student's error.

41. Use the map of Sacramento below. Tell whether the streets in each pair appear to be parallel or intersecting.

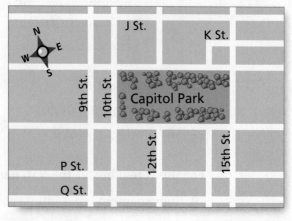

　a. P and 9th Streets　　　　　**d.** 9th and 12th Streets
　b. J and 15th Streets　　　　　**e.** J and 12th Streets
　c. K and J Streets　　　　　　**f.** P and 15th Streets

42. a. Suppose a town installs a mailbox at a point *P*. How many straight roads can the town plan that lead to *P*?

b. Suppose a town installs mailboxes at points *P* and *R*. How many straight roads might the town plan to build that pass by both mailboxes?

43. a. On a coordinate plane, draw a line through $\left(-\frac{1}{2}, -1\right)$ and $\left(1, 1\frac{1}{2}\right)$. Then draw a line through $(-1, 1)$ and $\left(\frac{1}{2}, 3\frac{1}{2}\right)$.

b. What appears to be true of the two lines that you drew in part (a)?

c. Find the slope of each line.

d. Inductive Reasoning Make a conjecture based on your answer to parts (b) and (c).

Multiple Choice Practice and Mixed Review

For Standards Tutorials, visit PHSchool.com. Web Code: bjq-9045

44. An artist wants to paint a rectangular mural in the space shown at the right. What is the length of the wall?

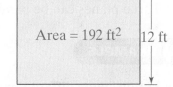

    Ⓐ 12 ft   Ⓒ 56 ft

    Ⓑ 16 ft   Ⓓ 180 ft

45. The population of Brazil is about 183,000,000. How is this number written in scientific notation?

    Ⓐ 1.83×10^{-8} Ⓒ 1.83×10^{8}

    Ⓑ 1.83×10^{-6} Ⓓ 183×10^{6}

46. $\triangle KLM$ is similar to $\triangle TUV$. Find the length of $\overline{UV}$.

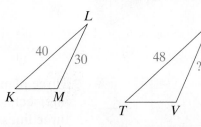

    Ⓐ 64 units   Ⓒ 36 units

    Ⓑ 38 units   Ⓓ 25 units

Lesson 8-7   **Graph each inequality in its own coordinate plane.**

47. $y \geq -2x + 6$ **48.** $y > x + 1$ **49.** $x \leq -4$

Lesson 5-3   **Simplify each expression.**

50. $\frac{3}{8} + \frac{7}{12}$ **51.** $2\frac{3}{4} - 1\frac{5}{6}$ **52.** $1\frac{1}{3} + 2\frac{1}{6}$ **53.** $2\frac{1}{2} - 3\frac{2}{3}$

54. $\frac{5}{8} \cdot \frac{3}{4}$ **55.** $2\frac{2}{3} \div \frac{3}{8}$ **56.** $1\frac{1}{4} \cdot 3$ **57.** $4\frac{3}{8} \div 4$

Develop Describe how two or more objects are related in space (e.g., the possible ways three planes might intersect).
Develop Develop generalizations of results obtained.

You can use the terms *parallel* and *intersecting* to describe the relationship between two or more planes in three-dimensional space.

When two planes have no points in common, they are parallel. When two planes intersect, their intersection is a line. When two planes have all points in common, they are *coincident*.

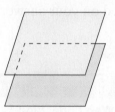
Parallel

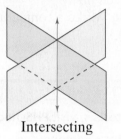
Intersecting

Coincident

Three planes can be parallel, intersecting, or coincident.

EXAMPLE

In how many different ways can three planes that are not coincident intersect in three-dimensional space?

Two planes intersect in a line. The third plane intersects the line at one point.

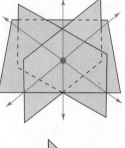

Three planes intersect in one line.

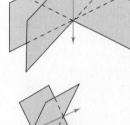

Two planes are parallel. The third plane intersects them in two lines.

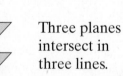

Three planes intersect in three lines.

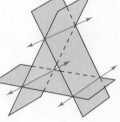

EXERCISES

1. Two lines are *skew* if they are not parallel and do not intersect. Is it possible for two planes to be considered skew? Explain.

2. In how many ways can a line and a plane intersect? Sketch an example of each.

Angle Relationships and Parallel Lines

What You'll Learn

- To identify adjacent and vertical angles
- To relate angles formed by parallel lines and a transversal

... And Why

To use the relationships of angles formed by parallel lines in real-world situations, such as setting leaded window panes

✓ Check Skills You'll Need

Solve.

1. $n + 45 = 180$

2. $75 + x = 90$

3. $3 = 2y + 90$

4. $2a + 15 = 45$

GO for Help
Lesson 7-1

🔊 New Vocabulary

- adjacent angles
- vertical angles
- congruent angles
- supplementary
- complementary
- transversal
- corresponding angles
- alternate interior angles

Develop Identify basic elements of geometric figures.

Adjacent and Vertical Angles

In this lesson you will learn to identify special pairs of angles. **Adjacent angles** share a vertex and a side but no points in their interiors.

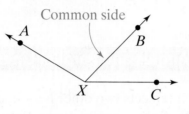

Common side

$\angle AXB$ and $\angle BXC$ are adjacent angles.

$\angle AXC$ and $\angle BXC$ are not adjacent angles.

Vertical angles are formed by two intersecting lines and are opposite each other. Vertical angles have the same measure.

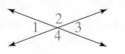

$\angle 1$ and $\angle 3$ are vertical angles.
$\angle 2$ and $\angle 4$ are vertical angles.

Angles that have the same measure are **congruent angles.** In the diagram above, $\angle 1$ is congruent to $\angle 3$. You can write this as $\angle 1 \cong \angle 3$. You can write *the measure of* $\angle 1$ as $m\angle 1$. Since $\angle 1 \cong \angle 3$, $m\angle 1 = m\angle 3$.

Recall that an *acute angle* measures less than 90°. A *right angle* measures 90°. An *obtuse angle* measures more than 90° but less than 180°. A *straight angle* measures 180°. Pairs of angles with certain measures also have special names.

If the sum of the measures of two angles is 180°, the angles are **supplementary.**

If the sum of the measures of two angles is 90°, the angles are **complementary.**

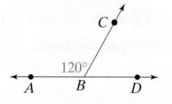

$\angle ABC$ and $\angle CBD$ are supplementary.

$\angle ABC$ and $\angle X$ are supplementary.
$\angle X$ and $\angle RQS$ are complementary.

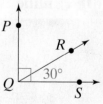

$\angle PQR$ and $\angle RQS$ are complementary.

1 EXAMPLE Finding the Measure of an Angle

Use the diagram at the left. Find the measure of ∠1 if $m\angle 4 = 135°$.

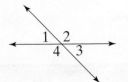

$$m\angle 1 + m\angle 4 = 180° \qquad \text{∠1 and ∠4 are supplementary.}$$

$$m\angle 1 + 135° = 180° \qquad \text{Replace } m\angle 4 \text{ with 135°.}$$

$$m\angle 1 + 135° - 135° = 180° - 135° \qquad \text{Solve for } m\angle 1.$$

$$m\angle 1 = 45°$$

✓ Quick Check

1. If $m\angle 8 = 20°$, find the measures of ∠5, ∠6, and ∠7.

Relating Angles and Parallel Lines

A line that intersects two other lines in different points is a **transversal.** Some pairs of angles formed by transversals and two lines have special names.

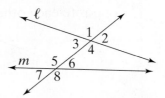

Corresponding angles lie on the same side of the transversal and in corresponding positions. ∠1 and ∠5, ∠3 and ∠7, ∠2 and ∠6, and ∠4 and ∠8 are corresponding angles.

Alternate interior angles are in the interior of a pair of lines and on opposite sides of the transversal. ∠3 and ∠6, and ∠4 and ∠5 are alternate interior angles.

When a transversal intersects two parallel lines, corresponding angles are congruent. Alternate interior angles are also congruent.

2 EXAMPLE Identifying Congruent Angles

GO ●nline

Video Tutor Help
Visit: PHSchool.com
Web Code: bje-0775

In the diagram, $\ell \parallel m$. Identify each of the following.

a. congruent corresponding angles

$\angle 1 \cong \angle 3,\ \angle 2 \cong \angle 4,\ \angle 8 \cong \angle 6,$
$\angle 7 \cong \angle 5$

b. congruent alternate interior angles

$\angle 3 \cong \angle 7,\ \angle 2 \cong \angle 6$

---

2. In the diagram, $a \parallel b$. Name four pairs of congruent corresponding angles and two pairs of congruent alternate interior angles.

When solving a problem that involves parallel lines, you can often choose whether to use corresponding angles or alternate interior angles.

More Than One Way

The windowpanes at the right are held in place by parallel strips of lead. Lines r and s are parallel and line q is a transversal. If $m\angle 1 = 65°$, what is $m\angle 4$?

Nicole's Method

Use corresponding angles.
$\angle 1 \cong \angle 3$ because they are corresponding angles, so $m\angle 3 = 65°$. $\angle 3$ and $\angle 4$ are supplementary, so $m\angle 3 + m\angle 4 = 180°$.

$$m\angle 3 + m\angle 4 = 180°$$
$$65° + m\angle 4 = 180°$$
$$65° + m\angle 4 - 65° = 180° - 65°$$
$$m\angle 4 = 115°$$

Eric's Method

Use alternate interior angles.
$\angle 1$ and $\angle 2$ are supplementary.

$$m\angle 1 + m\angle 2 = 180°$$
$$65° + m\angle 2 = 180°$$
$$65° + m\angle 2 - 65° = 180° - 65°.$$
$$m\angle 2 = 115°$$

$\angle 2$ and $\angle 4$ are alternate interior angles, so they are congruent. If $m\angle 2 = 115°$, then $m\angle 4 = 115°$.

Choose a Method

1. Which method do you prefer? Explain why.

2. What is another way to solve the problem?

Use the figure at the left for Exercises 1–4. Choose the term that best describes each pair of angles.

1. ∠1 and ∠3

2. ∠2 and ∠6

3. ∠5 and ∠8

4. ∠3 and ∠5

A. alternate interior
B. corresponding
C. supplementary
D. vertical

5. Draw an example of two corresponding angles that are also supplementary. Include angle measures.

Standards Practice

For more exercises, see *Extra Skills and Word Problem Practice.*

A **Practice by Example**

Example 1
(page 444)

GO for Help

Use the figure at the right for Exercises 6–8.

6. ∠1 and ∠2 are __?__ angles.

7. ∠1 and ∠3 are __?__ angles.

8. Find the measures of ∠1, ∠2, and ∠3 if $m\angle 4 = 100°$.

For Exercises 9 and 10, name the angle vertical to ∠1. Name an angle adjacent to ∠1. Then find $m\angle 1$.

9.

10.

Example 2
(page 444)

In the figure below, $\overleftrightarrow{AB} \parallel \overleftrightarrow{MN}$. Use the figure for Exercises 11–14.

11. Name four pairs of corresponding angles.

12. Name the alternate interior angles.

13. Name all angles congruent to ∠8.

14. **a.** List all angles that are congruent to ∠1.
    b. If $m\angle 5 = 45°$, what are the measures of the other angles?

B **Apply Your Skills**

15. Use the figure at the right. Find the sum of the measures of ∠1, ∠2, and ∠3.

16. Fill in the blank. The sum of the measures of two angles is 90°. The angles are __?__ angles.

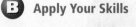
17. **Writing in Math** Describe how you will keep from confusing the definitions of supplementary angles and complementary angles.

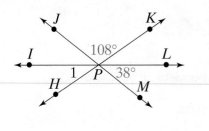

18. Use the figure at the left. Name the angle vertical to ∠1. Name an angle adjacent to ∠1. Then find $m\angle 1$.

19. Reasoning Angles on the "outside" of two lines and on opposite sides of a transversal are called *alternate exterior angles*. The transversal q intersects two parallel lines m and n. If $m\angle 1 = 84°$, what is the measure of ∠5? Explain your reasoning.

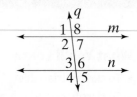

C Challenge

20. a. [Algebra] Write an equation and find the value of x.
   b. Find $m\angle KQB$.
   c. Find $m\angle KQR$.

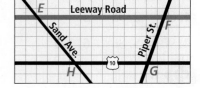

Multiple Choice Practice and Mixed Review

For Standards Tutorials, visit PHSchool.com. Web Code: bjq-9045

21. The length of $\overline{EF}$ along Leeway Road is 3 miles. The length of $\overline{FG}$ along Piper St. is 30% of $\overline{EF}$. The length of $\overline{GH}$ along Route 10 is 1.75 miles, and the length of $\overline{HE}$ along Sand Ave. is 75% of the length of $\overline{GH}$. Which expression is used to find the distance from E to F to G to H and back to E?

   Ⓐ $3 + 3.0(3) + 1.75 + 7.5(1.75)$
   Ⓑ $0.30(3 + 3) + 0.75(1.75 + 1.75)$
   Ⓒ $3 + 0.75 + 1.75 + 0.75$
   Ⓓ $3 + 0.30(3) + 1.75 + 0.75(1.75)$

22. Bill wants to buy cards with $20. Each card costs between $1.80 and $2.25. What is the maximum number of cards he can buy?
   Ⓐ 6   Ⓑ 8   Ⓒ 9   Ⓓ 11

23. Laura takes a random survey of the students in her school. Of the 48 students asked, 16 plan to go to the football game. There are 231 students in her school. To the nearest percent, what percent of the total number of students can she expect to attend the game?
   Ⓐ 7%   Ⓒ 33%
   Ⓑ 21%   Ⓓ 64%

GO for Help

Lesson 9-1   **Draw each figure.**

24. $\overline{AB}$ **25.** $\overrightarrow{CD}$ **26.** $\overrightarrow{DC}$ **27.** $\overleftrightarrow{EF}$ **28.** $\angle GHI$

Lesson 6-8   **Find the sale price.**

29. $25 at 10% discount   **30.** $324 at 20% discount

Classifying Polygons

Develop Use formulas routinely for finding the perimeter of basic two-dimensional figures.

Develop Identify basic elements of geometric figures.

What You'll Learn

- To classify triangles
- To classify quadrilaterals

. . . And Why

To use polygons in real-world situations involving design and construction

 **Check Skills You'll Need**

For the angle measures given, classify the angle as *acute*, *right*, or *obtuse*.

1. 85° **2.** 95° **3.** 160°

4. 90° **5.** 36° **6.** 127°

 **for Help**
Lesson 9-2

🔊 **New Vocabulary**

- polygon
- regular polygon

Classifying Triangles

A **polygon** is a *closed* plane figure with at least three *sides*. The sides meet only at their endpoints.

A triangle is a polygon with three sides. You can classify triangles by angle measures. You can also classify triangles by side lengths. Tick marks are used to indicate congruent sides of a figure.

Acute triangle
three acute angles

Right triangle
one right angle

Obtuse triangle
one obtuse angle

Equilateral triangle
three congruent sides

Isosceles triangle
at least two
congruent sides

Scalene triangle
no congruent sides

 1 **EXAMPLE** **Classifying a Triangle**

Classify the triangle by its sides and angles.

The triangle has two congruent sides and one right angle.

The triangle is an isosceles right triangle.

8 in.

8 in.

 Online active math

For: Triangle Activity
Use: Interactive Textbook, 9-3

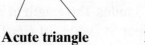 **Quick Check**

1. Judging by appearance, classify each triangle by its sides and angles.

a.

b.

c.

Classifying Quadrilaterals

You can also classify quadrilaterals by their sides and angles.

Vocabulary Tip

When you <u>classify</u> an item, you group it with other items that have similar characteristics.

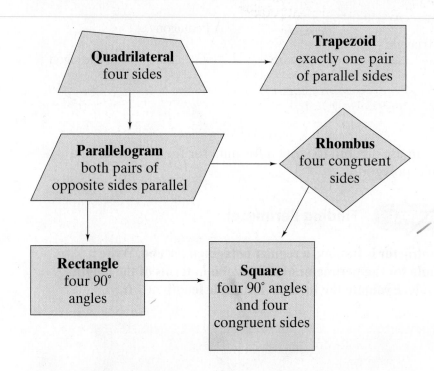

Quadrilateral
four sides

Trapezoid
exactly one pair
of parallel sides

Parallelogram
both pairs of
opposite sides parallel

Rhombus
four congruent
sides

Rectangle
four 90°
angles

Square
four 90° angles
and four
congruent sides

2 EXAMPLE **Classifying Quadrilaterals**

Name the types of quadrilaterals that have both pairs of opposite sides parallel.

All parallelograms have opposite sides parallel. Parallelograms include rectangles, rhombuses, and squares.

✓ Quick Check

2. Name the types of quadrilaterals that have four right angles.

In later math courses, you will prove that a parallelogram has opposite sides congruent and opposite angles congruent.

Polygons are named using their vertices. Start at one vertex and list them in consecutive order.

Vocabulary Tip

The plural of <u>vertex</u> is <u>vertices</u>.

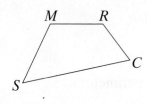

Starting from *M*, the name
of this figure is quadrilateral *MRCS*
or quadrilateral *MSCR*.

A **regular polygon** has all sides congruent and all angles congruent. Some regular polygons are shown below.

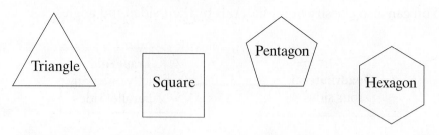

Triangle   Square   Pentagon   Hexagon

You can use algebra to write a formula for the perimeter of a regular polygon.

3 EXAMPLE   **Finding Perimeter**

A contractor is framing a regular octagonal gazebo. Write a formula for the perimeter of the gazebo in terms of the length of a side. Evaluate the formula for a side length of 7 ft.

Most gazebos are regular hexagonal or regular octagonal.

To write a formula, let $x =$ the length of each side. The perimeter of the regular octagon is

$x + x + x + x + x + x + x + x.$

The formula for the perimeter is $P = 8x$.

$P = 8x$ **Write the formula.**

$\quad = 8(7)$ **Substitute 7 for x.**

$\quad = 56$ **Simplify.**

For a side length of 7 ft, the perimeter is 56 ft.

✓ Quick Check

3. a. (Algebra) Write a formula to find the perimeter of a regular hexagon.
    b. Use the formula to find the perimeter if one side is 16 cm.

Open-Ended Sketch each figure.

1. an isosceles right triangle
2. a scalene obtuse triangle
3. an isosceles obtuse triangle
4. an isosceles acute triangle
5. a scalene right triangle
6. an equilateral triangle

7. **Reasoning** Your friend says that every square is a rectangle and every square is also a rhombus, so every rectangle must be a rhombus. Is your friend correct? Explain.

Standards Practice

For more exercises, see *Extra Skills and Word Problem Practice.*

A Practice by Example

Example 1 (page 448)

GO for Help

Judging by appearance, classify each triangle by its sides and angles.

8. 9. 10.

Example 2 (page 449)

Name the types of quadrilaterals that have the given property.

11. four congruent sides
12. exactly one pair of parallel sides
13. two pairs of parallel sides
14. opposite sides congruent
15. four congruent angles
16. opposite angles congruent

Example 3 (page 450)

Algebra **Write and use a formula for the perimeter of each figure. Use the formula to find the perimeter.**

17. an equilateral triangle with one side 3.5 cm

18. a square with one side 12.5 in.

19. a regular hexagon with one side $\frac{5}{8}$ in.

20. The Pentagon is a pentagon-shaped building near Washington, D.C., that is home to the United States Department of Defense. Write a formula for the perimeter of a regular pentagon in terms of the length of a side. Evaluate the formula to find the perimeter of the Pentagon, which has a side length of 921 ft.

B Apply Your Skills

21. Draw a parallelogram without a right angle but with four congruent sides. What is another name for this figure?

22. **Multiple Choice** What is the perimeter of an isosceles triangle with congruent sides of 16.2 cm and a third side half that length?
    Ⓐ 8.1 cm   Ⓑ 16.2 cm   Ⓒ 32.4 cm   Ⓓ 40.5 cm

Homework Video Tutor

Visit: PHSchool.com
Web Code: bje-0903

Name the types of quadrilaterals that do *not* have the given property.

23. four congruent sides
24. four 90° angles

25. Judging by appearance at the left, classify the triangle suggested by the edges of the piano, the piano lid, and the prop.

26. a. **Algebra** A decagon is a polygon with 10 sides. Write a formula for the perimeter of a regular decagon.
   b. Find the perimeter of a regular decagon with sides of 14.5 m.
   c. Find the length of a side of a regular decagon that has a perimeter of 22 ft.

27. **Writing in Math** Are all equilateral triangles isosceles? Are all isosceles triangles equilateral? Explain.

Name three different figures in each flag. For each triangle, state the type of triangle.

28.

Flag of Philippines

29.

Flag of Antigua

C Challenge

The lengths of two sides of an isosceles triangle are given. What is the perimeter? Explain.

30. 10 cm, 12 cm   31. 5 cm, 12 cm   32. 12 cm, 12 cm

Multiple Choice Practice and Mixed Review

For Standards Tutorials, visit PHSchool.com. Web Code: bjq-9045

33. To build a frame, a gardener wants to find the distance around the top of the greenhouse shown in the figure. What is the perimeter of the greenhouse?

   Ⓐ $142\frac{1}{2}$ in.   Ⓒ 231 in.
   Ⓑ $154\frac{1}{2}$ in.   Ⓓ 308 in.

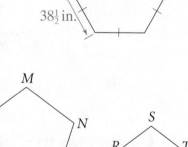

34. Regular pentagon *LMNOP* is similar to regular pentagon *RSTUV*. What scale factor was used to dilate pentagon *LMNOP* to pentagon *RSTUV*?

   Ⓐ 0.5   Ⓒ 1.25
   Ⓑ 0.6   Ⓓ 1.67

Lesson 9-2

35. A transversal intersects two parallel lines, forming eight angles. One angle measures 60°. Sketch a diagram showing the measures of all eight angles.

Angles of a Polygon

Develop Identify elements of geometric figures.
Develop Apply results from simpler problems to more complex problems.

In previous courses, you learned that the sum of the measures of the angles of a triangle is 180°. Now you have the tools to prove that this is true with deductive reasoning.

In the figure, $\overleftrightarrow{AC} \parallel \overleftrightarrow{DE}$. If two parallel lines are cut by a transversal, then alternate interior angles are congruent. Therefore, $\angle 1 \cong \angle 4$, or $m\angle 1 = m\angle 4$. Similarly, $m\angle 3 = m\angle 5$. $\angle ABC$ is a straight angle, so $m\angle 1 + m\angle 2 + m\angle 3 = 180°$. Substitute $m\angle 4$ for $m\angle 1$ and $m\angle 5$ for $m\angle 3$ and you get $m\angle 4 + m\angle 2 + m\angle 5 = 180°$. These are the angles of $\triangle DBE$.

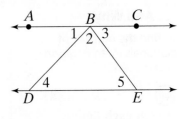

A **diagonal** of a polygon is a segment that connects two nonconsecutive vertices. You can use the triangles formed by diagonals to find the sum of the angle measures of any polygon.

EXAMPLE

Find the sum of the measures of the angles of a hexagon.

Sketch a hexagon. Draw the diagonals from vertex A.

The hexagon has **6** vertices.
From vertex A, there are **5** segments to the other vertices.
The segments determine **4** triangles.

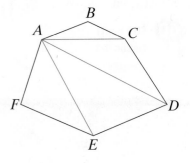

$$\begin{array}{ccccc} \text{number of} & & \text{number of degrees} & & \text{sum of measures of} \\ \text{triangles} & \cdot & \text{in angles of triangle} & = & \text{angles of hexagon} \\ 4 & \cdot & 180° & = & 720° \end{array}$$

EXERCISES

Find the sum of the measures of the angles of each polygon.

1. a quadrilateral

2. a decagon (10 sides)

3. an octagon

4. a dodecagon (12 sides)

5. Reasoning Write a formula for the sum of the measures of the angles s of an n-gon (n sides).

6. Find the value of x in the figure at the right.

7. Writing in Math The sum of the measures of the angles of a polygon is 1,260°. Explain how you can find the number of sides.

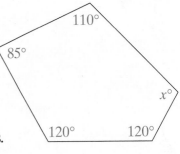

Find the number of sides in the polygon whose angle measures have the given sum.

8. 540°

9. 900°

10. 1,620°

11. 18,000°

Reasoning Strategy: Draw a Diagram

Develop Identify and construct basic elements of geometric figures (e.g., diagonals).

Develop Determine when and how to break a problem into simpler parts.

Develop Use a variety of methods, such as diagrams, to explain mathematical reasoning.

What You'll Learn

• To draw a diagram to solve a problem

. . . And Why

To find the number of diagonals in an octagon

 Check Skills You'll Need

Sketch each figure.

1. equilateral triangle

2. rectangle

3. pentagon

4. hexagon

5. octagon

GO for Help
Lesson 9-3

Draw a Diagram

Math Strategies in Action
One of the most important steps in a clothing designer's process is sketching possible designs. Designers can also translate their diagrams to computer-design programs to view their sketches on virtual models.

Drawing a diagram is an important problem-solving tool.

1 EXAMPLE **Drawing a Diagram**

How many diagonals does an octagon have?

Understand **Understand the problem.**

Make sure you understand the meaning of each term.

1. What is an octagon?

2. What is a diagonal?

Plan **Make a plan to solve the problem.**

One strategy for solving this problem is to draw a diagram and count the diagonals. An octagon has eight sides. You can draw five diagonals from one vertex of an octagon.

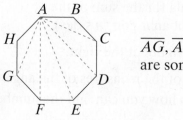

$\overline{AG}, \overline{AF}, \overline{AE}, \overline{AD}$, and $\overline{AC}$ are some of the diagonals.

3. There are 5 diagonals drawn from vertex *A*. Copy the diagram. Now find the number of diagonals you can draw from vertex *B*.

4. How many new diagonals can you draw from vertex *C*?

It may be helpful to organize your results as you count the diagonals.

Make a table similar to the one below and fill in the number of diagonals from each vertex. Do not count a diagonal twice. (The segment from A to C is the same segment as the one from C to A.)

Then add to find the total number of diagonals.

Vertex	Number of Diagonals
A	5
B	5
C	4
D	▪
E	▪
F	▪
G	▪
H	▪
Total	▪

Check **Check the answer to be sure it is reasonable.**

Counting the diagonals after they have all been drawn is not an easy task. To check your results, you may want to try a different approach.

Start with figures with fewer sides and see whether there is a pattern to the total numbers of diagonals as you increase the number of sides.

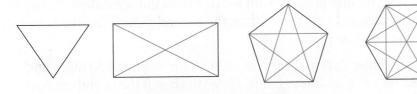

Figure	Number of Sides	Number of Diagonals
Triangle	3	0
Quadrilateral	4	2
Pentagon	5	5
Hexagon	6	9

Notice that the total number of diagonals increases as you increase the number of sides of the polygon. First the number increases by 2, then by 3, and then by 4. Continue this pattern to check your results.

✓ Quick Check

5. How many diagonals does a decagon have?

For more exercises, see *Extra Skills and Word Problem Practice.*

 Practice by Example

Example 1
(page 454)

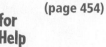 **for Help**

Solve by drawing a diagram.

1. A furniture delivery truck leaves the store at 8 A.M. It travels 6 miles east, then 4 miles south, then 2 miles west, and then 4 miles north. At the end of this route, how far is the truck from the store?

2. Bill is older than Jim and younger than Jose. Jose is older than Chris and younger than Tandala. Chris is older than Jim. Bill is younger than Tandala. Chris is older than Bill. Who is youngest?

3. **Geometry** How many triangles can you form in a hexagon if you draw all of the diagonals from only one vertex?

4. Eight soccer teams are to play each other two times in a season. How many games will be played?

5. There are 25 students in a math class. Ten students are in the math club. Twelve students are in the band. Five students are in both. How many students in the math class are members of neither club?

 Apply Your Skills

Solve using any strategy.

6. **Geometry** Snoozles are always born as twins, and each snoozle always moves in the opposite direction from its twin. Twin snoozles are at the origin of a coordinate plane. One follows the path $(0, 0)$ to $(1, 3)$ to $(2, 2)$ to $(4, 7)$. What path will its twin travel?

7. **Measurement** Maureen cut a 20-cm ribbon into exactly three pieces. The first piece is 3 cm shorter than the second piece. The third piece is 4 cm shorter than the second piece. Find the length of the shortest piece.

8. **Rental Rate** A rental car costs $34.95 for the first 150 miles and $.35 for each additional mile. How much will the rental car cost for driving 275 miles?

9. A student was standing in the middle of a line. Twenty-three students were ahead of her. How many students were in the line?

10. **Writing in Math** Suppose you want to find the thickness of one sheet of paper. Describe the problem solving method you would use.

11. Shana has three pets, a dog, a cat, and a bird. One of them is named Sammy. Noodles is younger than both the bird and the dog. Fluffy is green. Which pet has the name Sammy?

12. **Geometry** You can draw one segment to connect two points and three distinct segments to connect three named points. How many segments can you draw to connect five points if no three of the points lie on the same line?

STRATEGIES

- Act It Out
- Draw a Diagram
- Try, Test, Revise
- Look for a Pattern
- Make a Model
- Make a Table
- Simulate the Problem
- Solve by Graphing
- Use Multiple Strategies
- Work a Simpler Problem
- Work Backward
- Write an Equation
- Write a Proportion

 **Homework Video Tutor**

Visit: PHSchool.com
Web Code: bje-0904

13. Two friends rented a canoe for 10 days. One friend used the canoe for 6 days. The other friend used the canoe for 4 days. How much of the $150 rental fee should each friend pay?

C Challenge

14. Container A has twice the capacity of container B. Container A is full of sand and container B is empty. Suppose $\frac{1}{8}$ of the sand in container A is poured into container B. What fractional part of container B will contain sand?

15. Points P, Q, R, and S appear in that order on a line. The ratio $PQ : QR$ is 3 : 4, and the ratio $QR : RS$ is 2 : 5. The length PQ is 6 in. Find the length PS.

Multiple Choice Practice and Mixed Review

For Standards Tutorials, visit PHSchool.com. Web Code: bjq-9045

16. Which of the following is a diagonal of rectangle $ABCD$?

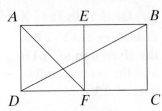

   Ⓐ $\overline{AB}$ Ⓒ $\overline{EF}$

   Ⓑ $\overline{AF}$ Ⓓ $\overline{DB}$

17. Notebooks cost $4 each. Which graph shows the relationship between the number of notebooks purchased and the total cost?

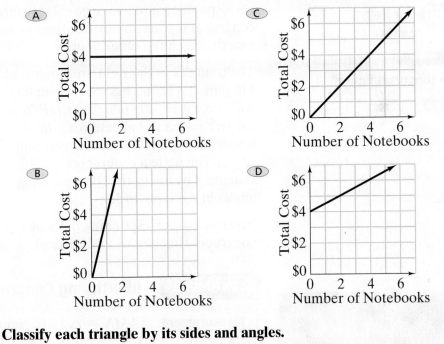

GO for Help   Lesson 9-3

Classify each triangle by its sides and angles.

18. no congruent sides and one right angle

19. three congruent sides

Lesson 6-4

Write each decimal as a fraction in simplest form and as a percent.

20. 0.14   **21.** 4.5   **22.** 0.11   **23.** 0.02   **24.** 0.125   **25.** 1

9-5 Congruence

Introduce, Develop Demonstrate an understanding of conditions that indicate two geometrical figures are congruent and what congruence means about the relationships between the sides and angles of the two figures.

What You'll Learn

• To identify corresponding parts of congruent triangles

• To determine whether triangles are congruent

. . . And Why

To use congruent figures for finding distance

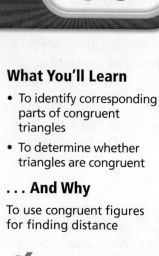

✓ Check Skills You'll Need

$\triangle ABC \sim \triangle XYZ$. For the given part of $\triangle ABC$, find the corresponding part of $\triangle XYZ$.

1. $\angle A$ 2. $\angle C$

3. $\overline{AB}$ 4. $\overline{CA}$

GO for Help

Lesson 6-3

🔊 New Vocabulary

• congruent figures

Identifying Corresponding Parts

Standards Investigation
Exploring Congruence

1. Have each member of your group cut plastic straws 3 cm, 6 cm, and 7 cm long. String an 18-cm string through the three straws. Tie the string just tight enough to form a strong triangle without bending any straws.

2. Hold the triangles up to one another to compare. Are they the same size and shape? Describe how the angle measures compare.

Congruent figures have the same size and shape, and their corresponding parts have equal measures. Two figures are congruent if you can flip, turn, and/or slide one figure to make it exactly match the other figure.

The triangles at the right are congruent. Flipping $\triangle ABC$ across the dashed line will make it exactly match $\triangle EDF$. You use tick marks to indicate congruent segments, and arcs to mark congruent angles. You write a congruence statement by listing the corresponding angles in the same order.

You can use corresponding parts of congruent triangles to find distance.

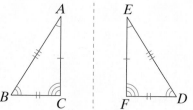

$\triangle ABC \cong \triangle EDF$

$\angle A \cong \angle E$	$\overline{AB} \cong \overline{ED}$
$\angle B \cong \angle D$	$\overline{BC} \cong \overline{DF}$
$\angle C \cong \angle F$	$\overline{AC} \cong \overline{EF}$

1 EXAMPLE   Identifying Congruent Parts

Measurement $\triangle AMN \cong \triangle ABC$. Name the corresponding parts.

a. **congruent angles**

$\angle M \cong \angle B$, $\angle N \cong \angle C$, $\angle MAN \cong \angle BAC$

b. **congruent sides**

$\overline{MN} \cong \overline{BC}$, $\overline{NA} \cong \overline{CA}$, $\overline{MA} \cong \overline{BA}$

c. **Find the distance from M to N.**

Since $\overline{MN} \cong \overline{BC}$ and $BC = 100$ yd, $MN = 100$ yd.

1. △*ABC* ≅ △*DEC*. List all pairs of congruent corresponding sides and angles. Then find *AC*.

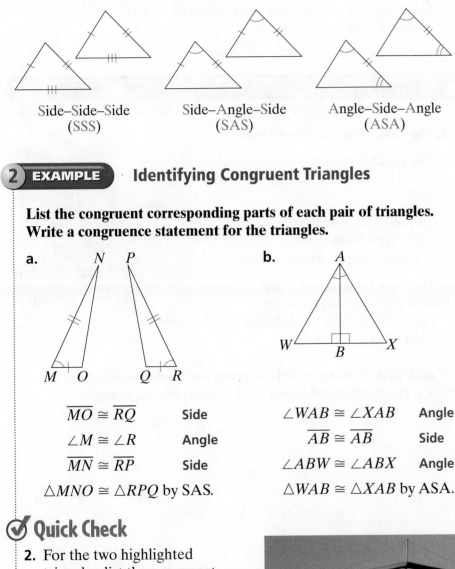

Identifying Congruent Triangles

You use corresponding parts of triangles to identify congruent triangles. Below are three of the ways to show that two triangles are congruent.

Side–Side–Side
(SSS)

Side–Angle–Side
(SAS)

Angle–Side–Angle
(ASA)

2 EXAMPLE **Identifying Congruent Triangles**

List the congruent corresponding parts of each pair of triangles. Write a congruence statement for the triangles.

a.

b.

$\overline{MO} \cong \overline{RQ}$ **Side**

∠*M* ≅ ∠*R*   **Angle**

$\overline{MN} \cong \overline{RP}$ **Side**

△*MNO* ≅ △*RPQ* by SAS.

∠*WAB* ≅ ∠*XAB*   **Angle**

$\overline{AB} \cong \overline{AB}$ **Side**

∠*ABW* ≅ ∠*ABX*   **Angle**

△*WAB* ≅ △*XAB* by ASA.

GO ●**nline**

Video Tutor Help

Visit: PHSchool.com
Web Code: bje-0775

✓ **Quick Check**

2. For the two highlighted triangles, list the congruent corresponding parts. Write a congruence statement (and reason) for the triangles.

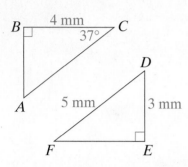

In the figure at the left, $\triangle ABC \cong \triangle DEF$. Use the figure for Exercises 1–13

1. $\angle A \cong$ ■

2. $\angle B \cong$ ■

3. $m\angle C =$ ■

4. $m\angle B =$ ■

5. $m\angle A =$ ■

6. $\overline{AC} \cong$ ■

7. $\overline{EF} \cong$ ■

8. $\overline{BA} \cong$ ■

9. $AC =$ ■

10. $FE =$ ■

11. $\triangle CBA \cong$ ■

12. $\triangle BAC \cong$ ■

13. Describe how you can flip, turn, and slide $\triangle ABC$ to make it exactly match $\triangle DEF$.

Standards Practice

For more exercises, see Extra Skills and Word Problem Practice.

(A) Practice by Example

Example 1
(page 458)

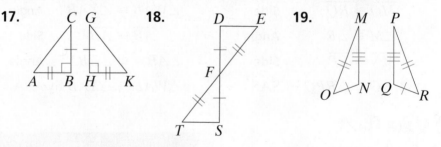

Use the design for Exercises 14–16.

14. The green triangles are congruent. Name the corresponding congruent angles.

15. The red-and-blue triangles are congruent. Name the corresponding congruent sides.

16. The dark blue triangles are isosceles and congruent, and $GD = 10$ in. Find the distance from G to I.

Example 2
(page 459)

For each pair of triangles, list the congruent corresponding parts. Write a congruence statement (and reason) for the triangles.

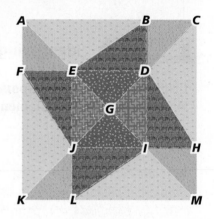

17.

18.

19.

(B) Apply Your Skills

Assume that $\triangle ABC \cong \triangle XYZ$. Answer the following.

20. Name the corresponding congruent angles.

Homework Video Tutor

Visit: PHSchool.com
Web Code: bje-0905

21. Name the corresponding congruent sides.

22. **Writing in Math** $\triangle ABC \cong \triangle XYZ$. What can you conclude about the perimeters of the triangles? Explain.

GO for Help

For a guide to reading the diagram in Exercise 23, see page 463.

For each pair of triangles, list the congruent corresponding parts. Write a congruence statement (and reason) for the triangles.

23.

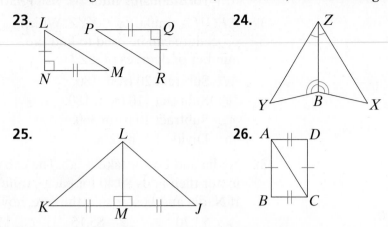

24.

25.

26.

Error Analysis The two figures in the diagram (left) are congruent. State whether each congruence statement is correct and explain.

27. $RAVK \cong NLUC$

28. $RKVA \cong ULNC$

29. $ARKV \cong CULN$

30. $\overline{NL} \cong \overline{KV}$

31. $\angle V \cong \angle C$

32. $\angle VAR \cong \angle LUC$

33. The end of the shipping container at the left is a rectangle. The diagonals are congruent and intersect at point H. $\overline{HB} \cong \overline{HD}$ and $\overline{AH} \cong \overline{CH}$. Which triangle is congruent to the given triangle? Explain.

    a. $\triangle ABH$ **b.** $\triangle ADC$

Explain why the triangles in each pair are congruent. Then find the missing measures in each diagram.

34.   **35.**

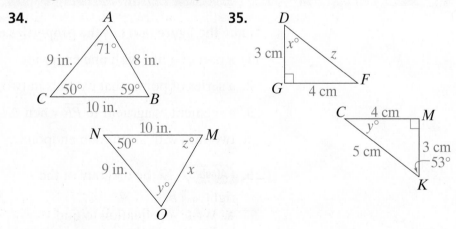

C Challenge

36. Reasoning $\triangle KWR$ is *equiangular* (all angles are congruent). $\triangle ABJ$ is also equiangular. Can you use **A**ngle-**A**ngle-**A**ngle (**AAA**) to show that two triangles are congruent? Use diagrams to justify your conclusion.

For Standards Tutorials, visit PHSchool.com. Web Code: bjq-9045

37. △*FGH* is similar to △*XYZ*. Which procedure can be used to find the number of degrees in ∠*Z*?

  Ⓐ Subtract 20 from 180.

  Ⓑ Subtract 110 from 180.

  Ⓒ Subtract 20 from 360.

  Ⓓ Divide 110 by 2.

38. Nadia and Foster take a cab. The cab meter starts at \$1.50. The meter then adds \$0.40 for each $\frac{1}{4}$ mile traveled. The trip is $5\frac{1}{2}$ mi. If Nadia and Foster split the fare, how much do they each pay?

  Ⓐ \$3.70 Ⓑ \$5.15 Ⓒ \$10.30 Ⓓ \$13.20

Lesson 9-4

39. Students are evenly spaced as they sit around a round table. The fourth student is directly across from the eleventh student. How many students are seated at the table?

Lesson 6-6 [Algebra] **Write and solve an equation.**

40. What percent of 50 is 20?

41. 15% of what number is 12?

42. Find 125% of 200.

Lesson 5-1 **Order from least to greatest.**

43. $\frac{1}{2}, \frac{5}{6}, \frac{3}{8}, \frac{2}{3}$ **44.** $\frac{3}{8}, \frac{2}{3}, \frac{3}{4}, \frac{4}{5}$ **45.** $\frac{1}{6}, \frac{1}{5}, \frac{1}{7}, \frac{1}{4}$

✓ Checkpoint Quiz 1

Name the figure that has the properties described.

1. a part of a line with one endpoint

2. a series of points that extends in two directions without end

3. a segment congruent to $\overline{PR}$ when △*LMN* ≅ △*PQR*

4. two rays with a common endpoint

5. [Algebra] In the diagram at the right, $a \parallel b$.

  a. Write an equation to find x.

  b. Find $m\angle TAV$.

  c. Find $m\angle TAN$.

  d. Find $m\angle DNK$.

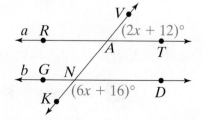

6. **Open-Ended** Draw a triangle that is scalene and has a right angle.

> **Develop** Demonstrate an understanding of what congruence means about the relationships between the sides and angles of two figures.
> **Develop** Note the method of deriving the solution.

Understanding Math Problems Read the problem below. Then let Shelley's thinking guide you through reading the diagram. Check your understanding with the exercises at the bottom of the page.

List the congruent corresponding parts of the triangles. Write a congruence statement (and reason) for the triangles.

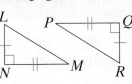

What Shelley Asks

What does the diagram show?

What congruent parts do I know?

What are the corresponding points?

Can I write a congruence statement?

Do I have SSS, SAS, or ASA?

Do I have SAS?

I must write the congruence statement (and reason).

What Shelley Thinks and Writes

Two triangles
The little squares show right angles.
The tick marks show congruent sides.

The single ticks show $\overline{LN} \cong \overline{RQ}$.
The double ticks show $\overline{NM} \cong \overline{QP}$.
I also know right angles are congruent.
I'll write:

$$\overline{LN} \cong \overline{RQ}$$
$$\overline{NM} \cong \overline{QP}$$
$$\angle N \cong \angle Q$$

Points L, N, M correspond to R, Q, and P.

I can write a congruence statement if I have SSS, SAS, or ASA.

I have congruence for two sides and an angle. SAS is the only possibility.

The angles have to be between the sides. They are! I have SAS.

I'll write:

$$\triangle LNM \cong \triangle RQP \text{ by SAS}$$

EXERCISES

Write a congruence statement (and reason) for the triangles.

1.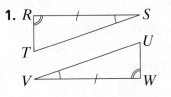

2.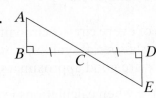

3.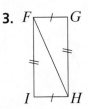

Circles

Develop Use formulas routinely for finding perimeter of basic geometric figures.
Develop Identify and construct basic elements of geometric figures.

✓ Check Skills You'll Need

Solve each proportion. Round to the nearest whole number where necessary.

1. $\frac{10}{100} = \frac{x}{360}$

2. $\frac{75}{100} = \frac{x}{360}$

3. $\frac{0.8}{5.3} = \frac{x}{360}$

4. $\frac{1.6}{5.3} = \frac{x}{360}$

GO for Help
Lesson 6-2

Finding Circumference

Standards Investigation
Exploring Pi

1. Work in groups. Each member of your group should have a ruler, string, and several circular objects, such as jar lids. Make a chart similar to the chart below. Record your results.

Object	Diameter	Circumference	Ratio $\frac{Circumference}{Diameter}$
▪	▪	▪	▪
▪	▪	▪	▪

2. Measure the diameter of each circle to the nearest millimeter.

3. Find the circumference of each circle by wrapping a string around the outside of the circle. Then straighten the string and measure its length to the nearest millimeter.

4. Calculate the ratio $\frac{circumference}{diameter}$ to the nearest tenth.

5. Make a conjecture about the relationship between the circumference of a circle and its diameter.

A **circle** is the set of all points in a plane that are the same distance from a given point, called the *center* of the circle.

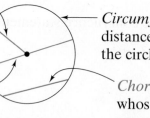

Radius is a segment that has one endpoint at the center and the other point on the circle.

Circumference is the distance around the circle.

Diameter is a chord that passes through the center of a circle.

Chord is a segment whose endpoints are on the circle.

The ratio of every circle's circumference C to its diameter d is the same. It has a special symbol, π, which is pronounced "pie." Both 3.14 and $\frac{22}{7}$ are good approximations for this ratio.

Use $\frac{22}{7}$ for π when calculations involve fractions, and use 3.14 when they do not.

If you multiply both sides of the equation $\frac{C}{d} = \pi$ by d, you get $C = \pi d$, which is a formula for the circumference of a circle.

Vocabulary Tip

The symbol π is a letter from the Greek alphabet. Leonhard Euler, an 18th-century Swiss mathematician, popularized the use of the symbol to represent the ratio of a circle's circumference to its diameter.

Take Note ✏️   Circumference of a Circle

The circumference of a circle is π times the diameter.

$$C = \pi d \qquad C = 2\pi r$$

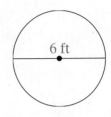

---

1 EXAMPLE   Finding Circumference

Find the circumference of the circle at the right.

$C = \pi d$ **Write the formula.**

$C = \pi(6)$ **Replace d with 6.**

≈ 18.84 **Use 3.14 for π.**

6 ft

The circumference of the circle is about 18.84 ft.

✅ Quick Check

1. Find the circumference of each circle.

   a. diameter $= 2\frac{4}{5}$ in.   **b.** radius $= 30$ mm   **c.** diameter $= 200$ mi

---

Making Circle Graphs

To make a circle graph, you find the measure of each *central angle*. A **central angle** is an angle whose vertex is the center of a circle. There are $360°$ in a circle.

2 EXAMPLE   Making a Circle Graph

Make a circle graph for Juan's weekly budget shown at the right.

Use proportions to find the measures of the central angles.

Juan's Weekly Budget	
Recreation (r)	20%
Lunch (ℓ)	25%
Clothes (c)	15%
Savings (s)	40%

$\dfrac{20}{100} = \dfrac{r}{360}$ $\dfrac{25}{100} = \dfrac{\ell}{360}$ $\dfrac{15}{100} = \dfrac{c}{360}$ $\dfrac{40}{100} = \dfrac{s}{360}$

   $r = 72°$ $\ell = 90°$ $c = 54°$ $s = 144°$

- Use a compass to draw a circle.
- Draw the central angles with a protractor.
- Label each section.
- Add a title and necessary information.

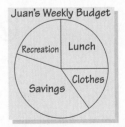

✅ Quick Check

2. Make a circle graph for the data. Round the measure of each central angle to the nearest degree.

Blood Types of Population

Type A	Type B	Type AB	Type O
40%	12%	5%	43%

3 **EXAMPLE**   **Reading a Circle Graph**

Quick Tip

When you use data to make a circle graph, your proportions will involve the total of the data, not 100. 0.3 + 0.4 + 1.3 + 1.8 = 3.8, so your proportions will compare 3.8 million visits to 360°.

Multiple Choice **Which circle graph best represents the data below?**

Visits to Kentucky's National Recreation Areas

Site	Visits (millions)
Abraham Lincoln's Birthplace	0.3
Big South Fork	0.4
Cumberland Gap	1.3
Mammoth Caves	1.8

Mammoth Caves have the most visits, so that section of the graph should be the largest. You can eliminate choices A and C. Abraham Lincoln's birthplace receives the fewest visits, so that section of the graph should be the smallest. You can eliminate choice D. The answer is B.

✅ Quick Check

3. Students at Western High School work in the following places: restaurants, 140; library, 15; auto shop, 60; retail stores, 75; and other places, 30. Draw a circle graph to show where students at Western High School work. Round the measures of the central angles to the nearest degree.

Refer to the circle graph and the information below for Exercises 1–4.

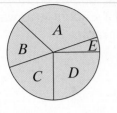

Nancy spends a third of her salary on rent, 20% on utilities, a fourth on food, 5% on transportation, and she saves a sixth.

1. About what percent of the circle graph does section D represent?

2. Which of Nancy's expenses could be represented by section D?

3. Which section of the circle graph can represent Nancy's rent?

4. **Writing in Math** You need to determine if Nancy spends more money on utilities or on savings. Will you refer to the problem or the circle graph to find information? Explain.

Standards Practice

For more exercises, see Extra Skills and Word Problem Practice.

A Practice by Example

Example 1 (page 465)

GO for Help

Find the circumference of each circle.

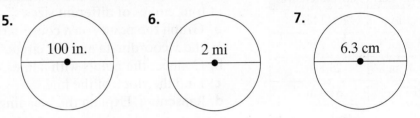

5. 100 in.   6. 2 mi   7. 6.3 cm

Find the circumference of each circle with the given radius or diameter.

8. radius = 3.5 cm   9. radius = $4\frac{2}{3}$ ft   10. diameter = 0.1 m

11. radius = 18 in.   12. radius = 90 ft   13. diameter = $\frac{1}{2}$ yd

Examples 2 and 3 (pages 465 and 466)

Find the measures of the central angles that you would draw to represent each percent in a circle graph. Round to the nearest degree.

14. 35%   15. 50%   16. 30%   17. 1%   18. 25%   19. 75%

20. Make a circle graph for the data.

What College Students Earn

Monthly Income from Jobs	No job	Less than $200	$200 to $399	$400 or over
Percent of Total Number of Students	33%	14%	25%	28%

B Apply Your Skills

21. The data below show how a group of students travel to school each day. Make a circle graph for the data.

How Students Travel to School

Transportation	Walk	Bicycle	Bus	Car	Other
Number of Students	55	80	110	40	15

22. In a recent survey, families were asked how they spend extra income. Twenty-two families said they went to the movies, 34 said they eat out, 83 went on vacations, and the remaining 75 put it into savings. Make a circle graph for the data.

23. **Writing in Math** Write a paragraph to a student who was not in class describing how to make a circle graph.

24. A *tangent* to a circle is a line, segment, or ray in the same plane as the circle and which intersects the circle in exactly one point. A *secant* is a line, segment, or ray that intersects a circle in two points. Use the diagram to identify the following.

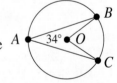

   a. one diameter   **b.** four radii
   c. two secants   **d.** three chords
   e. two tangents

Diameter	Circumference
1 in.	3.14 in.
5 in.	15.7 in.
8 in.	25.1 in.
10 in.	31.4 in.

25. The data at the left represent the circumference and the diameter of four circles of different sizes.
   a. Graph the points on a coordinate plane. Use the diameter as the x-coordinate and the circumference as the y-coordinate.
   b. Connect the points with a line.
   c. Find the slope of the line.
   d. **Reasoning** Explain the meaning of slope in this situation.

C **Challenge**

26. An *inscribed angle* is an angle with sides that are chords and its vertex on the circle. The measure of an inscribed angle is half the measure of the central angle with the same endpoint. Find $m\angle A$.

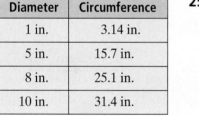

Multiple Choice Practice and Mixed Review

For Standards Tutorials, visit PHSchool.com. Web Code: bjq-9045

27. To the nearest degree, what is the measure of the central angle that represents 46% in a circle graph?
   Ⓐ 46°   Ⓑ 83°   Ⓒ 166°   Ⓓ 314°

28. What is the circumference of a circle with a radius of 2.5 cm?
   Ⓐ 1.25π cm   Ⓒ 5π cm
   Ⓑ 2.5π cm   Ⓓ 6.25π cm

29. What is the circumference of a circle with a diameter of 8 in.?
   Ⓐ 4π in.   Ⓒ 16π in.
   Ⓑ 8π in.   Ⓓ 64π in.

GO **for Help**   Lesson 6-2

30. **Rates** While exercising, your heart beats 32 times in 15 s. At this rate, how many times will it beat in 2 min?

Parts of a Circle

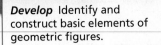

Develop Identify and construct basic elements of geometric figures.

An **arc** is part of a circle. An arc that is formed by half of a circle is called a **semicircle**. An arc that is shorter than a semicircle is a **minor arc**. An arc that is longer than a semicircle is a **major arc**.

Minor arcs are named with two letters. Semicircles and major arcs are named with three letters. In the circle at the right, $\overset{\frown}{AN}$ is a minor arc, $\overset{\frown}{MNV}$ is a semicircle, and $\overset{\frown}{AVM}$ is a major arc.

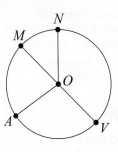

A central angle intersects a circle at two points to form a minor arc. $\angle AOM$ intersects circle O at points A and M. You say $\angle AOM$ *intercepts* $\overset{\frown}{AM}$. You can also say that $\overset{\frown}{AM}$ is *intercepted by* $\angle AOM$.

ACTIVITY

An organization drew the diagram below to plan the clean up of an oil spill that occurred at point O. The area inside circle O is affected. Points A and B represent lighthouses. Points X, Y, and Z represent ships.

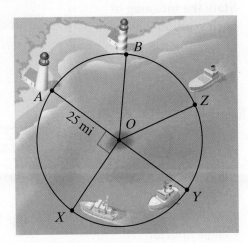

1. A ship leaves from lighthouse B and sails directly to point O. What kind of segment does its path form?

2. How far does the ship travel?

Ships X and Y are not equipped to travel through the oil spill. They travel the perimeter of the affected area.

3. Name the minor arc from ship X to lighthouse A. Name the major arc from ship X to lighthouse A.

4. What fraction of the circle's circumference does the length of the minor arc represent?

5. How far does ship X travel if it travels the path determined by the minor arc to lighthouse A? Round to nearest mile.

6. Ship Y can also travel one of two paths to lighthouse A. Name the two arcs. What type of arc does each path represent?

7. To the nearest mile, how far will ship Y travel to lighthouse A? Does this distance depend on which path ship Y travels? Explain.

The measure of an intercepted arc is equal to the measure of the central angle that intercepts it. For example, the measure of $\overset{\frown}{ZY}$ is equal to the measure of $\angle ZOY$.

8. What is the measure of $\overset{\frown}{XA}$?

9. The measure of $\angle YOB$ is 120°. What is the measure of $\overset{\frown}{AB}$?

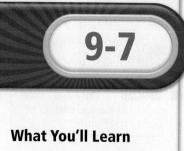

9-7 Constructions

Develop Identify and construct basic elements of geometric figures (e.g., midpoints, angle bisectors, and perpendicular bisectors) using a compass and straightedge.

What You'll Learn

- To construct a segment or an angle congruent to a given segment or angle
- To construct segment bisectors and angle bisectors

. . . And Why

To construct precise drawings such as those that architects use

✓ Check Skills You'll Need

State the meaning of each symbol.

1. B 2. $\overline{AB}$

3. $\overrightarrow{AB}$ 4. $\overleftrightarrow{AB}$

GO for Help

Lesson 9-1

◀)) New Vocabulary

- perpendicular lines
- segment bisector
- perpendicular bisector
- angle bisector

Congruent Segments and Angles

In constructions, you use only a *compass* and *straightedge* (an unmarked ruler) to accurately copy a segment or an angle, or draw an accurate bisector. A compass is a tool used to draw circles or parts of circles. An *arc* is part of a circle.

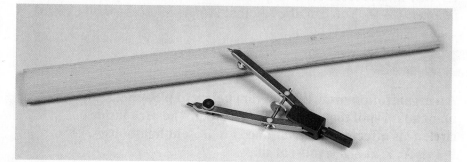

1 EXAMPLE   Constructing a Congruent Segment

Construct a segment congruent to $\overline{AB}$.

Step 1 Draw a ray with endpoint C.

Step 2 Open the compass to the length of $\overline{AB}$.

Step 3 With the *same* compass setting, put the compass tip on C. Draw an arc that intersects the ray. Label the intersection D.

$$\overline{CD} \cong \overline{AB}$$

✓ Quick Check

1. Draw a segment. Construct a segment twice the length of the segment you drew.

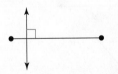

2 EXAMPLE Constructing a Congruent Angle

Construct an angle congruent to ∠E.

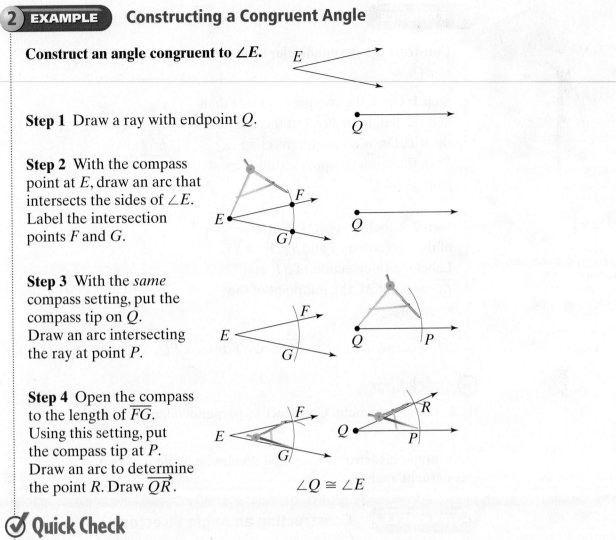

Step 1 Draw a ray with endpoint Q.

Step 2 With the compass point at E, draw an arc that intersects the sides of ∠E. Label the intersection points F and G.

Step 3 With the *same* compass setting, put the compass tip on Q. Draw an arc intersecting the ray at point P.

Step 4 Open the compass to the length of $\overline{FG}$. Using this setting, put the compass tip at P. Draw an arc to determine the point R. Draw $\overrightarrow{QR}$.

∠Q ≅ ∠E

✓ Quick Check

2. Draw an obtuse angle. Construct an angle congruent to the angle you drew.

Constructing Bisectors

The figures below show some special relationships intersecting lines may have.

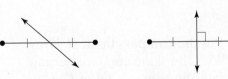

Perpendicular lines, segments, or rays intersect to form right angles.

A **segment bisector** is a line, segment, or ray that divides a segment into two congruent segments.

A **perpendicular bisector** is a line, segment, or ray that is perpendicular to the segment it bisects. The segment's *midpoint* is where the bisector intersects it.

Vocabulary Tip

To <u>bisect</u> means to divide into two equal parts. Therefore, a bisector divides a segment or angle into two congruent parts.

One way to hold a compass is shown above.

3 EXAMPLE **Constructing a Perpendicular Bisector**

Construct the perpendicular bisector of $\overline{PQ}$.

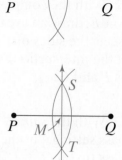

Step 1 Open the compass to more than half the length of $\overline{PQ}$. Put the compass tip at P. Draw an arc intersecting $\overline{PQ}$. With the same compass setting, repeat from point Q.

Step 2 Label the points of intersection of the two arcs as S and T. Draw $\overleftrightarrow{ST}$. Label the intersection of $\overleftrightarrow{ST}$ and $\overline{PQ}$ as point M, the midpoint of the segment.

$\overleftrightarrow{ST}$ is perpendicular to $\overline{PQ}$ and $\overleftrightarrow{ST}$ bisects $\overline{PQ}$.

✓ Quick Check

3. Draw a segment. Construct its perpendicular bisector.

An **angle bisector** is a ray that divides an angle into two congruent angles.

4 EXAMPLE **Constructing an Angle Bisector**

Construct the bisector of $\angle A$.

Step 1 Put the compass tip at A. Draw an arc that intersects the sides of $\angle A$. Label the points of intersection B and C.

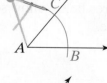

Step 2 Put the compass tip at B. Draw an arc. With the same compass setting, repeat with the compass tip at C. Make sure the arcs intersect. Label the intersection of the arcs D. Draw $\overrightarrow{AD}$.

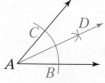

$\overrightarrow{AD}$ bisects $\angle BAC$.

✓ Quick Check

4. Draw an obtuse angle. Construct its angle bisector.

Choose the term that *best* matches each description.

1. bisects a segment
2. form a 90° angle
3. bisects a segment and forms a 90° angle

A. bisector
B. perpendicular bisector
C. perpendicular segments

4. Suppose you want to construct an angle congruent to an angle that measures 72.6°. Would you use a protractor or a compass and straightedge? Explain your choice.

5. **Reasoning** Do you need to know the length of a segment to construct a congruent segment? Explain.

Standards Practice

For more exercises, see *Extra Skills and Word Problem Practice*.

Ⓐ **Practice by Example**

For Exercises 6–10, draw a diagram similar to one that is given. Then construct each figure.

Example 1
(page 470)

GO for Help

6. $\overline{EF}$ congruent to $\overline{XY}$

7. $\overline{GH}$ twice the length of $\overline{XY}$

Example 2
(page 471)

8. $\angle D$ congruent to $\angle A$

9. $\angle Y$ congruent to $\angle X$

Example 3
(page 472)

10. the perpendicular bisector of $\overline{CD}$

11. Draw $\overline{DE}$ at least 4 in. long. Then construct its perpendicular bisector.

Example 4
(page 472)

For Exercises 12 and 13, first draw diagrams similar to ones shown.

12. Construct the bisector of $\angle J$.

13. Construct the bisector of $\angle K$.

Ⓑ **Apply Your Skills**

14. Use a protractor to draw a right angle. Construct its angle bisector.

For Exercises 15–17, draw a figure similar to the one that is given. Then construct each figure.

15. $\overline{MN}$ three times the length of $\overline{CD}$

16. $\overline{PQ}$ 1.5 times the length of $\overline{CD}$

17. $\triangle ABF$ with two angles congruent to $\angle X$

18. Draw an angle and label it $\angle A$. Then construct $\angle I$ so that $m\angle I = 2m\angle A$.

19. Construct a 90° angle.

20. **Writing in Math** How are constructing a segment bisector and constructing an angle bisector alike?

21. The bisector of $\angle XYZ$ is $\overrightarrow{YN}$. If the measure of $\angle XYN$ is 55°, what is the measure of $\angle XYZ$?

22. **a.** Draw a point and a line. Construct the perpendicular segment from the point to the line. (*Hint:* Place your compass tip at the point. Open your compass far enough to draw an arc that intersects the line in two points. Construct the perpendicular bisector of the segment between the two points.)

   b. An *altitude* of a triangle is a perpendicular segment from a vertex to a line containing the side opposite the vertex. Draw a large acute triangle. Construct its three altitudes.

C Challenge

23. Draw $\triangle PQR$. To construct $\triangle ABC$ congruent to $\triangle PQR$, first construct $\overline{AB}$ congruent to $\overline{PQ}$. Use a compass setting the length of $\overline{PR}$. Draw an arc with the compass tip at A. Then use a compass setting the length of $\overline{QR}$. With the compass tip at B draw an arc that intersects the first arc. Label the intersection C. Draw $\overline{AC}$ and $\overline{BC}$.

Multiple Choice Practice and Mixed Review

For Standards Tutorials, visit PHSchool.com. Web Code: bjq-9045

24. The table shows the results of a student survey about favorite classes. Which circle graph best represents the data?

Preferred Classes of Students

Class	Science	Math	Social Studies	Other
Percent	15	7	45	33

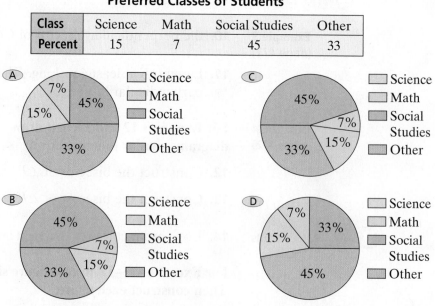

25. Find the measure of the central angle that would represent 12% in a circle graph. Round your answer to the nearest degree.

Prefixes and Common Meanings

Earlier in this book, you made index cards to learn new words and symbols. Here are two more strategies for learning new vocabulary.

Strategy 1 Break words apart into prefixes and roots. Then combine the meaning of the two parts.

Sample: *Bisector* has the prefix *bi* and the root *sector*.

Bi means "two" and sector means "section." So bisector means "two sections."

Here are some common prefixes and roots that you have used in this chapter.

deca (ten)	*dia* (through)	*equi* (equal)
gon (angle)	*hexa* (six)	*octa* (eight)
para (beside)	*penta* (five)	*poly* (many)
quadri (four)	*tri* (three)	

Strategy 2 Think about common meanings of words.

Sample: An acute pain is a sharp pain, and an acute angle makes a sharp point.

Connecting the word *acute* with the word *sharp* will help you remember that an acute angle measures less than 90°.

EXERCISES

Use a dictionary. Break each word into a prefix and a root. Then combine the meanings. Does the meaning you wrote make sense given the definition of the word? Explain.

1. hexagon
2. parallel
3. decagon
4. polygon
5. triangle
6. diagonal

Tell how the common word can help you remember the mathematical term.

7. interior (of your school); interior angles
8. (stand up) straight; straight angle

Tell how the words are related.

9. diagonal; diameter
10. vertex; vertical

Translations

Develop Use coordinate graphs to plot simple figures and determine their image under translations.

Develop Demonstrate an understanding of conditions that indicate two geometrical figures are congruent.

What You'll Learn

- To graph translations
- To describe translations

... And Why

To use translations in describing real-world situations, such as moves in a chess game

✓ Check Skills You'll Need

Graph each point.

1. $A(-4, 3)$ **2.** $B(0, 2)$

3. $C(1, 4)$ **4.** $D(4, -2)$

5. $E(-2, -3)$

GO for Help
Lesson 1-10

◀)) New Vocabulary

- transformation
- translation
- image

Graphing Translations

You can move pattern blocks by sliding them, flipping them, or turning them. Each of these moves is a type of transformation. A **transformation** is a change of position or size of a figure.

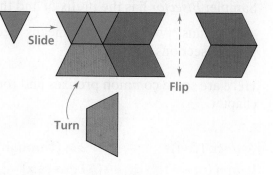

A **translation** is a transformation that moves points the same distance and in the same direction. A figure and its translated image are congruent. You can see examples of translations or slides in wallpaper, fabric, and wrapping paper.

The figure you get after a transformation is called the **image.** To name the image of a point, you use *prime* notation. The figure at the right shows the translation of A to its image A'.

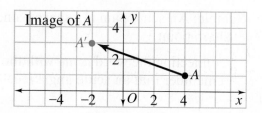

1 EXAMPLE Translating a Figure

Graph the image of $\triangle KRT$ after a translation 5 units to the right and 3 units down.

$\triangle KRT \cong \triangle K'R'T'$ because translating $\triangle KRT$ along the red arrows makes the figures exactly match.

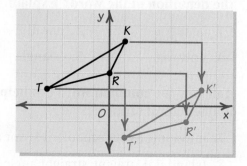

✓ Quick Check

1. On a coordinate plane, draw $\triangle KRT$. Graph the image of $\triangle KRT$ after each translation.

  a. 4 units to the left   **b.** 5 units down

Describing Translations

You can describe a transformation using arrow (→) notation, which describes the *mapping* of a figure onto its image.

2 EXAMPLE   Using Arrow Notation

The movement of point P is both horizontal and vertical. Use arrow notation to describe this translation.

The point moves from $P(-2, 2)$ to $P'(1, -1)$, so the translation is $P(-2, 2) \rightarrow P'(1, -1)$.

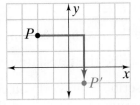

✓ Quick Check

2. Use arrow notation to describe a translation of $B(-1, 5)$ to $B'(3, 1)$.

You can also use arrow notation to write a general rule that describes a transformation. To write a rule for a translation, choose corresponding points on a figure and its image. Subtract the coordinates of the figure from the coordinates of its image.

3 EXAMPLE   Writing a Rule

Write a rule to describe the translation of △PQR to △P'Q'R'.

Use $P(3, 2)$ and its image $P'(-2, 5)$ to find the horizontal and vertical translations.

Horizontal translation: $-2 - 3 = -5$
Vertical translation: $5 - 2 = 3$

The rule is $(x, y) \rightarrow (x - 5, y + 3)$.

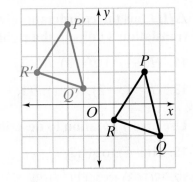

In chess, the move of a knight is a translation. The translation of piece A is $(x, y) \rightarrow (x + 1, y - 2)$.

✓ Quick Check

3. Write a rule to describe the translation of quadrilateral $ABCD$ to quadrilateral $A'B'C'D'$.

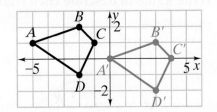

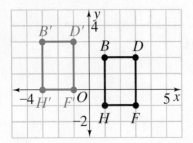

Use the diagram at the left for Exercises 1–5.

1. Compare the side lengths in *BDFH* to the side lengths in *B'D'F'H'*.

2. Compare the angle measures in *BDFH* to the angle measures in *B'D'F'H'*.

3. Are the two figures congruent? Explain how you know.

4. Describe the translation that maps *BDFH* onto *B'D'F'H'*.

5. Describe a method you could use to draw another figure congruent to *BDFH* on the same coordinate plane.

Standards Practice

For more exercises, see *Extra Skills and Word Problem Practice.*

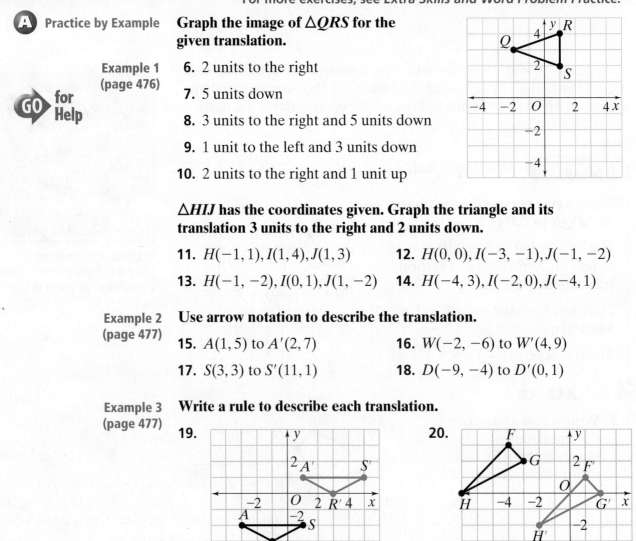

Ⓐ Practice by Example

Example 1
(page 476)

GO for Help

Graph the image of △*QRS* for the given translation.

6. 2 units to the right

7. 5 units down

8. 3 units to the right and 5 units down

9. 1 unit to the left and 3 units down

10. 2 units to the right and 1 unit up

△*HIJ* has the coordinates given. Graph the triangle and its translation 3 units to the right and 2 units down.

11. $H(-1, 1), I(1, 4), J(1, 3)$ 12. $H(0, 0), I(-3, -1), J(-1, -2)$

13. $H(-1, -2), I(0, 1), J(1, -2)$ 14. $H(-4, 3), I(-2, 0), J(-4, 1)$

Example 2
(page 477)

Use arrow notation to describe the translation.

15. $A(1, 5)$ to $A'(2, 7)$ 16. $W(-2, -6)$ to $W'(4, 9)$

17. $S(3, 3)$ to $S'(11, 1)$ 18. $D(-9, -4)$ to $D'(0, 1)$

Example 3
(page 477)

Write a rule to describe each translation.

19.

20.

Write a description of each rule.

21. $(x, y) \rightarrow (x - 11, y + 4)$ **22.** $(x, y) \rightarrow (x + 5, y - 2)$

23. $(x, y) \rightarrow (x - 6, y - 3)$ **24.** $(x, y) \rightarrow (x + 3, y + 9)$

B **Apply Your Skills**

Complete with *horizontal* or *vertical* to make a true statement.

25. In a __?__ translation, the *y*-coordinate changes and the *x*-coordinate stays the same.

26. In a __?__ translation, the *x*-coordinate changes and the *y*-coordinate stays the same.

The endpoints of a segment are given. Graph each segment and its image for the given translation.

27. $A(0, 0), B(0, 5)$; 2 units left   **28.** $C(0, 0), D(0, 1)$; 1 unit up

29. $E(0, 0), F(2, 0)$; 4 units down   **30.** $G(0, 0), H(-4, 0)$; 4 units up

31. $J(0, 0), K(5, 5)$; 1 unit right   **32.** $L(-1, 3), M(2, 1)$; 5 units left

Homework Video Tutor

Visit: PHSchool.com
Web Code: bje-0908

Write a rule to describe each translation.

33.

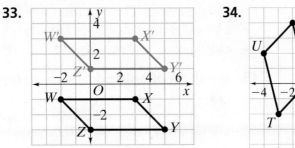

34.

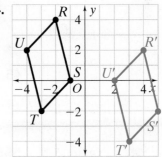

The endpoints of a segment are given. Graph each segment and its image for the given translation.

35. $N(3, 3), P(-3, 4)$;
3 units left, 2 units down

36. $Q(2, -1), R(-2, 1)$;
2 units right, 3 units up

37. $S(4, 3), T(1, -5)$;
4 units left, 1 unit up

38. $U(-4, -5), V(2, 1)$;
3 units right, 2 units down

39. Translate point $T(2, 5)$ 2 units to the right and 6 units up. Translate its image, point T', 4 units to the left and 1 unit down. What are the coordinates of the image of point T''?

40. **Writing in Math** Describe and explain the result of moving a figure *a* units horizontally and then $-a$ units horizontally.

41. You can use translations to draw three-dimensional figures. First draw a figure on graph paper. Translate the figure. Connect each vertex with its image. Use dashes for sides that are not visible. Try this, first with a rectangle; then with a triangle.

Challenge **42.** A rule like $(x, y) \rightarrow (2x, 2y)$ describes a dilation (see p. 300) of the coordinate plane. This dilation has center $(0, 0)$ and scale factor 2.
   a. $\overline{AB}$ has endpoints $A(4, 0)$ and $B(0, 3)$. Describe its image, $\overline{A'B'}$, for the dilation above. How do lengths AB and $A'B'$ compare?
   b. Describe a coordinate-plane dilation that has center $(0, 0)$ and scale factor $\frac{1}{2}$. Describe its effect on $\overline{AB}$ from part (a).

Multiple Choice Practice and Mixed Review

For Standards Tutorials, visit PHSchool.com. Web Code: bjq-9045

43. If rectangle *PRST* is translated 2 units to the right and 2 units down, what are the coordinates of point R'?

   Ⓐ $(-4, 1)$
   Ⓑ $(-4, -3)$
   Ⓒ $(-3, 0)$
   Ⓓ $(0, -3)$

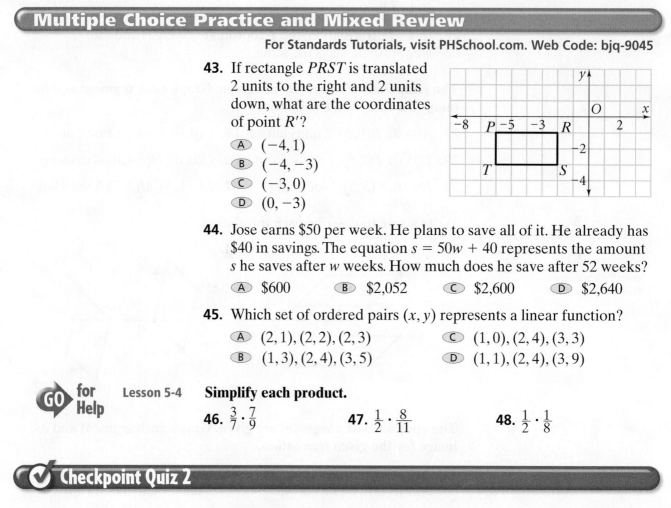

44. Jose earns $50 per week. He plans to save all of it. He already has $40 in savings. The equation $s = 50w + 40$ represents the amount s he saves after w weeks. How much does he save after 52 weeks?

   Ⓐ $600   Ⓑ $2,052   Ⓒ $2,600   Ⓓ $2,640

45. Which set of ordered pairs (x, y) represents a linear function?

   Ⓐ $(2, 1), (2, 2), (2, 3)$ Ⓒ $(1, 0), (2, 4), (3, 3)$
   Ⓑ $(1, 3), (2, 4), (3, 5)$ Ⓓ $(1, 1), (2, 4), (3, 9)$

GO for Help   Lesson 5-4

Simplify each product.

46. $\frac{3}{7} \cdot \frac{7}{9}$ **47.** $\frac{1}{2} \cdot \frac{8}{11}$ **48.** $\frac{1}{2} \cdot \frac{1}{8}$

✓ Checkpoint Quiz 2

Use the circle graph.

1. Eighty people attended a catered meal. Twenty-eight people ordered fish, half ordered chicken, and twelve ordered the vegetarian meal. Which section represents each of the meals?

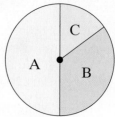

2. Determine the measure of the central angle of each section in the circle graph.

3. **Open-Ended** Draw a segment about $\frac{3}{4}$ in. long. Construct an equilateral triangle with sides of this length.

4. Graph $\overline{NR}$ with endpoints $N(2, 7)$ and $R(-4, 0)$. Then graph its image after a translation 4 units right and 3 units down.

Dilations in the Coordinate Plane

FOR USE WITH LESSON 9-8

Develop Construct drawings made to scale.

In Chapter 6, you used geometric software to make dilations of geometric figures. You can also dilate geometric figures in a coordinate plane.

ACTIVITY

Geometry $\triangle ABC$ has vertices $A(0, 0)$, $B(-1, 2)$, and $C(3, 3)$. Draw the triangle and its image under a dilation of scale factor 2 on the same coordinate plane.

Step 1 The scale factor is 2. Multiply the coordinates of each vertex by 2.

    $A(0, 0)$, so A' has coordinates $(0 \cdot 2, 0 \cdot 2)$, or $(0, 0)$.

    $B(-1, 2)$, so B' has coordinates $(-1 \cdot 2, 2 \cdot 2)$, or $(-2, 4)$.

    $C(3, 3)$, so C' has coordinates $(3 \cdot 2, 3 \cdot 2)$, or $(6, 6)$.

Step 2 Draw $\triangle ABC$ on a coordinate plane.

Step 3 Draw $\triangle A'B'C'$ with vertices $(0, 0)$, $(-2, 4)$, and $(6, 6)$.

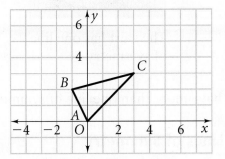

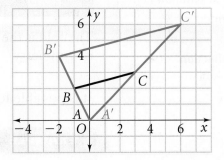

EXERCISES

Draw each figure and its image under the given dilation on the same coordinate plane.

1. $\triangle TRI$, vertices $T(-5, -5)$, $R(0, 0)$, and $I(-1, -3)$; scale factor 2

2. quadrilateral $MNPQ$, vertices $M(0, 0)$, $N(1, 4)$, $P(4, 5)$, and $Q(7, 0)$; scale factor 0.5

3. square $RECT$, vertices $R(0, 0)$, $E(2, -3)$, $C(5, -1)$, and $T(3, 2)$; scale factor 2

4. $\triangle NGL$, vertices $N(2, 2)$, $G(-2, 1)$, and $L(-1, -1)$; scale factor 3

Symmetry and Reflections

Develop Use coordinate graphs to plot simple figures and determine their image under reflections.

Develop Demonstrate an understanding of conditions that indicate two geometrical figures are congruent.

What You'll Learn

- To identify a line of symmetry
- To graph a reflection of a geometric figure

. . . And Why

To use symmetry and reflections in real-world situations, such as sewing

✓ Check Skills You'll Need
Graph each line.

1. $x = 0$ **2.** $y = 0$

3. $x = 3$ **4.** $y = 2$

5. $x = -1$ **6.** $x = y$

GO for Help
Lesson 8-3

◀)) New Vocabulary
- reflectional symmetry
- line of symmetry
- reflection
- line of reflection

Identifying Lines of Symmetry

A figure has **reflectional symmetry** when one half is a mirror image of the other half. A **line of symmetry** divides a figure with reflectional symmetry into two congruent halves.

A pattern for the back of a shirt is shown below. To make a shirt, you place the pattern on a folded piece of material, with the dashed lines of the pattern on the fold. After cutting the material, the back of the shirt will look like this.

The fold is the line of symmetry.

The shirt has one line of symmetry.

It is possible for a figure to have more than one line of symmetry.

1 EXAMPLE   Finding Lines of Symmetry

Draw the lines of symmetry. Tell how many there are.

a.

one line of symmetry

b.

six lines of symmetry

✓ Quick Check

1. Copy each figure. Draw all lines of symmetry.

a.

b.

A **reflection** is a transformation that flips a figure over a
line of reflection. The reflected figure, or image, is congruent to
the original figure. Together, an image and its reflection have line
symmetry, the line of reflection being the line of symmetry.

2 EXAMPLE   Reflecting Over an Axis

Graph the image of △ABC after a reflection over the y-axis.

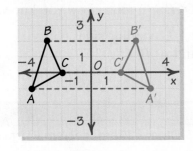

Since A is 4 units to the left
of the y-axis, A' is 4 units to the
right of the y-axis. Reflect the
other vertices. Draw △A'B'C'.

$△ABC \cong △A'B'C'$ because
reflecting △ABC across the y-axis
makes the figures exactly match.

GO Online

Video Tutor Help
Visit: PHSchool.com
Web Code: bje-0775

✓ Quick Check

2. Graph the image of △ABC after a reflection over the x-axis.

You can reflect images over lines other than the axes.

3 EXAMPLE   Reflecting Over a Line

Multiple Choice △PQR has vertices $P(-1, 3)$, $Q(1, 6)$, and $R(4, 5)$.
After a reflection over y = 2, what are the coordinates of Q?

(A) $(-1, 1)$ (B) $(1, -2)$ (C) $(1, -6)$ (D) $(4, -1)$

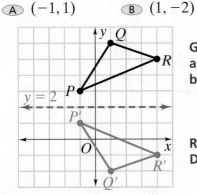

Graph y = 2. Since P is 1 unit
above the red line, P' is 1 unit
below the red line.

Reflect the other vertices.
Draw △P'Q'R'.

Quick Review

Remember that the
first number in an
ordered pair shows
position along the
x-axis. The second
number shows position
along the y-axis.

Point Q' has coordinates $(1, -2)$. The answer is B.

✓ Quick Check

3. Graph the image △ABC with vertices $A(3, 0)$, $B(2, 3)$, and
   $C(5, -1)$ after a reflection over each line.
   a. $x = 2$ **b.** $y = -1$

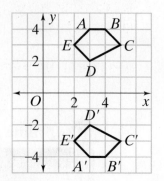

Use the figures at the left for Exercises 1–5.

1. Describe the transformation that maps $ABCDE$ onto $A'B'C'D'E'$.

2. Is $ABCDE$ congruent to $A'B'C'D'E'$? Explain how you know.

3. Graph the image of $A'B'C'D'E'$ after a reflection over the y-axis. Label the image $A''B''C''D''E''$.

4. Is $ABCDE$ congruent to $A''B''C''D''E''$? Explain how you know.

5. What is the relationship between corresponding sides and corresponding angles in $ABCDE$ and $A''B''C''D''E''$?

Standards Practice

For more exercises, see *Extra Skills and Word Problem Practice*.

A Practice by Example

Example 1
(page 482)

GO for Help

Copy each figure. Draw all lines of symmetry.

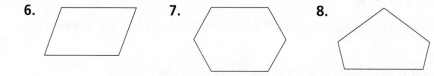

6.   7.   8.

Example 2
(page 483)

In Exercises 9–13, graph each figure and its image after a reflection over the given line.

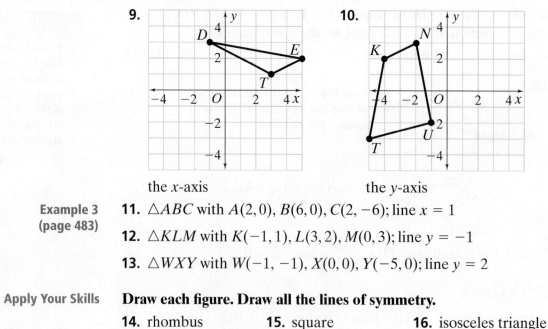

9.   10.

the x-axis   the y-axis

Example 3
(page 483)

11. $\triangle ABC$ with $A(2,0)$, $B(6,0)$, $C(2,-6)$; line $x = 1$

12. $\triangle KLM$ with $K(-1,1)$, $L(3,2)$, $M(0,3)$; line $y = -1$

13. $\triangle WXY$ with $W(-1,-1)$, $X(0,0)$, $Y(-5,0)$; line $y = 2$

B Apply Your Skills

Draw each figure. Draw all the lines of symmetry.

14. rhombus   15. square   16. isosceles triangle

17. **Writing in Math** Can a reflection image of an angle have a measure that is different from the original angle? Explain.

Graph each point and its image after a reflection over the given line. Name the coordinates of the image.

18. $H(-8, 3); y = 4$ **19.** $J(-8, 3); y = 2$ **20.** $V(5, 0); x = -2$

21. $A(2, 5); y = x$ **22.** $B(0, 3); y = 0$ **23.** $C(4, 0); x = 0$

Reasoning Decide whether each statement is *always* true, *sometimes* true, or *never* true.

24. When corresponding points of an original figure and its reflection are connected, the resulting segments are all perpendicular to the line of reflection.

25. When a point is reflected over a horizontal line, the y-coordinate of the point stays the same.

The given point is reflected over line 1. Then the image is reflected over line 2. Name the coordinates of the second image.

26. $A(3, -2)$
line 1: y-axis
line 2: x-axis

27. $B(-1, 5)$
line 1: x-axis
line 2: $y = 3$

28. $C(-5, -1)$
line 1: $x = 2$
line 2: y-axis

 Challenge

29. a. On a coordinate plane, graph the line $y = x$ and $\triangle ABC$ with vertices $A(5, 3)$, $B(6, -1)$, and $C(2, -1)$.

b. To graph the image of $\triangle ABC$ over the line $y = x$, trace the axes and $\triangle ABC$ on tracing paper. Fold the paper along $y = x$. Trace over the triangle so that it makes an impression on your original graph. Label A', B', and C' appropriately and draw $\triangle A'B'C'$.

c. Connect A to A', B to B', and C to C'. What do you notice about the line $y = x$ and these segments?

d. Complete: The line of reflection is the __?__ of the segment that connects a point to its image.

Multiple Choice Practice and Mixed Review

30. $\triangle EFG$ is shown on the coordinate grid. What are the coordinates of E' after $\triangle EFG$ is reflected over the x-axis?

Ⓐ $(2, -3)$
Ⓑ $(-2, 3)$
Ⓒ $(-2, -3)$
Ⓓ $(-3, 2)$

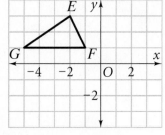

31. Which of the following is NOT a rational number?

Ⓐ -7 Ⓑ $1.234\ldots$ Ⓒ $2.\overline{4}$ Ⓓ $\dfrac{11}{3}$

for Help   Lesson 8-2   **32.** Graph $2y = x + 10$.

9-10 Rotations

Develop, Master Demonstrate an understanding of conditions that indicate two geometrical figures are congruent.

What You'll Learn

- To graph rotations
- To identify rotational symmetry

. . . And Why

To use rotations in describing real objects

✓ Check Skills You'll Need

Graph each triangle.

1. $A(1, 3)$, $B(4, 1)$, $C(3, -2)$

2. $J(-2, 1)$, $K(1, -3)$, $L(1, 4)$

3. $X(4, 0)$, $Y(0, 2)$ $Z(-2, -3)$

GO for Help
Lesson 1-10

🔊 New Vocabulary

- rotation
- center of rotation
- angle of rotation
- rotational symmetry

Graphing Rotations

A **rotation** is a transformation that turns a figure about a fixed point called the **center of rotation.** The angle measure of the rotation is the **angle of rotation.**

In the diagram, $\triangle QPR$ is rotated 90° about the center of rotation, point P. Notice that $m\angle QPQ' = 90°$ and $m\angle RPR' = 90°$. A figure and its rotation image are congruent.

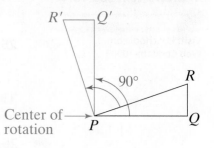

In the diagram, the direction of the rotation is *counterclockwise.* All rotations in this book will be counterclockwise.

You can graph a rotation on a coordinate plane.

1 EXAMPLE Finding a Rotation Image

Find the vertices of the image of $\triangle ABC$ after a rotation of 180° about the origin.

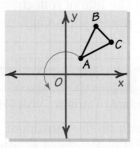 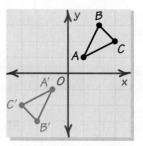

Step 1 Draw $\triangle ABC$. Place a piece of tracing paper over the graph. Trace the vertices of the triangle, the x-axis, and the y-axis. Then place your pencil at the origin to rotate the paper.

Step 2 Rotate the paper 180°. Make sure the axes line up. Mark the position of each vertex by pressing through the paper. Connect the vertices of the rotated triangle.

The vertices of the image are $A'(-1, -1)$, $B'(-2, -3)$, and $C'(-3, -2)$. $\triangle ABC$ can be rotated to exactly match $\triangle A'B'C'$, so $\triangle ABC \cong \triangle A'B'C'$ and corresponding sides and corresponding angles are congruent.

✓ Quick Check

1. Copy the graph of △*ABC* in Example 1. Draw its image after a rotation of 90° about the origin. Name the coordinates of the vertices of the image.

Identifying Rotational Symmetry

A figure has **rotational symmetry** if you can rotate it 180°, or less, so that its image matches the original figure. The angle (or its measure) through which the figure rotates is the angle of rotation.

The wheel at the right has rotational symmetry. You can turn the wheel from its original position to four other positions (five positions in all) and its picture will be as you see here. The smallest such turn moves *A* to *A'*. The angle of rotation is 360° ÷ 5, or 72°.

2 **EXAMPLE** **Identifying Rotational Symmetry**

Judging from appearance, state whether the flower has rotational symmetry. If so, what is the angle of rotation?

The flower can match itself in 3 positions.

The pattern repeats in 3 equal intervals. 360° ÷ 3 = 120°

The figure has rotational symmetry. The angle of rotation is 120°.

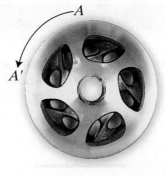

Online active math

For: Transformations Activity
Use: Interactive Textbook, 9-10

✓ Quick Check

2. Judging from appearance, tell whether each figure has rotational symmetry. If so, what is the angle of rotation?

a.   b.   c.

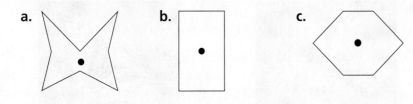

In the diagram below, $A'B'C'D$ is the image of rectangle $ABCD$ after a rotation about point D. Use the diagram for Exercises 1–5.

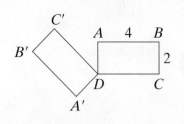

1. Estimate $m\angle C'DC$.

2. Estimate the angle of rotation for the transformation.

3. Is $ABCD$ congruent to $A'B'C'D$?

4. Find $A'D$.

5. Find $B'C'$.

Standards Practice

For more exercises, see *Extra Skills and Word Problem Practice*.

Ⓐ **Practice by Example**

Example 1
(page 486)

In Exercises 6–11, graph each figure and its image after a rotation of (a) 180° and (b) 90° about the origin.

6.

7.

8. point $D(-1, -3)$

9. point $E(3, 2)$

10. $\triangle KLM$ with $K(3, 0)$, $L(2, 4)$, $M(2, 2)$

11. $\triangle STU$ with $S(0, -4)$, $T(-4, -4)$, $U(-4, -3)$

Example 2
(page 487)

Judging from appearance, tell whether each figure has rotational symmetry. If so, what is the angle of rotation?

12.

13.

14.

15.

16. The vertices of a triangle are $V(0, 0)$, $W(2, 5)$, and $X(1, 5)$. On separate coordinate planes, graph the triangle and its images after rotations of (a) 90° and (b) 180° about $(1, 1)$.

17. ~~Writing in Math~~ Describe something in your classroom that has rotational symmetry. What is the angle of rotation?

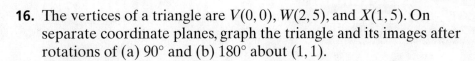

Homework Video Tutor

Visit: PHSchool.com
Web Code: bje-0910

In Exercises 18–21, does the figure have rotational symmetry? If so, what is the angle of rotation?

18. equilateral triangle
19. rectangle
20. regular pentagon
21. trapezoid

22. For Exercises 18–21, tell (a) whether each figure has line symmetry and (b) the number of lines of symmetry.

Each figure below is an image formed by rotating the figure at the left. What is each angle of rotation?

23.

24.

25.

26. $\triangle JKL$ has vertices $J(4, 4)$, $K(3, 2)$ and $L(5, 1)$.
   a. Graph its image, $\triangle J'K'L'$, after a rotation of 90° about the origin. Name the coordinates of the vertices of the image.
   b. Graph the image of $\triangle J'K'L'$ after a reflection over the y-axis.
   c. Is the image of $\triangle J'K'L'$ congruent to $\triangle JKL$? Explain.

27. **Reasoning** Is a rotation of 180° the same as a reflection over the y-axis? Justify your answer.

Multiple Choice Practice and Mixed Review

For Standards Tutorials, visit PHSchool.com. Web Code: bjq-9045

28. Figure $DEFG$ was dilated to form figure $LMNO$. What scale factor was used to change $DEFG$ into $LMNO$?

   Ⓐ $\frac{1}{4}$

   Ⓑ $\frac{1}{2}$

   Ⓒ 2

   Ⓓ 4

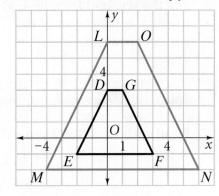

GO for Help   Lesson 9-9

The vertices of $\triangle ABC$ are $A(5, 6)$, $B(0, 3)$, and $C(3, 2)$. Graph $\triangle ABC$ and its image after a reflection over the given line.

29. $x = -2$
30. $y = -2$
31. x-axis

Sometimes for a problem, you may find it helpful to draw a diagram to keep track of the facts and actually see how the given information is related. Then you can use the diagram to help you solve the problem.

1 EXAMPLE

Shayna has nearly completed the annual Walk for Hunger. She began at the Start/Finish line and walked south for $\frac{1}{2}$ mile. Then she walked $1\frac{1}{2}$ miles east. She walked 1 mile north and then walked $\frac{1}{4}$ mile west. She turned right and walked $\frac{1}{4}$ mile. Then she turned left and walked $1\frac{1}{4}$ miles. Then she walked $\frac{1}{2}$ mile south. How far is it directly back to the Start/Finish line?

Ⓐ $\frac{1}{4}$ mile   Ⓑ $\frac{1}{2}$ mile   Ⓒ $1\frac{1}{4}$ miles   Ⓓ $1\frac{1}{2}$ miles

Draw a diagram on grid paper if possible. ⟶
Label each segment with its distance. If you draw the diagram carefully, it will show that Shayna is $\frac{1}{4}$ mile from the Start/Finish line. The correct choice is A.

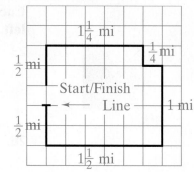

2 EXAMPLE

The endpoints of the diameter of a circle are at $(-4, 5)$ and $(4, 5)$ in a coordinate plane. What are the coordinates of the center of the circle?

Ⓐ $(0, 1)$ Ⓑ $(0, 9)$ Ⓒ $(0, 5)$ Ⓓ $(5, 0)$

On a coordinate plane, graph $(-4, 5)$ and $(4, 5)$. Sketch the circle and the segment from $(-4, 5)$ and $(4, 5)$. The midpoint of the segment is the center of the circle, which is located at $(0, 5)$. The correct answer is C.

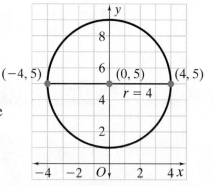

Multiple Choice Practice

Read each question. Then write the letter of the correct answer on your paper.

1. In Example 1, how far has Shayna walked?

Ⓐ $4\frac{1}{4}$ miles   Ⓑ $4\frac{1}{2}$ miles   Ⓒ $5\frac{1}{4}$ miles   Ⓓ $5\frac{1}{2}$ miles

2. On a coordinate plane, the vertices of rectangle $ABCD$ are located at $A(2, 1)$, $B(5, 1)$, and $C(5, 3)$. What are the coordinates of point D?

Ⓐ $(3, 5)$ Ⓑ $(3, 2)$ Ⓒ $(2, 3)$ Ⓓ $(5, 5)$

Chapter 9 Review

Vocabulary Review

🔊)) **English and Spanish Audio Online**

adjacent angles (p. 443)
alternate interior angles (p. 444)
angle bisector (p. 472)
angle of rotation (p. 486)
arc (p. 469)
center of rotation (p. 486)
central angle (p. 465)
circle (p. 464)
complementary (p. 443)
congruent angles (p. 443)
congruent figures (p. 458)
corresponding angles (p. 444)
image (p. 476)

line (p. 436)
line of reflection (p. 483)
line of symmetry (p. 482)
major arc (p. 469)
minor arc (p. 469)
parallel (p. 437)
perpendicular bisector (p. 471)
perpendicular lines (p. 471)
plane (p. 436)
point (p. 436)
polygon (p. 448)
ray (p. 436)
reflection (p. 483)

reflectional symmetry (p. 482)
regular polygon (p. 450)
rotation (p. 486)
rotational symmetry (p. 487)
segment (p. 436)
segment bisector (p. 471)
semicircle (p. 469)
skew (p. 437)
supplementary (p. 443)
transformation (p. 476)
translation (p. 476)
transversal (p. 444)
vertical angles (p. 443)

Match the vocabulary terms on the right with their descriptions on the left.

1. Angles that have the same measure, are opposite each other, and are formed by two intersecting lines

2. A flip of a figure over a line of reflection

3. A __?__ divides a figure with reflectional symmetry in half.

4. A location in space

5. A change of position or size of a figure

6. An angle whose vertex is the center of a circle

7. In a plane, all points the same distance from a given point

8. A line that intersects two other lines at different points

   A. central angle
   B. line of symmetry
   C. reflection
   D. transformation
   E. vertical angles
   F. transversal
   G. point
   H. circle

Go Online
PHSchool.com
For: Vocabulary quiz
Web Code: bjj-0951

Skills and Concepts

Lesson 9-1
- To name basic geometric figures
- To recognize intersecting lines, parallel lines, and skew lines

A **point** is a position in space. All geometric figures are made up of points. A **line** is a series of points that extend in two directions without end. A **segment** is a part of a line and has two endpoints. A **ray** is a part of a line with exactly one endpoint. An angle is two rays that intersect at their endpoints.

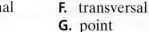

Name the following in the figure above.

9. 3 angles **10.** 3 rays **11.** a line **12.** 4 points **13.** 4 segments

Lesson 9-2

- To identify adjacent and vertical angles
- To relate angles formed by parallel lines and a transversal

Adjacent angles share a vertex and a side but no points in their interiors. **Vertical angles** are formed by intersecting lines and are **congruent.** If parallel lines are crossed by a **transversal** their **corresponding angles** are congruent. **Alternate interior angles** formed by a transversal and parallel lines are also congruent.

In the diagram at the right, $m \parallel n$.

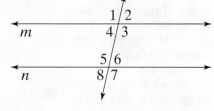

14. Name all angles congruent to $\angle 1$.

15. Name two pairs of supplementary angles.

16. Name all pairs of corresponding angles.

17. Name all pairs of alternate interior angles.

18. If $m\angle 2 = 75°$, find the measures of all the other angles.

Lessons 9-3 and 9-5

- To classify triangles
- To classify quadrilaterals
- To identify corresponding parts of congruent triangles
- To determine whether triangles are congruent

A **polygon** is a closed figure with at least three sides. Polygons with the same size and shape are **congruent.** A triangle can be classified by its angles and its sides. You can show two triangles are congruent using **Side-Side-Side, Side-Angle-Side,** and **Angle-Side-Angle.** You can classify some quadrilaterals as parallelograms, rectangles, squares, rhombuses, or trapezoids.

Use the most precise name for each figure described.

19. a triangle with all sides congruent

20. a parallelogram with all sides congruent and four 90° angles

21. a triangle with all acute angles and exactly two congruent sides

22. a quadrilateral with exactly one pair of parallel sides

List the congruent corresponding parts of each of the triangles below. Write a congruence statement (and reason) for the triangles.

23. **24.**

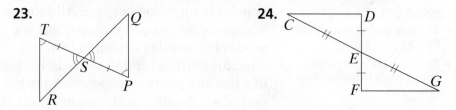

Lesson 9-4

- To draw a diagram to solve a problem

Drawing a diagram can help you visualize a problem.

25. A house is to be built on a lot 70 ft wide by 100 ft deep. The shorter side of the lot faces the street. The house must be set back from the street at least 25 ft. It must be 20 ft from the back lot line and 10 ft from each side lot line. What are the maximum length and width of the house?

Lesson 9-6

- To find circumferences
- To find central angles and to make circle graphs

You can use these formulas to find the circumference of a circle:
$$C = \pi d \text{ and } C = 2\pi r.$$
There are 360° in a circle. An angle whose vertex is the center of a circle is a **central angle.**

26. Find the circumference of a circle with a diameter of 14 cm.

27. Suppose a survey indicates that at 8 P.M. 40% of viewers watched channel X, 25% watched channel Y, and 35% watched channel Z. Make a circle graph of the data.

Lesson 9-7

- To construct a segment or an angle congruent to a given segment or angle
- To construct segment bisectors and angle bisectors

You can use a compass and straightedge to construct congruent segments, congruent angles, **segment bisectors,** and **angle bisectors.**

Draw $\triangle CDE$ with an obtuse $\angle D$.

28. Construct the bisector of $\angle D$.

29. Construct the perpendicular bisector of $\overline{DE}$.

Lessons 9-8, 9-9, and 9-10

- To graph translations
- To describe translations
- To identify a line of symmetry
- To graph a reflection of a geometric figure
- To graph rotations
- To identify rotational symmetry

A **transformation** is a change of position or size of a figure. The figure after the transformation is called the **image.** You can transform figures in a plane by a **translation,** a **reflection,** or a **rotation.**

What is the image of point $A(7, -2)$ after each transformation?

30. 4 units right, 3 units up

31. reflection over the y-axis

32. rotation of 90° about $(0, 0)$

33. reflection over the line $y = -1$

34. How do translations, reflections, and rotations affect the size and shape of an image? Explain.

Use the diagram to name the following.

1. all segments containing point G

2. all pairs of vertical angles

3. all rays containing point M

4. a line containing point T

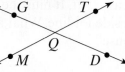

Use the diagram to name the following.

5. four segments that intersect $\overline{AB}$

6. three segments parallel to $\overline{AB}$

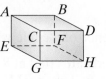

For Exercises 7 and 8, name all possible polygons for each description.

7. quadrilateral with at least one pair of parallel sides and at least two right angles

8. quadrilateral with one diagonal that divides it into two congruent equilateral triangles

9. Find the perimeter of an equilateral triangle that has a side measure of 60 cm.

10. Find the perimeter of a square that has a side measure of 60 cm.

11. The perimeter of a rectangle is 58 cm. One side is 18 cm. Find the lengths of the other three sides.

A segment has endpoints $A(-3, -6)$ and $M(-3, -4)$. Find the coordinates of the endpoints after each transformation.

12. a translation of 4 units right and 3 units up

13. a reflection over the y-axis

14. a rotation of 90° about the origin

15. Draw a segment. Construct its perpendicular bisector.

16. Draw an obtuse angle. Construct its angle bisector.

Use the diagram for Exercises 17 and 18.

17. If $m\angle 2 = 130°$, find $m\angle 4$.

18. **Writing in Math** Describe how you can find $m\angle 1$ if you know $m\angle 2$.

19. Forty two-year-old children were asked to name their favorite color. Five chose yellow, seven chose blue, and fourteen chose red. The rest chose other colors.
    a. To make a circle graph, what should be the measure of the central angle representing blue, red, and yellow? Round to the nearest degree.
    b. Make a circle graph for the information.

20. If $\overline{AB} \cong \overline{CD}$, $\angle A \cong \angle D$, and $\angle B \cong \angle C$, what method can you use to show that $\triangle ABE \cong \triangle DCF$?

21. **Open-Ended** Draw and describe a figure that has rotational symmetry.

22. a. The measures of two angles of a triangle are 50° and 35°. What is the measure of the third angle?
    b. Classify the triangle by its angles.

23. $\triangle CAB \cong \triangle DEB$. Find as many angle measures and side lengths as you can.

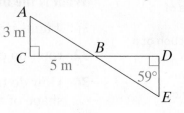

Some problems ask you to analyze a geometric transformation.

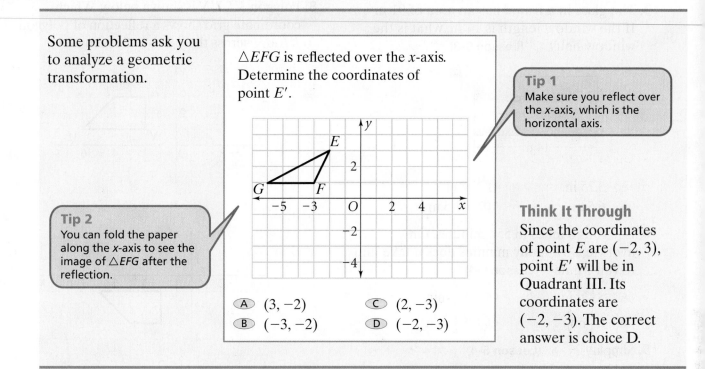

$\triangle EFG$ is reflected over the x-axis. Determine the coordinates of point E'.

Tip 1
Make sure you reflect over the x-axis, which is the horizontal axis.

Tip 2
You can fold the paper along the x-axis to see the image of $\triangle EFG$ after the reflection.

Ⓐ $(3, -2)$ Ⓒ $(2, -3)$
Ⓑ $(-3, -2)$ Ⓓ $(-2, -3)$

Think It Through
Since the coordinates of point E are $(-2, 3)$, point E' will be in Quadrant III. Its coordinates are $(-2, -3)$. The correct answer is choice D.

Vocabulary Review

As you solve problems, you must understand the meanings of mathematical terms. Choose the vocabulary term that correctly completes the sentence.

A. The (radius, diameter) of a circle is a chord that passes through the center of the circle.

B. A transformation that flips a figure over a line is a (translation, reflection).

C. A (circle, polygon) is a closed plane figure with at least three sides.

D. The figure you get after a transformation is an (image, area).

E. A (translation, dilation) is a transformation that moves points the same distance and in the same direction.

F. The set of all points in a plane that are the same distance from a given point is a (circle, translation).

Read each question. Then write the letter of the correct answer on your paper.

1. The distance from the center of the Ferris wheel to a passenger car is 328 feet. What is the approximate distance a passenger travels in 3 full rotations during the ride? **(Lesson 9-6)**

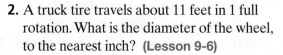

328 ft

passenger

Ⓐ 984 ft
Ⓑ 1,030 ft
Ⓒ 3,090 ft
Ⓓ 6,180 ft

2. A truck tire travels about 11 feet in 1 full rotation. What is the diameter of the wheel, to the nearest inch? **(Lesson 9-6)**

Ⓐ 3.5 in.   Ⓒ 94 in.
Ⓑ 42 in.   Ⓓ 132 in.

3. The glass in a frame has an area of 91 m². If the window length is 14 m, what is the window height? **(Lesson 3-3)**

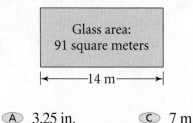

Glass area:
91 square meters

|←——14 m——→|

Ⓐ 3.25 in. Ⓒ 7 m
Ⓑ 6.5 m Ⓓ 31.5 m

4. Lee runs 6 miles in $55\frac{1}{2}$ minutes. On average, how many minutes does it take him to run 1 mile? **(Lesson 5-4)**

Ⓐ $8\frac{1}{2}$ min Ⓒ $9\frac{1}{4}$ min
Ⓑ $8\frac{3}{4}$ min Ⓓ $9\frac{1}{2}$ min

5. Simplify $2\frac{1}{2} \cdot 8$. **(Lesson 5-4)**

Ⓐ 8 Ⓒ 16
Ⓑ 12 Ⓓ 20

6. Simplify $2 - 1\frac{1}{8}$. **(Lesson 5-3)**

Ⓐ $\frac{3}{4}$ Ⓒ $1\frac{1}{8}$
Ⓑ $\frac{7}{8}$ Ⓓ $1\frac{7}{8}$

7. A circle with a radius of 3 units has its center at $(-2, 0)$ on a coordinate grid.

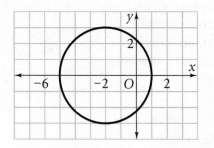

If the circle is translated 2 units to the left and 1 unit down, what will be the coordinates of the new center? **(Lesson 9-8)**

Ⓐ $(-4, -1)$ Ⓒ $(-1, -2)$
Ⓑ $(-4, 1)$ Ⓓ $(0, -1)$

8. Polygon *KLMN* is shown below. Which coordinate grid shows a reflection of polygon *KLMN* across the *y*-axis? **(Lesson 9-9)**

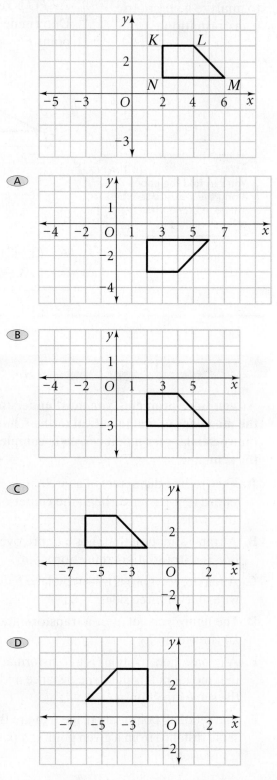

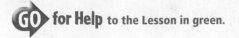
9. A nanometer is a unit equal to 0.000000001 meter. Which expression represents this number in scientific notation? **(Lesson 4-9)**

Ⓐ 1×10^{-10}
Ⓑ 1×10^{-9}
Ⓒ 1×10^{9}
Ⓓ 1×10^{10}

10. The Arctic tern, a sea bird, is the animal that migrates the longest distance each year. It flies 25,000 miles from the Arctic to the Antarctic and back. How is the distance expressed in scientific notation? **(Lesson 4-9)**

Ⓐ 25×10^{-3} mi
Ⓑ 2.5×10^{-4} mi
Ⓒ 2.5×10^{4} mi
Ⓓ 25×10^{4} mi

11. Complete: 3.15×10^{8} ▪ 2.1×10^{9}. **(Lesson 4-9)**

Ⓐ >   Ⓒ =
Ⓑ <   Ⓓ ≥

12. At a 25%-off sale, Andre bought a shirt that originally cost $30. How much was deducted from the original price? **(Lesson 6-8)**

Ⓐ $5.00
Ⓑ $7.50
Ⓒ $22.50
Ⓓ $25.00

13. The population of a town changed from 15,000 people to 18,000 people in one year. Find the percent of increase in population. **(Lesson 6-7)**

Ⓐ 6%   Ⓒ 17%
Ⓑ 12%   Ⓓ 20%

14. For which of the following figures is $\triangle DEF \cong \triangle ABC$? **(Lesson 9-5)**

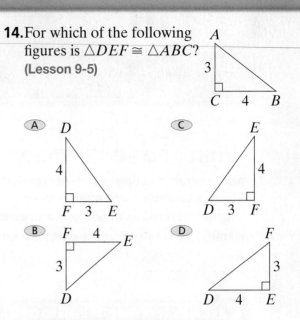

15. Carl made 210 phone calls in 3.5 months. Who made phone calls at the same rate? **(Lesson 6-1)**

Ⓐ Lucy: 120 calls in 3 months
Ⓑ Seth: 100 calls in 2.5 months
Ⓒ Amanda: 300 calls in 5 months
Ⓓ Matt: 75 calls in 1.5 months

16. Eleanor wants to purchase two art posters. One poster costs $4.85 and the other poster costs $15.00. There is sale at the store for 20% off each item, and there is 5% sales tax. Find the approximate amount that she has to pay for the two posters. **(Lesson 6-9)**

Ⓐ $16.67   Ⓒ $19.85
Ⓑ $20.05   Ⓓ $25.01

Area and Volume

What You've Learned

Add, subtract, multiply, and divide rational numbers and take positive rational numbers to whole number powers.

Use the correct order of operations to evaluate algebraic expressions.

Identify and construct basic elements of geometric figures.

Check Your Readiness **for Help** to the Lesson in green.

Finding the Areas of Rectangles and Squares (Geometric Formulas, p. 702)

Find the area of each figure.

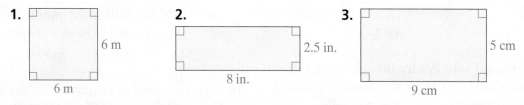

1. 6 m, 6 m

2. 8 in., 2.5 in.

3. 9 cm, 5 cm

Simplifying Expressions With Exponents (Lesson 4-7)

Simplify each product.

4. $5 \cdot 3^2$ **5.** $3.14 \cdot 5^2$ **6.** $6 \cdot 12^2$ **7.** $4^2 \cdot 3$ **8.** $10^2 \cdot 3$ **9.** $3.14 \cdot 12^2$

Multiplying by a Fraction (Lesson 5-4)

Find each product.

10. $\frac{1}{2} \cdot 12$

11. $\frac{1}{2} \cdot 13 \cdot 3$

12. $\frac{1}{2}(10 + 8)$

13. $\frac{1}{2} \cdot 20x$

14. $\frac{1}{2} \cdot 5x \cdot 2x$

15. $\frac{1}{2}(10)(6 + 5)$

16. $\frac{1}{2}(62)(30 + 14)$

17. $\frac{1}{3}(20)(35 + 40)$

18. $\frac{1}{3}(3)(5 + 3)$

Finding the Circumferences of Circles (Lesson 9-6)

Find the circumference of each circle. Use 3.14 for π.

19. $d = 50$ yd

20. $r = 100$ m

21. $d = 5.5$ in.

▲ You can use volume formulas to find the amount of space in a ship's hold.

What You'll Learn Next

Use formulas routinely for finding the area of basic two-dimensional figures and the surface area and volume of basic three-dimensional figures.

Estimate and compute the area of more complex or irregular two- and three-dimensional figures by breaking the figures down into more basic geometric objects.

Compute the length of the perimeter, the surface area of the faces, and the volume of a three-dimensional object built from rectangular solids.

10-1   Area: Parallelograms

Develop Use formulas routinely for finding the area of basic two-dimensional figures including rectangles, parallelograms, and squares.
Develop Identify basic elements of geometric figures.

What You'll Learn

• To find areas of rectangles
• To find areas of parallelograms

. . . And Why

To solve real-world problems involving area

✓ **Check Skills You'll Need**

Use $A = \ell w$ and find the third value.

1. $A = 54$ in.^{2}, $w = 6$ in.

2. $\ell = 35$ m, $w = 7$ m

3. $A = 25$ cm^2, $\ell = 2.5$ cm

4. $\ell = 7.2$ ft, $w = 7.2$ ft

GO for Help
Lesson 3-3

🔊 **New Vocabulary**

• area
• altitude

Finding Areas of Rectangles

Standards Investigation
Discovering an Area Formula

1. Use a 3 in.-by-5 in. index card. Find the area of the card.

2. Draw a line from one vertex to a point on another side to create a triangle. Cut along that line.

3. Use the pieces to form a parallelogram that is not a rectangle.

4. What is the area of your parallelogram? Explain.

The **area** of a figure is the number of square units it encloses. The rectangle outlined in red encloses 8 square units, each with area 1 cm^2 (1 square centimeter). So, the area of the rectangle is 8 cm^2.

You can use the formula $A = bh$ to find the area of a rectangle, where b is the length of one side and h is the length of the other. For the rectangle above, $A = 4 \cdot 2 = 8$. So, the area is 8 cm^2.

When you find area, the dimensions must be in the same unit.

---

1 EXAMPLE   Finding Area of a Rectangle

Find the area of the rectangular banner.

Step 1 Convert units.

$$24 \text{ in.} = 24 \text{ in.} \left(\frac{1 \text{ ft}}{12 \text{ in.}}\right) \quad \textbf{Convert 24 in.}$$

$$= 2 \text{ ft}$$

Step 2 Find the area.

$$A = bh \qquad \textbf{Use the formula for the area of a rectangle.}$$

$$= (2)(4) \quad \textbf{Substitute.}$$

$$= 8 \qquad \textbf{Simplify.}$$

The area of the banner is 8 ft^2.

1. Find the area of each rectangle.

a. 1 m
10 cm

b. 2 yd
2 ft

Finding Areas of Parallelograms

A rectangle is a special kind of parallelogram. The formula for the area of a parallelogram follows from the formula for the area of a rectangle. The height *h* of a parallelogram is the length of an *altitude*.

An **altitude** is a line segment perpendicular to the line containing a base of the figure and drawn from the side opposite that base.

Take Note   **Area of a Parallelogram**

The area of a parallelogram is the product of any base length *b* and the corresponding height *h*.

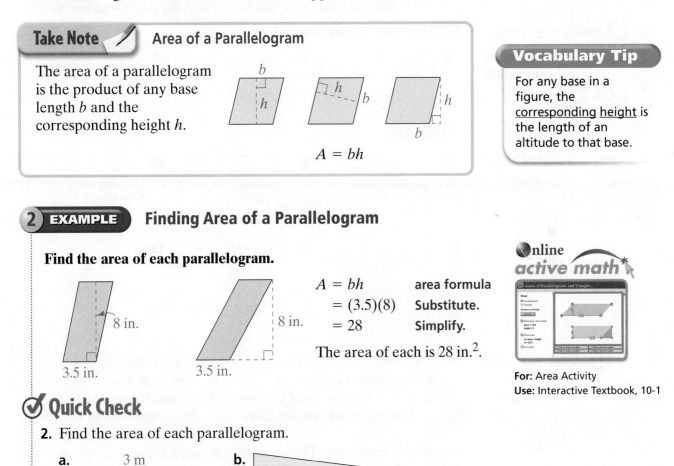

$$A = bh$$

> **Vocabulary Tip**
>
> For any base in a figure, the corresponding <u>height</u> is the length of an altitude to that base.

2 EXAMPLE   **Finding Area of a Parallelogram**

Find the area of each parallelogram.

8 in.

3.5 in.

8 in.

3.5 in.

$A = bh$ area formula
$ = (3.5)(8)$ Substitute.
$ = 28$ Simplify.

The area of each is 28 in.².

> **○**nline
> *active math*
>
> **For:** Area Activity
> **Use:** Interactive Textbook, 10-1

✓ **Quick Check**

2. Find the area of each parallelogram.

a.   3 m
2 m

b.   8 in.
3 in.

c. How do the areas of two parallelograms compare when the dimensions of one are twice the dimensions of the other?

Complete Exercises 1–4 to solve the problem below.

A football field is 300 ft long from goal line to goal line, and 160 ft wide from sideline to sideline. Find the area of the football field.

1. Draw a diagram of the football field. What shape is a football field?

2. Write the formula you can use to find the area of the football field.

3. What values will you substitute into the formula to find the area of the football field?

4. What is the area of the football field?

Standards Practice

For more exercises, see *Extra Skills and Word Problem Practice*.

A Practice by Example

Example 1
(page 500)

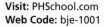 **for Help**

Example 2
(page 501)

Find the area of each parallelogram.

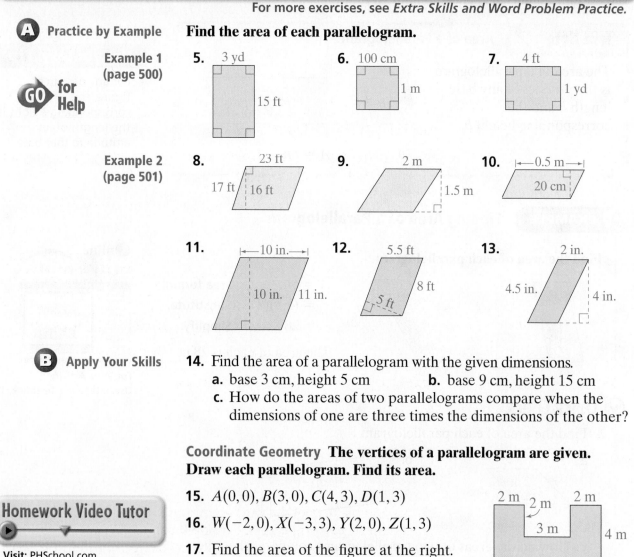

5. 3 yd / 15 ft

6. 100 cm / 1 m

7. 4 ft / 1 yd

8. 23 ft / 17 ft / 16 ft

9. 2 m / 1.5 m

10. 0.5 m / 20 cm

11. 10 in. / 10 in. / 11 in.

12. 5.5 ft / 8 ft / 5 ft

13. 2 in. / 4.5 in. / 4 in.

B Apply Your Skills

14. Find the area of a parallelogram with the given dimensions.
   a. base 3 cm, height 5 cm   b. base 9 cm, height 15 cm
   c. How do the areas of two parallelograms compare when the dimensions of one are three times the dimensions of the other?

Coordinate Geometry The vertices of a parallelogram are given. Draw each parallelogram. Find its area.

15. $A(0, 0)$, $B(3, 0)$, $C(4, 3)$, $D(1, 3)$

16. $W(-2, 0)$, $X(-3, 3)$, $Y(2, 0)$, $Z(1, 3)$

17. Find the area of the figure at the right. Assume that all angles are right angles.

2 m / 2 m / 2 m / 3 m / 4 m / 7 m

Homework Video Tutor

Visit: PHSchool.com
Web Code: bje-1001

Find the area of each parallelogram.

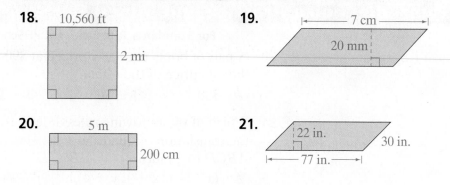

18. 10,560 ft   2 mi

19. 7 cm   20 mm

20. 5 m   200 cm

21. 22 in.   30 in.   77 in.

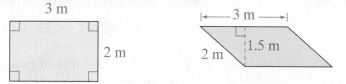

22. Construct an altitude using a compass and straightedge. Copy the parallelogram at the left. Construct the perpendicular bisector of a base. Extend the bisector to intersect the opposite base.

23. **Writing in Math** The two parallelograms below have the same perimeter. Are the areas the same? Explain.

3 m   2 m

3 m   2 m   1.5 m

Reasoning In Exercises 24 and 25, find the ratio of the areas of the parallelograms (smaller to larger). Justify each answer.

24. The bases are the same length. The height of one parallelogram is twice the height of the other.

25. The height and the length of a base of one parallelogram are both twice those of the other parallelogram.

26. **Open-Ended** You want to make a 400-ft² vegetable garden. You plan to build a fence to keep the rabbits out. To spend the least amount of money, you want to use as little fencing as possible.
  a. Draw and list three possible dimensions for your garden.
  b. Which of the three will need the least amount of fencing?

C Challenge   **Find the area of each shaded region. Assume that all angles that appear to be right angles are right angles.**

27. 8 ft   2 ft   4 ft   2 ft   2 ft   2 ft

28. 7 m   2.8 m 2.8 m   4 m   2.8 m 2.8 m

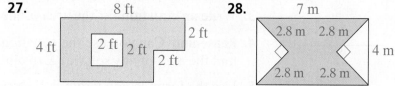

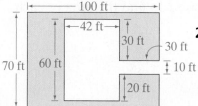

100 ft   42 ft   30 ft   30 ft   70 ft   60 ft   10 ft   20 ft

29. a. Find the area of the yard at the left. Assume that all angles that appear to be right angles are right angles.
  b. How many square yards of sod do you need to cover the yard?
  c. One bag of fertilizer covers approximately 2,000 ft². How many bags should you buy to cover the yard?

For Standards Tutorials, visit PHSchool.com. Web Code: bjq-9045

30. A pair of boots regularly priced at $90 is marked "$\frac{1}{3}$ off." What is the sale price of the boots?

   Ⓐ $30   Ⓑ $60   Ⓒ $90   Ⓓ $120

31. Which of the following rules describes the translation of quadrilateral $ABCD$ to quadrilateral $A'B'C'D'$?

   Ⓐ $(x, y) \rightarrow (x + 1, y + 4)$
   Ⓑ $(x, y) \rightarrow (x - 4, y - 1)$
   Ⓒ $(x, y) \rightarrow (x + 4, y + 1)$
   Ⓓ $(x, y) \rightarrow (x - 1, y - 4)$

GO for Help   Lesson 9-10   **The endpoints of a segment are given. Graph each segment and its image after a rotation of 90° about the origin.**

32. $A(5, 8), B(2, 4)$ **33.** $C(0, 3), D(3, -5)$ **34.** $E(-2, -3), F(-2, 4)$

Lesson 9-2   **35.** Find the measures of two supplementary angles if the difference of their measures is 56°.

Mathematical Reasoning

Develop Develop generalizations of the results obtained and the strategies used and apply them to new problem situations.

Area of a Square

You know that you can use the formula $A = bh$ to find the area of a parallelogram. Every square is a parallelogram. Follow the steps below to write a formula for the area of a square.

1. Use the formula $A = bh$ to find the area of the square at the right. What value will you substitute for b? What value will you substitute for h?

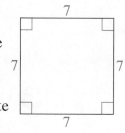

2. Use the formula $A = bh$ to find the area of the square at the left. What value will you substitute for b? What value will you substitute for h?

3. Write an equation for the area of the square at the left.

4. **Reasoning** Can you use the equation you found in Exercise 3 to find the area of any square? Explain.

5. Use the formula you wrote in Exercise 3 to find the area of each of the following squares.
   a. Side length is 5 yd.
   b. Side length is 6.2 cm.
   c. Perimeter is 9.6 m.

Develop Relate the changes in measurement with a change of scale to the units used.

When you know the perimeter of one of two similar figures, you can find the perimeter of the other figure.

1 ACTIVITY

- **On a piece of grid paper, draw a 3 unit-by-4 unit rectangle.**

- **Draw three different rectangles, each larger than but similar to the original rectangle. Label them I, II, and III.**

1. Use your rectangles to complete a table like the one below.

Rectangle	Perimeter	Area
Original	$2(3 + 4) = 14$	$3 \cdot 4 = 12$
I	■	■
II	■	■
III	■	■

2. Use the information in the table from Question 1 to complete a table like the one below.

Rectangles	Ratio of Corresponding Sides (in simplest form)	Ratio of Perimeters (in simplest form)	Ratio of Areas (in simplest form)
I: Original	■ : ■	■ : ■	■ : ■
II: Original	■ : ■	■ : ■	■ : ■
III: Original	■ : ■	■ : ■	■ : ■

3. Use the table from Question 2.
  a. Reasoning How is the ratio of perimeters related to the ratio of corresponding sides? Explain.
  b. How is the ratio of areas related to the ratio of corresponding sides? Explain.
  c. Without using grid paper, find the perimeter of a rectangle similar to the original rectangle you drew but with sides half as long.
  d. Find the area of the rectangle.

When you know the area of one of two similar figures, you can use a proportion to find the area of the other figure.

Parallelogram *GRAM* is similar to parallelogram *PQNO*. Parallelogram *GRAM* has an area of 54 in.².
Find the area of parallelogram *PQNO*.

The ratio of corresponding sides is $\frac{3}{9}$, or $\frac{1}{3}$. The ratio of the areas is $\frac{1^2}{3^2}$, or $\frac{1}{9}$.

$$\frac{1}{9} = \frac{A}{54}$$ Write a proportion.

$$9A = 54$$ Use cross-products.

$$A = 54 \div 9$$ Solve for *A*.

$$= 6$$

The area of parallelogram *PQNO* is 6 in.²

EXERCISES

Each pair of parallelograms is similar. Find the perimeter of each parallelogram.

1.
8.5 cm
a cm
2.8 cm
17 cm

2.
4.5 mm
4.5 mm
b mm
13.5 mm

Each pair of parallelograms is similar. Find the ratio of perimeters and the ratio of areas for each pair.

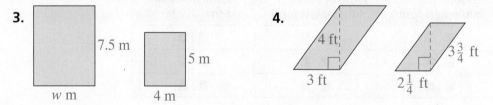

3.
7.5 m
5 m
w m
4 m

4.
4 ft
3 ft
$3\frac{3}{4}$ ft
$2\frac{1}{4}$ ft

Each pair of parallelograms is similar. Find the area of the larger parallelogram.

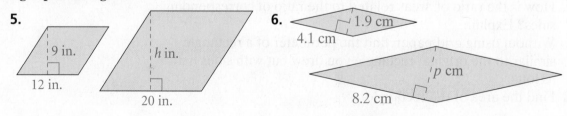

5.
9 in.
h in.
12 in.
20 in.

6.
1.9 cm
4.1 cm
p cm
8.2 cm

10-2 Area: Triangles and Trapezoids

Develop Use formulas routinely for finding the area of basic two-dimensional figures.

Introduce, Develop Compute the area of more complex two-dimensional figures.

Develop Identify basic elements of geometric figures.

What You'll Learn

• To find areas of triangles

• To find areas of trapezoids

. . . And Why

To find areas in real-world situations, such as construction

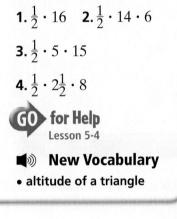

✓ Check Skills You'll Need

Find each product.

1. $\frac{1}{2} \cdot 16$ **2.** $\frac{1}{2} \cdot 14 \cdot 6$

3. $\frac{1}{2} \cdot 5 \cdot 15$

4. $\frac{1}{2} \cdot 2\frac{1}{2} \cdot 8$

GO for Help

Lesson 5-4

🔊 New Vocabulary

• altitude of a triangle

Finding Areas of Triangles

A diagonal divides a parallelogram into two congruent triangles.

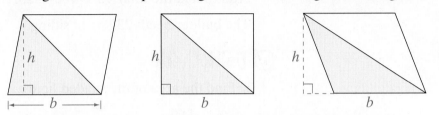

You can see that the area of a triangle is half the area of a parallelogram. An **altitude of a triangle** is the perpendicular segment from a vertex of a triangle to the line containing the opposite side. The height is the length of the altitude.

Take Note ✏️ **Area of a Triangle**

The area of a triangle equals half the product of any base length b and the corresponding height h.

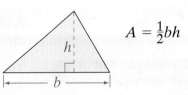

$$A = \frac{1}{2}bh$$

1 EXAMPLE Finding Area of a Triangle

Find the area of the triangle.

$A = \frac{1}{2}bh$ **Use the formula for the area of a triangle.**

$= \frac{1}{2} \cdot 8 \cdot 3$ **Replace *b* with 8 and *h* with 3.**

$= 12$ **Simplify.**

The area is 12 cm².

✓ Quick Check

1. Find the area of each triangle.

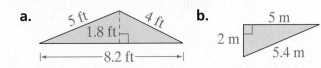

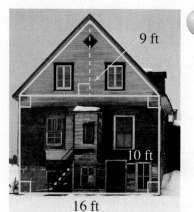

9 ft

10 ft

16 ft

2 EXAMPLE Finding Area of an Irregular Figure

How many square feet of siding does a builder need to cover the side of the house shown at the left?

Area of triangle	Area of rectangle
$A = \frac{1}{2}bh$	$A = bh$
$= \frac{1}{2} \cdot 16 \cdot 9$	$= 16 \cdot 10$
$= 72$	$= 160$

Add to find the total: $72 + 160 = 232$.

The builder needs 232 ft^2 of siding.

✓ Quick Check

2. Find the area of the shaded figure.

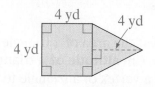

4 yd

4 yd

4 yd

Finding Areas of Trapezoids

A diagonal divides a trapezoid into two triangles. Notice that the triangles have the same height but different bases.

Quick Tip

To find the area of an irregular figure, you may need to use more than one area formula. Make sure you know the area formulas for triangles, parallelograms, and trapezoids.

You can add the areas of the triangles to find the area of the trapezoid.

A ——— 6 cm ——— D

4 cm

B ——— 9 cm ——— C

Area of $\triangle ABC$	Area of $\triangle ADC$
$A = \frac{1}{2}bh$	$A = \frac{1}{2}bh$
$= \frac{1}{2} \cdot 9 \cdot 4$	$= \frac{1}{2} \cdot 6 \cdot 4$
$= 18$	$= 12$

The areas of the two triangles are 18 cm^2 and 12 cm^2. The area of the trapezoid is the sum of the areas of the two triangles, 30 cm^2.

You can use this information to find a formula for the area of a trapezoid.

In a trapezoid, the parallel sides are its bases. For the figure at the right the bases are b_1 and b_2. The height is h.

The area of the trapezoid is $\frac{1}{2}b_1h + \frac{1}{2}b_2h$.

By using the Distributive Property, you can see that

$\frac{1}{2}b_1h + \frac{1}{2}b_2h$ is $\frac{1}{2}h(b_1 + b_2)$.

So, the area of the trapezoid is $\frac{1}{2}h(b_1 + b_2)$.

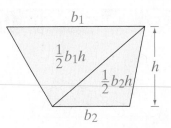

Take Note ✏️ **Area of a Trapezoid**

The area of a trapezoid is half the product of the height and the sum of the lengths of the bases.

$$A = \frac{1}{2}h(b_1 + b_2)$$

---

3 **EXAMPLE** **Finding Area of a Trapezoid**

The Erie Canal opened in 1825 and was hailed as an engineering marvel. Below is a cross section of the Erie Canal. Find the area of the trapezoidal cross section.

$A = \frac{1}{2}h(b_1 + b_2)$ Use the formula for the area of a trapezoid.

$A = \frac{1}{2} \cdot 4(28 + 40)$ Replace h with 4, b_1 with 28, and b_2 with 40.

$\quad = \frac{1}{2} \cdot 4(68)$ Simplify.

$\quad = 2 \cdot 68$

$\quad = 136$

The Erie Canal is 363 miles in length.

The area of the cross section is 136 ft^2.

✅ Quick Check

3. Find the area of each trapezoid.

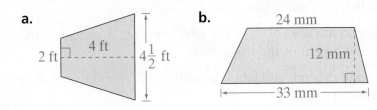

a.

b.

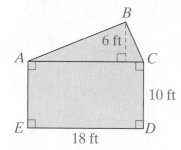

Use the figure at the left for Exercises 1–5.

1. What formula can you use to find the area of figure *ABC*?

2. What is the area of figure *ABC*?

3. What formula can you use to find the area of figure *ACDE*?

4. What is the area of figure *ACDE*?

5. What is the area of *ABCDE*?

Standards Practice

For more exercises, see *Extra Skills and Word Problem Practice.*

A Practice by Example

Example 1
(page 507)

GO for Help

Find the area of each triangle.

6.

7.

8.

Example 2
(page 508)

Find the area of each shaded figure.

9.

10.

Example 3
(page 509)

Find the area of each trapezoid.

11.

12.

13.

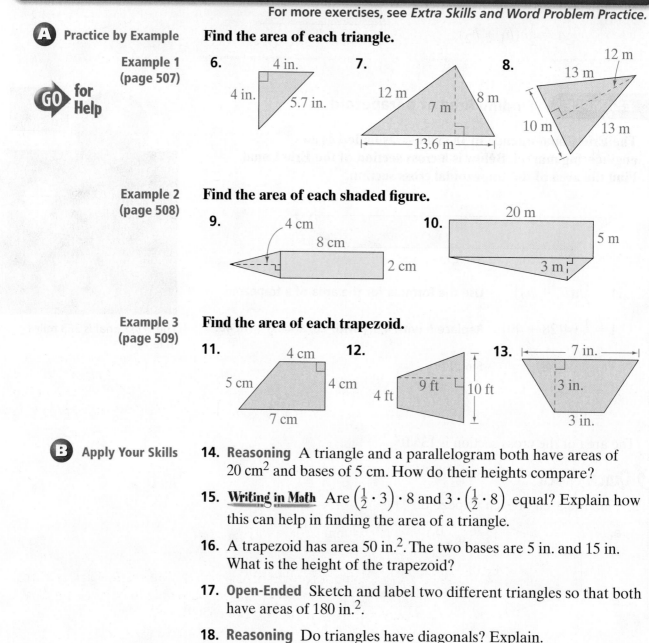

B Apply Your Skills

14. **Reasoning** A triangle and a parallelogram both have areas of 20 cm² and bases of 5 cm. How do their heights compare?

15. **Writing in Math** Are $\left(\frac{1}{2} \cdot 3\right) \cdot 8$ and $3 \cdot \left(\frac{1}{2} \cdot 8\right)$ equal? Explain how this can help in finding the area of a triangle.

16. A trapezoid has area 50 in.². The two bases are 5 in. and 15 in. What is the height of the trapezoid?

17. **Open-Ended** Sketch and label two different triangles so that both have areas of 180 in.².

18. **Reasoning** Do triangles have diagonals? Explain.

19. The altitude of isosceles triangle $\triangle ABC$ is the perpendicular bisector of its base $\overline{BC}$. Draw $\triangle ABC$. Use a compass and straightedge to construct its altitude.

Find the area of each shaded region.

20.

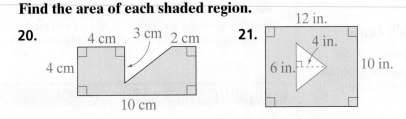

4 cm   3 cm   2 cm
4 cm
10 cm

21.

12 in.
4 in.
6 in.   10 in.

C Challenge

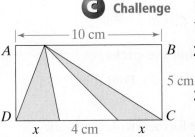

A ⟵ 10 cm ⟶ B
5 cm
D   x   4 cm   x   C

Reasoning In Exercises 22 and 23, find the ratios of the areas of the trapezoids (larger to smaller). Justify each answer.

22. The height and the lengths of the bases of one trapezoid are all twice those of the other trapezoid.

23. The trapezoids have the same height. One trapezoid has base lengths b and $2b$. The other has base lengths b and $4b$.

24. $ABCD$ (left) is a rectangle. What is the area of the shaded region?

Multiple Choice Practice and Mixed Review

For Standards Tutorials, visit PHSchool.com. Web Code: bjq-9045

25. The shaded area is a trapezoid with a 6-unit by 6-unit square hole in the middle. Which expression can be used to find the area of the shaded region?

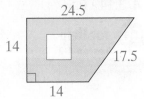

24.5
14   17.5
14

(A) $14 \cdot 14 + 10.5 \cdot 14 - 6 \cdot 6$

(B) $6 \cdot 6 + 14 \cdot (14 + 24.5)$

(C) $14 \cdot 14 + \dfrac{10.5 \cdot 14}{2} - 6 \cdot 6$

(D) $6 \cdot 6 + 14 \cdot (14 + 14.5)$

26. An arcade game awards players 5 tickets just for playing and an additional ticket for every 10 points scored. The equation $\dfrac{p}{10} + 5 = t$ represents the number of tickets t awarded for p points earned. How many tickets are awarded for 230 points earned?

(A) 18   (B) 28   (C) 2,295   (D) 2,305

Lesson 10-1

Find the area of each parallelogram.

27.

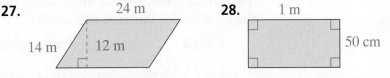

24 m
14 m   12 m

28.

1 m
50 cm

Lesson 6-10

29. Suppose you bought two books for \$15. The original prices of the two books were the same, but you were able to buy one for half price. What was the full price of each book?

Area: Circles

Develop Use formulas routinely for finding the area of basic two-dimensional figures including circles.

Develop Estimate and compute the area of more complex or irregular two-dimensional figures by breaking the figures down into more basic geometric objects.

What You'll Learn

- To find areas of circles
- To find areas of irregular figures that include parts of circles

. . . And Why

To use area formulas in real-world situations such as finding the amount of grass needed to cover a circular region

✓ Check Skills You'll Need

Simplify each expression.

1. $3.14 \cdot 4^2$

2. $3.14 \cdot 5^2$

3. $3.14 \cdot 9^2$

4. $3.14 \cdot 0.5^2$

GO for Help
Lesson 4-2

Finding Areas of Circles

Standards Investigation
Finding the Formula for Area of a Circle

1. Use a compass to draw a circle. Cut out the circle.

2. Fold the circle in half, and then in half again. Fold it in half a third and fourth time.

3. Cut out the 16 wedges that you have formed with the folds.

4. Arrange the wedges in a row as shown below.

5. Notice that the new shape resembles a parallelogram. How does the base of the parallelogram (the side shown in red) relate to the circumference of the circle? How does the height of the parallelogram relate to the radius of the circle?

6. Use the formula for the area of a parallelogram to estimate the area of your circle.

The diagram above shows the relationship between the area of a circle and a figure that is like a parallelogram. The height h of the parallelogram is about the same as the radius r of the circle. The base b is about half the circumference C of the circle.

You can use the formula for the area of a parallelogram to suggest the formula for the area of a circle.

$$A = bh \qquad \text{Use the formula for the area of a parallelogram.}$$

$$A = \left(\tfrac{1}{2}C\right)(r) \qquad \text{Substitute } \tfrac{1}{2}C \text{ for } b \text{ and } r \text{ for } h.$$

$$A = \tfrac{1}{2}(2\pi r) \cdot r \qquad \text{Substitute } 2\pi r \text{ for } C.$$

$$A = \pi r^2 \qquad \text{Simplify.}$$

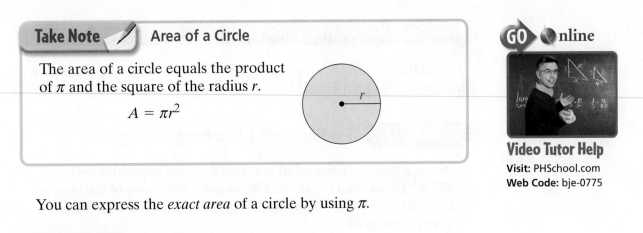
Take Note ✏ Area of a Circle

The area of a circle equals the product of π and the square of the radius r.

$$A = \pi r^2$$

You can express the *exact area* of a circle by using π.

1 EXAMPLE **Finding Area of a Circle**

Find the exact area of a circle with diameter 12 cm.

$A = \pi r^2$

$\quad = \pi(6)^2 \quad r = \frac{1}{2}d;\ r = 6$

$\quad = 36\pi \quad$ **Simplify.**

The area is 36π cm^2.

✓ Quick Check

● **1.** Find the exact area of a circle with radius 50 in.

For real-world situations, you usually want an approximate value for the area of a circle. If you are finding an approximate area, you can use 3.14 for π.

2 EXAMPLE **Estimating Area of a Circle**

The size of a mountain lion's territory depends on how much food is available. Where there is plenty of food, the circular territory of the mountain lion may be as small as 5 mi in diameter. Find the area of such a region to the nearest square mile.

$A = \pi r^2$

$\quad = \pi(2.5)^2 \quad\quad r = \frac{1}{2}d;\ r = 2.5$

$\quad = 6.25\pi \quad\quad$ **exact area**

$\quad \approx (6.25)(3.14) \quad$ **Use 3.14 for π.**

$\quad = 19.625 \quad\quad$ **approximate area**

The area of the region is about 20 mi^2.

The area of a mountain lion's territory ranges from 15 mi^2 to 30 mi^2.

✓ Quick Check

● **2.** Find the approximate area of a circle with radius 6 mi.

Finding Areas of Irregular Figures

To find the area of an irregular figure, you can sometimes separate it into figures with areas you know how to find.

3 EXAMPLE **Finding Area of an Irregular Figure**

Multiple Choice A pound of grass seed covers approximately 675 ft². Grass seed comes in 3-lb bags. Find the area of the lawn at the right below. How many bags of grass seed do you need to buy to cover the lawn?

Ⓐ 4 bags   Ⓒ 2 bags

Ⓑ 3 bags   Ⓓ 1 bag

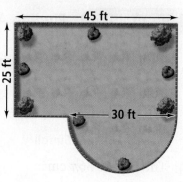

Quick Review

Remember to follow the order of operations when finding the area of a circle or half a circle. Square the radius first, and then multiply by an approximation of π.

Area of region that is one half of a circle

area of circle $= \pi r^2$

area of half circle $= \frac{1}{2}\pi r^2$

$A = \frac{1}{2}\pi(15)^2$ **$r = 15$**

$\quad = 112.5\pi$ **exact area**

$\quad \approx 353.25$ **Use 3.14 for π.**

Area of region that is a rectangle

area of rectangle $= bh$

$A = 45 \cdot 25$ **$b = 45; h = 25$**

$A = 1,125$

The area of the lawn is about 353 ft² + 1,125 ft² = 1,478 ft².

$1,478 \div 675 \approx 2.19$ **Divide to find the amount of seed.**

You need to buy one 3-lb bag of grass seed. The answer is D.

✓ Quick Check

3. Find the area of the shaded region to the nearest tenth.

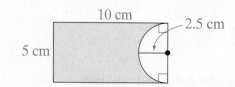

Number Sense **Match each object with its most likely area.**

1. dinner plate
2. quarter
3. 12-in. circular pizza
4. jar lid
5. center circle on a basketball court

A. 0.8 in.^{2}
B. 110 in.^{2}
C. 7 in.^{2}
D. 16,000 in.^{2}
E. 80 in.^{2}

6. What is the ratio of the area of a circle with a 12-in. diameter to the area of a circle with a 6-in. diameter?

Standards Practice

For more exercises, see *Extra Skills and Word Problem Practice*.

A **Practice by Example**
Examples 1 and 2
(page 513)

GO for Help

Find the area of each circle. Give the exact area and an approximate area to the nearest square unit.

7.

12 ft

8.
16 m

9.
60 cm

10. A standard dartboard has a diameter of 18 in. What is its area to the nearest square inch?

11. A culinary student decorates an 8-in.-diameter round cake. What is the approximate area of the top of the cake?

Example 3
(page 514)

Find the area of each figure to the nearest square unit.

12.
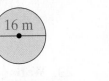
|←— 10 in. —→|
7 in.   3.5 in.

13.
|← 40 yd →|
40 yd

Find the area of each shaded region to the nearest square unit.

14.
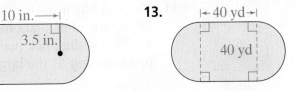
3 in.

15.
10 mi
20 mi

16.

12 mm
6 mm

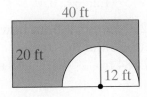
40 ft
20 ft
12 ft

17. A groundskeeper wants to use sod to cover the lawn shown in green in the diagram at the left. Each piece of sod covers 3 ft^2. About how many pieces of sod are needed?

18. Covering for the pool border is sold by the square yard (whole-number amounts only). It costs $20/yd^2.
   a. What is the area of the border in square feet?
   b. About how much will the covering cost?

Find the area of each circle. Give the exact area and an approximate area to the nearest tenth.

19. $r = 12$ mi **20.** $r = 0.3$ m **21.** $d = 1.5$ in. **22.** $d = 8.4$ mm

23. Open-Ended Describe a real-life situation, not used in this lesson, where you might use the formula for the area of a circle.

24. Which has a greater area, four circles, each with radius 1 m, or one circle with radius 4 m? Explain.

25. How many circles with radius 2 cm will have the same total area as a circle with radius 4 cm?

Find the area of each shaded region to the nearest square unit.

26.   **27.**   **28.**

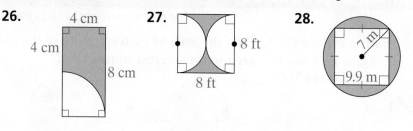

Homework Video Tutor

Visit: PHSchool.com
Web Code: bje-1003

29. Writing in Math What is the area of the largest circle that will fit in a square with area 64 cm^2? Explain.

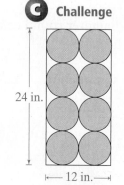

24 in.

12 in.

30. A manufacturer cuts lids for eight cans from one rectangular sheet of aluminum as shown at the left.
   a. What is the radius of each lid?
   b. How many square inches of aluminum do the lids require?
   c. How many square inches of aluminum are wasted?

31. You can buy a 10-in. diameter pizza for $6.50, a 12-in. pizza for $8.50, or a 14-in. pizza for $10.50.
   a. What is the price per square inch of each pizza?
   b. Reasoning Is the largest pizza the best buy? Explain.

Multiple Choice Practice and Mixed Review

For Standards Tutorials, visit PHSchool.com. Web Code: bjq-9045

32. Which numbers are in order from least to greatest?
   Ⓐ 0.7, $\frac{1}{5}$, 0, -1.2, $-\frac{1}{3}$ Ⓒ -1.2, $-\frac{1}{3}$, 0, $\frac{1}{5}$, 0.7
   Ⓑ 0.7, $\frac{1}{5}$, 0, $-\frac{1}{3}$, -1.2 Ⓓ -1.2, $-\frac{1}{3}$, 0, 0.7, $\frac{1}{5}$

33. A circular racetrack has a diameter of 200 meters. About how far does a car travel in three full revolutions around the track?
   Ⓐ 628 m   Ⓑ 942 m   Ⓒ 1,884 m   Ⓓ 3,768 m

34. Which ordered pair is *not* a solution of $y = 6x + 3$?

Ⓐ $(-1, -3)$ Ⓑ $(2, 15)$ Ⓒ $(0, 3)$ Ⓓ $(1, 6)$

GO for **Help** Lesson 10-2 **Find the area of each figure.**

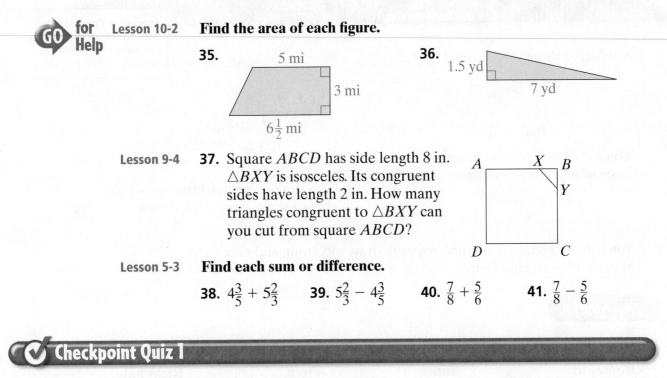

35.

5 mi

3 mi

$6\frac{1}{2}$ mi

36.

1.5 yd

7 yd

Lesson 9-4 **37.** Square $ABCD$ has side length 8 in. $\triangle BXY$ is isosceles. Its congruent sides have length 2 in. How many triangles congruent to $\triangle BXY$ can you cut from square $ABCD$?

Lesson 5-3 **Find each sum or difference.**

38. $4\frac{3}{5} + 5\frac{2}{3}$ **39.** $5\frac{2}{3} - 4\frac{3}{5}$ **40.** $\frac{7}{8} + \frac{5}{6}$ **41.** $\frac{7}{8} - \frac{5}{6}$

✓ Checkpoint Quiz 1

Find the area of each figure.

1. 10 in. 10 in.

2. 10 in. 10 in.

3. 20 in. 15 in.

4. 20 yd   12 yd   13 yd   30 yd

5. 35 cm   30 cm   70 cm

6. 15 m   25 m   20 m

Find the area of each figure. Give the exact area, and an approximate area to the nearest square unit.

7. 10 yd

8. 16 ft

9. 40 cm   20 cm

FOR USE WITH LESSON 10-4

Introduce Construct two-dimensional patterns for three-dimensional models.

A solid is a three-dimensional figure.

You can draw a solid *in perspective* (p. 523) to show that it is three-dimensional.

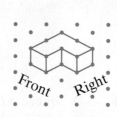

You can use isometric dot paper to draw a three-dimensional view.

You can use rectangular graph paper to draw top, front, and side views of three-dimensional figures.

EXAMPLE

Draw the top, front, and right-side views of the solid.

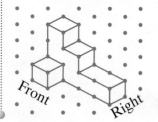

Isometric   Top   Front   Right Side

EXERCISES

Draw the top, front, and right-side views of each solid.

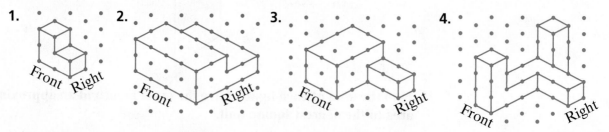

1.   2.   3.   4.

5. The top, front, and right-side views are given.
Draw an isometric view on isometric dot paper.

Top   Front   Right Side

10-4 Space Figures

Develop Construct two-dimensional patterns for three-dimensional models, such as cylinders, prisms, and cones.

Develop, Master Identify elements of three-dimensional objects.

What You'll Learn

- To identify common space figures
- To construct nets

. . . And Why

To identify space figures often used in constructing buildings

✓ Check Skills You'll Need

Judging by appearance, classify each polygon.

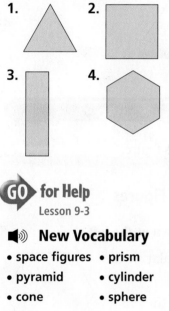

1.
2.
3.
4.

GO for Help
Lesson 9-3

🔊 New Vocabulary

- space figures
- prism
- pyramid
- cylinder
- cone
- sphere
- net

Naming Space Figures

The figures below are common three-dimensional figures, also called **space figures** or solids. The space figures you will study in this book are prisms, pyramids, cylinders, cones, and spheres.

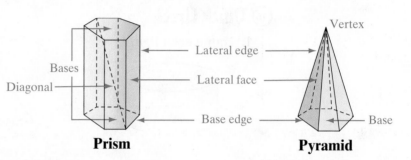

Prism

Pyramid

A **prism** has two parallel bases that are congruent polygons, and lateral faces that are parallelograms. A *diagonal* connects two nonconsecutive vertices.

A **pyramid** has a base that is a polygon. The lateral faces are triangles.

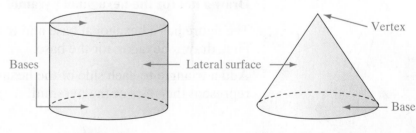

Cylinder

Cone

A **cylinder** has two parallel bases that are congruent circles.

A **cone** has one circular base and one vertex.

Sphere

A **sphere** is the set of all points in space that are a given distance from a given point called the center.

You can use the shape of a base to help you name a space figure.

1 EXAMPLE Naming Space Figures

For each figure, describe the bases and name the figure.

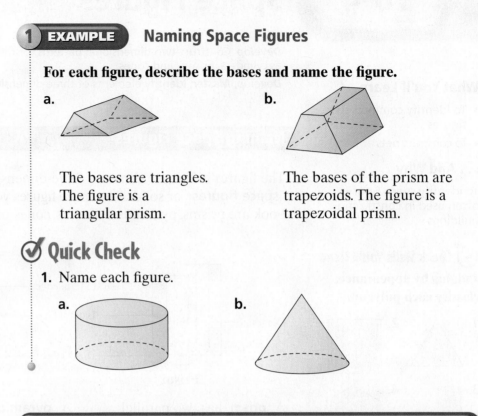

a.

The bases are triangles. The figure is a triangular prism.

b.

The bases of the prism are trapezoids. The figure is a trapezoidal prism.

✓ **Quick Check**

1. Name each figure.

a.

b.

Constructing Nets

A **net** is a pattern you can form into a space figure.

2 EXAMPLE Drawing Nets of Space Figures

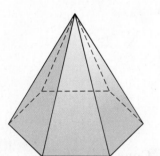

Draw a net for the hexagonal pyramid shown at the left.

The figure has a hexagonal base and triangular sides. First, draw a hexagon for the base.

Add a triangle to each side of the hexagon to represent the sides of the pyramid.

✓ **Quick Check**

2. Draw a net for the space figure shown at the right.

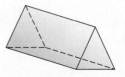

Match each container with the correct net.

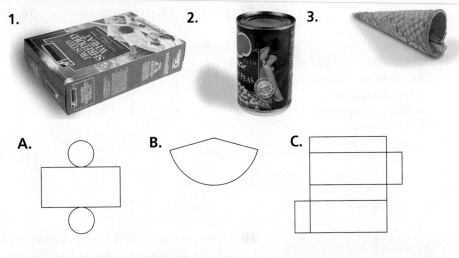

1.
2.
3.

A.
B.
C.

Standards Practice

For more exercises, see *Extra Skills and Word Problem Practice*.

A Practice by Example

Example 1
(page 520)

GO for Help

For each figure, describe the base(s), if any, and name the figure.

4.
5.
6.

7.
8.
9.

Example 2
(page 520)

Draw a net for each space figure in Exercises 10–12.

10.
11.
12.

B Apply Your Skills

Vocabulary Tip

Lateral means "on the side." The lateral faces of a prism or pyramid are the surfaces that connect with a base. See page 519.

For Exercises 13–15, write the most precise name for each space figure that has the given properties.

13. four lateral faces that are triangles

14. three lateral faces that are rectangles

15. a lateral surface and one circular base

16. What type of space figure does each object suggest?

    a. a shoe box   **b.** a teepee   **c.** a basketball

Open Ended **Draw a net for each space figure.**

17. pentagonal pyramid   **18.** an object in your classroom

19. Multiple Choice Which net can be folded to make a cube?

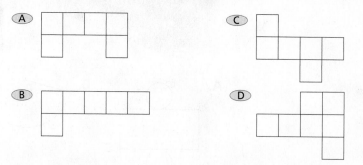

20. A net is made of 4 congruent rectangles and 2 congruent squares whose sides are the same length as the shorter sides of the rectangles. Name a space figure you can form from this net.

Name the space figure you can form from each net.

21.   **22.**   **23.**

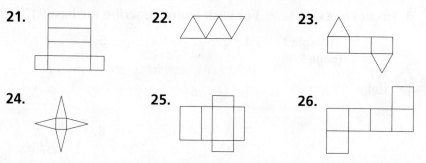

24.   **25.**   **26.**

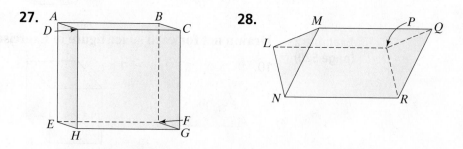

Copy each figure for Exercises 27–28. Name and sketch a diagonal.

27.   **28.**

29. <u>Writing in Math</u> Suppose you see a net for a rectangular prism and a net for a rectangular pyramid. Explain how you can match each net with its name.

30. Draw a net to represent a rectangular box that is 10 cm long, 8 cm wide, and 4 cm high. Label dimensions on the net.

31. A cube is easy to draw in *one-point perspective*. Draw a cube in one-point perspective by following the steps below.

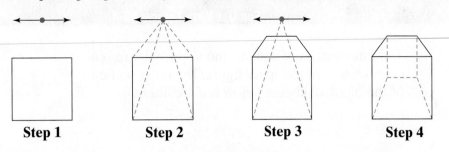

| Step 1 | Step 2 | Step 3 | Step 4 |

Step 1 Begin by drawing a square for the front. Draw a *horizon line* parallel to one horizontal edge of your square. Select a *vanishing point* on the horizon line.

Step 2 Draw lines, called *vanishing lines,* from the vertices of the square to the vanishing point.

Step 3 Draw a line segment parallel to the horizon line. Use this segment to determine the top and back edges.

Step 4 Draw dashed lines for the hidden back vertical and horizontal edges. Erase the horizon line and unnecessary parts of the vanishing lines.

32. Using steps like those suggested in Exercise 31, make a one-point perspective drawing of each figure.
a. triangular prism   **b.** cylinder

Multiple Choice Practice and Mixed Review

For Standards Tutorials, visit PHSchool.com. Web Code: bjq-9045

33. Joan earns $12.50 per hour after taxes. She knows she wants to buy $25.70 of sportswear, spend $8.00 on a movie, and pay $35.60 worth of bills. What is least number of hours she can work to cover her costs?
(A) 4   (B) 6   (C) 8   (D) 9

34. You want to determine the price of a tent that has been marked down 20%. The tent originally cost $80, and the sales tax is 5%. What is the first step to find the total cost of the tent?
(A) Find 15% of $80.   (C) Find 5% of $80.
(B) Find 20% of $80.   (D) Find 25% of $80.

 Lesson 10-3

For each circle, find the exact area and an approximate area.

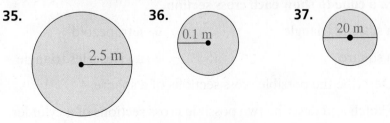

35. 2.5 m   **36.** 0.1 m   **37.** 20 m

Cross Sections of Space Figures

FOR USE WITH LESSON 10-4

Master Identify elements of three-dimensional objects and describe how two or more objects are related in space.

The intersection of a plane and a space figure is a *cross section* of the space figure. The cross section of the block of cheese below is a rectangle.

EXAMPLE

Sketch a plane intersecting a cube in three different ways to show a rectangular cross section.

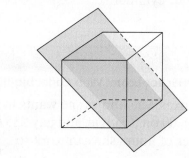 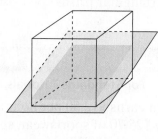 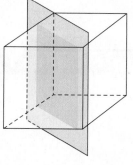

EXERCISES

Use the name of a polygon to describe each cross section of the cube. Points *M*, *N*, *P*, *Q*, and *R* are midpoints of edges.

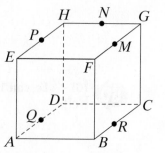

1. through *M*, *P*, *Q*, and *R*
2. through *E*, *A*, *C*, and *G*
3. through *B*, *E*, and *G*
4. through *M*, *N*, *D*, and *B*

Sketch a cube to show each cross section.

5. a scalene triangle
6. a trapezoid
7. a square
8. an isosceles triangle
9. Describe the possible cross sections of a sphere.
10. Sketch and describe two possible cross sections of a cylinder.

Surface Area of Rectangular Prisms

Introduce, Develop
Compute the length of the perimeter and the surface area of the faces of a three-dimensional object built from rectangular solids.

You can think of a cube, or any rectangular prism, as a solid made of small cubes. The *surface area* of the larger cube or prism is then the sum of the areas of the exposed faces of the small cubes.

Think of a cube that is formed from 27 centimeter cubes.

The front face of the cube contains nine exposed faces of the centimeter cubes. Its area is $9 \cdot 1$ cm^2, or 9 cm^2.

The six faces of the cube have the same area because they are identical. The surface area is $6 \cdot 9$ cm^2, or 54 cm^2.

You can find the surface area of a rectangular prism in a similar way.

1 ACTIVITY

The rectangular prism below is formed from 24 centimeter cubes. Follow steps 1–9 to find the prism's surface area.

1. What is the area of one exposed face of a centimeter cube?

2. How many centimeter-cube faces are exposed on the front face of the prism?

3. Based on your answers to Steps 1 and 2, what is the area of the front face of the prism?

4. How many centimeter-cube faces are exposed on the left face of the prism?

5. Based on your answers to Steps 1 and 4, what is the area of the left face of the prism?

6. How many centimeter-cube faces are exposed on the top face of the prism?

7. Based on your answers to Steps 1 and 6, what is the area of the top face of the prism?

8. Without calculating, determine the areas of the back, right, and bottom faces of the prism. Explain your reasoning.

9. What is the surface area of the rectangular prism? Explain your reasoning.

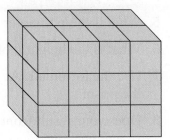

The *lateral area* of a cube or rectangular prism is the sum of the areas of the front, back, left, and right faces. The areas of the top and bottom faces are not included.

You can also find the lateral area (L.A.) of a cube or prism by calculating the product of the perimeter p of its base and its height h:

$$L.A. = ph$$

② ACTIVITY

The rectangular prism at the right is formed from 60 centimeter cubes. Follow Steps 1–8 to calculate the prism's lateral area.

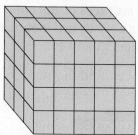

1. How many centimeter-cube faces are exposed on the front face of the prism? What is the area of the front face of the prism?

2. How many centimeter-cube faces are exposed on the left face of the prism? What is the area of the left face of the prism?

3. Based on your answers to Steps 1 and 2, what are the areas of the back and right faces of the prism? Explain.

4. Based on your answers to Steps 1, 2, and 3, what is the lateral area of the prism? Explain.

5. What is the perimeter p of the base of the prism?

6. What is the height h of the prism?

7. Use the formula L.A. = ph to calculate the lateral area L.A. of the prism.

8. Does your result from Step 7 agree with your result from Step 4?

EXERCISES

The retangular prism at the right is formed from 160 centimeter cubes.

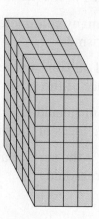

1. What is the surface area of the rectangular prism?

2. What is the lateral area of the rectangular prism?

3. If the top layer of cubes is removed from the prism, what are the surface area and the lateral area of the resulting prism?

4. If a cube is removed from one corner of the rectangular prism at the right, what is the surface area of the resulting solid? Explain your reasoning.

Surface Area: Prisms and Cylinders

Surface Area: Prisms and Cylinders

What You'll Learn

- To find surface areas of prisms
- To find surface areas of cylinders

. . . And Why

To find the amount of material needed in packaging

✓ Check Skills You'll Need

Find the circumference of each circle with the given radius or diameter.

1. $r = 5$ in.

2. $r = 4.2$ cm

3. $d = 8$ ft

4. $d = 6.8$ in.

for Help
Lesson 9-6

🔊 New Vocabulary

- surface area
- lateral area

Develop Use formulas routinely for finding the surface area of basic three-dimensional figures, including prisms and cylinders.

Finding Surface Areas of Prisms

Prisms and cylinders can be *right* or *oblique*.

Right prism   Oblique prism   Right cylinder   Oblique cylinder

In this text, you may assume that prisms and cylinders are right unless otherwise stated.

Surface area (S.A.) is the sum of the areas of the base(s) and the lateral faces of a space figure. One way to find the surface area of a space figure is to find the area of its net. You measure surface area in square units.

1 EXAMPLE   Finding Surface Area Using a Net

Find the surface area of the rectangular prism using a net.

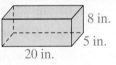

8 in.
5 in.
20 in.

| 40 in.² | ← 20 in. → | 40 in.² |

Draw and label a net.

8 in. | 160 in.²

5 in. | 100 in.²

Find the area of each rectangle in the net.

8 in. | 160 in.²

5 in. | 100 in.²

$40 + 40 + 160 + 100 + 160 + 100 = 600$ **Add the areas.**

The surface area is 600 in.²

✓ Quick Check

1. Find the surface area of the triangular prism.

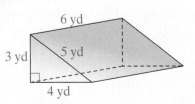

6 yd
3 yd   5 yd
4 yd

Lateral area (L.A.) of a prism is the sum of the areas of the lateral faces. The sum of the lateral areas and base areas of a prism equals the surface area.

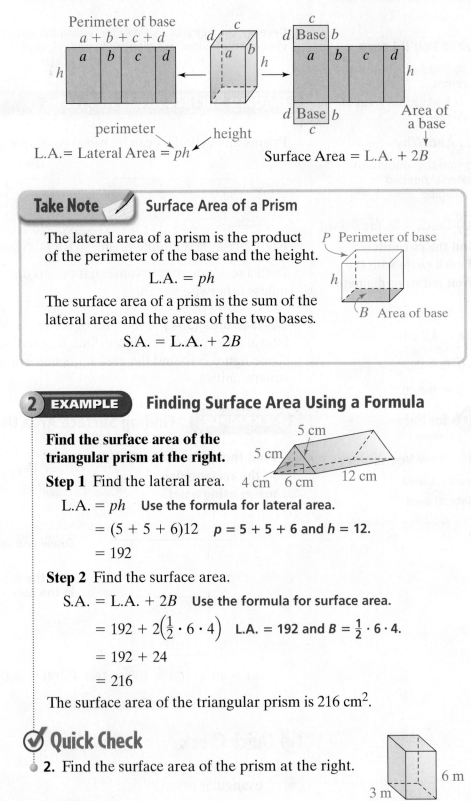

Perimeter of base
$a + b + c + d$

L.A.= Lateral Area = ph

Surface Area = L.A. + 2B

Take Note ✏ **Surface Area of a Prism**

The lateral area of a prism is the product of the perimeter of the base and the height.

$$L.A. = ph$$

The surface area of a prism is the sum of the lateral area and the areas of the two bases.

$$S.A. = L.A. + 2B$$

---

2 EXAMPLE **Finding Surface Area Using a Formula**

Find the surface area of the triangular prism at the right.

Step 1 Find the lateral area.

L.A. = ph Use the formula for lateral area.

= $(5 + 5 + 6)12$ $p = 5 + 5 + 6$ and $h = 12$.

= 192

Step 2 Find the surface area.

S.A. = L.A. + 2B   Use the formula for surface area.

= $192 + 2\left(\frac{1}{2} \cdot 6 \cdot 4\right)$ L.A. = 192 and $B = \frac{1}{2} \cdot 6 \cdot 4$.

= $192 + 24$

= 216

The surface area of the triangular prism is 216 cm².

✓ Quick Check

2. Find the surface area of the prism at the right.

6 m
3 m
4 m

Finding Surface Areas of Cylinders

If you cut a label from a soup can, you will see that the label is a rectangle. The height of the rectangle is the height of the can. The base length of the rectangle is the circumference of the can.

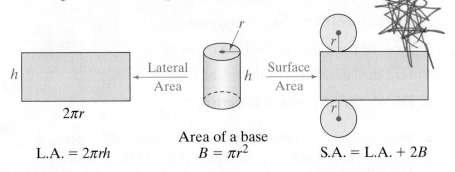

L.A. = $2\pi rh$

Area of a base
$B = \pi r^2$

S.A. = L.A. + $2B$

Online
active math

For: Surface Area Activity
Use: Interactive Textbook, 10-5

Take Note — Surface Area of a Cylinder

The lateral area of a cylinder is the product of the circumference of the base and the height of the cylinder.

$$\text{L.A.} = 2\pi rh$$

B is the area of a base.

The surface area of a cylinder is the sum of the lateral area and the areas of the two bases.

$$\text{S.A.} = \text{L.A.} + 2B$$

You can use 3.14 for π when an exact answer is not necessary.

---

3 EXAMPLE — Finding Surface Area of a Cylinder

Find the surface area of the can to the nearest square centimeter.

Step 1 Find the lateral area.

L.A. = $2\pi rh$ Use the formula for lateral area.

     = $2\pi(3.5)(11.5)$ $r = 3.5$ and $h = 11.5$.

     = 80.5π

Step 2 Find the surface area.

S.A. = L.A. + $2B$ Use the formula for surface area.

     = $80.5\pi + 2\pi(3.5)^2$ L.A. = 80.5π and $B = \pi(3.5)^2$.

     = $80.5\pi + 24.5\pi$

     = 105π

     ≈ 330   Use 3.14 for π. Round.

The surface area of the can is 105π cm^2, or about 330 cm^2.

3.5 cm

11.5 cm

✓ Quick Check

3. Find the surface area of a can with radius 5 cm and height 20 cm.

Use the triangular prism below for Exercises 1–6.

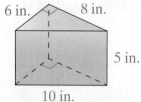

1. What shape is the base of the prism?

2. Find the area of the base of the prism.

3. Find the perimeter of the base of the prism.

4. Find the lateral area of the prism.

5. Find the surface area of the prism.

6. **Error Analysis** A student says that the height of the prism is the same as the height of triangular base. Is the student correct? Explain.

Standards Practice

For more exercises, see *Extra Skills and Word Problem Practice*.

A **Practice by Example**

Example 1
(page 527)

Find, to the nearest square unit, the surface area of the space figure represented by each net.

7.

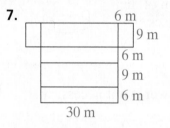

8.

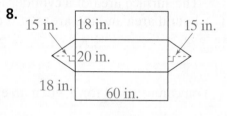

9. The base of a rectangular prism is 3 in. by 5 in. The height is 11 in.
   a. Draw and label a net for the prism.
   b. Find the surface area of the prism.

Example 2
(page 528)

Find the surface area of each prism.

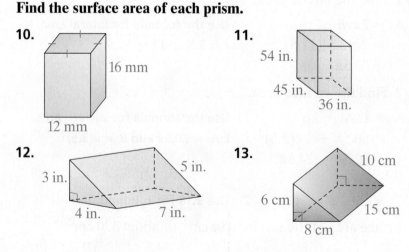

10.

11.

12.

13.

Example 3
(page 528)

Find the surface area of the cylinder shown or represented. Round to the nearest tenth.

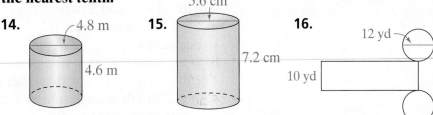

14. 4.8 m / 4.6 m

15. 5.6 cm / 7.2 cm

16. 12 yd / 10 yd

17. Juliet is trying to wrap a can of mixed nuts that is a birthday gift for her brother. The can has a radius of 8 cm and a height of 10 cm. Approximately how many square centimeters of wrapping paper will cover the gift?

 Apply Your Skills

18. A cylinder has radius 8 ft and height 12 ft. Draw and label a net for the cylinder. Find its exact and approximate surface areas.

19. Find the surface area of a square prism with base edge 7 m and height 15 m.

20. Find the area of the top and lateral surfaces of a cylindrical water tank with radius 20 ft and height 30 ft. Round to the nearest square foot.

Homework Video Tutor

Visit: PHSchool.com
Web Code: bje-1005

21. Multiple Choice A tent is approximately the shape of a triangular prism. Which is closest to the surface area of the tent?
  Ⓐ 10,800 in.²   Ⓒ 6,840 in.²
  Ⓑ 7,632 in.²   Ⓓ 1,020 in.²

42 in. / 36 in. / 72 in. / 44 in.

22. Estimate the lateral area of a cylinder with radius 10.3 cm and height 8.1 cm. Use 3 to approximate π.

23. The neighborhood swimming pool needs to be painted. The pool is 40 ft by 60 ft. The depth of the pool is 6 ft throughout.
  a. How many sides need to be painted?
  b. What is the total number of square feet to be painted?
  c. The materials for painting the pool cost $1.50 per square yard. What is the cost of the materials for painting the pool?

 **for Help**

For a guide to solving Exercise 24, see page 532.

24. Error Analysis A student explains that the two cylinders at the right have the same surface area. Explain the student's error.

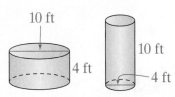

10 ft / 4 ft / 10 ft / 4 ft

25. Open-Ended Describe a real-world situation in which you need to know the surface area of a space figure.

26. Writing in Math In a triangular prism, what is the difference between the height of a base and the height of the prism?

27. You have made two boxes with lids. Which box required more cardboard, a box 8 in. by 6.25 in. by 10.5 in., or a box 9 in. by 5.5 in. by 11.75 in.? Explain.

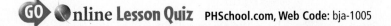

C Challenge

28. Reasoning Use the cubes with side
lengths of 1, 2, and 3 units.

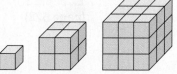

  a. Find the surface area of
    each cube.
  b. If the length of each side of a
    cube is doubled, how does that affect the surface area?
  c. If the length of each side of a cube is tripled, how does that
    affect the surface area?

29. The concrete figure at the left has a hole in it. The surface will be
painted except for the inside of the hole. Find the total surface
area to be painted to the nearest square foot.

30. Reasoning Which has the greater effect on the surface area of a
cylinder: doubling the base radius or doubling the height? Justify
your answer.

Multiple Choice Practice and Mixed Review

For Standards Tutorials, visit PHSchool.com. Web Code: bjq-9045

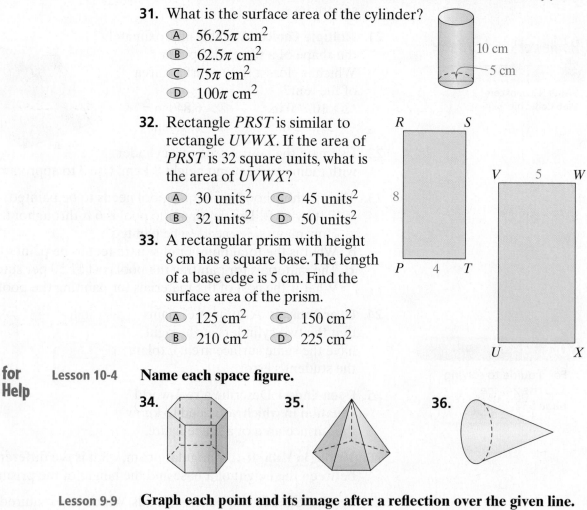

31. What is the surface area of the cylinder?

  Ⓐ 56.25π cm^2
  Ⓑ 62.5π cm^2
  Ⓒ 75π cm^2
  Ⓓ 100π cm^2

32. Rectangle *PRST* is similar to
rectangle *UVWX*. If the area of
PRST is 32 square units, what is
the area of *UVWX*?

  Ⓐ 30 units^2 Ⓒ 45 units^2
  Ⓑ 32 units^2 Ⓓ 50 units^2

33. A rectangular prism with height
8 cm has a square base. The length
of a base edge is 5 cm. Find the
surface area of the prism.

  Ⓐ 125 cm^2 Ⓒ 150 cm^2
  Ⓑ 210 cm^2 Ⓓ 225 cm^2

GO for Help

Lesson 10-4   **Name each space figure.**

34.   **35.**   **36.**

Lesson 9-9   **Graph each point and its image after a reflection over the given line.**

37. $A(0, 9)$; *x*-axis   **38.** $B(-3, 5)$; *y*-axis   **39.** $C(3, -1)$; $x = 2$

Understanding Math Problems For the problem below, let Diana's thinking guide you through using the formulas. Check your understanding with the exercises at the bottom of the page.

Error Analysis A student explains that the two cylinders at the right have the same surface area. Explain the student's error.

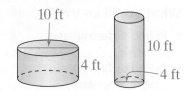

10 ft
10 ft
4 ft
4 ft

What Diana Thinks

First I need to use the formula for the surface area of a cylinder.

For L.A., use the formula $2\pi rh$. For B, use πr^2. r indicates the radius of each base and h indicates the height of each cylinder.

For the cylinder on the left, r is 5 and h is 4. Now I will substitute these values and simplify.

For the cylinder on the right, r is 2 and h is 10. I will substitute these values again and simplify.

Compare the surface areas. Then answer the question.

What Diana Writes

S.A. = L.A. + 2B

S.A. = $2\pi rh + 2(\pi r^2)$

<u>Cylinder on Left</u>
S.A. = $2(3.14)(5)(4) + 2(3.14)(5)^2$
    = 282.6

<u>Cylinder on Right</u>
S.A. = $2(3.14)(2)(10) + 2(3.14)(2)^2$
    = 150.72

The surface areas are not equal. The student incorrectly assumed that you can interchange diameter and height and have the same surface area.

EXERCISES

Write the formula you use to find the surface area of each figure. Give the meaning and value of each letter or letters in the formula.

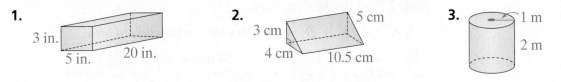

1.
3 in.
5 in.
20 in.

2.
5 cm
3 cm
4 cm
10.5 cm

3.
1 m
2 m

4. Error Analysis For Exercise 3, Hans says that the surface area of the cylinder is 12.56 m². What is his error?

Surface Area: Pyramids, Cones, and Spheres

What You'll Learn

- To find surface areas of pyramids
- To find surface areas of cones and spheres

. . . And Why

To find surface areas of real-world objects, such as a basketball

✓ Check Skills You'll Need

Use the Order of Operations to simplify each expression.

1. $\frac{2}{3}(9\pi) + \frac{1}{2}(8\pi)$

2. $\frac{3}{4}(12\pi) + \frac{2}{5}(15\pi)$

3. $\frac{1}{6}(24\pi) + \frac{1}{3}(3\pi)$

4. $\frac{5}{8}(32\pi) + \frac{1}{7}(14\pi)$

GO for Help
Lesson 5-4

🔊 New Vocabulary

- slant height

Develop Use formulas routinely for finding the surface area of basic three-dimensional figures.

Master Compute the area of more complex or irregular three-dimensional figures by breaking the figures down into more basic geometric objects.

Finding Surface Areas of Pyramids

In this text, all pyramids are *regular* pyramids. They have regular polygons for bases and congruent isosceles triangles for lateral faces. You can use the **slant height** ℓ, the height of a face, to find the area of the lateral faces. If n is the number of lateral triangular faces, L.A. is $n\left(\frac{1}{2}b\ell\right)$ or $\frac{1}{2}p\ell$.

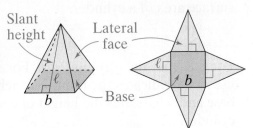

Take Note — Surface Area of a Pyramid

The lateral area of a pyramid is one half the product of the perimeter of the base and the slant height.

The surface area of a pyramid is the sum of the lateral area and the area of the base.

$$\text{L.A.} = \tfrac{1}{2}p\ell \qquad \text{S.A.} = \text{L.A.} + B$$

1 EXAMPLE — Finding Surface Area of a Pyramid

Find the surface area of the square pyramid.

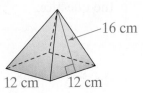

Step 1 Find the lateral area.

$$\text{L.A.} = \tfrac{1}{2}p\ell \qquad \text{Use the formula for lateral area.}$$

$$= \tfrac{1}{2} \cdot 48 \cdot 16 \qquad p = 4(12) \text{ and } \ell = 16.$$

$$= 384$$

Step 2 Find the surface area.

$$\text{S.A.} = \text{L.A.} + B \qquad \text{Use the formula for surface area.}$$

$$= 384 + 12^2 \qquad \text{L.A.} = 384 \text{ and } B = 12^2.$$

$$= 384 + 144$$

$$= 528$$

The surface area of the pyramid is 528 cm².

✔ Quick Check

1. A pyramid has a square base with edge 20 ft. The slant height is 8 ft. Find the surface area.

Finding Surface Areas of Cones and Spheres

In this text, every cone is a right circular cone with the vertex of the cone directly over the center of the circular base.

L.A. is $\frac{1}{2}(2\pi r)\ell$ or L.A. $= \pi r\ell$.

Take Note ✏ Surface Area of a Cone

The surface area (S.A.) of a cone is the sum of the lateral area and base area.

$$\text{L.A.} = \pi r\ell \qquad \text{S.A.} = \text{L.A.} + B$$

---

2 EXAMPLE   Finding Surface Area of a Cone

Find the surface area of the cone at the right.

L.A. $= \pi r\ell$ Use the formula for lateral area.
  $= \pi(4)(10)$ $r = 4$ and $\ell = 10$.
  $= 40\pi$

S.A. $=$ L.A. $+ B$ Use the formula for surface area.
  $= 40\pi + \pi(4)^2$ L.A. $= 40\pi$ and $B = \pi(4)^2$.
  $= 56\pi$
  ≈ 175.84 Use 3.14 for π.

The surface area of the cone is 56π cm², or about 176 cm².

✔ Quick Check

2. A cone has slant height 39 ft and radius 7 ft. Find its surface area to the nearest square foot.

A sphere has the same area as four circles with the same radius.

Take Note ✏ Surface Area of a Sphere

The surface area of a sphere of radius r is
$$\text{S.A.} = 4\pi r^2.$$

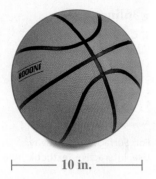

  Finding Surface Area of a Sphere

Calculate the surface area of a basketball.

$$\text{S.A.} = 4\pi r^2 \qquad \text{Use the formula for surface area.}$$

$$= 4\pi(5)^2 \qquad r = 5$$

$$= 100\pi \approx 314$$

The surface area is 100π in.^{2}, or about 314 in.^{2}.

⊢———— 10 in. ————⊣

✅ Quick Check

3. A sphere has a radius of 6 cm. Find its surface area. Use 3.14 for π.

You can find the surface area of a space figure that combines two or more figures you have studied.

More Than One Way

Find the surface area of the silo formed by a half sphere and a cylinder. The diameter of the silo is 20 ft.

↕10 ft

72 ft

Roberto's Method

Find the area of each space figure. Then find their sum.

One half sphere   Cylinder

$$\text{S.A.} = \frac{1}{2}(4\pi r^2) \qquad\qquad \text{L.A.} = 2\pi rh$$

$$\approx \frac{1}{2}(4)(3.14)(10^2) \qquad \approx 2(3.14)(10)(72)$$

$$= 628 \qquad\qquad\qquad = 4{,}521.6$$

Surface area of silo is about $628 + 4{,}521.6$, or $5{,}149.6$ ft^2.

Jasmine's Method

Combine formulas before substituting values.

$$\begin{array}{lll}
\text{Surface area} & = \frac{1}{2}\text{S.A.} & + \text{L.A.} \\
\text{of silo} & \quad\text{of sphere} & \quad\text{of cylinder}
\end{array}$$

$$= \frac{1}{2}(4\pi r^2) + 2\pi rh$$

$$= 2\pi r^2 + 2\pi rh$$

$$= 2\pi r(r + h)$$

$$\approx 2(3.14)(10)(10 + 72)$$

$$= 5{,}149.6$$

Surface area of silo is about $5{,}149.6$ ft^2.

Choose a Method

1. Which method do you prefer? Explain.

Use the pyramid at the left for Exercises 1–6.

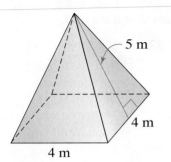

5 m

4 m

4 m

1. Draw a net for the pyramid.

2. What is the relationship between the lateral height of the pyramid and the heights of the lateral faces?

3. Find the total area of the triangles in your net.

4. Use the formula L.A. = $\frac{1}{2} p\ell$ to find the lateral area of the pyramid.

5. How are your results in Exercises 3 and 4 related?

6. Critical Thinking Explain why the formula L.A. = $4(\frac{1}{2} b\ell)$ gives the same lateral area as the formula L.A. = $\frac{1}{2} p\ell$. (*Hint*: Consider what the variables in each equation represent.)

Standards Practice

For more exercises, see *Extra Skills and Word Problem Practice*.

A Practice by Example

Examples 1–3
(pages 534–536)

GO for Help

Find the surface area of each space figure, to the nearest square unit.

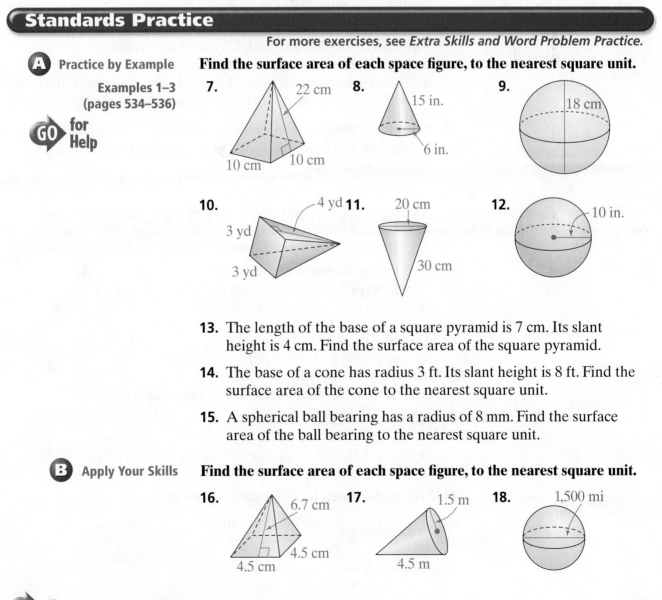

7. 22 cm
10 cm   10 cm

8. 15 in.
6 in.

9. 18 cm

10. 4 yd
3 yd
3 yd

11. 20 cm
30 cm

12. 10 in.

13. The length of the base of a square pyramid is 7 cm. Its slant height is 4 cm. Find the surface area of the square pyramid.

14. The base of a cone has radius 3 ft. Its slant height is 8 ft. Find the surface area of the cone to the nearest square unit.

15. A spherical ball bearing has a radius of 8 mm. Find the surface area of the ball bearing to the nearest square unit.

B Apply Your Skills

Find the surface area of each space figure, to the nearest square unit.

16. 6.7 cm
4.5 cm
4.5 cm

17. 1.5 m
4.5 m

18. 1,500 mi

19. Error Analysis A friend tells you that the surface area of a square prism with base length 4 m and height 5 m is the same as the surface area of a square pyramid with base length 4 m and height 5 m. Explain your friend's error.

Find the surface area of each figure to the nearest square unit.

20.   **21.**   **22.**

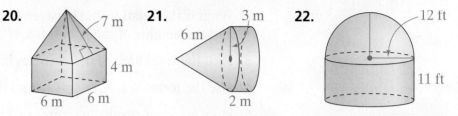

23. Writing in Math Write a paragraph explaining how to find the surface area of a cone with slant height 10 in. and base radius 8 in.

C Challenge

24. Approximately 70% of Earth's surface is covered by water. If the diameter of Earth is approximately 13,000 km, find the approximate surface area *not* covered by water.

25. The spherical planetarium at the American Museum of Natural History in New York City is 87 ft in diameter.
  a. What is the surface area of the sphere?
  b. The sphere is covered by 2,474 panels to absorb sound. What is the average area of each panel, to the nearest tenth of a square foot?

26. Reasoning Which has the greater surface area, a cylinder with height 2 in. and base radius of 2 in., or a sphere with radius 2 in.? Justify your answer.

Multiple Choice Practice and Mixed Review

For Standards Tutorials, visit PHSchool.com. Web Code: bjq-9045

27. Find the surface area of the figure.
  Ⓐ 2,150 in.^{2} Ⓒ 3,000 in.^{2}
  Ⓑ 2,600 in.^{2} Ⓓ 3,200 in.^{2}

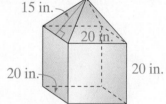

28. The salaries of 25 workers and a manager total $1,177,000. The manager's salary is $66,540. Which equation can be used to find a, a worker's salary?

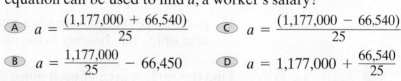

  Ⓐ $a = \dfrac{(1{,}177{,}000 + 66{,}540)}{25}$ Ⓒ $a = \dfrac{(1{,}177{,}000 - 66{,}540)}{25}$

  Ⓑ $a = \dfrac{1{,}177{,}000}{25} - 66{,}450$ Ⓓ $a = 1{,}177{,}000 + \dfrac{66{,}540}{25}$

GO for Help   Lesson 10-5

Find the surface area to the nearest square unit.

29.   **30.**

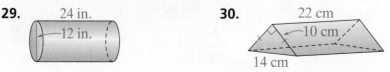

10-7 Volume: Prisms and Cylinders

Develop Use formulas routinely for finding the volume of basic three-dimensional figures, including prisms and cylinders.

Develop Compute the volume of a three-dimensional object built from rectangular solids.

What You'll Learn

- To find volumes of prisms
- To find volumes of cylinders

. . . And Why

To solve real-world problems such as finding volumes of containers

 Check Skills You'll Need

Find the area of each circle.

1. radius = 8 cm

2. radius = 12 cm

3. diameter = 20 cm

GO for Help
Lesson 10-3

🔊 **New Vocabulary**

- volume
- cubic unit

Finding the Volumes of Prisms

The **volume** of a three-dimensional figure is the number of cubic units needed to fill it. A **cubic unit** is the space occupied by a cube with edges one unit long.

Consider filling the rectangular prism at the right with centimeter cubes.

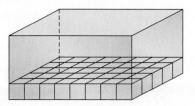

4 cm

5 cm

8 cm

The bottom layer of the prism contains $8 \cdot 5 = 40$ centimeter cubes, or a volume of 40 cm³ (cubic centimeters).

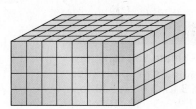

The prism has four layers of cubes, so it contains $4 \cdot 40$, or 160, centimeter cubes in all.

The volume of the prism is 160 cm³.

The volume found for the rectangular prism above suggests the following formula.

Take Note ✏ **Volume of a Prism**

The volume V of a prism is the product of the base area B and the height h.

$$V = Bh$$

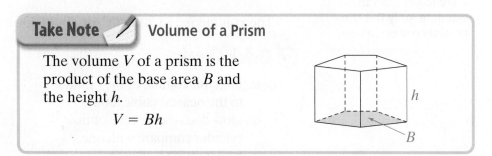

h

B

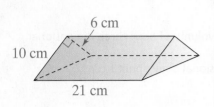
6 cm
10 cm
21 cm

① EXAMPLE Finding Volume of a Prism

Find the volume of the triangular prism at the left.

$$V = Bh \qquad \text{Use the formula for volume.}$$
$$= 30 \cdot 21 \quad B = \frac{1}{2} \cdot 10 \cdot 6 = 30$$
$$= 630 \qquad \text{Simplify.}$$

The volume is 630 cm³.

✓ Quick Check

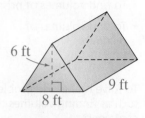
6 ft
9 ft
8 ft

1. Find the volume of the triangular prism.

Finding the Volumes of Cylinders

You can calculate the volume of a cylinder in much the same way that you calculate the volume of a prism.

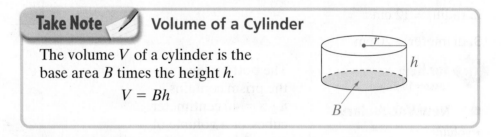

Take Note **Volume of a Cylinder**

The volume V of a cylinder is the base area B times the height h.
$$V = Bh$$

r
h
B

② EXAMPLE Finding Volume of a Cylinder

Problem Solving Tip

Estimate You can estimate by using 3 for π, 3 for 3.4, and 10 for 12. $V \approx 3 \cdot 3^2 \cdot 10$, or about 270. This estimate is lower than the actual volume because all values have been rounded down. Since choices A, B, and C are lower than this estimate, only D is the possible correct answer.

Multiple Choice **What is the volume of the juice can to the nearest cubic centimeter?**

Ⓐ 128 cm³   Ⓒ 256 cm³
Ⓑ 139 cm³   Ⓓ 436 cm³

$$V = Bh \qquad\qquad \text{Use the formula for volume.}$$
$$V = \pi r^2 h \qquad\qquad B = \pi r^2$$
$$= \pi \cdot 3.4^2 \cdot 12 \qquad r = 3.4; h = 12$$
$$= 138.72\pi$$
$$\approx 435.5808 \qquad \text{Use 3.14 for } \pi.$$

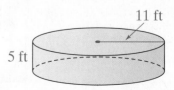
3.4 cm
12 cm

The volume is 138.72π cm³, or about 436 cm³. The answer is D.

✓ Quick Check

2. **a.** Find the volume of the cylinder to the nearest cubic foot.
   b. How does the volume of this cylinder compare with one having twice its dimensions?

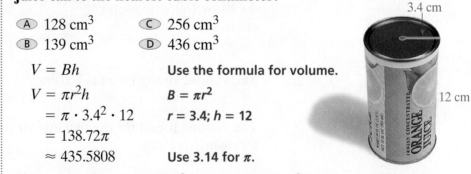
11 ft
5 ft

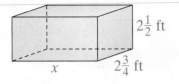

Use the figure at the left for Exercises 1–6.

1. What is the formula for the volume of the figure?

2. **Writing in Math** Describe what each variable in the formula represents.

3. Write an expression for the area of the base of the figure.

4. The volume of the figure is 38.5 ft^3. Explain how you can use this information to find the area of the base of the figure.

5. What is the area of the base of the figure?

6. Find x.

Standards Practice

For more exercises, see *Extra Skills and Word Problem Practice*.

A Practice by Example

Example 1 (page 540)

GO **for Help**

Find the volume of each prism.

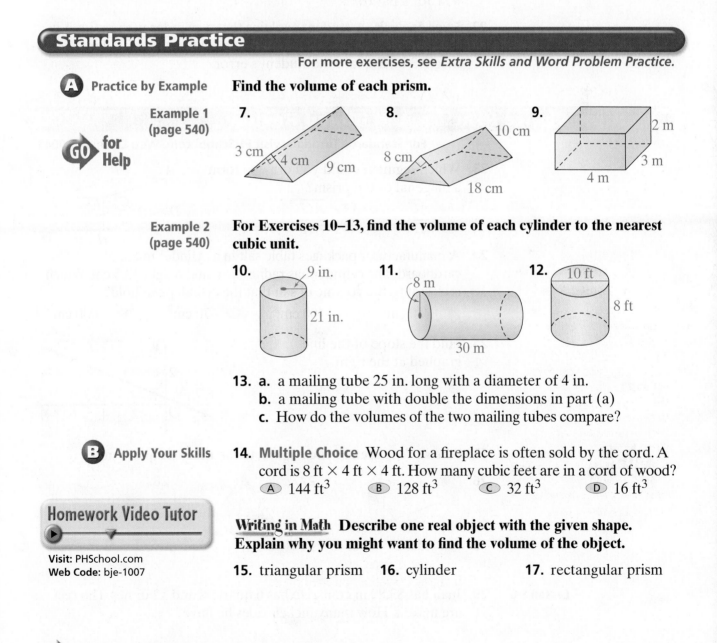

7.

8.

9.

Example 2 (page 540)

For Exercises 10–13, find the volume of each cylinder to the nearest cubic unit.

10.

11.

12.

13. **a.** a mailing tube 25 in. long with a diameter of 4 in.
    b. a mailing tube with double the dimensions in part (a)
    c. How do the volumes of the two mailing tubes compare?

B Apply Your Skills

14. **Multiple Choice** Wood for a fireplace is often sold by the cord. A cord is 8 ft × 4 ft × 4 ft. How many cubic feet are in a cord of wood?

    Ⓐ 144 ft^3 Ⓑ 128 ft^3 Ⓒ 32 ft^3 Ⓓ 16 ft^3

Homework Video Tutor

Visit: PHSchool.com
Web Code: bje-1007

Writing in Math **Describe one real object with the given shape. Explain why you might want to find the volume of the object.**

15. triangular prism   16. cylinder   17. rectangular prism

18. A storage box measures 24 in. by 12 in. by 3 in. Find its volume to the nearest cubic centimeter (1 in. = 2.54 cm).

Find each missing dimension. Use $\pi \approx 3.14$.

19.

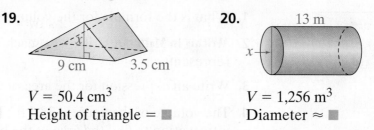

$V = 50.4$ cm^3
Height of triangle = ▪

20.

$V = 1,256$ m^3
Diameter $\approx$ ▪

C Challenge

21. Concrete is sold by the yard, which means by the cubic yard. It costs $70 per yard. How many cubic feet are in a cubic yard? How much would it cost to pour a slab that is 14 ft by 16 ft by 6 in. for a patio?

22. Error Analysis A student explains that a cylinder with radius 1 in. and height 3 in. has half the volume of one with radius 2 in. and height 3 in. Explain the student's error.

Multiple Choice Practice and Mixed Review

For Standards Tutorials, visit PHSchool.com. Web Code: bjq-9045

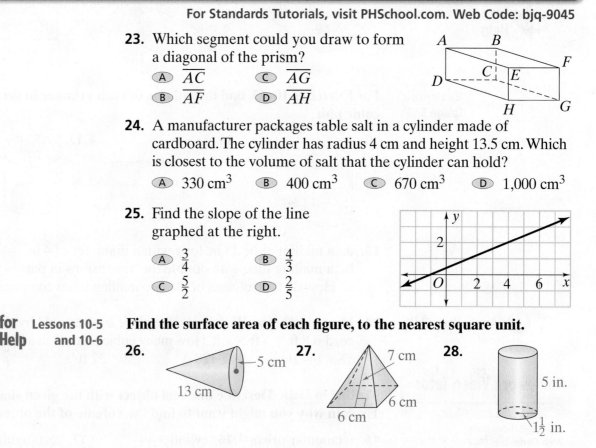

23. Which segment could you draw to form a diagonal of the prism?
- Ⓐ $\overline{AC}$
- Ⓒ $\overline{AG}$
- Ⓑ $\overline{AF}$
- Ⓓ $\overline{AH}$

24. A manufacturer packages table salt in a cylinder made of cardboard. The cylinder has radius 4 cm and height 13.5 cm. Which is closest to the volume of salt that the cylinder can hold?
- Ⓐ 330 cm^3
- Ⓑ 400 cm^3
- Ⓒ 670 cm^3
- Ⓓ 1,000 cm^3

25. Find the slope of the line graphed at the right.
- Ⓐ $\frac{3}{4}$
- Ⓑ $\frac{4}{3}$
- Ⓒ $\frac{5}{2}$
- Ⓓ $\frac{2}{5}$

GO for Help Lessons 10-5 and 10-6

Find the surface area of each figure, to the nearest square unit.

26.

27.

28.

Lesson 5-6

29. Juan has $3.80 in coins. He has 6 quarters and 12 dimes. The rest are nickels. How many nickels does he have?

> **Develop** Use formulas routinely for finding the volume of basic three-dimensional figures, including prisms and cylinders.

You can model prisms and cylinders using the movement of a two-dimensional figure along a line segment. For example, the figures below show that a circle moving along a line segment that is perpendicular to the circle forms a right cylinder. A circle moving along a line segment that is not perpendicular to the circle forms an oblique cylinder.

You have used the formula $V = Bh$ to find the volumes of right prisms and cylinders. You can use the same formula to find the volumes of oblique prisms and cylinders, where h is the length of the perpendicular segment that joins the planes on which its two bases lie. An oblique figure has the same volume as the corresponding right figure with a congruent base and equal height.

The following activity illustrates the relationship between right and oblique figures.

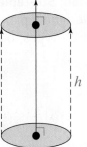
right cylinder

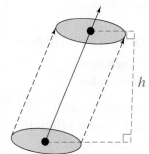
oblique cylinder

ACTIVITY

The stacks of paper below are made using sheets of identical sizes. They contain the same number of sheets of paper. The first stack forms an oblique prism. The second stack forms a right prism.

1. **Reasoning** Without calculating, explain how you know that the volumes of the two prisms formed by the stacks are equal.

2. A single sheet of paper is 3 in. wide and 4 in. long. Find the area of the base of each prism formed by the stacks.

3. The height of the stack of paper on the right is 3 in. Find the volume of the right prism formed by the second stack.

4. **Reasoning** Without calculating, find the height of the oblique prism formed by the first stack. Explain how you know.

5. Using your results in Steps 1 and 4, write and solve an equation to calculate the height of the oblique prism formed by the first stack.

EXERCISES

Use the figure at the right for Exercises 1–2.

1. Calculate the volume of the oblique cylinder shown at the right.

2. Sketch a right cylinder with the same volume. Include dimensions in your sketch.

2.5 in.

3 in.

Reasoning Strategy: Make a Model

Master Construct two-dimensional patterns for three-dimensional models.
Develop Apply strategies and results from simpler problems to more complex problems.

What You'll Learn

- To make a model

. . . And Why

To build the largest box possible from a rectangular piece of card board

 Check Skills You'll Need

Draw each figure described below.

1. a rectangle with small squares drawn in each corner

2. a rectangle divided into eight congruent rectangles

3. two parallelograms that have different shapes but the same perimeter

 for Help
Lesson 9-3

Make a Model

Math Strategies in Action When theater designers and product designers plan projects, they build models. They use different prototypes to compare sizes and layouts.

1 EXAMPLE   Making a Model

A box company makes boxes to hold popcorn. Each box is made by cutting the square corners out of a rectangular sheet of cardboard. The rectangle is $8\frac{1}{2}$ in. by 11 in. What are the dimensions of the box that will hold the most popcorn if the square corners have side lengths 1 in., 2 in., 3 in., and 4 in.?

Understand Understand the problem.

1. What is the goal of the problem?

2. What information do you have to help you build a model?

Plan Make a plan to solve the problem.

To find the size that will hold the greatest amount of popcorn, you must find the dimensions that will give you the greatest volume.

Build four boxes using sheets of $8\frac{1}{2}$ in.-by-11 in. paper. Test four whole-number lengths of cuts.

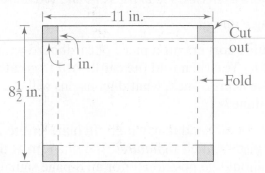

3. a. What are the dimensions of the box with corners 1 in. by 1 in.?
b. What is the volume of this box?

4. When you cut a 2 in.-by-2 in. square from each corner, what effect does that have on the length, width, and height of the box?

Carry Out **Carry out the plan.**

Measure to find the dimensions of each of your boxes. Then find the volume of each box.

5. Which box has the greatest volume?

6. Is it possible to create a box with 5 in.-by-5 in. corners? Explain.

Check **Check the answer to be sure it is reasonable.**

A table is another way to organize your information and solve the problem.

7. List the size of the cut, and then find the length, width, and height of the box. Find each volume.

Size of Cut	Length	Width	Height	Volume
1 in.	9 in.	6.5 in.	1 in.	58.5 in.^{3}
2 in.	▨ in.	▨ in.	▨ in.	▨ in.^{3}
3 in.	▨ in.	▨ in.	▨ in.	▨ in.^{3}
4 in.	▨ in.	▨ in.	▨ in.	▨ in.^{3}

✓ Quick Check

8. a. Use a table to find the volume of a box folded from an $8\frac{1}{2}$ in.-by-11 in. sheet of paper if the square corners have each of the following side lengths: $1\frac{1}{2}$ in., $2\frac{1}{2}$ in., and $3\frac{1}{2}$ in.

b. Did you find dimensions of a box that holds a greater volume than you did in Question 7? Which dimensions are they?

For more exercises, see *Extra Skills and Word Problem Practice*.

 A Practice by Example

Example 1
(page 544)

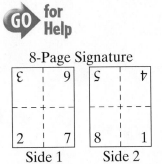 **GO** for Help

8-Page Signature

Side 1   Side 2

Solve by making a model.

1. You cut square corners off a piece of cardboard with dimensions 16 in. by 20 in. You then fold the cardboard to create a box with no lid. To the nearest inch, what dimensions will give you the greatest volume?

2. Newspapers, books, and magazines often are printed in groups of 8, 16, or 32 pages, called *signatures*. The diagram at the left shows how pages should be positioned for an 8-page signature. The pages are positioned to print on both sides of the paper that is fed through the printing press. When the paper is folded, the pages are in order. Make a model to show one way to position the pages in a 16-page book.

 B Apply Your Skills

Solve using any strategy.

3. The length of a rectangle is twice its width. The perimeter of the rectangle is 90 cm. What are the length and width?

4. A company packages snack mix in cylindrical tubes. Each tube is made from a rectangle of cardboard. The bases of the cylinder are plastic. The cardboard comes in $8\frac{1}{2}$ in.-by-11 in. sheets. To hold the greatest amount of mix, should the longer side or shorter side be the height? Justify your answer.

5. A dog owner wants to use 200 ft of fencing to enclose the greatest possible area for his dog. He wants the fenced area to be rectangular. What dimensions should he use?

6. **Writing in Math** You want to find how the length of a pendulum affects the time the pendulum takes to swing back and forth. Explain how you would model the situation.

7. An alphabet book will have one letter on each page. Eight pages will be printed on a single piece of paper. You fold the paper in half. Then you fold it in half again and trim the edges. The eight pages appear in order. Draw the layout for two sides of the large sheet for the letters A–H. Explain why two layouts are possible.

STRATEGIES

- Act It Out
- Draw a Diagram
- Try, Test, Revise
- Look for a Pattern
- Make a Model
- Make a Table
- Simulate the Problem
- Solve by Graphing
- Use Multiple Strategies
- Work a Simpler Problem
- Work Backward
- Write an Equation
- Write a Proportion

C Challenge

8. **Reasoning** In the parts (a)–(c), how many of the indicated cubes are there in this 3-by-3-by-3 cube?
    a. 1-by-1-by-1 cubes
    b. 2-by-2-by-2-cubes
    c. 3-by-3-by-3 cubes
    d. How many 3-by-3-by-3 cubes would be in a 5-by-5-by-5 cube?

9. One base of a trapezoid is twice as long as the other base. The height is the same as the shorter base. If the area is 24 cm², what is the height of the trapezoid?

Homework Video Tutor

Visit: PHSchool.com
Web Code: bje-1008

Multiple Choice Practice and Mixed Review

For Standards Tutorials, visit PHSchool.com. Web Code: bjq-9045

10. Which space figure below can you fold from the net at the right?

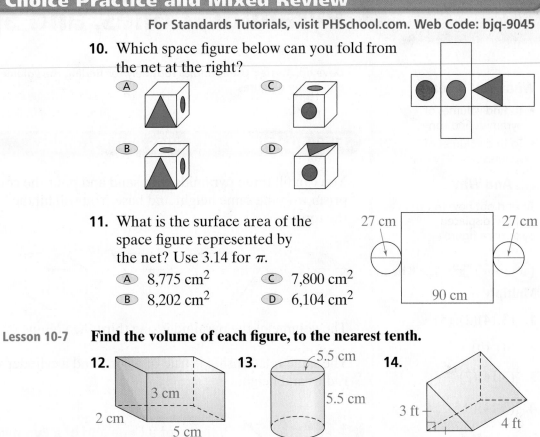

11. What is the surface area of the space figure represented by the net? Use 3.14 for π.

   Ⓐ 8,775 cm^2 Ⓒ 7,800 cm^2

   Ⓑ 8,202 cm^2 Ⓓ 6,104 cm^2

GO for Help   Lesson 10-7   **Find the volume of each figure, to the nearest tenth.**

12.   **13.**   **14.**

Lesson 8-2   **Find the solutions of each equation when x is 0, 1, and -1.**

15. $2x - y = 10$ **16.** $5x + y = 15$ **17.** $2x + 3y = 6$

✓ Checkpoint Quiz 2

Name each space figure. Find its surface area, to the nearest square unit.

1.   **2.**   **3.**

Find the volume of each figure to the nearest tenth.

4.   **5.**

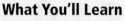

10-9

Volume: Pyramids, Cones, and Spheres

What You'll Learn

- To find volumes of pyramids and cones
- To find volumes of spheres

... And Why

To find out how much water is displaced by a space figure

✓ **Check Skills You'll Need**

Multiply

1. $\frac{1}{3}(3.14)(2)^2(5)$

2. $\frac{1}{3}(4)^2(6)$

3. $\frac{4}{3}(3.14)(2)^3$

4. $\frac{4}{3}(3.14)(0.5)^3$

GO for Help
Lesson 5-4

Develop, Master Use formulas routinely for finding the volume of basic three-dimensional figures.

Finding Volumes of Cones and Pyramids

You can fill three pyramids with sand and pour the contents into a prism with the same height and base. You will fill the prism evenly to the top.

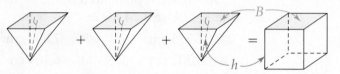

The volume of the pyramid is one third the volume of the prism.

The same relationship is true of a cone and a cylinder with the same radius and height.

Take Note 　　Volume of a Cone and of a Pyramid

The volume V of a cone or a pyramid is $\frac{1}{3}$ the product of the base area B and the height h.

$$V = \frac{1}{3}Bh$$

GO Online

Video Tutor Help
Visit: PHSchool.com
Web Code: bje-0775

1 EXAMPLE 　　Finding Volume of a Cone

Find the volume of the cone.

$V = \frac{1}{3}Bh$ 　　Use the formula for volume.

$V = \frac{1}{3}\pi r^2 h$ 　　$B = \pi r^2$

$= \frac{1}{3}\pi(3)^2(10)$ 　　Replace r with 3 and h with 10. Simplify.

$= 30\pi$

The volume of the cone is 30π ft³, or about 94 ft³.

✓ **Quick Check**

1. Find the volume, to the nearest cubic unit, of a cone with height 5 cm and radius of base 2 cm.

EXAMPLE **Finding Volume of a Pyramid**

Find the volume of the square pyramid.

$V = \frac{1}{3}Bh$ Use the formula for volume.

$V = \frac{1}{3}s^2h$ $B = s^2$

$= \frac{1}{3}(6)^2(10)$ Replace s with 6 and h with 10.

$= 120$ Simplify.

The volume of the pyramid is 120 ft^3.

10 ft

6 ft

✓ Quick Check

2. Find the volume of a square pyramid that has a side of 5 ft and a height of 20 ft.

Finding Volumes of Spheres

Below is the formula for the volume of a sphere.

Take Note **Volume of a Sphere**

The volume V of a sphere with radius r is $\frac{4}{3}\pi$ times the cube of the radius.

$$V = \frac{4}{3}\pi r^3$$

r

EXAMPLE **Finding Volume of a Sphere**

You build a snow statue with snow spheres. What is the volume of the snow in the bottom sphere?

$V = \frac{4}{3}\pi r^3$ Use the volume formula.

$= \frac{4}{3}\pi(1.5)^3$ Replace r with 1.5.

$= 4.5\pi$ Simplify.

The volume of the bottom snow sphere is 4.5π ft^3, or about 14 ft^3.

3 ft

✓ Quick Check

3. Find the volume of each sphere to the nearest whole number. Use 3.14 for π.

    a. radius = 15 m   **b.** diameter = 7 mi

Complete Exercises 1–4 to solve the problem below.

You place a steel ball with diameter 8 cm in a water-filled cylinder that is 10 cm in diameter and 10 cm high. Some of the water spills out. What is the volume of water left in the cylinder?

1. Find the volume of the water-filled cylinder.

2. Find the volume of the ball.

3. Find the difference of the two volumes.

4. What is the volume of the unspilled water left in the cylinder?

Standards Practice

For more exercises, see *Extra Skills and Word Problem Practice*.

A **Practice by Example**

Find the volume to the nearest cubic unit. Use 3.14 for π.

Example 1
(page 548)

GO for Help

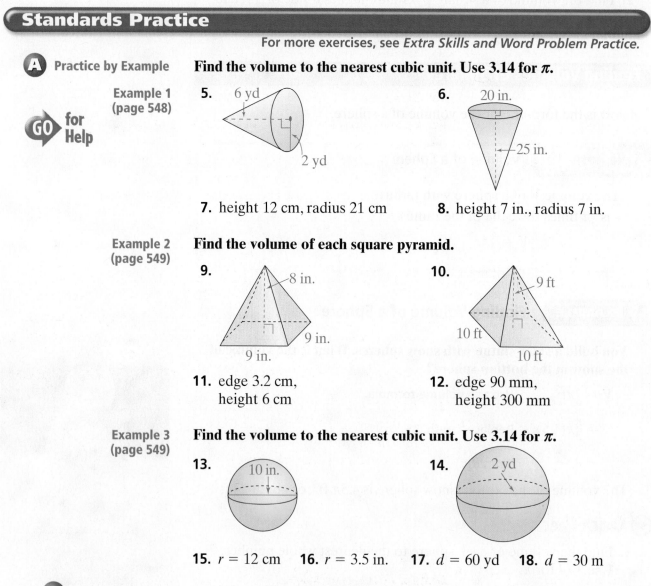

5. 6 yd / 2 yd

6. 20 in. / 25 in.

7. height 12 cm, radius 21 cm

8. height 7 in., radius 7 in.

Example 2
(page 549)

Find the volume of each square pyramid.

9. 8 in. / 9 in. / 9 in.

10. 9 ft / 10 ft / 10 ft

11. edge 3.2 cm, height 6 cm

12. edge 90 mm, height 300 mm

Example 3
(page 549)

Find the volume to the nearest cubic unit. Use 3.14 for π.

13. 10 in.

14. 2 yd

15. $r = 12$ cm   16. $r = 3.5$ in.   17. $d = 60$ yd   18. $d = 30$ m

B **Apply Your Skills**

19. A cone-shaped paper cup is 7 cm high with a diameter of 6 cm. If the ivy plant on Julia's desk needs 240 mL of water, about how many paper cups of water will she use to water it? (1 mL = 1 cm^3)

20. Tennis balls with a diameter of 2.5 in. are sold in cans of three (left). The can is a cylinder. To the nearest tenth, what is the volume of the space in the can not occupied by tennis balls? Assume the balls touch the can on the sides, top, and bottom.

21. To the nearest tenth, how much frozen yogurt can you pack inside a cone that is 5 in. high with a radius of 1.25 in?

22. <u>Writing in Math</u> Explain how you remember formulas for finding volumes of prisms and pyramids, cylinders and cones, and spheres.

Homework Video Tutor

Visit: PHSchool.com
Web Code: bje-1009

Find the missing dimension. Round to the nearest unit.

23.

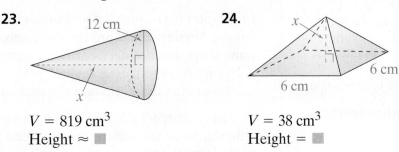

12 cm

x

$V = 819$ cm^3
Height ≈ ■

24.

x

6 cm

6 cm

$V = 38$ cm^3
Height = ■

25. Sphere: volume = 36π yd^3, diameter = ■

26. Cone: volume = 424 m^3, diameter = 18 m, height ≈ ■

C Challenge

27. You want to fill the top part of an hourglass $\frac{2}{3}$ full of salt. The height of the hourglass is 20 cm, and the radius of the base is 8 cm. Find the volume of salt needed.

Multiple Choice Practice and Mixed Review

For Standards Tutorials, visit PHSchool.com. Web Code: bjq-9045

28. A company charges Mae $625 to maintain 1,000 square feet of lawn. The company restores Walter's 800-square-foot lawn at the same rate. How much does Walter have to pay?

　Ⓐ $425.00　　Ⓑ $500.00　　Ⓒ $525.00　　Ⓓ $1,280.00

29. Abe uses the net to make a cardboard square pyramid. What is the total surface area of cardboard needed to make the pyramid?

　Ⓐ 104 in.^{2}
　Ⓑ 320 in.^{2}
　Ⓒ 576 in.^{2}
　Ⓓ 896 in.^{2}

$\ell = 10$ in.

16 in.

$\ell = 10$ in.

16 in.

Simplify each expression.

 for Help　Lesson 5-9　**30.** $(3ab^2)^3$　**31.** $-(4x)^2$　**32.** $(-2p^2)^4$　**33.** $\left(-\frac{3}{8}\right)^2$　**34.** $\left(\frac{2x}{y^3}\right)^2$

 Online Lesson Quiz PHSchool.com, Web Code: bja-1009

Scale Factors and Solids

Develop, Master Understand that when the lengths of all dimensions are multiplied by a scale factor, the surface area is multiplied by the square of the scale factor and the volume is multiplied by the cube of the scale factor.

Develop, Master Relate changes in measurement with a change of scale to the units used.

What You'll Learn

- To find dimensions of similar solids
- To find surface areas and volumes of similar solids

. . . And Why

To find surface areas and volume of real-world objects such as pitchers

 Check Skills You'll Need

Solve each proportion.

1. $\frac{x}{4} = \frac{7}{16}$

2. $\frac{9}{5} = \frac{m}{24}$

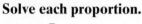 **for Help**
Lesson 6-2

◀)) **New Vocabulary**

- similar solids
- scale factor

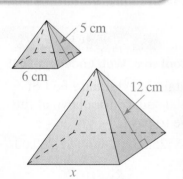

Finding Dimensions of Similar Solids

In Chapter 6, you studied properties of similar two-dimensional figures. **Similar solids** are three-dimensional figures that have the same shape but not necessarily the same size. As with similar polygons, corresponding angles have equal measures and the corresponding dimensions are in proportion.

You can construct similar solids by multiplying the lengths of all the dimensions by the same number, called the scale factor. The **scale factor** is the ratio of a length in one solid to the corresponding length in the similar solid.

You can find missing dimensions of similar solids.

1 **EXAMPLE** **Finding Dimensions of a Similar Solid**

The two pyramids shown at the left are similar. Find the length of the base edge *x*.

Method 1 Use the scale factor.

Write the ratio of the slant height of the large pyramid to the slant height of the small pyramid. The scale factor is $\frac{12}{5}$.

To find *x*, multiply the corresponding edge length by the scale factor.

$$6 \cdot \frac{12}{5} = 14.4$$

The base-edge length is 14.4 cm.

Method 2 Use corresponding parts to write a proportion.

$$\frac{x}{6} = \frac{12}{5} \quad \begin{array}{l} \longleftarrow \text{ dimensions of large pyramid} \\ \longleftarrow \text{ dimensions of small pyramid} \end{array}$$

$$6 \cdot \frac{x}{6} = 6 \cdot \frac{12}{5} \quad \text{Multiply each side by 6.}$$

$$x = 14.4 \quad \text{Simplify.}$$

The base-edge length is 14.4 cm.

✓ Quick Check

1. Two cylinders are similar. The small cylinder has a diameter of 4 m and a height of *h*. The large cylinder has a diameter of 5 m and height of 11 m. What is the value of *h*?

Finding Surface Area and Volume

You can use scale factors to find the surface area and volume of similar solids.

> **Take Note** ✎ **Surface Area and Volume of Similar Solids**
>
> If the scale factor of similar solids is $\frac{a}{b}$, then
> - the ratio of surface areas is $\frac{a^2}{b^2}$ and
> - the ratio of volumes is $\frac{a^3}{b^3}$

2 EXAMPLE **Surface Area and Volume of Similar Solids**

The surface area of the cylindrical pitcher is about 90 in.^{2}. Its volume is about 157 in.^{3}. The pitcher and creamer are similar. Find the surface area and volume of the creamer.

6 in.   3 in.

Pitcher   Creamer

The ratio of the diameters is $\frac{3}{6}$, or $\frac{1}{2}$.

So the ratio of the surface areas is $\frac{1^2}{2^2}$, or $\frac{1}{4}$.

$$\frac{\text{surface area of creamer}}{\text{surface area of pitcher}} = \frac{1}{4} \qquad \textbf{Write a proportion.}$$

$$\frac{S}{90} = \frac{1}{4} \qquad \textbf{Substitute the surface area of the pitcher.}$$

$$90 \cdot \frac{S}{90} = 90 \cdot \frac{1}{4} \qquad \textbf{Multiply each side by 90.}$$

$$S = 22.5 \qquad \textbf{Simplify.}$$

The surface area of the creamer is about 22.5 in.^{2}.

If the ratio of the diameters is $\frac{1}{2}$, the ratio of the volumes is $\frac{1^3}{2^3}$, or $\frac{1}{8}$.

$$\frac{\text{volume of creamer}}{\text{volume of pitcher}} = \frac{1}{8} \qquad \textbf{Write a proportion.}$$

$$\frac{V}{157} = \frac{1}{8} \qquad \textbf{Substitute the volume of the pitcher.}$$

$$157 \cdot \frac{V}{157} = 157 \cdot \frac{1}{8} \qquad \textbf{Multiply each side by 157.}$$

$$V = 19.625 \qquad \textbf{Simplify.}$$

The volume of the creamer is about 20 in.^{3}.

✓ Quick Check

2. A box has a surface area of about 54 in.^{2} and a volume of about 27 in.^{3}. The edge lengths of the box are about $\frac{1}{3}$ of the edge lengths of a larger box. Find the surface area and volume of the larger box.

1. **Vocabulary** What does it mean to say that two rectangular solids are similar?

Use the similar figures at the left for Exercises 2–4.

2. What proportion would you write to find *x*?

3. The surface area of the smaller cube is 6 cm². What is the surface area of the larger cube?

4. **Mental Math** The volume of the smaller cube is 1 cm³. What is the volume of the larger cube?

Standards Practice

For more exercises, see *Extra Skills and Word Problem Practice*.

Ⓐ Practice by Example

Example 1
(page 552)

GO for Help

For each pair of similar solids, find the value of the variable.

5.

6.

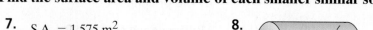

Example 2
(page 553)

Find the surface area and volume of each smaller similar solid.

7. S.A. = 1,575 m²
   V = 4,050 m³

   15 m   12 m

8.

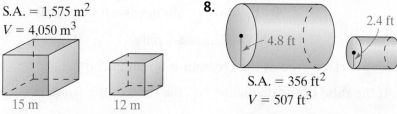

S.A. = 356 ft²
V = 507 ft³

9. Two similar cylindrical vases have diameters of 6 in. and 8 in. The smaller vase has a surface area of 1,960 in.² and a volume of 339 in.³. Find the surface area and volume of the larger vase.

Ⓑ Apply Your Skills

10. A glass cube has edges that are $\frac{3}{4}$ of the length of the edges of a larger cube. The larger cube has a surface area of 6,000 cm². What is the surface area of the smaller cube?

V = 64 ft³

2*v*   3*v*

11. The prisms at the left are similar. The volume of the small prism is 64 ft³. Find the volume of the large prism.

12. Two prisms are similar. The larger prism has a height of 18 m and a base-edge length of 20 m. The smaller prism has a height of 4.5 m. What is the base-edge length of the smaller prism?

13. **Number Sense** Amelia sees two cubic sculptures. She estimates the edge length of the larger sculpture is between 2.5 and 3 times the edge length of the smaller one. How much greater should she estimate the volume of the larger sculpture to be? Explain.

14. Gina used 78 square feet of plywood to build a storage bin to hold her gardening supplies. How much plywood will she need to build a similar box for her hand tools if the dimensions of the box are half the dimensions of the bin?

$V = 3.375 \text{ yd}^3$

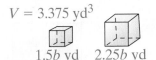

1.5*b* yd   2.25*b* yd

15. The prisms at the left are similar. The surface area of the small prism is 13.5 yd². The volume of the small prism is 3.375 yd³. Find the surface area and volume of the large prism.

16. **Writing in Math** Explain how to determine if two cones are similar.

17. Two prisms are similar. The surface area of one is four times the surface area of the other. What is the ratio of the corresponding dimensions?

C Challenge

18. How long is the edge of a cube with a volume that is twice that of the cube at the right? Round to the nearest tenth.

8 cm

Multiple Choice Practice and Mixed Review

For Standards Tutorials, visit PHSchool.com. Web Code: bjq-9045

19. The volume of the larger cube at the right is 216 cubic inches. What is the volume of the smaller cube?

   Ⓐ 6 in.³   Ⓒ 24 in.³
   Ⓑ 8 in.³   Ⓓ 72 in.³

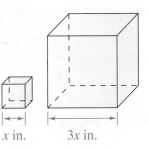

x in.   3*x* in.

20. There are 5.256 × 10⁵ minutes in a year. A teenager's heart beats about 80 times per minute. How many times does it beat per year?

   Ⓐ 6.57×10^7 Ⓒ 4.205×10^7
   Ⓑ 6.57×10^3 Ⓓ 4.205×10^7

21. Which of the following is an altitude of parallelogram *ABCD*?

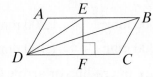

   Ⓐ $\overline{DE}$ Ⓑ $\overline{BC}$ Ⓒ $\overline{BD}$ Ⓓ $\overline{EF}$

 for Help   Lesson 4-9

Write each number in scientific notation.

22. 75,000   23. 0.00194   24. 0.000083

EXAMPLE

The net at the right forms a rectangular prism. Measure the dimensions in inches. Which is closest to the total surface area of the prism?

- Ⓐ 3 in.²
- Ⓒ 2 in.²
- Ⓑ $2\frac{1}{2}$ in.²
- Ⓓ $1\frac{1}{4}$ in.²

Use a customary ruler to measure the dimensions of the net in inches. You know that the surface area of the prism is the sum of the areas of each rectangle.

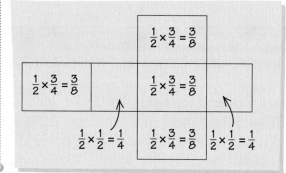

$$\text{S.A.} \approx \frac{3}{8} + \frac{1}{4} + \frac{3}{8} + \frac{3}{8} + \frac{3}{8} + \frac{1}{4}$$
$$= 2$$

The surface area of the prism is about 2 in.². The correct answer is C.

Multiple Choice Practice

Read each question. Then write the letter of the correct answer on your paper.

1. The net is a small model of a cylinder for an engine. Measure the dimensions in millimeters. Which is closest to the surface area of the model?

   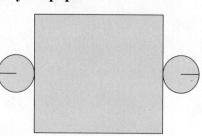

   - Ⓐ 2,900 mm²
   - Ⓒ 1,200 mm²
   - Ⓑ 1,300 mm²
   - Ⓓ 1,100 mm²

2. Measure the radius, or arrow length, of the spinner in centimeters. Which value is closest to the distance traveled by the tip of the arrow during three full rotations of the spinner?

   - Ⓐ 6 cm
   - Ⓑ 8 cm
   - Ⓒ 19 cm
   - Ⓓ 38 cm

Chapter 10 Review

Vocabulary Review

◀)) **English and Spanish Audio Online**

altitude (p. 501)
altitude of a triangle (p. 507)
area (p. 500)
cone (p. 519)
cubic unit (p. 539)
cylinder (p. 519)

lateral area (p. 528)
net (p. 520)
prism (p. 519)
pyramid (p. 519)
scale factor (p. 552)
similar solids (p. 552)

slant height (p. 534)
space figure (p. 519)
sphere (p. 519)
surface area (p. 527)
volume (p. 539)

Choose the vocabulary term that correctly completes the sentence.

1. The sum of the areas of the lateral faces of a prism is the __?__ of a prism.

2. A(n) __?__ is a space figure with one circular base and one vertex.

3. The __?__ of a parallelogram is a line segment that is drawn from the side opposite the base to the base and that is perpendicular to the base.

4. The __?__ of a three-dimensional figure is the number of cubic units needed to fill it.

5. The set of all points in space that are a given distance from a given point called the center is a(n) __?__.

6. A(n) __?__ has two parallel bases that are congruent circles.

7. The __?__ of a figure is the number of square units it encloses.

Go Online
PHSchool.com

For: Vocabulary quiz
Web Code: bjj-1051

Skills and Concepts

Lessons 10-1 and 10-2

- To find areas of rectangles
- To find areas of parallelograms
- To find areas of triangles
- To find areas of trapezoids

The **area** of a polygon is the number of square units enclosed by the polygon. To find the areas of parallelograms, triangles, or trapezoids, use the appropriate formulas.

parallelogram

$A = bh$

triangle

$A = \frac{1}{2}bh$

trapezoid

$A = \frac{1}{2}h(b_1 + b_2)$

Find the area of the shaded region in each figure.

8. Parallelogram   9. Trapezoid   10.

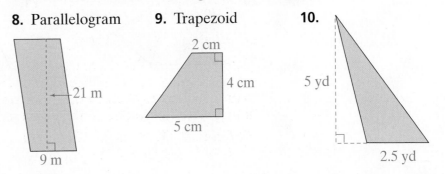

Lesson 10-3

- To find areas of circles
- To find areas of irregular figures that include parts of circles

To find the area of a circle, use the formula $A = \pi r^2$. Use 3.14 for π.

Find the area of each figure to the nearest square unit.

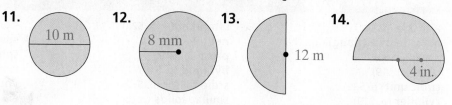

11.   10 m

12.   8 mm

13.   12 m

14.   4 in.

Lesson 10-4

- To identify common space figures
- To identify space figures from nets

Name **pyramids** and **prisms** by the shapes of their bases. A **cylinder** is a space figure with two circular bases. **Cones** have one circular base and one vertex. **Nets** are flat patterns for space figures.

Name the space figure represented by each net.

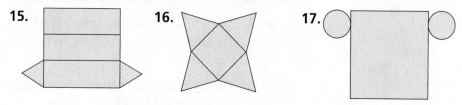

15.

16.

17.

Lessons 10-5 and 10-6

- To find surface areas of prisms
- To find surface areas of cylinders
- To find surface areas of pyramids
- To find surface areas of cones and spheres

The **lateral area** of a figure is the sum of the areas of the lateral faces. For pyramids and cones, use **slant height** ℓ to find the lateral area. The **surface area** of a figure is the sum of the lateral area and the area of the bases.

To find surface area, use the appropriate formula.

prisms and cylinders   pyramids and cones   sphere
S.A. = L.A. + 2B   S.A. = L.A. + B   S.A. = $4\pi r^2$

Find the surface area to the nearest square unit. Use 3.14 for π.

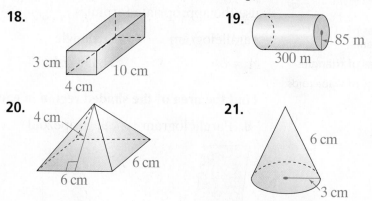

18.   3 cm   10 cm   4 cm

19.   85 m   300 m

20.   4 cm   6 cm   6 cm

21.   6 cm   3 cm

Lesson 10-8

• To make a model

To solve some problems, make a model.

22. A gift box measures 6 in. along each edge. You cut a rectangular sheet of wrapping paper to get a single piece with which you can cover the box without overlapping. What are the smallest possible dimensions of the original sheet of wrapping paper?

23. A 12 m-by-15 m rectangular garden has a walk 1 m wide around it. Describe how you would find the area of the walk.

Lessons 10-7 and 10-9

• To find volumes of prisms
• To find volumes of cylinders
• To find volumes of cones and pyramids
• To find volumes of spheres

Volume is the measure of how much a space figure can hold.

To find volume, use the appropriate formula.

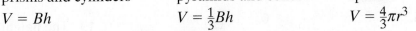

prisms and cylinders	pyramids and cones	spheres
$V = Bh$	$V = \frac{1}{3}Bh$	$V = \frac{4}{3}\pi r^3$

Find each volume to the nearest cubic unit.

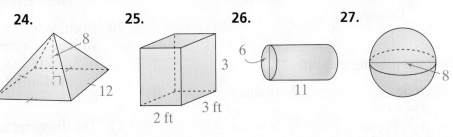

24. 8, 12

25. 3, 2 ft, 3 ft

26. 6, 11

27. 8

Lesson 10-10

• To find dimensions of similar solids
• To find surface areas and volumes of similar solids

Similar solids are solids with the same shape but not necessarily the same size. The scale factor is the ratio of a length in one solid to the corresponding length in a similar solid.

If the scale factor is $\frac{a}{b}$, then the ratio of the surface areas is $\frac{a^2}{b^2}$ and the ratio of the volumes is $\frac{a^3}{b^3}$.

Find the surface area and volume of the large solid in each pair of similar solids.

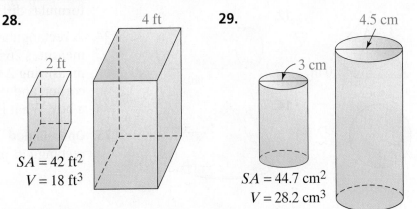

28. 2 ft, 4 ft
$SA = 42\ \text{ft}^2$
$V = 18\ \text{ft}^3$

29. 3 cm, 4.5 cm
$SA = 44.7\ \text{cm}^2$
$V = 28.2\ \text{cm}^3$

Use 3.14 for π as needed on this page.

Find the area of each figure.

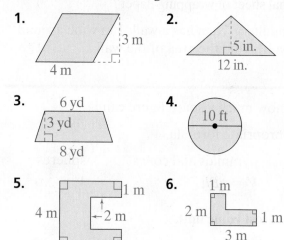

1.
3 m
4 m

2.
5 in.
12 in.

3.
6 yd
3 yd
8 yd

4.
10 ft

5.
1 m
4 m
2 m
4 m

6.
1 m
2 m
1 m
3 m

Find the missing measures.

7. circle
$d = 4$ cm
$A = \blacksquare$ cm^2

8. triangle
$b = 7$ m
$h = 4$ m
$A = \blacksquare$ m^2

Name the space figure for each net.

9.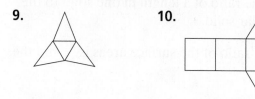

10.

Find the surface area of each figure.

11.
12 m
10 m

12.
2 cm
4 cm

13.
15 m

14.
2.5 cm
1.9 cm

Find the volume of each figure to the nearest cubic unit.

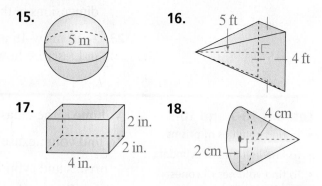

15.
5 m

16.
5 ft
4 ft

17.
2 in.
2 in.
4 in.

18.
4 cm
2 cm

19. The height of a rectangle is doubled while the base is unchanged. How does this affect the area? Explain.

20. In cubic feet, how much greater is the volume of a cone with height 10 ft and radius 6 ft than the volume of a square pyramid with height 10 ft and base edge length 6 ft?

21. The diameter of Mars is about 4,000 mi.
   a. Find the approximate surface area.
   b. Find the approximate volume.

22. A box is 25.5 cm by 17 cm by 5 cm.
   a. How much dry dishwashing detergent can it hold?
   b. Without overlap, how much cardboard is needed to make the box?

23. **Writing in Math** How is the formula for volume of a prism like the formula for volume of a pyramid? How are the formulas different?

24. A rectangular piece of sheet metal measures 26 in. by 20 in. A square measuring 2 in. by 2 in. is cut out of each corner, and the sides are folded to form a box. What is the volume of the box?

25. **Open-Ended** Draw a net for a rectangular prism.

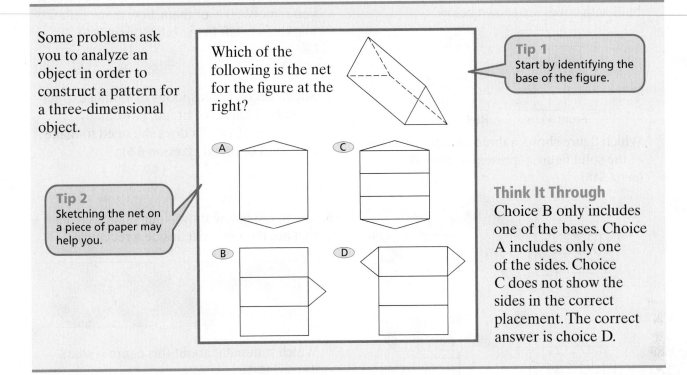

Some problems ask you to analyze an object in order to construct a pattern for a three-dimensional object.

Which of the following is the net for the figure at the right?

A

C

B

D

Tip 1
Start by identifying the base of the figure.

Tip 2
Sketching the net on a piece of paper may help you.

Think It Through
Choice B only includes one of the bases. Choice A includes only one of the sides. Choice C does not show the sides in the correct placement. The correct answer is choice D.

Vocabulary Review

As you solve problems, you must understand the meanings of mathematical terms. Choose the vocabulary term that correctly completes the sentence.

A. The (volume, surface area) of a three-dimensional figure is the number of cubic units needed to fill it.

B. A pattern that you can use to form a space figure is a (view, net).

C. A (prism, polygon) has two congruent parallel bases and lateral faces that are parallelograms.

D. A (rectangle, cube) is a quadrilateral with four 90° angles.

E. A (prism, cylinder) has two parallel bases that are congruent circles.

Read each question. Then write the letter of the correct answer on your paper.

1. The dimensions of two similar prisms are shown. What is the volume of the larger prism?
(Lesson 10-10)

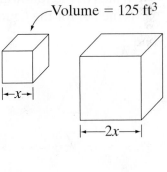

Volume = 125 ft³

   Ⓐ 800 ft³
   Ⓑ 1,000 ft³
   Ⓒ 3,500 ft³
   Ⓓ 6,000 ft³

2. A side length of cube B is three times a side length of cube A. If the volume of cube A is eight cubic meters, what is the volume of cube B? (Lesson 10-10)
   Ⓐ 24 m³   Ⓒ 216 m³
   Ⓑ 72 m³   Ⓓ 512 m³

3. The front view and right view of a solid figure built with cubes are shown below.

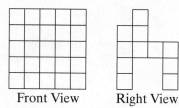

Front View   Right View

Which figure shows a three-dimensional view of the solid figure represented above? (page 518)

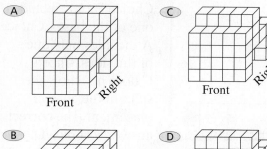

4. Which of the following is the net for the figure?

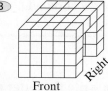

5. A package of 38 bulbs costs $19. Another package of 45 bulbs costs $27. How much money per bulb do you save when you buy the bulbs with the lower unit price? (Lesson 6-1)

  Ⓐ $0.01 Ⓑ $0.10 Ⓒ $0.70 Ⓓ $1.23

6. A bin of markers contains 20 yellow markers. If you remove 30% of them, how many yellow markers are left in the bin? (Lesson 6-5)

  Ⓐ 6   Ⓒ 16
  Ⓑ 14   Ⓓ 18

7. Sheila needs 12 teaspoons of vanilla extract to make 3 loaves of bread. How many teaspoons of vanilla does she need to make 20 loaves of bread? (Lesson 6-5)

  Ⓐ 80   Ⓒ 24
  Ⓑ 40   Ⓓ 5

8. The figure below shows four shaded circles that are the same size inside a rectangle.

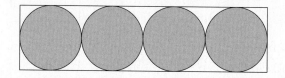

Which statement about this figure is true? (Lesson 10-3)

  Ⓐ The shaded area is less than half the total area of the rectangle.

  Ⓑ The unshaded area is more than 40% of the shaded area of the figure.

  Ⓒ The unshaded area is less than 25% of the shaded area of the figure.

  Ⓓ The shaded area is equal to the unshaded area of the figure.

9. From the table, which expression can be used to find the total cost, before tax, of r ruby gemstones, s sterling silver pendants, and b blue gemstones? (Lesson 1-1)

Jewelry	Cost ($)
Ruby Gemstones	35
Sterling Silver Pennants	30
Blue Gemstones	25

  Ⓐ $25r + 35s + 30b$
  Ⓑ $35r + 30s + 25b$
  Ⓒ $r + s + b$
  Ⓓ $(25 + 35 + 30)(r + s + b)$

10. Stewart rents a computer. The rate is $40 for a 2-week rental. What is the cost of a 9-week rental? **(Lesson 6-1)**
  Ⓐ $40   Ⓒ $160
  Ⓑ $80   Ⓓ $180

11. A hummingbird can flap its wings 3,000 times in a minute. At that rate, how many times can it flap its wings in 2 hours? **(Lesson 6-1)**
  Ⓐ 1.8×10^3 Ⓒ 1.8×10^5
  Ⓑ 6×10^3 Ⓓ 3.6×10^5

12. It takes about 27.3 days for the moon to orbit Earth. About how many times will the moon orbit the Earth in 2 years? **(Lesson 6-1)**
  Ⓐ 13.4   Ⓒ 26.7
  Ⓑ 13.6   Ⓓ 54.6

13. What is the volume of the hollow region of the concrete cylinder shown below? **(Lesson 10-7)**

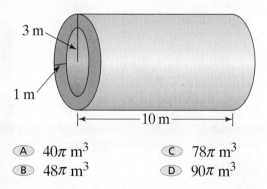

  Ⓐ 40π m^3 Ⓒ 78π m^3
  Ⓑ 48π m^3 Ⓓ 90π m^3

14. Add the lengths 3.25 cm, 10.8 cm, and 0.425 cm. Round the sum to the appropriate place value. **(page 156)**
  Ⓐ 14.475 cm   Ⓒ 14.47 cm
  Ⓑ 14.48 cm   Ⓓ 14.5 cm

15. How can you prove that the triangles below are congruent? **(Lesson 9-5)**

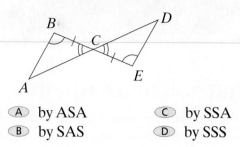

  Ⓐ by ASA   Ⓒ by SSA
  Ⓑ by SAS   Ⓓ by SSS

16. Find the volume of the rectangular prism below. **(Lesson 10-7)**

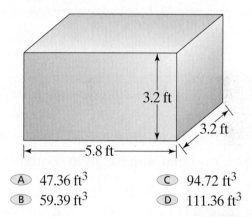

  Ⓐ 47.36 ft^3 Ⓒ 94.72 ft^3
  Ⓑ 59.39 ft^3 Ⓓ 111.36 ft^3

Irrational Numbers and Nonlinear Functions

What You've Learned

Identify and construct basic elements of geometric figures.

Demonstrate an understanding of the conditions that indicate two geometrical figures are congruent and what congruence means about the relationships between the sides and angles of the two figures.

Identify elements of three-dimensional geometric objects (e.g., diagonals of rectangular solids) and describe how two or more objects are related in space.

✓ **Check Your Readiness**   **GO for Help** to the Lesson in green.

Understanding Coordinates (Lesson 1-10)

Name the point with the given coordinates.

1. $(0, 3)$ **2.** $(1, -4)$ **3.** $(-2, 2)$

4. $(-5, -1)$ **5.** $(3, 5)$ **6.** $(6, -4)$

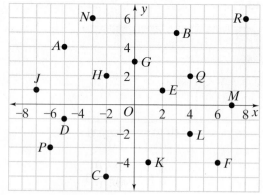

Write the coordinates of each point.

7. A **8.** E **9.** M

10. J **11.** L **12.** P

Simplifying Numbers With Exponents (Lesson 4-2)

Simplify each expression.

13. 10^2 **14.** 6^2 **15.** 2^2 **16.** 9^2 **17.** 11^2

18. 0.2^2 **19.** 7^2 **20.** 2.3^2 **21.** 4^2 **22.** 5^2

Solving Proportions (Lesson 6-2)

Solve each proportion.

23. $\frac{1}{3} = \frac{a}{12}$ **24.** $\frac{h}{5} = \frac{20}{25}$ **25.** $\frac{24}{6} = \frac{4}{x}$ **26.** $\frac{2}{7} = \frac{c}{35}$

27. $\frac{e}{5} = \frac{32}{80}$ **28.** $\frac{18}{g} = \frac{3}{10}$ **29.** $\frac{4}{11} = \frac{28}{m}$ **30.** $\frac{21}{13} = \frac{42}{a}$

31. $\frac{2}{15} = \frac{c}{75}$ **32.** $\frac{1}{4} = \frac{8}{x}$ **33.** $\frac{13}{p} = \frac{39}{51}$ **34.** $\frac{x}{20} = \frac{40}{100}$

▲ You can use the Pythagorean Theorem to solve problems involving distance.

What You'll Learn Next

Differentiate between rational and irrational numbers.

Use the inverse relationship between raising to a power and extracting the root of a perfect square integer; for an integer that is not a square, determine without a calculator the two integers between which its square root lies and explain why.

Understand and use coordinate graphs to plot simple figures and determine lengths and areas related to them.

Know and understand the Pythagorean theorem and its converse and use it to find the length of the missing side of a right triangle and the lengths of other line segments.

New Vocabulary

🔊 **English and Spanish Audio Online**

- **cubic function** (p. 592)
- **distance** (p. 579)
- **hypotenuse** (p. 570)
- **irrational number** (p. 567)

- **legs** (p. 570)
- **midpoint** (p. 581)
- **monomial** (p. 590)
- **perfect square** (p. 566)

- **quadratic function** (p. 591)
- **square root** (p. 566)

Academic Vocabulary
- **verify** (p. 584)

11-1

Square Roots and Irrational Numbers

Develop, Master Differentiate between rational and irrational numbers.

Develop Know that every rational number is a terminating or repeating decimal.

Introduce, Develop Use the inverse relationship between raising to a power and extracting the root of a perfect square integer; for an integer that is not square, determine the two integers between which its square root lies.

What You'll Learn

- To find square roots of numbers
- To classify real numbers

. . . And Why

To use square roots in real-world situations such as finding the distance to the horizon

✓ Check Skills You'll Need

Write the numbers in each list without using exponents.

1. $1^2, 2^2, 3^2, \ldots, 12^2$

2. $10^2, 20^2, 30^2, \ldots, 120^2$

GO for Help
Lesson 4-2

🔊 New Vocabulary

- perfect square
- square root
- irrational number

Finding Square Roots

Consider the squares at the right.

Each square has sides with integer length. The area of a square is the *square* of the length of a side. The square of an integer is a **perfect square.**

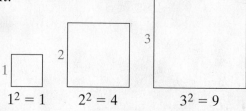

$1^2 = 1 \qquad 2^2 = 4 \qquad 3^2 = 9$

The inverse of squaring a number is finding a **square root.** The square-root radical, $\sqrt{}$, indicates the nonnegative square root of a number. In this book, you may assume that an expression under a square-root radical is greater than or equal to zero.

1 EXAMPLE   Simplifying Square Roots

Simplify each square root.

a. $\sqrt{64}$

$\sqrt{64} = 8$

b. $-\sqrt{121}$

$-\sqrt{121} = -11$

✓ Quick Check

1. Simplify each square root.   **a.** $\sqrt{100}$ **b.** $-\sqrt{16}$

The first thirteen perfect squares are

0, 1, 4, 9, 16, 25, 36, 49, 64, 81, 100, 121, and 144.

For an integer that is not a perfect square, you can estimate a square root. For example, 8 is between the perfect squares 4 and 9.

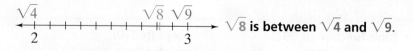

$\sqrt{8}$ is between $\sqrt{4}$ and $\sqrt{9}$.

Since 8 is closer to 9 than to 4, $\sqrt{8}$ is closer to 3 than to 2. So, $\sqrt{8} \approx 3$.

2 EXAMPLE   Estimating a Square Root

Multiple Choice You can use the formula $d = \sqrt{1.5h}$ to estimate the distance d, in miles, to a horizon line when your eyes are h feet above the ground. Estimate the distance to the horizon seen by a parasailer whose eyes are 90 feet above the ground.

  Ⓐ 15.5 mi   Ⓑ 14 mi   Ⓒ 12 mi   Ⓓ 10 mi

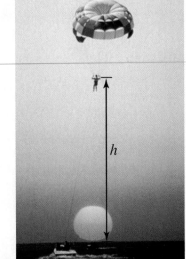

$d = \sqrt{1.5h}$	Use the formula.
$d = \sqrt{135}$	Replace h with 90 and multiply.
$\sqrt{121} < \sqrt{135} < \sqrt{144}$	Find perfect squares close to 135.
$\sqrt{144} = 12$	Find the square root of the closest perfect square.

The parasailer can see about 12 miles to the horizon. The correct answer is C.

✓ Quick Check

2. Estimate to the nearest integer.   **a.** $\sqrt{50}$ **b.** $-\sqrt{22}$

Classifying Real Numbers

You can express a rational number as the ratio of two integers $\frac{a}{b}$, with $b \neq 0$. In decimal form, a rational number either terminates or repeats. An **irrational number** has decimal form that neither terminates nor repeats, and it cannot be written as the ratio of two integers. Together, rationals and irrationals form the real numbers.

If an integer is not a perfect square, its square root is irrational.

3 EXAMPLE   Identifying Irrational Numbers

Identify each number as rational or irrational.

  a. $\sqrt{18}$ irrational, because 18 is not a perfect square

  b. 432.8   rational, because it is a terminating decimal

  c. 0.1212 . . .   rational, because it is a repeating decimal

  d. 0.120120012 . . .   irrational; it neither terminates nor repeats

  e. π irrational; it cannot be represented as $\frac{a}{b}$, where a and b are integers

For: Square Root Activity
Use: Interactive Textbook, 11-1

✓ Quick Check

3. Identify each number as rational or irrational. Explain.

  a. $\sqrt{2}$ **b.** $-\sqrt{81}$ **c.** 0.53   **d.** $\sqrt{42}$

Vocabulary Match each term with its meaning.

1. perfect square
2. square root
3. irrational number
4. area of a square

A. the square of the length of a side of a square
B. a decimal form that neither terminates or repeats
C. the inverse of squaring a number
D. the square of an integer

5. Name a rational and an irrational number between 10 and 20.

Standards Practice

For more exercises, see *Extra Skills and Word Problem Practice*.

A Practice by Example

Example 1
(page 566)

GO for Help

Simplify each square root.

6. $\sqrt{4}$ 7. $-\sqrt{36}$ 8. $\sqrt{1}$ 9. $\sqrt{25}$
10. $-\sqrt{49}$ 11. $\sqrt{81}$ 12. $-\sqrt{9}$ 13. $-\sqrt{169}$

Example 2
(page 567)

Estimate to the nearest integer.

14. $\sqrt{10}$ 15. $\sqrt{17}$ 16. $-\sqrt{39}$ 17. $-\sqrt{55}$

18. The top of the Transamerica Pyramid in San Francisco, California, is 853 ft high. Using the formula $d = \sqrt{1.5h}$ from Example 2, estimate the distance you could see to the horizon from the top of the building.

Example 3
(page 567)

Identify each number as rational or irrational. Explain.

19. 4.1010010001 . . .   20. $\sqrt{87}$
21. $-\sqrt{16}$ 22. $-0.\overline{3}$
23. $\sqrt{5}$ 24. 2,222,222
25. $\sqrt{144}$ 26. 0.31311 . . .

B Apply Your Skills

Simplify each square root.

27. $\sqrt{196}$ 28. $\sqrt{\frac{4}{9}}$ 29. $\sqrt{\frac{25}{49}}$ 30. $\sqrt{\frac{36}{64}}$

31. **Reasoning** What do you get when you square $\sqrt{x}$?

Estimate to the nearest integer.

32. $\sqrt{7}$ **33.** $\sqrt{2}$ **34.** $\sqrt{40}$ **35.** $-\sqrt{80}$

36. $\sqrt{58}$ **37.** $-\sqrt{98}$ **38.** $\sqrt{14}$ **39.** $\sqrt{105}$

Identify each number as rational or irrational. Explain.

40. $\sqrt{0}$ **41.** 1.001001001 . . .   **42.** 2.3010010001 . . .

43. Writing in Math A classmate was absent for today's lesson. Explain to him or her how to estimate $\sqrt{30}$.

44. a. Patterns You can create irrational numbers. For example, the number 1.010010001 . . . shows a pattern, yet it is irrational. What pattern do you see?

     b. Open-Ended Name three irrational numbers between 9 and 10.

Algebra **Find two integers that make each equation true.**

45. $a^2 = 9$ **46.** $b^2 = 25$ **47.** $y^2 = 100$ **48.** $m^2 = \frac{100}{25}$

49. Geometry Estimate the radius of the circle to the nearest inch.

50. Geometry Find the length of a side of a square with area 81 cm^2.

$A = 12$ in.^{2}

C Challenge

If a number is the product of three identical factors, each factor is the *cube root* of the number. Since $2^3 = 8$, 2 is the cube root of 8. In Exercises 51–54, find the number n that makes each equation true.

51. $n^3 = -8$ **52.** $n^3 = 27$ **53.** $n^3 = -27$ **54.** $n^3 = 343$

Multiple Choice Practice and Mixed Review

For Standards Tutorials, visit PHSchool.com. Web Code: bjq-9045

55. The area of a square is 17 square units. Which is closest to the length of a side?

     Ⓐ 3 units   Ⓒ 250 units

     Ⓑ 4 units   Ⓓ 290 units

56. Which is an irrational number?

     Ⓐ $\sqrt{4}$ Ⓑ $\sqrt{6}$ Ⓒ 0   Ⓓ 3.7

57. Which fraction is the same as 2.16?

     Ⓐ $\frac{54}{25}$ Ⓑ $\frac{45}{25}$ Ⓒ $\frac{13}{5}$ Ⓓ $\frac{11}{5}$

GO for Help   Lesson 6-5

58. Shannon scored 17 correct on a 25-item test. The passing grade was 65%. Did Shannon pass? Explain.

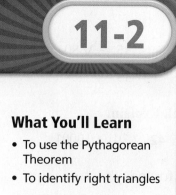

11-2 · The Pythagorean Theorem

Develop For an integer that is not square, determine the two integers between which its square root lies.

Introduce, Develop Know and understand the Pythagorean theorem and its converse and use it to find the length of the missing side of a right triangle.

What You'll Learn

- To use the Pythagorean Theorem
- To identify right triangles

. . . And Why

To use the Pythagorean Theorem in real-world situations, such as carpentry

Check Skills You'll Need

Simplify.

1. $4^2 + 6^2$ 2. $5^2 + 8^2$

3. $7^2 + 9^2$ 4. $9^2 + 3^2$

GO for Help

Lesson 4-2

New Vocabulary

- **legs**
- **hypotenuse**

Using the Pythagorean Theorem

Standards Investigation
Exploring Right Triangles

1. On graph paper, draw right triangles with sides a and b. Measure the length of the third side c with another piece of graph paper.

   Copy and complete the table below.

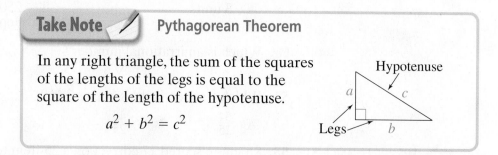

a	b	c	a²	b²	c²
3	4	▪	9	16	▪
5	12	▪	25	144	▪
9	12	▪	81	144	▪

2. Based on your table, use >, <, or = to complete the following statement.

$$a^2 + b^2 \; \blacksquare \; c^2$$

Vocabulary Tip

A <u>right</u> <u>triangle</u> is a triangle with a 90° angle.

In a right triangle, the two shortest sides are **legs.** The longest side, which is opposite the right angle, is the **hypotenuse.** The Pythagorean Theorem shows how the legs and hypotenuse of a right triangle are related.

Take Note   Pythagorean Theorem

In any right triangle, the sum of the squares of the lengths of the legs is equal to the square of the length of the hypotenuse.

$$a^2 + b^2 = c^2$$

You will prove the Pythagorean Theorem in a future math class. For now, you will use the theorem to find the length of a leg or the length of a hypotenuse.

570   Chapter 11   Irrational Numbers and Nonlinear Functions

1 EXAMPLE   Using the Pythagorean Theorem

Find c, the length of the hypotenuse, in the triangle at the right.

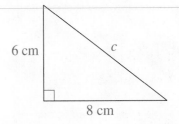

6 cm

c

8 cm

$c^2 = a^2 + b^2$ Use the Pythagorean Theorem.

$c^2 = 6^2 + 8^2$ Replace a with 6 and b with 8.

$c^2 = 100$ Simplify.

$c = \sqrt{100} = 10$ Find the positive square root of each side.

The length of the hypotenuse is 10 cm.

✓ Quick Check

1. The lengths of two sides of a right triangle are given. Find the length of the third side.

   a. legs: 3 ft and 4 ft   **b.** leg: 12 m; hypotenuse: 15 m

You can use estimation or a table of square roots to find approximate values for square roots.

2 EXAMPLE   Finding an Approximate Length

Find the value of x in the triangle at the right. Round to the nearest inch.

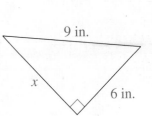

9 in.

x

6 in.

$a^2 + b^2 = c^2$ Use the Pythagorean Theorem.

$6^2 + x^2 = 9^2$ Replace a with 6, b with x, and c with 9.

$36 + x^2 = 81$ Simplify.

$x^2 = 45$ Subtract 36 from each side.

$x = \sqrt{45}$ Find the positive square root of each side.

Then use one of the two methods below to approximate $\sqrt{45}$.

Method 1 Use estimation.
The number 45 lies between the perfect squares 36 and 49. Since 45 is closer to 49 than to 36, $\sqrt{45}$ is closer to 7. So, $\sqrt{45} \approx 7$.

Method 2 Use a table of square roots.
Use the table on page 701. Find 45 in the N column. Then find the corresponding value in the $\sqrt{N}$ column. It is 6.708.

$x \approx 7$ Round to the nearest whole number.

The value of x is about 7 in.

✓ Quick Check

2. In a right triangle, the length of the hypotenuse is 15 m and the length of a leg is 8 m. What is the length of the other leg, to the nearest meter?

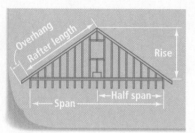

3 EXAMPLE   Finding the Length of the Hypotenuse

Multiple Choice The carpentry terms *span*, *rise*, and *rafter length* are illustrated in the diagram at the left. A carpenter wants to make a roof that has a span of 24 ft and a rise of 8.5 ft. What should the rafter length be?

Ⓐ 14.7 ft   Ⓑ 15.5 ft   Ⓒ 20.5 ft   Ⓓ 32.5 ft

$c^2 = a^2 + b^2$	Use the Pythagorean Theorem.
$c^2 = 12^2 + 8.5^2$	Use half the span, 12 ft. Replace a with 12 and b with 8.5.
$c^2 = 144 + 72.25$	Square 12 and 8.5.
$c^2 = 216.25$	Add.
$c = \sqrt{216.25}$	Find the positive square root.
$c \approx 14.7$	Round to the nearest tenth.

The rafter length should be about 14.7 ft. The answer is A.

✅ Quick Check

3. What is the rise of a roof if the span is 22 feet and the rafter length is 14 feet? Round to the nearest tenth of a foot.

Identifying Right Triangles

The *Converse of the Pythagorean Theorem* allows you to substitute the lengths of the sides of a triangle into the equation $a^2 + b^2 = c^2$ to check whether a triangle is a right triangle. If the equation is true, the triangle is a right triangle.

4 EXAMPLE   Finding a Right Triangle

Is a triangle with sides 12 m, 15 m, and 20 m a right triangle?

$a^2 + b^2 = c^2$	Write the equation for the Pythagorean Theorem.
$12^2 + 15^2 \stackrel{?}{=} 20^2$	Replace a and b with the shorter lengths and c with the longest length.
$144 + 225 \stackrel{?}{=} 400$	Simplify.
$369 \neq 400$	

The triangle is not a right triangle.

✅ Quick Check

4. Can you form a right triangle with the three lengths given? Explain.

   a. 7 in., 8 in., $\sqrt{113}$ in.   **b.** 5 mm, 6 mm, 10 mm

For: Right Triangle Activity
Use: Interactive Textbook, 11-2

Name the hypotenuse and legs of each right triangle.

Copy and complete each step to find the missing length, in inches, in the triangle below.

3. $6^2 + b^2 = \blacksquare^2$

4. $\blacksquare + b^2 = 100$

5. $b^2 = \blacksquare^2$

6. $b = \blacksquare$

For more exercises, see *Extra Skills and Word Problem Practice*.

Ⓐ Practice by Example

Examples 1 and 2
(page 571)

GO for Help

In each right triangle, find each missing length to the nearest tenth.

7.
5 cm   c
12 cm

8.
8 m   8 m
k

The lengths of two sides of a right triangle are given. Find the length of the third side. Round to the nearest tenth where necessary.

9. legs: 12 in. and 16 in.

10. legs: 21 ft and 28 ft

11. leg: 48 ft; hypotenuse: 50 ft

12. leg: 33 ft; hypotenuse: 55 ft

Example 3
(page 572)

Use the Pythagorean Theorem to solve each problem.

13. A painter places an 11-ft ladder against a house. The base of the ladder is 3 ft from the house. How high on the house does the ladder reach?

14. Darla hikes due north for 6 km. She then turns due east and hikes 3 km. What is the direct distance between her starting point and stopping point, rounded to the nearest tenth of a kilometer?

Example 4
(page 572)

Can you form a right triangle with the three lengths given? Explain.

15. 4 m, 6 m, 7 m

16. 4 mi, 5 mi, 6 mi

17. 7 in., 24 in., 25 in.

18. 6, 7, $\sqrt{85}$

19. 8 in., 10 in., 12 in.

20. 5 cm, 12 cm, 13 cm

Use the triangle at the right.
Find the missing length to
the nearest tenth of a unit.

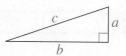

21. $a = 2$ in., $b = 4$ in., $c = \blacksquare$ **22.** $a = 1.4$ m, $b = 2.8$ m, $c = \blacksquare$

23. $a = 3$ ft, $c = 5$ ft, $b = \blacksquare$ **24.** $b = 2.7$ km, $c = 3.4$ km, $a = \blacksquare$

Homework Video Tutor

Visit: PHSchool.com
Web Code: bje-1102

Any three positive integers that make $a^2 + b^2 = c^2$ true form
a *Pythagorean triple*. Does each group of three integers below
form a Pythagorean triple? Show your work.

25. $3, 4, 5$ **26.** $7, 24, 25$ **27.** $10, 24, 25$ **28.** $5, 12, 13$

29. For each group in Exercises 25–28 that forms a Pythagorean
triple, multiply the integers by 2. Do the three new numbers form
a Pythagorean triple? Show your work.

30. Jim works for a landscaping company. He must plant and stake a
tree as shown at the left. If there is 6 in. of extra length at both
ends of each wire, how long must each wire be, to the nearest
tenth of a foot?

31. <u>Writing in Math</u> Can you form a right triangle with side lengths of
$3p$ ft, $4p$ ft, and $5p$ ft? Explain.

5 ft

2 ft

Can you form a right triangle with the three given lengths? Explain.

32. $\sqrt{5}$ yd, $\sqrt{3}$ yd, $\sqrt{2}$ yd   **33.** 1 m, 0.54 m, 0.56 m

Find the value of n in each diagram. Give your answer as a square root.

34.

35.

36.

37.

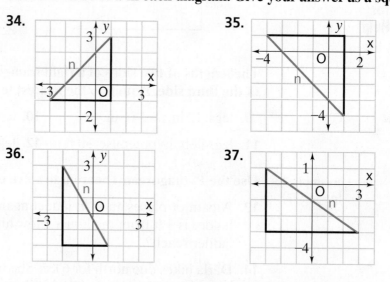

38. The triangle at the left has sides of length $a, b,$ and c.
   a. Which is greater, the area of an equilateral triangle with side
   length a, or the area of an equilateral triangle with side length c?
   Justify your answer.
   b. The formula for the area of an equilateral triangle is $A = \frac{s^2\sqrt{3}}{4}$.
   Find the ratio of the area of an equilateral triangle with side
   length a to the area of an equilateral triangle with side length b.

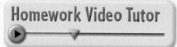

c
a
b

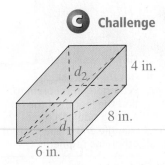

C Challenge

4 in.

8 in.

6 in.

39. Geometry In the rectangular prism at the left, d_1 is the diagonal of the base of the prism, and d_2 is the *diagonal of the prism*.
   a. Find d_1.
   b. The triangle formed by d_1, d_2, and the side that is 4 in. is a right triangle. Use your answer to part (a) to find d_2.
   c. Find the diagonal of a rectangular prism with dimensions 9 in., 12 in., and 5 in.

Multiple Choice Practice and Mixed Review

For Standards Tutorials, visit PHSchool.com. Web Code: bjq-9045

40. Which figure best represents a triangle with sides $a, b,$ and c in which the relationship $a^2 + b^2 = c^2$ is always true?

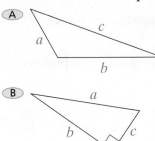

Ⓐ
Ⓒ
Ⓑ
Ⓓ

41. An airplane takes off in a straight path. When it has traveled 5 km, it is 3 km high. To the nearest kilometer, what is the horizontal distance d that the airplane has flown over?

5 km   3 km d

   Ⓐ 2 km   Ⓒ 6 km
   Ⓑ 4 km   Ⓓ 8 km

GO for Help   Lesson 11-1   **Identify each number as rational or irrational.**

42. $\sqrt{36}$ **43.** $0.\overline{6}$ **44.** $-\sqrt{12}$ **45.** -33.3 **46.** $0.\overline{654}$

✓ Checkpoint Quiz 1

Estimate to the nearest integer.

   1. $-\sqrt{3}$ **2.** $\sqrt{14}$ **3.** $\sqrt{27}$ **4.** $\sqrt{90}$ **5.** $-\sqrt{45}$ **6.** $\sqrt{105}$

The lengths of two legs of a right triangle are given. Find the length of the hypotenuse. Round to the nearest tenth.

   7. 6 ft, 8 ft   **8.** 8 m, 14 m   **9.** 7 yd, 24 yd   **10.** 5 cm, 5 cm

Can you form a right triangle with the three lengths given? Explain.

   11. 8 in., 10 in., 12 in.   **12.** 5 cm, 12 cm, 13 cm

13. Open-Ended Name three irrational numbers between 10 and 20.

The Pythagorean Theorem and Circles

> **Develop** Use the Pythagorean theorem to find the length of the missing side of a right triangle and the lengths of other line segments.

Follow the steps below to discover a characteristic of chords and their perpendicular bisectors.

Step 1 With a compass, construct a large circle. Label the center O.

Step 2 Draw a chord $\overline{AB}$ that is not a diameter.

Step 3 Construct the perpendicular bisector of the chord with a compass and straightedge or by folding the circle so that A lies on B.

Step 4 Label the point where the perpendicular bisector intersects the chord D.

Step 5 Write a conjecture about the perpendicular bisector of a chord and the center of the circle.

Step 6 Classify $\triangle AOD$ by its angles.

The distance from the center of a circle to a chord is the length of the perpendicular segment with endpoints at the center of the circle and on the chord. You can use the radius of a circle and the length of a chord to find the distance from the center of a circle to the chord.

1 EXAMPLE

Circle O at the right has a radius of 10 cm. Chord $\overline{FG}$ is 12 cm long. How far is $\overline{FG}$ from O?

Since $\overline{MO}$ is perpendicular to $\overline{FG}$ and passes through the center of the circle, $\overline{MO}$ is the perpendicular bisector of $\overline{FG}$. So $MG = \frac{1}{2}FG$. Therefore $MG = 6$ cm. Use the Pythagorean Theorem to find the distance x from the center O to the chord $\overline{FG}$.

$$10^2 = x^2 + 6^2$$
$$100 = x^2 + 36$$
$$100 - 36 = x^2 + 36 - 36$$
$$64 = x^2$$
$$8 = x$$

The distance from the center O to the chord $\overline{FG}$ is 8 cm.

For a given circle, you can also find the length of a chord or the length
of the radius if you know two other lengths.

2 EXAMPLE

**Chord $\overline{PT}$ is 24 in. long and 5 in. from the center of
circle O at the right. Find the length of the radius.**

$\overline{MO}$ is the perpendicular bisector of $\overline{PT}$. So $PM = \frac{1}{2}(PT) = 12$.

Use the Pythagorean Theorem to find the radius r.

$$r^2 = 12^2 + 5^2$$
$$r^2 = 144 + 25$$
$$r^2 = 169$$
$$r = 13$$

The radius is 13 in.

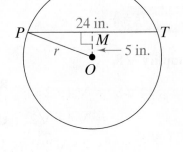

EXERCISES

**Find x, the distance from the center O of each circle to chord $\overline{JK}$.
Round to the nearest tenth.**

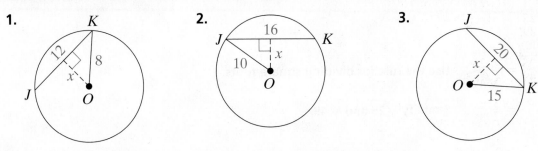

1.

2.

3.

**Find the length of x in each circle O. If your answer is not an integer,
round to the nearest tenth.**

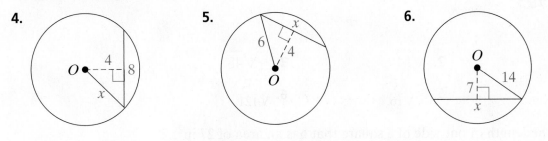

4.

5.

6.

Develop Use the inverse relationship between raising to a power and extracting the root of a perfect square integer.
Develop Apply strategies from simpler problems to more complex problems.
Develop Note the method of deriving the solution and demonstrate a conceptual understanding of the derivation by solving similar problems.

The rules for multiplying and dividing square roots will help you work more efficiently with square roots.

For nonnegative numbers, the square root of a product equals the product of the square roots. Algebraically, if $a \geq 0$ and $b \geq 0$, then $\sqrt{ab} = \sqrt{a} \cdot \sqrt{b}$.

1 EXAMPLE

Simplify $\sqrt{8}$.

$$\sqrt{8} = \sqrt{4 \cdot 2}$$ Rewrite 8 as the product of 4, its perfect square factor, and 2.

$$= \sqrt{4} \cdot \sqrt{2}$$ Use the rule for multiplying square roots.

$$= 2 \cdot \sqrt{2}$$ Simplify $\sqrt{4}$.

$$= 2\sqrt{2}$$

For nonnegative numbers, the square root of a quotient equals the quotient of the square roots. Algebraically, if $a \geq 0$ and $b \geq 0$, then $\sqrt{\frac{a}{b}} = \frac{\sqrt{a}}{\sqrt{b}}$.

2 EXAMPLE

Simplify $\sqrt{\frac{25}{49}}$.

$$\sqrt{\frac{25}{49}} = \frac{\sqrt{25}}{\sqrt{49}}$$ Use the rule for dividing square roots.

$$= \frac{5}{7}$$ Simplify $\sqrt{25}$ and $\sqrt{49}$.

Sometimes you need to use both rules in order to simplify a square root.

EXERCISES

Simplify.

1. $\sqrt{12}$ **2.** $\sqrt{54}$ **3.** $-\sqrt{48}$

4. $\sqrt{\frac{25}{36}}$ **5.** $-\sqrt{\frac{5}{16}}$ **6.** $\sqrt{\frac{75}{121}}$

7. Find the length of one side of a square that has an area of 27 in.^{2}.

11-3

Distance and Midpoint Formulas

What You'll Learn

- To find the distance between two points using the Distance Formula
- To find the midpoint of a segment using the Midpoint Formula

. . . And Why

To find the perimeters of figures on the coordinate plane

✓ Check Skills You'll Need

Write the coordinates of each point.

1. A **2.** D **3.** G **4.** J

GO for Help
Lesson 1-10

🔊 New Vocabulary

- distance
- midpoint

Develop Identify basic elements of geometric figures (midpoints).

Develop Use coordinate graphs to determine lengths and areas related to figures.

Develop Use the Pythagorean theorem to find the length of the missing side of a right triangle.

Finding Distance

In the graph at the right, you can locate point $C(7, 1)$ to form a right triangle with points $A(2, 1)$ and $B(7, 3)$. Using the Pythagorean Theorem, you can find AB.

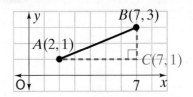

$$(AB)^2 = (AC)^2 + (BC)^2$$

$(AB)^2 = (7 - 2)^2 + (3 - 1)^2$ **AC equals the difference in x values.** **BC equals the difference in y values.**

$(AB)^2 = 5^2 + 2^2$ **Simplify.**

$AB = \sqrt{25 + 4} = \sqrt{29} \approx 5.4$ **Find the square root.**

The Distance Formula is based on the Pythagorean Theorem.

Take Note 📝   Distance Formula

You can find the **distance** d between any two points (x_1, y_1) and (x_2, y_2):

$$d = \sqrt{(x_2 - x_1)^2 + (y_2 - y_1)^2}$$

① EXAMPLE   Using the Distance Formula

Find the distance between $A(6, 3)$ and $B(1, 9)$.

$d = \sqrt{(x_2 - x_1)^2 + (y_2 - y_1)^2}$ **Use the Distance Formula.**

$d = \sqrt{(1 - 6)^2 + (9 - 3)^2}$ **Replace (x_2, y_2) with (1, 9) and (x_1, y_1) with (6, 3).**

$d = \sqrt{(-5)^2 + 6^2}$ **Simplify.**

$d = \sqrt{61}$ **Find the exact distance.**

$d \approx 7.8$ **Round to the nearest tenth.**

The distance between A and B is about 7.8 units.

✓ Quick Check

1. Find the distance between the two points in each pair. Round to the nearest tenth.

    a. $(3, 8), (2, 4)$ **b.** $(10, -3), (1, 0)$

You can also use the Distance Formula to solve geometry problems. Wait until the last step to round your answer.

2 EXAMPLE   Finding Area and Perimeter

Find the area and perimeter of rectangle *ABCD*.

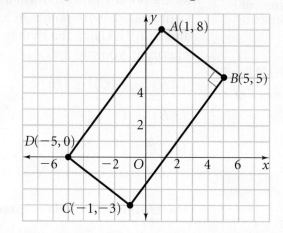

Use the Distance Formula to find two side lengths.

$$AB = \sqrt{(5 - 1)^2 + (5 - 8)^2}$$ Replace (x_2, y_2) with $(5, 5)$ and (x_1, y_1) with $(1, 8)$.

$$= \sqrt{16 + 9} = \sqrt{25} = 5$$ Simplify.

$$BC = \sqrt{(-1 - 5)^2 + (-3 - 5)^2}$$ Replace (x_2, y_2) with $(-1, -3)$ and (x_1, y_1) with $(5, 5)$.

$$= \sqrt{36 + 64} = \sqrt{100} = 10$$ Simplify.

area $= 5 \cdot 10 = 50$

perimeter $= 2(5) + 2(10) = 30$

The area of rectangle *ABCD* is 50 square units and the perimeter of rectangle *ABCD* is 30 units.

✓ Quick Check

2. Find the area and perimeter of △*DEF* at the right. Round to the nearest tenth.

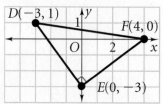

Finding the Midpoint

The **midpoint** of a segment $\overline{AB}$ is the point M on $\overline{AB}$ halfway between the endpoints A and B where $AM = MB$.

Take Note ✎ **Midpoint Formula**

You can find the midpoint of a line segment with endpoints $A(x_1, y_1)$ and $B(x_2, y_2)$:

$$M\left(\frac{x_1 + x_2}{2}, \frac{y_1 + y_2}{2}\right)$$

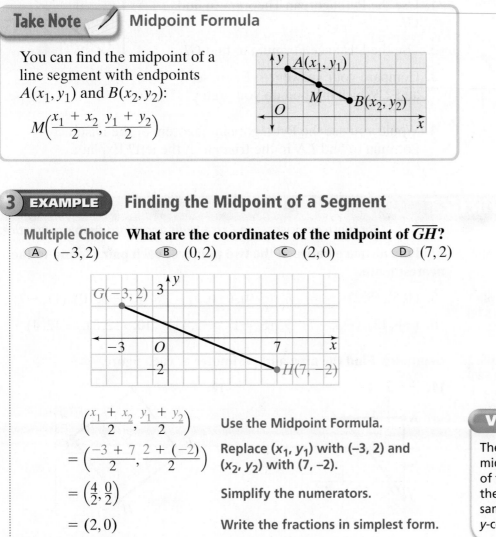

---

3 **EXAMPLE** **Finding the Midpoint of a Segment**

Multiple Choice **What are the coordinates of the midpoint of $\overline{GH}$?**

Ⓐ $(-3, 2)$ Ⓑ $(0, 2)$ Ⓒ $(2, 0)$ Ⓓ $(7, 2)$

$$\left(\frac{x_1 + x_2}{2}, \frac{y_1 + y_2}{2}\right) \quad \text{Use the Midpoint Formula.}$$

$$= \left(\frac{-3 + 7}{2}, \frac{2 + (-2)}{2}\right) \quad \text{Replace } (x_1, y_1) \text{ with } (-3, 2) \text{ and } (x_2, y_2) \text{ with } (7, -2).$$

$$= \left(\frac{4}{2}, \frac{0}{2}\right) \quad \text{Simplify the numerators.}$$

$$= (2, 0) \quad \text{Write the fractions in simplest form.}$$

The coordinates are $(2, 0)$. The answer is C.

Vocabulary Tip

The x-coordinate of the midpoint is the mean of the x-coordinates of the endpoints. The same is true for the y-coordinate.

✓ **Quick Check**

3. Find the midpoint of each segment.

a.   b.

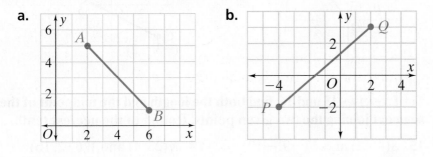

Use the graph at the right for Exercises 1–3. Round to the nearest tenth.

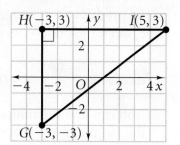

1. Use the Pythagorean Theorem to find *GI*.

2. Use the Distance Formula to find *GI*.

3. Compare your answers to Exercises 1 and 2. Which method do you prefer?

4. Would you use the Pythagorean Theorem or the Distance Formula to find *LN* in the triangle at the left? Explain.

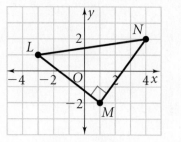

For more exercises, see *Extra Skills and Word Problem Practice.*

Ⓐ Practice by Example

GO for Help

Example 1 (page 579)

Find the distance between the two points of each pair. Round to the nearest tenth.

5. $(1, 5), (5, 2)$
6. $(6, 0), (-6, 5)$
7. $(-5, 10), (11, -7)$

8. $(-6, 12), (-3, -7)$
9. $(8, -1), (-5, 11)$
10. $(12, 3), (-12, 4)$

Example 2 (page 580)

Geometry Find the area and perimeter of each figure.

11.

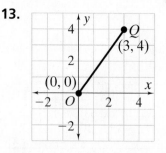

12.

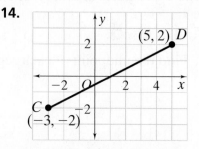

Example 3 (page 581)

Find the coordinates of the midpoint of each segment.

13.

14.

Ⓑ Apply Your Skills

For Exercises 15 and 16, find both the length and the midpoint of the segment joining the two given points. Round to the nearest tenth.

15. $S(9, 12)$ and $U(-9, -12)$
16. $K(23, 4)$ and $W(-2, 16)$

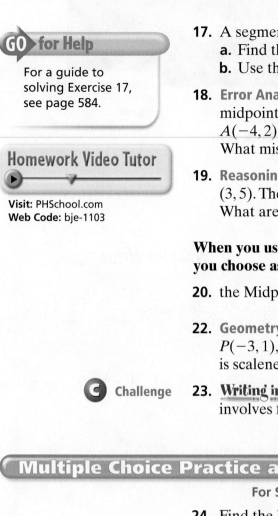

GO for Help

For a guide to solving Exercise 17, see page 584.

Homework Video Tutor

Visit: PHSchool.com
Web Code: bje-1103

17. A segment has endpoints $A(-3, 5)$ and $B(2, 1)$.
   a. Find the midpoint M of the segment.
   b. Use the Distance Formula to verify that $AM = MB$.

18. Error Analysis A student's calculation of the midpoint of the segment with endpoints $A(-4, 2)$ and $B(6, 6)$ is shown at the right. What mistake did the student make?

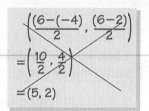

19. Reasoning The midpoint of $\overline{AB}$ is $(3, 5)$. The coordinates of A are $(-6, 1)$. What are the coordinates of B?

When you use the indicated formula, does it matter which point you choose as (x_1, y_1)? Explain.

20. the Midpoint Formula   **21.** the Distance Formula

22. Geometry The three vertices of a triangle have coordinates $P(-3, 1)$, $Q(2, -5)$, and $R(4, 6)$. Determine whether the triangle is scalene, isosceles, or equilateral. Show your work.

C Challenge   **23. Writing in Math** Explain how using the Midpoint Formula involves finding averages.

Multiple Choice Practice and Mixed Review

For Standards Tutorials, visit PHSchool.com. Web Code: bjq-9045

24. Find the length of a side of square *JKLM*.
  Ⓐ 5   Ⓒ 100
  Ⓑ 6.25   Ⓓ 625

25. Starting at the third floor, an elevator goes down two floors and up seven floors. What number represents the floor where the elevator stops?
  Ⓐ 6   Ⓒ 8
  Ⓑ 7   Ⓓ 12

26. The figure shows a ramp used for skateboarding. What horizontal distance h does the ramp cover?

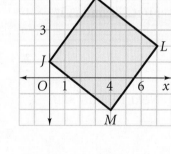

  Ⓐ 8 ft   Ⓑ 12 ft   Ⓒ 14 ft   Ⓓ 18 ft

Can you form a right triangle with the lengths given?

GO for Help

Lesson 11-2

27. 8 m, 15 m, 17 m   **28.** 5 in., 8 in., 5 in.   **29.** 20 yd, 12 yd, 16 yd

Lesson 10-4

30. Geometry Draw a net to represent a rectangular prism that is 4 in. long, 3 in. wide, and 2 in. high. Label dimensions on the net.

Develop Identify basic elements of geometric figures.

Understanding Math Problems Read the problem below. Then let Leo's thinking guide you through the solution. Check your understanding with the exercises at the bottom of the page.

A segment has endpoints $A(-3, 5)$ and $B(2, 1)$.
a. Find the midpoint M of the segment.
b. Use the Distance Formula to verify that $AM = MB$.

What Leo Thinks

First I need to find the midpoint of $\overline{AB}$. I'll use the Midpoint Formula. Substitute.

Simplify.

Next I need to verify that this is the midpoint M by showing that $AM = MB$. Since *verify* means "prove," I need to show a reason for each step.

First I'll find AM.

Next I'll find MB.

I need to summarize my findings.

What Leo Writes

$$\left(\frac{x_1 + x_2}{2}, \frac{y_1 + y_2}{2}\right) = \left(\frac{-3 + 2}{2}, \frac{5 + 1}{2}\right)$$

$$= \left(-\frac{1}{2}, 3\right) \text{ or } (-0.5, 3)$$

Step	Reason

$AM = \sqrt{(-0.5 - (-3))^2 + (3 - 5)^2}$
           Distance Formula

$AM = \sqrt{10.25}$ Simplify.

$MB = \sqrt{(2 - (-0.5))^2 + (1 - 3)^2}$
           Distance Formula

$MB = \sqrt{10.25}$ Simplify.

$AM = MB = \sqrt{10.25}$, so $(-0.5, 3)$ is the midpoint of $\overline{AB}$.

EXERCISES

Solve each problem. Justify your steps to verify your answer.

1. Find the perimeter of the triangle with vertices located at $(5, 9)$, $(7, 4)$, and $(-3, 7)$.

2. The vertices of a triangle are located at $(-1, 5), (2, 5)$, and $(2, 1)$. Show that this is a right triangle. (*Hint:* Use the Distance Formula and the Converse of the Pythagorean Theorem.)

Area of an Equilateral Triangle

Develop Use formulas routinely for finding the area of basic two-dimensional figures.

Develop Know and understand the Pythagorean theorem and use it to find the length of the missing side of a right triangle.

Develop Develop generalizations of the results obtained and the strategies used and apply them to new problem situations.

In an equilateral triangle, an altitude is also the perpendicular bisector of the side to which it is perpendicular. For example, in equilateral $\triangle XYZ$ below, $\overline{YW}$ is an altitude of the triangle. It is also the perpendicular bisector of $\overline{XZ}$.

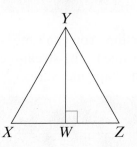

You can use this information to find a formula for the area of an equilateral triangle in terms of its side length s.

ACTIVITY

Triangle ABC is an equilateral triangle. The altitude of $\triangle ABC$ is $\overline{BF}$.

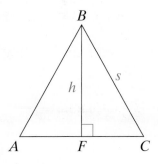

1. How is AF related to FC? How are AF and FC related to AC?

2. Write an expression for FC in terms of s.

3. Identify two right triangles in the diagram.

4. Use the Pythagorean Theorem to write an equation in terms of h^2 and s^2 that you can use to find h.

5. Solve the equation you wrote in Exercise 4 for h. Simplify all square roots.

6. Use your result from Exercise 5 to write an equation in terms of s that you can use to find the area of $\triangle ABC$.

7. **Reasoning** Can you use the equation you wrote in Exercise 6 to find the area of any equilateral triangle? Explain.

Use your results from Exercise 6 to answer the following questions.

8. Triangle KYL is an equilateral triangle with a side length of 4 cm. What is the area of $\triangle KYL$?

9. Triangle TIF is an equilateral triangle with a side length of $2n$. What is the area of $\triangle TIF$ in terms of n?

10. Triangle CRL is an equilateral triangle with a side length of s. Its area is 12 in^2. What is s?

11-4

Reasoning Strategy: Write a Proportion

Develop Construct and read drawings and models made to scale.
Develop Apply strategies from simpler problems to more complex problems.

What You'll Learn

To write a proportion from similar triangles

. . . And Why

To solve problems of unknown distance

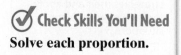

Check Skills You'll Need

Solve each proportion.

1. $\frac{1}{3} = \frac{a}{12}$ **2.** $\frac{h}{5} = \frac{20}{25}$

3. $\frac{1}{4} = \frac{8}{x}$ **4.** $\frac{2}{7} = \frac{c}{35}$

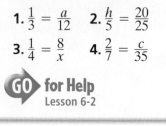

for Help
Lesson 6-2

Write a Proportion

Math Strategies in Action You can't measure the distance from the Auburn-Foresthill Bridge to the streambed of the North Fork of the American River with a tape measure.

Surveyors sometimes find such distances indirectly using similar triangles and proportions.

1 EXAMPLE   **Writing a Proportion**

To find *RS*, the distance from the deck of the bridge to the river, a surveyor picks one pier of the bridge, $\overline{QT}$, which he knows is perpendicular to the deck of the bridge. The two triangles, $\triangle PRS$ and $\triangle PQT$, are similar. He then measures $\overline{QT}$, $\overline{QP}$, and $\overline{QR}$. What is the distance *RS* from the deck of the bridge to the river?

Problem Solving Tip

If problems involving distance do not include diagrams, draw your own to help you solve the problem.

Understand   **Understand the problem.**

   1. What information is given?

   2. What are you asked to find?

Plan **Make a plan to solve the problem.**

Since $\triangle PQT \sim \triangle PRS$ and you know three lengths, writing and solving a proportion is a good strategy to use. It is helpful to draw the triangles as separate figures.

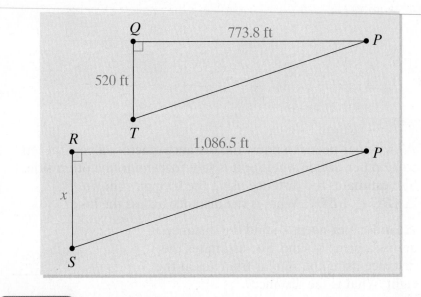

Carry Out **Carry out the plan.**

Write a proportion using the legs of the similar right triangles.

$\dfrac{773.8}{520} = \dfrac{1,086.5}{x}$ **Write a proportion.**

$773.8x = 520(1,086.5)$ **Write cross products.**

$773.8x = 564,980$ **Multiply.**

$x \approx 730.14$ **Divide each side by 773.8.**

The distance RS from the deck of the bridge to the river is about 730 ft.

Check **Check the answer to be sure it is reasonable.**

Solving problems that involve indirect measurement often makes use of figures that *overlap*. Use the diagram on page 586 to answer the following questions.

✓ Quick Check

3. Which segments overlap?

4. A common error students make is to use part of a side in a proportion. For example, some students might think $\dfrac{773.8}{520}$ is equal to $\dfrac{312.7}{x}$. How does drawing the triangles as separate figures help you avoid this error?

Standards Practice

For more exercises, see *Extra Skills and Word Problem Practice*.

A Practice by Example

Example 1
(page 586)

 for Help

In Exercises 1–2, write a proportion and find the value of each x.

1. △*ABE* ~ △*ACD*

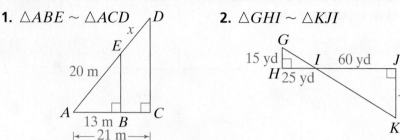

2. △*GHI* ~ △*KJI*

3. A swimmer needs to know the distance *x* across a lake (at left) to help her decide whether it is safe to swim to the other side. She estimates the distance using the triangles shown. △*ABC* ~ △*EDC*. What is the distance across the lake?

4. A landscaper needs to find the distance *x* across a piece of land. She estimates the distance using the similar triangles at the right. What is the distance?

B Apply Your Skills

5. Indirect Measurement To estimate the height of a tree, Milton positions a mirror on the ground so he can see the top of the tree reflected in it. His height, his distance from the mirror, and his line of sight to the mirror determine a triangle. The tree's height, its distance from the mirror, and the distance from the top of the tree to the mirror form a similar triangle. Use the measurements shown to determine the height of the tree.

STRATEGIES

- Act It Out
- Draw a Diagram
- Try, Test, Revise
- Look for a Pattern
- Make a Model
- Make a Table
- Simulate the Problem
- Solve by Graphing
- Use Multiple Strategies
- Work a Simpler Problem
- Work Backward
- Write an Equation
- Write a Proportion

Solve using any strategy.

6. There are 30 students in a math class. Twelve belong to the computer club, and eight belong to the photography club. Three belong to both clubs. How many belong to neither club?

7. Jake spent $\frac{3}{8}$ of his money on a book and $\frac{1}{2}$ of what was left on a magazine. He now has $6.25. How much money did he start with?

8. Hai takes 12 minutes to walk to school. He wants to get there 15 minutes early to meet with his lab partner. What time should he leave his house if school starts at 8:10 A.M.?

9. Number Sense Christa thought of a number. She added 4, multiplied the sum by −5, and subtracted 12. She then doubled the result and got −34. What number did Christa start with?

Homework Video Tutor

Visit: PHSchool.com
Web Code: bje-1104

10. The height of the Eiffel Tower is 984 ft. A souvenir model of the tower is 6 in. tall. At 5 P.M. in Paris, the shadow of the souvenir model is 8 in. long. The Eiffel Tower and its shadow determine two legs of a right triangle that are similar to the two legs of a right triangle determined by the souvenir model and its shadow. About how long is the shadow of the Eiffel Tower?

11. Madison Square Garden in New York City is built in the shape of a circle. Its diameter is 404 ft and it accommodates 20,234 spectators. To the nearest tenth of a square foot, how much area is there for each spectator?

12. Algebra You serve a tennis ball from one end of a tennis court, 39 ft from the net. You hit the ball at 9 feet above the ground. It travels in a straight path down the middle of the court, and just clears the top of the 3-ft net. This is illustrated in the diagram. $\triangle PQR \sim \triangle MQS$. How far from the net does the ball land?

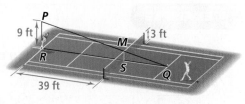

Madison Square Garden

Multiple Choice Practice and Mixed Review

For Standards Tutorials, visit PHSchool.com. Web Code: bjq-9045

13. In the diagram at the right, the triangles are similar. What is x?

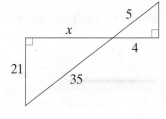

- Ⓐ 43.75
- Ⓒ 26.25
- Ⓑ 28
- Ⓓ 17

14. What is 80% of 75?

- Ⓐ 6
- Ⓒ 93
- Ⓑ 60
- Ⓓ 600

15. What is the surface area of the cylinder below?

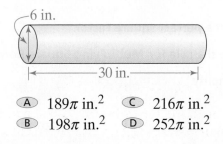

- Ⓐ 189π in.^{2}
- Ⓒ 216π in.^{2}
- Ⓑ 198π in.^{2}
- Ⓓ 252π in.^{2}

 for Help   Lesson 11-3

Find the midpoint of each segment with given endpoints.

16. $A(2, 3)$ and $B(4, 7)$ **17.** $L(-1, 2)$ and $M(2, 6)$

Lesson 7-4   **18.** Keith collected twice as much money as Lucy for a walkathon. Together they collected $120. How much money did each person collect?

Monomials

Develop Extend the process of taking powers and extracting roots to monomials when the latter results in a monomial with an integer exponent.

A **monomial** is a real number, a variable, or a product of a real number and variables with whole-number exponents.

You can simplify square roots of monomials. Assume that the value of each variable is not negative.

1 EXAMPLE

Write each square root without a radical sign.

a. $\sqrt{25x^2}$

$\sqrt{25x^2} = \sqrt{(5x)^2}$ Write $25x^2$ as the square of $5x$.

$\qquad\quad = 5x$ Simplify.

b. $\sqrt{p^6}$

$\sqrt{p^6} = \sqrt{(p^3)^2}$ Use the rule for the Power of a Power.

$\qquad = p^3$ Simplify.

You can also simplify expressions that have nonsquare factors by using the rule for Multiplying Square Roots.

2 EXAMPLE

Simplify each square root.

a. $\sqrt{x^9}$

$\sqrt{x^9} = \sqrt{x^8 \cdot x}$ Use the rule for Multiplying Powers With the Same Base.

$\qquad = \sqrt{x^8} \cdot \sqrt{x}$ Use the rule for Multiplying Square Roots.

$\qquad = x^4\sqrt{x}$ Simplify.

b. $\sqrt{48x}$

$\sqrt{48x} = \sqrt{16 \cdot 3x}$ Find a perfect square factor.

$\qquad\; = \sqrt{16} \cdot \sqrt{3x}$ Use the rule for Multiplying Square Roots.

$\qquad\; = 4\sqrt{3x}$ Simplify.

EXERCISES

Write each square root without the radical sign.

1. $\sqrt{49y^2}$ **2.** $\sqrt{100m^{12}}$ **3.** $-\sqrt{25x^6}$ **4.** $\sqrt{a^2b^{10}}$ **5.** $-\sqrt{169w^{26}}$

Simplify each square root.

6. $\sqrt{a^{12}}$ **7.** $\sqrt{36x^4}$ **8.** $\sqrt{81b^8}$ **9.** $-\sqrt{64a^{16}}$ **10.** $-\sqrt{x^4y^{12}}$

11. $\sqrt{c^7}$ **12.** $\sqrt{x^{23}}$ **13.** $-\sqrt{20m}$ **14.** $\sqrt{27b^{11}}$ **15.** $-\sqrt{72a^{19}}$

Graphing Nonlinear Functions

Introduce Graph functions of the form $y = nx^2$ and $y = nx^3$ and use in solving problems.

Introduce Plot the values from the volumes of three-dimensional shapes for various values of the edge lengths (e.g., cubes with varying edge lengths or a triangle prism with a fixed height and an equilateral triangle base of varying lengths).

What You'll Learn

- To graph quadratic functions
- To graph cubic functions

. . . And Why

To use nonlinear functions to model volume

✓ Check Skills You'll Need

Find the y values of each equation for $x = -2, 0,$ and 2.

1. $y = 5x - 1$

2. $y = \frac{1}{2}x + 3$

3. $y = 3x + 2$

4. $y = \frac{1}{4}x - 5$

GO for Help
Lesson 8-2

🔊 New Vocabulary

- quadratic function
- cubic function

Graphing Quadratic Functions

Standards Investigation
Graphing Data

You can graph the area of a square as a function of the length of a side of the square.

1. Copy and complete the table at the right.

2. Draw a graph of the data. Does your graph appear to be a linear function? Explain.

Side x	Area y
1	1
2	■
3	■
4	■
5	■
6	36

In a **quadratic function,** the input variable is squared. The simplest quadratic function can be written as $y = nx^2$, where n is a nonzero constant. The graph of a quadratic function is a U-shaped curve called a *parabola*. The curve may open upward or downward.

1 EXAMPLE Graphing a Quadratic Function

For the function $y = 2x^2$, make a table with integer values of x from -2 to 2. Then graph the function.

Make a table.

x	$2x^2 = y$	(x, y)
-2	$2(-2)^2 = 8$	$(-2, 8)$
-1	$2(-1)^2 = 2$	$(-1, 2)$
0	$2(0)^2 = 0$	$(0, 0)$
1	$2(1)^2 = 2$	$(1, 2)$
2	$2(2)^2 = 8$	$(2, 8)$

Make a graph.

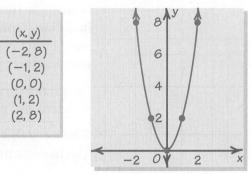

✓ Quick Check

1. Make a table with integer values of x from -2 to 2 for $y = -2x^2$. Graph the function.

Graphing a Cubic Function

In a **cubic function,** the input variable is *cubed*, or raised to the third power. The simplest cubic function can be written as $y = nx^3$, where n is a nonzero constant.

2 **EXAMPLE** **Graphing a Cubic Function**

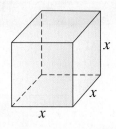

The function $y = x^3$ models the volume y of a cube with side length x, as shown at the left. Graph the function.

Make a table.

x	$x^3 = y$	(x, y)
-2	$(-2)^3 = -8$	$(-2, -8)$
-1	$(-1)^3 = -1$	$(-1, -1)$
0	$(0)^3 = 0$	$(0, 0)$
1	$(1)^3 = 1$	$(1, 1)$
2	$(2)^3 = 8$	$(2, 8)$

Make a graph.

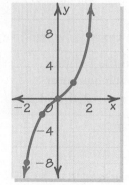

Neither volume nor side length can have negative values. In the context of the situation, only the part of the graph that falls in the first quadrant represents the volume function.

✔ Quick Check

2. Graph the function $y = 3x^3$.

You can use the graph of a function to estimate solutions to problems.

3 **EXAMPLE** **Using a Graph to Solve a Problem**

A manufacturer uses the function $y = \frac{1}{4}x^3$ to estimate the profit y, in dollars, from selling a single product for x dollars. The maximum possible profit is $3. Estimate the amount the manufacturer should charge to make the maximum profit.

Graph the function. Since the charge cannot be negative, use positive values of x.

When $y = 3$, x is more than 2 but less than 2.5. The manufacturer should charge about $2.25.

✔ Quick Check

3. Use the equation $y = 2x^3$. Estimate the value of x when $y = 3$.

More Than One Way

The equation $d = \frac{1}{2}t^2$ gives the distance d, in feet, that a ball rolling down a ramp travels in t seconds. Estimate the time the ball takes to roll 7 ft.

Tina's Method

I can graph the parabola $d = \frac{1}{2}t^2$. Since t represents time, I will use positive values of t. I will make a table using values of t from 0 to 4 and plot the points.

t	$\frac{1}{2}t^2 = d$	(t, d)
0	$\frac{1}{2}(0)^2 = 0$	$(0, 0)$
1	$\frac{1}{2}(1)^2 = \frac{1}{2}$	$(1, \frac{1}{2})$
2	$\frac{1}{2}(2)^2 = 2$	$(2, 2)$
3	$\frac{1}{2}(3)^2 = \frac{9}{2}$	$(3, \frac{9}{2})$
4	$\frac{1}{2}(4)^2 = 8$	$(4, 8)$

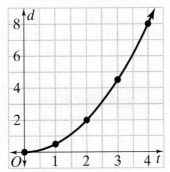

I will use the graph to estimate the value of t when $d = 7$. When $d = 7$, the value of t is between 3 and 4. I can see from the graph that the value is closer to 4 than 3, so 4 seconds is a reasonable estimate.

Kevin's Method

I can solve the equation $7 = \frac{1}{2}t^2$.

$$7 = \frac{1}{2}t^2$$
$$2 \cdot 7 = 2 \cdot \frac{1}{2}t^2 \quad \text{Multiply each side by 2.}$$
$$14 = t^2 \quad \text{Simplify.}$$
$$\sqrt{14} = \sqrt{t^2} \quad \text{Find the positive square root of each side.}$$
$$\sqrt{14} = t \quad \text{Simplify.}$$

14 is between the perfect squares 9 and 16. Since 14 is closer to 16 than to 9, $\sqrt{14}$ is closer to $\sqrt{16}$ than to $\sqrt{9}$. Since $\sqrt{16} = 4$, a reasonable estimate for t is 4 seconds.

Choose a Method

1. Which method do you prefer to use to estimate a solution? Explain.

For Exercises 1–3, state whether the function is a quadratic function or a cubic function. Explain your reasoning.

1. $y = 25x^2$ **2.** $y = -8x^3$ **3.** $y = \frac{2}{5}x^2$

4. Compare the graphs of quadratic functions and cubic functions. How are they different? How are they alike?

5. On a clear day, the distance d in miles you can see across the ocean from a height of h feet is given by the function $h = \frac{2}{3}d^2$. Make a table that illustrates the distances you can see from a height of 10 to 100 ft at 10-ft intervals.

Standards Practice

For more exercises, see *Extra Skills and Word Problem Practice.*

A Practice by Example

Example 1
(page 591)

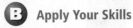

For each function, make a table with integer values of x from -2 to 2. Then graph the function.

6. $y = 4x^2$ **7.** $y = -x^2$ **8.** $y = -3x^2$ **9.** $y = 5x^2$

10. $y = -\frac{1}{2}x^2$ **11.** $y = 0.25x^2$ **12.** $y = -\frac{1}{3}x^2$ **13.** $y = -\frac{1}{5}x^2$

Example 2
(page 592)

Graph each function.

14. $y = -x^3$ **15.** $y = -3x^3$ **16.** $y = \frac{1}{2}x^3$

17. $y = -\frac{1}{4}x^3$ **18.** $y = \frac{1}{3}x^3$ **19.** $y = 0.25x^3$

Example 3
(page 592)

For Exercises 20–22, estimate the value of x for the given y-value of each cubic function.

20. $y = -\frac{1}{6}x^3; y = -11$ **21.** $y = -2x^3; y = -7$ **22.** $y = \frac{3}{4}x^3; y = 20$

23. A community planning group uses the function $y = \frac{1}{10}x^3$ to estimate the total number of new homes y built in a community after x months. The maximum number of homes that can be built is 13. In about how many months will the maximum number of homes be built in the community?

Homework Video Tutor

Visit: PHSchool.com
Web Code: bje-1105

B Apply Your Skills

24. a. Graph $y = x^2$, $y = 2x^2$, and $y = \frac{1}{2}x^2$ on the same coordinate plane.
    b. Describe how the coefficients of x^2 affect the graphs.

25. Writing in Math Describe how the graphs of the functions $y = x^3$, $y = -x^3$, and $y = -2x^3$ are alike and how they are different.

26. The equation $d = \frac{1}{10}s^2$ relates the depth d of the ocean in meters to the speed s at which tsunamis travel in meters per second. Make a graph to show the depth d for varying values of speed s.

27. Make a graph to show the volume V of an equilateral triangular prism with height 3 m with varying values of side s. Use the formula for the area of an equilateral triangle $A = \frac{s^2\sqrt{3}}{4}$.

28. The rectangular prism at the left has a square base. Sketch a graph to show its volume V for varying values of s. Estimate s when $V = 10$ in^3.

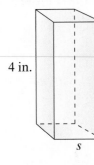

4 in.

s

29. A cube has side length x.
   a. Write a function that relates the volume y_1 of the cube to its side length x. Write a function that relates the surface area y_2 of the cube to its side length x.
   b. Estimate the value of x that makes the cube's volume y_1 equal to its surface area y_2.

C Challenge

30. A car-washing business uses the equation $p = -4c^2 + 40c$ to predict the profit p, in dollars, they can make with the cost c, in dollars, of a car wash. How much should the business charge to generate the most profit?

Multiple Choice Practice and Mixed Review

For Standards Tutorials, visit PHSchool.com. Web Code: bjq-9045

31. What is the slope of the line?
   A. -3 C. 2
   B. $\frac{1}{2}$ D. 3

32. Of 150 shoes, 2% are defective. About how many of 200 shoes would you predict to be defective?
   A. 2 C. 4
   B. 3 D. 5

GO for Help Lesson 4-9

33. Greenland is the world's largest island and has an area of 2,175,600 km^2. Express this area in scientific notation.

✓ Checkpoint Quiz 2

Find AB and the midpoint of $\overline{AB}$. Round AB to the nearest tenth.

1. $A(0, -2)$ and $B(-6, -9)$ **2.** $A(8, 11)$ and $B(-5, 2)$

Graph each function.

3. $y = 3x^2$ **4.** $y = -2x^2$ **5.** $y = -2x^3$ **6.** $y = 4x^3$

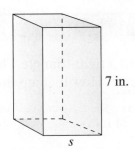

7 in.

s

7. The prism at the left has a square base. For what value of s will the volume be 49 in.^{3}?

You can solve many problems by letting a variable represent an unknown quantity you want to find.

1 EXAMPLE

José saw the original model of the Statue of Liberty. On that day, the shadow of the model measured 100 feet. A nearby pole measured 4 feet and its shadow was 5 feet. How tall was the model?

Ⓐ 80 ft   Ⓑ 99 ft   Ⓒ 101 ft   Ⓓ 125 ft

Sketch similar triangles (not to scale). Let h be the height. Then write a proportion using h.

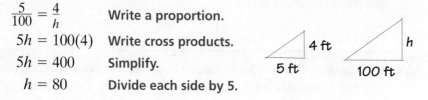

$\dfrac{5}{100} = \dfrac{4}{h}$	**Write a proportion.**
$5h = 100(4)$	**Write cross products.**
$5h = 400$	**Simplify.**
$h = 80$	**Divide each side by 5.**

The model was 80 ft tall. The correct answer is A.

2 EXAMPLE

Eva dives into a pool from a diving board that is 8 feet high. She lands in the water 6 feet horizontally from where she dives. What is the distance from the edge of the diving board to where Eva lands in the pool?

Ⓐ 5 ft   Ⓑ 10 ft   Ⓒ 14 ft   Ⓓ 20 ft

The distance from where Eva dives to where she lands is unknown. Let c represent this distance. Use a diagram with a right triangle.

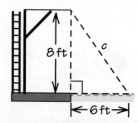

$c^2 = a^2 + b^2$	**Use the Pythagorean Theorem.**
$= 8^2 + 6^2$	**Replace a with 8 and b with 6.**
$= 100$	**Simplify.**
$c = \sqrt{100} = 10$	**Find the positive square root of each side.**

The distance is 10 feet. The correct answer is B.

Multiple Choice Practice

A 15-ft ladder leaning against a house forms a right triangle. The base of the ladder is 9 ft from the base of the house. How high up the house does the ladder reach?

Ⓐ 6 ft   Ⓑ 12 ft   Ⓒ 24 ft   Ⓓ 144 ft

Chapter 11 Review

cubic function (p. 592)
distance (p. 579)
hypotenuse (p. 570)
irrational number (p. 567)

legs (p. 570)
midpoint (p. 581)
monomial (p. 590)

perfect square (p. 566)
quadratic function (p. 591)
square root (p. 566)

Match the vocabulary terms on the right with their descriptions on the left.

1. the two shortest sides of a right triangle

2. the square of an integer

3. the point halfway between the endpoints of a segment

4. the longest side of a right triangle, opposite the right angle

5. a number that cannot be expressed as a ratio of two integers

6. the inverse of the square of a number

A. irrational number
B. square root
C. legs
D. midpoint
E. hypotenuse
F. perfect square

Go Online
PHSchool.com
For: Vocabulary quiz
Web Code: bjj-1151

Skills and Concepts

Lesson 11-1
• To find square roots of numbers
• To classify real numbers

The square of an integer is a **perfect square.** The inverse of squaring a number is finding a **square root.** The symbol $\sqrt{\ }$ indicates the positive square root of a number. A number that cannot be expressed as the ratio of two integers $\frac{a}{b}$, where b is not zero, is **irrational.** If a positive integer is not a perfect square, its square root is irrational.

Simplify each square root.

7. $\sqrt{1}$ **8.** $-\sqrt{16}$ **9.** $\sqrt{49}$ **10.** $\sqrt{64}$ **11.** $-\sqrt{36}$

Estimate to the nearest integer.

12. $\sqrt{5}$ **13.** $\sqrt{11}$ **14.** $\sqrt{33}$ **15.** $\sqrt{62}$ **16.** $\sqrt{91}$

Identify each number as rational or irrational. Explain.

17. 0.55 **18.** $\sqrt{64}$ **19.** $0.\overline{45}$ **20.** $\sqrt{15}$ **21.** $0.123123\ldots$

22. Explain why $0.12122122212222\ldots$ is an irrational number.

Chapter Review (continued)

Lesson 11-2

- To use the Pythagorean Theorem
- To identify right triangles

In a right triangle, the two shortest sides are the **legs.** The longest side, which is opposite the right angle, is the **hypotenuse.** The Pythagorean Theorem states that in any right triangle the sum of the squares of the lengths of the legs is equal to the square of the length of the hypotenuse ($a^2 + b^2 = c^2$).

Can you form a right triangle with the three lengths given? Show your work.

23. 1 mi, 3 mi, 3 mi

24. 8 yd, 15 yd, 17 yd

25. $\sqrt{6}$ ft, $\sqrt{10}$ ft, 4 ft

26. 30 m, 40 m, 50 m

The lengths of two sides of a right triangle are given. Find the length of the third side to the nearest tenth of a unit.

27. legs: 30 mi, 60 mi

28. legs: 6.9 km and 10.4 km

29. leg: 10 in.; hypotenuse: 18 in.

30. leg: 2 ft; hypotenuse: 3.5 ft

31. A baseball diamond is really a square. The length of each side is 90 ft. How far does a ball thrown along the diagonal of the square travel? Round your answer to the nearest tenth.

Lesson 11-3

- To find the distance between two points using the Distance Formula
- To find the midpoint of a segment using the Midpoint Formulai

The Distance Formula states that the **distance** d between any two points (x_1, y_1) and (x_2, y_2) is $d = \sqrt{(x_2 - x_1)^2 + (y_2 - y_1)^2}$.

The Midpoint Formula states that the **midpoint** of a line segment with endpoints $A(x_1, y_1)$ and $B(x_2, y_2)$ is $\left(\dfrac{x_1 + x_2}{2}, \dfrac{y_1 + y_2}{2}\right)$.

Find the distance between each pair of points. Round to the nearest tenth.

32. $(3, 0), (0, 2)$

33. $(-1, 7), (3, 10)$

34. $(4, -5), (-8, -1)$

35. $(-10, -12), (-8, -11)$

36. $(2, -14), (9, -20)$

37. $(10, 4), (-2, -2)$

Find the midpoint of each segment with the given endpoints.

38. $H(0, 1)$ and $J(4, 7)$

39. $K(2, 6)$ and $L(4, 2)$

40. $M(-7, 8)$ and $P(3, -4)$

41. $A(4, 9)$ and $B(5, 11)$

42. $X(-15, -12)$ and $Y(-9, -4)$

43. $D(20, 18)$ and $E(-15, -19)$

Lesson 11-4

- To write a proportion from similar triangles

You can write a proportion to solve indirect measurement problems using similar triangles.

44. An engineer needs to know what length to plan for a bridge across a river. She estimates the distance using the similar triangles $\triangle ABC$ and $\triangle DEC$ in the figure below. What is the distance a across the river?

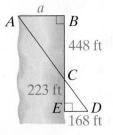

45. Kallie feeds her dog $1\frac{1}{8}$ cans of dog food each day Sunday through Friday. On Saturday, she feeds the dog half as much. How many cans of dog food does Kallie feed her dog in a week?

Lesson 11-5

- To graph quadratic functions
- To graph cubic functions

In a **quadratic function,** the input variable is squared. The simplest quadratic function can be written as $y = nx^2$, where $n \neq 0$.

In a **cubic function,** the input variable is cubed. The simplest cubic function can be written as $y = nx^3$, where $n \neq 0$.

Complete each table with integer values for the given function. Then graph each function.

46. $y = -6x^2$

x	$-6x^2 = y$	(x, y)
-2		
-1		
0		
1		
2		

47. $y = \frac{1}{6}x^2$

x	$\frac{1}{6}x^2 = y$	(x, y)
-9		
-6		
0		
6		
9		

Sketch the graph of each function.

48. $y = \frac{1}{8}x^3$

49. $y = -5x^3$

Simplify each square root.

1. $\sqrt{25}$ 2. $-\sqrt{81}$

3. $\sqrt{100}$ 4. $-\sqrt{4}$

5. $\sqrt{16}$ 6. $\sqrt{49}$

Estimate to the nearest integer.

7. $\sqrt{6}$ 8. $\sqrt{12}$

9. $\sqrt{45}$ 10. $\sqrt{78}$

11. $\sqrt{85}$ 12. $\sqrt{118}$

Identify each number as rational or irrational.

13. $0.999\ldots$ 14. $\sqrt{24}$

15. $\sqrt{100}$ 16. $420{,}420$

Find each missing length to the nearest tenth of a unit.

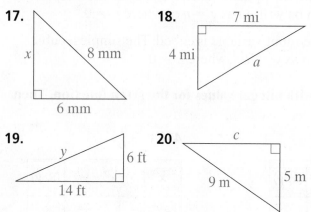

17. (triangle with sides x, 8 mm, 6 mm, right angle)

18. (triangle with 7 mi, 4 mi, a, right angle)

19. (triangle with y, 6 ft, 14 ft, right angle)

20. (triangle with c, 9 m, 5 m, right angle)

Find the distance between each pair of points. Round to the nearest tenth.

21. $(0,0), (4,6)$

22. $(5,-3), (-6,2)$

23. $(-8,-9), (1,2)$

24. $(-1,-3), (-4,-7)$

Find the midpoint of each segment with the given endpoints.

25. $C(5,0)$ and $D(3,6)$

26. $M(9,-4)$ and $P(2,8)$

27. To estimate the height of a tree, Joan positions a mirror on the ground so she can see the top of the tree reflected in it. Joan's height, her distance from the mirror, and her line of sight to the mirror determine a triangle. The tree's height, its distance from the mirror, and the distance from the top of the tree to the mirror determine a similar triangle. Use the measurements below to find the height of the tree.

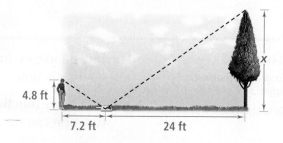

4.8 ft   7.2 ft   24 ft   x

Find the missing lengths.

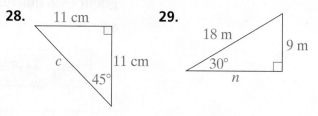

28. (triangle with 11 cm, 11 cm, c, $45°$)

29. (triangle with 18 m, 9 m, $30°$, n)

Graph each function.

30. $y = 6x^2$ 31. $y = \frac{2}{3}x^2$

32. $y = -5x^2$ 33. $y = 5x^3$

34. $y = -\frac{3}{8}x^3$ 35. $y = 10x^3$

Some problems ask you to identify information that you need to solve a problem. Sometimes the needed information is in a diagram.

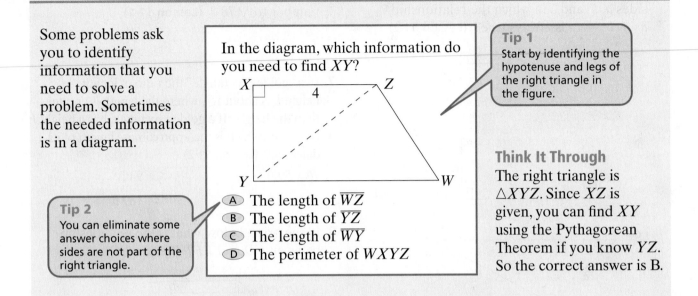

In the diagram, which information do you need to find XY?

Ⓐ The length of $\overline{WZ}$
Ⓑ The length of $\overline{YZ}$
Ⓒ The length of $\overline{WY}$
Ⓓ The perimeter of $WXYZ$

Tip 1
Start by identifying the hypotenuse and legs of the right triangle in the figure.

Think It Through
The right triangle is $\triangle XYZ$. Since XZ is given, you can find XY using the Pythagorean Theorem if you know YZ. So the correct answer is B.

Tip 2
You can eliminate some answer choices where sides are not part of the right triangle.

Vocabulary Review

As you solve problems, you must understand the meanings of mathematical terms. Match each term with its mathematical meaning.

A. Pythagorean Theorem

B. legs

C. hypotenuse

D. surface area

E. cylinder

F. lateral area

I. the two shorter sides of a right triangle

II. the sum of the areas of the base(s) and the lateral faces of a space figure

III. the sum of the areas of the lateral faces of a space figure

IV. In a right triangle, the sum of the squares of the legs is equal to the square of the hypotenuse.

V. the longest side of a right triangle that is opposite the right angle

VI. a space figure with two circular, parallel, and congruent bases

Read each question. Then write the letter of the correct answer on your paper.

1. The figure shows a glass prism that is used to display puppies at a pet store. **(Lesson 10-5)**

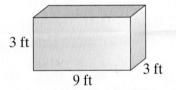

If the prism has an open top and a wooden floor, how many square inches of glass are needed for the lateral area of the display?
Ⓐ 24 ft²   Ⓑ 36 ft²   Ⓒ 72 ft²   Ⓓ 126 ft²

2. The steamroller wheel shown is a cylinder that has a radius of 1 meter and a height of 2 meters. Estimate the area covered by one rotation of the wheel. **(Lesson 10-5)**

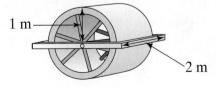

Ⓐ 6 m²   Ⓑ 12 m²   Ⓒ 18 m²   Ⓓ 360 m²

3. Which figure best represents a triangle with sides a, b, and c in which the relationship $a^2 + b^2 = c^2$ is always true? **(Lesson 11-2)**

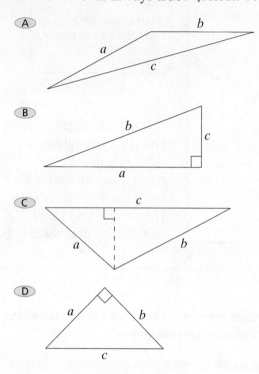

Ⓐ

Ⓑ

Ⓒ

Ⓓ

4. The area of a square is 30 square centimeters. To the nearest centimeter, what is the length of one side? **(Lesson 11-1)**

Ⓐ 5 cm   Ⓒ 15 cm

Ⓑ 8 cm   Ⓓ 90 cm

5. What is the length of side $\overline{AB}$, in units, of the square? **(Lesson 11-1)**

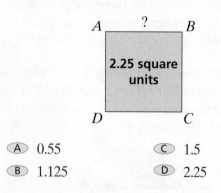

Ⓐ 0.55   Ⓒ 1.5

Ⓑ 1.125   Ⓓ 2.25

6. What is the closest whole number to $\sqrt{78}$? **(Lesson 11-1)**

Ⓐ 8   Ⓒ 70

Ⓑ 9   Ⓓ 80

7. In a "golden rectangle" the ratio of length ℓ to height h is about 1.7, where the length is greater than the height. If a golden rectangle has a height h of 35 feet, which is the approximate length of its diagonal? **(Lesson 11-2)**

Ⓐ 59 ft   Ⓒ 94 ft

Ⓑ 69 ft   Ⓓ 189 ft

8. In the prism below, what is the relationship between $\overline{CD}$ and $\overline{EF}$? **(Lesson 9-1)**

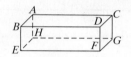

Ⓐ parallel

Ⓑ intersecting

Ⓒ skew

Ⓓ perpendicular

9. The table shows an approximate conversion between feet and meters.

Meters	Feet
1	3.3
2	6.6
3	9.8
4	13.0

About how many feet are in 16 meters? **(page 288)**

Ⓐ 5 ft   Ⓒ 52 ft

Ⓑ 17 ft   Ⓓ 64 ft

10. Tristan runs 5 kilometers in 45 minutes. His goal is to run the same distance in 40 minutes by next year. How many kilometers per hour does he need to run next year to reach his goal? **(Lesson 3-3)**

Ⓐ 3.3 km/h   Ⓒ 7.5 km/h

Ⓑ 6.7 km/h   Ⓓ 15 km/h

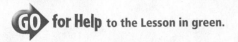
11. Which graph best represents the graph of the function $y = \frac{1}{4}x^3$? **(Lesson 11-5)**

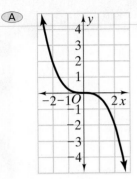

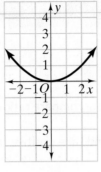

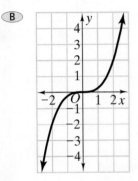

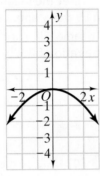

12. The volume of the prism is shown.

$$V = 216 \text{ m}^3$$

The area of the prism's base is 18 m². What is x? **(Lesson 10-7)**

Ⓐ 6 m

Ⓑ 12 m

Ⓒ 72 m

Ⓓ 108 m

13. Find the midpoint W of a segment with endpoints $X(4, 4)$ and $Y(2, 2)$. **(Lesson 11-3)**

Ⓐ $W(-1, -1)$

Ⓑ $W(1, 1)$

Ⓒ $W(2, 2)$

Ⓓ $W(3, 3)$

14. The average person needs $2\frac{1}{2}$ qt of water each day. How many gallons does the average person need per week? **(Lesson 5-5)**

Ⓐ $4\frac{3}{8}$ gallons

Ⓑ $9\frac{1}{2}$ gallons

Ⓒ 10 gallons

Ⓓ $17\frac{1}{2}$ gallons

15. Line h is drawn in each figure. Which figure shows enough information to find the length of h? **(Lesson 11-2)**

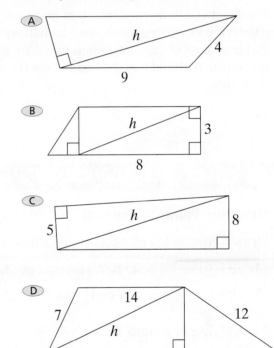

16. How many centimeters equal 20 meters? **(Lesson 3-6)**

Ⓐ 0.02 centimeters

Ⓑ 0.2 centimeters

Ⓒ 200 centimeters

Ⓓ 2,000 centimeters

17. The product of 13 and a number n is 156. Which equation shows this relationship? **(Lesson 2-4)**

Ⓐ $13 + n = 156$

Ⓑ $13n = 156$

Ⓒ $156 - n = 13$

Ⓓ $\frac{156}{n} = 13$

Data Analysis

What You've Learned

Read, write, and compare numbers in scientific notation, compare rational numbers in general.

Add, subtract, multiply, and divide rational numbers and take positive rational numbers to whole-number powers.

Represent quantitative relationships graphically and interpret the meaning of a specific part of the graph in the situation represented by the graph.

Plot the values of quantities whose ratios are always the same. Fit a line to the plot and understand that the slope of the line equals the ratio of the quantities.

 **Check Your Readiness**   **GO** for **Help** to the Lesson in green.

Graphing Points (Lesson 1-10)

Draw a coordinate plane. Graph each point.

1. $A(1,0)$ **2.** $B(0,1)$ **3.** $C(2,5)$ **4.** $D(3,3)$

5. $E(-1,1)$ **6.** $F(-1,-1)$ **7.** $G(2,-3)$ **8.** $H(-3,2)$

Multiplying Fractions (Lesson 5-4)

Find each product.

9. $\frac{2}{3} \cdot \frac{1}{2}$ **10.** $\frac{7}{8} \cdot \frac{6}{7}$ **11.** $\frac{9}{10} \cdot \frac{8}{9}$ **12.** $\frac{5}{6} \cdot \frac{4}{5}$

13. $\frac{3}{4} \cdot \frac{2}{3}$ **14.** $\frac{7}{8} \cdot \frac{6}{7} \cdot \frac{5}{6}$ **15.** $\frac{3}{5} \cdot \frac{5}{6} \cdot \frac{2}{7}$ **16.** $\frac{7}{8} \cdot \frac{4}{5} \cdot \frac{3}{7}$

Fractions, Decimals, and Percents (Lesson 6-4)

Write each percent as a decimal, and each decimal or fraction as a percent.

17. 50%   **18.** 36%   **19.** 20%   **20.** 5%

21. $\frac{1}{5}$ **22.** $\frac{7}{8}$ **23.** 0.28   **24.** 0.3

▲ You can use graphs to display data related to sports.

What You'll Learn Next

Know various forms of display for data sets, including a stem-and-leaf plot or box-and-whisker plot; use the forms to display a single set of data or to compare two sets of data.

Represent two numerical variables on a scatter plot and informally describe how the data points are distributed and any apparent relationship that exists between the two variables.

Understand the meaning of, and be able to compute, the minimum, the lower quartile, the median, the upper quartile, and the maximum of a data set.

New Vocabulary

◀)) English and Spanish Audio Online

- **box-and-whisker plot** (p. 617)
- **frequency table** (p. 612)
- **histogram** (p. 613)
- **line plot** (p. 612)
- **mean** (p. 606)
- **measures of central tendency** (p. 606)
- **median** (p. 606)
- **mode** (p. 606)
- **negative correlation** (p. 630)
- **no correlation** (p. 630)
- **outlier** (p. 607)
- **positive correlation** (p. 630)
- **quartiles** (p. 617)
- **range** (p. 606)
- **scatter plot** (p. 628)
- **stem-and-leaf plot** (p. 622)
- **trend line** (p. 635)

Mean, Median, and Mode

Introduce Understand the meaning of, and be able to compute, the median of a data set.

Develop Express the solution clearly and logically; support solutions with evidence in both verbal and symbolic work.

Finding Mean, Median, Mode, and Range

Mean, *median*, and *mode* are **measures of central tendency** of a collection of data. Consider the data 2, 3, 4, 5, 8, 8, and 12.

The **mean** is the sum of the data values divided by the number of data values.

$$\text{mean} = \frac{2 + 3 + 4 + 5 + 8 + 8 + 12}{7}$$
$$= \frac{42}{7} = 6 \qquad \uparrow \text{number of data values}$$

The **median** is the middle number when data values are written in order and there is an odd number of data values. For an even number of data values, the median is the mean of the two middle numbers.

2 3 4 **5** 8 8 12
↑
median

The **mode** is the data item that occurs most often. There can be one mode, more than one mode, or no mode.

2 3 4 5 **8 8** 12
mode

The **range** of a set of data is the difference between the greatest and least values.

range = 12 − 2 = 10
greatest ⌐   ⌐ least
value   value

1 EXAMPLE Finding Mean, Median, Mode, and Range

Use the Readathon graph. Find the (a) mean, (b) median, (c) mode, and (d) range.

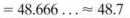

a. **Mean:** $\dfrac{\text{sum of data values}}{\text{number of data values}}$

$$= \frac{40 + 45 + 48 + 50 + 50 + 59}{6}$$

$$= \frac{292}{6}$$

$$= 48.666\ldots \approx 48.7$$

b. **Median:** 40 45 48 50 50 59   Write the data in order.

$\dfrac{48 + 50}{2} = 49$ Find the mean of the two middle numbers.

c. **Mode:** Find the data value that occurs most often. The mode is 50.

d. **Range:** Greatest value − least value = 59 − 40 = 19.

✅ Quick Check

1. Find the mean, median, mode, and range: 2.3 4.3 3.2 2.9 2.7 2.3

2 EXAMPLE   Identifying Modes

How many modes, if any, does each have?

a. $1.50 $2.00 $2.25 $2.40 $3.50 $4.00

No values are the same, so there is no mode.

b. 2 3 6 _8_ _8_ 10 11 12 _14_ _14_ 18 20

Both 8 and 14 appear the same number of times, and most often. There are two modes.

c. grape, grape, banana, nectarine, <u>strawberry</u>, <u>strawberry</u>, <u>strawberry</u>, orange, watermelon

Strawberry appears most often. There is one mode.

✅ Quick Check

2. Find the number of modes.

   a. 11 9 7 7 8 8 13 11   **b.** 38.5 55.4 45.3 38.5 68.4

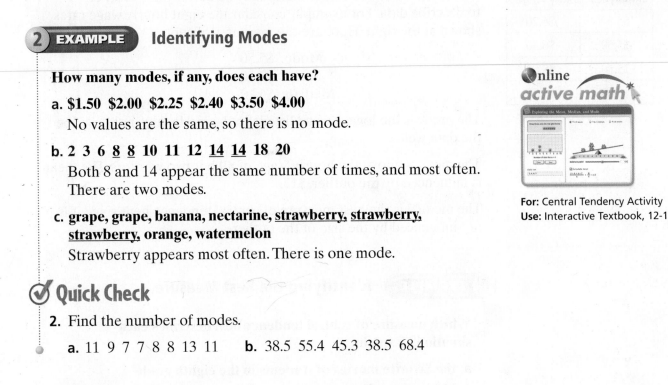

Online
active math

For: Central Tendency Activity
Use: Interactive Textbook, 12-1

An **outlier** is a data value that is much greater or less than the other data values. An outlier can affect the mean of a group of data.

3 EXAMPLE   Identifying Outliers

Use the map of Central America at the right.

a. Which data value is an outlier?

The data value for Honduras, 6,500 mi^2, is an outlier. It is an outlier because it is 1,500 mi^2 away from the closest data value.

b. How does the outlier affect the mean?

$\dfrac{21,700}{7} = 3,100$ Find the mean with the outlier.

$\dfrac{15,200}{6} \approx 2,500$ Find the mean without the outlier.

$3,100 - 2,500 = 600$

The outlier raises the mean by about 600 mi^2.

Approximate Land Areas That Can Be Farmed in Central American Countries

Guatemala 5,000 mi^2
Belize 200 mi^2
Honduras 6,500 mi^2
Nicaragua 4,500 mi^2
El Salvador 2,200 mi^2
Costa Rica 1,200 mi^2
Panama 2,100 mi^2

SOURCE: *The New York Times Almanac*

✅ Quick Check

3. Find an outlier in each group of data below and tell how it affects the mean. Round to the nearest tenth.

   a. 9 10 12 13 8 9 31 9   **b.** 1 17.5 18 19.5 16 17.5

Employees' Hourly Wages	
$5.50	$6.20
$5.50	$6.30
$5.50	$8.00
$6.00	$17.00

One measure of central tendency may be better than another to describe data. For example, consider the eight hourly wage rates shown at the right. Here are the measures of central tendency.

Mode: $5.50
Mean: $7.50
Median: $6.10

The mode is the lowest wage listed. So the mode does not describe the data well.

The mean is above the hourly wage of all but two workers. The mean is influenced by the outlier, $17.

The median is the best measure of central tendency here since it is not influenced by the size of the outlier.

4 EXAMPLE **Identifying the Best Measure**

Which measure of central tendency best describes each situation? Explain.

a. the favorite movies of students in the eighth grade

Mode; since the data are not numerical, the mode is the appropriate measure. When determining the most frequently chosen item, or when the data are not numerical, use the mode.

b. the daily high temperatures during a week in July

Mean; since daily high temperatures in July are not likely to have an outlier, mean is the appropriate measure. When the data have no outliers, use the mean.

c. the distances students in your class travel to school

Median; since one student may live much farther from school than the majority of students, the median is the appropriate measure. When an outlier may significantly influence the mean, use the median.

Vocabulary Tip

To help you recall that median means "middle number," think of the green, grassy median strip in the middle of a divided highway.

✔ Quick Check

4. a. Toshio found the following prices for sport shirts:
$20, $26, $27, $28, $21, $42, $18, and $20.
Find the mean, median, and mode for the shirt prices.

b. Reasoning Which measure of central tendency best describes the data? Justify your reasoning.

Use the data below for Exercises 1–2.

17 10 14 24 15 19 13 20 17 23

1. Calculate the mean and the median. Does one measure of central tendency describe the data better than the other?

2. Suppose 48 is added to the data set. How does it affect the mean and the median?

3. Describe a set of data that would best be described by the median.

4. **Error Analysis** Use the restaurant review at the left. Your friend says that no meal costs less than $10 at Robert's. Is your friend correct? Explain.

Restaurant Reviews ✴

Robert's Bistro
Experience fine dining at Robert's Bistro, where the mean cost of a meal in the dining room is $20.

Standards Practice

For more exercises, see *Extra Skills and Word Problem Practice*.

A **Practice by Example**

GO for **Help**

Example 1 (page 606)

Find the mean, median, mode, and range of each group of data. If an answer is not a whole number, round to the nearest tenth.

5. 47 56 57 63 89 44 56

6. 4 5 2 3 2 3 3 3 1 1 3

7. 1 2 4 5 5 6 9

8. 2.8 3.6 3.8 4.1 2.8 3.7 4.3

9. Mia's workouts lasted 1.0 h, 1.5 h, 2.25 h, 1.5 h, 2.4 h, and 2.1 h. Find the mean, median, and mode of these times. If the answer is not an integer, round to the nearest tenth.

Example 2 (page 607)

How many modes, if any, does each group of data have?

10. 31 44 44 31 38

11. 4.3 4.9 4.9 5.2

12. 64 68 64 65 68 65 72 61

13. Bob, Ana, Ron, Bob, Kay

Example 3 (page 607)

Find the outlier in each group of data and tell how it affects the mean.

14. 37 4 7 3 11 9 13 5

15. 126 123 115 125 123

16. Rita's quiz scores are 72, 96, 74, 80, and 79. Find the outlier and tell how it affects Rita's mean quiz score.

Example 4 (page 608)

Which measure of central tendency best describes each situation? Explain.

17. numbers of apples in 2-lb bags

18. favorite brands of jeans of 14-year-olds

19. ages of students in a fifth-grade classroom

Homework Video Tutor

For Exercises 20–24, find mean, median, mode, and range. Which measure best describes each group of data? Explain.

20. 3,456 560 435 456

21. 5.6 6.8 1.2 6.5 7.9 6.5

22. 33 76 86 92 86

23. 8 2 4 9 16

24. resting heart rate in beats per minute: 79 72 80 81 40 72

Which measure of central tendency best describes each situation? Explain.

25. shoe colors in a classroom

26. widths of computer screens at a bank

27. numbers of pets owned by classmates

Fat and Calorie Content
(per 2-tablespoon serving)

Seed or Nut	Fat (g)	Calories
Peanut	8.9	104
Pecan	9.1	90
Pistachio	7.9	92
Pumpkin	7.9	93
Sunflower	8.9	102
Walnut	7.7	80

For Exercises 28–30, use the table at the left. Round answers to the nearest tenth.

28. **Data Analysis** You make a mixture using the same amount of each kind of seed and nut.
   a. What is the mean number of grams of fat in a 2-tablespoon serving of the mixture?
   b. What is the mean number of Calories in a 2-tablespoon serving?

29. **Writing in Math** Describe two mixtures that each use a total of 8 tablespoons. Do the two parts of Exercise 28 for your mixtures.

C Challenge

30. A mixture of equal amounts of pumpkin seeds, sunflower seeds, and pistachios contains 12 tablespoons in all. How many grams of fat and how many Calories does the mixture have?

Multiple Choice Practice and Mixed Review

For Standards Tutorials, visit PHSchool.com. Web Code: bjq-9045

31. The table shows the distance Maggie ran each month. She ran 12 mi. in June. Find the median distance she ran in 6 months.

Month	January	February	March	April	May
Distance (mi)	28.5	32.0	30.0	29.5	31.5

   Ⓐ 29.5 mi   Ⓑ 29.75 mi   Ⓒ 30 mi   Ⓓ 31 mi

32. Which integer is closest to $\sqrt{52}$?
   Ⓐ 5   Ⓑ 7   Ⓒ 8   Ⓓ 10

GO for Help Lesson 3-2

Estimate each product or quotient.

33. $9.01 ÷ $1.42   **34.** 7.5 · 89.1   **35.** 12.6 · $2.99

Bar Graphs

Develop Know various forms of display for data sets; use the forms to compare two sets of data.

You can use a spreadsheet program to make a double bar graph. First enter the data in a spreadsheet. Then use a graphing tool to draw a double bar graph.

EXAMPLE

The spreadsheet gives population data (in thousands) for five states. Graph the data.

	A	B	C
1		Age 25 to 34	Age 75 to 84
2	California	5,297	1,357
3	Florida	2,112	1,068
4	Illinois	1,805	544
5	New York	2,671	896
6	Texas	3,284	741

Bar graphs are often useful in comparing amounts. Since the data show populations for two age ranges, use a double bar graph.

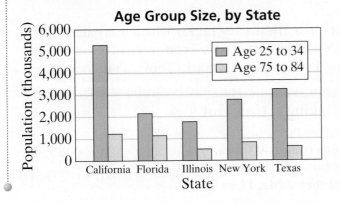

EXERCISES

1. a. Use a spreadsheet to make a double bar graph of the postage rate data below.

Postage Rates

Sent From the United States to	First Class 1-oz Letter (¢)	Postcard (¢)
United States	39	24
Canada	60	50
Mexico	60	50
All other countries	80	70

SOURCE: U.S. Postal Service. Go to **PHSchool.com** for a data update. Web Code: bjg-2041

b. Data Analysis Use the graph you made in part (a). Which bar is tallest? Explain.

12-2

Frequency Tables, Line Plots, and Histograms

What You'll Learn

- To display data in frequency tables and line plots
- To display data in histograms

. . . And Why

To solve real-world problems involving battery life

✓ **Check Skills You'll Need**

Find the median and mode of each data set.

1. 6, 9, 9, 5, 9

2. 73, 78, 77, 73, 79

3. 300, 100, 200, 150, 300

4. 3, 5, 7, 9, 3, 4, 6, 3, 7

GO for Help
Lesson 12-1

🔊 **New Vocabulary**

- frequency table
- line plot
- histogram

Develop Know various forms of display for data sets.

Using Frequency Tables and Line Plots

Standards Investigation
Exploring Frequency Tables

Many people have favorite colors. Do people also have favorite numbers? Take a survey of your classmates.

1. Ask each person to choose an integer from 0 to 9. Use a table to record the responses.

2. Which number was chosen most frequently? How many times was each of the other numbers chosen?

3. Suppose you want to continue your survey. Looking back, would you use the same type of table you used for Question 1? Can you make improvements? Explain.

You can display data in a **frequency table,** which lists each data item with the number of times it occurs. Then you can use a **line plot,** which displays data with X marks above a number line.

1 EXAMPLE **Making a Line Plot**

A number cube was rolled 20 times. The results are at the right. Display the data in a frequency table. Then make a line plot.

5	2	5	4	1	6	5	2	5	1
3	6	1	3	4	5	3	5	3	4

Use a tally mark for each result.

Count the tally marks and record the frequency.

Number	Tally	Frequency
1	III	3
2	II	2
3	IIII	4
4	III	3
5	HHI I	6
6	II	2

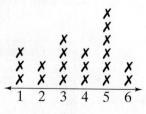

✅ Quick Check

1. Display the data below in a frequency table.
   10 12 13 15 10 11 14 13 10 11 11 12 10 10 15

Using Histograms to Display Data

A **histogram** shows the frequencies of data items as a graph. The data are often grouped into intervals. The intervals are of equal size and do not overlap. The height of each bar shows the frequency of the data in a given interval.

Online
active math

For: Histogram Activity
Use: Interactive Textbook, 12-2

② EXAMPLE   Making a Histogram

The results of testing 12 batteries of the same type are shown at the right. Use the data to make a histogram.

Hours of Battery Life

9	12	14	10	15	10
18	23	10	14	22	11

Step 1 Decide on the interval size. The data start at 9 hours and go to 24 hours. A possible interval choice is 4 hours.

Step 2 Make a frequency table.

Hours	Tally	Frequency
9–12	ⵌ I	6
13–16	III	3
17–20	I	1
21–24	II	2

Step 3 Make a histogram. Include a title and label the axes.

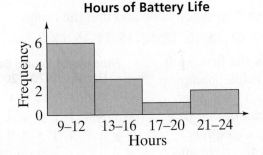

Hours of Battery Life

✅ Quick Check

2. **a.** Display the data for battery life in a histogram with intervals of 3 hours.
   b. Is the range of the data 14 or 4? Explain.

1. Vocabulary How is a histogram different from a bar graph?

Use the line plot below for Exercises 2 and 3.

2. Reasoning Explain why the number line for the line plot starts at 25 instead of 0.

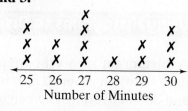

3. Find the median of the data set.

Standards Practice

For more exercises, see *Extra Skills and Word Problem Practice*.

A Practice by Example

Example 1
(page 636)

GO for Help

Display each set of data in a frequency table and a line plot.

4. 25 29 28 28 30 25 26 28 27 29 26 30

5. rolls of a number cube: 4 1 3 4 2 1 2 5 2 3 5 1 6 1 3 5 6

6. test scores: 100 90 70 60 95 65 85 70 70 75 80 85 75 70 100 90

Example 2
(page 637)

Draw a histogram for each frequency table.

7.

Interval	1–2	3–4	5–6	7–8
Frequency	7	10	4	5

8.

Interval	5–8	9–12	13–16
Frequency	12	8	2

9. A company asked its employees to keep track of the number of minutes they spend online checking e-mail each day. The responses are shown at the right.
  a. What intervals would you use to make a histogram?
  b. Make a frequency table for the data.
  c. Make a histogram.

Minutes Checking E–mail

25	35	24	27	42
45	36	38	62	84
72	33	44	27	54
28	33	65	71	24
54	47	36	71	29

B Apply Your Skills

10. Display the data in a frequency table and find the range.
14 16 14 16 14 13 12 15 16 12 12 15 14 15 15

Homework Video Tutor

Visit: PHSchool.com
Web Code: bje-1202

11. In the World Series, the first team to win four games is the champion. Sometimes the series ends after four games, but it can last up to seven games. Make a frequency table of the data at the right and use the table to find the mode.

Number of World Series Games, 1970—2004

5 7 7 7 5 7 4 6 6 7 6 6
7 5 5 7 7 7 5 4 4 7 6 6
0 6 6 7 4 4 5 7 7 6 4

A frequency table or line plot may allow you to readily "see" the mode and find the median. Find the mode and the median for the data set in each exercise.

12. Exercise 4   **13.** Exercise 5   **14.** Exercise 6

15. Writing in Math A magazine line plot shows results of a survey. Explain how to use the line plot to find each of the following.
   a. the number of people who answered the survey
   b. the mode, median, and mean

C Challenge
16. Open-Ended Describe a set of data that would be easier to display with a frequency table than with a histogram.

Multiple Choice Practice and Mixed Review

For Standards Tutorials, visit PHSchool.com. Web Code: bjq-9045

17. What is the length of the hypotenuse of a right triangle with side lengths of 3 in. and 4 in.?

   Ⓐ 4 in.   Ⓑ 5 in.   Ⓒ 7 in.   Ⓓ 25 in.

18. Which number best represents the scale factor used to dilate △*ABC* into △*TUV*?

   Ⓐ $\frac{1}{3}$ Ⓒ 2

   Ⓑ $\frac{2}{3}$ Ⓓ 3

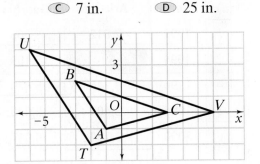

 for Help   Lesson 12-1

Find the mean, median, and mode for each data set.

19. 12 13 14 16 16 17 18 18   **20.** 8 15 22 9 11 16 20 10

Checkpoint Quiz 1

Use the data below for Exercises 1–3.
   47 51 50 52 50 47 48 50 49 51 48 52

1. Display the data in a frequency table.

2. Display the data in a line plot.

3. Find the mean, median, and mode of the data. Round to the nearest tenth.

The data below gives the heights, in inches, of plants grown for a science project. Use the data for Exercises 4–6.
   25 25 20 25 16 20 25 30 25 31 26 28 30

4. Display the data in a histogram.

5. Find the mean, median, and mode of the data. Round to the nearest tenth.

6. Identify the outlier in the data.

> *Develop* Know various forms of display; use the forms to compare two sets of data.

You can use a spreadsheet program to make double line graphs.

EXAMPLE

The spreadsheet gives the voting-age populations in thousands for two states. Graph the data in the spreadsheet.

	A	B	C
1	Year	Arizona	Georgia
2	1992	2,812	5,006
3	1994	2,923	5,159
4	1996	3,245	5,420
5	1998	3,405	5,620
6	2000	3,764	6,017

Row 3 contains voting-age populations of both states in 1994.

Cell B3 contains the voting-age population of Arizona in 1994.

— **Column B contains the voting-age population of Arizona.**

Choose an appropriate type of graph from your spreadsheet program. Line graphs are often useful to display changes in data over a period of time. Since the data show changes over time for two states, use a double line graph.

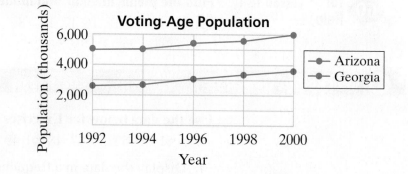

Voting-Age Population

EXERCISES

1. Use a spreadsheet to graph the data below.

Average Prices Farmers Received

Year	1996	1997	1998	1999	2000	2001	2002	2003
Price for Turkey (¢/lb)	43.3	38.9	38.0	40.8	40.6	39.0	36.5	36.0
Price for Chicken (¢/lb)	38.1	37.7	39.3	37.1	33.6	39.3	30.5	34.6

SOURCE: U.S. Department of Agriculture.
Go to **PHSchool.com** for a data update.
Web Code: bjg-2041

2. **Writing in Math** Explain when you would use a line graph and when you would use a bar graph to display a data set.

12-3 Box-and-Whisker Plots

Develop Know various forms of display for data sets, including a box-and-whisker plot; use the forms to display a single set of data or to compare two sets of data.

Develop, Master Understand the meaning of, and be able to compute, the minimum, the lower quartile, the median, the upper quartile, and the maximum of a data set.

What You'll Learn

- To make box-and-whisker plots
- To analyze data in box-and-whisker plots

. . . And Why

To solve real-world problems involving large data sets

✔ **Check Skills You'll Need**

Find each median.

1. 12, 10, 11, 7, 9, 8, 10, 5

2. 4.5, 3.2, 6.3, 5.2, 5, 4.8, 6, 3.9

3. 55, 53, 67, 52, 50, 49, 51, 52, 52, 52

4. 101, 100, 100, 105, 102, 101

GO **for Help**

Lesson 12-1

🔊 **New Vocabulary**

- box-and-whisker plot
- quartiles

Crops Harvested

Year	Acres (millions)	Year	Acres (millions)
1988	298	1995	314
1989	318	1996	326
1990	322	1997	333
1991	318	1998	326
1992	317	1999	327
1993	308	2000	323
1994	321		

SOURCE: *Statistical Abstract of the United States.* Go to to **PHSchool.com** for a data update. Web Code: bjg-2041

Making Box-and-Whisker Plots

A **box-and-whisker plot** displays the distribution of data items along a number line. **Quartiles** divide the data into four equal parts. The median is the middle quartile.

Box-and-Whisker Plot

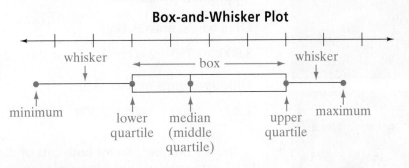

1 EXAMPLE **Making a Box-and-Whisker Plot**

The table, below left, shows United States crops harvested from 1988 to 2000. Make a box-and-whisker plot.

Step 1 Arrange the data in order from least to greatest. Find the median.

298 308 314 317 318 318 321 322 323 326 326 327 333

Step 2 Find the lower quartile and upper quartile, which are the medians of the lower and upper "halves."

298 308 314 317 318 318 321 322 323 326 326 327 333

$$\text{lower quartile} = \frac{314 + 317}{2} = \frac{631}{2} = 315.5$$

$$\text{upper quartile} = \frac{326 + 326}{2} = \frac{652}{2} = 326$$

Step 3 Draw a number line. Mark the minimum and maximum, the median, and the quartiles. Draw a box from the first to the third quartiles. Mark the median with a vertical segment. Draw whiskers to the minimum and maximum.

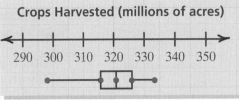

Crops Harvested (millions of acres)

290 300 310 320 330 340 350

✅ Quick Check

1. Draw a box-and-whisker plot for the distances of migration of birds (thousands of miles): 5, 2.5, 6, 8, 9, 2, 1, 4, 6.2, 18, 7.

You can compare two sets of data by making two box-and-whisker plots below one number line.

2 EXAMPLE **Comparing Sets of Data**

Use box-and-whisker plots to compare orca whale masses and hippopotamus masses.

Orca whale masses (kg)

3,900 2,750 2,600 3,100 4,200 2,600 3,700 3,000 2,200

Hippopotamus masses (kg)

1,800 2,000 3,000 2,500 3,600 2,700 1,900 3,100 2,300

Draw a number line for both sets of data. Use the range of data points to choose a scale.

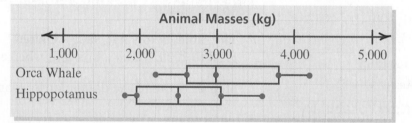

Draw the second box-and-whisker plot below the first one.

✅ Quick Check

2. Compare annual video sales and CD sales by making two box-and-whisker plots below one number line.

videos (millions of units): 28, 24, 15, 21, 22, 16, 22, 30, 24, 17

CDs (millions of units): 16, 17, 22, 16, 18, 24, 15, 16, 25, 18

An orca whale can weigh from 2,500 kg to 4,500 kg. A hippopotamus can weigh from 1,400 kg to 3,200 kg.

Online
active math

For: Box-and-Whisker Activity
Use: Interactive Textbook, 12-3

Analyzing Box-and-Whisker Plots

Although you cannot see every data point in a box-and-whisker plot, you can use the quartiles and the maximum and minimum values to analyze and describe a data set.

3 EXAMPLE **Describing Data**

Describe the data in the box-and-whisker plot.

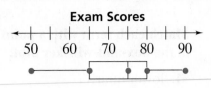

Exam Scores

The highest score is 90 and the lowest is 50. At least half of the scores are within 10 points of the median, 75. Since the quartiles and the median are not evenly spaced, the data is not evenly distributed.

✓ Quick Check

3. Describe the data in the box-and-whisker plot.

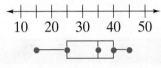

You can compare box-and-whisker plots to analyze two sets of data.

4 EXAMPLE **Comparing Sets of Data**

The box-and-whisker plot below compares the percents of the United States voting-age population who said they registered to vote to the percents who said they voted. What conclusions can you draw?

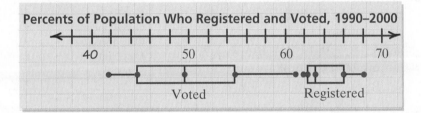

Percents of Population Who Registered and Voted, 1990–2000

The percent registered was fairly constant, since the box-and-whisker plot is narrow. The percent who voted varied more, but it was always less than the percent who registered. Therefore, you can conclude that many who were registered did not vote.

Problem Solving Tip

Understand the data before you work on a problem. When you analyze a box-and-whisker plot, ask yourself questions such as "How many sets of data are displayed?"

✓ Quick Check

4. Use the box-and-whisker plots below. What conclusions can you draw about heights of Olympic basketball players?

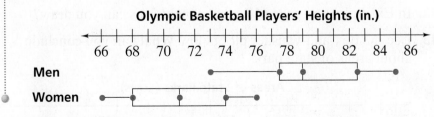

Olympic Basketball Players' Heights (in.)

Match each term with a point in the box-and-whisker plot.

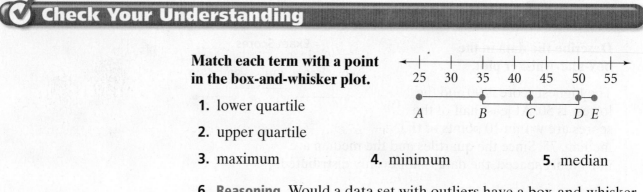

1. lower quartile

2. upper quartile

3. maximum
4. minimum
5. median

6. **Reasoning** Would a data set with outliers have a box-and-whisker plot with long whiskers or short whiskers? Explain.

Standards Practice

For more exercises, see *Extra Skills and Word Problem Practice*.

A Practice by Example

Example 1
(page 617)

GO for Help

7. Use the data at the right to make a box-and-whisker plot for the maximum speeds of animals.

8. Make a box-and-whisker plot for this set of data:
16, 18, 59, 75, 30, 34, 25, 49, 27, 16, 21, 58, 71, 19, 50

Example 2
(page 618)

9. Compare the data sets by making two box-and-whisker plots below one number line.
set A: 3, 7, 9, 12, 2, 1, 6, 5, 4, 3, 7, 10, 13, 8, 1, 9
set B: 9, 8, 1, 7, 6, 3, 7, 9, 8, 6, 4, 7, 8, 9, 10, 10

Maximum Speeds of Animals for a Quarter Mile

Animal	Maximum Speed (mi/h)
Cheetah	70
Lion	50
Quarter horse	47.5
Coyote	43
Hyena	40
Rabbit	35
Giraffe	32
Grizzly bear	30
Cat (domestic)	30
Elephant	25
Squirrel	12

SOURCE: *The World Almanac*

Example 3
(page 619)

Answer each question for the data in the box-and-whisker plot below.

10. What are the highest and lowest prices for the CD players?

11. About half of the prices are within what amount of the median?

Prices of Portable CD Players ($)

Example 4
(page 619)

12. In Example 2 on page 618, what conclusions can you draw?

13. Use the box-and-whisker plot below. What can you conclude about areas of state parks?

Areas of State Parks (acres)

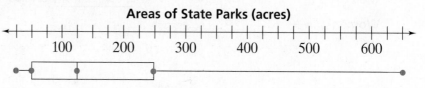

14. a. Compare the ages of male and female soccer players by making two box-and-whisker plots below one number line.

Ages of U.S. Olympic Soccer Team Players

men: 22, 21, 22, 26, 20, 26, 23, 21, 22, 22, 22, 22, 21, 22, 23, 21, 20, 22

women: 30, 27, 28, 25, 31, 24, 31, 24, 21, 23, 27, 18, 19, 24, 23, 20

b. Compare the box-and-whisker plots. What can you conclude?

15. Writing in Math Explain how you can find the quartiles of a set of data.

16. Error Analysis A student made a box-and-whisker plot. The student marked the maximum and minimum data values and then divided the distance between those points into four equal parts. What error did the student make?

17. Open-Ended Write a set of data whose box-and-whisker plot has a long box and short whiskers.

C Challenge

18. Reasoning Can you find the mean, median, and mode of a set of data by looking at a box-and-whisker plot? Explain.

Homework Video Tutor

Visit: PHSchool.com
Web Code: bje-1203

Multiple Choice Practice and Mixed Review

For Standards Tutorials, visit PHSchool.com. Web Code: bjq-9045

19. The table shows maximum life spans of different animals. Which box-and-whisker plot best represents these data?

A 10 20 30 40 50 60 70 80 90

B 8 16 24 32 40 48 56 64 72

C 16 24 32 40 48 56 64 72 80

D 5 15 25 35 45 55 65 75

Animals' Maximum Life Spans

Animal	Years
Beaver	50
Black bear	36
Chimpanzee	53
Chipmunk	8
Elephant	77
Goat	18
Horse	50
Mouse	6
Squirrel	23
Tiger	26

Display each set of data in a frequency table.

for Help Lesson 12-2

20. 6 8 7 6 5 8 5 6 4 8 7 5 4 7 6 8 6 7

21. 32 31 29 33 31 32 35 33 32 31 32 30

12-4 Stem-and-Leaf Plots

Develop Know various forms of display for data sets, including a stem-and-leaf plot; use the forms to display a single set of data or to compare two sets of data.

What You'll Learn

- To make stem-and-leaf plots
- To use stem-and-leaf plots to compare data sets

. . . And Why

To analyze data from real-world situations, such as comparing race times

✓ Check Skills You'll Need

Use the data below for Exercises 1–3. Round to the nearest tenth.

10, 20, 40, 50, 30, 30, 20, 40, 40, 10, 20, 40

1. Find the mean.

2. Find the median.

3. Find the mode.

GO for Help
Lesson 12-1

🔊 New Vocabulary

- stem-and-leaf plot

Making Stem-and-Leaf Plots

A **stem-and-leaf plot** is a graph that displays numerical data arranged in order. Each data item is broken into a stem and a leaf.

The stem is the digit or digits on the left and the leaf is the digit or digits on the right.

1|0 ← leaf
↑
stem

5.|52 ← leaf
↑
stem

5.5|2 ← leaf
↑
stem

① EXAMPLE Making a Stem-and-Leaf Plot

Make a stem-and-leaf plot for the data in the table below.

Prices of Digital Music Players (dollars)
189, 214, 200, 195,
190, 192, 193, 211,
201, 196, 195, 194,
205, 198, 208, 201

Step 1 Choose the stems. The least value is 189. The greatest value is 214. For this data, use the first two digits as the stems. The stems in this case are 18, 19, 20, and 21.

Step 2 Draw the stem-and-leaf plot. Include a key.

stems   leaves
↓   ↓

18	9
19	0 2 3 4 5 5 6 8
20	0 1 1 5 8
21	1 4

Key: 19 | 2 means $192

The leaves are the ones place written in increasing order.

The key explains what the stems and leaves represent.

✓ Quick Check

High Temperatures (°F) Death Valley, California
87 91 101 111 120
125 134 126 120
113 97 86

1. The monthly high temperatures for Death Valley, California, are shown at the left. Make a stem-and-leaf plot for the data.

Using Stem-and-Leaf Plots to Compare Data

A back-to-back stem-and-leaf plot shows two sets of data in the same graph. The side-by-side display makes it easy to compare the data visually. The plot also makes it easier to "see" the median and the mode of a data set.

2 EXAMPLE Comparing Sets of Data

The winning times in the Olympic 100-m dash are shown at the right. Draw a back-to-back stem-and-leaf plot for the data. Use the median and mode of each data set to compare the data.

Use seconds for the stems and tenths of seconds for the leaves. Put the leaves in ascending order starting at the stems.

Winning Times, 100-m Dash

Men's Times (tenths of second)	Stem (seconds)	Women's Times (tenths of second)
9 9 9 9 8	9	
3 2 1 1 0 0 0	10	5 8 8 9 9
	11	0 0 0 1 1 1 4

means 10.0 ←— 0 | 10 | 5 —→ means 10.5

Show the stems in the middle of the plot with the leaves to the left and right.

Include a key for each side of the stem-and-leaf plot.

Winning Times, 100-m Dash (seconds)

Year	Men	Women
1960	10.2	11.0
1964	10.0	11.4
1968	9.9	11.0
1972	10.1	11.1
1976	10.1	11.1
1980	10.3	11.1
1984	10.0	11.0
1988	9.9	10.5
1992	10.0	10.8
1996	9.8	10.9
2000	9.9	10.8
2004	9.9	10.9

SOURCE: *Sports Illustrated Sports Almanac*

The back-to-back stem-and-leaf plot gives the impression that the women's winning times are greater than the men's winning times.

The median of the times for men is 10.0 s. The median of the times for women is 11.0 s. The mode of the times for men is 9.9 s. The mode of the times for women is 10.0 s. Based on the measures of central tendency, the women's winning times tend to be greater than the men's winning times.

✓ Quick Check

2. Draw a back-to-back stem-and-leaf plot for the annual sales data in the table below. Use the median and the mode of each data set to compare the data.

Annual Sales (millions)

Year	1	2	3	4	5	6	7	8	9	10
Videos	28	24	15	21	22	16	22	30	24	17
CDs	16	17	22	16	18	24	15	16	25	18

Online active math

For: Stem-and-Leaf Plot Activity
Use: Interactive Textbook, 12-4

Because stem-and-leaf plots display data items in numerical order, they are useful tools for finding median and mode.

More Than One Way

The table shows the annual percent change in the United States Consumer Price Index. The Consumer Price Index measures the average change in how much you pay for things. Find the median and mode.

United States Consumer Price Index

Year	Percent Change
1993	3.0
1994	2.6
1995	2.8
1996	3.0
1997	2.3
1998	1.6
1999	2.2
2000	3.4
2001	2.8
2002	1.6
2003	2.3
2004	2.7

SOURCE: Bureau of Labor Statistics. Go to **PHSchool.com** for a data update. Web Code: bjg-9041

Michelle's Method

A stem-and-leaf plot is an appropriate way to organize the data to find the median and mode.

```
1 | 6 6
2 | 2 3 3 6 7 8 8
3 | 0 0 4
```

Key: 3 | 0 means 3.0%

$$\frac{2.6 + 2.7}{2} = 2.65$$

The median is the mean of the sixth and seventh leaves.

The median change in the United States Consumer Price Index is 2.65%. The modes are 1.6%, 2.3%, 2.8%, and 3.0%.

Eric's Method

To find the median and mode, I need to put the data items in order.

1.6 1.6 2.2 2.3 2.3 2.6 2.7 2.8 2.8 3.0 3.0 3.4

The median is the mean of the sixth and seventh items, which is 2.65.

The median change in the United States Consumer Price Index is 2.65%.

The modes are 1.6%, 2.3%, 2.8%, and 3.0%.

Choose a Method

The table shows the average amount of time drivers in different cities spend in traffic annually. Find the median and mode of the data. Explain why you chose the method you used.

City	Hours	City	Hours
Los Angeles	56	Denver	45
Phoenix	31	Houston	50
Seattle	53	New York	34
Las Vegas	21	Miami	42
Chicago	34	Detroit	41

SOURCE: *Time Almanac*

Use the stem-and-leaf plot below for Exercises 1–4.

1. What numbers make up the stems?

2. What are the leaves for the first stem?

3. How many data items are shown in the stem-and-leaf plot?

4. Find the median and mode of the data.

Test Scores	
6	8 8
7	8 8 8 8 9
8	1 2 2 4 4 4 5 5 6 7 7
9	2 2 5 5 5 8

Key: 7 | 8 means 78%

For more exercises, see *Extra Skills and Word Problem Practice.*

A Practice by Example

Example 1
(page 622)

GO for Help

Make a stem-and-leaf plot for each set of data.

5. 54 48 52 53 67 61 68 49 40 50 69 73 74 76 78

6. 124 129 131 116 138 107 105 116 122 137 138 134

7. 3.7 5.0 6.9 3.2 4.5 6.3 6.7 5.8 5.2 6.9 5.0 4.3 4.1

Example 2
(page 623)

Use the stem-and-leaf plot below for Exercises 8 and 9.

8. The plot at the right shows the blood pressure of 40 men and women of the same age. Find the mean and median of each data set.

9. **Reasoning** What conclusions can you draw about men's blood pressure compared to women's blood pressure? Explain.

		Blood Pressure	
Men			Women
8	6	5 5 6 8	
9 7 7 6	7	0 1 1 2 5 6 8 8 9	
9 9 8 7 4 4 1	8	0 0 3 5 6	
8 5 4 2 0 0	9	0 1	
2 0	10		

Key: means 94 ← 4 | 9 | 1 → means 91

Vocabulary Tip

In a stem-and-leaf plot of two sets of data, 8 |6| 5 means that both 8 and 5 are leaves of the stem 6.

B Apply Your Skills

10. Make a back-to-back stem-and-leaf plot for the data sets below. Then find the median and mode.

Length of Wood Boards (in.)

Saw A	Saw B
64 58 63 57 54 61 52 54	72 63 52 57 64 49 45 43

11. **Writing in Math** A set of data contains numbers in the 30s, 40s, and 60s only. Is it necessary to put a 5 on the stem of a stem-and-leaf plot? Justify your answer.

Homework Video Tutor

Visit: PHSchool.com
Web Code: bje-1204

Squirrel monkeys have a lifespan of about 20 years.

12. **a.** Use the data below on the life spans of different animals (in years) to make a stem-and-leaf plot.

1 10 3 10 4 12 13 15 15 20 40 6 7 10 15 18 22 20
25 7 12 5 15 20 25 20 15

b. Number Sense If you add the data values 13. 2, 14. 5, 13.5, 15.6, 18.2, 19.7, 21.3, 35.6, 40.2, 13.7, and 12.8, why might you choose different stems in your stem-and-leaf plot?

13. In golf, a player's score is based on the total number of strokes needed to get the ball into the holes. Use the mean, median, and mode of each set of data below to compare men's scores to women's scores.

U.S. Open 1983–2004

Men's Scores		Women's Scores
9 9 9 9 8 8 8 7 7 6 6 6 6 2 2 2	27	2 2 3 4 4 6 7 7 8 8
5 2 0 0 0 0	28	0 0 0 2 3 3 4 5 7
	29	0 0 0

Key: means 276 ← 6 | 27 | 2 → means 272

SOURCE: *Sports Illustrated 2005 Almanac*

 Challenge

14. The data sets below have the same mean, median, mode, and range. Copy and complete the back-to-back stem-and-leaf plot.

7 6 ■	3	1 2 3
6 5 4 3 1	4	2 ■ ■ 6
■ 0	5	0 0 1

Key: means 3■ ← ■ | 3 | 1 → means 31

Multiple Choice Practice and Mixed Review

For Standards Tutorials, visit PHSchool.com. Web Code: bjq-9045

15. What is the median of the data at the right?

Ⓐ 3.0

Ⓑ 3.05

Ⓒ 3.15

Ⓓ 3.5

1	4 7
2	9
3	0 1 2 2 2
4	

1 | 2 means 1.2

16. Which list shows the numbers in order from least to greatest?

Ⓐ $9.25, 9\frac{1}{3}, 9\frac{5}{6}, 10, 10\frac{1}{6}$ Ⓒ $10, 9.25, 9\frac{1}{3}, 10\frac{1}{6}, 10, 9\frac{5}{6}$

Ⓑ $9.25, 9\frac{1}{3}, 9\frac{5}{6}, 10\frac{1}{6}, 10$ Ⓓ $9\frac{1}{3}, 9.25, 9\frac{5}{6}, 10, 10\frac{1}{6}$

 Lesson 12-1

17. Find the mean, median, mode, and range of the set of data.

178 179 180 182 177 183 185 180 180 179

Choosing the Best Graph

Develop Know various forms of display for data sets.

Sometimes you have to choose which type of graph to use to represent a set of data. Knowing the differences among the types of graphs can help you make the best choice.

You use a bar graph to compare amounts. One axis shows the categories and the other axis shows the amounts. A multiple-bar graph includes a key.

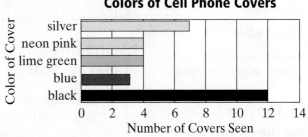

Colors of Cell Phone Covers

You use a line graph to show the changes in a set of data over a period of time. A multiple-line graph shows changes in more than one category of data. You can use a line graph to look for trends and make predictions.

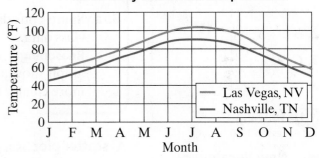

Mean Daily Maximum Temperatures

Circle graphs show data as percents or fractions of a whole. The total must be 100% or 1. The angles at the center are central angles, and each angle is proportional to the percent or fraction of the total.

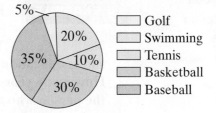

Selected Students' Favorite Sports

- Golf
- Swimming
- Tennis
- Basketball
- Baseball

EXERCISES

Choose a bar graph, line graph, or circle graph to display each set of data. Explain your choice.

1. **List and Sale Prices**

Item	List Price	Sale Price
Digital camera	$279	$223
Headphone radio	$40	$32
Smartphones	$195	$156

2. **Costs of Owning a Car**

Category	Percent
Financing	52
Insurance	20
Gas, oil, and maintenance	25
Registration	3

12-5 Scatter Plots

Master Know various forms of display for data sets; use the forms to display a single set of data or to compare two sets of data.

Introduce, Develop Represent two numerical variables on a scatterplot and informally describe how the data points are distributed and any apparent relationship that exists between the two variables.

What You'll Learn

- To interpret and draw scatter plots
- To use scatter plots to find trends

. . . And Why

To solve real-world problems involving trends

✓ Check Skills You'll Need

Write the coordinates of each point.

1. A
2. B
3. C
4. D

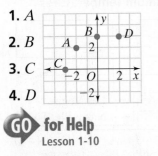

GO for Help
Lesson 1-10

◀》 New Vocabulary

- scatter plot
- positive correlation
- negative correlation
- no correlation

Interpreting and Drawing Scatter Plots

Standards Investigation
Making Scatter Plots

1. **Data Collection** For each person in your group, measure the height and *hand span,* the greatest distance possible between the tips of the thumb and little finger on one hand.

2. Graph the lengths as ordered pairs (height, hand span).

3. **a.** Share your data with the class. Make a graph of the class data.

   b. Reasoning Compare the two graphs you made. Does one graph show a relationship between heights and hand spans more clearly than the other? Explain.

A **scatter plot** is a graph that shows the relationship between two sets of data. To make a scatter plot, graph the data as ordered pairs.

1 EXAMPLE Interpreting Scatter Plots

Multiple Choice The scatter plot shows education and income data. How many years of education does the person who earns $100,000 have?

Ⓐ 12 years   Ⓒ 15 years

Ⓑ 14 years   Ⓓ 16 years

The point (16, 100) has income coordinate 100. The person earning $100,000 in a year has 16 years of education. The answer is D.

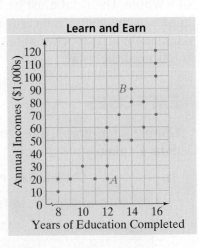

✓ Quick Check

1. a. Describe the person represented by point *A* in the example.

   b. Describe the person represented by point *B*.

   c. How many people have exactly 12 years of education?

Making a Scatter Plot

Use the table to make a scatter plot of the latitude and temperature data.

Climate Data

City	Location (degrees north latitude)	Daily Mean Temperature (°F)	Mean Annual Precipitation (inches)
Atlanta, GA	34	61	51
Boston, MA	42	51	42
Chicago, IL	42	49	36
Duluth, MN	47	39	30
Honolulu, HI	21	77	22
Houston, TX	30	68	46
Juneau, AK	58	41	54
Miami, FL	26	76	56
Phoenix, AZ	33	73	8
Portland, ME	44	45	44
San Diego, CA	33	64	10
Wichita, KS	38	56	29

SOURCES: *The World Almanac* and *The Statistical Abstract of the United States*. Go to **PHSchool.com** for a data update. Web Code: bjg-2041

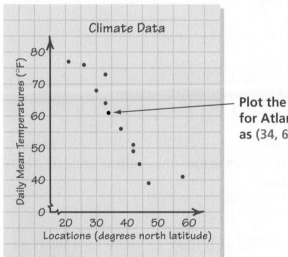

Plot the data for Atlanta as (34, 61).

> **Quick Tip**
>
> Remember that in a scatter plot one *y*-value can correspond to more than one *x*-value.

✅ Quick Check

2. Use the table in Example 2.

   a. Make a scatter plot of the latitude and precipitation data.

   b. Make a scatter plot of the temperature and precipitation data. Plot temperatures along the horizontal axis of the graph.

You can use scatter plots to look for trends. The next three scatter plots show the types of relationships two sets of data may have.

Vocabulary Tip

"Positive slope" in a scatter plot suggests a positive correlation. "Negative slope" suggests a negative correlation.

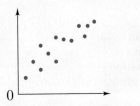

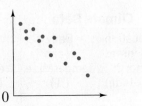

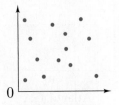

Positive correlation
As one set of values increases, the other set tends to increase.

Negative correlation
As one set of values increases, the other set tends to decrease.

No correlation
The values show no relationship.

3 EXAMPLE **Finding a Trend**

Use the scatter plot below. Is there a *positive correlation*, a *negative correlation*, or *no correlation* between the years and the winning times? Explain.

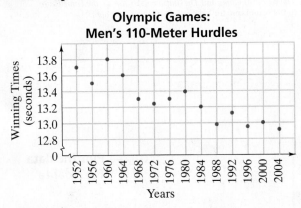

Since 1952, the winning times have generally decreased. There is a negative correlation.

✓ Quick Check

3. Use the scatter plot below. Is there a *positive correlation*, a *negative correlation*, or *no correlation* between the years and the winning distances? Explain.

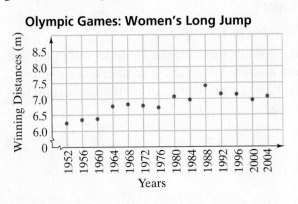

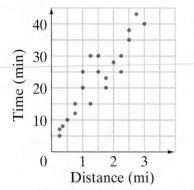

Use the scatter plot at the left. It shows distances and travel times for students going to school.

1. As the distance from school increases, what happens to the amount of time it takes to get to school?

2. Is there a *positive correlation*, a *negative correlation*, or *no correlation* between the distance and the time?

3. Explain what the point (0.5, 10) represents.

4. How many students take longer than 35 min to get to school?

Standards Practice

For more exercises, see *Extra Skills and Word Problem Practice.*

A Practice by Example
Example 1
(page 628)

GO for Help

For a guide to reading and solving Exercises 5–7, see page 634.

Statistics The scatter plot shows the average times that 15 students spent watching television and doing physical activities in a day.

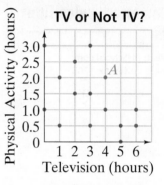

5. Describe the student represented by point *A*.

6. How many students averaged 1 hour of physical activity?

7. How many students averaged 5 hours of watching television?

Example 2
(page 629)

For Exercises 8–10, use the table below. Make a scatter plot for the data indicated. Graph calories on the horizontal axis.

Nutritional Values for 100 Grams of Food

Food	Fat (grams)	Protein (grams)	Carbohydrate (grams)	Energy (calories)
Bread	4	8	50	267
Cheese	33	25	1	403
Chicken	4	31	0	165
Eggs	11	13	1	155
Ground beef	19	27	0	292
Milk	3	3	5	61
Peanuts	49	26	16	567
Pizza	5	12	33	223
Tuna	1	26	0	116

SOURCE: U. S. Department of Agriculture Nutrient Database for Standard Reference

8. calories and grams of protein

9. calories and grams of fat

10. calories and grams of carbohydrates

Example 3
(page 630)

Is there a *positive correlation*, a *negative correlation*, or *no correlation* between the sets of data in each scatter plot? Explain.

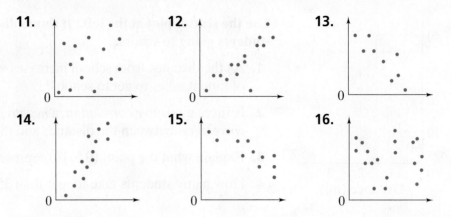

11. **12.** **13.**

14. **15.** **16.**

B **Apply Your Skills**

Would you expect a *positive correlation*, a *negative correlation*, or *no correlation* between each pair of data sets? Explain.

Homework Video Tutor

Visit: PHSchool.com
Web Code: bje-1205

17. the age of pets in a home and the number of pets in that home

18. the temperature outside and the number of layers of clothing

19. your grade on a test and the amount of time you studied

20. the shoe sizes and the shirt sizes for men

21. the number of students in a school and the number of stores nearby

22. **Writing in Math** Describe a pair of data sets, different from any in this lesson, for which you would expect to see a scatter plot with a negative correlation. Explain.

23. The table at the right shows the average prices of movie tickets and the numbers of movie admissions.
  a. Make a scatter plot of the data in the table. Graph prices on the horizontal axis.
  b. **Data Analysis** Is there a *positive correlation*, a *negative correlation*, or *no correlation* between the numbers of admissions and the prices of tickets?
  c. **Reasoning** Would your answer to part (b) be the same if you graphed ticket prices on the vertical axis instead? Explain.

Year	Number of Admissions (millions)	Average Ticket Price
1990	1,189	$4.23
1992	1,173	$4.15
1994	1,292	$4.18
1996	1,339	$4.42
1998	1,481	$4.69

SOURCE: Motion Picture Association of America

C **Challenge**

24. The scatter plot at the right shows the number of person-hours y needed by a bakery to fill an order for x pies. Write an equation for the line. Use it to predict the number of person-hours needed to fill an order for 15 pies.

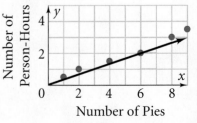

Multiple Choice Practice and Mixed Review

For Standards Tutorials, visit PHSchool.com. Web Code: bjq-9045

25. As the numbers of pages in magazines increase, the weights of the magazines increase. Which scatter plot represents the situation?

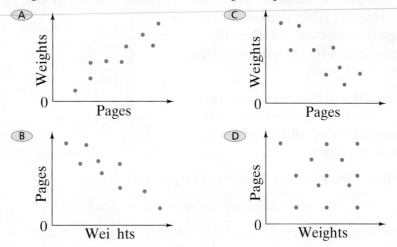

26. The table shows the number of minutes Tan works out at the gym from Monday through Thursday.

Tan's Workout Times

Day	Monday	Tuesday	Wednesday	Thursday
Time (minutes)	90	75	80	85

Tan exercises for only 35 minutes on Friday. What is the median of Tan's workout times?

    Ⓐ 35 minutes   Ⓒ 80 minutes

    Ⓑ 73 minutes   Ⓓ 90 minutes

27. Which equation is represented by the graph at the right?

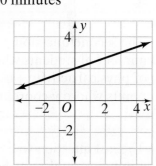

    Ⓐ $\frac{1}{3}x - y = -2$

    Ⓑ $-\frac{1}{3}x - y = 2$

    Ⓒ $y = 3x + 2$

    Ⓓ $3x - y = 2$

Lesson 7-6   **Solve each formula for the variable indicated in red.**

28. $V = \frac{1}{3}Bh$ **29.** $A = \frac{1}{2}(b + c)h$ **30.** $S = \frac{a}{1 - r}$

Lesson 6-6   **31.** Ms. Jimenez earns $27,000 per year. She is paid weekly. She puts 8% of her salary in a retirement fund. How much money goes into this fund each week?

Analyzing Data Read the problems below. Then let Will's thinking guide you through the solutions. Check your understanding with the exercise at the bottom of the page.

Statistics The scatter plot shows the average times that 15 students spent watching television and doing physical activities in a day.

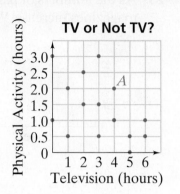

TV or Not TV?

> **Master** Know various forms of display for data sets.
> **Develop** Represent two numerical variables on a scatter plot and informally describe how the data points are distributed and any apparent relationship that exists between the two variables.

5. Describe the student represented by point A.

6. How many students averaged 1 hour of physical activity?

7. How many students averaged 5 hours of watching television?

What Will Thinks	What Will Writes
Before I begin, I need to read and understand the graph.	Horizontal axis = hours of TV Vertical axis = hours of physical activity Each point is (TV hours, activity hours).
The first question wants me to describe the student represented by point A. I need to find the coordinates of the point and state what the coordinates mean in this situation.	Point A has coordinates (4, 2). (4, 2) means (4 TV hours, 2 activity hours). The student averaged 4 hours of TV viewing and 2 hours of physical activity each day.
The second question wants me to find the number of students who averaged 1 hour of physical activity. I need to find the points whose y-coordinate is 1.	Points with y-coordinate 1: (0, 1) (4, 1) (6, 1) Three students averaged 1 hour of physical activity.
The last question wants me to find the number of students who averaged 5 hours of watching TV. I need to find the points whose x-coordinate is 5.	Points with x-coordinate 5: (5, 0) (5, 0.5) Two students averaged 5 hours of TV.

EXERCISE

1. Would you expect there to be a positive correlation, a negative correlation, or no correlation between hours of physical activity and hours of watching television? Justify your choice.

2. Does the scatter plot suggest a correlation? Explain.

Reasoning Strategy: Solve by Graphing

What You'll Learn

- To solve problems by graphing

. . . And Why

To solve real-world problems involving wildlife populations

 **Check Skills You'll Need**

Find the slope of each line.

1.

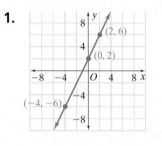

2.

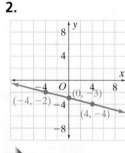

 **for Help**
Lesson 8-3

🔊 **New Vocabulary**

- trend line

Online active math

For: Writing Equations Activity
Use: Interactive Textbook, 12-6

Develop, Master Represent two numerical variables on a scatterplot and informally describe how the data points are distributed.

Develop Estimate unknown quantities graphically and solve for them by using logical reasoning and arithmetic and algebraic techniques.

Solve by Graphing

Math Strategies in Action

Businesses and government agencies use scatter plots to make predictions. For example, the park service at Isle Royale, Michigan, surveys the moose and wolf populations each spring. They use a scatter plot to show the relationship between them.

On the scatter plot they draw a **trend line** that closely fits the data points in the scatter plot. Using the trend line, they can predict the size of one population from the size of the other.

Wolves are predators of moose.

1 EXAMPLE **Solving by Graphing**

Use the data in the table below. About how many moose would you expect to be on the island in a year when there are 18 wolves?

Isle Royale Populations

Year	Wolf	Moose	Year	Wolf	Moose	Year	Wolf	Moose
1982	14	700	1988	12	1,653	1994	15	1,800
1983	23	900	1989	11	1,397	1995	16	2,400
1984	24	811	1990	15	1,216	1996	22	1,200
1985	22	1,062	1991	12	1,313	1997	24	500
1986	20	1,025	1992	12	1,600	1998	14	700
1987	16	1,380	1993	13	1,880	1999	25	750

SOURCE: Isle Royale National Park Service

Understand **Understand the problem.**

1. What are the two variables?

2. What are you trying to predict?

Make a plan to solve the problem.

You can graph the data in a scatter plot. If the points show a correlation, you can draw a trend line. You can then use the line to predict other data values.

Carry Out Carry out the plan.

Step 1 Make a scatter plot by graphing the (wolf, moose) ordered pairs. Use the *x*-axis for wolves and the *y*-axis for moose.

Step 2 Sketch a trend line. The line should be as close as possible to the data points. There should be about as many points above the trend line as below it.

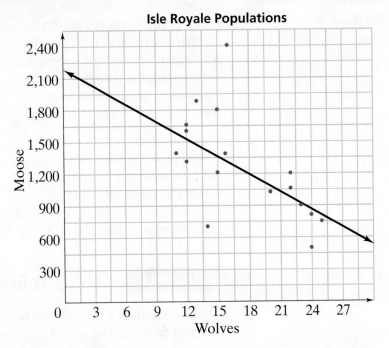

Step 3 To predict the number of moose when there are 18 wolves, find the point on the trend line that corresponds to 18 wolves.

There will be about 1,200 moose when there are 18 wolves.

Check Check the answer to be sure it is reasonable.

You can write an equation for a trend line. You can use the equation to make predictions.

✓ Quick Check

3. a. What is the *y*-intercept of the trend line above?
   b. Find the slope of the trend line.
   c. Write an equation for the trend line in slope-intercept form.
   d. Use the equation you wrote in part (c). Find the solution of the equation when $x = 18$.

A Practice by Example

Example 1
(page 635)

for Help

Solve each problem by graphing.

For Exercises 1 and 2, use the table below that shows the populations of some states and the numbers of cars registered in those states.

State Populations and Cars

State	Population (millions)	Registered Cars (millions)	State	Population (millions)	Registered Cars (millions)
FL	14.4	7.2	NY	18.1	7.9
GA	7.3	3.8	OH	11.2	6.6
IL	11.8	6.2	PA	12.0	5.9
KS	2.6	1.2	SC	3.7	1.8
ME	1.2	0.6	TN	5.3	3.0
MS	2.7	1.3	TX	19.1	7.4
NV	1.6	0.6	WA	5.5	2.6

SOURCE: *Statistical Abstract of the United States*. Go to **PHSchool.com** for a data update. Web Code: bjg-2041

1. a. Make a scatter plot of the data. Graph population on the horizontal axis.
  b. Draw a trend line.
  c. Predict how many cars are registered by the 32.2 million people in California.
  d. Write an equation for your trend line. Predict the number of cars registered by the 7.3 million people in North Carolina.

2. Writing in Math Is there a correlation between the two data sets? Explain.

3. Data Analysis Use the data in the table below. Predict the number of gallons bought for $15.

Gasoline Purchases

Dollars Spent	12	14	11	12	10	6	10	8
Gallons Bought	7.3	8.0	5.9	6.5	5.7	3.5	5.1	4.4

STRATEGIES

• Act It Out
• Draw a Diagram
• Try, Test, Revise
• Look for a Pattern
• Make a Model
• Make a Table
• Simulate the Problem
• Solve by Graphing
• Use Multiple Strategies
• Work a Simpler Problem
• Work Backward
• Write an Equation
• Write a Proportion

B Apply Your Skills

Solve using any strategy.

4. A supermarket charges $1.17 for a 12-oz jar of salsa and $1.89 for a 20-oz jar. Now the producer is introducing a 16-oz jar of the same salsa. What do you think would be a fair price for this new size? Justify your answer to the manager of the store.

Homework Video Tutor

▶ ────────

Visit: PHSchool.com
Web Code: bje-1206

5. (**Algebra**) A plumber charges $45 for a service call, plus $70/h for her time.
  a. Find the cost of a two-hour service call.
  b. How long was a service call that cost $150?

6. To provide wheelchair access, a ramp with a slope of $\frac{1}{15}$ is being built to a door of a building. The bottom of the door is 3 ft above street level. How far will the ramp extend from the building?

C Challenge

7. The data table on page 635 shows 18 data pairs. Its scatter plot (page 636) shows 17 plotted points. Make a conjecture as to why this is so. Study the table to verify or disprove your conjecture.

Multiple Choice Practice and Mixed Review

For Standards Tutorials, visit PHSchool.com. Web Code: bjq-9045

8. Simplify $a^{-4} \cdot a^2$.

  Ⓐ a^{-8} Ⓑ a^{-2} Ⓒ a^2 Ⓓ a^8

9. Which of the following is an irrational number?

  Ⓐ $-\sqrt{4}$ Ⓑ $1.\overline{6}$ Ⓒ $\left(\frac{1}{5}\right)^2$ Ⓓ $\sqrt{7}$

10. A linear graph shows the cost of phone calls. The y-values represent total cost. The x-values represent time, in minutes. What does the slope of the line represent?

  Ⓐ duration of call   Ⓒ total cost

  Ⓑ cost per minute   Ⓓ minutes per dollar

GO for Help   Lesson 8-2

Find the solutions of each equation for $x = -3, 0,$ and 2.

11. $y = -3x$ **12.** $y = \frac{1}{3}x + 4$ **13.** $y = 0.5x - 2$

✓ Checkpoint Quiz 2

1. Compare the following data sets by making two box-and-whisker plots below one number line.

  Set A: 12, 13, 9, 14, 5, 4, 10, 10, 14, 10

  Set B: 4, 9, 7, 5, 12, 13, 6, 8, 10, 6

The table shows the number of cups of lemonade sold by a vendor on days with the given outside temperatures. Use the data for Exercises 2 and 3.

2. Make a scatter plot for the data. Graph temperature on the horizontal axis.

3. Use a trend line to predict the number of cups that will be sold when the temperature is 75°F.

Temp. (°F)	Number of Cups
60	10
65	12
70	22
80	30
85	35

```
3 | 0 2 2
4 | 1 3 5 7 7
5 | 4 4 4 5 6 8 9

3 | 2 means 3.2
```

Use the stem-and-leaf plot at the left.

4. Which numbers are the stems?

5. What is the mode for the data set?

6. What is the range for the data set?

Measuring Bounce Height

When you drop a tennis ball, how high will it bounce on the first bounce? Does the height you drop it from affect how high it bounces? Scientists collect data and use scatter plots to determine answers to questions like these.

> **Develop, Master** Represent two numerical variables on a scatterplot and informally describe how the data points are distributed and any apparent relationship that exists between the two variables.
> **Develop** Estimate unknown quantities graphically and solve for them by using logical reasoning and arithmetic and algebraic techniques.

ACTIVITY

You will need a meter stick and a tennis ball. Drop the ball from various heights and record the height of the first bounce in a table like the one below. (*Hint:* You will get more accurate measurements if you tape the meter stick to the wall and drop the ball close to it.)

Drop height (cm)	100	90	80	70	60	50	40
Bounce height (cm)	▪	▪	▪	▪	▪	▪	▪
Bounce height (cm)	▪	▪	▪	▪	▪	▪	▪
Bounce height (cm)	▪	▪	▪	▪	▪	▪	▪
Average bounce height (cm)	▪	▪	▪	▪	▪	▪	▪

1. **a.** Drop the tennis ball three times from each height. Record your results.
   b. Take an average of the three bounce heights. Record the average bounce height for each drop height.

2. Use the data in your table to make a scatter plot. Graph drop height along the *x*-axis and average bounce height along the *y*-axis.

3. **a.** Draw a trend line on your scatter plot. You should have about the same number of data points above and below your trend line.
   b. Write an equation for your trend line.

4. **Predict** Use your trend line to predict the bounce height of a tennis ball dropped from a height of 200 cm and from 250 cm.

5. The first bounce of a tennis ball reaches a height of 125 cm. Use your trend line. Estimate the drop height.

Many questions involve interpreting data in a graph. Before you answer the question, be sure you understand the information the graph displays.

1 EXAMPLE

Chen surveyed students about their age and the average number of hours they study. The scatter plot shows the results. How old is the person who spends the longest time on homework?

(A) 13   (B) 14   (C) 15   (D) 16

The scatter plot relates students' ages to the number of hours they spend on homework each night. The highest value on the *y*-axis, about 4 hours, corresponds to the *x*-value of 16 years old. The correct answer is D.

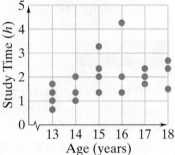

Students' Ages and Study Time

Multiple Choice Practice

Read each question. Then write the letter of the correct answer on your paper.

1. The diagram below shows the number of eighth graders who volunteer for the newspaper and the yearbook. Based on the data, how many students out of a group of 100 would you expect to volunteer for both the newspaper and the yearbook?

  (A) 13

  (B) 15

  (C) 25

  (D) 31

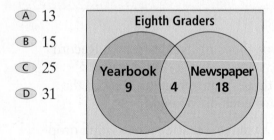

2. The scatter plot at the right shows the number of pets owned by people of different ages. Based on the scatter plot, what conclusion can you draw?

  (A) As the age of pet owners increases, the number of pets owned increases.

  (B) As the age of pet owners increases, the number of pets owned decreases.

  (C) There is no relationship between age and number of pets owned.

  (D) People over 40 years old do not purchase pets.

Pet Ownership

Chapter 12 Review

Vocabulary Review

🔊 **English and Spanish Audio Online**

box-and-whisker plot (p. 617)
frequency table (p. 612)
histogram (p. 613)
line plot (p. 612)
mean (p. 606)
measures of central tendency (p. 606)

median (p. 606)
mode (p. 606)
negative correlation (p. 630)
no correlation (p. 630)
outlier (p. 607)
positive correlation (p. 630)
quartiles (p. 617)

range (p. 606)
scatter plot (p. 628)
stem-and-leaf plot (p. 622)
trend line (p. 635)

Choose the vocabulary term that correctly completes the sentence.

1. The sum of a group of data items divided by the number of data items is the __?__ .

2. Numbers that describe groups of data items are called __?__ .

3. Numbers that divide a data set into four equal parts are __?__ .

4. The difference between the greatest and the least values in a data set is the __?__ of the data set.

5. A listing of a data set that shows the number of times each data item occurs is a(n) __?__ .

Go Online
PHSchool.com
For: Vocabulary quiz
Web Code: bjj-1251

Skills and Concepts

Lesson 12-1

- To find mean, median, mode, and range of a set of data
- To choose the best measure of central tendency

You can use a **measure of central tendency** to describe a collection of data. The **mean** is the sum of the data items divided by the number of data items. The **median** is the middle value or the mean of the two middle values when the data are written in order. The **range** is the difference between the greatest and least values in a data set. The **mode** is the data item that occurs most often. An **outlier** is a data item that is much greater or much less than the rest of the data items.

Find the mean, median, and mode. When an answer is not an integer, round to the nearest tenth. Identify any outliers.

6. 2, 3, 6, 2, 8, 9, 5, 10, 4, 5   7. 16.1, 16.3, 15.9, 16.2, 16.3, 16.3, 15.8

8. 32, 35, 31, 57, 33, 30, 34   9. 0.1, 7.9, 0.2, 0.3, 0.1, 0.2, 0.1, 0.1, 0.3

Which measure of central tendency best describes each situation? Explain.

10. the favorite radio stations of teenagers in your neighborhood

11. the numbers of videos owned by students in your class

12. the prices of 8-oz containers of yogurt at six local grocery stores

Lesson 12-2

- To display data in frequency tables and line plots
- To display data in histograms

You can show data in a **frequency table,** which lists each data item with the number of times it occurs, or a **line plot,** which displays data with **X** marks on a number line. A **histogram** shows the frequencies of data items as a graph.

Display each set of data in a frequency table and a line plot.

13. 11 10 12 10 12 11 13 12 11 9 12 10

14. 47 48 46 47 45 49 46 48 50 48 46 49

Draw a histogram for each frequency table.

15.

Interval	1–3	4–6	7–9	10–12
Frequency	6	4	5	2

16.

Interval	2–3	4–5	6–7	8–9
Frequency	2	8	6	7

Lesson 12-3

- To make box-and-whisker plots
- To analyze data in box-and-whisker plots

A **box-and-whisker plot** displays data items below a number line. **Quartiles** divide the data into four parts. The median is the middle quartile. You can compare two sets of related data by making two box-and-whisker plots on one number line.

Make a box-and-whisker plot for each set of data.

17. 6 9 6 5 8 2 3 9 4 8 5 7 12 9 4

18. 21 35 26 32 24 30 29 38 27 32 51

19. 27 25 23 29 25 28 26 27 23 21 20 24 25 28 30 19 25

20. 2 6 3 9 15 4 9 20 6 7 2 3 8 4 1 5 6 8 5 4 9 3 2 8 7

Lesson 12-4

- To make stem-and-leaf plots
- To use stem-and-leaf plots to compare data sets

A **stem-and-leaf plot** is a graph that shows numerical data arranged in order. Each data item is broken into a stem and leaf. Stem-and-leaf plots can help you to compare data.

The data below show different juice prices (in cents) at various stores.

89 79 85 79 85 67 75 99 79 63 90 72 78 65 78

21. Make a stem-and-leaf plot for the data.

22. Find the mode and the median of the data.

The stem-and-leaf plot shows the time spent on homework by students in two classes. Use the data for Exercises 23–25.

Time Spent on Homework (min)

Class A		Class B
7 4 3	6	1 1 3 5 5
9 9 8 5 4 4	7	0 2 2 4
5 2 1 0	8	4 5 8 9
7 6 6 4 2	9	3 6 7 9 9 9

means 63 ◄— 3 │6│1 —► means 61

23. Which numbers are the stems?

24. What is the range for each set of data?

25. Find the median and the mode for each set of data.

Lessons 12-5 & 12-6

- To interpret and draw scatter plots
- To use scatter plots to find trends
- To solve problems by graphing

A **scatter plot** is a graph that shows the relationship between two sets of data. A scatter plot can help you find trends between sets of data.

Use the scatter plot below for Exercises 26–29.

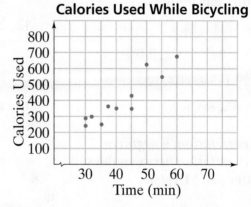

Calories Used While Bicycling

26. How long did the person who used 240 calories ride a bicycle?

27. How many calories did the person who bicycled 50 minutes use?

28. **Data Analysis** Is there a positive correlation, a negative correlation, or no correlation between the time spent bicycling and the calories used? Explain.

29. **Data Analysis** Carefully place a straightedge (preferably transparent) on the scatter plot to serve as a trend line. Use the trend line to predict the number of calories a person uses on a 70-min bicycle ride.

For Exercises 1 and 2, use the box-and-whisker plot below.

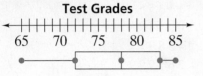

Test Grades

65   70   75   80   85

1. What is the median grade on the test?

2. What is the range in grades?

3. Make a box-and-whisker plot for the data.
   75, 70, 80, 85, 85, 55, 60, 60, 65, 85, 75, 95, 50

4. Use the data below.
   8, 4, 5, 1, 8, 4, 7, 9, 10, 5, 0, 5, 3, 4, 2
   a. Display the data in a frequency table.
   b. Display the data in a line plot.
   c. Find the range of the data.

Find the mean, median, mode, and range. When an answer is not an integer, round to the nearest tenth. Identify any outliers.

5. 11, 12, 9, 13, 10, 12, 11, 14, 12

6. 5.3, 5.6, 5.2, 5.0, 5.4, 5.6, 5.1, 5.0

7. 10.6, 9.8, 11.6, 29.1, 3.4, 11.4, 12.7

8. 8.7, 8.5, 8.7, 8.5, 8.6, 8.5, 8.7, 8.6

Is there a *positive correlation*, a *negative correlation*, or *no correlation* between the sets of data in each scatter plot? Explain.

9.

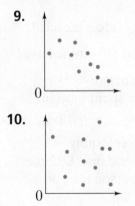

10.

11. Use the data in the table below.

New York Thruway Tolls

Distance (miles)	Toll (dollars)	Distance (miles)	Toll (dollars)
112	3.50	125	3.90
137	3.75	100	3.10
112	3.40	22	0.70
69	1.65	58	1.80
69	2.15	137	4.25
169	5.70	43	1.80
90	2.80	84	3.05
188	5.85	164	5.10

   a. Make a (distance, toll) scatter plot.
   b. Draw a trend line. Predict the toll if a car travels 200 mi on the toll road.
   c. Use your trend line to predict how far a car traveled on the toll road if there was a $4.50 toll.
   d. Write an equation of your trend line.

12. Make a stem-and-leaf plot for the number of subscribers (in millions) of ten cable television networks: 81.8, 81.3, 81.3, 81.0, 82.5, 83.3, 82.1, 81.9, 81.8, 81.0.

13. a. The data below show the career earnings in millions of dollars of the top male and female golfers. Use a single number line to make a box-and-whisker plot for each set of data.

   Male: 21.9, 18.0, 17.8, 15.3, 14.6, 14.5, 14.7

   Female: 10.2, 8.5, 7.6, 7.3, 6.9, 6.7, 6.3

   b. **Writing in Math** Write a paragraph comparing the sets of data.

14. **Data Analysis** Which measure of central tendency best describes the weights of the dogs in one neighborhood?

   15 lb, 20 lb, 18 lb, 27 lb, 15 lb, 70 lb

   Ⓐ mean   Ⓒ mode
   Ⓑ median   Ⓓ all of the above

Standards Mastery

Read each question. Then write the letter of the correct answer on your paper.

1. Lilly's survey results of her classmate's favorite season are shown in the table below.

Favorite Season

Season	Spring	Summer	Fall	Winter
Number of Students	8	16	4	3

Which circle graph best represents the information given in the table?
(Lesson 9-6)

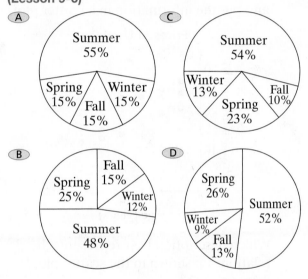

A

Summer 55%
Spring 15% / Fall 15% / Winter 15%

C

Summer 54%
Winter 13% / Spring 23% / Fall 10%

B

Fall 15%
Spring 25% / Winter 12%
Summer 48%

D

Spring 26%
Winter 9% / Fall 13% / Summer 52%

2. The figure shows a circle inside of a square. Which procedure should be used to find the area of the shaded region?
(Lesson 10-1)

Ⓐ Find the area of the circle and subtract it from the area of the square.

Ⓑ Find the circumference of the circle and subtract it from the perimeter of the square.

Ⓒ Find the area of the square and subtract it from the area of the circle.

Ⓓ Find the perimeter of the square and subtract it from the circumference of the circle.

3. A school group is taking a trip to the state capital. The cost is $50 for the bus driver plus $2.50 per mile for gasoline and maintenance of the bus. The total cost is $67.50. How many miles did the group travel?
(Lesson 7-1)

Ⓐ 5 mi   Ⓒ 7 mi
Ⓑ 6 mi   Ⓓ 8 mi

4. The solid below is made of 8 cubes with edge lengths of 1 cm. What is its surface area?
(page 525)

Ⓐ 4 cm^2 Ⓒ 16 cm^2
Ⓑ 8 cm^2 Ⓓ 24 cm^2

5. How does the graph of $y = -2x^2$ compare to the graph of $y = x^2$? **(Lesson 11-5)**

Ⓐ The graph of $y = -2x^2$ is more narrow than $y = x^2$ and opens downward.

Ⓑ The graph of $y = -2x^2$ is wider than $y = x^2$ and opens downward.

Ⓒ The graph of $y = -2x^2$ is more narrow than $y = x^2$ and opens upward.

Ⓓ The graph of $y = -2x^2$ is wider than $y = x^2$ and opens upward.

6. Kendra drove 580 miles in 550 minutes. At this rate, about how many hours did it take her to drive 200 miles? **(Lesson 6-1)**

Ⓐ 1.5 h   Ⓒ 2.5 h
Ⓑ 1.8 h   Ⓓ 3 h

7. Galeno uses the expression $0.75q + 0.25h$ to find his final grade, where q is the mean quiz score and h is the mean homework score. Galeno's mean quiz score is 88 and his final grade is 91. What is his mean homework score? **(Lesson 7-1)**

Ⓐ 88   Ⓒ 97
Ⓑ 91   Ⓓ 100

8. Which number is between 7 and 8?
(Lesson 11-1)

Ⓐ $\sqrt{45}$ Ⓒ $\sqrt{66}$

Ⓑ $\sqrt{53}$ Ⓓ $\sqrt{80}$

9. The graph below represents the volume V, in cubic inches, of a rectangular prism with a square base side length s in. and height 1 in. What is the approximate value of s when $V = 10$? (Lesson 11-5)

Ⓐ 1

Ⓑ 2

Ⓒ 3

Ⓓ 4

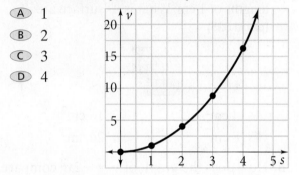

10. Jan is twice as old as Wendy. Wendy is 3 years older than Bart. Bart is one year younger than David. David is 8 years old. How old is Jan?
(Lesson 8-6)

Ⓐ 10 years old   Ⓒ 20 years old

Ⓑ 12 years old   Ⓓ 22 years old

11. A 10-foot ladder rests against a house. The base of the ladder is 6 feet from the house. How high is the top of the ladder?
(Lesson 11-2)

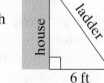

Ⓐ 6 ft

Ⓑ 8 ft

Ⓒ 10 ft

Ⓓ 16 ft

12. Simplify $\dfrac{4^{-3}}{3^{-4}}$. (Lesson 4-8)

Ⓐ $-\dfrac{64}{81}$ Ⓒ $-\dfrac{81}{64}$

Ⓑ $\dfrac{64}{81}$ Ⓓ $\dfrac{81}{64}$

13. Which of the following are skew segments in the rectangular prism? (Lesson 9-1)

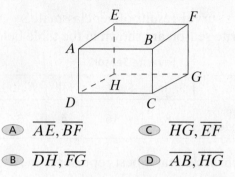

Ⓐ $\overline{AE}, \overline{BF}$ Ⓒ $\overline{HG}, \overline{EF}$

Ⓑ $\overline{DH}, \overline{FG}$ Ⓓ $\overline{AB}, \overline{HG}$

14. Mr. James researched the price of used cars and put the information in a scatter plot.

Which description best represents the relationship shown in the scatter plot?
(Lesson 12-5)

Ⓐ Positive trend

Ⓑ No trend

Ⓒ Negative trend

Ⓓ Cannot be determined

15. Daisy has three hours to mow her grandparents' backyard, which measures 58 feet by 44 feet. About how many square feet should Daisy mow each hour?
(Lesson 6-1)

Ⓐ 34 ft^2 Ⓒ 290 ft^2

Ⓑ 70 ft^2 Ⓓ 850 ft^2

16. Point B has coordinates $(-2, 3)$. It is translated 5 units to the left and 2 units up. What are the coordinates of B'? **(Lesson 9-8)**

   Ⓐ $(-4, 8)$ Ⓒ $(3, 1)$

   Ⓑ $(-7, 5)$ Ⓓ $(0, -2)$

17. Which of the following is a rational number? **(Lesson 11-1)**

   Ⓐ $\sqrt{6}$ Ⓒ $\sqrt{8}$

   Ⓑ $\sqrt{7}$ Ⓓ $\sqrt{9}$

18. Meredith had 3 m of ribbon. She used 95 cm wrapping a present for her mother, 40 cm wrapping a present for her father, and 80 cm wrapping a present for her sister. How much ribbon does she have left? **(Lesson 3-6)**

   Ⓐ 85 cm   Ⓒ 0.85 cm

   Ⓑ 8.5 cm   Ⓓ 0.085 cm

19. Refer to the triangle. Which equation is true? **(Lesson 11-2)**

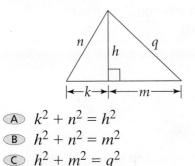

   Ⓐ $k^2 + n^2 = h^2$

   Ⓑ $h^2 + n^2 = m^2$

   Ⓒ $h^2 + m^2 = q^2$

   Ⓓ $m^2 + q^2 = h^2$

20. At a school, students' overall averages are determined using their math, science, and language grades. The language grade counts twice toward the average, and the math and science grades each count once. Gary earned a 96 in math and a 91 in language. Overall, he earned a 93. What was his science grade? **(Lesson 7-2)**

   Ⓐ 91   Ⓒ 93

   Ⓑ 92   Ⓓ 94

21. A lion runs across a field at an average rate of 200 yards in 16 seconds. Which of the following represents the same unit rate in yards per second? **(Lesson 6-1)**

   Ⓐ Cape hunting dog:
     150 yards in 12 seconds

   Ⓑ Gazelle:
     100 yards in 12 seconds

   Ⓒ Gray fox:
     160 yards in 15 seconds

   Ⓓ Elk:
     300 yards in 32 seconds

22. Which of the following statements is NOT true? **(Lesson 1-4)**

   Ⓐ $|-9 + 4| = 5$

   Ⓑ $|-5| \le |0 - 6|$

   Ⓒ $|-7| \le 0$

   Ⓓ $|-9| \le |-10|$

23. Name the three-dimensional figure that you can form from the net below. **(Lesson 10-4)**

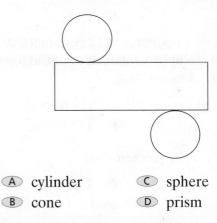

   Ⓐ cylinder   Ⓒ sphere

   Ⓑ cone   Ⓓ prism

24. How many cubes with edge lengths of 1 in. are needed to fill a box that is 10 inches by 14 inches by 12 inches? **(Lesson 10-7)**

   Ⓐ 428   Ⓒ 856

   Ⓑ 560   Ⓓ 1,680

25. The graph below represents the cost c in dollars per month for using t minutes of airtime on a mobile phone plan. What is the cost per minute? **(Lesson 8-3)**

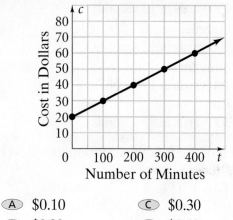

Number of Minutes

Ⓐ $0.10   Ⓒ $0.30
Ⓑ $0.20   Ⓓ $0.40

26. The volume of a box is 13,824 in.^{3}. How many cubic feet is this? **(Lesson 5-5)**

Ⓐ 4   Ⓒ 96
Ⓑ 8   Ⓓ 1,152

27. A CD has a diameter of 12 centimeters. What is the approximate area of the top of the CD? **(Lesson 10-3)**

Ⓐ 18.84 cm^2 Ⓒ 113.04 cm^2
Ⓑ 37.68 cm^2 Ⓓ 452.16 cm^2

28. Simplify $\sqrt{4^2}$. **(Lesson 11-1)**

Ⓐ 2   Ⓒ 8
Ⓑ 4   Ⓓ 16

29. A Ferris wheel is 40 feet in diameter. Which is closest to the distance traveled in three rotations by a point on the Ferris wheel? **(Lesson 9-6)**

Ⓐ 125.6 ft   Ⓒ 376.8 ft
Ⓑ 251.2 ft   Ⓓ 753.6 ft

30. Which expression is equivalent to $\frac{1}{27} + \frac{1}{9}$? **(Lesson 4-8)**

Ⓐ $\frac{1}{27 + 9}$

Ⓑ $\left(\frac{1}{3}\right)^3 + \left(\frac{1}{3}\right)^2$

Ⓒ $\left(\frac{1}{3}\right)^6$

Ⓓ $\left(\frac{1}{3}\right)^3 + \left(\frac{1}{3}\right)^3$

31. Nadia swims 18 laps in 12 minutes and Raef swims 16 laps in 8 minutes. Which of the following statements is true? **(Lesson 6-1)**

Ⓐ Nadia swims 0.5 lap per minute faster than Raef.

Ⓑ They both swim the same number of laps per minute.

Ⓒ Raef swims 0.5 lap per minute faster than Nadia.

Ⓓ Raef swims 2 laps per minute faster than Nadia.

32. Which is an irrational number? **(Lesson 11-1)**

Ⓐ $\sqrt{9}$

Ⓑ $\frac{3}{5}$

Ⓒ π

Ⓓ 2.75

33. What is the next step in simplifying $\frac{3}{20} - \frac{7}{24}$ using the least common denominator? **(Lesson 5-3)**

Ⓐ $\frac{3}{20} \cdot \frac{6}{6} - \frac{7}{24} \cdot \frac{5}{5}$

Ⓑ $\frac{3}{20} \cdot \frac{1}{6} - \frac{7}{24} \cdot \frac{1}{5}$

Ⓒ $\frac{3}{20} \cdot \frac{5}{5} - \frac{7}{24} \cdot \frac{6}{6}$

Ⓓ $\frac{3}{20} \cdot \frac{1}{5} - \frac{7}{24} \cdot \frac{1}{6}$

34. Which expression is equivalent to $\frac{12x^8}{3x^4}$?
(Lesson 4-8)

Ⓐ $9x^2$

Ⓑ $9x^4$

Ⓒ $4x^2$

Ⓓ $4x^4$

35. Denise makes a circle graph that shows her average monthly expenditures. She earns $800 per month tutoring. Which conclusion is NOT valid based on the data?
(Lesson 9-6)

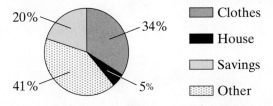

Clothes
House
Savings
Other

Ⓐ For house expenses, she spends about $40 per month.

Ⓑ She spends about $\frac{1}{3}$ of her money on clothes.

Ⓒ More than $\frac{1}{5}$ of her expenditures are for other activities.

Ⓓ She saves more than 0.30 of her money.

36. Which of the following is the net for a pentagonal pyramid? (Lesson 10-4)

Ⓐ
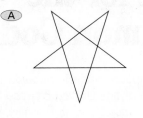

Ⓑ
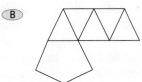

Ⓒ
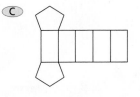

Ⓓ
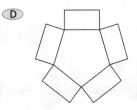

Chapter Projects

Cure for the Common Code

A special sculpture stands outside the headquarters of the United States Central Intelligence Agency (CIA) in Langley, Virginia. Carved in the copper sculpture is a message in secret code. The code is so complex that for many years even CIA agents could not figure it out. The sculptor, James Sandborn, provided the secret agents with a challenge they could appreciate.

Chapter 1 *Algebraic Expressions and Integers*

Invent a Secret Code For the chapter project, you will decode computer writing and write in a code used by Julius Caesar. Then you'll invent a code of your own.

For: Information about secret codes
Web Code: bjd-0161

DON'T LOSE YOUR BALANCE!

Have you ever used a balance in your science class? Balances make very precise measurements in science, industry, and government. The United States Mint, for example, ensures that the coins it produces meet exact specifications. You can make your own version of a balance and use it to compare the masses of different objects.

Chapter 2 *Solving One-Step Equations and Inequalities*

Make a Balance Scale For the chapter project, you will make a simple balance scale. You will use it to write and solve equations and inequalities for the masses of different coins.

Go Online
PHSchool.com

For: Information about balances
Web Code: bjd-0261

CURRENCY EVENTS

Chapter 3 *Decimals and Equations*

When you are shopping, of course you want to know how much an item costs before you decide to buy it! When you travel in another country, you need to "translate" the cost into its value in U.S. dollars.

Compare Currencies For the chapter project, you will research currency exchange rates and calculate prices in different currencies. You will make a poster that shows prices in U.S. dollars and in the currencies of three other countries.

Go Online
PHSchool.com

For: Information about currencies
Web Code: bjd-0361

TIME AFTER TIME

Chapter 4 *Factors, Fractions, and Exponents*

On the morning of the summer solstice, the sun rises directly over one of the stones at Stonehenge in southern England. Just as a sundial tells the time of day, Stonehenge tells the time of year.

A calendar may involve several astronomical events. For example, our day is based on Earth's rotation, whereas our year is based on Earth's movement around the sun. Over the centuries, people have come up with many different calendars.

Design a Calendar For the chapter project, you will investigate calendars and adjustments to calendars. Then you will design your own calendar. Your final project will be a sample and an explanation of your calendar.

Go Online
PHSchool.com

For: Information about calendars
Web Code: bjd-0461

If the Shoe Fits

What size shoe do you wear? As you grow, your shoe size can change rapidly. If your foot grows half an inch, does that mean you should get shoes that are a half-size larger?

The scale we use for sizing shoes is from the *duodecimal*, or base 12, number system. For that reason, a size chart could come in handy.

Chapter 5 Operations With Fractions

Make a Comparison Chart For the chapter project, you will make measurements and calculations that relate women's shoe sizes, men's shoe sizes, and shoe lengths. Your final project will be a convenient comparison chart that you can distribute to your friends and family and to shoe stores.

For: Information about shoe sizes
Web Code: bjd-0561

STRING BAND

Guitars, fiddles, harps . . . people have been enjoying stringed instruments for thousands of years. The music from a stringed instrument follows rules of mathematics that you will learn in this chapter.

Chapter 6 Ratios, Proportions, and Percents

Make a Musical Instrument For the chapter project, you will construct and play a simple stringed instrument. You will make measurements that can be applied to a real instrument. Your final project will consist of drawings that show how to play notes on both instruments.

Go Online
PHSchool.com

For: Information about stringed instruments
Web Code: bjd-0661

Have you ever wondered why some objects sink while others float? People float in the salt water of the Dead Sea. Pebbles sink when tossed into a river. The densities of a liquid and an object influence whether the object sinks or floats in the liquid. Similarly, the densities of two liquids influence whether they combine or separate.

Chapter 7 *Solving Equations and Inequalities*

Find the Densities of Liquids For the chapter project, you will measure the masses and volumes of several liquids. You will use your measurements and an equation to calculate the density of each liquid.

Go Online
PHSchool.com

For: Information about densities
Web Code: bjd-0761

Rental Math

Your school is planning its graduation ceremony. Hundreds of people will be coming, and they need places to sit. Your school has some chairs, but not enough for this crowd! Better call a rental company.

Chapter 8 *Linear Functions and Graphing*

Compare Prices For the chapter project, you will research the cost of renting folding chairs. You do not yet know how many chairs you will need, so you will investigate the price per chair, as well as delivery charges. For your report to the graduation committee, you will write and graph equations to show the total costs of renting chairs from different companies.

Go Online
PHSchool.com

For: Information about chair rentals
Web Code: bjd-0861

TREASURE HUNT!

A mysterious map has come into your possession. The map shows the Sea Islands off the coast of Georgia. But that's not all! The map also contains three clues that tell where a treasure is supposedly buried.

Draw a Treasure Map Your project for this chapter will be to find the location of the treasure. Trace the map provided, and then add to the drawing by following the clues in the activities.

Go Online
PHSchool.com

For: Information about treasure maps
Web Code: bjd-0961

MAKING A SPLASH

When you jump into a pool or step into a bathtub, you cause the water level to rise. That's an example of water displacement. The volume of water displaced is equal to the volume of the object submerged—you.

Use Water Displacement to Find Volume For your chapter project, you will build a prism and a cylinder. You will calculate their volumes by using formulas. Then you will find their volumes by using water displacement.

Go Online
PHSchool.com

For: Information about water displacement
Web Code: bjd-1061

Big Trees

Chapter 11 *Irrational Numbers and Nonlinear Functions*

A giant sequoia in California is the largest living thing on Earth. It weighs about as much as 15 blue whales. What is the largest tree in your neighborhood? Maybe it is the largest of its species. You could nominate it to be in the National Register of Big Trees.

Measure a Big Tree The National Register of Big Trees has a formula to compare the sizes of trees of the same species: Big Tree Points = $C + H + \frac{S}{4}$, where C is the

circumference in inches of the trunk at $4\frac{1}{2}$ feet above the ground, H is the tree's height in feet, and S is the average spread in feet of the tree's crown of branches.

For the chapter project, you will measure a tree and calculate its score in Big Tree Points.

Go Online
PHSchool.com

For: Information about tree sizes
Web Code: bjd-1161

The Good Times Poll

Chapter 12 *Data Analysis*

Do you participate in an organized extracurricular activity, such as a sport or a club? How much time do you devote to such activities each week? How does the amount of time you spend compare to the averages for students in your class and your school?

Conduct a Survey For the chapter project, you will do a survey of your class and a survey of your school. You will use statistical measures and graphs to analyze and display the results.

Go Online
PHSchool.com

For: Information about surveys
Web Code: bjd-1261

Skills and Word Problems

● **Lesson 1-1** Write a variable expression for each word phrase.

1. 6 less than x

2. y less than 12

3. the sum of z and 2

4. a number m increased by 34

5. the product of 8 and p

6. t divided by 5

● **Lesson 1-2** Simplify each expression.

7. $15 + 20 \cdot 3$

8. $46 - 4(2 + 8)$

9. $16 \div 4 + 10 \div 2$

10. $100 \div (30 + 20)$

11. $5(8 + 4) \div 6 \div 2$

12. $9 \cdot 6 - 12 \div 2$

● **Lesson 1-3** Evaluate each expression.

13. $3x + 6$, for $x = 12$

14. $15a - 2a$, for $a = 20$

15. $38 - 3y$, for $y = 9$

16. $25 - (t + 18)$, for $t = 7$

17. $\dfrac{x + y}{10}$, for $x = 35$ and $y = 65$

● **Lesson 1-4** Compare. Use >, <, or = to complete each statement.

18. $-12 \ \blacksquare \ -9$

19. $|-4| \ \blacksquare \ |4|$

20. $-|-7| \ \blacksquare \ |-7|$

21. $0 \ \blacksquare \ -100$

● **Lessons 1-5 and 1-6** Simplify each expression.

22. $-56 + 60$

23. $18 + (-25)$

24. $-34 + (-36)$

25. $19 - (-5)$

26. $80 - (-125)$

27. $-82 - (-50)$

28. $-7 + 35 + (-22)$

29. $-44 - 20 - 80$

30. $-8 + (-13) - (24)$

● **Lesson 1-7** Write a rule for continuing each pattern. Find the next three numbers in the pattern.

31. $-12, -3, 6, 15, 24, \ldots$

32. $0.15, 0.3, 0.45, 0.6, \ldots$

33. $1, 1, 2, 3, 5, 8, 13, \ldots$

● **Lesson 1-9** Simplify each expression.

34. $-4 \cdot 12$

35. $-15(-8)$

36. $30 \cdot (-5)$

37. $-1(-2)(-3)(-4)$

38. $-78 \div (-3)$

39. $-150 \div 25$

40. $\dfrac{120}{-15}$

41. $-1{,}125 \div (-125)$

● **Lesson 1-10** Draw a coordinate plane. Graph each point.

42. $A(0, 9)$

43. $B(-3, -5)$

44. $C(-9, 5)$

45. $D(7, 2)$

46. $E(0, 0)$

47. $F(8, 0)$

48. $G(7, -8)$

49. $H(1, 1)$

50. $K(-2, -2)$

● **Lesson 1-1** **Write an expression for each statement.**

51. Shari has g gel pens, and Jennifer has 8 fewer gel pens.

52. A stock starts Friday at a price p, and ends the day $2.50 higher.

● **Lesson 1-2** **Write and simplify a numerical expression for the phrase.**

53. the quotient of twenty-eight and seven, minus two

● **Lesson 1-3** **Write an expression for each statement. Then evaluate it for the given value.**

54. A video store pays $30 for each movie m that it purchases. How much does it pay for 15 movies?

55. A pizza store charges $3 for delivery and $10 per pizza p. How much does it cost to have three pizzas delivered?

● **Lesson 1-4** **Write an expression to represent each quantity.**

56. a payment of d dollars on a credit card with a balance of $165

57. The temperature on top of a mountain is 4°C lower than the temperature t at the base of the mountain.

● **Lessons 1-5 and 1-6** **Write a numerical expression for each statement. Then find the sum or difference.**

58. Your savings account had a balance of $175 before you deposited $250.

59. A hot-air balloon descends 450 ft from a height of 1,000 ft.

● **Lesson 1-7** **Is each conjecture correct or incorrect? If incorrect, give a counterexample.**

60. The difference of two numbers is always less than their sum.

61. The sum of two numbers is always greater than zero.

● **Lesson 1-8** **Look for a pattern to help you solve the problem.**

62. You owe a friend $42. You repay the friend $2 the first day, $4 the second day, $6 the third day, and so on. How many days will you take to pay your friend back?

● **Lesson 1-9** **Simplify each expression.**

63. thirty-six divided by three

64. four times six, divided by twelve

● **Lesson 1-10** **Write the coordinates of each point.**

65. three units left of the y-axis and six units below the x-axis

66. five units right of the y-axis and two units above the x-axis

Skills and Word Problems

● **Lesson 2-1** Simplify each expression. Justify each step.

1. $99 + (-46) + (-99) + 45$

2. $225 + 320 + 75$

3. $18 + 12 + (-25) + 13$

4. $5 \cdot 678 \cdot 2$

5. $58 \cdot 2 \cdot 50$

6. $20 \cdot 4 \cdot 5 \cdot 25$

● **Lessons 2-2 and 2-3** Use the Distributive Property to simplify.

7. $7(5) - 3(5)$

8. $3 \cdot 6 + 7 \cdot 6$

9. $15 \cdot 32 - 12 \cdot 32$

10. $7b + 25 - 4b$

11. $3(a - 2c)$

12. $3q + 2(q + 1)$

13. $-3(4y - 1) + 5(7 - y)$

14. $41 - 2(m + 1) - m$

15. $12 + 5x - 2(3x + 5)$

● **Lesson 2-4** Write an equation for each sentence. Is each equation *true*, *false*, or an *open sentence*?

16. Twice the sum of a number and one is twenty-two.

17. Negative three divided by negative one is three.

18. Forty-five plus five equals negative fifty.

● **Lessons 2-5 and 2-6** Solve each equation.

19. $40 + x = 25$

20. $-5 = y - 12$

21. $z + (-23) = -47$

22. $14 = a - 9$

23. $t - 453 = -520$

24. $78 = b + 100$

25. $4k = 96$

26. $300 = -15j$

27. $-12c = 180$

28. $\frac{d}{7} = -14$

29. $-4 = \frac{w}{6}$

30. $\frac{k}{-9} = -20$

● **Lesson 2-8** Graph the solutions of each inequality.

31. $x > -12$

32. $y \le 3$

33. $0 \ge z$

34. $p < -9$

35. $7 < n$

36. $f \le -3$

● **Lessons 2-9 and 2-10** Solve each inequality.

37. $a + 3 < -1$

38. $-2 > b - 4$

39. $5 + x > -8$

40. $-12 < -2 + y$

41. $w - 32 \le 15$

42. $-20 \ge z - 13$

43. $\frac{c}{5} \le -3$

44. $8p \ge -96$

45. $0 < 8r$

46. $\frac{t}{-6} < -3$

47. $\frac{a}{11} > -22$

48. $-12k \ge -144$

Lesson 2-1 Name each property shown.

49. Seven plus twelve equals twelve plus seven.

50. Thirty-four times one is thirty-four.

Lesson 2-2 Use the Distributive Property to solve each problem.

51. A sports stadium holds 14,600 people. There are eight home games in a season. Find the total number of people who could attend home games in one season.

52. Janet drives 36 miles Monday through Friday to work and back. How many miles does she drive in one week?

Lesson 2-3 Write and simplify a variable expression.

53. A family ordered four dinners at d dollars each and a $7 side dish from a local restaurant. There is a $3 delivery charge.

Lesson 2-4 Write an equation to solve each problem.

54. Michelle wants to run a total of 15 miles per week. She runs 3 miles each day d that she runs. Will she meet her goal by running 5 days per week?

55. Suppose you want to save $105. You put $15 per week w into a savings account. Will you have $105 in 6 weeks?

Lessons 2-5 and 2-6 Write and solve an equation.

56. Jake bought five books at a yard sale. He now has 44 books. How many books did Jake have before?

57. A painter pays $15 per can of paint. How many cans of paint can she buy with $165?

Lesson 2-7 Use *Try, Test, and Revise* to solve each problem.

58. Sara bought some tapes for $8 each and some books for $5 each. She paid a total of $39. How many of each did she buy?

59. The sum of the ages of two brothers is 22 and the product of their ages is 120. How old are the brothers?

Lesson 2-8 Write and graph an inequality for each sentence.

60. A number d plus fifteen is no more than 12.

61. Seven times a number p is more than forty-two.

Lessons 2-9 and 2-10 Write and solve an inequality.

62. Four times a number r is no more than sixty-five.

63. You want to save at least $100. How much do you need to save if you start with $37?

Skills and Word Problems

● **Lesson 3-1 Estimate. State the method you used.**

1. $5.35 + 7.953$

2. $25.68 - 3.7$

3. $6.877 + 3.521 + 8.5$

4. $103.890 - 25.6$

5. $42.875 + 36.982 + 45.7$

6. $42.651 - 12.8$

● **Lesson 3-2 Estimate each product or quotient.**

7. $9.5(12.31)$

8. $24.8 \div 5.03$

9. $2.8 \cdot 6.11$

10. $-5.78 \div 1.95$

11. $(-2.468)(-9.031)$

12. $-19.32 \div 4.025$

● **Lesson 3-3 Evaluate each formula for the values given.**

13. perimeter of a rectangle: $P = 2\ell + 2w$
when $\ell = 45$ yd and $w = 20$ yd

14. circumference of a circle: $C = 2\pi r$
when $r = 6.8$ in.; use 3.14 for π

15. distance traveled: $d = rt$
when $r = 50$ mi/h and $t = 3.5$ h

16. perimeter of a square: $P = 4s$
when $s = 12$ cm

● **Lessons 3-4 and 3-5 Solve each equation.**

17. $t + 4.5 = 17.2$

18. $15.5 + y = 10.5$

19. $x - 70.2 = 23.6$

20. $1.2b = 6$

21. $c \div 5.3 = 12$

22. $-21.2 = p - 12.7$

23. $f \div 5.25 = 7.8$

24. $6.4m = 38.4$

25. $-3.1 = -31a$

26. $h + 25.8 = 76$

27. $101.5 = j - 82.8$

28. $-50.8 = d + 36.2$

29. $4.5v = 13.5$

30. $s \div 10.5 = 42$

31. $26.2 = z - 6.55$

32. $42.3 = m + 17.8$

● **Lesson 3-6 Complete each statement.**

33. 0.95 m = ■ cm

34. 250 mL = ■ L

35. 2.5 kg = ■ g

36. 60 g = ■ kg

37. 0.54 L = ■ mL

38. 5.62 m = ■ cm

39. 58 cm = ■ m

40. 564 mm = ■ m

41. 345 g = ■ mg

42. 36 mg = ■ g

43. 234 cm = ■ m

44. 567 mg = ■ g

Lessons 3-1 and 3-2 Estimate each amount.

45. Four packages of ground beef weigh 1.94 lb, 1.82 lb, 2.21 lb, and 2.03 lb.

46. You buy three items that cost $4.85, $7.45, and $8.99.

47. Your class is on a field trip. Thirty students buy lunches that cost $4.95 each.

48. A car holds 12 gallons of gasoline. Gas costs $2.29/gal. About how much will it cost to fill the car up?

49. A fund drive for a charity raised $2,450. If 120 people donated, about how much did each person donate on average?

Lesson 3-3 Use the distance formula $d = rt$ (where d is the distance, r is rate, or speed, and t is time spent traveling) to answer each question.

50. The length of Michelle's commute to work is 35 mi. It takes her 54 min to get to work. What is her average speed?

51. Sam runs 6 mi/h. How many minutes will it take him to run 4 mi?

52. A train travels 70 mi/h. How far does it travel in 45 min?

53. Janelle pedals her bicycle at a rate of 12 mi/h. How far does she travel in 25 minutes?

54. Mike walks 3 mi/h. How many minutes will it take him to walk 1 mi?

Lessons 3-4 and 3-5 Write and solve an equation.

55. Karenna spent $8.75 at a video store. She had $16.65 when she left the video store. How much money, m, did she start with?

56. At the deli, 1.5 lb of turkey cost $5.64. What is the cost per pound, c, of the turkey?

Lesson 3-6 Convert each unit.

57. A bag of potato chips has 400 mg of sodium per serving. How many grams of sodium does it have?

58. Julius is training to run a 10-km race. How many meters long is the race?

59. A box of fruit cookies weighs 340 g. What is the weight of the box in milligrams?

60. The distance from Sacramento to Fresno is about 190 km. What is this distance in meters?

Lesson 3-7 Solve the problem by *Acting It Out*.

61. A class has 15 students. How many handshakes are there if each person in the class shakes hands once with everyone else?

Skills and Word Problems

● **Lesson 4-1** **List all the factors of each number.**

1. 60   **2.** 45   **3.** 64   **4.** 46   **5.** 36   **6.** 100

● **Lesson 4-2** **Evaluate each expression.**

7. x^2, for $x = 8$ **8.** $-2v^3$, for $v = 2$ **9.** $5t^2 - 4$, for $t = 4$

10. $a^3 + 10$, for $a = -5$ **11.** mn^2, for $m = 3$ and $n = 4$ **12.** $6(2r - 4)^2$, for $r = 7$

● **Lesson 4-3** **Is each number _prime_, _composite_, or _neither_? For each composite number, write the prime factorization. Use exponents where possible.**

13. 25   **14.** 36   **15.** 47   **16.** 38   **17.** 1   **18.** 117

Find the GCD.

19. 20, 30   **20.** 8, 12, 18   **21.** $5x, 40x$ **22.** $6y, 108$

● **Lesson 4-4** **Write in simplest form.**

23. $\frac{12}{20}$ **24.** $\frac{4}{20}$ **25.** $\frac{35}{80}$ **26.** $\frac{18}{36}$

27. $\frac{13}{52}$ **28.** $\frac{75}{100}$ **29.** $\frac{16}{50}$ **30.** $\frac{5x}{65x^2}$

31. $\frac{3x^2}{45x}$ **32.** $\frac{50a^2}{5a}$ **33.** $\frac{36x}{16}$ **34.** $\frac{100pq}{625q}$

● **Lesson 4-6** **Order each set of numbers from least to greatest.**

35. $0.2, \frac{3}{10}, -2, -1, -\frac{1}{2}, -0.3$ **36.** $\frac{4}{5}, 0, -0.8, -\frac{2}{3}, 1, -2$

Evaluate each expression for $a = 10$ and $b = -4$. Write in simplest form.

37. $\frac{a + b}{a}$ **38.** $\frac{b}{a}$ **39.** $\frac{a - b}{3a}$ **40.** $\frac{b^2}{a^2}$

● **Lessons 4-7 and 4-8** **Simplify each expression.**

41. $8a^2 \cdot 3a^4$ **42.** $3y^2 \cdot 2y^3$ **43.** $(p^5)^6$ **44.** $(x^3)(y)(x^5)$

45. $\frac{6x^2}{2x^5}$ **46.** $\frac{18t^{20}}{6t^5}$ **47.** $\frac{b^2}{b^3}$ **48.** 12^0

● **Lesson 4-9** **Multiply. Express each result in scientific notation.**

49. $(5 \times 10^4)(8 \times 10^9)$ **50.** $(1.1 \times 10^6)(6 \times 10^{10})$ **51.** $(3 \times 10^{12})(4 \times 10^8)$

Lesson 4-1 Use divisibility rules to answer each question.

52. A restaurant serves a 12-piece appetizer. What sizes of groups can split the appetizer evenly?

53. How many six-slice pizzas must you order for five people to get the same number of slices with none left over?

Lesson 4-2 Write a variable expression.

54. seven minus j times j plus four

Lesson 4-3 Solve each problem.

55. A teacher divides 27 students into groups of at least two students. All the groups are the same size. What is the greatest possible number of groups?

56. Lucia is reading a book with 25 chapters. She reads the same number of chapters each day. Can she finish the book in exactly six days? Explain.

Lesson 4-4 Write a fraction in simplest form for each statement.

57. A chef used four eggs from a carton of twelve.

58. Twenty-five of thirty students went on a field trip.

Lesson 4-5 Solve by simplifying each problem.

59. Thirty-two teams are going to play in a single-elimination tournament. How many games will be played in the tournament?

60. How many digits are used to write the numbers 90 through 110?

Lesson 4-6 Use the acceleration formula, $a = \dfrac{f - i}{t}$ (where a is acceleration, f is final speed, i is initial speed, and t is time) to answer each question.

61. A car goes from an initial speed of 46 ft/s to a final speed of 71 ft/s in 5 s. What is the acceleration?

62. A bicyclist went from a complete stop to 18 ft/s in 6 s. What was her acceleration?

Lessons 4-7 and 4-8 Write an exponential expression for each phrase. Then simplify.

63. x cubed to the fourth power

64. four times y to the fourth power divided by y squared

Lesson 4-9 Write the population in scientific notation.

65. The population of the United States increased by approximately 32,700,000 people between 1990 and 2000.

Skills and Word Problems

● **Lesson 5-1** Find the LCM of each group of numbers or expressions.

1. $15, 30$ **2.** $4, 8, 10$ **3.** $8x, 12y$ **4.** $3t^2, 5t$

Compare. Use >, <, or = to complete each statement.

5. $\frac{5}{8} \blacksquare \frac{3}{5}$ **6.** $\frac{3}{10} \blacksquare \frac{1}{3}$ **7.** $\frac{3}{4} \blacksquare \frac{6}{8}$ **8.** $-\frac{1}{5} \blacksquare -\frac{1}{4}$

● **Lesson 5-2** Write each fraction or mixed number as a decimal.

9. $\frac{7}{8}$ **10.** $2\frac{3}{5}$ **11.** $\frac{3}{11}$ **12.** $\frac{16}{5}$ **13.** $-\frac{7}{10}$ **14.** $-2\frac{1}{9}$

Write each decimal as a fraction or mixed number in simplest form.

15. 1.3 **16.** 0.605 **17.** $0.\overline{6}$ **18.** $-0.\overline{15}$ **19.** 0.35 **20.** 5.4

● **Lesson 5-3** Add or subtract.

21. $\frac{2}{5} + \frac{3}{5}$ **22.** $3\frac{3}{4} - 1\frac{5}{6}$ **23.** $-\frac{5}{8} + \frac{1}{4}$ **24.** $\frac{10}{x} - \frac{12}{x}$

25. $\frac{1}{2} - \frac{3}{4}$ **26.** $4\frac{5}{6} + 5\frac{2}{9}$ **27.** $\frac{5}{t} + \frac{3}{4}$ **28.** $5\frac{1}{3} - \frac{7}{8}$

● **Lesson 5-4** Find each product or quotient.

29. $\frac{3}{5} \cdot \frac{2}{3}$ **30.** $\frac{5}{6} \div 1\frac{2}{3}$ **31.** $-\frac{7}{10} \cdot 1\frac{3}{7}$ **32.** $\frac{5y}{6} \div \frac{2y}{3}$ **33.** $-\frac{2}{3} \cdot \left(-\frac{9}{22}\right)$

34. $-\frac{3}{8} \div \frac{1}{4}$ **35.** $\frac{5x}{7} \cdot \frac{1}{5}$ **36.** $\left(-\frac{1}{2}\right)\left(-\frac{3}{4}\right)$ **37.** $\frac{2}{5} \div \left(-\frac{1}{5}\right)$ **38.** $\frac{6}{7} \cdot \frac{3}{7}$

● **Lesson 5-5** Complete each statement.

39. $60 \text{ in.} = \blacksquare \text{ ft}$ **40.** $15 \text{ qt} = \blacksquare \text{ pt}$ **41.** $4 \text{ lb} = \blacksquare \text{ oz}$

● **Lessons 5-7 and 5-8** Solve each equation.

42. $\frac{3}{5} + a = 1\frac{2}{3}$ **43.** $b - 3\frac{1}{2} = 5$ **44.** $-\frac{4}{5}c = \frac{7}{10}$

45. $5d = \frac{3}{4}$ **46.** $1\frac{4}{7} = f + \frac{3}{14}$ **47.** $\frac{7}{8} = g - \frac{2}{3}$

● **Lesson 5-9** Simplify each expression.

48. $(8a^3)^2$ **49.** $(x^2y^3)^4$ **50.** $(-2v)^3$ **51.** $(abc^3)^5$ **52.** $(f^2g^3)^6$

53. $(2xy)^3$ **54.** $\left(\frac{2}{5}\right)^3$ **55.** $\left(\frac{2c}{d^3}\right)^2$ **56.** $\left(\frac{3t}{4v}\right)^2$ **57.** $\left(\frac{1}{4}\right)^3$

● **Lesson 5-1 Use the LCM to answer each question.**

58. A store sells T-shirts in packages of three, and pairs of socks in packages of five. What is the least number of packages you can buy to have equal numbers of pairs of socks and T-shirts?

59. Pietro and Nancy are working on class projects. One week before it is due, Pietro has completed $\frac{5}{7}$ of his project and Nancy has completed $\frac{2}{3}$ of her project. Who has completed more?

● **Lesson 5-2 Write a fraction to answer each question.**

60. A $20 shirt is on sale for $16. What fraction of the original price is the sale price?

61. Steve found a dime and a quarter on the ground. What fraction of a dollar did he find?

● **Lessons 5-3 and 5-4 Write and simplify an expression.**

62. the quotient of one half and two fifths

63. Suppose you are packing a box that measures $1\frac{3}{4}$ ft by $1\frac{1}{2}$ ft. How much longer is the box than it is wide?

● **Lesson 5-5 Use dimensional analysis to answer each question.**

64. In gym class you are going to run a half-mile. How many feet will you run?

65. Jacques has a gallon jug of milk that is $\frac{1}{4}$ full. How many cups of milk does he have?

● **Lesson 5-6 Work backward to solve each problem.**

66. Suppose you want to finish running some errands by 4:00 P.M. Shopping will take 20 min. Eating will take 25 min. You will meet with a friend for 15 min. And your travel time will be a total of 20 min. When should you start your errands?

67. Molly has $3.50. She spent $5, $6.50, and $3.20. How much money did Molly have originally?

● **Lessons 5-7 and 5-8 Write and solve an equation.**

68. You have read $\frac{2}{7}$ of a book. How much of the book remains?

69. A building is made of bricks that are $\frac{3}{5}$ ft tall. The building is 60 bricks high. Find the height of the building, h.

● **Lesson 5-9 Use the formula for volume of a cube, $V = s^3$.**

70. Find the volume of a cube with side length $5d$ cm.

Extra Practice

Skills and Word Problems

● **Lesson 6-1** Write each ratio as a fraction in simplest form.

1. 15 : 30   **2.** 25 to 10   **3.** 4 out of 16   **4.** $\frac{15}{35}$

Find each unit rate.

5. 40 mi/h = ■ ft/s   **6.** 8 cm/s = ■ m/h   **7.** 5.5 qt/min = ■ gal/h

● **Lesson 6-2** Solve each proportion. Round to the nearest tenth where necessary.

8. $\frac{3}{5} = \frac{a}{60}$ **9.** $\frac{8}{7} = \frac{96}{b}$ **10.** $\frac{8}{c} = \frac{40}{85}$ **11.** $\frac{d}{36} = \frac{2}{3}$

12. $\frac{105}{200} = \frac{x}{40}$ **13.** $\frac{8}{15} = \frac{y}{50}$ **14.** $\frac{z}{40} = \frac{11}{15}$ **15.** $\frac{t}{2} = \frac{1.5}{8}$

● **Lesson 6-3** The scale of a map is 4 in. : 25 mi. Find the actual distance for each map distance. Round to the nearest tenth where necessary.

16. 10 in.   **17.** 5.5 in.   **18.** $\frac{1}{2}$ in.   **19.** 3 in.

● **Lesson 6-4** Write each percent as a fraction in simplest form and as a decimal.

20. 10%   **21.** 200%   **22.** 6%   **23.** 1.75%   **24.** 8.5%

Write each number as a percent. Where necessary, round to the nearest tenth of a percent.

25. 0.15   **26.** 1.2   **27.** $\frac{5}{12}$ **28.** $\frac{1}{8}$ **29.** 0.345

● **Lessons 6-5 and 6-6** Solve each percent problem by using a proportion or an equation.

30. Find 12% of 80.   **31.** 30% of x is 12. What is x?

32. What percent of 50 is 2.5?   **33.** Find 30% of 121.

34. 60% of m is 24. What is m?   **35.** What percent of 30 is 9?

● **Lesson 6-7** Find each percent of change. Tell whether the change is an increase or a decrease.

36. 120 to 80   **37.** 40 to 100   **38.** 175 to 231   **39.** $4 to $3.50

● **Lesson 6-8** Find each sale price.

40. regular price, $100; discount, 20%   **41.** regular price, $60; discount, 25%

● **Lesson 6-9** Use fractions or decimals to estimate each percent.

42. 27% of 88   **43.** 99% of 20   **44.** 32% of 66

Lesson 6-1 Find the unit rate.

45. A person runs 40 yd in 6 s.

46. A car backs up 15 ft in 5 s.

Lessons 6-2 and 6-3 Use a proportion to answer each question.

47. An athlete measures her heart rate while exercising. Her heart beats 32 times in 15 seconds. Find her heart rate per minute.

48. A map has a scale of 1 cm : 5 km. Two cities are 4.5 cm apart on the map. What is the actual distance between the cities?

49. A car is 15 ft long. A model of the car has a scale of 1 in. : 2 ft. How long is the model?

Lesson 6-4 Write a percent to represent each situation.

50. Three students in a class of 25 are absent.

51. A baseball player has a batting average of 0.275.

Lesson 6-5 Write and solve a proportion.

52. Out of 120 people who saw a movie, 40% of them enjoyed it. How many people liked the movie?

Lesson 6-6 Write and solve an equation.

53. Forty-five percent of a number n is eighty.

54. Find the final price of a $25 item after 6% sales tax.

Lesson 6-7 Find each percent of change.

55. Last year 150 people attended a school dance. This year 175 people attended.

56. A bicycle sold for $200 last month. The same model was on sale for $170 this month.

Lesson 6-8 Find each selling price.

57. A $12 DVD is marked up 15%.

58. A $65 pair of shoes is discounted 20%.

Lesson 6-9 Use rational numbers to estimate each solution.

59. A pair of shoes is on sale for 30% off the regular price of $39.95. After the discount, 6% sales tax is added. Is $30.00 enough money to buy the pair of shoes?

60. Estimate a 20% tip on a dinner bill of $24.30.

Lesson 6-10 Make a table to solve the problem.

61. An investment account returns 7% each year. An investor deposits $2,500 into the account. Find the balance in the account at the end of each of the next ten years.

Skills and Word Problems

● **Lessons 7-1, 7-2, and 7-3 Solve and check each equation.**

1. $10 - 5x = 15$

2. $3y + 17 = -13$

3. $62 = -12z + 14$

4. $6x - 2x = 12$

5. $t + 5 - 2t = -10$

6. $24 = 2(b - 2) - 4b$

7. $5 - 2(y - 5) = 27$

8. $-56a + 90 + 58a = 92$

9. $8 = 3(c + 8)$

10. $8 - \frac{t}{2} = 53$

11. $75 = \frac{m}{3} + 10$

12. $\frac{3}{5}p + 18 = 24$

13. $0.05x - 0.08 + x = 0.97$

14. $2.5y + 3.5 = -1.5$

15. $6.3p + 1.2p = 22.5$

16. $2x + 6 = 5$

17. $3a + 2 = -8$

18. $3(b - 2) = 9$

19. $8(f + 3) = -32$

20. $\frac{1}{4}(x - 8) = \frac{3}{4}$

21. $4(w - 2.1) = 0.6$

● **Lesson 7-5 Solve and graph each inequality.**

22. $3x + 18 > 12$

23. $4 + 9a \geq -23$

24. $10.5 < -4y + 2.5$

25. $19 - 3x \geq -2$

26. $-5(a - 3) \leq 45$

27. $\frac{1}{2}(t - 6) \leq 22$

28. $\frac{y}{4} - 6 < -9$

29. $-31.4 \leq 2x + 1$

30. $5.8 > 1 + 0.2m$

● **Lesson 7-6 Solve for the variable indicated in red.**

31. $s = p + c$

32. $x + y = 180$

33. $a - b = c$

34. $I = prt$

● **Lesson 7-7 Find the simple interest.**

35. $450 deposited at an interest rate of 2% for 4 years

36. $3,000 deposited at an interest rate of 3% for 10 years

37. $10,000 deposited at an interest rate of 9% for 5 years

Find each balance.

38. $9,000 at 6% compounded annually for 5 years

39. $25,000 at 7% compounded semiannually for 10 years

40. $12,000 at 3% compounded semiannually for 8 years

41. $1,000 at 4% compounded annually for 10 years

42. $500 at 1.5% compounded annually for 4 years

43. $2,000 at 5% compounded semiannually for 2 years

● **Lessons 7-1, 7-2, 7-3, and 7-4 Write and solve an equation.**

44. Three fourths of a number n plus four is ten.

45. Negative three times a number n plus four equals two.

46. Darryl had $265 in his checking account. He spent $60 dollars and deposited d dollars each week for 5 weeks. His final balance was $330. Find the amount of money he deposited each week.

47. Lila has a collection of 85 coins. She adds six coins to the collection and gives away two coins from the collection each week. Find the number of coins in her collection after 8 weeks.

48. Mr. Maxwell's phone service costs $40 per month plus $.10 for each minute of long-distance calls. His bill for January was $52.20. How many long-distance minutes did he use?

49. Suppose you have $70 in your savings account. If you deposit $20 each week, in how many weeks will you have $250?

50. A car rental company charges $20 per day plus $.15 per mile. The bill for two days was $49.75. How many miles did the customer drive?

51. Jane leaves school and walks home at a rate of 4 mi/h. 15 minutes later, Bill finds a book that Jane forgot and runs at a rate of 8 mi/h. How many minutes will it take Bill to catch up with Jane?

● **Lesson 7-5 Write and solve an inequality.**

52. A student received grades of 75, 90, and 83 on three math tests. What grade does the student need on the fourth test to have an average test score of at least 85?

● **Lesson 7-6 Use the distance formula $d = rt$, where d is distance, r is rate, or speed, and t is time spent traveling.**

53. A car travels 35 miles in 50 minutes. What is the speed of the car in mi/h?

54. A runner signed up for a 10-mile race. How long will it take the runner to complete the race if he runs at a rate of 8 mi/h?

● **Lesson 7-7 Use the compound interest formula $B = p(1 + r)^n$, where B is the final balance, p is the principal, r is the interest rate for each period, and n is the number of interest periods.**

55. Ms. Simpson takes out a $1,200 loan that charges 8% interest compounded annually. Suppose she makes no payments on the loan for 6 years. Find the balance after 6 years.

56. A savings account with a balance of $150 earns 2% interest compounded semiannually. No deposits or withdrawals are made. Find the balance in the account after 5 years.

Extra Practice

Skills and Word Problems

● **Lesson 8-1 Is each relation a function? Explain.**

1. $\{(3, 5), (4, 7), (4, 8), (6, 10)\}$ **2.** $\{(0, -1), (1, 3), (-2, 4), (3, 6)\}$

3. $\{(4, 5), (5, 2), (1, -3), (-2, -3), (0, 2)\}$ **4.** $\{(1.5, 0.6), (1.5, 1.1), (2, 1.9), (1, 3.2)\}$

● **Lesson 8-2 Find the solution of each equation for $x = -3, 0,$ and 2.**

5. $y = 3x - 2$ **6.** $y = 2x + 5$ **7.** $y = \frac{1}{2}x + 8$ **8.** $x = 3 - y$

9. $y = -4$ **10.** $2y = 6x - 10$ **11.** $x - 2y = 3$ **12.** $y = -x - 1.5$

Is each ordered pair a solution of $4x + 3y = 9$?

13. $(-3, 1)$ **14.** $(3, -1)$ **15.** $(0, 3)$ **16.** $(0, -3)$

● **Lesson 8-3 Find the slope and y-intercept of the graph of each equation.**

17. $y = 5x - 4$ **18.** $y = 10 - 3x$ **19.** $2y = 3x + 12$ **20.** $4x + y = 16$

21. $y = \frac{3}{5}x - 1$ **22.** $12x - 6y = 30$ **23.** $y = x - \frac{1}{2}$ **24.** $x - y = -2$

Graph each line.

25. slope 3, through $(0, -5)$ **26.** slope -1, through $(3, 5)$ **27.** no slope, through $(2, -1)$

28. $y = 2x + 1$ **29.** $x + y = 4$ **30.** $y = \frac{1}{2}x - 1$

● **Lesson 8-4 Write an equation for the direct variation in each table.**

31.

x	y
0	0
2	3
4	6
6	9

32.

x	y
-2	-4
-1	-2
0	0
1	2

33.

x	y
-4	-2
0	0
4	2
8	4

Write an equation for the direct variation that includes each point.

34. $A(6, 4)$ **35.** $M(9, 3)$ **36.** $P(4, 12)$ **37.** $R(14, 2)$

● **Lessons 8-6 and 8-7 Solve each system by graphing.**

38. $y = x + 3$
$3x - y = 1$ **39.** $x + y = -7$
$x - y = 1$ **40.** $y > 2x - 4$
$y < -3x + 6$ **41.** $x + y < 10$
$x - y < -5$

Is (2, 1) a solution of each system of equations?

42. $2x + 3y = 7$
$-3x + 2y = -4$ **43.** $3x - 2y = 4$
$4x + 2y = 8$ **44.** $-4x + 9y = 1$
$3x - 7y = -1$ **45.** $5x + 3y = 16$
$-2x + 3y = -1$

Lesson 8-1 Is each relation a function? Explain.

46. Is the number of miles driven a function of the amount of gasoline used?

47. Is the time it takes to build a house a function of the number of people working on it?

Lesson 8-2 Use the formula $F = \frac{9}{5}C + 32$, where F is the temperature in Fahrenheit and C is the temperature in Celsius.

48. The boiling point of a chemical is 35°C. Find the equivalent temperature in degrees Fahrenheit.

Lesson 8-3 Find each slope.

49. The top of a roof is 8 ft higher than the edge, 6 feet away.

50. An airplane climbs 2,000 ft over a distance of 10 miles.

Lesson 8-4 Solve using a direct variation model.

51. A recipe for 8 dozen cookies calls for $2\frac{1}{4}$ cups of flour. The number of cookies you make is directly proportional to the amount of flour you have. How many cookies can you make with 9 cups of flour?

52. A salesman's monthly commission is directly proportional to his sales. In January his commission was $1,250, and his sales were $5,000. What will his commission be in a month when his sales are $8,000?

Lesson 8-5 Solve using any strategy.

53. A student is planning an outfit to wear to school. She has five pairs of pants, eight shirts and three pairs of shoes to choose from. How many possible outfits does she have to choose from?

54. Billy buys a candy bar and a soda for $2.00. Rafael buys a soda and a bag of chips for $2.25. Sal buys a candy bar and a bag of chips for $1.75. Find the cost of each item.

Lesson 8-6 Write and solve a system of equations.

55. A bag contains red and blue marbles. There are 20 fewer blue marbles than red marbles, and twice as many red marbles as blue marbles. How many marbles are in the bag?

56. A phone company offers two service plans. One plan costs $10 per month and $.09 per minute. The other plan costs $15 per month and $.05 per minute. For what number of minutes will the cost of the plans be the same?

Lesson 8-7 Write and graph a linear inequality.

57. A grocery store charges $3/lb for chicken and $5/lb for beef. How many pounds of each can you buy for less than $15?

Extra Practice

Skills and Word Problems

● **Lesson 9-1 Use the figure at the right.**

1. Name the line in three ways.
2. Name four different rays.

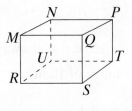

Use the figure at the right. Name each of the following.

3. four segments that intersect $\overline{MR}$
4. three segments parallel to $\overline{MR}$
5. three segments skew to $\overline{MR}$

● **Lesson 9-2 In the figure at the right, $x \parallel y$.**

6. List all angles that are congruent to $\angle 1$.
7. If $m\angle 5 = 67°$, what are the measures of the other angles?

● **Lesson 9-3 Classify each figure.**

8.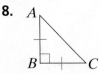

9.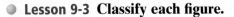

10.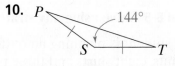

● **Lesson 9-5**

11. $\triangle XYZ \cong \triangle STU$. Which of the following must be true?
    a. $\overline{YZ} \cong \overline{TU}$ b. $\angle X \cong \angle T$ c. $\overline{ZX} \cong \overline{TS}$
    d. $\angle YZX \cong \angle STU$ e. $\triangle YZX \cong \triangle UTS$

● **Lesson 9-6 Find the circumference of each circle with the given radius or diameter. Use 3.14 for π. Round to the nearest tenth.**

12. radius = 4 in.   13. diameter = 25 ft   14. radius = 7.8 cm   15. diameter = 100 m

● **Lesson 9-7 Draw $\triangle XYZ$ with acute $\angle Y$.**

16. Construct the angle bisector of $\angle Y$.   17. Construct a bisector of $\overline{XY}$.

● **Lessons 9-8, 9-9 and 9-10 Graph the image of $\triangle CDG$ with vertices $C(1, 3)$, $D(3, 5)$, and $G(5, 1)$ after each transformation.**

18. 3 units left, 2 units down   19. reflected over the x-axis   20. rotated 90° about the origin

- **Lesson 9-1** Use *always*, *sometimes*, or *never* to complete each statement.

  21. Parallel lines are ___?___ in the same plane.

  22. Skew lines ___?___ intersect.

- **Lesson 9-2**

  23. Two roads intersect. One corner of the intersection has an angle of 65°. Find the measure of the adjacent angle.

- **Lesson 9-3** **Find each perimeter.**

  24. A pond in the shape of a regular hexagon has a side length of 3 ft.

  25. A plaza forms an isosceles triangle with two congruent sides 25 yd long, and the third side 10 yd long.

- **Lesson 9-4** **Solve by drawing a diagram.**

  26. Tom leaves his house and walks 3 blocks east, 6 blocks south, 2 blocks east, 4 blocks north, and 4 blocks west. How many blocks and in which direction(s) does Tom need to walk to get home?

- **Lesson 9-5**

  27. Suppose you draw a diagonal line in the sand between opposite corners in a rectangular sandbox. Does the line form two congruent triangles? Explain.

- **Lesson 9-6** **Find the circumference.**

  28. A circular flower garden has a radius of 12 ft.

- **Lesson 9-7** **Construct the figure.**

  29. Draw $\angle DEF$. Then construct the angle bisector $\overrightarrow{EG}$.

- **Lesson 9-8** **Write the translation in arrow notation.**

  30. A city is moving a historic building. The building is 1.5 mi east and 2 mi south of the center of town. It is moving to a point 1 mi west and 0.4 mi south of the center of town.

- **Lesson 9-9** **Decide whether the statement is *always* true, *sometimes* true, or *never* true. Explain.**

  31. The image of a point reflected over a vertical line will have the same *y*-coordinate.

- **Lesson 9-10**

  32. Do isosceles triangles have rotational symmetry? Do equilateral triangles? Explain.

Skills and Word Problems

● **Lessons 10-1 and 10-2** Find the area of each figure.

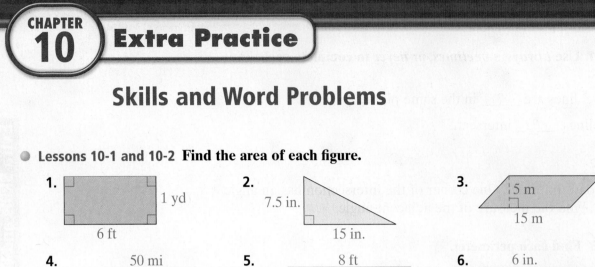

1.

6 ft, 1 yd

2.

7.5 in.
15 in.

3.

5 m
15 m

4.

50 mi
30 mi
80 mi

5.

8 ft
3 ft ←4 ft→ 1 ft
1 ft

6.

6 in.
3 in.
8 in.

● **Lesson 10-3** Find the area of each figure. Give an exact answer and an approximate answer to the nearest tenth using 3.14 for π.

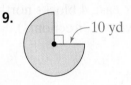

7.

52 m

8.

5 cm

9.

10 yd

● **Lesson 10-4**

10. Draw a net to represent a rectangular box that is 3 ft long, 5 ft wide, and 2 ft high. Find the surface area.

● **Lessons 10-5, 10-6, 10-7, and 10-9** Find the surface area and volume of each space figure, to the nearest tenth. Use 3.14 for π.

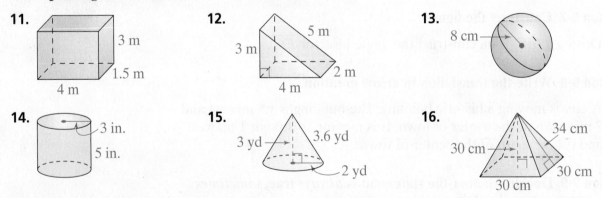

11.

3 m
1.5 m
4 m

12.

5 m
3 m
2 m
4 m

13.

8 cm

14.

3 in.
5 in.

15.

3 yd 3.6 yd
2 yd

16.

34 cm
30 cm
30 cm
30 cm

● **Lesson 10-10** Each pair of prisms is similar. Find the volume of the larger prism.

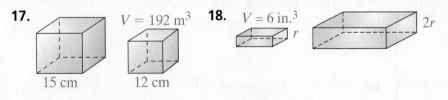

17.

$V = 192$ m^3
15 cm
12 cm

18. $V = 6$ in.^{3}
r
2r

- **Lessons 10-1, 10-2, and 10-3 Find the area of each figure.**

  19. a rectangular football field 360 ft long by 160 ft wide

  20. a pool shaped like a parallelogram with a base of 30 yd and a height of 12 yd

  21. the square infield of a baseball diamond, 90 ft on each side

  22. a triangular garden with a base of 15 m and a height of 20 m

  23. a water treatment plant with circular pools 125 ft in diameter

- **Lesson 10-4 Write the most precise name for each space figure with the given properties.**

  24. three lateral surfaces that are triangles

  25. one surface with no vertices or bases, all points equidistant from point p

  26. two hexagonal bases and six lateral surfaces

- **Lessons 10-5 and 10-6 Find the surface area of each figure.**

  27. a can of soup with a diameter of 4 in. and a height of 5 in.

  28. a sugar cube with a side length of 1.5 cm

  29. a ball with a diameter of 25 cm

  30. a silo formed by a cylinder with a height of 150 ft and a half sphere with a radius of 35 ft

- **Lessons 10-7 and 10-9 Find the volume of each figure.**

  31. a racquetball court shaped like a rectangular prism with length 30 ft, width 20 ft, and height 40 ft

  32. a hockey puck 1 in. thick and 3 in. in diameter

  33. a globe with a diameter of 20 cm

- **Lesson 10-8 Solve by making a model.**

  34. Suppose you cut 5-cm squares out of the corners of a 20 cm-by-30 cm piece of cardboard to make a box with no top. How much wrapping paper will you need to cover the box?

- **Lesson 10-10**

  35. A child's basketball has a radius that is $\frac{2}{3}$ the radius of a regulation size basketball with a radius of 12.4 cm. Find the volume and surface area of the child's basketball. Use 3.14 for π.

Skills and Word Problems

● **Lesson 11-1** Simplify each square root.

1. $\sqrt{4}$ **2.** $\sqrt{100}$ **3.** $-\sqrt{36}$ **4.** $\sqrt{121}$ **5.** $\sqrt{25}$

Estimate to the nearest integer.

6. $\sqrt{50}$ **7.** $\sqrt{12}$ **8.** $\sqrt{40}$ **9.** $\sqrt{105}$ **10.** $\sqrt{55}$

Identify each number as rational or irrational.

11. $\sqrt{9}$ **12.** 0.6 **13.** $\sqrt{5}$ **14.** $0.\overline{6}$ **15.** $0.010010001\ldots$

● **Lesson 11-2** Find each missing length, to the nearest tenth of a unit.

16.

30 in. x 40 in.

17.

28 yd   29 yd x

18.

38.5 m   45 m a

● **Lesson 11-3** Find the distance between each pair of points. Round to the nearest tenth.

19. $(4, 6), (8, 2)$ **20.** $(0, -4), (-5, 1)$ **21.** $(20, -5), (10, -8)$

Find the midpoint of each segment with the given endpoints.

22. $A(5, 4)$ and $B(3, 0)$ **23.** $C(-2, -4)$ and $D(3, 1)$ **24.** $E(-1, 5)$ and $F(2, -1)$

● **Lesson 11-4** Write a proportion and find the value of x.

25. $\triangle ABE \sim \triangle ACD$

5 m A E B x D C 12 m   8 m

26. $\triangle GHI \sim \triangle KJI$

G K 5 yd   4 yd H I J 6 yd x

● **Lessons 11-5** Graph each function.

27. $y = 2x^2$ **28.** $y = -4x^2$ **29.** $y = -\frac{1}{2}x^2$

Estimate the value of x for the given y-value of each cubic function.

30. $y = \frac{1}{4}x^3; y = 2$ **31.** $y = -4x^3; y = 4$ **32.** $y = \frac{3}{4}x^3; y = 21$

Lesson 11-1 Use the formula $d = \sqrt{1.5h}$, where h is the height above ground in feet and d is the distance to the horizon in miles.

33. At the top of a Ferris wheel, Jose is 395 ft above the ground. About how far can Jose see to the horizon?

34. The observation deck of a skyscraper is 950 ft above the ground. About how far can Suzette see from the deck?

Lesson 11-2 Use the Pythagorean Theorem to answer each question.

35. The top of a straight slide is 3 m above the ground. The end of the slide is 4 m from the ladder. How long is the slide?

36. Three friends are trying to stand at the points of a right triangle. The distances between them are 10 yd, 24 yd, and 29 yd. Did they form a right triangle? Explain.

Lesson 11-3 Use the distance formula, $d = \sqrt{(x_2 - x_1)^2 + (y_2 - y_1)^2}$.

37. Samir's house is 3 miles east and 2 miles south of his school. Find the shortest distance between his house and the school.

38. The vertices of a triangle are $L(8, 1)$, $M(2, 1)$, $N(5, 5)$. Determine whether the triangle is scalene, isosceles, or equilateral.

Lesson 11-4 Write and solve a proportion.

39. LaTanya is using a mirror to measure the height of a tree indirectly. She positions the mirror 0.75 m away from her on the ground so that she can see the top of the tree. Her eyes are 1.5 m above the ground. The tree is 10 m behind her. How tall is the tree?

40. Michael is using shadows to measure the height of a tree indirectly. He positions himself 15 ft from the base of the tree so that his shadow and the tree's shadow end at the same point. Michael is 5 ft tall, and his shadow is 6 ft long. What is the height of the tree?

Lesson 11-5 Use quadratic and cubic functions.

41. The equation $d = \frac{1}{2}t^2$ gives the distance d, in feet, that a ball rolls down a ramp in t seconds. Estimate the time it takes a ball to roll down a 33-ft ramp.

42. A software development company uses the formula $y = \frac{1}{8}x^3$ to estimate the number of new games y that they can produce in x years. The maximum number of games that can be produced is 26. In about how many years will the maximum number of games be produced?

Skills and Word Problems

Lesson 12-1 Find the mean, median, and mode. When the answer is not an integer, round to the nearest tenth. Identify any outliers.

1. 10 13 10 15 12 11 12 19 14

2. 85 86 80 85 90 90 50 88

3. $25 $30 $32 $28 $30 $15 $28 $30

4. 6.2 4.5 4.8 12.3 5.7 4.8 6.0

Which measure of central tendency best describes each group of data?

5. minutes watching television

56 36 95 58 267 84

6. number of books read

1 5 7 8 5 5 2

Lesson 12-2 Display each set of data in a frequency table. Then draw a line plot for each frequency table. Find the range.

7. 21 22 20 21 21 20 23 22 21 21

8. 95 100 95 95 90 80 85 80 95 100

Display the data in a histogram.

9. The numbers of letters in each of the first 25 words in a book are shown below. Display the data in a histogram.

4 6 3 4 3 8 2 7 8 2 1 10 2 4 8 3 4 3 3 4 2 3 3 3 2 3

Lesson 12-3 Use box-and-whisker plots to compare data sets. Use a single number line.

10. 1st set: 26 60 36 44 62 24 29 50 37 52 40 41 18 39 64 42
2nd set: 78 22 29 67 10 62 50 72 8 63 35 80 52 60 18 65 61

Lesson 12-4 Make a stem-and-leaf plot for each set of data. Then find the median, the mode, and the range.

11. 15, 22, 25, 10, 36, 15, 28, 35, 18

12. 47, 41, 60, 75, 85, 53, 57, 76, 79, 81, 84, 86

13. 785, 785, 776, 772, 792, 788, 761, 768, 768

14. 4.5, 4.3, 0.8, 3.5, 2.6, 1.4, 0.2, 0.8, 4.3, 6.0

Lesson 12-5 Use the table below to complete Exercises 15 and 16.

15. Make a scatter plot of (time studying, test grade).

16. Is there a positive correlation, negative correlation, or no correlation between the sets of data? Explain.

Study Time

Time Spent Studying (minutes)	40	30	20	50	75
Test Grade	85	80	60	80	90

Lesson 12-1 Find the mean, median, mode, and range of each group of data. Then identify which measure of central tendency best describes the data set.

17. The daily balance in a checking account for 5 days is $30, $42, $25, $25, $34.

18. The heights in centimeters of ten people are 168, 160, 164, 166, 180, 178, 165, 166, 160, and 166.

Lesson 12-2 Display the data in a line plot.

19. A class survey asked students how many pens they had. Five people had one pen, 8 people had two pens, 4 people had three pens, 2 people had four pens, and 3 people had no pens.

Lesson 12-3 Make a box-and-whisker plot for each set of data.

20. ages of members of the drama club: 13, 18, 16, 13, 14, 14, 14, 15, 18, 17, 15, 16, 16, 15, 16, 16, 14, 14, 17, 17, 19

21. number of students in various clubs: 5, 20, 30, 12, 10, 15, 20, 6, 10, 8, 9, 17, 18, 4, 22, 27

Lesson 12-4 Use the stem-and-leaf plot at the right. The plot shows the age at death for presidents who died before 1900 and those who died after 1900.

22. Which numbers are the stems?

23. What is the youngest age at which a president died for each set of data?

24. What is the median for each set of data?

25. What is the mode for each set of data?

26. What is the range for each set of data?

Age of U.S. Presidents at Death

Before 1900		After 1900
9	4	6
7 6 3	5	7 8
8 7 6 5 4 3	6	0 0 3 4 7 7
9 8 7 4 3 1 0	7	1 2 8
3 5 0	8	1 8
0	9	0 3

means 49 ⟵ 9 | 4 | 4 ⟶ means 46

Lesson 12-5 Would you expect a *positive correlation*, a *negative correlation*, or *no correlation* between each pair of data sets? Explain.

27. grades on homework and grades on tests

28. price of a television and number sold

Lesson 12-6 Solve each problem by graphing.

29. A car gets 28 mi/gal in highway driving. How many gallons of gasoline does the car need to drive 150 mi?

30. A builder constructs a skateboard ramp with a slope of $\frac{1}{8}$. Find the length of a ramp that increases 5 ft in height.

Comparing and Ordering Whole Numbers

The numbers on a number line are in order from least to greatest.

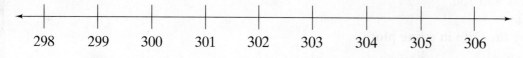

You can use a number line to compare whole numbers. Use the symbols > (is greater than) and < (is less than).

1 EXAMPLE

Use > or < to compare the numbers.

a. 303 ■ 299

303 is to the right of 299.

303 > 299

b. 301 ■ 305

301 is to the left of 305.

301 < 305

The value of a digit depends on its place in a number. Compare digits starting from the left.

2 EXAMPLE

Use > or < to compare the numbers.

a. 12,060,012,875 ■ 12,060,012,675

8 hundreds > 6 hundreds, so

12,060,012,875 > 12,060,012,675.

b. 465,320 ■ 4,653,208

0 millions < 4 millions, so

465,320 < 4,653,208.

EXERCISES

Use > or < to compare the numbers.

1. 3,660 ■ 360

2. 74,328 ■ 74,238

3. 88,010 ■ 8,101

4. 87,524 ■ 9,879

5. 295,286 ■ 295,826

6. 829,631 ■ 842,832

7. 932,401 ■ 932,701

8. 60,000 ■ 500,009

9. 1,609,372,002 ■ 609,172,002

10. 45,248,315,150 ■ 45,283,718,150

Write the numbers from least to greatest.

11. 3,747; 3,474; 3,774; 3,347; 3,734

12. 70,903; 70,309; 73,909; 73,090

13. 32,056,403; 302,056,403; 30,265,403; 30,256,403

14. 884,172; 881,472; 887,142; 881,872

Rounding Whole Numbers

You can use number lines to help you round numbers.

1 EXAMPLE

a. Round 7,510 to the nearest thousand.

7,510 is between 7,000 and 8,000
and closer to 8,000.
7,510 rounds to 8,000.

b. Round 237 to the nearest ten.

237 is between 230 and 240
and closer to 240.
237 rounds to 240.

To round a number to a particular place, look at the digit to the right
of that place. If the digit is less than 5, round down. If the digit is 5 or
greater, round up.

2 EXAMPLE

Round to the place of the underlined digit.

a. 3,4**6**3,280
The digit to the right of the 6 is 3, so
3,463,280 rounds down to 3,460,000.

b. 28**9**,543
The digit to the right of the 9 is 5, so
289,543 rounds up to 290,000.

EXERCISES

Round to the nearest ten.

1. 42   **2.** 89   **3.** 671   **4.** 3,482   **5.** 7,029   **6.** 661,423

Round to the nearest thousand.

7. 5,800   **8.** 3,100   **9.** 44,280   **10.** 9,936   **11.** 987   **12.** 313,591

13. 5,641   **14.** 37,896   **15.** 82,019   **16.** 808,155   **17.** 34,501   **18.** 650,828

Round to the place of the underlined digit.

19. 68,**8**52   **20.** **4**51,006   **21.** 3,40**7**,481   **22.** 2**8**,512,030   **23.** 71,2**2**5,003

24. 96,**4**49   **25.** 4**0**1,223   **26.** **8**,902   **27.** 3,6**7**7   **28.** 2,551,**7**50

29. 68,**6**63   **30.** 70**1**,803,229   **31.** 56**5**,598   **32.** 32,**8**10   **33.** 1,**4**46,300

Multiplying Whole Numbers

When you multiply by a two-digit number, first multiply by the ones and then multiply by the tens. Add the products.

1 EXAMPLE

Multiply 62 × 704.

Step 1	Step 2	Step 3
704	704	704
× 62	× 62	× 62
1408	1408	1 408
	42240	+ 42 240
		43,648

2 EXAMPLE

Find each product.

a. 93 × 6

$$\begin{array}{r} 93 \\ \times\ 6 \\ \hline 558 \end{array}$$

b. 25 × 48

$$\begin{array}{r} 48 \\ \times\ 25 \\ \hline 240 \\ +\ 960 \\ \hline 1,200 \end{array}$$

c. 80 × 921

$$\begin{array}{r} 921 \\ \times\ 80 \\ \hline 73,680 \end{array}$$

EXERCISES

Find each product.

1. 74 × 6
2. 35 × 9
3. 53 × 7
4. 80 × 8
5. 98 × 4
6. 65 × 8

7. 512 × 3
8. 407 × 9
9. 225 × 6
10. 340 × 5
11. 816 × 7
12. 603 × 3

13. 70 × 36
14. 41 × 55
15. 38 × 49
16. 601 × 87
17. 271 × 34
18. 450 × 67

19. 6 × 82
20. 405 × 5
21. 81 × 9
22. 3 × 274
23. 552 × 4

24. 60 × 84
25. 52 × 17
26. 31 × 90
27. 78 × 52
28. 43 × 66

29. 826 × 3
30. 702 × 4
31. 8 × 180
32. 6 × 339
33. 781 × 7

Dividing Whole Numbers

First estimate the quotient by rounding the divisor, the dividend, or both. When you divide, after you bring down a digit, you must write a digit in the quotient.

EXAMPLE

Find each quotient.

a. $741 \div 8$

Estimate:

$720 \div 8 \approx 90$

$$
\begin{array}{r}
92 \text{ R5} \\
8\overline{)741} \\
-72 \\
\hline
21 \\
-16 \\
\hline
5
\end{array}
$$

b. $838 \div 43$

Estimate:

$800 \div 40 \approx 20$

$$
\begin{array}{r}
19 \text{ R21} \\
43\overline{)838} \\
-43 \\
\hline
408 \\
-387 \\
\hline
21
\end{array}
$$

c. $367 \div 9$

Estimate:

$360 \div 9 \approx 40$

$$
\begin{array}{r}
40 \text{ R7} \\
9\overline{)367} \\
-360 \\
\hline
7
\end{array}
$$

EXERCISES

Divide.

1. $4\overline{)61}$ **2.** $8\overline{)53}$ **3.** $7\overline{)90}$ **4.** $3\overline{)84}$ **5.** $6\overline{)81}$

6. $6\overline{)469}$ **7.** $3\overline{)653}$ **8.** $8\overline{)645}$ **9.** $9\overline{)231}$ **10.** $4\overline{)415}$

11. $60\overline{)461}$ **12.** $40\overline{)213}$ **13.** $70\overline{)517}$ **14.** $30\overline{)432}$ **15.** $80\overline{)276}$

16. $43\overline{)273}$ **17.** $52\overline{)281}$ **18.** $69\overline{)207}$ **19.** $38\overline{)121}$ **20.** $81\overline{)433}$

21. $94\overline{)1,368}$ **22.** $62\overline{)1,147}$ **23.** $55\overline{)2,047}$ **24.** $85\overline{)1,450}$ **25.** $46\overline{)996}$

26. $94 \div 4$ **27.** $66 \div 9$ **28.** $90 \div 5$ **29.** $69 \div 6$ **30.** $58 \div 8$

31. $323 \div 5$ **32.** $849 \div 7$ **33.** $404 \div 8$ **34.** $934 \div 3$ **35.** $619 \div 6$

36. $777 \div 50$ **37.** $528 \div 20$ **38.** $443 \div 70$ **39.** $312 \div 40$ **40.** $335 \div 60$

41. $382 \div 72$ **42.** $580 \div 68$ **43.** $279 \div 43$ **44.** $232 \div 27$ **45.** $331 \div 93$

46. $614 \div 35$ **47.** $423 \div 28$ **48.** $489 \div 15$ **49.** $1,134 \div 51$ **50.** $1,103 \div 26$

Decimals and Place Value

Each digit in a whole number or a decimal has both a place and a value. The value of any place is one tenth the value of the place to its left. The chart below can help you read and write decimals.

Billions	Hundred millions	Ten millions	Millions	Hundred thousands	Ten thousands	Thousands	Hundreds	Tens	Ones	.	Tenths	Hundredths	Thousandths	Ten-thousandths	Hundred-thousandths	Millionths
2	4	0	1	2	6	2	8	3	0	.	7	5	0	1	9	1

EXAMPLE

a. What is the value of the digit 8 in the number above?
The digit 8 is in the hundreds place.
So, its value is 8 hundreds.

b. Write 2.006 in words.
The digit 6 is in the thousandths place.
So, 2.006 is read two and six thousandths.

c. Write five and thirty-four ten-thousandths as a decimal.
Ten-thousandths is 4 places to the right of the decimal point.
So, the decimal will have 4 places after the decimal point.
The answer is 5.0034.

EXERCISES

Use the chart above. Write the value of each digit.

1. the digit 9
2. the digit 7
3. the digit 5
4. the digit 6
5. the digit 4
6. the digit 3

Write a decimal for the given words.

7. forty-one ten-thousandths
8. eighteen and five hundred four thousandths
9. eight millionths
10. seven and sixty-three hundred-thousandths
11. thirteen thousandths
12. sixty-five and two hundred one thousandths

Write each decimal in words.

13. 0.06
14. 4.7
15. 0.00011
16. 0.9
17. 0.012
18. 0.000059
19. 0.0042
20. 6.020

Comparing and Ordering Decimals

To compare two decimals, use the symbols > (is greater than), < (is less than), or = (is equal to). When you compare, start at the left and compare the digits.

1 EXAMPLE

Use >, <, or = to compare the decimals.

a. 0.1 ■ 0.06
   1 tenth > 0 tenths, so
   0.1 > 0.06.

b. 2.4583 ■ 2.48
   5 hundredths < 8 hundredths,
   so 2.4583 < 2.48.

c. 0.30026 ■ 0.03026
   3 tenths > 0 tenths, so
   0.30026 > 0.03026.

2 EXAMPLE

Draw number lines to compare the decimals.

a. 0.1 ■ 0.06

b. 2.4583 ■ 2.48

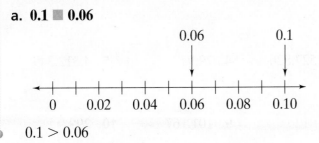

0.1 > 0.06

2.4583 < 2.48

EXERCISES

Use >, <, or = to compare the decimals. Draw number lines if you wish.

1. 0.003 ■ 0.02
2. 84.2 ■ 842
3. 0.162 ■ 0.106
4. 0.0659 ■ 0.6059

5. 2.13 ■ 2.99
6. 3.53 ■ 3.529
7. 2.01 ■ 2.010
8. 0.00072 ■ 0.07002

9. 0.458 ■ 0.4589
10. 8.627 ■ 8.649
11. 0.0019 ■ 0.0002
12. 0.19321 ■ 0.19231

Write the decimals in order from least to greatest.

13. 2.31, 0.231, 23.1, 0.23, 3.21
14. 1.02, 1.002, 1.2, 1.11, 1.021

15. 0.02, 0.002, 0.22, 0.222, 2.22
16. 55.5, 555.5, 55.555, 5.5555

17. 0.07, 0.007, 0.7, 0.71, 0.72
18. 2.78, 2.7001, 2.701, 2.71, 2.7

19. 7, 7.3264, 7.3, 7.3246, 7.0324
20. 0.0101, 0.0099, 0.011, 0.00019

Rounding

When you round to a particular place, look at the digit to the right of that place. If it is 5 or greater, you increase the digit in the place you are rounding to by 1. If it is less than 5, you leave the digit in the place you are rounding to unchanged.

EXAMPLE

a. **Round 1.627 to the nearest whole number.**
The digit to the right of the units place is 6, so 1.627 rounds up to 2.

b. **Round 12,034 to the nearest thousand.**
The digit to the right of the thousands place is 0, so 12,034 rounds down to 12,000.

c. **Round 2.7195 to the nearest hundredth.**
The digit to the right of the hundredths place is 9, so 2.7195 rounds up to 2.72.

d. **Round 0.060521 to the nearest thousandth.**
The digit to the right of the thousandths place is 5, so 0.060521 rounds up to 0.061.

EXERCISES

Round to the nearest thousand.

1. 105,099
2. 10,400
3. 79,527,826
4. 79,932
5. 4,312,349

Round to the nearest whole number.

6. 135.91
7. 3.001095
8. 96.912
9. 101.167
10. 299.9

Round to the nearest tenth.

11. 82.01
12. 4.67522
13. 20.397
14. 399.95
15. 129.98

Round to the nearest hundredth.

16. 13.458
17. 96.4045
18. 0.699
19. 4.234
20. 12.09531

Round to the place of the underlined digit.

21. 7.0615
22. 5.77125
23. 1,522
24. 0.91952
25. 4.243
26. 236.001
27. 352
28. 3.495366
29. 8.07092
30. 0.6008
31. 409
32. 23,951,888
33. 2.5784
34. 862
35. 19.32
36. 918
37. 7.735
38. 25.066047
39. 983,240,631
40. 27
41. 0.003771
42. 0.0649
43. 12.777
44. 1,759,230
45. 20,908

Adding and Subtracting Decimals

Add or subtract decimals just as you would whole numbers. You line up
the decimal points and then add or subtract. If you wish, you can use
zeros to make the columns even.

EXAMPLE

Find each sum or difference.

a. 37.6 + 8.431

$$\begin{array}{r} 37.6 \\ + \ 8.431 \\ \hline \end{array} \rightarrow \begin{array}{r} 37.600 \\ + \ 8.431 \\ \hline 46.031 \end{array}$$

b. 8 − 4.593

$$\begin{array}{r} 8 \\ - \ 4.593 \\ \hline \end{array} \rightarrow \begin{array}{r} 8.000 \\ - \ 4.593 \\ \hline 3.407 \end{array}$$

c. 8.3 + 2.99 + 17.5

$$\begin{array}{r} 8.3 \\ 2.99 \\ + \ 17.5 \\ \hline \end{array} \rightarrow \begin{array}{r} 8.30 \\ 2.99 \\ + \ 17.50 \\ \hline 28.79 \end{array}$$

EXERCISES

Find each sum or difference.

1.
$$\begin{array}{r} 39.7 \\ - \ 36.03 \\ \hline \end{array}$$

2.
$$\begin{array}{r} 1.08 \\ - \ 0.9 \\ \hline \end{array}$$

3.
$$\begin{array}{r} 6.784 \\ + \ 0.528 \\ \hline \end{array}$$

4.
$$\begin{array}{r} 5.01 \\ - \ 0.87 \\ \hline \end{array}$$

5.
$$\begin{array}{r} 13.02 \\ + \ 23.107 \\ \hline \end{array}$$

6.
$$\begin{array}{r} 8.634 \\ + \ 1.409 \\ \hline \end{array}$$

7.
$$\begin{array}{r} 2.1 \\ - \ 0.5 \\ \hline \end{array}$$

8.
$$\begin{array}{r} 8.23 \\ - \ 3.1 \\ \hline \end{array}$$

9.
$$\begin{array}{r} 1.05 \\ + \ 12.9 \\ \hline \end{array}$$

10.
$$\begin{array}{r} 2.6 \\ + \ 0.003 \\ \hline \end{array}$$

11.
$$\begin{array}{r} 0.1 \\ 58.21 \\ + \ 1.9 \\ \hline \end{array}$$

12.
$$\begin{array}{r} 12.2 \\ 3.06 \\ + \ 0.5 \\ \hline \end{array}$$

13.
$$\begin{array}{r} 9.42 \\ 3.6 \\ + \ 21.003 \\ \hline \end{array}$$

14.
$$\begin{array}{r} 15.22 \\ 7.4 \\ + \ 8.125 \\ \hline \end{array}$$

15.
$$\begin{array}{r} 3.7 \\ 20.06 \\ + \ 16.19 \\ \hline \end{array}$$

16. 76.39 − 8.47

17. 8.7 + 17.03

18. 32.403 + 12.06

19. 20.5 + 11.45

20. 8.9 − 4.45

21. 1.245 + 5.8

22. 3.9 + 6.57

23. 14.81 − 8.6

24. 11.9 − 2.06

25. 3.45 + 4.061

26. 8.29 + 4.3

27. 7.06 − 4.235

28. 6.02 + 4.005

29. 7.05 − 3.5

30. 1.18 + 3.015

31. 2.304 − 0.87

32. 5.002 − 3.45

33. 6.8 + 3.57

34. 0.23 + 0.091

35. 0.5 − 0.18

36. 8.3 + 2.99 + 17.52

37. 9.5 + 12.32 + 6.4

38. 4.521 + 1.8 + 3.07

39. 3.602 + 9.4 + 24

40. 11.6 + 8.05 + 5.13

41. 7.023 + 1.48 + 3.9

42. 57 + 0.6327 + 189.007

43. 741 + 6.08 + 0.0309

44. 0.045 + 16.32 + 8.6

45. 4.27 + 6.18 + 0.91

46. 3.856 + 14.01 + 1.72

47. 11.45 + 3.79 + 23.861

Multiplying Decimals

Multiply decimals as you would whole numbers. Then place the decimal point in the product. To do this, add the number of decimal places in the factors.

1 EXAMPLE

Multiply 0.068 × 2.3.

Step 1 Multiply.

```
  0.068
× 2.3
  204
+ 1360
  1564
```

Step 2 Place the decimal point.

```
  0.068   ← three decimal places
× 2.3     ← one decimal place
  204
+ 1360
  0.1564  ← four decimal places
```

2 EXAMPLE

Find each product.

a. **3.12 × 0.9**

```
  3.12
× 0.9
  2.808
```

b. **5.75 × 42**

```
   5.75
×  42
  11 50
+ 230 00
 241.50
```

c. **0.964 × 0.28**

```
   0.964
×  0.28
   7712
+ 19280
 0.26992
```

EXERCISES

Multiply.

1.
```
  1.48
× 3.6
```

2.
```
  191.2
× 3.4
```

3.
```
  0.05
× 43
```

4.
```
  0.27
× 5
```

5.
```
  1.36
× 3.8
```

6.
```
  6.23
× 0.21
```

7.
```
  0.512
× 0.76
```

8.
```
  0.04
× 7
```

9.
```
  0.136
× 8.4
```

10.
```
    3
× 0.05
```

11. 2.07×1.004

12. 0.12×6.1

13. 3.2×0.15

14. 0.74×0.23

15. 2.6×0.14

16. 0.77×51

17. 9.3×0.706

18. 71.13×0.4

19. 0.42×98

20. 6.3×85

21. 45×0.028

22. 76×3.3

23. 9×1.35

24. 4.56×7

25. 5×2.41

26. 704×0.3

27. 8.003×0.6

28. 42.2×0.9

29. 0.6×30.02

30. 0.05×11.8

Zeros in a Product

When you multiply with decimals, you may have to write one or more zeros to the left of a product before you can place the decimal point.

1 EXAMPLE

Multiply 0.06 × 0.015.

Step 1 Multiply.

$$\begin{array}{r} 0.015 \\ \times\ 0.06 \\ \hline 90 \end{array}$$

Step 2 Place the decimal point.

$$\begin{array}{r} 0.015 \\ \times\ 0.06 \\ \hline 0.00090 \end{array}$$

← The product should have 5 decimal places, so you must write three zeros before placing the decimal point.

2 EXAMPLE

a. 0.02 × 1.3

$$\begin{array}{r} 1.3 \\ \times\ 0.02 \\ \hline 0.026 \end{array}$$

b. 0.012 × 2.4

$$\begin{array}{r} 2.4 \\ \times\ 0.012 \\ \hline 48 \\ +\ 240 \\ \hline 0.0288 \end{array}$$

c. 0.022 × 0.051

$$\begin{array}{r} 0.051 \\ \times\ 0.022 \\ \hline 102 \\ +\ 1020 \\ \hline 0.001122 \end{array}$$

EXERCISES

Multiply.

1. $\begin{array}{r} 0.03 \\ \times\ 0.9 \end{array}$
2. $\begin{array}{r} 0.06 \\ \times\ 0.5 \end{array}$
3. $\begin{array}{r} 2.4 \\ \times\ 0.03 \end{array}$
4. $\begin{array}{r} 7 \\ \times\ 0.01 \end{array}$
5. $\begin{array}{r} 0.05 \\ \times\ 0.05 \end{array}$

6. $\begin{array}{r} 0.016 \\ \times\ 0.12 \end{array}$
7. $\begin{array}{r} 0.031 \\ \times\ 0.08 \end{array}$
8. $\begin{array}{r} 0.03 \\ \times\ 0.2 \end{array}$
9. $\begin{array}{r} 0.27 \\ \times\ 0.033 \end{array}$
10. $\begin{array}{r} 0.014 \\ \times\ 0.25 \end{array}$

11. 0.003 × 0.55
12. 0.01 × 0.74
13. 0.47 × 0.08
14. 0.76 × 0.1
15. 0.3 × 0.27
16. 0.19 × 0.05
17. 0.018 × 0.04
18. 0.43 × 0.2
19. 0.03 × 0.03
20. 4.003 × 0.02
21. 0.5 × 0.08
22. 0.06 × 0.7
23. 0.047 × 0.008
24. 0.05 × 0.06
25. 0.03 × 0.4
26. 0.05 × 0.036
27. 0.4 × 0.23
28. 0.3 × 0.017
29. 0.3 × 0.24
30. 0.67 × 0.09
31. 3.02 × 0.006
32. 0.31 × 0.08
33. 0.14 × 0.05
34. 0.07 × 0.85

Dividing Decimals by Whole Numbers

When you divide a decimal by a whole number, the decimal point in the quotient goes directly above the decimal point in the dividend. You may need extra zeros to place the decimal point.

1 EXAMPLE

Divide 2.432 ÷ 32.

Step 1 Divide.

```
      76
32)2.432
  - 2 24
     192
   - 192
       0
```

Step 2 Place the decimal point.

```
    0.076    ← Put extra zeros to the left.
32)2.432       Then place the decimal point.
  - 2 24
     192
   - 192
       0
```

2 EXAMPLE

a. **37.6 ÷ 8**

```
     4.7
8)37.6
 - 32
   5 6
 - 5 6
     0
```

b. **39.33 ÷ 69**

```
      0.57
69)39.33
  - 34 5
    4 83
  - 4 83
      0
```

c. **4.482 ÷ 54**

```
      0.083
54)4.482
  - 4 32
     162
   - 162
       0
```

EXERCISES

Divide.

1. 7)17.92
2. 5)16.5
3. 9)6.984
4. 6)91.44
5. 4)35.16

6. 56)8.848
7. 22)2.42
8. 26)1,723.8
9. 83)15.272
10. 39)26.91

11. 14.49 ÷ 7
12. 10.53 ÷ 9
13. 17.52 ÷ 2
14. 37.14 ÷ 6

15. 0.1352 ÷ 8
16. 0.0324 ÷ 9
17. 0.0882 ÷ 6
18. 0.8682 ÷ 6

19. 12.342 ÷ 22
20. 29.792 ÷ 32
21. 22.568 ÷ 26
22. 11.340 ÷ 36

23. 45.918 ÷ 18
24. 79.599 ÷ 13
25. 58.5 ÷ 15
26. 74.664 ÷ 12

27. 21.0 ÷ 84
28. 89.378 ÷ 67
29. 0.0672 ÷ 48
30. 171.031 ÷ 53

Multiplying and Dividing by Powers of Ten

You can use shortcuts to multiply or divide by powers of ten.

When you multiply by	Move the decimal point	When you divide by	Move the decimal point
10,000	4 places to the right	10,000	4 places to the left
1,000	3 places to the right	1,000	3 places to the left
100	2 places to the right	100	2 places to the left
10	1 place to the right	10	1 place to the left
0.1	1 place to the left	0.1	1 place to the right
0.01	2 places to the left	0.01	2 places to the right
0.001	3 places to the left	0.001	3 places to the right

EXAMPLE

Multiply or divide.

a. 0.7×0.001

Move the decimal point 3 places to the left.

0.000.7

$0.7 \times 0.001 = 0.0007$

b. $0.605 \div 100$

Move the decimal point 2 places to the left.

0.00.605

$0.605 \div 100 = 0.00605$

EXERCISES

Multiply or divide.

1. $10,000 \times 0.056$
2. 0.001×0.09
3. 5.2×10
4. $0.03 \times 1,000$

5. $236.7 \div 0.1$
6. $45.28 \div 10$
7. $0.9 \div 1,000$
8. $1.07 \div 0.01$

9. 100×0.08
10. $1.03 \times 10,000$
11. 1.803×0.001
12. 4.1×100

13. $13.7 \div 0.001$
14. $203.05 \div 0.01$
15. $4.7 \div 10$
16. $0.05 \div 100$

17. 23.6×0.01
18. $1,000 \times 0.12$
19. 0.41×0.001
20. 0.01×6.2

21. $42.3 \div 0.1$
22. $0.4 \div 10,000$
23. $5.02 \div 0.01$
24. $16.5 \div 100$

25. $0.27 \div 0.01$
26. 1.05×0.001
27. 10×0.04
28. $2.09 \div 100$

29. 0.65×0.1
30. $0.03 \div 100$
31. $2.6 \div 0.1$
32. $12.6 \times 10,000$

33. $0.3 \div 1,000$
34. 0.01×6.7
35. 100×0.158
36. $23.1 \div 10$

Dividing Decimals by Decimals

To divide with a decimal divisor, multiply it by the smallest power of ten that will make the divisor a whole number. Then multiply the dividend by that same power of ten.

EXAMPLE

Find each quotient.

a. $3.348 \div 6.2$
Multiply by 10.

$$
\begin{array}{r}
0.54 \\
6.2.\overline{)3\,3.48} \\
-3\,1\,0 \\
\hline
2\,48 \\
-2\,48 \\
\hline
0
\end{array}
$$

b. $2.4885 \div 0.35$
Multiply by 100.

$$
\begin{array}{r}
7.11 \\
0.35.\overline{)2\,48.85} \\
-2\,45 \\
\hline
3\,8 \\
-3\,5 \\
\hline
35 \\
-35 \\
\hline
0
\end{array}
$$

c. $0.0576 \div 0.012$
Multiply by 1,000.

$$
\begin{array}{r}
4.8 \\
0.012.\overline{)0.057.6} \\
-48 \\
\hline
96 \\
-96 \\
\hline
0
\end{array}
$$

EXERCISES

Divide.

1. $3.2\overline{)268.8}$ **2.** $1.9\overline{)123.5}$ **3.** $0.3\overline{)135.6}$ **4.** $2.3\overline{)170.2}$ **5.** $7.9\overline{)252.8}$

6. $5.7\overline{)10.26}$ **7.** $2.3\overline{)71.53}$ **8.** $3.1\overline{)16.12}$ **9.** $7.8\overline{)24.18}$ **10.** $6.3\overline{)14.49}$

11. $134.42 \div 5.17$ **12.** $89.96 \div 3.46$ **13.** $160.58 \div 5.18$ **14.** $106.59 \div 6.27$

15. $62.4 \div 3.9$ **16.** $260.4 \div 8.4$ **17.** $316.8 \div 7.2$ **18.** $162.4 \div 2.9$

19. $1.512 \div 0.54$ **20.** $3.225 \div 0.43$ **21.** $2.484 \div 0.69$ **22.** $511.5 \div 5.5$

23. $0.992 \div 0.8$ **24.** $4.53 \div 0.05$ **25.** $3.498 \div 0.06$ **26.** $59.2 \div 0.8$

27. $2.198 \div 0.07$ **28.** $14.28 \div 0.7$ **29.** $1.98 \div 0.5$ **30.** $26.36 \div 0.04$

31. $3.922 \div 7.4$ **32.** $23.52 \div 0.98$ **33.** $71.25 \div 7.5$ **34.** $114.7 \div 3.7$

35. $0.832 \div 0.52$ **36.** $1.125 \div 0.09$ **37.** $9.666 \div 2.7$ **38.** $1.456 \div 9.1$

39. $0.4374 \div 1.8$ **40.** $2.3414 \div 0.46$ **41.** $0.07224 \div 0.021$ **42.** $0.1386 \div 0.18$

43. $0.16926 \div 0.091$ **44.** $0.6042 \div 5.3$ **45.** $2.3374 \div 0.62$ **46.** $1.0062 \div 0.078$

Zeros in Decimal Division

When you are dividing by a decimal, sometimes you need to use extra zeros in the dividend or the quotient, or both.

1 EXAMPLE

Divide $0.045 \div 3.6$.

Step 1 Multiply by 10.

$$3.6\overline{)0.0.45}$$

Step 2 Divide.

$$
\begin{array}{r}
125 \\
3.6\overline{)0.0.4500} \\
-36 \\
\hline
90 \\
-72 \\
\hline
180 \\
-180 \\
\hline
0
\end{array}
$$

Step 3 Place the decimal point.

$$
\begin{array}{r}
0.0125 \\
3.6\overline{)0.0.4500} \\
-36 \\
\hline
90 \\
-72 \\
\hline
180 \\
-180 \\
\hline
0
\end{array}
$$

2 EXAMPLE

Find each quotient.

a. $0.4428 \div 8.2$
   Multiply by 10.

$$
\begin{array}{r}
0.054 \\
8.2\overline{)0.4.428}
\end{array}
$$

b. $0.00434 \div 0.07$
   Multiply by 100.

$$
\begin{array}{r}
0.062 \\
0.07\overline{)0.00.434}
\end{array}
$$

c. $0.00306 \div 0.072$
   Multiply by 1,000.

$$
\begin{array}{r}
0.0425 \\
0.072\overline{)0.003.0600}
\end{array}
$$

EXERCISES

Divide.

1. $0.05\overline{)0.0023}$
2. $0.02\overline{)0.000162}$
3. $0.12\overline{)0.009}$
4. $2.5\overline{)0.021}$

5. $0.0019 \div 0.2$
6. $0.9 \div 0.8$
7. $0.000175 \div 0.07$
8. $0.142 \div 0.04$

9. $0.0017 \div 0.02$
10. $0.003 \div 0.6$
11. $0.0105 \div 0.7$
12. $0.034 \div 0.05$

13. $0.00056 \div 0.16$
14. $0.0612 \div 7.2$
15. $0.217 \div 3.1$
16. $0.052 \div 0.8$

17. $0.000924 \div 0.44$
18. $0.05796 \div 0.63$
19. $0.00123 \div 8.2$
20. $0.0954 \div 0.09$

21. $0.0084 \div 1.4$
22. $0.259 \div 3.5$
23. $0.00468 \div 0.52$
24. $0.104 \div 0.05$

25. $0.00063 \div 0.18$
26. $0.011 \div 0.25$
27. $0.3069 \div 9.3$
28. $0.00045 \div 0.3$

Writing Equivalent Fractions

If you multiply or divide both the numerator and the denominator of a fraction by the same number, you get an equivalent fraction.

1 EXAMPLE

a. Find the missing number in $\frac{5}{6} = \frac{20}{\blacksquare}$.

$$\frac{5}{6} \overset{\times 4}{=} \frac{20}{\blacksquare}$$

$$\frac{5}{6} = \frac{20}{24}$$
$$\scriptstyle \times 4$$

b. Find the missing number in $\frac{12}{30} = \frac{\blacksquare}{15}$.

$$\frac{12}{30} \overset{\div 2}{=} \frac{\blacksquare}{15}$$

$$\frac{12}{30} = \frac{6}{15}$$
$$\scriptstyle \div 2$$

To write a fraction in simplest form, divide both the numerator and the denominator by the greatest common factor.

2 EXAMPLE

a. Write $\frac{6}{15}$ in simplest form.

3 is the greatest common factor.

$$\frac{6}{15} = \frac{6 \div 3}{15 \div 3} = \frac{2}{5}$$

The simplest form of $\frac{6}{15}$ is $\frac{2}{5}$.

b. Write $\frac{36}{42}$ in simplest form.

6 is the greatest common factor.

$$\frac{36}{42} = \frac{36 \div 6}{42 \div 6} = \frac{6}{7}$$

The simplest form of $\frac{36}{42}$ is $\frac{6}{7}$.

EXERCISES

Find each missing number.

1. $\frac{1}{3} = \frac{\blacksquare}{6}$
2. $\frac{3}{4} = \frac{\blacksquare}{16}$
3. $\frac{18}{30} = \frac{6}{\blacksquare}$
4. $\frac{2}{3} = \frac{\blacksquare}{21}$
5. $\frac{3}{4} = \frac{9}{\blacksquare}$

6. $\frac{3}{10} = \frac{9}{\blacksquare}$
7. $\frac{4}{5} = \frac{\blacksquare}{30}$
8. $\frac{2}{3} = \frac{8}{\blacksquare}$
9. $\frac{33}{55} = \frac{\blacksquare}{5}$
10. $\frac{27}{72} = \frac{9}{\blacksquare}$

11. $\frac{2}{3} = \frac{\blacksquare}{24}$
12. $\frac{11}{12} = \frac{55}{\blacksquare}$
13. $\frac{3}{5} = \frac{18}{\blacksquare}$
14. $\frac{60}{72} = \frac{10}{\blacksquare}$
15. $\frac{7}{8} = \frac{\blacksquare}{24}$

Write each fraction in simplest form.

16. $\frac{12}{36}$
17. $\frac{25}{30}$
18. $\frac{14}{16}$
19. $\frac{27}{36}$
20. $\frac{21}{35}$
21. $\frac{40}{50}$

22. $\frac{24}{40}$
23. $\frac{32}{64}$
24. $\frac{15}{45}$
25. $\frac{27}{63}$
26. $\frac{44}{77}$
27. $\frac{45}{75}$

28. $\frac{60}{72}$
29. $\frac{77}{84}$
30. $\frac{12}{24}$
31. $\frac{24}{32}$
32. $\frac{7}{21}$
33. $\frac{18}{42}$

Mixed Numbers and Improper Fractions

A fraction, such as $\frac{10}{7}$, in which the numerator is greater than or equal to the denominator is an improper fraction. You can write an improper fraction as a mixed number that shows the sum of a whole number and a fraction.

Sometimes it is necessary to do the opposite and write a mixed number as an improper fraction.

EXAMPLE

a. Write $\frac{11}{5}$ as a mixed number.

$$\frac{11}{5} \rightarrow \begin{array}{r} 2 \\ 5\overline{)11} \\ -10 \\ \hline 1 \end{array}$$ ← whole number

← remainder

$$\frac{11}{5} = 2\frac{1}{5}$$ ← whole number + $\frac{\text{remainder}}{\text{denominator}}$

b. Write $2\frac{5}{6}$ as an improper fraction.

$$2\frac{5}{6} = 2 + \frac{5}{6}$$

$$= \frac{12}{6} + \frac{5}{6}$$ ← Write 2 as $\frac{12}{6}$.

$$= \frac{12 + 5}{6}$$ ← Add the numerators.

$$2\frac{5}{6} = \frac{17}{6}$$

EXERCISES

Write each improper fraction as a mixed number.

1. $\frac{7}{5}$
2. $\frac{9}{2}$
3. $\frac{13}{4}$
4. $\frac{21}{5}$
5. $\frac{13}{10}$
6. $\frac{49}{5}$

7. $\frac{21}{8}$
8. $\frac{13}{7}$
9. $\frac{17}{5}$
10. $\frac{49}{6}$
11. $\frac{17}{4}$
12. $\frac{5}{2}$

13. $\frac{27}{5}$
14. $\frac{12}{9}$
15. $\frac{30}{8}$
16. $\frac{37}{12}$
17. $\frac{8}{6}$
18. $\frac{19}{12}$

19. $\frac{45}{10}$
20. $\frac{15}{12}$
21. $\frac{11}{2}$
22. $\frac{20}{6}$
23. $\frac{34}{8}$
24. $\frac{21}{9}$

Write each mixed number as an improper fraction.

25. $1\frac{1}{2}$
26. $2\frac{2}{3}$
27. $1\frac{1}{12}$
28. $3\frac{1}{5}$
29. $2\frac{2}{7}$
30. $4\frac{1}{2}$

31. $2\frac{7}{8}$
32. $1\frac{2}{9}$
33. $5\frac{1}{5}$
34. $4\frac{7}{9}$
35. $9\frac{1}{4}$
36. $2\frac{3}{8}$

37. $7\frac{7}{8}$
38. $1\frac{5}{12}$
39. $3\frac{3}{7}$
40. $6\frac{1}{2}$
41. $3\frac{1}{10}$
42. $4\frac{6}{7}$

Adding and Subtracting Fractions With Like Denominators

When you add or subtract fractions with the same denominator, add or subtract the numerators and then write the answer over the denominator.

1 EXAMPLE

Add or subtract. Write each answer in simplest form.

a. $\frac{5}{8} + \frac{7}{8}$

$$\frac{5}{8} + \frac{7}{8} = \frac{5+7}{8}$$
$$= \frac{12}{8} = 1\frac{4}{8} = 1\frac{1}{2}$$

b. $\frac{11}{12} - \frac{2}{12}$

$$\frac{11}{12} - \frac{2}{12} = \frac{11-2}{12}$$
$$= \frac{9}{12} = \frac{3}{4}$$

To add or subtract mixed numbers, add or subtract the fractions first. Then add or subtract the whole numbers.

2 EXAMPLE

Add or subtract. Write each answer in simplest form.

a. $3\frac{4}{6} + 2\frac{5}{6}$

$$\begin{array}{r} 3\frac{4}{6} \\ + 2\frac{5}{6} \\ \hline 5\frac{9}{6} = 5 + 1 + \frac{3}{6} = 6\frac{1}{2} \end{array}$$

b. $6\frac{1}{4} - 1\frac{3}{4}$

$$\begin{array}{r} 6\frac{1}{4} \rightarrow \\ -1\frac{3}{4} \\ \hline \end{array} \quad \begin{array}{r} 5\frac{5}{4} \quad \leftarrow \text{Rewrite 1 unit as } \frac{4}{4} \text{ and add it to } \frac{1}{4}. \\ -1\frac{3}{4} \\ \hline 4\frac{2}{4} = 4\frac{1}{2} \end{array}$$

EXERCISES

Add or subtract. Write each answer in simplest form.

1. $\frac{4}{5} + \frac{3}{5}$ 2. $\frac{2}{6} - \frac{1}{6}$ 3. $\frac{2}{7} + \frac{2}{7}$ 4. $\frac{7}{8} + \frac{2}{8}$ 5. $1\frac{2}{5} - \frac{1}{5}$

6. $\frac{3}{6} - \frac{1}{6}$ 7. $\frac{6}{8} - \frac{3}{8}$ 8. $\frac{2}{9} + \frac{1}{9}$ 9. $\frac{4}{5} - \frac{1}{5}$ 10. $\frac{5}{9} + \frac{7}{9}$

11. $9\frac{1}{3} - 8\frac{1}{3}$ 12. $8\frac{6}{7} - 4\frac{2}{7}$ 13. $3\frac{1}{10} + 1\frac{3}{10}$ 14. $2\frac{2}{9} + 3\frac{4}{9}$

15. $4\frac{5}{12} - 3\frac{1}{12}$ 16. $9\frac{5}{9} + 6\frac{7}{9}$ 17. $5\frac{7}{8} + 2\frac{3}{8}$ 18. $4\frac{4}{7} - 2\frac{1}{7}$

19. $9\frac{3}{4} + 1\frac{3}{4}$ 20. $8\frac{2}{3} - 4\frac{1}{3}$ 21. $8\frac{7}{10} + 2\frac{3}{10}$ 22. $1\frac{4}{5} + 3\frac{3}{5}$

23. $7\frac{1}{5} - 2\frac{3}{5}$ 24. $4\frac{1}{3} - 1\frac{2}{3}$ 25. $4\frac{3}{8} - 3\frac{5}{8}$ 26. $5\frac{1}{12} - 2\frac{7}{12}$

Multiplying and Dividing Fractions

To multiply fractions, multiply the numerators and the denominators.
To divide fractions, multiply by the reciprocal of the divisor.

EXAMPLE

Multiply. Write each answer in simplest form.

a. $\dfrac{8}{9} \times \dfrac{3}{10} = \dfrac{\overset{4}{\cancel{8}}}{\underset{3}{\cancel{9}}} \times \dfrac{\overset{1}{\cancel{3}}}{\underset{5}{\cancel{10}}} = \dfrac{4}{15}$

b. $3\dfrac{1}{8} \times 1\dfrac{3}{4} = \dfrac{25}{8} \times \dfrac{7}{4}$

$\qquad = \dfrac{175}{32} = 5\dfrac{15}{32}$ $\longleftarrow$ Rewrite as a mixed number.

Divide. Write each answer in simplest form.

c. $\dfrac{2}{3} \div \dfrac{4}{5} = \dfrac{2}{3} \times \dfrac{5}{4}$

$\qquad = \dfrac{\overset{1}{\cancel{2}}}{3} \times \dfrac{5}{\underset{2}{\cancel{4}}} = \dfrac{5}{6}$

d. $3\dfrac{1}{8} \div 1\dfrac{3}{4} = \dfrac{25}{8} \div \dfrac{7}{4}$

$\qquad = \dfrac{25}{\underset{2}{\cancel{8}}} \times \dfrac{\overset{1}{\cancel{4}}}{7} = \dfrac{25}{14} = 1\dfrac{11}{14}$ $\longleftarrow$ Rewrite as a mixed number.

EXERCISES

Multiply. Write each answer in simplest form.

1. $\dfrac{3}{4} \times \dfrac{3}{5}$

2. $\dfrac{2}{3} \times \dfrac{3}{4}$

3. $6 \times \dfrac{2}{3}$

4. $\dfrac{3}{4} \times \dfrac{5}{6}$

5. $\dfrac{5}{8} \times \dfrac{2}{3}$

6. $\dfrac{9}{16} \times \dfrac{2}{3}$

7. $\dfrac{3}{10} \times \dfrac{2}{15}$

8. $\dfrac{3}{4} \times \dfrac{1}{6}$

9. $\dfrac{1}{4} \times \dfrac{5}{20}$

10. $\dfrac{9}{10} \times \dfrac{1}{3}$

11. $1\dfrac{1}{3} \times 2\dfrac{2}{3}$

12. $\dfrac{3}{5} \times 2\dfrac{3}{4}$

13. $2\dfrac{1}{4} \times 3\dfrac{1}{3}$

14. $\dfrac{1}{4} \times 3\dfrac{1}{3}$

15. $6\dfrac{1}{4} \times 7$

16. $1\dfrac{3}{4} \times 2\dfrac{1}{5}$

17. $2\dfrac{3}{4} \times \dfrac{1}{2}$

18. $3\dfrac{4}{5} \times 2\dfrac{1}{3}$

Divide. Write each answer in simplest form.

19. $\dfrac{5}{8} \div \dfrac{5}{7}$

20. $\dfrac{5}{7} \div \dfrac{5}{8}$

21. $\dfrac{3}{4} \div \dfrac{6}{11}$

22. $\dfrac{1}{9} \div \dfrac{1}{9}$

23. $\dfrac{1}{9} \div 9$

24. $\dfrac{9}{10} \div \dfrac{3}{5}$

25. $\dfrac{2}{3} \div \dfrac{1}{9}$

26. $\dfrac{4}{5} \div \dfrac{5}{6}$

27. $\dfrac{1}{5} \div \dfrac{8}{9}$

28. $\dfrac{7}{8} \div \dfrac{1}{3}$

29. $4\dfrac{1}{5} \div 2\dfrac{2}{5}$

30. $6\dfrac{1}{4} \div 4\dfrac{3}{8}$

31. $2\dfrac{1}{3} \div 5\dfrac{5}{6}$

32. $1\dfrac{1}{2} \div 4\dfrac{1}{2}$

33. $15\dfrac{2}{3} \div 1\dfrac{1}{3}$

34. $10\dfrac{1}{3} \div 2\dfrac{1}{5}$

35. $6\dfrac{1}{4} \div 1\dfrac{3}{4}$

36. $6\dfrac{2}{3} \div 3\dfrac{1}{8}$

Working With Integers

Quantities less than zero can be written using negative integers. For example, a temperature of 5 degrees below zero can be written as −5. Positive integers are used for quantities greater than zero.

① EXAMPLE

Write an integer for each situation.

a. **10 degrees above zero**
+10, or 10

b. **a loss of $20**
−20

c. **15 yards lost**
−15

A number line can be used to compare integers. The integer to the right is greater.

② EXAMPLE

Compare. Use >, <, or = to complete each statement.

a. **0 ■ −3**
0 is to the right, so it is greater.
0 > −3

b. **−2 ■ −6**
−2 is to the right, so it is greater.
−2 > −6

c. **−7 ■ 3**
−7 is to the left, so it is less.
−7 < 3

EXERCISES

Write an integer for each situation.

1. 6 yards gained
2. 10 yards lost
3. 5 steps forward
4. 4 steps backward
5. find $3
6. lose $8
7. 12 floors up
8. 4 floors down

Compare. Use >, <, or = to complete each statement.

9. 0 ■ −1
10. −9 ■ 0
11. −3 ■ 3
12. 7 ■ −3
13. 0 ■ 1
14. 3 ■ 0
15. 1 ■ −4
16. −2 ■ −9
17. 6 ■ −1
18. 3 ■ −10
19. −7 ■ 3
20. 4 ■ 6
21. −16 ■ −25
22. −15 ■ −12
23. 7 ■ −8
24. 2 ■ 3
25. −7 ■ −8
26. 35 ■ −40
27. −30 ■ −20
28. 25 ■ −25
29. 9 ■ −9
30. −6 ■ −5
31. −23 ■ −15
32. −17 ■ −19
33. −15 ■ −25

Table 1 Measures

Metric

Length

10 millimeters (mm) = 1 centimeter (cm)

100 cm = 1 meter (m)

1,000 m = 1 kilometer (km)

Area

100 square millimeters (mm^2) =
  1 square centimeter (cm^2)

10,000 cm^2 = 1 square meter (m^2)

1,000,000 m^2 = 1 square kilometer (km^2)

Volume

1,000 cubic millimeters (mm^3) =
  1 cubic centimeter (cm^3)

1,000,000 cm^3 = 1 cubic meter (m^3)

Mass

1,000 milligrams (mg) = 1 gram (g)

1,000 g = 1 kilogram (kg)

Volume (Capacity)

1,000 milliliters (mL) = 1 liter (L)

1 mL = 1 cm^3

Customary

Length

12 inches (in.) = 1 foot (ft)

3 ft = 1 yard (yd)

36 in. = 1 yd

5,280 ft = 1 mile (mi)

1,760 yd = 1 mi

Area

144 square inches (in.^{2}) = 1 square foot (ft^2)

9 ft^2 = 1 square yard (yd^2)

4,840 yd^2 = 1 acre

Volume

1,728 cubic inches (in.^{3}) = 1 cubic foot (ft^3)

27 ft^3 = 1 cubic yard (yd^3)

Weight

16 ounces (oz) = 1 pound (lb)

2,000 lb = 1 ton (t)

Volume (Capacity)

8 fluid ounces (fl oz) = 1 cup (c)

2 c = 1 pint (pt)

2 pt = 1 quart (qt)

4 qt = 1 gallon (gal)

Time

1 minute (min) = 60 seconds (s)

1 hour (h) = 60 min

1 day (d) = 24 h

1 year (yr) = 365 d

Table 2 📖 Reading Math Symbols

$>$	is greater than	p. 102
$<$	is less than	p. 102
$\geq$	is greater than or equal to	p. 102
$\leq$	is less than or equal to	p. 102
$=$	is equal to	p. 82
$\neq$	is not equal to	p. 82
$\approx$	is approximately equal to	p. 128
$\stackrel{?}{=}$	is this statement true?	p. 83
$+$	plus (addition)	p. 5
$-$	minus (subtraction)	p. 5
$\times, \cdot$	times (multiplication)	p. 5
$\div, \overline{)}$	divide (division)	p. 5
$\sqrt{x}$	nonnegative square root of x	p. 566
$^{\circ}$	degrees	p. 443
$\%$	percent	p. 306
$(\ )$	parentheses for grouping	p. 9
$\lvert a \rvert$	absolute value of a	p. 19
$a:b, \frac{a}{b}$	ratio of a to b	p. 284
(a, b)	ordered pair with x-coordinate a and y-coordinate b	p. 52
$\cong$	is congruent to	p. 443
$\sim$	is similar to	p. 295
$\parallel$	is parallel to	p. 437
π	pi, an irrational number approximately equal to 3.14	p. 464
b	y-intercept	p. 401
m	slope of a line	p. 401
$-a$	opposite of a	p. 19
$\frac{1}{a}$	reciprocal of a	p. 244
a^n	nth power of a	p. 178
d	diameter	p. 464
	distance	pp. 137, 579
A'	image of A, A prime	p. 476

A	Area	p. 500
b_1, b_2	base lengths of a trapezoid	p. 509
b	base length	p. 501
h	height	p. 501
p or P	perimeter	p. 138
ℓ	length	p. 138
	slant height	p. 534
w	width	p. 138
C	circumference	p. 464
S.A.	surface area	p. 527
L.A.	lateral area	p. 528
B	area of a base	p. 528
V	volume	p. 539
r	rate	p. 137
	radius	p. 465
$\overline{AB}$	segment AB	p. 436
$\overrightarrow{AB}$	ray AB	p. 436
$\overleftrightarrow{AB}$	line AB	p. 436
$\triangle ABC$	triangle with vertices A, B, and C	p. 295
$\angle A$	angle with vertex A	p. 443
$\angle ABC$	angle with sides $\overrightarrow{BA}$ and $\overrightarrow{BC}$	p. 443
$m\angle ABC$	measure of angle ABC	p. 443
AB	length of segment $\overline{AB}$	p. 436

Table 3 Squares and Square Roots

N	N^2	$\sqrt{N}$	N	N^2	$\sqrt{N}$
1	1	1	51	2,601	7.141
2	4	1.414	52	2,704	7.211
3	9	1.732	53	2,809	7.280
4	16	2	54	2,916	7.348
5	25	2.236	55	3,025	7.416
6	36	2.449	56	3,136	7.483
7	49	2.646	57	3,249	7.550
8	64	2.828	58	3,364	7.616
9	81	3	59	3,481	7.681
10	100	3.162	60	3,600	7.746
11	121	3.317	61	3,721	7.810
12	144	3.464	62	3,844	7.874
13	169	3.606	63	3,969	7.937
14	196	3.742	64	4,096	8
15	225	3.873	65	4,225	8.062
16	256	4	66	4,356	8.124
17	289	4.123	67	4,489	8.185
18	324	4.243	68	4,624	8.246
19	361	4.359	69	4,761	8.307
20	400	4.472	70	4,900	8.367
21	441	4.583	71	5,041	8.426
22	484	4.690	72	5,184	8.485
23	529	4.796	73	5,329	8.544
24	576	4.899	74	5,476	8.602
25	625	5	75	5,625	8.660
26	676	5.099	76	5,776	8.718
27	729	5.196	77	5,929	8.775
28	784	5.292	78	6,084	8.832
29	841	5.385	79	6,241	8.888
30	900	5.477	80	6,400	8.944
31	961	5.568	81	6,561	9
32	1,024	5.657	82	6,724	9.055
33	1,089	5.745	83	6,889	9.110
34	1,156	5.831	84	7,056	9.165
35	1,225	5.916	85	7,225	9.220
36	1,296	6	86	7,396	9.274
37	1,369	6.083	87	7,569	9.327
38	1,444	6.164	88	7,744	9.381
39	1,521	6.245	89	7,921	9.434
40	1,600	6.325	90	8,100	9.487
41	1,681	6.403	91	8,281	9.539
42	1,764	6.481	92	8,464	9.592
43	1,849	6.557	93	8,649	9.644
44	1,936	6.633	94	8,836	9.695
45	2,025	6.708	95	9,025	9.747
46	2,116	6.782	96	9,216	9.798
47	2,209	6.856	97	9,409	9.849
48	2,304	6.928	98	9,604	9.899
49	2,401	7	99	9,801	9.950
50	2,500	7.071	100	10,000	10

Formulas and Properties

Geometric Formulas

Perimeter and Circumference

Rectangle

$P = 2\ell + 2w$

Circle

$C = \pi d$ or $C = 2\pi r$

Area

Square

$A = s^2$

Parallelogram and Rectangle

$A = bh$

Triangle

$A = \frac{1}{2}bh$

Trapezoid

$A = \frac{1}{2}h(b_1 + b_2)$

Circle

$C = \pi r^2$

Triangle Formulas

Pythagorean Theorem

In a right triangle with legs of lengths a and b and hypotenuse of length c, $a^2 + b^2 = c^2$.

Triangle Angle Sum

For any $\triangle ABC$,

$m\angle A + m\angle B + m\angle C = 180°$.

Surface Area

Rectangular Prism

L.A. $= ph$

S.A. $=$ L.A. $+ 2B$

Cylinder

L.A. $= 2\pi rh$

S.A. $=$ L.A. $+ 2B$

Pyramid

L.A. $= \frac{1}{2}p\ell = n\left(\frac{1}{2}b\ell\right)$, where n is the number of faces

S.A. $=$ L.A. $+ B$

Cone

L.A. $= \pi r\ell$

S.A. $=$ L.A. $+ B$

Sphere

S.A. $= 4\pi r^2$

Volume

Prism

$V = Bh$

Cylinder

$V = Bh$, or $\pi r^2 h$

Pyramid

$V = \frac{1}{3}Bh$

Cone

$V = \frac{1}{3}Bh$, or $\frac{1}{3}\pi r^2 h$

Sphere

$V = \frac{4}{3}\pi r^3$

Properties of Real Numbers

Unless otherwise stated, $a, b, c,$ and d are real numbers.

Identity Properties

Addition $a + 0 = a$ and $0 + a = a$

Multiplication $a \cdot 1 = a$ and $1 \cdot a = a$

Commutative Properties

Addition $a + b = b + a$

Multiplication $a \cdot b = b \cdot a$

Associative Properties

Addition $(a + b) + c = a + (b + c)$

Multiplication $(a \cdot b) \cdot c = a \cdot (b \cdot c)$

Inverse Properties

Addition

$a + (-a) = 0$ and $-a + a = 0$

Multiplication

$a \cdot \frac{1}{a} = 1$ and $\frac{1}{a} \cdot a = 1 (a \neq 0)$

Distributive Properties

$a(b + c) = ab + ac \qquad (b + c)a = ba + ca$

$a(b - c) = ab - ac \qquad (b - c)a = ba - ca$

Properties of Equality

Addition If $a = b$, then $a + c = b + c$.

Subtraction If $a = b$, then $a - c = b - c$.

Multiplication If $a = b$, then $a \cdot c = b \cdot c$.

Division If $a = b$, and $c \neq 0$, then $\frac{a}{c} = \frac{b}{c}$.

Substitution If $a = b$, then b can replace a in any expression.

Reflexive $a = a$

Symmetric If $a = b$, then $b = a$.

Transitive If $a = b$ and $b = c$, then $a = c$.

Zero-Product Property

If $ab = 0$ then $a = 0$ or $b = 0$.

Zero Property of Multiplication

$a \cdot 0 = 0 \cdot a = 0$

Cross Product Property

$\frac{a}{b} = \frac{c}{d}$ is equivalent to $ad = bc$.

Closure Properties

$a + b$ is a unique real number.

ab is a unique real number.

Density Property

Between any two rational numbers, there is at least one other rational number.

Properties of Inequality

Addition If $a > b$, then $a + c > b + c$.
If $a < b$, then $a + c < b + c$.

Subtraction If $a > b$, then $a - c > b - c$.
If $a < b$, then $a - c < b - c$.

Multiplication

If $a > b$ and $c > 0$, then $ac > bc$.

If $a < b$ and $c > 0$, then $ac < bc$.

If $a > b$ and $c < 0$, then $ac < bc$.

If $a < b$ and $c < 0$, then $ac > bc$.

Division

If $a > b$ and $c > 0$, then $\frac{a}{c} > \frac{b}{c}$.

If $a < b$ and $c > 0$, then $\frac{a}{c} < \frac{b}{c}$.

If $a > b$ and $c < 0$, then $\frac{a}{c} < \frac{b}{c}$.

If $a < b$ and $c < 0$, then $\frac{a}{c} > \frac{b}{c}$.

Transitive If $a > b$ and $b > c$, then $a > c$.

Comparison If $a = b + c$ and $c > 0$, then $a > b$.

Properties of Exponents

For $a \neq 0$ and any integers m and n:

Zero Exponent $a^0 = 1$

Negative Exponent $a^{-n} = \frac{1}{a^n}$

Product of Powers $a^m \cdot a^n = a^{m+n}$

Quotient of Powers $\frac{a^m}{a^n} = a^{m-n}$

Power of a Power $(a^m)^n = a^{m \cdot n}$

English/Spanish Illustrated Glossary

Absolute value (p. 19)   Absolute value is the distance of a number from zero on a number line. You write *the absolute value* of -3 as $|-3|$.

The absolute value of -3 is 3 because -3 is 3 units from zero on a number line.

Valor absoluto (p. 19)   El valor absoluto de un número es la distancia desde cero hasta ese número en una recta numérica. Escribe "el valor absoluto de -3" como $|-3|$.

Acute angle (p. 443)   An acute angle is an angle with a measure less than 90°.
EXAMPLE $0° < m\angle 1 < 90°$

Ángulo agudo (p. 443)   Un ángulo agudo es cualquier ángulo que mide menos de 90°.

Acute triangle (p. 448)   An acute triangle is a triangle with three acute angles.
EXAMPLE $\angle 1, \angle 2,$ and $\angle 3$ are acute.

Acutángulo (p. 448)   Acutángulo es un triángulo que tiene tres ángulos agudos.

Addition Property of Equality (p. 90)   If $a = b$ then $a + c = b + c$.

$8 = 2(4),$ so $8 + 3 = 2(4) + 3$

Propiedad aditiva de la igualdad (p. 90)   Si $a = b$, entonces $a + c = b + c$.

Addition Property of Inequality (p. 107)   If $a > b$, then $a + c > b + c$. If $a < b$, then $a + c < b + c$.

$7 > 3,$ so $7 + 4 > 3 + 4$
$2 < 5,$ so $2 + 6 < 5 + 6$

Propiedad aditiva de la desigualdad (p. 107)   Si $a > b$, entonces $a + c > b + c$. Si $a < b$, entonces $a + c < b + c$.

Additive identity (p. 69)   The additive identity is zero. When you add a number and 0, the sum equals the original number.

$a + 0 = a$

Identidad aditiva (p. 69)   La identidad aditiva es cero. Cuando se suman un número y 0, la suma es idéntica al número original.

Additive inverses (p. 24)   Additive inverses are two numbers with a sum of zero.

23 and -23 are additive inverses because $-23 + 23 = 0$.

Inversos aditivos (p. 24)   Se llaman inversos aditivos a los números cuya suma es igual a cero.

Adjacent angles (p. 443)   Adjacent angles are two angles that share a vertex and a side but no points in their interiors.

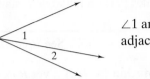

$\angle 1$ and $\angle 2$ are adjacent angles.

Ángulos adyacentes (p. 443)   Ángulos adyacentes son dos ángulos que tienen un mismo vértice y un lado común, pero no tienen puntos interiores comunes.

Algebraic expression (p. 4)   An algebraic expression is a mathematical phrase that uses variables, numbers, and operation symbols.

$7 + x, 2y - 4, \frac{3}{5}z$, and $\frac{7}{k}$ are algebraic expressions.

Expresión algebraica (p. 4)   Una expresión algebraica es un enunciado matemático en el cual intervienen variables, números, y símbolos de operaciones.

Alternate interior angles (p. 444)   Alternate interior angles are angles between two lines and on opposite sides of a transversal.

EXAMPLE $\angle 2$ and $\angle 3$ are alternate interior angles. $\angle 1$ and $\angle 4$ are also alternate interior angles.

Ángulos alternos internos (p. 444)   Ángulos alternos internos son los pares de ángulos no adyacentes, ambos interiores, en lados opuestos de una transversal.

Altitude (p. 501)   An altitude is any segment perpendicular to the line containing the base of a figure, and drawn from the side opposite the base.

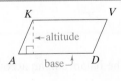

Altura (p. 501)   La altura es cualquier segmento perpendicular a la recta de la base de la figura y se dibuja desde el lado opuesto a la base.

Angle (p. 443)   An angle is a figure formed by two rays with a common endpoint.

EXAMPLE $\angle 1$ is made up of $\overrightarrow{GP}$ and $\overrightarrow{GS}$ with common endpoint G.

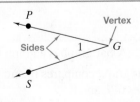

Ángulo (p. 443)   Un ángulo es una figura formada por dos rayos que parten de un origen común.

Angle bisector (p. 472)   An angle bisector is a ray that divides a given angle into two congruent angles, each half the size of the given angle.

EXAMPLE $\overrightarrow{BD}$ is the angle bisector of $\angle ABC$.

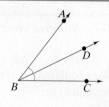

Bisectriz de un ángulo (p. 472)   La bisectriz de un ángulo es el rayo que divide un ángulo dado en dos ángulos congruentes, cada uno de los cuales tiene la mitad de tamaño que el ángulo dado.

Angle of rotation (p. 486)   See *Rotation*.

Ángulo de rotación (p. 486)   Ver *Rotation*.

Arc (p. 469)   An arc is part of a circle.

Arco (p. 469)   Un arco es una parte de la circunferencia de un círculo.

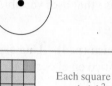

Area (p. 500)   The area of a figure is the number of square units it encloses.

EXAMPLE $b = 4$ ft and $h = 6$ ft, so the area is 24 ft^2.

Área (p. 500)   El área de una figura es el número de unidades cuadradas en su interior.

Each square equals 1 ft^2.

Associative Properties of Addition and Multiplication (p. 68)
For any numbers $a, b,$ and $c, (a + b) + c = a + (b + c)$ and $(ab)c = a(bc)$.

$(2 + 7) + 3 = 2 + (7 + 3)$
$(9 \cdot 4)5 = 9(4 \cdot 5)$

Propiedad asociativa de la suma y de la multiplicación (p. 68)   Para cualesquiera números a, b y $c, (a + b) + c = a + (b + c)$ y $(ab)c = a(bc)$.

B

Balance (p. 372)   The balance in an account is the principal plus the earned interest.

See *Compound interest*.

Balance (p. 372)   El balance de una cuenta es el capital más el interés ganado.

Bar graph (p. 51)   A bar graph is a graph that compares amounts.

EXAMPLE This bar graph compares the numbers of students in grades 6, 7, and 8.

Gráfica de barras (p. 51)   Una gráfica de barras es una gráfica que compara cantidades.

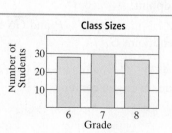

Base (p. 178)   The base is the repeated factor of a number written in exponential form.

$5^4 = 5 \cdot 5 \cdot 5 \cdot 5$
5 is the base.

Base (p. 178)   La base es el factor repetido de un número que se escribe en forma exponencial.

Bases of three-dimensional figures (p. 519)   See *Cone, Cylinder, Prism,* and *Pyramid.*

Bases de figuras tridimensionales (p. 519)   Ver *Cone, Cylinder, Prism* y *Pyramid.*

Bases of two-dimensional figures (pp. 501, 507)   See *Parallelogram, Triangle,* and *Trapezoid.*

Bases de figuras bidimensionales (pp. 501, 507)   Ver *Parallelogram, Triangle,* y *Trapezoid.*

Box-and-whisker plot (p. 617)   A box-and-whisker plot is a graph that shows the distribution of data along a number line. Quartiles divide the data into four equal parts.

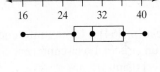

EXAMPLE   The box-and-whisker plot at the right is for the data
16 19 26 27 27 29 30 31 34 35 37 39 40.

The lower quartile is 26.5. The median is 30. The upper quartile is 36.

Gráfica de caja y brazos (p. 617)   Una gráfica de caja y brazos presenta la distribución de datos en una recta numérica. Los cuartiles dividen los datos en cuatro partes iguales.

Center of rotation (p. 486)   See *Rotation.*

Centro de rotación (p. 486)   Ver *Rotation.*

Central angle (p. 465)   A central angle is an angle whose vertex is the center of a circle.

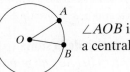

$\angle AOB$ is a central angle.

Ángulo central (p. 465)   Un ángulo central es un ángulo cuyo vértice está en el centro del círculo.

Chord (p. 464)   A chord of a circle is a segment whose endpoints are on the circle.

EXAMPLE $\overline{AB}$ is a chord of circle O.

Cuerda (p. 464)   Una cuerda es un segmento cuyos extremos se hallan en un círculo.

English/Spanish Glossary

Circle (p. 464) A circle is the set of all points in a plane that are equidistant from a given point, called the center.

EXAMPLE Circle O

Círculo (p. 464) Un círculo es un conjunto de puntos en un plano que se hallan a la misma distancia de un punto dado llamado el centro.

$O \bullet \leftarrow$ ─── Center

Circle graph (p. 465) A circle graph is a graph that represents parts of a whole. The total must be 100% or 1.

EXAMPLE This circle graph represents the different types of plays that William Shakespeare wrote.

Gráfica circular (p. 465) Una gráfica circular es la gráfica que representa partes de un todo. El total debe ser cien por ciénto o uno.

Shakespeare's Plays

Histories 26% — Tragedies 26%
Romances 13% — Comedies 35%

Circumference (p. 464) Circumference is the distance around a circle. You calculate the circumference of a circle by multiplying the diameter by π.

Circunferencia (p. 464) La circunferencia es la distancia alrededor de un círculo. La circunferencia de un círculo se calcula multiplicando el diámetro por π.

10 cm   about 31.4 cm
O

The circumference of the circle is 10π cm, or approximately 31.4 cm.

Coefficient (p. 78) A coefficient is a number that multiplies a variable.

Coeficiente (p. 78) Un coeficiente es el número que multiplica una variable.

In the expression $2x + 3y - 16$, 2 is the coefficient of x and 3 is the coefficient of y.

Commission (p. 312) Commission is pay that is equal to a percent of sales.

Comisión (p. 312) Una comisión es un pago que equivale a un porcentaje de las ventas.

A saleswoman received a 5% commission on sales of $120. Her commission was $6.

Commutative Properties of Addition and Multiplication (p. 68) For any numbers a and b, $a + b = b + a$ and $ab = ba$.

Propiedad conmutativa de la suma (p. 68) Para cualquier número a y b, $a + b = b + a$, y $ab = ba$.

$6 + 4 = 4 + 6$
$9 \cdot 5 = 5 \cdot 9$

Compass (p. 470) A compass is a geometric tool used to draw circles and arcs.

Compás (p. 470) Un compás es un instrumento de geometría que se emplea para trazar círculos y arcos.

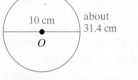

Compatible numbers (p. 133)   Compatible numbers are numbers that are close in value to the numbers you want to add, subtract, multiply, or divide, and for which the operation is easy to perform mentally. Estimating sums, differences, products, and quotients is easy to do mentally when you use compatible numbers.

Estimate $151 \div 14.6$.

$151 \approx 150$

$14.6 \approx 15$

$150 \div 15 = 10$

$151 \div 14.6 \approx 10$

For $155 \div 14.6$, 150 and 15 are compatible numbers.

Números compatibles (p. 133)   Los números compatibles son aquéllos con un valor cercano a los números que deseas sumar, restar, multiplicar o dividir, y con los cuales es fácil hacer los cálculos mentalmente. Cuando calculas sumas, diferencias, productos y cocientes, te resulta más fácil utilizar números compatibles.

Complementary angles (p. 443)   Complementary angles are two angles whose measures add to 90°.

EXAMPLE $\angle BCA$ and $\angle CAB$ are complementary angles.

Ángulos complementarios (p. 443)   Dos ángulos son complementarios cuando la suma de sus medidas es 90°.

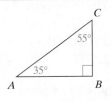

Composite number (p. 182)   A composite number is an integer greater than 1 with more than two positive factors.

24 is a composite number that has 1, 2, 3, 4, 6, 8, 12, and 24 as factors.

Número compuesto (p. 182)   Un número compuesto es el número entero mayor que uno, que tiene más de dos factores positivos.

Compound interest (p. 372)   Compound interest is interest paid on both the principal and the interest earned in previous interest periods. You can use the formula $B = p(1 + r)^n$ where B is the final balance, p is the principal, r is the interest rate for each interest period, and n is the number of interest periods.

You deposit $500 in an account earning 5% annual compound interest. The balance after six years is $500(1 + 0.05)^6$, or $670.05. The compound interest is $670.05 - 500$, or $170.05.

Interés compuesto (p. 372)   Interés compuesto es el interés pagado sobre el principal y sobre el interés ganado en previos períodos de interés. Para calcular el interés compuesto, se puede usar la formula $B = p(1 + r)^n$, en donde B es el balance en la cuenta, p es el principal, r es la tasa de interés para cada período y n es el número de períodos de interés.

Cone (p. 519)   A cone is a space figure with one circular base and one vertex.

Cono (p. 519)   Un cono es una figura tridimensional con una base circular y un vértice.

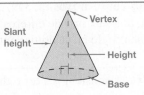

Congruent angles (p. 443)   Congruent angles are angles that have the same measure.

EXAMPLE $\angle B \cong \angle C$

Ángulos congruentes (p. 443)   Ángulos congruentes son los ángulos que tienen la misma medida.

Congruent figures (p. 458)   Congruent figures are figures that have the same size and shape. Congruent polygons have congruent corresponding sides and congruent corresponding angles. The symbol $\cong$ means "is congruent to."

EXAMPLE $\overline{AB} \cong \overline{QS}$, $\overline{BC} \cong \overline{SR}$, and $\overline{AC} \cong \overline{QR}$.
   $\angle A \cong \angle Q$, $\angle B \cong \angle S$, and $\angle C \cong \angle R$.
   Triangles ABC and QSR are congruent.
   $\triangle ABC \cong \triangle QSR$

Figuras congruentes (p. 458)   Figuras congruentes son las figuras que tienen el mismo tamaño y la misma forma. Los polígonos congruentes tienen lados correspondientes congruentes y ángulos correspondientes congruentes. El símbolo $\cong$ significa "es congruente con."

Congruent segments (p. 470)   Congruent segments are segments that have the same length.

Segmentos congruentes (p. 470)   Segmentos congruentes son aquéllos que tienen la misma longitud.

$$\overline{AB} \cong \overline{WX}$$

Conjecture (p. 35)   A conjecture is a conclusion reached through inductive reasoning.

Conjectura (p. 35)   Una conjetura es una conclusión obtenida usando el razonamiento inductivo.

A dropped piece of toast always lands with its buttered side down.

Consecutive integers (p. 349)   Consecutive integers are a sequence of integers obtained by counting by ones from any integer.

Numeros enteros consecutivos (p. 349)   Los números enteros consecutivos son una sucesión de enteros que se obtiene al contar en unidades comenzando en cualquier entero.

Three consecutive integers are $-5, -4,$ and -3.

Constant (p. 78)   A constant is a term that has no variable.

Constante (p. 78)   Constante es un término que no tiene variable.

In the expression $4x - 13y + 17$, 17 is the constant.

Constant of variation (p. 405)   The constant of variation is the nonzero constant k in the direct variation function $y = kx$.

Constante de variación (p. 405)   Una constante de variación es la constante k, no igual a 0, en la variación directa, $y = kx$.

In the direct variation $y = 2x$, 2 is the constant of variation.

Coordinate plane (p. 52) The coordinate plane is the plane formed by two number lines that intersect at their zero points. The horizontal number line is called the *x*-axis. The vertical number line is called the *y*-axis. The two axes meet at the origin, $O(0, 0)$, and divide the coordinate plane into four quadrants.

Plano de coordenadas (p. 52) El plano de coordenadas está formado por la intersección de una recta numérica horizontal, llamada el eje de *x*, y una recta numérica vertical, llamada el eje de *y*. Los dos ejes se intersecan en el origen, $O(0, 0)$, y divide el plano de coordenadas en cuatro cuadrantes.

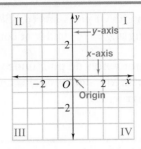

Coordinates (p. 52) Coordinates are ordered pairs (x, y) that identify points in a coordinate plane. The *x*-coordinate (the first coordinate) shows the horizontal position. The *y*-coordinate (the second coordinate) shows the vertical position.

Coordenadas (p. 52) Las coordenadas son pares ordenados (x, y), que identifican puntos en el plano de coordenadas. La coordenada *x*, (la primera coordenada) muestra la posición horizontal. La coordenada *y* (la segunda coordenada) muestra la posición vertical.

The ordered pair $(-2, 1)$ describes the point that is found by moving 2 units to the left from the origin and one unit up from the *x*-axis.

Correlation (p. 429) A correlation is a relation between two sets of data. The data have a *positive correlation* if, as one set of values increases, the other set tends to increase. The data have a *negative correlation* if, as one set of values increases, the other set tends to decrease. The data have little or *no correlation* if the values show no relationship.

Correlación (p. 429) Una correlación es la relación que hay entre dos conjuntos de datos. Los datos tienen una *correlación positiva* si, a medida que aumenta un conjunto de valores, el otro conjunto tiende a aumentar. Los datos tienen una *correlación negativa* si, a medida que aumenta un conjunto de valores, el otro conjunto tiende a disminuir. Los datos tienen correlación débil o *no tienen correlación* si los valores no muestran relación entre ellos.

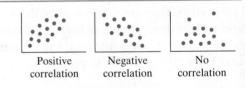

Positive correlation   Negative correlation   No correlation

Corresponding angles (p. 470) Corresponding angles are pairs of nonadjacent angles that lie on the same side of a transversal of two lines and in corresponding positions.

EXAMPLE $\angle 1$ and $\angle 3$ are corresponding angles.
$\angle 2$ and $\angle 4$ are corresponding angles.

Ángulos correspondientes (p. 470) Ángulos correspondientes son los pares de ángulos no adyacentes, uno interior y el otro exterior, en el mismo lado de la transversal.

Corresponding angles of polygons (p. 458) Corresponding angles are matching angles of similar or congruent figures.

Ángulos correspondientes de polígonos (p. 458) Ángulos correspondientes son los ángulos equivalentes de figuras semenjantes o congruentes.

Corresponding
angles of
similar trapezoids

Corresponding
angles of
congruent triangles

Corresponding sides of polygons (p. 458) Corresponding sides are matching sides of similar or congruent figures.

Lados correspondientes de polígonos (p. 458) Lados correspondientes son los lados equivalentes de figuras semejantes o congruentes.

Corresponding
sides of
similar polygons

Corresponding
sides of
congruent triangles

Counterexample (p. 37) A counterexample is an example that proves a statement false.

Contraejemplo (p. 37) Contraejemplo es todo ejemplo que pruebe la falsedad de un enunciado.

Statement: Motor vehicles have four wheels.

Counterexample: A motorcycle is a motor vehicle with two wheels.

Cross products (p. 290) Cross products are products formed from a proportion. They are the product of the numerator of the first ratio and the denominator of the second ratio, and the product of the denominator of the first ratio and the numerator of the second ratio. For a proportion, these products are equal.

Productos cruzados (p. 290) Los productos cruzados son los productos formados a partir de una proporción. Son el producto del numerador de la primera razón y del denominador de la segunda razón, y el producto del denominador de la primera razón y del numerador de la segunda razón. Para una proporción, estos productos son iguales.

The cross products for the proportion $\frac{3}{4} = \frac{6}{8}$ are $3 \cdot 8$ and $4 \cdot 6$.
$3 \cdot 8 = 24$ and $4 \cdot 6 = 24$.

Cross section (p. 524) A cross section is the intersection of a plane and a space figure.

Sección de corte (p. 524) Una sección de corte es la intersección de un plano y una figura tridimensional.

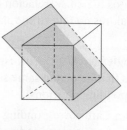

Cube (p. 520) A cube is rectangular prism with six congruent faces.

Cubo (p. 520) Un cubo es un prisma rectangular con seis caras congruentes.

Face

Cube root (p. 569)   The cube root of a given number is a number whose third power is the given number. The symbol for the cube root of a number is $\sqrt[3]{}$.

$\sqrt[3]{8} = 2$ because $2^3 = 8$.
$\sqrt[3]{-8} = -2$ because $(-2)^3 = -8$.

Raíz cúbica (p. 569)   La raíz cúbica de un número dado es un número cuya tercera potencia es el número dado. El símbolo de la raíz cúbica de un número es $\sqrt[3]{}$.

Cubic function (p. 592)   A cubic function is a function based on cubing the input variable.

$y = 5x^3$

Función cúbica (p. 592)   Una función cúbica es una función en la cual la mayor potencia de la variable es 3.

Cubic unit (p. 539)   A cubic unit is the amount of space occupied by a cube with edges one unit long.

Unidad cúbica (p. 539)   Una unidad cúbica es el espacio que ocupa un cubo cuyos lados tienen una unidad de longitud.

Cylinder (p. 519)   A cylinder is a space figure with two circular, parallel, and congruent bases.

Cilindro (p. 519)   Un cilindro es una figura tridimensional con dos bases circulares, paralelas y congruentes.

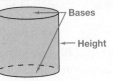

D

Decagon (p. 452)   A decagon is a polygon with ten sides.

See *Polygon*.

Decágono (p. 452)   Un decágono es un polígono que tiene diez lados.

Deductive reasoning (p. 57)   Deductive reasoning is the process of reasoning logically from given facts to a conclusion.

EXAMPLE Deductive reasoning is used to simplify the expression $4c + 3(3 + c)$.

$$4c + 3(3 + c) = 4c + 9 + 3c$$
$$= 4c + 3c + 9$$
$$= (4 + 3)c + 9$$
$$= 7c + 9$$

Razonamiento deductivo (p. 57)   El razonamiento deductivo es el proceso de razonar lógicamente para llegar a una conclusión a partir de datos dados.

Diagonal (p. 453)   A diagonal of a polygon is a segment that connects two nonconsecutive vertices.

Diagonal (p. 453)   Una diagonal de un polígono es un segmento que conecta dos vértices no consecutivos.

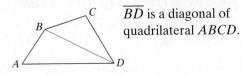

$\overline{BD}$ is a diagonal of quadrilateral $ABCD$.

English/Spanish Glossary

Diameter (p. 464)   A diameter of a circle is a chord that passes through the center of the circle.
EXAMPLE $\overline{RS}$ is a diameter of circle O.

Diámetro (p. 464)   Un diámetro de un círculo es una cuerda que pasa a través del centro de un círculo.

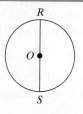

Dilation (p. 300)   A dilation is a transformation that results in a size change. The scale factor, r, describes the size of the change from the original figure to its image. If $r > 1$, the dilation is an enlargement. If r is positive and $r < 1$, the dilation is a reduction.

Dilatación (p. 300)   Una dilatación es una transformación que da como resultado un cambio de tamaño. El factor de escala r describe el tamaño del cambio de la figura original a su reproducción. Si $r > 1$, la dilatación es un agrandamiento. Si $r < 1$, la dilatación es una reducción.

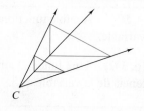

The blue triangle is an enlargement of the red triangle. The red triangle is a reduction of the blue triangle.

Dimensional analysis (p. 248)   Dimensional analysis is a method of manipulating units in a calculation to determine the units of the result.

Análisis dimensional (p. 248)   Análisis dimensional es el proceso de analizar las unidades en un cálculo para determinar las unidades del resultado.

$$\frac{225 \text{ mi}}{1 \text{ h}} \cdot \frac{1 \text{ h}}{3{,}600 \text{ s}} \cdot \frac{5{,}280 \text{ ft}}{1 \text{ mi}} = 330 \text{ ft/s}$$

Direct variation (p. 405)   A direct variation is a linear function modeled by the equation $y = kx$, where $k \neq 0$.

Variación directa (p. 405)   Una variación directa es una función lineal $y = kx$, en la cual $k \neq 0$.

$y = 16x$

Discount (p. 320)   A discount is the amount by which a price is decreased.

Descuento (p. 320)   Descuento es la cantidad en la cual un precio es reducido.

The price of a $10 book is reduced by a discount of $1.50 to sell for $8.50.

Distance Formula (p. 579)   The distance d between any two points (x_1, y_1) and (x_2, y_2) is $d = \sqrt{(x_2 - x_1)^2 + (y_2 - y_1)^2}$.

Fórmula de distancia (p. 579)   La distancia d entre cualesquiera dos puntos (x_1, y_1) y (x_2, y_2) es $d = \sqrt{(x_2 - x_1)^2 + (y_2 - y_1)^2}$.

The distance between $(6, 3)$ and $(1, 9)$ is d:

$$d = \sqrt{(1 - 6)^2 + (9 - 3)^2}$$
$$= \sqrt{(-5)^2 + 6^2}$$
$$= \sqrt{61}$$
$$\approx 7.8$$

Distributive Property (p. 73)   For any numbers a, b, and c, $a(b + c) = ab + ac$ and $a(b - c) = ab - ac$.

$$2\left(3 + \tfrac{1}{2}\right) = 2 \cdot 3 + 2 \cdot \tfrac{1}{2}$$
$$8(5 - 3) = 8(5) - 8(3)$$

Propiedad distributiva (p. 73)   Para cualquier número a, b y c, $a(b + c) = ab + ac$ y $a(b - c) = ab - ac$

Divisible (p. 172)   Divisible means that the remainder is 0 when you divide one integer by another.

15 is divisible by 5 because $15 \div 5 = 3$ with remainder 0.

Divisible (p. 172)   Un número entero es divisible por otro número si el residuo es cero.

Division Property of Equality (p. 94)   If $a = b$ and $c \neq 0$, then $\dfrac{a}{c} = \dfrac{b}{c}$.

$6 = 3(2)$, so $\dfrac{6}{3} = \dfrac{3(2)}{3}$

Propiedad de igualdad en la división (p. 94)   Si $a = b$ y $c \neq 0$, entonces $\dfrac{a}{c} = \dfrac{b}{c}$.

Division Properties of Inequality (p. 110)   If $a < b$ and c is positive, then $\dfrac{a}{c} < \dfrac{b}{c}$. If $a > b$ and c is positive, then $\dfrac{a}{c} > \dfrac{b}{c}$.

If you divide each side of an inequality by a negative number, you reverse the inequality symbol.

If $a < b$ and c is negative, then $\dfrac{a}{c} > \dfrac{b}{c}$.

If $a > b$ and c is negative, then $\dfrac{a}{c} < \dfrac{b}{c}$.

$3 < 6$, so $\dfrac{3}{3} < \dfrac{6}{3}$

$8 > 2$, so $\dfrac{8}{2} > \dfrac{2}{2}$

$6 < 12$, so $\dfrac{6}{-3} > \dfrac{12}{-3}$

$16 > 8$, so $\dfrac{16}{-4} < \dfrac{8}{-4}$

Propiedad de división de la desigualdad (p. 110)   Si $a < b$ y c es positivo, entonces $\dfrac{a}{c} < \dfrac{b}{c}$. Si $a > b$ y c es positivo, entonces $\dfrac{a}{c} > \dfrac{b}{c}$. Si se divide cada lado de una desigualdad por un número negativo, se invierte la dirección del símbolo de desigualdad.

Si $a < b$, y c es negativo, entonces $\dfrac{a}{c} > \dfrac{b}{c}$.

Si $a > b$, y c es negativo, entonces $\dfrac{a}{c} < \dfrac{b}{c}$.

Domain (p. 388)   A domain is the set of first coordinates of the ordered pairs of a relation.

In the relation $\{(0, 1), (-3, 2), (0, 2)\}$, the domain is $\{0, -3\}$.

Dominio (p. 388)   Un dominio es el conjunto que comprende todas las primeras coordenadas de los pares ordenados de una relación.

E

Edge (p. 519)   An edge is the intersection of two faces of a space figure.

Arista (p. 519)   Un arista es el segmento en donde se intersecan dos caras de una figura tridimensional.

English/Spanish Glossary

Equation (p. 82)   An equation is a mathematical sentence with an equal sign, =. An equation says that the side to the left of the equal sign has the same value as the side to the right of the equal sign.

$2(6 + 17) = 46$

Ecuación (p. 82)   Una ecuación es un enunciado matemático que contiene un signo igual, =. Una ecuacíon dice que el lado izquierdo del signo igual tiene el mismo valor que el lado derecho del signo igual.

Equilateral triangle (p. 448)   An equilateral triangle is a triangle with three congruent sides.

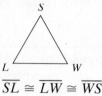

Triángulo equilátero (p. 448)   Un triángulo es equilátero cuando sus tres lados son congruentes.

$\overline{SL} \cong \overline{LW} \cong \overline{WS}$

Equivalent fractions (p. 188)   Equivalent fractions are fractions that describe the same part of a whole.

$\frac{3}{4}$ and $\frac{6}{8}$

Fracciones equivalentes (p. 188)   Fracciones equivalentes son fracciones que describen la misma parte de un todo.

Evaluate an expression (p. 14)   To evaluate an expression is to replace each variable with a number, and then follow the order of operations.

To evaluate the expression $3x + 2$ for $x = 4$, substitute 4 for x.
$3x + 2 = 3(4) + 2 = 12 + 2 = 14$

Evaluación de una expresión (p. 14)   Una expresión se evalúa, sustituyendo cada variable con un número. Luego se sigue el órden de las operaciones.

Exponent (p. 178)   An exponent is a number that shows how many times a base is used as a factor.

$3^4 = 3 \cdot 3 \cdot 3 \cdot 3$
4 is the exponent.

Exponente (p. 178)   Un exponente es un número que indica las veces que una base se usa como factor.

Face (p. 519)   A face is a surface of a space figure.

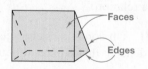

Cara (p. 519)   Cara es la superficie plana de una figura tridimensional.

Factor (p. 173)   A factor of a nonzero integer is an integer that divides the nonzero integer with remainder zero.

1, 2, 3, 4, 6, 9, 12, 18, and 36 are factors of 36.

Factor (p. 173)   Un número entero es factor de otro número entero distinto de cero, cuando lo divide y el residuo es cero.

Formula (p. 137)   A formula is an equation that shows a relationship between quantities that are represented by variables.

Fórmula (p. 137)   Una fórmula es una ecuación que muestra una relación entre las cantidades que representan las variables.

The formula $P = 4s$ gives the perimeter of a square in terms of the length s of a side.

Frequency table (p. 612)   A frequency table is a list of items that shows the number of times, or frequency, with which they occur.

EXAMPLE   This frequency table shows the number of household telephones for the students in one school class.

Tabla de frecuencia (p. 612)   Una tabla de frecuencia registra el número de veces, o frecuencia, con que se ha producido un determinado tipo de resultado.

Household Telephones

Phones	Tally	Frequency
1	卌 |||	8
2	卌		6
3						4

Front-end estimation (p. 128)   Front-end estimation is a way to estimate a sum. First add the front-end digits. Round to estimate the sum of the remaining digits. Then combine estimates.

Estimación por la izquierda (p. 128)   La estimación por la izquierda se emplea para estimar sumas. Primero, se suman los dígitos delanteros. Luego, se redondea para estimar la suma de los dígitos restantes. Por último se combinan las estimaciones.

Estimate $3.49 + $2.29.
$3 + 2 = 5$
$0.49 + 0.29 \approx 0.50 + 0.30 = 0.80$
$\$3.49 + \$2.29 \approx \$5 + \$0.80 = \$5.80$

Function (p. 388)   A function is a relationship in which each member of the domain is paired with exactly one member of the range. A number of the domain is an input and the related number of the range is an output.

Función (p. 388)   Una función es una relación en la que a cada miembro de un dominio le corresponde exactamente un miembro dominio. Un número del dominio es el valor de entrada y el número relacionado del dominio es el valor de salida.

Earned income is a function of the number of hours worked (n). If you earn $5/h, then your income is expressed by the function $f(n) = 5n$.

Greatest common divisor (GCD) (p. 183)   The greatest common divisor of two or more numbers is the greatest divisor that the numbers have in common.

Máximo común divisor (MCD) (p. 183)   El máximo común divisor de dos o más números es el mayor divisor que los números tienen en común.

The greatest common divisor (GCD) of 12 and 30 is 6.

Greatest common factor (GCF) (p. 183)   See *Greatest common divisor*.

Máximo común divisor (MCD) (p. 183)   Ver *Greatest common divisor*.

Greatest possible error (p. 252)   The greatest possible error of a measurement is half the unit used for measuring.

The measurement 400 kg is rounded to the nearest hundred kilograms. So, the greatest possible error is 50 kg.

Máximo error posible (p. 252)   El máximo error posible de una medida es la mitad de la unidad usada para medir.

▼ **H**

Height of a three-dimensional figure (pp. 528, 529, 548)
See *Cone*, *Cylinder*, *Prism*, and *Pyramid*.

Altura de figuras tridimensionales (pp. 528, 529, 548)
Ver *Cone*, *Cylinder*, *Prism* y *Pyramid*.

Height of a two-dimensional figure (pp. 501, 507, 509)
See *Parallelogram*, *Triangle*, and *Trapezoid*.

Altura de figuras bidimensionales (pp. 501, 507, 509)
Ver *Parallelogram*, *Triangle* y *Trapezoid*.

Hexagon (p. 450)   A hexagon is a polygon with six sides.

See *Polygon*.

Hexágono (p. 450)   Un hexágono es un polígono que tiene seis lados.

Histogram (p. 613)   A histogram is a bar graph in which the heights of the bars give the frequencies of the data. There are no spaces between bars.

EXAMPLE This histogram gives the frequencies of board-game purchases at a local toy store.

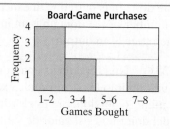

Histograma (p. 613)   Un histograma es una gráfica de barras en la cual la altura de las barras representa la frecuencia de los datos. No hay espacio entre las barras.

Hypotenuse (p. 570)   In a right triangle, the hypotenuse is the longest side, which is opposite the right angle.

See *Right triangle*.

Hipotenusa (p. 570)   La hipotenusa es el lado más largo de un triángulo rectángulo. Es el lado opuesto al ángulo recto.

▼ **I**

Identity Properties of Addition and Multiplication (p. 69)   For any number *a*, the sum of *a* and 0 is *a*. The product of *a* and 1 is 1.

$a + 0 = a$
$a \cdot 1 = a$

Propiedad de identidad de la suma y de la multiplicación (p. 69)
La suma de cero y cualquier número *a* es *a*. El producto de cualquier número *a* y uno es *a*.

Image (p. 476)   An image is the result of the transformation of a point, line, or figure to a new set of coordinates.

See *Transformation*.

Imagen (p. 476)   Una imagen es el resultado de la transformación de un punto, una recta o una figura a un nuevo conjunto de coordenadas.

Improper fraction (p. 238)   An improper fraction is a fraction with a numerator that is greater than or equal to the denominator.

$\frac{24}{15}$ and $\frac{16}{16}$ are improper fractions.

Fracción impropia (p. 238)   Una fracción impropia es una fracción cuyo numerador es mayor o igual que su denominador.

Indirect measurement (p. 296)   Indirect measurement is a method of determining length or distance without measuring directly.

EXAMPLE   By using the distances shown in the diagram and using properties of similar figures, you can find the height of the taller tower.

$$\frac{240}{540} = \frac{x}{1,192} \rightarrow x \approx 529.8 \text{ ft}$$

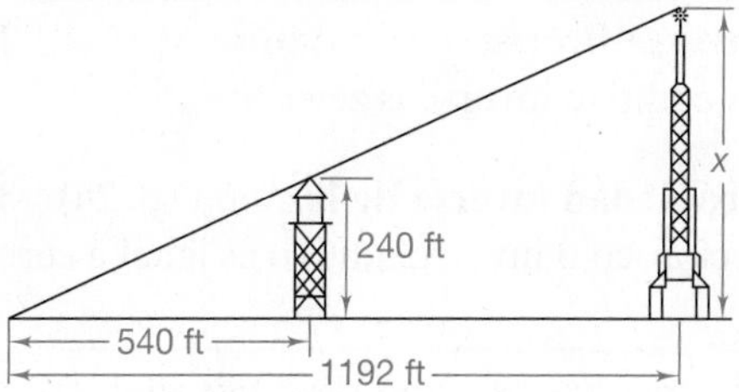

Medición indirecta (p. 296)   La medición indirecta es un método para determinar la longitud o distancia sin medir directamente.

Inductive reasoning (p. 35)   Inductive reasoning is making conclusions based on patterns you observe.

By inductive reasoning, the next number in the pattern 2, 4, 6, 8, . . . is 10.

Razonamiento inductivo (p. 35)   El razonamiento inductivo es sacar conclusiones a partir de patrones observados.

Inequality (p. 102)   An inequality is a sentence that uses one of the symbols $>, <, \geq, \leq,$ or $\neq$.

$0 \leq 2, k > -3, 10 < t$

Desigualdad (p. 102)   Una desigualdad es un enunciado que usa uno de los siguientes símbolos $>, <, \geq, \leq,$ o $\neq$.

Integer (p. 19)   Integers are the whole numbers and their opposites.

$-45, 0,$ and 289 are integers.

Números enteros (p. 19)   Los números enteros son el conjunto de los números enteros positivos (naturales) y sus opuestos.

Interest (p. 371)   See *Compound interest* and *Simple interest*.

Interés (p. 371)   Ver *Compound interest* y *Simple interest*.

Interest rate (p. 371)   An interest rate is the percentage of the balance that an account or investment earns in a fixed period of time.

A savings account pays $2\frac{1}{4}\%$ per year.

Tasa de interés (p. 371)   Una tasa de interés es el porcentaje del saldo que gana una cuenta o inversión durante un período fijo.

Inverse operations (p. 88)   Inverse operations are operations that undo each other.

Multiplication and division are inverse operations.

Operaciones inversas (p. 88)   Operaciones inversas son las operaciones que se cancelan una a la otra.

Inverse Property of Addition (p. 24)   The sum of an integer and its additive inverse is zero.

$17 + (-17) = 0$

Propiedad inversa de la suma (p. 24)   La suma de un número y su recíproco o inverso aditivo es igual a cero.

Inverse Property of Multiplication (p. 244)   The product of a nonzero rational number and its multiplicative inverse is 1.

$7 \cdot \left(\frac{1}{7}\right) = 1$

Propiedad inversa de la multiplicación (p. 244)   El producto de un número por su recíproco o inverso multiplicativo es igual a 1.

Irrational number (p. 567)   An irrational number is a number whose decimal form neither terminates nor repeats.

The number π, which is approximately equal to 3.141592654, is an irrational number.

Número irracional (p. 567)   Un número irracional es aquél cuyas cifras decimales son infinitas y no se repiten.

Isosceles triangle (p. 448)   An isosceles triangle is a triangle with at least two congruent sides.
EXAMPLE $\overline{LM} \cong \overline{LB}$
$\triangle MLB$ is an isosceles triangle.

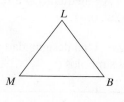

Triángulo isósceles (p. 448)   Un triángulo isósceles es aquel que tiene al menos dos lados congruentes.

L

Lateral area (p. 528)   The lateral area of a prism is the sum of the areas of the lateral faces.

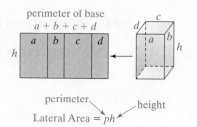

Área lateral (p. 528)   El área lateral de un prisma es la suma de las áreas de las caras laterales.

Lateral face (p. 519)   See *Prism* and *Pyramid*.

Cara lateral (p. 519)   Ver *Prism* y *Pyramid*.

Least common denominator (LCD) (p. 228)   The least common denominator of two or more fractions is the least common multiple (LCM) of their denominators.

Mínimo común denominador (MCD) (p. 228)   El mínimo común denominador de dos o más fracciones es el mínimo común múltiplo (mcm) de sus denominadores.

The least common denominator (LCD) of the fractions $\frac{3}{8}$ and $\frac{7}{10}$ is $2 \cdot 2 \cdot 2 \cdot 5$, or 40.

Least common multiple (LCM) (p. 226)   The least common multiple of two or more numbers is the least number that is a common multiple.

Mínimo común múltiplo (MCM) (p. 226)   El número menor que es múltiplo común de dos o más números es el mínimo común múltiplo.

The least common multiple (LCM) of 6 and 15 is $2 \cdot 3 \cdot 5$, or 30.

Legs of a right triangle (p. 570)   The legs of a right triangle are the two shorter sides of the triangle.

Catetos de un triángulo rectángulo (p. 570)   Los catetos de un triángulo rectángulo son los lados más cartos del triángulo.

See *Right triangle*.

Like terms (p. 78)   Like terms are terms with the same variable(s), raised to the same power(s).

EXAMPLE $3b$ and $12b$ are like terms. Like terms can be combined by using the Distributive Property.

Términos semejantes (p. 78)   Términos semejantes son aquellos que tienen la o las mismas variables elevadas a las mismas potencias.

$3b + 12b = (3 + 12)b$
$\qquad\quad\; = 15b$

Line (p. 436)   A line is a series of points that extends in opposite directions without end.

EXAMPLE $\overleftrightarrow{AB}, \overleftrightarrow{BA}$, or *n* represent a line.

Recta (p. 436)   Una recta es una serie de puntos que se extiende infinitamente en direcciones opuestas.

Line graph (p. 51)   A line graph is a graph that shows a relationship between two quantities.

EXAMPLE   This line graph shows the change in the number of listeners to station KLZR during the day.

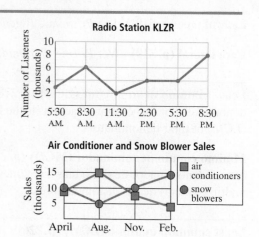

EXAMPLE   This multiple line graph represents seasonal air conditioner and snowblower sales (in thousands) for a large chain of stores.

Gráfica lineal (p. 51)   Una gráfica lineal representa la relación que existe entre dos cantidades.

Line of reflection (p. 483)   A line of reflection is a line across which a figure is reflected.

See *Reflection*.

Eje de reflexión (p. 483)   Un eje de reflexión es una recta sobre la cual una figura es reflejada.

Line of symmetry (p. 482)   A line of symmetry is a line that divides a figure with reflectional symmetry into two congruent halves.

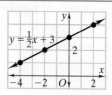

Eje de simetría (p. 482)   Un eje de simetría es una recta que divide una figura que tiene simetría de reflexión en dos mitades congruentes.

Line plot (p. 612)   A line plot is a graph that displays data by using X's above a number line.

EXAMPLE   This line plot shows the numbers of girls on a field hockey team who are at the indicated heights.

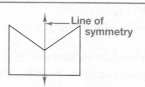

Diagrama de puntos (p. 612)   Un diagrama de puntos es una gráfica que muestra datos marcando una X sobre una recta numérica.

Linear equation (p. 394)   A linear equation is any equation whose graph is a line.

EXAMPLE $y = \frac{1}{2}x + 3$ is linear because its graph is a line.

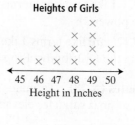

Ecuación lineal (p. 394)   Una ecuación lineal es cualquier ecuación cuya gráfica de todas sus soluciones es una recta.

Linear inequality (p. 420)   A linear inequality is a number sentence in which the equal sign of a linear equation is replaced with $>$, $<$, $\geq$, or $\leq$.

$$y \geq 2x + 3$$
$$y < -4x - 1$$

Desigualdad lineal (p. 420)   Una desigualdad lineal es una proposición numérica en la cual el signo igual de una ecuación lineal se reemplaza con un signo $>$, $<$, $\geq$ o $\leq$.

Lower quartile (p. 617)   The lower quartile is the median of the lower half of a data set.

See *Box-and-whisker plot.*

Cuartil inferior (p. 617)   El cuartil inferior es la mediana de la mitad inferior del conjunto de datos.

▼M

Major arc (p. 469)   A major arc of a circle is an arc that is longer than a semicircle.

Arco mayor (p. 469)   Un arco mayor de un círculo es cualquier arco más grande que un semicírculo.

Markup (p. 320)   Markup is the amount of increase in price. Markup is added to the cost of merchandise to arrive at the selling price.

A store buys a coat for $60 and sells it for $100. The markup is $40.

Sobrecosto (p. 320)   El sobrecosto es la cantidad que se aumenta en precio. El sobrecosto se agrega al costo de la mercadería y eso da el precio de venta.

Mean (p. 606)   The mean of a collection of data is the sum of the data items divided by the number of data items.

The mean temperature (°F) for the temperatures 44, 52, 48, 55, 61, 67, and 58 is 55.

Media (p. 606)   La media de un conjunto de datos resulta de la suma de los datos dividida entre el número de componentes de los datos.

Measures of central tendency (p. 606)   Measures of central tendency in statistics are *mean*, *median*, and *mode*.

See *Mean, Median,* and *Mode.*

Medidas de tendencia central (p. 606)   En la estadística, la *media*, la *mediana* y la *moda* son medidas de tendencia central.

Median (p. 606)   The median of a collection of data is the middle number when there is an odd number of data items and they are written in order. For an even number of data items, the median is the mean of the two middle numbers.

The median temperature (°F) for the temperatures 44, 48, 52, 55, 58, 61, and 67 is 55.

Mediana (p. 606)   La mediana es el número central de un conjunto de datos, cuando hay un número impar de datos y éstos están dispuestos en orden. Si hay un número par de datos, la mediana es la media de los dos números centrales.

English/Spanish Glossary

Midpoint Formula (p. 581)   The midpoint of a line segment with endpoints $A(x_1, y_1)$ and $B(x_2, y_2)$ is $\left(\frac{x_1 + x_2}{2}, \frac{y_1 + y_2}{2}\right)$.

The midpoint of $A(-3, 2)$ and $B(7, -2)$ is $\left(\frac{-3 + 7}{2}, \frac{2 + -2}{2}\right)$, or $(2, 0)$.

Fórmula del punto medio (p. 581)   El punto medio de un segmento con puntos extremos $A(x_1, y_1)$ y $B(x_2, y_2)$ es $\left(\frac{x_1 + x_2}{2}, \frac{y_1 + y_2}{2}\right)$.

Minor arc (p. 469)   A minor arc of a circle is an arc that is smaller than a semicircle.

Arco menor (p. 469)   Un arco menor de un círculo es un arco más corto que un semicírculo.

Mixed number (p. 231)   A mixed number is the sum of a whole number and a fraction.

$3\frac{11}{16}$ is a mixed number.
$3\frac{11}{16} = 3 + \frac{11}{16}$

Número mixto (p. 231)   Un número mixto es la suma de un número entero y una fracción.

Mode (p. 606)   The mode of a collection of data is the data item that occurs most often. There can be no mode, one mode, or more than one mode.

The mode of the collection of numbers $3, 4, 1, 3, 2, 2, 5, 3$ is 3.

Moda (p. 606)   La moda de un conjunto de datos es el dato que se presenta con mayor frecuencia. Puede no haber moda, una moda o más de una moda.

Monomial (p. 590)   A monomial is a real number, a variable, or a product of a real number and variables with whole number exponents.

$5x$, -4, and y^3 are all monomials.

Monomio (p. 590)   Un monomio es un número real, una variable o el producto de un número real y variables con exponentes que sean números enteros.

Multiple (p. 226)   A multiple of a number is the product of that number and any nonzero whole number.

The multiples of 13 are $13, 26, 39, 52$, and so on.

Múltiplo (p. 226)   El múltiplo de un número es el producto de dicho número y cualquier otro número entero distinto de cero.

Multiple line graph (p. 616)   A multiple line graph is a graph that shows more than one data set changing over time.

See *Line graph*.

Gráfica multilineal (p. 616)   Una gráfica multilineal representa las variaciones de más de un conjunto de datos en el tiempo.

Multiplication Property of Equality (p. 95)   If $a = b$, then $ac = bc$. $12 = 3(4)$, so $12 \cdot 2 = 3(4) \cdot 2$

Propiedad multiplicativa de la igualdad (p. 95)   Si $a = b$, entonces $ac = bc$.

Multiplication Properties of Inequality (p. 111)   If $a < b$, and c is positive, then $ac < bc$. If $a > b$, and c is positive, then $ac > bc$.

If you multiply each side of an inequality by a negative number, you reverse the inequality symbol.

If $a < b$, and c is negative, then $ac > bc$. If $a > b$, and c is negative, then $ac < bc$.

$3 < 4$, so $3(5) < 4(5)$
$7 > 2$, so $7(6) > 2(6)$

$6 < 9$, so $6(-2) > 9(-2)$
$7 > 5$, so $7(-3) < 5(-3)$

Propiedad multiplicativa de la desigualdad (p. 111)   Si $a < b$, y c es positivo, entonces $ac < bc$. Si $a > b$, y c es positivo, entonces $ac > bc$. Si se multiplica cada lado de una desigualdad por un número negativo, se invierte la dirección del signo de la desigualdad. Si $a < b$, y c es negativo, entonces $ac > bc$. Si $a > b$, y c es negativo, entonces $ac < bc$.

Multiplicative identity (p. 69)   The multiplicative identity is 1. For any number a, the product of a and 1 is a. $a \cdot 1 = a$

Identidad multiplicativa (p. 69)   La identidad multiplicativa es 1. Cuando se multiplica un número por uno, el producto es igual al número original.

Multiplicative inverse (p. 244)   The multiplicative inverse of a number is its reciprocal.   The multiplicative inverse of $\frac{4}{9}$ is $\frac{9}{4}$.

Inverso multiplicativo (p. 244)   El inverso multiplicativo de un número es su recíproco.

N

Negative correlation (p. 630)   See *Correlation*.

Correlación negativa (p. 630)   Ver *Correlation*.

Net (p. 520)   A net is a pattern that can be folded to form a space figure.
EXAMPLE This net can be folded to form a cube.

Plantilla (p. 520)   Una plantilla es un patrón que se puede doblar para formar una figura tridimensional.

No correlation (p. 630)   See *Correlation*.

Sin correlación (p. 630)   Ver *Correlation*.

English/Spanish Glossary

EXAMPLES

O

Obtuse angle (p. 443)   An obtuse angle is an angle with a measure greater than 90° and less than 180°.

Ángulo obtuso (p. 443)   Un ángulo obtuso es un ángulo que mide más de 90° y menos de 180°.

Obtuse triangle (p. 448)   An obtuse triangle is a triangle with one obtuse angle.

EXAMPLE   △*NJX* is an obtuse triangle, since ∠*J* is an obtuse angle.

Triángulo obtusángulo (p. 448)   Un triángulo es obtusángulo cuando contiene un ángulo obtuso.

Octagon (p. 454)   An octagon is a polygon with eight sides.

Octágono (p. 454)   Un octágono es un polígono que tiene ocho lados.

See *Polygon.*

Open sentence (p. 82)   An open sentence is an equation with one or more variables.

Proposición abierta (p. 82)   Una proposición abierta es una ecuación con una o más variables.

$3a = 5a + 8$

Opposites (p. 19)   Opposites are numbers that are the same distance from zero on the number line but in opposite directions.

Números opuestos (p. 19)   Números opuestos son los números que se hallan a la misma distancia de cero en una recta numérica pero en direcciones opuestas.

−17 and 17 are opposites because they are both 17 units from zero on the number line.

Order of operations (pp. 8, 179)
  1. Work inside grouping symbols.
  2. Simplify any terms with exponents.
  3. Multiply and divide in order from left to right.
  4. Add and subtract in order from left to right.

Orden de las operaciones (pp. 8, 179)
  1. Efectúa las operaciones que están dentro de los signos de agrupación.
  2. Trabaja con los exponentes.
  3. Multiplica y divide en orden de izquierda a derecha.
  4. Suma y resta en orden de izquierda a derecha.

$2^3(7 - 4) = 2^3(3) = 8 \cdot 3 = 24$

Ordered pair (p. 52)   An ordered pair is a pair of numbers that gives the location of a point in a coordinate plane. The first number is the x-coordinate and the second number is the y-coordinate.

See *Coordinates*

Par ordenado (p. 52)   Un par ordenado es un par de números que describe la localización de un punto en un plano de coordenadas. El primer número es la coordenada x y el segundo número es la coordenada y.

Origin (p. 52)   The origin is the intersection of the x-axis and the y-axis in a coordinate plane. The ordered pair $(0, 0)$ describes the origin.

See *Coordinate plane.*

Origen (p. 52)   El origen es el punto de intersección de los ejes de x y de y en un plano de coordenadas. El par ordenado $(0, 0)$ describe el origen.

Outlier (p. 607)   An outlier is a data value that is much higher or lower than the other data values in a collection of data.

An outlier in the data 1, 1, 2, 3, 4, 4, 6, 7, 7, 52 is 52.

Extremo (p. 607)   Un extremo es un valor de un conjunto de datos que es mucho mayor o menor que el resto de los datos.

P

Parabola (p. 591)   A parabola is the graph of a quadratic function. It is U-shaped.

EXAMPLE This parabola is the graph of the equation $y = x^2 - 2$.

Parábola (p. 591)   Una parábola es la gráfica de una ecuación cuadrática. Tiene la forma de U.

Parallel lines (p. 437)   Parallel lines are lines that lie in the same plane and do not intersect. The symbol $\parallel$ means "is parallel to."

EXAMPLE $\overleftrightarrow{EF} \parallel \overleftrightarrow{HI}$

Rectas paralelas (p. 437)   Rectas paralelas son las rectas que se encuentran en un mismo plano y no se cortan. El símbolo de dos rectas verticales paralelas significa "es paralelo a".

Parallelogram (p. 449)   A parallelogram is a quadrilateral with both pairs of opposite sides parallel.

EXAMPLE $KVDA$ is a parallelogram.

$\overline{KV} \parallel \overline{AD}$ and $\overline{AK} \parallel \overline{DV}$.

Paralelogramo (p. 449)   Un paralelogramo es un cuadrilátero en el cual los lados opuestos son paralelos.

English/Spanish Glossary

Pentagon (p. 450)   A pentagon is a polygon with five sides.

See *Polygon*.

Pentágono (p. 450)   Un pentágono es un polígono que tiene cinco lados.

Percent (p. 301)   A percent is a ratio that compares a number to 100. The symbol for percent is %.

$\dfrac{50}{100} = 50\%$

Porcentaje (p. 301)   Un porcentaje es una razón que compara un número con cien. El símbolo de porcentaje es %.

Percent of change (p. 316)   Percent of change is the percent something increases or decreases from its original amount.

A school's population increases from 500 to 520 students. The percent of change is $\dfrac{520 - 500}{500} = 4\%$.

Porcentaje de cambio (p. 316)   El porcentaje de cambio es el porcentaje en que algo aumenta o disminuye en relación con su valor original.

Perfect square (p. 566)   A perfect square is the square of an integer.

$3^2 = 9$, so 9 is a perfect square.

Cuadrado perfecto (p. 566)   Un cuadrado perfecto es un número natural que es igual a la segunda potencia de un número entero.

Perimeter (p. 138)   The perimeter of a figure is the distance around the figure. To find the perimeter of a rectangle, find the sum of the lengths of all its sides, or use the formula $P = 2\ell + 2w$.

EXAMPLE   The perimeter of *ABCD* is 12 ft.

Perímetro (p. 138)   El perímetro de una figura es la suma de las longitudes de sus lados. Para hallar el perímetro de un rectángulo, halla la suma de los largos de todos los lados o usa la fórmula $P = 2\ell + 2w$.

Perpendicular bisector (p. 471)   A perpendicular bisector is a line, segment, or ray that is perpendicular to a segment at its midpoint.

EXAMPLE $\overleftrightarrow{FG}$ is the perpendicular bisector of $\overline{DE}$.

Mediatriz (p. 471)   Una mediatriz es una recta, segmento o rayo que es perpendicular a un segmento en su punto medio.

Perpendicular lines (p. 471)   Perpendicular lines are lines that intersect to form right angles.

Rectas perpendiculares (p. 471)   Rectas perpendiculares son aquellas que se cortan para formar ángulos rectos.

$\overleftrightarrow{DE} \perp \overleftrightarrow{RS}$

Pi (p. 464)   Pi (π) is the name for the ratio of the circumference C to the diameter d of a circle.

Pi (p. 464)   Pi (π) es el nombre de la razón de la circumferencia C al diámetro d de un círculo.

Plane (p. 436)   A plane is a flat surface that has no thickness and extends without end in the directions of all the lines it contains.

Plano (p. 436)   Un plano es una superficie plana que no tiene grosor y que se extiende indefinidamente en las direcciónes de todas las líneas que contiene.

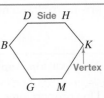

$ABCD$ or M is a plane.

Point (p. 436)   A point is a location in space that has no size.

Punto (p. 436)   Un punto es una posición en el espacio. No tiene dimensiones, solamente tiene localización.

$\cdot\,A$

A is a point

Polygon (p. 448)   A polygon is a closed plane figure with at least three sides.

Polígono (p. 448)   Un polígono es una figura plana cerrada formada por tres o más lados.

Positive correlation (p. 630)   See *Correlation*.

Correlación positiva (p. 630)   Ver *Correlation*.

Power (p. 178)   A power is any expression in the form a^n. *Power* is also used to refer to the exponent.

Potencia (p. 178)   Una potencia es cualquier expresión de la forma a^n. La potencia también se usa para referirse al exponente.

5^4 is a power and can be read as "five to the fourth power."

Precision in measurement (p. 156)   The precision of a measurement is its exactness. A measurement cannot be more precise than the precision of the measuring tool used.

Precisión de una medición (p. 156)   La precisión de una medición se refiere a su grado de exactitud. Una medida no puede ser más precisa que la precisión del instrumento de medida utilizado.

A hundredth of a meter is a smaller unit than a tenth of a meter. So, 2.72 m is more precise than 2.7 m.

Prime factorization (p. 183)   The prime factorization of a number is the expression of the number as the product of its prime factors.

Descomposición en factores primos (p. 183)   La descomposición en factores primos de un número es la expresión de dicho número como el producto de sus factores primos.

The prime factorization of 30 is $2 \cdot 3 \cdot 5$.

English/Spanish Glossary

Prime number (p. 182)   A prime number is an integer greater than 1 with only two positive factors, 1 and itself.

13 is a prime number because its only factors are 1 and 13.

Número primo (p. 182)   Un número primo es un número natural que tiene exactamente dos factores positivos, 1 y él mismo.

Principal (p. 371)   The principal is the initial amount of an investment or loan.

See *Simple interest*.

Capital (p. 371)   El capital es el monto inicial de una inversión o préstamo.

Prism (p. 519)   A prism is a space figure with two parallel and congruent polygonal faces, called bases, and lateral faces that are parallelograms. A prism is named for the shape of its base.

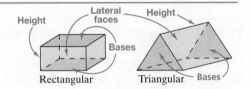

Prisma (p. 519)   Un prisma es una figura tridimensional con dos caras poligonales congruentes y paralelas llamadas bases, y caras laterales paralelas. Un prisma recibe su nombre de acuerdo a la forma de las bases.

Proportion (p. 290)   A proportion is an equality of two ratios.

$\frac{3}{12} = \frac{12}{48}$ is a proportion.

Proporción (p. 290)   Una proporción es una igualdad de dos razones.

Pyramid (p. 519)   A pyramid is a space figure with triangular faces that meet at a vertex, and a base that is a polygon. A pyramid is named for the shape of its base.

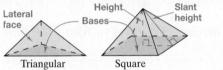

Pirámide (p. 519)   Una pirámide es una figura tridimensional con caras triangulares que convergen en un vértice, y una base que es un polígono. Una pirámide recibe su nombre de acuerdo a la forma de la base.

Pythagorean Theorem (p. 570)   In any right triangle, the sum of the squares of the lengths of the legs (a and b) is equal to the square of the length of the hypotenuse (c): $a^2 + b^2 = c^2$.

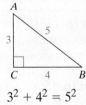

$3^2 + 4^2 = 5^2$

Teorema de Pitágoras (p. 570)   Para cualquier triángulo rectángulo, la suma del cuadrado de las longitudes de los catetos (a y b) es igual al cuadrado de la longitud de la hipotenusa (c): $a^2 + b^2 = c^2$.

Q

Quadrants (p. 52)   Quadrants are the four regions determined by the x- and y-axes of the coordinate plane.

See *Coordinate plane*.

Cuadrantes (p. 52)   El eje de x y el eje de y dividen el plano de coordenadas en cuatro regiones llamadas cuadrantes.

Quadratic function (p. 591) A quadratic function is a function based on squaring the input variable. The graph of a quadratic function is a parabola.

See *Parabola*.

Función cuadrática (p. 591) Una función cuadrática es la función que tiene una variable elevada a la segunda potencia. La gráfica de una función cuadrática es una párabola.

Quadrilateral (p. 449) A quadrilateral is a polygon with four sides.

See *Polygon*.

Cuadrilátero (p. 449) Un cuadrilátero es un polígono con cuatro lados.

Quartiles (p. 617) Quartiles are numbers that divide a data set into four equal parts.

See *Box-and-whisker plot*.

Cuartiles (p. 617) Los cuartiles son números que dividen un conjunto de datos en cuatro partes iguales.

R

Radius (plural is radii) (p. 464) A radius of a circle is a segment that has one endpoint at the center of the circle and the other endpoint on the circle.

EXAMPLE $\overline{OA}$ is a radius of circle O.

Radio (p. 464) El radio de un círculo es un segmento que tiene un extremo en el centro y el otro en el círculo.

Range of a relation (p. 388) A range is the set of second coordinates of the ordered pairs of a relation.

In the relation $\{(0, 1), (-3, 2), (0, 2)\}$, the range is $\{1, 2\}$.

Recorrido de una relación (p. 388) Un recorrido es el conjunto que comprende todas las segundas coordenadas de los pares ordenados de una relación.

Range of a set of data (p. 606) The range is the difference between the greatest and least values in a set of data.

The range of the data 7 9 15 3 18 2 16 14 14 20 is $20 - 2 = 18$.

Amplitud de un conjunto de datos (p. 606) La amplitud es la diferencia entre los valores mayor y menor de un conjunto de datos.

Rate (p. 284) A rate is a ratio that compares quantities measured in different units.

A student typed 1,100 words in 50 minutes for a typing rate of 1,100 words per 50 minutes, or 22 words/minute.

Tasa (p. 284) Una tasa es una razón que compara dos cantidades medidas en unidades diferentes.

English/Spanish Glossary

Ratio (p. 284) A ratio is a comparison of two quantities by division.

Razón (p. 284) Una razón es la comparación de dos números mediante una división.

There are three ways to write a ratio: 72 to 100, 72 : 100, and $\frac{72}{100}$.

Rational number (p. 197) A rational number is any number you can write as a quotient of two integers $\frac{a}{b}$, where b is not zero.

Número racional (p. 197) Un número racional es cualquier número que puede escribirse como el cociente de dos enteros $\frac{a}{b}$, donde b es distinto de cero.

$\frac{3}{5}, -8, 8.7, 0.333\ldots, -5\frac{3}{11}, 0,$ and $\frac{17}{4}$ are rational numbers.

Ray (p. 436) A ray is a part of a line. It has exactly one endpoint. Its endpoint is named first.

Rayo (p. 436) Un rayo es una parte de una recta. Tiene exactamente un extremo. El extremo se nombre primero.

$\overrightarrow{SW}$ represents a ray.

Real number (p. 567) A real number is a rational number or an irrational number.

Números reales (p. 567) Un número real es un número racional o un número irracional.

$3, -5.25, 3.141592653\ldots,$ and $\frac{7}{8}$ are real numbers.

Reciprocal (p. 244) Reciprocals are two numbers with a product of 1.

Recíprocos (p. 244) Dos números son recíprocos cuando su producto es 1.

$\frac{4}{9}$ and $\frac{9}{4}$ are reciprocals.

$\frac{4}{9} \cdot \frac{9}{4} = 1.$

Rectangle (p. 449) A rectangle is a parallelogram with four right angles.

EXAMPLE $RSWH$ is a rectangle.

Rectángulo (p. 449) Un rectángulo es un paralelogramo con cuatro ángulos rectos.

Reflection (p. 483) A reflection is a transformation that flips a figure over a line of reflection.

EXAMPLE $K'L'M'N'$ is the reflection of $KLMN$ across the y-axis. The y-axis is the line of reflection.

Reflexión (p. 483) Una reflexión es una transformación que invierte una figura a través de un eje de reflexión.

Reflectional symmetry (p. 482) A figure has reflectional symmetry when one half of the figure is a mirror image of the other half. The line of reflection is also called the line of symmetry.

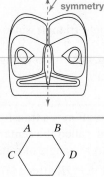

Line of symmetry

Simetría de reflexión (p. 482) Una figura tiene simetría de reflexión cuando la mitad de la figura es una imagen refleja de la otra mitad. El eje de reflexión también se llama el eje de simetría.

Regular polygon (p. 450) A regular polygon is a polygon with all its sides congruent and all its angles congruent.

EXAMPLE *ABDFEC* is a regular hexagon.

Polígono regular (p. 450) Un polígono regular tiene todos sus lados congruentes y todos sus ángulos son congruentes.

Relation (p. 388) A relation is a set of ordered pairs.

$\{(0, 2), (-3, 2), (0, 1)\}$ is a relation.

Relación (p. 388) Una relación es un conjunto de pares ordenados.

Relatively prime (p. 186) Two numbers are relatively prime if their GCD is 1.

9 and 20 are relatively prime.

Números primos entre sí (p. 186) Dos números son primos entre sí, si su máximo común divisor es 1.

Repeating decimal (p. 232) A repeating decimal is a decimal in which the same block of digits repeats without end. The symbol for a repeating decimal is a bar drawn over the digit or digits that repeat.

$0.8888\ldots = 0.\overline{8}$

Decimal periódico (p. 232) Un decimal periódico es un decimal cuyos dígitos se repiten indefinidamente. El símbolo de un decimal periódico es una raya trazada encima del dígito o dígitos que se repiten.

Rhombus (p. 449) A rhombus is a parallelogram with four congruent sides.

EXAMPLE *GHJI* is a rhombus.
$GH = HJ = IJ = GI$

Rombo (p. 449) Un rombo es un paralelogramo con cuatro lados congruentes.

Right angle (p. 443) A right angle is an angle with a measure of 90°.
EXAMPLE $\angle CDE$ is a right angle.

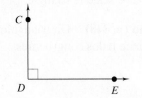

Ángulo recto (p. 443) Un ángulo recto es un ángulo que mide 90°.

English/Spanish Glossary

Right triangle (p. 448)   A right triangle is a triangle with one right angle.

EXAMPLE $\triangle ABC$ is a right triangle, since $\angle B$ is a right angle.

Triángulo rectángulo (p. 448)   Un triángulo rectángulo es aquél que posee un ángulo recto.

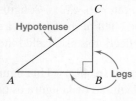

Rotation (p. 486)   A rotation is a transformation that turns a figure about a fixed point, called the center of rotation. The angle measure of the rotation is the angle of rotation.

EXAMPLE   The image of $\triangle PQR$ after a 90° rotation is $\triangle PQ'R'$. Point P is the center of rotation.

Rotación (p. 486)   Una rotación es una transformación en la cual una figura se mueve sin deformación alrededor de un punto fijo, llamado centro de rotación. La medida del ángulo de la rotación es el ángulo de rotación.

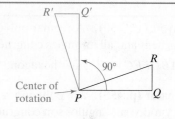

Rotational symmetry (p. 487)   A figure has rotational symmetry if the figure can be rotated 180° or less and match the original figure.

Simetría rotacional (p. 487)   Una figura tiene simetría rotacional si la figura se puede rotar 180° o menos y coincide exactamente con la figura original.

This figure has 60° rotational symmetry.

Scale drawing (p. 296)   A scale drawing is an enlarged or reduced drawing that is similar to an actual object or place.

Dibujo a escala (p. 296)   Un dibujo a escala es un dibujo aumentado o reducido que es similar al objeto o lugar real.

A map is a scale drawing.

Scale factor (pp. 300, 552)   A scale factor is the number that describes the size change from an original figure to its image.

Factor de escala (pp. 300, 552)   El factor de escala es el número que describe la relación entre los tamaños de las partes del dibujo de un objeto y los tamaños reales de ese objeto.

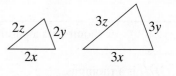

The scale factor is $\frac{3}{2}$.

Scalene triangle (p. 448)   A scalene triangle is a triangle with no congruent sides.

EXAMPLE $\triangle NPO$ is a scalene triangle.

Triángulo escaleno (p. 448)   Un triángulo escaleno es un triángulo que no tiene lados congruentes.

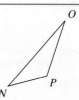

Scatter plot (p. 628)   A scatter plot is a graph that displays data from two related sets as ordered pairs.

EXAMPLE   This scatter plot displays the amount various companies spent on advertising (in dollars) versus product sales (in thousands of dollars).

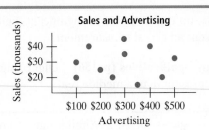

Diagrama de dispersión (p. 628)   Un diagrama de dispersión es una gráfica que muestra datos de dos conjuntos relacionados, como pares ordenados.

Scientific notation (p. 210)   Scientific notation is a way of expressing a number. A number is expressed in scientific notation when it is written as the product of a number greater than or equal to 1 and less than 10, and a power of 10.

In scientific notation, 37,000,000 is written as 3.7×10^7.

Notación científica (p. 210)   La notación científica es una forma de expresar un número. Un número se expresa en notación científica cuando se escribe como el producto de un número mayor o igual a 1 y menor que 10 y el segundo es una potencia de 10.

Segment (p. 436)   A segment is part of a line. It has two endpoints.

Segmento (p. 436)   Un segmento es parte de una recta. Tiene dos puntos extremos.

$\overline{CB}$ represents the segment shown.

Segment bisector (p. 471)   A segment bisector is a line, segment, or ray that separates a segment into two congruent segments.

Mediatriz de un segmento (p. 471)   La mediatriz de un segmento es una recta, segmento o rayo que divide el segmento en dos segmentos congruentes.

Line ℓ bisects $\overline{KJ}$.

Semicircle (p. 469)   A semicircle is half of a circle.

Semicírculo (p. 469)   Un semicírculo es la mitad de un círculo.

Side (pp. 443, 448)   See *Angle* and *Polygon*.

Cara (p. 443, 448)   Ver *Angle* y *Polygon*.

English/Spanish Glossary

Significant digits (p. 156) Significant digits are the digits that represent an actual measurement.

Dígitos significativos (p. 156) Dígitos significativos son los dígitos que representan una medida real.

Similar figures (p. 295) Similar figures are figures with corresponding angles that have equal measures and corresponding sides that have proportional lengths. The symbol ~ means "is similar to."

EXAMPLE $\triangle ABC \sim \triangle RTS$

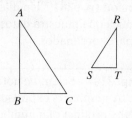

Figuras semejantes (p. 295) Figuras semejantes son figuras con ángulos correspondients que tienen la misma medida y lados correspondientes que tienen longitudes proporcionales. El símbolo ~ significa "es semejante a."

Similar solids (p. 552) Two solids are similar if they have the same shape and if all corresponding dimensions are proportional.

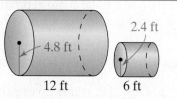

Sólidos semejantes (p. 552) Dos sólidos son semejantes si tienen la misma forma y si sus dimensiones correspondientes son proporcionales.

Simple interest (p. 371) Simple interest is interest paid only on the principal, the initial amount of money invested or borrowed. The formula for simple interest is $I = prt$, where I is the interest, p is the principal, r is the interest rate per year, and t is the time in years.

The simple interest on $1,000 at 5% for 2 years is $1,000 · 0.05 · 2, or $100.

Interés simple (p. 371) Interés simple es aquel que se paga sólo por el capital, el monto inicial de dinero que se invierte o se pide prestado. La fórmula de interés simple es $I = prt$, donde I es el interés, p es el capital, r es la tasa de interés anual y t es el tiempo en años.

Simplest form of a fraction (p. 188) The simplest form of a fraction is the form in which the only common factor of the numerator and denominator is 1.

The simplest form of the fraction $\frac{15}{20}$ is $\frac{3}{4}$.

Mínima expresión de una fracción (p. 188) La mínima expresión de una fracción es la expresión en que el único factor común del numerador y del denominador es 1.

Simplify a variable expression (p. 78)   To simplify a variable expression is to replace it with an equivalent expression having as few terms as possible.

$2x + 5 + 4x$ simplifies to $6x + 5$.

Simplificar una expresión variable (p. 78)   Se simplifica una expresión variable al reemplazarla con una expresión equivalente que tiene el menor número posible de términos.

Skew lines (p. 437)   Skew lines are lines in space that do not intersect and are not parallel. They do not lie in the same plane. Skew segments must be parts of skew lines.

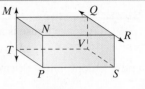

Rectas cruzadas (p. 437)   Las rectas cruzadas son rectas en el espacio, que no se intersecan y que no son paralelas. No están en el mismo plano. Los segmentos cruzados son partes de rectas cruzadas.

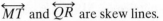

$\overleftrightarrow{MT}$ and $\overleftrightarrow{QR}$ are skew lines.

Slant height (p. 534)   See *Cone* and *Pyramid*.

Altura inclinada (p. 534)   Ver *Cone* y *Pyramid*.

Slope (p. 399)   Slope is a ratio that describes the tilt of a line.

$$\text{slope} = \frac{\text{vertical change}}{\text{horizontal change}} = \frac{\text{difference in } y\text{-coordinates}}{\text{difference in } x\text{-coordinates}}$$

Pendiente (p. 399)   La pendiente de una recta es la razón que describe su inclinación.

$$\text{Pendiente} = \frac{\text{variación vertical}}{\text{variación horizontal}} = \frac{\text{diferencia en las coordenadas } y}{\text{diferencia en las coordenadas } x}$$

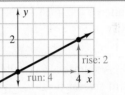

The slope of the given line is $\frac{2}{4}$, or $\frac{1}{2}$.

Slope-intercept form of an equation (p. 401)   The slope-intercept form of an equation is $y = mx + b$, where m is the slope and b is the y-intercept of the line.

The equation $y = 2x + 1$ is in slope-intercept form with $m = 2$ and $b = 1$.

Forma pendiente-intercepto de una ecuación (p. 401)   La forma pendiente-intercepto de una ecuación es $y = mx + b$ donde m es la pendiente y b es el intercepto en y de la recta.

Solid (p. 519)   A solid is a three-dimensional figure.

See *Space figure*.

Sólido (p. 519)   Un sólido es una figura tridimensional.

Solution (p. 83)   A solution is any value or values that make an equation or an inequality true.

Solución (p. 83)   Una solución es cualquier valor o valores que hacen verdadera una ecuación o una desigualdad.

4 is the solution of $x + 5 = 9$.

$(8, 4)$ is a solution of $y = -1x + 12$ because $4 = -1(8) + 12$.

-4 is a solution of $2x < -3$, because $2 \cdot -4 < -3$.

$(-1, 3)$ is a solution of $y > x - 4$, because $3 > -1 - 4$.

Space figure (p. 519)   A space figure is a three-dimensional figure, or solid.

EXAMPLE   A cylinder, a cone, and a prism are space figures.

Cuerpo geométrico (p. 519)   Un cuerpo geométrico es una figura tridimensional o sólido.

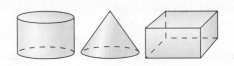

Sphere (p. 519)   A sphere is the set of points in space that are a given distance from a point, called the center.

Esfera (p. 519)   Una esfera es el conjunto de todos los puntos del espacio que se hallan a una misma distancia de un punto dado llamado el centro.

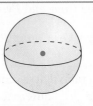

Square (p. 449)   A square is a parallelogram with four right angles and four congruent sides.

EXAMPLE   *QRTS* is a square.
$\angle Q, \angle R, \angle T$, and $\angle S$ are right angles.
$QR = RT = ST = SQ$

Cuadrado (p. 449)   Un cuadrado es un paralelogramo con cuatro ángulos rectos y cuatro lados congruentes.

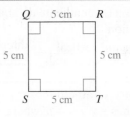

Square root (p. 566)   The square root of a given number is a number that when multiplied by itself equals the given number.

The symbol for the nonnegative square root of a number is $\sqrt{\ }$.

Raíz cuadrada (p. 566)   La raíz cuadrada de un número dado es un número que cuando es multiplicado por sí mismo, es igual al número dado.

$\sqrt{25} = 5$ because $5^2 = 25$.

Standard notation (p. 211)   Standard notation is the usual form for representing a number.

Notación normal (p. 211)   La notación normal es la forma común de representar un número.

The standard notation of 8.9×10^5 is 890,000.

Stem-and-leaf plot (p. 622)   A stem-and-leaf plot is a display that shows numeric data arranged in order. The leaf of each data item is its last digit. The stem is its other digits. The stems are stacked in order and the leaves are arranged in order to the side of each stem.

```
Stem  Leaf
 27 | 7
 28 | 5 6 8
 29 | 6 9
 30 | 8
```
27 | 7 means 27.7.

EXAMPLE   This stem-and-leaf plot displays recorded times in a race. The stem records the whole number of seconds. The leaf represents tenths of a second. So, 27 | 7 represents 27.7 seconds.

Diagrama de tallo y hojas (p. 622)   Un diagrama de tallo y hojas es una representación que muestra datos numéricos en orden de valor relativo. La hoja de cada dato es su último dígito. El tallo es sus otros dígitos. Los tallos están organizados en columnas ordenadas y las hojas están organizadas en orden al lado de cada tallo.

Straight angle (p. 443)   A straight angle is an angle with a measure of 180°.

Ángulo llano (p. 443)   Un ángulo llano es un ángulo cuya medida es 180°.

Subtraction Property of Equality (p. 88)   If $a = b$, then $a - c = b - c$.

$10 = 2(5)$, so $10 - 5 = 2(5) - 5$

Propiedad sustrativa de la igualdad (p. 88)   Si $a = b$, entonces $a - c = b - c$.

Subtraction Property of Inequality (p. 106)   If $a > b$, then $a - c > b - c$. If $a < b$, then $a - c < b - c$.

$7 > 4$, so $7 - 3 > 4 - 3$
$6 < 9$, so $6 - 2 < 9 - 2$

Propiedad sustractiva de la desigualdad (p. 106)   Si $a > b$, entonces $a - c > b - c$. Si $a < b$, entonces $a - c < b - c$.

Supplementary angles (p. 443)   Supplementary angles are two angles whose measures add to 180°.

130° 50°
  A   D

Ángulos suplementarios (p. 443)   Dos ángulos son suplementarios si la suma de sus medidas es 180°.

$\angle A$ and $\angle D$ are supplementary.

Surface area (p. 527)   Surface area is the sum of the areas of the base(s) and lateral faces of a space figure.

Each square = 1 in.^{2}

EXAMPLE   The surface area of the prism is the sum of the areas of its faces.
$(12 + 12 + 12 + 12 + 9 + 9)$ in.$^2 = 66$ in.^{2}

Área total (p. 527)   El área total es la suma de las áreas de la o las bases y de las caras laterales de una figura tridimesional.

English/Spanish Glossary

System of linear equations (p. 414)   A system of linear equations is two or more linear equations.

$y = 3x + 1$ and $y = -2x - 3$ form a system of linear equations.

Sistema de ecuaciones lineales (p. 414)   Dos o más ecuaciones lineales forman un sistema de ecuaciones lineales.

System of linear inequalities (p. 422)   A system of linear inequalities is two or more linear inequalities.

$y \geq 3x + 1$ and $y < -2x - 3$ form a system of linear inequalities.

Sistema de desigualdades lineales (p. 422)   Dos o más desigualdades lineales forman un sistema de desigualdades lineales.

T

Term of an expression (p. 78)   A term is a number, a variable, or the product of a number and variable(s).

The expression $7x + 12 + (-9y)$ has three terms: $7x$, 12, and $-9y$.

Término de una expresión (p. 78)   Un término es un número, una variable o el producto de un número y una o mas variables.

Terminating decimal (p. 231)   A terminating decimal is a decimal with a finite number of digits.

Both 0.6 and 0.7265 are terminating decimals.

Decimal finito (p. 231)   Un decimal finito es un decimal que tiene un número finito de digitos.

Three-dimensional figure (p. 519)   A three-dimensional figure is a figure that does not lie in a plane.

See *Space figure*.

Figura tridimensional (p. 519)   Una figura tridimensional es una figura que no está situada en un plano.

Transformation (p. 476)   A transformation is a change of position or size of a figure. Four types of transformations are translations, reflections, rotations, and dilations.

EXAMPLE $K'L'M'N'$ is a reflection of $KLMN$ across the y-axis.

Transformación (p. 476)   Una transformación es un cambio de posición o tamaño de una figura. Una transformación puede ser una traslación, una reflexión, una rotación o una dilatación.

Translation (p. 476) A translation is a transformation that moves points the same distance and in the same direction.

EXAMPLE $A'B'C'D'$ is the translation image of $ABCD$.

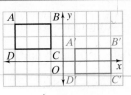

Traslación (p. 476) Una traslación es una transformación que mueve puntos la misma distancia y en la misma dirección.

Transversal (p. 444) A transversal is a line that intersects two other lines in different points.

EXAMPLE $\overleftrightarrow{RI}$ is a transversal of $\overleftrightarrow{QS}$ and $\overleftrightarrow{HJ}$.

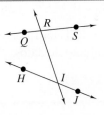

Transversal (p. 444) Un transversal es una recta que interseca a otras dos rectas en puntos distintos.

Trapezoid (p. 449) A trapezoid is a quadrilateral with exactly one pair of parallel sides.

EXAMPLE $UVYW$ is a trapezoid.

$$\overleftrightarrow{UV} \parallel \overleftrightarrow{WY}$$

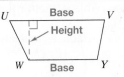

Trapecio (p. 449) Un trapecio es un cuadrilátero que tiene exactamente un par de lados paralelos.

Tree diagram (p. 41) A tree diagram is a diagram that displays all the possible outcomes of an event.

EXAMPLE There are for 4 possible outcomes for tossing 2 coins: HH, HT, TH, and TT.

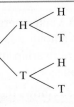

Diagrama de árbol (p. 41) Un diagrama de árbol presenta todos los resultados posibles de un suceso.

Trend line (p. 635) A trend line is a line that closely fits the data points in a scatter plot.

Línea de tendencia (p. 635) Una línea de tendencia es la recta que más corresponde con los puntos de los datos en una diagrama de dispersión.

Triangle (p. 450) A triangle is a polygon with three sides.

Triángulo (p. 450) Un triángulo es un polígono con tres lados.

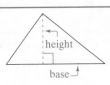

Unit rate (p. 284)   A unit rate is a rate that has denominator 1.

Tasa unitaria (p. 284)   Una tasa unitaria es la tasa cuyo denominador es 1.

If you drive 165 mi in 3 h, your unit rate of travel is 55 mi in 1 h or 55 mi/h.

Upper quartile (p. 617)   The upper quartile is the median of the upper half of a data set.

Cuartil superior (p. 617)   El cuartil superior es la mediana de la mitad superior de un conjunto de datos.

See *Quartile*.

Variable (p. 4)   A variable is a letter that stands for a number.

Variable (p. 4)   Una variable es una letra que representa a un número.

x is a variable in the equation $9 - x = 3$.

Variable expression (p. 4)   See *Algebraic expression*.

Expresión variable (p. 4)   Ver *Algebraic expression*.

Venn diagram (p. 187)   A Venn diagram is a diagram that illustrates the relationships among collections of objects or numbers. The intersection, or overlap, of two circles indicates what is common to both collections.

EXAMPLE   The Venn diagram shows the activities of 67 music students.

Diagrama Venn (p. 187)   Un diagrama Venn es un diagrama que muestra la relación entre dos conjuntos de objectos o números. La intersección o sobreposición de dos círculos indica lo que tienen en común ambos conjuntos.

Vertex (pp. 443, 449)   See *Angle* and *Polygon*.

Vértice (pp. 443, 449)   Ver *Angle* y *Polygon*.

Vertical angles (p. 443)   Vertical angles are angles formed by two intersecting lines, and are opposite each other. Vertical angles are congruent.

Ángulos verticales (p. 443)   Ángulos verticales son aquellos formados por dos rectas que se intersecan y que son opuestos entre sí. Los ángulos verticales son congruentes.

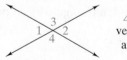

$\angle 1$ and $\angle 2$ are vertical angles, as are $\angle 3$ and $\angle 4$.

Vertical-line test (p. 389) The vertical-line test is a test that allows you to describe graphically whether a relation is a function.

EXAMPLE Since the vertical line $x = 2$ passes through two points of the graph, the relation is not a function.

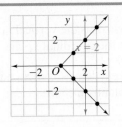

Prueba de la línea vertical (p. 389) Método que permite determinar gráficamente si una relación es o no es una función.

Volume (p. 539) The volume of a space figure is the number of cubic units needed to fill it.

EXAMPLE The volume of the rectangular prism is 36 in.^{3}.

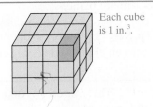

Each cube is 1 in.^{3}.

Volumen (p. 539) El volumen de una figura tridimensional es el número de unidades cúbicas necesarias para llenar el espacio interior de dicha figura.

X

x-axis (p. 52) The x-axis is the horizontal number line that, together with the y-axis, establishes the coordinate plane.

See *Coordinate plane*.

Eje de x (p. 52) El eje de x es la recta numérica horizontal que, junto al eje de y, forma el plano de coordenadas.

x-coordinate (p. 52) The x-coordinate is the horizontal position of a point in the coordinate plane.

See *Coordinates*.

Coordenada x (p. 52) La coordenada x muestra la ubicación horizontal de un punto en el plano de coordenadas.

x-intercept (p. 397) The x-intercept of a line is the x-coordinate of the point where the line crosses the x-axis.

EXAMPLE The x-intercept is 2. The y-intercept is −3.

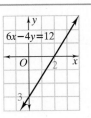

$6x - 4y = 12$

Intercepto x (p. 397) El intercepto x de una recta es la coordenada x del punto de intercepción de la recta con el eje de x.

y-axis (p. 52)   The y-axis is the vertical number line that, together with the x-axis, forms the coordinate plane.

See *Coordinate plane*.

Eje de y (p. 52)   El eje de y es la recta numérica vertical que, junto al eje de x, forma el plano de coordenadas.

y-coordinate (p. 52)   The y-coordinate is the vertical position of a point in the coordinate plane.

See *Coordinates*.

Coordenada y (p. 52)   La coordenada y muestra la ubicación vertical de un punto en el plano de coordenadas.

y-intercept (p. 401)   The y-intercept of a line is the y-coordinate of the point where the line crosses the y-axis.

See *x-intercept*.

Intercepto y (p. 401)   El intercepto y de una recta es la coordenada y del punto de intercepción de la recta con el eje de y.

Z

Zero pair (p. 23)   A zero pair is a positive unit paired with a negative unit.

← A zero pair

Par nulo (p. 23)   Un par nulo es el emparejamiento de una unidad positiva con una unidad negativa.

Chapter 1

Check Your Readiness p. 2

1. 1 **2.** 11 **3.** 11 **4.** 19 **5.** 13 **6.** 40 **7.** 17 **8.** 44
9. 176 **10.** 28 **11.** 166 **12.** 75 **13.** > **14.** >
15. < **16.** < **17.** < **18.** = **19.** 12 **20.** 30 **21.** 28
22. 5 **23.** 96 **24.** 5 **25.** 200 **26.** 80 **27.** 31
28. 13 **29.** 480 **30.** 12 **31.** 1 **32.** 4 **33.** 7 **34.** 10

Lesson 1-1 pp. 4–7

Check Skills You'll Need 1. 7 **2.** 12 **3.** 5 **4.** 4 **5.** 3

Standards Check 1a. Algebraic expression; x is the variable. **b.** numerical expression **c.** Algebraic expression; d is the variable **2a.** $0.50b$ **b.** $\frac{m}{60}$

Check Your Understanding 1. the cost of the sports cards **2.** The number of sports cards Jose has **3.** multiplication, addition **4.** $2x + 4$

Lesson 1-2 pp. 8–12

Check Skills You'll Need 1. 82 **2.** 43 **3.** 71 **4.** 19 **5.** 14
6. 26

Standards Check 1a. 17 **b.** 3 **c.** 3 **2a.** 4 **b.** 12 **3.** 3

Check Your Understanding 1. C **2.** A **3.** D **4.** B

Lesson 1-3 pp. 14–17

Check Skills You'll Need 1. 60 **2.** 18 **3.** 29 **4.** 32

Standards Check 1a. 28 **b.** 45 **2a.** 90 **b.** 23 **c.** 12
3. $29c$; $145 **4.** $146

Check Your Understanding 1. Work within grouping symbols. **2.** Multiply and divide in order from left to right. **3.** Multiply and divide in order from left to right. **4.** Add and subtract in order from left to right. **5.** Add.

Lesson 1-4 pp. 18–22

Check Skills You'll Need 1. $m - 3$ **2.** $8 \div 2$ **3.** $8 + 7$

Standards Check

1.

$-6, 0, 2$ **2.** the absolute value of negative ten; 10
3. 20

Check Your Understanding 1. 2 **2.** 5 **3.** -4 **4.** $-48°C$
5. $58°C$ **6.** 5

Checkpoint Quiz 1 1. $f + 23$ **2.** $\frac{g}{34}$ **3.** $9p$ **4.** 20 **5.** 2
6. 19 **7.** 0 **8.** 54 **9.** 15

10a.

b. Tuesday, Wednesday, Monday, Thursday

Lesson 1-5 pp. 24–29

Check Skills You'll Need 1. < **2.** > **3.** < **4.** = **5.** > **6.** >

Standards Check 1a. 3 **b.** 4 **c.** -4 **2a.** -4 **b.** 5
c. -6 **3a.** -38 **b.** 47 **c.** -90 **4.** 1,280 m **5a.** -10
b. 70

Check Your Understanding 1. C **2.** E **3.** A **4.** D **5.** B
6. negative **7.** positive **8.** negative

Lesson 1-6 pp. 30–34

Check Skills You'll Need 1. -1 **2.** -29 **3.** -10 **4.** 11
5. 0 **6.** -23

Standards Check 1a. -5 **b.** -1 **c.** -3 **2a.** -4
b. -6 **c.** 5 **3a.** 35 **b.** -106 **c.** -46 **d.** $-81°C$

Check Your Understanding 1. $-9 - (-2) = -7$ **2.** $3 + (-8) = -5$ or $3 - 8 = -5$ **3.** $6 + (-4)$ **4.** $-5 + 10$
5. $14 + 2$ **6.** $20 + (-4) + 7$ **7.** $1 + (-18) + 3$
8. $-2 + (-3) + (-5)$

Lesson 1-7 pp. 35–39

Check Skills You'll Need 1. -7 **2.** -11 **3.** -15 **4.** -19

Standards Check 1. A six-sided figure with all vertices on a circle. **2.** Start with 4 and add 5 repeatedly. **3.** Start with 1 and add 2 repeatedly; 9, 11. **4.** Answers may vary. Sample: No; if the coin is fair, the coin can come up tails on any toss. **5a.** correct **b.** Incorrect; 8 and $|8|$ are not opposites. **c.** correct

Check Your Understanding 1. 3 **2.** 6 **3.** 8 **4.** 7 **5.** 4
6. 5 **7.** Answers may vary. Sample: No; the pattern 2, 4, 7 could be 2, 4, 6 or 2, 4, 8.

Lesson 1-8 pp. 40–43

Check Skills You'll Need 1. Start with 8 and add 3 repeatedly; 20, 23, 26 **2.** Start with 1, then alternately add 4 and subtract 1; 11, 10, 14 **3.** Start with 3, then alternately add 2 and multiply by 2; 26, 52, 54 **4.** Start with 1, then add 3 repeatedly; 13, 16, 19

Standards Check 8. 127 students

Lesson 1-9 pp. 44–49

Check Skills You'll Need 1. 20 **2.** 24 **3.** 25 **4.** 28 **5.** 30
6. 140

Standards Check 1a. −12 **b.** −12 **c.** −14 **2.** 12
3a. 64 **b.** −90 **c.** 0 **4a.** −4 **b.** 8 **c.** 14 **d.** −2

Check Your Understanding 1. $5 \cdot (-2) = -10$ **2.** $4(-9) =$
-36 **3.** $5(-5)$ **4.** Positive; the integers have the
same sign. **5.** Negative; the integers have
opposite signs. **6.** Negative; the integers have
opposite signs. **7.** Positive; the first product is
negative, so the second is the product of integers
with the same sign.

Checkpoint Quiz 2 1. −8 **2.** 20 **3.** −45 **4.** 8 **5.** −12
6. 72 **7–9.** Answers may vary. Samples are given.
7. $3 + (-10) = -7$ **8.** $2 - (-20) = 22$
9. $8 \cdot (-5) = -40$ **10.** 13, 18, 23 **11.** 81, 243, 729

Lesson 1-10   pp. 52–56

Check Skills You'll Need

1.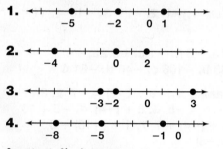

2.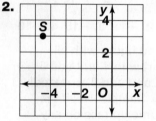

3.

4.

Standards Check 1. (2, −3); (3, 3)

2.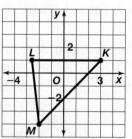

3. triangle

Check Your Understanding 1. (0, 0) **2.** −5
3. y-coordinate **4a.** origin **b.** 5 **c.** up

Chapter 2

Check Your Readiness   p. 66

1. 1.1, 1.1 **2.** 0.3, 0.3 **3.** 0.7, 0.7 **4.** 5.8, 5.8
5. 2.5, 2.5 **6.** 6, 6 **7.** 0.6, 0.6 **8.** 0.07, 0.07 **9.** <
10. > **11.** < **12.** > **13.** < **14.** = **15.** = **16.** <

17. > **18.** < **19.** < **20.** > **21.** 25 **22.** 28 **23.** 15
24. −110 **25.** 36 **26.** 16 **27.** −24 **28.** 45
29. −20 **30.** −27 **31.** −5 **32.** −45

Lesson 2-1   pp. 68–72

Check Skills You'll Need 1. −25 **2.** 35 **3.** −7 **4.** −46

Standards Check
1. $18; 6 + 8 + 4$
$\quad = 6 + (8 + 4)$ Assoc. Prop. of Add.
$\quad = 6 + (4 + 8)$ Comm. Prop. of Add.
$\quad = (6 + 4) + 8$ Assoc. Prop. of Add.
$\quad = 10 + 8$ Add within parentheses.
$\quad = 18$ Add.
2a. Comm. Prop. of Add **b.** Ident. Prop of Mult.
c. Assoc. Prop. of Mult. **3a.** 27 **b.** 3 **c.** 40 **d.** 10
4. $6.30 **5a.** 300 **b.** −120 **c.** 240 **d.** 540

Check Your Understanding 1. Comm. Prop. of Add.
2. Assoc. Prop. of Mult. **3.** 5 + 95 **4.** 2 · 5
5. Answers may vary. Sample: Reordering and
regrouping can put numbers in positions in which
they are easier to combine. Example: 83 +
194 + 17 is easier to simplify if 83 and 17 are
added first.

Lesson 2-2   pp. 73–77

Check Skills You'll Need 1. 12 **2.** 24 **3.** 20 **4.** 6 **5.** 8 **6.** 4

Standards Check 1. 1,791 **2.** $1,428 **3a.** 210
b. −120 **c.** 35 **4a.** $8x - 12$ **b.** $3x + 12$ **c.** $6x + 2$
5a. $14 - 6d$ **b.** $18m + 3$ **c.** $-15t + 6$

Check Your Understanding 1. 12; 12 **2.** z; z **3.** a; a **4.** b

---

Lesson 2-3   pp. 78–81

Check Skills You'll Need 1. $5b + 20$ **2.** $-6x - 15$
3. $-32 - 12q$ **4.** $-12b + 42$

Standards Check 1a. 2, 4; $2s$, $4s$; 6 **b.** −4; none;
none **c.** 9, 2, −2, 1; $9m$ and $-2m$, $2r$ and r; none
2. $7a + 1$ **3a.** $2b$ **b.** $-13m$ **c.** $3p$ **4.** $-y + 5m$

Check Your Understanding 1. opposites **2.** Distributive
3. $5c$

Checkpoint Quiz 1 1. Comm. Prop of Mult.
2. Assoc. Prop. of Mult. **3.** Ident. Prop. of Mult.
4. Comm. Prop. of Add. **5.** Comm. Prop. of Mult.
6. Dist. Prop. **7.** $9a$ **8.** $18y$ **9.** $16w - 6$

Lesson 2-4   pp. 82–85

Check Skills You'll Need 1. $x + 46$ **2.** $g - 4$ **3.** $t - 5$
4. $\dfrac{z}{26}$

Standards Check 1a. false; $2 \neq 3$ **b.** open; has a
variable **c.** true; $20 = 20$ **2.** $20 - x = 3$; open
because there is a variable **3a.** no **b.** yes

---

4. $b + 6 = 33$; $27 + 6 = 33$; Yes, the backpack weighs 27 lb.

Check Your Understanding 1. True; for example, $3 + 2 = 7$. **2.** False, $3w - 7$ is not an equation. **3.** True; by definition an open sentence is one that contains a variable. **4.** True, for example $x = x$. **5.** Answers may vary. Sample: An algebraic expression may use variables. A numerical expression does not.

Lesson 2-5   pp. 88–92

Check Skills You'll Need 1. 3 **2.** 9 **3.** 8 **4.** 6

Standards Check 1a. −5 **b.** 4 **c.** −1 **2.** $123 = r + 55$; 68 beats/min **3a.** 13 **b.** 72 **c.** 112 **4.** $17 ≈ $15; $9 ≈ $10; $10 ≈ n − 15$; $25

Check Your Understanding 1. $−6 + y = 18$ **2.** $a − 5 = 23$ **3.** Subtract 8. **4.** Subtract 54. **5.** Add 19. **6.** 35; 35; −125 **7.** 86; 86; −236

Lesson 2-6   pp. 94–97

Check Skills You'll Need 1. 1 **2.** −1 **3.** −1 **4.** 1

Standards Check 1. 21 **2a.** −8 **b.** −12 **c.** 14 **3a.** −50 **b.** 324 **c.** −600

Check Your Understanding 1. $\frac{x}{25} = 125$ **2.** $−15t = −75$ **3.** Divide by 6. **4.** Divide by 3. **5.** Multiply by 5. **6.** yes; $\frac{−3}{−3} = 1$ **7.** no; $\frac{−18}{−3} ≠ −6$ **8.** no; $3(−3) ≠ 9$

Lesson 2-7   pp. 98–101

Check Skills You'll Need 1. 178 **2.** 188 **3.** 183 **4.** 180 **5.** 180 (Ex. 4)

Standards Check 6. 53 adult tickets, 80 student tickets

Lesson 2-8   pp. 102–105

Check Skills You'll Need

1. −9, −3, 7

2. −10, −8, −2

3. −5, 0, 3

4. −6, 3, 10

Standards Check

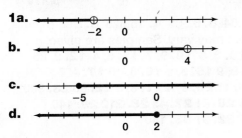
1a.
b.
c.
d.

---

2. $x ≥ 3$ **3.** $n < 5$

Check Your Understanding 1. D **2.** A **3.** B **4.** C **5.** Answers may vary. Sample: Use solid dot for ≥ and ≤; use open dot for > and <. **6.** Answers may vary. Sample: Graphing can show infinitely many solutions.

Lesson 2-9   pp. 106–109

Check Skills You'll Need 1. −2 **2.** 19 **3.** 9 **4.** 29

Standards Check 1a. $m > 3$

b. $t < 7$

c. $x ≥ −10$

2. ≤ 28 lb **3a.** $m > 42$ **b.** $v ≤ 11$ **c.** $t ≥ 16$

Check Your Understanding 1. Comm. Prop. of Add. **2.** Add. **3.** Subtract 10 from each side. **4.** Subtract.

Checkpoint Quiz 2 1. true; $19 = 19$ **2.** open; variable **3.** false; $1 ≠ −1$ **4.** −4 **5.** 4 **6.** 6 **7.** −32 **8.** −9 **9.** $a ≥ 6$ **10.** $r < 19$ **11.** $m > −19$ **12.** 1 quarter, 5 dimes, 2 pennies

Lesson 2-10   pp. 110–114

Check Skills You'll Need 1. 4 **2.** −9 **3.** −20 **4.** 288

Standards Check 1a. $x > 10$ **b.** $m < −7$ **c.** $t > −4$ **2a.** $m ≥ 8$ **b.** $t > −21$ **c.** $r > 35$

Check Your Understanding 1. unchanged **2.** unchanged **3.** reverses **4.** reverses **5.** Divide by 4. **6.** Divide by −4.

Chapter 3

Check Your Readiness   p. 124

1. 40 **2.** 10 **3.** 0 **4.** 600 **5.** 830 **6.** 6,010 **7.** < **8.** > **9.** < **10.** < **11.** > **12.** > **13.** 8.349, 8.35, 8.351, 9.25 **14.** 0.017, 0.02, 0.0201, 0.201 **15.** −14.1, −1.401, −1.4, −1.04 **16.** −3.2, −3.19, −2.8, −2.3 **17.** 11.49 **18.** 3.07 **19.** 3.65 **20.** 1.206 **21.** 6.7067 **22.** 6.9 **23.** 55.12 **24.** 10.6 **25.** 98.7 **26.** 532 **27.** 300 **28.** 154,070 **29.** 0.08 **30.** 0.0842 **31.** 0.0161 **32.** 0.001209

Lesson 3-1   pp. 127–131

Check Skills You'll Need 1. 2 tens **2.** 3 tenths **3.** 8 hundredths **4.** 6 thousandths

Standards Check 1a. tenths; 38.4 **b.** ones; 1 **c.** tenths; 7,098.6 **d.** thousandths; 274.943

e. tenths; 5.0 f. hundredths; 9.85 **2a.** about 560
b. about 220 **3a.** about 18.6 **b.** about $11
4. about 125

Check Your Understanding 1. exact **2.** estimate
3. estimate **4.** exact

Lesson 3-2   pp. 132–135

Check Skills You'll Need 1. 146 **2.** 199 **3.** 101 **4.** 28

Standards Check 1a. about 10 **b.** about 68
c. about 160 **2.** about $40 **3a.** about 20
b. about 6 **c.** about 20 **4a.** Yes; 0.68 is close to
an estimate of 0.8. **b.** No; 52.3 is not close to an
estimate of 5.

Check Your Understanding 1. 4(14.95) **2.** Rounding; I
am multiplying. I use compatible numbers for
division. **3.** Answers may vary. Sample: $60
4. No **5.** No. The total is too low.

Lesson 3-3   pp. 137–140

Check Skills You'll Need 1. 14 **2.** 10 **3.** 14 **4.** 3.5

Standards Check 1a. $r = 28$ mi/h **b.** $t = 51.5$ yr
2a. 61°F **b.** 59°F **c.** 53.5°F **3a.** 88.2 cm **b.** 52 in.

Check Your Understanding 1. 2,730 **2.** r **3.** division
4. 280 mi/h

Checkpoint Quiz 1 1. 15.66 **2.** 0.891 **3.** 7,023 **4.** 345.7
5. about 32 **6.** about 24 **7.** about −1 **8.** about 6
9. 8.5 h

Lesson 3-4   pp. 142–145

Check Skills You'll Need 1. 9.86 **2.** 2.45 **3.** 2.04 **4.** 3.08

Standards Check 1a. 13.9 **b.** 38.96
2. $35.48 + m = 70$; $34.52 **3a.** 21.1 **b.** −7.4
4. $x − 14.95 = 12.48$; $27.43

Check Your Understanding 1. yes **2.** no **3.** yes **4.** 1.2,
1.2, Subtract 1.2 from each side; 13.8, Simplify.
5. 3.33, 3.33, Add 3.33 to each side; 15.75,
Simplify.

Lesson 3-5   pp. 146–149

Check Skills You'll Need 1. 11.7 **2.** 0.48 **3.** 6.618
4. 4.8018

Standards Check 1a. −2 **b.** 0.5 **c.** 90.9
2. $5.5p = 7.70$; $1.40 **3a.** −3 **b.** 12.5 **c.** −360
4. 12 hits

Check Your Understanding 1. reasonable **2.** not
reasonable **3.** not reasonable **4.** reasonable
5. The student multiplied 30 by 3 instead of
dividing.

Lesson 3-6   pp. 150–155

Check Skills You'll Need 1. 500 **2.** 0.01406 **3.** 2.94
4. 0.009

Standards Check 1. Answers may vary. Samples are
given. **a.** Centimeter; a meter is too large unless
you use fractional parts of a meter; millimeters
are too small. **b.** Gram; an energy bar has a mass
of several grams, but it is much less than 1
kilogram. **c.** Kilogram; a horse is very heavy, so
grams are too small. **d.** Liter; a gas tank
holds several liters, so milliliters are too small.
2a. 50 km; millimeters are used to measure very
small lengths. **b.** 10 mL; the eyedropper holds
several drops of water but much less than a quart.
3a. 0.035 **b.** 250,000 **c.** 6,000 **4a.** 3,800 m
b. 250 mL

Check Your Understanding 1. C **2.** F **3.** B **4.** E **5.** A **6.** D

Checkpoint Quiz 2 1. 0.25 **2.** 8.55 **3.** 130 **4.** 3.05
5. 6.5 **6.** 129.6 **7.** 1.5 m; 1.5 cm is a little wider
than the width of a thumbnail. **8.** 500 mL; 500 L
would be about 500 qt. **9.** 0.095 **10.** 7,650,000
11. 0.675 **12.** 7,100 **13.** 9,100 g

Lesson 3-7   pp. 158–161

Check Skills You'll Need 1. Start with 0 and add 6
repeatedly; 24, 30, 36 **2.** Start with −18 and add 9
repeatedly; 18, 27, 36 **3.** Start with 0. Alternately
add 2 and subtract 1; 5, 4, 6 **4.** Start with 7.
Alternately subtract 1 and add 2; 9, 11, 10

Standards Check

5.

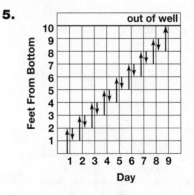

Chapter 4

Check Your Readiness   p. 170

1. 1,728 **2.** −64 **3.** 6,561 **4.** 15,625 **5.** 512 **6.** 64
7–12. Answers may vary. Samples are given.
7. 2, 6 **8.** 9, 5 **9.** 3, 6 **10.** 9, 7 **11.** 6, 4 **12.** 2, 25
13. 16, 2 **14.** 9, 9 **15.** 6, 9 **16.** 6, 10 **17.** 4, 7
18. 7, 8 **19.** 4, 11 **20.** 9, 4 **21.** 8, 9 **22.** 90 **23.** 900
24. 22 **25.** 49 **26.** 21 **27.** 45 **28.** 212 **29.** 140
30. 23 **31.** 27 **32.** 91 **33.** 130

Lesson 4-1 ～ pp. 172–175

Check Skills You'll Need **1.** 160 **2.** 73 **3.** 51 **4.** 48 **5.** 177 **6.** 118

Standards Check **1a.** Yes; 160 ends in 0. **b.** No; 56 does not end in 0. **c.** No; 53 does not end in 0, 2, 4, 6, or 8. **d.** Yes; 1,118 ends in 8. **2a.** No; the sum of the digits, 10, is not divisible by 9. **b.** No; the sum of the digits, 13, is not divisible by 3. **c.** Yes; the sum of the digits, 12, is divisible by 3. **d.** Yes; the sum of the digits, 18, is divisible by 9. **3a.** 1, 2, 5, 10 **b.** 1, 3, 7, 21 **c.** 1, 2, 3, 4, 6, 8, 12, 24 **d.** 1, 31 **e.** 1 row of 36 students, 2 rows of 18 students, 3 rows of 12 students, 4 rows of 9 students, or 6 rows of 6 students

Check Your Understanding **1–3.** Answers may vary. Samples are given. **1.** 5 **2.** 12 **3.** 20 **4.** 5 **5.** 2

Lesson 4-2 pp. 178–181

Check Skills You'll Need **1.** 81 **2.** 144 **3.** −64 **4.** 10,000

Standards Check **1a.** 6^3 **b.** $4xy^2$ **2a.** 49 **b.** −16, 16 **3a.** −58 **b.** 81

Check Your Understanding **1.** power/exponent **2.** exponent **3.** base **4.** No; $-8^2 = -64$. $(-8)^2 = 64$.

Lesson 4-3 pp. 182–186

Check Skills You'll Need **1.** 1, 3, 5, 15 **2.** 1, 5, 7, 35 **3.** 1, 7 **4.** 1, 2, 4, 5, 10, 20 **5.** 1, 2, 4, 5, 10, 20, 25, 50, 100 **6.** 1, 11, 121

Standards Check **1.** 11, 13, 17, 19; 10, 12, 14, 15, 16, 18, 20 **2a.** $2^3 \cdot 3^2$ **b.** 11^2 **c.** $3^2 \cdot 5^2$ **b.** $2^2 \cdot 59$ **3a.** 4 **b.** 3 **c.** $4r$ **d.** $15m$

Check Your Understanding **1–3.** Answers may vary. Samples are given. **1.** 31, 37 **2.** 44, 48 **3.** Yes; they both multiply to equal 225 and factor to $3^2 \cdot 5^2$.

Lesson 4-4 pp. 188–191

Check Skills You'll Need **1.** 7 **2.** 12 **3.** $5mn$ **4.** 3

Standards Check **1a–c.** Answers may vary. Samples are given. **1a.** $\frac{1}{3}$, $\frac{10}{30}$ **b.** $\frac{5}{6}$, $\frac{20}{24}$ **c.** $\frac{7}{10}$, $\frac{28}{40}$ **2a.** $\frac{3}{4}$ **b.** $\frac{3}{4}$ **c.** $\frac{4}{5}$ **3a.** $\frac{1}{ac}$ **b.** $\frac{n}{3}$ **c.** $3x$

Check Your Understanding **1–3.** Answers may vary. **4.** B

Checkpoint Quiz 1 **1.** 2, 3, 5, 10 **2.** 2, 3, 9 **3.** 2, 3 **4.** none **5.** 3, 9 **6.** 64 **7.** 125 **8.** −18 **9.** $\frac{1}{2}$ **10.** $\frac{2}{3}$ **11.** $\frac{4}{7}$ **12.** $\frac{1}{4}$ **13.** $2y$ **14.** Answers may vary. Samples: $5a^2$, $10a^2$; $25a^3b$, $30a^2$

Lesson 4-5 pp. 193–196

Check Skills You'll Need **1.** > **2.** > **3.** < **4.** <

Standards Check **6.** 45 pictures

Lesson 4-6 pp. 197–200

Check Skills You'll Need **1.** $\frac{1}{5}$ **2.** $\frac{2}{3}$ **3.** $\frac{4}{5}$ **4.** $\frac{3}{4}$

Standards Check **1.** Answers may vary. Sample: $-\frac{8}{10}$, $\frac{-4}{5}$, $\frac{4}{-5}$

2.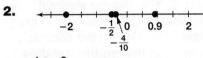

3a. $-\frac{1}{3}$ **b.** $\frac{2}{3}$ **c.** −3

Check Your Understanding **1.** −1 **2.** $\frac{1}{5}$ **3.** 0.8 **4.** $\frac{-3}{5}$ **5.** yes **6.** yes **7.** yes **8.** no

Lesson 4-7 pp. 201–204

Check Skills You'll Need **1.** k^4 **2.** m^2n^2 **3.** 2^4 **4.** 5^3

Standards Check **1a.** 0.00032 **b.** m^{12} **2a.** $18a^4$ **b.** $15c^9$ **c.** $12x^6$ **3a.** 256 **b.** c^{20} **c.** m^6

Check Your Understanding **1.** D **2.** B **3.** C **4.** A

Lesson 4-8 pp. 205–209

Check Skills You'll Need **1.** x **2.** $\frac{1}{y}$ **3.** $\frac{2x}{3}$ **4.** $\frac{ab}{4}$

Standards Check **1a.** 1,000 **b.** x^7 **2a.** 1 **b.** 5 **c.** y^3 **d.** $\frac{1}{5}$ **3a.** $\frac{1}{16}$ **b.** $\frac{1}{a^2}$ **c.** $\frac{1}{3y^4}$ **4a.** b^{-6} **b.** $m^{-3}n^{-6}$ **c.** $x^{-4}y^2$

Check Your Understanding **1.** $\frac{2 \cdot 2 \cdot 2 \cdot 2 \cdot 2 \cdot 2}{2 \cdot 2 \cdot 2 \cdot 2 \cdot 2} = 2$ **2.** $\frac{\frac{1}{3} \cdot \frac{1}{3} \cdot \frac{1}{3} \cdot \frac{1}{3}}{\frac{1}{3} \cdot \frac{1}{3}} = \left(\frac{1}{3}\right)^2$ **3.** $\frac{0.08 \cdot 0.08 \cdot 0.08 \cdot 0.08 \cdot 0.08}{0.08 \cdot 0.08} = (0.08)^3$ **4.** $3^{-2} = \frac{1}{3^2} = \frac{1}{9}$

Checkpoint Quiz 2 **1–5.** Answers may vary. Samples are given. **1.** $\frac{1}{4}$, $\frac{-1}{-4}$, $\frac{2}{8}$ **2.** $\frac{1}{3}$, $\frac{-1}{-3}$, $\frac{2}{6}$ **3.** $\frac{7}{10}$, $\frac{-7}{-10}$, $\frac{14}{20}$ **4.** $\frac{9}{14}$, $\frac{-9}{-14}$, $\frac{-18}{-28}$ **5.** $\frac{8}{10}$, $\frac{-8}{-10}$, $\frac{-4}{-5}$ **6.** $-\frac{1}{3}$ **7.** $-\frac{1}{2}$ **8.** $\frac{2}{3}$ **9.** $-\frac{5}{8}$ **10.** $\frac{1}{4}$

11–15.

16. 128 **17.** x^{50} **18.** $6a^2$ **19.** $\frac{1}{x^5}$ **20.** $\frac{1}{a^6}$

Check Skills You'll Need 1. 10^8 2. 10^{16} 3. 10^2 4. 10^{-3}

Standards Check 1a. 5.45×10^7 b. 7.23×10^5 2a. 2.1×10^{-4} b. 5×10^{-8} 3a. 32,100,000 b. 0.000000059 c. 10,060,000,000 4a. 1.6×10^6 b. 2.03×10^5 c. 7.243×10^{15} 5a. 18.3×10^6, 0.098×10^9, 526×10^7 b. 0.22×10^{-10}, 8×10^{-9}, 14.7×10^{-7} 6a. 2.4×10^{11} b. 5.68×10^{-3} 7. 1.002×10^{-23} kg

Check Your Understanding 1. 1 2. No; the decimal point moves 5 place values. Only three zeros are needed. 3. Less than zero. Moving the decimal point places the number in the ten-thousandths place. 4. The numbers are equal. 5. Numbers can be grouped together and powers of 10 can be grouped together for easier calculation.

Chapter 5

1. 1.2 2. 60 3. −45 4. −40 5. 1.5 6. 74 7. 8 8. −1.78 9. 3 10. 4 11. 12 12. 1 13. 10 14. 5 15. 9 16. 1 17. 10 18. 14 19–21. Answers may vary. Samples are given. 19. $\frac{1}{2}, \frac{3}{6}$ 20. $\frac{8}{12}, \frac{2}{3}$ 21. $\frac{3}{4}, \frac{6}{8}$ 22. $\frac{5}{6}$ 23. $\frac{2}{5}$ 24. −2 25. $\frac{1}{4}$ 26. $-\frac{24}{25}$ 27. $\frac{1}{3}$ 28. $\frac{4}{15}$ 29. $\frac{4}{31}$ 30. $-\frac{2}{9}$ 31. $-\frac{2}{13}$ 32. $\frac{1}{6}$ 33. $\frac{5}{7}$ 34. 5.4 35. 0.6 36. 0.625 37. 0.75 38. 0.375

Check Skills You'll Need 1. $2^2 \cdot 5$ 2. 5^3 3. $3^2 \cdot 5$ 4. $2 \cdot 3 \cdot 31$ 5. $3^3 \cdot 23$ 6. $3^2 \cdot 5^2 \cdot 7$

Standards Check 1a. 12 b. 20 c. 60 2a. 48 b. 45 c. 180 3a. $60xy$ b. $56m^4$ c. $75xy^2$ 4a. $\frac{4}{9} > \frac{2}{9}$ b. $-\frac{4}{9} < -\frac{2}{9}$ c. $-\frac{4}{9} < \frac{2}{9}$ 5a. $\frac{6}{7} > \frac{4}{5}$ b. $\frac{2}{3} < \frac{3}{4}$ c. $-\frac{3}{4} < -\frac{7}{10}$ 6. $\frac{1}{6} < \frac{5}{12} < \frac{2}{3} < 1$

Check Your Understanding 1. 30: 30, 60, 90, 120, 150, 180; 24: 24, 48, 72, 96, 120, 144 2. the number of salt or pepper shakers in a set of boxes 3. the least number of salt and pepper shakers you can buy to have an equal amount 4. 4 boxes of salt shakers and 5 boxers of pepper shakers

Check Skills You'll Need 1. 0.241, 2.41, 12.4, 24.1 2. 1.003, 1.030, 1.300, 13.03 3. −0.1, −0.01, 0.01, 0.1

Standards Check 1a. 0.75 b. 1.875 c. 3.3 d. 0.6 2a. $0.\overline{7}$; repeating 7 b. $0.9\overline{54}$; repeating; 54 c. 1.375; terminating d. $0.\overline{72}$; repeating; 72

3. 0.2, 0.5, $\frac{7}{10}, \frac{4}{5}$ 4a. $1\frac{3}{4}$ b. $2\frac{8}{25}$ c. $\frac{13}{20}$ 5a. $\frac{7}{9}$ b. $\frac{6}{11}$ c. $\frac{71}{333}$

Check Your Understanding 1. rational 2. D 3. A 4. E 5. B 6. C

Check Skills You'll Need 1. 8 2. 18 3. $10n$ 4. 18 5. 40 6. $10n$

Standards Check 1a. $\frac{4}{7}$ b. $\frac{5}{k}$ 2a. $-\frac{1}{8}$ b. $\frac{3m - 14}{7m}$ 3a. $-\frac{5}{24}$ b. $\frac{1}{36}$ 4a. $6\frac{5}{8}$ b. $2\frac{1}{18}$ c. $1\frac{17}{36}$

Check Your Understanding 1. D 2. B 3. C 4. E 5. A

Checkpoint Quiz 1 1. > 2. = 3. < 4. < 5. 0.51 6. $\frac{3}{250}$ 7. 1.25 8. $\frac{1}{3}$ 9. $0.8\overline{3}$ 10. $\frac{17}{33}$ 11. $\frac{11}{13}$ 12. $\frac{5}{36}$ 13. $4\frac{19}{40}$ 14. $\frac{2}{3}$

Check Skills You'll Need 1. $\frac{7}{3}$ 2. $\frac{33}{10}$ 3. $\frac{13}{9}$ 4. $\frac{24}{5}$ 5. $\frac{63}{8}$ 6. $\frac{36}{7}$

Standards Check 1a. $\frac{2}{15}$ b. $-\frac{5}{9}$ c. $\frac{35}{72}$ d. $\frac{3}{32}$ 2a. $\frac{4}{7}$ b. $-\frac{7}{25}$ c. $\frac{x}{6}$ 3a. $1\frac{1}{2}$ b. $\frac{6}{7}$ c. $-4\frac{8}{15}$ 4a. $-\frac{1}{2}$ b. $\frac{15a}{16}$ c. $\frac{b}{2}$

Check Your Understanding 1. multiplicative inverse 2. $\frac{3}{2}$ 3. $-\frac{1}{2}$ 4. 3 5. −3 6. $-\frac{5}{9}$ 7. 1 8. $\frac{5}{2}$ 9. $\frac{1}{4}$ 10. $\frac{2}{9}$

Check Skills You'll Need 1. $\frac{1}{3}$ 2. 52 3. 10 4. $1\frac{1}{2}$

Standards Check 1a. Feet or yards; inches are too small and miles are too large. b. Pounds; the weight is too great to measure in ounces. c. Inches; the length is too small to measure in feet. d. Fluid ounces; the capacity of a cup is too large. 2. $\frac{7}{8}$ 3. $10\frac{1}{2}$

Check Your Understanding 1. G 2. A 3. C 4. F 5. D 6. B 7. E 8. < 9. > 10. =

Check Skills You'll Need 1. $\frac{1}{10}, \frac{1}{5}, \frac{1}{4}, \frac{1}{3}, \frac{1}{2}$ 2. $\frac{3}{3}, \frac{5}{3}, \frac{7}{3}, \frac{13}{3}$ 3. $\frac{3}{13}, \frac{3}{7}, \frac{3}{5}, \frac{3}{3}$ 4. $-\frac{3}{3}, -\frac{3}{5}, -\frac{3}{7}, -\frac{3}{13}$

Standards Check 7. 3 h 55 min

Check Skills You'll Need 1. $-1\frac{1}{8}$ 2. $8\frac{5}{24}$ 3. $2\frac{5}{8}$ 4. $-7\frac{7}{18}$

Standards Check 1. $-\frac{1}{3}$ 2. $1\frac{1}{7}$ 3a. $2\frac{1}{18}$ b. Answers may vary. Sample: I subtracted the mixed number $1\frac{1}{3}$ from both sides of the equation to solve for z.

Check Your Understanding 1. Add $\frac{3}{4}$ to each side.
2. $2 \cdot 3$ **3.** Write each fraction using common denominators. **4.** $\frac{9}{12}$ **5.** $\frac{11}{12}$

Lesson 5-8   pp. 262–266

Check Skills You'll Need 1. $\frac{5}{14}$ **2.** $-1\frac{1}{2}$ **3.** $6\frac{1}{4}$ **4.** 3

Standards Check 1. $\frac{7}{18}$ **2.** 1 **3a.** $-\frac{7}{8}$ **b.** $\frac{13}{15}$ **c.** $-\frac{1}{14}$
4a. 8 **b.** $-\frac{3}{10}$ **c.** $4\frac{6}{11}$

Check Your Understanding
1.
$$-\frac{7}{10}h = 5\frac{3}{5}$$
$$-\frac{10}{7} \cdot \left(\frac{-7}{10}h\right) = -\frac{10}{7} \cdot 5\frac{3}{5}$$
$$h = -\frac{10}{7} \cdot \frac{28}{5}$$
$$h = -8$$

2. negative **3.** positive **4.** zero **5.** zero

Checkpoint Quiz 2 1. 14 **2.** $\frac{1}{2}$ **3.** $-\frac{4}{27}$ **4.** $1\frac{1}{3}$ **5.** -2
6. 34 **7.** $2\frac{1}{4}$ **8.** 90 **9.** $1\frac{1}{2}$ **10.** $\frac{1}{3}$ **11.** $\frac{1}{5}$ **12.** $1\frac{5}{8}$ **13.** $11\frac{1}{4}$
14. $\frac{6}{35}$ **15.** $\frac{7}{15}$ **16.** $-17\frac{1}{3}$ **17.** $-\frac{27}{40}$ **18.** $3\frac{3}{5}$ **19.** $\frac{5}{33}$
20. 6 miles **21.** 55 mi/h **22.** \$12 **23.** Answers may vary. Sample: A desktop can be measured in inches; 48 inches.

Lesson 5-9   pp. 270–273

Check Skills You'll Need 1. 64 **2.** 81 **3.** 1 **4.** x^{18} **5.** b^{10}
6. a^{28}

Standards Check 1a. 216 **b.** $16p^4$ **c.** x^5y^{10} **d.** $25x^6$
2a. $16y^4$ **b.** $-16y^4$ **3a.** $\frac{16}{81}$ **b.** $\frac{8x^6}{27}$

Check Your Understanding 1. $(5x^2)^2$ **2.** $(5x \cdot x) \cdot (5x \cdot x)$
$= 25x^4$ **3.** $25x^4$; yes **4.** Answers may vary.
Sample: Yes; because $20 < 25$, $20x^4 < 25x^4$, so the area of the tablecloth is greater.

Chapter 6

Check Your Readiness   p. 282

1. 16 **2.** 13.5 **3.** $\frac{7}{8}$ **4.** 2.5 **5.** $1\frac{1}{4}$ **6.** 27.5
7–12. Answers may vary. Samples are given.
7. $\frac{2}{8}, \frac{4}{16}$ **8.** $\frac{2}{5}, \frac{8}{20}$ **9.** $\frac{3}{7}, \frac{12}{28}$ **10.** $\frac{4}{18}, \frac{6}{27}$ **11.** $\frac{6}{16}, \frac{9}{24}$
12. $\frac{10}{12}, \frac{15}{18}$ **13.** $\frac{1}{4}$ **14.** $\frac{1}{4}$ **15.** $\frac{4}{5}$ **16.** $\frac{3}{8}$ **17.** $\frac{3}{7}$ **18.** $\frac{1}{8}$ **19.** $\frac{5}{6}$
20. $\frac{1}{25}$ **21.** 0.35 **22.** $\frac{3}{50}$ **23.** 3.75 **24.** $\frac{7}{20}$ **25.** $\frac{7}{8}$
26. 3.6 **27.** $1\frac{7}{100}$ **28.** $0.\overline{6}$ **29.** $11.\overline{1}$ **30.** $\frac{4}{5}$ **31.** 6.25
32. $3\frac{49}{50}$

Lesson 6-1   pp. 284–287

Check Skills You'll Need 1. $\frac{6}{7}$ **2.** $\frac{3}{5}$ **3.** $\frac{9}{10}$ **4.** $\frac{4}{5}$ **5.** $\frac{1}{3}$ **6.** $\frac{5}{3}$, or $1\frac{2}{3}$

Standards Check 1. 34 mi/gal **2.** 52.5 **3.** 9 workers

Check Your Understanding 1. $\frac{7}{8}$ **2.** $\frac{8}{15}$ **3.** \$.05 **4.** 315

Lesson 6-2   pp. 290–294

Check Skills You'll Need 1. 13 **2.** 6 **3.** 15 **4.** 3

Standards Check 1a. 6 **b.** 44 **c.** 77 **2a.** yes, cross products equal **b.** no, cross products not equal **c.** yes, cross products equal **3.** 87 nautical miles

Check Your Understanding 1. $\frac{6}{8}$ **2.** $\frac{6}{8} = \frac{\ell}{24}$ **3.** 18
4. Answers may vary. Sample: The units in his fractions do not form a proportion.

Lesson 6-3   pp. 295–299

Check Skills You'll Need 1. 14 **2.** 133.3 **3.** 6.7 **4.** 3.6

Standards Check 1. 15.8

2. 28 ft

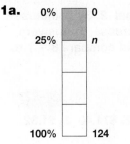

3. $2\frac{3}{4}$ in.

Check Your Understanding 1. 4.5 **2.** 4.5 in. **3.** Answers may vary. Sample: It's important because you know the map is not in proportion.

Checkpoint Quiz 1 1. 4 mi/h **2.** 6 gal/min **3.** 48 ft/s
4. 4.5 **5.** 42 times **6.** 6.6 in.

Lesson 6-4   pp. 301–305

Check Skills You'll Need 1. 0.625 **2.** 0.45 **3.** 0.75
4. $0.8\overline{3}$ **5.** $0.\overline{6}$ **6.** $0.\overline{72}$

Standards Check 1a. $\frac{29}{50}$ **b.** $\frac{18}{25}$ **c.** $1\frac{11}{25}$ **2a.** 0.625
b. 0.45, $\frac{9}{20}$ **3a.** 40% **b.** 23% **c.** 175% **4.** 27%

Check Your Understanding 1. D **2.** C **3.** A **4.** B **5.** 0.5; Answers may vary. Sample: $0.5 = 50\%$, $50\% > 4\%$.

Lesson 6-5   pp. 306–310

Check Skills You'll Need 1. 7 **2.** 230 **3.** 25 **4.** 18

Standards Check

1a.

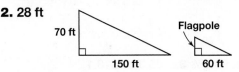

b.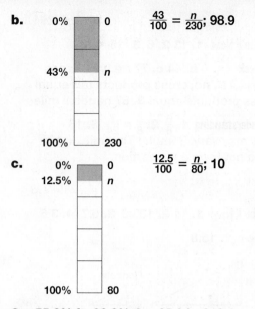

0% — 0
43% — n
100% — 230

$$\frac{43}{100} = \frac{n}{230}; 98.9$$

c.

0% — 0
12.5% — n
100% — 80

$$\frac{12.5}{100} = \frac{n}{80}; 10$$

2a. 55.2% **b.** 93.3% **3a.** 25.3 **b.** 313.1
4. about 3,567 screens

Check Your Understanding 1. B **2.** C **3.** A **4.** Answers may vary.

Lesson 6-6   pp. 311–314

Check Skills You'll Need 1. 0.48 **2.** 0.05 **3.** 0.238
4. 0.7225 **5.** 1.36 **6.** 1.785

Standards Check 1a. $0.96 = n \cdot 10$; 9.6%
b. $19.2 = 0.32 \cdot n$; 60 **2a.** $n = 1.455 \cdot 20$; 29.1
b. $380 = 1.25n$; 304 **3.** $.85 **4.** 1,400 people

Check Your Understanding 1. 28 **2.** Greater; 44 is the part. **3.** Answers may vary. Sample: Change the percent to a decimal, $0.32 \cdot n$. Change the percent to a fraction, $\frac{32}{100} \cdot n$.

Lesson 6-7   pp. 316–319

Check Skills You'll Need 1. 46% **2.** 247% **3.** 3%
4. 523.6%

Standards Check 1a. 14% **b.** 60% **c.** 112.5%
2. 26% **3a.** 50% **b.** 5.0% **c.** 92.9%

Check Your Understanding 1. original **2.** 30%, increase **3.** 19%, increase **4.** 43%, decrease **5.** Answers may vary. Sample: Jessi should compare $8 - 7$ to 7, not 8.

Lesson 6-8   pp. 320–323

Check Skills You'll Need 1. $61.50 **2.** $71.40 **3.** $1.32
4. $12.79

Standards Check 1. $42 **2.** $8.50 **3.** $3.30

Check Your Understanding 1. C **2.** A **3.** D **4.** B **5.** $32.13

Checkpoint Quiz 2 1. = **2.** < **3.** > **4.** $0.33 \cdot 120 = n$;
39.6 **5.** $1.25 \cdot 42 = n$; 52.5 **6.** $n \cdot 5.6 = 1.4$; 25%
7. $0.15 \cdot q = 9.75$; 65 **8.** $9,600

Lesson 6-9   pp. 325–329

Check Skills You'll Need 1. 80% **2.** 53% **3.** 62.5%
4. 60% **5.** 58.$\overline{3}$% **6.** 12.5%

Standards Check 1. food, 40% **2.** The second copier is faster. **3.** about 1 mg **4.** Explanations may vary. Sample: The total cost is about $396. $350 is not enough.

Check Your Understanding 1. 148.5 mi **2.** 156 mi
3. 156 mi; 7.5 mi **4.** The student wrote 1.5% as $\frac{15}{100}$. Sample correction: Use $\frac{2}{100}$ as an estimate of 1.5%.

$$1.5\% < \frac{2}{100} \cdot 90$$
$$= \frac{1,800}{100}$$
$$= 1.8$$

Lesson 6-10   pp. 330–333

Check Skills You'll Need 1. $163.83

Standards Check 11. about 299 million people

Chapter 7

Check Your Readiness   p. 342

1. $p + 3$ **2.** $q - 6$ **3.** $12y$ **4.** $10d$ **5.** $2b$ **6.** $n - 8$
7. $4n$ **8.** $-3b + 10$ **9.** $19c + 13$ **10.** $-7x - 5y$
11. $2a + 6$ **12.** $9m - 35$ **13.** 11 **14.** -21 **15.** -98
16. 5 **17.** 8 **18.** 9 **19.** -32 **20.** -8 **21.** $c \geq 1$
22. $y < 2$ **23.** $b < 4$ **24.** $x > 0$ **25.** $x \geq -6$
26. $x \leq 15$ **27.** $b \leq 19$ **28.** $m \geq 80$

Lesson 7-1   pp. 344–347

Check Skills You'll Need 1. 8 **2.** 11 **3.** 1 **4.** -12 **5.** -10

Standards Check 1a. 3 **b.** 16 **2a.** -2 **b.** 21 **3.** $11

Check Your Understanding 1. C **2.** B **3.** A **4.** D **5.** The order of operations is reversed when you solve an equation. You add and subtract first.

Lesson 7-2   pp. 348–352

Check Skills You'll Need 1. $5x + 4$ **2.** $6y$ **3.** $3a$ **4.** $2 + c$
5. $2x - 7$

Standards Check 1. 92 points **2a.** 88, 89, 90, 91
b. 32, 34 **3a.** $4\frac{2}{3}$ **b.** -14

Check Your Understanding 1. Distributive Prop.
2. Comm. Prop. of Add. **3.** Combine like terms.
4. Subtract −6 from each side. **5.** Simplify.

Lesson 7-3 — pp. 353–357

Check Skills You'll Need 1. −3 **2.** $2\frac{1}{4}$ **3.** −4 **4.** $\frac{2}{3}$

Standards Check 1a. 50 **b.** $10\frac{1}{2}$ **2.** $\frac{3}{4}$ **3.** 4

Check Your Understanding 1. D **2.** E **3.** C **4.** A **5.** B

Lesson 7-4 — pp. 358–361

Check Skills You'll Need 1. $p - 21 = 48$ **2.** $b + 6 = 33$
3. $140 + d = 192$

Standards Check 5a. $2 \cdot 29.95 + 0.12m = 76.34$
b. 137 mi **c.** $29.95 \approx 30$; $0.12 \approx 0.1$; $137 \approx 140$;
$2 \cdot 30 + 0.1 \cdot 140 = 60 + 14 = 74$; Since $74 \approx 76.34$,
137 mi is a reasonable answer. **6.** 122 mi

Checkpoint Quiz 1 1. 20 **2.** 11 **3.** −18 **4.** 4 **5.** 28
6. −48 **7.** 2 **8.** 1.3 **9.** −6 **10.** 0 **11.** 1 **12.** 6
13. $p - 0.25p = 82.50$; $110 **14.** $n + (n + 1) + (n + 2) = 132$; 43, 44, 45

Lesson 7-5 — pp. 363–366

Check Skills You'll Need

1. $w \geq -9$
$\underset{-10\,-9\,-8\,-7\,-6\,-5\,-4\,-3\,-2\,-1\ \ 0}{\bullet\!-\!-\!-\!-\!-\!-\!-\!-\!-\!\longrightarrow}$

2. $z > 10$
$\longleftarrow\!\underset{4\ \ 5\ \ 6\ \ 7\ \ 8\ \ 9\ 10\ 11\ 12\ 13\ 14}{\circ\!-\!\longrightarrow}$

3. $a < -2$
$\longleftarrow\!\underset{-5\,-4\,-3\,-2\,-1\ \ 0\ \ 1\ \ 2\ \ 3\ \ 4\ \ 5}{\circ}$

4. $x \leq -1$
$\longleftarrow\!\underset{-5\,-4\,-3\,-2\,-1\ \ 0\ \ 1\ \ 2\ \ 3\ \ 4\ \ 5}{\bullet}$

Standards Check

1. $x \leq -8$
$\underset{-10\quad-8\quad-8\quad-4\quad-2}{\bullet}$

2. $m \geq -15$
$\underset{-15\ \ -10\ \ -5\quad 0\quad 5\quad 10}{\bullet\!-\!-\!-\!-\!-\!\longrightarrow}$

3. $\geq \$7,500$

Check Your Understanding 1. $\frac{x}{-4} - 2$ **2.** $\leq$ **3.** $\frac{x}{-4} - 2$
≤ -18; $x \geq 64$ **4.** No; $-12 \not\geq 64$.

Lesson 7-6 — pp. 367–370

Check Skills You'll Need 1. 320 km **2.** 32 m **3.** 48 ft²

Standards Check 1a. $s = p + c$ **b.** $k = hj$
c. $p = \frac{I}{rt}$ **2a.** $a = \frac{1}{5}b - \frac{7}{5}$ **b.** $w = \frac{1}{2}P - \ell$
c. $x = 3(y - 8)$ **3.** $r = \frac{d}{t}$ **4.** $h = an$; 11 hits

Check Your Understanding 1. 3; 3; 6, 6; 6, c **2.** j; h; g; j

Checkpoint Quiz 2 1. −2 **2.** −6 **3.** $\frac{2}{9}$ **4.** 4 **5.** 3 **6.** 5
7. $y > -\frac{9}{10}$ **8.** $x > -56$ **9.** $x > 5$ **10.** $h = s - g$
11. $r = \frac{1}{3}k - \frac{4}{3}$ **12.** $t = \frac{I}{pr}$

Lesson 7-7 — pp. 371–375

Check Skills You'll Need 1. $24 **2.** $1,100 **3.** $31.50
4. $17.88

Standards Check 1a. $30 **b.** $4.38

2a.

Bal. at Yr Start	Interest	Bal. at Yr End
$500.00	$15.00	$515.00
$515.00	$15.45	$530.45

2b.

Bal. at Yr Start	Interest	Bal. at Yr End
$625.00	$12.50	$637.50
$637.50	$12.75	$650.25
$650.25	$13.01	$663.26
$663.26	$13.27	$676.53

3a. $955.09 **b.** $955.37

Check Your Understanding 1. C **2.** B **3.** D **4.** A **5.** The
compound-interest account; it has a balance of
$1,169.86. The simple-interest account has a
balance of $1,160.

Chapter 8

Check Your Readiness — p. 384

1. −4, −7 **2.** 19, 13 **3.** 10.5, 12 **4.** −11, −13
5. (5, 2) **6.** (−3, 4) **7.** (4, 0) **8.** (6, −3) **9.** (−4, −3)
10. (0, 3) **11–16.**
17. $-\frac{1}{18}$ **18.** 3 **19.** 1 **20.** $\frac{1}{3}$
21. $y = -4x + 3$
22. $y = -2x + 4$
23. $y = 2x - 6$
24. $y = -6x - 8$
25. $y = -x + 12$
26. $y = -\frac{1}{2}x + \frac{5}{2}$
27. $y = \frac{1}{5}x + 4$
28. $y = -\frac{3}{4}x + 3$

Lesson 8-1 — pp. 388–392

Check Skills You'll Need 1–6.

Standards Check 1a. No; there are two range values for the domain value 2. **b.** Yes; there is one range value for each domain value.
2a. No; a specific postage cost (domain value) can mail packages of different weights (range values). **b.** Yes; for each package weight (domain value) there is one postage cost to the same zip code (range value).
3a. A function; no vertical line passes through two graphed points.
b. Not a function; a vertical line passes through both $(-1, -1)$ and $(-1, 3)$.

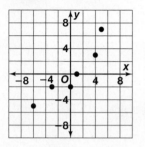

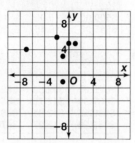

c. A function; no vertical line passes through two graphed points.

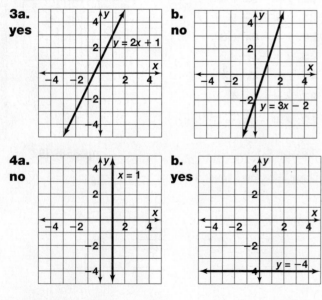

Check Your Understanding 1. $(-1, 0, 1, 2, 4)$ **2.** $(-1, 1, 4)$
3. yes **4.** no **5.** Yes, 2 is added to the range. **6.** no

Lesson 8-2   pp. 393–397

Check Skills You'll Need 1. 4 **2.** -10 **3.** 3 **4.** 6

Standards Check 1a. $(-3, -5)$ **b.** $(-3, 15)$
c. $(-3, -4)$ **2.** $14°C$

3a. yes

b. no

4a. no

b. yes

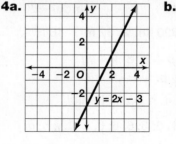

---

c. no

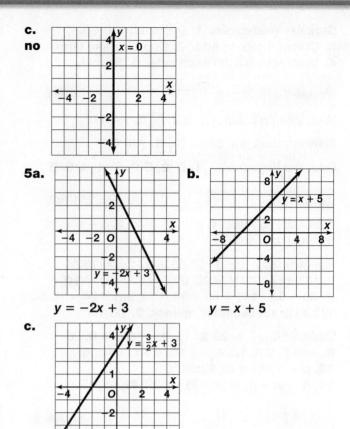

5a. $y = -2x + 3$

b. $y = x + 5$

c. $y = \frac{3}{2}x + 3$

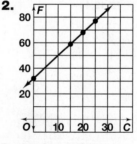

Check Your Understanding 1. 32; 59; 68; 77
2.

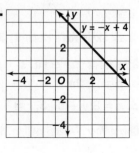

3. no **4.** no **5.** yes

Lesson 8-3   pp. 399–404

Check Skills You'll Need 1. -9 **2.** 5 **3.** -3 **4.** 0

Standards Check 1. $-\frac{3}{4}$ **2.** $\frac{3}{4}$ **3.** $\frac{1}{12}$

4a.   **b.**

Check Your Understanding 1. 4, 3; 2, 3 **2.** $\frac{2}{3}$ **3.** Yes, the slope between any two points is constant.

Checkpoint Quiz 1 1. Answers may vary. Sample: $(0, -9), (2, 0), (1, -4\frac{1}{2})$ **2.**
3. Yes; there is one range value for each domain value.
4. Answers may vary. Sample: If every vertical line passes through just one graphed point, then the relation is a function.
5. 5 **6.** −1 **7.** undefined
8. 2 **9.** −2, 5

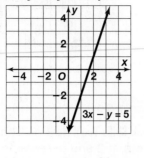

Lesson 8-4   pp. 405–408

Check Skills You'll Need 1. 0 **2.** $-1\frac{3}{4}$ **3.** 7

Standards Check

1.

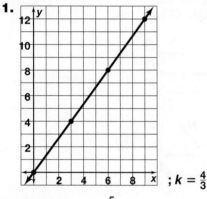

$; k = \frac{4}{3}$

2. 225 lb **3.** $y = -\frac{5}{3}x$

Check Your Understanding 1. $\frac{1}{2}$ **2.** 0.945 **3.** $y = 0.945x$
4. 7.56

Lesson 8-5   pp. 410–413

Check Skills You'll Need 1. $7(-12) = -84$ **2.** $11x = 132$
3. $\frac{x}{45} = 3$

Standards Check 3. $18 = 12 + 2 \cdot 3$ **4.** $3 + 18 = 21$

Lesson 8-6   pp. 414–419

Check Skills You'll Need

1.

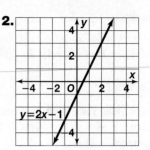

2.

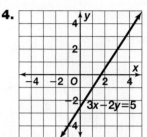

3.

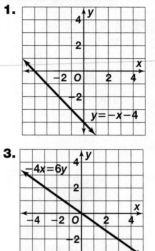

4.

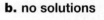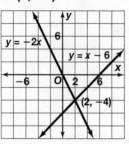

Standards Check

1. $(2, -4)$

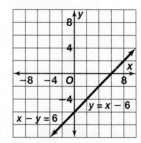

2a. infinitely many solutions   **b.** no solutions

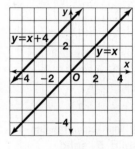

3. −3, −5

Check Your Understanding 1. $x + y = 4$ **2.** $y = 3x$
3.

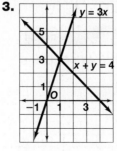

4. The lengths of the pieces that satisfy both equations. **5.** 1 ft, 3 ft

Checkpoint Quiz 2

1. $y = -8x$ **2.** $y = -3x$ **3.** $(-2, 8)$ **4.** $(-3, -4)$
5. $(1, 3)$ **6.** $(-2\ -1)$ **7.** $231g = c$ **8.** $3, -7$

Lesson 8-7   pp. 420–425

Check Skills You'll Need 1. yes; $-5 + 3 \geq -2$
2. no; $5 - 1 \not< 4$ **3.** yes; $-2 - 2(-4) \leq 6$
4. no; $4(-2) + 1 \not> -7$

Standards Check

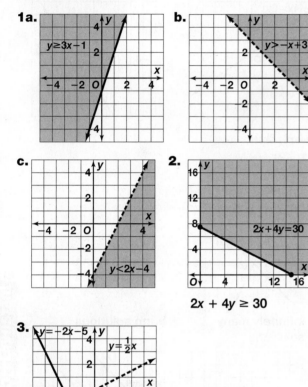

1a. $y \geq 3x - 1$
b. $y > -x + 3$
c. $y < 2x - 4$
2. $2x + 4y = 30$

$2x + 4y \geq 30$

3. $y = -2x - 5$; $y = \frac{1}{2}x$

Check Your Understanding 1. C **2.** C **3.** dashed
4. solid **5.** solid

Chapter 9

Check Your Readiness   p. 434

1. 25 cm **2.** 14.4 in. **3.** 100.8 m **4.** 6.4 ft **5.** 6 cm
6. $\frac{1}{2}$ in. **7.** 2.8 cm **8.** 7.5 ft

9–18.

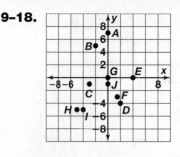

Lesson 9-1   pp. 436–441

Check Skills You'll Need 1. The graph is a line that starts at 3 and extends to the right without end.
2. The graph is a line that starts at 0 and extends to the left without end. **3.** The graph is a line that starts at 5 and extends to the left without end.
4. The graph is a line that starts at -2 and extends to the right without end.

Standards Check 1a. C, N, V **b.** $\overline{NC}, \overline{NV}$
c. $\overrightarrow{NC}, \overrightarrow{NV}$ **2a.** $\overline{EH}, \overline{FG}, \overline{AE}, \overline{BF}$
b. $\overline{HG}, \overline{DC}, \overline{AB}$ **c.** $\overline{DH}, \overline{CG}, \overline{AD}, \overline{BC}$

3a.

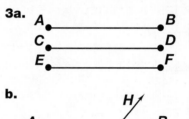

b.

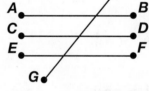

c.

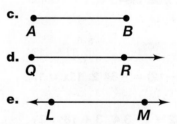

d.

e.

Check Your Understanding 1. A, B, C **2.** $\overline{AB}, \overline{BC}, \overline{AC}$
3. $\overrightarrow{AC}, \overrightarrow{BC}, \overrightarrow{BA}, \overrightarrow{CA}$ **4.** Z, R, F **5.** $\overline{ZR}, \overline{RF}, \overline{ZF}$
6. Answers may vary. Sample: $\overrightarrow{ZR}, \overleftrightarrow{RF}, \overrightarrow{ZF}$ **7.** No; two lines that are not in the same plane are skew, and skew lines cannot be parallel.

Lesson 9-2   pp. 443–447

Check Skills You'll Need 1. 135 **2.** 15 **3.** -43.5 **4.** 15

Standards Check 1. $160°, 20°, 160°$ **2.** $\angle 1 \cong \angle 5$, $\angle 2 \cong \angle 6, \angle 3 \cong \angle 7, \angle 4 \cong \angle 8; \angle 3 \cong \angle 5, \angle 4 \cong \angle 6$

Check Your Understanding 1. D **2.** B **3.** C **4.** A
5. Answers may vary.

Lesson 9-3   pp. 448–452

Check Skills You'll Need 1. acute **2.** obtuse **3.** obtuse
4. right **5.** acute **6.** obtuse

Standards Check 1a. scalene right triangle
b. isosceles obtuse triangle **c.** scalene obtuse
triangle **2.** rectangles and squares **3a.** $P = 6x$
b. 96 cm

Check Your Understanding

1–6. Answers may vary. Samples are given.

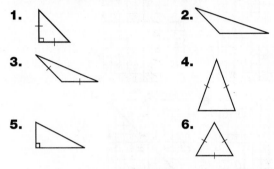

7. No. A rectangle that has four congruent sides
(a square) is a rhombus. Not every rectangle
is a square.

Lesson 9-4   pp. 454–457

Check Skills You'll Need 1. **2.**

3. **4.** **5.**

Standards Check 5. 35

Lesson 9-5   pp. 458–462

Check Skills You'll Need 1. $\angle X$ **2.** $\angle Z$ **3.** $\overline{XY}$ **4.** $\overline{ZX}$

Standards Check 1. $\overline{AB} \cong \overline{DE}$, $\overline{BC} \cong \overline{EC}$, $\overline{AC} \cong \overline{DC}$,
$\angle A \cong \angle D$, $\angle B \cong \angle E$, $\angle BCA \cong \angle ECD$, $AC = 50$ m
2. $\overline{FJ} \cong \overline{FG}$, $\overline{JI} \cong \overline{GH}$, $\overline{FI} \cong \overline{FH}$, $\triangle JFI \cong \triangle GFH$
by SSS

Check Your Understanding 1. $\angle D$ **2.** $\angle E$ **3.** $m\angle F$, or 37°
4. $m\angle E$, or 90° **5.** $m\angle D$, or 50° **6.** $\overline{DF}$ **7.** $\overline{BC}$
8. $\overline{ED}$ **9.** DF, or 5 mm **10.** CB, or 4 mm **11.** $\triangle FED$
12. $\triangle EDF$ **13.** Answers may vary. Sample: Flip
$\triangle ABC$ over $\overline{AC}$. Rotate it until $\overline{CB} \cong \overline{FE}$. Slide it
until it exactly matches $\triangle DEF$.

Checkpoint Quiz 1 1. ray **2.** line **3.** $\overline{LN}$ **4.** angle
5a. $6x + 16 + 2x + 12 = 180$, $x = 19$ **b.** 50°
c. 130° **d.** 130° **6.** Answers may vary.
Sample:

Lesson 9-6   pp. 464–468

Check Skills You'll Need 1. 36 **2.** 270 **3.** 54 **4.** 109

Standards Check 1a. about $8\frac{4}{5}$ in. **b.** about 188.4 mm
c. about 628 mi

2. Blood Types of Population

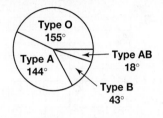

3. Student Jobs at Western High School

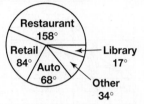

Check Your Understanding 1. 25% **2.** food **3.** section A
4. Answers may vary. Sample: It is easier to view
the circle graph to compare information.

Lesson 9-7   pp. 470–474

Check Skills You'll Need 1. point B **2.** a line segment
with endpoints A and B **3.** a ray with endpoint A
and containing B **4.** a line containing point A and
point B

Standards Check

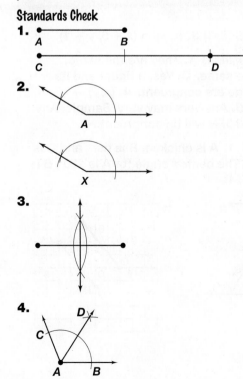

Instant Check System Answers

Check Your Understanding 1. A **2.** C **3.** B **4.** Answers may vary. Sample: Compass and straightedge; it is difficult to measure 72.6° with a protractor. **5.** Answers may vary. Sample: No, you only need to open the compass to the length of the segment.

Lesson 9-8 pp. 476–480

Check Skills You'll Need 1–5.

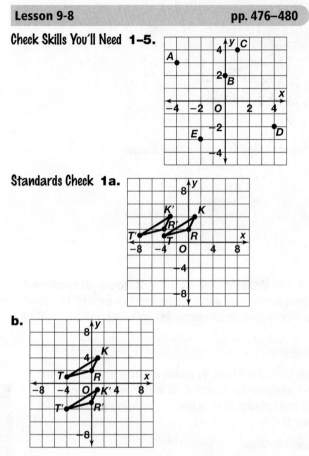

Standards Check 1a.

b.

2. $B(-1, 5) \rightarrow B'(3, 1)$ **3.** $(x, y) \rightarrow (x + 5, y - 1)$

Check Your Understanding 1. They are the same. **2.** They are the same. **3.** Yes, a figure and its translated image are congruent. **4.** $(x, y) \rightarrow (x - 4, y + 1)$ **5.** Answers may vary. Sample: Any translation of *BDFH* will be congruent.

Checkpoint Quiz 2 1. A is chicken, B is fish, and C is vegetarian. **2.** The central angle for A is 180°, B is 126°, and C is 54°.

3.

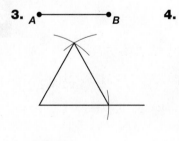

4.

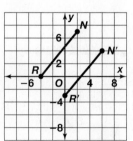

Lesson 9-9 pp. 482–485

Check Skills You'll Need

1. **2.**

3. **4.**

5. **6.**

Standards Check

1a. **b.**

2. **3a.**

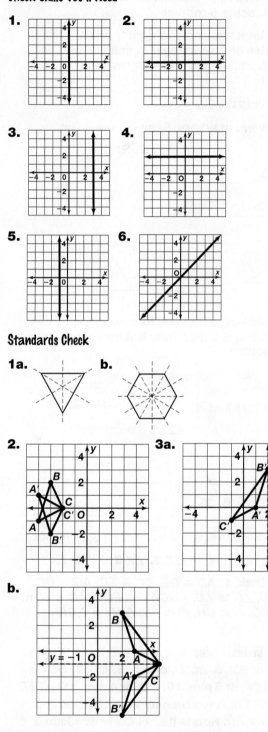

b.

Check Your Understanding 1. a reflection over the *x*-axis **2.** Yes, a figure and its reflection are congruent.

3.

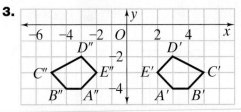

4. Yes; $ABCDE \cong A'B'C'D'E'$ and $A'B'C'D'E' \cong A''B''C''D''E''$, so $ABCDE \cong A''B''C''D''E''$.
5. They are congruent.

Lesson 9-10   pp. 486–489

Check Skills You'll Need

1. **2.**

3.

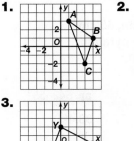

Standards Check

1.

2a. no **b.** yes, 180°
c. yes, 180°

The vertices of the image are $A'(-1, 1)$, $B'(-3, 2)$, and $C'(-2, 3)$.

Check Your Understanding **1.** 1,358 **2.** 1,358 **3.** yes
4. 2 **5.** 2

Chapter 10

Check Your Readiness   p. 498

1. 36 m² **2.** 20 in.² **3.** 45 cm² **4.** 45 **5.** 78.5
6. 864 **7.** 48 **8.** 300 **9.** 452.16 **10.** 6 **11.** $19\frac{1}{2}$
12. 9 **13.** 10x **14.** 5x² **15.** 55 **16.** 1,364 **17.** 500
18. 8 **19.** 157 yd **20.** 628 m **21.** 17.27 in.

Lesson 10-1   pp. 500–504

Check Skills You'll Need **1.** $\ell = 9$ in. **2.** $A = 245$ m²
3. $w = 10$ cm **4.** $A = 51.84$ ft²

Standards Check 1a. 1,000 cm², or 0.1 m²
b. 12 ft², or $1\frac{1}{3}$ yd² **2a.** 6 m² **b.** 24 in.² **c.** The area
of the larger parallelogram is 4 times the area of
the smaller parallelogram.

Check Your Understanding **1.** Rectangle **2.** $A = bh$
3. $b = 300$; $h = 160$ **4.** 48,000 ft²

Lesson 10-2   pp. 507–511

Check Skills You'll Need **1.** 8 **2.** 42 **3.** $37\frac{1}{2}$ **4.** 10

Standards Check 1a. 7.38 ft² **b.** 5 m² **2.** 24 yd²
3a. 13 ft² **b.** 342 mm²

Check Your Understanding **1.** $A = \frac{1}{2} bh$ **2.** 54 ft²
3. $A = bh$ **4.** 180 ft² **5.** 234 ft²

Lesson 10-3   pp. 512–517

Check Skills You'll Need **1.** 50.24 **2.** 78.5 **3.** 254.34
4. 0.785

Standards Check 1. $2,500\pi$ in.² **2.** about
113 mi² **3.** 40.2 cm²

Check Your Understanding **1.** E **2.** A **3.** B **4.** C **5.** D
6. 4 to 1

Checkpoint Quiz 1 **1.** 100 in.² **2.** 50 in.² **3.** 300 in.²
4. 300 yd² **5.** 2,100 cm² **6.** 150 m² **7.** 100π yd²;
314 yd² **8.** 64π ft²; 201 ft² **9.** $(800 + 50\pi)$ cm²;
957 cm²

Lesson 10-4   pp. 519–523

Check Skills You'll Need **1.** triangle **2.** square
3. rectangle **4.** hexagon

Standards Check 1a. cylinder **b.** cone

2.

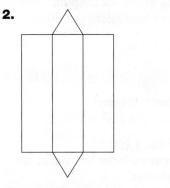

Check Your Understanding **1.** C **2.** A **3.** B

Lesson 10-5   pp. 527–532

Check Skills You'll Need **1.** 31.4 in. **2.** 26.4 cm
3. 25.1 ft **4.** 21.4 in.

Standards Check 1. 84 yd² **2.** 108 m²
3. 250π cm², about 785 cm²

Check Your Understanding 1. triangle **2.** 24 in.^{2} **3.** 24 in. **4.** 120 in.^{2} **5.** 168 in.^{2} No; the height of the prism is the length of the segment that joins the two triangular bases, or 5 in. The height of the triangular base of the prism is the height of the triangle, or 8 in.

Lesson 10-6   pp. 534–538

Check Skills You'll Need 1. 10π **2.** 15π **3.** 5π **4.** 22π

Standards Check 1. 720 ft^2 **2.** about 1,011 ft^2 **3.** about 452.16 cm^2

Check Your Understanding
1.

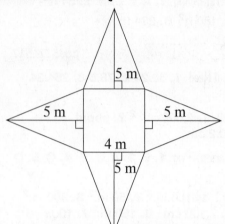

2. They are the same. **3.** 40 m^2 **4.** 40 m^2 **5.** They are the same. **6.** In the formula L.A. = $4(\frac{1}{2} b\ell)$, b represents the length of the base of a rectangular pyramid. The product $4b$ represents the perimeter of the rectangular base of the pyramid. In the formula L.A. = $\frac{1}{2} p\ell$, p represents the perimeter of the base of the rectangular pyramid. The formulas are equivalent because $4b = p$.

Lesson 10-7   pp. 539–542

Check Skills You'll Need 1. about 201 cm^2 **2.** about 452 cm^2 **3.** about 314 cm^2

Standards Check 1. 216 ft^3 **2a.** 1,900 ft^3 **b.** The volume of the larger cylinder is 8 times the volume of the smaller cylinder.

Check Your Understanding 1. $V = bh$ **2.** V represents the volume of the prism. B represents the area of the base of the prism. h represents the height of the prism. **3.** $2\frac{3}{4} \cdot x$ **4.** Answers may vary. Sample: In the formula $V = Bh$, substitute 38.5 for V and $2\frac{1}{2}$ for h. Solve the equation. **5.** $15\frac{2}{5}$ ft^2 **6.** $5\frac{3}{5}$ ft^2.

Lesson 10-8   pp. 544–547

Check Skills You'll Need

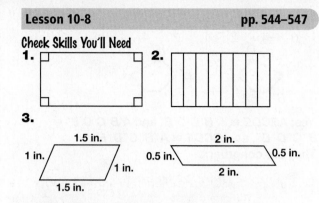

Standards Check 8a. 66 in.^{3}; 52.5 in.^{3}; 21 in.^{3} **b.** Yes; $5\frac{1}{2}$ in. by 8 in. by $1\frac{1}{2}$ in.

Checkpoint Quiz 2 1. square prism, 56 cm^2 **2.** cylinder, 207 in.^{2} **3.** square pyramid, 85 cm^2 **4.** 78.1 cm^3 **5.** 169.6 in.^{3}

Lesson 10-9   pp. 548–551

Check Skills You'll Need 1. $20.9\overline{3}$ **2.** 32 **3.** $33.49\overline{3}$ **4.** $0.52\overline{3}$

Standards Check 1. 21 cm^3 **2.** $166.\overline{6}$ ft^3 **3a.** 14,130 m^3 **b.** 180 mi^3

Check Your Understanding 1. about 785 cm^3 **2.** about 113 cm^3 **3.** about 672 cm^3 **4.** about 672 cm^3

Lesson 10-10   pp. 552–555

Check Skills You'll Need 1. $\frac{7}{4}$ **2.** $\frac{216}{5}$

Standards Check 1. 8.8 m **2.** S.A. = 486 in.^{2}; $V = 729$ in.^{3}

Check Your Understanding 1. Two solids are similar if their corresponding angles are congruent and their corresponding dimensions are proportional. **2.** $\frac{1}{3} = \frac{1}{x}$ **3.** 54 cm^2 **4.** 27 cm^3

Chapter 11

Check Your Readiness   p. 564

1. G **2.** K **3.** H **4.** D **5.** B **6.** F **7.** $(-5, 4)$ **8.** $(2, 1)$ **9.** $(7, 0)$ **10.** $(-7, 1)$ **11.** $(4, -2)$ **12.** $(-6, -3)$ **13.** 100 **14.** 36 **15.** 4 **16.** 81 **17.** 121 **18.** 0.04 **19.** 49 **20.** 5.29 **21.** 16 **22.** 25 **23.** 4 **24.** 4 **25.** 1 **26.** 10 **27.** 2 **28.** 60 **29.** 77 **30.** 26 **31.** 10 **32.** 32 **33.** 17 **34.** 8

Lesson 11-1   pp. 566–569

Check Skills You'll Need **1.** 1, 4, 9, 16, 25, 36, 49, 64, 81, 100, 121, 144 **2.** 100; 400; 900; 1,600; 2,500; 3,600; 4,900; 6,400; 8,100, 10,000; 12,100; 14,400

Standards Check 1a. 10 **b.** −4 **2a.** 7 **b.** −5
3a. irrational; because 2 is not a perfect square
b. rational; because 81 is a perfect square
c. rational; because it is a terminating decimal
d. irrational; because 42 is not a perfect square

Check Your Understanding 1. D **2.** C **3.** B **4.** A
5. Answers may vary. Sample: rational number 13.27; irrational number $\sqrt{177}$

Lesson 11-2   pp. 570–575

Check Skills You'll Need 1. 52 **2.** 89 **3.** 130 **4.** 90

Standards Check 1a. 5 ft **b.** 9 m **2.** 13 m
3. 8.7 ft **4a.** Yes, $7^2 + 8^2 = 113$.
b. No, $5^2 + 6^2 \neq 10^2$.

Check Your Understanding 1. legs: $\overline{AC}$, $\overline{BC}$; hypotenuse: $\overline{AB}$ **2.** legs: $\overline{XY}$, $\overline{YZ}$; hypotenuse: $\overline{XZ}$
3. 10 **4.** 36 **5.** 64 **6.** 8

Checkpoint Quiz 1 1. −2 **2.** 4 **3.** 5 **4.** 9 **5.** −7 **6.** 10
7. 10 ft **8.** 16.1 m **9.** 25 yd **10.** 7.1 cm **11.** No, $8^2 + 10^2 \neq 12^2$. **12.** Yes, $5^2 + 12^2 = 13^2$.
13. Answers may vary. Sample: $\sqrt{120}$, $\sqrt{299}$, 15.010010001 . . .

Lesson 11-3   pp. 579–583

Check Skills You'll Need 1. (−3, 4) **2.** (0, 3) **3.** (−4, −2)
4. (3, −1)

Standards Check 1a. 4.1 **b.** 9.5 **2.** area = 12.5 square units, perimeter = 17.1 units
3a. (4, 3) **b.** (−1, 0.5)

Check Your Understanding 1. 10 **2.** 10 **3.** The answers are the same. Explanations may vary. **4.** Answers may vary. Sample: Distance formula; it is not easy to calculate *LM* and *MN*.

Lesson 11-4   pp. 586–589

Check Skills You'll Need 1. 4 **2.** 4 **3.** 32 **4.** 10

Standards Check 3. $\overline{RQ}$ and $\overline{RP}$, $\overline{ST}$ and $\overline{SP}$
4. It allows you to draw the entire 312.7 + 773.8 side to complete the larger triangle.

Lesson 11-5   pp. 591–595

Check Skills You'll Need 1. −11, −1, 9 **2.** 2, 3, 4
3. −4, 2, 8 **4.** $-5\frac{1}{2}$, −5, $-4\frac{1}{2}$

Standards Check

1.

x	$-2x^2 = y$	(x, y)
−2	$-2(-2)^2 = -8$	(−2, −8)
−1	$-2(-1)^2 = -2$	(−1, −2)
0	$-2(0)^2 = 0$	(0, 0)
1	$-2(1)^2 = -2$	(1, −2)
2	$-2(2)^2 = -8$	(2, −8)

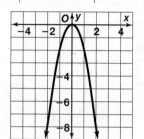

2.

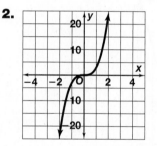

3. $x \approx 1$

Check Your Understanding 1. Quadratic; it can be written as $y = nx^2$, where $n = 25$. **2.** Cubic; it can be written as $y = nx^3$, where $n = -8$. **3.** Quadratic; it can be written as $y = nx^2$, where $n = \frac{2}{5}$.
4. Answers may vary. Sample: The graph of a quadratic function in the form $y = nx^2$ is a U-shaped curve in Quadrants I and II with vertex at (0, 0). The graph of a cubic function in the form $y = nx^3$ has a curve similar to a quadratic function, but the left half of the curve is flipped over the *x*-axis.

5.

d	$\frac{2}{3}d^2 = h$	(d, h)
10	$\frac{2}{3}(10)^2 \approx 67$	$(10, 67)$
20	$\frac{2}{3}(20)^2 \approx 267$	$(20, 267)$
30	$\frac{2}{3}(30)^2 = 600$	$(30, 600)$
40	$\frac{2}{3}(40)^2 \approx 1,067$	$(40, 1067)$
50	$\frac{2}{3}(50)^2 \approx 1,667$	$(50, 1667)$
60	$\frac{2}{3}(60)^2 = 2,400$	$(60, 4200)$
70	$\frac{2}{3}(70)^2 \approx 3,267$	$(70, 3267)$
80	$\frac{2}{3}(80)^2 \approx 4,267$	$(80, 2467)$
90	$\frac{2}{3}(90)^2 = 5,400$	$(90, 5400)$
50	$\frac{2}{3}(100)^2 \approx 6,667$	$(100, 6667)$

6.

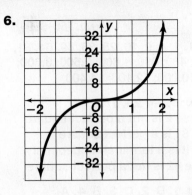

7. $s \approx 2.6$

Chapter 12

Check Your Readiness p. 604

1–8.

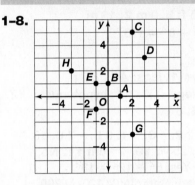

9. $\frac{1}{3}$ **10.** $\frac{3}{4}$ **11.** $\frac{4}{5}$ **12.** $\frac{2}{3}$ **13.** $\frac{1}{2}$ **14.** $\frac{5}{8}$ **15.** $\frac{1}{7}$ **16.** $\frac{3}{10}$
17. 0.50 **18.** 0.36 **19.** 0.20 **20.** 0.05 **21.** 20%
22. 87.5% **23.** 28% **24.** 30%

Lesson 12-1 pp. 606–610

Check Skills You'll Need 1. 3, 4, 5, 6, 6, 8, 9
2. 68, 69, 71, 72, 72 **3.** 98, 101, 101, 112, 120
4. 3, 3.3, 3.7, 3.74, 37

Standards Check 1. 2.95, 2.8, 2.3, 2 **2a.** 3 modes
b. 1 mode **3a.** 31; raises the mean by 2.6
b. 1; lowers the mean by 2.8 **4a.** $25.25, $23.50,
$20 **b.** Answers may vary. Sample: Median; the
mode is equal to two of the smaller data values,
and the outlier ($42) affects the mean too much.

Check Your Understanding 1. Mean 17.2, median 17; no
2. The mean becomes 20. The median remains
17. **3.** Answers may vary. Sample: data sets that
include outliers **4.** Answers may vary. Sample:
No, the restaurant could serve a $9 and a $31
meal.

Checkpoint Quiz 2 1. $AB = 9.2$; $(-3, -\frac{11}{2})$
2. $AB = 15.8$; $(\frac{3}{2}, \frac{13}{2})$
3.

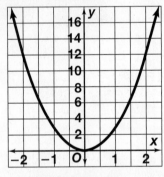

4.

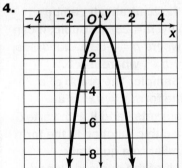

5.

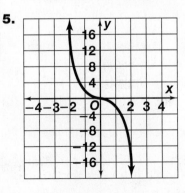

Lesson 12-2   pp. 612–615

Check Skills You'll Need **1.** 9; 9 **2.** 77; 73 **3.** 200; 300
4. 5; 3

Standards Check

1.

Number	Frequency
10	5
11	3
12	2
13	2
14	1
15	2

2a.

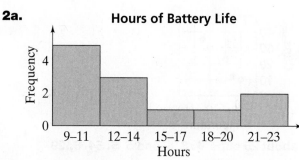

Hours of Battery Life

b. 14; the hours of battery life are the data, so the range is $23 - 9 = 14$.

Check Your Understanding **1.** Answers may vary.
Sample: A histogram uses the width of the bars to show interval size. **2.** There are no data items less than 25. **3.** 27

Checkpoint Quiz 1

1.

Number	Frequency
47	2
48	2
49	1
50	3
51	2
52	2

2.

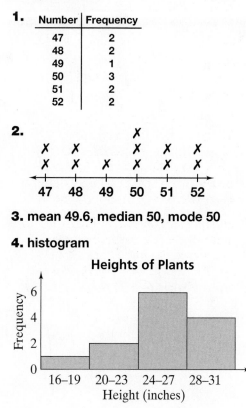

```
                X
  X   X        X   X   X
  X   X    X   X   X   X
 ─┼───┼───┼───┼───┼───┼─
  47  48  49  50  51  52
```

3. mean 49.6, median 50, mode 50

4. histogram

Heights of Plants

---

5. mean 25.1, median 25, mode 25 **6.** 16

Lesson 12-3   pp. 617–621

Check Skills You'll Need **1.** 9.5 **2.** 4.9 **3.** 52 **4.** 101

Standards Check

1.

Migrations of Birds (thousands of miles)
```
 ─┼─┼─┼─┼─┼─┼─┼─┼─┼─┼─┼─┼─┼─┼─┼─┼─┼─┼─
  1 2 3 4 5 6 7 8 9 10 11 12 13 14 15 16 17 18
```

2.

Annual Sales (millions of units)
```
 15 16 17 18 19 20 21 22 23 24 25 26 27 28 29 30
              Videos
              CDs
```

3. The highest value is 45 and the lowest is 15. The median is 35. At least half of the values are within 10 units of the median. **4.** The women's heights have a median of 71 in. and a range of 10 in. The men's heights have a median of 79 in. and a range of 12 in. Most of the men are taller than the tallest woman.

Check Your Understanding **1.** B **2.** D **3.** E **4.** A **5.** C
6. Long whiskers; there will be a large difference between the minimum or maximum and the other values.

Lesson 12-4   pp. 622–626

Check Skills You'll Need **1.** 29.2 **2.** 30 **3.** 40

Standards Check

1.   Monthly High
      Temperatures

```
  8 | 6 7
  9 | 1 7
 10 | 1
 11 | 1 3
 12 | 0 0 5 6
 13 | 4
```
Key: 13 | 4 means 134

2.

Videos (millions)		CDs (millions)
7 6 5	1	5 6 6 6 7 8 8
8 4 4 2 2 1	2	2 4 5
0	3	

means 21 → 1 | 2 | 2 ← means 22

Median for videos: 22   Median for CDs: 17.5
Modes for videos: 24 and 22   Modes for CDs: 16

Check Your Understanding **1.** 6, 7, 8, 9 **2.** 8, 8 **3.** 24
4. median 84%, mode 78%

Lesson 12-5   pp. 628–633

Check Skills You'll Need 1. (−2, 2) **2.** (0, 3) **3.** (−3, 0)
4. (2, 3)

Standards Check 1a. This person has 12 years of
education and earns $20,000 in a year. **1b.** The
person has 14 years of education and earns
$90,000 in a year. **c.** 4 people

2a.

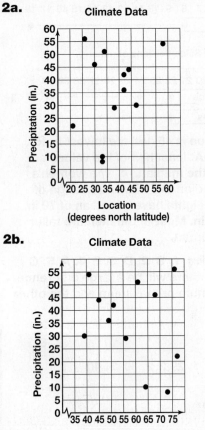

2b.

Climate Data

3a. Positive correlation; as time goes by, the
winning distances have tended to increase.

Check Your Understanding 1. Amount of time increases.
2. positive correlation **3.** A student who lives
0.5 mi away takes 10 min to get to school.
4. 3 students

Lesson 12-6   pp. 635–638

Check Skills You'll Need 1. 2 **2.** −$\frac{1}{4}$

Standards Check 3a–d. Answers may vary.
Samples are given. **a.** about 2,175 **b.** about −55
c. $y = -55x + 2,175$ **d.** 1,185

Checkpoint Quiz 2
1.

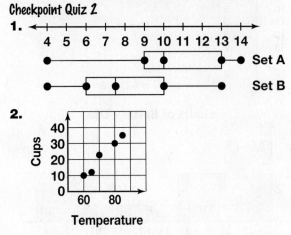

2.

3. about 25 cups **4.** 3, 4, and 5 **5.** 54 **6.** 29

Selected Answers

Chapter 1

Lesson 1-1   pp. 6–7

STANDARDS PRACTICE 5. Variable expression; b is the variable. **7.** Variable expression; n is the variable. **9.** Variable expression; x is the variable. **11.** $m + 16$ **13.** $\frac{n}{3}$ **15.** $3c$ **17.** $2 \cdot 12$ **19.** $5 \cdot 7$ **21.** Variable expression; d is the variable. **23.** Variable expression; g is the variable. **25.** $7 \cdot 4$ **27.** $\frac{160}{16}$ **29.** $d - 20$ **31.** $300m + 80b$ **33.** C **35.** A **37.** Answers may vary. Sample: The student confused the positions of n and 5. **39.** D **41.** B **43.** 72 **45.** 75 **47.** 2

Lesson 1-2   pp. 11–12

STANDARDS PRACTICE 5. 27 **7.** 2 **9.** 31 **11.** 13 **13.** 49 **15.** 13 **17.** 33 **19.** 4 **21.** We must agree on an order of operations to ensure that everyone gets the same value for an expression. **23.** 24 **25.** 16 **27.** 25 **29.** > **31.** < **33.** $7 \cdot (8 - 6) + 3 = 17$ **35.** $5 + (4 \cdot 9)$; 41 **37.** $17 - (25 \div 5)$; 12 **39.** $4 + 7 \cdot 3$; 25 hours **41.** Answers may vary. Sample: $(6 \times 6) - (2 \times 2)$ and $(2 \times 6) + (2 \times 6) + (2 \times 2) + (2 \times 2)$; 32 m² **43.** Answers may vary. Sample: Payton bought 4 pairs of blue socks and 3 pairs of red socks at $3 a pair. She also bought a hat for $2. What was the total cost of her purchases? $23 **45.** C **47.** D **49.** $\frac{k}{20}$ **51.** $10d$

Lesson 1-3   pp. 16–17

STANDARDS PRACTICE 7. 2 **9.** 23 **11.** 107 **13.** 12 **15.** 10 **17.** 6 **19.** 65 **21.** 15 **23.** 11 **25.** 91 **27.** 99 **29.** 2 **31a.** $153w$ **b.** 306 Calories **33.** Answers may vary. Sample: You did not work within the grouping symbols first. **35.** 8.9 **37.** 0 **39.** Answers may vary. Sample: Liam has 5 fewer than 3 times the number of cards that Jamie has. Jamie has 5 cards. How many cards does Liam have? **41.** D **43.** D **45.** $\frac{d}{20}$

Lesson 1-4   pp. 20–22

STANDARDS PRACTICE
7. $-9, -2, 8$ [number line: −9, −2, 0, 8]

9. $-6, 0, 6$ [number line: −6, 0, 6]

11. 2, 2 **13.** 7, 7 **15.** 4, 4 **17.** 3 **19.** 17 **21.** Answer may vary. Sample: 28 golf strokes over par **23.** 6 **25.** 2 **27.** 0 **29.** −13 **31.** −23

33. < **35.** < **37.** < **39.** = **41.** > **43.** $r + n$
45. Answers may vary. Sample: My friend did not take into account the signs of the numbers.
47. positive

49a.

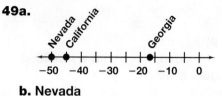

   b. Nevada

51. Explanations may vary. Sample: If x and y have opposite signs, $|x + y| \neq |x| + |y|$. For $x = -1$ and $y = 3$, $|-1 + 3| = 2$ while $|-1| + |3| = 4$. **53.** −2, −1 **55.** D **57.** B **59.** 14 **61.** 440 **63.** <

Lesson 1-5   pp. 27–29

STANDARDS PRACTICE 9. $-4 + 7$; 3 **11.** $-4 + (-2)$; −6 **13.** −3 **15.** 3 **17.** 3 **19.** −13 **21.** 53 **23.** 2,620 m **25.** 12 **27.** 12 **29.** > **31.** > **33.** 0 **35.** 16 **37.** Positive; the number with greater absolute value is positive. **39.** Negative; all numbers are negative. **41.** −8 **43.** $-20 + 18$; −2 **45.** $120 + (-25)$; 95 **47.** 1 **49.** $158 **51.** Answers may vary. Sample: First find the difference of the absolute values of the two numbers. Then give the answer the sign of the number with the greater absolute value. **53.** positive **55.** positive **57.** B **59.** B **61.** >

Lesson 1-6   pp. 32–34

STANDARDS PRACTICE 9. −4 **11.** 1 **13.** −6 **15.** −1 **17.** −12 **19.** $6 + 2$; 8 **21.** $2 + (-6)$; −4 **23.** $-2 + (-6)$; −8 **25.** $75 + 25$; 100 **27.** −124 **29.** 19 **31.** 913 **33.** −83 **35.** −52 **37.** 850 **39.** 66 **41–45.** Answers may vary. Samples are given. **41.** $15 - 5 = 10$; $-5 - (-15) = 10$ **43.** $5 - 20 = -15$; $-20 - (-5) = -15$ **45.** $12 - 1 = |11|$; $-5 - (-16) = |11|$ **47.** −24°C **49.** 2 **51.** −7 **53.** 10 **55.** 12 **57.** 0 **59.** −30 **61.** $-2 - 4$; −6; $6 **63.** $0 + 15 - 25$; −10; −10°F **65–69.** Answers may vary. Samples are given. **65.** −280 **67.** −110 **69.** 80 **71a.** 16, 20, 24, 28 **b.** 28 **c.** 24

73. −3;

5	−9	1
−5	−1	3
−3	7	−7

75. 6;

9	−5	−4	6
−2	4	3	1
2	0	−1	5
−3	7	8	−6

77. D **79.** B **81.** 7 **83.** −11 **85.** 11 **87.** 3
89. −6

Lesson 1-7   pp. 38–39

STANDARDS PRACTICE

9. a six-sided figure with a six-sided figure inside it

11. Start with −10 and add 6 repeatedly; 14, 20
13. Answers may vary. Sample: No. Mario's catching a cold could be due to many different reasons. **15.** correct

17. a square inside a circle inside a triangle inside a diamond

19. Incorrect; some have 4. **21.** correct **23.** Start with −1.1 and repeatedly add −1.1. **25.** Start with 1 and alternately subtract and add consecutive multiples of 3; 10, −11, 13 **27.** D **29.** −7 **31.** 103

Lesson 1-8   pp. 42–43

STANDARDS PRACTICE 1. 36 laps/day **3.** $10.23
5. 11 pieces; 16 pieces **7a.** $59; $21 **b.** 10 people
9. 3 mi **11.** A **13.**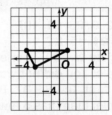

Lesson 1-9   pp. 47–49

STANDARDS PRACTICE 9. −9 **11.** −24 **13.** −18
15. −81 **17.** −48 **19.** −60 **21.** −360 **23.** −96
25. −18 **27.** −7 **29.** 10 **31.** 2 yd **33.** $92 **35.** D
37. B **39.** −14 **41.** −21,384 **43.** 216 **45.** −20
47a. −36 **b.** $40 per share **49.** < **51.** < **53.** <
55. −15 **57.** −15, 5 **59–61.** Answers may vary.
Samples are given. **59.** 3 and −2; −1 **61.** −11
and 0; −6 **63.** Negative; the numerator is positive, and the denominator is negative, so the quotient is negative. **65a.** $\frac{1}{2}$ **b.** Answers may vary.
Sample: Draw a number line from 0 to 1 in eighths.
Find and number halfway between 0 and $\frac{1}{4}$. **67.** C
69. 37 **71.** > **73.** 50 − n

Lesson 1-10   pp. 54–56

STANDARDS PRACTICE 5. III **7.** IV **9.** II
11. (0, −7) **13.** (−2, 4) **15.** (−8, 3)

17–23.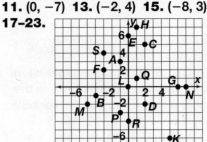

25.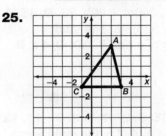

27.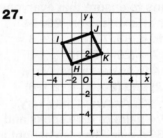

29. F **31.** P **33.** (−2, 3) **35.** (6, 6) **37.** y-axis
39. y-axis
41. triangle   **43.** parallelogram

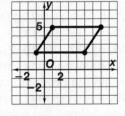

45. (0, −5) **47.** about 122° W, 38° N
49. Carson City, Nevada
51.

53. Answers may vary. Sample: 52a flips the figure across the y-axis. 52b flips the figure across the x-axis. 52c flips the figure across one axis and then the other. **55.** I **57.** III **59.** Explanations may vary. Sample: No; since a and b describe positions on two number lines, (a, b) and (b, a) describe different points (unless a = b). **61.** 8 units^2 **63.** A **65.** −95 **67.** 20 **69.** 3

Chapter 1 Review   pp. 59–61

1. origin **2.** variable **3.** y-axis **4.** quadrants **5.** integers **6.** x-coordinate **7.** absolute value **8.** x − 25 **9.** 3n **10.** 10 − t **11.** $\frac{x}{4}$ **12.** n + 5 **13.** y + 2 **14.** 24 **15.** 12 **16.** 37 **17.** 19 **18.** 17 **19.** 20 **20.** 40 **21.** 450 **22.** 16 **23.** −17 **24.** 1,000 **25.** 9 **26.** −12 **27.** > **28.** > **29.** < **30.** = **31.** −30 **32.** −7 **33.** 12 **34.** 14 **35.** −15 **36.** −27 **37.** −11 **38.** −1 **39.** −20 ft **40.** Start with 0 and add 6 repeatedly; 24, 30, 36 **41.** Start with −18 and add 9 repeatedly; 18, 27, 36 **42.** Start with $\frac{1}{2}$ and add $\frac{1}{2}$ repeatedly; $2\frac{1}{2}$, 3, $3\frac{1}{2}$ **43.** 8 weeks **44.** $112 **45.** −42 **46.** −5 **47.** 72 **48.** 7 **49.** −3 **50.** −165 **51.** −8 **52.** 35 **53.** 102 **54.** (1, −3) **55.** (−2, 1) **56.** (−3, −3) **57.** (2, 2)

Chapter 2

Lesson 2-1   pp. 71–72

STANDARDS PRACTICE 7. (5 + 91) + 11; 5 + (91 + 11) **9.** Comm. Prop. of Add. **11.** Assoc. Prop. of Mult. **13.** Ident. Prop. of Mult. **15.** 93 **17.** 29 **19.** 37 **21.** 7.88 **23.** −70 **25.** −320 **27.** 107 **29.** −10,000 **31.** Answers may vary. Sample: Combine 3 and 27 first since their sum is 30, a multiple of 10. It is easier to add mentally if you look for numbers whose sum is a multiple of 10. **33.** 540 **35.** No; for subtraction 6 − 4 ≠ 4 − 6 and 6 − (3 − 1) ≠ (6 − 3) − 1; for division, 12 ÷ 3 ≠ 3 ÷ 12; and (20 ÷ 4) ÷ 2 ≠ 20 ÷ (4 ÷ 2). **37.** a = 1, c = 0 **39.** B **41.** III **43.** II **45.** 12h

Lesson 2-2   pp. 76–77

STANDARDS PRACTICE 5. 138 **7.** 336 **9.** 936 **11.** 784 **13.** 1,176 people **15.** −9 **17.** 21 **19.** 150 **21.** 3(3x − 1); 9x − 3 **23.** 4v − 12 **25.** −14z − 6 **27.** 12a + 36 **29.** −5m − 30 **31.** −7t + 28 **33.** 2y − 12 **35.** −18 **37.** −104 **39.** 1,792 miles **41.** 21n − 14 **43.** 5m − 30 **45.** −15y − 24 **47.** Comm. Prop. of Add. **49.** Assoc. Prop. of Add. **51.** My friend didn't distribute the 7 to the t. **53.** 3 (7x + 8) **55.** D **57.** 1 **59.** −3

Lesson 2-3   pp. 80–81

STANDARDS PRACTICE 5. 2; none; −7 **7.** 6, −5; 6xy, −5xy; none **9.** 1, 2, 3, −4; a, 2a, 3a, −4a; none **11.** 7x − 2 **13.** 8x − 3 **15.** 13a **17.** 6w **19.** 9a − 3 **21.** 5z + 8y **23.** 3t + 1 **25.** 4 **27.** −4r + 3 **29.** 3 **31.** 4b − 6 **33.** 4p + 10 + 3, or 4p + 13 **35.** The variables are not separated by plus or minus signs. **37.** −82x **39.** 78u − 50k + 42 **41.** D

Lesson 2-4   pp. 84–85

STANDARDS PRACTICE 7. open; variable **9.** false; 7 ≠ 8 **11.** false; 27 ≠ 30 **13.** 25 = v + 15; open; variable **15.** no **17.** yes **19.** no **21.** 850 + x = 1,200; no **23.** open; variable **25.** open sentence; contains a variable **27.** 15 + n = 50; open; contains a variable **29.** yes; no; yes; no. Explanations may vary. **31.** yes; −9 = −9 **33.** no; −6 ≠ 6 **35–37.** Answers may vary. Samples are given. **35.** London is the capital of England. Water is made of hydrogen and oxygen. **37.** She has new shoes. It has six legs. **39.** A **41.** −4t −19 **43.** 25 mi **45.** 0

Lesson 2-5   pp. 91–92

STANDARDS PRACTICE 9. 11 **11.** −3 **13.** −15 **15.** 5,200 = s + 2,520; 2,680 m/s **17.** 54 **19.** 11 **21.** 6 **23.** 44 **25.** 40 **27.** −20 **29.** A **31.** −20 **33.** −300 **35.** Yes; subtracting a number gives the same result as adding its opposite. **37.** 113 **39.** −75 **41.** 140 **43.** open; variable **45.** false; 2 ≠ 3

Lesson 2-6   pp. 96–97

STANDARDS PRACTICE 9. 16 **11.** 14 **13.** 19 **15.** −6 **17.** −5 **19.** −10 **21.** 36 h **23.** 42 **25.** 105 **27.** −16 **29.** 40 **31.** 13 **33.** 42 **35.** 300 **37.** 5 **39.** Dividing by 0 would result in 4 = 5, which is not a true statement. **41.** $\frac{n}{10}$ = 100; 1,000 **43.** C **45.** You do something to each side of the equation. You divide by 3 in the first equation; you subtract 3 in the second. **47.** −100 **49.** 382,300 **51.** 3, −3 **53.** b + a **55.** $\frac{b}{a}$, a ≠ 0 **57.** D **59.** −11 **61.** −19 **63.** increase of 1,765 ft **65.** 7n

Lesson 2-7   pp. 100–101

STANDARDS PRACTICE 1. Answer may vary. Samples: 14 dimes, 2 nickels; 2 quarters, 6 dimes, 8 nickels **3.** 11 years and 12 years

5. 16 ft² 7. −10 9. 122, 123 11. 2,750 m, 2,250 m
13. 3,200 cells 15. A 17. −6 19. 2 21. Identity Property of Multiplication

Lesson 2-8   pp. 104–105

STANDARDS PRACTICE

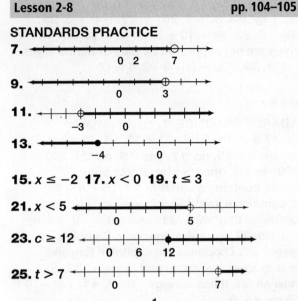

7.
9.
11.
13.

15. $x \le -2$ 17. $x < 0$ 19. $t \le 3$
21. $x < 5$
23. $c \ge 12$
25. $t > 7$

27. $x \le -10$ 29. $x < -\frac{1}{2}$ 31. Answers may vary. Sample: To go to a movie rated PG-13, you have to be 13 years old or older; $a \ge 13$ 33. $f \ge 5$
35. 40 and 50 37. $y > a - b$ 39. D 41. 34 43. 72
45. $3n + 6$

Lesson 2-9   pp. 108–109

STANDARDS PRACTICE

5. $w < 7$
7. $x \ge 1$
9. $m \le 0$
11. $t \le -15$

13. 64,000 lb 15. $x \ge 11$ 17. $r \le 7$ 19. $c > 14$
21. $w < 11$ 23. $y \le 8$ 25. Add 3 to each side.

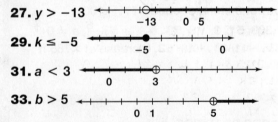

27. $y > -13$
29. $k \le -5$
31. $a < 3$
33. $b > 5$

35. $13 + n > 15$; $n > 2$ 37. ≤ $49 39. Subt. within parentheses. Simplify. Add. Prop. of Inequality Simplify. 41. $12d + 8 < 50$. $d < 3.5$. At most, you can buy 3 DVDs. 43. B

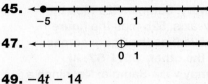

45.
47.

49. $-4t - 14$

Lesson 2-10   pp. 113–114

STANDARDS PRACTICE 7. $t > 7$ 9. $x > -2$
11. $x \le 3$ 13. $k \le -8$ 15. at least 72 hours
17. $m \le -108$ 19. $y > 12$ 21. $q > -18$ 23. $b \ge 12$
25. $r \le -21$ 27. $b \ge -93$ 29. $b > -18$ 31. $x \ge 4$
33. You reversed the inequality symbol when dividing each side by a positive number.
35. $7t \le 21$; $t \le 3$ 37. $\frac{v}{-5} < 9$; $v > -45$
39. Div. Prop. of Ineq. Simplify. 41. Mult. Prop. of Ineq. Simplify. 43. 4 teachers 45. Yes; if 12 is less than x, x must be greater than 12. 47. C 49. $t > 11$
51. $v < 23$ 53. Comm. Prop. of Add.

Chapter 2 Review   pp. 117–119

1. D 2. B 3. E 4. A 5. C 6. H 7. J 8. F 9. G
10. I 11. 80 12. 700 13. 547 14. 6,500 15. 300
16. 105 17. 864 18. 496 19. 387 20. $4w + 36$
21. $24 + 48a$ 22. $-42 + 14m$ 23. You can write 15 as $5 \cdot 3$. $5x + 5 \cdot 3 = 5(x + 3)$ by the Distributive Property. 24. $-3a + 7$ 25. $7w + 9$
26. $9 - 3x$ 27. $15 - 24n$ 28. k 29. $-17r + 31$
30. They have the same variable or no variable and are separated by addition or subtraction signs. 31. $32 + 5 = 6 \cdot 6$; false 32. $\frac{t}{17} = -3$; open
33. $4 \cdot 20 = 80$; true 34. $p + 1.75 = 6.50$ 35. 11
36. 8 37. −5 38. 27 39. 128 40. −8 41. $6.50
42.
43.
44.
45.
46. $t < 0$ 47. $h > 12$ 48. $n > 14$ 49. $k \ge 2$
50. $s \le 3$ 51. $m < -6$ 52. $d < -14$ 53. $c \le 36$

Chapter 3

Lesson 3-1   pp. 130–131

STANDARDS PRACTICE 5. hundredths; 27.39
7. ones; 1,046 9. 345.7 11. 215 13-17. Answers may vary. Samples are given. 13. about $10
15. about 40 17. about $30 19. about $13.90
21. about 20.7 23. about 7.10 miles 25. Answers may vary. Sample: about 80 27. about 44 in.

29–35. Answers may vary. Samples are given.
29. about 11.1 **31.** about $480 **33.** about 9.2
35. about 3,200 **37.** about 22,000 mi^2 **39.** You
subtracted 219 instead of 21.9. **41.** A **43.** 4
45. −4 **47.** $x \le 3$ **49.** $y \ge 0$

| Lesson 3-2 | pp. 134–135 |

STANDARDS PRACTICE 7. about 44 **9.** about
100 **11.** about 4 **13.** about $60 **15.** about 2
17. about $50 **19.** about 8 **21.** No; 45.6 is not
close to an estimate of 5. **23.** about 380
25. about 3 **27.** about $6 **29.** not reasonable;
$47 \times 2 = 94$ **31.** Answers may vary: Samples are
given. elem. school teacher: about $45.50/h in
Detroit, about $32.50/h in Lincoln; secretary:
about $18/h in Detroit, about $12.75/h in Lincoln;
truck driver: about $17.50/h in Detroit, about
$15.75/h in Lincoln. **33.** about $5 **35.** You
rounded to $20 \div 4$. Your friend used compatible
numbers, $21 \div 3$. **37.** C **39.** 7:20 P.M.

| Lesson 3-3 | pp. 139–140 |

STANDARDS PRACTICE 5. $d = 481.25$ m
7. $t = 259.3$ s **9.** $d = 539.5$ mi **11.** 67°F **13.** 60°F
15. 52°F **17.** 55.4 mm **19.** 136.4°F **21.** 161.6°F
23. −128.2°F **25.** 22 m; 27.01 m^2 **27.** about
4,200 mi^2 **29.** C **31.** about 700 ft^2 **33.** B
35. $n = 2t$; each n value is twice the t value
below it.

| Lesson 3-4 | pp. 144–145 |

STANDARDS PRACTICE 7. 15.4 **9.** 3.54 **11.** 8.8
8. $c + 1,855.3 = 4,360.3$; 2,505 lb **13.** 23.7 **15.** −0.8
17. 5.3 **19.** $584.43 **21.** $t + 17.8 \approx 18$; about
0.2 mi/h **23.** 0 **25.** 1.2 **27.** 11 **29.** Answers may
vary. Sample: $7.24 **31.** Add −1.8 to each side.
33. 35.773 **35.** C **37.** 369.72 in.^{2}

| Lesson 3-5 | pp. 148–149 |

STANDARDS PRACTICE 7. 0.6 **9.** −2.44 **11.** 8.6
13. 1.2 **15.** 9 days **17.** −1.94 **19.** 456 **21.** −708
23. 0.0804 **25.** 179 hits **27.** 30 **29.** 0.9912
31. −5.4 **33.** $-7.3n = 30.66$; −4.2 **35. a.** 20 hits
b. You can have only a whole number of hits.
37. 25 onions **39.** $x = 0.6$, $y = 0.7$ (or $x = 0.7$,
$y = 0.6$) **41.** D **43.** −5.3 **45.** 7.285

| Lesson 3-6 | pp. 153–155 |

STANDARDS PRACTICE 1. C **3.** B **5.** A
7. Gram; a banana is well under a kilogram, so
kilograms are too large. **9.** Centimeter; the length
is much less than a meter and much more than a

millimeter, so meters are too large and millimeters
are too small. **11.** Meter; the width is much less
than a kilometer and much more than a centimeter,
so kilometers are too large and centimeters are too
small. **13.** 5 kg; the mass of a dog is much greater
than the mass of 5 paper clips. **15.** 350 g; 350 mg
is less than the mass of a paper clip. **17.** 0.234
19. 3,010 **21.** 7,300 **23.** 0.035 **25.** 5.18 m
27. Camille multiplied 6,392 g by 1,000, so she
changed grams to milligrams. To change grams to
kilograms she should have *divided* 6,392 by 1,000
to get 6.392 kg. **29.** m **31a.** 48,000 L **b.** 2,880,000 L
33. Answers may vary. Sample: 2 km; 2 m can be
walked in 3 or 4 steps. **35.** 90.05 **37.** 0.62
39. 900,000 **41.** 1,300,000 **43.** 5.623 **45.** 3.048 m
47. E **49.** F **51.** D **53. a.** 4 to 5 km
b. 4,000 to 5,000 m **55.** A **57.** C **59.** about 7
61. about 10 **63.** $n < -15$

| Lesson 3-7 | pp. 160–161 |

STANDARDS PRACTICE 1. 66 matches **3.** 12 ways
5. 3.25 ft **7.** 80 sketches **9.** 1,320 pieces **11.** 10
different ways **13.** A **15.** 0.27 **17.** 2 **19.** 300

| Chapter 3 Review | pp. 163–165 |

1. significant digits **2.** compatible numbers
3. formula **4.** perimeter **5–14.** Answers may vary.
Samples are given. **5.** about 10; front–end
6. about 24; rounding **7.** about 60; clustering
8. about 11.7; front-end **9.** about 18; clustering
10. about 4; rounding **11.** about 10; rounding
13. about 6; rounding **14.** about 6; rounding
15. Answers may vary. Sample: you use rounding
when only a rough answer is needed and the
numbers are not clustered. You use front-end
estimation when you need a better estimate of a
sum. You use clustering when there are 3 or
more numbers and there is one number that they
are all close to. **16.** about 40 feet **17.** about 48
18. about 4 **19.** about 10 **20.** about 5 **21.** about 12
22. about 5 **23.** about −8 **25.** about 12
26. about 24 **27.** 70 mi **28.** 384 mm^2 **29.** 37.68 in.
30. 52 cm **31.** 7.1 **32.** 9.25 **33.** −2.01 **34.** 26.2
35. −9.1 **36.** 10.6 **37a.** $3.2 + x = 2.64$ **b.** −$.56
38. 2.5 **39.** 40.817 **40.** 11.3 **41.** 968.75 **42.** −19.4
43. −185.0125 **44a.** $3.5m = 5.60$ **b.** $1.60
45. Meter; a kilometer is too large unless you
use fractional parts of a kilometer; centimeters
are too small. **46.** Kilogram; a bicycle is heavy, so
grams are too small. **47.** Milliliter; a liter is about
the same as a quart, so liters are too large. **48.** 85
49. 0.16 **50.** 230 **51.** 1,600 **52.** 620 **53.** 0.08
54. A mature oak tree would be a number of
meters tall. Centimeters is too small a unit.

55. 24 days **56.** 24; Answers may vary. Sample: If you were hiking by yourself, you would greet 6 people. 4 hikers × 6 greetings per hiker = 24 greetings.

Chapter 4

Lesson 4-1 pp. 174–175

STANDARDS PRACTICE **7.** yes; ends in 0 **9.** no; does not end in 0 **11.** yes; ends in 5 **13.** no; does not end in 0, 2, 4, 6, or 8 **15.** yes; sum of digits is divisible by 3 **17.** yes; sum of digits is divisible by 3 **19.** yes; sum of digits is divisible by 9 **21.** yes; sum of digits is divisible by 3 **23.** 1, 2, 4, 8 **25.** 1, 3, 5, 15, 25, 75 **27.** 2; the number ends in 2. **29.** 5; the number ends in 5. **31a.** 66 and 4,710 **b.** 66 and 4,710 **c.** An integer is divisible by 6 if it is an even number and the sum of its digits is divisible by 3. **33.** $1 \cdot 28, 2 \cdot 14, 4 \cdot 7$ **35.** $1 \cdot 35, 5 \cdot 7$ **37.** $1 \cdot 50, 2 \cdot 25, 5 \cdot 10$ **39.** $1 \cdot 72, 2 \cdot 36, 3 \cdot 24, 4 \cdot 18, 6 \cdot 12, 8 \cdot 9$ **41.** 8 **43.** 5 **45a.** 2 plates of 21 cookies, 3 plates of 14 cookies, 6 plates of 7 cookies **b.** 2 plates of 28 cookies, 4 plates of 14 cookies, 7 plates of 8 cookies, 8 plates of 7 cookies **c.** 2 plates of 30 cookies, 3 plates of 20 cookies, 4 plates of 15 cookies, 5 plates of 12 cookies, 6 plates of 10 cookies **d.** 2 plates of 72 cookies, 3 plates of 48 cookies, 4 plates of 36 cookies, 6 plates of 24 cookies, 8 plates of 18 cookies, 9 plates of 16 cookies, 12 plates of 12 cookies, 16 plates of 9 cookies, 18 plates of 8 cookies

47a.

Number	Last two digits	Are last two digits divisible by 4?	Is the number divisible by 4?
136	36	Yes	Yes
1,268	68	Yes	Yes
314	14	No	No
1,078	■ 78	■ No	■ No
696	■ 96	■ Yes	■ Yes

b. An integer is divisible by 4 if its last 2 digits are divisible by 4. **49.** Answers may vary. Sample: 21, 24, 33 **51.** D **53.** g

Lesson 4-2 pp. 180–181

STANDARDS PRACTICE **5.** r^4s^2 **7.** 9^5 **9.** $-7a^2b$ **11.** 10,000 **13.** 64 **15.** −64 **17.** 1,000,000 **19.** 31 **21.** 73 **23.** −9 **25.** $-15x^2y$ **27.** $8ab^2$ **29.** 35 **31.** 27 **33.** 7.2 **35.** 243 **37.** 5.96 **39.** a. 10,000 times **b.** Answers may vary. Sample: I would use 10^4 because other microscopes may have powers described in powers of 10. **41.** 25 cm^2 **43.** 8 in.

45. $x = y$ or $x = 0$ or $y = 0$; $5(-2)^2(-2) = 5(-2)(-2)^2$ or $5(0)^2y = 5(0)y^2$ or $5x^2(0) = 5x(0)^2$ **47.** Answers may vary. Sample: A number *squared* is the area of a square. A number *cubed* is the volume of a cube. **49.** $3^0 = 1$; $3^{-1} = \frac{1}{3}$ **51.** A **53.** 3, 5, 9 **55.** 2, 5, 10

Lesson 4-3 pp. 185–186

STANDARDS PRACTICE **5.** Prime; it has only two factors, 1 and 31. **7.** Prime; it has only two factors, 1 and 53. **9.** Prime; it has only two factors, 1 and 19. **11.** Composite; it has more than two factors, 1, 3, 31, and 93. **13.** $2^3 \cdot 3^2 \cdot 5$ **15.** $2 \cdot 3 \cdot 31$ **17.** 7^2 **19.** $3^3 \cdot 23$ **21.** 3 **23.** $2mn$ **25.** neither **27.** composite; $2 \cdot 3^2 \cdot 29$ **29.** 1 **31.** 4 **33.** $30a$ **35.** c^2df **37.** C **39.** Yes; the GCD is 1. **41.** No; the GCD is 13. **43.** No; the GCD is 13. **45.** Yes; the GCD is 1. **47.** Answers may vary. Sample: Divide 50 by the prime factor 5, and then divide the quotient, 10, by the prime factor 5 in a factor tree. Write the prime factorization $2 \cdot 5^2$. **49.** D **51.** 20 **53.** 29 **55.** 1.8 **57.** 2.7

Lesson 4-4 pp. 190–191

STANDARDS PRACTICE **5.** $\frac{1}{4}, \frac{4}{16}$ **7.** $\frac{1}{3}, \frac{2}{6}$ **9.** $\frac{1}{3}, \frac{12}{36}$ **11.** $\frac{1}{3}$ **13.** $\frac{1}{4}$ **15.** $\frac{1}{3}$ **17.** $\frac{1}{3}$ **19.** $\frac{m^2}{3}$ **21.** $\frac{3x}{2}$ **23.** $\frac{7a}{12}$ **25.** $8b$ **27.** $\frac{2}{5}, \frac{8}{20}$ **29.** $\frac{5}{8}, \frac{20}{32}$ **31.** No; the GCF of 65 and 91 is 13. The fraction can be simplified to $\frac{5}{7}$. **33.** $\frac{9}{16}$ **35.** $\frac{3}{4}$ **37.** 8 **39.** $\frac{r^3}{9t}$ **41.** $\frac{x^2}{3z}$ **43.** $\frac{2m}{3}$ **45.** Answers may vary. Sample: $\frac{6x}{10}, \frac{3xy}{5y}$ **47.** $\frac{28}{55}$ **49a.** $\frac{28}{31}$ **b.** 2003; $\frac{28}{31}$ is about $\frac{7}{8}$, while $\frac{25}{28}$ is about $\frac{5}{6}$. **51.** $7\frac{8}{25}$ **53.** B **55.** 12.03

Lesson 4-5 pp. 195–196

STANDARDS PRACTICE **1.** 107 digits **3.** 15 pizzas **5.** 6 gardens **7.** B **9.** 10 color combinations **11.**

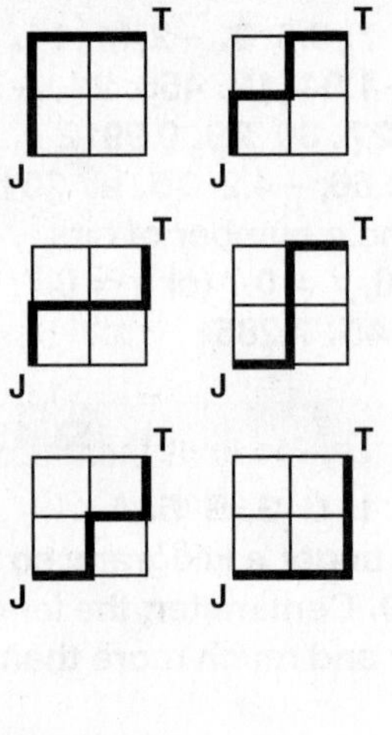

Answers may vary. Sample: Draw line segments for all 4-block routes. **13.** $76; Tyrek: $51; Zeroy: $23 **15.** D **17.** B **19.** $\frac{1}{4}$ **21.** $\frac{a}{2}$ **23.** Start with 8; subtract 3 repeatedly.

Lesson 4-6   pp. 199–200

STANDARDS PRACTICE 9–13. Answers may vary. 9. $\frac{2}{12}, \frac{-2}{-12}, \frac{-1}{-6}$ **11.** $-\frac{10}{18}, \frac{-5}{9}, \frac{5}{-9}$ **13.** $\frac{-4}{6}, \frac{-2}{3}, \frac{2}{-3}$ **15.** $-0.75, \frac{-3}{5}, -0.3, \frac{1}{10}, \frac{2}{3}, 2$ **17.** $\frac{2}{3}$ **19.** $\frac{5}{6}$ **21.** $-\frac{1}{8}$ **23.** 44 ft/s² **25.** Answers may vary. Sample answer: $\frac{8}{8}$ **27.** $\frac{4}{5}$ **29.** $\frac{3}{4}$ **31.** $-\frac{2}{27}$ **33. a.** Answers may vary. Sample: $\frac{1}{3}, \frac{1}{4}$ **b.** Infinitely many. Between any two rational numbers, you can find another rational number. **35.** 64 **37.** $-\frac{2}{3}, \frac{2}{3}$ **39.** $\frac{4}{5}, \frac{4}{5}$ **41.** $-\frac{3}{5}, \frac{3}{5}$ **43.** Not always true; for $a = 1, \frac{1}{1} = \frac{1}{1}$ **45.** Not always true; for $a = 1 = b, \frac{1^2}{1^2} = \frac{1}{1}$ **47.** C **49.** 40 three-piece outfits

Lesson 4-7   pp. 203–204

STANDARDS PRACTICE 5. $\frac{1}{64}$ **7.** $x^9 y^2$ **9.** 0.216 **11.** $28b^7$ **13.** $10x^9$ **15.** $-30d^7$ **17.** 1,000,000 **19.** 64 **21.** x^{35} **23.** 7 **25.** 4 **27.** 3 **29.** = **31.** > **33.** Both $x^8 \cdot x^2$ and $x^5 \cdot x^5$ are equivalent to x^{10}. **35.** $15x^3$ **37.** $2x^4$; the two terms are being added, not multiplied. **39a.** a^{12} **b.** $\frac{a^n}{b^n}$ **41.** B **43.** −4

Lesson 4-8   pp. 208–209

STANDARDS PRACTICE 5. 8 **7.** $\frac{5y^5}{3}$ **9.** 6 **11.** x^4 **13.** 1 **15.** c **17.** $\frac{1}{5a^3}$ **19.** $\frac{1}{b^3}$ **21.** y^{-3} **23.** $m^{-2}n^{-2}$ **25.** The student thought that the base was −5. **27.** $\frac{1}{6}$ **29.** $\frac{1}{4}$ **31.** 2 **33.** 5 **35.** Negative; $-3^{-2} = -\frac{1}{3^2} = -\frac{1}{9}$ **37.** a^2b^{-5} **39.** b^5c^{-9} **41.** b^{-5} **43.** r^{-3} **45.** $\frac{4}{5}$ **47.** $\frac{x^5}{y^8}$ **49.** B **51.** x^9

Lesson 4-9   pp. 214–215

STANDARDS PRACTICE 7. 5.559×10^8 **9.** 6×10^{-6} **11.** 4.09×10^{-3} **13.** 59,400,000 **15.** 120,000 **17.** 275,000,000 **19.** 9×10^{10} **21.** 5.28×10^{10} **23.** $0.065 \times 10^{11}, 16 \times 10^9, 2.3 \times 10^{12}$ **25.** $2.996 \times 10^4, 432 \times 10^3, 65 \times 10^4$ **27.** 8.6×10^{-5} **29.** 6×10^4 **31.** 900 **33.** 0.000000602 **35.** B **37. a–b.** Answers may vary. Samples are given. Move the decimal point 4 places to the right and write 4.3×10^{-4}. Write $523.4 \times 10^5 = 5.234 \times 10^2 \times 10^5 = 5.234 \times 10^7$.

39. about 2.76×10^{12} **41.** D **43.** C **45.** x^2 **47.** $\frac{3m^2}{n}$

Chapter 4 Review   pp. 217–219

1. factor **2.** simplest form **3.** rational number **4.** scientific notation **5.** exponents **6.** prime number **7.** 1, 2, 3, 4, 6, 12 **8.** 1, 2, 3, 5, 6, 10, 15, 30 **9.** 1, 2, 3, 6, 7, 14, 21, 42 **10.** 1, 2, 3, 4, 6, 8, 9, 12, 18, 24, 36, 72 **11.** 1, 3, 37, 111 **12.** 1, 2, 3, 4, 6, 7, 9, 12, 14, 18, 21, 28, 36, 42, 63, 84, 126, 252 **13.** 8 **14.** 27 **15.** 172 **16.** −25 **17.** 121 **18.** 58 **19.** 49 **20.** 16 **21.** prime **22.** composite; $2^2 \cdot 5$ **23.** prime **24.** composite; $2 \cdot 5 \cdot 11$ **25.** composite; $3 \cdot 29$ **26.** 4 **27.** 9 **28.** 1 **29.** $3x^2$ **30.** $2ab$ **31.** $3cd$ **32.** No factor of a positive integer is greater than the integer. **33.** $\frac{1}{5}$ **34.** $\frac{1}{2}$ **35.** $\frac{4}{13}$ **36.** $\frac{7}{10}$ **37.** $\frac{7}{11}$ **38.** $\frac{1}{6}$ **39.** x **40.** 5 **41.** $\frac{1}{4}$ **42.** $\frac{2}{5}$ **43.** $\frac{x}{3}$ **44.** $4b$ **45.** 1, 4, 9, 16, 25, 36, 49, 64, 81, 100

46–49.

50. $\frac{2}{5}$ **51.** $\frac{7}{8}$ **52.** −1 **53.** $-\frac{4}{5}$ **54.** 128 **55.** $21a^6$ **56.** b^7c^4 **57.** x^{15} **58.** y^{20} **59.** 4,096 **60.** $\frac{1}{b^2}$ **61.** $\frac{7}{8y^5}$ **62.** 2×10^6 **63.** 4.58×10^8 **64.** 7×10^{-7} **65.** 5.9×10^{-9} **66.** 800,000,000,000 **67.** 0.0000032 **68.** 11,190,000 **69.** 0.000000000005 **70.** $4.3 \times 10^{10}, 12 \times 10^{11}, 3,644 \times 10^9$ **71.** $8 \times 10^{-10}, 58 \times 10^{-10}, 716 \times 10^{-10}$ **72.** 2.4×10^{16} **73.** 1.8×10^{11}

Chapter 5

Lesson 5-1   pp. 229–230

STANDARDS PRACTICE 5. 180 **7.** 30 **9.** in 21 days **11.** 60 **13.** $24a^3$ **15.** $-\frac{2}{3} < -\frac{1}{3}$ **17.** $\frac{11}{12} > \frac{7}{12}$ **19.** $\frac{6}{8} < \frac{7}{9}$ **21.** $-\frac{5}{18} > -\frac{1}{3}$ **23.** $\frac{3}{9} < \frac{5}{9} < \frac{7}{9}$ **25.** $\frac{2}{7} < \frac{2}{5} < \frac{2}{3} < 2$ **27.** < **29.** > **31.** = **33.** < **35.** 1,800 **37.** $120x$ **39.** $72xy$ **41.** $20g^2j^4$ **43.** 5 packages of hot dogs and 9 packages of buns **45.** < **47.** > **49.** > **51.** < **53.** 20 in. by 20 in. The length of the sides of the square must be a multiple of 4 and 5. The LCM of 4 and 5 is 20. **55.** D **57.** D **59.** 1.394×10^{-3} **61.** 5×10^{-6}

Lesson 5-2   pp. 234–235

STANDARDS PRACTICE 7. 0.28 **9.** 1.45 **11.** Yes; $\frac{5}{16} = 5 \div 16 = 0.3125$, so $10\frac{5}{16} = 10.3125$.
13. $-0.1\overline{6}$; repeating; 6 **15.** $0.\overline{81}$; repeating; 81
17. $0.3, \frac{1}{2}, \frac{3}{2}, \frac{5}{2}$ **19.** $0.06, \frac{2}{5}, \frac{6}{5}, \frac{3}{2}$ **21.** $3\frac{2}{5}$ **23.** $7\frac{3}{20}$
25. $\frac{14}{111}$ **27.** $-\frac{1}{3}$ **29.** = **31.** < **33a.** Sarah: 0.286;
Lizzie: 0.302 **b.** Lizzie; $0.302 > 0.286$ **35.** $\frac{1}{15}$
37. $\frac{272,727}{1,000,000}$ **39.** No; there is no block of digits
that repeats. **41.** $4 \div 99$ since $0.\overline{04} = \frac{4}{99}$ **43.** D
45. C

Lesson 5-3   pp. 240–241

STANDARDS PRACTICE 7. $\frac{4}{z}$ **9.** $\frac{9}{11}$ **11.** $1\frac{1}{2}$ **13.** $\frac{5}{x}$
15. $\frac{7}{20}$ **17.** $\frac{30 - 2x}{5x}$ **19.** $\frac{5}{8}$ **21.** $1\frac{5}{24}$ **23.** $3\frac{5}{8}$ **25.** $-\frac{7}{8}$
27–29. Answers may vary. Samples are given.
27. 9 **29.** 48 **31.** A good way to check your work
is to see whether your answer is close to your
estimate. **33.** $1\frac{3}{10}$ **35.** $\frac{21 + 20d}{30}$ **37.** $1\frac{3}{8}$ **39.** $\frac{x}{2}$
41. $\frac{1}{8}$ **43.** $\frac{9}{98}$ **45.** C **47.** D **49.** $0.6, 0.66, \frac{2}{3}$

Lesson 5-4   pp. 245–246

STANDARDS PRACTICE 11. $\frac{2}{15}$ **13.** $\frac{12}{35}$ **15.** $\frac{7}{10}$
17. $\frac{9x}{2}$ **19.** $5\frac{1}{28}$ **21.** $-3\frac{1}{5}$ **23.** $1\frac{1}{4}$ hours **25.** $\frac{5}{6}$
27. $-1\frac{1}{21}$ **29.** $1\frac{1}{2}$ **31.** $\frac{1}{3}$ **33.** $-2\frac{4}{7}$ **35.** 2 **37.** $-\frac{3}{5}$
39. $-8\frac{1}{3}$ **41.** $1\frac{1}{3}$ **43.** $-1\frac{1}{5}$ **45.** $\frac{4}{9}$ **47.** $3\frac{43}{144}$
49. $1\frac{1}{4}$ **51.** 40 **53.** $1\frac{1}{24}$ **55.** $\frac{12}{49}$
57a. $3\left(\frac{1}{2}a\right) - \frac{a}{-4}$ **b.** $5\frac{1}{4}$ **59.** 6 rest stops
61a. $\frac{1}{4}, \frac{1}{6}, \frac{1}{8}, \frac{1}{10}$ **b.** The quotients decrease.
63. Answers may vary. Sample: $\frac{2}{3}, \frac{4}{7}$ **65.** C
67. $1\frac{23}{35}$ **69.** $\frac{1}{21}$

Lesson 5-5   pp. 249–251

STANDARDS PRACTICE 11–13. Explanations
may vary. Samples are given. **11.** Ounces; it is
closest to the weight of a paper clip. **13.** Miles;
distances to continents would be measured in
miles. **15.** $\frac{3}{4}$ **17.** $\frac{1}{2}$ **19.** 2,640 **21.** Julia **23.** A
25. C **27.** 9,560 ft **29.** weight **31.** weight
33. capacity **35–37.** Explanations may vary.
Samples are given. **35.** Pounds or ounces; tons
are too large. **37.** Gallons; quarts or ounces are
too small. **39a.** mile; about 3,740 mi **b.** Answers
may vary. Sample: rod; about 1,196,800 rods
41. yes **43.** no; 2 in. **45.** $2\frac{1}{3}$ **47.** 10,000 **49.** $1\frac{1}{2}$
51. A quarter pound is $\frac{1}{4}$ of 16 oz, or 4 oz, and
4 oz < 6 oz. **53.** gal **55.** D **57.** $\frac{9}{29}$ **59.** $1\frac{1}{5}$

Lesson 5-6   pp. 255–256

STANDARDS PRACTICE 1. 8:30 A.M. **3.** the 12:15 P.M.
bus **5.** 6 different amounts; \$.40, \$.45, \$.50, \$.55,
\$.60, \$.65 **7.** \$30 **9.** 60 freshmen **11.** B
13. C **15.** $\frac{2}{5}$ **17.** 2 **19.** −120 **21.** about \$48

Lesson 5-7   pp. 260–261

STANDARDS PRACTICE 7. $-\frac{1}{5}$ **9.** $\frac{1}{6}$ of the book
11. $1\frac{1}{9}$ **13.** $1\frac{1}{8}$ **15.** $3\frac{5}{8}$ **17.** $2\frac{3}{4}$ **19.** 0 **21.** $-2\frac{7}{8}$
23. Explanation may vary. Sample given.
23. Negative; $\frac{9}{10} > \frac{1}{2}$, so $\frac{1}{2} - \frac{9}{10} < 0$. **25.** $13\frac{3}{8}$ lb
27a. $64\frac{1}{4}$ in. **b.** $60\frac{7}{8}$ in. **29.** $-\frac{19}{24}$ **31.** 3 **33.** $-\frac{1}{10}$
35. Answers may vary. Sample: Your house plant
grows $\frac{1}{2}$ in. in the month after you buy it. If it is 7 in.
tall now, how tall was the plant when you bought it?
$x = 6\frac{1}{2}$ in. **37.** A **39.** D **41.** c **43.** pt **45.** yd

Lesson 5-8   pp. 264–266

STANDARDS PRACTICE 7. $\frac{2}{15}$ **9.** $\frac{3}{56}$ **11.** $\frac{4}{21}$ **13.** $\frac{5}{63}$
15. 1 **17.** 4 **19.** $\frac{2}{3}$ **21.** $7\frac{1}{2}$ **23.** $-\frac{1}{7}$ **25.** −12 **27.** 2
29. $\frac{1}{4}$ **31.** $-\frac{2}{33}$ **33.** $2\frac{8}{27}$ **35.** 10 weeks
37. 261,000 mi **39.** $-1\frac{7}{26}$ **41.** $3\frac{9}{13}$ **43.** $-\frac{5}{12}$
45. $-1\frac{19}{81}$ **47.** 6 **49.** 4 **51.** 10 min **53.** $1\frac{2}{15}$ mi; 100 ft
55. 12 **57.** $-1\frac{1}{6}$ **59.** D

Lesson 5-9   pp. 272–273

STANDARDS PRACTICE 5. 36 **7.** r^4s^{12} **9.** $16a^{10}$
11. $8x^6$ **13.** $8a^{15}$ **15.** $8b^3$ **17.** $10,000x^{12}$
19. $-125b^3$ **21.** $25c^6$ **23.** $-27a^{12}b^3$ **25.** $\frac{4}{25}$
27. $\frac{16}{49y^2}$ **29.** $\frac{16}{81}$ **31.** $\frac{m^6}{b^{18}}$ **33.** $-\frac{27}{64}$ **35.** 2
37. 4 **39.** 5 **41.** 81 **43.** 1 **45.** $16c^2$ units^2
47. $\frac{343}{1,000}$ units^3 **49.** $\frac{343a^3}{8c^3}$ units^3 **51.** 100
53. $4a^2b^6$ **55.** $-\frac{32}{x^{15}}$ **57.** $-\frac{27a^3}{b^6}$ **59.** $\frac{16c^4}{d^8}$ **61.** $\frac{32y^{20}}{x^{10}}$
63. 4 **65.** 3; 6 **67.** C **69.** D **71.** B **73.** $\frac{2}{9}$
75. $-1\frac{21}{22}$

Chapter 5 Review   pp. 275–277

1. f **2.** c **3.** a **4.** b **5.** g **6.** d **7.** e **8.** 36 **9.** $56m^2$
10. 105 **11.** $30xy$ **12.** > **13.** < **14.** > **15.** =
16. 0.6 **17.** $0.1\overline{6}$ **18.** 0.625 **19.** $0.\overline{3}$ **20.** 0.07
21. $\frac{1}{4}$ **22.** $\frac{5}{6}$ **23.** $5\frac{3}{5}$ **24.** $2\frac{4}{99}$ **25.** $3\frac{1}{12}$ **26.** $7\frac{2}{15}$
27. $\frac{30 + 3x}{5x}$ **28.** $\frac{7}{8}$ **29.** $\frac{7}{12}$ ft, or 7 in. **30.** $\frac{7}{40}$
31. $-\frac{4}{5}$ **32.** $1\frac{1}{5}$ **33.** $3\frac{3}{4}$ **34.** $\frac{1}{2}$ **35.** $2\frac{1}{2}$ **36.** $3\frac{3}{8}$
37. 60 **38.** 24 **39.** 96 **40.** 5,500 **41.** 2:30 P.M.
42. 15 buses **43.** \$45.50 **44.** $2\frac{3}{8}$ **45.** $1\frac{2}{15}$ **46.** $1\frac{1}{3}$

47. $\frac{1}{54}$ 48. $-\frac{8}{21}$ 49. $\frac{2}{9}$ 50. $16d^4$ 51. 36 52. $a^{10}b^5$
53. $-\frac{1}{8}$ 54. $\frac{x^2}{9}$ 55. $\frac{16a^4}{c^8}$

Chapter 6

Lesson 6-1   pp. 286–287

STANDARDS PRACTICE 5. 48 ft/s 7. 52 mi/h 9. $\frac{1}{2}$
11. 19.2 13. $117\frac{1}{3}$ 15a. 12 b. 36 17. $985.50
19. 235 m/s 21. class A: $\frac{6}{30}$ or $\frac{1}{5}$; class B: $\frac{4}{24}$ or $\frac{1}{6}$
23. Answers may vary. Sample: Usually not;
adding 1 to both the numerator and the
denominator leaves the ratio unchanged only
when $a = b$; $\frac{1}{1} = \frac{1+1}{1+1}$, but $\frac{1}{2} \neq \frac{1+1}{2+1}$, or $\frac{2}{3}$.
25. 7.5 h 27. Patrice should receive $42; Tatiana
should receive $35. 29. D 31. −1,728 33. $-\frac{b^6}{a^3}$

Lesson 6-2   pp. 292–294

STANDARDS PRACTICE 5. 16 7. 5 9. 8 11. 72
13. 20 15. 20 17. no, cross products not equal
19. no, cross products not equal 21. no, cross
products not equal 23. yes, cross products equal
25. $2.40 27. 15 posters 29. no, cross products
not equal 31. no, cross products not equal
33. yes, cross products equal 35. no, cross
products not equal 37. 10 39. 72 41. 28 43. 6.7
45. 77.2 47. 16.9 49–51. Answers may vary.
Samples are given. 49. 20 51. 3 53. $36.67
55. Yes; multiply each side by $\frac{b}{c}$. 57. B 59. 15 s
61. 30 more times 63. $\frac{25}{2.5} = \frac{100}{x}$; 10 s
65. $\frac{3\frac{1}{2}}{4} = \frac{x}{1}$; 0.875 lb. 67. $\frac{6}{2} = \frac{y}{10}$; 30 lb
69. $\frac{5.76}{2.25} = \frac{c}{1}$; $2.56 71. 12 ft wide and 15 ft long
73. B 75. $\frac{1}{100}$ 77. $\frac{25}{14}$

Lesson 6-3   pp. 297–299

STANDARDS PRACTICE 5. $2\frac{1}{2}$ ft 7. 9 cm 9. 5.7
11. 12 ft 13. 18 km 15. 51 km 17. 1.2 m
19. about 11 in.; 6 in. 21. 36 in. 23. perimeter
1 in. : 9 ft; area 1 in.^{2} : 81 ft^2 25. 7.5 ft by 7.5 ft
27. 243.75 ft^2 29. 2 in. 31. $1\frac{3}{4}$ in. 33. Answers
may vary. 35. N scale 37. B 39. 2 41. $2\frac{2}{5}$
43. 0.375 45. 0.4375

Lesson 6-4   pp. 303–305

STANDARDS PRACTICE 7. $\frac{7}{25}$ 9. $\frac{11}{20}$ 11. $\frac{3}{50}$
13. $3\frac{3}{20}$ 15. $1\frac{1}{50}$ 17. 0.044 19. 0.063 21. 0.797
23. 0.52 25. 0.0003 27. 168% 29. 70% 31. 6%

33. 259% 35. 15.6% 37. 23% 39. 55% 41. 62.5%
43. 16.7% 45. 22.2% 47. 13% 49. 83.3%
51. 450% 53. < 55. > 57. about 30%
59. $\frac{1}{10}$; 10% 61. 0.75; 75% 63. $\frac{1}{4}$; 0.25
65. No; it is not possible to answer more items
than are on the test. 67. Yes; the test had 300
items and the student answered 288 of them
correctly. 69. −0.09, −1%, 0.093, 11%, $\frac{1}{8}$
71. Yes; $\frac{32}{45} = 71.\overline{1}\%$, and $71.\overline{1}\% > 70\%$.
73. Answers may vary. Sample: Move the
decimal point two places to the right and add
a percent sign. 0.25 = 25%, 1.35 = 135%,
75. Explanations may vary. Sample: 0.25 is 25%
and 0.25% is 0.0025. 77. 125 79. A 81. 47

Lesson 6-5   pp. 309–310

STANDARDS PRACTICE 5. $\frac{75}{100} = \frac{n}{560}$; 420
7. $\frac{80}{100} = \frac{n}{20}$; 16 9. $\frac{53}{100} = \frac{n}{70}$; 37.1 11. $\frac{16}{100} = \frac{n}{75}$; 12
13. $\frac{n}{100} = \frac{16}{20}$; 80% 15. $\frac{n}{100} = \frac{30}{40}$; 75 17. $\frac{n}{100} = \frac{13}{25}$; 52
19. $\frac{n}{100} = \frac{17}{92}$; 18.5 21. $\frac{25}{100} = \frac{8}{n}$; 32 23. $\frac{49}{100} = \frac{31}{n}$; 63.3
25. $\frac{2}{100} = \frac{1}{n}$; 50 27. 663,000 people 29. $\frac{300}{100} = \frac{n}{50}$;
150 31. $\frac{60}{100} = \frac{n}{15}$; 9 33. $\frac{35}{100} = \frac{52.5}{n}$; 150
35a. Nevada: $975; Kansas: $795; Pennsylvania:
$900; New Mexico: $750; California: $1,087.50
b. Nevada: $15,975; Kansas: $15,795;
Pennsylvania: $15,900; New Mexico: $15,750;
California: $16,087.50 37. 50 members 39. Pacs;
$\frac{1}{3} \approx 33.3\%$. Since 33.3 > 30, $\frac{1}{3}$ is the greater
discount rate. 41. 6 43. B 45. 8% 47. 58.3%

Lesson 6-6   pp. 313–314

STANDARDS PRACTICE 5. $n = 0.3 \cdot 30$; 9
7. $120 = 0.15 \cdot n$; 800 9. $n = 0.56 \cdot 75$; 42
11. $n \cdot 4 = 9$; 225% 13. $n \cdot 150 = 96$; 64%
15. $n \cdot 1 = 4.7$; 470% 17. $.96 19. about 98
million households 21a. False; 63 is not less than
10% of 88. b. True; 88 is greater than 50% of 63.
23. $n = 0.055 \cdot 44$; 2.4 25. $0.092 \cdot b = 27.6$; 300
27. $n = 2.64 \cdot 12$; 31.7 29. Answers may vary.
Sample: A toy company makes 125% of the profit
it expected for the year. 31. 100 33. 20% 35. 1.8
37. C 39. $\frac{n}{100} = \frac{45}{360}$; 12.5 41. $\frac{1.5}{100} = \frac{45}{n}$; 3,000
43. $9y^9$

Lesson 6-7   pp. 318–319

STANDARDS PRACTICE 7. 32% 9. 25%
11. 10% 13. 150% 15. 64% 17. 70% 19. 55%
21. 16.7% 23. 26.2% 25. 9.1% 27. 18.8%
decrease 29. 18.8% increase 31. 166.7%
increase 33. 24.1% increase 35. 83.1% decrease

37a. 305% **b.** 1,329% **c.** 5,685% **39.** 12.5% increase **41.** 1.1% increase **43.** 20% decrease **45.** 460 **47.** B **49.** 94% **51.** 3,600

Chapter 7

Lesson 6-8   pp. 322–323

STANDARDS PRACTICE 7. $22.04 **9.** $10.50 **11.** $27.75 **13.** $.42; $8.07 **15.** $12.74 **17a.** Find 10% of $11 to get the discount and subtract the result from $11; or find 90% of $11. **b.** $9.90 **19.** The sweater at Store A; its sale price of $17.50 is less than the sale price of $18 at Store B. **21.** $y - x, \frac{y-x}{x}(100)$ **23.** $364.36 **25.** C **27.** 66.7%

Lesson 6-9   pp. 328–329

STANDARDS PRACTICE 5. They drove the farthest the first day before dinner. **7.** the second worker **9.** about $6.00 **11.** The mid-size car; it gets 34 mi/gal. The van only gets 25.8 mi/gal. **13.** about $.90 **15.** about $2.86 **17.** about 15 **19.** < **21.** It took Ron 30 min and Isabella 32 min. Ron won the race. **23.** C **25.** 23 mi

Lesson 6-10   pp. 332–333

STANDARDS PRACTICE 1. about 8,934 people **3.** 24 orders **5.** 16 outfits **7.** 8 and 26 **9.** 1 adult, 5 children; 3 adults, 2 children **11.** 50 acre-feet **13.** C **15.** B

Chapter 6 Review   pp. 335–337

1. C **2.** B **3.** A **4.** D **5.** G **6.** E **7.** F **8.** 50 mi/h **9.** $1.89/lb **10.** 90 words/min **11.** 7.5 **12.** 0.5 **13.** 35 **14.** 0.7 **15.** 49 **16.** 126 **17.** 45 **18.** 35 **19.** 0.5 cm **20.** $\frac{6}{25}$; 0.24 **21.** $\frac{18}{25}$; 0.72 **22.** $\frac{2}{25}$; 0.08 **23.** $\frac{1}{200}$; 0.005 **24.** 30% **25.** 33% **26.** 33.3% **27.** 35% **28.** 88.9% **29.** 2.1% **30.** 240% **31.** 0.6% **32.** $\frac{15}{100} = \frac{n}{48}$; 7.2 **33.** $\frac{20}{100} = \frac{30}{x}$; 150 **34.** $\frac{n}{100} = \frac{90}{300}$; 30% **35.** $\frac{125}{100} = \frac{100}{y}$; 80 **36.** $0.35 \cdot a = 70$; 200 **37.** $n = 0.68 \cdot 300$; 204 **38.** $n \cdot 180 = 9$; 5% **39.** $n \cdot 56 = 3.5$; 6.25% **40.** 25% decrease **41.** 75% decrease **42.** 20% increase **43.** 75% decrease **44.** $8.75 **45.** $1.70/lb **46.** The soup kitchen received $200. **47.** about 16 **48.** about 76 **49.** about 41 **50.** 30 mi **51.** Answers may vary.

Chapter 7

Lesson 7-1   pp. 346–347

STANDARDS PRACTICE 7. 6 **9.** −3 **11.** 15 **13.** −70 **15.** 16 weeks **17.** −9 **19.** 12 **21.** −3 **23.** −60 **25.** 15 **27.** 15 weeks **29.** The first problem requires an initial step of adding 2 to each side. **31.** 2 **33.** 14 **35.** B **37.** B **39.** 25%

Lesson 7-2   pp. 351–352

STANDARDS PRACTICE 7. 6 **9.** Jasmine 30 marbles, Bill 64 marbles **11.** 18, 20, 22 **13.** 10 **15.** 1 **17.** −5 **19.** −12 **21.** $5\frac{1}{3}$ **23.** −15, −14, −13, −12, −11 **25.** A **27.** First, use the Distributive Property and combine like terms. Next, subtract 8 from each side. Finally, divide each side by 12. **29.** 2 **31.** 36 **33.** −21, −19, −17, −15 **35.** D **37.** $\frac{2}{5}$ **39.** 48

Lesson 7-3   pp. 356–357

STANDARDS PRACTICE 7. Subtract 2 from each side or multiply each side by 5. **9.** 32 **11.** 12 **13.** 15 **15.** −5 **17.** $3\frac{1}{2}$ **19.** 5.5 **21.** 2 **23.** −3.2 **25.** $7\frac{1}{5}$ **27.** 36 **29.** $\frac{2}{5}$ **31.** −7.6 **33.** −14 **35.** 2 **37.** $\frac{c}{6} + 25.75 = 90.30$; $387.30 **39.** $66.60 **41.** −4 **43.** A **45.** C **47.** 0 **49.** 4 **51.** 3

Lesson 7-4   pp. 360–361

STANDARDS PRACTICE 1. $60 **3.** 20 cm by 12 cm **5.** 3.5 h **7.** 28 posts **9.** 8 quarters and 8 dimes **11.** $1\frac{1}{2}h$ **13.** A **15.** 60

Lesson 7-5   pp. 365–366

STANDARDS PRACTICE 5. Add 2 to each side, simplify, divide each side by 4, and simplify.

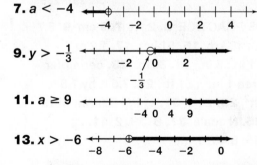

7. $a < -4$

9. $y > -\frac{1}{3}$

11. $a \geq 9$

13. $x > -6$

15. $y \le 2$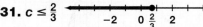
(number line) −4 −2 0 2 4

17. $y \le -5$
(number line) −20 −15 −10 −5 0

19. $8r \ge 420$; $r \ge 52.5$; at least 52.5 mi/h
21. $c \le 72$ **23.** $y > 4\frac{4}{5}$ **25.** $c < -1$ **27.** The student simplified $\frac{-36}{-12}$ to −3 instead of 3.
29. 5.6 mi **31.** 13 months **33.** D **35.** $276.14

Lesson 7-6   pp. 369–370

STANDARDS PRACTICE 3. $w = \frac{V}{\ell h}$ **5.** $p = qd$
7. $m = \frac{3}{2}n + \frac{15}{2}$ **9.** $s = \frac{C}{0.04}$; $4,900 **11.** $h = \frac{2V}{\pi r^2}$
13. $h = \frac{2A}{a + b}$ **15.** Answers may vary. Sample: Solve the equation for h and substitute the known values. **17a.** $v = \frac{p}{1.5w} - \frac{h}{1.5}$ **b.** 3.5 h
19. B **21.** $x > 2$ **23.** $b > 24$ **25.** 31.25

Lesson 7-7   pp. 374–375

STANDARDS PRACTICE 7. $19.58; $889.58
9. $600.00 $10,600.00 $10,600.00 $636.00 $11,236.00 $11,236.00 $674.16 $11,910.16
11. $17,057.71 **13.** $71,250.06 **15.** A
17. Answers may vary. Sample: Simple interest is computed only on the original principal. Compound interest is computed on both the principal and the interest. **19a.** $1,400 and $1,469.33 **b.** about 9 years **c.** about 11.1%
21. A **23.** $m = \frac{fa}{15}$ **25.** $k = \frac{8}{5}d - \frac{8}{5}$

Chapter 7 Review   pp. 377–379

STANDARDS PRACTICE 1. compound interest **2.** principal **3.** balance **4.** consecutive integers **5.** interest rate **6.** simple interest **7.** interest **8.** −4 **9.** 2 **10.** 48 **11.** 3 **12.** 21 **13.** $1\frac{2}{3}$ **14.** $\frac{4}{5}$
15. −2 **16.** 15 **17.** 8 **18.** −18, −17, −16, −15
19. $6\frac{3}{8}$ **20.** 16 **21.** $6\frac{1}{4}$ **22.** 3 **23.** 2.992 **24.** $1.34\overline{81}$
25. $24.95 + 6.95p = 45.80$; 3 channels
26. $p - 0.15p = 29.74$; $34.99 **27.** $10n + 20n + 147 = 1,167$; 34 tens, 34 twenties **28.** $a + 0.08a = 1,296$; $1,200 **24.** 3 **25.** −4
29. $a > 7$
(number line) −4 0 4 7

30. $y \le -3$
(number line) −3 −1 0 1

31. $c \le \frac{2}{3}$
(number line) −2 0 $\frac{2}{3}$ 2

32. $x < -4$
(number line) −4 −2 0 2

33. $x < -9$
(number line) −9 −4 0 4

34. $b < 2$
(number line) −2 0 2

35. $x < 6$
(number line) −2 0 2 6

36. $x \ge -\frac{3}{5}$
(number line) −2 −$\frac{3}{5}$ 0 2

37. $799 + 25\left(\frac{c}{8}\right) \le 1,000$; about 64 megabytes
38. $m = \frac{r}{6k}$ **39.** $y = \frac{4}{3}x$ **40.** $g = \frac{Q}{p}$ **41.** $b = a + 2c$
42. $a = \frac{1}{3}w - \frac{5}{3}n$ **43.** $h = 6e - 66$ **44.** $13.50
45. $252.50 **46.** $90.00 **47.** $8,489.66
48. $22,464.38 **49.** $27,917.68 **50.** $40,203.22
51. Answers may vary. Sample: Yes; with more interest periods, the interest would start earning interest earlier.

Chapter 8

Lesson 8-1   pp. 391–392

STANDARDS PRACTICE 7. Yes; there is one range value for each domain value. **9.** No; there are two range values for the domain value 6.
11. No; subscribers of a specific age (domain value) may pay different subscription prices (range values). **13.** Not a function; a vertical line passes through both (2, −1) and (2, 4).

(graph)

15. Not a function; domain value −1 has two range values 4 and 9.

(graph)

17. A function; no vertical line passes through two points on the graph.

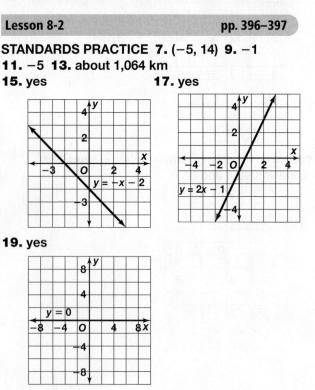

19. Not a function; a vertical line passes through both (−7, 3) and (−7, −3) and through both (−5, 1) and (−5, −1).

21. No; yes; a relation can have more than one range value for a domain value and thereby not be a function. A function is a relation by definition. **23.** A function can have the same *y*-coordinate with different *x*-coordinates, but it cannot have the same *x*-coordinate with different *y*-coordinates. **25.** Each range value is the absolute value of its domain value. **27.** Each range value is the square of its domain value. **29.** A **31.** D **33.** 12 **35.** 0.65

Lesson 8-2   pp. 396–397

STANDARDS PRACTICE 7. (−5, 14) **9.** −1
11. −5 **13.** about 1,064 km
15. yes   **17.** yes

19. yes

21. $y = -x + 3$

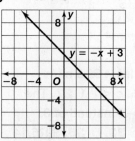

23. Answers may vary. Sample: If you can solve the equation for *y*, you have a function.
25. $(-2, 5\frac{1}{2})$, $(1, 6\frac{1}{4})$, (4, 7) **27.** The student forgot to divide −3*x* by 4. **29a.** (0, 30) and (40, 0); you burn 360 cal by swimming only the butterfly stroke for 30 min or only the backstroke for 40 min.

b.

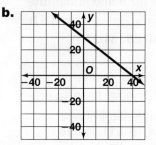

c. (0, 30) is the point at which the graph and the *y*-axis intercept each other; (40, 0) is the point at which the graph and the *x*-axis intercept each other. **d.** about 27 min **31.** C **33.** Yes, there is one range value for each domain value.

Lesson 8-3   pp. 402–404

STANDARDS PRACTICE 5. −1 **7.** −2 **9.** 2
11. 0.65
13. −1; 0   **15.** 2; 1

17. 1; −4   **19.** −3; 3

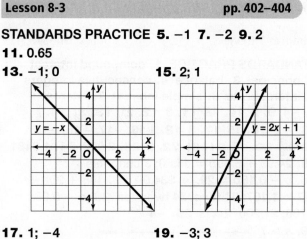

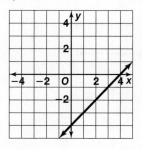

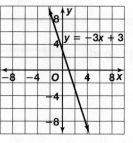

21. The student could have calculated $\frac{\text{difference in } x\text{-coordinates}}{\text{difference in } y\text{-coordinates}}$. **23.** $-\frac{1}{3}$ **25.** The upper roof has the steeper pitch because it has the greater slope. **27.** 0 **29.** undefined

31. $y = 2x + 4$

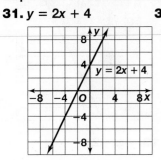

33. $y = -x + 1$

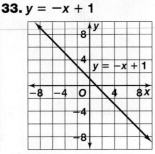

35. $y = \frac{1}{2}x$

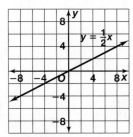

37. $y = \frac{1}{2}x - 4$

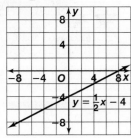

39. $y = \frac{2}{3}x + 5$

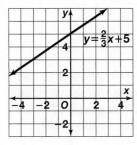

41. yes; $2(-4) - 6(-2) = 4$

43a.

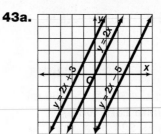
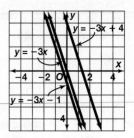

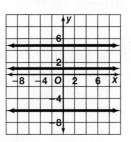

b. The lines are parallel. Explanations may vary. Sample: Their $\frac{\text{rise}}{\text{run}}$ ratios are the same, so they never meet.

c. 0

45. C

47. $x < 3$

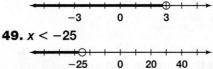

49. $x < -25$

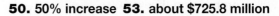

50. 50% increase **53.** about $725.8 million

Lesson 8-4 pp. 407–408

5.

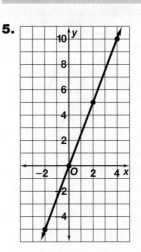

7.

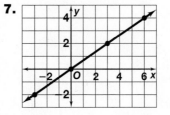

9. 34 h **11.** $Y = -\frac{1}{2}x$ **13a.** $d - 3.5f$ **b.** 52.5 in.
15. 54 **17.** A **19.** $\frac{3}{2}$ **21.** 1

Lesson 8-5   pp. 412–413

STANDARDS PRACTICE 1a. 4:30 P.M. **b.** 180 mi
3. 30 ft **5.** Sandy 101 g, White Ears 108 g,
Sport 115 g **7.** 64 choices **9.** $24 **11a.** the
clerk **b.** after 5 years **13.** 10 ways **15.** C
17. A

Lesson 8-6   pp. 417–419

STANDARDS PRACTICE 7. no **9.** (4, 5) **11.** (4, 6)
13. no solution **15.** −2, −6 **17.** yes **19.** (1, 5)
21. 20 ft² **23a.** $y = 200 + 0.10x$ and
$y = 150 + 0.20x$
b. $500

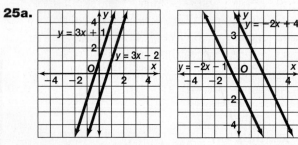

c. If weekly sales are about $600, you would earn
more money at the position that pays $150/wk
plus 20% commission. If $x = 600$,
$y = 270$. If $x = 600$ in the other equation,
$y = 260$, which is less than 270.

25a.

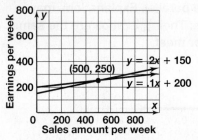

**b. Conjectures may vary. Sample: A system of
equations with the same slope but different
y-intercepts has no solutions.**
27. Answers may vary. Sample: $y = 3x, y = 3x + 2$
29. Answers may vary. Sample: $y - x = 2$,
$y = x + 2$ **31.** B **33.** D **35.** $x > -4$ **37.** $c \le 1$
39. $w \le -\frac{1}{2}$

Lesson 8-7   pp. 423–425

STANDARDS PRACTICE

7. 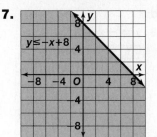   **9.**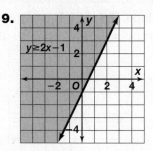

11. 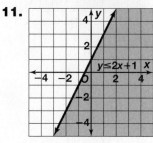   **13.** $y \ge -2x$

15. $y \ge 3x$ **17.**

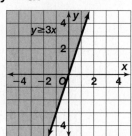   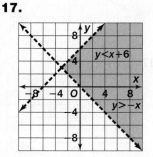

19.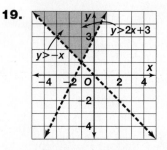

21. Multiply both sides of $-y < x$ by −1 to get
$y > -x$. The graph of $y < -x$ is the set of points
below the graph of $y = -x$. The graph of
$y > -x$ is the set of points above the graph
of $y = -x$.

23.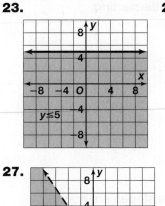
25.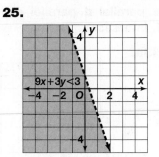

27.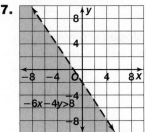

29. $y = -x - 3$; dashed **31.** $y = -4x$; dashed
33. $y = -\frac{5}{3}x + 3$; solid **35.** $2x + 3y \geq 60$

37. 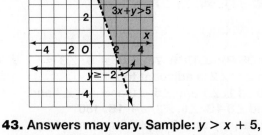 **39.**

41.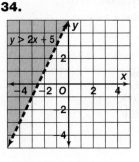

43. Answers may vary. Sample: $y > x + 5$,
$y < x + 3$ **45.** Answers may vary. Sample: $y \geq 0$,
$y \leq 0$ **47.** $y \leq x - 1$; $y > -2x - 4$ **49.** D
51. (3, 5) **53.** (3, −3) **55.** $\frac{5}{6}$ **57.** $\frac{3}{20}$ **59.** $-3\frac{1}{2}$
61. 6

Chapter 8 Review   pp. 427–429

1. slope **2.** vertical-line test **3.** direct variation
correlation **4.** function **5.** linear equation
6. domain **7.** range **8.** solution **9.** Yes; there is

one range value for each domain value. **10.** Yes;
there is one range value for each domain value.
11. No; there are domain values for which there
is more than one range value. **12.** No; one length
of time (for different distances) could result in
different costs. **13.** (−3, 2), (0, 5), (2, 7)
14. (−3, 12), (0, 0), (2, −8) **15.** (−3, $1\frac{1}{2}$), (0, 3),
(2, 4) **16.** (−3, 12), (0, 6), (2, 2)

17. −1, 7   **18.** 1, 2

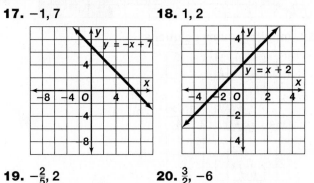

19. $-\frac{2}{5}$, 2   **20.** $\frac{3}{2}$, −6

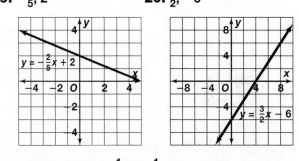

21. −2 **22.** 3 **23.** $-\frac{1}{2}$ **24.** $\frac{1}{2}$ **25.** −1 **26.** 60.96 cm
27. 2,401 ft² **28.** Answers may vary. Sample: A
diagram gives a visual picture of the problem. A
table organizes possible dimensions and their
related areas. Looking for a pattern leads to the
answer. **29.** (4, −1) **30.** (4, −3) **31.** (2, −3)
32. (1, 5) **33.** The graphs could be parallel lines,
so there is no common solution.

34.   **35.**

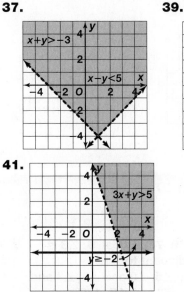 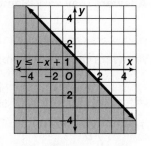

36.

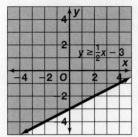

37.

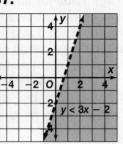

38. infinitely many solutions

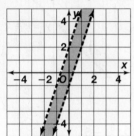

39.

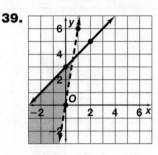

c. parallel **d.** parallel **e.** intersecting
f. intersecting

43a.

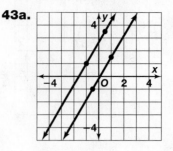

b. parallel **c.** $\frac{5}{3}, \frac{5}{3}$ **d.** If the slopes are equal, the lines are parallel. **45.** C

47.

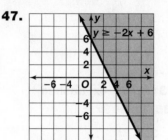

49.

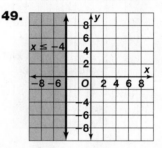

51. $\frac{11}{12}$ **53.** $-1\frac{1}{6}$ **55.** $7\frac{1}{9}$ **57.** $1\frac{3}{32}$

Chapter 9

Lesson 9-1   pp. 439–441

STANDARDS PRACTICE 9. Answers may vary.
Sample: $\overrightarrow{DA}$ **11.** $\overrightarrow{CH}, \overrightarrow{CW}$ **13.** $\overline{KD}, \overline{DG}, \overline{EH}, \overline{EF}$
15. $\overline{GJ}, \overline{FI}, \overline{KJ}, \overline{HI}$ **17.** $\overrightarrow{RS}, \overrightarrow{QP}, \overrightarrow{LK}$
19. $\overline{AB}, \overline{AD}, \overline{EF}, \overline{EH}$ **21.** $\overline{FG}, \overline{BC}, \overline{DC}, \overline{HG}$
23. Answers may vary. Sample:

25. Answers may vary. Sample:

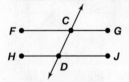

27. Answers may vary. Sample: Not possible; $\overrightarrow{AB}$
and $\overline{BC}$ both contain point B. **29.** $\overline{WZ}$ **31.** $\overline{ST}$
33. sometimes **35.** always **37.** never **39.** $\overline{AB}$ is
the segment from A to B. AB is a number, the
length of $\overline{AB}$. **41a.** intersecting **b.** intersecting

Lesson 9-2   pp. 446–447

STANDARDS PRACTICE 7. vertical **9.** ∠3 is
vertical to ∠1. ∠2 is adjacent to ∠1.
m∠1 = 40° **11.** ∠1 and ∠5, ∠2 and ∠6, ∠3 and
∠7, ∠4 and ∠8 **13.** ∠6, ∠2, ∠4 **15.** 180°
17. Answers may vary. Sample: Supplementary
angles can form a straight angle and both
supplementary and straight begin with "s".
19. Answers may vary. Sample: ∠1 ≅ ∠3 because
they are corresponding angles. So m∠3 = 84°.
∠5 ≅ ∠3, so m∠5 = 84°. **21.** D **23.** C

25.

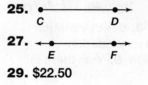

27.

29. $22.50

STANDARDS PRACTICE 9. isosceles right triangle **11.** square, rhombus **13.** parallelogram, rhombus, square, rectangle **15.** rectangle, square **17.** $P = 3x$; 10.5 cm **19.** $P = 6x$; $3\frac{3}{4}$ in. **21.** rhombus

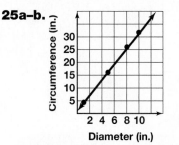

23. trapezoid, parallelogram, rectangle
25. scalene acute triangle **27.** Yes; if a triangle is equilateral, then it is also isosceles because it has at least two congruent sides. No, if a triangle is isosceles, then it is not necessarily equilateral because it may have exactly two congruent sides.
29. Answers may vary. Sample: trapezoid, isosceles triangle, right triangle **31.** The congruent sides must be 12 cm, so the perimeter is 29 cm. If the congruent sides were 5 cm, then the base could not be 12 cm because the third side would have to be less than 10 cm to form a triangle. **33.** C
35.

```
        120°/60°
        60°/120°
      120°/60°
      60°/120°
```

STANDARDS PRACTICE 1. 4 mi **3.** 4 triangles **5.** 8 students **7.** 5 cm **9.** 47 students **11.** the dog **13.** $90, $60 **15.** 34 in. **17.** B **19.** equilateral triangle **21.** $4\frac{1}{2}$, 450% **23.** $\frac{1}{50}$, 2% **25.** 1,100%

STANDARDS PRACTICE 15. $\overline{EB} \cong \overline{JF} \cong \overline{IL} \cong \overline{DH}$, $\overline{BD} \cong \overline{FE} \cong \overline{LJ} \cong \overline{HI}$, $\overline{DE} \cong \overline{EJ} \cong \overline{JI} \cong \overline{ID}$
17. $\overline{BC} \cong \overline{HG}$, $\overline{AB} \cong \overline{KH}$, $\angle B \cong \angle H$, $\triangle ABC \cong \triangle KHG$ by SAS **19.** $\overline{ON} \cong \overline{RQ}$, $\overline{OM} \cong \overline{RP}$, $\overline{NM} \cong \overline{QP}$, $\triangle ONM \cong \triangle RQP$ by SSS **21.** $\overline{AB} \cong \overline{XY}$, $\overline{BC} \cong \overline{YZ}$, $\overline{AC} \cong \overline{XZ}$ **23.** $\overline{NL} \cong \overline{QR}$, $\overline{NM} \cong \overline{QP}$, $\angle N \cong \angle Q$, $\triangle LNM \cong \triangle RQP$ by SAS **25.** $\overline{KM} \cong \overline{JM}$, $\overline{ML} \cong \overline{ML}$, $\angle KML \cong \angle JML$, $\triangle KML \cong \triangle JML$ by SAS
27. Incorrect: $\angle R$ does not correspond with $\angle N$.
29. Incorrect: $\angle A$ does not correspond with $\angle C$.
31. Incorrect: $\angle V$ and $\angle C$ are not corresponding angles. **33a.** $\triangle CDH$; congruent by SSS or by SAS **b.** $\triangle CBA$; congruent by SSS or by SAS
35. congruent by SAS; $\angle D \cong \angle K$, so $x = 53$. Because the sum of the angle measures in a triangle is 180°, $y = 37$ and $z = 5$ cm. **37.** B

39. 14 students **41.** $0.15 \cdot x = 12$, 80 **43.** $\frac{3}{8}$, $\frac{1}{2}$, $\frac{2}{3}$, $\frac{5}{6}$ **45.** $\frac{1}{7}$, $\frac{1}{6}$, $\frac{1}{5}$, $\frac{1}{4}$

STANDARDS PRACTICE 5. about 314 in.
7. about 19.8 cm **9.** about $29\frac{1}{3}$ ft **11.** about 113 in. **13.** about $1\frac{4}{7}$ yd **15.** 180° **17.** 4° **19.** 270°
21.

How Students Travel to School

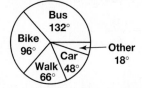

23. Answers may vary. Sample: Draw a circle using a compass. Then, use proportions to find the central-angle measures of all the sections of your circle graph. Use a protractor to draw the angles accurately. Finally, label each section and add a title and other necessary information.

25a–b.

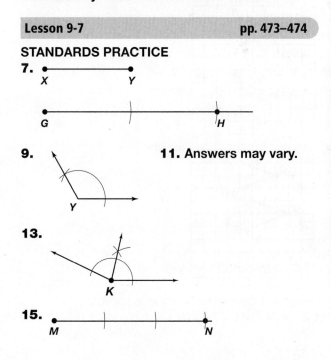

c. 3.14 **d.** The slope is the value of π. For every increase of 1 in. diameter, the circumference increases by about 3.14 in. **27.** C **29.** B

STANDARDS PRACTICE
7.
```
X ●————————————● Y
```
```
G ●————/————————|——— H
```
9.

11. Answers may vary.

13.

15.
```
M ●————/————|————● N
```

17.

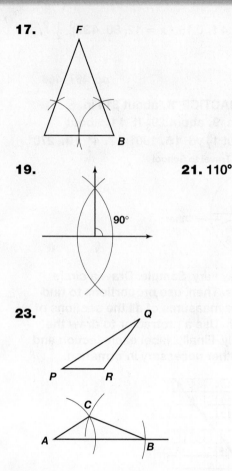

19.

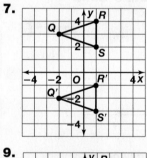

21. 110°

23.

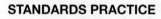

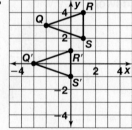

25. 43°

Lesson 9-8   pp. 478–480

STANDARDS PRACTICE

7.

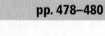

9.

11.

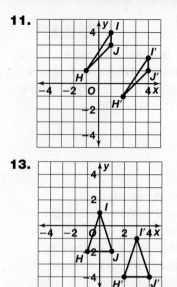

13.

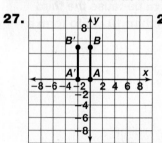

15. $A(1, 5) \rightarrow A'(2, 7)$ **17.** $S(3, 3) \rightarrow S'(11, 1)$
19. $(x, y) \rightarrow (x + 4, y + 3)$ **21.** translation 11 units to the left and 4 units up **23.** translation 6 units to the left and 3 units down **25.** vertical

27.

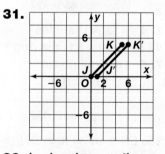

29.

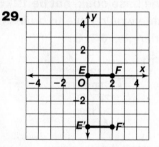

31.

33. $(x, y) \rightarrow (x, y + 4)$

35.

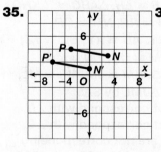

37.

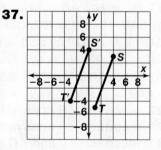

41.

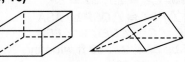

43. D **45.** B **47.** $\frac{4}{11}$

Lesson 9-9   pp. 484–485

STANDARDS PRACTICE

7.

9.

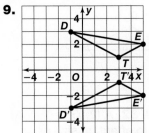

11.

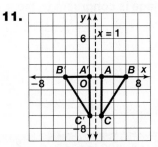

13.

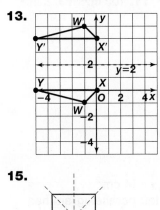

15.

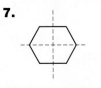

17. No, a figure and its reflection image are congruent.

19. $J'(-8, 1)$

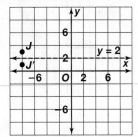

21. $A'(5, 2)$

23. $C'(-4, 0)$

25. sometimes **27.** (−1, 11)

29a–b.

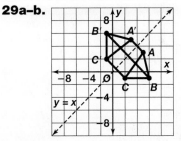

c. They are perpendicular. **d.** perpendicular bisector **31.** B

Lesson 9-10   pp. 488–489

STANDARDS PRACTICE

7a.   **b.**

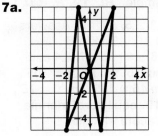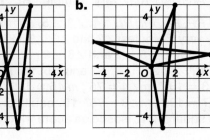

Selected Answers

9a.
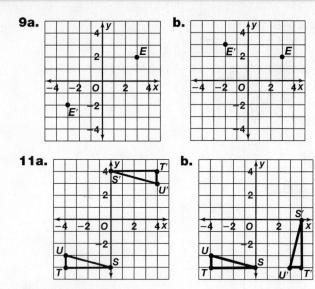
b.

11a.
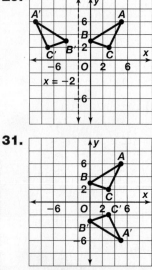
b.

13. yes, 60°
15. no
17. Answers may vary. **19.** yes, 180° **21.** no
23. 90° **25.** 180° **27.** No; the reflection of (2, 5) across the y-axis is (−2, 5). A 180° rotation image of (2, 5) is (−2, −5).

29.

31.

Chapter 9 Review   **pp. 491–493**

1. E **2.** C **3.** B **4.** G **5.** D **6.** A **7.** H **8.** F
9. ∠RPD, ∠DPL, ∠RPL **10.** $\overrightarrow{PR}$, $\overrightarrow{PD}$, $\overrightarrow{PL}$

11. Answers may vary. Sample: $\overleftrightarrow{RL}$ **12.** R, P, D, L

13. $\overline{RP}$, $\overline{PD}$, $\overline{PL}$, $\overline{RL}$ **14.** ∠3, ∠5, ∠7 **15.** Answers may vary. Samples: ∠2 and ∠3, ∠5 and ∠6
16. ∠1 and ∠5, ∠2 and ∠6, ∠3 and ∠7, ∠4 and ∠8 **17.** ∠4 and ∠6, ∠3 and ∠5 **18.** m∠1 = 105°, m∠3 = 105°, m∠4 = 75°, m∠5 = 105°, m∠6 = 75°, m∠7 = 105°, m∠8 = 75° **19.** equilateral triangle
20. square **21.** isosceles acute triangle

22. trapezoid **23.** ∠T ≅ ∠P, $\overline{ST}$ ≅ $\overline{SP}$, ∠RST ≅ ∠QSP, △RST ≅ △QSP by ASA
24. $\overline{DE}$ ≅ $\overline{FE}$, $\overline{CE}$ ≅ $\overline{GE}$, ∠DEC ≅ ∠FEG, △CDE ≅ △GFE by SAS **25.** 50 ft wide by 55 ft long **26.** about 43.96 cm
27. Television Programming

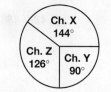

28–29. Drawings may vary. Samples:

28.
29.

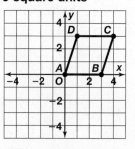

30. A′(11, 1) **31.** A′(−7, −2) **32.** A′(2, 7)
33. A′(7, 0) **34.** They have no effect on size or shape. In each case the image is congruent to the original figure.

Chapter 10

Lesson 10-1   **pp. 502–504**

STANDARDS PRACTICE 5. 135 ft², or 15 yd²
7. 12 ft², or $1\frac{1}{3}$ yd² **9.** 3 m² **11.** 100 in.² **13.** 8 in.²
15. 9 square units

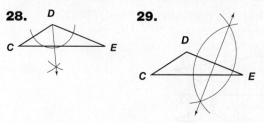

17. 22 m² **19.** 1,400 mm², or 14 cm²
21. 1,694 in.² **23.** No; the left parallelogram has an area of 6 m² while the right parallelogram has 4.5 m². **25.** $\frac{1}{4}$; the area of a parallelogram is bh, so doubling both dimensions quadruples the area. **27.** 24 ft² **29a.** 4,180 ft² **b.** 464.$\overline{4}$ yd²
c. 3 bags **31.** C

33.

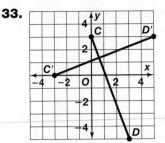

35. 118°, 62°

Lesson 10-2   pp. 510–511

STANDARDS PRACTICE 7. 47.6 m² **9.** 20 cm²
11. 22 cm² **13.** 15 in.² **15.** Yes, by the
Commutative and Associative Properties.
Regrouping factors can make it easier to find the
area by mental math. **17.** Answers may vary.
Samples:

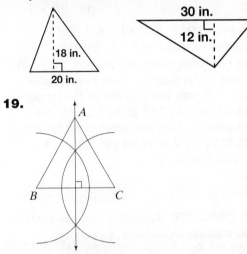

19.

21. 108 in.² **23.** $\frac{1}{2}h(b + 4b) : \frac{1}{2}h(b + 2b) = 5b : 3b =$
5 : 3 **25.** C **27.** 288 m² **29.** $10

Lesson 10-3   pp. 515–517

STANDARDS PRACTICE 7. 144π ft²; 452 ft²
9. 900π cm²; 2,826 cm² **11.** 50 in.² **13.** 2,856 yd²
15. 357 mi² **17.** about 191 pieces **19.** 144π mi²;
452.2 mi² **21.** 0.5625π in.²; 1.8 in.² **23.** Answers
may vary. Sample: Find the area of a circular
stage for a play. **25.** 4 circles **27.** 14 ft²
29. 16π cm²; the square will have a side length of
8 cm. The radius of the circle inside is $\frac{1}{2} \cdot 8 =$
4 cm. The area is π(4)², or 16π. **31a.** about
$.082/in.², about $.075/in.², about $.068/in.²
b. Yes; it has the lowest cost per square inch of
all the pizzas. **33.** C

Lesson 10-4   pp. 521–523

STANDARDS PRACTICE 5. The bases are
triangles. The figure is a triangular prism. **7.** The
base is a rectangle. The figure is a rectangular
pyramid. **9.** There are no bases. The figure is a
sphere.

11.

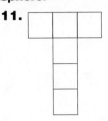

13. pyramid **15.** cone

17.

19. C **21.** square prism **22.** triangular prism
23. rectangular prism
27. Answers may vary. Sample:

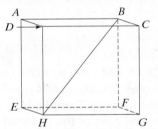

29. Answers may vary. Sample: A net for a
rectangular prism has two rectangular bases
with four rectangular faces attached. A net for a
rectangular pyramid has one rectangular base
with four triangular faces attached. **31.** Answer
may vary. **33.** B **35.** 6.25π m²; 20 m².

Lesson 10-5   pp. 530–532

STANDARDS PRACTICE 7. 1,008 m²

9a.

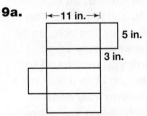

b. 206 in.² **11.** 11,988 in.² **13.** 408 cm²
15. 175.8 cm² **17.** 904 cm² **19.** 518 m² **21.** A
23a. 5 sides **b.** 3,600 ft² **c.** $600 **25.** Answers
may vary. Sample: When you paint a room, you

Selected Answers

need to find the surface area of the walls to buy the correct amount of paint. **27.** The first box requires 399.25 in.^{2} of cardboard. The second requires 439.75 in.^{2} of cardboard. So the second box requires more cardboard. **29.** 658 ft^2 **31.** B **33.** C **35.** pentagonal pyramid

37.

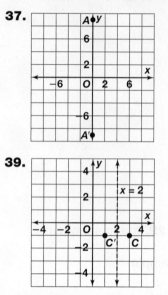

39.

Imagine the fold is the spine of a book. Letter the "pages" A through H. Unfold the paper.

C	F	E	D
B	G	H	A

9. 4 cm **11.** A **13.** 130.6 cm^3 **15.** −10, −8, −12
17. 2, $1\frac{1}{3}$, $2\frac{2}{3}$

Lesson 10-9   pp. 550–551

STANDARDS PRACTICE 5. 25 yd^3 **7.** 5,539 cm^3
9. 216 in.^{3} **11.** 20.48 cm^3 **13.** 523 in.^{3}
15. 7,235 cm^3 **17.** 113,040 yd^3 **19.** 4 cups
21. about 8.2 in.^{3} **23.** 22 cm **25.** 6 yd **27.** about 447 cm^3 **29.** C **31.** −16x^2 **33.** $\frac{9}{64}$

Lesson 10-10   pp. 554–555

STANDARDS PRACTICE 5. 8.4 in **7.** 1,008 m^2;
2,074 m^3 **9.** 3,484 in.^{2}; 804 in.^{3} **11.** 216 ft^3
13. Since the two sculptures are similar, the ratio of their volumes is the cube of their scale factor. So she should estimate the volume of the larger sculpture to be between 2.5^3 and 3^3, or 15.625 and 27, times greater than the smaller sculpture.
15. S.A. = 30.375 yd^2, V = 11.39 yd^3 **17.** 2 : 1
19. B **21.** D **23.** 1.94 × 10^{-3}

Chapter 10 Review   pp. 557–559

STANDARDS PRACTICE 1. lateral area **2.** cone
3. altitude **4.** volume **5.** sphere **6.** cylinder
7. area **8.** 189 m^2 **9.** 14 cm^2 **10.** 6.25 yd^2
11. 79 m^2 **12.** 201 mm^2 **13.** 57 m^2 **14.** 31 in.^{2}
15. triangular prism **16.** square pyramid
17. cylinder **18.** 164 cm^2 **19.** 205,513 m^2
20. 84 cm^2 **21.** 85 cm^2 **22.** Answers may vary. Sample: 24 in. by 18 in. **23.** Find the area of the walk and garden, and then subtract the area of the garden. **24.** 384 units^3 **25.** 18 ft^3 **26.** 311 units^3
27. 268 units^3 **28.** S.A. = 168 ft^2; V = 144 ft^3
29. S.A. = 100.575 cm^2, V = 95.175 cm^3.

Chapter 11

Lesson 11-1   pp. 568–569

STANDARDS PRACTICE 7. −6 **9.** 5 **11.** 9
13. −13 **15.** 4 **17.** −7 **19.** irrational; it neither terminates nor repeats **21.** rational; because 16 is a perfect square **23.** irrational; because 5 is not a perfect square **25.** rational; because 144 is a perfect square **27.** 14 **29.** $\frac{5}{7}$ **31.** x **33.** 1
35. −9 **37.** −10 **39.** 10 **41.** rational; repeating

Lesson 10-6   pp. 537–538

STANDARDS PRACTICE 7. 540 cm^2 **9.** 1,017 cm^2
11. 1,256 cm^2 **13.** 105 cm^2 **15.** about 804 mm^2
17. 28 m^2 **19.** Answers may vary. Sample: My friend forgot that the lateral area of the pyramid is half of the lateral area of the prism. Also, it is necessary to add the area of the second base of the prism. **21.** 122 m^2 **23.** Use the slant height to find the lateral area using the formula L.A. = $\pi r \ell$ = 3.14 · 8 · 10, then add the area of the base, 3.14 · 8^2, to the lateral area to find the surface area.
25a. about 23,800 ft^2 **b.** 9.6 ft^2 **27.** B **29.** 1,130 in.^{2}.

Lesson 10-7   pp. 541–542

STANDARDS PRACTICE 7. 54 cm^3 **9.** 24 m^3
11. 6,029 m^3 **13a.** 314 in.^{3} **b.** 2,512 in.^{3} **c.** The volume of the larger tube is 8 times the volume of the smaller tube. **15–17.** Answers may vary. Samples are given. **15.** A tent; you may need to see how many of your friends can fit in a tent on a camping trip. **17.** A large box; you may need to find how much the box can hold when you store items. **19.** 3.2 cm **21.** 27; $290.37 **23.** C **25.** D
27. 120 cm^2 **29.** 22 nickels

Lesson 10-8   pp. 546–547

STANDARDS PRACTICE 1. 10 in. by 14 in. by 3 in.
3. 30 cm, 15 cm **5.** 50 ft by 50 ft **7.** Answers may vary. Sample: Fold a sheet of paper in quarters.

decimal **43.** Answers may vary. Sample: Think of the perfect squares closest to 30, one less than 30 and one greater than 30. Take the square root of the one closest to 30. **45.** 3, −3 **47.** 10, −10 **49.** 2 in. **51.** −2 **53.** −3 **55.** B **57.** A

Lesson 11-2   pp. 573–575

STANDARDS PRACTICE 7. 13 cm **9.** 20 in.
11. 14 ft **13.** about 10.6 ft **15.** no; $4^2 + 6^2 \neq 7^2$
17. yes; $7^2 + 24^2 = 25^2$ **19.** no; $8^2 + 10^2 \neq 12^2$
21. 4.5 in. **23.** 4 ft **25.** yes; $3^2 + 4^2 = 5^2$
27. no; $10^2 + 24^2 \neq 25^2$ **29.** yes, $6^2 + 8^2 = 10^2$;
yes, $14^2 + 48^2 = 50^2$; yes, $10^2 + 24^2 = 26^2$
31. Yes; $(3p)^2 + (4p)^2 = (5p)^2$ for any value of p.
33. no; $0.56^2 + 0.54^2 \neq 1^2$ **35.** $\sqrt{50}$ **37.** $\sqrt{52}$
39a. 10 in. **b.** about 10.8 in. **c.** about 15.8 in.
41. B **43.** rational **45.** rational

Lesson 11-3   pp. 582–583

STANDARDS PRACTICE 5. 5 **7.** 23.3
9. 17.7 **11.** 10 unit^2; 15.4 units **13.** (1.5, 2)
15. 30; (0,0) **17a.** (−0.5, 3)
b. $AM = \sqrt{(-3 - (-0.5))^2 + (5 - 3)^2} = \sqrt{10.25}$
$MB = \sqrt{(2 - (-0.5))^2 + (1 - 3)^2} = \sqrt{10.25}$
19. (12, 9) **21.** No; the square of a number $(x_1 - x_2)$ and the square of its opposite $(x_2 - x_1)$ are equal. **23.** Each coordinate of the midpoint is the average of the corresponding coordinates of the endpoints. **25.** C **27.** yes; $8^2 + 15^2 = 17^2$
29. yes; $12^2 + 16^2 = 20^2$

Lesson 11-4   pp. 588–589

STANDARDS PRACTICE 1. $\frac{20}{x + 20} = \frac{13}{21}$; 12.3 m
3. 1.2 mi **5.** 28 ft **7.** \$20 **9.** −3 **11.** 6.3 ft^2 **13.** B
15. B **17.** (0.5, 4)

Lesson 11-5   pp. 594–595

STANDARDS PRACTICE

7.

x	$-x^2$	y	(x, y)
−2	$-(-2)^2$	−4	(−2, −4)
−1	$-(-1)^2$	−1	(−1, −1)
0	$-(0)^2$	0	(0, 0)
1	$-(1)^2$	−1	(1, −1)
2	$-(2)^2$	−4	(2, −4)

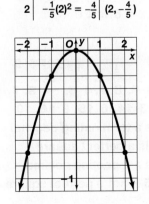

9.

x	$5x^2 = y$	(x, y)
−2	$5(-2)^2 = 20$	(−2, 20)
−1	$5(-1)^2 = 5$	(−1, 5)
0	$5(0)^2 = 0$	(0, 0)
1	$5(1)^2 = 5$	(1, 5)
2	$5(2)^2 = 20$	(2, 20)

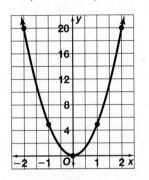

11.

x	$0.25x^2 = y$	(x, y)
−2	$0.25(-2)^2 = 1$	(−2, 1)
−1	$0.25(-1)^2 = 0.25$	(−1, 0.25)
0	$0.25(0)^2 = 0$	(0, 0)
1	$0.25(1)^2 = 0.25$	(1, 0.25)
2	$0.25(2)^2 = 1$	(2, 1)

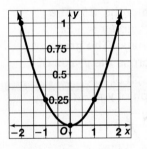

13.

x	$-\frac{1}{5}x^2 = y$	(x, y)
−2	$-\frac{1}{5}(-2)^2 = -\frac{4}{5}$	$(-2, -\frac{4}{5})$
−1	$-\frac{1}{5}(-1)^2 = -\frac{1}{5}$	$(-1, -\frac{1}{5})$
0	$-\frac{1}{5}(0)^2 = 0$	(0, 0)
1	$-\frac{1}{5}(1)^2 = -\frac{1}{5}$	$(1, -\frac{1}{5})$
2	$-\frac{1}{5}(2)^2 = -\frac{4}{5}$	$(2, -\frac{4}{5})$

15.

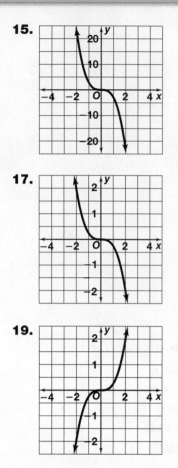

17.

19.

21. $x \approx 1.5$ **23.** about 5 months **25.** The graphs of $y = x^3$, $y = -x^3$, and $y = -2x^3$ have the same general shape. The graph of $y = -x^3$ is a reflection across the y-axis of the graph $y = x^3$. The graph of $y = -2x^3$ is narrower than the graph of $y = -x^3$.

27.

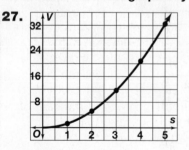

29a. $y_1 = x^3$; $y_2 = 6x^2$ **b.** $x = 6$ **31.** C
33. $2.1756 \times 10^6 \text{ km}^2$

Chapter 11 Review   pp. 597–599

1. C **2.** F **3.** D **4.** E **5.** A **6.** B **7.** 1 **8.** −4 **9.** 7
10. 8 **11.** −6 **12.** 2 **13.** 3 **14.** 6 **15.** 8 **16.** 10
17. rational; because it is a terminating decimal
18. rational; because 64 is a perfect square
19. rational; because it is a repeating decimal
20. irrational; because 15 is not a perfect square

21. rational; because it is a repeating decimal
22. It is irrational because the decimal neither terminates nor repeats. **23.** no; $1^2 + 3^2 \neq 3^2$
24. yes; $8^2 + 15^2 = 17^2$ **25.** yes;
$(\sqrt{6})^2 + (\sqrt{10})^2 = 4^2$ **26.** yes; $30^2 + 40^2 = 50^2$
27. 67.1 mi **28.** 12.5 km **29.** 15 in **30.** 2.9 ft
31. 127.3 ft **32.** 3.6 **33.** 5 **34.** 12.6 **35.** 2.2
36. 9.2 **37.** 13.4 **38.** (2, 4) **39.** (3, 4) **40.** (−2, 2)
41. (4.5, 10) **42.** (−12, −8) **43.** (2.5, −0.5)
44. about 337.5 ft **45.** $7\frac{5}{16}$ cans

46.

x	$-6x^2 = y$	(x, y)
−2	$-6(-2)^2 = -24$	$(-2, -24)$
−1	$-6(-1)^2 = -6$	$(-1, -6)$
0	$-6(0)^2 = 0$	$(0, 0)$
1	$-6(1)^2 = -6$	$(1, -6)$
2	$-6(2)^2 = -24$	$(2, -24)$

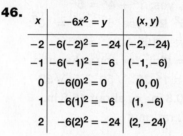

47.

x	$\frac{1}{6}x^2 = y$	(x, y)
−9	$\frac{1}{6}(-9)^2 = 13.5$	$(-9, 13.5)$
−6	$\frac{1}{6}(-6)^2 = 6$	$(-6, 6)$
0	$\frac{1}{6}(0)^2 = 0$	$(0, 0)$
6	$\frac{1}{6}(6)^2 = 6$	$(6, 6)$
9	$\frac{1}{6}(9)^2 = 13.5$	$(9, 13.5)$

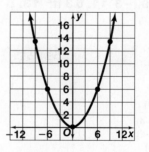

48.

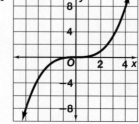

49.

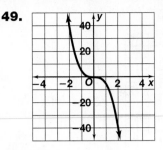

Chapter 12

STANDARDS PRACTICE 5. 58.9, 56, 56, 45 **7.** 4.6, 5, 5, 8 **9.** 1.8 h, 1.8 h, 1.5 h **11.** 1 mode **13.** 1 mode **15.** 115; lowers mean by about 1.9 **17.** Mean; there likely are no outliers. **19.** Mean; there likely are no outliers. **16.** Median; there is no mode, and the outlier (367) affects the mean too much. **17.** Mean, median, or mode since they are all about equal. **21.** 5.8, 6.5, 6.5, 6.7; median (or mode); the outlier (1.2) affects the mean too much. **23.** 7.8, 8, none, 14; mean (or median); there is no mode and the mean and median are nearly the same. **25.** Mode; the data are not numerical. **27.** Median; there could easily be outliers. **29.** Answers may vary. Sample: Two tablespoons each of peanuts, pecans, pistachios, and pumpkin seeds; 8.45 g; 94.75 Calories; two tablespoons each of walnuts, sunflower seeds, pumpkin seeds, and pistachios; 8.1 g; 91.75 Calories. **31.** B **33.** about 6 **35.** about $39.00

STANDARDS PRACTICE

5. Rolls of a Number Cube

Number	Frequency
1	4
2	3
3	3
4	2
5	3
6	2

```
X
X X X   X
X X X X X
X X X X X
1 2 3 4 5 6
```

7.

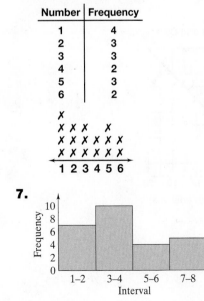

9a. Answers may vary. Sample: the greatest value is 84 and the least value is 24. So intervals could be 24-35, 36-47, 48-59, 60-71, and 72-83.

b.

Hours	Tally	Frequency
24–31	IIII II	7
32–39	IIII I	6
40–47	IIII	4
48–55	II	2
56–63	I	1
64–71	III	3
72–79	I	1
80–87	I	1

c.

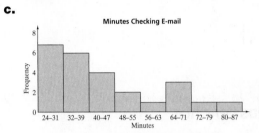

Minutes Checking E-mail

11. World Series Games, 1970-2002

Number of Games	Frequency
0	1
1	0
2	0
3	0
4	6
5	6
6	9
7	13

; 7

13. 1; 3 **15. a.** Count the x's. **b.** Answers may vary. Sample: For mode, find the value of the stack with the most x's. For median, find the middle value or the average of the two middle values. For mean, multiply the number of x's in a stack by the value of each stack. Find the sum of the products. Divide by the number of x's from part (a). **17.** B **19.** 15.5, 16, 16 and 18

STANDARDS PRACTICE

7. Maximum Speeds of Animals (mi/h)

9.

set A
set B

11. $15 **13.** The acreages vary considerably, from about 25 acres to about 650 acres. However, about half of the parks are between 50 and 250 acres, with a median of 125 acres. **15.** The lower quartile is the median of the lower half of the data; the upper quartile is the median of the upper half of the data. The middle quartile is the median of the data. **17.** Answers may vary. Sample: 10, 12, 12, 30, 31, 45, 47 **19.** D

21.

Number	Frequency
29	1
30	1
31	3
32	4
33	2
34	0
35	1

Lesson 12-4   pp. 625–626

STANDARDS PRACTICE

5.
```
4 | 0  8  9
5 | 0  2  3  4
6 | 1  7  8  9
7 | 3  4  6  8
Key: 4 | 8 means 48
```

7.
```
3 | 2  7
4 | 1  3  5
5 | 0  0  2  8
6 | 3  7  9  9
Key: 3 | 2 means 3.2
```

9. Both measures of central tendency indicate that the women's blood pressure in the survey was considerably less than the men's blood pressure. **11.** Answers may vary. Sample: it is not necessary, but it would help show the range of data. **13.** The mean, median, and mode for the men's golf scores are around 278 strokes, while the women's scores were around 280. This indicates that the difference in scores isn't very large. However, the fact that one of the modes for the women's scores was 290 shows that women frequently do have a higher number of strokes. **15.** B **17.** 180.3, 180, 180, 8

Lesson 12-5   pp. 631–633

STANDARDS PRACTICE 5. averaged 4 h watching television and 2 h of physical activity daily **7.** 2 students

9.

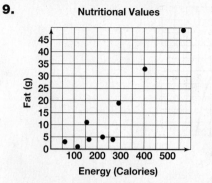

Nutritional Values

11. No correlation; there is no apparent relationship. **13.** Negative correlation; as one set of values increases, the other set tends to decrease. **15.** Negative; as one set of values increases, the other set tends to decrease. **17.** No correlation; the sets of data are not related. **19.** Positive; the more you study, the better your grade will be. **21.** No correlation; the sets of data are not related.

23a.

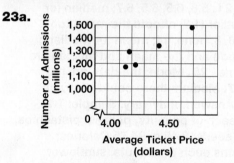

b. positive correlation **c.** Yes; interchanging the axes doesn't affect the relationship between the variables. **25.** A **27.** A **29.** $h = \frac{2A}{b + c}$ **31.** $41.54

Lesson 12-6   pp. 637–638

STANDARDS PRACTICE 1. a–b. Trend lines may vary. Sample given.

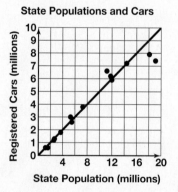

State Populations and Cars

c. about 16 million cars **d.** $y = 0.5x$; about 3.6 million cars **3.** Answers may vary. Sample: 8.4 gal **5. a.** $185 **b.** 1.5 h **7.** The 1982 and 1998 values are the same. **9.** D **11.** (−3, 9), (0, 0), (2, −6) **13.** (−3, −3.5), (0, −2), (2, −1)

Chapter 12 Review   pp. 641–643

1. mean **2.** measures of central tendency **3.** quartlies **4.** range **5.** frequency table **6.** 5, 2 and 5; no outliers **7.** 16.1, 16.2, 16.3 no outliers **8.** 36, 33, none; outlier: 57 **9.** 1.0, 0.2, 0.1 outliers: 7.9 **10.** Mode; the data are not numerical. **11.** Median; there could easily be outliers. **12.** Mean; there are likely no outliers.

13.

Number	Frequency
9	1
10	3
11	3
12	4
13	1

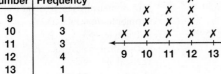

14.

Number	Frequency
45	1
46	3
47	2
48	3
49	2
50	1

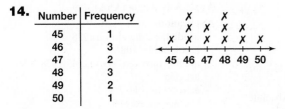

15.

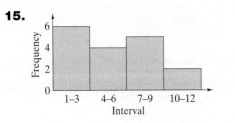

16.

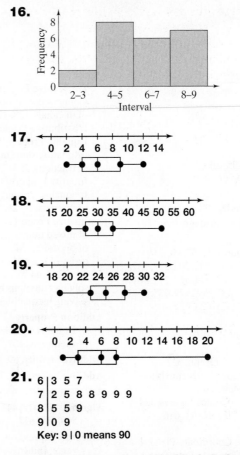

17.

18.

19.

20.

21.
```
6 | 3 5 7
7 | 2 5 8 8 9 9 9
8 | 5 5 9
9 | 0 9
Key: 9 | 0 means 90
```

22. mode: 79, median: 79 **23.** 6, 7, 8, 9 **24.** class A: 34; class B: 38 **25.** median: class A 79.5, class B 84; mode: class A 74, 79, and 96, class B 99 **26.** 30 min **27.** about 620 Calories **28.** Positive correction; as the time bicycling increase, the Calories used increases. **29.** about 800 Calories

Index

R

Radical symbol, 566

Radius
- of circle, 464
- of cone, 535, 548
- of cylinder, 540
- defined, 464
- of sphere, 536, 549

Rafter length, 572

Range
- of data, 613, 641
- defined, 606, 641
- finding, 606
- of function, 388, 389, 427
- of relation, 388, 389, 427

Rates,
- converting, 285
- defined, 284, 335
- exercises that use, 265, 328, 329, 380, 412, 424, 468
- finding, 285
- unit, 284, 335

Ratio
- of circumference to diameter, 464–465
- defined, 284, 335
- proportions and, 290–291
- scales and, 296
- writing, 284

Rational numbers, 197–198. *See also* Decimals; Fraction(s); Mixed numbers; Whole numbers
- absolute value of, 200
- comparing, 198
- converting to decimals, 276
- defined, 197, 219
- dividing, 244, 276
- evaluating fractions containing variables, 198
- graphing, 198
- identifying, 197, 597
- integers as, 197
- multiplying, 242–243
- simplest form of, 188–189, 218
- solving equations with, 258–259

Ray, 436, 491

Real numbers, 567

Reasonableness
- checking problem solutions for, 41, 99, 151, 159, 194, 254, 348, 359
- of estimation, 128, 133, 236

Reasoning, 8, 23, 28, 39, 49, 56, 72, 77, 96, 114, 149, 175, 181, 190, 200, 204, 218, 235, 245, 266, 300, 304, 305, 310, 314, 319, 323, 375, 387, 424, 447, 468, 473, 485, 489, 503, 505, 510, 511, 516, 532, 538, 543, 546, 583, 608, 614, 621, 625, 632. *See also* Conjectures; Deductive reasoning; Error analysis; Inductive reasoning; Logical reasoning; Mathematical reasoning

Reasoning Strategies
- Act It Out, 158–159, 165
- Draw a Diagram, 454–455, 493
- Look for a Pattern, 40–41, 61
- Make a Model, 544–545, 559
- Make a Table, 330–331, 337
- Solve a Simpler Problem, 193–194, 218
- Solve by Graphing, 635–636, 643
- Try, Test, Revise, 98–99, 119
- Use Multiple Strategies, 410–411, 429
- Work Backward, 253–254, 277
- Write a Proportion, 586–587, 599
- Write an Equation, 358–359, 378

Reciprocals
- defined, 244
- multiplying by, 244, 262, 263, 276, 353
- negative, 263

Rectangles
- area of, 10, 12, 73, 203, 243, 367, 500–501, 505, 508, 514
- defined, 449
- formulas for, 138, 702
- modeling factors, 173, 182, 242
- perimeter of, 138, 505, 580

Rectangular graph paper, 518

Rectangular prism, 539, 702

Reductions (dilations), 300, 481

Reflection(s), 483, 493

Reflectional symmetry, 482–483

Reflexive Property of Equality, 703

Regular polygon
- defined, 450
- diagonals in, 454–455, 508, 574

Regular pyramid, 534

Relations
- defined, 388, 427
- domain, 388, 389, 427
- mapping, 389–390
- range of, 388, 389, 427
- vertical-line test of, 389–390

Relatively prime numbers, 186

Repeated addition, 44

Repeated multiplication, 178

Repeating decimal, 232, 233, 235, 276

Review. *See* Assessment; Mixed Review; Skills Handbook

Rhombus, 449

Right cylinder, 527

Right prism, 527

Right triangles, 448
- finding, 572
- hypotenuse of, 570, 598
- identifying, 572
- legs of, 570, 598
- Pythagorean Theorem and, 570–572, 598

Rise, 399, 572

Roots
- cube, 569
- square. *See* Square roots

Rotation(s)
- angle of, 486
- center of, 486
- defined, 486, 493
- graphing, 486–487

Rotation image, 486

Rotational symmetry, 487

Rounding
- compatible numbers, 133, 164
- decimals, 127–129, 163–164, 686
- fractions, 236
- percents, 307, 308
- whole numbers, 681, 686

Rules
- for adding integers, 25–26
- for dividing integers, 46
- of divisibility, 172–173
- function, 388, 427
- for multiplying integers, 45
- for patterns, 35–36
- for raising a product to a power, 270, 277
- for subtracting integers, 31
- writing, 477

Run, 399

S

Same sign, 25, 45, 46, 60

SAS (Side-Angle-Side), 459

Scale(s)
- computer software for, 300
- dilations, 300, 481
- drawing to, 296, 300, 336
- of model, 296, 336

Scale drawings
- exercise that use, 304
- using, 296, 336

Scale factor, 300

Scalene triangle, 448

Scatter plots
- defined, 628–630, 643
- finding trends with, 630
- interpreting and drawing, 628–629
- making, 629
- predictions and, 628–630

Scientific notation, 210–213, 219
- calculating with, 213
- changing to, 212
- comparing and ordering numbers with, 212
- converting to standard notation with, 211–212, 219
- defined, 210, 219
- multiplying with, 213
- writing in, 211–212, 219

Secant, 468

Segment(s)
- congruent, 470
- defined, 436, 491
- endpoint of, 436, 479, 491
- midpoint of, 581, 598
- perpendicular, 471
- skew, 437, 438

Substitution Property of Equality, 703

Subtraction
  of decimals, 142–143, 687
  Distributive Property and, 74
  of fractions, 237–238, 258, 276, 696
  of integers, 30–31, 60
  of mixed numbers, 236, 238–239, 276
  modeling, 30–31
  order of operations and, 8–10
  rules for, 31
  solving equations with, 88–89,
    142–143, 258
  solving inequalities with, 106–107,
    363–364

Subtraction Property
  of Equality, 88, 703
  of Inequality, 106, 703

Sum(s). *See also* Addition
  estimating, 128
  of measures of angles of a polygon,
    453

Summation. *See* Addition

Supplementary angles, 443

Surface area (S.A.)
  of cone, 535, 559, 702
  of cylinder, 529, 536, 558, 702
  defined, 527, 558
  formulas for, 528, 529, 536, 558
  of prism, 527–528, 558
  of pyramid, 534, 558, 702
  of rectangular prism, 702
  of sphere, 535–536, 559, 702
  of triangular prism, 528

Surveys
  exercises that use, 312, 612

Symbols
  approximately equal to, 128
  arrow, 477
  congruence, 443
  greater than, 102
  greater than or equal to, 102
  grouping, 9–10
  less than or equal to, 103
  for multiplication, 45
  order of operations and, 9–10
  radical, 566
  for similarity, 295, 700
  square root, 566, 700
  table of, 700

Symmetric Property
  of Equality, 703
  of Inequality, 703

Symmetry
  line of, 482
  reflectional, 482–483
  rotational, 487

Systems of linear equations, 414–416, 429

Systems of linear inequalities, 422, 429

T _____

Tables
  conjectures in, 99
  data in, 41, 136

estimating from, 136
  frequency, 612–613, 642
  for graphing linear equations, 394, 395
  nonlinear functions in, 591–593
  problem solving with, 330–331, 337
  reading, 136

Take Note, 9, 24, 25, 31, 45, 46, 69, 73, 88,
  90, 94, 95, 106, 107, 110, 111, 150,
  172, 173, 179, 201, 202, 205, 206,
  207, 244, 270, 271, 311, 371, 373,
  465, 501, 507, 509, 513, 529, 534,
  535, 539, 540, 548, 549, 553, 570,
  579, 581

Tangent, to circle, 468

Technology, *See also* Computers
  software, 300, 611, 616

Temperature
  exercises involving, 20, 22, 368
  formula for, 137, 139, 368

Ten, powers of, 691

Term(s)
  defined, 78
  like, 78, 79, 348–349, 377

Terminating decimal, 231, 276

Test-Taking Strategies
  Answering the Question Asked, 274
  Choosing the Process, 162
  Drawing a Diagram, 490
  Eliminating Answers, 376
  Finding Needed Information, 58
  Interpreting Data, 640
  Measuring to Solve, 556
  Reading Comprehension Questions,
    216
  Using a Variable, 596
  Using Estimation, 334
  Using Mental Math, 116
  Work Backward, 426

Thinking Skills. *See* Conjectures; Error
  Analysis; Reasoning

Three-dimensional figures. *See* Space
  figures

Time, 253–254, 368, 699

Transformations
  defined, 476, 493
  dilation, 300
  reflection, 483, 493
  rotation, 486–487, 493
  translation. *See* Translations

Transitive Property
  of Equality, 703
  of Inequality, 703

Translations, 476–477, 493

Transversal, 444, 492

Trapezoid(s)
  area of, 508–509, 557
  defined, 449

Trapezoidal prism, 520

Tree diagram, 41, 183

Trend
  negative, 630, 643
  no trend, 630, 643

positive, 630, 643
  scatter plots to find, 630, 643

Trend line, 635–636, 643

Triangles
  acute, 448
  altitude of, 474, 507
  angle sums, 702
  area of, 507–508, 557
  base of, 507
  classifying, 448, 492
  congruent, 459, 492
  defined, 448
  equilateral, 448
  formulas for, 702
  height of, 507
  isosceles, 448
  obtuse, 448
  perimeter of, 580
  Pythagorean Theorem for, 570–572,
    598
  right. *See* Right triangles
  scalene, 448
  similar, 295, 296
  vertices of, 486–487

Triangular prism, 520
  surface area of, 528
  volume of, 540

Try, Test, Revise **reasoning strategy,**
  98–99, 119

Turn (rotation), 458, 486–487, 493

Two-step equations, 344–345, 377, 378

Two-step inequalities, 363–364, 378

Two-variable equation, 393–395, 428

U _____

Unit rate, 284, 335

Units of measure. *See* Customary units
  of measure; Metric system

Unlike denominators, 237–238

Upper Quartile, 617

Use Multiple Strategies **reasoning**
  strategy, 410–411, 429

V _____

Vanishing point, 523

Variable(s)
  defined, 4, 59
  equations with two variables, 393–395
  evaluating fractions containing, 198
  in expressions. *See* Algebraic
    expressions
  in test taking, 596

Variable expressions, *See* Algebraic
  expression

Venn diagrams, 187

Vertex
  in naming polygons, 449
  of space figure, 519
  of triangle, 486–487

Index

Acknowledgments

Staff Credits

The people who made up the Mathematics team—representing design services, editorial, editorial services, education technology, image services, marketing, market research, production services, publishing processes, and strategic markets—are listed below. Bold type denotes the core team members.

Dan Anderson, Scott Andrews, Carolyn Artin, Beth Blumberg, Kyla Brown, Judith D. Buice, Kerry Cashman, Sarah Castrignano, Allison Cook, Bob Craton, Patrick Culleton, Sheila Defazio, Kathleen Dempsey, Emily Dumas, Frederick Fellows, **Suzanne Finn,** Patricia Fromkin, Sandy Graff, Shelby Gragg, **Ellen Welch Granter,** Etta Jacobs, Linda D. Johnson, Gillian Kahn, Jonathan Kier, Betsy Krieble, Mary Landry, Christopher Langley, Lisa LaVallee, Christine Lee, **Elizabeth Lehnertz,** Sara Levendusky, Cheryl Mahan, **Ann Mahoney,** Constance McCarty, Patricia K. McDonald, Carolyn McGuire, Anne McLaughlin, Richard McMahon, Eve Melnechuk, Terri Mitchell, Hope Morley, Michael Oster, Jeffrey Paulhus, Marcy Rose, Rashid Ross, Carol Roy, Irene Rubin, Siri Schwartzman, Vicky Shen, Jewel Simmons, **Dennis Slattery,** Nancy Smith, Richard Sullivan, Dan Tanguay, Tiffany Taylor-Sullivan, Mark Tricca, Paula Vergith, Teresa Whitney, Merce Wilczek, Joe Will, Kristin Winters, Heather Wright, Allison Wyss, Helen Young

Additional Credits: Sarah J. Aubry, Nicholas Cronin, Patty Fagan, Tom Greene, Karmyn Guthrie, Mary Beth McDaniel, Cynthia Metallides, Christine Nevola, Ted Smykal, Steve Thomas, Michael Torocsik, Alwyn Velasquez

Cover Design

Nancy Smith

Cover Image

Bridge, Roger Ressmeyer/Corbis; landscape, Fritz Poelking/DRK Photo.

Illustration

XNR Production

Photo Research

Heather Wright

Photography

Front Matter Pages vii, © Jorge Moro/Fotolia; **viii,** © Ambrose/Fotolia; **ix,** © Helder Almeida/Fotolia; **x,** © Creatas Images/Thinkstock; **xi,** © Stockbyte/Thinkstock; **xii,** © Andy/Fotolia; **xiii,** © Michael Ireland/Fotolia; **xiv,** © simonkr/Fotolia; **xv,** © IT Stock/Thinkstock; **xvi,** © Marika Eglite/Fotolia; **xvii,** © dzain/Fotolia; **xviii,** © Igor Mojzes/Fotolia; **xix,** © Tom Brakefield/Thinkstock;

Chapter 1 Pages 3, © Terrance Emerson/Fotolia; **5,** © Ambrose/Fotolia; **10 m,** © Monkey Business/Fotolia; **10 b,** © Yuri Arcurs/Fotolia; **10 t,** © thomas bredenfeld/Fotolia; **15,** © Kelpfish/Fotolia; **17,** © Tom Brakefield/Thinkstock; **18,** © Brand X Pictures/Thinkstock; **26,** © Jason Reed/Thinkstock; **31,** © Fabrice BEAUCHENE/Fotolia; **42,** © Prentice Hall; **44,** © Goodshoot/Thinkstock;

Chapter 2 Pages 67, © Getty Images/Jupiterimages/Thinkstock; **74,** © Jean-Michel LECLERCQ/Fotolia; **83,** © Getty Images/Jupiterimages/Thinkstock; **88 ml & mr,** © Ron Chapple Stock/© Superstock; **89,** © Duncan Smith/Thinkstock; **98,** © Michael Blann/Thinkstock; **104 r,** © Amy Green/Fotolia; **104 l,** © Getty Images/Jupiterimages/ Thinkstock; **107,** © Helder Almeida/Fotolia; **111,** © Keith Brofsky/ Thinkstock;

Chapter 3 Pages 125, © Superstock; **132,** © Creatas Images/Thinkstock; **133,** © MP/Fotolia; **137,** © Wild Geese/Fotolia; **144,** © Wolfgang Kruck/Fotolia; **145 t,** © Karen Roach/Fotolia; **152,** © Jgz/Fotolia; **154,** © urosr/Fotolia; **158,** © Comstock/Thinkstock;

Chapter 4 Pages 171, © Getty Images/Photos.com/Thinkstock; **179 b,** © Steve Young/Fotolia; **179 t & m,** © Duncan Smith/Thinkstock; **189,** © Getty Images/Hemera Technologies/Thinkstock; **193,** © KaYann/Fotolia; **198,** © Stephen Coburn/Fotolia; **207,** © Michael Ireland/Fotolia; **208,** © Fingolfin/Fotolia; **211,** © Charlie Borland/Superstock; **213,** © Czanner/Fotolia; **215,** © Stockbyte/Thinkstock;

Chapter 5 Pages 225, © Superstock; **228,** © Jetta Productions/Thinkstock; **231,** © Getty Images/Jupiterimages/Thinkstock; **238,** © mvkazit/Fotolia; **243,** © Andy/Fotolia; **253,** © Dawn/Fotolia; **260,** © Mat Hayward/Fotolia; **265,** © Tim Markley/Fotolia;

Chapter 6 Pages 283, © Albo/Fotolia; **291,** © NASA/Thinkstock; **293 m,** © Artur Golbert/Fotolia; **298,** © FikMik/Fotolia; **301,** © Michael Ireland/Fotolia; **319,** © Eric Isselée/Fotolia; **321 m,** © Lisa F. Young/Fotolia; **321 b,** © Jaimie Duplass/Fotolia; **330,** © K. Geijer/Fotolia; **332,** © Alexander Raths/Fotolia;

Chapter 7 Pages 343, © Kelpfish/Fotolia; **345,** © wabkmiami/Fotolia; **357,** © simonkr/Fotolia; **358 m,** © 18percentgrey/Fotolia; **364,** © Karl Weatherly/Thinkstock; **368,** © Getty Images/Jupiterimages/Thinkstock;

Chapter 8 Pages 385, © Creatas Images/Thinkstock; **389,** © Getty Images/Jupiterimages/Thinkstock; **393,** © Getty Images/Jupiterimages/Thinkstock; **399,** © Getty Images/Jupiterimages/Thinkstock; **403,** © Susan Caranci/Fotolia; **403,** © Karin Lau/Fotolia; **410,** © Gail Johnson/Fotolia; **416 t & b,** © Monkey Business/Fotolia; **421,** © Stockbyte/Thinkstock;

Chapter 9 Pages 435, © skyphoto/Fotolia; **436,** © Marika Eglite/Fotolia; **445 b,** © Lisa F. Young/Fotolia; **445 m,** © Monkey Business/Fotolia; **445 t,** © xmasbaby/Fotolia; **450,** © James Steidl/Fotolia; **452,** © Kwest/Fotolia; **454,** © Getty Images/Jupiterimages/Thinkstock; **458,** © Maslov Dmitry/Fotolia; **459,** © thomas hansson/Fotolia; **461,** © WMP/Fotolia; **482 bl,**